PETER THE GREAT

'A biography almost as massive as its gigantic protagonist . . . This epic task must have exhausted the author, but is in no way daunting to the reader. The familiar but still incredible story is told with a verve and sympathy that have deservedly made it a bestseller.' Nikolai Tolstoy

'Vividly describes the life and times of one of the grandfathers of modern Russia, and traces the origins and many traits of the current Russian life and character' *Sunday Express*

'By taking an enormous canvas and filling every inch of it with action and description, Massie has placed Peter clearly in perspective among his contemporaries, and in measuring him by the yardstick of that age has shown better than any other biographer precisely why this 6ft 7inch epileptic was hailed as "Petrus Magnus Imperator"' *Sunday Times*

Robert K. Massie was born in Lexington, Kentucky in 1929. He studied American History at Yale University and Modern European History at Oxford University, which he attended as a Rhodes Scholar. He lives in Irvington, New York.

Also by Robert K. Massie

Dreadnought: Britain, Germany and the
Coming of the Great War

Nicholas and Alexandra

The Romanovs

Last Courts of Europe: Royal Family Album, 1860–1914

Journey (with Suzanne Massie)

PETER THE GREAT

His Life and World

Robert K Massie

**PHOENIX
PRESS**

5 UPPER SAINT MARTIN'S LANE
LONDON
WC2H 9EA

A PHOENIX PRESS PAPERBACK

First published in Great Britain
by Victor Gollancz Ltd in 1981
Abacus edition published in 1982
This paperback edition published in 2001
by Phoenix Press,
a division of The Orion Publishing Group Ltd,
Orion House, 5 Upper St Martin's Lane,
London WC2H 9EA

A CIP catalogue record for this book is available
from the British Library.

Printed and bound in Great Britain by
Clays Ltd, St Ives plc

ISBN 1 84212 116 2

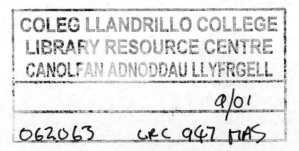

For
MARY KIMBALL TODD
and
JAMES MADISON TODD
and in memory of
ROBERT KINLOCH MASSIE

Contents

Part One: Old Muscovy

1	Old Muscovy	3
2	Peter's Childhood	18
3	"A Maiden of Great Intelligence"	31
4	The Revolt of the Streltsy	38
5	The Great Schism	53
6	Peter's Games	65
7	The Regency of Sophia	79
8	Sophia Overthrown	95
9	Gordon, Lefort and the Jolly Company	108
10	Archangel	124
11	Azov	134

Part Two: The Great Embassy

12	The Great Embassy to Western Europe	155
13	"It Is Impossible to Describe Him"	168
14	Peter in Holland	178
15	The Prince of Orange	190
16	Peter in England	203
17	Leopold and Augustus	217
18	"These Things Are in Your Way"	234
19	Fire and Knout	244

20 Among Friends   262
21 Voronezh and the Southern Fleet   275

Part Three: The Great Northern War

22 Mistress of the North   289
23 Let the Cannon Decide   302
24 Charles XII   312
25 Narva   323
26 "We Must Not Lose Our Heads"   339
27 The Founding of St. Petersburg   355
28 Menshikov and Catherine   367
29 The Hand of the Autocrat   383
30 Polish Quagmire   397
31 Charles in Saxony   413
32 The Great Road to Moscow   427
33 Golovchin and Lesnaya   439
34 Mazeppa   455
35 The Worst Winter Within Memory   467
36 The Gathering of Forces   479
37 Poltava   490
38 Surrender by the River   507
39 The Fruits of Poltava   516

Part Four: On the European Stage

40 The Sultan's World   529
41 Liberator of the Balkan Christians   539
42 Fifty Blows on the Pruth   552
43 The German Campaign and Frederick William   567
44 The Coast of Finland   581
45 The Kalabalik   591
46 Venice of the North   602
47 An Ambassador Reports   613

48 The Second Journey West 624

49 "The King Is a Mighty Man . . ." 635

50 A Visitor in Paris 644

51 The Education of an Heir 657

52 A Paternal Ultimatum 669

53 Flight of the Tsarevich 681

54 The Future on Trial 692

55 Charles' Last Offensive 711

56 King George Enters the Baltic 724

57 Victory 735

Part Five: The New Russia

58 In the Service of the State 747

59 Commerce by Decree 770

60 Supreme Under God 783

61 The Emperor in St. Petersburg 795

62 Along the Caspian 818

63 Twilight 828

Epilogue 846

Genealogy of the Romanov Dynasty, 1613–1917 858

Acknowledgments 861

Selected Bibliography 863

Notes 869

Index 887

Maps

Russia during the youth of Peter the Great 1672–1696   14

Moscow   40

The Swedish Empire at the beginning of the Great Northern War   293

The Battle of Narva I   331

The Battle of Narva II   335

The Swedish invasion of Russia, 1708–1709   441

Poltava I   488

Poltava II   496

Poltava III   499

Poltava IV   503

The Pruth campaign   555

Europe in the time of Peter the Great   910–911

Plan of St. Petersburg, 1716   912–913

Part One

OLD
MUSCOVY

1

OLD MUSCOVY

ROUND MOSCOW, the country rolls gently up from the rivers winding in silvery loops across the pleasant landscape. Small lakes and patches of woods are sprinkled among the meadowlands. Here and there, a village appears, topped by the onion dome of its church. People are walking through the fields on dirt paths lined with weeds. Along the riverbanks, they are fishing, swimming and lying in the sun. It is a familiar Russian scene, rooted in centuries.

In the third quarter of the seventeenth century, the traveler coming from Western Europe passed through this countryside to arrive at a vantage point known as the Sparrow Hills. Looking down on Moscow from this high ridge, he saw at his feet "the most rich and beautiful city in the world." Hundreds of golden domes topped by a forest of golden crosses rose above the treetops; if the traveler was present at a moment when the sun touched all this gold, the blaze of light forced his eyes to close. The white-walled churches beneath these domes were scattered through a city as large as London. At the center, on a modest hill, stood the citadel of the Kremlin, the glory of Moscow, with its three magnificent cathedrals, its mighty bell tower, its gorgeous palaces, chapels and hundreds of houses. Enclosed by great white walls, it was a city in itself.

In summer, immersed in greenery, the city seemed like an enormous garden. Many of the larger mansions were surrounded by orchards and parks, while swaths of open space left as firebreaks burst out with grasses, bushes and trees. Overflowing its own walls, the city expanded into numerous flourishing suburbs, each with its own orchards, gardens and copses of trees. Beyond, in a wide circle around the city, the manors and estates of great nobles and the white walls and gilded cupolas of monasteries were scattered among meadows and tilled fields to stretch the landscape out to the horizon.

Entering Moscow through its walls of earth and brick, the traveler plunged immediately into the bustling life of a busy commercial city. The streets were crowded with jostling humanity. Tradespeople, artisans, idlers

and ragged holy men walked beside laborers, peasants, black-robed priests and soldiers in bright-colored caftans and yellow boots. Carts and wagons struggled to make headway through this river of people, but the crowds parted for a fat-bellied, bearded boyar, or nobleman, on horseback, his head covered with a fine fur cap and his girth with a rich fur-lined coat of velvet or stiff brocade. At street corners, musicians, jugglers, acrobats and animal handlers with bears and dogs performed their tricks. Outside every church, beggars clustered and wailed for alms. In front of taverns, travelers were sometimes astonished to see naked men who had sold every stitch of clothing for a drink; on feast days, other men, naked and clothed alike, lay in rows in the mud, drunk.

The densest crowds gathered in the commercial districts centered on Red Square. The Red Square of the seventeenth century was very different from the silent, cobbled desert we know today beneath the fantastic, clustered steeples and cupolas of St. Basil's Cathedral and the high Kremlin walls. Then it was a brawling, open-air marketplace, with logs laid down to cover the mud, with lines of log houses and small chapels built against the Kremlin wall where Lenin's tomb now stands, and with rows and rows of shops and stalls, some wood, some covered by tent-like canvas, crammed into every corner of the vast arena. Three hundred years ago, Red Square teemed, swirled and reverberated with life. Merchants standing in front of stalls shouted to customers to step up and inspect their wares. They offered velvet and brocade, Persian and Armenian silk, bronze, brass and copper goods, iron wares, tooled leather, pottery, innumerable objects made of wood, and rows of melons, apples, pears, cherries, plums, carrots, cucumbers, onions, garlic and asparagus as thick as a thumb, laid out in trays and baskets. Peddlers and pushcart men forced their way through the crowds with a combination of threats and pleas. Vendors sold pirozhki (small meat pies) from trays suspended by cords from their shoulders. Tailors and street jewelers, oblivious to all around them, worked at their trades. Barbers clipped hair, which fell to the ground unswept, adding a new layer to a matted carpet decades in the forming. Flea markets offered old clothes, rags, used furniture and junk. Down the hill, nearer the Moscow River, animals were sold, and live fish from tanks. On the riverbank itself, near the new stone bridge, rows of women bent over the water washing clothes. One seventeenth-century German traveler noted that some of the women selling goods in the square might also sell "another commodity."

At noon, all activity came to a halt. The markets would close and the streets empty as people ate dinner, the largest meal of the day. Afterward, everyone napped and shopkeepers and vendors stretched out to sleep in front of their stalls.

With the coming of dusk, swallows began to soar over the Kremlin battlements and the city locked itself up for the night. Shops closed behind

heavy shutters, watchmen looked down from the rooftops and bad-tempered dogs paced at the end of long chains. Few honest citizens ventured into the dark streets, which became the habitat of thieves and armed beggars bent on extracting by force in the dark what they had failed to get by pleading during the daylight hours. "These villains," wrote an Austrian visitor, "place themselves at the corners of streets and throw swinging cudgels at the heads of those that pass by, in which practice they are so expert that these mortal blows seldom miss." Several murders a night were common in Moscow, and although the motive for these crimes was seldom more than simple theft, so vicious were the thieves that no one dared respond to cries for help. Often, terrorized citizens were afraid even to look out their own doors or windows to see what was happening. In the morning, the police routinely carried the bodies found lying in the streets to a central field where relatives could come to check for missing persons; eventually, all unidentified corpses were tumbled into a common grave.

Moscow in the 1670's was a city of wood. The houses, mansions and hovels alike, were built of logs, but their unique architecture and the superb carved and painted decoration of their windows, porches and gables gave them a strange beauty unknown to the stolid masonry of European cities. Even the streets were made of wood. Lined with rough timbers and wooden planks, thick with dust in summer or sinking into the mud during spring thaws and September rains, the wood-paved streets of Moscow attempted to provide footing for passage. Often, they failed. "The autumnal rains made the streets impassable for wagons and horses," complained an Orthodox churchman visiting from the Holy Land. "We could not go out of the house to market, the mud and clay being deep enough to sink in overhead. The price of food rose very high, as none could be brought in from the country. All the people, and most of all ourselves, prayed to God that He would cause the earth to freeze."

Not unnaturally in a city built of wood, fire was the scourge of Moscow. In winter when primitive stoves were blazing in every house, and in summer when the heat made wood tinder-dry, a spark could create a holocaust. Caught by the wind, flames leaped from one roof to the next, reducing entire streets to ashes. In 1571, 1611, 1626 and 1671, great fires destroyed whole quarters of Moscow, leaving vast empty spaces in the middle of the city. These disasters were exceptional, but to Muscovites the sight of a burning house with firemen struggling to localize the fire by hastily tearing down other buildings in its path was a part of daily life.

As Moscow was built of logs, Muscovites always kept spares on hand for repairs or new construction. Logs by the thousand were piled up between houses or sometimes hidden behind them or surrounded by fences as protection from thieves. In one section, a large wood market kept thousands of prefabricated log houses of various sizes ready for sale; a buyer had only

to specify the size and number of rooms desired. Almost overnight, the timbers, all clearly numbered and marked, would be carried to his site, assembled, the logs chinked with moss, a roof of thin planks laid on top and the new owner could move in. The largest logs, however, were saved and sold for a different purpose. Cut into six-foot sections, hollowed out with an axe and covered with lids, they became the coffins in which Russians were buried.

RISING FROM A HILL 125 feet above the Moscow River, the towers, cupolas and battlements of the Kremlin dominated the city. In Russian, the word "kreml" means "fortress," and the Moscow Kremlin was a mighty citadel. Two rivers and a deep moat rippled beneath its powerful walls. These walls, twelve to sixteen feet thick and rising sixty-five feet above the water, formed a triangle around the crest of the hill, with a perimeter of a mile and a half and a protected enclosure of sixty-nine acres. Twenty massive towers studded the wall at intervals, each a self-contained fortress, each designed to be impregnable. The Kremlin was not impregnable; archers and pikemen and later musketeers and artillerymen could be made to surrender to hunger if not to assault, but the most recent siege, early in the seventeenth century, had lasted two years. Ironically, the besiegers were Russian and the defenders Poles, supporters of a Polish claimant, the False Dmitry, who temporarily occupied the throne. When the Kremlin finally fell, the Russians executed Dmitry, burned his body, primed a cannon on the Kremlin wall and fired his ashes back toward Poland.

In normal times, the Kremlin had two masters, one temporal, the other spiritual: the tsar and the patriarch. Each lived within the fortress and governed his respective realm from there. Crowding around the Kremlin squares were government offices, lawcourts, barracks, bakeries, laundries and stables; nearby stood other palaces and offices and more than forty churches and chapels of the patriarchate of the Russian Orthodox Church. At the center of the Kremlin, on the crest of the hill around the edges of a wide square, stood four magnificent buildings—three superb cathedrals and a majestic, soaring bell tower—which, then and now, may be considered the physical heart of Russia. Two of these cathedrals, along with the Kremlin wall and many of its towers, had been designed by Italian architects.

The largest and most historic of these cathedrals was the Assumption Cathedral (Uspensky Sobor), in which every Russian tsar or empress from the fifteenth century to the twentieth was crowned. It had been built in 1479 by Ridolfo Fioravanti of Bologna but reflected many essential Russian features of church design. Before beginning its construction, Fioravanti had visited the old Russian cities of Vladimir, Yaroslavl, Rostov and Novgorod

to study their beautiful cathedrals, and then produced a Russian church with far more space inside than any Russian had ever seen. Four huge circular columns supported the onion-shaped central dome and its four smaller satellite domes without the complicated webbing of walls and buttressing previously thought necessary. This gave an airiness to the ceiling and a spaciousness to the nave entirely unique in Russia, where the power as well as the beauty of the Gothic arch were unknown.

Across the square from the Assumption Cathedral stood the Cathedral of the Archangel Michael, where the tsars were entombed. Built by Alvesio Novy of Milan, it was considerably more Italianate than either of its two sisters. Inside, amidst its several chapels, the deceased rulers were clustered in groups. In the middle of one small room, three carved stone coffins held Ivan the Terrible and his two sons. Other tsars lay in rows along the walls, their coffins of brass and stone covered with embroidered velvet cloths with inscriptions sewn in pearls around the hems. Tsar Alexis, father of Peter the Great, and two of his sons, Fedor and Ivan VI, also both tsars, would lie in this small room, but they would be the last. Alexis' third son, Peter, would build a new cathedral in a new city on the Baltic where he and all the Romanovs who followed would be entombed.*

The smallest of the three cathedrals, the Cathedral of the Annunciation, had nine towers and three porches, and was the only one designed by Russian architects. Its builders came from Pskov, which was famous for its carved stone churches. Used extensively as a private chapel by the tsars and their families, its iconostasis was set with icons by the two most famous painters of this form of religious art in Russia, Theophanes the Greek, who came from Byzantium, and his Russian pupil Andrei Rublev.

On the eastern side of the square, towering above the three cathedrals, stood the whitewashed brick bell towers of Ivan the Great, the Bono Tower and the Tower of the Patriarch Philaret, now joined into a single structure. Beneath its highest cupola, 270 feet in the air, rows of bells hung in laddered niches. Cast in silver, copper, bronze and iron, in many sizes and timbres (the largest weighed thirty-one tons), they rang with a hundred messages: summoning Muscovites to early mass or vespers, reminding them of fasts and festivals, tolling the sadness of death, chiming the happiness of marriage, jangling warnings of fire or booming the celebration of victory. At times, they rang all night, driving foreigners to consternation. But Russians loved their bells. On holidays, the common people crowded to the belfries to take turns pulling the ropes. The first bells usually sounded from the Kremlin, then the sound was taken up by all the bells of Moscow's

---

* Except Peter II, whose body is in the Kremlin, and Nicholas II, the last tsar, whose body was destroyed in a pit outside Ekaterinburg in the Urals.

"forty times forty" churches. Before long, waves of sound passed over the city and "the earth shook with their vibrations like thunder" according to one awed visitor.

From building cathedrals, the Italian architects turned to building palaces. In 1487, Ivan the Great commissioned the first stone palace of the Kremlin, the Palace of Facets (Granovitaya Palata), so named because its gray stone exterior walls were cut prismatically to resemble the surface of facet-cut jewels. Its most notable architectural feature was a throne room seventy-seven feet on each side, whose roof was supported by a single, massively arched column in the middle. When foreign ambassadors were being received, and on other state occasions, a small curtained window near the ceiling permitted the cloistered women of the tsar's family to peek down and watch.

The Palace of Facets was primarily an official state building, and thus, in 1499, Ivan the Great ordered another palace of brick and stone in which to live. This five-story building, called the Terem Palace, contained a honeycomb of low-ceilinged, vaulted apartments for himself and the many women—wives, widows, sisters, daughters—of the royal family. The building was badly damaged by fire several times during the sixteenth and early seventeenth centuries, but both of the first Romanov tsars, Michael and his son Alexis, lavished great efforts to restore the building. In Alexis' time, the doors, windows, parapets and cornices were made of white stone carved into foliage and figures of birds and animals, then painted bright colors. Alexis devoted special effort to refurbishing the fourth floor as a dwelling for himself. The five principal rooms—anteroom, throne room (known as the Golden Hall), study, bedroom and private chapel—were fitted with wooden walls and floors to prevent the dampness caused by moisture condensing on brick and stone, and the walls were covered with hangings of embroidered silk, woolen tapestries or tooled leather, depicting scenes from the Old and New Testaments. The arches and ceilings were intersected by curving arabesques and Eastern versions of plants and fairy-tale birds, all done in brilliant colors with lavish inlays of silver and gold. The furnishing of the tsar's apartment was partly traditional and partly modern. The old, carved oaken benches and chests and polished wooden tables were there, but so also were upholstered armchairs, elaborate gilded and ebony tables, clocks, mirrors, portraits and bookcases filled with books of theology and history. One window of the tsar's study was known as the Petitioner's Window. Outside was a small box which could be lowered to the ground, stuffed with petitions and complaints, then raised to be read by the sovereign. The tsar's bedroom was upholstered with Venetian velvet and contained an intricately carved four-poster oak bed, curtained and canopied with brocade and silk and heaped with furs, eiderdown and cushions to ward off the icy currents of winter air that blasted against the windows and

eddied under the doors. All these rooms were simultaneously heated and decorated by huge stoves of glazed, colored tiles whose radiant warmth also kept Russia's rulers warm. The major drawback to these splendid chambers was their lack of light. Little sunlight could filter through the narrow windows with their double sheets of mica separated by strips of lead. Not only at night and on the short, gray days of winter, but even in summertime, most of the illumination in the Terem Palace came from the light of flickering candles in the alcoves and along the walls.

IN THE THIRD QUARTER of the seventeenth century, the royal chambers were occupied by the second tsar of the Romanov dynasty, "the Great Lord, Tsar and Grand Duke, Alexis Mikhailovich, of all Great and Little and White Russia, Autocrat." Remote and inaccessible to his subjects, this august figure was enclosed in an aura of semi-divinity. An embassy of Englishmen, come in 1664 to thank the Tsar for his constant support of their once-exiled monarch, Charles II, was deeply impressed by the sight of Tsar Alexis seated on his throne:

> The Tsar like a sparkling sun darted forth most sumptuous rays, being most magnificently placed upon his throne, with his scepter in his hand and having his crown on his head. His throne was of massy silver gilt, wrought curiously on top with several works and pyramids; and being seven or eight steps higher than the floor, it rendered the person of the Prince transcendently majestic. His crown (which he wore upon a cap lined with black sables) was covered quite over with precious stones, terminating toward the top in the form of a pyramid with a golden cross at the spire. The scepter glittered also all over with jewels, his vest was set with the like from the top to the bottom and his collar was answerable to the same.

From infancy, Russians had been taught to regard their ruler as an almost god-like creature. Their proverbs embodied this view: "Only God and the tsar know," "One sun shines in heaven and the Russian tsar on earth," "Through God and the tsar, Russia is strong," "It is very high up to God; it is a very long way to the tsar."

Another proverb, "The sovereign is the father, the earth the mother," related the Russian's feeling for the tsar to his feeling for the land. The land, the earth, the motherland, "rodina," was feminine. Not the pure maiden, the virgin girl, but the eternal, mature woman, the fertile mother. All Russians were her children. In a sense, long before communism, the Russian land was communal. It belonged to the tsar as father, but also to

the people, his family. Its disposal belonged to the tsar—he could give away vast tracts to favored noblemen—yet it still remained the joint property of the national family. When it was threatened, all were willing to die for it. The tsar, in this familial scheme, was the father, "Batushka," of the people. His autocratic rule was patriarchal. He addressed his subjects as his children and had the same unlimited power over them that a father has over his children. The Russian people could not imagine any limitation of the power of the tsar, "for how can a father's authority be limited except by God?" When he commanded, they obeyed for the same reason that when a father commands, the child must obey, without question. At times, obeisance before the tsar took on a slavish, Byzantine quality. Russian noblemen, when greeting or receiving favors from the tsar, prostrated themselves in front of him, touching the ground with their foreheads. When addressing his royal master, Artemon Matveev, who was Tsar Alexis' leading minister and close friend, declared, "We humbly beseech you, we your slave Artemushka Matveev, with the lowly worm, my son Adrushka, before the high throne of Your Royal Majesty, bowing our faces to the earth. . . ." In addressing the tsar, his whole lengthy official title had to be used. In so doing, the accidental omission of a single word could be considered an act of personal disrespect almost equivalent to treason. The tsar's own conversation was sacrosanct: " 'Tis death for anyone to reveal what is spoken in the tsar's palace," declared an English resident.

In fact, the demi-god who bore these titles, who wore a crown braided with "tufts of diamonds as big as peas, resembling bunches of glittering grapes" and the imperial mantle embroidered with emeralds, pearls and gold, was a relatively unassuming mortal. Tsar Alexis was recognized in his own time as "tishaishy tsar," the quietest, gentlest and most pious of all the tsars, and when he succeeded his father on the throne in 1645 at the age of sixteen, he was already known as "the Young Monk." In manhood, he grew taller than most Russians, about six feet, well built, inclined to fat. His roundish face was framed by light-brown hair, a mustache and a flowing brown beard. His eyes also were brown, their tone ranging from hardness in anger to warmth in affection and religious humility. "His Imperial Majesty is a goodly person, about two months older than King Charles II," reported his English physician, Dr. Samuel Collins, adding that his patron was "severe in his chastisements but very careful of his subjects' love. Being urged by a stranger to make it [punishable by] death for any man to desert his colors, he answered, 'It was a hard case to do that, for God has not given courage to all men alike.' "

Although he was tsar, Alexis' life inside the Kremlin was more like that of a monk. At four a.m., the Tsar threw aside his sable coverlet and stepped from his bed clad in shirt and drawers. He dressed and went immediately to

the chapel next to his bedroom for twenty minutes of prayers and readings from devotional books. When he had kissed the icons and been sprinkled with holy water, he emerged and sent a chamberlain to bid the Tsaritsa good morning and ask after her health. A few minutes later, he went to her chamber to escort her to another chapel, where together they heard morning prayers and early mass.

Meanwhile, boyars, government officials and secretaries had gathered in a public anteroom awaiting the arrival of the Tsar from his private chambers. As soon as they saw "the bright eyes of the Tsar," they began to bow to the ground, some as many as thirty times, in gratitude for favors granted. For a while, Alexis listened to reports and petitions; then, at about nine a.m., the entire group went to hear a two-hour mass. During the service, however, the Tsar continued to converse quietly with his boyars, conducting public business and issuing instructions. Alexis never missed any divine service. "If he be well, he goes to it," said Dr. Collins. "If sick, it comes to him in his chamber. On fast days he frequents midnight prayers, standing four, five, or six hours together, prostrating himself on the ground, sometimes a thousand times, and on great festivals, fifteen hundred."

Following morning mass, the Tsar returned to administrative work with his boyars and secretaries until time for dinner at noon. He ate alone at a high table surrounded by boyars who dined at lower tables along the walls of the room. He was served only by special boyars, who tasted his food and sipped his wine before offering the cup. Meals were gargantuan; on festival days, as many as seventy dishes might be served at the Tsar's table. Zakuski, or hors d'oeuvres, included raw vegetables, especially cucumbers, salted fish, bacon and innumerable pirozhki, sometimes stuffed with egg, fish, rice or cabbage and herbs instead of meat. Then came soups and roasts of beef, mutton and pork, seasoned with onion, garlic, saffron and pepper. There were dishes of game and fish such as salmon, sturgeon and sterlet. Dessert was cakes, cheeses, preserves, fruits. Russians drank mostly vodka, beer or a milder drink called kvas, made of fermented black bread, variously flavored with raspberry, cherry or other fruits.

But Alexis rarely touched any of the succulent dishes that were presented to him. Instead, he sent them as presents to various boyars to show special favor. His own palate was monastically simple. He ate only plain rye bread and drank light wine or beer, perhaps with a few drops of cinnamon added; cinnamon, Dr. Collins reported, was the "aroma imperiale." During periods of religious fasting, said Dr. Collins, the Tsar "eats but three meals a week; for the rest, he takes a piece of brown bread and salt, a pickled mushroom or cucumber and drinks a cup of small beer. He eats fish but twice in Lent and observes it seven weeks altogether. . . . In fine, no monk is more observant of canonical hours than he is of fasts. We may reckon he fasts almost eight months in twelve."

Following dinner, the Tsar slept for three hours until time to return to church for vespers, again with his boyars, again to consult on affairs of state during the religious service. Supper and the end of the day were spent either with his family or with intimate friends playing backgammon or chess. Alexis' special pleasure during these hours was to listen to people read or tell stories. He liked hearing passages from books of church history, or the lives of saints, or the presentation of religious dogma, but he also liked to hear the reports of Russian ambassadors traveling abroad, extracts from foreign newspapers or simple tales told by pilgrims and wanderers who had been brought to the palace to entertain the monarch. In warmer weather, Alexis left the Kremlin to visit his country mansions outside Moscow. One of these at Preobrazhenskoe on the Yauza River was the center of Alexis' favorite sport, falconry. Over the years, the enthusiastic huntsman built up an immense establishment of 200 falconers, 3,000 falcons and 100,000 pigeons.

Most of the time, however, Alexis prayed and worked. He never questioned his own divinely granted right to rule; in his mind, he and all monarchs were chosen by God and responsible only to God.* Beneath the tsar stood the nobility, divided into almost a dozen ranks. The greatest noblemen held the highest rank, that of boyar, and were members of the old princely families who held hereditary landed estates. Below were the lesser aristocracy and gentry who had been given estates in return for service. There was a small middle class of merchants, artisans and other townspeople and then—the huge base of the pyramid—the peasants and serfs who made up the overwhelming mass of Russian society; their conditions of life and methods of farming were roughly similar to those of the serfs of medieval Europe. Most Muscovites used the title "boyar" to include all noblemen and high officials. Meanwhile, the actual daily work of administering the tsar's government was in the hands of between thirty and forty departments known as Prikazy. Generally speaking, they were inefficient, wasteful, overlapping, difficult to control and corrupt—in brief, a bureaucracy which nobody had designed and over which no one had any real control.

FROM HIS DIMLY LIT, incense-scented Kremlin rooms and chapels, Tsar Alexis ruled the largest nation on earth. Vast plains, endless tracts of dark

---

* When the English Parliamentarians cut off the head of King Charles I, in 1649, Tsar Alexis was so shocked and personally outraged that he expelled all English merchants from the interior of Russia, a move which gave great advantage to Dutch and German merchants. While King Charles II remained in exile, Alexis sent him money and his tenderest wishes for "the disconsolate widow of that glorious martyr, King Charles I."

forest and boundless expanses of desert and tundra stretched from Poland to the Pacific. Nowhere in this immensity of space was the wide horizon broken by more than shallow mountains and rolling hills. The only natural barriers to movement on the broad plain were the rivers, and from the earliest times these had been converted into a network of watery highways. In the region around Moscow, four great rivers had their tributary headwaters: the Dnieper, the Don and the mighty Volga flowed south to the Black and the Caspian seas; the Dvina flowed north to the Baltic and the frozen Arctic.

Scattered over this immense landscape was a thin sprinkling of human beings. At the time of Peter's birth—near the end of Tsar Alexis' reign—the population of Russia was roughly eight million people. This was about the same as that of Russia's western neighbor, Poland, although the Russians were dispersed over a far greater area. It was much larger than the population of Sweden (less than two million) or England (slightly more than five million), but less than half that of the most populous and powerful state in Europe, the France of Louis XIV (nineteen million). A fraction of the Russian population lived in the old Russian towns—Nizhni-Novgorod, Moscow, Novgorod, Pskov, Vologda, Archangel, Yaroslavl, Rostov, Vladimir, Suzdal, Tver, Tula—and in the more recently acquired Kiev, Smolensk, Kazan and Astrachan. Most of the people lived on the land, where they wrenched a living from the earth, the forest and the waters.

Enormous though Alexis' tsardom was, Russia's boundaries were fragile and under pressure. In the east, under Ivan the Terrible and his successors, Muscovy had conquered the middle Volga and the khanate of Kazan, extending the Russian empire to Astrachan and the Caspian Sea. The Urals had been crossed and the immense, largely empty spaces of Siberia added to the tsar's domain. Russian pioneers had penetrated to the northern Pacific and established a few bleak settlements there, although a clash with the aggressive Manchu Dynasty of China had forced a withdrawal of Russian outposts along the Amur River.

To the west and the south, Russia was ringed by enemies who struggled to keep the giant landlocked and isolated. Sweden, then reigning as Mistress of the Baltic, stood guard across this seaborne road to the West. Westward lay Catholic Poland, the ancient enemy of Orthodox Russia. Only recently, Tsar Alexis had reconquered Smolensk from Poland, although that Russian fortress town lay a mere 150 miles from Moscow. Late in his reign, Alexis had won back from Poland the shining prize of Kiev, mother of all Russian cities and the birthplace of Russian Christianity. Kiev and the fertile regions both east and west of the Dnieper were the lands of the Cossacks. These were Orthodox people, originally vagabonds, freebooters and runaways who had fled the onerous conditions of life in old Muscovy to form bands of irregular cavalry and then to become pioneers, colonizing farms, villages

RUSSIA DURING THE YOUTH OF PETER THE GREAT, 1672-1696

ARCTIC OCEAN

Kola

WHITE SEA

Solovetsky Monastery

Archangel

SWEDEN

N. Dvina R.

GULF OF BOTHNIA

FINLAND

KARELIA

Vasa

Lake Onega

Abo

Helsingfors

Vyborg

Lake Ladoga

Vologda

Stockholm

GULF OF FINLAND

Reval

INGRIA

Noteborg

ESTONIA

Narva

Novgorod

N

BALTIC SEA

L. Peipus

Dorpat

Pskov

Tver

Yaroslavl

LIVONIA

Riga

Volga R.

Pereslavl-Zalessky

Kazan

DUCHY OF COURLAND

Troitse Monastery

Suzdal

W. Dvina R.

Moscow

Vladimir

Nishni-Novgorod

Kama

Danzig

Königsberg

LITHUANIA

Moscow R.

Kama R.

PRUSSIA

Vilna

Smolensk

Oka R.

Grodno

Minsk

Tula

Sama

POLAND

Orel

RUSSIA

Warsaw

Pripet R.

Saratov

Bug R.

Desna

Kursk

Voronezh

Cracow

Don R.

Tsaritsyn

Lemberg

Kiev

UKRAINE

Poltava

Kharkov

Volga R.

Dniester R.

Dnieper R.

Donets R.

HUNGARY

MOLDAVIA

Bender

Rostov

Tagonrog

Astrachan

Prut R.

Ochakov

Kazikerman

Azov

CASPIAN SEA

Perekop Isthmus

SEA OF AZOV

WALACHIA

CRIMEA

Kerch

Kuban

Danube R.

OTTOMAN EMPIRE

Bakhchisarai

BULGARIA

BLACK SEA

Adrianople

SCALE of MILES

Constantinople

0   40

and towns throughout the upper Ukraine. Gradually, this line of Cossack settlements was spreading southward, but the limits still were 300 or 400 miles above the shores of the Black Sea.

The ground in between, the famous black-earth steppe of the lower Ukraine, was empty. Here, tall grasses grew so high that sometimes only the head and shoulders of a man on horseback could be seen moving along above the grass. In Alexis' day, this steppe was the hunting and grazing ground of the Crimean Tatars, Islamic descendants of the old Mongol conquerors and vassals of the Ottoman sultan, who lived in villages along the slopes and among the crags of the mountainous Crimean peninsula. Every spring and summer, they brought their cattle and horses down to feed on the steppe grasslands. Often enough, they strapped on their bows, arrows and scimitars and rode north to raid and plunder among the Russian and Ukrainian villages, sometimes storming the wooden stockade of a town and leading the entire population off into slavery. These massive raids, bringing thousands of Russian slaves annually into the Ottoman slave markets, were a source of embarrassment and anguish to the tsars in the Kremlin. But there was nothing so far that anyone could do. Indeed, twice, in 1382 and 1571, the Tatars had sacked and burned Moscow itself.

BEYOND THE MASSIVE white Kremlin battlements, beyond the gilt and blue onion domes and the wooden buildings of Moscow lay the fields and the forest, the true and eternal Russia. For centuries, everything had come from the forest, the deep, rich, virgin forest which stretched as far as an ocean. Amidst its birches and firs, its bushes with berries, its mosses and soft ferns, the Russian found most of what he needed for life. From the forest came logs for his house and firewood for warmth, moss to chink his walls, bark for his shoes, fur for his clothing, wax for his candles, and meat, sweet honey, wild berries and mushrooms for his dinner. Through most of the year, the forest groves rang with the sound of axes. On lazy summer days, men, women and children searched beneath the dark trunks for mushrooms, or brushed through the high grasses and flowers to pick wild raspberries and red and black currants.

Russians are a communal people. They did not live alone deep in the forest, contesting the primeval weald with wolf and bear. Rather they chose to cluster in tiny villages built in forest clearings, or on the edges of lakes or the banks of slow-moving rivers. Russia was an empire of such villages: lost at the end of a dusty road, surrounded by pasture and meadowland, a collection of simple log houses centered on a church whose onion dome gathered up the prayers of the villagers and passed them along to heaven. Most of the houses had only a single room without a chimney; smoke from the fire burning inside the stove found its way outdoors as best it could,

through cracks in the logs. Usually, as a result, everything and everyone inside was black with soot. For this reason, too, public baths were a common institution in Russia. Even the smallest village had its steaming bathhouse where men and women together could scrub themselves clean and then go outside, even in winter, to permit the wind to cool and dry their heated, naked bodies.

When the Russian peasant dressed, first combing his beard and hair, he put on a shirt of rough cloth which hung over his waist and was tied with a string. His trousers were loose and were stuffed into boots if he owned them, or, more often, into cloth leggings tied with heavy threads. "Their hair is cropt to their ears and their heads covered winter and summer with a fur cap," wrote a Western visitor. "Their beards remain yet untouched. . . . Their shoes are tied together with bast. About their neck they wear from the time of their baptism a cross, and next to it their purse, though they commonly keep the small money, if it be not much, a good while in their mouth, for as soon as they receive any, either as a present, or as their due, they put it into their mouths and keep it under their tongue."

Few people in the world live in such harmony with nature as the Russians. They live in the North, where winter comes early. In September, the light is fading by four in the afternoon and an icy rain begins. Frost comes quickly, and the first snow falls in October. Before long, everything vanishes beneath a blanket of whiteness: earth, rivers, roads, fields, trees and houses. Nature takes on not only a majesty but a frightening omnipotence. The landscape becomes a broad white sea with mounds and hollows rising and falling. On days when the sky is gray, it is hard, even straining the eye, to see where earth merges with air. On brilliant days, when the sky is a gorgeous azure, the sunlight is blinding, as if millions of diamonds were scattered on the snow, refracting light.

After 160 days of winter, spring lasts only for several weeks. First the ice cracks and breaks on rivers and lakes, and the murmuring waters, the dancing waves return. On land, the thaw brings mud, an endless, vast sea of mud through which man and beast must struggle. But every day the dirty snow recedes, and soon the first sprouts of green grass appear. Forest and meadows turn green and come to life. Animals, larks and swallows reappear. In Russia, the return of spring is greeted with a joy inconceivable in more temperate lands. As the warming rays of the sun touch meadow grass and the backs and faces of peasants, as the days rapidly grow longer and the earth everywhere is coming to life, the glad feeling of revival, of deliverance, urges people to sing and celebrate. The 1st of May is an ancient holiday of rebirth and fertility when people dance and wander in the woods. And while youth revels, the older people thank God that they have lived to see this glory again.

Spring races quickly into summer. There is great heat and choking dust,

but there is also the loveliness of an immense sky, the calm of the great land rolling gently to the horizon. There is the freshness of early morning, the coolness of shade in groves of birches or along the rivers, the mild air and warm wind of night. In June, the sun dips beneath the horizon for only a few hours and the red of sunset is followed quickly by the delicate rose-and-blue blush of dawn.

Russia is a stern land with a harsh climate, but few travelers can forget its deep appeal, and no Russian ever finds peace in his soul anywhere else on earth.

2

PETER'S CHILDHOOD

In March 1669, when Tsar Alexis was forty, his first wife, the Tsaritsa Maria Miloslavskaya, died in the attempted performance of her essential dynastic function: that is, in giving birth to a child. She was greatly mourned, not only by her husband, but also by her numerous Miloslavsky relatives whose power at court had rested on her marriage to the Tsar. Now, all this was over, and through their tears for their departed sister and niece they watched and worried.

Their uneasy situation was worsened by the fact that, despite all her efforts, Maria had not left behind her the certainty of a Miloslavsky heir. During her twenty-one years of marriage to Alexis, Maria, four years older than her husband, had done her best: thirteen children—five sons and eight daughters—were born before the attempt to produce a fourteenth killed her None of Maria's sons was strong; four survived her, but within six months two of these were gone, including the sixteen-year-old heir to the throne, named Alexis after his father. Thus, on the death of his wife, the Tsar was left with only two sons of the Miloslavsky marriage—two sons, unfortunately, whose prospects were poor. Fedor, then ten, was frail, and Ivan, aged three, was half blind and had a speech impediment. If both died before their father, or soon after him, the succession would be open, and no one knew who might lunge for the throne. In short, all Russia except the Miloslavskys hoped that Alexis would find a new wife and do so quickly.

If the Tsar did select a new tsaritsa, it was understood that his choice would be a daughter of the Russian nobility and not one of the available foreign princesses. The intermarriage of dynasties for the advancement or protection of state interests was common in most parts of seventeenth-century Europe, but in Russia the practice was abhorred and avoided. Russian tsars chose Russian consorts, or, more specifically, an Orthodox tsar could choose only an Orthodox tsaritsa. The Russian church, the nobility, the merchants and the mass of simple Russian people would look with horror at a foreign princess bringing in her train Catholic priests or

Protestant pastors to corrupt the pure Orthodox faith. This ban helped to isolate Russia from most of the effects of intercourse with foreign nations and ensured the keenest jealousy and competition among those noble Russian families who had among their daughters a potential tsaritsa.

Within a year of Maria Miloslavskaya's death, Alexis had found her successor. Depressed and lonely, he spent frequent evenings at the home of his intimate friend and chief minister, Artemon Matveev, an unusual man for seventeenth-century Muscovy. He was not from the highest boyar class, but had risen to power on merit. He was interested in scholarly subjects and was fascinated by Western culture. At the regular receptions which he held in his house for foreigners living in or visiting Moscow, he questioned them intelligently on the state of politics, art and technology in their homelands. Indeed, it was in the German Suburb, the settlement just outside the city where all foreigners were required to live, that he found his own wife, Mary Hamilton, the daughter of a Scots royalist who had left Britain after the beheading of Charles I and the triumph of Cromwell.

In Moscow, Matveev and his wife lived as much as possible like modern seventeenth-century Europeans. They hung their walls with paintings and mirrors in addition to icons; inlaid cabinets displayed Oriental porcelains and chiming clocks. Matveev studied algebra and dabbled in chemistry experiments in his home laboratory, and concerts, comedies and tragedies were performed in his small private theater. To traditional Muscovites, the behavior of Matveev's wife was shocking. She wore Western dresses and bonnets; she refused to seclude herself on an upper floor of her husband's house like most Moscow wives, but appeared freely among his guests, sitting down with them at dinner and sometimes even joining in the conversation.

It was during one of these unconventional evenings in the presence of the unusual Mary Hamilton that the eye of the widower Tsar Alexis fell on a second remarkable woman in Matveev's household. Natalya Naryshkina was then nineteen years old, a tall, shapely young woman with black eyes and long eyelashes. Her father, Kyril Naryshkin, a relatively obscure landowner of Tatar origins, lived in Tarus province, far from Moscow. In order to lift his daughter above the life of the rural gentry, Naryshkin had persuaded his friend Matveev to accept Natalya as his ward and raise her in the atmosphere of culture and freedom that characterized the minister's house in Moscow. Natalya had profited from her opportunity. For a Russian girl, she was well educated, and by watching and assisting her foster mother she had learned to receive and entertain male guests.

One evening when the Tsar was present, Natalya came into the room with Mary Hamilton to serve cups of vodka and plates of caviar and smoked fish. Alexis stared at her, noticing her healthy, glowing good looks, her black, almond-shaped eyes and her serene but modest behavior. When

she stood before him, he was impressed by the blend of respect and good sense in her brief replies to his questions. Leaving Matveev's house that night, the Tsar was much cheered up, and in saying good night he asked Matveev whether he was looking for a husband for this appealing young woman. Matveev replied that he was, but that, as neither Natalya's father nor he himself was rich, the dowry would be small and suitors doubtless few. Alexis declared that there were still a few men who valued a woman's qualities higher than her fortune, and he promised to help his minister find one.

Not long after, the Tsar asked Matveev whether he had had any success. "Sire," replied Matveev, "young men come every day to see my charming ward, but none seem to think of matrimony."

"Well, well, so much the better," said the Tsar. "Perhaps we shall be able to do without them. I have been more fortunate than you. I have found a gentleman who will probably be agreeable to her. He is a very honorable man with whom I am acquainted, is not destitute of merit and has no need of a dowry. He loves your ward and is inclined to marry her and make her happy. Though he has not yet disclosed his sentiments, she knows him, and if she is consulted, I think she will accept him."

Matveev declared that of course Natalya would accept anyone "proposed by Your Majesty. However, before she gives her consent, she may probably desire to know who he is. And this appears to me no more than what is reasonable."

"Well, then," announced Alexis, "tell her it is me, and that I am determined to marry her."

Matveev, overwhelmed by the implications of this declaration, threw himself at his sovereign's feet. He recognized instantly both the glittering prospects and the unfathomable dangers of Alexis' decision. To have his ward elevated to tsaritsa would seal his own success: her relatives and friends would rise along with her; they and he would replace the Miloslavskys as the ruling power at court. But it also meant dangerously stimulating the antagonism of the Miloslavskys, as well as the jealousy of many of the powerful boyar families who already were suspicious of his role as favorite. If, somehow, the choice was announced and then the match misfired, Matveev would be ruined.

With this in mind, Matveev begged that even if determined on his choice, the Tsar would nevertheless submit to the traditional process of publicly picking his bride from a flock of assembled candidates. The ceremony, which had its antecedents in Byzantium, decreed that women of marriageable age from all parts of Russia should assemble at the Kremlin for the tsar's inspection. In theory, the women were to come from every class of Russian society, including serfs, but in practice this fairy tale

never came true. No tsar ever gazed on a beautiful serf maiden and, smitten, led the blushing creature off to become his tsaritsa. However, the assembly did include daughters of the lesser nobility, and Natalya Naryshkina's rank made her perfectly eligible. At court, the frightened young women, pawns in the ambitions of their families, were examined by court officials to certify virginity. Those who survived this scrutiny were summoned to the Kremlin palace to await the smile or nod of the boy or man who could place one of them on the throne.

A game played for the highest stakes also entails high risks. Within that same century, there had been grim examples of the lengths to which ambitious families would go to prevent a girl from another family becoming the new tsaritsa. In 1616, Maria Khlopfa, the known choice of nineteen-year-old Michael Romanov, had so displeased the Saltykov family, then predominant at court, that they drugged the girl, presented her to Michael in this state, told the Tsar that she was incurably ill and then, as punishment for daring to present herself as a potential bride, dispatched Maria and all her family to exile in Siberia. In 1647, Alexis himself, at the age of eighteen, had chosen Euphemia Vsevolozhska to be his first wife. But when she was being dressed, a group of court ladies twisted her hair so tightly that in Alexis' presence she fainted. The court physicians were persuaded to declare that she had epilepsy, and she and her relatives were also dispatched to Siberia. Maria Miloslavskaya had been Alexis' second choice.

Now, for Natalya Naryshkina and for Matveev, who stood behind her, similar dangers loomed. The Miloslavskys knew that if Natalya was chosen, their influence would be undermined. This reversal would affect not only the male Miloslavskys who held high office and wielded power, but the females as well. All of the royal princesses, Tsar Alexis' daughters, were Miloslavskys, and they did not at all like the prospect of a new tsaritsa actually younger than some of them.

Nevertheless, Natalya and Matveev really had no choice: Alexis was determined. Notice had been given that on February 11, 1670, the preliminary inspection of all eligible young women would take place, and Natalya Naryshkina was commanded to be present. A second inspection, by the Tsar himself, was scheduled for April 28. But, soon after the first assembly, rumors spread that Natalya Naryshkina had been chosen. The inevitable counterattack was prepared, and, four days before the second inspection, anonymous letters were found in the Kremlin accusing Matveev of using magic herbs to make the Tsar desire his ward. An investigation was necessary, and the marriage was postponed for nine months. But nothing was proved, and finally, on February 1, 1671, to the joy of most Russians and the chagrin of the Miloslavskys, Tsar Alexis and Natalya Naryshkina were married.

FROM THE DAY OF THEIR MARRIAGE, it was clear to everyone that the forty-one-year-old Tsar was deeply in love with his handsome, black-haired young wife. She brought him freshness, happiness, relaxation and a sense of renewal. He wanted her constantly by his side and took her with him wherever he went. The first spring and summer of their marriage, the newly-weds moved happily from one to another of the Tsar's summer palaces around Moscow, including Preobrazhenskoe, where Alexis rode with his falcons.

At court, the new Tsaritsa quickly became an agent of change. With her semi-Western upbringing in Matveev's house, Natalya loved music and theater. Early in his reign, Alexis had issued an edict sternly forbidding his subjects to dance, to play games or watch them, at wedding feasts either to sing or play on instruments, or to give one's soul to perdition in such pernicious and lawless practices as word play, farces or magic. "Offenders for the first and second offenses are to be beaten with rods; for the third and fourth to be banished to the border towns." But when Alexis married Natalya, an orchestra played at his wedding banquet, mingling its new polyphonic Western harmonies with the strains of a Russian choir chanting in unison. The blend of sounds was far from perfect; Dr. Collins described the cacophony as being like "a flight of screech owls, a nest of jackdaws, a pack of hungry wolves, and seven hogs on a windy day."

Royal sponsorship of the theater soon followed. To please his young bride, the Tsar began to patronize playwriting and ordered construction of a stage and hall in the former house of a boyar inside the Kremlin and another at the summer retreat of Preobrazhenskoe. The Lutheran pastor in the German Suburb, Johannes Gregory, was asked by Matveev to recruit actors and produce plays. On October 17, 1672, the first production, a Biblical drama, was ready. It was presented in the presence of Tsar and Tsaritsa with a cast of sixty, all of whom were foreigners except a few boys and young men from the court. The play lasted all day and the Tsar watched the performance for ten hours straight without rising from his seat. Four additional plays and two ballets soon followed.

Alexis' delight in his new Tsaritsa increased even more when, in the fall of 1671, he learned that she was pregnant. Both father and mother prayed for a son, and on May 30, 1672, at one o'clock in the morning, she delivered a large, apparently healthy boy. The child was named Peter after the apostle. Along with good health, his mother's black, vaguely Tatar eyes, and a tuft of auburn hair, the royal infant entered the world at normal size. In accordance with the old Russian custom of "taking the measure," an image of Peter's patron saint was painted on a board of exactly the same dimensions as the infant, and the resultant image of St. Peter with the Holy

Trinity measures nineteen and a quarter inches long and five and a quarter inches wide.

Moscow rejoiced when the booming of the great bell in the Tower of Ivan the Great on the Kremlin square announced the birth of this new Tsarevich. Messengers galloped to carry the news to other Russian towns, and special ambassadors were dispatched to Europe. From the white ramparts of the Kremlin, cannon thundered in salute for three days, while the bells of the city's 1,600 churches pealed continuously.

Alexis was overjoyed with his new son, and personally arranged every detail of a service of public thanksgiving in the Assumption Cathedral. Afterward, Alexis raised Kyril Naryshkin, Natalya's father, and Matveev, her foster father, in rank, and then himself handed vodka and wines from trays to his guests.

The baby Peter, four weeks old, was christened on June 29, the holy day of St. Peter in the Orthodox calendar. Wheeled into church in a rolling cradle along a path sprinkled with holy water, the child was held over the font by Fedor Naryshkin, the Tsaritsa's eldest brother, and christened by Alexis' private confessor. The following day, a royal banquet was offered to delegations of boyars, merchants and other citizens of Moscow who thronged to the Kremlin with congratulatory gifts. The tables were decorated with enormous blocks of sugar sculpted into larger-than-life statues of eagles, swans and other birds. There was even an intricate sugar model of the Kremlin, with figures of tiny people coming and going. In her private apartments above the banqueting halls, the Tsaritsa Natalya gave a separate reception for the wives and daughters of the boyars, handing plates of sweets to her guests on their departure.

Soon afterward, the subject of all this celebration, surrounded by his own small, private household staff, was moved into his suite of rooms. He had a governess, a wet nurse—"a good and clean woman with sweet and healthy milk"—and a staff of dwarfs especially trained to act as servants and playmates to the royal children. When Peter was two, he and his retinue, now grown to include fourteen attending gentlewomen, moved into a grander Kremlin apartment—the walls hung with deep red fabrics, the furniture upholstered in crimson and embroidered with threads of gold and bright blue. Peter's clothes—miniature caftans, shirts, vests, stockings and caps—were cut from silk, satin and velvet, embroidered with silver and gold, buttoned and tasseled with sewn clusters of pearls and emeralds.

A doting mother, a proud father and a pleased Matveev competed to lavish gifts on the child, and Peter's nursery soon overflowed with elaborate models and toys. In one corner stood a carved wooden horse with a leather saddle studded with silver nails and a bridle decorated with emeralds. On a table near the window rested an illuminated picture book,

painstakingly made for him by six icon painters. Music boxes and a small, elegant clavichord with copper strings were brought from Germany. But Peter's favorite toys and his earliest games were military. He liked to bang on cymbals and drums. Toy soldiers and forts, model pikes, swords, arquebuses and pistols spread across his tables and chairs and floor. Next to his bed, Peter kept his most precious toy, given to him by Matveev, who had bought it from a foreigner: a model of a boat.

Intelligent, active and noisy, Peter grew rapidly. Most children walk at around one year; Peter walked at seven months. His father liked taking this healthy little Tsarevich with him on excursions around Moscow and to the royal villas outside the capital. Sometimes he went to Preobrazhenskoe, the informal retreat where Matveev had built a summer theater; this quiet place on the banks of the Yauza River beyond the German Suburb was Natalya's favorite. But more often he was taken to the architectural marvel of Alexis' reign, the huge palace at Kolomenskoe.

This immense building, constructed entirely of wood, was regarded by Russian contemporaries as the Eighth Wonder of the World. Standing on a bluff overlooking a bend in the Moscow River, it was an exotic jumble of shingled onion domes, tent roofs, steep pyramidal towers, horseshoe arches, vestibules, latticed stairways, balconies and porches, arcades, courtyards and gateways. A separate three-storied building, with two peaked towers, served as the private apartment of Peter and his half-brother Ivan. Although from the outside it seemed a crazy quilt of old Russian architecture, the palace had many modern features. There were baths not only for members of the family, but also for the servants (the palace of Versailles, constructed at roughly the same time, was built without either baths or toilets). The wooden walls of the Kolomenskoe palace were pierced by 3,000 mica-paned windows, and light streamed in on 270 rooms decorated in modern, secular style. Brightly painted scenes decorated the ceilings, mirrors and velvet drapes hung on the walls, interspersed with portraits of Julius Caesar and Alexander the Great. The silver throne, studded with gems, on which Alexis received his visitors was flanked by two giant bronze lions. When the Tsar pushed a lever, the eyes of these mechanical beasts would roll, their jaws would open, and from their throats came a hoarse, brassy roar.*

Natalya preferred the less formal daily routine in these suburban palaces to that in the Kremlin. Hating the stuffy air of the Tsaritsa's closed carriage, she raised its curtains—in public—and was soon riding to and from the country, and once even in a state procession, in an uncovered carriage with her husband and child. Because it was easier for her to watch, Alexis re-

---

* In 1771, exactly 100 years after it was built, the great wooden palace was torn down by Catherine the Great.

ceived foreign ambassadors at Kolomenskoe rather than at the Kremlin. In 1675, the procession of the arriving Austrian ambassador was deliberately slowed as it passed the window where the Tsaritsa sat, so that she might have more time to observe. This same diplomat, waiting to be presented to the Tsar, caught a glimpse of Peter: "The door opened suddenly and Peter, three years old, a curly-headed boy, was seen for a moment holding his mother's hand."

Later that year, Peter was regularly seen in public. Alexis had ordered several of the large, gilded court carriages used by other contemporary European monarchs. Matveev, knowing exactly how to please, thereupon ordered a miniature copy of one of these carriages and presented it to Peter. This tiny coach, "inset with gold ornament, drawn by four dwarf ponies, with four dwarfs riding at the side and another dwarf behind," became a favorite sight on state occasions.

Alexis had five years with Natalya Naryshkina. A second child, named Natalya after her mother, was born and lived; a third child, again a daughter, was born and died. At court, the effect of the marriage had been strongly felt. The austere, painfully religious quality of Alexis' earlier years gave way to a new, more relaxed spirit, a greater readiness to accept Western ideas, entertainments and techniques. But the greatest effect was on the Tsar himself. Marriage to this young wife revived and delighted him. The last years of his life were the happiest.

SUDDENLY, WHEN PETER was only three and a half, the serenity of his nursery life was shattered. On Epiphany in January 1676, Tsar Alexis, at forty-seven, healthy and active, took part in the annual ceremony of the blessing of the waters of the Moscow River. Standing in the frozen winter air during the long ceremony, he caught a chill. A few days later, in the middle of the performance of a play, the Tsar left the Kremlin theater and went to bed. At first, the illness did not seem dangerous. Nevertheless, it grew steadily worse, and after ten days, on February 8, Tsar Alexis died.

At a stroke, Peter's world changed. He had been the adored small son of a father who doted on his mother; now he was the potentially troublesome offspring of his dead father's second wife. The successor to the throne was fifteen-year-old Fedor, the semi-invalid eldest surviving son of Maria Miloslavskaya. Although Fedor had never been well, in 1674 Alexis had formally declared him to be of age, recognized him as heir and presented him as such to his subjects and the foreign ambassadors. At that time, it had seemed only a formality; Fedor's health was so delicate and Alexis' so good that few thought the delicate son would live to succeed the robust father.

But now it had happened: Fedor was Tsar, and the great pendulum of

power had swung back again from Naryshkin to Miloslavsky. Although his legs were so swollen that he had to be carried to his coronation, Fedor was crowned without opposition. The Miloslavskys came flooding triumphantly back to office. Fedor himself bore no ill-will against his stepmother, Natalya, or his little half-brother, Peter, but he was only fifteen and could not completely resist the power of his Miloslavsky relatives.

At the head of this clan stood his uncle Ivan Miloslavsky, who had hastened back from his post as Governor of Astrachan to replace Matveev as chief minister. That Matveev himself, as effective leader of the Naryshkin party, would in turn be banished to some ceremonial post was expected; it was an accepted accompaniment to the swing of the pendulum; it would balance the sending of Miloslavsky to Astrachan. The Tsaritsa Natalya, therefore, was saddened but resigned when her foster father was ordered to depart for Siberia to become Governor of Verkoture, a province in the northwestern part of that immense territory. But she was shocked and terrified when she learned that, en route to his new post, Matveev had been overtaken by new orders from Ivan Miloslavsky: Matveev was to be arrested, stripped of all his property and conducted as a state prisoner to Pustozersk, a remote town north of the Arctic Circle. (Actually, Ivan Miloslavsky's fear of his powerful rival had driven him even further: he had tried to have Matveev condemned to death, charging him with theft from the Treasury, the use of magic and even an attempt to poison Tsar Alexis. Ivan Miloslavsky pressed young Fedor hard, but the Tsar refused the death sentence and Miloslavsky had to settle for Matveev's imprisonment.)

Deprived of their powerful champion, and with their other supporters pushed from office, Natalya and her two children faded from public view. At first, Natalya feared for her children's physical safety; her son, three-and-a-half-year-old Peter, remained the Naryshkin party's hope for the future. But as time passed, the Tsaritsa relaxed; the life of a royal prince was still considered sacred, and Tsar Fedor never exhibited toward his newly poor relations anything but sympathy and kindness. They remained in the Kremlin, cloistered in their private apartments. There Peter began his education. At that time in Muscovy, most people, even among the gentry and the clergy, were illiterate. In the nobility, education rarely consisted of more than reading, writing and a smattering of history and geography. Instruction in grammar, mathematics and foreign languages was reserved for religious scholars who needed these tools to grapple with theology. There were exceptions: two of Tsar Alexis' children, Fedor and his sister the Tsarevna Sophia, had been placed in the hands of famous theological scholars from Kiev, had received a thorough classical education and could speak the foreign languages of a truly learned seventeenth-century Muscovite, Latin and Polish.

Peter's education began simply. At three, when his father was still alive, he had been given a primer to start learning the alphabet. When he reached five, Tsar Fedor, who was his godfather as well as his half-brother, said to Natalya, "Madam, it is time our godson started his lessons." Nikita Zotov, a clerk who worked in the tax-collection department, was selected as Peter's tutor. Zotov, an amiable, literate man who knew the Bible well but was not a scholar, was overwhelmed at being chosen for his role. Trembling, he was led to the Tsaritsa, who received him with Peter at her side. "You are a good man well versed in the Holy Writ," she said, "and I entrust to you my only son." Whereupon Zotov flung himself on the ground and burst into tears. "Matushka," he cried, "I am not worthy to look after such a treasure!" The Tsaritsa gently raised him up and told him that Peter's lessons would begin the next day. To encourage Zotov, the Tsar gave him a suite of apartments and raised him to the rank of minor nobleman, the Tsaritsa presented him with two complete sets of new clothes and the Patriarch gave him 100 roubles.

On the following morning, with both Tsar and Patriarch present to watch, Zotov gave Peter his first lesson. The new schoolbooks were sprinkled with holy water, Zotov bowed low to his small pupil and the lesson began. Zotov started first with the alphabet and, as time passed, went on to the Prayer Book and the Bible. Long passages of Holy Scripture, drilled into Peter's early memory, remained with him permanently; forty years later, he could recite them by heart. He was taught to sing the magnificent Russian choral litany, and he took great pleasure in this talent. In later years, traveling through Russia, Peter often attended services in country churches. His practice on these occasions was to stride straight up to the choir and sing along in a loud voice.

Zotov's assignment had been only to teach Peter to read and write, but he found his pupil eager to go further. Peter constantly urged Zotov to tell him more stories of Russian history, of battles and heroes. When Zotov mentioned the boy's enthusiasm to Natalya, she commissioned master engravers from the Ordnance Office to compose books of colored drawings depicting foreign cities and palaces, sailing ships, weapons and historical events. Zotov placed this collection in Peter's room so that when the boy was bored with his regular lessons, these books could be brought out, looked at and discussed. A giant globe, taller than a man, sent to Tsar Alexis from Western Europe, was brought to the schoolroom for Peter to study. Its depiction of the geography of Europe and Africa was remarkably accurate. The details of the eastern coast of North America were also correct—Chesapeake Bay, Long Island and Cape Cod were all precisely drawn—but farther west the lines became more inexact. California, for example, was shown as separate from the rest of the continent.

In the schoolroom, Zotov won Peter's deep affection, and for as long

as the tutor lived, Peter kept him close. Zotov has been criticized for giving his pupil an inferior education, inadequate to the needs of a boy who would be tsar, yet at the time of these lessons Peter stood behind his two half-brothers, Fedor and Ivan, in the succession. His education, though less severely classical than that given to Fedor and Sophia, was far better than that of the average Russian nobleman. Most important, it was perhaps the best education for a mind like Peter's. He was not a scholar, but he was unusually open and curious, and Zotov stimulated this curiosity; it is doubtful that anyone could have done better. Strange though it may seem, when this royal prince who was to become an emperor reached manhood, he was, in large part, a self-taught man. From his earliest years, he himself had chosen what he wished to learn. The mold which created Peter the Great was not made by any parent, tutor or counselor; it was cast by Peter himself.

BETWEEN CLASSROOM AND PLAY in the Kremlin and at Kolomenskoe, Peter's life passed uneventfully during the six years (1676–1682) of Fedor's reign. Fedor seemed very much his father's son—mild-mannered, indulgent and relatively intelligent, having been educated by the leading scholars of the day. Unfortunately, his scurvy-like disease frequently forced him to rule Russia lying on his back.

Nevertheless, Fedor did carry out one great reform, the abolition of the medieval system of precedence, a crushing weight on public administration, which decreed that noblemen could only accept state offices or military commands according to their rank. And to prove his rank, every boyar jealously guarded his family records. There were endless squabbles, and it became impossible to put capable men in key positions because others, citing higher rank, would refuse to serve under them. This system enshrined incompetence, and in the seventeenth century, in order to field an army at all, the tsars had been forced to set the system aside temporarily and declare that wartime commands would be assigned "without precedence."

Fedor wanted to make these temporary waivers permanent. He appointed a commission which recommended the permanent abolition of precedence; then he called a special council of boyars and clergy and personally urged the abolition for the welfare of the state. The Patriarch enthusiastically supported him. The boyars, suspicious and reluctant to give up the hallowed prerogatives of rank, grudgingly agreed. Fedor ordered that all family documents, service books and anything pertaining to previous precedence and rank be surrendered. Before the eyes of the Tsar, the Patriarch and the council, these were wrapped in bundles, carried into a Kremlin courtyard and tossed into the flames of a bonfire. Fedor decreed that thereafter offices and power would be distributed on a basis of merit

and not of birth, a principle which Peter would subsequently make the foundation of his own military and civilian administration. (Ironically, many boyars, seeing their ancient privileges go up in smoke, silently cursed Fedor and the Miloslavskys and thought of the young Peter as a potential savior of the old ways.)

Although he had married twice in his brief life, Fedor died without an heir. His first wife died in childbirth, followed a few days later by her newborn son. The death of this infant and Fedor's declining health increased the uneasiness of the Miloslavskys, who urged Fedor to marry again. He agreed, despite the warnings of doctors that the exertions of marriage would kill him, because he had fallen in love with a beautiful, high-spirited, fourteen-year-old girl. Martha Apraxina was not the choice of the Miloslavskys; rather she was a goddaughter of Matveev, and she asked, as a condition of her marriage, that the imprisoned statesman be pardoned and his property restored. Fedor agreed, but before the godfather could arrive in Moscow to congratulate the bride in person, the Tsar, two and a half months after his wedding, was dead.

Since Michael Romanov's accession in 1613, each tsar had been succeeded by his eldest surviving son: Michael had been succeeded by his eldest surviving son, Alexis, and Alexis by his eldest surviving son, Fedor. In each case, before his own death, the tsar had formally presented this eldest son to the people and officially designated him the heir to the throne. But now Fedor had died without leaving a son or designating an heir.

The two surviving candidates were Fedor's sixteen-year-old brother, Ivan, and his ten-year-old half-brother, Peter. Normally, Ivan, who was six years older than Peter as well as being the son of Alexis' first wife, would have been the uncontested choice. But Ivan was nearly blind, lame and spoke with difficulty, whereas Peter was active, glowing and big for his age. More important, the boyars knew that, whichever boy ascended the throne, the actual power would be in the hands of a regent. By now, most of them were antagonistic to Ivan Miloslavsky and preferred Matveev, who, under the nominal regency of the Tsaritsa Natalya, would wield power if Peter became tsar.

The decision came immediately after the boyars' final leavetaking of Tsar Fedor. One by one, the boyars passed the bed on which the dead Tsar lay, stopping to kiss the cold white hand. Then the Patriarch Joachim and his bishops entered the crowded room, and Joachim posed the formal question, "Which of the two princes shall be tsar?" Arguments followed; some supported the Miloslavskys, saying that Ivan's claim was strongest; others urged that it was impractical and foolish to continue the rule of the Russian state from a sickbed. The discussion grew hot, and finally, out of the uproar, the cry was heard: "Let the people decide!"

In theory, "the people" meant that the tsar should be elected by a

Zemsky Sobor, an Assembly of the Land, a gathering of noblemen, merchants and townspeople from all parts of the Muscovite state. It was an Assembly of the Land which in 1613 had persuaded the first Romanov, sixteen-year-old Michael, to accept the throne, and which had ratified the succession of Alexis. But such an assembly could not be gathered for weeks. Thus, at that moment, "the people" meant the Moscow crowd massed outside the palace windows.

The bells of the Ivan the Great bell tower sounded, and the Patriarch, the bishops and the boyars walked to the porch at the top of the Red Staircase overlooking Cathedral Square. Looking out over the crowd, the Patriarch cried, "The Tsar Fedor Alexeevich of blessed memory is dead. He leaves no heirs but his brothers, the Tsarevich Ivan Alexeevich and the Tsarevich Peter Alexeevich. To which of the two princes do you give the rule?" There were loud shouts of "Peter Alexeevich" and a few cries of "Ivan Alexeevich," but the shouts for Peter became louder and drowned out the others. The Patriarch thanked and blessed the crowd. The choice was made.

Inside, the newly elected ten-year-old sovereign waited. His short, curly hair framed his round, tanned face with the large black eyes, the full lips, the wart on the right cheek. He reddened with self-consciousness when the Patriarch approached and began to speak. The churchman formally announced the death of the Tsar, his own election, and concluded, "In the name of the whole people of the Orthodox Faith, I beg you to be our tsar." Peter refused at first, saying that he was too young and that his brother would be better able to rule. The Patriarch insisted, saying, "Lord, reject not our petition." Peter was silent, his blush grew deeper. Minutes passed. Gradually, the people in the room understood that Peter's silence meant that he had accepted.

The crisis had passed. Peter was tsar, his mother would be regent and Matveev would rule. This is what everyone present believed at the end of that tumultuous day. But they had reckoned without the Tsarevna Sophia.

3

"A MAIDEN
OF GREAT INTELLIGENCE"

THERE WAS NO TYPICAL Russian woman; Russian blood was a mixture of Slav, Tatar, Balt and others. Ideally, perhaps, a Russian woman was fair and comely, with light chestnut hair, and her figure, once past girlhood, was generous. In part, this was because Russian men liked strong women with big bosoms, and in part because their shapes, unmolded by stays, were free to expand as nature decreed. Western visitors, accustomed to the corseted waists of Versailles, St. James's, and the Hofburg, found Russian women bulky.

They were not uninterested in appearing beautiful. They dressed in long, flowing bright-colored sarafans embroidered with golden threads. Billowing sleeves flared out from the shoulders and would have covered the hands had they not been held at the wrist by glittering bracelets. The gowns worn over these sarafans were of velvet, taffeta or brocade. Girls wore their hair in a single long braid with a ring of flowers or a ribbon. A married woman was never bareheaded. Indoors, she wore a cloth headdress; when she went out, she donned a kerchief or a rich fur hat. They daubed their cheeks with red to enhance their beauty, and wore the handsomest earrings and most valuable rings which their husbands could afford.

Unfortunately, the higher a lady's rank and the more gorgeous her wardrobe, the less likely she was to be seen. The Muscovite idea of women, derived from Byzantium, had nothing of those romantic medieval Western conceptions of gallantry, chivalry and the Court of Love. Instead, a woman was regarded as a silly, helpless child, intellectually void, morally irresponsible and, given the slightest chance, enthusiastically promiscuous. This puritanical idea that an element of evil lurked in all little girls affected their earliest childhood. In good families, children of opposite sexes were never allowed to play together—to preserve the boys from contamination. As they grew older, girls, too, were subject to contamination, and even the most innocent contact between youths and maidens was forbidden. Instead, to preserve their purity while teaching them prayer, obedience and a few

useful skills such as embroidery, daughters were kept under lock and key. A song described them "sitting behind thirty locked doors, so that the wind may not ruffle their hair, nor the sun burn their cheeks, nor the handsome young men entice them." Thus they waited, ignorant and undefiled, until the day came to thrust them into the hands of a husband.

Usually, a girl was married in the full bloom of adolescence to a man she had not met until all the major parties to the marriage—her father, the bridegroom and the bridegroom's father—had made the decision final. The negotiations might have been lengthy; they involved critical matters such as the size of the dowry and guarantees of the bride's virginity. If, subsequently, in the not necessarily expert opinion of the young bridegroom, the girl had had previous experience, he could ask that the marriage be voided and the dowry returned. This meant a messy lawsuit; far better to examine carefully in advance and be absolutely sure.

When everything was settled, the young wife-to-be, her face covered with a linen veil, was summoned into her father's presence to be introduced to her future husband. Taking a small whip, the father struck his daughter lightly on the back, saying, "My daughter, this is the last time you shall be admonished by the authority of your father beneath whose rule you have lived. Now you are free of me, but remember that you have not so much escaped from my sway as passed beneath that of another. Should you not behave as you ought to toward your husband, he in my stead will admonish you with this whip." Whereupon the father handed the whip to the bridegroom, who, according to custom, nobly declared that he "believes he will have no need of this whip." Nevertheless, he accepted it as a gift from his father-in-law, and attached it to his belt.

On the wedding eve, the bride was brought by her mother to the bridegroom's house with her trousseau and the nuptial bed. In the morning, heavily veiled, she went through the ceremony, pledging fidelity by exchanging rings and then falling at her husband's feet, touching her forehead to his shoes in a gesture of subjugation. With his wife on the floor beneath him, the bridegroom benevolently covered her with the hem of his coat, acknowledging his obligation to support and protect this humble creature. Then, while the guests began to banquet, the newlyweds went straight to bed. They were given two hours, after which the doors of their room flew open and the guests crowded around, wanting to know whether the husband had found his wife a virgin. If the answer was yes, congratulations were lavished upon them, they were led to a bath of sweet-smelling herbs and then to the banquet hall to join in the feast. If the answer was no, everyone, but most of all the bride, suffered.

Once married, the new wife assumed her place in her husband's home, as an animate domestic chattel, and possessed no rights except through him. Her functions were to look after his house, see to his comfort and

bear his children. If she had sufficient talent, she ruled as mistress over the servants; if not, in the master's absence the servants took charge without asking or telling her anything. When her husband had an important guest, she was permitted to appear before dinner, dressed in her best ceremonial robes, bearing a welcoming cup on a silver tray. Standing before the guest, she bowed, handed the cup, offered her cheek for a Christian kiss and then wordlessly withdrew. When she bore a child, those who feared her husband or wanted his patronage came to congratulate him and present a gold piece for the newborn. If the gift was generous, the husband had good reason to be happy with his excellent wife.

If the husband was not happy, there were procedures for improving his situation. In most cases, where only a mild correction was necessary, he could beat her. The *Domostroy* or Household Management Code, dating from 1556 and attributed to a monk named Sylvester, gave specific advice to the heads of Muscovite families on numerous domestic matters, from preserving mushrooms to disciplining wives. On the latter issue, it recommended that "disobedient wives should be severely whipped, though not in anger." Even a good wife should be taught by her husband "by using the whip to her from time to time, but nicely, in secret, and in a polite fashion, avoiding blows of the fist which cause bruises." In the lower classes, Russian men beat their wives on the slightest pretext. "Some of these barbarians will tie up their wives by the hair of their head, and whip them stark naked," wrote Dr. Collins. Sometimes the beatings were so severe that the woman died; then the husband was free to remarry. Inevitably, a few wives, tormented beyond endurance, struck back and murdered their husbands. The number was small because a new law, published early in Alexis' reign, dealt harshly with such criminals: a wife guilty of murdering her husband was buried alive in the earth with only her head protruding above the ground, and left to die.

In serious cases, where a wife was so hopelessly unsatisfactory that she was not worth beating, or where the husband had found another woman whom he preferred, the solution was divorce. To divorce his wife, an Orthodox husband had simply to thrust her, willing or not, into a convent. There, her hair was sheared off, she was dressed in a long black gown with wide sleeves and enshrouding hood and she became, in the eyes of the world, dead. For the rest of her life, she lived amid the crowds of women in nunneries, some of them young girls forced to abandon life by greedy brothers or relatives who wished to avoid sharing an estate or paying a dowry, others simply wives who had run away and preferred anything to going back to their husbands.

Once his wife was "dead," a husband was free to remarry, but this freedom was not unlimited. The Orthodox Church permitted a man two dead wives or two divorces, but his third wife had to be his last. Thus, a

husband who had violently abused his first two wives was likely to handle his third with care; if she died or ran away, he could never marry again.

This isolation of women and disdain for their companionship had a grim effect on seventeenth-century Russian men. Family life was stifled, intellectual life was stagnant, the coarsest qualities prevailed and men, deprived of the society of women, found little else to do but drink. There were exceptions. In some households, intelligent women played a key role, albeit behind the scenes; in a few, strong women even dominated weak husbands. Ironically, the lower a woman stood in the social scale, the greater her chance for equality. In the lower classes, where life was a struggle for simple existence, women could not be pushed aside and treated as useless children; their brains and muscle were needed. They were considered inferior, but they lived side by side with men. They bathed with men, and ran laughing through the snow with men, completely naked. On endless winter evenings, they joined the men in feasting and drinking around the stove, packed together, allowing embraces from whoever was next to them, laughing, crying and finally falling asleep in drunken communion. If a husband was cruel, still he had once been kind; if he beat her, it permitted her to forgive again. "Yes, he beats me, but then he falls on his knees with tears in his eyes and begs my forgiveness. . . ."

At the summit of the female social order stood the tsaritsa, the wife of the tsar. Her life, although more comfortable than that of her lesser sisters, was no more independent. She devoted her time to her family, to prayer and to good deeds and charities. Within the palace, she directed the household, seeing to her own wardrobe and watching over that of her husband and children. Usually, the tsaritsa herself was skilled with a needle and embroidered robes and vestments, either for the tsar or the church; in addition, she supervised the labor of many seamstresses. It was her duty to give generously to the poor and to oversee the marriages and ensure the dowries of the numerous young women of her household. Like her husband, the tsaritsa spent much time in church, but, even with all her duties, there were many empty hours. To pass the time, the tsaritsa played cards, listened to stories, watched the singing and dancing of her maidens and laughed at the clowning of her dwarfs dressed in bright-pink costumes with red leather boots and green cloth caps. At the end of the day, after vespers and when the tsar had finished his work, the tsaritsa might be summoned to visit her husband.

Whether or not marriage was a desirable state for a seventeenth-century Russian woman was arguable. But there were some women in Russian society who would never know. By rank, they were at the very top, the sisters and daughters of the tsar. By fortune, who can say? None of these princesses, called tsarevnas, would ever meet a man, fall in love, marry

and have children. Similarly, none would ever be haggled over, marketed, legally raped, beaten or divorced. The barrier was their rank. They could never marry Russians beneath their own royal rank (although the tsar could choose a wife from the nobility), and they were barred by religion from marrying foreigners—by definition, infidels or heretics. Therefore, from birth they were doomed to live their lives in the narrow gloom of the terem, an apartment, usually at the top of a large Russian house, reserved for women. There, they passed their time in prayer, embroidery, gossip and boredom. They would never know anything of the wider world, and the world would notice their existence only when it was announced that they had been born or died.

Except for their close male relatives and the patriarch and a few selected priests, no man ever set eyes on these shadowy royal recluses. The terem itself was an exclusively female world. When a tsarevna was ill, the shutters were drawn and the curtains closed to darken the room and hide the patient. If it was necessary to take her pulse or examine her body, it had to be done through a covering of gauze so that no male fingers would touch the naked female skin. Early in the morning or late at night, the tsarevnas went to church, hurrying through closed corridors and secret passageways. In cathedrals or chapels, they stood screened behind red silk curtains in a dark part of the choir to avoid the gaze of male eyes. When they walked in state processionals, it was behind the moving silken walls of closed canopies. When they left the Kremlin on pilgrimage to a convent, it was in specially constructed bright-red carriages or sledges, closed like movable cells, surrounded by maids and men on horseback to clear the roads.

THE TEREM SHOULD HAVE BEEN Sophia's world. Born in 1657, she lived there in early childhood, one of a dozen princesses—the sisters, aunts and daughters of Tsar Alexis—all caged behind its tiny windows. There seemed no reason for her rare and extraordinary quality. She was simply the third of Alexis' eight daughters by Maria Miloslavskaya; she was one of six who survived. Like her sisters, she should have been equipped with a rudimentary female education and passed her life in anonymous seclusion.

And yet Sophia was different. That strange alchemy which, for no apparent reason, lifts one child out of a large family and endows it with a special destiny had created Sophia. She had the intelligence, the ambition, the decisiveness which her feeble brothers and anonymous sisters so overwhelmingly lacked. It was almost as if her siblings had been drained of normal health, vitality and purpose in order to magnify these qualities in Sophia.

From an early age, it was apparent that Sophia was exceptional. As a child, she somehow persuaded her father to break the terem tradition and

permit her to share the lessons of her brother Fedor, who was four years younger. Her tutor was the eminent scholar Simeon Polotsky, a monk of Polish ancestry from the famous academy in Kiev. Polotsky found her "a maiden of great intelligence and the most delicate understanding, with an accomplished masculine mind." Together with a younger monk, Sylvester Medvedev, Polotsky taught his pupil theology, Latin, Polish and history. She became acquainted with poetry and drama and even performed in religious plays. Medvedev shared Polotsky's view that the Tsarevna was a student with "marvelous understanding and judgment."

Sophia was nineteen when her father died and her fifteen-year-old brother became Tsar Fedor II. Soon after Fedor's coronation, the Tsarevna began to emerge from the obscurity of the terem. Increasingly throughout his reign, she was seen in circumstances hitherto wholly unknown to women. She attended sessions of the boyar council. Her uncle Ivan Miloslavsky and the leading minister, Prince Vasily Golitsyn, included her in their conversations and decisions, so that her political views matured and she learned to judge the character of men. Gradually, she came to realize that her intellectual attainments and strength of will matched and even surmounted those of the men around her, that there was no reason, except her sex and the unbroken tradition in Muscovy that the autocrat be a man, to bar her from supreme power.

During the last week of Fedor's life, Sophia stayed at his bedside, acting as comforter, confidante and messenger, and became deeply involved in affairs of state. Fedor's death and the sudden elevation to the throne of her half-brother, Peter, rather than her full brother, Ivan, were terrible blows to Sophia. She genuinely mourned Fedor, who had been her classmate and friend as well as her brother; further, the promise of a Naryshkin restoration at court meant the end of any special status for her, a Miloslavsky princess. She would certainly have less contact with high officers of state like Prince Vasily Golitsyn, whom she had come to admire. Worse, because she and the new regent, the Tsaritsa Natalya, disliked each other, she might even be sent back to the terem.

Desperately, Sophia sought another solution. She hurried to the Patriarch to complain of Peter's quick election to the throne. "This election is unjust," she protested. "Peter is young and impetuous. Ivan has reached his majority. *He* must be the tsar." Joachim said that the decision could not be changed. "But at least let both rule!" begged Sophia. "No," decreed the Patriarch, "joint rule is ruinous. Let there be one tsar. It is thus pleasing to God." For the moment, Sophia had to retreat. A few days later, however, at Fedor's funeral, she made her feelings public. Peter, accompanied by his mother, followed the bier in the procession to the cathedral. Walking along, Natalya heard loud noises behind her and turned to find that Sophia had joined the procession without the moving canopy which traditionally screened a

daughter of a tsar from the public. In the open, only partially veiled, Sophia was weeping theatrically and calling on the crowd to witness her grief.

Sophia's act was unprecedented, and at the crowded cathedral Natalya retaliated. During the long burial service, Natalya took Peter by the hand and walked out. Later, she explained that her son was exhausted and hungry and to have remained would have been bad for his health, but the Miloslavskys were scandalized. The situation was made worse by Natalya's arrogant younger brother Ivan Naryshkin, only just recalled to court. "The dead," he said, referring to the entire Miloslavsky clan, "should bury the dead."

On leaving the cathedral, Sophia again gave vent to her grief, now mingled with bitter rage. "You see how our brother Tsar Fedor has suddenly gone from this world. His enemies have poisoned him. Have pity on us orphans. We have no father, nor mother, nor brother. Our elder brother, Ivan, has not been elected tsar, and if we are to blame, let us go live in other lands which are ruled over by Christian kings."

4

THE REVOLT
OF THE STRELTSY

THROUGHOUT THE FIRST HALF of Peter's life, the key to power in Russia was the Streltsy, the shaggy, bearded pikemen and musketeers who guarded the Kremlin and were Russia's first professional soldiers. They were sworn to protect "the government" in a crisis but often had difficulty deciding where the legitimate government lay. They were a kind of collective dumb animal, never quite sure who was its proper master, but ready to rush and bite anyone who challenged its own privileged position. Ivan the Terrible had formed these regiments to give a permanent professional core to the unwieldy feudal host which previous Muscovite rulers had led into battle. These older armies, consisting of squadrons of mounted noblemen and a horde of armed peasants, were summoned in the spring and sent home in the autumn. Usually, these summer soldiers, untrained and undisciplined, clutching whatever spear or axe lay at hand when they were mustered, fared badly against their better-equipped Western enemies, the Poles or the Swedes.

On guard or on parade, the Streltsy were a colorful sight. Each regiment had its own vivid colors: a caftan or full-length coat of blue, green or cherry, a fur-trimmed hat of the same color, breeches tucked into yellow boots turned up at the toe. Over the caftan, each soldier buckled a black leather belt from which to sling his sword. In one hand, he carried a musket or arquebus, in the other a halberd or pointed battle-axe.

Most of the Streltsy were simple Russians, living by the old ways, revering both tsar and patriarch, hating innovation and opposing reforms. Both officers and men were suspicious and resentful of the foreigners brought in to train the army in new weapons and tactics. They were ignorant of politics, but when they believed the country was veering from proper traditional paths, they easily convinced themselves that duty demanded their interference in affairs of state.

In peacetime, they had not enough to do. A few detachments were stationed on the Polish and Tatar frontiers, but the bulk was concentrated in Moscow, where they lived in special quarters near the Kremlin. By 1682,

they numbered 22,000—divided into twenty-two regiments of 1,000 men each—who with their wives and children were an enormous mass of idle soldiery and dependents quartered in the heart of the capital. They were coddled: the tsar provided the handsome log houses in which they lived, the tsar furnished their food, their clothing and their pay. In return they served as sentries in the Kremlin and guards at the city gates. When the tsar traveled in Moscow, the Streltsy lined his route; when he left the city, they provided an escort. They served as policemen, carrying small whips to break up fights. When the city caught fire, the Streltsy became firemen.

Gradually, with so much extra time on their hands, the Streltsy drifted into trade. Individual Strelets opened shops. As members of the army, they paid no taxes on their profits and became rich. Membership in the regiments became desirable and enlistment a privilege passed down on an almost hereditary basis. As soon as a boy was old enough, he was enrolled in his father's regiment. Naturally, the richer the Streltsy became, the more reluctant they were to resume their primary duties as soldiers. A Strelets with a profitable shop was likely to offer bribes rather than accept some arduous assignment. The Streltsy officers also profited from this large pool of manpower. Some used the idle musketeers as servants, others to build their houses or tend their gardens. Sometimes the officers embezzled the soldiers' pay, and soldiers' formal complaints to the government were usually ignored and the petitioners punished.

This is exactly what had happened in May 1682, as the young Tsar Fedor lay on his deathbed. The Griboyedov Regiment presented a formal petition accusing their colonel, Semyon Griboyedov, of withholding half their pay and forcing them to work during Easter Week on a house he was building outside Moscow. The commander of the Streltsy, Prince Yury Dolgoruky, ordered the soldier presenting the petition to be whipped for insubordination. But this time, as the petitioner was being led to the knout, he passed a watching group of his regimental comrades. "Brothers," he cried, "why do you give me up? I gave the petition by your orders and for you!" Aroused, the Streltsy fell upon the guards and liberated the prisoner.

This incident inflamed the Streltsy Quarter. Seventeen regiments immediately accused their colonels of cheating or maltreatment and demanded punishment. The Regent Natalya's fledgling government, just taking office, inherited the crisis and floundered badly. Many boyars of the oldest families of Russia—the Dolgorukys, Repnins, Romodanovskys, Sheremetevs, Sheins, Kurakins and Urusovs—had rallied behind Peter and his mother, but none knew how to placate the Streltsy. In the end, desperate to blunt the soldiers' hostility, Natalya sacrificed the colonels. Without investigation, she ordered the colonels arrested and stripped of rank, and their property and wealth divided to meet the soldiers' claims. Two of the colonels, one of them Semyon Griboyedov, were publicly knouted, while twelve others were given

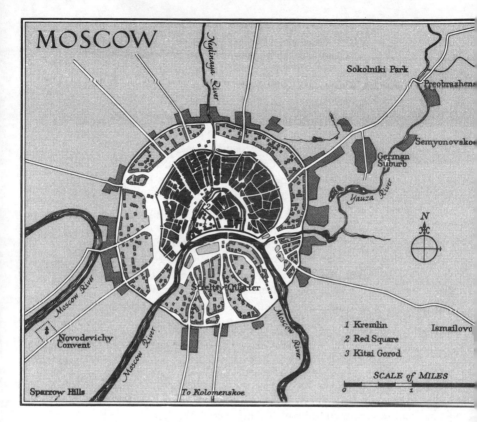

MOSCOW

Nalinaya River

Sokolniki Park

Preobrazhens

Semyonovskoe

German Suburb

Yauza River

N

Moscow River

Streltsy Quarter

Moscow River

Moscow River

Novodevichy Convent

1 Kremlin
2 Red Square
3 Kitai Gorod

Ismailovo

SCALE of MILES

0   1

Sparrow Hills   To Kolomenskoe

the lesser punishment of being beaten with sticks, called batogs, at the direction of the Streltsy themselves. "Beat them harder," they urged, until their officers fainted. Then, the Streltsy grumbled with satisfaction. "They have had enough. Let them go."

Allowing a mutinous soldiery to beat its officers was a risky way of restoring discipline. For the moment, the Streltsy were appeased, but in fact their new sense of power, their increased assurance that they were entitled and even obligated to purge the state of its enemies, had made them far more dangerous.

The Streltsy thought they knew who these enemies were: the boyars and the Naryshkins. Sinister stories had been passed among them. It was rumored that Fedor had not died naturally, as had been announced, but had been poisoned by foreign doctors with the connivance of the boyars and the Naryshkins. These same enemies had then pushed aside Ivan, the rightful heir, in favor of Peter. Now that their diabolical schemes had succeeded,

foreigners would be given power in the army and government, Orthodoxy would be degraded and trampled, and, worst of all, those faithful defenders of the old values in Muscovy, the Streltsy, would be horribly punished. These were stories which played on the traditional prejudices of the Streltsy. And other events were described in a manner calculated to arouse the soldiery. On taking office, Natalya had distributed wholesale new promotions in rank to all her Naryshkin relatives, even elevating her arrogant twenty-three-year-old younger brother Ivan to the rank of boyar. Ivan Naryshkin already was an object of dislike for his remark at Fedor's funeral. Now, fresh rumors spread: that he had rudely pushed the Tsarevna Sophia to the ground; that he had taken the crown and placed it on his own head, declaring that it looked better on him than on anyone else.

But the stories had a source, the rumors a purpose. Who was behind this effort to arouse the Streltsy? One instigator was Ivan Miloslavsky, who was keenly anxious to overthrow Peter, Natalya and the Naryshkin party. Having already been exiled himself during the previous period of Naryshkin dominance at court, he had retaliated by sending Matveev to six years of harsh internment in the Arctic; now, Matveev was returning to Moscow to act as chief advisor to the new Regent—Tsaritsa Natalya Naryshkina—and Ivan Miloslavsky knew what he could expect in this latest shift of power. Another plotter was Prince Ivan Khovansky, a vain, incessantly noisy man whose soaring ambitions were constantly thwarted by his own incompetence. Relieved of his post as Governor of Pskov, he was called before Tsar Alexis, who told him, "Everybody calls you a fool." Never willing to accept this valuation, convinced by the Miloslavskys that high office awaited him at their hands, he was an active supporter of their cause.

Surprisingly, the plot also involved Prince Vasily Golitsyn, a man of Western tastes, caught on the Miloslavsky side because of the enemies he had made. During Fedor's reign, Golitsyn had urged reforms. It was he who drew up the new organization of the army and proposed the abolition of precedence, and for this the boyars hated him. As the boyars now supported Natalya and the Naryshkins, Golitsyn was thrown among the Miloslavskys.

Ivan Miloslavsky, Ivan Khovansky and Vasily Golitsyn all had motives for inciting the Streltsy, but, should such a revolt succeed, none of them could step forward and rule the Russian state. Only one person was a member of the royal family, had been the confidante of Tsar Fedor and could act as regent if young Ivan mounted the throne. Only one person was now threatened with complete seclusion in a convent or terem and the extinction of all meaningful political or personal existence. Only one person had the intelligence and courage to attempt to overthrow an elected tsar. No one knows the exact extent of her involvement in the plot and the terrible events that followed; some say it was done on her behalf but without her

knowledge. But the circumstantial evidence is strong that the chief conspirator was Sophia.

Meanwhile, completely unaware, Natalya waited anxiously in the Kremlin for Matveev's return. On the day of Peter's election as tsar, she had sent messengers urging him to come quickly to Moscow. He started back, but his trip turned into a triumphal progress. Every town through which he passed offered thanksgiving services and a feast for the rehabilitated statesman. Finally, on the evening of May 11, after six years in exile, the old man reentered Moscow. Natalya greeted him as her savior and presented him to the ten-year-old Tsar, whom he had last seen as a child of four. Matveev's hair was white and his step was slow, but Natalya was certain that, with his experience and wisdom, with the prestige he enjoyed among both boyars and Streltsy, the old man would soon be able to establish order and harmony.

So it seemed for three days. During this time, Matveev's house was crowded with welcoming boyars, merchants and foreign friends from the German Suburb. The Streltsy, remembering him as an honorable former commander, sent delegations from the regiments to pay their respects. Even members of the Miloslavsky family came, with the exception of Ivan Miloslavsky, who sent word that he was ill. Matveev received them all with happy tears streaming down his face, while his house, cellars and courtyard overflowed with welcoming gifts. Peril seemed distant, but Matveev, newly arrived on the scene and still not in full control, underestimated the danger. Sophia and her party never relaxed, and the spark of revolt remained alive among the regiments. Matveev and Natalya, isolated in the Kremlin and enveloped in their happiness, did not feel the mounting tension, but others did. Baron Van Keller, the Dutch ambassador, wrote: "The discontent of the Streltsy continues. All public affairs are at a stand still. Great calamities are feared and not without cause, for the might of the Streltsy is great and no resistance can be opposed to them."

AT NINE O'CLOCK on the morning of May 15, the smoldering spark burst into flame. Two horsemen, Alexander Miloslavsky and Peter Tolstoy, both members of Sophia's intimate circle, galloped into the Streltsy Quarter, shouting, "The Naryshkins have murdered the Tsarevich Ivan! To the Kremlin! The Naryshkins will kill the whole royal family. To arms! Punish the traitors!"

The Streltsy Quarter erupted. Bells tolled urgently, battle drums began to beat. Men in caftans buckled on their armor and their sword belts, grasped their halberds, spears and muskets and assembled in the streets ready for battle. Some of the musketeers chopped off the handles of their long spears and halberds to make weapons deadlier at close range. Unfurling their broad regimental banners embroidered with pictures of the Virgin, and

beating their drums, they began to advance through the streets toward the Kremlin. As they approached, terrified citizens scurried out of their path. "We are going to the Kremlin to kill the traitors and murderers of the Tsar's family!" the soldiers shouted.

Meanwhile, within the offices and palaces of the Kremlin, the day was proceeding normally. No one had the slightest idea of what was happening in the city or of the doom moving toward them. The great gates of the citadel were wide open, with only a scattering of sentries. A meeting of the council of boyars had just ended and the boyars were sitting quietly in their offices and in the public rooms of the palaces, or strolling and talking while waiting for their midday dinner. Matveev was just leaving the council chamber and coming out onto the staircase leading to the bedchamber when he saw Prince Fedor Urusov running toward him, out of breath.

Urusov gasped out the news: The Streltsy had risen! They were marching through the city toward the Kremlin! Matveev, astounded and alarmed, returned to the palace to warn the Tsaritsa Natalya; he ordered the Patriarch to come immediately, the Kremlin gates to be closed, the duty regiment of Streltsy, the Stremyani Regiment, to man the walls and prepare to defend Peter, his family and the government.

Scarcely had Matveev finished speaking when three messengers arrived one after another, each bringing worse news than his predecessor. The first announced that the Streltsy were already nearing the Kremlin walls; the second, that the gates could not be closed so quickly; and the third, that everything was too late, for the Streltsy were already inside the Kremlin. As he spoke, hundreds of rebellious musketeers were surging through the open gates, up the hill and into Cathedral Square in front of the Facets Palace. As they came, the soldiers of the Stremyani Regiment were swept along with them, abandoning their posts and joining their comrades from other regiments.

At the top of the hill, the Streltsy poured into the square surrounded by the three cathedrals and the Ivan Bell Tower. Massed before the Red Staircase, which led from the square into the palace, they shouted, "Where is the Tsarevich Ivan? Give us the Naryshkins and Matveev! Death to the traitors!" Inside, the terrified boyars of the council, still uncertain as to what had provoked this violent assault, collected in the palace banquet hall. Prince Cherkassky, Prince Golitsyn and Prince Sheremetev were chosen to go out and ask the Streltsy what they wanted. They learned from the cries: "We want to punish the traitors! They have killed the Tsarevich and will kill the whole royal family! Give us the Naryshkins and the other traitors!" Understanding that in part the mutiny was due to a mistake, the delegation returned to the banquet hall and told Matveev. He in turn went to Natalya and advised her that the only way to calm the soldiers would be to show them that the Tsarevich Ivan was still alive and the royal family united. He

asked that she take both Peter and Ivan to the top of the Red Staircase and show them to the Streltsy.

Natalya trembled. To stand with her ten-year-old son in front of a howling mob of armed men calling for the blood of her family was an appalling assignment. Yet she had no choice. She took Peter by one hand and Ivan by the other and stepped onto the porch at the head of the staircase. Behind her stood the Patriarch and the boyars. When the Streltsy saw the Tsaritsa and the two boys, the shouting died and a confused murmur filled the square. In the hush, Natalya raised her voice and cried out, "Here is the Lord Tsar Peter Alexeevich. And here is the Lord Tsarevich Ivan Alexeevich. Thanks be to God, they are well and have not suffered at the hands of traitors. There are no traitors in the palace. You have been deceived."

A new clamor arose from the Streltsy. This time, the soldiers were arguing among themselves. A few, curious and bold, climbed the staircase or placed ladders against the porch and mounted to get a closer look at the helpless trio standing bravely before them. They wanted to be sure that Ivan was still truly alive. "Are you really Ivan Alexeevich?" they asked the pathetic boy. "Yes," he stammered in an almost inaudible voice. "Are you really Ivan?" they asked again. "Yes, I am Ivan," said the Tsarevich. Peter, standing only a few feet from the Streltsy, their faces and weapons level with his eyes, said nothing. Despite the tremble in his mother's hand, he remained rigid, staring calmly, showing no sign of fear.

Thoroughly bewildered by this confrontation, the Streltsy retreated down the steps. Obviously, they had been deceived—Ivan had not been murdered. There he stood, his hand held protectively by the Naryshkin Tsaritsa, whose family was supposed to have murdered him. There was no need for vengeance; all their glorious patriotic feelings began to seem foolishly out of place. A small group of Streltsy, not to be deterred from private vengeance against certain arrogant boyars, began to shout their names, but most stood silent and confused, staring uncertainly at the three figures on the porch above them.

Natalya stood there for another minute, gazing down at the sea of pikes and halberds before her. Then, having done what she could, she turned and led the two boys back into the palace. As soon as she disappeared, Matveev with his white beard and long robes stepped forward to the head of the staircase. Under Tsar Alexis, he had been a popular commander of the Streltsy, and many still remembered him favorably. He began to speak to them quietly, confidently, in a tone both proprietary and paternal. He reminded them of their loyal service in the past, of their reputation as defenders of the tsar, of their victories in the field. Without condemning them, more in sorrow than in anger, he asked how they could stain their great reputation by this rebellious tumult which was all the more lamentable

as it was based on rumor and falsehood. He stressed that there was no need for them to protect the royal family, which, as they had just seen with their own eyes, was unharmed and safe. There was no need to threaten murder or violence to anyone. Quietly, he advised them to disperse, go home and ask pardon for their actions of the day. He promised that such petitions would be accepted and the outburst explained as excessive, misplaced loyalty to the throne.

These confident, friendly words made a deep impression. The soldiers in front, who could hear them best, listened carefully and nodded in approval. In the rear, there still were loud arguments, while some shouted for silence so that they could hear Matveev. Gradually, as Matveev's words sank in, the entire mob became quiet.

When Matveev had finished, the Patriarch also spoke briefly, calling the Streltsy his children, admonishing them gently for their behavior, suggesting that they ask pardon and disperse. These words, too, were soothing, and it seemed that the crisis had passed. Matveev, sensing the better mood, saluted the Streltsy, turned and walked back into the palace to bring the good news to the distraught Tsaritsa. His departure was a fatal mistake.

As soon as Matveev disappeared, Prince Michael Dolgoruky, the son of the Streltsy commander, appeared at the top of the Red Staircase. Humiliated by the mutinous behavior of the troops, he was now in a towering rage and foolishly chose this moment to attempt to reestablish military discipline. In the roughest language, he cursed the men and commanded them to return to their homes. Otherwise, he threatened, the knout would fly.

Instantly, the calm created by Matveev dissolved in a roar of anger. The infuriated Streltsy remembered all their reasons for marching on the Kremlin: The Naryshkins were to be punished, hated boyars like Dolgoruky were to be destroyed. A torrent of frenzied Streltsy charged up the Red Staircase toward their commander. They seized him by his robe, lifted him above their heads and threw him over the balustrade onto the pikes of their comrades below. The crowd roared its approval, shouting, "Cut him to pieces!" Within a few seconds, the quivering body was butchered, bespattering everyone around with blood.

This first violent act unleashed savagery and madness. Brandishing sharp steel, lusting for more blood, the entire raging mass of the Streltsy stormed up the Red Staircase and into the palace itself. Their next victim was Matveev. He was standing in an anteroom of the banqueting hall talking to Natalya, who still held the hands of Peter and Ivan. Seeing the Streltsy rushing toward her shouting for Matveev, Natalya dropped Peter's hand and instinctively threw her arms around Matveev to protect him. The Streltsy pushed the two boys aside, tore the old man from Natalya and hurled her aside. Prince Cherkassky threw himself into the struggle, trying to pull Matveev free of his captors, but they flung him away. Before the eyes of

Peter and Natalya, Matveev was dragged out of the room and across the porch to the balustrade at the head of the Red Staircase. There, with exultant cries, they lifted him high in the air and hurled him down onto the upraised blades. Within seconds, the closest friend and prime minister of Peter's father, the guardian, confidant and chief support of Peter's mother, was hacked to pieces.

With Matveev dead, there was nothing to stop the Streltsy. They ran unopposed through the state halls, private apartments, churches, kitchens and even the closets of the Kremlin, clamoring for the blood of Naryshkins and boyars. Fleeing, the terrified boyars hid where they could. The Patriarch escaped into the Cathedral of the Assumption. Only Natalya, Peter and Ivan remained exposed, huddled together in a corner of the banqueting hall.

For most, there was no escape. The Streltsy hammered down locked doors, looked under beds and behind altars, thrusting their pikes into every dark space where a human being might be hiding. Those who were caught were dragged to the Red Staircase and thrown over the balustrade. Their bodies were dragged from the Kremlin through the Spassky Gate into Red Square, where they were tossed onto a growing pyramid of dismembered human parts. With sharp blades at their throats, the court dwarfs were forced to help find the Naryshkins. One of Natalya's brothers, Afanasy Naryshkin, was hidden behind the altar in the Church of the Resurrection. A dwarf leading a pack of Streltsy pointed him out, and the victim was dragged by his hair to the steps of the chancel, where he was cut to pieces. The Privy Councillor and Director of Foreign Affairs, Ivanov, his son Vasily and two colonels were killed on the porch between the banqueting hall and the Cathedral of the Annunciation. The aged boyar Romodanovsky was caught between the Patriarch's palace and the Miracle Monastery, dragged by his beard to the Cathedral Square and there raised and tossed onto spear points.

From the palace square inside the Kremlin, the bodies and pieces of bodies, often with swords and spears still sticking in them, were dragged through the Spassky Gate into Red Square. The passage of these grisly remains was accompanied by jeering cries of "Here comes the Boyar Artemon Sergeevich Matveev! . . . Here comes a Privy Councillor. Make way for him!" As the hideous pile in front of St. Basil's Cathedral grew higher and higher, the Streltsy shouted to the watching crowds, "These boyars loved to exalt themselves! This is their reward!"

By nightfall, even the Streltsy had begun to tire of the butchery. There was no place for them to sleep in the Kremlin, and most began to stream back through the city to their own houses. Despite the bloodshed, their day had been only a partial success. Only one Naryshkin, Natalya's brother Afanasy, had been found and killed. The chief object of their hatred, her brother Ivan, was still at large. Accordingly, they posted a heavy guard at

all the gates of the Kremlin, sealing off escape, and swore to return to continue the search the following day. Inside the Kremlin, Natalya, Peter and their Naryshkin relatives spent a night of terror. Kyril Naryshkin, the Tsaritsa's father, her brother Ivan and three younger brothers remained concealed in the room of Peter's eight-year-old sister, Natalya, where they had been hiding all day. They had not been found, but they could not escape. At dawn, the Streltsy marched again with beating drums into the Kremlin. Still looking for Ivan Naryshkin, the two foreign doctors who supposedly had poisoned Tsar Fedor, and other "traitors," they entered the Patriarch's house on Cathedral Square. Looking through his cellars and under his beds, they threatened his servants with spears and demanded to see the Patriarch himself. Joachim came out, dressed in his most glittering ceremonial robes, to tell them that there were no traitors to be found in his house and that if they wished to kill someone there, they should kill him.

And so the search went on, with the Streltsy continuing to hunt through the palace, and their prey, the Naryshkins, continuing to elude them. After two days spent in the dark closets of Peter's small sister's bedroom, Natalya's father, Kyril Naryshkin, three of his sons and the young son of Matveev moved to the apartments of Tsar Fedor's young widow, the Tsaritsa Martha Apraxina. There, Ivan Naryshkin cropped his long hair, and then the small group followed an old bedchamber woman down into a dark underground storeroom. It was the old woman's idea to bolt the door, but young Matveev said, "No. If you fasten the door, the Streltsy will suspect something, break down the door, find us and kill us." The refugees therefore made the room as dark as possible and crouched in the darkest corner, leaving the door open. "We had scarcely got there," said young Matveev, "before several Streltsy passed and looked quickly around. Some of them peered in through the open door, struck their spears into the darkness, but left quickly, saying, 'It is plain our men have already been here.'"

On the third day, when the Streltsy came again to the Kremlin, they were determined to wait no longer. Their leaders mounted the Red Staircase and delivered an ultimatum: Unless Ivan Naryshkin was surrendered immediately, they would kill every boyar in the palace. They made it clear that the royal family itself was in danger.

Sophia took charge. In front of the terrified boyars, she marched up to Natalya and declared in a loud voice, "Your brother will not escape the Streltsy. Nor is it right that we should perish on his account. There is no way out. To save the lives of all of us, you must give up your brother."

It was a tragic moment for Natalya. She had seen Matveev dragged away and slaughtered. Now she was asked to yield her brother to a frightful death. Terrible though the decision was, Natalya had no real choice. She ordered the servants to bring her brother to her. He came, and she led him into a palace chapel, where he received Holy Communion and the last rites, accepting her

decision and his coming death with great bravery. Weeping, Natalya handed him a holy icon of the Mother of God to hold in his hands when he went to meet the Streltsy.

Meanwhile, in the face of growing threats from the impatient Streltsy, the boyars became desperate. Why was Ivan Naryshkin lingering? At any moment, the Streltsy might carry out their threats. The aged Prince Jacob Odoevsky, gentle but frightened, came up to the weeping Natalya and Ivan and said, "How long, my lady, are you keeping your brother? For you must give him up. Go on quickly, Ivan Kyrilovich, and don't let us all be killed on your account."

Following Natalya and holding the icon, Ivan Naryshkin walked to the door where the Streltsy were waiting. As he appeared, the mob uttered a hoarse shout of triumph and surged forward. Before his sister's eyes, they seized their victim and began to beat him. He was dragged by his feet down the Red Staircase, through the palace square and into a torture room, where for a number of hours they kept him in agony, trying to extract a confession that he had murdered Tsar Fedor and plotted to take the throne. Through it all, Naryshkin clenched his teeth, groaned and said not a word Then Dr. Van Gaden, the alleged poisoner of Fedor, was brought in. Under torture, he promised to name accomplices, but as his words were being written down, his torturers, realizing the state he was in, cried, "What's the use of listening to him? Tear up the paper," and stopped the farce.

Ivan Naryshkin was now nearly dead; both his wrists and ankles had been snapped, and his hands and feet hung at strange angles. He and Van Gaden were dragged to Red Square and raised on the points of spears for a last presentation to the crowd. Lowered to earth, their hands and feet were chopped off with axes, the rest of their bodies cut into pieces and, in a final orgy of hate, the bloody remains were trampled into the mud.

The slaughter was over. One final time, the Streltsy assembled before the Red Staircase. Satisfied that they had avenged the "poisoning" of Tsar Fedor, stifled the plot of Ivan Naryshkin and killed all the men who they believed were traitors, they wished to proclaim their loyalty. From the courtyard, they cried, "We are now content. Let Your Tsarish Majesty do with the other traitors as may seem good. We are ready to lay down our heads for the Tsar, the Tsaritsa, the Tsarevich and the Tsarevnas."

Calm returned quickly. That same day, permission was given to bury the bodies which had been lying in Red Square since the first day of the massacre. Matveev's faithful servant trudged out carrying a sheet, in which he carefully collected all he could find of the mutilated body of his master. He washed the pieces and carried them on pillows to the parish church of St. Nicholas, where they were buried. The remaining Naryshkins went unharmed and unpursued. Three surviving brothers of Natalya and Ivan had escaped the Kremlin disguised as peasants. The Tsaritsa's father, Kyril

Naryshkin, was forced by Streltsy pressure to shave his head and take the vows of a monk, and, as Father Cyprian, was sent to a monastery 400 miles north of Moscow.

As part of the settlement, the Streltsy demanded their back pay, a sum of twenty roubles per man. Although it had no power to resist, the council of boyars could not grant this; there simply was no money. A compromise was reached by granting ten roubles per man. To raise this amount, the property of Matveev, Ivan Naryshkin and other boyars who had been killed was auctioned off, much of the Kremlin palace's silver plate was melted down and a general tax was placed on the population.

The Streltsy also demanded complete amnesty for their behavior and even a triumphal column in Red Square to honor their recent deeds. Inscribed on the column were to be the names of all their victims, who were to be labeled as criminals. Once again, the government dared not refuse, and the column was quickly erected.

Finally, in a move designed not only to conciliate the Streltsy but also to regain control over them, the musketeers were formally designated the Palace Guard. At the rate of two regiments a day, they were summoned to the Kremlin, where they were feasted as heroes in the banqueting hall and corridors of the palace. Sophia appeared before them to praise their loyalty and devotion to the throne. To honor them, she herself walked among the soldiers and handed them cups of vodka.

THUS, SOPHIA came to power. Now there was no opposition: Matveev was dead, Natalya was overwhelmed by the tragedy that had engulfed her family, Peter was a boy of ten. Yet Peter was still tsar. As he grew older, he would doubtless assert his power; the Naryshkins would wax in influence, and this Miloslavsky victory would prove only temporary. Accordingly, Sophia's plan required another step. On May 23, prompted by her agents, the Streltsy demanded a change in the occupancy of the Russian throne. In a petition sent to Khovansky, whom Sophia already had appointed as their commander, the Streltsy pointed out that there was a certain illegality to Peter's election as tsar; he was the son of the second wife, while Ivan, the son of the first wife and the older of the two boys, had been shunted aside. It was not proposed that Peter be dethroned; he was the son of a tsar, he had been elected and then proclaimed by the Patriarch. Instead, the Streltsy demanded that Peter and Ivan rule jointly as co-tsars. If the petition was not granted, they threatened to attack the Kremlin again.

The Patriarch, the archbishops and the boyars assembled in the Facets Palace to consider this new demand. In fact, they had no choice: The Streltsy could not be opposed. Besides, it was argued, to have two tsars might even be an advantage: while one went to war, the other could stay home and

govern the state. It was formally agreed that the two Tsars should reign jointly. The bells in the Ivan the Great Bell Tower were rung, and in the Assumption Cathedral prayers were sent up for the long life of the two most Orthodox Tsars Ivan Alexeevich and Peter Alexeevich. Ivan's name was mentioned first, as the Streltsy petition had asked that he be considered the senior of the two.

Ivan himself was dismayed by this new development. Handicapped both in speech and in sight, he was reluctant to take any part in government. He argued with Sophia that he much preferred a quiet, peaceful life, but under pressure he agreed that he would appear with his half-brother on state occasions and occasionally in council. Outside the Kremlin, the population, in whose name the Streltsy supposedly put forward the new joint arrangement, was astonished. Some laughed aloud at the idea of Ivan—whose infirmities were well known—being tsar.

There was the final, crucial question: As both boys were young, someone else would actually have to govern the state. Who would this be? Two days later, on May 29, another delegation of Streltsy appeared with a last demand: that because of the youth and inexperience of the two Tsars, the Tsarevna Sophia become the regent. The Patriarch and the boyars quickly consented. That same day, a decree announced that the Tsarevna Sophia Alexeevna had replaced the Tsaritsa Natalya as regent.

Thus, Sophia assumed the leadership of the Russian state. Although she was filling a vacancy which she and her agents had created, Sophia was now in fact the natural choice. No male Romanov had reached sufficient age to master the government, and she surpassed all the other princesses in education, talent and strength of will. She had shown that she knew how to launch and to ride the whirlwind of the Streltsy revolt. The soldiers, the government, even the people now looked to her. Sophia accepted, and for the next seven years this extraordinary woman governed Russia.

To CONFIRM and entrench her triumph, Sophia moved rapidly to institutionalize the new structure of power. On July 6, only thirteen days after the outbreak of the Streltsy revolt, the double coronation of the two boy Tsars, Ivan and Peter, took place. This hurriedly arranged ceremony was a curiosity unprecedented not only in the history of Russia but in the whole history of European monarchy. Never before had two co-equal male sovereigns been crowned. The day began at five a.m. when Peter and Ivan, dressed in long robes of cloth of gold embroidered with pearls, went to morning prayer in a palace chapel. From there they proceeded to the banqueting hall, where they solemnly promoted in rank a number of Sophia's lieutenants, including Ivan Khovansky and two Miloslavskys. The formal coronation procession moved out onto the porch and down the Red Staircase, two boys walking side by

side, ten-year-old Peter already taller than limping sixteen-year-old Ivan. Preceded by priests sprinkling holy water, Peter and Ivan made their way through the vast crowd packed into Cathedral Square to the door of the Assumption Cathedral, where the Patriarch, wearing a dazzling golden robe sewn with pearls, greeted the two Tsars and held out his cross for them to kiss. Inside, the lofty cathedral glowed with light filtering down from the high cupolas, flickering from hundreds of candles, reflected on the surfaces of thousands of jewels.

In the middle of the cathedral, directly under the enormous image of Christ with his hand upraised in blessing, on a raised platform covered with crimson cloth, a double throne awaited Ivan and Peter. It had been impossible in the short time available to create two exactly equal thrones, and so the silver throne of Tsar Alexis had been divided by a bar. Behind the seat on which both boys would sit, a curtain cloaked a small hiding place for their monitor, who, through a hole, could whisper the necessary instructions and responses during the ceremony.

The ceremony began with the two Tsars approaching the iconostasis and kissing the holiest of the icons. The Patriarch asked them to declare their faith, and each replied, "I belong to the Holy Orthodox Russian Faith." Then a series of lengthy prayers and hymns prepared for the supreme moment of the ceremony, the placing on the heads of the Tsars the golden crown of Monomakh.

This ancient, sable-fringed cap which supposedly had been given by an Emperor of Constantinople to Vladimir Monomakh, twelfth-century Grand Prince of Kiev, had been used in the coronation ceremonies of all Grand Princes of Moscow and, after Ivan IV took the new title of tsar, all the tsars of Russia.* Ivan was crowned, then Peter, then the cap was returned to Ivan's head and a replica, made especially for Peter, was placed on the brow of the younger Tsar. At the end of the service, the new rulers again kissed the cross, the holy relics and icons, and moved in procession to the Cathedral of the Archangel Michael to pay homage at the tombs of previous tsars, then to the Cathedral of the Annunciation and so back to the banqueting hall to feast and receive congratulations.

---

* The dual coronation of Ivan and Peter was the last time the Cap of Monomakh was used to crown a Russian autocrat. Peter's eighteenth- and nineteenth-century successors all took the imperial title as emperors and empresses. Many of them had new, much larger crowns made for themselves, culminating in the Imperial Crown of Russia ordered by Catherine the Great and used to crown the last seven Russian monarchs. Nevertheless, the Cap of Monomakh still carried enormous symbolic power, and although it was never again placed on a sovereign's head, it was carried in every coronation procession to symbolize the unbroken line which traced from the new monarch back to the Eastern Empire of Constantinople.

THE UPHEAVAL was over. In rapid and bewildering succession, a tsar had died; a ten-year-old boy, the minor child of a second wife, had been elected in his place; a savage military revolt had overthrown this election and spattered the young Tsar and his mother with the blood of their own family; and then, with all the jeweled panoply of state, the boy was crowned jointly with a frail and helpless older half-brother. Through all the horror, although he had been elected tsar, he was powerless to intervene.

The Streltsy revolt marked Peter for life. The calm and security of his boyhood were shattered, his soul was wrenched and seared. And its impact on Peter had, in time, a profound impact on Russia.

Peter hated what he had seen: the maddened, undisciplined soldiery of the old medieval Russia running wild through the Kremlin; statesmen and nobles dragged from their private chambers and bloodily massacred; Moscow, the Kremlin, the royal family, the Tsar himself at the mercy of ignorant, rioting soldiers. The revolt helped create in Peter a revulsion against the Kremlin with its dark rooms and mazes of tiny apartments lit by flickering candles, its population of bearded priests and boyars, its pathetically secluded women. He extended his hatred to Moscow, the capital of the Orthodox tsars, and to the Orthodox Church, with its chanting priests, wafting incense and oppressive conservatism. He hated the ancient Muscovite pomp and ceremony which could call him "next to God" but could not protect him or his mother when the Streltsy turned against them.

While Sophia ruled, Peter left Moscow, growing up in the countryside outside the city. Later, when Peter was master of Russia, his aversions had significant consequences. Years were to pass when the Tsar never set foot in Moscow, and, ultimately, Peter stripped Moscow of its rank. The ancient capital was replaced by a new city created by Peter on the Baltic. In a way, the Streltsy revolt helped to inspire the building of St. Petersburg.*

---

* A striking parallel to Peter's hatred of Moscow can be found in Louis XIV's abhorrence of Paris. In 1648, when Louis (like Peter in 1682) was ten years old, the revolt of the French parliament and nobility known as the Fronde erupted. Armies were raised to suppress the upheaval and then subsequently turned against the crown. At the height of the tumult, the boy King and his mother were besieged by a Paris mob. At night, with the sound of angry cries and the rattle of muskets in his ears, Louis was spirited out of Paris to Saint-Germain, where the King spent the night on a bed of straw.

Louis' biographers stress the powerful and lasting impression made on the boy by this event. Thereafter, he despised Paris and rarely set foot in the city. He built Versailles, and the great château became the capital of France, just as Peter avoided Moscow and built a new capital on the Neva. But as Peter's childhood ordeal was worse, so his reaction to it was far more sweeping. Louis built a great château close to Paris from which to rule; Peter built an entire city, far away.

5

THE GREAT SCHISM

SOPHIA WAS REGENT, and her regency began with an immediate test of her talent for rule. The Streltsy, who had brought her to power, now swaggered arrogantly through Moscow, assuming that any demand they might make would be instantly granted. The schismatic members of the Orthodox Church, or Old Believers, assumed that the triumph of the Streltsy over the government would bring a return to the old religion, a revival of the traditional Russian ritual and liturgy which had been condemned two decades before by the church establishment and suppressed by the power of the state. Sophia, no less than her father, Alexis, and her brother, Fedor, regarded the Old Believers as heretics and rebels. Yet, because many of the Streltsy—including their new commander, Prince Ivan Khovansky—were fervent Old Believers, it seemed likely that these two forces would combine to press their will on the fledgling regime.

Sophia handled the situation with courage and skill. She received the leaders of the Old Believers in the banqueting hall of the Kremlin palace and from her throne argued and shouted them into silence before dismissing them. Then, calling the Streltsy into her presence in detachments of a hundred at a time, she bribed them with money, with promises and with wine and beer which she herself served them from a silver tray. With these blandishments, she weaned the soldiers away from their aggressive support of the schismatic clergy, and once the Streltsy were pacified, Sophia ordered the leaders of the Old Believers seized. One was executed and the others dispersed into exile. Within nine weeks, Prince Khovansky was arrested, charged with insubordination and his head lay on the block.

This time Sophia had triumphed, but the struggle between the Old Believers and the established powers in church and state was not concluded; it persisted not only through her regency and the reign of Peter, but until the end of the imperial dynasty. It was rooted in the deepest religious feelings of the people, and is known in the history of the church and of Russia as the Great Schism.

CHRISTIANITY, if practiced in the ideal, seems especially suited to the Russian character. Russians are preeminently a pious, compassionate and humble people, accepting faith as more powerful than logic and believing that life is controlled by superhuman forces, be they spiritual, autocratic or even occult. Russians feel far less need than most pragmatic Westerners to inquire why things happen, or how they can be made to happen (or not to happen) again. Disasters occur and they accept; orders are issued and they obey. This is something other than brute docility. It stems rather from a sense of the natural rhythms of life. Russians are contemplative, mystical and visionary. From their observations and meditations, they have produced an understanding of suffering and death which gives a meaning to life not unlike that affirmed by Christ.

In Peter's time, the Russian believer exhibited a piety of behavior as complicated and rigorous as his piety of belief was simple and profound. His calendar was filled with saints' days to be observed, and with innumerable rites and fasts. He worshipped with endless signs of the cross and genuflections before altars in church and before icons which he hung in a corner of his house. Before sleeping with a woman, a man would remove the crucifix around her neck and cover all the icons in the room. Even in winter, a married couple who made love would not attend church before taking a bath. Thieves on the point of theft bowed to icons and asked forgiveness and protection. There could be no oversight or error on these matters, for what was at stake was far more important than anything that could happen on earth. Punctiliousness in religious observance guaranteed eternal life.

During two centuries of Mongol domination, the church became the nucleus of Russian life and culture. A vigorous religious life flourished in the towns and villages, and numerous monasteries were founded, especially in the remote forests of the north. None of these efforts was impeded by the Mongol khans, who traditionally cared little about the religious practices of their vassal states as long as the required taxes and tribute continued to flow to the Golden Horde. In 1589, the first patriarch of Moscow was created, signaling the final emancipation from the primacy of Constantinople.

Moscow and Russia had achieved independence—and isolation. Confronted on the north by Lutheran Sweden, on the west by Catholic Poland and on the south by the Islamic Turks and Tatars, the Russian church adopted a defensive stance of xenophobic conservatism. All change became abhorrent, and huge energies were devoted to the exclusion of foreign influences and heretical thoughts. As Western Europe moved through the Reformation and the Renaissance and into the Enlightenment, Russia and her church remained pure—petrified in their medieval past.

By the middle of the seventeenth century—twenty years before the birth of Peter—the weight and strain of this cultural backwardness began to tell on Russian society. Despite the objections of the church, foreigners were

coming to Russia, bringing new techniques and ideas in war, commerce, engineering and science. Inevitably, other principles and concepts crept in with them. The Russian church, suspicious and frightened, reacted with such extreme hostility that wary foreigners were forced to seek the protection of the tsar. Yet, the intellectual ferment continued to bubble. It was not long before Russians themselves, including some within the church, began to look with doubtful eyes on their orthodoxy. Questions were raised: The church challenged the church, and the church challenged the tsar. Separately, each of these struggles was a disaster for the church; together, they led to a catastrophe—the Great Schism—from which the Russian Orthodox Church would never recover.

IN PERSONAL TERMS, these struggles took the form of a dramatic three-way confrontation among the Tsar Alexis and two extraordinary churchmen, the overbearing, iron-willed Patriarch Nikon and the fanatical, fundamentalist Archpriest Avvakum. Ironically, Tsar Alexis was the most pious of all the tsars; he surrendered more power to a man of the church—Nikon—than any tsar before or since. Yet, before the end of his reign the Russian church was fatally divided and weakened and Nikon was draped with chains in a cold stone cell. Even more ironic was the struggle between Nikon and Avvakum. Both were men of simple origins from the forests of northern Russia. Both rose quickly in the church, came to Moscow in the 1640's and became friends. Both saw as the great goal of their lives the purification of the Russian church. Disagreeing violently as to what constituted purity, each passionately convinced that he alone was correct, the two great antagonists flailed and thundered at each other like mighty prophets. And then, almost simultaneously, both fell before the reasserted power of the state. In exile, each still believed himself the dedicated servant of Christ, had visions and worked miraculous cures. Death found one at the stake and the other by the side of a lonely road.

Nikon was the tall, rough-hewn son of a Russian peasant from the trans-Volga region of the northeast. Originally ordained a secular priest of the "white" clergy, he had married, but later he separated from his wife and became a monk. Shortly after arriving in Moscow as archimandrite or abbot of the New Monastery of the Savior, the six-feet-five-inch monk was introduced to the youthful Tsar Alexis. Awed by Nikon's spiritual intensity as well as his physical presence, Alexis began to meet him regularly every Friday. In 1649, Nikon became Metropolitan of Novgorod, one of the most ancient and powerful sees of Russia. Then, in 1652, when the incumbent Patriarch died, Alexis asked Nikon to accept the patriarchal throne.

Nikon did not accept until the twenty-three-year-old Tsar fell on his knees and begged him tearfully. Nikon agreed on two conditions: He de-

manded that Alexis follow his leadership "as your first shepherd and father in all that I shall teach on dogma, discipline and custom." And he asked the Tsar's support in all major attempts to reform the Russian Orthodox Church. Alexis swore, and Nikon took the throne determined on a broad program of reform. He intended to rid the clergy of drunkenness and other vices, establish church supremacy over the state and then, at the head of this pure and powerful Russian church, assert its preeminence over the entire Orthodox world. His initial move was to attempt to change the liturgy and ritual by which millions of Russian people worshipped daily, purging all sacred books and printed liturgies of the many deviations, alterations and simple errors that had crept into them over centuries of use, and making them consistent with scholarly Greek doctrine. The old, uncorrected books were to be destroyed.

Changing the ritual and liturgy provoked a storm of controversy. Devout Russians considered crucial such matters as how many hallelujahs were to be shouted at various points in the service, how many consecrated loaves were to be at the offertory or on the altar, the spelling of Jesus' name (from Isus to Iisus) and, most notably, whether, in making the sign of the cross, one extended the newly decreed three fingers (symbolizing the Trinity) or the traditional two fingers (symbolizing the dual nature of Christ). If one was convinced that the world was only a preparation for paradise or the inferno, and that personal salvation depended on the punctilious observance of church ritual, then crossing oneself with two fingers instead of three could mean the difference between spending eternity in heaven or in hellfire. Besides, the fundamentalist clergy argued, why accept the practices and wording of the Greek church over the Russian? Since Moscow had succeeded Constantinople as the Third Rome and Russian Orthodoxy had become the true faith, why bow to the Greeks in matters of ritual, dogma or anything else?

In 1655, Nikon sought and received support from a source outside Russia. He invited Macarius, Patriarch of Antioch, to come to Moscow, and the Syrian churchman made the long journey, bringing with him his son and secretary, Paul of Aleppo. Paul kept a diary of the journey, and from it we have many firsthand views of Nikon and Alexis.* They arrived in January

---

* Paul of Aleppo's journal, *The Travels of Macarius,* is an extraordinarily rueful catalogue of lamentations, grumbles, groans, sulks and whines at having to put up with the hardships of life in seventeenth-century Russia.

Worst of all were the length and conditions of the Russian church services which they, as visiting churchmen, were required to attend. "All their churches are void of seats," complained Paul. "There is not one, even for the Bishop. You see the people all through the service standing like rocks, motionless, or incessantly bending with their devotions. God help us for the length of their prayers and chants and masses. . . .'. Custom has made them insensible of weariness. . . . We never left the church but tottering on our legs after so much standing. . . . We remained very weak with pains in our

1655 and were greeted by the regal figure of the Russian Patriarch, Nikon, "robed in a green velvet mandya embroidered with figures in red velvet, with cherubim in the center in gold and pearls. On his head was a white latia of damask, surmounted with a gold arch bearing a cross of jewels and pearls. Above his eyes were cherubim in pearls; the edges of the latia were laced with gold and set with pearls."

From the beginning, the travelers were as much impressed by the piety and deferential humility of the young Tsar as by the commanding magnificence of the Russian Patriarch. On his own, Alexis made "a habit of attending on foot the festivals of the principal saints in their own churches, abstaining from the use of his carriage. From the beginning of the mass to the end, he stands with his head uncovered, bowing continually, striking his forehead on the ground in weeping and lamentation before the saint's icon; and this in the presence of the whole assembly." On one occasion, Alexis accompanied Macarius on a visit to a monastery thirty miles from Moscow, and there "the Emperor took our master [Macarius] by the arm and led him to the temporary hospital that he might bless and pray over the paralyzed and sick. On entering the place, some of us were unable to remain there for the disagreeable, putrid smell, nor could we endure to look upon the afflicted inmates. But the Emperor's only thought was his wish that our master should pray over and bless them. And as the Patriarch blessed each, the Emperor followed him, and kissed the patient's head, mouth and hands, from the first to the last. Wonderful indeed appear to us such holiness and humility while we thought of nothing but escaping from the place."

On the matter of changing the ritual and liturgy which had so stirred up the Russian church, Macarius stood firmly behind Nikon. At a church synod summoned by Nikon in the fifth week of Lent 1655, Nikon pointed out the errors to his fellow Russian churchmen and repeatedly called upon Macarius to confirm his judgment. Macarius invariably sided with Nikon, and the Russian clergy, whether convinced or not in their hearts, publicly were forced to agree.

backs and legs for some days. . . . We suffered from the severe cold, enough to kill us as we had to stand upon the iron pavement. What surprised us most was to see the boys and little children of the great officers of state standing bareheaded and motionless without betraying the smallest gesture of impatience." In one service all the names of all the soldiers who died fighting against the Poles over the past two years were read. "The archdeacon read with great slowness and composure while the singers continually chanted 'Everlasting Remembrance' until we were ready to drop with the fatigue of standing, our legs being frozen under us."

In conclusion, Paul decided, "anyone wishing to shorten his life by five or ten years should go to Muscovy and walk there as a religious man."

LIKE OTHER LORDLY MONARCHS—for such he had become—Nikon was a great builder. As Metropolitan of Novgorod, he founded convents and rebuilt monasteries throughout his vast northern see. In Moscow, using tiles and stones given him by the Tsar, he constructed a magnificent new patriarchal palace inside the Kremlin. It had seven halls, broad balconies, great windows, comfortable apartments, three private chapels and a rich library of books in Russian, Slavonic, Polish and other languages. In one of these halls, Nikon dined on a raised platform while the other clergy were served at lower tables, exactly as, not far away, the Tsar was dining surrounded by his boyars.

Nikon's greatest architectural monument was his huge Monastery of the Resurrection, known as "The New Jerusalem," constructed on the Istra River thirty miles west of Moscow. The Patriarch meant the parallels to be exact: the monastery was erected on the "Hill of Golgotha," the stretch of river nearby was renamed the Jordan and the central cathedral of the monastery was modeled after the Church of the Resurrection which houses the Holy Sepulcher in Jerusalem itself. On the cathedral, with its dome 187 feet high, its twenty-seven chapels, its bell tower, its high brick walls, gilded gates and dozens of other buildings, Nikon spared no expense, proclaiming in architecture what he was also proclaiming in other ways: that Moscow was the true site of the New Jerusalem.

Nikon was a stern enforcer of discipline on both laity and clergy. Attempting to regulate the daily life of the common people, he banned cursing, card playing, sexual promiscuity and even drinking. Further, he insisted that every faithful Russian spend four hours a day in church. Against the erring clergy, he was relentless. Paul of Aleppo reported: "Nikon's janissaries are perpetually going the rounds of the city, and whenever they find any priest or monk in a state of intoxication, he is taken to prison. We saw his prison full of them in the most wretched condition, galled with heavy chains and with logs of wood on their necks and legs. When any of the higher clergy or a superior of a monastery has committed a crime, he is sentenced to irons and condemned to sift flour for the bakehouse day and night until he has completed his sentence. Whereas formerly the Siberian convents were empty, this Patriarch has filled them with the heads of monasteries and higher clergy and with dissolute and wretched monks. Lately, the Patriarch has gone so far as to deprive the High Steward of the Supreme Convent of Troitsky of his great dignity, although he ranked as the third dignitary of the kingdom after the Emperor and the Patriarch. He has sentenced him to be a corn grinder in the convent of Sievsk for the crime of taking bribes from the rich. By his severities, Patriarch Nikon makes all fear him and his word prevails."

For six years, Nikon acted as virtual ruler of Russia. He not only shared with the Tsar the title of "Great Sovereign," but he often exercised purely political power over temporal affairs. When Alexis left Moscow to campaign

in Poland, he left Nikon behind as regent, ordering that "no affair great or small should be determined without his advice." Given this authority, Nikon did everything possible to exalt the supremacy of the church at the expense of the state. Within the Kremlin, he behaved more regally than the Tsar; not only churchmen and commoners but the great nobles of Russia came beneath his sway.

Paul of Aleppo described Nikon's imperious treatment of Alexis' ministers of state: "We observed that, when the council met in the council chamber, and when the Patriarch's bell rang for them to come to his palace, those officials who were too late were made to wait outside his door in the excessive cold until he should order them to be admitted. When they were allowed to enter, Patriarch Nikon would turn to the icons while all the state officers bowed before him to the ground, bareheaded. They remained uncovered until he left the hall. To each he gave his decision on every affair, commanding them how to act." The truth, Paul concluded, was that "the grandees of the Empire do not entertain much dread of the Tsar; they rather fear the Patriarch and by many more degrees."

For a while, Nikon ruled serenely and it began to seem that the exercise of power gave him the power itself. But this assumption had a fatal weakness: True power still rested with the Tsar. As long as the Patriarch retained the Tsar's devotion and support, no one could stand against him. But his enemies continued to accumulate, like the slow piling up of an avalanche, and they worked to stir up the Tsar's jealousy and distrust.

In time, signs of friction between Nikon and Alexis became more numerous. Even as Macarius and Paul were leaving Moscow to return to Antioch, they were overtaken by a royal courier summoning Macarius to return. On the road back, they met a group of Greek merchants who reported that on Good Friday the Tsar and the Patriarch had had a public argument in church on a point of ceremony. Alexis angrily called the Patriarch a "stupid clown," whereupon Nikon retorted, "I am your spiritual father. Why then do you revile me?" Alexis shot back, "It is not you who are my father but the holy Patriarch of Antioch, and I will send to bring him back." Macarius returned to Moscow and managed to close the breach temporarily.

By the summer of 1658, however, Nikon's position had been severely weakened. When the Tsar began to ignore him, Nikon attempted to force Alexis' hand. Following a service in the Assumption Cathedral, he dressed as a simple monk, left Moscow and retired to the New Jerusalem Monastery, asserting that he would not return until the Tsar reaffirmed confidence in him. But he had miscalculated. The Tsar, now a mature twenty-nine, was not unhappy to be rid of the imperious Patriarch. Not only did he let the surprised Nikon wait in his monastery for two years, but then he called a synod of churchmen to accuse the Patriarch of having "of his own will abandoned the most exalted patriarchal throne of Great Russia and so having aban-

doned his flock and thus having caused confusion and interminable contention." In October 1660, this synod declared that "by his conduct the Patriarch had absolutely abdicated and thereby ceased to be Patriarch." Nikon rejected the synod's decision, sprinkling his rebuttal with abundant references to the Holy Scriptures. Alexis sent both the accusations and Nikon's replies to the four Orthodox Patriarchs of Jerusalem, Constantinople, Antioch and Alexandria, pleading with them to come to Moscow "to review and confirm the case of the ex-Patriarch Nikon, who had ill-administered the stewardship of the patriarchal power." Two of the Patriarchs, Pasius of Alexandria and Macarius of Antioch, agreed to come, although they did not arrive until 1666. In December of that year, the trial of Nikon was convened with the two foreign Patriarchs presiding over a synod of thirteen metropolitans, nine archbishops, five bishops and thirty-two archimandrites.

The trial was held in a hall of the new patriarchal palace which Nikon had built in the Kremlin. Nikon was charged with exalting the church above the state, illegally deposing bishops and "having left the church to nine years of widowhood caused by his disorderly departure from his chair." Nikon defended himself by arguing that his office was clearly superior to that of the temporal ruler: "Has thou not learned that the highest authority of the priesthood is not received from kings and tsars, but contrariwise it is by the priesthood that rulers are anointed? Therefore it is abundantly plain that the priesthood is a very much greater thing than royalty. For this reason, manifestly, the tsar must be less than the bishop and owe him obedience." The synod, however, rejected this view and reasserted the traditional balance of church-state power: the tsar was supreme over all his subjects, clergy and patriarch included, except in matters of church doctrine. At the same time, the synod confirmed and sustained Nikon's changes in the Russian ritual and liturgy.

Nikon himself was condemned to exile. Until the last days of his life, he lived as a monk in a remote monastery, in a tiny cell at the top of a winding staircase so narrow that a single man could scarcely pass. His bed was a square of granite covered with a blanket of cut rushes. In mortification, he wore a heavy iron plate on his chest and chains attached to his arms and legs.

In time, Alexis' anger faded. He did not overturn the decision of the synod, but he wrote to Nikon to ask his blessing, sent gifts of food and, when Peter was born, a sable coat in the name of his new son. Nikon's final years were spent as a healer; reportedly, he achieved 132 miraculous cures within one three-year period. On Alexis' death, young Tsar Fedor tried to befriend Nikon. When, in 1681, it was reported that the aging monk was dying, Fedor granted him a partial pardon and freed him to return to his New Jerusalem Monastery. Nikon died peacefully on the road home in August 1681. Afterward, Fedor obtained from the four Eastern patriarchs letters of posthumous rehabilitation, and in death Nikon regained the title of patriarch.

Nikon's legacy was the opposite of that he had intended. Never again would a patriarch wield such power; thereafter the Russian church would be clearly subordinate to the state. Nikon's successor, the new Patriarch Joachim, well understood his designated role when he addressed the Tsar saying: "Sovereign, I know neither the old nor the new faith, but whatever the Sovereign orders, I am prepared to follow and obey in all respects."

NIKON HAD BEEN DEPOSED, but the religious upheaval he brought to Russia was only beginning. The same synod which condemned the Patriarch for attempting to raise church power over royal power had also endorsed the revisions in liturgy and ritual which Nikon had sponsored. Throughout Russia, the lower clergy and the common people cried out in anguish at this decision. People who cherished the old Russian practices of their fathers, who had been taught that theirs was the only true, uncontaminated faith, refused to accept the changes. For them, the old forms were the key to salvation; any suffering on earth was preferable to damnation of their eternal souls. These new changes in their services in church were the work of foreigners. Had not Nikon himself admitted, even proclaimed, "I am Russian, the son of a Russian, but my faith and religion are Greek"? The foreigners were bringing the Devil's works to Russia: tobacco ("bewitched grass"), representational art and instrumental music.* Now, bolder and more wicked than ever, the foreigners were trying to subvert the Russian church from within. It was said that Nikon's New Jerusalem Monastery was filled with Moslems, Catholics and Jews busily rewriting the sacred Russian books. It was even said that Nikon (some said it was Alexis) was the Antichrist whose reign presaged the end of the world. In essence, the religion these Russians wanted was that preached by an earlier fundamentalist priest: "Thou simple, ignorant and humble Russia, stay faithful to the plain, naïve gospel wherein eternal life is found." Now under attack, devout Russian believers could only cry out, "Give us back our Christ!"

The result was that Nikon's attempt to reform the church produced—even after Nikon himself was gone—a full-scale religious rebellion. Thousands of people who refused to accept the reforms became known as Old Believers or Schismatics. Because the state was supporting the church reforms, revolt against the church widened into revolt against the state, and the Old Believers refused to obey either authority. Neither persuasion by the church nor repression by the government could move them.

---

* During the anti-foreign riots of 1649, six carriages of musical instruments had been found and burned by the mob. This prejudice was not new, nor has it changed. The Russian Orthodox Church, believing that God should be praised only by the human voice, still does not permit instrumental music in its services. The result is its superb a cappella choirs.

To escape the rule of the Antichrist and the persecution of the state, whole villages of Old Believers fled to the Volga, the Don, the shores of the White Sea and beyond the Urals. Here, deep in the forest or on remote river-banks, they formed new settlements, enduring the hardships of pioneers to build their communities. Some did not flee far enough. When the soldiers followed, the Old Believers declared themselves ready to be engulfed in purifying flames rather than renounce the ritual and liturgy of their fathers. Children were heard saying, "We shall be burned at the stake. In the next world, we shall have little red boots and shirts embroidered with golden thread. They will serve us with as much honey, nuts and apples as we want. We will not bow down to the Antichrist." Some communities, tired of wait-ing, crowded together—men, women and children—into their wooden churches, barricaded the doors and, singing the old liturgies, burned the buildings down over their own heads. In the far north, the monks of the powerful Solovetsky Monastery won over the garrison of soldiers to fight for the Old Beliefs (in part by stressing the Nikonian ban on drink). To-gether, monks and soldiers endured an eight-year siege, repelling all the might that the Moscow government could send against them.

The most commanding, incandescent figure among the Old Believers was the Archpriest Avvakum. At once heroic, passionate and fanatical, he possessed a physical courage to match and sustain his puritanical faith. He wrote in his autobiography, "A woman came to confess to me, burdened with many sins, guilty of fornication and of all the sins of the flesh, and, weeping, she began to acquaint me with them all, leaving nothing out, standing before the Gospels. And I, thrice accursed, fell sick myself. I inwardly burned with a lecherous fire, and that hour was bitter to me. I lit three candles and fixed them to the lectern and placed my right hand in the flame, and held it there till the evil passion was burned out, and when I had dismissed the young woman and laid away my vestments, I prayed and went to my house, grievously humbled in spirit."

Avvakum was the most vivid writer and preacher of his day—when he preached in Moscow, people flocked to hear his eloquence—and, among the leading clergymen, the one most outraged by Nikon's reforms. Bitterly, he condemned all change and any compromise, and denounced Nikon as a heretic and tool of Satan. Raging against such changes as the realistic por-trayal of the Holy Family in newly made icons, he thundered, "They paint the image of Immanuel the Savior with plump face, red lips, dimpled fingers and large fat legs, and altogether make him look like a German, fat-bellied, corpulent, omitting only to paint the sword at his side. And all this was invented by the dirty cur Nikon."

In 1653, Nikon banished his erstwhile friend Avvakum to Tobolsk in Siberia. Nine years later, with the Patriarch himself in disgrace, Avvakum's powerful friends in Moscow persuaded the Tsar to recall the priest and

establish him once again in a Kremlin church. For a while, Alexis was a frequent and respectful member of Avvakum's audience, even referring to the priest as an "Angel of God." But Avvakum's stubborn fundamentalism kept intruding. Defiantly, he announced that newborn babies knew more about God than all the scholars of the Greek church, and declared that, in order to be saved, all who had accepted the heretical Nikonian reforms must be rebaptized. These outbursts led to a second banishment, this time to far-off Pustozersk on the shores of the Arctic Ocean. From this remote spot, Avvakum managed to remain the leader of the Old Believers. Unable to preach, he wrote eloquently to his followers, urging them to preserve the old faith, not to compromise, to defy their persecutors and to accept suffering and martyrdom gladly in imitation of Christ. "Burning your body," he said, "you commend your soul to God. Run and jump into the flames. Say, 'Here is my body, Devil. Take and eat it; my soul you cannot take.' "

Avvakum's final act of defiance assured his fiery destiny. From exile, he wrote to young Tsar Fedor declaring that Christ had appeared to him in a vision and revealed that Fedor's dead father, Tsar Alexis, was in hell, suffering torments because of his approval of Nikonian reforms. Fedor's response was to condemn Avvakum to be burned alive. In April 1682, Avvakum achieved his long-desired martyrdom, bound to a stake in the marketplace of Pustozersk. Crossing himself a last time with two fingers, he shouted joyfully to the crowd, "There is terror in the stake until thou art bound to it, but, once there, embrace it and all will be forgotten. Thou wilt behold Christ before the heat has laid hold upon thee, and thy soul, released from the dungeon of the body, will fly up to heaven like a happy little bird."

Across Russia, the example of Avvakum's death inspired thousands of his followers. During a six-year period, from 1684 to 1690, 20,000 Old Believers voluntarily followed their leader into the flames, preferring martyrdom to accepting the religion of the Antichrist. Sophia's government seemed to fit this image as well as that of Alexis or Fedor; indeed, she was even harsher on Schismatics than her father or her brother had been. Provincial governors were instructed to provide whatever troops were necessary to help the provincial metropolitan enforce the established religion. Anyone failing to attend church was questioned, and those suspected of heresy were tortured. Those who gave shelter to Schismatics suffered loss of all their property and exile. Yet, despite torture, exile and the stake, the Old Beliefs continued strong.

Not all the Old Believers submitted to persecution or cremated themselves. Those who had fled to refuges in the northern forests organized life there along new lines, not unlike the Protestant religious dissenters who in this same period were leaving Europe to found religious communities in New England. Keeping to themselves, the Old Believers established farming and fishing communities and laid the foundations of a future prosperity. A gen-

eration later, in Peter's time, the Old Believers were already recognized as sober, industrious workers. Peter, appreciating these qualities, told his officials, "Leave them alone."

In the long run, it was the established church and therefore Russia itself which suffered most from the Great Schism. The reforms which Nikon had hoped would purify the church and prepare it for leadership of the Orthodox world had shattered it instead. The two antagonists, Nikon and Avvakum, and the two factions, the reformers and the Old Believers, fought each other to exhaustion, draining the energy of the church, alienating its most zealous members and leaving it permanently subordinate to the temporal power. When Peter arrived, he would look upon the church in much the same light Nikon had: as a disorganized, lethargic body whose corruption, ignorance and superstition must be vigorously purged. Setting about this task (and not completing it until near the end of his reign), Peter had two overwhelming advantages over Nikon: He had greater power, and he was dependent on no one to approve his reforms. Even so, he attempted less. Peter never tampered with ritual, liturgy or doctrine as Nikon had. Peter enforced the authority of the established church against the Schismatics, but he did not broaden the religious schism. Peter's schisms lay in other realms.

6

PETER'S GAMES

DURING THE YEARS SOPHIA RULED, there were certain ceremonial functions which only Peter and Ivan could perform. Their signatures were required on important public documents, and their presence was necessary at state banquets, religious festivals and ceremonial receptions of foreign ambassadors. In 1683, when Peter was eleven, the two co-Tsars received the ambassador of King Charles XI of Sweden. The ambassador's secretary, Engelbert Kampfer, recorded the scene:

> Both Their Majesties sat . . . on a silver throne like a bishop's chair, somewhat raised and covered with red cloth. . . . The Tsars wore robes of silver cloth woven with red and white flowers, and, instead of scepters, had long golden staves bent at the end like bishops' croziers, on which, as on the breastplate of their robes, their breasts and their caps, glittered white, green and other precious stones. The elder drew his cap down over his eyes several times and, with looks cast down on the floor, sat almost immovable. The younger had a frank and open face, and his young blood rose to his cheeks as often as anyone spoke to him. He constantly looked about, and his great beauty and his lively manner—which sometimes brought the Muscovite magnates into confusion—struck all of us so much that had he been an ordinary youth and no imperial personage we would gladly have laughed and talked with him. The elder was seventeen, and the younger sixteen years old.* When the Swedish ambassador gave his letters of credence, both Tsars rose from their places . . . but Ivan, the elder, somewhat hindered the proceedings through not understanding what was going on, and gave his hand to be kissed at the wrong time. Peter was so eager that he did not give the secretaries the usual time for raising

---

* A measure of Peter's size and vitality was that, although he was only eleven, the Swedes took him for sixteen.

him and his brother from their seats and touching their heads. He jumped up at once, put his own hand to his hat and began quickly to ask the usual question: "Is His Royal Majesty, Charles of Sweden, in good health?" He had to be pulled back until the elder brother had a chance to speak.

In 1684, when Peter was twelve, a German physician reported:

Then I kissed the right hand of Peter, who with a half-laughing mouth gave me a friendly and gracious look and immediately held out to me his hand; while the hands of the Tsar Ivan had to be supported. He [Peter] is a remarkably good-looking boy, in whom nature has shown her power; and has so many advantages of nature that being the son of a king is the least of his good qualities. He has a beauty which gains the heart of all who see him and a mind which, even in his early years, did not find its like.

Van Keller, the Dutch ambassador, writing in 1685, was effusive:

The young Tsar has now entered his thirteenth year. Nature develops herself with advantage and good fortune in his whole personality; his stature is great and his mien is fine; he grows visibly and advances with as much in intelligence and understanding as he gains the affection and love of all. He has such a strong preference for military pursuits that when he comes of age we may surely expect from him brave actions and heroic deeds.

Ivan made a woeful contrast. In 1684, when Peter was ill with measles, the Austrian ambassador was received only by Ivan, who had to be supported under the arms by two servants and whose responses were in a voice barely audible. When General Patrick Gordon, a Scottish soldier in Russian service, was received in the presence of Sophia and Vasily Golitsyn, Ivan was so sickly and weak that during the interview he did nothing but stare at the ground.

Throughout Sophia's regency, and although they saw each other only on formal occasions, Peter's relations with Ivan remained excellent. "The natural love and intelligence between the two Lords is even better than before," wrote Van Keller in 1683. Naturally, Sophia and the Miloslavskys worried about Ivan. He was the foundation of their power, and from him must come their future. His life might be short, and unless he produced an heir, they would be cut off from the succession. Thus, in spite of Ivan's infirmities of eyes, tongue and mind, Sophia decided that he must marry and attempt to father a child. Ivan bowed and took as his wife Praskovaya

Saltykova, the spirited daughter of a distinguished family. In their initial
effort, Ivan and Praskovaya were partially successful: they conceived a
daughter; perhaps next time it would be a son.
For the Naryshkins, who found a grim satisfaction in Ivan's debilities,
these developments were cause for gloom. Peter was still too young to
marry and compete with Ivan in producing an heir. Their hope lay in
Peter's youth and health; in 1684, when Peter had measles and high fever,
they were in despair. They could only wait and endure Sophia's rule while
Natalya's tall, bright-faced son grew to manhood.

THE POLITICAL EXILE of the Naryshkins had been Peter's personal good
fortune. Sophia's coup d'état and the expulsion of his party from power had
freed him from all but occasional ceremonial duties. He was at liberty to
grow in the free, unrestricted, fresh-air life of the country. For a while after
the Streltsy revolt, the Tsaritsa Natalya had remained with her son and
daughter in the Kremlin, keeping the same apartments she had occupied
since her husband's death. But increasingly, with Sophia in power, the
atmosphere seemed narrow and oppressive. Natalya still resented bitterly
the murder of Matveev and her brother Ivan Naryshkin, and she was never
certain that Sophia might not take some new action against her and her
children. But there was little danger of this; for the most part, Sophia simply
ignored her stepmother. Natalya was given a small allowance to live on; it
was never enough, and the humbled Tsaritsa was forced to ask the Patriarch
or other members of the clergy for more.

To escape the Kremlin, Natalya began to spend more time at Tsar
Alexis' favorite villa and hunting lodge at Preobrazhenskoe on the Yauza
River, about three miles northeast of Moscow. In Alexis' time, it had been
part of his huge falconry establishment, and it still included rows of stables
and hundreds of coops for the falcons and for the pigeons who were their
prey. The house itself, a rambling wooden structure with red curtains at
the windows, was small, but it stood in green fields patched with trees.
From the crest of a hill, Peter could gaze on rolling meadowlands, fields of
barley and oats, a silvery river looping through groves of birch trees, small
villages dominated by white-walled churches and a blue or green onion
church dome.

Here, in the fields and woods of Preobrazhenskoe and along the banks
of the Yauza, Peter could ignore the classroom and do nothing but play. His
favorite game, as it had been from earliest childhood, was war. During
Fedor's reign, a small parade ground had been laid out for Peter in the
Kremlin where he could drill the boys who were his playmates. Now, with
the open world of Preobrazhenskoe around him, there was infinite space for
these fascinating games. And, unlike most boys who play at war, Peter could

draw on a government arsenal to supply his equipment. The arsenal records show that his requests were frequent. In January 1683, he ordered uniforms, banners and two wooden cannon, their barrels lined with iron, mounted on wheels to allow them to be pulled by horses—all to be furnished immediately. On his eleventh birthday, in June 1683, Peter abandoned wooden cannon for real cannon with which, under the supervision of artillerymen, he was allowed to fire salutes. He enjoyed this so much that messengers came almost daily to the arsenal for more gunpowder. In May 1685, Peter, nearing thirteen, ordered sixteen pairs of pistols, sixteen carbines with slings and brass mountings and, shortly afterward, twenty-three more carbines and sixteen muskets.

By the time Peter was fourteen and he and his mother had settled permanently at Preobrazhenskoe, his martial games had transformed the summer estate into an adolescent military encampment. Peter's first "soldiers" were the small group of playmates who had been appointed to his service when he reached the age of five. They had been selected from the families of boyars to provide the Prince with a personal retinue of young noblemen who acted the roles of equerry, valet and butler; in fact they were his friends. Peter also filled his ranks by drawing from the enormous, now largely useless group of attendants of his father, Alexis, and his brother Fedor. Swarms of retainers, especially those involved in the falconry establishment of Tsar Alexis, remained in the royal service with nothing to do. Fedor's health had prevented him from hunting, Ivan was even less able to enjoy the sport and Peter disliked it. Nevertheless, all these people continued to receive salaries from the state and be fed at the Tsar's expense, and Peter decided to employ some of them in his sport.

The ranks were further swelled by other young noblemen presenting themselves for enrollment, either on their own impulse or on the urging of fathers anxious to gain the young Tsar's favor. Boys from other classes were allowed to enroll, and the sons of clerks, equerries, stable grooms and even serfs in the service of noblemen were set beside the sons of boyars. Among these young volunteers of obscure origin was a boy one year younger than the Tsar named Alexander Danilovich Menshikov. Eventually, 300 of these boys and young men had mustered on the Preobrazhenskoe estate. They lived in barracks, trained like soldiers, used soldiers' talk and received soldiers' pay. Peter held them as his special comrades, and from this collection of young noblemen and stableboys he eventually created the proud Preobrazhensky Regiment. Until the fall of the Russian monarchy in 1917, this was the first regiment of the Russian Imperial Guard, whose colonel was always the Tsar himself and whose proudest claim was that it had been founded by Peter the Great.

Soon, all the quarters available in the little village of Preobrazhenskoe were filled, but Peter's boy army kept expanding. New barracks were built

in the nearby village of Semyonovskoe; in time, this company developed into the Semyonovsky Regiment, and it became the second regiment of the Russian Imperial Guard. Each of these embryo regiments numbered 300 and was organized into infantry, cavalry and artillery—just like the regular army. Barracks, staff offices and stables were built, more harnesses and caissons were drawn from the equipment of the regular horse artillery, five fifers and ten drummers were detached from regular regiments to pipe and beat the tempo of Peter's games. Western-style uniforms were designed and issued: black boots, a black three-cornered hat, breeches and a flaring, broad-cuffed coat which came to the knees, dark bottle green for the Preobrazhensky company and a rich blue for the Semyonovsky. Levels of command were organized, with field officers, subalterns, sergeants, supply and administrative staffs and even a pay department, all drawn from the ranks of boys. Like regular soldiers, they lived under strict military discipline and underwent rigorous military training. Around their barracks they mounted guard and stood watches. As their training advanced, they set off on long marches through the countryside, making camp at night, digging entrenchments and setting out patrols.

Peter plunged enthusiastically into this activity, wanting to participate fully at every level. Rather than taking for himself the rank of colonel, he enlisted in the Preobrazhensky Regiment at the lowest grade, as a drummer boy, where he could play with gusto the instrument he loved. Eventually, he promoted himself to artilleryman or bombardier, so that he could fire the weapon which made the most noise and did the most damage. In barracks or field, he allowed no distinction between himself and others. He performed the same duties, stood his turn at watch day and night, slept in the same tent and ate the same food. When earthworks were built, Peter dug with a shovel. When the regiment went on parade, Peter stood in the ranks, taller than the others but otherwise undistinguished.

Peter's boyhood refusal to accept senior rank in any Russian military or naval organization became a lifelong characteristic. Later, when he marched with his new Russian army or sailed with his new fleet, it was always as a subordinate commander. He was willing to be promoted from drummer boy to bombardier, from bombardier to sergeant and eventually up to general or, in the fleet, up to rear admiral and eventually vice admiral, but only when he felt that his competence and service merited promotion. In part, at the beginning, he did this because in peacetime exercises drummer boys and artillerymen had more fun and made more noise than majors and colonels. But there was also his continuing belief that he should learn the business of soldiering from the bottom up. And if he, the Tsar, did this, no nobleman would be able to claim command on the basis of title. From the beginning, Peter set this example, degrading the importance of birth, elevating the necessity for competence, instilling in the

Russian nobility the concept that rank and prestige had to be earned anew by each generation.

As Peter grew older, his war games became more elaborate. In 1685, in order to practice the building, defense and assault of fortifications, the boy soldiers worked for almost a year to construct a small fort of earth and timber on the bank of the Yauza at Preobrazhenskoe. As soon as it was finished, Peter bombarded it with mortars and cannon to see whether he could knock it down. In time, the rebuilt fort would grow into a little fortified town called Pressburg with its own garrison, administrative offices, court of justice and even a play "King of Pressburg" who was one of Peter's comrades, and whom Peter himself pretended to obey.

For a military game of this complexity, Peter needed professional advice; even the most eager boys cannot build and bombard fortresses by themselves. The technical knowledge came from foreign officers in the German Suburb. Increasingly, these foreigners, originally summoned to act as temporary instructors, stayed on to act as permanent officers of the boy regiments. By the early 1690's, when the two companies were formally transformed into the Preobrazhensky and Semyonovsky Guards Regiments, nearly all the colonels, majors and captains were foreigners; only the sergeants and the men were Russians.

It has been suggested that Peter's motive in developing these youthful companies was to build an armed force which might one day be used to overthrow Sophia. This is unlikely. Sophia was fully aware of what was going on at Preobrazhenskoe and was not seriously concerned. If she had thought that there was danger, Peter's requests for arms from the Kremlin arsenal would not have been fulfilled. As long as Sophia possessed the loyalty of the 20,000 Streltsy in the capital, Peter's 600 boys meant nothing. Sophia even loaned Peter regiments of Streltsy to participate in his mock battles. But in 1687, just as Peter was preparing a large-scale field exercise, Sophia embarked on the first campaign against the Crimean Tatars. The Streltsy, the regular soldiers and the foreign officers loaned to Peter were ordered to rejoin the regular army, and Peter's maneuvers were canceled.

DURING THOSE YEARS, everything attracted Peter's curiosity. He asked for a dining-room clock, a statue of Christ, a Kalmuck saddle, a large globe, a performing monkey. He wanted to know how things worked, he loved the sight and the feel of tools in his large hands; he watched craftsmen use these tools, then he copied them and savored the sensation of biting into wood, chipping stone or molding iron. At the age of twelve, he ordered a carpenter's bench and mastered the use of axes, chisels, hammers and nails. He became a stonemason. He learned the delicate business of turning a

lathe and became an excellent turner in wood and later in ivory. He learned how type was set and books were bound. He loved the clang of hammers on glowing red iron in the blacksmith's shop.

One consequence of this free, open-air boyhood at Preobrazhenskoe was that Peter's formal education was discontinued. When he left the Kremlin, hating the memories associated with it, he cut himself off from the learned tutors who had trained Fedor and Sophia, and from the customs and traditions of a tsar's education. Bright and curious, he escaped to the out-of-doors to learn practical rather than theoretical subjects. He dealt with meadows and rivers and forests rather than classrooms; with muskets and cannon rather than paper and pens. The gain was important, but the loss was serious, too. He read few books. His handwriting, spelling and grammar never advanced beyond the abominable level of early childhood. He learned no foreign language except the smattering of Dutch and German he later picked up in the German Suburb and on his travels abroad. He was untouched by theology, his mind was never challenged or expanded by philosophy. Like any willful, intelligent child taken out of school at the age of ten and given seven years of undisciplined freedom, his curiosity led him in many directions; even unguided, he learned much. But he missed the formal, disciplined training of the mind, the steady, sequential advance from the lower to the higher disciplines until one reached what in the Greek view was the highest art, the art of governing men.

Peter's education, directed by curiosity and whim, a blend of useful and useless, set the man and the monarch on his course. Much that he accomplished might never have happened had Peter been taught in the Kremlin and not at Preobrazhenskoe; formal education can stifle as well as inspire. But later Peter himself felt and lamented the lack of depth and polish in his own formal education.

His experience with a sextant is typical of his enthusiastic, self-guided education. In 1687, when Peter was fifteen, Prince Jacob Dolgoruky, about to leave on a diplomatic mission to France, mentioned to the Tsar that he had once owned a foreign instrument "by which distance and space could be measured without moving from the spot." Unfortunately, the instrument had been stolen, but Peter asked the Prince to buy him one in France. On Dolgoruky's return to Moscow in 1688, Peter's first question was whether he had brought the sextant. A box was produced and a parcel inside unwrapped; it was a sextant, elegantly made of metal and wood, but no one present knew how to use it. The search for an expert began; it led quickly to the German Suburb and soon produced a graying Dutch merchant named Franz Timmerman, who picked up the sextant and quickly calculated the distance to a neighboring house. A servant was sent to pace the distance and came back to report a figure similar to Timmerman's. Peter eagerly asked to be taught. Timmerman agreed, but declared that his pupil would

first need to learn arithmetic and geometry. Peter had once learned basic arithmetic, but the skill had fallen into disuse; he did not even remember how to subtract and divide. Now, spurred by his desire to use the sextant, he plunged into a variety of subjects: arithmetic, geometry and also ballistics. And the further he went, the more paths seemed to open before him. He became interested again in geography, studying on the great globe which had belonged to his father the outlines of Russia, Europe and the New World.

Timmerman was a makeshift tutor; he had spent twenty years in Russia and was out of touch with the latest technology of Western Europe. Yet to Peter he became a counselor and friend, and the Tsar kept the pipe-smoking Dutchman constantly at his side. Timmerman had seen the world, he could describe how things worked, he could answer at least some of the questions constantly posed by this tall, endlessly curious boy. Together, they wandered through the countryside around Moscow, visiting estates and monasteries or poking through small villages. One of these excursions in June 1688 led to a famous episode which was to have momentous consequences for Peter and for Russia. He was wandering with Timmerman through a royal estate near the village of Ismailovo. Among the buildings behind the main house was a storehouse which, Peter was told, was filled with junk and had been locked for years. His curiosity aroused, Peter asked that the doors be opened and, despite the musty smell, he began to look around inside. In the dim light, a large object immediately caught his eye: an old boat, its timbers decaying, turned upside down in a corner of the storehouse. It was twenty feet long and six feet wide, about the size of a lifeboat on a modern ocean liner.

This was not the first boat Peter had ever seen. He knew the cumbersome, shallow-draft vessels which Russians used to transport goods along their wide rivers; he also knew the small craft used for pleasure boating at Preobrazhenskoe. But these Russian boats were essentially river craft: barge-like vessels with flat bottoms and square sterns, propelled by oars or ropes pulled by men or animals on the riverbank, or simply by the current itself. This boat before him now was different. Its deep, rounded hull, heavy keel and pointed bow were not meant for rivers.

"What kind of boat is it?" Peter asked Timmerman.

"It is an English boat," the Dutchman replied.

"What is it used for? Is it better than our Russian boats?" asked Peter.

"If you had a new mast and sails on it, it would go not only with the wind, but against the wind," said Timmerman.

"Against the wind?" Peter was astonished. "Can it be possible?"

He wanted to try the boat at once. But Timmerman looked at the rotting timbers and insisted on major repairs; meanwhile, a mast and sails could be made. With Peter constantly pressing him to hurry, Timmerman

found another elderly Dutchman, Karsten Brandt, who had arrived from Holland in 1660 to build a ship on the Caspian Sea for Tsar Alexis. Brandt, who lived as a carpenter in the German Suburb, came to Ismailovo and set to work. He replaced the timbers, calked and tarred the bottom, set a mast and rigged sails, halyards and sheets. The boat was taken on rollers down to the Yauza and launched. Before Peter's eyes, Brandt began to sail on the river, tacking to right and left, using the breeze to sail not only into the wind, but against the lazy current. Overwhelmed with excitement, Peter shouted to Brandt to come to shore and take him aboard. He jumped in, took the tiller and, under Brandt's instruction, began to beat into the wind. "And mighty pleasant it was to me," the Tsar wrote years later in the preface to his *Maritime Regulations*.*

Thereafter, Peter went sailing every day. He learned to work the sails and use the wind, but the Yauza was narrow, the breeze was often too light to provide maneuverability and the boat constantly went aground. The nearest really large body of water, nine miles across, was Lake Pleschev, near Pereslavl, eighty-five miles northeast of Moscow. Peter might be an irresponsible youth larking about in the fields, but he was also a tsar and he could not travel so far from his capital without some serious purpose. He quickly found one. There was a June festival at the great Troitsky Monastery, and Peter begged his mother's permission to go there and participate in the religious ceremony. Natalya agreed, and once the service was over, Peter, now beyond the reach of any restrictive authority, simply headed northwest through the forest to Pereslavl. By prearrangement, Timmerman and Brandt were with him.

Standing on the lake bank, with the summer sun beating down on his

---

* The true origin of this famous boat, which Peter called "The Grandfather of the Russian Navy," is unknown. Peter believed that it was English; one legend says that originally it was sent as a gift to Ivan the Terrible by Queen Elizabeth I. Others think that it was built in Russia by Dutch carpenters during the reign of Tsar Alexis. What is important is that it was a small sailing ship of Western design.

Recognizing its significance in his own life, Peter was determined that the boat be preserved. In 1701, it was taken into the Kremlin and kept in a building near the Ivan Bell Tower. In 1722, when the long war with Sweden was finally over, Peter commanded that the boat be brought from Moscow to St. Petersburg. Weighing a ton and a half, it would have to be dragged partway over log corduroy roads, and Peter's orders for its care were specific: "Bring the boat to Schlüsselburg. Be careful not to destroy it. For this reason, go only in daytime. Stop at night. When the road is bad, be especially careful." On May 30, 1723, Peter's fifty-first birthday, the celebrated boat sailed down the Neva and out into the Gulf of Finland to be met there by its "grandchildren," the men-of-war of the Russian Baltic Fleet. In August of that year, the boat was placed in a special building inside the Fortress of Peter and Paul, where it remained for over two centuries. Today, Peter's boat is the most prized exhibit of the Navy Museum of the U.S.S.R. in the former Stock Exchange building on the point of Leningrad's Vasilevsky Island.

shoulders and sparkling on the water, Peter looked out across the lake. Only dimly, in the distance, could he make out the farther shore. Here, he could sail for an hour, for two hours, without having to tack. He longed to sail at once, but there were no boats, nor did it seem possible to drag the English boat this far from Ismailovo. He turned to Brandt and asked whether it would be possible to build new boats here on the shores of the lake.

"Yes, we can build boats here," replied the old carpenter. He looked around at the empty shoreline and the virgin forest. "But we shall need many things."

"No matter," said Peter excitedly. "We shall have whatever we need."

Peter's intention was to help build the boats at Lake Pleschev. This meant not just another quick, unauthorized visit to the lake, but obtaining permission to live there for an extended period. He returned to Moscow and laid siege to his mother. Natalya resisted, insisting that he remain in Moscow at least until the formal celebration of his name day. Peter stayed, but the day afterward he and Brandt and another old Dutch shipbuilder named Kort hurried back to Lake Pleschev. They chose a site for their boatyard on the eastern shore of the lake, not far from the Moscow-Yaroslavl road, and began building huts and a dock beside which to moor the future boats. Timber was cut, seasoned and shaped. Working from dawn until dark, with Peter and other workmen sawing and hammering vigorously under the direction of the Dutchmen, they laid the keels for five boats—two small frigates and three yachts, all to have rounded bows and sterns in the Dutch style. In September, the skeletons of the boats began to rise, but none was finished when Peter was forced to return to Moscow for the winter. He left unwillingly, asking the Dutch shipwrights to stay behind and work as hard as possible in order to have the boats ready by spring.

THE CHANCE DISCOVERY of this old boat and Peter's first sailing lessons on the Yauza were the beginning of two compulsive themes in his personality and his life: his obsession for the sea and his desire to learn from the West. As soon as he was tsar in power as well as name, he turned toward the sea, first south to the Black Sea, then northwest to the Baltic. Impelled by the will of this strange sea-dreamer, the huge landlocked nation stumbled toward the oceans. It was strange and yet it was also partly inevitable. No great nation has survived and flourished without access to the sea. What is remarkable is that the drive sprang from the dreams of an adolescent boy.

As Peter sailed on the Yauza with Brandt beside him at the tiller, his new fascination for the water coincided and intermingled with his ad-

miration for the West. He knew that he was in a foreign boat, taking lessons from a foreign instructor. These Dutchmen who had repaired the boat and were showing him how to use it came from a technically advanced civilization, compared to Muscovy. Holland had hundreds of ships and thousands of seamen; for the moment, Timmerman and Brandt represented all this. They became heroes to Peter. He wanted to be near the two old men so they could teach him. At that moment, they were the West. And, one day, he would be Russia.

BY THE END OF 1688, Peter was sixteen and a half and no longer a boy. Whether wearing a robe of cloth of gold and sitting on the throne or digging trenches, pulling ropes and hammering nails in a sweat-stained green tunic while swapping earthy technical talk with carpenters and soldiers, physically he was a man. In an age when life was short and generations succeeded each other rapidly, men often became fathers at sixteen and a half. This was especially true of princes, for whom the need to provide for the succession was a first great responsibility. Peter's duty was clear: It was time to marry and beget a son. Peter's mother felt this keenly, and by this time even Sophia did not object. It was not simply a matter of Naryshkin versus Miloslavsky, it was a question of ensuring the Romanov succession. The Tsarevna could not marry; Tsar Ivan had produced only daughters.

Natalya also had more personal reasons. She was annoyed by her son's growing interest in foreigners; this preference far surpassed anything she had known in the moderately Westernized atmosphere of Matveev's house or the increasingly liberalized atmosphere of the court in the last years of Tsar Alexis. Peter was spending *all* of his time with these Dutchmen, and they treated him as an apprentice, not an autocrat. They had introduced him to drinking, to smoking a pipe and to foreign girls who behaved very differently from the secluded daughters of the Russian nobility. Besides, Natalya was seriously worried about Peter's safety. His firing of cannon, his sailing in boats was dangerous. He was away for long periods, he was out of her control, he was consorting with unsuitable people, he was endangering his life. A wife would change all this. A beautiful Russian girl, shy, simple and loving, would distract him and give him something more interesting to do than running through the fields and splashing about in rivers and lakes. A good wife could convert Peter from an adolescent into a man. With luck, she could also quickly make the man a father.

Peter accepted his mother's wish without argument—not because he had suddenly become a dutiful son, but because the whole matter was of minimal interest to him. He agreed that the traditional collection of eligible

young women be assembled at the Kremlin; he agreed that his mother should sort them out and choose the likeliest. Once this was done, he looked at the prospect, made no complaint and thereby ratified his mother's choice. Thus, painlessly, Peter acquired a wife and Russia a new tsaritsa. Her name was Eudoxia Lopukhina. She was twenty—three years older than Peter—and was said to be pretty, although no portrait of Eudoxia at this age has survived. She was shy and totally deferential, which recommended her to her new mother-in-law. She was well born, being the daughter of an old, strongly conservative Muscovite family which traced its origins to the fifteenth century and was now linked by marriage with the Golitsyns, Kurakins and Romodanovskys. She was devoutly Orthodox, almost completely uneducated, shuddered at all things foreign and believed that, to please her husband, she had only to become his principal slave. Pink, hopeful and helpless, she stood beside her tall, young bridegroom and became his wife on January 27, 1689.

Even for a time when all marriages were arranged, the match was a disaster. Peter, whatever his physical readiness for fatherhood, was still bursting with the excitement of his new discoveries, still caring more about how things work than how people behave. Not many seventeen-year-old boys of any epoch, even if forced to marry, can be expected to abandon all they love and tamely settle into domesticity. And, certainly, Eudoxia was ill-equipped to perform such a miracle with Peter. Modest, conventional, scarcely more than a shy child, overwhelmingly aware of her husband's rank, eager to please but uncertain how to do it, she might have made a model tsaritsa for a conventional Muscovite tsar. She was prepared to give what she could, but her husband's wild, impetuous spark of genius left her confused, and his boisterous masculine world frightened her. She was prepared to assist at great ceremonies of state, but not at boat building. Her dislike of foreigners increased. She had been taught that they were evil; now they were stealing her husband from her. She could not talk to Peter; she knew nothing of carpentry or rigging. From the beginning, her conversation bored him; soon, so did her lovemaking; before long, he could barely stand the sight of her. Yet, they were married and they slept together, and within two years two sons were born. The eldest was the Tsarevich Alexis, whose tragic life would torment Peter. The second, an infant named Alexander, died after seven months. When this happened, scarcely three years after his marriage, Peter was so estranged from his wife and so unfeeling that he did not bother to attend the infant's funeral.

EVEN THE HONEYMOON was brief. In early spring, only a few weeks after his marriage, Peter was restlessly watching the ice beginning to break on the Yauza at Preobrazhenskoe. Knowing that soon it would be melting on Lake

Pleschev, he strained to get away from his wife, his mother and his responsibilities. At the beginning of April 1689, he burst free and hurried to the lake, anxious to see how Brandt and Kort had progressed. He found the lake ice breaking, most of the boats finished, ready to be launched and needing only some coils of good rope for rigging the sails. On the same day, he wrote exuberantly to his mother, asking for ropes, slyly stressing that the sooner the ropes arrived, the sooner he would be able to come home to her:

> To my beloved little mother, Lady Tsaritsa and Grand Duchess Natalya Kyrilovna: Your little son, Petrushka, now here at work, asks your blessing and desires to hear about your health. We, through your prayers, are well. The lake is all clear of ice today, and all the boats except the big ship are finished, only we are waiting for ropes. Therefore, I beg your kindness that these ropes, seven hundred fathoms long [about 4,200 feet], be sent from the Artillery Department without delay, for the work is held up waiting for them, and our stay here is prolonged. I ask your blessing.

Natalya understood and was angry. She replied not by sending ropes, but by ordering Peter to return immediately to Moscow to attend a memorial service for Tsar Fedor; his absence would be considered a shocking disrespect to his brother's memory. Miserable at the idea of leaving his boats, Peter tried again to resist his mother's command. His next letter to her was a mixture of forced cheerfulness and bland evasion:

> To my most beloved mother, Lady Tsaritsa Natalya Kyrilovna, Your unworthy son, Petrushka, desires greatly to know about your health. As to your orders to me to return to Moscow, I am ready, only there is work to do here and the man you sent me has seen it himself, and will explain more clearly. We through your prayers are in perfect health. About my coming I have written at length to Lev Kyrilovich [Peter's uncle and the Tsaritsa's brother] and he will report to you. Therefore, I must humbly surrender myself to your will. Amen!

But Natalya was adamant: Peter had to come. He arrived in Moscow only the day before the memorial service, and a month passed before he could again escape; this time, when he returned to Lake Pleschev, he found that Kort had died. Working beside Brandt and the other shipbuilders, Peter helped finish the boats. Soon after, he wrote again to his mother, using as his courier the boyar Tikhon Streshnev, whom Natalya had sent to Pereslavl to see what was going on. "Hey!" Peter saluted his mother:

I wish to hear about your health, and beg your blessing. We are all well. As to the boats, I say again that they are very good about which Tikhon Nikitich will tell you himself. Thy unworthy Petrus.

The signature "Petrus" is revealing. The rest of this letter was in Peter's uncertain Russian, but he wrote his name in Latin, using the unfamiliar, and to him exotically appealing, Western alphabet. In addition, along with Latin, Peter was learning Dutch from his fellow workers.

In these spring months at Pereslavl just after his marriage, Peter wrote five letters to his mother but none to his wife. Nor did he mention her at all when he wrote to Natalya. This failure of attention was readily accepted by Natalya. In the small court at Preobrazhenskoe, where both wife and mother-in-law were living, tensions already existed. Natalya, who had chosen this girl for Peter, quickly saw her limitations, disdained her and accepted Peter's negative evaluation. Eudoxia, installed in this friendless place, pathetically hoped that Peter would come home and create harmony, and wrote him begging him to remember her, pleading for some sign of love and tenderness:

I salute my lord, the Tsar Peter Alexeevich. May you be safe, my light, for many years. We beg your mercy. Come home to us, O Lord, without delay. I, thanks to your mother's kindness, am safe and well. Your little wife, Dunka, bows low before you.

Then, once again, Peter was commanded to return for a public ceremony in Moscow. Once again, he reluctantly abandoned his boats, but this time, when he appeared in the capital, his mother insisted that he stay. A crisis was coming: Members of the boyar aristocratic party gathered around Peter and his mother were preparing to challenge the government of the Regent Sophia. After seven years of unassailably competent rule, Sophia's administration was foundering. There had been two disastrous military campaigns. Now, the Regent, carried away by her passion for Vasily Golitsyn, commander of the beaten armies, was trying to persuade Muscovites to treat her lover as a conquering hero. It was too much to swallow, and Peter's adherents believed that the end was near. But they needed the symbol of their cause close at hand. Clothed in majesty, he might step easily into the full omnipotence of being tsar. Clothed in knickers, sitting on a log in a shipyard two days' journey from Moscow, he remained the boy Sophia knew: an outlandish lad whose exotic tastes she regarded with a blend of indulgent amusement and contempt.

7

THE REGENCY
OF SOPHIA

SOPHIA WAS TWENTY-FIVE when she became regent and only thirty-two when her title and office were stripped away. A portrait shows a brown-eyed girl with a round face, pink cheeks, ash-blond hair, a long chin and a cupid-bow mouth. She is plump but not unattractive. On her head she wears a small crown with an orb cross; around her shoulders she wears a red, fur-trimmed robe. The features in this portrait have never been challenged; the painting is generally used by both Western and Soviet scholars to depict Sophia. Nevertheless, the picture is inadequate. This is a portrait of any pleasant, modestly pretty young woman; it reveals none of the fierce energy and determination that enabled Sophia to ride the whirlwind of the Streltsy revolt and then to rule Russia for seven years.

A quite different, thoroughly grotesque account of her physical appearance was supplied by a French diplomatic agent named De Neuville who was sent to Moscow by the Marquis de Béthune, French ambassador to Poland, in 1689. In one of the most ungallant descriptions of a lady ever offered by a man—certainly by a Frenchman—he wrote of Sophia:

> Her mind and her great ability bear no relation to the deformity of her person, as she is immensely fat, with a head as large as a bushel, hairs on her face, and tumors on her legs, and at least forty years old. But in the same degree that her stature is broad, short and coarse, her mind is shrewd, subtle, unprejudiced and full of policy. And though she has never read Machiavelli, nor learned anything about him, all his maxims come naturally to her.

Had Sophia truly been this hideous, however, others would certainly have mentioned it. And De Neuville was in Moscow at the end of Sophia's regency, when her policy was to align Russia on the side of France's enemy, Austria, in a war against France's secret friend, the Ottoman Empire. He was seriously wrong about Sophia's age—he added eight years;

but this may have been part of his insult. Surely, at least one item in his dreadful catalogue sprang entirely from imagination, for De Neuville was certainly never an observer of Sophia's legs. Nevertheless, whatever his motive, this Frenchman has had his effect. His description will continue to afflict Sophia for as long as her history is written.

WHEN SOPHIA BECAME REGENT in 1682, she quickly installed her own lieutenants in office. Her uncle Ivan Miloslavsky remained a leading advisor until his death. Fedor Shaklovity, the new commander of the Streltsy, who won the respect of the restless soldiers and reinstilled firm discipline in the Moscow regiments, was another supporter. He was a man from the Ukraine, of peasant stock and barely literate, but he was dedicated to Sophia and ready to see that any order of hers was carried out. As the regency progressed, he became even closer to Sophia, eventually rising to be secretary of the boyar council, whose members hated him fiercely because of his low origins. To balance Shaklovity, Sophia also took counsel from the learned young monk, Sylvester Medvedev, whom she had known while still a girl in the terem. A zealous disciple of Sophia's tutor, Simeon Polotsky, Medvedev was considered to be the most learned theologian in Russia.

Miloslavsky, Shaklovity and Medvedev were important, but the greatest figure of Sophia's regency—her advisor, her principal minister, her strong right arm, her comforter and eventually her lover—was Prince Vasily Vasilievich Golitsyn. A scion of one of the oldest aristocratic houses of Russia, Golitsyn in his tastes and ideas was even more Western and revolutionary than Artemon Matveev. An experienced statesman and soldier, an urbane lover of the arts and a cosmopolitan political visionary, Golitsyn was perhaps the most civilized man Russia had yet produced. Born in 1643, he was educated far beyond the custom of the Russian nobility. As a boy, he studied theology and history and learned to speak and write Latin, Greek and Polish.

In Moscow, in his great stone palace roofed with heavy brass sheets, Golitsyn lived like a grand seigneur on the Western model. Visitors, expecting the usual primitive Muscovite furnishings, were astonished at its splendor: carved ceilings, marble statues, crystal, precious stones and silver plate, painted glass, musical instruments, mathematical and astronomical devices, gilded chairs and ebony tables inlaid with ivory. On the walls were Gobelin tapestries, tall Venetian mirrors, German maps in gilt frames. The house boasted a library of books in Latin, Polish and German, and a gallery of portraits of all Russia's tsars and many reigning monarchs of Western Europe.

Golitsyn found great stimulus in the company of foreigners. He was a

constant visitor in the German Suburb, dining there regularly with General Patrick Gordon, the Scottish soldier who had been an advisor and collaborator in his efforts to reform the army. Golitsyn's house in Moscow became a gathering place for foreign travelers, diplomats and merchants. Even Jesuits, whom most Russians rigorously avoided, found a welcome. A French visitor was struck by the sensitive manner in which Golitsyn, instead of heartily urging him to drink the glass of vodka presented on arrival in the manner of most Muscovite hosts, gently advised him not to take it as it was usually not pleasant for foreigners. During the leisurely after-dinner discussions in Latin, topics ranged from the merits of new firearms and projectiles to European politics.

Golitsyn passionately admired France and Louis XIV; he insisted that his son constantly wear a miniature portrait of the Sun King. To the French agent in Moscow, De Neuville, he revealed his hopes and dreams. He talked of further reforms in the army, of trading across Siberia, of establishing permanent relations with the West, of sending young Russians to study in Western cities, of stabilizing money, proclaiming freedom of worship and even emancipating the serfs. As Golitsyn talked, his vision expanded: He dreamed of "peopling the deserts, of enriching the beggars, turning savages into men and cowards into heroes and shepherds' huts into palaces of stone."

Sophia met this unusual man when she was twenty-four, in the full bloom of her rebellion against the terem. Golitsyn was thirty-nine, blue-eyed, wore a small mustache, a neatly trimmed Van Dyke beard and, over his shoulders, an elegant fur-lined cape. Among a crowd of conventional Muscovite boyars in their heavy caftans and bushy beards, he looked like a dashing earl just arrived from England. With her intelligence, her taste for learning and her ambition, it was natural that Sophia should see in Golitsyn the personification of an ideal and the attraction was inevitable.

Golitsyn had a wife and grown children, but it did not matter. Strong-minded and passionate, now plunging into life with abandon, Sophia had cast caution to the winds in her move for power. She would do no less for love. What is more, she would combine the two. With Golitsyn she would share power and love, and together they would rule: He, with his vision, would propose ideas and policies; she, with her authority, would see that they were executed. On her proclamation as regent, she named Golitsyn head of the Foreign Office. Two years later, she conferred on him the rare distinction of Keeper of the Great Seal; in effect, prime minister.

In her early years as regent, Sophia's role was difficult. In private she ruled the state, but in public she shielded her person and her activities behind the ceremonial figures of the two boy Tsars and the administrative offices of Golitsyn. People rarely saw her. Her name appeared on public documents only as "The Most Orthodox Princess, the Sister of Their Majesties." When she did appear in public, it was separately from her

brothers and in a manner which made her appear at least co-equal with them. An example was the farewell for departing Swedish ambassadors taking home from Moscow a reconfirmation of the treaty of peace between Russia and Sweden. In the morning, the ambassadors were summoned to watch the formal ceremony in which the boy Tsars pledged their oath on the Holy Gospel to keep the terms of the treaty. The ambassadors arrived in royal carriages to be greeted by Prince Golitsyn, who escorted them between lines of red-coated Streltsy up the Red Staircase into the banqueting hall, where Peter and Ivan sat on their double throne. Benches along the walls of the room were lined with boyars and state officials. The Tsars and the ambassadors exchanged formal greetings, and both sides pledged to keep the peace. Then Peter and Ivan rose, removed the crowns from their heads, walked to a table holding the Holy Gospels and a document containing the text of the treaty, and there, invoking God as a witness, promised that Russia would never break the treaty and attack Sweden. The Tsars kissed the Gospels, and Golitsyn handed the treaty document to the ambassadors.

The official ceremony was thus concluded. The real farewell audience for the ambassadors came later the same day. Once again, the ambassadors were conducted through lines of Streltsy armed with gleaming halberds. At the entrance to the Golden Hall, two chamberlains announced that the great lady, the Noble Tsarevna, the Grand Duchess Sophia Alexeevna, Imperial Highness of all Great and Little and White Russia, was prepared to receive them. The ambassadors bowed and entered the hall. Sophia sat on the Diamond Throne presented to her father by the Shah of Persia. She wore a robe of silver cloth embroidered with gold, lined with sables and covered with mantles of fine lace. On her head was a crown of pearls. Her attendants —the wives of boyars and two female dwarfs—stood nearby. Before the throne stood Vasily Golitsyn and Ivan Miloslavsky. When the ambassadors had saluted her, Sophia beckoned them forward and spoke to them for a few minutes. They kissed her hand, she dismissed them, and subsequently, in the gesture of a Russian autocrat, sent them dinner from her own table.

Under Sophia's regency, Golitsyn prided himself on administering "a reign based on justice and general consent." The people of Moscow seemed content; on holidays, crowds strolled through the public gardens and along the banks of the river. Among the nobility, a strong Polish influence was felt; Polish gloves, fur caps and soap were in demand. Russians became fond of tracing genealogies and creating family coats of arms. Sophia herself continued her intellectual life, writing verses in Russian and even plays, some of which were performed in the Kremlin.

The appearance as well as the manners of Moscow began to change. Golitsyn was interested in architecture, and the number of devastating fires in Moscow cleared wide areas for him to exercise his influence. In the autumn of 1688, the Treasury was temporarily unable to pay the

salaries of foreign officers, for every rouble had been advanced in loans to help citizens rebuild houses destroyed by flames. To combat fire, a decree ordered that wooden roofs be covered with earth to reduce burnable surface. Golitsyn urged Muscovites to build of stone, and during his administration all new public buildings and a bridge across the Moscow River were erected of stone.

But Kremlin theatricals, Polish gloves and even new stone buildings in Moscow did not mean a real reform of Russian society. As the years went by, the regime increasingly was forced to content itself with keeping order at home, and Golitsyn's larger dreams remained unrealized. The army seemed to improve under the leadership of foreign officers, but it was to fail miserably when put to the test of war. The colonization of distant Siberian provinces was halted as all the state's military resources were thrown into war against the Tatars. Russia's trade remained in foreign hands, and amelioration of the lot of the serfs was never mentioned outside Golitsyn's elegant salon. "Peopling the deserts, enriching the beggars, turning savages into men and cowards into heroes" remained the stuff of fantasy.

The one great achievement of the regency lay in the realm of foreign policy. From the beginning, Sophia and Golitsyn had resolved on a policy of peace with all of Russia's neighbors. Large pieces of formerly Russian territory were still in foreign hands: The Swedes held the southern coast of the Gulf of Finland, the Poles occupied White Russia and Lithuania. But Sophia and Golitsyn decided not to contest these conquests. Thus, as soon as her government was firmly established, Sophia sent embassies to Stockholm, Warsaw, Copenhagen and Vienna, declaring Russia's willingness to accept the status quo by confirming all existing treaties.

In Stockholm, King Charles XI was pleased to hear that Tsars Ivan and Peter would make no attempt to recover the Russian Baltic provinces surrendered to Sweden in 1661 by Tsar Alexis in the Treaty of Kardis. In Warsaw, Sophia's embassy confronted a more complicated situation. Poles and Russians were traditional enemies. For two centuries they had warred, with Poland generally having the upper hand. Polish armies had penetrated deep into Russia, Polish troops had occupied the Kremlin, a Polish tsar had even been placed on the Russian throne. The most recent war had ended, after twelve years of fighting, with a truce signed in 1667. By its terms, Tsar Alexis established Russia's western frontier at Smolensk and won title to all the Ukraine east of the Dnieper River. He was also permitted to keep, for two years only, the ancient city of Kiev; at the end of two years, it was to be returned to Poland.

It was a promise impossible to keep. Years passed, the truce was maintained, but Alexis and, after him, his son Fedor found themselves unable to give up Kiev. Kiev meant too much: it was one of the oldest of Russian cities, it was the capital of the Ukraine, it was Orthodox. To surrender it

back to Catholic Poland was difficult, painful and, finally, unthinkable. Therefore, in negotiations Moscow hedged, argued and delayed, while the Poles stubbornly refused to give up their claim. It was here that matters stood when Sophia's peace proposals arrived.

In the meantime, however, a new crisis had arisen to confront the Poles. Poland and Austria were at war with the Ottoman Empire. In 1683, the year after Peter's accession, the Ottoman tide reached its high-water mark in Europe as Turkish armies besieged Vienna. It was the King of Poland, Jan Sobieski, who led the Christian armies to victory under the city's walls. The Turks retreated down the Danube, but the war continued, and both Poland and Austria were eager for Russian help. In 1685, the Poles were severely defeated by the Turks, and the following spring a splendid Polish embassy with 1,000 men and 1,500 horses arrived in Moscow to seek a Russo-Polish alliance. Golitsyn received them royally; they were escorted through the streets by special detachments of Streltsy and feasted by the highest Russian nobility. After prolonged negotiations, both sides achieved their objectives. Both sides also paid a heavy price.

Poland formally ceded Kiev to Russia, giving up forever her claim to the great city. For Russia, for Sophia, for Golitsyn, this was the greatest triumph of the Tsarevna's regency. The Russian negotiators, led by Golitsyn, were lavishly rewarded with praise, gifts, serfs and estates; the two Tsars themselves handed them goblets from which to drink. In Warsaw, King Jan Sobieski was desolate at losing Kiev; when he agreed to the treaty, tears flowed from his eyes. Nevertheless, Russia paid for this triumph: Sophia had agreed to declare war on the Ottoman Empire and launch an attack on the Sultan's vassal, the Khan of the Crimea. For the first time in Russian history, Muscovy would join a coalition of European powers in fighting a common enemy.*

War with the Turks meant an abrupt change in Russian foreign policy.†

---

* It is important to note that this first Russian war with Turkey was not inspired by either of the objectives generally attributed to Russian aggression in this area. It was not motivated by a drive for a warm-water port, and it was not a holy crusade to free Constantinople from the infidels. Rather, it was a war that Russia entered unwillingly as an unwelcome obligation of a treaty with Poland. In fact, Russia first attacked Turkey not to acquire Constantinople, but to gain unimpeachable title to Kiev.

† One consequence of Sophia's decision to make war in the south still affects the modern world. Remote in time though it may seem, her decision to attack the Tatars had an important bearing on, and even helped to originate, the Far Eastern boundary dispute between the Soviet Union and China. Having decided to make a maximum effort against the Tatars, Sophia and Golitsyn suspended all other Russian territorial ambitions. The momentum of the advance to the Pacific was abruptly halted. By the mid-seventeenth century, Russian soldiers traders, hunters and pioneers had reached and conquered the basin of the Amur River, which makes a vast looping circle around the territory now known as Manchuria. For years, under increasing Chinese pressure, frontier soldiers had been sending desperate appeals to Moscow for reinforcements. But

Up to this time, there had never been hostilities between sultan and tsar. Relations between Moscow and Constantinople were so friendly that Russian ambassadors at the Sublime Porte (the palatial building in which the Sultan's chief minister, the Grand Vizier, had his offices) had always been treated with greater respect than the embassies of other powers. And the Ottoman Empire was still a dynamic force in the world. The Grand Vizier, Kara Mustapha, had been hurled back from Vienna, and the Janissaries had retreated down the Danube, but the Sultan's empire was so vast and his army so large that Sophia was reluctant to challenge him. Before she and Golitsyn agreed to sign the treaty, they summoned General Gordon repeatedly to ask his opinion about the state of the army and the size of the military risk. Solemnly, the experienced Scottish soldier declared that he thought the time was favorable for war.

It was not the Turks whom Sophia and Golitsyn were asked to attack, but their vassals, the Crimean Tatars. Russian fear of these Moslem descendants of the Mongols was deep-rooted. Year after year, Tatar horsemen rode north out of their Crimean stronghold across the grazing lands of the Ukrainian steppe and, in small bands or large armies, swooped down on Cossack settlements or Russian towns to ravage and plunder. In 1662, Tatars captured the town of Putivl and carried off all the 20,000 inhabitants into slavery. By the end of the seventeenth century, Russian slaves thronged Ottoman slave markets. Russian men were seen chained to the oars of galleys in every harbor in the eastern Mediterranean; young Russian

---

Sophia, reducing her commitments, sent, not reinforcements, but a diplomatic mission headed by Fedor Golovin to work out a peace with the Manchu Dynasty. The negotiations took place in the Russian frontier post of Nerchinsk on the upper Amur River. Golovin was at a disadvantage; not only had Sophia ordered him to make peace, but the Chinese brought up a large fleet of heavily armed junks and surrounded the fort with 17,000 soldiers. In the end, Golovin signed a paper which gave the whole of the Amur basin to China.

Subsequently, the Russians claimed that the treaty had been based not on justice, but on the presence of so much menacing Chinese military force. In 1858 and 1860, the tables were turned, and Russia took back 380,000 square miles of territory from an impotent China. Not all Russians approved this claim. After all, the Treaty of Nerchinsk had been honored for 180 years; all that time, the territory had been Chinese. But Tsar Nicholas I approved, proclaiming, "Where the Russian flag has once been hoisted, it must never be lowered."

This is the essence of the Soviet-Chinese dispute: The Russians argue that the vast region was taken from them unfairly during Sophia's regency and that, as *Izvestia* put it in 1972, "this provided the grounds for Russian diplomacy in the mid-nineteenth century to review the treaty by peaceful means and to establish the final Russian-Chinese border in the Far East." In reply, the Chinese argue that the Treaty of Nerchinsk was the legitimate treaty and that the Russians simply stole the territory from them in the nineteenth century. Today, the territory is Russian. But on Chinese maps it is Chinese. Today, along the Amur River, several million Russian and Chinese soldiers face each other across this disputed border.

boys made a welcome gift from the Crimean Khan to the Sultan. So numerous, in fact, were the Russian slaves in the East that it was asked mockingly whether any inhabitants still remained in Russia. There seemed no way to stop these devastating Tatar raids. The frontier was too broad, the Russian defenses too scanty; the Tatars' objectives could not be known in advance, and their mobility could not be equaled. The Tsar was reduced to paying an annual sum to the Khan, protection money which the Khan called a tribute and the Russians preferred to describe as a gift. But this did not stop the raids.

Although Moscow was far away and in the capital the raids were considered as harassment rather than aggression, nevertheless they were an affront to the national honor. In carrying out the terms of the treaty with Poland, Moscow would attempt to snuff out the Tatar raids at their source. But, despite Gordon's optimism, the campaign would not be easy. Bakhchisarai, the Khan's capital in the mountains of the Crimea, was a thousand miles from Moscow. To get there, the army would have to march south across the breadth of the Ukrainian steppe, force the Perekop Isthmus at the entrance to the Crimea, then advance across the wasteland of the northern Crimea. Many of the boyars who would serve as officers in the army reacted unenthusiastically to this prospect. Some were suspicious of the treaty with Poland, preferring, if there was to be war, to fight against, rather than support, the Poles. Others feared the long, hazardous march. And many opposed the campaign simply because Golitsyn had proposed it. Prince Boris Dolgoruky and Prince Yury Shcherbatov threatened to present themselves and their retainers for military service dressed in black, as a protest against the treaty, the campaign and Golitsyn himself.

Nevertheless, through the autumn and winter, Russia mobilized an army. Recruits were mustered, special taxes collected, thousands of horses, oxen and wagons assembled, and in early spring a commander was chosen. To his own dismay, the generalissimo of this expedition was none other than Vasily Golitsyn. Golitsyn had some military experience, but essentially he considered himself a statesman rather than a military commander. He would have preferred to remain in Moscow, to keep control of the government and a close eye on his numerous enemies. But his opponents argued loudly that the minister who had made the commitment to attack the Tatars should be required to lead the expedition. Golitsyn was caught; there was nothing he could do but accept.

In May 1687, a Russian army of 100,000 men began marching southward along the road to Orel and Poltava. Golitsyn moved cautiously, afraid that the mobile Tatar cavalry would ride around his columns and strike him in the rear. On June 13, he was camped on the lower Dnieper, 150 miles above Perekop, and there was still no Tatar opposition, not even a sign of

the Khan's scouts. But Golitsyn's men saw something worse: smoke along the horizon. The Tatars were burning the steppe to deny forage to the horses and oxen of the Russians. As the lines of fire advanced through the tall grass, they left behind a landscape of blackened, smoldering stubble. Sometimes, the flames approached the army itself, engulfing men and animals in smoke and threatening to burn the cumbersome baggage train. Thus afflicted, the Russian army stumbled forward until, at a point sixty miles above Perekop, Golitsyn decided to go no farther. The army began to retreat. In the heat and dust of July and August, unable to find food or forage, the army staggered homeward. In his reports to Moscow, however, Golitsyn described the campaign as a success. The Khan, he declared, had been so terrified by the advance of the Muscovite army that he had fled into hiding in the remote mountain fastnesses of the Crimea.

Golitsyn returned to Moscow late in the evening of September 14 to be hailed as a hero. The next morning, he was admitted to kiss the hands of the Regent and the two Tsars. Sophia issued a proclamation announcing a victory and heaping her favorite with praise and rewards. New estates and monies were lavished on him, and smaller gold medals bearing the likenesses of Sophia, Peter and Ivan were given to his officers. In fact Golitsyn had marched for four months, lost 45,000 men and returned to Moscow without ever sighting, much less engaging, the main Tatar army.

It did not take long for the true facts to be perceived in the capitals of Russia's allies. The reaction was disgust and anger. As it happened, that year, 1687, the Poles had had little success, but the Austrians and Venetians had been more fortunate, dislodging the Turks from important towns and fortresses in Hungary and on the Aegean. The following year, 1688, Russia mounted no campaign at all against the common enemy, and the situation worsened for her allies. Large Turkish armies concentrated to attack Poland, while, in Germany, Louis XIV of France attacked the Hapsburg empire in the rear. In the face of these new threats, both King Jan Sobieski and Emperor Leopold considered making peace with the Turks. Eventually, they agreed to continue the war only if Russia would meet its obligations and renew its attack on the Crimea.

Sophia and Golitsyn would have been happy to end the war at once, had they been allowed to keep Kiev. What they could not face was the withdrawal of Russia's allies, leaving Muscovy alone to face the whole might of the Ottoman Empire. Reluctantly, therefore, they faced the necessity of organizing another expedition to the Crimea. In the spring of 1688, the Tatar Khan provided a further stimulus to action. Launching a campaign of his own, he ravaged the Ukraine, threatening the cities of Poltava and Kiev and advancing almost to the Carpathians. When he retired to the Crimea in the autumn, 60,000 prisoners stumbled behind his horsemen.

Forced to continue the war, Golitsyn proclaimed a second campaign against the Crimea, declaring that he would make peace only when all the Black Sea coast was ceded to Russia and the Tatars were entirely removed from the Crimea and resettled on the opposite side of the Black Sea in Turkish Anatolia. This declaration, extravagant to the point of nonsense, indicated the increasingly desperate personal position of Golitsyn. By now, it was essential that he defeat the Tatars in order to repulse the domestic criticism from his political and personal enemies in Moscow. Before he left for the campaign, he was attacked by an unsuccessful assassin; on the very eve of his departure, he found a coffin left outside his door with a note warning that if this second campaign were not more successful than the first, the coffin would be his home.

The new campaign was to be launched earlier than the last: "before the ice broke." Troops began assembling in December, and in early March Golitsyn started to the south with 112,000 men and 450 cannon. A month later, he was reporting to Sophia that his progress was impeded by snow and extreme cold, then by swollen rivers, broken bridges and thick mud. At the Samara River, Mazeppa, Hetman of the Cossacks, joined the army with 16,000 horsemen. Once again, the advance was slowed by steppe fires, but this time they were less serious. Golitsyn had already sent his own men ahead to burn the steppe so that when the main army arrived they would find new shoots of tender grass springing up.

In mid-May, as the army approached the Perekop Isthmus, a mass of 10,000 Tatar cavalry suddenly appeared from nowhere and attacked the Kazan Regiment commanded by Boris Sheremetev, the future field marshal. Overwhelmed, the Russians broke and ran. The Tatars galloped toward the baggage train, but Golitsyn was able to align his artillery and halt the charge with cannon fire. The following day, May 16, during a drenching rainstorm, another Tatar charge swirled in on Golitsyn's rear. Once again, artillery managed to beat off the attackers. Thereafter, the Russian army was never without a menacing Tatar escort on the horizon.

On May 30, the Russians arrived before the dirt wall which stretched four miles across the Isthmus of Perekop. Behind a deep ditch stood a rampart lined with cannon and Tatar warriors; beyond that, a fortified citadel contained the rest of the Khan's army. Golitsyn was in no mood to launch an assault. His men were tired, his water was short, he lacked the necessary siege equipment. Instead, while his exhausted men camped beneath the wall, he tried his diplomatic skill in negotiations. His terms were much lighter than those proclaimed in Moscow. Now, he asked only that the Tatars promise not to attack the Ukraine and Poland, give up their demand for Russian tribute and release Russian prisoners. The Khan, feeling his strength, refused the first two demands and replied to the third by saying that many of the prisoners were already free but "had accepted the Mohammedan faith."

Golitsyn, unable to make an agreement and unwilling to attack, decided once again to retreat.

Again, reports of brilliant victories were sent to Moscow, again Sophia accepted them and hailed the returning general as a conqueror. And not only as a conqueror of Tatars, but of herself. Her letters are less those of a queen welcoming one of her generals than of a woman crying out to her lover to hurry home:

> Oh, my joy, light of my eyes, how can I believe my heart that I am going to see you again, my love. That day will be great to me when you, my soul, shall come to me. If it were only possible for me, I would place you before me in a single day. Your letters, confided to God's care, have all reached me in safety. I was going on foot and had just arrived at the Monastery of St. Sergius, at the holy gates themselves, when your letter about the battles came. I do not know how I went in. I read as I walked. What you have written, little father, about sending to the monasteries, that I have fulfilled. I have myself made pilgrimages to all the monasteries on foot.

Meanwhile, the army was struggling homeward. Francis Lefort, a Swiss officer in Russian service, wrote to his family in Geneva that the campaign cost 35,000 men: "20,000 killed and 15,000 taken prisoners. Besides that, seventy cannon were abandoned, and all the war material."

Despite these losses, Sophia again welcomed her lover as a hero. When Golitsyn arrived in Moscow on July 8, Sophia broke protocol by greeting him not in the Kremlin palace, but at the gates of the city. Together, they rode to the Kremlin, where Golitsyn was received and publicly thanked by Tsar Ivan and the Patriarch. By Sophia's command, special thanksgiving services were held in all Moscow churches to celebrate the safe and victorious return of the Russian army. Two weeks later, the rewards for the campaign were announced: Golitsyn was to receive an estate in Suzdal, a large sum of money, a gold cup and a caftan of cloth of gold lined with sables. Other officers, Russian and foreign, were given silver cups, extra wages, sables and gold medals.

The joy of these celebrations was marred by only one thing: Peter's disapproval. From the beginning, he refused to accept the charade of "victory." He declined to greet the returning "hero" in the Kremlin with Ivan and the Patriarch. For a week, he withheld his consent to the rewards. Finally prevailed upon to acquiesce, he was bitter. Etiquette prescribed that Golitsyn go to Preobrazhenskoe to thank the Tsar for his generosity. When Golitsyn arrived, Peter refused to see him. It was not only an affront, it was a challenge.

In his diary, Gordon described the growing tension:

Everyone saw plainly and knew that the consent of the younger Tsar had not been extorted without the greatest difficulty and that this merely made him more excited against the generalissimo and the most prominent members of the other party at court; for it was now seen that an open breach was imminent. . . . Meanwhile everything was, as far as possible, held secret in the great houses, but yet not with such silence and skill but that everyone knew what was going on.

THE PROCLAMATION of a second campaign against the Tatars had sent a new wave of resentment through the growing number of people opposed to Sophia's rule. Already, there was discontent over Sophia's administration, and her favorite, Golitsyn—unpopular as the man who had abolished precedence and who preferred Western ways to traditional Russian customs —was now marked as an unsuccessful general about to set out on another unpopular campaign. Victory, of course, would lay much of this antagonism to rest, but not all of it. For, simply with the passage of time, a new element was coming into play: Peter was growing up.

Judging that it would not be long before this active young Tsar would be ready to take some more important role in the government, the party of boyars gathered around Peter and Natalya at Preobrazhenskoe began to measure its strength. It counted some of the greatest names in Russia: Urusov, Dolgoruky, Sheremetev, Romodanovsky, Troekurov, Streshnev, Prozorovsky, Golovkin and Lvov, not to mention the families of Peter's mother and wife, Naryshkin and Lopukhin. It was this aristocratic party, as it was called, which insisted that Golitsyn, having made the treaty with Poland, be the one to lead the armies on the second campaign.

In defending himself against these waiting foes, Golitsyn had a single ally, Fedor Shaklovity. The most decisive and ruthless of Sophia's advisors, his feelings toward the opposition aristocratic party, and indeed toward all boyars, were clear: He hated them as they hated him. Beginning in 1687, when he told a group of Streltsy disdainfully that the boyars were like a lot of "withered, fallen apples," he had done his best to rouse the soldiers against the noblemen. He, more clearly than anyone else in Sophia's party, saw that once Peter was grown, the aristocrats would be too strong. The time to destroy them completely, he insisted, was now.

Once Golitsyn left for the south, he had no one but Shaklovity to guard his interests; and the boyars began to move. A Naryshkin was promoted to boyar; Golitsyn's old enemy Prince Michael Cherkassky was nominated for important office. Plaintively, Golitsyn wrote from the steppe to Shaklovity, begging for help:

We always have sorrow and little joy, not like those who are always joyful and have their own way. In all my affairs, my only hope is in thee. Write me, pray, whether there are not any devilish obstacles coming from those people [the boyars]. For God's sake, keep a sleepless eye on Cherkassky, and don't let him have that office, even if you have to use the influence of the Patriarch or the Princess [Sophia] against him.

Peter's public rebuff of Sophia's lover shocked, angered and worried the Regent. It was the first direct challenge to her position, the first clear signal that the young Naryshkin Tsar would not automatically do whatever he was told to do. The truth that Peter was no longer a boy, that he was growing up and would one day be of age and that then the regency would become superfluous, was evident to everyone. Sophia scoffed at Peter's adolescent war games and boat building, but foreign observers, whose governments wanted an objective forecast of Russia's future, watched carefully what happened at Preobrazhenskoe. Baron Van Keller, the Dutch ambassador, had written The Hague praising Peter's demeanor, intellectual capacity and enormous popularity: "Taller than his courtiers, the young Peter attracts everyone's attention. They praise his intelligence, the breadth of his ideas, his physical development. It is said that he will soon be admitted to sovereign power, and affairs cannot then but take a very different turn."

Sophia did nothing to restrain or suppress her half-brother. Busy with state affairs, finding the boy and his mother no threat to her government, she simply left them alone. When Peter was twelve, she presented him with a collection of stars, buttons and diamond clasps. As he grew older, she put no restrictions on his demands for real muskets and cannon to be sent from the armory for use in his violently realistic war games. The flow of weapons was constant, but Sophia ignored it. In January 1689, he was allowed to sit for the first time at a meeting of the Council of Boyars. He found the discussion boring and did not often return. Beneath the surface, however, Sophia felt a growing sense of insecurity and anxiety. After seven years of wielding power, she had not only grown accustomed to it, she could not imagine giving it up. Yet she was well aware that she was a woman, and that the role of regent was a temporary one. Unless, somehow, her own position was formally changed, she would have to step aside when her brothers came of age. Now, that moment was close at hand. Ivan was married, with daughters, but he, of course, was not the problem. He was not only content but anxious that someone should lift from him the burden of rule. But Peter was entering manhood, as his marriage to Eudoxia Lopukhina had given strong evidence.

It was a painful situation for Sophia; unless something was done, a crisis resulting in her own repudiation was inevitable.

In fact, Sophia had already taken some steps to improve her position, and had tried and been rebuffed in an attempt to take others. Three years before, in 1686, on the conclusion of the treaty of peace with Poland, Sophia had taken advantage of the general approval of her policies to begin to use the title of autocrat, normally reserved for tsars. Thereafter, this title was applied to her name in all official documents and at all public ceremonies, placing her on an equal status with her brothers, Ivan and Peter. Everyone knew, however, that Sophia was not equal because, unlike her brothers, she had not been crowned. Sophia hoped that this, too, would be possible. In the summer of 1687, she instructed Shaklovity to determine whether, in the event Golitsyn won a great victory over the Crimean Khan, she would have the support of the Streltsy if she had herself crowned. Shaklovity did as he was told; he urged the Streltsy to petition the two Tsars to allow the coronation of their sister. But the Streltsy, conservative in outlook, were opposed, and the project was temporarily laid aside. Nevertheless, the idea was kept alive by the appearance of an astonishing portrait of Sophia. Drawn by a Polish artist, it depicted the Regent seated alone, wearing the crown of Monomakh on her head and holding the orb and scepter in her hands, exactly as crowned male autocrats were usually painted. Her title was given as Grand Duchess and Autocrat. Beneath the picture was a twenty-four-line verse, composed by the monk Sylvester Medvedev, lauding the regal qualities of the lady portrayed and comparing her favorably to Semiramis of Assyria, the Empress Pulcheria of Byzantium and Queen Elizabeth I of England. Copies of the picture, printed on satin, silk and paper, circulated in Moscow, while others went to Holland with the request that the verses be translated into Latin and German and distributed throughout Europe.

To the boyars gathered around Peter and his mother, Sophia's assumption of the title was intolerable and her distribution of her portrait clothed in the Russian state regalia was menacing. They surmised that she meant to have herself crowned, marry her favorite, Vasily Golitsyn, and then either dethrone the two Tsars or dispose of Peter by whatever means were necessary. Whether in fact this was in Sophia's mind, no one can say. She had already achieved so much that perhaps she did indeed dream of formal, unchallenged rule with her loved one sitting at her side. There is no evidence, however, that she was prepared to depose Peter, and Golitsyn, for his part, was extremely circumspect on the matter of marriage: There was still a Princess Golitsyn.

The one member of Sophia's party who was not shy about his hopes or intentions was Fedor Shaklovity. Repeatedly, he pressed upon her the necessity of crushing the Naryshkin party before Peter came of age. More than once, he urged groups of Streltsy to kill the leaders of Peter's party and

perhaps even the Tsaritsa Natalya. He failed; Sophia was unwilling to take such drastic steps, and Golitsyn shrank from any violence. Yet, Shaklovity's devotion stirred Sophia. During the long weeks when Golitsyn was far away on his second fruitless campaign against the Crimea, even as she was writing her passionate letters to her "Little Father," Sophia may temporarily have taken Shaklovity as her lover.

INEVITABLY, time would have changed the relations between Peter and Sophia, but their confrontation was precipitated by the disastrous outcome of the second Crimean campaign. As long as Sophia's government was successful, it was difficult to challenge her, but Golitsyn's two campaigns revealed more than military failures: By calling attention to the relationship between the Regent and the army commander, they gave Sophia's enemies something specific to attack.

Peter himself had taken no part in either the peace treaty with Poland or the military campaigns against the Tatars, but he was keenly interested in military affairs and was as anxious as any other Russian to put an end to the Tatar raids into the Ukraine. Accordingly, he had followed with excitement the course of Golitsyn's military campaigns. When, in June 1689, Golitsyn returned from his second disastrous campaign, Peter was angry and contemptuous. On July 18, an incident brought this growing antagonism to public attention. At the festival celebrating the miraculous appearance of the icon of Our Lady of Kazan, Sophia appeared with her two brothers in the Assumption Cathedral, just as she had done in preceding years. When the service was over, Peter, after a whispered remark from one of his companions, walked over to Sophia and asked her to step out of the procession. This was an open challenge: to prevent the Regent from walking with the Tsars was to strip away her authority. Sophia understood the implication and refused to obey. Instead, she personally took the icon from the Metropolitan and, carrying it, defiantly continued to walk in the procession. Incensed and frustrated, Peter immediately left the procession and returned to fume and sulk in the country.

The tension between the two parties was mounting; rumors filled the air, each side feared a sudden move by the other and each was convinced that its own best strategy was to remain on the defensive. Neither party wished to forfeit the moral advantage by striking the first blow. Outwardly, Peter had no good reason to attack his half-sister and half-brother in the Kremlin. They were ruling according to the agreement of the 1682 coronation of the two Tsars; they had not in any way repudiated that agreement or infringed his prerogative. Similarly, Sophia could find no public excuse to attack Peter at Preobrazhenskoe; he was an anointed tsar. Although the Streltsy, on Shaklovity's urging, might support her against an attack by the

Naryshkins and Peter's play troops, persuading them to march on Preobrazhenskoe to attack the Lord's anointed would be far more difficult. These same considerations made both sides unsure of their actual strength. In numbers, Sophia held a great advantage; she had most of the Streltsy behind her, along with the foreign officers in the German Suburb. Peter's numerical strength was small: He had only his family, his companions, his play troops, who numbered about 600, and the probable support of the Sukharev Regiment of the Streltsy. Yet, though her physical strength was greater, it was based on weakness; Sophia could never be sure how deeply the loyalty of the Streltsy ran, and she had an exaggerated fear of even the small number of armed men gathered around Peter. That summer, wherever the Regent went, she was always surrounded by a strong guard of her own Streltsy. She lavished on them gifts of money and plied them with pleas and exhortations: "Do not abandon us. May we depend on you? If we are unnecessary, my brother and I will take refuge in a monastery."

As Sophia struggled to maintain her influence, Vasily Golitsyn, the returning "hero" of Perekop, remained silent, unwilling to become involved in any attack or open opposition to Peter and the boyars around him. Sophia's other admirer and lieutenant, Shaklovity, was more determined. Frequently, he went among the Streltsy and openly denounced the members of Peter's party; he did not mention Peter's name, but talked of eliminating his leading supporters and sending the Tsaritsa Natalya to a convent.

July ended and August began, the tension in Moscow rising with the heat. On July 31, Gordon noted in his diary: "The heat and bitterness are ever greater and greater and it appears that they must break out soon." A few days later, he referred to "rumors unsafe to be uttered." Both sides waited nervously through the midsummer days and nights. The situation was layered with powdery, dry tinder. Any rumor could become the spark.

8

SOPHIA OVERTHROWN

THE CRISIS EXPLODED on August 17, 1689. Earlier that summer, while Golitsyn was still in the south, Sophia had developed the habit of making pilgrimages on foot to churches and monasteries in the vicinity of Moscow. On the afternoon of the 17th, she asked Shaklovity to provide an escort of Streltsy to accompany her the following morning to the Donskoy Monastery about two miles from the Kremlin. Because a murder had recently occurred near the monastery, the company of Streltsy which Shaklovity ordered into the Kremlin was larger and better armed than usual. The march through the streets of this column of heavily armed musketeers did not go unnoticed. Then, as the detachment was making its bivouac inside the Kremlin, an anonymous letter began to circulate in the palace warning that on that very night Peter's Preobrazhenskoe play soldiers would attack the Kremlin and attempt to kill Tsar Ivan and the Regent Sophia. No one took time to investigate the authenticity of the letter; it may even have been contrived by Shaklovity. Understandably, Sophia became extremely upset. To calm her, Shaklovity ordered the great Kremlin gates closed and summoned more Streltsy to garrison the citadel. Scouts were posted along the road to Preobrazhenskoe to report any sign of soldiers moving from Peter's camp in the direction of Moscow. Inside the Kremlin, a long rope was attached to the alarm bell of the cathedral so that it could be pulled from within the palace; a man running out to pull it might be cut down by pre-assigned assassins.

The people of Moscow watched the mobilization of the Streltsy with alarm and dread. They remembered the bloodbath seven years before, and now a new upheaval seemed very near. Even the Streltsy were uneasy. They assumed that they would be ordered to march on the Naryshkin court at Preobrazhenskoe, and, for many, the prospect was troubling. Peter, after all, was an anointed tsar whom they were sworn to defend, just as they were sworn to defend Tsar Ivan and the Regent Sophia. It was an unhappy

business of mixed and hesitating loyalties. And, most important, no one wanted to be on the losing side.

Meanwhile, at Preobrazhenskoe, news of the tumult in Moscow caused excitement but no special precautions. During the evening, one of Peter's chamberlains rode into the city carrying a routine dispatch from the Tsar to the Kremlin. His arrival, however, was misinterpreted by some of the nervous and overexcited Streltsy. Knowing that he was from Peter, they pulled the chamberlain from his horse, beat him and dragged him into the palace to see Shaklovity.

This bit of violence had immediate and unexpected repercussions. During the preceding weeks, the older and more experienced of Peter's adherents, his uncle Lev Naryshkin and Prince Boris Golitsyn, a cousin of Sophia's favorite, Vasily Golitsyn, aware that a confrontation with Sophia and Shaklovity was coming, had been working quietly to gain informers among the Streltsy. Seven men had been won over, the chief of whom was Lieutenant Colonel Larion Elizarov, and their standing orders were to report any decisive move made by Shaklovity. Alerted by the mobilization of the Streltsy, Elizarov was watching closely for a sign that the soldiers would be ordered to march on the Naryshkin camp at Preobrazhenskoe. On learning that Peter's messenger had been dragged from his horse, beaten and taken to Shaklovity, he assumed that the attack on Peter was beginning. Two horses had been saddled, and two of Elizarov's fellow conspirators were ordered to ride urgently to warn the Tsar.

At Preobrazhenskoe, all was quiet when, a little after midnight, the two messengers galloped into the courtyard. Peter was asleep, but an attendant burst into his room and shouted that he must run for his life, the Streltsy were on the march, coming for him. Peter leaped from his bed and, still in his nightgown and with bare feet, ran to the stables, mounted a horse and galloped to a temporary hiding place in a nearby grove of trees where he waited while his companions brought his clothes. Then he dressed quickly, remounted and, accompanied by a small band, set off on the road to the Troitsky Monastery, forty-five miles northeast of Moscow. The trip took the rest of the night. When Peter arrived at six in the morning, he was so tired that he had to be lifted from his horse.

To those who saw him, it was apparent that the terror of the night had taken a toll on the highly strung seventeen-year-old. For seven years, the nightmare of the Streltsy hunting down Naryshkins had been a part of Peter's dreams. To be startled awake with the news that they were actually coming was to mingle nightmare with reality. At Troitsky, he was carried to bed, but he was so exhausted and overwrought that he burst into tears and sobbed convulsively, telling the abbot between sobs that his sister had planned to kill him with all his family. Gradually, as weariness overcame him, he dropped into a deep sleep. While Peter slept, there were other

arrivals at Troitsky. Within two hours, Natalya and Eudoxia reached the monastery, both aroused and hurried away from Preobrazhenskoe, and accompanied by the soldiers of Peter's play regiments. Later that day, the entire Sukharev Regiment of Streltsy arrived from Moscow to rally to the younger Tsar.

The nature of what had happened—Peter pulled from his bed and fleeing—suggests that the decision to seek sanctuary was taken in panic. This was not the case; indeed, the decision to go was not Peter's. As part of their overall plan for confronting Sophia, Lev Naryshkin and Boris Golitsyn had worked out in advance an escape route for Peter and all the court at Preobrazhenskoe: If and when an emergency made it necessary, the entire party would flee to Troitsky. Thus, Peter's arrival and the rapid assembly of his forces inside the powerful walls of the fortified monastery had been carefully prearranged. Peter, however, had not been told about this plan and, when he was awakened in the middle of the night and told to run for his life, he was terrified. Later, the story that an anointed tsar had had to flee in his nightshirt from the approach of his enemies lent weight to the charges against Sophia. Unwittingly, Peter had played his role perfectly.

In fact, he had not been in any danger at all, because the Streltsy had never been ordered to march against Preobrazhenskoe and, when news of Peter's flight to Troitsky reached the Kremlin, no one knew what to make of it. Sophia, hearing the report as she emerged from matins, was convinced that Peter's behavior implied some threat to her. "Except for my precautions, they would have murdered all of us," she said to the Streltsy around her. Shaklovity was contemptuous. "Let him run," he said. "He has plainly gone mad."

As she studied the new situation, however, Sophia became uneasy. More clearly than Shaklovity, she realized the significance of what had happened. Spurred by a false danger, Peter had taken a decisive step. The Troitsky Monastery was more than an impregnable fortress; it was perhaps the holiest place in Russia, a traditional sanctuary for the royal family in time of greatest danger. Now, if Peter's adherents were able to paint a picture of the Tsar fleeing to Troitsky to rally all Russians against a usurper, they would gain an enormous advantage. It would be impossible to persuade the Streltsy to march against the Troitsky Monastery, and to the people Peter's flight would signify that the Tsar's life was in danger. Her position, Sophia realized, was seriously threatened, and unless she moved very carefully, she could lose everything.

THE FAMOUS MONASTERY of Troitskaya-Sergeeva, or, to use its full name, the Laurel of St. Sergius under the Blessing of the Holy Trinity, was about forty-five miles northeast of Moscow on the Great Russian Road that leads

from the capital to Great Rostov and then to Yaroslavl on the Volga. The origins of this hallowed and historic place lay in the fourteenth century, when it became the site of a small wooden church and monastery founded by a monk named Sergius who blessed Russian arms before the great Battle of Kulikovo against the Tatars. When the Russians won, the monastery became a national shrine. In the sixteenth century, Troitsky became rich and powerful: dying tsars and noblemen in hope of salvation bequeathed their wealth to the monastery, and its treasure vaults were choked with gold, silver, pearls and jewels. Huge white walls, from thirty to fifty feet high and twenty feet thick, circled the monastery for a mile in circumference, making it impregnable. From the ramparts and from the immense round towers which stood at the corners, the muzzles of scores of brass cannon looked out on the countryside. In 1608–1609, during the Time of Troubles, Troitsky withstood a siege by 30,000 Poles, whose cannonballs simply bounded off the monastery's massive walls.*

Safe within this mighty bastion, the huge ramparts garrisoned by play soldiers and loyal Streltsy, Peter and his party planned their counterattack. Their first move was to send a messenger to Sophia asking why so many Streltsy had gathered the previous day in the Kremlin. It was a difficult question for Sophia to answer. With the two sides still outwardly observing all formal courtesies, Sophia could not reply that she had mobilized the Streltsy because she expected an attack by her brother Peter. The answer she gave—that she had summoned the soldiers to escort her on her walk to the Donskoy Monastery—seemed flimsy; thousands of armed men were unnecessary for this purpose, and Peter's supporters were further convinced of her bad faith.

Peter's next move was to order the colonel of the elite Stremyani Regiment, Ivan Tsykler, to come to Troitsky with fifty of his men. To Sophia, this summons seemed ominous; Tsykler had been one of the leaders of the 1682 Streltsy revolt and thereafter one of her most loyal officers. If he was allowed to go, and if under torture he told what he knew about Shaklovity's schemes for suppressing the Naryshkins, the breach with Peter would be irreparable. Yet, again, she had no choice. Peter was tsar, it was a royal command, to defy it meant an open challenge. When Tsykler arrived, he told everything he knew without torture. Observing

---

* Today, the monastery is commonly called Zagorsk after the industrial town which now spreads beneath its walls. An oasis of religious life in Soviet Russia, it is, as it has been for centuries, an attraction for pilgrims from all over Russia. As one of the richest assemblages of religious architecture to be found in the Soviet Union, it has also become a regular stop for most foreign tourists who visit Moscow. Happily, even now, Troitsky still exudes something of the beauty, the grandeur and the holiness of its past.

Peter's star ascending, he had offered to come to Peter's side if only the Tsar would protect him by issuing a royal command.

From the beginning, Sophia understood the weakness of her position. If it came to a fight, Peter would surely overwhelm her; her only chance of survival lay in reconciliation. However, if she could persuade Peter to leave Troitsky and return to Moscow, stripping him of the sanctity and protection of those powerful walls, then she could deal with his advisors, Peter himself could be sent back to play with his soldiers and boats, and her authority as regent would be reestablished. Accordingly, she dispatched Prince Ivan Troekurov, whose son was an intimate friend of Peter's, to persuade Peter to return. Troekurov's mission failed. Peter clearly understood the advantage of remaining at Troitsky, and he sent Troekurov back with the message that he would no longer consent to be governed by a woman.

It was Peter's move. In his own hand, he wrote letters to the colonels of all the Streltsy regiments, commanding them to come to Troitsky with ten men from each regiment. When this news reached the Kremlin, Sophia reacted violently. She summoned the Streltsy colonels and warned them not to become involved in the dispute between her brother and herself. When the colonels hesitated, telling her that they had orders from the Tsar himself which they dared not disobey, Sophia declared passionately that any man attempting to leave for Troitsky would be beheaded. Vasily Golitsyn, still commander of the army, ordered that no foreign officer leave Moscow for any reason. Under these threats, the Streltsy colonels and the foreign officers remained in Moscow.

The following day, Peter increased the pressure by sending official notice to Tsar Ivan and Sophia that he had commanded the Streltsy colonels to come to Troitsky. He asked that Sophia, as regent, see that his orders were obeyed. In reply, Sophia sent Ivan's tutor and Peter's confessor to Troitsky to explain that the soldiers were delayed and to beg for reconciliation. These two returned to Moscow two days later, empty-handed. Meanwhile, Shaklovity sent spies to Troitsky to observe the activity there and count the numbers of Peter's adherents. They came back with fresh reports of Peter's growing strength and confidence, and, in fact, Shaklovity had only to muster his own men every morning to realize that growing numbers were deserting at night and taking the road to Troitsky.

Sophia appealed to the Patriarch Joachim to go to Troitsky and use the great weight of his office to attempt a reconciliation with Peter. The Patriarch agreed, and promptly, on arriving, cast in his lot with Peter. Subsequently, when new defectors from Moscow arrived at Troitsky, they were received by Peter and Joachim, the Tsar and the Patriarch, standing side by side.

Joachim's act was not, as he saw it, a betrayal. Although he had submitted to Sophia as regent, he was from a boyar family that opposed her government. Personally, he disliked Sophia and Golitsyn for their Western manners, and he had resisted her ambition to be crowned. More important, he detested the monk Sylvester Medvedev for trespassing on church matters which he insisted lay within the province of the Patriarch. Until this moment of crisis, he had supported the Regent, not out of sympathy, but in recognition of her authority; his change of allegiance was a clear sign that power and authority were being transferred.

The defection of the Patriarch was a massive blow to Sophia. His departure encouraged others to follow. But still the mass of the Streltsy and the leading citizens of Moscow remained in the city, uncertain what to do, awaiting some further indication as to who was likely to win.

On August 27, Peter moved again. He sent stern letters repeating his command that all the Streltsy colonels and ten soldiers from each regiment report immediately to Troitsky. A similar order summoned numerous representatives of the people of Moscow. This time, all who failed to obey were threatened with death. These letters, threatening explicit punishment, had a great impact, and a disorganized mass of Streltsy led by five colonels immediately set out to submit to the Tsar.

Sophia, sitting in the Kremlin, powerless to halt the continuing exodus to Troitsky, was becoming desperate. In a final effort to resolve the crisis by conciliation, she decided to go to Troitsky herself and confront Peter personally. Accompanied by Vasily Golitsyn, Shaklovity and a guard of Streltsy, she set out along the Great Russian Road. At the village of Vozdvizhenskoe, about eight miles from the great monastery, she was met by Peter's friend Ivan Buturlin and a company of soldiers with loaded muskets. Aligning his men across the road, Buturlin ordered the Regent to halt. He told her that Peter refused to see her, forbade her coming to Troitsky and commanded that she return immediately to Moscow. Insulted and angry, Sophia declared, "I shall certainly go to Troitsky!" and ordered Buturlin and his men out of her path. At this moment, another of Peter's supporters, the younger Prince Troekurov, arrived with the Tsar's command that his sister must definitely be prevented from coming, if necessary by force.

Frustrated and humiliated, Sophia retreated. Returning to the Kremlin before dawn on September 11, she sent for the dwindling circle of her supporters. Her tone was near hysterical: "They almost shot me at Vozdvizhenskoe. Many people rode out after me with muskets and bows. It was with difficulty I got away and hastened to Moscow in five hours. The Naryshkins and Lopukhins are making a plot to kill the Tsar Ivan Alexeevich, and are even aiming at my head. I will collect the regiments and talk to them myself. Obey us and do not go to Troitsky. I trust in you. In

whom should I trust rather than you, O faithful supporters? Will you also run away? Kiss the cross first"—and Sophia held out the cross for each one to kiss. "Now if you try to run away, the cross will not let you go. When letters come from Troitsky, do not read them. Bring them to the palace."

Having gained the initiative, Peter and his advisors were not to give it up. Within a few hours of Sophia's return to Moscow, Colonel Ivan Nechaev arrived from Troitsky with official letters addressed to Tsar Ivan and the Regent Sophia. These letters formally announced the existence of a plot against the life of Tsar Peter and declared the leading plotters to be Shaklovity and Medvedev—traitors who were to be arrested immediately and sent to Peter at Troitsky for judgment.

These letters, delivered first to a palace clerk at the foot of the Red Staircase, produced a shock wave which rolled through the palace. Officials and officers who had stood by Sophia expecting either that she would win or that there would be a compromise understood now that they faced ruin or death. Those Streltsy still partially loyal to the Regent began to grumble that they would not protect traitors and that the plotters must be surrendered. Sophia ordered that Colonel Nechaev, the bearer of these unwelcome letters, be brought to her, and he received the full force of her seething emotions. Raging, trembling, she asked him, "How dare you take upon yourself such a duty?" Nechaev answered that he did not dare to disobey the Tsar. In a fury, Sophia ordered his head cut off. Luckily for Nechaev, no executioner could be found at that moment, and in the ensuing uproar he was forgotten.

Sophia, alone and at bay, tried one final time to rally her supporters. Going out to the top of the Red Staircase, she addressed a crowd of Streltsy and citizens in the palace square. Her head high, she hurled defiance at the Naryshkins and begged her audience not to desert her:

"Evil-minded people . . . have used all means to make me and the Tsar Ivan quarrel with my younger brother. They have sown discord, jealousy and trouble. They have hired people to talk of a plot against the life of the younger Tsar and of other people. Out of jealousy of the great services of Fedor Shaklovity and of his constant care, day and night, for the safety and prosperity of the empire, they have given him out to be the chief of the conspiracy, as if one existed. To settle the matter and to find out the reason for this accusation, I went myself to Troitsky, but was kept back by the advice of the evil counselors whom my brother has about him and was not allowed to go farther. After being insulted in this way, I was obliged to come home. You all well know how I have managed these seven years; how I took on myself the regency in the most unquiet times; how I have concluded a famous and true peace with the Christian rulers, our neighbors, and how the enemies of the Christian religion have been brought by my arms into terror and confusion. For your services you have received great

reward and I have always shown you my favor. I cannot believe that you will betray me and will believe the inventions of enemies of the general peace and prosperity. It is not the life of Fedor Shaklovity that they want, but my life and that of my brother."

Three times that day, Sophia made this speech, first to the Streltsy, then to the leading citizens of Moscow, finally to a large crowd which included a number of foreign officers summoned from the German Suburb. Her exhortations had an effect: "It was a long and fine speech," said Gordon, and the mood of the crowd seemed much improved. At his sister's command, Tsar Ivan descended into the crowd to hand cups of vodka to the boyars, officials and Streltsy. Sophia was pleased. In a generous mood, she sent for Colonel Nechaev, forgave him and handed him a cup of vodka.

In this interim, Prince Boris Golitsyn, one of the dominant leaders in Peter's party at Troitsky, tried to win the support of his cousin Vasily. Boris sent a messenger asking Vasily to come to Troitsky to seek the Tsar's favor. Vasily replied by asking Boris to help him mediate between the two parties. Boris refused and suggested again that Vasily come to Troitsky, promising that he would be favorably received by Peter. Honorably, Vasily refused, saying that duty required him to remain at Sophia's side.

It was again Peter's move, and again he increased the pressure on Sophia. On September 14, a written order from Peter arrived in the German Suburb. Addressed to all the generals, colonels and other officers residing there, it restated the existence of a plot, named Shaklovity and Medvedev as the chief conspirators and commanded that all foreign officers come to Troitsky, fully armed and on horseback. For these foreign soldiers, this order posed a dangerous dilemma. They had contracted to serve the government, but, in this chaotic situation, who was the government? Already, in an effort to avoid taking sides in a family quarrel between brother and sister, General Gordon, the leader of the foreign officers, had declared that without an order from both Tsars none of his officers would stir. Now Peter's command forced the issue for Gordon. Personally, aside from all threats, Gordon was embarrassed by the need to choose a side: He was fond of Peter and had often helped him in his games with artillery and fireworks, and he was even closer to Golitsyn, with whom he had worked for years to reform the Russian army and whom he had followed on the two disastrous campaigns to the Crimea. Thus, when Peter's letter was opened and read in the presence of all the senior foreign officers, Gordon's reaction was to report Peter's command to Golitsyn and ask his advice. Golitsyn was distressed and said that he would discuss the matter immediately with Sophia and Ivan. Gordon reminded Golitsyn that all the foreigners, through no fault of their own, risked their heads if they made the wrong move. Golitsyn understood and said that he would give them an answer by evening. He asked that Gordon send his son-in-law to the palace to receive the Regent's answer.

Gordon, however, made his own decision as soon as he saw Golitsyn's hesitation. If the Regent's favorite, the Keeper of the Great Seal, the commander-in-chief of the army, could not issue a command, then the regime in Moscow was obviously near collapse. Gordon saddled his horse and told his officers that, no matter what orders came from the Kremlin, he meant to leave for Troitsky. That night, a long cavalcade of foreign officers rode out of the capital and reached the monastery at dawn. Peter arose to greet them and give them his hands to kiss.

The departure of the foreign officers was, as Gordon himself noted in his diary, "the decisive break." The Streltsy remaining in Moscow realized that Peter had won. To save themselves, they crowded in front of the palace demanding that Shaklovity be surrendered to them so that they could take him to Troitsky and hand him over to Peter. Sophia refused, where-upon the Streltsy began to shout, "You had better finish this matter at once! If you do not give him up, we shall sound the alarm bell!" Sophia understood what this meant: another riot, with soldiers running wild, slaughtering whoever they decided was a traitor. In this violence, anyone— even she—might die. She was beaten. She sent for Shaklovity, who, like Ivan Naryshkin seven years before, had been hiding in the palace chapel. Tearfully, she gave him up, and that night he was taken in chains to Troitsky.

The struggle was over, the regency was concluded, Peter had won. After victory came vengeance. The first blows fell swiftly on Shaklovity. Upon his arrival at Troitsky, he was interrogated under the knout. After fifteen blows, he admitted that he had considered the murder of Peter and his mother, Natalya, but he denied making any specific plans. In the course of his confession, he completely exonerated Vasily Golitsyn from any knowledge of, or participation in, his activities. Golitsyn himself was now also at Troitsky. On the morning of Shaklovity's arrival, Golitsyn had voluntarily appeared outside the monastery walls, asking permission to enter and pay homage to Tsar Peter. His request to enter was denied and he was com-manded to wait in the village until a decision about him had been made. How to handle him was a difficult problem for Peter and his supporters. On the one hand, he had been Sophia's principal minister, general and lover for the seven years of the regency and therefore must be degraded along with the Regent's other intimate advisors. On the other hand, it was widely recognized that the intent of Golitsyn's service had been honorable even when he failed in execution. Shaklovity had stated that Golitsyn had had no part in any plot. Most important, Golitsyn was a member of one of Russia's preeminent families, and his cousin Prince Boris Golitsyn was anxious to spare the family the disgrace of a charge of treason.

In trying to spare Vasily, Boris Golitsyn risked the anger of the Tsaritsa Natalya and others of Peter's advisors. At one point, they even

threatened to implicate him along with his cousin. This moment came after Shaklovity had written a nine-page confession in the presence of Boris Golitsyn. It was after midnight when Shaklovity finished, and Peter had gone to bed, so Boris took the confession to his own room, intending to hand it to Peter in the morning. But someone rushed to the Tsar, awakened him and reported that Boris Golitsyn had taken Shaklovity's confession to his room so that he could remove anything in it detrimental to his cousin. Peter immediately sent a messenger to ask Shaklovity whether he had written a confession and, if so, where it was. Shaklovity replied that he had given it to Prince Boris Golitsyn. Golitsyn, luckily, was warned by a friend that Peter was awake and hurried to present the confession to the Tsar. Sternly, Peter asked why he had not been given the papers immediately. When Golitsyn replied that it was late and he had not wished to wake the Tsar, Peter accepted the explanation and, on the basis of Shaklovity's exoneration, decided to spare Vasily Golitsyn's life.

At nine that evening, Vasily Golitsyn was summoned. Expecting to see Peter in person, he had prepared a statement reciting his services to the state as a preface to asking for pardon. But no audience was granted. Golitsyn was left to stand in the middle of a crowded anteroom while a clerk appeared on a staircase and read his sentence aloud. He was charged with reporting only to the Regent and not to the Tsars in person, with writing Sophia's name on official documents in equality with those of the Tsars, and with causing harm and burdens to the government and people by his bad generalship of the two Crimean campaigns. Although his life was spared, his sentence was harsh: He was deprived of the rank of boyar, stripped of all property and exiled with his family to a village in the Arctic. He set out, miserable and newly impoverished. Along the way, he was cheered by a courier from Sophia who brought him a packet of money and her promise to procure his release through the intercession of Tsar Ivan. It was perhaps the last good news Golitsyn ever received. Soon, Sophia was unable to help anyone, not even herself, and the handsome, urbane Golitsyn began twenty-five years of exile. He was forty-six in that summer of 1689 when Sophia was overthrown, and he lived a wretched existence in the Arctic until he died in 1714 at the age of seventy-one.

It is ironic that a man so advanced for the Russia of his day, one who might have been so useful to Peter in the Tsar's effort to modernize the state, should have found himself in the party opposing Peter, should have lost everything in the shift of power and thus been condemned to sit out most of the Great Reformer's reign in an Arctic hut. And it was equally ironic that the Muscovite boyars should have rallied to Peter in opposition to Golitsyn. By helping Peter overthrow Sophia and Golitsyn, they believed they were rejecting the dangerous intrusion of Western culture. In fact, they

had cleared away the major obstacles to the rise of the greatest Westernizer in Russia's history.

GOLITSYN'S END seems wretched, but it was mild in comparison to the fate of other members of Sophia's inner circle. Although, according to Gordon, Peter was reluctant to impose the ultimate penalty upon his opponents, the older leaders of his party, and especially the Patriarch, insisted on it. Shaklovity was condemned to death, and four days after his arrival at Troitsky he was beheaded outside the great wall of the monastery. Two others died with him. Three Streltsy were knouted, their tongues were torn out and they were exiled to Siberia. Sylvester Medvedev had fled from Moscow, hoping to find asylum in Poland, but he was intercepted, brought to Troitsky and interrogated under torture. He admitted that he had heard vague talk against the lives of some of Peter's adherents and that he had written the damningly complimentary verses inscribed beneath Sophia's portrait, but he denied that he had been involved in any conspiracy against either Peter or the Patriarch. He was held, then denounced again, severely tortured with fire and hot irons, and finally, two years later, he was executed.

With Sophia's supporters annihilated, there still remained the central problem of what to do with Sophia herself. Alone and friendless, she waited in the Kremlin to learn her fate. None of the testimony given under torture by Shaklovity had implicated her in a conspiracy to remove Peter from the throne, much less to murder him. The most that could be said was that she was aware of designs against certain members of Peter's party and that she had been ambitious to share power with her brothers by right as autocrat rather than by delegation as regent. This, however, was enough for Peter. From Troitsky, he wrote to Ivan declaring his grievances against Sophia and proposing that henceforth the two of them alone should rule the state. He pointed out that in their coronation God had given the crown to two, not three, persons; the presence of their sister Sophia and her claims to equality with the two anointed by God were a trespass on God's will and their rights. He proposed that they govern jointly, without the disagreeable interference of "this shameful third person." He asked Ivan's permission to appoint new officials without Ivan's specific consent to each one, and concluded that Ivan should still be the senior Tsar—"I shall be ready to honor you as I would my father."

Powerless to disagree, Ivan agreed. An order was given that Sophia's name be excluded from all official documents. Soon afterward, Peter's emissary, Prince Ivan Troekurov, arrived in the Kremlin to ask Tsar Ivan to request Sophia to leave the Kremlin for the Novodevichy Convent on the city's outskirts. She was not required to take the veil as a nun, and a suite

of comfortable, well-furnished apartments was assigned to her; a large number of servants was to accompany her, and she was to live a comfortable life, restricted only in the fact that she could not leave the convent and could be visited only by her aunts and sisters. But Sophia immediately understood that this kind of confinement, however luxurious, meant the end of everything in life that held meaning for her. Power, action, excitement, intellect and love were to be stripped away. She resisted, refusing for more than a week to leave the Kremlin palace, but the pressure became too great and she was escorted ceremonially to the convent, within the walls of which she would pass the remaining fifteen years of her life.

Peter refused to return to Moscow until Sophia had left the Kremlin. Once his sister was safely incarcerated, he rode south from Troitsky, but delayed for a week en route, passing the time with General Gordon, who exercised his infantry and cavalry under the eye of the Tsar. Finally, on October 16, Peter reentered the capital, riding along a road lined with Streltsy regiments kneeling to ask his pardon. Entering the Kremlin, he went to the Uspensky Cathedral to embrace his brother, Ivan; then, dressed in robes of state, he presented himself at the top of the Red Staircase. For the first time, the young man who stood there, very tall, with round face and dark eyes, was the master of the Russian state.

THUS FELL SOPHIA, the first woman to rule in Moscow. Her achievements as a ruler have been exaggerated. Prince Boris Kurakin strained the truth when he said, "Never had there been such wise government in the Russian state. During the seven years of her rule, the whole state did come to a flower of great wealth." On the other hand, she was not, as some admirers of Peter have depicted her, simply the last ruler of the old order, a final reactionary stumbling block before the path of Russian history smoothed and broadened into the new modern avenue of the Petrine era. The truth is that Sophia was competent and, on the whole, ruled well. During the years she guided the state, Russia was in transition. Two tsars, Alexis and Fedor, had instituted mild changes and reforms in Russian policies. Sophia neither slowed nor hurried this pace, but she did allow it to continue and, in so doing, helped prepare the way for Peter. In the light of what had begun under Alexis and continued under Fedor and Sophia, even the striking changes made by Peter take on more of an evolutionary than a revolutionary character.

It was not as a Russian ruler but as a Russian woman that Sophia was remarkable. Over the centuries, Russian women had been degraded into domestic chattels hidden away in the dark chambers of the terem. Sophia stepped into the light of day and seized control of the state. Regardless of how well she exercised power once she had it, the simple fact of taking

power in that era was enough to make of her a historic figure. Unfortunately, Sophia's womanhood was not only her distinction, it was also her undoing. When the crisis came, Muscovites were still unwilling to follow a woman in opposition to a crowned tsar.

Peter put Sophia in Novodevichy, and the gates of the convent closed permanently behind her. But in the century that followed, the role of royal women in Russia changed. Four female sovereigns succeeded Peter on the throne. An immense distance lay between the secluded creatures of the seventeenth-century terem and these spirited eighteenth-century empresses. And the greater part of the journey was made by a single woman, the Regent Sophia. Cut from the same cloth as these empresses, with the same determination and drive to rule, it was she who showed the way.

Peter himself, long after her deposing, described Sophia to a foreigner as "a princess endowed with all the accomplishments of body and mind to perfection, had it not been for her boundless ambition and insatiable desire for governing." In the forty-two years of his reign, only one Russian stood up to challenge his right to the throne: Sophia. Twice, in 1682 and 1689, she pitted her strength against his. In the third and final domestic challenge to Peter's omnipotence, the Streltsy uprising in 1698, the one opponent whom Peter feared was Sophia. She had then been locked in a convent for nine years, but Peter instantly assumed that she was behind the uprising. In his mind, she was the only person strong enough to dream of overthrowing him.

That Sophia possessed such qualities—that she could frighten Peter, that she had the audacity to challenge him and the strength of personality to worry him even from inside convent walls—should not be surprising. She was, after all, his sister.

9

GORDON, LEFORT
AND THE JOLLY COMPANY

BY TRADITIONAL COUNTING, the reign of Peter the Great lasted for forty-two years, beginning in 1682, when he was crowned as a boy of ten, and continuing until his death in 1725 at the age of fifty-two. Nevertheless, as we have seen, during the first seven of these years the two boy Tsars, Peter and Ivan, were removed from all practical state affairs while the real power of government resided with their sister Sophia. One might assume, therefore, that Peter's reign could more truly be reckoned as beginning in the summer of 1689 when he and his partisans seized power from the Regent and the tall young Tsar rode in triumph into Moscow with his title secure and his people on their knees before him. But, surprisingly, the triumphant young autocrat still did not begin to rule. For five more years, the Tsar turned his back on governing Russia, blithely returning to the adolescent life he had made for himself before the flight to Troitsky—of Preobrazhenskoe and Lake Pleschev, of soldiers and boats, of informality and lack of responsibility. All he wanted was to be left alone to enjoy his freedom. He was completely indifferent to government and affairs of state; later, he confessed that he had nothing on his mind during these years except his own amusement. In this sense, then, the true beginning of Peter's reign can be said to have been not in 1682, when he was ten, or in 1689, when he was seventeen, but in 1694, when he was twenty-two.

In the meantime, the government was administered by the small group which had supported and guided Peter in the confrontation with the Regent. His mother, Natalya, now forty, was the nominal leader, but she was not as independent as Sophia and she was easily swayed by the men around her. The Patriarch Joachim, a conservative churchman unrelenting in his hostility to all foreigners, stood at her elbow, determined to expunge the Western viruses which had crept into Russia under Sophia and Vasily Golitsyn. The Tsar's uncle, Natalya's brother Lev Naryshkin, received the vital office of Director of Foreign Affairs; in effect, he was the new prime minister. He was an amiable man of unexceptional intelligence whose joy was his new

authority to give dazzling receptions and glorious banquets, served on gold and silver plates, for the foreign ambassadors. In actual negotiations with these ambassadors and in the practical running of his office, he was greatly and necessarily assisted by one of Russia's few professional diplomats, Emilian Ukraintsev. The boyar Tikhon Streshnev, an old friend of Tsar Alexis and Peter's formal guardian, was entrusted with the conduct of all home affairs. The third of the governing trio was Boris Golitsyn, who had successfully survived the lingering suspicion hanging over him for his effort to brake the fall of his cousin Vasily. Other famous names appeared in government: Urusov, Romodanovsky, Troekurov, Prozorovsky, Golovkin, Dolgoruky. Some who had been prominent under Sophia—Repnin and Vinius—kept their posts. Boris Sheremetev remained as commander of the southern army facing the Tatars. In addition, more than thirty Lopukhins of both sexes, the relatives of Peter's young wife, Eudoxia, arrived at court ready to pluck what advantage they could from their relative's position.

For Russia, the change in government was for the worse. The new administrators lacked both the skill and the energy of their predecessors. Not a single important law was made in these five years. Nothing was done to defend the Ukraine against the devastating raids of the Tatars. There was brawling at court and corruption in government. Law and order decayed in the countryside. There was an outburst of popular hatred against all foreigners: One decree, influenced by the Patriarch, ordered all Jesuits to leave the country within two weeks. Another commanded that all foreigners be halted at the frontier and thoroughly questioned as to their origins and their reasons for visiting Russia. Their answers were to be sent to Moscow and the foreigners held at the frontier until permission for them to enter was granted by the central government. Simultaneously, the Director of the Posts, Andrew Vinius, was instructed to have his officials open and read all letters which crossed the frontier. The Patriarch even wanted to have all the Protestant churches in the German Suburb destroyed and was forestalled only when its inhabitants produced a document from Tsar Alexis containing written permission for the existence of these churches. At the height of this xenophobia, a foreigner was seized by a mob on a Moscow street and burned alive.

Nevertheless, for all his effort, there was one Russian whose habits the Patriarch could not change. Joachim's despair was Peter himself, who passed so much of his time in the German Suburb among those very foreigners whom the Patriarch feared. Still, while Joachim lived, Peter kept his behavior under control. On March 10, 1690, the Tsar invited General Gordon to dine at court in honor of the birth of his son, the Tsarevich Alexis. Gordon accepted, but the Patriarch intervened, protesting vehemently at the inclusion of a foreigner at a celebration honoring the heir to the Russian throne. Furious, Peter deferred and the invitation was withdrawn, but the

following day he invited Gordon to his country house, dined with him there and then rode back to Moscow with the Scot, conversing publicly throughout the ride. The problem resolved itself a week later, on March 17, when Joachim suddenly died. He left a testament urging the Tsar to avoid contact with all heretics, Protestant or Catholic, to drive them out of Russia and to eschew personally all foreign clothes and customs. Above all, he demanded that Peter appoint no foreigners to official positions in the state or army where they would be in a position to give orders to the Orthodox faithful. Peter's response, once Joachim was buried, was to order himself a new set of German clothes and, a week later, go for the first time to dine as Gordon's guest in the German Suburb.

The choice of a new patriarch turned on the same issues that Joachim himself had provoked: liberalism versus conservatism, toleration of foreigners versus a fierce defense of traditional Orthodoxy. Some of the more educated clergy, supported by Peter, favored Marcellus, Metropolitan of Pskov, a scholarly churchman who had traveled abroad and spoke several languages, but the Tsaritsa Natalya, the ruling group of boyars, the monks and most of the lower clergy preferred the more conservative Adrian, Metropolitan of Kazan. The contest within the church was heated, with the partisans of Adrian charging that Marcellus had too much learning, would favor Catholics and had already trod on the fringes of heresy. After five months of debate, Adrian was chosen, because, said a disappointed Patrick Gordon, of the new patriarch's "ignorance and simplicity."

Peter was stung by this rebuff. Seven years later, he described the election of Adrian with bitter disgust to a foreign host. "The Tsar told us," said the foreigner, "that when the Patriarch in Moscow was dead, he designed to fill that place with a learned man who had traveled, who spoke Latin, Italian and French. [But] the Russians petitioned him in a tumultuous manner not to set such a man over them, alleging three reasons: first, because he spoke barbarous languages; second, because his beard was not big enough for a patriarch; and third, because his coachman sat upon the coach seat and not upon the horses as was usual."

IN FACT, despite the wish or decree of any patriarch, the West was already firmly installed only three miles from the Kremlin. Outside Moscow, on the road between the city and Preobrazhenskoe, stood a remarkable, self-contained Western European town known as the German Suburb.* Visitors

---

* The German Suburb—in Russian "Nemetskaya Sloboda"—derived its name from the Russian word for "German," which is "Nemets." To most Russians, unable to distinguish between different foreign tongues, all foreigners were "Germans"—"Nemtsy."

strolling along its broad, tree-lined avenues, past its two- and three-story brick houses with large European-style windows, or through its stately squares with splashing fountains, could scarcely believe that they were in the heart of Russia. Behind the stately mansions decorated with columns and cornices lay precisely arranged European gardens studded with pavilions and reflecting pools. Along the streets rolled carriages made in Paris or London. Only the onion domes of Moscow's churches rising across the fields in the distance reminded visitors that they were a thousand miles from home.

In Peter's day, this prosperous foreign island was relatively new. A previous settlement for foreigners founded by Ivan the Terrible inside the city had been dispersed during the Time of Troubles. After the advent of the first Romanov in 1613, foreigners settled wherever they could throughout the city. This development angered Muscovite conservatives who believed that their holy Orthodox city was being profaned, and in the uprising of 1648 bands of Streltsy made random attacks on foreign dwellings. In 1652, Tsar Alexis decreed that foreigners were forbidden to live or have churches within the walls of Holy Moscow, but he permitted a new foreign settlement, the German Suburb, to be laid out on the banks of the Yauza with plots of ground allotted on the basis of rank to all foreign officers, engineers, artists, doctors, apothecaries, merchants, schoolmasters and others in Russian service.

Originally, the colony had been made up predominantly of Protestant Germans, but by the middle of the seventeenth century there were numerous Dutchmen, Englishmen and Scots. The Scots, mostly royalists and Catholics in flight from Oliver Cromwell, were assured a refuge despite their religion because of Tsar Alexis' violent anger at the beheading of King Charles I. Among the Scottish Jacobite names prominent in the German Suburb were Gordon, Drummond, Hamilton, Dalziel, Crawford, Graham and Leslie. In 1685, Louis XIV revoked the Edict of Nantes, ending France's official toleration of Protestantism. The Regent and Vasily Golitsyn permitted a number of French Huguenot refugees, fleeing the new persecution in France, to come to Russia. By Peter's adolescence, accordingly, the German Suburb had become an international colony of 3,000 West Europeans, where royalists mingled with republicans and Protestants with Catholics, their national, political and religious differences softened by distance and exile.

Enclosure in a separate suburb made it easy for them to maintain the habits and traditions of the West. The inhabitants wore foreign clothing, read foreign books, had their own Lutheran and Calvinist churches (Catholics were not permitted a church, but priests could say mass in a private home), spoke their own languages and educated their children. They kept up a constant correspondence with their native countries. One of the most respected foreigners, the Dutch resident Van Keller, sent and received news

from The Hague every eight days, keeping the Suburb closely informed of all that was happening beyond Russia's frontiers. General Patrick Gordon waited eagerly for the scientific reports of London's Royal Society. English wives received volumes of poetry along with their fine china and scented soap. Then, too, the Suburb contained a seasoning of actors, musicians and adventurers who helped produce the repertory theater, the concerts, balls, picnics, as well as the love affairs and duels which kept the Suburb distracted and amused.

Obviously, this foreign island, a nucleus of a more advanced civilization, did not remain untouched by the Russian sea around it. The houses and gardens of the German Suburb bordered the royal lands at Sokolniki and Preobrazhenskoe, and eventually, despite the Patriarch's ban, bolder Russians, thirsty for knowledge and intelligent conversation, began to mingle socially with the foreigners who lived only a few hundred yards away. Through them, foreign habits began to permeate Russian life. Soon, Russians who had laughed at foreigners for eating "grass" were also eating salads. The habit of smoking tobacco and taking snuff, anathematized by the Patriarch, began to spread. Some Russians like Vasily Golitsyn even began to trim their hair and beards and converse with Jesuits.

Contact rubbed both ways, and many foreigners adopted Russian qualities. Lacking foreign women to marry, they took Russian wives, learned the Russian language and allowed their children to be baptized in the Orthodox Church. Nevertheless, as a result of their enforced residency in the German Suburb, most maintained their own Western style of life, language and religion. A marriage in the opposite direction was still rare, as few Western women were willing to marry a Russian and accept the inferior status of Russian women. But this was changing. Mary Hamilton had married Artemon Matveev and presided over the household in which Tsar Alexis had met Natalya Naryshkina. As Russian gentlemen became more Westernized, they had no trouble finding Western wives, a practice which flourished happily until the very end of imperial Russia in 1917. Peter's son Alexis married a Western wife, and every tsar thereafter who reached the age to marry chose or had selected for him a princess from Western Europe.

FROM CHILDHOOD PETER HAD been curious about the German Suburb. As he passed along the road, he had seen its handsome brick houses and shaded gardens. He had come to know Timmerman and Brandt, and the foreign officers who supervised the building of his play forts and the firing of his artillery, but until the death of the Patriarch Joachim in 1690 his contacts with the foreign suburb were restricted. After the old churchman's death, Peter's visits became so frequent that he seemed almost to live there.

In the German Suburb, the young Tsar found a heady combination of good wine, good talk and fellowship. When Russians spent an evening together, they simply drank until everyone was asleep or there was nothing more to drink. The foreigners also drank deeply, but amidst the haze of tobacco smoke and over the clank of beer tankards there was also conversation about the world, its monarchs and statesmen, scientists and warriors. Peter was excited by these discussions. When news reached the German Suburb of the victory of the English fleet over the French at La Hogue in 1694, he was enthusiastic. He asked for the original message, had it translated immediately and then, leaping up and shouting for joy, ordered an artillery salute to King William III of England. In these long evenings, he also listened to a wealth of advice about Russia: to institute more frequent drill for his army, to give his soldiers sterner discipline and regular pay, to capture the Orient trade by diverting it from the Ottoman-dominated Black Sea to the Caspian Sea and the Volga River.

Once the inhabitants of the Suburb understood that this tall young monarch liked them, they invited him everywhere and competed for his company. He was asked to participate in weddings, baptisms and other family celebrations. No merchant married a daughter or baptized a son without asking the Tsar to join the feast. Peter often served as a godfather, holding Lutheran and Catholic children at the font. He was best man at numerous foreign marriages, and in the dancing afterward he became an enthusiastic participant in the rollicking country dance known as the Grossvater.

In a society which mingled Scottish soldiers, Dutch merchants and German engineers, Peter naturally found many whose ideas fascinated him. One was Andrew Vinius, a middle-aged Russian-Dutchman who had one foot in each of the two cultures. Vinius' father was a Dutch engineer-merchant who had established an ironworks in Tula south of Moscow in the time of Tsar Michael and become wealthy. His mother, a Russian woman, had brought up her son in the Orthodox religion. Speaking both Russian and Dutch, Vinius had served first in the Ministry of Foreign Affairs and then been given charge of the Post Office. He had written a book on geography, spoke Latin and was a student of Roman mythology. From him, Peter began to learn Dutch and a smattering of Latin. In writing to Vinius, the Tsar signed himself Petrus and he referred to his "games of Neptune and Mars" and to the celebrations he held "in honor of Bacchus."

It was in the German Suburb also that Peter met two other foreigners, widely divergent in background and style, who became even more important to him. These were the stern old Scottish mercenary soldier General Patrick Gordon and the charming Swiss adventurer Francis Lefort.

Patrick Gordon was born in 1635 on his family estate of Auchleuchries near Aberdeen in the Scottish Highlands. His family was illustrious and

fiercely Catholic, being connected with the first Duke of Gordon and the Earls of Errol and Aberdeen. The English Civil War had disrupted Gordon's youth. His family was staunchly royalist, and when Oliver Cromwell severed King Charles I's head, he also laid low the fortunes of all devoted Stuart followers; thereafter, a Scottish Catholic boy had no chance of entering a university or finding a useful career in military or public service, and, at sixteen, Patrick went abroad to seek his fortune. After two years in a Jesuit college in Brandenburg, he ran away to Hamburg and joined a group of Scottish officers recruited by the Swedish army. Gordon served the King of Sweden with distinction, but when he was captured by the Poles, he had no qualms about switching sides. It was the normal procedure for mercenary soldiers of fortune—changing masters from time to time was not considered disgraceful either by them or by the governments who hired them. A few months later, Gordon was recaptured and was persuaded to rejoin the Swedes. Later still, he was re-recaptured, and once again he joined the Poles. Before the age of twenty-five, Patrick Gordon had changed sides four times.

In 1660, the new Stuart king, Charles II, was restored to the throne of England, and Gordon was ready to go home. Before he sailed, however, a Russian diplomat in Europe made him a glittering offer: three years' service in the Russian army, beginning with a commission as a major. Gordon accepted, only to find, on reaching Moscow, that the time clause of his contract was meaningless; as a useful soldier, he would not be allowed to leave. When he applied, he was threatened with denunciation as a Polish spy and a Roman Catholic and menaced with Siberia. Temporarily accepting his fate, he settled into Moscow life. Learning quickly that his best chance of promotion lay in marrying a Russian woman, he found one, and together they produced a family. The years went by and Gordon served Tsar Alexis, Tsar Fedor and the Regent Sophia, fighting against Poles, Turks, Tatars and Bashkirs. He became a general and twice returned to England and Scotland, although the Muscovites made sure that this enormously valuable personage would come back to them by keeping his wife and children in Russia. In 1686, James II personally asked Sophia to release Gordon from Russian service so that he might return home; this royal request was refused, and for a while the Regent and Vasily Golitsyn were so angry with the General that there was more talk of ruin and Siberia. Then King James wrote again declaring that he wished to appoint Gordon as his ambassador in Moscow; the appointment was also refused by the Regent, who declared that General Gordon could not serve as ambassador because he was still on service with the Russian army and, indeed, was about to leave on a campaign against the Tatars. Thus, in 1689, Gordon, at fifty-four, was respected by all, enormously rich (his salary was a thousand roubles a year, whereas the Lutheran pastor was paid only sixty) and the preeminent foreign soldier

in the German Suburb. When, as head of the foreign-officer corps, he mounted his horse and rode to Troitsky to join Peter, it was the final blow to Sophia's hopes.

It is not surprising that Gordon—courageous, widely traveled, battle-seasoned, loyal and canny—would appeal to Peter. What is surprising is that eighteen-year-old Peter appealed to Gordon. Peter was tsar, to be sure, but Gordon had served other tsars without any special feelings of friendship. In Peter, however, the old soldier found an adept and admiring pupil, and, acting as a kind of unofficial military tutor, he instructed Peter in all aspects of warfare. During the five years after Sophia's fall, Gordon became not only Peter's hired general, but a friend.

For Gordon, as it turned out, Peter's friendship was decisive. Now the intimate friend and counselor of the youthful monarch, he gave up his dream of going back to pass his final years in the Highlands. He accepted the fact that he would die in Russia, and indeed, in 1699, when the old soldier finally died, Peter stood by his bed and closed his eyes.

In 1690, soon after Sophia's overthrow, Peter became friendly with another foreigner of a quite different kind, the gay and gregarious Swiss soldier of fortune Francis Lefort. Over the next decade, Lefort was to become Peter's boon companion and friend of the heart. In 1690, when Peter was eighteen, Francis Lefort was thirty-four, almost as tall as Peter, but huskier than the narrow-shouldered Tsar. He was handsome with a large, sharp nose and expressive and intelligent eyes. A portrait made of him a few years later shows him against a background of Peter's ships; he is clean-shaven, with a lace scarf around his neck, and his full, curled wig falls onto the shoulders of a finely wrought armor breastplate which bears the crested insignia of Peter's double-headed eagle.

Francis Lefort was born in Geneva in 1656, the son of a prosperous merchant, and through his charm and wit he soon became a member of its amiable society. His taste for the merry life quickly snuffed out any desire to become a merchant like his father, and an enforced term as a clerk to another merchant in Marseilles made him so unhappy that he fled to Holland to join the Protestant armies fighting Louis XIV. There, still only nineteen, the young adventurer heard tales of opportunity in Russia, and he embarked for Archangel. Arriving in Russia in 1675, he found no office available and lived for two years without work in the German Suburb. He was never dull—people liked his irrepressible gaiety, and eventually his career picked up. He became a captain in the Russian army, married a cousin of General Gordon and was noticed by Prince Vasily Golitsyn. He served in Golitsyn's two campaigns against the Crimea, but when Gordon led the foreign officers away from Sophia to join Peter at Troitsky, Lefort was in the van. Soon after the Regent's fall, the thirty-four-year-old Lefort was important enough to be promoted to major general.

Peter was captivated by this formidably charming man of the world. Here was someone who sparkled in precisely the way to catch Peter's youthful eye. Lefort was not profound, but his mind worked quickly and he loved to talk. His speech was filled with the West, its life, manners and technology. As a drinking companion and ballroom cavalier, Lefort had no equal. He excelled at organizing banquets, suppers and balls, with music, drink and female dancing partners. From 1690 on, Lefort was constantly in Peter's company; they dined together two or three times a week and saw each other daily. Increasingly, Lefort endeared himself by his frankness, openness and generosity. Where Gordon gave Peter seasoned advice and sensible counsel, Lefort gave gaiety, friendship, sympathy and understanding. Peter relaxed in Lefort's affection, and when the Tsar became suddenly inflamed at someone or something, lashing out physically at all around him, only Lefort was able to approach and seize the young monarch, gripping Peter in his powerful arms and holding him until he calmed.

In considerable part, Lefort's success was due to his unselfishness. Although he loved luxury and its trappings, he was never grasping and took no steps to ensure that he would not be impoverished on the following day—a quality that endeared him even more to Peter, who saw to it that all Lefort's needs were amply cared for. Lefort's debts were paid, he was presented with a palace and funds to run it, and he was promoted rapidly to full general, admiral and ambassador. Most important to Peter, Lefort genuinely loved his life in Russia. He returned as a visitor to his native Geneva, bearing many titles and the Tsar's personal testimony to the city fathers of the esteem in which he held this Genevois. But, unlike Gordon, Lefort never dreamed of returning permanently to his birthplace. "My heart," he told his fellow Swiss, "is wholly in Moscow."

For Peter, walking into Lefort's house was like stepping onto a different planet. Here were wit, charm, hospitality, entertainment, relaxation and usually the exciting presence of women. Sometimes, they were the respectable wives and pretty daughters of the foreign merchants and soldiers, dressed in the latest Western gowns. More often, they were rollicking, unshockable wenches whose role was to see that no man was gloomy; buxom, sturdy women who did not take offense at barracks language or the admiring touch of rough male hands. Peter, knowing only the stiffly wooden female creatures produced by the terem, entered this world with delight. Guided by Lefort, he soon found himself contentedly sitting in a haze of tobacco smoke, a tankard of beer on the table, a pipe in his mouth and his arm around the waist of a giggling girl. His mother's remonstrances, the Patriarch's censure, his wife's tears were all forgotten.

Before long, Peter's eye fell on a particular one of these young women. She was a flaxen-haired German girl named Anna Mons, the daughter of a Westphalian wine merchant. Her reputation was blemished; she had al-

ready been conquered by Lefort. Alexander Gordon, the general's son, described her as "exceedingly beautiful" and when Peter revealed his interest in her blond hair, bold laugh and flashing eyes, Lefort readily ceded his conquest to the Tsar. The easy-mannered beauty was exactly what Peter wanted: She could match him drink for drink and joke for joke. Anna Mons became his mistress.

There was little substance behind Anna's spontaneous laughter, and her fondness for Peter was powerfully stimulated by her ambition. She used her favors to obtain his favors, and Peter showered her with gems, a country palace and an estate. Blinded to protocol, he appeared with her in the company of Russian boyars and foreign diplomats. Naturally, Anna began to hope for more. She knew that Peter could not bear the sight of his wife, and with the passage of time she grew to believe that she might one day replace the Tsaritsa on the throne. Peter thought of it, but saw no need for marriage. The liaison was enough; as it was, it lasted twelve years.

Most of Peter's companions, of course, were not foreigners but Russians. Some were friends of his childhood who had stayed at his side through the long exile at Preobrazhenskoe. Others were older men with distinguished service and ancient names, attracted to Peter despite his wild behavior and foreign friends because he was the anointed Tsar. Prince Michael Cherkassky, an elderly, bearded man devoted to the old ways, sought Peter out of a sense of patriotism, unwilling to watch from a distance while the youthful autocrat flung himself about with foreigners. A similar spirit motivated Prince Peter Prozorovsky, another austere and elderly sage, and Fedor Golovin, Russia's most experienced diplomat, who had negotiated the Treaty of Nerchinsk with China. When Prince Fedor Romodanovsky attached himself to the youthful Tsar, it was with a sense of devotion which would know no limit. He hated the Streltsy, who had murdered his father in the bloodbath of 1682. Later, as Governor of Moscow and as Chief of Police, he would rule with an iron hand. And when the Streltsy rose again in 1698, Romodanovsky would descend on them like a pitiless avenging angel.

It was a strange assortment at first, this motley collection of distinguished graybeards, youthful roisterers and foreign adventurers. But time shaped them into a cohesive group that called itself the Jolly Company and went everywhere with Peter. It was a vagabond, itinerant sort of life, roaming the countryside, dropping in unannounced to eat and sleep with a surprised nobleman. In Peter's wake were anywhere from 80 to 200 followers.

An average banquet for the Jolly Company began at noon and ended at dawn. The meals were gargantuan, but there were intervals between courses for smoking, for games of bowls and ninepins, for archery matches and shooting at targets with muskets. Speeches and toasts were accompanied not only by cheers and shouts but by blasts of trumpets and salvos of artillery. When a band was present, Peter played the drums. In the evenings, there

was dancing and, often, an exhibition of fireworks. When sleep overcame a reveler, he simply rolled off his bench onto the floor and snored away. Half the company might sleep while the rest roared. Sometimes, these parties extended into a second or third day, with guests sleeping side by side on the floor, rising to consume further prodigious quantities of food and drink and then sinking back again into lazy slumber.

AN OBVIOUS REQUISITE for membership in Peter's Jolly Company was a capacity for drink, but there was nothing new or abnormal about this intemperance in Peter's friends. Since time immemorial, drink had been—in the words of the Grand Prince Vladimir of Kiev in the tenth century—"the joy of the Russes." Successive generations of Western travelers and residents had found drunkenness almost universal in Russia. Peasants, priests, boyars, tsar: all were participants. According to Adam Olearius, who visited Muscovy in the time of Peter's grandfather Tsar Michael, no Russian ever willingly missed a chance to take a drink. To be drunk was an essential feature of Russian hospitality. Proposing toasts that no one dare refuse, host and guests gulped down cup after cup, turning their beakers upside down on their heads to prove that they were empty. Unless the guests were sent home dead drunk, the evening was considered a failure.

Peter's father, Tsar Alexis, his piety notwithstanding, was as Russian as the next man. Dr. Collins, Alexis' physician, noted how pleased his employer was to see his boyars "handsomely fuddled." The boyars, in turn, were always eager to see foreign ambassadors as drunk as possible. Common people drank also, less to be sociable than to forget. Their goal was to reach a stupor of unconsciousness, putting the unhappy world around them out of mind as rapidly as possible. In grimy taverns, men and women alike pawned their valuables and even their clothes to keep the vodka mugs coming. "Women," reported another Westerner, "are often the first to become raving mad with immoderate draughts of brandy and are to be seen, half-naked and shameless, in almost all the streets."

Alexis' roistering son and his Jolly Company fully upheld these Russian traditions. Although much of the alcohol consumed at their revels was in the milder form of beer or kvas, the intake was vast and continuous—Gordon in his diary speaks often of the amount Peter has drunk and of the difficulties that he, a middle-aged man, is having in keeping up. But it was Lefort who taught Peter to drink really heavily. Of Lefort, the German philosopher Leibniz, who observed the Swiss when he traveled to the West with Peter on the Great Embassy, was to write, "[Alcohol] never overcomes him, but he always continues master of his reason . . . no one can rival him . . . he does not leave his pipe and glass till three hours after sunrise." Eventually, this drinking took its toll. Lefort died a relatively young man of forty-three;

Peter died at fifty-two. When he was young, though, these wild bacchanalia did not leave Peter exhausted and debauched, but actually seemed to refresh him for the next day's work. He could drink all night with his comrades and then, while they snored in drunken slumber, rise at dawn and leave them to begin work as a carpenter or shipbuilder. Few could match his pace.

In time, Peter decided not to leave the arrangements for these banquets to chance. He enjoyed dining two or three times a week at Lefort's house, but it was impossible for Lefort with his limited income to arrange the complicated and expensive entertainment which the Tsar expected, so Peter built for him a larger hall to accommodate several hundred guests. Eventually, even this became too small, and the Tsar therefore erected a handsome stone mansion, magnificently furnished with tapestries, wine cellars and a banqueting hall large enough for 1,500 people. Lefort was the nominal owner, but in fact the mansion became a kind of clubhouse for the Jolly Company. When Peter was absent, and even when Lefort was absent, those members of the Jolly Company remaining in Moscow gathered at this house to dine, drink and pass the night, their expenses defrayed by the Tsar.

Gradually, from spontaneous drinking bouts and banquets, the Company proceeded to more organized buffoonery and masquerades. To most of his comrades Peter had, in sportive moments, given nicknames, and these nicknames were gradually elevated into masquerade titles. The boyar Ivan Buturlin was given the title "The Polish King" because in one of the military maneuvers at Preobrazhenskoe he was commander of the "enemy" army. Prince Fedor Romodanovsky, the other commander and defender of the play fortress town of Pressburg, was promoted to "King of Pressburg" and then to "Prince-Caesar." Peter addressed him as "Your Majesty" and "My Lord King" and signed his letters to Romodanovsky, "Your bondsman and eternal slave, Peter." This charade, in which Peter mocked his own autocratic rank and title, continued throughout the reign. After the Battle of Poltava, the defeated Swedish officers were led into the presence of the "Tsar"—who was in fact Romodanovsky. Only a few of the Swedes, none of whom had ever seen the real Peter, wondered who was the extremely tall Russian officer standing behind the Mock–Prince-Caesar.

But Peter's parody of temporal power was mild compared to the bizarre mockery he and his comrades appeared to make of the church. The Jolly Company was organized into "The All-Joking, All-Drunken Synod of Fools and Jesters," with a Mock–"Prince-Pope," a college of cardinals and a suite of bishops, archimandrites, priests and deacons. Peter himself, although only a deacon, took charge of drawing up the rules and instructions for this strange assembly. With the same enthusiasm with which he was later to draw up laws for the Russian empire, he carefully defined the rituals and ceremonies of the Drunken Synod. The first commandment was that "Bacchus be worshipped with strong and honorable drinking and receive his just

dues." In practical terms, this meant that "all goblets were to be emptied promptly and that members were to get drunk every day and never go to bed sober." At these riotous "services," the Prince-Pope, who was Peter's old tutor, Nikita Zotov, drank everyone's health and then blessed the kneeling congregation by making the sign of the cross over them with two long Dutch pipes.

On church holidays, the games become more elaborate. At Christmas, more than 200 men, singing and whistling, would travel around Moscow leaning out of overcrowded sleighs. At their head, riding in a sleigh drawn by twelve bald men, rode the Mock–Prince-Pope. His costume was sewn with playing cards, he wore a tin hat and he was perched atop a barrel. Choosing the richer noblemen and merchants to honor with their caroling, they swarmed into their houses, expecting food and drink as thanks for their uninvited songs. During the first week of Lent, another procession, this time of "penitents," followed the Prince-Pope through the city. The Company, wearing outlandish costumes inside out, rode on the backs of donkeys and bullocks or sat in sleighs pulled by goats, pigs or even bears.

A marriage in Peter's circle stirred the Jolly Company to special efforts. In 1695, when Peter's favorite jester, Jacob Turgenev, married a sexton's daughter, the feasts and celebrations lasted three days. The wedding took place in a field outside Preobrazhenskoe, and Turgenev and his bride arrived for the ceremony in the Tsar's finest court carriage. Behind them came a procession of leading boyars wearing fantastic costumes—hats of birchbark, boots of straw, gloves made of mouse skins, coats covered with squirrel tails and cats' paws; some were on foot and others rode in carts drawn by oxen, goats or pigs. The celebrations ended with a triumphal entry into Moscow with the newly married couple mounted together on the back of a camel. "The procession," Gordon comments, "was extraordinary fine," but the joke may have been carried too far because a few days later the bridegroom, Turgenev, suddenly died in the night.

The Drunken Synod, created when Peter was eighteen, continued its tipsy existence until the end of the Tsar's reign, with the mature man who had become an emperor continuing to engage in the same coarse buffoonery begun by an unbridled adolescent. This behavior, which foreign diplomats found vulgar and scandalous, seemed blasphemous to many of Peter's subjects. It added substance to the growing belief of the conservative Orthodox faithful that Peter was himself the Antichrist, and they waited eagerly for the bolt from heaven which would strike down the blasphemer. In fact, it was partially in order to provoke, dismay and degrade the hierarchy of the church, and especially the new Patriarch Adrian, that Peter had originally instituted the Drunken Synod. His mother and the conservative boyars had had their victory over his own candidate, the more enlightened Marcellus of Pskov—so be it!—but Peter retaliated by appoint-

ing his own Mock-Patriarch. The parody of the church hierarchy not only gave vent to his own resentment, but, as the years went by, reflected his continuing impatience with the whole institution of the church in Russia. Nevertheless, Peter learned to be careful. The Drunken Synod did not directly insult the Russian Orthodox Church because Peter quickly steered the parody to a safer mimicry of the Roman Catholic Church. The original leader of the masquerade, the Prince-Patriarch, became the Prince-Pope, he was surrounded by a College of Cardinals, and the ceremonies and language of the charade were borrowed not from the Russian liturgy but from the Roman. To this game, of course, fewer Russians objected.

In Peter's own eyes, the buffoonery of the Mock-Synod was not blasphemous. Certainly, God was too majestic a being to be offended by his little parodies and games. Ultimately, that was what the revels of the Mock-Synod were: games. They were a form of relaxation—clownish perhaps, ridiculous, even gross—but for the most part, the Company were not men of refined sensibilities. They were men of action, engaged in building and governing a state. Their hands were stained with blood, mortar and dust, and they needed to relax. Their pleasures were true to their character: They drank, they laughed, they shouted, they dressed in costumes, danced, played practical jokes, made fun of one another and of whatever passed beneath their eyes—especially the church, which resisted everything they were trying to do.

To CONTEMPORARY RUSSIANS, it was not only Peter's soul that seemed in danger during these years, but his body as well. He experimented continually with ever more elaborate and dangerous fireworks. During the Shrovetide celebrations of 1690, when Peter was also honoring the birth of his son Alexis, a display lasted five hours. One five-pound rocket, instead of bursting in the air, fell back to earth, landing on the head of a boyar and killing him. As Peter became more proficient, these pyrotechnical displays became more spectacular. In 1693, following a long salute from fifty-six cannon, there appeared the image of a flag of white flame bearing on it in Dutch letters the monogram of Prince Romodanovsky, followed by a tableau of a fiery Hercules tearing open the jaws of a lion.

And there was the game of war. During the winter of 1689–1690, Peter waited impatiently for spring to begin maneuvers with his play regiments. The Tsar's suppers with General Gordon were filled with discussions of new European drills and tactics to be taught to the troops. The test came in the summer, in an exercise during which the Preobrazhensky Regiment attacked the fortified camp of the Semyonovsky Regiment. Hand grenades and fire pots were used which, though they were made of pasteboard and clay, still were dangerous when tossed into a group of men. Peter himself was hurt

when, during the storming of an earthwork, a clay pot filled with gunpowder burst near him, burning his face.

Through the summer of 1691, the regiments prepared for a large-scale sham battle to be waged in the autumn. Romodanovsky, the mock King of Pressburg, commanded an army which consisted of the two play regiments and other troops and was pitted against a Streltsy army commanded by Prince Ivan Buturlin, the mock King of Poland. The battle, which began at dawn on October 6, was fought bitterly two days, and ended in victory of the "Russian" army commanded by Romodanovsky. But Peter, not satisfied, ordered a second round, which took place in high wind, rain and mud on October 9. Romodanovsky's army was again victorious, but there were real casualties. Prince Ivan Dolgoruky was shot in the right arm, the wound became infected and nine days later he died. Gordon himself was wounded in the thigh and his face so severely burned that he spent a week in bed.

During this period, Peter did not forget his boats. To speed the work at Pereslavl, twenty Dutch shipwrights from the famous shipyard at Zaandam in Holland had been contracted early in 1691 to come to Russia. When Peter returned to Lake Pleschev, he found these men working with Karsten Brandt on two small thirty-gun frigates and three yachts. Peter stayed with them only three weeks, but the following year he visited the lake four times, twice remaining for more than a month. Equipped with an "imperial decree" from Prince-Caesar Romodanovsky to build a warship from the keel up, Peter worked from dawn to dusk, eating in the boatyard and sleeping only when he was too tired to work. Oblivious to everything else, he refused to go to Moscow to receive the visit of an ambassador from Persia. Only when two senior members of his government, his uncle Lev Naryshkin and Boris Golitsyn, traveled to the lake to persuade him of the importance of the event did Peter reluctantly consent to lay down his tools and go with them to Moscow. Within a week, he was back at the lake.

In August, he persuaded his mother and sister Natalya to visit his boat-yard and fleet. His wife, Eudoxia, came with the other ladies, and during the month they were there Peter enthusiastically maneuvered his little flotilla of twelve ships before their eyes. Sitting on the small hill that rises from the shore, the ladies could see the Tsar, dressed in a crimson coat, standing on deck, waving his arms, pointing and shouting orders—all thoroughly mysterious and disquieting to women not far removed from the terem.

Peter remained at the lake that year until November. When he did finally return to Moscow, an attack of dysentery kept him in bed for six weeks. He became so feeble that there were fears for his life. His comrades and followers were alarmed: If Peter died, nothing could prevent the return of Sophia and exile or even death for themselves. But the Tsar was only twenty-one, his constitution was strong, and toward Christmas he began to

recover. By late January he was once again spending his evenings in the German Suburb. Near the end of February, Lefort gave a banquet in Peter's honor, and at dawn the next day, without having slept, Peter rode off to Pereslavl to work on his boats through the whole of Lent.

His visits that year, 1693, were to be Peter's last extended periods at Lake Pleschev. Twice, in subsequent years, he passed by the lake on his way to the White Sea, and still later he went there to check on artillery materials for the Azov campaign. But after 1697 he did not return until he was en route to Persia in 1722. After a quarter of a century, he found boats and buildings neglected and rotted. He gave orders that what remained should be carefully preserved, and for a while an effort was made by the local nobility. In the nineteenth century, every spring, all the clergy of Pereslavl would board a barge and, attended by a crowd of people in many boats, sail to the middle of the lake to bless the water in memory of Peter.

10

ARCHANGEL

LIKE A GIANT closed up in a cave with only a pinhole for light and air, the great land mass of the Muscovite empire possessed but a single seaport: Archangel, on the White Sea. This unique harbor, remote from the Russian heartland, is only 130 miles south of the Arctic Circle. Six months of the year, it is frozen in ice. Yet, despite its drawbacks, Archangel was Russian. It was the one place in the entire realm where a young monarch intoxicated by the idea of ships and oceans could actually see great ships and breathe salt air. No tsar had even been to Archangel, but no tsar had ever been interested in ships. Peter himself explained it in his preface to the *Maritime Regulations,* written twenty-seven years later in 1720:

> For some years I had the fill of my desires on Lake Pleschev, but finally it got too narrow for me. . . . I then decided to see the open sea, and began often to beg the permission of my mother to go to Archangel. She forbade me such a dangerous journey, but, seeing my great desire and unchangeable longing, allowed it in spite of herself.

Before Natalya bowed to his pleas, however, she extracted from her son—"my life and my hope"—a promise that he would not sail on the ocean.

On July 11, 1693, Peter left Moscow for Archangel with more than 100 people, including Lefort and many of his Jolly Company, as well as eight singers, two dwarfs and forty Streltsy to act as guards. The distance from the capital was 600 miles as the crow flies, but as humans traveled, by road and river, it was almost 1,000 miles. The first 300 were up the Great Russian Road, past the Troitsky Monastery, Pereslavl and Rostov, across the Volga at Yaroslavl to the busy town of Vologda, the southern transshipment center for the Archangel trade, where they boarded a fleet of large, colorfully painted barges which had been prepared for them. The rest of the trip lay down the River Suhona to its junction with the River Dvina, and, from there, north on the Dvina itself to Archangel. The barges moved

slowly, even though they were traveling downstream. In spring w[ ]
river was in flood from melting snows, Peter's boats could have
easily, but now it was midsummer, the rivers had dropped and sometimes
the barges scraped bottom and had to be dragged. In two weeks, the
flotilla reached Kholmogory, the administrative capital and seat of the
archbishop of the northern region. Here, the Tsar was welcomed with
clanging churchbells and banquets; with difficulty he broke away and continued the last few miles downriver. At last, he saw the watchtowers, the
warehouses, the docks and anchored ships which made up the port of
Archangel.

Archangel did not lie directly on the coast of the White Sea. Rather, it
was situated thirty miles up the river, where the ice formed even more
quickly than in the salt water of the ocean itself. From October to
May, the river running past the town was frozen hard as steel. But in the
spring, when the ice began to melt first along the White Sea coasts, then
along the rivers inland, Archangel began to stir. Barges loaded in the interior of Russia with furs, hides, hemp, tallow, wheat, caviar and potash
floated in an endless procession north down the Dvina. At the same time,
the first merchant ships from London, Amsterdam, Hamburg and Bremen,
convoyed by warships to guard against the roving French corsairs, pushed
their way through the melting ice floes around the North Cape to Archangel.
In their holds, they brought wool and cotton cloth, silk and lace, gold and
silver objects, wines, and chemicals for dying cloth. In Archangel, during the
hectic summer months, as many as a hundred foreign ships might be seen
lying in the river, discharging their Western cargoes and taking on Russian
ones.

The days were feverishly busy, but life was pleasant for foreigners during an Archangel summer. In late June there were twenty-one hours of sunlight a day, and people slept little. The town was splendidly supplied with
fresh fish and game. Salmon was brought from the sea to be smoked or
salted and sent to Europe or the interior, but there was plenty to eat fresh in
Archangel. The rivers were stocked with fresh-water fish, including perch,
pike and delicious small eels. Poultry and wild deer were numerous and cheap,
and a partridge the size of a turkey could be had for two English pence.
There were hares, ducks and geese. Because so many ships arrived from
Europe, Dutch beer, French wine and cognac were plentiful, although
Russian customs duties made them expensive. There were a Dutch Reformed church and a Lutheran church; there were balls and picnics and a
constant stream of new captains and officers.

For a young man like Peter, fascinated by the West and Westerners and
magnetized by the sea, everything here was exciting: the ocean itself
stretching over the horizon, the tide rising and falling twice a day, the
smell of salt sea air and of rope and tar around the wharves, the sight of so

many ships at anchor, their great oaken hulls, their tall masts and furled sails, the bustle of the busy port with small boats crisscrossing the harbor, the wharves and warehouses piled with interesting goods, the merchants, sea captains and sailors from many lands.

Peter could see most of the activity in the port from the house prepared for him on Moiseev Island. Already, on the first day of his arrival, he was anxious to put to sea, his promise to Natalya forgotten. He hurried to the quay where lay a small twelve-gun yacht, the *St. Peter,* which had been built for him. He boarded her, studied her hull and rigging and waited impatiently for a chance to test her qualities beyond the mouth of the Dvina on the open sea.

His opportunity came soon after. A convoy of Dutch and English merchantmen was sailing for Europe. Peter aboard the *St. Peter* would escort it through the White Sea to the edge of the Arctic Ocean. On a favorable wind and tide, the ships weighed anchor, unfurled canvas and steered down the river, past the two low forts which guarded the approaches from the sea. By midday, for the first time in history, a Russian tsar was on salt water. As the low hills and forests receded into the distance, Peter was surrounded only by the dancing waves, the ships rising and falling on the deep green water of the White Sea, the creak of timbers and the whistle of wind in the rigging.

All too soon for Peter, the convoy reached the extreme northern point where the White Sea, still relatively landlocked, broadens out into the vast Arctic Ocean. Here Peter reluctantly turned back. On returning to Archangel, knowing that word of his voyage would soon reach Moscow, he wrote to his mother. Without actually mentioning the trip, he sought to calm her in advance:

> You have written, O Lady, that I have saddened you by not writing of my arrival. But even now I have no time to write in detail because I am expecting some ships, and as soon as they come—when no one knows, but they are expected soon as they are more than three weeks from Amsterdam—I shall come to you immediately, travelling day and night. But I beg for mercy for one thing: Why do you trouble yourself about me? You have deigned to write that you have given me unto the care of the Virgin. When you have such a guardian for me, why do you grieve?

It was a resourceful argument, but it made no difference to Natalya. She wrote to Peter, begging him to remember his promise to remain on shore and urging him to return to Moscow. She even enclosed a letter from his three-year-old son, Alexis, endorsing her plea. Peter replied several times that she must not worry: "If you are grieved, what pleasure

have I? I beg you make my wretched self happy by not grieving about me" and "You have deigned to write to me . . . to say that I should write to you oftener. Even now I write by every post and my only fault is that I do not come myself."

In fact, Peter had no intention of quitting Archangel until the expected fleet of Dutch merchantmen arrived from Amsterdam. Meanwhile, his days passed joyfully. From the window of his house on Moiseev Island he could see ships arriving and departing on the river. Eagerly, he boarded and inspected every ship in port, questioning the captains for hours, climbing the masts to study the rigging and examining the construction of the hulls. The Dutch and English captains lavished hospitality on the youthful monarch, inviting him to drink and dine with them on board. They talked of the wonders of Amsterdam, the great shipbuilding center of Zaandam, the courage of Dutch seamen and soldiers in resisting the ambitions of Louis XIV of France. Soon, Holland became Peter's passion, and he walked the streets of Archangel dressed in the costume of a Dutch sea captain. He sat in taverns smoking a clay pipe and emptying bottle after bottle with grizzled Dutch captains who had sailed with the legendary admirals Tromp and de Ruyter, and with Lefort and his comrades he attended endless dinners and dances at the houses of foreign merchants. And he also found time to work at forge and lathe. It was during this visit that he began turning the elaborate ivory chandelier made from walrus tusks that now hangs in the Peter Gallery of the Hermitage. He went frequently to the Church of the Prophet Elijah, and worshippers learned to accept the sight of the Tsar reading the epistle or standing and singing with the choir. He liked the Archbishop of Kholmogory, Afanasy, and enjoyed talking to him after his midday dinner.

Even as the summer was ending, Peter had decided to return to Archangel the following year, but there were things he wanted to change. It depressed him that, except for his own small yacht, there was in this Russian port no Russian ship manned by Russian seamen. With his own hands, he laid the keel of a vessel larger than the little *St. Peter,* and commanded that it be finished during the winter. In addition, wanting a truly ocean-going Western ship, he asked Lefort and Vinius to order a Dutch-built frigate from Nicholas Witsen, Burgomaster of Amsterdam.

In mid-September, the Dutch merchant convoy arrived. Peter welcomed it and at the same time said goodbye to Archangel with a huge celebration organized by Lefort. There were banquets lasting a week, balls and salvos of artillery from the forts and the ships at anchor. The return to Moscow was slow. The barges were moving upriver now, dragged not by animals but by men pulling ropes along the shore. While the watermen strained and the barges moved slowly, the passengers got out and walked along at the edge of the forest, sometimes shooting wild ducks and pigeons for their

dinner. Whenever the flotilla passed a village, the priest and peasants came to the royal barge to present fish, gooseberries, chickens and fresh eggs. Sometimes, standing on the barges at night, the travelers would see a wolf on the bank. By the time they reached Moscow in mid-October, the first snow had fallen in Archangel. The harbor was closed for winter.

THAT SAME WINTER, after his return to Moscow, Peter suffered a heavy blow. On February 4, 1694, after an illness of only two days, his mother, the Tsaritsa Natalya, died at forty-two. Natalya had not been well since her month-long visit to Peter's regatta at Lake Pleschev in 1693. In the winter, she was dangerously stricken. Peter was at a banquet when he received a message that his mother was failing; he jumped up and hurried to her bed-chamber. He had spoken with her and received her last blessing when the Patriarch appeared and began to berate him for coming in the Western clothes which Peter now customarily wore; it was disrespectful and in-sulting to the Tsaritsa, the Patriarch declared. Furious, Peter replied that a patriarch, as head of the church, should have weightier matters to attend to than the business of tailors. Not wanting to continue the argument, Peter stormed out. He was at his house in Preobrazhenskoe when the news came that his mother was dead.

Natalya's death plunged Peter into grief. For several days, he could not speak without bursting into tears. Gordon went to Preobrazhenskoe to find Peter "exceeding melancholy and dejected." The Tsaritsa's funeral was a magnificent state pageant, but Peter refused to attend. Only after her burial did he come to her grave to pray, alone. To Fedor Apraxin in Arch-angel he wrote:

> I dumbly tell my grief and my last sorrow about which neither my hand nor my heart can write in detail without remembering what the Apostle Paul says about not grieving for such things, and the voice of Edras, "Call me again the day that is past." I forget all this as much as possible, as being above my reasoning and mind, for thus it has pleased the Almighty God, and all things are according to the will of their Creator. Amen. Therefore, like Noah, resting awhile from my grief, and leaving aside that which can never return, I write about the living.

The rest of the letter went on to give instructions about the ship being built at Archangel, clothing for the sailors and other practical matters. At twenty-two, life moves swiftly and wounds heal quickly. Within five days, Peter appeared at Lefort's house. There were no ladies, no music, no dancing and no fireworks, but Peter did begin to talk about the world.

Within the family, Natalya's place in Peter's affections was taken by his younger sister, Natalya, a cheerful girl who, without understanding all of her brother's objectives, always supported him wholeheartedly. She belonged to his generation, and she was curious about everything that came from abroad. Nevertheless, with the Tsaritsa's death, all the strong members of Peter's family were gone: his father and mother dead, his half-sister Sophia locked into a convent. His wife, Eudoxia, was there, but he seemed utterly oblivious to her feelings or even her existence. Gone with the Tsaritsa were the last bonds of restraint on Peter's actions. He had loved his mother and tried to please her, but increasingly he had been impatient. In recent years, her constant effort to restrict his movements and curtail his desire for novelty and contact with foreigners had weighed on him. Now, he was free to live as he wished. For Natalya's life, although influenced by her years in Matveev's Westernized house, had remained essentially that of a Muscovite woman of the older type. Her passing was the breaking of the last powerful link which had bound Peter to the traditions of the past. It was only Natalya who had kept Peter in touch with Kremlin ritual; after her death, he quickly ceased to take part in it. Two and a half months after Natalya's death, Peter appeared with Ivan in the great court Easter procession, but this was the last time he participated in Kremlin ceremonies. After that, no one possessed the strength to force him to do what he was not inclined to do.

IN THE SPRING OF 1694, Peter returned to Archangel. This time, twenty-two barges were needed to carry the 300 people of Peter's suite down the river. The barges also carried twenty-four cannon for the ships, 1,000 muskets, many barrels of powder and even more barrels of beer. In high spirits at the thought of going to sea again, Peter promoted several of his older comrades to high naval ranks: Fedor Romodanovsky was made an admiral, Ivan Buturlin a vice admiral and Patrick Gordon a rear admiral. None except Gordon had ever been on a boat, and Gordon's nautical experience had been as a passenger on ships crossing the English Channel. Peter himself took the title of skipper, intending to captain the Dutch frigate ordered from Witsen.

In Archangel, Peter gave thanks at the Church of the Prophet Elijah, and then rushed to the river to see his ships. His little yacht, *St. Peter*, lay at the jetty, rigged and ready for sea. The Dutch frigate had not arrived, but the new ship which he had begun the summer before was finished and waiting in stocks for him to launch. Peter grabbed a sledgehammer, knocked away the props and delightedly watched the hull splash down into the water. While the new ship, christened *St. Paul,* was being fitted with masts and sails, Peter decided to pass the time by visiting the Solovetsky Monastery,

which lay on an island in the White Sea. On the night of June 10, he boarded the *St. Peter,* taking with him the Archbishop Afanasy, a few comrades and a small group of soldiers. They left on the tide, but at the mouth of the Dvina the wind dropped, and it was not until the following morning that they sailed, on a freshening wind, out into the White Sea. During the day, the sky darkened and the wind began to rise. Eighty miles out from Archangel, a full gale burst over the tiny ship. Howling wind ripped the sails from masts and booms, and mountainous green seas rolled over the deck. The yacht pitched and rolled in giant waves, threatening to capsize; the crew, experienced sailors, huddled together, praying. The passengers, assuming that they were doomed, crossed themselves and prepared to drown. Drenched, the Archbishop struggled to pass among them on the rolling deck, giving the Last Sacrament.

Peter, braced at the helm in the wind and spray, received the Last Sacrament, but did not give up hope. Each time the ship rose on one great wave and fell into the deep trough that followed, Peter struggled with the rudder, trying to keep the bow into the wind. His determination had an effect. The pilot crept aft and shouted in Peter's ear that they should try to make for the harbor of Unskaya Gulf. With the pilot assisting him at the helm, they steered through a narrow passage, past rocks over which huge seas were boiling and hissing, into the harbor. At about noon on June 12, after twenty-four hours of terror, the little yacht anchored in calm waters off the small Pertominsk Monastery.

The entire ship's company rowed ashore to give thanks for their salvation in the monastery chapel. Peter rewarded the pilot with money and presented the monks with gifts and additional grants of revenue. Then, as his personal thanksgiving, he made with his own hands a wooden cross ten feet high and carried it on his shoulder to the spot on the shore where he had landed after his ordeal. It bore his inscription in Dutch: "This cross was made by Captain Peter in the summer of 1694."*

Outside the anchorage, the storm raged for three more days. On the 16th, the wind dropped, and Peter again set sail for the Solovetsky Monastery, the most famous in northern Russia. He spent three days at Solovetsky, pleasing the monks by his devotions before their holy relics.

---

* A few years later, Peter ingeniously used his near-miraculous escape in this storm to reinforce his case that he must visit the West, an idea which most Russians opposed. He was dining with a group at the home of Boris Sheremetev when he revealed that during the height of the tempest he had vowed to St. Peter, his patron saint, that if his life was saved he would travel to Rome to give thanks at the tomb of his namesake apostle in the Holy City. Now, he declared, he had to fulfill his vow.

Peter's visit to Rome, scheduled for the last part of the Great Embassy, never took place. He was en route in 1698 when he was called hurriedly back to Moscow by news of the last revolt of the Streltsy.

His return to Archangel was on calm seas, and his arrival was hailed with jubilation by his anxious friends, who knew about the storm and feared for the survival of the *St. Peter* and its passenger.

A few weeks later, the new ship which Peter had launched was ready for sea. Now, with the smaller *St. Peter,* Peter had two ocean-going ships, and when the new Dutch-built frigate arrived from Amsterdam, his flotilla would increase to three. This happy event took place on July 21, when the frigate *Holy Prophecy* sailed into the estuary of the Dvina and anchored off Solombola. Under the command of Captain Jan Flam, who had already made thirty voyages to Archangel, she was a sturdy, round-nosed Dutch warship with forty-four cannon ranged along her upper and middle decks. Burgomaster Witsen, hoping to please the Tsar, had seen to it that the cabins were wood-paneled, with elegant polished furniture, silk hangings and handsomely woven carpets.*

Peter was wild with excitement. He rushed to the river when the ship was sighted, hurried on board and climbed or crawled through every inch of rigging and lower deck. That night, the new skipper of the *Holy Prophecy* celebrated on board, and the following day he wrote ecstatically to Vinius:

Min Her:

What I have so long desired has come about. Jan Flam has arrived all right with forty-four cannon and forty sailors, on his ship. Congratulate all of us! I shall write more fully by the next post, but now I am beside myself with joy and cannot write at length. Besides, it is impossible, for Bacchus is always honored in such cases and with his vine leaves he dulls the eyes of those who wish to write at length.

Skipper of the Ship Holy Prophecy

Within a week, the new frigate was ready to sail under the command of her new captain. Peter had arranged that his small Russian flotilla should accompany to the Arctic Ocean a convoy of Dutch and English merchantmen returning home. Before sailing, Peter had arranged that the

---

* Along with her cannon and luxurious furnishings, the *Holy Prophecy* brought another Western gift to Russia. When the ship anchored at Archangel, the great red-white-and-blue banner of Holland floated from her stern. Peter, admiring the ship and everything about her, immediately decided that his own naval flag should be modeled after it. Accordingly, he took the Dutch design—three broad horizontal stripes, red on top, white in the middle and blue on the bottom—and simply changed the sequence. In the Russian flag, white was on top, then blue, then red. This naval flag quickly became the flag of the Russian empire (as distinct from the imperial standard of the tsar, which was the double eagle) and remained so until the fall of the dynasty in 1917.

disposition of the fleet and the signals for directing its movements should be according to techniques which he himself had devised. The newly commissioned *St. Paul,* with Vice Admiral Buturlin aboard, was in the van, followed by four Dutch ships laden with Russian cargoes. Then came Peter's new frigate, with Admiral Romodanovsky and the Tsar himself as captain (although Jan Flam was at his elbow). After this, four English merchantmen and, in the rear, the yacht *St. Peter,* bearing General Gordon, the new rear admiral. Gordon's seamanship was meager; he almost steered his ship aground on a small island, thinking that the crosses in a cemetery on shore were the masts and yardarms of the vessels ahead of him.

Peter's flotilla escorted the convoy as far as Svyatoy Nos on the Kola Peninsula, east of Murmansk. Here, the White Sea broadened out into the gray waters of the Arctic Ocean. Peter had hoped to sail farther, but a strong wind was blowing, and after his earlier experience, he allowed himself to be persuaded to turn back. Five guns were fired to signal that the escort was turning back, and the Western ships disappeared over the northern horizon. Peter's three small ships returned to Archangel, the Tsar held a farewell banquet and, on September 3, reluctantly started back for Moscow.

IN SEPTEMBER of that year, 1694, a wide valley near the village of Kozhukhovo on the bank of the Moscow River was the site of Peter's last and greatest peacetime army maneuvers. This time, 30,000 men were involved, including infantry, cavalry, artillery and long columns of supply wagons. The combatants were divided into two armies. One, commanded by Ivan Buturlin, consisted of six Streltsy regiments plus numerous squadrons of cavalry. The opposing side was commanded by Fedor Romodanovsky, the mock King of Pressburg, who commanded Peter's two Guards regiments, the Preobrazhensky and Semyonovsky, plus two additional regular regiments and a number of companies of militia summoned from towns as far from Moscow as Vladimir and Suzdal. In essence, the war game revolved around an assault by Buturlin's army on a riverbank fort to be defended by Romodanovsky's force.

Before the maneuvers began, Moscow was treated to the excitement of seeing the two armies in parade uniforms, accompanied by scribes, musicians and the special troop of dwarf cavalry, marching through the city streets on their way to the maneuver ground. As the Preobrazhensky Regiment approached, Muscovites gasped: In front of the troops, dressed as a regular artilleryman, marched the Tsar. For a population accustomed to glimpsing tsars at a distance in all their majesty, it was an unbelievable sight.

In the maneuvers, the fighting was conducted with zest, inspired by the

natural rivalry between the Streltsy regiments and the Guards, both determined to prove their merit before the Tsar. Bombs and cannon were fired, and although there was no ball and shot, faces were burned and bodies maimed. The assaulting army threw a bridge across the Moscow River and began to mine the Pressburg fort. Peter had counted on a long siege in which all the Western arts of mining and countermining under fortifications could be practiced, but, unfortunately, Bacchus also was on the scene, and most days ended with huge banquets and drinking bouts. After one of these, the attacking force, flushed with confidence, decided to make a sudden assault. The defenders, equally flushed, were in no state to resist, and the fort was easily taken. Peter was furious at this hasty conclusion. The following day, he ordered the victors out of the fort and all prisoners returned, and commanded that the fort not be stormed again until the walls had been properly mined and had properly caved in. He was obeyed, and this time it took three weeks to subdue the fort in the textbook manner.

The Kozhukhovo maneuvers were concluded late in October, and as the regiments returned to their barracks for winter, Peter began to discuss with his advisors how he might best employ them in the coming year. Perhaps the moment had come to stop playing at war; perhaps it was time to turn this new weapon he had forged against the Turks, with whom Russia was still technically at war. That some action of this kind was being considered that winter is revealed in a letter written by Gordon in December 1694. "I believe and hope," the Scot wrote to a friend in the West, "that this coming summer we shall undertake something for the advantage of Christianity and our allies."

11

AZOV

PETER WAS NOW TWENTY-TWO, in the prime of his young manhood. To those who were seeing the Tsar for the first time, his most awesome physical characteristic was his height: at six feet seven inches, the monarch towered over everyone around him, the more so because in those days the average man was shorter than today. Tall as he was, however, Peter's body was more angular than massive. His shoulders were unusually thin for a man of his height, his arms were long and his hands, which he was eager to display, were powerful, rough and permanently callused from his work in the shipyard. Peter's face in these years was round, still youthful and almost handsome. He wore a small mustache and no wig; instead, he let his own straight, auburn-brown hair hang halfway between his ears and his shoulders.

His most extraordinary quality, even more remarkable than his height, was his titanic energy. He could not sit still or stay long in the same place. He walked so quickly with his long, loose-limbed stride that those in his company had to trot to keep up with him. When forced to do paperwork, he paced around a stand-up desk. Seated at a banquet, he would eat for a few minutes, then spring up to see what was happening in the next room or to take a walk outdoors. Needing movement, he liked to burn off his energy in dancing. When he had been in one place for a while, he wanted to leave, to move along, to see new people and new scenery, to form new impressions. The most accurate image of Peter the Great is of a man who throughout his life was perpetually curious, perpetually restless, perpetually in movement.

It was, however, during these same years that a worrisome, often mortifying physical disorder began to afflict the young Tsar. When he was emotionally agitated or under stress from the pressure of events, Peter's face sometimes began to twitch uncontrollably. The disorder, usually troubling only the left side of his face, varied in degree of severity: Sometimes the tremor was no more than a facial tic lasting only a second or

two; at other times, there would be a genuine convulsion, beginning with a contraction of the muscles on the left side of his neck, followed by a spasm involving the entire left side of his face and the rolling up of his eyes until only the whites could be seen. At its worst, when violent, disjointed motion of the left arm was also involved, the convulsion ended only when Peter had lost consciousness.

With only unprofessional descriptions of Peter's symptoms available, neither the precise nature of his illness nor its cause will ever be known. Most likely, he suffered from focal epileptic seizures, among the milder of a range of neurological disorders whose most severe form is grand-mal epilepsy. There is no evidence that Peter suffered from this extreme condition; there are no reports that he collapsed totally unconscious on the floor, foamed at the mouth or lost control of his bodily functions. In Peter's case, the disturbance began in a part of the brain affecting muscles of the left side of his neck and face. If the provocation continued without alleviation, the focus of the disturbance could spread to adjacent parts of the brain affecting the motion of the left shoulder and arm.

Not knowing the exact nature of the affliction, it is even more difficult to pinpoint the cause. At the time, and in subsequent historical writing, a wide range of opinions has been offered. Peter's convulsions have been ascribed to the traumatic horror he suffered in 1682 when, as a ten-year-old boy, he stood by his mother and watched the massacre of Matveev and the Naryshkins by the rampaging Streltsy. By others, his condition has been traced to the shock of being awakened in the middle of the night at Preobrazhenskoe seven years later and told that the Streltsy were coming to kill him. Some have blamed it on the excessive drinking which the Tsar learned at Lefort's elbow and practiced with the Jolly Company. There was even a rumor, passed to the West in correspondence from the German Suburb, that the Tsar's affliction had been caused by poison administered by Sophia endeavoring to clear her path to the throne. The most likely cause of this kind of epilepsy, however, especially in the absence of a hard blow which could leave permanent scar tissue on the brain, is high fever over an extended period. Peter suffered such a fever during the weeks between November 1693 and January 1694 when he became so ill that many believed he would die. A fever of this kind in the nature of encephalitis can cause local scarring of the brain; subsequently, when specific psychological stimuli disturb this damaged area, a seizure of the kind which Peter suffered can be triggered.

The psychological impact of this illness upon Peter was profound; it accounts in large part for his unusual shyness, especially with strangers who were not familiar with his convulsions and therefore unprepared to witness them. For paroxysms of this kind, as disturbing to those around him as to Peter himself, there was no real treatment, although what was done

then would still be considered eminently reasonable today. When the tremor was no more than a tic, Peter and those in his company tried to proceed as if nothing had happened. If the convulsion became more pronounced, his friends or orderlies quickly brought someone to him whose presence he found relaxing. Eventually, whenever she was nearby, this was his second wife, Catherine, but before Catherine appeared, or if she was not present, it was some young woman who could soothe the Tsar. "Peter Alexeevich, here is the person to whom you wished to speak," his worried orderly would say and then withdraw. The Tsar would lie down and place his shaking head on the woman's lap and she would stroke his forehead and temples, speaking to him softly and reassuringly. Peter would fall asleep, his loss of consciousness clearing the electrical disturbances in his brain, and when he awoke an hour or two later, he was always refreshed and in far better humor than he had been before.

IN THE WINTER OF 1695, Peter sought some new outlet for his energy. His two summers in Archangel, his brief cruises on the White Sea, his long talks with English and Dutch sea captains had stimulated him. Now, he wanted to travel farther, to see more, to sail more ships. One recurring idea was an expedition to Persia and the East. This subject came up often during winter evenings in the German Suburb, where Dutch and English merchants talked grandly of the Europe-to-Persia and Europe-to-India trade which could be developed along the rivers to Russia. From Archangel, Lefort had written to his family in Geneva that "there was talk of a journey in about two years' time to Kazan and Astrachan." Later, the Swiss wrote, "Next summer we are going to construct five large ships and two galleys which, God willing, will go two years hence to Astrachan for the conclusion of important treaties with Persia." "There is also an idea of constructing some galleys and going to the Baltic Sea," wrote Lefort.

With talk of Persia and the Baltic in the air, Moscow was surprised in the winter of 1695 at the announcement that Russia would embark the following summer on a renewed war against the Tatars and their overlords, the Ottoman Empire. We do not know exactly why Peter decided that winter to attack the Turkish fortress of Azov. It has been suggested that this sudden plunge into active war stemmed entirely from Peter's restlessness and that it served mainly as an outlet for his energy and curiosity. Thus, seen in retrospect, it becomes another step in the great maritime adventure of his life: first the Yauza, then Lake Pleschev, then Archangel—so the sequence runs. Now, he dreamed of creating a fleet. But Russia's only seaport was frozen solid six months of the year. The nearest sea, the Baltic, was still firmly gripped by Sweden, the dominant military power in Northern

Europe. Only one avenue to salt water remained: to the south and the Black Sea.

Or, if this new adventure was not a Game of Neptune, perhaps it was a Game of Mars. For twenty years, Peter had been playing with soldiers; first toys, then boys, then grown men. His games had grown from drills involving a few hundred idle stable boys and falconers to 30,000 men involved in the assault and defense of the river fort of Pressburg. Now, seeking the excitement of real combat, he looked for a fortress to besiege, and Azov, isolated at the bottom of the Ukrainian steppe, suited admirably.

Unquestionably, Peter's compulsion to reach the sea and his desire to test his army both played a part in the Azov decision. But there were other reasons, too. Russia was still at war with the Ottoman Empire, and every summer the horsemen of the Tatar Khan rode north to raid the Ukraine. In 1692, an army of 12,000 Tatar cavalry appeared before the town of Neimerov, burned it to the ground and carried away 2,000 prisoners to be sold in the Ottoman slave marts. A year later, the number of Russian prisoners mounted to 15,000.

Since Sophia's fall, Moscow had done little to defend these southern border regions, despite their appeals to the capital. Indeed, the Tsar's indifference had led to a stinging jibe from Dositheus, the Orthodox Patriarch of Jerusalem. "The Crimean Tatars are but a handful," he wrote to Peter, "and yet they boast that they receive tribute from you. The Tatars are Turkish subjects, so it follows that you are Turkish subjects. Many times you have boasted that you will do such and such, but all finished with words only and nothing in fact is done."

In addition, there was a diplomatic reason for a resumption of hostilities with the Turks and Tatars. Moscow's ally King Jan Sobieski of Poland, judging that Russia had contributed nothing of consequence in the common war against Turkey, had threatened to make a separate peace with the Ottoman Empire which would ignore Russia's interests completely. Indeed, the King complained to the Russian resident in Warsaw, he could scarcely be blamed for abandoning Moscow's interests since no one had troubled to explain to him exactly what Moscow's interests were.

The Azov campaign, then, was more than an elaborate war game mounted for the Tsar's private education and amusement. The desire to suppress the Tatar raids and the need to make a military effort to satisfy the Poles were serious pressures to which any Russian government would have had to respond. These two factors happened to dovetail perfectly with Peter's private desires.

The decision remained as to where the campaign would take place. There were two objectives: to harry the Turk and to suppress the Tatar. Golitsyn's two unhappy campaigns had left the Russians wary of still

another direct attack across the steppe toward Perekop. Instead, this time the two prongs of the Russian attack would fall on either side of the peninsular stronghold. The dual objectives would be the mouths of the rivers Dnieper and Don, where Turkish forts blocked Ukrainian Cossack or Russian access to the Black Sea. This time, instead of marching across the dry steppe, trundling supplies in thousands of wagons, the Russian army would travel south by water, using barges as vehicles of supply.

Two very different Russian armies were formed to make the double offensive. The eastern army was to move down the Don to attack the powerful Turkish fortress of Azov and was composed of Peter's play soldiers, the men who had attacked or defended Pressburg in the previous autumn games at Kozhukhovo. They included the new Preobrazhensky and Semyonovsky Guards Regiments, the Streltsy and the Western-trained artillery and cavalry—31,000 men in three divisions, commanded by Lefort, Golovin and Gordon. To avoid jealousy, none of the three was named supreme commander; each division was to operate independently, and the three generals were to make overall decisions in council in the presence of the twenty-three-year-old Bombardier Peter.

The second or western prong of the Russian offensive, which would move down the Dnieper to attack the major Turkish forts at Ochakov and Kazikerman and three smaller forts guarding the mouth of the river, was made up of a much larger, more traditional Russian army, commanded by the boyar Boris Sheremetev. This army was reminiscent of the huge forces which Golitsyn had led south: 120,000 men, most of them peasant levies called up in the old Russian style for a single summer of campaigning: In the overall plan, Sheremetev's effort was to be subsidiary to Peter's; its purpose was not simply to capture the Dnieper forts but also to distract the main army of Tatar horsemen from riding east to attack Peter's troops before Azov. In addition, Peter hoped that the presence of this huge covering force would sever the communications between the Crimea and the European Ottoman provinces to the west, thus obstructing the customary annual movement of Tatar cavalry to join the Sultan's army in the Balkans. This would be a direct contribution to Russia's hard-pressed allies. Further, the mere presence of this vast Russian army in the Ukraine would strengthen the Tsar's influence among the volatile, impressionable Cossacks.

Once the plan of campaign was decided, Peter plunged into preparations. Exuberantly, he wrote to Apraxin in Archangel, "At Kozhukhovo we jested. Now we are going to play the real game before Azov."

Gordon's division was ready first and left Moscow in March, moving south across the steppe "full of flowers and herbs, asparagus, wild thyme, marjoram, tulips, pinks, meliot and maiden gilly flowers," according to the commander's diary. The main body with Peter, Lefort and Golovin left in May, embarking directly onto barges in the Moscow River and

moving downstream to join the Volga. It followed the great river as far as Tsaritsyn (later Stalingrad, now Volgograd), then dragged the cannon and supplies across to the lower Don, where it reembarked on other boats. Progress was slow because of the leaky barges and inexperienced boatmen and Peter angrily wrote to Vinius: "Most of all the delay was caused by stupid pilots and workmen who call themselves masters, but in reality are as far from being so as the earth is from heaven." On June 29, the main body of 21,000 men reached Azov to find Gordon's 10,000 soldiers entrenched before the city.

The fortress town of Azov stood on the left bank of the southernmost branch of the Don about fifteen miles upstream from the Sea of Azov. In 500 B.C., a Greek colony, one of a number of Greek settlements around the coast of the Black Sea, had occupied the site. Later, the town, commanding the entrance to the great river and its trade, had been a colony of the merchant state of Genoa. Taken by the Turks in 1475, it became the northeastern link in their absolute control of the Black Sea and served as a barrier to any Russian advance down the Don. They had fortified the town with towers and walls, and, as part of the barrier system, two Turkish watchtower forts were situated a mile upriver from the city, with iron chains stretched between them across the river to prevent the light Cossack galleys slipping past the town and out into the sea.

With Peter present before the town, the Russian cannon opened fire, and for fourteen weeks the bombardment continued. There were many problems. Experienced engineers were lacking, and in Peter's day a siege was as much a matter for engineers as for artillerymen or foot soldiers. The Russian supply organization was unable to cope with the problem of feeding 30,000 men in the open air for so long a time, and the army quickly denuded the meager countryside around Azov. The Streltsy were unwilling to follow orders given by European officers and were often useless. Of the overall situation, Gordon said, "We sometimes acted as if we were not in earnest."

At first, the two Turkish watchtower forts above the town prevented the passage of Russian barges down the river with supplies for the army. The supplies had to be unloaded above this point and carried in wagons overland to the troops, and the wagons were exposed to swooping attacks from the Tatar cavalry which hovered on the periphery of the Russian camp. Capture of the two forts became a primary objective, and the army was cheered when the Don Cossacks stormed one of the forts; soon after, under intense artillery fire, the Turks abandoned the other fort.

Peter's happiness at this success was quickly spoiled by an episode of treachery in his own camp. A Dutch sailor named Jacob Jensen defected from the Russians to the Turks carrying important information. Originally a seaman on a Dutch ship in Archangel, Jensen had entered Russian service, accepted the Orthodox faith and served in the new Russian artillery. Peter,

liking both Dutchmen and artillery, had kept Jensen near him and, during the days and nights before Azov, had confided in him. When Jensen deserted, he betrayed to the Pasha in Azov the numbers and disposition of the Russian troops, the strengths and weaknesses of the siege works and what he knew of Peter's intentions. He also made a suggestion based on the immutable habit of all Russians, including soldiers, of taking a nap after the big midday meal. A few days later, at exactly this hour, a formidable Turkish sortie into the Russian trenches was launched. At first, the sleepy Russians ran, but Gordon managed to rally them, and after a desperate three-hour battle the Turks were driven back. The thrust was costly to the besiegers: 400 Russians were killed and 600 wounded, and many of the siege works were wrecked.

Even more damaging than Jensen's treachery was the inability of the Russian army to cut off and isolate the fortress. Gordon, the most experienced soldier present, wanted a total investiture of the town, but, for lack of men, the Russian siege works did not even completely encircle the land side of Azov. Between the end of the Russian trenches and the river was an open gap through which Tatar cavalry maintained communication with the Azov garrison. And the siege was rendered even less effective by lack of ships to control the river. Peter could only watch helplessly when twenty Turkish galleys came upstream and anchored near the town to deliver supplies and reinforcements to the Turkish garrison.

Through the long weeks of the siege, Peter himself toiled indefatigably. He continued to play two roles. As a common artilleryman, the bombardier who called himself Peter Alexcev helped load and fire the siege mortars that hurled bombs and shells into the town. As Tsar, he presided over the senior war council and discussed and reviewed all plans and operations. In addition, he kept up a constant correspondence with his friends in Moscow. Endeavoring to raise his own drooping spirits, he maintained his jesting tone, addressing Romodanovsky in Moscow as "My Lord King" and signing himself with expressions of great respect as "Bombardier Peter."

Increasingly, the problem of divided command hampered the Russian siege operation. Lefort and Golovin both resented General Gordon's superior military experience and tended to side together in council to overrule the veteran Scot. Peter also grew impatient with the course of the siege and, together with Lefort and Golovin, forced a decision to launch a sudden major assault in an effort to take the town by storm. Gordon argued that to take a fortress of this strength they must advance the trenches closer to the walls so that the troops could be protected until the moment of attack and not be lengthily exposed on the open ground before the walls. His warnings were brushed aside, and on August 15 the attack was made and it failed, as predicted. "Such was the result of this ill-timed and rash undertaking," wrote Gordon in his diary. "Of the four regiments, 1,500 men

were killed, not including officers. About 9 o'clock, His Majesty sent for me and the other officers. There was nothing to be seen but angry looks and sad countenances." The Russian adversity continued. Two huge land mines, intended to be placed under the Turkish walls, blew up while still inside the Russian trenches with further heavy casualties. Autumn was beginning. Peter knew that he could not leave his men in the trenches throughout the winter; either he would have to take the town or retreat. But a final attack was no more successful than the first, and on October 12, with the soldiers' morale very low and the weather growing colder, Peter raised the siege. That he planned to return the following year, however, was indicated by the fact that he left the two watchtower forts strongly garrisoned by 3,000 men.

The retreat northward was a disaster, more costly in lives and equipment than the entire summer siege. For seven weeks, through heavy rains, the Russians trudged and stumbled north across the steppe, hotly pursued and harried by Tatar horsemen. The rivers were swollen by the rains, the grass had been burned in the summer and now was sodden, there was nothing for the animals to eat, and the men had difficulty finding dry wood to start a fire. The Austrian diplomat Pleyer was accompanying the army, and his report to Vienna was a tale of calamity: "Great quantities of provisions, which could have kept a large army [were] either ruined by bad weather, or lost by the barges going to the bottom. . . . It was impossible to see without tears how through the whole steppe for five hundred miles men and horses lay half-eaten by the wolves, and many villages were full of sick, some of whom died."

On December 2, the army reached Moscow. Peter, imitating the precedent of Sophia and Golitsyn which he himself had condemned, attempted to mask his defeat by staging a triumphal entry into the capital. He marched through the city with a single pathetic Turkish prisoner walking ahead of him. No one was fooled, and the grumbling against the Tsar's foreign military advisors increased. How could an Orthodox army expect to conquer when it was commanded by foreigners and heretics?

This argument was given additional weight by the fact that Sheremetev's army, an old-style Russian host entirely officered by Russians, had achieved considerable success on the lower Dnieper. Together with the horsemen of the Cossack Hetman Mazeppa, Sheremetev's troops had stormed two of the Turkish fortresses along the river, after which the Turks had withdrawn from two others. This achievement gave the Russians control of the whole line of the Dnieper almost down to its estuary on the Black Sea.

But, despite Sheremetev's successes, Peter's own campaign against Azov had been a failure. His vaunted "Western-style" army had been held at bay and had suffered disastrously in retreat. Yet, if defeat was a shock for the exuberant twenty-three-year-old, it did not discourage him. Peter meant to

return. Making no excuses, acknowledging failure, Peter threw himself into preparations for a second attempt. He had been thwarted by three mistakes: divided command, a lack of skilled engineers to construct efficient siege works and an absence of control of the sea at the river mouth to seal off the fortress from outside help.

The first defect was easiest to rectify: The following summer, a supreme military commander would be named. Peter attempted to remedy the second problem by writing to the Austrian Emperor and the Elector of Brandenburg for competent siege experts to aid in defeating the infidel Turk. Far more difficult was the third factor, a fleet to control the river. And yet Peter decided he had to provide one, and demanded that by May—in five short months—a war fleet of twenty-five armed galleys and 1,300 new river barges be built for transporting troops and supplies. The galleys were to be not merely shallow-draft river craft but respectable sea-going men of war fit to defeat Turkish warships on the estuary of the Don or even on the open waters of the Sea of Azov.

The effort appeared impossible. Not only was the time ridiculously short, but these particular five months were the worst time of the year. Rivers and roads were frozen by ice and snow, the days were short as winter night came early, men working in the open air would hammer and saw with fingers numbed by cold. And there was no seaport, no shipbuilding site. Peter would have to build his ships somewhere in the interior of Russia and float them downriver to bring them into position to fight the Turks. Moreover, in the Russian heartland there were no real shipwrights. Russians knew only how to make river boats, simple craft 100 feet long by 20 feet wide, fitted together without the use of a single nail, used for one voyage down the river and then broken up for timber or firewood. Peter's plan, then, was to build the shipyards, assemble the workmen, teach them to mark, cut and hew the timber, lay the keels, build the hulls, step the masts, shape the oars, weave the ropes, sew the sails, train the crews and sail the whole massive fleet down the River Don to Azov. All within five winter months!*

He went to work. As a shipbuilding site, he chose the town of Voronezh on the upper Don, about 300 miles below Moscow and 500 miles above the sea. The town had several advantages. Sheer distance made it secure from the threat of Tatar raids. It was situated above the line of the treeless steppe and lay in a belt of thick virgin forest where timber was readily available. For these reasons, since the reign of Alexis and the adherence of

---

* Naval shipbuilding began in Russia and America at about the same time. In 1690, five years before Peter commenced his urgent shipbuilding program at Voronezh, a small man of war, the *Falkland*, was built for the British navy at Portsmouth, New Hampshire. The vessel, constructed entirely by colonial shipwrights, was the first warship built in North America.

the Ukraine to Russia, Voronezh had been a site for building the simple barges which carried goods to the Don Cossacks. On the low eastern bank of the river at Voronezh, Peter built new shipyards, expanded the old ones and summoned huge numbers of conscripted unskilled laborers. Belgorod province, where Voronezh lay, was commanded to send 27,828 men to work in the shipyards. Peter sent to Archangel for skilled carpenters and shipbuilders, routing foreign and Russian artisans out of their winter indolence, promising that they would finish by summer. He appealed to the Doge of Venice to send him experts in the construction of galleys. A galley ordered from Holland and newly arrived at Archangel was cut into sections and brought to Moscow, where it served as a model for others being built that winter at Preobrazhenskoe. These one- and two-masted vessels, constructed at Preobrazhenskoe or Lake Pleschev, were built in sections like modern prefabricated ships; then the sections were mounted on sledges and dragged over the snowy roads for final assembly at Voronezh.

IN THE MIDDLE of Peter's Herculean effort, on February 8, 1696, Tsar Ivan suddenly died. Feeble, uncomprehending and harmless, gentle Ivan had passed most of his twenty-nine years as a living icon, presented at ceremonies or dragged forward in moments of crisis to calm an angry mob. The difference between restless, energetic Peter and his silent, passive half-brother and co-Tsar was so great that there remained great affection between them. By keeping the royal title, Ivan had lifted many wearisome burdens of state ceremony from the royal bombardier and skipper. During his travels, Peter had always written tender and respectful letters to his brother and co-monarch. Now that Ivan was gone, buried in state in the Kremlin's Archangel Michael Cathedral, Peter took Ivan's young widow, the Tsaritsa Praskovaya, and her three daughters under his care. Praskovaya, in gratitude, remained loyal to Peter for the rest of her life.

Ivan's death had no active political significance, but it put a final, formal seal on Peter's sovereignty. He was now sole Tsar, the single, supreme ruler of the Russian state.

WHEN PETER RETURNED to Voronezh, he found vast activity and confusion. Mountains of timber had been cut and dragged to the building yards, and dozens of barges had already taken shape. But there were endless problems: Many of the ship's carpenters were slow in arriving from Archangel; many unskilled laborers, improperly housed and badly fed, deserted; the weather varied between thaws which turned the ground to mud and sudden new freezes which turned the river and the roads to ice.

Peter hurled himself into action. He slept in a small log house next to

the shipyard and rose before dawn. Warming himself by a fire next to his carpenters, surrounded by the sound of blows of axe, hammer and mallet, Peter worked on a galley, the *Principium*, which he was building along Dutch lines. He reveled in the work. "According to the divine decree to our grandfather Adam, we are eating our bread in the sweat of our face," he wrote.

In March, the weather improved, and in mid-April three galleys, including the *Principium*, were launched. Hundreds of new barges were already moored in the river, ready for loading. To crew this new armada, Peter sent for boatmen from even the most distant Russian rivers and lakes. To man the war galleys, he created a special marine force of 4,000 men culled from many regiments, with a heavy proportion coming from his own Preobrazhensky and Semyonovsky Guards.

The overall mobilization was smaller than it had been the previous summer—in this second campaign there would be no march on the Dnieper —but the force destined to make the second assault on Azov would be double the size of the previous summer. Forty-six thousand Russian soldiers would be bolstered by 15,000 Ukrainian Cossacks, 5,000 Don Cossacks and 3,000 Kalmucks—wiry, brown-skinned, semi-Asiatic horsemen who could ride with any Tatar. A single officer, the boyar Alexis Shein, had been appointed commander-in-chief of the expedition. Shein was not an experienced military commander, but he came from a distinguished family, his judgment was considered sound and his appointment silenced those conservative Muscovites who grumbled that a Russian army commanded by a foreigner could never succeed. Lefort, although no seaman, was made admiral of the new fleet, while Peter, shifting his interest from Mars to Neptune, took the title of naval captain rather than artillery bombardier.

On May 1, Shein, the generalissimo, boarded his commander's galley and raised on its stern a great embroidered banner bearing the Tsar's arms. Two days later, the first ships weighed anchor and the long procession of galleys and barges began the voyage down the Don. Peter, starting later with a battle squadron of eight fast galleys, overtook the main fleet on May 26. By the end of the month, the entire fleet of barges and galleys had reached the Russian-held watchtower forts above Azov.

Fighting began immediately. On May 28, the leader of the Don Cossacks, who had gone ahead with 250 men to reconnoiter the mouth of the river, sent back word that two large Turkish ships were anchored there. Peter decided to attack. Nine galleys were selected, and one of Gordon's best regiments embarked in them. They were accompanied down the river by forty Cossack boats, each carrying twenty men. In unfamiliar waters and with unfavorable winds, the galleys began to go aground and were ordered to turn back. Peter transferred into one of the lighter Cossack boats and continued down the river, but at its mouth he found not two but thirty

Turkish craft, including warships, barges and lighters. This force he judged too strong for his small boats, and he returned upstream to the Russian camp; the Cossacks, however, remained in the vicinity of the Turkish ships. The following night, while the Turks were still moving supplies from the sea-going ships to the shore, the Cossack raiders attacked and captured ten of the smaller Turkish boats. The remainder of the Turkish force fled back to the main anchorage, where the Turkish captains became so alarmed that, although their unloading was still incomplete, the entire Turkish fleet weighed anchor and sailed the open sea. This was the last succor the city of Azov was to receive.

A few days later, Peter returned to the mouth of the river, bringing his entire force of twenty-nine galleys safely past the fortress of Azov. The city was now isolated, and any help sent by the Sultan would have to fight its way upriver through Peter's flotilla. To strengthen his grip, Peter landed troops at the mouth of the river and constructed two small forts containing artillery. When these were finished, he wrote to Romodanovsky, "We are now completely out of danger of the Turkish fleet." On June 14, a number of ships appeared and attempted to land troops to attack the Russian forts, but the approach of Peter's galleys quickly frightened them away. Two weeks later, the Turks tried again, but again the arrival of the Russian galleys forced them to withdraw.

Meanwhile, with the sea secure and the city isolated, Peter's generals and engineers could proceed with the siege. Fortunately for them, the Turkish garrison of Azov, not expecting the Russians to return after their previous failure, had done little to improve its situation. The Turks had not bothered to level the Russian earth siege works or fill in the Russian trenches of the previous summer, and Peter's returning soldiers reoccupied them quickly with a minimum of fresh digging. With twice its former numbers, the Russian army was now able to spread its siege lines completely around the land side of the city.

Once his artillery was in place, Peter called on the Turkish Pasha in Azov to surrender. On June 26, when the Tsar's demand was refused, the Russian cannon opened fire. Through the days that followed, Peter lived primarily on his galley anchored at the mouth of the Don, coming upstream at times to watch the bombardment. When news of his activities reached Moscow, his sister Natalya, alarmed by reports that he was exposing himself to enemy fire, wrote and begged him not to go near enemy cannonballs and bullets. Lightheartedly, Peter replied, "It is not I who go near to cannonballs and bullets, but they come near to me. Send orders for them to stop it."

As all hope of reinforcement from the sea was gone, Peter repeated his offer of good surrender terms to the garrison. A Russian archer fired an arrow over the walls bearing a written offer of honorable terms, granting

the garrison the right to depart the fortress with all its arms and baggage if it surrendered before the coming assault. The answer was a billowing line of smoke from the walls as all the Turkish cannon fired back in unison. Meanwhile, the siege works progressed. Under Gordon's direction, 15,000 Russians toiled with shovels, filling baskets of earth and piling up dirt higher and higher, and nearer and nearer the Turkish walls, until at last a vast earth platform had been built from which it was possible to see and fire directly down into the streets of the town. By mid-July, the Austrian siege engineers sent by the Emperor Leopold arrived. They had been four months en route, having understood that the campaign would not begin until late summer. When Peter discovered that their ignorance was due to the unwillingness of Ukraintsev at the Foreign Ministry in Moscow to reveal the army's plan to Austria for fear it would leak to the Turks, he wrote in fury to Vinius, the culprit's brother-in-law: "Has he any healthy good sense? Entrusted with state matters, yet he conceals what everybody knows. Just tell him that what he does not write on paper I shall write on his back!"

The Austrian engineers were impressed by the magnitude of the Russian earth mound, but suggested a more scientific approach, using mines, trenches and well-placed siege cannon. Nevertheless, it was the earth mound that resulted in the taking of the town. A number of Cossacks, disgusted by the endless work with shovels and baskets and finding carrying earth a poor substitute for fighting, determined to attack the town on their own. On July 27, without orders from their generals, 2,000 Cossacks stormed down from the earth mound onto the walls and into the streets of the town. Had they been supported by regular soldiers or Streltsy, they would have been successful. As it was, a desperate Turkish counterattack forced them back, but they managed to keep control of one of the corner towers of the wall, where they were finally reinforced by soldiers sent by Golovin. The following day, to exploit the breakthrough, Shein ordered a general assault, but before it could begin, the Turks signaled by lowering and waving their banners that they were ready to surrender. The Pasha, seeing his wall breached, had decided to accept the Russian offer of surrender under honorable conditions.

The terms allowed the Turks to withdraw with all their arms and baggage, along with their wives and children, but Peter insisted that the Dutch traitor Jensen be delivered. The Pasha hesitated as Jensen screamed at him, "Cut off my head, but don't give me up to Moscow!" But the Tsar insisted, and Jensen was brought, tied hand and foot, into the Russian camp.

The following day, with banners flying, the Turkish garrison marched out of Azov and through the Russian lines to board the Turkish ships which had been permitted to approach. Shein, the victorious commander, waited on horseback by the embarkation point. The Pasha thanked him for keeping his word, lowered his banner in respect, boarded his ship and

sailed away. Ten Russian regiments marched into the empty city, which was found heavily damaged by the bombardment. The Cossacks could not be restrained and looted the empty houses while the Russian commanders sat down to a victory banquet which spared "neither drink nor powder."

Azov was now a Russian town, and Peter ordered the immediate razing of all the siege works. Under the supervision of the Austrian engineers, he began reconstruction of the town's own fortified walls and bastions. The streets were cleared of ruins and rubble, and the mosques were transformed into Christian churches. Peter heard mass in one new church before he left the city.

Now he needed a harbor for his new Don River fleet. Azov itself was too far upstream, and the mouths of the Don were treacherous: too shallow in some spots, too deep in others. For a week, Peter cruised along the nearby coasts of the Sea of Azov seeking an anchorage, sleeping on a bench of one of his new galleys. Finally, he decided to build a harbor on the north shore of the sea, thirty miles from the mouth of the Don. The site lay behind a point known to the Cossacks as Tagonrog, and here Peter ordered the construction of a fort and harbor which were to become the first real naval base in Russian history.

News of the Azov victory astonished Moscow. For the first time since the reign of Alexis, a Russian army had won a victory. "When your letter came," Vinius reported to Peter, "there were many guests at the house of Lev Kyrilovich [Naryshkin, Peter's uncle]. He immediately sent me with it to the Patriarch. His Holiness, on reading it, burst into tears, ordered the great bell to be rung and, in the presence of the Tsaritsa and the Tsarevich, gave thanks to the Almighty. All talked with astonishment of the humility of their lord, who, after such a great victory, has not lifted up his own heart, but has ascribed all to the Creator of Heaven and has praised only his assistants, although everyone knows that it was by your plan alone, and by the aid you got from the sea, that such a noted town has bowed down to your feet."

Peter sent word to Vinius that if "the laborer is worthy of his hire" it would be appropriate to honor him and the commander-in-chief with a triumphal arch and a victory parade. Vinius immediately began to make preparations while, to allow him time, Peter delayed his homeward journey. He inspected the ironworks of Tula and worked with the famous blacksmith Nikita Demidov, whose later family fortune rested on the Tsar's immense grants to him of mining territory in the Urals.

On October 10, the Tsar joined his troops at Kolomenskoe for the triumphal march into the capital. To the bewilderment of the Muscovites, it was staged not in the traditional Orthodox religious setting which had greeted Alexis' triumphs with holy icons borne by church dignitaries but

with new pagan pageantry inspired by Greek and Roman mythology. The triumphal arch erected by Vinius near the Moscow River was classically Roman, with massive statues of Hercules and Mars supporting it and the Turkish Pasha depicted lying in chains beneath it.

The procession itself stretched several miles. At its head rode eighteen horsemen, followed by a six-horse carriage bearing Peter's aged tutor, the Prince-Pope Nikita Zotov, dressed in armor and bearing sword and buckler. Then came fourteen more horsemen before the gilded carriage of Admiral Lefort, who was wearing a crimson coat trimmed with gold. Fedor Golovin and Lev Naryshkin were next, then thirty cavalrymen in silver cuirasses. Two companies of trumpeters preceded the royal standard of the Tsar, which was surrounded by guards with pikes. Behind the standard, in another gilded carriage, rolled the commander-in-chief, Alexis Shein, followed by sixteen captured Turkish standards, their shafts reversed and their banners trailing in the dirt. A grim warning followed: a simple peasant cart containing the trussed-up figure of the traitor Jensen. Around his neck he wore a sign proclaiming EVILDOER; by his side stood two executioners surrounded with axes, knives, whips and pincers, to give lurid display to the fate that awaited Jensen and other traitors.

And where, amidst all this gorgeous assemblage of flashing colors, of prancing horses and marching men, was the Tsar? To their amazement, Muscovites finally saw Peter not on a white horse or in a golden carriage at the head of his army, but walking with other galley captains behind the carriage of Admiral Francis Lefort. He was recognizable by his great height and by his German captain's uniform, with foreign breeches, a black coat and a wide black hat in which, as a single sign of special rank, he had placed a white feather. On foot, in this fashion, the victorious Tsar walked through his capital the nine miles from Kolomenskoe south of the city to Preobrazhenskoe on the northeast.

NEWS OF THE YOUNG TSAR'S TRIUMPH reverberated quickly through Europe, causing astonishment and admiration. Vinius wrote directly to Witsen, Burgomaster of Amsterdam, asking that he pass the news of the victory to Peter's hero, King William III of England. In Constantinople, the news brought consternation. The weary Turkish soldiers returning home from the long siege were arrested, three officials were executed and the Pasha who had surrendered the town was forced to flee for his life.

Azov was only a beginning. Those Russians who hoped that now after a great victory, the first in three decades, Peter would quietly settle down to rule as his father, Alexis, and brother Fedor had done soon learned of the new projects and ideas bubbling in their master's mind. The first was

construction of a sea-going fleet. What Peter wanted were real ships, not just the galleys he had built for the single purpose of supporting a land campaign and sealing off a fortress from the sea. By taking Azov, Peter had won access only to the Sea of Azov; entry into the Black Sea itself was still blocked by the powerful Turkish fortress at Kerch astride the strait between the Sea of Azov and the Black Sea, and to force this strait, Peter would need a fleet of sea-going ships.

Scarcely had the Moscow triumph been celebrated when Peter summoned his council of boyars to Preobrazhenskoe and announced his plans to colonize Azov and Tagonrog and begin the construction of a navy. A stream of edicts flowed from this historic meeting. Three thousand peasant families and 3,000 Streltsy with their wives and children were uprooted and dispatched to Azov as military colonizers. Twenty thousand Ukrainian laborers were drafted and sent to Tagonrog to build the naval harbor. The new ships themselves were to be built at Voronezh, where the present shipyards would be vastly expanded; from there, the finished vessels would be floated down the Don. Responsibility for building the ships was allocated. All who could afford to help—church, landowners, merchants—would join the state in paying the costs. The state itself would build ten large ships. Every great landowner would build one ship. Every large monastery would build one ship. All these ships were to be fully constructed, equipped and armed within eighteen months. The government would provide the timber, but the landowners or church officials were to provide everything else: ropes, sails, cannon, fittings.

The order was harshly enforced. Failure meant immediate confiscation of property. When the merchants of Moscow and other cities, feeling that their allocation of twelve ships was too much for them, petitioned the Tsar for a lighter burden, their share was increased to fourteen. Usually, the ships were built at Voronezh without the landowners or merchants actually taking personal charge of construction. They simply paid the necessary costs and hired foreign shipbuilders from the German Suburb to perform the skilled work.

Shipbuilders from Europe began to arrive; the thirteen galley experts requested of the Doge of Venice came and were set to work; fifty other Western shipwrights arrived in Moscow and were sent to Voronezh. But these foreigners were only a cadre. To construct the fleet that Peter envisaged would require many more shipbuilders and, once the ships were afloat, many naval officers to command them. At least some of these would have to be Russian. On November 22, 1696, a few weeks after the shipbuilding effort was announced, Peter declared that he was sending more than fifty Russians, most of them young and sons of the noblest families, to Western Europe to study seamanship, navigation and shipbuilding.

Twenty-eight were sent to Venice to study the famed Venetian galleys; the rest were dispatched to Holland and England to study the larger ships of the two great maritime powers. Peter himself drew up the syllabus for study: The Russian students were to familiarize themselves with charts and compasses and other tools of seafaring, to learn the art of shipbuilding, to serve on foreign ships, starting at the bottom as common sailors, and, if possible, to participate in naval warfare. None was to return to Russia without a certificate signed by a foreign master attesting to the student's proficiency.

Peter's command fell on horrified ears. Some of those selected were already married—Peter Tolstoy, the oldest of the students, was fifty-two when sent abroad—and they would be uprooted from wives and children and sent into the temptations of the Western world. Their parents feared the corrupting effect of Western religion, and their wives feared the seductive arts of Western women. And all had to travel at their own expense. But there was no recourse; they had to go. None returned to Russia to become distinguished admirals, but their years abroad were not wasted. Tolstoy employed his knowledge of the West and his facility in the Italian language to effective use as ambassador to Constantinople. Boris Kurakin became Peter's leading ambassador in Western Europe. Yury Trubetskoy and Dmitry Golitsyn became senators, Golitsyn being regarded as one of the most erudite men in Peter's Russia. And these fifty were but the first wave. In the years that followed, scores of Russian youths, commoners as well as noblemen, were routinely sent abroad for naval training. The knowledge they brought home helped to change Russia.

The massive building program for the Azov fleet and the sending of dozens of young Russians abroad to learn seamanship were not the greatest shocks that awaited Russia in the wake of Peter's victory over the Turks. Two weeks after the dispatch of the first naval apprentices, Councilor Ukraintsev of the Foreign Ministry made another, even more dramatic announcement:

> The Sovereign has directed for his great affairs of state that to the neighboring nations, to the Emperor, to the Kings of England and Denmark, to the Pope of Rome, to the Dutch states, to the Elector of Brandenburg, and to Venice shall be sent his great Ambassadors and Plenipotentiaries: the General and Admiral Francis Lefort, General Fedor Golovin and Councilor Prokofy Voznitsyn.

The Great Embassy, as it came to be called, would number more than 250 people, and it would be absent from Russia for more than eighteen months. As well as giving its members an opportunity to study the West at first hand and to enlist officers, sailors, engineers and shipwrights to build and

man a Russian fleet, it would enable Westerners to see and report their impressions of the leading Russians who made the trip. Soon after the announcement, two almost unbelievable rumors raced through Moscow: the Tsar himself meant to accompany the Great Embassy to the West, and he meant to go not as Great Lord and Tsar, autocrat and sovereign, but as a mere member of the ambassadors' staff. Peter, who stood six feet seven inches, intended to travel incognito.

Part Two

THE GREAT
EMBASSY

12

THE GREAT EMBASSY
TO WESTERN EUROPE

HE GREAT EMBASSY was one of the two or three overwhelming events in Peter's life. The project amazed his fellow countrymen. Never before had a Russian tsar traveled peacefully abroad; a few had ventured across the border in wartime to besiege a city or pursue an enemy army, but not in time of peace. Why did he want to go? Who would rule on his behalf? And why, if he must go, did he plan to travel incognito?

Many of the same questions were to be asked by Europeans, not in anguish but in sheer fascination. What was the reason for this mysterious journey by the reigning monarch of a vast, remote, semi-Oriental land, a monarch traveling incognito, disdaining ceremony and refusing honors, curious to see everything and to understand how everything worked? As news of the journey spread, speculation as to its purpose was rife. Some believed with Pleyer, the Austrian agent in Moscow, that the Embassy was "merely a cloak to allow . . . the Tsar to get out of his own country and divert himself a little, and has no other serious purpose." Others (such as Voltaire, who wrote about it later) thought that Peter's purpose was to learn what ordinary life was like, so that when he remounted the throne he would be a better ruler. Still others believed Peter's claim that he was fulfilling the vow he had taken, at the time of his near-shipwreck, to visit the tomb of St. Peter in Rome.

In fact, there was a sound diplomatic reason for the Embassy. Peter was anxious to renew and if possible strengthen the alliance against the Turks. As he saw it, the capture of Azov was only a beginning. He hoped now to force the Strait of Kerch with his new fleet and attain mastery of the Black Sea, and to accomplish this he must not only acquire technology and trained manpower, he must have reliable allies; Russia could not fight the Ottoman Empire alone. Already, the solidarity of the alliance was threatened. King Jan Sobieski of Poland had died in June 1696, and with his death most of the anti-Turkish fervor had gone out of that nation. Louis XIV

of France was maneuvering to place French princes on the thrones of Spain and Poland, ambitions which were likely to provoke new wars with the Hapsburg empire; the Emperor, in consequence, was eager for peace in the East. To prevent any further crumbling of the alliance, the Russian Embassy intended to visit the capitals of its allies: Warsaw, Vienna and Venice. It would also visit the chief cities of the Protestant maritime powers, Amsterdam and London, in search of possible help. Only France, friend of the Turk and enemy of Austria, Holland and England, would be avoided. The ambassadors were to look for capable shipwrights and naval officers, men who had reached command by merit and not through influence; and they were to purchase ship's cannon, anchors, block and tackle, and instruments of navigation which could be copied and reproduced in Russia.

But even such serious objectives could have been attained by Peter's ambassadors without the physical presence of the Tsar himself. Why, then, did he go? The simplest answer seems the best: He went because of his desire to learn. The visit to Western Europe was the final stage of Peter's education, the culmination of all he had learned from foreigners since boyhood. They had taught him all that they could in Russia, but there was more, and Lefort was constantly urging him to go. Peter's overriding interest was in ships for his embryo navy, and he was well aware that in Holland and England lived the greatest shipbuilders in the world. He wanted to go to those countries, where dockyards turned out the dominant navies and merchant fleets of the world, and to Venice, which was supreme in the building of multi-oared galleys for use in inland seas.

The best authority on his motive is Peter himself. Before his departure, he had a seal engraved for himself which bore the inscription, "I am a pupil and need to be taught." Later, in 1720, he wrote a preface to a set of newly issued *Maritime Regulations* for the new Russian navy, and in it described the sequence of events during this earlier part of his life:

> He [Peter was describing himself in the third person] turned his whole mind to the construction of a fleet . . . A suitable place for ship-building was found on the River Voronezh, close to the town of that name, skillful shipwrights were called from England and Holland, and in 1696 there began a new work in Russia—the construction of great warships, galleys and other vessels. And so that this might be forever secured in Russia, and that he might introduce among his people the art of this business, he sent many people of noble families to Holland and other states to learn the building and management of ships; and that the monarch might not be shamefully behind his subjects in that trade, he himself undertook a journey to Holland; and in Amsterdam at the East India wharf, giving himself

up, with other volunteers, to the learning of naval architecture, he got what was necessary for a good carpenter to know, and, by his own work and skill, constructed and launched a new ship.

As for his decision to travel incognito—implemented by his command that all mail leaving Moscow be censored to prevent leakage of his plan— it was intended as a buffer, a façade, to protect him and give him freedom. Anxious to travel, yet hating the formality and ceremony that would inevitably inundate him should he journey as a reigning monarch, he chose to travel "invisibly" within the Embassy ranks. By giving the Embassy distinguished leadership, he could assure a reception consistent with persons of rank; by pretending that he himself was not present, he gave himself freedom to avoid wasted hours of numbing ceremony. In honoring his ambassadors, his hosts would be honoring the Tsar, and meanwhile Peter Mikhailov could come and go, and see whatever he liked.

If Peter's purpose seems narrow, the impact of this eighteen-month journey was to be immense. Peter returned to Russia determined to remold his country along Western lines. The old Muscovite state, isolated and introverted for centuries, would reach out to Europe and open itself to Europe. In a sense, the flow of effect was circular: the West affected Peter, the Tsar had a powerful impact upon Russia, and Russia, modernized and emergent, had a new and greater influence on Europe. For all three, therefore—Peter, Russia and Europe—the Great Embassy was a turning point.

THE EUROPE which Peter was setting out to visit in the spring of 1697 was dominated by the power and glory of a single man, His Most Christian Majesty, Louis XIV of France. Called the Sun King, and represented in both pageantry and art as Apollo, his rays reached out to affect every corner of European politics, diplomacy and civilization.

When Peter was born, and through all but the last ten years of his life, Louis was the most influential man in Europe. It is impossible to understand the Europe which Russia was entering without first considering the French monarch. Few kings in any epoch have exceeded his majesty. His reign of seventy-two years was the longest in the history of France; his French contemporaries considered him a demi-god. "His slightest gesture, his walk, his bearing, his countenance; all was measured, appropriate, noble, majestic," wrote the court diarist, Saint-Simon. His presence was overwhelming. "I never trembled like this before Your Majesty's enemies," confessed one of Louis' marshals on entering the royal presence.

Although Louis was born to the throne, the sweep of his majesty depended more on his character—his massive ego and absolute self-assurance

—than on his physical or political inheritance. In physical stature, he was short even for that day—only five feet four inches. He had a robust figure and powerful, well-muscled legs which he loved to display in tight silk stockings. His eyes were brown, he had a long, thin, arched nose, a sensuous mouth and chestnut hair, which, as he grew older, was hidden in public beneath a wig of long black curls. The smallpox which had afflicted him when he was nine had left his cheeks and chin covered with pits.

Louis was born September 5, 1638, the belated first fruit of a marriage which had been barren for twenty-three years. The death of his father, Louis XIII, made the boy King of France at four. During his childhood, France was ruled by his mother, Anne of Austria, and her chief minister (who was perhaps also her lover), Cardinal Mazarin, the protégé of and successor to the great Richelieu. When Louis was nine, France erupted into the limited revolution known as the Fronde. This humiliation scarred the boy King, and even before the death of Mazarin he was determined to be his own master, to allow no minister to dominate him as Richelieu had dominated his father and Mazarin his mother. Nor, for the rest of his life, did Louis ever willingly set foot in the narrow, turbulent streets of Paris.

Louis was always a country man. In the first years of his reign, he traveled with the court back and forth between the great royal châteaux outside Paris, but kings of France, especially great kings, built their own palaces to reflect their personal glory. In 1668, Louis chose the site of his own palace, the land of his father's small hunting château at Versailles, twelve miles west of Paris. Here, on a sandy knoll rising only slightly above the rolling woodland of the Ile de France, the King ordered his architect, Le Vau, to build. For years, the work continued. Thirty-six thousand men labored on the scaffolding which surrounded the building or toiled in the mud and dust of the developing gardens, planting trees, laying drainpipes, erecting statues of marble and bronze. Six thousand horses dragged timbers or blocks of stone on carts and sledges. The mortality rate was high. Nightly, wagons carried away the dead who had fallen from a scaffolding or been crushed by the unexpected sliding of a heavy piece of stone. Malarial fever raged through the crude barracks of the workmen, killing dozens every week. In 1682, when the château was finally finished, Louis had built the greatest palace in the world. It had no ramparts: Louis had built his seat undefended, in the open country, to demonstrate the power of a monarch who had no need of moats and walls to protect his person.

Behind a façade one fifth of a mile in length were enormous public galleries, council chambers, libraries, private apartments for the royal family, boudoirs and a private chapel, not to mention corridors, stairways, closets and kitchens. In decoration, Versailles has been said to represent the most conspicuous consumption of art and statuary since the days of the Roman empire. Throughout the palace, the high ceilings and great doors were

emblazoned in gold with the mark of Apollo, the sign of the flaming sun, the symbol of the builder and occupant of this enormous palace. The walls were covered with patterned velvet, paneled in marble or hung with tapestries, the windows curtained with embroidered velvet in winter and flowered silk in summer. At night, thousands of candles flickered in hundreds of glass chandeliers and silver candelabra. The rooms were furnished with exquisite inlaid furniture—gilded tables whose legs were scrolled or decorated with flowers and leaves, and broad-backed chairs upholstered with velvet. In the private apartments, rich carpets were laid over inlaid floors and the walls were hung with huge paintings by Andrea del Sarto, Titian, Raphael, Rubens and Van Dyck. In Louis' bedroom hung the "Mona Lisa."

The gardens, designed by Le Nôtre, were as spectacular as the palace. Millions of flowers, bushes and trees were laid out with precise geometrical precision amidst grassy avenues, terraces, ramps and staircases, ponds, lakes, fountains and cascades. The fountains, with 1,500 jets of water spouting from octagonal lakes, became—and remain—the envy of the world. Tiny clipped hedges curved into ornate designs, separating flowers of every color and description, many of them changed daily. The King was especially fond of tulips, and every year (when he was not at war with Holland) four million tulip bulbs were imported from Dutch nurseries to turn Versailles flaming crimson and brilliant yellow in spring. The King's passion for orange trees led Le Nôtre to design a huge orangery, depressed below the open air so that the trees would be protected from the wind. Even this was not enough, and Louis brought some of his orange trees indoors and kept them by the windows of his private rooms, planted in silver tubs.

Standing at the tall windows of the Galeries des Glaces in the palace's western façade, the King could look down long prospects of grass, stone and water, adorned with sculpture, to the Grand Canal. This body of water, constructed in the shape of a huge cross, was more than a mile long. Here the King was taken to boat and sail. On summer evenings, the entire court boarded gondolas sent as a gift from the Doge of Venice, and spent hours floating and drifting beneath the stars while Lully and the court orchestra, on a raft nearby, filled the air with music.

Versailles became the symbol of the supremacy, wealth, power and majesty of the richest and most powerful prince in Europe. Everywhere on the continent, other princes recorded their friendship, their envy, their defiance of Louis by building palaces in emulation of his—even princes who were at war with France. Each of them wanted a Versailles of his own, and demanded that his architects and craftsmen create palaces, gardens, furniture, tapestries, carpets, silver, glass and porcelain in imitation of Louis' masterpiece. In Vienna, Potsdam, Dresden, at Hampton Court and later in St. Petersburg, buildings arose and were decorated under the stimulus of Versailles. Even the long avenues and stately boulevards of

Washington, D.C., which was laid out over a century later, were geometrically designed by a French architect in imitation of Versailles.

Louis loved Versailles, and when distinguished visitors were present, the King personally conducted them through the palace and gardens. But the palace was much more than Europe's most gorgeous pleasure dome; it had a serious political purpose. The King's philosophy rested on total concentration of power in the hands of the monarch; Versailles became the instrument. The vast size of the palace made it possible for the King to summon and house there all the important nobility of France. Into Versailles, as if drawn by an enormous magnet, came all the great French dukes and princes; the rest of the country, where the heads of these ancient houses had lands, heritage, power and responsibilities, was left deserted and ignored. At Versailles, with power out of their reach, the French nobility became the ornament of the king, not his rival.

Louis drew the nobles to him, and once they were there, he did not abandon them to dreariness and boredom. At the Sun King's command, Versailles blazed with light. A ceaseless round of intricate protocol and brilliant entertainment kept everyone busy from morning until night. Everything revolved in minute detail around the King. His bedroom was placed at the very center of the palace, looking eastward over the Cours de Marbre. From eight o'clock in the morning, when the curtains of the royal bed were drawn aside and Louis woke to hear, "Sire, it is time," the monarch was on parade. He rose, was rubbed down with rosewater and spirits of wine, was shaved and dressed, observed by the most fortunate of his subjects. Dukes helped him to pull off his nightshirt and pull on his breeches. Courtiers argued over who was to bring the King his shirt. They jostled for the privilege of presenting the King with his chaise percée (his "chair with a hole in it"), then crowded around while the King performed his daily natural functions. There was a throng in his chamber when he prayed with his chaplain, and when he ate. It followed as he walked through the palace, strolled through the gardens, went to the theater or rode to his hounds. Protocol determined who had a right to sit in the King's presence and whether on a chair with a back or only on a stool. So glorified was the monarch that even when his dinner was passing by, courtiers raised their hats and swept them on the ground in salute, declaring respectfully, "La viande du roi" ("The King's dinner").

Louis loved to hunt. Every day in good weather, he rode with sword or spear in hand, following baying dogs through the forest in pursuit of boar or stag. Every evening, there was music and dancing and gambling at which fortunes were won and lost. Every Saturday night, there was a ball. Often, there were masquerades, elaborate three-day festivals when the entire court dressed up as Romans, Persians, Turks or Red Indians. The feasts at Versailles were gargantuan. Louis himself ate for two men.

Wrote the Princess Palatine: "I have often seen the King eat four different plates of soup of different kinds, a whole pheasant, a partridge, a large plate of salad, two thick slices of ham, a dish of mutton in garlic-flavored sauce, a plateful of pastries, and then fruit and hard-boiled eggs. Both the King and 'Monsieur' [Louis' younger brother] are exceedingly fond of hard-boiled eggs." The King's grandchildren later were taught the polite innovation of using a fork to eat with, but when they were invited to dine with the monarch, he would have none of it and forbade them using these tools, declaring, "I have never in my life used anything to eat with but my knife and my fingers."

The main feast at Versailles was a feast of love. The enormous palace with its numberless rooms to slip away to, its crisscrossing alleys of trees, its statues to hide behind, made a gorgeous stage. In this, as in everything, the King played the leading role. Louis' wife, Maria Theresa, who had come to him as an infanta of Spain, was a simple, child-like creature with large blue eyes. She surrounded herself with half a dozen dwarfs and dreamed of Spain. As long as she lived, Louis upheld his marriage duties, finding his way into her bed eventually every night, dutifully making love to her twice a month. The court always knew these occasions by the fact that the Queen went to confession the following day and her face had a special glow. But the Queen was not enough for Louis. He was highly sexed, always inclined to go to bed with any woman who was handy and relentless in pursuit. "Kings who have a desire, seldom sigh for long," said the courtier Bussy-Rabutin, but there is no record that Louis was ever seriously rebuffed. On the contrary, the court was filled with beautiful women, most of them married but still ambitious, who flaunted their availability. The three successive Maîtresses en Titre (the acknowledged royal mistresses), Louise de La Vallière, Madame de Montespan and Mademoiselle de Fontanges, were but the tip of the iceberg, although with Madame de Montespan it was a grand passion which lasted twelve years and resulted in seven children. No one was disturbed about these arrangements except perhaps the Marquis de Montespan, who angered the King by making a jealous fuss and referring to his wife through all these years as "the late Madame de Montespan."

Whomever the King chose, the court honored. Duchesses rose when a new mistress entered the room. In 1673, when Louis went to war, he took with him the Queen, Louise de la Vallière and Madame de Montespan, then extremely pregnant. All three ladies lumbered along after the army in the same carriage. On campaign, Louis' military tent was made of Chinese silk and had six chambers, including three bedrooms. War, for the Sun King, was not all hell.

Even in France, the view of Louis as a gracious, majestic monarch was not universally held. There were those who found him inconsiderate: he

would set off on long carriage rides of five or six hours, insisting that ladies ride with him even when they were pregnant, and then would absolutely refuse to halt so that they might relieve themselves. He seemed unconcerned about the common people: those who tried to speak to him of the poverty his wars were inflicting were excluded from his presence as persons of bad taste. He was stern and could be ruthless: after the Affaire des Poisons, in which numerous court personages who had recently died were alleged to have been poisoned and a plot against the life of the King was hinted, thirty-six of the accused were tortured and burned at the stake, while eighty-one men and women were chained up for life at the bottom of French dungeons, their jailors commanded that if they spoke, they were to be whipped. The story of the Man in the Iron Mask, whose identity was known only to the King, and who was held for life in solitary confinement, was whispered at court.

Outside France, few in Europe regarded the Sun King's rays as wholly beneficial. To Protestant Europe, Louis was an aggressive, brutal Catholic tyrant.

The instrument of Louis' wars was the army of France. Created by Louvois, it numbered 150,000 in peacetime, 400,000 in wartime. The cavalry wore blue, the infantry pale red, and royal guards—the famed Maison du Roi—scarlet. Commanded by the great marshals of France, Condé, Turenne, Vendôme, Tallard and Villars, the army of France was the envy—and menace—of Europe. Louis himself was not a warrior. Although as a young man he went to war, making a dashing figure on horseback in a gleaming breastplate, a velvet cape and a plumed three-cornered hat, the King did not actually participate in battles, but he became quite expert in the details of strategy and military administration. When Louvois died, the King assumed his role and became his own minister of war. It was he who discussed the grand strategy of campaigns with his marshal and saw to the raising of supplies, the recruiting, training and allocation and the collection of intelligence.

Thus the century unrolled, and the prestige of the Sun King and the power and glory of France mounted year by year. The splendor of Versailles aroused the admiration and envy of the world. The French army was the finest in Europe. The French language became the universal language of diplomacy, society and literature. Anything, everything, was possible, it seemed, if beneath the paper bearing the command there appeared the tall, shaky signature "Louis."

AT THE TIME of the Great Embassy, the gap between Russia and the West seemed far wider than anything measurable in terms of sea-going ships or superior military technology. From the West, Russia appeared dark and

medieval—the glories of its architecture, its icons, its church music and its folk art were unknown, ignored or despised—whereas, to its own educated inhabitants at least, late-seventeenth-century Europe seemed a brilliant, modern community. New worlds were being explored not only across the oceans but also in science, music, art and literature. New instruments to meet practical needs were being invented. Today, many of these achievements have become the necessities and treasures of modern man—the telescope, the microscope, the thermometer, the barometer, the compass, the watch, the clock, champagne, wax candles, street lighting and the general use of tea and coffee all made their first appearance in these years. Fortunate men already had heard the music of Purcell, Lully, Couperin and Corelli; within a few years, they would listen also to the works of Vivaldi, Telemann, Rameau, Handel, Bach and Scarlatti (the last three all born in the same year, 1685). At court and in the ballrooms of the nobility, ladies and gentlemen danced the gavotte and the minuet. France's trio of immortal playwrights, Molière, Corneille and Racine, probed deep into the foibles of human nature, and their plays, first performed before their royal patron at Versailles, spread rapidly in performance and reading to every corner of Europe. England was giving to literature Thomas Hobbes, John Locke, Samuel Pepys and John Evelyn, the poets John Dryden and Andrew Marvell and, above all, John Milton. In painting, most of the mid-seventeenth-century giants—Rembrandt, Rubens, Van Dyck, Vermeer, Frans Hals and Velásquez—had departed, but in France distinguished men and women still had their portraits painted by Mignard and Rigaud, or in London by Sir Godfrey Kneller, a pupil of Rembrandt, who painted ten reigning sovereigns, including the youthful Peter the Great.

In their libraries and laboratories, the scientists of Europe, liberated from obeisance to religious doctrine, were plunging forward, deducing conclusions from observed facts, shrinking from no result because it might be unorthodox. Descartes, Boyle and Leeuwenhoek produced scientific papers on coordinate geometry, the relation between the volume, pressure and density of gases, and the astonishing world that could be seen through a 300-power microscope. The most original of these minds ranged over multiple fields of intellect; for example, Gottfried von Leibniz, who discovered the differential and integral calculus, also dreamed of drawing up social and governmental blueprints for an entirely new society; for years, he was to pursue Peter of Russia in hopes that the Tsar would allow him to use the Russian empire as an enormous laboratory for his ideas.

The greatest scientific mind of the age, spanning mathematics, physics, astronomy, optics, chemistry and botany, belonged to Isaac Newton. Born in 1642, Member of Parliament for Cambridge, knighted in 1705, he was fifty-five when Peter arrived in England. His greatest work, the majestic *Principia Mathematica*, formulating the law of universal gravitation, was

already behind him, published in 1687. Newton's work, in the appraisal of Albert Einstein, "determined the course of Western thought, research and practice to an extent that nobody before or since his time can touch." With the same passion for discovery, other seventeenth-century Europeans were setting out on other oceans to explore and colonize the globe. Most of South America and much of North America were ruled from Madrid. English and Portuguese colonies had been planted in India. The flags of half a dozen European nations flew over settlements in Africa; even so unlikely and non-maritime a state as Brandenburg had established a colony on the Gold Coast. In the most promising of all the new regions being explored, the eastern half of North America, two European states, France and England, had established colonial empires. France's was much larger in territory: from Quebec and Montreal, the French had penetrated through the Great Lakes into the heartland of modern America. In 1672, the year of Peter's birth, Jacques Marquette explored the region around Chicago. A year later, he and Father Louis Jolliet descended the Mississippi in canoes as far as Arkansas. In 1686, when Peter was sailing boats on the Yauza, the Sieur de La Salle claimed the entire Mississippi Valley for France, and in 1699 the lands at the mouth of the great river were named Louisiana in honor of Louis XIV.

The English settlements scattered along the Atlantic seaboard from Massachusetts through Georgia were more compact, more densely settled and therefore more tenacious in times of trouble. The Dutch New Netherlands—absorbed into today's New York and New Jersey—and the colony of New Sweden, near modern Wilmington, Delaware, both had fallen as spoils to England during the Anglo-Dutch naval wars of the 1660's and 1670's. By the time of Peter's Great Embassy, New York, Philadelphia and Boston were substantial towns of more than 30,000 inhabitants.

Around the globe, the majority of mankind lived near the earth. Life on the land was a struggle for survival. Wood, wind, water and the straining muscles of men and beasts were the sources of energy. Most men and women talked only about people or events within the horizon of field and village; things that happened elsewhere were beyond their ken and interest. When the sun went down, the world—its plains and hills and valleys, its cities, towns and villages—was plunged into darkness. Here and there, a fire might burn or a candle flicker, but most human activity stopped and people went to sleep. Staring into the darkness, they warmed themselves with private hopes or wrestled with personal despair, and then they slept to ready themselves for the coming day.

All too often, life was not only hard but short. The rich might live to fifty, while the life of a poor man terminated, on the average, somewhere between thirty and forty. Only half of all infants survived their first year and the toll in palaces was as heavy as in cottages. Of the five children born to

Louis XIV and his Queen, Maria Theresa, only the Dauphin survived. Queen Anne of England, desperately trying to produce an heir, gave birth sixteen times; not one of these children lived beyond ten years. Peter the Great and his second wife, Catherine, were to produce twelve children, but only two daughters, Anne and Elizabeth, reached adulthood. Even the Sun King was to lose his only son, his eldest grandson and his eldest great-grandson, all prospective kings of France, to measles within a span of fourteen months.

In fact, through the seventeenth century, the population of Europe actually declined. In 1648, it was estimated at 118 million; by 1713 the estimate had fallen to 102 million. Primarily, the causes were the plagues and epidemics that periodically devastated the continent. Sweeping through a city, borne by fleas in the fur of rats, plague left behind a carpet of human corpses. In London in 1665, 100,000 died; nine years before in Naples, 130,000. Stockholm lost one third of its population to plague in 1710–1711 and Marseilles half of its inhabitants in 1720–1721. Bad harvests and consequent famine also killed hundreds of thousands. Some died directly from starvation, but most were prey to illnesses whose task was easier because of lowered resistance due to malnutrition. Poor public sanitation was also responsible for many deaths. Lice carried typhus, mosquitoes carried malaria, and the piles of horse manure in the streets attracted flies that bore typhoid and infantile diarrhea to carry off thousands of children. Smallpox was almost universal—some died and some survived, marked by deep pits across the face and body. The dark face of Louis XIV was marred by the pox, as were the fair features of Charles XII of Sweden. Not until 1721 was the dread disease partially contained by the development of an inoculation. Then, the brave decision of the Princess of Wales to submit to the procedure not only stirred the courage of others, but even made it fashionable.

INTO THIS MODERN seventeenth-century world, with all its radiance and energies and all its ills, those few Russians who traveled abroad emerged blinking like creatures of the dark led into the light. They disbelieved in or disapproved of most of what they saw. Foreigners, of course, were heretics, and contact with them was likely to contaminate; indeed, the whole process of conducting relations with foreign governments was at best a necessary evil. The Russian government had always been reluctant to receive permanent foreign embassies in Moscow. Such embassies would only "bring harm to the Muscovite state and embroil it with other nations," explained one of Tsar Alexis' leading officials. And the same blend of disdain and distrust governed Russian attitudes toward sending their own embassies abroad. Russian envoys journeyed westward only when there were compelling reasons. Even then, such envoys customarily were ignorant of

foreign countries, knew little about European politics or culture and spoke only Russian. Sensitive about their inadequacies, they compensated by paying elaborate attention to matters of protocol, titles and modes of address. They demanded that they be allowed to deliver all communications from their master into the hands of the foreign monarch himself. Further, they demanded that when this foreign monarch received them, he should inquire formally after the health of the Tsar and, while so doing, rise and remove his hat. Needless to say, this was not a ceremony that greatly appealed to Louis XIV or even to lesser European princes. When offended hosts suggested that Russian ambassadors conform to Western practices, the Russians coldly answered, "Others are not our model."

In addition to being ignorant and arrogant, Russian envoys were rigidly limited as to their freedom of action. Nothing could be agreed to in negotiation unless it had been foreseen and accepted in their advance instructions. Anything new, even of the least importance, had to be cleared with Moscow although this effort required weeks of waiting while couriers rode. Thus, few courts welcomed the prospect of a Russian mission, and those foreign officials detailed to deal with a party of visiting Muscovites considered themselves to be powerfully unlucky.

Such an encounter occurred in 1687 when the Regent Sophia sent Prince Jacob Dolgoruky and a Russian embassy to Holland, France and Spain. In Holland, they were well received, but in France everything possible went wrong. The courier sent ahead to Paris to announce their arrival had refused to deliver his message to anyone except the King in person. As neither the Minister of Foreign Affairs nor anyone else could wrench this adamant Russian from his purpose, he was sent back without anyone in Paris opening and reading his letter. The embassy proceeded from Holland toward France anyway. On reaching the French frontier at Dunkirk, all embassy baggage was sealed by customs men with the explanation that it would be opened, examined and passed by more qualified officials once it reached Paris. The Russians promised to leave the customs seals intact, but the moment they reached Saint-Denis on the outskirts of Paris, they broke the seals, opened the baggage and spread its contents, mostly valuable Russian furs, out on tables for sale. French merchants thronged about and business was brisk. Subsequently, horrified French court officials sniffed that the Russians had forgotten "their dignity as ambassadors, that they might act as retail merchants, preferring their profit and private interests to the honor of their masters."*

---

* The apparent brazenness of Russian behavior was the result of the normal arrangements made for any Russian diplomatic mission traveling abroad. Russian ambassadors were paid little or no salary, but instead were supplied by the state with goods, primarily furs, which were much in demand in Europe. They were expected to sell

The ambassadors were received by the King at Versailles and things went well until another customs official arrived to examine the baggage. When the Russians refused to allow this, the police arrived, accompanied by locksmiths. The enraged Russians shouted insults, and one of the ambassadors actually drew his knife, whereupon the French withdrew, reporting the matter to the King. Louis indignantly ordered the Russians to leave France, telling them to take back to the two Tsars the presents they had sent to him. When the ambassadors refused to go before having another audience with the King, French officials removed all furniture from the house in which the Russians were staying and cut off their supply of food. Within a day, the Russians capitulated, pleading for an audience, claiming that if they returned to Moscow without one, they would lose their heads. This time, they tamely agreed to allow their baggage to be examined and to conduct their negotiations with lesser officials if only Louis would receive them. Two days later, the King invited them to dine at Versailles and personally showed them the gardens and fountains. The ambassadors were so entranced that they did not wish to leave and began producing imaginative reasons for prolonging their stay. Upon returning home, however, they complained loudly of their treatment in Paris, and Russian umbrage over this diplomatic fracas was a partial factor in the subsequent poor relations between Russia and France. Along with French support of Turkey, with which Russia was at least nominally at war until 1712, it influenced Peter's decision not to travel to Paris until after the Sun King's death. And thus it was that as the Great Embassy prepared to leave Russia, it did not contemplate a visit to the greatest monarch of the West, and, sadly for both history and legend, the two royal colossi of the age, Peter and Louis, never stood in the same room.

---

these furs to pay their expenses and to obtain their own recompense. Naturally, since the furs were in effect their salary, Russian diplomats were anxious to get their baggage through customs without paying duty.

13

"IT IS IMPOSSIBLE
TO DESCRIBE HIM"

As CHIEF of the Great Embassy, with the rank of First Ambassador, Peter named Lefort, now titled Governor-General of Novgorod as well as General-Admiral. Lefort's two fellow ambassadors both were Russian: Fedor Golovin, the Governor-General of Siberia, and Prokofy Voznitsyn, Governor of Bolkhov. Golovin was one of Russia's first professional diplomats. At the age of thirty-seven, he had negotiated for Sophia the Treaty of Nerchinsk with China, and since Peter's assumption of power he had become one of the Tsar's close companions and most useful servants. Conduct of foreign affairs was entrusted to him, and eventually he was granted the title of General-Admiral. In 1702, he was created a Count of the Holy Roman Empire and became, in effect, Peter's prime minister. Voznitsyn also had previous diplomatic experience, having served on missions to Constantinople, Persia, Venice and Poland.

Chosen to escort the ambassadors were twenty noblemen and thirty-five young Russian "volunteers" who, like those dispatched in previous months, were going to England, Holland and Venice to learn shipbuilding, navigation and other nautical sciences. Many of the noblemen and "volunteers" were Peter's comrades from the play regiments at Preobrazhenskoe, his boat-building days at Pereslavl, the visits to Archangel and the campaigns against Azov. Prominent among these were his childhood friend Andrei Matveev and the brash young Alexander Menshikov. To complete the Embassy, there were chamberlains, priests, secretaries, interpreters, musicians (including six trumpeters), singers, cooks, coachmen, seventy soldiers and four dwarfs, bringing the total above 250. And somewhere in the ranks was a tall young man, brown-haired, dark-eyed, with a wart on the right side of his face, whom the others addressed simply as Peter Mikhailov. For members of the Embassy to address him as anything else, to reveal that he was the Tsar or even to mention that the Tsar was present with the Embassy, was punishable by death.

To govern Russia in his absence, Peter established a three-man regency council. The first two were his uncle Lev Naryshkin and Prince Boris Golitsyn, both faithful and trusted older men who had advised his mother during the years of exile at Preobrazhenskoe and who had guided his party during the final crisis with Sophia. The third regent was Prince Peter Prozorovsky, the Tsar's treasurer, who suffered from the strange malady of being unwilling to touch the hand of another person or even to open a door lest he contaminate himself. Nominally subordinate to these three men, but in fact the real viceroy of Russia during Peter's absence, was Prince Fedor Romodanovsky, the Governor-General of Moscow, commander of the four regiments of the Guard and Prince-Caesar of the Jolly Company. Given supreme jurisdiction in all civil and military cases and charged with maintaining order, Romodanovsky was sternly commanded to deal in the severest manner with any flickerings of discontent or rebellion. Alexis Shein, the generalissimo of the successful Azov expedition, was left in command of Azov, while Boris Sheremetev, leaving on his own private three-year journey to Rome, was replaced on the Dnieper frontier by Prince Jacob Dolgoruky.

On the eve of the Embassy's departure, Peter was happily celebrating at a banquet at Lefort's mansion when a messenger brought disquieting news. As Gordon wrote in his diary, "A merry night has been spoiled by an accident of discovering treason against his Majesty." Three men—a colonel of the Streltsy, Ivan Tsykler, and two boyars—were seized and accused of plotting against Peter's life. The evidence was thin. Tsykler had been one of the first of Sophia's officers to go to Troitsky and cast in his lot with Peter. For this switch of alliance he had expected great rewards, and had been disappointed; now, he was being sent to serve in the garrison at Azov. Disgruntled, he may have expressed his discontent too publicly. The two boyars involved were outspoken men who were representative of a rising tide of complaint about the style and direction of Peter's rule: The Tsar had deserted his wife and the Kremlin; he maintained his shameful relations with foreigners in the German Suburb; he had lowered the dignity of the throne by walking in the Azov victory parade behind the carriage of the Swiss Lefort; now he was abandoning them to spend many months with foreigners in the West.

Unfortunately, their grumbling touched a raw nerve in Peter's character: Once again, the Streltsy were mixed up in charges of treason. His fear and loathing of them boiled forth. The three men were bloodily executed on Red Square, losing first their arms and legs to the axe, and then their heads. In addition, Peter's fear that their dissent might be only the prelude to an attempted Miloslavsky restoration stirred him to a lurid act of contempt against that family. The coffin of Ivan Miloslavsky, who had been dead for fourteen years, was placed on a sledge, yoked to a team of swine and

dragged into Red Square. There, the coffin was opened beneath the execution block, so that the blood of the newly condemned men would spatter the face of the corpse.

Five days after this barbaric scene in Moscow, the Great Embassy set out to study the civilization and technology of the West. On March 20, 1697, the Embassy departed for Novgorod and Pskov in a long procession of sledges and baggage wagons. Among the bulky carts were gorgeous costumes of silk and brocade sewn with pearls and jewels for use by Lefort and the other ambassadors in formal audiences, a large consignment of sable furs to be used to cover expenses where gold, silver or bills on Amsterdam would not suffice, an immense supply of honey, salmon and other smoked fish, and Peter's personal drum.

Crossing the Russian frontier, the Great Embassy entered the Swedish-held Baltic province of Livonia (whose territory was generally that of modern Latvia). Unfortunately, the Swedish governor of Riga, Eric Dahlberg, was completely unprepared for so large a group and especially for the distinguished visitor concealed in its ranks. For this, the Russian Governor of Pskov, the Russian town nearest the frontier, was partly at fault. He had been ordered to make arrangements, but in his letter to Dahlberg he neglected to mention either the size of the visiting Embassy or, more importantly, what august personage would be traveling incognito along with it. Dahlberg had replied with a formal letter of welcome, saying he would do everything possible "with neighborly friendliness." He pointed out, however, that his reception would necessarily be pinched because of a disastrous harvest that had brought the province to the brink of famine. To make matters worse, in addition to inadequate advance warning, there was a missed connection. Dahlberg sent carriages with an escort of cavalry to the frontier to bring the Tsar's ambassadors into Riga in diplomatic style. Because the important members of the Embassy, Peter included, were traveling ahead of the main party, they missed this welcome. Just outside Riga, when the carriages and escort finally caught up with the ambassadors, the Swedes offered a second reception and staged a military parade to make amends.

Had this been the only mishap and had Peter been able to pass through Riga quickly and cross the River Dvina* as intended, all might still have been well. But he arrived in early spring just as the ice was breaking in the river, which flowed beneath the city walls. There was no bridge, and the large ice floes in the river made crossing by boat impossible. For seven days, Peter and the Russian party were forced to wait in the city for the ice to melt. Although impatient and anxious to leave, Peter initially was pleased by

---

* The river emptying into the White Sea at Archangel is also called Dvina. The Archangel Dvina is often called the North Dvina and the river at Riga, the West Dvina.

the honor done to his ambassadors. Every time they came or went from the citadel, a salute of twenty-four guns roared out.

Riga, the capital of Livonia, was a Protestant Baltic city of of tall, thin church spires, gabled roofs, cobbled streets and thriving independent merchants, totally different from Pskov and Russia not far away. Riga was also a major citadel and a powerful anchor of the Swedish Baltic empire, and, with this in mind, the Swedish hosts were nervous about these Russian visitors and especially about the presence of the inquisitive twenty-four-year-old Tsar. Predictably, Peter was determined to study the city's fortifications. Riga was a modern fortress, carefully constructed on the latest Western lines by Swedish military engineers. As such, it was far more powerful and thus more interesting to Peter than the old-style fortifications of simple walls and towers which characterized all Russian fortresses, including the Kremlin, and which Peter had faced and conquered at Azov. Here were stone-faced bastions and palisaded contrescarpes built after the model of the French master Vauban. To Peter, it was a rare opportunity and he meant to make the most of it. He climbed over the ramparts, made pencil sketches, measured the depth and width of the moats, and studied the angles of fire of the cannon at the embrasures.

Peter regarded his own activity as that of a student studying a modern fortress in the abstract, but the Swedes understandably saw it somewhat differently. To them, Peter was a monarch and military commander whose father's army had besieged this city only forty years before. The fortress which Peter was examining and measuring with such care had been erected specifically to protect the city from the Russians and to prevent Russian penetration to the Baltic coast. Thus, the sight of the tall young man standing on their ramparts working with his sketch pad and measuring tapes was unnerving. In addition, there was the problem of Peter's incognito. One day, a Swedish sentry, observing the foreigner copying details into a notebook, ordered him away. Peter ignored the sentry and persisted in his activity. Raising his musket, the Swedish soldier threatened to fire. Peter was outraged, regarding this not so much as an insult to rank as a breach of hospitality. Lefort, as First Ambassador, protested to Dahlberg. The Swedish Governor, whatever his private feelings at this reconnaissance of his fortifications, apologized and assured the ambassador that no discourtesy had been intended. Lefort accepted the explanation and agreed that the soldier should not be punished for doing his duty.

Nevertheless, relations between the Swedish hosts and Russian guests continued to deteriorate. Dahlberg was in a difficult position. The Russian Great Embassy was not officially accredited to the Swedish court. In addition, the fact that the Tsar was present but did not wish his presence acknowledged created thorny protocol problems. Dahlberg, therefore, was formally polite, doing what protocol demanded for important ambassadors

of a neighboring monarch, but nothing more. No entertainment was planned; there were no banquets, no fireworks, no amusements of the sort Peter enjoyed. The stiff, cold Swedish commander simply withdrew and—it seemed to the Russians—ignored them. Also, as the Embassy was not bound for Sweden itself, but only in transit through Swedish territory, the normal diplomatic procedure by which the host country paid the expenses of diplomatic visitors was not observed. The Russians were left to pay for their own food, lodgings, horses and fodder, and for these the ambassadors paid a price inflated by famine and the desire of Riga merchants to extract as much as they could from the visitors.

In addition to feeling these grievances, Peter was increasingly irritated by the crowds that came to stare at him. When finally, after a week, the ice was sufficiently melted so that they could cross the river, Dahlberg attempted to send his visitors off in style. Boats carrying the royal yellow-and-blue flag of Sweden ferried the Russian Embassy across the river while, from the fortress, cannon thundered in salute. But it was too late. In Peter's mind, Riga was a city of meanness, inhospitality and insults. As he traveled around Europe, Riga suffered further by contrast. In most of the other cities Peter visited, the reigning sovereign was there to greet him, and even though Peter insisted on his incognito, these electors, kings and even the Austrian Emperor always found a way to meet him privately, to entertain him lavishly and to pay his bills.

Peter's antagonism toward Riga rankled deeply. Three years later, needing excuses for beginning the Great Northern War against Sweden, he cited his rude reception by Riga. And thirteen years later, in 1710, when Russian troops surrounded the city and began the siege that led to its capture and incorporation for over two centuries into the Russian empire, Peter himself was present to fire the first three shells into the city. "Thus," he wrote to Menshikov, "the Lord God has enabled us to see the beginning of our revenge on this accursed place."

ONCE ACROSS the Dvina, Peter entered the Duchy of Courland, whose capital, Mitau, was thirty miles south of Riga. Nominally a fief of the Polish kingdom, Courland was sufficiently distant from Warsaw to maintain a practical autonomy, and with Poland now disintegrating, the Duke of Courland was almost his own master. Here, there was no question of making the mistake that Dahlberg had made in Riga. The Tsar was the Tsar; the incognito would be respected, but everyone would know *who* was incognito. Thus, although his duchy was poor, Duke Frederick Casimir honored the Embassy with lavish entertainment. "Open tables were kept everywhere with trumpets and music attended by feasting and excessive drinking as if His Tsarish Majesty had been another Bacchus. I have not yet seen such

hard drinkers," wrote one of the Duke's ministers. Lefort's drinking was especially notable. "It never overcomes him, but he always continues master of his reason." The Russians, it was whispered by the foreigners among them, were really no more than "baptized bears."

Knowing that the Tsar loved the water, the Duke of Courland arranged to charter a yacht so that his guest could make the next stage of his journey by sea. Peter's destination was Königsberg, then a town in the large and powerful North German electoral state of Brandenburg. On hand in the town to welcome the Tsar was the Elector himself, Frederick III. A member of the ambitious House of Hohenzollern, Frederick had expansive plans for himself and his domains. His dream was to transform his electorate into a powerful kingdom to be known as Prussia, and to transform himself into Frederick I, King of Prussia. The title could be granted by the Hapsburg Emperor in Vienna, but the real augmentation of power could come only at the expense of Sweden, whose fortresses and territories were spread along the coast of North Germany. Frederick was anxious for Russian support as a counterweight to Sweden. And here, as if in answer to his need, came the Tsar himself, intending to pass through the territory of Brandenburg. Naturally, Frederick was in Königsberg to greet him.

Peter, traveling by sea, slipped into Königsberg and came ashore at night. He took a modest lodging and made a private visit to the Elector. The first conversation lasted an hour and a half while the two rulers discussed ships, gunnery and navigation. Thereafter, Frederick took Peter hunting near his country house, and together they watched a fight between two bears. Peter astonished his hosts by playing loudly on the trumpet and drum, and his curiosity, liveliness and readiness to be pleased made a favorable impression.

Eleven days later, the horsemen and wagons of the Russian Great Embassy arrived by road, and Peter watched from a window to see how they were received. Frederick granted them a handsome expense allowance for their visit and served a magnificent welcoming dinner, followed by fireworks. Peter along with the other young noblemen of the Embassy attended in a scarlet coat with gold buttons. Later, Frederick confessed that he had had to struggle to keep a straight face when, as dictated by protocol, he had asked the ambassadors for news of the Tsar and whether they had left him in excellent health.

In their negotiations, Frederick was anxious to reconfirm an old alliance which Tsar Alexis had made with Brandenburg against Sweden, but Peter, still at war with Turkey, was unwilling to do anything which might provoke the Swedes. Finally, in talks aboard the Elector's yacht, the two monarchs agreed on a new treaty, promising generally to help each other against their mutual enemies. Frederick also asked the Tsar to assist in his campaign to promote himself to king. Peter agreed to treat the Elector's ambassadors in

Moscow at the same level as that accorded to his own ambassadors in Brandenburg; this was vague, but it was something that Frederick could use in making his case to the Emperor in Vienna.

Although anxious to leave for Holland, Peter lingered in Königsberg until the situation in Poland became clearer. In June 1696, when Jan Sobieski died, the Polish throne became vacant, and two contenders, Augustus, Elector of Saxony, and the Bourbon Prince de Conti, the nominee of Louis XIV, were competing for it. Russia, Austria and most of the German states were firmly opposed to Conti's election. A French king on the Polish throne meant an immediate end to Polish participation in the war against Turkey, a Franco-Polish alliance and the extension of French power into Eastern Europe. To prevent this, Peter was prepared to fight, and he moved Russian troops to the Polish border. With the issue still cloudy, the two parties still maneuvering and the Diet still not prepared to vote, Peter decided to wait in Königsberg before proceeding westward. While he waited, Peter examined things in Königsberg which interested him. With Colonel Streltner von Sternfeld, chief engineer of the army of Brandenburg and an expert in the science of artillery, Peter studied both the theory and the practice of ballistics. He fired cannon of various sizes at targets while Von Sternfeld corrected his aim and explained his mistakes. When Peter left, Von Sternfeld made out a certificate attesting to the knowledge and skill of his pupil Peter Mikhailov.

Unfortunately, in Königsberg as in Riga, Peter got into trouble. This time, his hasty temper rather than his curiosity was responsible. On his Name Day, more important than a birthday to all Russians, Peter had counted on a visit from Frederick, and had planned his own fireworks display for the Elector's benefit. But Frederick, not realizing the significance of the day, had left Königsberg to meet the Duke of Courland, delegating several of his ministers to represent him at the Tsar's celebration. Peter was hurt and publicly humiliated when Frederick failed to appear, and showed his pique openly to the representatives, saying loudly in Dutch to Lefort, "The Elector is very good, but his ministers are the devil." Thinking he saw one of the ministers smile at his words, Peter flew into a rage, rushed at the Brandenburger, cried, "Get out! Get out!" and pushed him out of the room. After his anger cooled, he wrote a letter to his "dearest friend" Frederick. The letter was an apology, but into it crept the nature of his complaint. On departure, Peter made further amends by sending Frederick a large ruby.

IN MID-AUGUST, after Peter had spent seven weeks in Königsberg, the news came that Augustus of Saxony had arrived in Warsaw and been elected King of Poland. Peter was pleased by this outcome and anxious to leave immediately by sea for Holland, but the presence of a squadron of French

warships in the Baltic forced him to change his plans; he had no wish to wind up an involuntary guest aboard a vessel flying the great white fleur-de-lis banner of the King of France. Disappointed, he took the only path open to him: by land, across the German electoral states of Brandenburg and Hanover.

Peter's disappointment at not being able to travel by ship was compounded by a new problem he now faced in traveling by land: all along his route, people wanted to see him. The long delay in Königsberg had provided ample time for news of his presence with the Embassy to spread across Europe, and everywhere there was great excitement and curiosity: For the first time, a Muscovite tsar, the ruler of a dimly perceived, exotic land, was traveling in Europe, where he might be seen, examined and marveled at. The Tsar was upset by attentions of this kind.

Having left Königsberg in secret, he urged his coachman to hurry, hoping to avoid notice and detection. He passed through Berlin quickly, sitting far back in a corner of the coach to avoid recognition. This speed and reclusiveness carried him rapidly across North Germany, but he was not to avoid an encounter with two redoubtable ladies who had laid plans to waylay him. These were Sophia, the widowed Electress of Hanover, and her daughter Sophia Charlotte, Electress of Brandenburg. The two Electresses were eager to examine for themselves the much-talked-about Tsar. The younger Electress, Sophia Charlotte, who had been visiting her mother in Hanover while her husband, the Elector Frederick, was welcoming Peter in Königsberg, was especially intrigued. She had expected to meet him in Berlin, and now, determined to overtake him as he approached Hanover, she packed her mother, her brothers and her children into carriages and hurried to intercept the Russian party at the town of Koppenbrügge. Arriving just ahead of Peter, she sent a chamberlain to invite the Tsar to dinner.

At first, seeing the size of the ladies' retinue and the crowd of local citizens milling curiously outside the gate, Peter refused to come. The chamberlain persisted, and Peter yielded on the assurance that, apart from Sophia Charlotte and her mother, there would be only her brothers, her children and the important members of Peter's suite. Ushered into the presence of the two royal ladies, Peter faltered, blushed and was unable to speak. They were, after all, the first aristocratic, intellectually inclined Western ladies he had ever met; his only previous contact with Western women had been with the middle-class wives and daughters of the Western merchants and soldiers in the German Suburb. But these two ladies were exceptional even among European aristocracy. Sophia of Hanover, then sixty-seven, was the vigorous, commonsensical, successful ruler of that thriving North German state. A few years after this meeting with Peter, she, as the granddaughter of King James I of England, would be picked by the British parliament to succeed Queen Anne and thereby secure the Protestant

succession in England.* Her daughter, twenty-nine-year-old Sophia Charlotte of Brandenburg, was equally strong-minded and made a dazzling figure among the ladies of the North German courts. For a while, she had been the designated bride of Louis XIV's grandson, the Duke of Burgundy, before politics had dictated that Burgundy should marry Marie Adelaide of Savoy. During the two years Sophia Charlotte had lived at Versailles, her wit and beauty had attracted the admiration of the Sun King himself. She was well educated, and Leibniz had become her friend as well as her tutor. Indeed, so delightful and appealing was Sophia Charlotte that her husband, who built the Charlottenburg Palace for her in Berlin, was actually in love with her. Naturally, in deference to the august example set for lesser monarchs by Louis XIV, Frederick felt that he must have a mistress, but he vastly preferred his charming and clever wife.

Peter, confronted by these poised and elegant ladies, simply covered his face with his hands and muttered in German, "I don't know what to say." Realizing his difficulty, Sophia Charlotte and her mother put their guest at ease by placing him between them at the table and beginning to talk to him. Before long, his shyness began to pass and he started speaking so freely that the two women had to compete for his attention. The dinner lasted four hours and both Electresses were eager to go on plying him with questions, but Sophia Charlotte was afraid that he was bored and called for music and dancing. Peter at first refused to dance, saying that he had no gloves, but once again the ladies changed his mind and soon he was performing heartily. Turning them around the floor, he felt strange things under their dresses: the whalebones in their corsets. "These German women have devilish hard bones," he shouted to his friends. The ladies were delighted.

Peter was enjoying himself immensely. This party was gayer than those in the German Suburb, gayer even than the roaring banquets of the Jolly Company. He overflowed with good spirits. He ordered his dwarfs to dance. He kissed and pinched the ear of his favorite dwarf. He planted kisses on the head of the ten-year-old Princess Sophia Dorothea, the future mother of Frederick the Great, destroying her coiffure. He also embraced and kissed the fourteen-year-old Prince George, who would later become King George II of England.

In the course of the evening, the two Electresses closely observed the Tsar. He was, they found, far from the uncivilized young barbarian described by rumor. "He has a natural, unconstrained air which pleased me," wrote Sophia Charlotte. His grimaces and facial contortions were not as bad as they had expected and, Sophia Charlotte added sympathetically,

---

* Sophia did not live to wear the British crown. She died before Queen Anne, and both her Hanoverian and English titles passed to her son, George Louis, who ruled the two simultaneously as Elector of Hanover and King George I of England.

"Some are not in his power to correct." The elder Electress, an experienced judge of men, described the evening and the guest of honor in detail:

> The Tsar is very tall, his features are fine, and his figure very noble. He has great vivacity of mind, and a ready and just repartee. But, with all the advantages with which nature has endowed him, it could be wished that his manners were a little less rustic. We immediately sat down to table. Herr Koppenstein, who did the duty as marshal, presented the napkin to His Majesty, who was greatly embarrassed, for at Brandenburg, instead of a table napkin, they had given him a ewer and basin [to clean his hands] after the meal. He was very gay, very talkative, and we established a great friendship for each other, and he exchanged snuff-boxes with my daughter. We stayed in truth a very long time at table, but we would gladly have remained there longer still without feeling a moment of boredom, for the Tsar was in very good humor, and never ceased talking to us. My daughter had her Italians sing. Their song pleased him though he confessed to us that he did not care much for music.
>
> I asked him if he liked hunting. He replied that his father had been very fond of it, but that he himself, from his earliest youth, had had a real passion for navigation and fireworks. He told us that he worked himself in building ships, showed us his hands, and made us touch the callous places that had been caused by work. He brought his musicians, and they played Russian dances, which we liked better than the Polish ones. . . .
>
> We regretted that we could not stay much longer, so that we could see him again, for his society gave us much pleasure. He is a very extraordinary man. It is impossible to describe him, or even to give an idea of him, unless you have seen him. He has a very good heart, and remarkably noble sentiments. I must tell you also, that he did not get drunk in our presence, but we had hardly left when the people of his suite began to make ample amends.
>
> He is a prince at once very good and very bad; his character is exactly that of his country. If he had received a better education, he would be an exceptional man, for he has great qualities and unlimited natural intelligence.

Peter signaled his own pleasure at the evening by sending each of the Electresses a trunkful of Russian sables and brocade. Then he left immediately, ahead of the main party. For Holland was only a few miles farther down the Rhine.

14

PETER
IN HOLLAND

IN THE SECOND HALF of the seventeenth century, Holland, a term used to describe the seven United Provinces of the Northern Netherlands, was at the peak of its world power and prestige. With its dense, teeming population of two million hard-working Dutchmen crowded into a tiny area, Holland was by far the richest, most urbanized, most cosmopolitan state in Europe. Not surprisingly, the prosperity of this small state was a source of wonder and envy to its neighbors, and often this envy turned to greed. On such occasions, the Dutch drew on certain national characteristics to defend themselves. They were valiant, obstinate and resourceful, and when they fought—first against the Spaniards, then against the English and finally against the French—they fought in a way which was practical and, at the same time, desperately and sublimely heroic. To defend their independence and their democracy, a people of two million maintained an army of 120,000 and the second-largest navy in the world.

Holland's prosperity, like its freedom, rested on ingenuity and hard work. In most European nations of the day, the vast majority of the people were tied to the land, engaged in the simple process of feeding themselves and creating a small surplus to feed the towns and cities. In Holland, one Dutch peasant, by producing larger crop yields per acre, by somehow extracting more milk and butter from his cows and more meat from his pigs, was able to feed two of his non-farming fellow citizens. Thus, in Holland more than half the population was freed for other activities, and they bustled into commerce, industry and shipping.

Commerce and shipping were the source of Holland's enormous wealth. The seventeenth-century Dutch were a trading, sea-faring people. The great sister ports of Amsterdam and Rotterdam, situated at the twin mouths of the Rhine, were at the junction of Europe's canals, its most important rivers and the oceans of the world. Almost everything passing in and out of Europe, up and down Europe's coast and across the sea passed through Holland. English tin, Spanish wool, Swedish iron, French wines, Russian

furs, Indian spices and teas, Norwegian timber and Irish wool flowed into the Netherlands to be graded, finished, woven, blended, sorted and shipped out again on the watery highways. To carry these goods, the Dutch had a near-monopoly on the world's shipping. Four thousand Dutch merchantmen—more merchant ships than those possessed by the rest of the world combined—sailed the world's oceans. The Dutch East India Company, founded in 1602, and the newer West India Company had offices in every major port in the world. Dutch seamen, combining the vigor of the explorer with the calculation of the trader, were always seeking new markets and new ports. As ships sailed ceaselessly to and fro, goods and profits piled up and the Dutch merchant republic became richer and richer. New services were developed in the city of Amsterdam to protect and encourage trade: insurance was devised to spread the risks; banks and the stock exchange found ways to deal in credit and to float public loans on an unprecedented scale to finance great commercial enterprises; printers printed contracts and bills of lading and all the multiple paper forms necessary to organize, advertise and confirm the thousands of business transactions occurring daily. Wealth bred confidence, confidence bred credit, credit bred more wealth, and Holland's power and fame spread farther. Holland was the true model of the rich, successful mercantile state, a commercial paradise to which young men came from all over Protestant Europe, especially England and Scotland, to learn the commercial and financial techniques of Holland's supremacy.

It was to this glittering mecca of commerce, sea power, culture and world empire that an eager young Russian named Peter Mikhailov was hurrying across Germany in the late summer of 1697.

AT PERESLAVL, at Archangel, at Voronezh, talking with Dutch shipwrights and sea captains, Peter had often heard the name of Zaandam. This Dutch town on the banks of the great gulf of the Ij, ten miles north of Amsterdam, was said to build the finest ships in Holland. In the fifty private shipbuilding yards in and around the town, as many as 350 ships a year were constructed, and so rapid and expert were the Zaandamers reputed to be that from the moment a keel was laid until the vessel was ready for sea, not more than five weeks were allowed to pass. Over the years, Peter's desire to visit and learn to build ships in Zaandam had taken firm root. Now, as he traveled across Germany, he told his comrades that he meant to remain in Zaandam through the autumn and winter learning shipbuilding. When he reached the Rhine at Emmerich near the Dutch frontier, he was so impatient that he hired a boat and, leaving most of the Embassy behind, sailed straight down the river, passing through Amsterdam without even stopping to rest.

Early on Sunday morning, August 18, Peter and his six companions were sailing along a canal approaching Zaandam when the Tsar noticed a familiar figure sitting in a rowboat, fishing for eels. It was Gerrit Kist, a Dutch blacksmith who had worked with Peter in Moscow. Overjoyed to see a familiar face, Peter boomed out a greeting. Kist, snatched from his thoughts and raising his eyes to see the Tsar of Russia sailing by, almost fell out of his boat. Steering for the bank and jumping from his boat, Peter hugged Kist excitedly and swore him to secrecy regarding his presence. Then, finding that Kist lived nearby, the Tsar immediately announced that he would stay with the blacksmith. Kist had many objections, arguing that his house was too small and plain for a monarch, and proposing instead the house of a widow who lived just behind his own house. With an offer of seven florins, the widow was persuaded to move in with her father. Thus, within a few hours Peter was happily settled into a tiny wooden house consisting of two small rooms, two windows, a tiled stove and a curtained, airless sleeping closet so small that he could not fully stretch out. Two of his companions stayed with him; the other four found nearby quarters.

Because it was Sunday, the shipyards were closed, but Peter was intensely excited and found it impossible to sit quietly and do nothing. He went out into the streets, which were filled with people strolling on a summer Sunday afternoon. The crowd, attracted by the news that a strange boat had arrived carrying foreigners in exotic costumes, began to notice him. Annoyed, he tried to find refuge at the Otter Inn, but there also people stared at him. It was only the beginning.

Early Monday morning, Peter hurried to a store on the dike and bought carpenter's tools. Then he went to the private shipyard of Lynst Rogge and, under the name Peter Mikhailov, signed himself up as a common workman. He began working happily, shaping timbers with his hatchet and constantly asking the foreman the name of every object he saw. After work, he began visiting the wives and parents of Dutch shipbuilders still in Russia, explaining to them that he worked side by side with their sons and husbands, declaring with pleasure, "I, too, am a carpenter." He called on the widow of a Dutch carpenter who had died in Russia, to whom he had previously sent a gift of 500 florins. The widow told him that she had often prayed for a chance to tell the Tsar how much his gift had meant to her. Touched and pleased, Peter sat down and had supper with her.

On Tuesday, anxious to be out on the water, Peter bought a small rowboat, having haggled over the price in the best Dutch fashion. He obtained it for forty florins, and then he and the seller went to a tavern and shared a pitcher of beer.

Despite Peter's wish that no one learn his identity, the secret quickly began to evaporate. On Monday morning, Peter had ordered his com-

panions to shed their Russian robes for the red jackets and white canvas trousers of Dutch workmen, but, even so, the Russians did not look like Dutchmen. Peter's own great height made real anonymity impossible, and by Tuesday everyone in Zaandam knew that "a person of great importance" was in town. This was confirmed by an incident on Tuesday afternoon when Peter, walking down a street and eating plums from his hat, offered some to a group of boys he encountered. There was not enough fruit to go around, and the boys began to follow him. When he tried to chase them away, they pelted him with stones and mud. Peter took shelter in the Three Swans Inn and sent for help. The Burgomaster himself came and Peter was forced to explain who he was and why he was there. The Burgomaster immediately issued an order forbidding Zaandamers to trouble or insult "distinguished persons who wish to remain unknown."

Soon, the most "distinguished person" was precisely identified. A Zaandam shipwright working in Russia had written home to his father that the Great Embassy was coming to Holland and that the Tsar would probably be with it, traveling incognito. He advised his father that Peter would be easy to recognize because of his great height, the shaking or twitching of his head and left arm, and the small wart on his right cheek. The father had just read this letter aloud on Wednesday to everyone in Pomp's barber shop when a tall man with exactly those distinguishing marks walked in. Like barbers everywhere, Pomp regarded it as part of his calling to pass along all local gossip, and he forthwith broadcast the news that the tallest of the strangers was the Tsar of Muscovy. To verify Pomp's report, people hurried to Kist, who was harboring the stranger and who was known to be familiar with the Tsar from his years in Russia. Kist, faithful to Peter's wish, stoutly denied his guest's identity until his wife said, "Gerrit, I cannot stand it any longer. Stop lying."

Even though Peter's secret was out, he still tried to maintain his incognito. He refused an invitation to dine with the leading merchants of Zaandam and declined to eat fish cooked in the special Zaandam style with the Burgomaster and his councilors. To both these invitations, Peter replied that there was no one of importance present; the Tsar had not yet come. When one leading merchant came to Peter's comrades to offer a larger house with a garden filled with fruit trees which would be more suitable for them and their master, they replied that they were not noblemen but servants, and that their present accommodations were ample.

News of the Tsar's appearance in Zaandam spread rapidly across Holland. Many people flatly refused to believe it, and numerous bets were placed. Two merchants who had met Peter at Archangel hurried to Zaandam. Seeing him at his house on Thursday morning, they came out, pale with emotion, and declared, "Certainly, it is the Tsar, but how and why is

he here?" Another acquaintance from Archangel told Peter of his amazement at seeing him in Holland in workman's clothes. Peter replied simply, "You see it," and refused to say anything else on the subject.

On Thursday, Peter bought a sailboat for 450 florins and installed a new mast and bowsprit with his own hands. When the sun rose on Friday, he was sailing on the Ij, tiller in hand. That afternoon, after dinner, he went sailing again, but as he cruised on the Ij, he saw a large number of boats putting out from Zaandam to join him. To escape, he steered for shore and jumped out, only to find himself in the middle of another curious crowd, pushing to see him and staring at him as if he were an animal in the zoo. In anger, Peter cuffed one spectator on the head, provoking the crowd to shout at the victim, "Bravo! Marsje, now you have been knighted!" By this time, the numbers of people in boats and on the shore had grown so great that Peter secluded himself in an inn and would not return to Zaandam until darkness fell.

The following day, Saturday, Peter had intended to observe the interesting and delicate mechanical operation by which a large, newly constructed ship was dragged across the top of a dike by means of rollers and capstans. To protect him, a space had been enclosed with a fence so that he could watch without being crushed by the crowd. By Saturday morning, however, the news of Peter's anticipated presence had brought even larger crowds of people from as far as Amsterdam; there were so many that the fences were trampled down. Peter, seeing the windows and even the roofs of the surrounding houses jammed with spectators, refused to go, even though the Burgomaster came in person to urge him. In Dutch, Peter replied, "Too many people. Too many people."

On Sunday, crowds came from Amsterdam, boatload after boatload. In desperation, the guards on the Zaandam bridges were doubled, but the crowd merely pushed them aside. Peter did not dare step outside all day. Pent up indoors, his anger and frustration smoldering, he pleaded with the embarrassed town council for help, but it could do nothing with the torrent of strangers which was growing every minute. As a last resort, he decided to leave Zaandam. His boat was brought from its normal mooring to a place near the house. By vigorous use of his knees and elbows, Peter managed to force his way through the crowd and climb on board. Although a high wind which had been blowing since morning had now reached the proportions of a storm, he insisted on leaving. A stay in the rigging parted as he cast off, and for a moment the boat was in danger of foundering. Nevertheless, despite the urging of experienced seamen, Peter sailed away, arriving three hours later in Amsterdam. Here, too, a crowd of Dutchmen pressed against one another to see him. Once again, several of them caught blows from the angry Tsar. Finally, he made his way to an inn which had been reserved for the Great Embassy.

This was the end of Peter's long-dreamed-of visit to Zaandam. Trying to work in an open shipyard or move freely about the town was plainly impossible, and Peter's intended stay of several months was reduced to an actual stay of a single week. Later, he sent Menshikov and two other members of his party back to Zaandam to learn the special technique of making masts, and he himself returned for two brief visits, but the education in Dutch shipbuilding that Peter had planned for himself was to take place not in Zaandam but in Amsterdam.

AMSTERDAM, in Peter's time, was the greatest port in Europe and the wealthiest city in the world. Built where two rivers, the Amstel and the Ij, flowed into the Zuider Zee, the city rose up from the water. Piles had been driven into the marshy ground to give it a footing, and the water flowed through the city in concentric rings of canals—five such rings in Peter's day. Each canal was bisected and trisected by smaller canals, so that the entire city was practically afloat, an archipelago of seventy islands, linked by 500 bridges arching over the canals to allow boats and barges to pass beneath. The city walls were constructed just inside the outermost canal so that the canal itself made a natural moat. Embedded in these ramparts were sturdy, round defensive watchtowers which—typically—the utilitarian Dutch had put to a second use. On top of the towers they set windmills, whose rotating vanes supplied energy to pumps working constantly to drain the water from small patches of dry ground. Standing on the fortifications, a watcher gazed out across a wide expanse of flat, watery countryside studded in every direction with other windmills, great and small, turning ceaselessly to pump out the sea.

The city's buildings proclaimed its wealth. Seen from the harbor, Amsterdam was a panorama of red-brick church towers, symmetrical and practical, designed in the distinctive rounded Dutch style. The city fathers were enormously proud of their City Hall, regarding the building, which rested on 13,659 piles, as the Eighth Wonder of the World. (Today, the building is a royal palace.) Throughout the city, there were breweries, sugar refineries, tobacco warehouses, storehouses for coffee and spices, bakeries, slaughterhouses and ironworks, each contributing by its shape or its pungent smell to a scene of enormous variety and richness. But mostly it was in the stately homes built along the canals by the city's prosperous merchants that Amsterdam's wealth was displayed. Set back from the canals, on streets lined with elms and linden trees, these red-brick mansions remain today Amsterdam's handsomest feature. Very narrow (because the owners were taxed on the basis of the width of their houses), they rose four or five stories to an elegant, pointed gable at the peak. From this peak, a beam usually projected out over the street and was used as an

anchor for block and tackle to haul heavy furniture and other objects up from the street and in through the windows of the upper floors, the stairs being too narrow for this purpose. Through these tall windows the owner could look down on the street, the trees, the elegant iron lampposts and the shaded, rippling water of the canals.

Water and ships were everywhere. Turning every corner, a visitor caught sight of masts and sails. The waterfront was a forest of spars. Along the canals, pedestrians stepped over ropes, iron rings for mooring boats, pieces of timber, barrels, anchors, even cannon. The whole city was a semi-shipyard. And the harbor itself was crowded with ships of every size—the small, gaff-rigged fishing boats just back at midday from an early morning's catch on the Zuider Zee; the big, three-masted East India Company merchantmen and seventy- or eighty-gun ships-of-the-line, all showing the typical Dutch design with round, turned-up bows, broad-beamed hulls and shallow bottoms, looking exactly like outsized Dutch wooden shoes equipped with masts and sails; the elegant state yachts, with bulbous Dutch bows and large, ornate after-cabins with leaded windows opening over the stern. And at the eastern end of the harbor, in a section called Ostenburg, lay the Dutch East India Company dockyards with the great wharves and shipbuilding ramps where the company's ships were constructed. Row on row, the great, round, bulbous hulls of the East Indiamen took shape, up from the keel, rib by rib, plank by plank, deck by deck. Nearby, veteran ships returning from long voyages were overhauled— first, the rigging and masts were removed, then the hulls were dragged into shallow tidal water and rolled on their sides. There they lay like beached whales while carpenters, fitters and other workmen swarmed over them, scraping their bottoms of rich layers of marine growth, replacing their rotten planks and melting fresh tar into the seams to keep out the sea.

It was to this dockyard, a special seamen's paradise within the larger paradise that was all of Amsterdam, that Peter came to spend four months.

PETER'S RETURN to Amsterdam had been forced by the crowds in Zaandam, but he would have returned in any case to greet his own Great Embassy, which was just arriving. The ambassadors had been received in royal style at Cleves near the frontier, and four large yachts and numerous carriages had been placed at their disposal. The city fathers of Amsterdam, understanding the potential significance of this Embassy in terms of future trade with Russia, decided to receive it with extraordinary honors.

The reception included ceremonial visits to the City Hall, the Admiralty and the docks, special performances of opera and ballet, and a major banquet which ended with a display of fireworks set off from a raft in the Amstel. During these festivities, Peter had a chance to talk to the ex-

traordinary man who was Burgomaster of Amsterdam, Nicholas Witsen. Cultured, wealthy, respected for his character as well as his achievements, he was an explorer, a patron of the arts and an amateur scientist, as well as a public official. One of his passions was ships, and he took Peter to see his collections of ship models, navigational instruments and tools used in shipbuilding. Witsen was fascinated by Russia and for a long time, along with his other duties and interests, Witsen had acted as the unofficial minister of Muscovy in Amsterdam.

During the months that Peter was in Amsterdam, the Tsar and the Burgomaster spoke daily and Peter turned to Witsen with the problem of the crowds in Zaandam and Amsterdam. How could he work quietly, learning to build ships, surrounded by curious, staring strangers? Witsen had an immediate suggestion. If Peter remained in Amsterdam, he could work in the shipyards and docks of the East India Company, which were enclosed by walls and barred to the public. Peter was delighted by the idea, and Witsen, a director of the company, undertook to arrange it. The following day, the board of directors of the East India Company resolved to invite "a high personage present here incognito" to work in its shipyard and, for his convenience, to set aside for him the house of the master ropemaker so that he could live and work undisturbed inside the shipyard. In addition, to assist him in learning shipbuilding, the board ordered the laying of the keel of a new frigate, 100 feet or 130 feet long, whichever the Tsar preferred, so that he and his comrades could work on it and observe Dutch methods from the very beginning.

That night, at the formal state banquet given the Embassy by the city of Amsterdam, Witsen told Peter of the decision reached by the directors earlier in the day. Peter was enthusiastic and, although he loved fireworks, he could scarcely restrain himself through the rest of the meal. When the last skyrocket had burst, the Tsar jumped to his feet and announced that he was leaving for Zaandam right then, in the middle of the night, to fetch his tools so that he could start work in the morning. Attempts by both Russians and Dutchmen to stop him were useless, and at eleven p.m. he boarded his yacht and sailed away. The following morning, he was back and went straight to the East India Company shipyard in the Ostenburg section. Ten Russian "volunteers" including Menshikov went with him, while the rest of the "volunteers" were scattered by Peter's command around the harbor, learning the trades of sailmaker, ropemaker, mast turning, the use of block and tackle, and seamanship. Prince Alexander of Imeritia was dispatched to The Hague to study artillery. Peter himself enrolled as a carpenter under the master shipwright, Gerrit Claes Pool.

The first three weeks were spent in collecting and preparing the necessary timbers and other materials. So that the Tsar could see exactly what was being done, the Dutch gathered and laid out all the pieces before

even laying the keel. Then, as each piece was fastened into place, the ship was assembled rapidly, almost like a huge model made from a kit. The frigate, 100 feet long, was called *The Apostles Peter and Paul,* and Peter worked enthusiastically on every stage of its assembly.

Every day, Peter arrived at the shipyard at dawn, carrying his axe and tools on his shoulders as the other workmen did. He allowed no distinction between himself and them, and strictly refused to be addressed or identified by any title. In his afternoon leisure hours, he liked sitting on a log, talking to sailors or shipbuilders or anyone who addressed him as "Carpenter Peter" or "Baas [Master] Peter." He ignored or turned away from anyone who addressed him as "Your Majesty" or "Sire." When two English noblemen came to catch a glimpse of the Tsar of Muscovy working as a laborer, the foreman, in order to point out which one was Peter, called to him, "Carpenter Peter, why don't you help your comrades?" Without a word, Peter walked over and put his shoulder beneath a timber which several men were struggling to raise and helped lift it into place.

Peter was happy with the house assigned to him. Several of his comrades lived there with him in the manner of a group of common workmen. Originally, the Tsar's meals were prepared by the staff of the inn at which the Embassy was staying, but this bothered him; he wanted an entirely independent household. He had no fixed hours for meals; he wished to be able to eat whenever he was hungry. It was arranged that he should be supplied with firewood and foodstuffs and then left alone. Thereafter, Peter lighted his own fire and cooked his own meals like a simple carpenter.

But although he was in a foreign land, wearing the clothes and practicing the trade of a laborer, neither Peter nor his countrymen ever forgot who he really was or the awesome power he wielded. His viceroys in Moscow were reluctant to act without his consent, and every post brought him thick bundles of letters asking for guidance, requesting favors or passing on news. Peter himself, in a shipyard a thousand miles from his capital, took far more interest in his own government than ever before. He insisted on being informed of even the smallest details of those public affairs which he had once so happily neglected. He wanted to know everything that was happening: How are the Streltsy behaving? What progress is being made on the two Azov forts? What about the harbor and the forts at Tagonrog? What is happening in Poland? When Shein wrote about a victory over the Turks outside Azov, Peter celebrated by giving a magnificent banquet for the principal merchants of Amsterdam, followed by a concert, a ball and fireworks. When Peter learned of the climactic victory Prince Eugene of Savoy won over the Turks at Zenta, he sent the news to Moscow along with the fact that he had given another banquet to honor this success. He tried to reply every Friday to the letters from Moscow, although, as he wrote

to Vinius, "sometimes from weariness, sometimes from absence, sometimes from Khmelnitsky [drink], we cannot accomplish it."

On one occasion, Peter's power over two of his subjects, both noblemen serving with the Embassy in Holland, was stayed. Hearing that these Russians had criticized his behavior, saying that he should make less of a spectacle of himself and act more in keeping with his rank, Peter flew into a fury. Presuming that he wielded in Holland as he did in Russia the power of life and death over his subjects, he ordered the pair placed in irons as a preliminary to their execution. Witsen interfered, asking Peter to remember that he was in Holland, where no execution could take place except by sentence of a Dutch court. Gently, Witsen suggested that the men be freed, but Peter was adamant. Finally, he reluctantly agreed to a compromise which saw the two unfortunates exiled to the farthest overseas colonies of Holland: one to Batavia, the other to Surinam.

Outside the shipyard, Peter's curiosity was insatiable. He wanted to see everything with his own eyes. He visited factories, sawmills, spinning mills, paper mills, workshops, museums, botanical gardens and laboratories. Everywhere he asked, "What is that for? How does it work?" Listening to the explanations, he nodded: "Very good. Very good." He met architects, sculptors and Van der Heyden, the inventor of the fire pump, whom he tried to persuade to come to Russia. He visited the architect Simon Schnvoet, the museum of Jacob de Wilde, and learned to sketch and draw under the direction of Schonebeck. He engraved a plate depicting a tall young man, who closely resembled himself, holding the cross high, standing on the fallen crescent and banners of Islam. At Delft, he visited engineer Baron von Coehorn, the Dutch Vauban, who gave him lessons in the science of fortifications. He visited Dutchmen in their homes, especially Dutchmen engaged in the Russian trade. He became interested in printing when he met the Tessing family, and granted one of the brothers the right to print books in Russian and to introduce them into Russia.

Several times, Peter left the shipyard to visit the lecture hall and dissecting room of Professor Fredrik Ruysch, the renowned professor of anatomy. Ruysch was famous throughout Europe for his ability to preserve parts of the human body and even whole corpses by injection of chemicals. His magnificent laboratory was considered one of the marvels of Holland. One day, Peter was present in front of the body of a small child so perfectly preserved that it seemed alive and smiling. Peter gazed at it a long time, marveling, and finally could not resist leaning forward and kissing the cold forehead. Peter became so interested in surgery that he had difficulty leaving the laboratory; he wanted to stay and observe more. He dined with Ruysch, who advised him on his choice of surgeons to take back to Russia for service with his army and fleet. He was intrigued by

anatomy and thereafter considered himself qualified as a surgeon. After all, he was able to ask, how many others in Russia had studied with the famous Ruysch?

In later years, Peter always carried two cases with him, one filled with mathematical instruments to examine and verify construction plans presented to him, the other filled with surgical instruments. He left instructions that he was to be informed whenever an interesting operation was to be performed in a hospital in his vicinity, and he was usually present, frequently lending assistance and acquiring sufficient skill to dissect, to bleed, to draw teeth and to perform minor operations. Those of his servants who fell ill tried to keep it a secret from the Tsar lest he appear at their bedsides with his case of instruments to offer—and even insist on their acceptance of—his services.

In Leyden, Peter visited the famous Dr. Boerhaave, who supervised a celebrated botanical garden. Boerhaave also lectured on anatomy, and when he asked Peter what hour he would like to visit, the Tsar chose six o'clock the following morning. He also visited Boerhaave's dissection theater, where a corpse was lying on a table with some of its muscles exposed. Peter was studying the corpse with fascination when he heard grumbles of disgust from some of his squeamish Russian comrades. Furious, and to the horror of the Dutch, he ordered them to approach the cadaver, bend down and bite off a muscle of the corpse with their teeth.

In Delft, he visited the celebrated naturalist Anton van Leeuwenhoek, inventor of the microscope. Peter spent more than two hours talking with him and looking through the miraculous instrument by which Leeuwenhoek had discovered the existence of spermatozoa and had studied the circulation of blood in fish.

On free days in Amsterdam, Peter wandered the city on foot, watching the citizens bustling by, the carriages rattling over the bridges, the thousands of boats rowing up and down the canals. On market days, the Tsar went to the great open-air market, the Botermarket, where goods of every kind were piled up in the open or under arcades. Standing next to a woman buying cheeses, or a merchant choosing a painting, Peter observed and studied. He especially enjoyed watching street artists performing before a crowd. One day, he watched a celebrated clown juggling while standing on top of a cask, and Peter stepped forward and tried to persuade the man to come back with him to Russia. The juggler refused, saying he was having too much success in Amsterdam. In the market, the Tsar witnessed a traveling dentist who pulled aching teeth with unorthodox instruments such as the bowl of a spoon or the tip of a sword. Peter asked for lessons and absorbed enough to experiment on his servants. He learned to mend his own clothes and, from a cobbler, how to make himself a pair of slippers. In winter, when the skies were eternally gray and the Amstel

and the canals were frozen, Peter saw women dressed in furs and woolens and men and boys in long cloaks and scarves go speeding by on ice skates with curved blades. The warmest places, he found, and the places where he was happiest, were the beer houses and taverns where he relaxed with his Dutch and Russian comrades.

Observing Holland's immense prosperity, Peter could not escape asking himself how it was that his own people, with an endless stretch of steppe and forest at their disposition, produced only enough to feed themselves, whereas here in Amsterdam, with its wharves and warehouses and forest of masts, more convertible wealth had been accumulated than in all the expanse of Russia. One reason, Peter knew, was trade, a mercantile economy, the possession of ships; he resolved to dedicate himself to achieving these things for Russia. Another reason was the religious toleration in Holland. Because international trade could not flourish in an atmosphere of narrow religious doctrine or prejudice, Protestant Holland practiced the widest religious toleration in the Europe of that day. It was to Holland that the dissenters fled from James I's Calvinist England in 1606, from there to sail a decade later to Plymouth Bay. It was to Holland also that the French Protestant Huguenots swarmed by the thousands when Louis XIV revoked the Edict of Nantes. Throughout the seventeenth century, Holland served as Europe's intellectual and artistic clearinghouse as well as its commercial center. It was to defend their religious liberties as much as their commercial supremacy that the Dutch resisted so fiercely the aggrandizements of Louis XIV's Catholic France. Peter was intrigued by this atmosphere of religious toleration. He visited many Protestant churches in Holland and asked questions of the pastors.

One brilliant facet of Holland's seventeenth-century culture did not much interest him. This was the new and remarkable painting of the great masters of the Dutch School—Rembrandt, Vermeer, Frans Hals and their contemporaries and successors. Peter bought paintings and took them back to Russia, but they were not the Rembrandts and other masterpieces which later were collected by Catherine the Great. Instead, Peter collected pictures of ships and the sea.

15

THE PRINCE
OF ORANGE

IN A PREDATORY WORLD, Holland's wealth and power were neither gained nor maintained without a struggle. The republic had been born in the sixteenth-century struggle of the Protestant provinces of the northern Netherlands to break the grip of their Spanish master, Philip II. In 1559, they finally achieved independence. With skill and determination, the Dutchmen developed the sea power that defeated the Spanish admirals, inherited Spain's worldwide ocean trade routes and laid the foundation for Holland's overseas empire. But as the republic waxed in prosperity, it aroused the envy and greed of its two most powerful neighbors, England and France. Coveting the Dutch near-monopoly on European trade, the English under both Oliver Cromwell and Charles II assaulted Holland, and three Anglo-Dutch naval wars resulted. It was in the second of these wars that an English fleet commanded by the King's brother, the Duke of York (later to become King James II), seized the harbor of New Amsterdam and named the village at the tip of Manhattan Island "New York" after himself. Later, the Dutch retaliated with a daring naval raid up the Thames estuary, thrusting into the main British naval base at Chatham, burning four ships-of-the-line at anchor and sailing away with the *Royal Charles*, the pride of the Royal Navy, in tow. In these wars at sea between two seafaring peoples, the Dutch more than held their own. Led by two superb admirals, Tromp and de Ruyter, the Dutch sailed their smaller, round-nosed warships against the larger, heavier English ships with such bravery and seamanship that Holland became the only nation ever consistently to defeat the British navy.

Holland's wars against England were fought at sea and in the colonies. A far deadlier threat to the United Provinces was to come by land from Holland's mighty neighbor, the France of Louis XIV. To the men gathered around Louis at Versailles, the success of the tiny Protestant republic was an affront to France's greatness, a sin against her religion and, most important, a barrier and competitor to her commerce. The King, his finance minister Colbert and his war minister Louvois were united in their desire to crush

the remarkable, upstart Dutchmen. In 1672, with the largest and finest army in the history of Western Europe and the Sun King in personal command, France swept across the Rhine to within sight of the steeples of Amsterdam. Holland was finished . . . or would have been if not for the emergence into history of one of the seventeenth century's most extraordinary figures, William of Orange.

WILLIAM, Prince of Orange, simultaneously Stadholder of Holland and the United Netherlands and King William III of England, was perhaps the most interesting political figure Peter was to meet in his lifetime. Two dramatic, almost miraculous events had set the direction of William's life. At twenty-one, at a moment when an apparently invincible French army had swallowed half the Dutch republic, William was handed supreme military and political power and asked to repel the aggressors. He succeeded. Fifteen years later, at thirty-six, without relinquishing his Dutch offices and titles, he conducted the only successful invasion of England since the days of William the Conqueror.

Physically, William of Orange was not blessed. Slender and unusually short, with a slight deformity of the spine which crooked his back, he had a thin, dark face, black eyes, a long, aquiline nose, full lips and black hair hanging in heavy curls which gave him an appearance more Spanish or Italian than Dutch. In fact, William possessed very little Dutch blood. He was born into a curious European family, a princely house whose history is integral to the struggle for independence of the Netherlands, and yet whose hereditary principality of Orange lies hundreds of miles to the south, in the Rhône Valley of France, a few miles north of Avignon. Since the days of William the Silent, who led the Dutch to freedom against Spain in the sixteenth century, the House of Orange had furnished the republic with elected leaders—stadholders—in times of danger. The family's blood was good enough for marriage into other royal families, and half of William's ancestors were Stuarts. His grandfather was King Charles I of England, his mother was an English princess, her brothers—his uncles—two Kings of England: Charles II and James II.

William became the head of the House of Orange at the moment of birth; his father had died of smallpox a week before. Brought up by his grandmother, he suffered severely from asthma, and through his childhood he was lonely, delicate and unhappy. In those years, the office of stadholder was vacant and Holland was ruled by an oligarchy led by two brothers, John and Cornelius De Witt, who believed that by careful conciliation they could placate Louis XIV. Then, in 1672, the year of Peter's birth, came the first crisis of William's life. In that spring, Louvois presented Louis with a magnificent new French army of 110,000 men massed at Charleroix on the

northern frontier. Louis, arriving to assume personal command of the blow which was to destroy the Protestant republic, expected no difficulty. "I now possess an escort which will allow me to take a quiet little journey into Holland," he said contentedly. Although the Sun King was in nominal command, the experienced Marshal Turenne and the Prince de Condé gave the actual orders. Louis' army easily forced the Rhine on new copper pontoon bridges, and Dutch cities and fortresses fell like ninepins. Seeing the French implacably advancing, the people of Holland panicked. There were riots against the De Witts, who were held personally responsible for the country's plight. In The Hague, a frenzied mob burst in upon the brothers and lynched them.

It was at this moment of crisis that the Dutch suddenly turned like terrified children to the House of Orange, which had provided salvation a century before. William was only twenty-one, but on July 8 he was appointed Stadholder of Holland and Captain General of the Army for life. His program was straightforward and bleak: "We can die in the last ditch." Immediately, he began to demonstrate the qualities for which he was to become famous. He took the field wearing the commander's garb which was to be his attire for many years: the azure uniform of the Dutch Blue Guards, light armor covering his back and chest, a full cravat of Brussels lace, an orange sash and scarf, high boots, fringed braided gloves and belt, a broad-brimmed hat with feathers. Remaining on horseback from dawn until nightfall, indifferent to fatigue, the slight young prince threw down the gauntlet before Louis and his veteran marshals.

Within a week of taking command, William was forced to make an appalling decision. Despite his efforts, his army could not hold the French, who thrust swiftly forward into the heart of the United Netherlands. Arnhem fell and Utrecht, only twenty-two miles from Amsterdam. Then, when the French were only a day's march away from the great Dutch port, the Dutch obeyed William's command and cut the dikes. The sea rolled in, flooding crops and meadows, engulfing rich country houses and gardens, drowning cattle and pigs, and undoing the labor of many generations. As soldiers opened the sluices and cut the dikes, desperate farmers, unwilling to see their farms disappear beneath the onrushing waters, fought to prevent them. Amsterdam, hitherto almost defenseless, now became an island. The French, lacking boats, could only stare at the great city from a distance.

To Louis' chagrin, although the Dutch army was beaten and half of Holland inundated, William refused to yield. The Dutch battalions, unable to defeat the more numerous French, nevertheless remained in the field, waiting. Condé settled into winter quarters in Utrecht, hoping that when winter came he could attack Amsterdam across the ice. But the winter was mild, and Louis, who never liked to have French armies operating far from France, became nervous. Meanwhile, William had been active diplomatically.

To the Hapsburg Emperor, to Brandenburg, Hanover, Denmark and Spain, he pointed out that Louis' power and ambition were a threat not just to Holland but to other states as well. All were impressed by the argument, and even more by the continuing Dutch resistance. In the spring, the war widened. William's small army began to attack the French lines of communication, and Louis became more nervous. At last, systematically destroying the towns they had occupied, the French withdrew. This partial victory—the survival of Holland—was almost solely the achievement of a twenty-one-year-old soldier and statesman who in those few months became the second most important national leader in Europe.

Peace finally came in 1678, but the suspicions raised in William by Louis' ambitions were never assuaged. Opposition to the great French King became William's obsession. He understood that the power of France could never be matched by any other single power; therefore, his life work became the tireless weaving of coalitions of European states strong enough to repulse the Sun King's ambition, which was, as William saw it, to establish in Europe "a universal monarchy and a universal religion."

The young hero grew quickly into an experienced statesman and warrior. Physically courageous and energetic, a ruthless disciplinarian of himself and his men, William was nevertheless not a great soldier. Although he commanded Dutch and English armies for almost three decades, he never rose above the second rank as a military commander; he certainly was not to be compared with the lieutenant who succeeded him as generalissimo of the anti-French coalition, John Churchill, first Duke of Marlborough. William's talent lay not in winning battles—he was frequently beaten—but in surviving defeat, in remaining in the field, in pulling back, enduring, and preparing for the next campaign. His genius lay in diplomacy. Stern, unlovable, impatient, self-willed, passionate, his true nature was to tolerate no obstruction, smashing through everything to his objective. But because Holland had not the power to indulge this side of his character, he was forced to suppress these feelings, to compromise with his allies, to make concessions, to soothe and to wait.

William was a Calvinist, but he tolerated all religions: The Pope was his ally, so was the Catholic Emperor; there were Catholic officers in his army. Every other prejudice and antagonism was set aside; his sole vendetta was with Louis. At bottom, however, his life was guided by a steely Calvinist belief in predestination. He was convinced that he, like others in his family before him, was acting as an instrument of God. The Deity, he believed, had chosen his family and now himself to save the Netherlands and the Protestant cause in Europe. He even saw his mission as personal: himself and Louis locked in single combat for the future of Europe. Given this granite foundation to his faith, it did not dismay William when his armies failed in battle: Everything was preordained by God, and defeat was only a

challenge to his worthiness, a test of his ability to continue as God's champion. Although William sometimes doubted and even despaired, he never gave up, believing that somehow, through miracles if necessary, God would save his cause. Thus, although his power was much less than Louis', William, unlike Louis, was prepared to run great risks. It was a risk of this magnitude, a second miracle almost, which in 1688 suddenly catapulted William onto the throne of England.

For years, William's primary diplomatic objective, after the safeguarding of Holland, had been to pull his cynical uncle, Charles II of England, away from France, and to attach England to Holland in alliance against France. He never entirely succeeded, but after 1672 England remained neutral in the uneasy peace that followed. In 1677, to further his policy, twenty-six-year-old William married his first cousin, Charles II's niece, the fifteen-year-old Princess Mary of England. It was not a love match, as women in general meant little to William, and the marriage was childless. The Princess, however, was a devoted wife who gave up England and dedicated herself to becoming a Princess of Holland, not even visiting her own country for ten years after her marriage. She became much beloved by the Dutch people, and she returned their affection. She had no expectation of ever mounting the English throne: Before her stood first the incumbent king, her uncle Charles II, then any legitimate male heirs whom he might sire, then her father, the Duke of York, followed by *his* legitimate male heirs.

In 1685, however, after twenty-five years on the English throne, Charles II died, leaving no legitimate child, and the throne passed to his younger brother, England's finest admiral, James, Duke of York. This change of monarchs greatly altered England's position. James was honest, blunt, proud, single-minded and devoid of subtlety. Born a Protestant, he had converted to Catholicism at the age of thirty-five, displaying thereafter all the special fanaticism of the convert, a trait in which he was enthusiastically encouraged by his Catholic second wife, Mary of Modena. On the decks of his ships or in a special little wooden chapel mounted on wheels and trundled along in the midst of his army, James heard mass twice a day.

Once on the throne, James moved quickly to change the balance of political forces in England. His first objective was simply to remove the restrictions placed on English Catholics by the strongly anti-Catholic Protestant majority. Increasingly, however, Catholics were promoted into key positions. Catholic governors were installed in the Channel ports and a Catholic admiral was given command of the Channel fleet. Although Protestant anxiety and opposition mounted swiftly, one important fact stifled overt action: James had no son, and his two daughters, Mary and Anne, were both Protestants. English Protestants, thus, were prepared to await James' death and Mary's succession. And Mary's husband, who would succeed with her to the throne, was William of Orange. William's title to

rule came only partially from his status as Mary's husband; in his own right he was also, as the only nephew of both King Charles II and King James II, the next heir after Mary and Anne.

William did not dislike his uncle, but he deeply feared the presence of a Catholic monarch on the English throne, with its implications of an alignment of Catholic France and Catholic England against Protestant Holland. Nevertheless, he, too, was prepared to wait for James to die and his own wife, Mary, to come to the throne. But on June 20, 1688, James' Queen, Mary of Modena, produced a son. The Catholic King had a Catholic heir. This challenge flung down before the Protestants of England turned them immediately to William. Although what happened next was seen by James' supporters (who came to be called Jacobites) as a stroke of monstrous ambition by a ruthless nephew and son-in-law usurping the throne of England, the motive for William's action had almost nothing to do with England and everything to do with France and Europe. It was not that William wanted to be King of England or cared about preserving the liberties of Englishmen or the rights of Parliament; what he wanted was to keep England in the Protestant camp.

The invitation to William to replace his uncle on the English throne was sent to William by seven of the most respected Protestant leaders in England, including both Whigs and Tories. Obtaining the support and permission of the States General of Holland, William embarked a Dutch army of 12,000 men on 200 merchant vessels escorted by 49 warships, almost the entire Dutch fleet. Slipping past the watching English and French fleets, he landed at Torbay on the Devonshire coast. He came ashore behind a banner carrying the ancient creed of the House of Orange, "Je maintiendrai" ("I shall maintain"), to which William had added the words: "the liberties of England and the Protestant religion."

James sent his most skilled military commander and his intimate personal friend, John Churchill, then Earl of Marlborough, to confront William's army, but Marlborough, himself a Protestant, promptly defected to the invaders. So did James' other daughter, Princess Anne, along with her husband, Prince George of Denmark. This broke the King's spirit. Crying, "God help me! Even my own children have deserted me!" he fled unshaven from London, throwing the Great Seal into the river as he crossed the Thames and embarked for France. There, in the château of St. Germain-en-Laye, where he now lies buried, the proud and obstinate monarch lived for thirteen years as a pensioner of Louis. He kept a shadow court and a handful of Irish Guards, all dependent for their daily bread on Louis, whose vanity was gratified by the presence at his feet of a suppliant exiled monarch.

Mary's position in the quarrel between her father and her husband was painful, but, as a Protestant and a wife, she supported William. When she arrived in England, she quickly rejected proposals that she become the sole

monarch to the exclusion of her husband. William and Mary were proclaimed joint sovereigns by a Parliament which, in turn, extracted from them a Bill of Rights and other privileges which are today the centerpieces of the British constitution.

Ironically, although the events of 1688 marked an overwhelming change in the political and constitutional history of England, and are referred to as the Glorious Revolution, William did not much care about them. He acquiesced in whatever Parliament asked, in order to keep its support for the struggle in Europe. He left domestic policy in the hands of others while striving to control England's foreign policy himself, coordinating it with Dutch policy and even merging the Dutch and English diplomatic services to act as one. His foreign policy was, simply, war with France, and in taking William, England also took his war. In essence, a trade had been made: Parliament accepted William's war in order to protect the Protestant religion and assert its supremacy; William accepted Parliament's supremacy in order to keep England's support in fighting Louis.

William did not feel at home among the islanders. He hated the English weather, which aggravated his asthma, and he disliked the English people: "I am sure that this people has not been made for me, nor I for it." He longed for Holland. In 1692, when The Hague was holding its annual fair, he sighed, "I wish I were a bird and could fly over." On another occasion, he spoke of Holland, "for which I am longing as a fish for water."

And the English heartily returned William's dislike. They commented on his unsociability, his silence and his surliness toward his English subjects, as well as on his distaste for their habits, their traditions, their parties and politics, and for London. But although he took the witty Elizabeth Villiers as his mistress, Queen Mary remained devoted to him, ruling England in his behalf whenever he was absent from the realm and retiring from politics completely whenever he returned. When she died of smallpox at the age of thirty-two, William mourned her bitterly. He continued on as sole monarch, a childless, lonely man whose heir was Mary's sister, Princess Anne. The French, ever ready to believe the worst of the strange little man who so desperately opposed them, spread rumors that he was in love with the Earl of Albemarle.

What William most disliked about the English was what he regarded as their naïve disregard of their own long-term interests and their selfish lack of concern about what happened to Europe; in other words, their wavering commitment to his great cause. As King of England, he bound English interests to the Dutch, but he did not subordinate the one to the other. Instead, as leader of the coalition of Europe, he took an overall view of his role. He began to speak of Europe as an entity, and in his correspondence the objective became "the general interest of Europe."

Predictably, within two years of William's coronation, England was at

war with France. The war lasted nine years, the result was inconclusive and the Treaty of Ryswick, being drawn up at The Hague in 1697 at the moment of Peter's visit to Holland, altered no boundaries, although by its terms Louis finally recognized William as King of England. Thereafter, in a brief interlude of peace, Louis and William even worked together to head off the international crisis which would inevitably be precipitated when the feeble King of Spain, Carlos II, died without an heir. The agreed solution was partition, but Carlos upset their plans by leaving his kingdom and empire to Louis' grandson, and the Sun King tore up his treaty with William. William, naturally, refused to accept this merger of the territory and power of France and Spain, and tirelessly began once again to assemble an anti-French coalition.

The great war which followed, called the War of the Spanish Succession, lasted eleven years and marked the dividing line between seventeenth-century and eighteenth-century Europe. In immediate terms, the war was won and William's goal achieved: France was held within its boundaries, Holland preserved its freedom and the Protestant religion was maintained in Europe. But William did not live to see it. In the spring of 1702, on the eve of his declaration of war, the King went for a ride on Sorrel, his favorite horse, in the park at Hampton Court. The horse stumbled, pitching William out of the saddle, breaking his collarbone. At first, the accident did not seem serious, but William, at fifty, was exhausted. His eyes were deeply sunken, his asthmatic cough never stopped. His emaciated body lacked the strength to resist, and on March 19, 1702, he died.

IT WAS Peter's good fortune that William happened to be in Holland when the Great Embassy arrived. Ever since the Tsar's adolescence, William had been his foremost hero among Western leaders. Through the long evenings in the German Suburb, talking with Hollanders, Germans and other foreigners, most of them adherents to William's Protestant, anti-French cause, Peter had listened to innumerable tales about the dauntless, skillful and persistent Dutchman. In 1691, at Pereslavl, he had ordered the cannon of his ships on the lake fired in salute when he heard of the English and Dutch victory over the French fleet at La Hogue. Predisposed to value all things Dutch, wanting to learn the secrets of Dutch shipwrights, hoping to enlist Dutch help in his war against the Turks, Peter was eager to meet the King and Stadholder whom he so admired.

Their first encounter took place at Utrecht, Peter being escorted there by Witsen and Lefort. The meeting was completely private and informal, as both monarchs always preferred. They were an unlikely pair: the small, coldly disciplined Dutchman with his bent back and asthmatic wheeze, and the towering, youthful, impulsive Russian. Peter's proposal that William

join him in a Christian alliance against the Turks drew no response. William, although negotiating peace with France, wanted no major war in the East which could distract and divert his Austrian ally and tempt Louis XIV to renew his adventures in the West. In any case, Peter's appeal was to be officially delivered not by himself to William, but by the Russian ambassadors to the formal rulers of Holland, Their High Mightinesses the States General, who sat in the national capital, The Hague. It was to them that the Great Embassy would present its credentials and state its business, and Peter took this event extremely seriously. As Russia had no permanent ambassadors or embassies abroad, the arrival of this large delegation headed by three leading men of the Russian state (even apart from the unacknowledged presence of the sovereign) and the manner of its reception were matters of great importance to Peter. He was eager that the Embassy's debut be auspicious, and for this purpose Ryswick provided an excellent stage. The most celebrated statesmen and diplomats of all the major European powers were present to conduct or oversee the crucial peace negotiations; anything that happened in Ryswick would be carefully noted and reported back to every capital and monarch in Europe.

The Russian ambassadors fussed for days in Amsterdam preparing themselves for their audience. They ordered three magnificent state carriages, new wardrobes for themselves and new liveries for their servants. Meanwhile, in The Hague, two hotels were readied for them and stocked with large quantities of wine and food. As the Embassy prepared, Peter told Witsen that he wanted to accompany his ambassadors incognito to observe how they were received. This request was difficult for Witsen to comply with, but even harder to refuse. Peter went along in one of the lesser carriages, insisting that his favorite dwarf accompany him even though the coach was crowded. "Very well," he said, "then I'll put him on my knees." All along the road from Amsterdam to The Hague, Peter kept seeing new things. Passing a mill, Peter asked, "What is this for?" Told it was a mill to cut stones, he declared, "I want to see it." The carriage stopped, but the mill was locked. Even at night, crossing a bridge, Peter wanted to study its construction and take measurements. The carriage stopped again, lanterns were brought and the Tsar measured the bridge's length and width. He was measuring the depth of its pontoons when the wind blew out the lights.

At The Hague, Peter was taken to the Hotel Amsterdam, where he was shown a beautiful room with a luxurious bed. He rejected both, choosing instead a small room at the top of the hotel with a simple camp bed. A few minutes later, however, he decided that he wanted to be with his ambassadors. It was after midnight, but he insisted that the horses be put back in the carriage and driven to the Hotel des Doelens. Here, again, he was shown a handsome apartment which did not please him and he went in search of his own accommodations. Spotting one of the Embassy servants fast asleep on

a bearskin, Peter pushed him with his feet, saying, "Come on, come on, get up!" The servant rolled over, growling. Peter kicked him a second time, crying, "Quickly, quickly, I want to sleep there." This time, the servant understood and leaped to his feet. Peter threw himself on the warm bearskin and went to sleep.

On the day the ambassadors were received by the States General, Peter was dressed in European style as a gentleman of the court. He wore a blue suit with gold ornaments, a blond wig and a hat with white plumes. Witsen ushered him into a chamber next to the hall in which the reception would take place; through a window, Peter was able to observe and hear everything. There he stood and waited for the ambassadors to appear. "They are late," he complained. His impatience grew as he saw everyone turning constantly to look at him and heard the growing buzz of excitement as whispers passed that the Tsar was in the next room. He wanted to escape, but could not without crossing the crowded audience hall. Distraught, he asked Witsen to command the members of the States General to turn their heads away in order not to see him as he crossed. Witsen told him that he could not command these gentlemen who were the sovereigns in Holland, but that he would ask them. They replied that they would be willing to rise in the presence of the Tsar but would not consent to turn their backs. On hearing this, Peter covered his face with his wig and walked rapidly across the hall into the vestibule and down the stairs.

A few minutes later, the ambassadors arrived in the hall and the audience took place. Lefort made a speech in Russian which was translated into French, and presented Their High Mightinesses with a large collection of sables. Lefort, who wore European clothes in Moscow, was dressed for the occasion in Muscovite robes of cloth of gold, bordered with furs. His hat and sword sparkled with diamonds. Golovin and Voznitsyn were dressed in black satin sewn with gold, pearls and diamonds; on their breasts they wore medallions enclosing a portrait of the Tsar, and their shoulders were covered with a gold embroidery of the double eagle. The ambassadors made a good impression, the Russian costumes were much admired and everyone talked about the Tsar.

While in The Hague, Peter maintained his official incognito, meeting privately with Dutch statesmen but refusing any public recognition. He attended a banquet for the diplomatic corps, sitting next to Witsen. He continued to meet privately with William, although no record of their conversations has remained. Finally, satisfied with the reception of his ambassadors and leaving them to conduct the actual negotiations with the States General, he returned to his work in the shipyard at Amsterdam. The Embassy had limited success. The Dutch were not interested in a crusade against the Turks, and because of the debts piled up from their war against France and the need to rebuild their own navy, they rejected the Russian

request for help in building and arming seventy warships and more than one hundred galleys for use on the Black Sea.

During the autumn, often escorted by Witsen, Peter made frequent excursions by carriage across the flat Dutch countryside. Rolling along through regions once at the bottom of a shallow sea, he looked out at a landscape dotted with windmills and brick church spires, meadows filled with grazing cows, and little brick towns with brick streets. The rivers and canals packed with boats and barges were a delight for Peter. Often, when the water was hidden by the flatness of the landscape, it seemed as if the brown sails and masts were moving independently across the wide fields.

Aboard a state yacht, Witsen took Peter to the island of Texel on the North Sea coast to watch the return of the Greenland whaling fleet. The place was remote, with long, rolling dunes and scrub trees growing at the edge of the white sand. In the harbor, Peter boarded one of the sturdy, three-masted vessels, examined everything and asked many questions about whales. To demonstrate, the whaler lowered a whaleboat and the crew demonstrated attacking a whale with a harpoon. Peter marveled at their precision and coordination. Then, although the ship reeked of whale blubber, the Tsar descended belowdecks to see the rooms where the whales were butchered and the blubber was boiled for its precious oil.

Several times, Peter returned quietly to Zaandam to visit his comrades who were still working there. Menshikov was learning to make masts, Naryshkin was learning navigation, Golovkin and Kurakin were working on hull construction. Usually, he traveled there by water, or went sailing during his visit. Once, when he was sailing during a storm against advice, his boat capsized. Peter clambered out and patiently sat on the upturned bottom, waiting to be rescued.

Although his privacy was protected as long as he worked on the docks, it was impossible to isolate him when he sailed on the Ij. Small boats filled with curious people regularly tried to accost him. This always made Peter angry. Once, at the urging of several lady passengers, the captain of a mail boat tried to draw alongside Peter's craft. In a fury, Peter threw two empty bottles at the captain's head. He missed, but the mail boat reversed course and left him alone.

Early in his visit, Peter met the leading Dutch admiral of the day, Gilles Schey, a pupil of de Ruyter's. It was Schey who offered him the most striking and agreeable spectacle of his visit: a great sham naval battle on the Ij. The boat owners in northern Holland were invited to attend, and cannon were placed on all the craft able to carry them. Companies of volunteer soldiers were distributed among the decks and riggings of the larger boats, charged to simulate the fire of musketeers during the battle. On a Sunday morning, under a cloudless sky with a fresh wind, hundreds of boats assembled along the edge of a dike lined with thousands of spectators.

Peter and members of his Embassy boarded the grand yacht of the East India Company and sailed toward the two fleets already ranged in opposing lines of battle. After a salute to the guest, the battle began. First, the two lines of ships fired salvos at each other; then a number of individual ship-to-ship engagements commenced. The battle, with its advance and retreat, its grappling and boarding, its smoke and noise, pleased the Tsar so much that he made his own ship steer for the place of hottest action. With the cannon thundering continually so that no one could hear, "the Tsar was in a state of rapture difficult to describe." In the afternoon, a number of collisions forced the Admiral to signal both sides to break off the action.

Peter dined often with Schey and tried to persuade the Admiral to come to Russia to supervise construction of the Russian fleet and to take command when it put to sea. He offered Schey all the titles he might want, a pension of 24,000 florins, more for his wife and children in case they preferred to remain behind in Holland, and promised to make the arrangements himself with William. Schey declined, which did not in any way diminish Peter's respect for him, and proposed another admiral to Peter as a man capable of supervising and commanding a navy. This was Cornelius Cruys, born in Norway of Dutch parents. With the rank of rear admiral, he was Chief Inspector of Naval Stores and Equipment of the Dutch Admiralty at Amsterdam, and in this capacity had already been advising the Russians in their purchases of naval equipment. He was exactly the kind of man Peter wanted, but, like Schey, Cruys showed little enthusiasm for Peter's offer. Only the united efforts of Schey, Witsen and other prominent persons who understood that Cruys in Russia would have a powerful influence on Russian trade persuaded the reluctant Admiral to accept.

Except for the time needed for his visit to The Hague and his trips to see various places and people in other parts of Holland, Peter worked steadily in the shipyard for four months. On November 16, nine weeks after the laying of his frigate's keel, the hull was ready for launching, and at the ceremony Witsen, in the name of the city of Amsterdam, presented the vessel to Peter as a gift. The Tsar, deeply moved, embraced the Burgomaster and immediately named the frigate *Amsterdam*. Later, loaded with many of the objects and machines Peter had purchased, she was dispatched to Archangel. Pleased as he was with the ship, Peter was even prouder of the piece of paper he received from Gerrit Pool, the master shipwright, certifying that Peter Mikhailov had worked four months in his dockyard, was an able and competent shipwright and had thoroughly mastered the science of naval architecture.

Nevertheless, Peter was disturbed by his instruction in Holland. What he had learned had been little more than ship's carpentry—it was better than the ship's carpentry he had learned in Russia, but it was not what he was seeking. Peter wanted to grasp the basic secrets of ship design; in effect,

naval architecture. He wanted blueprints, made scientifically, controlled by mathematics, not simply a greater handiness with axe and hammer. But the Dutch were empirical in shipbuilding as in everything else. Each Dutch shipyard had its own individual rule-of-thumb design, each Dutch shipwright built what had worked for him before and there were no basic principles which Peter could carry back to Russia. In order to build a fleet a thousand miles away on the Don with a force of largely unskilled laborers, he needed something which could be easily explained, understood and copied by men who had never seen a ship before.

Peter's growing dissatisfaction with Dutch methodology in shipbuilding expressed itself in several ways. First, he sent word back to Voronezh that Dutch shipwrights working there were no longer to be allowed to build as they pleased, but were to be placed under the supervision of Englishmen, Venetians or Danes. Second, now that his frigate was finished, he resolved to go to England to study English shipbuilding techniques. In November, in one of his interviews with William, Peter mentioned his desire to visit England. When the king returned to London, Peter sent Major Adam Weide after him with a formal request that the Tsar be allowed to come to England incognito. William's response elated Peter. The King replied that he was making a present to the Tsar of a superb new royal yacht, still unfinished, which, when completed, would be the most gracefully proportioned and fastest yacht in England. In addition, King William announced that he was sending two warships, *Yorke* and *Romney*, with three smaller ships, commanded by Vice Admiral Sir David Mitchell, to escort the Tsar to England. It was Peter's decision that he should come alone, except for Menshikov and several of the "volunteers," leaving Lefort and the majority of the Embassy in Holland to continue negotiating with the Dutch.

On January 7, 1698, after almost five months in Holland, Peter and his companions boarded the *Yorke*, Admiral Mitchell's flagship, and early the next morning set sail across the narrow strip of gray sea that separates the continent from England.

16

PETER IN ENGLAND

AT THE TIME of Peter's visit, London and Paris were the two most populous cities in Europe. In commercial wealth, London ranked second to Amsterdam, which it was soon to succeed. What made London unique, however, was the degree to which it dominated the nation in which it lay. Like Paris, London was the national capital and seat of government, and, like Amsterdam, it was the country's greatest port, the center of its commerce, art and culture. In England, however, the size of the city dwarfed all else. London, counting its immediate environs, had 750,000 inhabitants; the next largest city in England, Bristol, had a mere 30,000. Or, to put it differently, one Englishman in ten was a Londoner; only one Frenchman in forty lived in Paris.

London in 1698 lay mainly on the north bank of the Thames, stretching from Tower Hill to the Houses of Parliament. The great boulevard of the city, spanned by a single bridge, London Bridge, was the Thames. The river, 750 feet across, flowed between marshy banks thick with reeds, interspersed with trim gardens and green meadows—its stone embankments came later. The Thames played a key role in the city's life. Always crowded with ships, it was used as a thoroughfare for getting from one part of the city to another. Hundreds of watermen rowing little boats provided a quicker, cleaner and safer service than could be had by traveling through the crowded streets. In autumn and winter, great mists and fogs swirled up from the Thames to roll through the streets, shrouding everything in a thick, brown, poisonous vapor created by the fog mixing with the smoke pouring from thousands of chimneys.

The London that Peter visited and explored on foot was rich, vital, dirty and dangerous. The narrow streets were piled with garbage and filth which could be dropped freely from any overhanging window. Even the main avenues were dark and airless because greedy builders, anxious to gain more space, had projected upper stories out over the street. Through these Stygian alleys, crowds of Londoners jostled and pushed one another.

Traffic congestion was monumental. Lines of carriages and hackney cabs cut deep ruts into the streets, so that passengers inside were tossed about, arriving breathless, nauseated and sometimes bruised. When two coaches met in a narrow street, fearful arguments ensued, with the two coachmen "saluting each other with such diabolical titles and bitter execrations as if every one was striving which should go to the Devil first." For short distances, to avoid the mud and pushing of the crowds, sedan chairs carried by two strong men were popular. Biggest of all were the overland coaches which rolled into London from the highroads, carrying commercial travelers and visitors from the country. Their destinations were the inns, where weary passengers could dine on cabbage and a pudding, Westphalian ham, chicken, beef, wine, mutton steaks and pigeons, and rise the next morning to a breakfast of ale and toast.

London was a violent city with coarse, cruel pleasures which quickly crushed the unprotected innocent. For women, the age of consent was twelve (it remained twelve in England until 1885). Crimes were common, and in some parts of the city people could not sleep for the cries of "Murder!" rising from the streets. Public floggings were a popular sight, and executions drew vast crowds. On "Hanging Day," workmen, shopkeepers and apprentices left their jobs to jam the streets, joking and laughing, and hoping to catch a glimpse of the condemned's face. Wealthy ladies and gentlemen paid for places in windows and balconies overlooking the route from Newgate Prison to Tyburn, where executions took place, or, best of all, in wooden stands especially erected to provide an unobstructed view. The most ghastly execution was the penalty for treason: hanging, drawing and quartering. The condemned man was strung up until he was almost dead from strangulation, then cut down, disemboweled while still alive, beheaded, and his trunk was then chopped into quarters.

Sports were heavily stained with blood. Crowds paid to see bulls and bears set upon by enraged mastiffs; often, the teeth of the bear had been filed down and the cornered beast could only swat with his great paws at the mastiffs that leaped and tore at him. Cockfights attracted gamblers, and large purses were wagered on the specially trained fowl.

But, for all its violence, London was also a city where grace, beauty and civilized life were important. It was during this age that Sir Christopher Wren, the greatest of English architects, erected fifty-two new parish churches in London on sites wiped clean by the Great Fire. Their thin, glittering steeples gave London a breathtakingly distinctive skyline, dominated by Wren's masterpiece, the gigantic domed structure of St. Paul's Cathedral. The church was forty-one years in building; on the eve of Peter's arrival, the choir had just been opened for public worship.

For intelligent men, life in London centered on hundreds of coffee houses where the conversation could center on anything under the sun.

Gradually, the different houses began to specialize in talk about politics, religion, literature, scientific ideas, business, shipping or agriculture. Choosing the house by the talk he wished to hear, a visitor could step in, sit by the fire, sip coffee and listen to every shade of opinion expressed in brilliant, learned and passionate terms. Good conversationalists could sharpen their wits, writers could share their dilemmas, politicians could arrange compromises, the lonely could find simple warmth. In Lloyd's coffee house, marine insurance had its beginnings. At Will's, Addison was to have his chair by the fire in winter and by the window in summer.

THIS WAS LONDON in 1698. As for the larger polity, England itself, the seventeenth century was a time of transition from the small, relatively insignificant sixteenth-century island kingdom of Queen Elizabeth I to the great European power and world empire of the eighteenth and nineteenth centuries. When Elizabeth died in 1603, and with her the Tudor Dynasty, England was free of the ambitions of Spain, having beaten off Philip II and his armada. But England remained a peripheral factor in the affairs of Europe. The dynastic question was settled when King James VI of Scotland, son of Mary Queen of Scots, came down from Edinburgh to take the English throne as James I and begin a century of Stuart rule. During the first half of this century, England was absorbed in its own problems, trying to sort out the tangled strands of religious conscience and the relative power of crown and Parliament. When the debate burst into civil war, the second Stuart, Charles I, lost his head, and for eleven years England was ruled under the stern eye of the Lord Protector, Oliver Cromwell. Even when Charles II was restored to the throne in 1660, religious tension remained acute. The nation was divided between Catholic and Protestant, and, among the Protestants, between Church of England and Nonconformists.

Yet, England's power and ambitions were growing. In the mid-seventeenth century, the Dutch dominated the world's trade routes, but English seamen and merchants were eager to compete, and three naval wars with Holland jarred this Dutch supremacy. Later, during the War of the Spanish Succession, John Churchill, Duke of Marlborough, won four major victories over the French armies in the field, besieged and captured supposedly invincible fortresses and was on the verge of driving the Sun King out of Versailles itself when victory was snatched from him by a government decision to end the war. England triumphed, nevertheless, not only over France but also over its own ally, Holland. The long war had overstrained even the superbly organized resources of the wealthy Dutch. The Dutch position on the continent was far more vulnerable than that of England, and during the struggle Holland's vast ocean trade was heavily restricted while that of England flourished and grew. The status of the two powers, nearly

equal in the seventeenth century, changed rapidly in the eighteenth. Dutch power waned quickly and Holland slipped to the rank of a lesser state. England emerged from Marlborough's wars supreme on the oceans, and its maritime power led to world empire with colonies in every corner of the globe.

Peter's visit to England came at a pivotal moment of this transition to world power. The Treaty of Ryswick ended the first great war against Louis, with the Sun King's power held in check. The final struggle, the War of the Spanish Succession, was four years off, but already England was bustling with the energy which would fuel Marlborough's victories on land and make the Royal Navy mistress of the seas. The wealth of England's commerce still could not compete with the fertile soil of France, but England had an insuperable advantage: it was an island. Its security lay not in the chain of fortresses that Holland maintained in the Spanish Netherlands, but in the waves and its fleet. And although fleets were expensive, they cost less than armies and fortresses. Louis raised dozens of magnificent French armies, but to do so left his people crushed by taxes. In England, the taxes voted by Parliament hurt but did not crush. Europe was amazed by the resilience of the English economy and by the apparent wealth of the English Treasury. It was a system which could not fail to impress a visiting monarch anxious to lift his people up from a simple agrarian economy and into the modern world.

H.M.S. *Yorke* was the largest warship Peter had yet sailed on, and during his twenty-four-hour trip across the Channel he watched the handling of the ship with interest. Although the weather was stormy, the Tsar remained on deck through the entire voyage, constantly asking questions. The ship was pitching and rolling in the heavy seas, but Peter insisted on going aloft to study the rigging.

Early the next morning, the little squadron arrived off the Suffolk coast and was saluted by the guns of the coastal forts. At the mouth of the Thames, Peter and Admiral Mitchell transferred from the *Yorke* onto the smaller yacht *Mary*. This yacht, escorted by two others, sailed up the Thames and, on the morning of January 11, anchored near London Bridge. Here, Peter transferred onto a royal barge and was rowed upriver to a landing quay on the Strand. He was met by a court chamberlain with a welcome from King William. Peter replied in Dutch, and Admiral Mitchell, who spoke Dutch, acted as translator. Peter admired Mitchell, and his first request to the King was that Mitchell be assigned as his official escort and translator throughout his stay.

Peter spent his first days in London in a house at 21 Norfolk Street. At his request, the building selected was small and simple, with a door opening

directly onto the riverbank. Two days after the Tsar's arrival, the King himself paid an informal visit. Arriving in a small, unmarked carriage, William found the Tsar still in shirt sleeves in the bedroom he shared with four other Russians. The two rulers began to talk, but William soon found the air in the tiny room too warm and heavy for his asthma—on arrival, Peter had closed the window in the fashion of Moscow, where double windows are sealed against the cold from early autumn until late spring. Unable to breathe, William begged that the window be opened, and when it was, he inhaled deeply the fresh, cold air that poured into the room.

On the 23rd, Peter, accompanied by Admiral Mitchell and two Russian companions, drove to Kensington Palace to pay his first visit to William as King of England, and this meeting was longer than the brief conversations in Holland or the short interview in Peter's stifling room on Norfolk Street. Although the relationship between Peter and William never became intimate —the gap between the exuberant, rough-mannered, autocratic twenty-five-year-old and the lonely, weary, melancholy King being far too wide— William nevertheless was interested in Peter. Apart from being impressed by the Tsar's energy and curiosity, he could not help being flattered by Peter's admiration of him and the achievements of his career, and, as a life-long builder of alliances, he was pleased by the Tsar's animosity against his own antagonist, Louis XIV. As for Peter, neither William's age nor his personality made friendship easy, but the Tsar continued to respect his Dutch hero.

After his talk with the King, Peter was introduced to the heir to the throne, the thirty-three-year-old Princess Anne, who would succeed William within four years. At William's persuasion, the Tsar stayed on to witness a ball, although, to preserve his incognito, he watched through a small window in the wall of the room. He was fascinated by the construction of a wind dial which had been installed in the main gallery of Kensington Palace. Through connecting rods with a weathervane on the roof, the dial indicated which way the wind was blowing. Later, Peter would install an identical device in his own small summer palace by the Neva in St. Petersburg.

It was also at this meeting that William persuaded Peter to sit for a portrait by Sir Godfrey Kneller which contemporaries considered a remarkable likeness. Today, the original hangs in the King's Gallery of Kensington Palace, where its being painted was suggested almost 300 years ago.

Peter's one visit to Kensington Palace was the full extent of his ceremonial life in London. Stubbornly maintaining his incognito, he went about London as he pleased, frequently on foot even on wintry days. As in Holland, he visited workshops and factories, continually asking to be shown how things worked, even demanding drawings and specifications. He looked in on a watchmaker to buy a pocket watch and stayed to learn to dismantle, repair and reassemble the intricate mechanism. Impressed by

the carpentry in English coffins, he ordered one shipped to Moscow to serve as a model. He bought a stuffed crocodile and a stuffed swordfish, outlandish creatures never seen in Russia. He made a single visit to a London theater, but the crowd stared more at him than at the stage and he retreated to hide behind his comrades. He met the man who had designed the yacht *Royal Transport,* being readied for him by the King, and was astonished to find the designer to be a young, hard-drinking English nobleman, very much a man after his own heart. Peregrine Osborne, Marquis of Carmarthen, was the son of Charles II's great minister Danby, now the Duke of Leeds. He happened also to be a superb seaman and an original designer as well as a majestic drinker. It was Carmarthen who introduced Peter to his favorite drink, a cup of brandy laced with peppers. Together, the two went so often to a tavern in Great Tower Street that it was renamed the Czar of Muscovy. With Carmarthen, Peter met Laetitia Cross, a leading actress of the day. He took pleasure in her company, and, with the understanding that some reward would come her way, she moved in with him for the duration of his stay in England.

The sight in London that most attracted Peter, of course, was the forest of masts belonging to the ships moored in rows in the great merchant-fleet anchorage known as the Pool of London. In the Pool alone, Daniel Defoe one day counted no less than 2,000 ships. But Peter, anxious to begin his course in shipbuilding amidst the docks and shipyards of the lower Thames, was temporarily frustrated by ice on the river. As it happened, the winter of 1698 was exceptionally cold. The upper Thames was partly frozen, and people were able to walk from Southwark across to London. Piemen, jugglers and small boys plied their wares and played games on the ice, but it made travel by water impossible and delayed Peter's project.

For greater convenience and to escape the crowds that were now beginning to dog his excursions, he moved his lodgings to Deptford, staying at Sayes Court, a large, elegantly furnished house provided for him by the English government. The house belonged to John Evelyn, the celebrated essayist and diarist, and it was Evelyn's pride; he had spent forty-five years laying out its gardens, its bowling green, its gravel paths and groves of trees. To make room for Peter and his comrades, another tenant, Admiral Benbow, had been moved out, and the house had been especially re-decorated. For Peter, its attractions were its size (it was large enough to hold his entire suite), the garden in which he could relax in privacy, and the door at the foot of the garden which opened directly onto the dockyard and the river.

Unfortunately for Evelyn, the Russians cared little for his reputation or for his lifelong effort to create beauty. They vandalized his house. Even while they were still there, Evelyn's horrified steward wrote to his master:

There is a house full of people and right nasty. The Tsar lies next to the library and dines in the parlour next your study. He dines at ten o'clock and six at night, is very seldom at home a whole day, very often in the King's yard [the shipyard], or by water, dressed in several dresses. The King is expected here this day; the best parlour is pretty clean for him to be entertained in. The King pays for all he [the Tsar] has.

But it was not until the Russians had left at the end of their three-month stay and Evelyn came to see his once-beautiful home that the full extent of the damage became apparent. Appalled, Evelyn hurried off to the Royal Surveyor, Sir Christopher Wren, and the Royal Gardener, Mr. London, to ask them to estimate the cost of the repairs. They found floors and carpets so stained and smeared with ink and grease that new floors had to be installed. Tiles had been pulled from the Dutch stoves and brass door locks pried open. The paintwork was battered and filthy. Windows were broken, and more than fifty chairs—every one in the house—had simply disappeared, probably into the stoves. Featherbeds, sheets and canopies were ripped and torn as if by wild animals. Twenty pictures and portraits were torn, probably used for target practice. Outside, the garden was ruined. The lawn was trampled into mud and dust, "as if a regiment of soldiers in iron shoes had drilled on it." The magnificent holly hedge, 400 feet long, 9 feet high and 5 feet thick, had been flattened by wheelbarrows rammed through it. The bowling green, the gravel paths, the bushes and trees, all were ravaged. Neighbors reported that the Russians had found three wheelbarrows, unknown in Russia, and had developed a game with one man, sometimes the Tsar, inside the wheelbarrow and another racing him into the hedges. Wren and his companions noted all this and made a recommendation which resulted in a recompense to Evelyn of 350 pounds and ninepence, an enormous sum for that day.

NOT SURPRISINGLY in an age of religious struggle, the Protestant missionary spirit was awakened by the presence of the curious young monarch who meant to import Western technology into his backward kingdom. If ship-building techniques, why not religion? Rumors that Peter was not devoted to traditional Orthodoxy and was interested in other faiths opened broad visions in the heads of aggressive Protestants. Would it be possible to convert the young monarch and, through him, his primitive people? Could there at least be a union of the Anglican and Orthodox churches? The Archbishop of Canterbury was inspired by the prospect, and even King William lent an ear. On the command of the King and the Archbishop, an

eminent English churchman, Gilbert Burnet, Bishop of Salisbury, was instructed to call upon the Tsar "and to offer him such information of our religion and constitution as he was willing to receive."

On February 15, Peter received Burnet and a formal delegation of Anglican churchmen. Peter liked Burnet and they met several times for dialogues lasting several hours, but Burnet, who had come to instruct and persuade, found the chances of conversion to be nil; Peter was only the first of many Russians whose interest in importing Western technology was mistaken by naïve Westerners for an opportunity also to export Western philosophy and ideas. His interest in Protestantism was purely clinical. Skeptical of all religions, including Orthodoxy, he was seeking, amidst the forms and doctrines of each, that which could be useful to him and his state. After their conversations, Burnet took the Tsar to visit the Archbishop of Canterbury at Lambeth Palace. Invited to attend services at St. Paul's, Peter refused because of the large crowds, but he did take Anglican communion in the Archbishop's private chapel before a breakfast at which the two had a lengthy discussion.

Long after the Tsar had returned to Russia, Burnet set down his impressions of the tall young Russian sovereign with whom he had talked so earnestly:

> I waited often on him, and was ordered both by the King and the archbishop and bishops to attend upon him. I had good interpreters, so I had much free discourse with him. He is a man of very hot temper, soon inflamed, and very brutal in his passion; he raises his natural heat by drinking much brandy, which he rectified himself with great application. He is subject to convulsive motions all over his body, and his head seems to be affected with these. He wants not capacity, and has a larger measure of knowledge than might be expected from his education, which was very indifferent; a want of judgment with an instability of temper, appear in him too often and too evidently. He is mechanically turned, and seems designed by nature rather to be a ship-carpenter than a great prince. This was his chief study and exercise while he stayed here. He wrought much with his own hands, and made all about him work at the models of ships. He told me how he designed a great fleet at Azov, and with it to attack the Turkish empire; but he did not seem capable of conducting so great a design, though his conduct in his wars since this has discovered a greater genius in him than appeared at that time. He was desirous to understand our doctrine, but he did not seem disposed to mend matters in Moscovy; he was, indeed, resolved to encourage learning, and to polish his people by sending some of them to travel in other countries, and to draw strangers to come and live among them.

He seemed apprehensive still of his sister's intrigues. There is a mixture both of passion and severity in his temper. He is resolute but understands little of war, and seems not at all inquisitive that way. After I had seen him often, and had conversed much with him, I could not but adore the depth of the providence of God, that had raised up such a furious man to so absolute authority over so great a part of the world.

Peter's interest in church affairs extended beyond the established Church of England. Tales of his curiosity about Protestantism inspired all kinds of sects, fanatical and otherwise, to hope that they might gain a convert or supporter. Reformers, extremists, philanthropists and simple quacks approached the Tsar, hoping to use him as a means of introducing their particular beliefs into Peter's far-off country. Most of these Peter ignored. But he was fascinated by the Quakers. He went to several Quaker meetings and eventually met William Penn, to whom the huge proprietary colony of Pennsylvania had been granted by Charles II in exchange for cancellation of an enormous loan to the crown. Penn had actually spent only two years in his "holy experiment," a territory devoted to religious toleration in the New World, and now, during Peter's visit, he was preparing to depart again. Hearing that Peter had already attended a Quaker service, Penn went to Deptford to see the Tsar on April 3. They talked in Dutch, which Penn spoke, and Penn presented Peter with a number of his writings in that language. After Penn's visit, Peter continued to go to Quaker meetings in Deptford. Following the service as best he could, standing up, sitting down, observing long periods of silence, he constantly looked about to see what others were doing. The experience stayed with him. Sixteen years later, in the North German province of Holstein, he found a Quaker meetinghouse and attended with Menshikov, Dolgoruky and others. The Russians, except for Peter, understood nothing of the words being spoken, but they sat in silence and occasionally the Tsar leaned over and interpreted. When the service was over, Peter declared to his followers that "whoever could live according to such a doctrine would be happy."

During the same weeks that Peter was in conversation with English church leaders, he also consummated a business deal which, as he well knew, would sadden the hearts of his own Orthodox churchmen. Traditionally, the Orthodox Church forbade the use of that "ungodly herb," tobacco. In 1634, Peter's grandfather Tsar Michael had forbidden smoking or any other use of tobacco ón pain of death; subsequently, the penalty was reduced and Russians caught smoking merely had their nostrils slit. Nevertheless, the influx of foreigners into Russia had spread the habit, and punishment was rare; Tsar Alexis had even licensed tobacco for a short period, making its sale a state monopoly. But the church and all conservative Russians still

deeply disapproved. Peter, of course, ignored this disapproval; as a youth, he had been introduced to tobacco and was seen nightly smoking a long clay pipe with his Dutch and German friends in the German Suburb. Before departing Russia with the Great Embassy, Peter had issued a decree authorizing both the sale and the smoking of tobacco.

In England, whose colonies included the great tobacco-growing plantations of Maryland, Virginia and North Carolina, this sudden potential of opening a vast new market for tobacco caused great excitement. Already, tobacco merchants had petitioned the King to intercede with the Tsar on their behalf. As it happened, no one was more interested in this matter, or better positioned to do something about it, than Carmarthen, Peter's new comrade. When Carmarthen brought to him a proposal from a group of English merchants for a tobacco monopoly in Russia, Peter was instantly attracted. Not only did he see smoking as a Western habit whose wider use would help to loosen the iron grip of the Orthodox Church. There was an even greater immediate attraction: money. By this time, Peter and his Embassy desperately needed funds. The costs of supporting 250 Russians abroad, even with the subsidies received from the host countries, were enormous. In addition, Peter's agents in Holland were recruiting seamen, ships' officers, shipwrights and other personnel. They had to pay initial subscription fees, down payments of salaries and travel expenses. The agents were busy buying so many articles, instruments, machines and models that ten ships had to be chartered to carry this cargo along with the recruits back to Russia. The treasury of the Embassy was repeatedly drained, and Moscow was repeatedly called upon to send huge sums. But there was never enough.

This situation made Carmarthen's proposal irresistible. He offered to pay 28,000 English pounds in return for permission to import a million and a half pounds of tobacco into Russia free of customs duties and to sell it on the Russian market free of all restrictions. Most important from Peter's point of view, Carmarthen was prepared to pay cash in advance to Peter in London. The contract was signed on April 16, 1698. Peter's pleasure can be measured in Lefort's reply to the Tsar's jubilant announcement: "On your orders, we [in Holland] did not open your letter until we had drained three goblets, and after we read it we drank three more. . . . In truth, I believe it's a fine stroke of business."

When not working at the dockyards, Peter hurried about London and its vicinity trying to see all the interesting places. He visited the Greenwich Naval Hospital, designed by Christopher Wren and called "one of the most sublime sights English architecture affords." Peter approved of William III's simple style of living in the red-brick, oak-paneled palace at Kensington, but the majestic hospital with its twin colonnades facing the Thames had an effect on him. Going to dine with the King after his visit to Greenwich, the Tsar could not help saying, "If I were to advise Your Majesty, it

would be to move your court to the hospital and bring the patients to your palace." Peter saw the tombs of England's monarchs (and also the apple and oyster sellers) inside Westminster Abbey. He visited Windsor Castle and Hampton Court, but royal palaces were less interesting to him than functioning scientific or military institutions. At the Greenwich Observatory, he discussed mathematics with the Royal Astronomer. At the Woolwich Arsenal, England's main cannon foundry, Peter discovered in Master of the Ordnance Romney a fellow spirit with whom he could share his delight in artillery and fireworks. The Tower of London at that time served as arsenal, zoo, museum and site of the Royal Mint. Touring the museum of medieval armor, Peter was not shown the axe which, fifty years earlier, had beheaded Charles I. His hosts remembered that Peter's father, Tsar Alexis, hearing that the English people had beheaded their sovereign, had furiously stripped English merchants in Russia of all their privileges. Thus, the axe was kept hidden from Peter, "as it was feared that he would throw it into the Thames." For Peter, the most interesting part of the Tower was the mint. Struck by the excellence of English coinage, and the technique by which the coins were made, he went back repeatedly. (Unfortunately, the Warden of the Royal Mint, Sir Isaac Newton, lived and worked at Trinity College, Cambridge.) Peter was impressed by the reform of English coinage instituted by Newton and John Locke. To prevent the constant degrading of the coinage by people snipping little bits of silver off the edges, English coins had milled edges. Two years later, when Peter began to reform Russia's badly irregular coinage, the English system served as a model.

Throughout his stay in England, Peter was always on the lookout for qualified men for service in Russia. Aided in his recruiting by Carmarthen, he interviewed scores and finally persuaded about sixty Englishmen to follow him. Among them were Major Leonard van der Stamm, the master shipwright at Deptford; Captain John Perry, a hydraulic engineer to whom Peter assigned responsibility for building the Volga-Don canal; and Professor Henry Farquharson, a mathematician from the University of Aberdeen who was to open a School of Mathematics and Navigation in Moscow. Peter also wrote to a friend in Russia that he had recruited two barbers "for purposes of future demands," a hint that had ominous portents for those in Moscow whose pride lay in the length of their beards.

PETER'S FEELING for William and his gratitude to the King grew even greater when the regal gift of the yacht *Royal Transport* was handed over to him on March 2. He sailed in her the following day and as often thereafter as he could. In addition, William ordered that Peter be shown everything he wished to see of the English fleet. The climax came when the Tsar was invited to a special review of the fleet and a mock engagement off Spithead

near the Isle of Wight. A naval squadron consisting of the *Royal William*, the *Victory* and the *Association* took Peter and his suite on board in Portsmouth and carried them into The Solent off the Isle of Wight. There, Peter transferred to Admiral Mitchell's flagship, *Humber*. On exercise day, the fleet weighed anchor; the great ships set their sails and formed opposing lines of battle. Broadsides roared out, shrouding the fleets in smoke and flame just as they would in a real battle, but on this day no cannonballs flew. Nevertheless, as the great ships maneuvered through the smoke, turning in unison to attack each other, Peter was jubilant. He tried to see and note down everything: the scurrying of the seamen to dress the sails, the orders to the helmsmen, the number and caliber and serving of the guns, the signals from the flagship to her sisters in the line. It was a momentous day for a young man who, scarcely ten years before, had first seen a sailboat and learned to tack it back and forth on the narrow Yauza. When the ships returned at night to their anchorage, their guns thundered a twenty-one-gun salute and the seamen roared out cheers for the youthful monarch who dreamed of the day he would fly his own banner in the van of a Russian fleet.

William invited him to the Houses of Parliament. Not wishing to be stared at, Peter chose as his vantage point a window outside an upper gallery, and from there the Tsar observed the King on his throne surrounded by the English peerage on benches. This episode led to the remark by an anonymous observer which went around London, "Today, I have seen the rarest thing in the world: one monarch on the throne and another on the roof." Peter listened to the debate with an interpreter and then, to the Russians who were with him, declared that, while he could not accept the limitation by parliaments of the power of kings, still "it is good to hear subjects speaking truthfully and openly to their king. This is what we must learn from the English!" While Peter was there, William gave his formal assent to a number of bills, including a land tax which it was estimated would produce 1.5 million pounds in revenue. When Peter expressed surprise that Parliament could raise so much by passage of a single bill, he was told that, the year before, Parliament had passed a bill which had collected three times as much.

As Peter's visit neared its end, his presence in London came to be accepted as almost normal. The imperial ambassador Hoffman wrote to his master in Vienna:

> The court here is well contented with [Peter], for he now is not so afraid of people as he was at first. They accuse him of a certain stinginess only, for he has been in no way lavish. All the time here he went about in sailor's clothing. We shall see in what dress he presents himself to Your Imperial Majesty. He saw the King very rarely, as he did not wish to change his manner of life, dining at

eleven o'clock in the morning, supping at seven in the evening, going to bed early, and getting up at four o'clock, which very much astonishes those Englishmen who kept company with him. They say that he intends to civilize his subjects in the manner of other nations. But from his acts here, one cannot find any other intention than to make them sailors.

The ambassador's report was intended as a last-minute briefing for the Emperor, as Peter was expected to depart any day for Holland, and the next stop on his tour was Vienna. But the Tsar's departure was repeatedly postponed. He had come for only a short visit, but had found so much to see and do, not only at the Deptford shipyard but also at Woolwich and the mint, that he constantly delayed. This stirred anxiety in those members of the Embassy left behind in Amsterdam. They not only worried about the Tsar's whereabouts and intentions, but they had received news from Vienna that the Emperor was about to make a separate peace with their common enemy, the Turks. The ostensible purpose of the Great Embassy being to strengthen the alliance, news of its impending disintegration did not make the Russians happy. As these messages arrived and the pressures on him grew, Peter reluctantly decided that he must leave.

On April 18, Peter paid his farewell visit to the King. Relations between the two had chilled somewhat when Peter learned that William had had a hand in the forthcoming peace between the Emperor and the Sultan. For William, of course, it was essential to help disengage the Hapsburg empire from its war in the Balkans and turn it around to prepare against the only enemy William cared about: France. Nevertheless, the final meeting at Kensington Palace was amicable. The Tsar distributed 120 guineas among the King's servants who had waited on him, which, according to one observer, "was more than they deserved, they being very rude to him." To Admiral Mitchell, his escort and translator, he gave forty sables and six pieces of damask, a handsome gift. It was on this occasion, too, that Peter supposedly took from his pocket a small object wrapped in brown paper which he gave to the King as a token of friendship and appreciation. William unwrapped it, the story goes, and found a magnificent uncut diamond. Another account says that it was a huge, rough ruby fit to be "set upon the top of the Imperial Crown of England."

On May 2, Peter reluctantly left London. He paid a final visit to the Tower and the mint on the day of his departure while his companions were waiting for him aboard the *Royal Transport,* and when the yacht moved down the river, Peter stopped and anchored at Woolwich so that he could go ashore and say goodbye to Romney at the arsenal. Under way once again, the *Royal Transport* reached Gravesend at dusk, where the Tsar anchored again. In the morning, accompanied by Carmarthen sailing in his

own yacht, *Peregrine,* Peter made for Chatham, the naval harbor. There he transferred to the *Peregrine* and cruised through the port, admiring the giant, three-decked ships-of-the-line lying at anchor. With Carmarthen, he boarded three men-of-war, the *Britannia,* the *Triumph* and the *Association,* and then was rowed ashore to visit the naval-stores depot.

The following morning, the *Royal Transport* weighed anchor and made for Margate, where the Thames estuary meets the sea. There, he found an English naval squadron, again commanded by Admiral Mitchell, waiting to escort him back to Holland. The crossing was stormy and exciting, more so than most of the Russians on board could have wished, but Peter relished the waves seething over the decks.*

Although he never returned to England, Peter had enjoyed his taste of English life. He found there much that he liked: informality, a practical, efficient monarch and government, good drinking and good talk about ships, gunnery and fireworks. Although he was not intimate with William, the King had opened every door, he had given Peter access to his shipyards, mint and gun foundries, he had displayed his fleet, he had allowed the Russians to talk with everyone and make notes. Peter was grateful and carried away the highest respect not only for English ship design and workmanship, but for the island as a whole. In Russia, he once said to Perry that "if he had not come to England he had certainly been a bungler." Further, continued Perry, "His Majesty has often declared to his lords, when he has been a little merry, that he thinks it a much happier life to be an admiral in England than a tsar in Russia." "The English island," Peter said, "is the best and most beautiful in the world."

* Sadly, Peter never sailed again on his splendid English yacht. She was loaded at Amsterdam with Peter's own collection of instruments and curiosities bought during his tour, and sent back to Archangel. There, on Peter's orders, she was met by Franz Timmerman, who was commanded to bring her through the network of rivers and lakes in northern Russia to Yaroslavl and thence down the Volga. One day, when his Volga-Don canal was finished, Peter hoped to bring her down the Don to Azov and sail her on the Black Sea. But the *Royal Transport* drew eight feet and Timmerman could not bring her even as far as the Volga. She returned to Archangel, where she remained for fifteen years. In 1715, when Russia had become a Baltic naval power, Peter ordered her refitted and sailed around the North Cape to join him in the Baltic. She entered the Baltic and was lost in a storm off the coast of Sweden.

17

LEOPOLD AND AUGUSTUS

IN AMSTERDAM, the Embassy was overjoyed to see the Tsar again; they had felt themselves abandoned as Peter's visit of weeks in England extended over four months. They had spent the winter traveling around the small country, gaining everywhere a formidable reputation as drinkers. They tried on ice skates, unknown in Russia—but, not realizing that the ice in Holland was thinner than the winter ice of Russia, they frequently fell through. When this happened, the Dutch were amazed that, rather than change out of their icy, dripping clothes, the Russians were content with another drink. But, despite their revels, the winter had not been wasted. Peter returned to find large piles of materiel, weapons, special instruments and naval stores waiting. More important, the Embassy had recruited 640 Dutchmen, among them Rear Admiral Cruys and other naval officers (eventually, Cruys persuaded 200 Dutch naval officers to come to Russia), seamen, engineers, technicians, shipwrights, physicians and other specialists. To carry them and the equipment purchased back to Russia, ten ships had been chartered.

On May 15, 1698, Peter and the Great Embassy left Amsterdam for Vienna, their route lying through Leipzig, Dresden and Prague. In Dresden, capital of the electoral state of Saxony and a city so rich in architecture and art treasures that it was called "the Florence on the Elbe," Peter was received especially warmly. The Elector Augustus was now also King Augustus II of Poland, and, on Peter's arrival, he was away in his new kingdom, but he had left instructions that the Tsar, to whom in part he owed his new throne, be handsomely welcomed as a royal guest.

Peter's initial reaction to Dresden hospitality was hostile. As he entered the city, he saw people staring at him, not only because of his rank but also because of his unusual height. His sensitivity to these stares had grown, not diminished, during his months in the West, and he threatened to leave Dresden immediately unless they could be stopped. Prince Fürstenberg, the Elector's representative and Peter's host, attempted to calm the Tsar. When,

on the night of his arrival and despite the hour, Peter asked to visit the famous Dresden Kunstkammer Museum and the special private treasury known as the Green Vault, Fürstenberg quickly agreed. After midnight, the Tsar, the Prince and the museum's curator entered the Elector's palace, where the museum was housed in seven rooms on the top floor. The Kunstkammer, or "cabinet of curiosities," had been founded more than a century before to gather and display both natural wonders and man-made objects of special interest. Its collection of elaborate clocks and mechanical instruments, mining and manufacturing tools, along with rare books, parade armor and portraits of notables, was open to all scholars and persons of good birth and was exactly the kind of thing to fascinate Peter. He resolved, one day, to create a similar Kunstkammer in Russia. The Green Vault, so named because its walls were painted the national color of Saxony, was a secret storehouse, accessible through a single door in the Elector's living quarters. Here the rulers of Saxony kept a collection of jewels and precious objects which were among the richest in Europe. Peter was absorbed by both collections and remained, examining one instrument or object after another, until dawn.

The following evening, Fürstenberg gave a small private dinner that expanded into the kind of noisy, boisterous party the Russians loved. Trumpeters, oboists and drummers were called in to provide music. At Peter's request, five ladies were also invited, including the beautiful Countess Aurora von Königsmark, mistress of the Elector and mother of the future great marshal of France, Maurice de Saxe. The party went on until three a.m. with Peter exuberantly taking the drumsticks and playing "with a perfection that far surpassed the drummers." After this night of drinking, music and dancing, Peter set off in a light-hearted mood for Prague and Vienna, and as soon as the Tsar was out of town, the relieved and weary Prince Fürstenberg wrote to the Elector: "I thank God that all has gone off so well, for I feared that I could not fully please this fastidious gentleman."

FOUR MILES NORTH of the old city of Vienna rise the twin hills of the Kahlenberg and the Leopoldsberg; east of the city, the Danube flows southward toward Budapest; to the west lie the rolling meadows and forests of the Vienna Woods. Yet, for all its magnificent setting, Vienna did not compare in size with London, Amsterdam, Paris or even with Moscow. Primarily, this was because Vienna, unlike the other great cities of Europe, was not a great port or commercial trading center. Its sole function was to be the seat of the imperial House of Hapsburg, the crossroads and administrative center of the vast sweep of territory from the Baltic to Sicily which owed allegiance to the Emperor Leopold I. In fact, in Peter's time, the Emperor ruled two

empires. The first was the old Holy Roman Empire, a loosely bound union of almost independent states in Germany and Italy, whose ties and ancient traditions went back through a thousand years to the empire of Charlemagne. The other empire, quite separate and distinct, was the collection of traditional Hapsburg lands in Central Europe—the Archduchy of Austria, the Kingdom of Bohemia, the Kingdom of Hungary and other territories in the Balkans recently conquered from the Turks.

It was the first empire, the Holy Roman Empire of the German Nation, which gave the Emperor his title and immense prestige and justified the enormous size and magnificence of his court. In fact, however, the title was hollow and the empire itself was almost wholly façade. The rulers of this congerie of disparate states, the hereditary electors,* margraves, landgraves, princes and dukes, determined for themselves the religion of their subjects, the size of their armies and whether, when war came, they would fight beside the Emperor, against him, or remain neutral. None of these great lords gave more than a passing thought to their ties to their imperial master when it came to matters of serious policy. They, or their representatives, sat in the Imperial Diet at Regensburg, originally the empire's legislative organ, now purely consultative and decorative. The Emperor could make no law without the Diet's consent, and the discussions never reached consent, as the envoys argued endlessly over precedence. When an emperor died, the Diet met and automatically elected the next head of the House of Hapsburg. This was traditional, and tradition was the single feature of the ancient empire which had not been allowed to die.

Despite the hollowness of his imperial title, the Emperor was not unimportant. The strength of the House of Hapsburg, its revenues, its army and its power, stemmed from the states and territories it really ruled: Austria, Bohemia, Moravia, Silesia, Hungary and new claims and conquests which stretched across the Carpathians into Transylvania and across the Alps to the Adriatic. There were also Hapsburg claims to the throne of Spain with all of Spain's possessions in Europe, including Spain itself, the Spanish Netherlands, and Naples, Sicily and Sardinia. This second empire looked to the south and east for dangers and opportunities. Lying as a barrier between Western Europe and the Balkans, it believed in its holy mission to defend Christianity against the advance of the Ottoman Empire. The Protestant princes to the north had no interest in the Emperor's fears or ambitions in the Balkans; they saw these matters as private enterprises of the House of Hapsburg, and if the Emperor wanted their support in any of them, he usually had to buy it.

Austria was the center and Vienna the heart of the Hapsburg world.

---

* The title "elector" was given to the seven Germanic princes who held the privilege of electing the Holy Roman Emperor.

It was a Catholic world, heavy with tradition and elaborate ceremony, actively guided by the Jesuits who were never far from the deliberations of the councils of state. Or from the elbow of the imperial personage in whom God, they assured him, had placed a special trust.

HIS MOST CATHOLIC MAJESTY Leopold I, Emperor of the Holy Roman Empire, Archduke of Austria, King of Bohemia and King of Hungary, admitted no mortal man to be his equal except the Pope. In the eyes of the Hapsburg Emperor, His Most Christian Majesty the King of France was no more than an arriviste, an upstart of mediocre genealogy and odious pretensions. The Tsar of Muscovy was scarcely more notable than other Eastern princes who lived in tents.

Leopold was unshakably certain of his position. The House of Hapsburg was the oldest reigning dynasty in Europe. For 300 years, in unbroken succession, the family had worn the crown of the Holy Roman Empire, whose history and prerogatives traced back to Charlemagne. By the end of the seventeenth century, the Reformation and the Thirty Years' War had diminished the Imperial power, but in name, the Emperor was still the preeminent secular ruler of Christendom. His actual power might have faded in comparison to that of the King of France, but a sense of superiority —shadowy, medieval, semi-ecclesiastical—still prevailed. To preserve that sense of rank was one of Leopold's principal concerns. He maintained a staff of industrious historians and librarians who had managed by their research to link the Emperor's genealogy back through innumerable heroes and saints to Noah.

The man who bore this heavy weight of genealogical responsibility was swarthy, of middling height, with the projecting lower jaw and protruding lower lip which traditionally marked (if not disfigured) the Hapsburgs. Although in 1698 he had already occupied the imperial throne for forty years and would sit on it seven years more, he had not been born to the crown. Instead, Leopold was a younger brother, bred for the church, who had been snatched from his theological studies only by the death of his older brother, Ferdinand. Elected emperor at eighteen, Leopold throughout his long reign preferred the quieter things: theology, the arts, court ceremony and the study of genealogy; he especially loved music and himself composed operas. He was not a warrior, although under him the empire was almost continually at war. When the Ottoman armies surrounded and besieged Vienna in 1683, the Emperor quietly departed, returning only after the Turks had been repelled and driven down the Danube. His character was melancholy, apathetic and obstinate. Yet, in his lethargy he somehow projected an austere dignity which was not without grandeur,

part of which lay in his attitude toward himself. To be the emperor, he knew, was to stand at the summit of mankind. Every detail of daily life at the imperial court was designed to proclaim that sublime rank. In the chambers and corridors of his ancient Viennese palace, the Hofburg, the Emperor was the object of a rigid protocol more akin to Byzantium than to Versailles. Normally, the Emperor wore Spanish court dress: black velvet with white point lace, a short cloak, his brimmed hat turned up at one side, the red stockings worn only by Hapsburg emperors, and red shoes. On ceremonial days—which were frequent—he appeared in almost Eastern splendor, covered with scarlet-and-gold brocade embroidered with diamonds, surrounded by his Knights of the Golden Fleece, each wearing a long cloak of crimson velvet embroidered with gold. Thus attired, on religious feast days the Emperor went on foot to mass, marching at the head of a long procession. Whenever the Emperor and his family passed, courtiers bowed low and dropped to one knee. If his name was mentioned, even when he was in another room, all who heard it performed a similar genuflection. When Their Majesties dined alone, their dishes passed through twenty-four hands before reaching the imperial table. Wine was poured by a steward who filled the imperial glass while on one knee.

The center of this stultifying ceremony was the Hofburg Palace, a confusing maze of buildings constructed over centuries, linked by corridors and dark staircases, tiny courtyards and grand hallways. Into this jumble of stone and masonry, which had none of the symmetry and elegance of Versailles, the Emperor, his court of 2,000 noblemen and 30,000 servants were crammed alongside numerous government offices, a museum and even a hospital. Except when on occasional visits to the Favorits Palace just outside the city, where he hunted stags, or the Laxenburg Palace twenty miles away, where he set his falcons on the herons, Leopold ruled his empire from the Hofburg.

In fact, the chaos of the Hofburg was symbolic of the chaos of the empire. The administration of the Hapsburg emperors was not effective. They could never weld together all the chanceries, councils, treasuries and other diverse organs of the Holy Roman Empire and the Hapsburg domains into a single cohesive structure of central government. Leopold himself, trained for theology, was an indecisive autocrat. Timid, apathetic, uncertain which course to take, he preferred to listen to advice, to mull endlessly over the contradictory recommendations of his advisors. A French diplomat described him as "a clock which always required rewinding." By the 1690's he was enveloped in a many-layered cocoon of committees, all quietly and vigorously warring with one another behind his back. Policy was made by default.

At heart, Leopold and after him his two sons, the Emperors Joseph I and Charles VI, did not believe that a chaotic administration was a fundamental defect. The three of them, over almost a century, shared the view that the administration of government was a minor matter, infinitely less important not only for their own souls but for the future of the Hapsburg House than belief in God and support of the Catholic Church. If God was satisfied with them, He would ensure that the House continued and prospered. This, then, was the basis of their political theory and their practice of government: that the throne and empire had been fixed on them by God, and that "Our House, its interests and its destiny, were being watched over and would be upheld by a power grander than any on earth."

During Leopold's long reign, despite the apathy of the Emperor and the stifling quality of his bureaucracy, the fortunes of the empire actually rose. This may have been due to the influence of God, as Leopold believed, but more immediately, in the last decades of his reign, Leopold's prospects and power rested on the shining sword of Prince Eugene of Savoy. The slight, stooping Prince was a Field Marshal of the Holy Roman Empire, commander of the Imperial armies, and—with the Duke of Marlborough and King Charles XII of Sweden—one of the most famous and successful military commanders of his age.

Eugene was Italian and French by birth, his title stemming from a grandfather who was Duke of Savoy. He was born in Paris in 1663, the son of Olympia Mancini, one of the famous beauties of Louis XIV's court, and the Comte de Soissons. Because his face and frail body were so nondescript, his application to serve in the French army was rejected and he was designated for an ecclesiastical career; indeed, Louis XIV took to calling Eugene in public "Le Petit Abbé." The Sun King's gibes were to cost France dearly. At twenty Eugene made his way to the Emperor to ask for a command in the Imperial army. Leopold's somber court appealed to Eugene and his own personal intensity and lack of frivolity—qualities that had earned him mockery at Versailles—gained him favor in Vienna. Eugene's arrival coincided with the Turkish siege and, still only twenty, he took command of a dragoon regiment. In the years that followed, he gave up his desire for a principality in Italy and dedicated his life to the army. At twenty-six, he was a general of cavalry; at thirty-four, he was commander of the Imperial army in Hungary. There, on September 11, 1697, while Peter was at work in an Amsterdam shipyard, Eugene crushed the Sultan's main army, three times larger than his own, in a desperate battle at Zenta. The peace was brief. Soon he was fighting the Emperor's enemies in the Low Countries, on the Rhine, in Italy and on the Danube. He participated in two of the Duke of Marlborough's greatest victories, at Blenheim and at Oudenard, modestly accepting the role of vice-commander. His military genius has been shaded by Marlborough's, but while Marlborough's reputation rests on ten

years of command during the War of the Spanish Succession, Eugene was a soldier for fifty years, a commander-in-chief for thirty.

On behalf of their august potentate, the Emperor's counselors and advisors, historians and genealogists, fought tenaciously over matters of protocol. The Tsar of Muscovy, however vast the size of his domains, could not conceivably be received as the equal of God's personal steward, the Emperor. The matter was further complicated by the fact that, officially, the Tsar would not be present. Yet somehow some notice had to be taken of the tall young man whose incognito was Peter Mikhailov. Such weighty problems took time to resolve; it required four days to work out the details of the Embassy's entry into Vienna, and an entire month of negotiations to agree to the manner in which the Emperor would receive the ambassadors. Meanwhile, Peter was anxious to meet the Emperor personally. The Austrian court officials were adamant that a Tsar incognito could not be publicly received by His Imperial Majesty, but Lefort's persistence bore fruit in a private meeting.

The informal interview was held in the Favorits Palace, Leopold's summer villa on the outskirts of the city. Peter, in keeping with his incognito, was taken through a small door in the garden and up a back spiral staircase into the audience chamber. He had been carefully briefed by Lefort as to the agreed-on protocol for the meeting: the two monarchs were to enter the long audience hall simultaneously from doors at opposite ends; walking slowly, they were to meet exactly halfway, at the fifth window. Unfortunately, Peter, on opening the door and seeing Leopold, forgot what he had been told and, bounding toward the Emperor in long, quick strides, reached Leopold by the third window. The Austrian courtiers gasped. Protocol had been upset! What would happen to Peter? What would happen to them? But as the two sovereigns drew apart into a window recess to talk, with only Lefort as their interpreter, the courtiers were relieved to see that the Tsar was treating their master with great respect and deference. The two made quite a contrast: the short, pale, fifty-eight-year-old Emperor with his narrow, gloomy face framed by a large wig and a thick mustache hanging over his pendulous lower lip; and the abnormally tall, twenty-six-year-old Tsar with his vigorous, imperious, sometimes jerky gestures. The meeting was actually only an exchange of compliments and lasted fifteen minutes. Afterward, Peter descended into the palace garden and cheerfully rowed himself around a lake in a little rowboat.

This first meeting set the tone for Peter's two-week stay in Vienna, his only visit to the imperial capital. Despite the annoying cluckings of the Austrian protocol officers, Peter remained in a good-natured and deferential mood. He called on the Empress and the imperial princesses and tried to be pleasant. He genially refused the allotment by the imperial court of 3,000 gulden a week for the Russian Embassy's expenses in Vienna. This

sum, Peter protested, was far too much for his "dear brother" to pay, having just borne the burden of long wars; Peter reduced the sum by half. The Austrians, who had been fully informed as to Peter's character both in Moscow and throughout the tour, could scarcely believe that the subdued, modest figure before them was the man they had heard about. Foreign ambassadors spoke of his "delicate and polished manners." The Spanish ambassador wrote to Madrid, "Here he appears quite unlike the description of other courts and far more civilized, intelligent, with excellent manners and modest."

In one important quarter in Vienna, Peter's surprising amiability and curiosity raised high hopes. The Catholic Church, especially the Jesuit College of Vienna, was aware from the reports of the imperial ambassador in London of Peter's lack of attachment to doctrinaire Orthodoxy and his interest in other religions. As the Archbishop of Canterbury and other Protestants had begun to think of converting the Tsar to Protestantism, so the Catholics began to hope that the monarch and, after him, his realm might be brought home to the Mother Church. These hopes were embodied in the Emperor's personal advisor, Father Woolf, a Jesuit priest who spoke some Russian. On St. Peter's Day, after attending an Orthodox service conducted by his own Russian priest traveling with the Embassy, Peter attended mass at the Jesuit College. There he heard Father Woolf preach "that the keys would be bestowed a second time, upon a new Peter, that he might open another door." Soon after, Peter attended a second mass, celebrated this time by Cardinal Kollonitz, the Primate of Hungary, and then joined the Cardinal for a lunch in the college refectory. From their conversation, it became clear that Peter was not thinking of conversion and the rumors that he was planning to go to Rome to be accepted into the church by the Pope himself were false. He was going to Venice to study galley building; if he went to Rome at all, it would be as a tourist, not as an applicant. After their meeting, the Cardinal described his visitor:

> The Tsar is a tall young man from twenty-eight to thirty years of age, with a dark complexion, proud and grave, and with an expressive countenance. His left eye, his left arm and left leg were injured by the poison given him during the life of his brother; but there remains of this now only a fixed look in his eye and a constant movement of his arm and leg. To hide this, he accompanies this involuntary motion with continual movements of his entire body, which by many people, in the countries which he has visited, have been attributed to natural causes, but really they are artificial. His wit is alert and quick; his manners, closer to civil than savage. The journey he has made has improved him greatly, and the difference from the beginning of his present travels and the present time is obvious,

although his native coarseness still appears; chiefly in his relations with his followers, whom he holds in check with great severity. He has a knowledge of history and geography and he desires to know more about these subjects; but his strongest interest is in the sea and ships, on which he himself works manually.

In the course of Peter's visit, Leopold staged one of his famous masked balls of the Viennese court. The setting was a supposed country inn, with the Emperor and Empress as innkeepers, and the court and foreign ambassadors all dressed as peasants in native costume. Prince Eugene of Savoy was there. Peter was dressed for the evening as a Frisian peasant, and his partner drawn by lot, Fräulein Johanna von Thurn, was dressed as his Frisian mate. At dinner, all precedence was discarded and the Emperor and Empress sat where they liked at the table. During the toasts, Leopold found a happy formula for toasting his distinguished guest who was not officially there. Rising to face the masked young visitor, the Emperor said, "I believe you know the Tsar of Russia. Let us drink to his health." The following morning, the cup that the Emperor had used for the toast arrived at Peter's door as a gift. It was inlaid with rock crystal and worth 2,000 florins. The Tsar's pleasure in the company of his supper partner was measured the following day when she received a gift of four pairs of sables and 250 ducats.

Returning this hospitality, on St. Peter's Day the Russian Embassy entertained its hosts by giving an all-night ball for one thousand guests. Fireworks lit by the Tsar's own hand, dancing, drinking and chases through the summer gardens brought a touch of the German Suburb to Vienna. At a state dinner given after the Emperor's reception of the Embassy, the health of the two consorts, the Empress and the Tsaritsa, was not drunk. This omission, arranged at the request of the Russians, was a sign of what was in store for Eudoxia when Peter returned to Moscow. During the dinner, when the talk turned to wine, Baron Königsacker insisted that Lefort immediately taste six specimens he recommended. When the wine arrived and Lefort had tasted it, he asked that his tall friend standing as a servant behind his chair might taste it, too.

DESPITE all the public amiability, Peter's mission to Vienna was a diplomatic failure. The Great Embassy had come to engage Austria's interest in resuming a more vigorous war against the Turks. Instead, they found themselves struggling to prevent an Austrian acceptance of a Turkish offer of peace which was highly favorable to Austria but not to Russia—a peace with all combatants agreeing to establishing the current status quo, each one keeping the territory he had won. For the Hapsburg monarch, this

was a favorable settlement: Hungary and parts of Transylvania would remain under Hapsburg control. The idea of peace was enormously tempting. Besides, the shadow of Louis loomed once again in the West. It was time to disengage in the East, accept the fruits of victory, regroup and turn to face the Sun King.

The only party not happy about the prospect of peace was Peter. Having renewed the war against Turkey himself in 1695 and 1696 with his campaigns against Azov, having captured that fortress and tasted the ambition to sail on the Black Sea, having moved mountains to build a fleet at Voronezh and come himself to Europe to learn shipbuilding and hire shipwrights, naval captains and seamen to build and man his Black Sea fleet, he could not permit the war to end until he had at least acquired Kerch and Turkish acceptance of his right to sail on the Black Sea.

Peter expressed this demand personally to the imperial Foreign Minister, Count Kinsky, and through Kinsky to the Emperor. Understanding that the Austrians were determined to make peace, Peter concentrated on the terms of that peace. Primarily, he wanted to make certain the Emperor would insist that Turkey cede to Russia the fortress of Kerch, which commanded the junction of the Black Sea with the Sea of Azov. Without Kerch, Peter's new fleet could not gain entry into the Black Sea, but would be confined on the vast but essentially useless Sea of Azov. Kinsky replied that the peace congress, to which Russia would naturally be invited, had not yet begun. If Peter wanted Kerch, he had best seize it quickly before the treaty was signed; he doubted that the Turks could be forced to hand it over merely by diplomatic pressures at a conference table, "for the Turks are not accustomed to give up their fortresses without a fight." The Emperor promised at least that he would sign no treaty without the Tsar's full knowledge of its terms.

This was the best that could be done, and Peter was impatient to leave: Vienna was an inland city with no docks or ships, and his next stop was to be Venice, where he hoped to learn the secrets of the marvelously efficient Venetian war galleys. By July 15, everything was arranged, the Embassy's passports were ready and some members of the suite were already on the road to Venice. Peter himself had just come away from his farewell audience with the Emperor when, at the moment of departure, the latest post from Moscow arrived, bringing an urgent letter with disturbing news from Romodanovsky. Four regiments of Streltsy, upon being ordered to march from Azov to the Polish frontier, had revolted and were instead marching on Moscow. As Romodanovsky was writing, they were only sixty miles from the capital, and loyal troops under Shein and Patrick Gordon had gone out to block their path. Nothing was said of the cause or extent of the revolt, and there was no further news as to what had happened. The letter had been a month on the way. Peter realized that

while he had been dancing in peasant costume at a masked ball, the Streltsy might have occupied the Kremlin, his sister Sophia seized the Russian throne and he himself been branded a traitor. At once, he decided to abandon the rest of the tour, cancel the visit to Venice and return directly to Moscow to face whatever awaited him there. Hoping and trusting that his regents were still in power, he wrote to Romodanovsky:

I have received your letter in which your grace writes that the seed of Ivan Mikhailovich [Miloslavsky] is sprouting. I beg you to be severe; in no other way is it possible to put out the flame. Although we are sorry to give up our present profitable business, yet, for the sake of this, we shall be with you sooner than you think.

In terminating the Embassy, Peter decided to take with him the first two ambassadors, Lefort and Golovin, to help in dealing with the situation in Moscow and leave the third, Voznitsyn, in Vienna to act as Russian representative at the coming peace negotiations with the Turks.

On July 19, Peter left Vienna on the road to Poland, astonishing the Austrians, who knew nothing of his news and expected to see him depart in the direction of Venice. He traveled day and night, stopping only to eat and change horses. He had reached Cracow when a messenger, forwarded along to him at a gallop by Voznitsyn, brought fresh and brighter news. Shein had met and subdued the rebels; 130 had been executed and 1,860 were prisoners. Peter was relieved, and considered turning around for his intended visit to Venice. But he was halfway home, he had been away for a year and a half and there was much he wanted to do in Moscow. He continued eastward, slowing his pace, proceeding in a leisurely fashion toward the town of Rawa in Galicia. Here, for the first time, the Tsar met an extraordinary figure in whose diplomatic and military machinations Peter and Russia were to become deeply involved. This was Augustus, Elector of Saxony and now also, thanks to the support of both the Emperor and the Tsar, King of Poland.

POLAND, through whose territory the Tsar was journeying homeward, was the weakest and most vulnerable of all the great European states in Peter's day. In physical size and in population, it was a giant: Its frontiers sprawled from Silesia to the Ukraine, from the Baltic to the Carpathians; its population was eight million, one of the largest in Europe, yet, politically and militarily, Poland was insignificant. Indeed, the vast state remained intact only because its neighbors were too busy or too weak themselves to bother pulling it apart. For the full twenty years of the Great Northern War which

was about to begin, Poland lay prostrate, its unhappy function being to provide a battleground for invading foreign armies. Before the military power of aggressive Sweden, whose entire empire counted only two and a half million subjects, giant Poland lay helpless.

A number of factors were responsible for Poland's impotence. The first was an absence of any real racial or religious cohesion. Only half of Poland's people were actually Polish, and this half tended to be Catholic. The other half—Lithuanians, Russians, Jews and Germans—were a mixture of Protestant, Russian Orthodox and Jewish faiths. Among these richly varied strains, political and religious antagonism flourished. The Lithuanians fought among themselves and united only in common hatred of the Poles. The Jews, who made up a large percentage of the town populations, tended to dominate trade and finance, thus incurring the fear and envy of the Poles. The Cossacks, whose nominal allegiance was to the Ukrainian Hetman, himself now a nominal subject of the Tsar, refused all orders from a Polish king.

If the racial and religious situation was confused, the political situation was chaotic. Poland was a republic which had a king. The king was an elective, not a hereditary, monarch, exercising only such power as the nobility chose to grant to him—which usually was none. The monarch therefore became little more than a state ornament. Thus, at a time when France was leading most European nations toward centralization of power and royal absolutism, Poland was headed in the opposite direction, toward political disintegration and anarchy. The true rulers of Poland were the great Polish and Lithuanian lords who ruled over immense territories where no central authority was permitted to penetrate. In Lithuania, the mighty Sapieha family, dreaming of the throne themselves, categorically defied all kings of Poland.

It was the Polish and Lithuanian land-owning aristocrats who, in 1572, had insisted that the crown be made an elective office. It was they who at the end of the seventeenth century owned all the nation's wealth and exported flax, grain and timber from their vast estates down the Vistula to the Baltic. They kept all political power, not only electing their sovereign but imposing on him a formal pact, to be signed by the elected candidate before his coronation, setting forth the terms on which he could rule. The embodiment of their ideal was reached when the Diet, or Polish parliament, finally agreed that no bill could pass if a single member objected. Nor did king or Diet have any machinery for authorizing or collecting taxes. There was no systematic Polish foreign policy. "This unsettled nation [is] like the sea," complained an English diplomat. "It foams and roars . . . [but it] only moves when it is agitated by some superior power."

The Polish army operated on a similar basis. Its cavalry was always superbly brave and gorgeously equipped: diamonds flashed on the breast-

plates and swords of the gallant horsemen. But discipline was nonexistent. At any moment, a Polish army in the field might be swollen or diminished by the arrival or departure of a great nobleman and his armed retainers. It was up to these gentlemen alone to decide whether and when they should participate in a campaign. If they wearied or were irked, they simply withdrew, no matter what the perils of their action to the other troops of the Polish army. At times, also, the Polish king would be at war, but the Polish republic, as represented by the Diet, would be at peace. It was in this kind of kaleidoscopic confusion with an ornamental king, a hamstrung parliament, an individualistic feudal army, that the vast, tumultuous Polish nation stumbled and lurched in the general direction of anarchy.

With such a system, Poland's sole hope of unity and order lay in a strong monarch somehow superimposing himself on the chaos. The choice, however, was not simply up to the Polish nobility. By this time, the election of a new Polish king who would hold even limited power over the vast nation was a European concern. Every monarch in Europe yearned to win the Polish crown for his own house, or at least for a prince favorable to his house. Peter of Russia, as Poland's eastern neighbor, was especially concerned. Fearing that a French candidate might win the throne, Peter had been prepared if necessary to invade Poland. To influence the election or be ready if the Frenchman won, Peter moved Russian troops to the Polish frontier. (It was a command to regiments of Streltsy to shift from Azov to the Polish border which had precipitated their revolt and thus recalled the Tsar from Vienna.) And on the other side of the continent, the Sun King desired to see the creation of a Poland friendly to France rising up behind the Hapsburg Emperor's back. Louis' candidate was François Louis de Bourbon, Prince de Conti, a French Prince of the Blood, whose battlefield exploits, powerful charm and sexual ambivalence had made him the darling of the French court. Conti was not enthusiastic about accepting the royal title, hating to leave his friends and the delights of Versailles for the barbarian wastes of Eastern Europe. But the King was determined and opened his purse, sending three million gold pounds to buy the votes of as many members of the Diet as were necessary. The effort was successful, and with the support of most of the Polish nobility, including the Sapieha family of Lithuania, Conti was elected and sailed for Danzig with a powerful French naval squadron commanded by the famous admiral Jean Bart.

Conti arrived in Poland to find that the election had been overturned. The disappointed candidate, Augustus of Saxony, supported by the Tsar and the Emperor, had simply refused to accept the Diet's decision and had marched into Poland at the head of a Saxon army. Arriving in Warsaw before Conti, Augustus converted his personal religion to Catholicism,

persuaded the Diet to change its mind and had himself crowned King of Poland on September 15, 1697. Conti quite happily returned to Versailles, and Augustus began a reign which lasted for thirty-six years. Thus, Augustus had been on the Polish throne for less than a year when Peter passed through the country on his way back to Moscow. Augustus was also Elector of Saxony, although the union of Saxony and Poland was only through his own person. The two states lacked even a common frontier, being separated by the Hapsburg province of Silesia and the territories of Brandenburg on the Oder River. Saxony was Lutheran, Poland was predominantly Catholic. Augustus' power, like that of all Polish kings, was limited, but already he was eagerly seeking ways to improve this situation.

When Peter arrived at Rawa, where the new King was staying, he found in Augustus a young man physically exceptional like himself. Augustus was tall (except in the presence of Peter, whose height was abnormal) and powerfully built; he was called Augustus the Strong, and it was said that he could bend a horseshoe with his bare hands. At twenty-eight, he was bluff and hearty, and had red cheeks, blue eyes, a strong nose, a full mouth and exceptionally heavy and bushy black eyebrows. His wife, a Hohenzollern, had left him when he became a Catholic, but this mattered little to Augustus, whose sensuality and philandering were on a gargantuan scale. Even in a time when he had many competitors, Augustus' efforts were remarkable; he collected women, and from his enjoyment of his collection Augustus was reported to have left 354 bastards. One of his favorite mistresses was the beautiful Countess Aurora von Königsmark, whom Peter had already met in Dresden; another, years later, would be the Countess Orzelska, who happened also to be his daughter.

Enjoying the flesh, Augustus also loved practical jokes which celebrated this taste. He gave Peter a gold box with a secret spring, ornamented by two portraits of another mistress. The portrait on the cover showed the lady in rich and formal dress, wearing an expression of proper dignity. The second picture, revealed when the spring was touched and the lid popped open, showed the same lady in a state of voluptuous, passionate disorder after she had yielded to the advances of her lover.*

In the bluff, hearty, fun-loving young Augustus, Peter recognized a

---

* On another occasion, indulging this same humor, Augustus was escorting Frederick William of Prussia and his sixteen-year-old son, the future Frederick the Great, on a tour of his palace in Dresden. They entered a bedchamber and were admiring the ceiling when suddenly a curtain around the bed was lifted, revealing a naked woman on the bed. Horrified, the stern and prudish Frederick William rushed from the room, dragging his son after him. Augustus, roaring with laughter, apologized, but later during the visit he sent the same woman to the youthful Frederick to enjoy. Out of politeness, the young man took her, although his own preference was not for women.

kindred spirit. They spent four days at Rawa, dining, reviewing the Saxon infantry and cavalry, and drinking together in the evenings. Peter showed his affection by frequently embracing and kissing his new friend. "I cannot begin to describe to you the tenderness between the two sovereigns," wrote a member of Peter's suite. The impression made on Peter by Augustus was deep and lasting, and he proudly wore the royal arms of Poland, which Augustus had presented to him. On returning to Moscow, when receiving his own welcoming boyars and friends on the day after his return, he flaunted his new friendship before them. "I prize him [Augustus] more than the whole of you together," he announced, "and that not because of his royal preeminence over you, but merely because I like him."

The days at Rawa and Peter's new friendship had momentous results for Russia. It was during these days that Augustus, who had already profited from Peter's support in winning his crown, used the Tsar's enthusiastic friendship to press another of his own ambitious projects: a joint attack on Sweden. The Swedish King, Charles XI, had died, leaving the throne to his fifteen-year-old son. The moment seemed ripe for an attempt to wrest away the Baltic provinces which Sweden used to block Polish and Russian access to the Baltic Sea. Augustus was shrewd and deceitful; in time, he was to earn a reputation for double-dealing second to none among European rulers. It was like him to propose that, to better ensure success, the attack be planned in secret and delivered by surprise.

Peter listened sympathetically to his boisterous and conniving new friend. He had his own reasons for being attracted to the scheme: in Vienna, he had been made to realize that the war in the south against Turkey was coming to an end. The door to the Black Sea was closing just as his own appetite for maritime adventure was growing. He had returned from Holland and England imbued with the spirit of ships, navies, trade and the sea. So it is not surprising that a proposal to break through to the Baltic, opening a direct maritime route to the West, appealed to him. Further, the Swedish provinces which would be attacked had once been Russian. They had fallen once as plums in one direction; so be it: Let them now be plucked by another hand. Peter nodded when Augustus spoke. Twenty-five years later, writing an introduction to the official Russian history of the Great Northern War, the Tsar confirmed that at this meeting at Rawa the initial agreement for an attack on Sweden had been made.

THE GREAT EMBASSY was over. The first peacetime journey out of Russia by a Russian tsar had taken eighteen months, cost two and a half million roubles, introduced the carpenter Peter Mikhailov to electors, princes, kings and an emperor, and proved to Western Europe that Russians did not eat

raw meat and wear only bearskins. What were the substantive results? In terms of its avowed, overt purpose, the reinvigoration and enlargement of the alliance against the Turks, the Embassy failed. Peace was coming in the East as Europe prepared for new and different wars. Wherever he went for help, in The Hague, in London, in Vienna, Peter found the looming shadow of Louis XIV. It was the Sun King and not the Sultan who frightened Europe. European diplomacy, money, ships and armies were being mobilized for the impending crisis when the throne of Spain would become vacant. Russia, left to make peace or fight the Turks alone, had no choice but to make peace.

In terms of practical, useful results, however, the Embassy was a considerable success. Peter and his ambassadors had succeeded in recruiting more than 800 technically skilled Europeans for Russian service, the bulk of them Dutchmen, but also Englishmen, Scots, Venetians, Germans and Greeks. Many of these men remained in Russia for years, made significant contributions to the modernization of the nation and left their names permanently inscribed in the history of Peter's reign.

More important was the profound and enduring impression that Western Europe made on Peter himself. He had traveled to the West in order to learn how to build ships, and this he had accomplished. But his curiosity had carried him into a wide range of new fields. He had probed into everything that caught his eye—had studied microscopes, barometers, wind dials, coins, cadavers and dental pliers, as well as ship construction and artillery. What he saw in the thriving cities and harbors of the West, what he learned from the scientists, inventors, merchants, tradesmen, engineers, printers, soldiers and sailors, confirmed his early belief, formed in the German Suburb, that his Russians were technologically backward—decades, perhaps centuries, behind the West.

Asking himself how this had happened and what could be done about it, Peter came to understand that the roots of Western technological achievement lay in the freeing of men's minds. He grasped that it had been the Renaissance and the Reformation, neither of which had ever come to Russia, which had broken the bonds of the medieval church and created an environment where independent philosophical and scientific inquiry as well as wide-ranging commercial enterprise could flourish. He knew that these bonds of religious orthodoxy still existed in Russia, reinforced by peasant folkways and traditions which had endured for centuries. Grimly, Peter resolved to break these bonds on his return.

But, curiously, Peter did not grasp—perhaps he did not wish to grasp—the political implications of this new view of man. He had not gone to the West to study "the art of government." Although in Protestant Europe he was surrounded by evidence of the new civil and political rights of in-

dividual men embodied in constitutions, bills of rights and parliaments, he did not return to Russia determined to share power with his people. On the contrary, he returned not only determined to change his country but also convinced that if Russia was to be transformed, it was he who must provide both the direction and the motive force. He would try to lead; but where education and persuasion were not enough, he would drive—and if necessary flog—the backward nation forward.

18

"THESE THINGS
ARE IN YOUR WAY"

AT FIRST LIGHT on the morning of September 5, 1698, Moscow awoke to learn that the Tsar had returned. Peter had arrived the night before with Lefort and Golovin, made a brief visit to the Kremlin, stopped at the houses of several friends and then gone to spend the night in his wooden house at Preobrazhenskoe with Anna Mons. As the news spread quickly across the city, a crowd of boyars and officials flocked to Peter's door to welcome him home, hoping, says an observer, "to prove by the promptitude of their obsequiousness, the constancy of their loyalty." Peter received them all with enthusiastic pleasure. Those who threw themselves on the ground at his feet in the old Muscovite fashion, he "lifted up graciously from their groveling posture and embraced with a kiss, such as is due only among private friends."

That very day, even as one grandee was elbowing the next aside to come closer to the Tsar, the warmth of their welcome was put to an extraordinary test. After passing among them and exchanging embraces, Peter suddenly produced a long, sharp barber's razor and with his own hands began shaving off their beards. He began with Shein, the commander of the army, who was too astonished to resist. Next came Romodanovsky, whose deep loyalty to Peter surmounted even this affront to his Muscovite sensibility. The others were forced, one by one, to submit until every boyar present was beardless and none could laugh and point a shocked finger at the others. Only three were spared: the Patriarch, watching the proceedings with horror, in respect for his office; Prince Michael Cherkassky, because of his advanced age; and Tikhon Streshnev, in deference to his role as guardian of the Tsaritsa.

The scene was remarkable: at a stroke the political, military and social leaders of Russia were bodily transformed. Faces known and recognized for a lifetime suddenly vanished. New faces appeared. Chins, jaws, cheeks, mouths, lips, all hidden for years, emerged, giving their owners a wholly

new look. It was comical, but the humor of it was mixed with nervousness and dread. For most Orthodox Russians, the beard was a fundamental symbol of religious belief and self-respect. It was an ornament given by God, worn by the prophets, the apostles and by Jesus himself. Ivan the Terrible expressed the traditional Muscovite feeling when he declared, "To shave the beard is a sin that the blood of all the martyrs cannot cleanse. It is to deface the image of man created by God." Priests generally refused to bless men without beards; they were considered shameful and beyond the pale of Christendom. Yet, as more beardless foreign merchants, soldiers and engineers arrived in Moscow in the mid-seventeenth century, Peter's father, Tsar Alexis, had relaxed the rule, declaring that Russians might shave if they wished. Few did so, and even those drove the Patriarch Adrian to fresh condemnation: "God did not create men beardless, only cats and dogs. Shaving is not only foolishness and dishonor; it is a mortal sin." Such sentiments rang in the boyars' ears even as they obeyed the Tsar's command.

Peter, beardless himself, regarded beards as unnecessary, uncivilized and ridiculous. They made his country a subject of mirth and mockery in the West. They were a visible symbol of all he meant to change, and, typically, he attacked, wielding the razor himself. Thereafter, whenever Peter attended a banquet or ceremony, those who arrived with beards departed without them. Within a week of his return, he went to a banquet given by Shein and sent his court fool, Jacob Turgenev, around the room in the role of barber. The process was often uncomfortable; shaving long, thick beards with a dry razor left many gouges and cuts where the sharp blade came too close. But no one dared object; Peter was there to box the ears of any who showed reluctance.

Although the cutting of beards began in Peter's intimate circle to ridicule the old Russian way and to show that those who wished the Tsar's favor would thereafter appear beardless in his presence, the ban against beards soon became serious and general. By decree, all Russians except the clergy and the peasants were ordered to shave. To ensure that the order was carried out, officials were given the power to cut the beard off any man, no matter how important, whom they encountered. At first, horrified and desperate Russians bribed these officials to let them go, but as soon as they did, they would fall into the hands of another official. Before long, wearing a beard became too expensive a luxury.

Eventually those who insisted on keeping their beards were permitted to do so on paying an annual tax. Payment entitled the owner to a small bronze medallion with a picture of a beard on it and the words TAX PAID, which was worn on a chain around the neck to prove to any challengers that his beard was legal. The tax was graduated; peasants paid only two kopeks a year, wealthy merchants paid as much as a hundred roubles. Many were

willing to pay this tax to keep their beards, but few who came near Peter were willing to risk his wrath with a chin that was not hairless. Finding men in his presence still bearded, Peter sometimes, "in a merry humor, pulled out their beards by the roots or took it off so roughly [with a razor] that some of the skin went with it."

Although Peter was merry about it, most Russians considered beard-cutting an act of aggression and humiliation. Some would rather give up anything than lose the beards which they had worn through life, expected to carry to the grave and thus arrive, proudly wearing them, in the next world. They could not resist; Peter's will was too strong. But they tried pathetically to atone for what they had been taught was a mortal sin. John Perry, the English engineer whom Peter signed up for service during his trip to London, described an aged Russian carpenter whom he met on the wharves of Voronezh.

About this time the Tsar came down to Voronezh where I was on service, and a great many of my men who had worn their beards all their lives were now obliged to part with them, amongst whom, just coming from the hands of the barber, was an old Russ carpenter . . . a very good workman with his hatchet and whom I always had a friendship for. I jested a little with him . . . telling him that he was become a young man and asked him what he had done with his beard. . . . He put his hand in his bosom and pulled it out and showed it to me; further telling me that when he came home, he would lay it up to have it put in his coffin and buried along with him, that he might be able to give an account of it to St. Nicholas, when he came to the other world, and that all his brothers [fellow workers] had taken the same care.*

PETER'S MOOD on his return was cheerful and enthusiastic. He was happy to be back in the company of his friends and so eager to start making changes that he scarcely knew where to begin. Impulsively, he went one place, then rushed off to another. On his second day in Moscow, he reviewed his troops—and was immediately displeased. "Seeing at a glance

---

* After Peter, beards returned very slowly to the upper levels of Russian society. Through the eighteenth and the first half of the nineteenth century, all public officials and officers and soldiers of the army were required to be shaved. In the 1860's and 1870's, under Alexander II, this rule was relaxed and many government ministers and Russian soldiers—with the exception of members of the Imperial Guard—again began to wear beards. All the tsars who followed Peter were clean-shaven except the last two, Alexander III and Nicholas II, who both wore beards in order to manifest their strong Slavophile tastes.

how backward they were as compared with other soldiers," said Johann Korb, an Austrian diplomat,

> he went himself through all the attitudes and movements of the manual exercises, teaching them by his own motions how they should endeavor to form their heavy, clumsy bodies. Tired at last with the uncouth horde, he went off with a bevy of boyars to a dinner which he had ordered at his Ambassador Lefort's. Salvos of artillery mingled with the shouts of the drinkers, and the pleasures of the table were protracted to a late hour of the evening. Then, taking advantage of the shades of night, attended by a very few of those in whom he reposes most confidence, he went to the Kremlin, where he indulged a father's affection in seeing his darling little son [the Tsarevich Alexis], kissed him thrice, and leaving many other pledges of endearment, returned to his wooden dwelling in Preobrazhenskoe, fleeing the sight of his wife, the Tsaritsa [Eudoxia], whom he dislikes with a loathing of old date.

A few days later, Peter celebrated the Russian New Year — which, according to the calendar of Old Muscovy, began September 1—with a huge banquet at General Shein's house. The guests included a large crowd of boyars, officers and others, among them a group of common sailors from the infant fleet. Peter particularly honored the sailors, spending much of the evening with them, halving apples and giving one part to a sailor while eating the other himself. He threw his arm around one sailor and called him "brother." Toast followed toast, and each lifting of the glasses provoked a salute of twenty-five guns.

Still another "sumptuous entertainment" took place two weeks after the Tsar's return, and although Peter arrived with "his gums swollen with toothache," the Austrian ambassador reported that he had never seen him happier. General Patrick Gordon arrived to present himself to the Tsar for the first time since Peter's return, excusing himself for the delay by saying that he had been at his country house and had been held back by bad weather and storms. The old soldier twice bowed low and was about to go on his knees to embrace the Tsar around the knees when Peter extended his hand and clasped it warmly.

Not long after Peter compelled his boyars to shave their beards, he also began to insist they change from traditional Russian clothing to Western dress. Some had already done so; Polish costume had appeared at court and was regularly worn by progressive figures such as Vasily Golitsyn. In 1681, Tsar Fedor had insisted that his courtiers shorten their long robes so as to permit them to walk. But most continued to wear the traditional Russian national costume: embroidered shirt, wide breeches tucked into floppy

boots brilliantly colored in red or green with turned-up toes and gold trim, and on top of that a caftan reaching to the ground with a straight collar of velvet, satin or brocade and sleeves of exaggerated length and width. To go outdoors, another long garment was added, light in summer, fur-lined in winter, with high, square collar and even longer sleeves which fell to the bottom of the heels. Walking in procession in Moscow in their long, flowing robes and tall, fur-lined hats, a group of Russian boyars made an opulent, almost Oriental picture.

Peter detested this national dress because it was impractical. In his own active life, working in a shipyard, sailing, marching with his soldiers, the long, bulky robes got in the way and he could scarcely walk. Nor did he like the expressions of curiosity, amusement and contempt which he saw on Western faces when a group of Russians in national costumes walked through the streets of a Western town. Back in Moscow, he resolved on change. Among the most persistent wearers of the old dress was the stern Prince Romodanovsky. When Romodanovsky was told that Fedor Golovin, an ambassador of the Great Embassy, had taken off his Russian clothes in the West and put on fashionable foreign garments, Romodanovsky said, "I do not believe Golovin to be such a brainless ass as to despise the dress of his fatherland." Yet on October 30, when Peter ordered that Golovin and Lefort be received in state to acknowledge the Embassy's return, and that only those in Western dress be allowed to appear, Romodanovsky himself was obliged to conform.

That winter, in the course of a two-day banquet and celebration to dedicate Lefort's new palace, Peter took a pair of long cutting shears and clipped the wide sleeves of the boyars around him at the table. "See," he said, "these things are in your way. You are safe nowhere with them. At one moment you upset a glass, then you forgetfully dip them in the sauce." He handed the sheared-off sleeves to the astonished guests, suggesting, "Get gaiters made of them."

A year later, in January 1700, Peter transformed persuasion into decree. With rolling drums in the streets and squares, it was proclaimed that all boyars, government officials and men of property, both in Moscow and in the provinces, were to abandon their long robes and provide themselves with Hungarian or German-style caftans. The following year, a new decree commanded men to wear a waistcoat, breeches, gaiters, boots and a hat in the French or German style, and women to put on petticoats, skirts, bonnets and Western shoes. Later decrees prohibited the wearing of high Russian boots and long Russian knives. Models of the new approved costumes were hung at Moscow's gates and in public places in the city for people to observe and copy. All who arrived at the gates in traditional dress except peasants were permitted to enter only after paying a fine. Subsequently, Peter in-structed the guards at the city gates to force to their knees all visitors arriving

in long, traditional coats and then to cut off the coats at the point where the lowered garment touched the ground. "Many hundreds of coats were cut accordingly," says Perry, "and being done with good humor it occasioned mirth among the people and soon broke the custom of wearing long coats, especially in places near Moscow and those towns wherever the Tsar came." Not surprisingly, Peter's sartorial transformation was much more readily accepted by women than by men. His sister Natalya and his widowed sister-in-law, Praskovaya, were the first to set the example, and many Russian noblewomen hurried to follow. Seeing great possibilities in foreign dress, anxious to be à la mode, they sent to the West for examples of the gowns, shoes and hats being worn at Versailles.

As time passed, subsequent decrees further extended and refined Peter's will that the new clothes be worn "for the glory and comeliness of the state and the military profession." Resistance was never so strong as that which had greeted his condemnation of beards; priests might still berate clean-shaven men, but the church did not rise to the defense of the traditional robes. Fashion has its own authority, and lesser men scurried to adopt the dress of their superiors. Within five years, Whitworth, the English ambassador, reported from Moscow that "in all this great city not a single person of importance is to be met dressed otherwise than in the German manner."

In the country, however, fashion still bowed to age-old habit. Those of the nobility, the bureaucracy and the merchants who fell under Peter's eye dressed as he desired, but other gentry living on their far-off estates still serenely wore their long robes. In a way, this first and most obvious of Peter's reforms on his return from the West was typical of what followed. In his impatience to apply Western customs to Russian society, he jettisoned Russian habits whose existence was based on common sense. It was true that the old Russian clothing was bulky and made walking difficult; limbs were certainly freer once the long robes and coats were cast off. But in the rigorous cold of Russian winter, the freer limbs were also more likely to be frostbitten. When the temperature sank to twenty or thirty below zero, the old Russian in his warm boots, his greatcoat rising above his ears and reaching down to the ground, with his bushy beard protecting his mouth and cheeks, could look with satisfaction at that poor Westernized fellow whose face was purple in the cold and whose knees, showing beneath his shortened coat, knocked together in a futile effort to keep warm.

PETER'S ARDENT DETERMINATION to rid himself quickly of all appurtenances and reminders of the old Muscovite customs and traditions had bleak results for his wife, Eudoxia. The autumn of his return from the West marked the final break between the twenty-six-year-old Tsar and the twenty-nine-year-old Tsaritsa.

Peter had long wished to end his marriage and to shed this sad and cloying woman whom he had never loved and whom he had been forced to marry. From the beginning, it had been no secret that Peter went out of his way to avoid his wife. She was simple and uneducated. She feared his enthusiasms and disliked his friends—particularly Lefort—and the foreigners who thronged into Peter's life. A good Orthodox woman who believed that foreigners were the source of heresy and contamination, she could not bear to see her husband adopting their clothes, their language, their habits and their ideas. Inevitably, by trying to come between her enthusiastic, headstrong husband and the glittering life he had found with his new friends, Eudoxia only made her own position weaker. She also knew that Peter was unfaithful, that he kept Anna Mons in handsome style. Foolishly, she showed her jealousy openly, which angered Peter, while her own attempts to please him with letters or marks of affection merely wearied him. In short, he was bored with her, embarrassed by her and longed to be free of her.

While still in the West, dining, dancing and making conversation with the fascinating ladies he met everywhere, Peter resolved to be rid of his own helpless, uninteresting and possessive wife. He did not write a single line to Eudoxia during his eighteen months abroad, but his letters to his friends in Russia contained broad hints of his intentions. From London he wrote to his uncle Lev Naryshkin and to Tikhon Streshnev, urging that they persuade his wife to take religious vows and become a nun. Once she took the veil, all earthly relationships, including marriage, were null and void. On returning to Amsterdam, Peter increased the pressure, asking Romodanovsky to intervene and use his influence on the reluctant Tsaritsa. Even the Patriarch was induced to work on Peter's behalf, although he tried to avoid the unwelcome task. By the time he reached Vienna, Peter had made up his mind. His refusal to offer a toast to the Empress, which would require him to drink the reciprocal toast that would be offered to the Tsaritsa, was a clear signal of his hardened purpose.

On returning to Moscow, Peter at first refused to see Eudoxia. Instead, he angrily asked Naryshkin and the others why his orders regarding her had not been carried out. They replied that in so delicate a matter the sovereign himself must handle the arrangements. Thus, after he had been in Moscow for several days, Peter summoned Eudoxia to meet him at Vinius' house. For four hours they argued, Peter insisting furiously that she must accept the veil and release him. Eudoxia, finding strength in desperation, steadfastly refused, pleading that her duty as a mother made it impossible for her to leave the world. Once incarcerated in a convent, she predicted (accurately, as it turned out), she would never see her son again. Therefore, she declared that she would never voluntarily abandon either the palace or her marriage.

Peter left the interview determined to have his way. First, Alexis, then eight and a half, was forcibly taken from his mother and put in the care of Peter's younger sister, Natalya, at Preobrazhenskoe. One morning soon after, a simple postal carriage, without ladies-in-waiting or servants, was sent to the palace. Eudoxia was bundled into it and the cart rattled off to the Pokrovsky Monastery in Suzdal. There, ten months later, Eudoxia's head was shaved and she was forced to take a new name as a nun, Helen. Later in Peter's life, she would reappear in a surprising way, but, for the moment, Peter's wish was accomplished: he at last was free.

IN THE MONTHS that followed Peter's return from the West, he imposed other changes on Russian life. Most were superficial and symbolic; like the cutting of beards and the trimming of clothes, they were harbingers of the deeper institutional reforms to come in the decades ahead. These early transformations really changed nothing fundamental in Russian society. Yet, to Russians they seemed very strange, for they had to do with the commonest ingredients of everyday life.

One of these changes had to do with the calendar. Since the earliest times, Russians had calculated the year not from the birth of Christ but from the moment when they believed the world had been created. Accordingly, by their reckoning, Peter returned from the West not in the year 1698 but in the year 7206. Similarly, Russians began the New Year not on January 1, but on September 1. This stemmed from their belief that the world was created in autumn when the grain and other fruits of the earth had ripened to perfection and were ready to pluck, rather than in the middle of winter when the earth was covered with snow. Traditionally, New Year's Day, September 1, was celebrated with great ceremony, with the tsar and the patriarch seated on two thrones in a courtyard of the Kremlin surrounded by crowds of boyars and people. Peter had suspended these rites as obsolete, but September 1 still remained the beginning of the New Year.

Anxious to bring both the year and New Year's Day into line with the West, Peter decreed in December 1699 that the next new year would begin on January 1 and that the coming year would be numbered 1700. In his decree, the Tsar stated frankly that the change was made in order to conform to Western practice.* But to blunt the argument of those who said that God

---

* In choosing to follow the Julian calendar then in use in England, Peter brought Russia into line with the West just before the West itself changed. In 1752, England adopted the Gregorian calendar, but Russia refused to change a second time, with the result that until the Revolution the Russian calendar was behind the West, eleven days in the eighteenth century, twelve in the nineteenth and thirteen in the twentieth. In 1918, the Soviet government finally accepted the Gregorian calendar, which now is standard throughout the world.

could not have made the earth in the depth of winter, Peter invited them "to view the map of the globe, and, in a pleasant temper, gave them to understand that Russia was not all the world and that what was winter with them was, at the same time, always summer in those places beyond the equator." To celebrate the change and impress the new day on the Muscovites, Peter ordered special New Year's services held in all the churches on January 1. Further, he instructed that festive evergreen branches be used to decorate the doorposts in interiors of houses, and he commanded that all citizens of Moscow should "display their happiness by loudly congratulating" one another on the New Year. All houses were to be illuminated and open for feasting for seven days.

Peter also altered Russian money. He had returned ashamed of the haphazard, informal, almost Oriental monetary system in use within his realm. Up to that point, a substantial amount of the currency circulating in Russia consisted of foreign coins, usually German or Dutch, with an M stamped on them to denote "Muscovy." The only Russian coins in general circulation were small oval bits of silver called kopeks, stamped on one side with an image of St. George and on the other with the title of the tsar. The quality of the silver and the size of the coins differed greatly, and to make change, Russians simply sliced them into pieces with a heavy blade. Peter, influenced by his visit to the Royal Mint in England, had come to understand that in order to promote a growth of trade, he must have an adequate supply of official money, issued and protected by the government. He therefore ordered the production of large, handsomely made copper coins which could be used as change for the existing kopeks. Subsequently, he coined gold and silver pieces in higher denominations up to the rouble, which equaled 100 kopeks. Within three years, this new coinage had reached such an impressive scale that nine million roubles' worth of specie had been issued and was circulating.

Another foreign idea was presented to Peter in an anonymous letter found one morning on the floor of a government office. Normally, unsigned missives contained denunciations of high officials, but this letter was a proposal that Russia adopt a system of using stamped paper, that all formal agreements, contracts, petitions and other documents be required to be written on official paper bearing the duty-paid mark of an eagle in the upper left-hand corner. The paper should be sold only by the government; the income would accrue to the state Treasury. Enormously pleased, Peter enacted the measure at once and instituted a search for the anonymous writer. He was found to be a serf named Alexis Kurbatov, who, as steward to Boris Sheremetev, had accompanied his master to Italy, where he had observed the use of Italian stamped paper. Peter handsomely rewarded Kurbatov and gave him a new government post, where his duty was to find further ways of increasing government revenues.

It was Peter himself who carried home another Western practice which simultaneously broadened the sophistication of Russian society and saved the state land and money. The traditional Russian manner of rewarding important services to the tsar had been the bestowal of large estates or gifts of money. In the West, Peter discovered the thriftier device of awarding decorations—orders, crosses and stars. Imitating such foreign decorations as England's Order of the Garter and the Hapsburg Order of the Golden Fleece, Peter created an exclusive order of Russian knighthood, the Order of St. Andrew, named after the patron saint of Russia. The new knights were distinguished by a broad light-blue ribbon worn diagonally across the chest and the cross of St. Andrew in black on white enamel. The first recipient was Fedor Golovin, Peter's faithful companion and ambassador on the Great Embassy and now, to all intents and purposes, the unofficial prime minister. The Tsar also named Mazeppa, Hetman of the Cossacks, and Boris Sheremetev, who was to succeed Shein as commander of the army. Twenty-five years later, at Peter's death, the Order of St. Andrew numbered thirty-eight members, twenty-four of them Russians and fourteen foreigners. This order remained the highest and most coveted of all the honors conferred by a Russian sovereign until the fall of the empire. Thus, for over two centuries, human nature being what it is, these pieces of colored ribbon and bits of silver and enamel became worth as much to Russian generals, admirals, ministers and other officials as thousands of acres of good Russian earth.

19

FIRE AND KNOUT

ONCE THE BEARDS WERE SHAVED and the first reunion toasts drunk, the smile faded from Peter's face. There was grimmer work to be done: it was time for a final reckoning with the Streltsy.

Ever since Sophia's downfall, the former elite troops of the old Muscovite armies had been deliberately humiliated. In Peter's sham battles at Preobrazhenskoe, the Streltsy regiments always made up the "enemy" whose role was always to lose. More recently, in real combat beneath the walls of Azov, the Streltsy had suffered heavy losses. They resented being made to dig like laborers, piling up earth for the siege works; they disliked being forced to obey the commands of foreign officers, and they grumbled at seeing their young Tsar so eager to follow the advice of these Westerners speaking incomprehensible tongues.

Unfortunately for the Streltsy, the two Azov campaigns had conclusively demonstrated to Peter how inferior in discipline and fighting quality they were to his own new regiments, and he announced his intention to model his army along Western lines. After the capture of Azov, it was the new regiments which returned to Moscow with the Tsar to make a triumphal entry and be granted honors, while the Streltsy were left behind to rebuild the fortifications and to garrison the conquered town. This violated all precedents; the Streltsy's traditional place in peacetime was Moscow, where they guarded the Kremlin, kept their wives and families and ran profitable businesses on the side. Now, some of the soldiers had been away from home for almost two years, and this, too, was by design. Peter and his government wanted as few of them as possible in the capital, and the best way to keep them away was to assign them to permanent service on a distant frontier. Thus, wanting at one point to reinforce the Russian army on the Polish border, the government ordered 2,000 Streltsy of the regiments in Azov dispatched there. They were to be replaced in Azov by some of the Streltsy remaining in Moscow, while the Guards and other Western-style troops would remain in the capital to protect the government.

The Streltsy marched, but their discontent mounted. They were furious at having to walk from one distant outpost to another hundreds of miles away, and even angrier that they were not allowed to pass through Moscow to see their families. Along the route, some of the soldiers actually deserted to reappear in Moscow, presenting petitions for back pay and asking permission to remain in the capital. Their petitions were rejected and they were ordered to return to their regiments immediately or face punishment. They returned to their comrades, telling them how badly they had been received. They also brought the latest news and gossip of the Moscow streets, much of it centered on Peter and his long absence in the West. Even before his departure, his preference for foreigners and his elevation of foreign officers to high places in the state and army had angered the Streltsy. Now their anger was fueled by fresh rumors. Peter was said to have become a German, to have given up the Orthodox faith, even to be dead.

As the Streltsy conferred excitedly among themselves, their personal grievances began to expand into a larger, political grievance against the Tsar: their faith and their country were being subverted; the Tsar was no longer a tsar! A true tsar sat enthroned in the Kremlin, remote, appearing only in great processions covered with jewels and robes. This tall Peter who shouted and drank with carpenters and foreigners all night in the German Suburb, who walked in triumphal processions in the wake of foreigners whom he had made generals and admirals, could not be a true tsar. If he was really the son of Alexis—and many doubted it—then he had been bewitched; and they pointed to his epileptic seizures as evidence that he was a child of the Devil. As all this boiled in their minds, the Streltsy realized their duty: to overthrow this changeling tsar, this false tsar, and reestablish the old traditional ways.

Just at this moment, a new decree arrived from Moscow: The companies were to disperse themselves into garrisons in towns between Moscow and the Polish-Lithuanian border, and the deserters who had come to Moscow were to be arrested and exiled. This decree was the catalyst. Two thousand Streltsy decided to march on Moscow. On June 9, at a dinner at the Austrian embassy in Moscow, Korb, the newly arrived secretary to the embassy, noted, "Today for the first time a vague rumor of the revolt of the Streltsy struck terror." People remembered the revolt sixteen years before, and now, fearing a repetition of that slaughter, those who could began leaving the capital.

In this atmosphere of panic, the Tsar's government met to face the danger. No one knew how many rebels there were, or how close they were to the city. The troops in Moscow were commanded by the boyar Alexis Shein, and at Shein's elbow, as he had been at Azov, was the old Scot, General Patrick Gordon. Shein agreed to accept the responsibility for suppressing the mutiny, but he asked that all members of the boyar council

approve the decision unanimously and signify their approval by signing or setting their seals to the document. The boyars refused, probably in recognition that if the Streltsy should win, their signatures would doom them. Nevertheless, they agreed that it was essential to prevent the Streltsy from entering Moscow and inciting a larger rebellion. Whatever loyal troops could be found would be assembled and marched out to meet the Streltsy before they reached the city.

The two Guards regiments, the Preobrazhensky and the Semyonovsky, were ordered to prepare to march on an hour's notice. To stamp out any sparks of rebellion that might have spread to them, the order declared that those who refused to march against the traitors would be proclaimed traitors themselves. Gordon went among the troops, exhorting them and assuring them that there was no more glorious and noble combat than that undertaken to save the sovereign and the state against traitors. Four thousand loyal troops mustered and marched westward out of the city, Shein and Gordon riding at their head. Most important, Colonel de Grage, an Austrian artillery officer, was there with twenty-five field cannon.

The confrontation took place thirty miles northwest of Moscow near the Patriarch Nikon's famous New Jerusalem Monastery. Everything—numbers, leadership, artillery, even timing—favored the loyal forces. Had the Streltsy arrived only an hour earlier, they might have occupied the powerful monastery and been able to withstand a siege long enough to dishearten the loyal soldiers and persuade some of them to join the revolt; and the walled fortress would have been a tactical buttress to their position. As it was, the two sides met in open, rolling countryside.

Near the monastery ran a small stream. Shein and Gordon took up a commanding position on the eastern bank, blocking the road to Moscow. Soon afterward, the long lines of Streltsy carrying their muskets and halberds began to appear, and the vanguard started to ford the river. To discover whether there was any chance of ending the rebellion peaceably, Gordon walked down to the riverbank to talk to the mutineers. As the first of the Streltsy emerged from the water, he advised them, as an old soldier, that night was close and Moscow too far to reach that day; it would be better to camp for the night on the far side of the river, where there was plenty of room. There they could rest and decide what to do on the following day. The Streltsy, exhausted and uncertain, not having expected to have to fight before reaching Moscow but now seeing the government troops drawn up against them, accepted Gordon's advice and began to make camp. To Gordon the Streltsy spokesman, Sergeant Zorin, handed an unfinished petition which complained:

> That they had been ordered to serve in different towns for a year at a time, and that, when they were in front of Azov, by the device of

a heretic and foreigner, Fransko Lefort, in order to cause great harm to Orthodoxy, he, Fransko Lefort, had led the Moscow Streltsy under the wall at the wrong time, and by putting them in the most dangerous and bloody places many of them had been killed; that by his device a mine had been made under the trenches, and that by this mine he had also killed three hundred men and more.

The petition continued with other complaints, including "that they had heard that Germans are coming to Moscow to have their beards shaved and publicly smoke tobacco to the discredit of Orthodoxy." Meanwhile, as Gordon parleyed with the rebels, Shein's troops had quietly entrenched themselves on the commanding high ground on the eastern bank and De Grage had placed his cannon on the height, their muzzles pointing down across the stream at the Streltsy.

At dawn the following day, satisfied that his own position was as strong as he could make it, Gordon again went down to talk to the Streltsy, who demanded that their petition be read to the loyal army. Gordon refused; the petition was actually a call to arms against Tsar Peter and a condemnation of Peter's closest friends, especially Lefort. Instead, Gordon spoke of Peter's clemency. He urged the Streltsy to return peacefully and resume their garrison duties, as no good could come of mutiny. He promised that if they would present their requests peacefully and with proper expressions of loyalty, he would see that they received satisfaction for their grievances and pardon for their disobedience up to that point. Gordon failed. "I used all the rhetoric I was master 'of, but all in vain," he wrote. The Streltsy answered only that they would not go back to their posts "until they had been allowed to kiss their wives in Moscow and had received their arrears in pay."

Gordon reported this to Shein, then returned a third time with a final offer to pay their salaries and grant pardon. By this time, however, the Streltsy were restless and impatient. They warned Gordon, their former commander but also a foreigner, that he must leave immediately or get a bullet for his efforts. They shouted that they recognized no master and would take orders from no one, that they would not go back to their garrisons, that they must be admitted to Moscow, and that if their way was blocked, they would open the road with cold steel. Furious, Gordon returned to Shein, and the loyal troops prepared to fight. On the western bank, the Streltsy troops, too, formed ranks, knelt and asked the blessing of God. On both sides of the stream, countless signs of the cross were made as Russian soldiers prepared for battle against each other.

The first shots came on Shein's command. With a roar, smoke billowed out from the cannon muzzles, but no harm was done. De Grage's guns had fired powder but not shot; Shein had hoped that this display of force might

awe the Streltsy into submission. Instead, the blank volley had the opposite effect. Hearing the noise, but seeing no damage among their ranks, the Streltsy were emboldened to think that they were the stronger party. Beating their drums and waving their banners, they advanced across the river. At this, Shein and Gordon ordered De Grage to bring his guns into action in earnest. The cannon roared again, this time sending ball and shot whistling into the lines of the Streltsy. Over and over, De Grage's twenty-five guns fired into the mass of men before them. Cannonballs volleyed into the lines, lopping off heads, arms and legs.

In an hour it was over. While the cannon still boomed, the Streltsy lay down on the ground to escape the fire, begging to surrender. From the loyal side, commands to throw down their arms were shouted. The Streltsy quickly obeyed, but even so, the artillery continued to fire, Gordon reasoning that if he silenced his guns, the Streltsy might gain courage and be persuaded to attack again before they could be properly disarmed. And so the cowed and terrified Streltsy allowed themselves to be fettered and bound until they were truly harmless.

With the rebels in chains, Shein was merciless. On the spot, with the entire body of mutinous Streltsy in chains and under guard on the battlefield, he ordered an investigation of the rebellion. He wanted to know the cause, the instigators, the objectives. To a man, each Strelets whom he questioned admitted his own involvement and agreed that he himself deserved death. But, equally to a man, all refused to give any details as to their goals or to betray any of their fellows as instigators or leaders. Accordingly, in the pleasant countryside near the New Jerusalem Monastery, Shein ordered the Streltsy put to torture. Knout and fire did their work, and at last one soldier was persuaded to speak. Agreeing that he and all his fellows deserved death, he admitted that had the rebellion been successful, they had intended first to sack and burn the entire German Suburb and massacre all its inhabitants, then to enter Moscow, kill all who resisted, seize the leading boyars, kill some and exile others. Following this, they would announce to the people that the Tsar, who had gone abroad on the malicious advice of the foreigners, had died in the West and the Princess Sophia would be called upon to act as regent again until the Tsarevich Alexis, Peter's son, should reach his majority. To advise and support Sophia, Vasily Golitsyn would be recalled from exile.

Perhaps this was true or perhaps Shein had simply extracted by torture what he wished to hear. In any case, he was satisfied and, on the basis of this confession, ordered the executioners to begin their work. Gordon protested—not to save the lives of the condemned men, but to preserve them for more thorough interrogation in the future. Anticipating Peter's intense desire to get to the bottom of the matter on his return, he pleaded with Shein. But Shein was the commander and he insisted that immediate

executions were necessary to make the proper impression on the rest of the Streltsy—and on the nation—as to how traitors were dealt with. One hundred and thirty were executed in the field and the rest, nearly 1,900, were brought back to Moscow in chains. There they were turned over to Romodanovsky, who distributed them in the cells of various fortresses and monasteries around the countryside to await Peter's return.

PETER, rushing home from Vienna, had been informed along the way of the easy victory over the Streltsy and been assured that "not one got away." Yet, despite the quick snuffing out of the revolt which had never seriously threatened his throne, the Tsar was profoundly disturbed. His first thought, after the anxiety and humiliation of having his army rebel while he was traveling abroad, was—exactly as Gordon had known it would be—to wonder how far the roots of the rebellion had spread and what high persons might have been involved. Peter doubted that the Streltsy had acted alone. Their demands and charges against his friends, himself and his way of life seemed too broad for simple soldiers. But who had instigated them? On whose behalf?

None of his boyars or officers could give him a satisfactory answer. They said that the Streltsy had been too strong under torture and that answers could not be forced out of them. Angry and suspicious, Peter ordered the Guards regiments to collect the hundreds of prisoners from cells around Moscow and bring them to Preobranzhenskoe. There, in the interrogation that followed, Peter resolved to discover whether, as he had written to Romodanovsky, "the seed of the Miloslavskys had sprouted again." And even if this had not been a full-fledged plot to overthrow his government, he was determined to put an end to those "begetters of evil." Since his childhood, the Streltsy had opposed and threatened him—they had murdered his friends and relations, they had supported the claims of the usurper Sophia and they continued to scheme against him; only two weeks before his departure abroad, the plot of the Streltsy Colonel Tsykler had been discovered. Now, once again they had used violent language against his foreign friends and himself and had marched on Moscow intending to overthrow the state. Peter was weary of it all: the nuisance as well as the danger, the arrogant claims to special privilege and to fight only when and where they wished, the poor performance as soldiers, the fact that they were semimedieval figures in a modern world. Once and for all, one way or another, he would be rid of them.

INTERROGATION meant questioning under torture. Torture in Russia in Peter's day was used for three purposes: to force men to speak; as punish-

ment, even when no information was desired; and as a prelude to or refinement of death by execution. Traditionally, three general methods of torture were used in Russia: the batog, the knout and fire.

A batog was a small rod or stick about the thickness of a man's finger, commonly used to beat an offender for lesser crimes. The victim was spread on the floor, lying on his stomach, his back bared and his legs and arms extended. Two men applied batogs simultaneously to the bare back, one sitting or kneeling on the victim's head and arms, the other on his legs and feet. Facing each other, the two punishers wielded their sticks rhythmically in turn, "keeping time as smiths do at an anvil until their rods were broken in pieces and then they took fresh ones until they were ordered to stop." Laid on indiscriminately over a prolonged time with a weakened victim, the batogs could cause death, although this was not usually the case.

More serious punishment or interrogation called forth the knout, a savage but traditional method of inflicting pain in Russia. The knout was a thick, hard leather whip about three and a half feet long. A blow from the knout tore skin from the bare back of a victim and, when the lash fell repeatedly in the same place, could bite through to the bone. The degree of punishment was determined by the number of strokes inflicted; fifteen to twenty-five was considered standard; more than that often led to death.

Applying the knout was skilled work. The wielder, observed John Perry, applied "so many strokes on the bare back as are appointed by the judges, first making a step back and giving a spring forward at every stroke, which is laid on with such force that the blood flies at every stroke and leaves a weal behind as thick as a man's finger. And these [knout] masters as the Russians call them, are so exact in their work that they very rarely strike two strokes in the same place, but lay them on the whole length and breadth of a man's back, by the side of each other with great dexterity from the top of a man's shoulders down to the waistband of his breeches."

Normally, to receive the knout, the victim was lifted and spread across the back of another man, frequently some strong fellow selected by the knoutmaster from among the spectators. The victim's arms were tied over the shoulders of his stationary porter and his legs around the porter's knees. Then, one of the knoutmaster's assistants grabbed the victim by the hair, pulling his head out of the way of the rhythmic strokes of the lash that were falling on the outspread, heaving back.

If desired, the knout could be applied in an even more terrible way. The victim's hands were tied behind his back and a long rope was tied to his wrists and then passed over the branch of a tree or an overhead beam. Pulling down on the rope meant hoisting the victim into the air with his arms revolving backward the wrong way in their shoulder sockets. To make sure that the arms were pulled completely out of joint, a heavy log or other weight was sometimes tied to the victim's feet. With the victim already in agony,

the knoutmaster then flailed the distended back with the designated number of strokes, whereupon the victim was lowered to the ground and his arms were wrenched back into joint again. In some cases, this torture would be repeated on a weekly basis until the victim confessed.

Torture by fire was common—sometimes alone, sometimes in combination with other tortures. In its simplest form, interrogation by fire meant that the victim's "hands and feet are tied and he is fixed on a long pole, as upon a spit, and he has his raw back roasted over the fire and he is examined and called upon to confess." In some cases, a man who had just been knouted was taken down and tied to this kind of pole, so that the back being roasted was already raw and bleeding from the whip. Or a man still suspended in the air after receiving the knout would have his bleeding back touched and probed with a red-hot iron.

In general, executions in Russia were similar to those in other countries. Offenders were burned to death, hanged or beheaded. Victims were burned in the middle of a pile of logs filled with straw. Beheading required the victim to place his head on a block and submit to the blow of an axe or sword. This easy, instant death was sometimes made harder by first lopping off the hands and feet. Executions of this kind were so common, wrote one Dutch traveler, "that if one is performed at one end of town, in the other they seldom know anything of it." Counterfeiters were punished by taking their false coins, melting them down and pouring the molten metal down their throats. Rapists were castrated.

Although public torture and execution were no novelty to any seventeenth-century European, what struck most visitors to Russia was the stoicism, "the unconquerable stubbornness" with which most Russians accepted these terrible agonies. They steadfastly resisted hideous pain, refusing to betray friends, and when condemned to death they went meekly and calmly to the gallows or block. An observer in Astrachan saw thirty rebels beheaded in less than half an hour. There was no noise or clamor. The condemned men simply went to the block and laid their heads in the pools of blood left by their predecessors. None even had his hands tied behind him.

This incredible hardiness and unconquerable endurance of pain astonished not only foreigners but also Peter himself. Once, after a man had been tortured four times by knout and fire, Peter approached him in sheer wonder and asked how he could stand such great pain. The man was happy to talk about it and revealed to Peter the existence of a torture society of which he was a member. He explained that nobody was admitted without first being tortured, and that thereafter promotion within the society rested on being able to accept higher grades of torture. To this bizarre group, the knout was nothing. "The sharpest pain of all," he explained to Peter, "is when a burning coal is placed in the ear; nor is it less painful when the head is

shaved and extremely cold water is let fall slowly drop by drop upon it from a height."

More astonishing and even touching was the fact that sometimes the same Russians who could withstand the knout and fire and remain mute until death would break if handled with kindness. This happened with the man who told Peter of the torture society. He had refused to utter a word of confession although he had been tortured four times. Peter, seeing that he was invulnerable to pain, walked up to him and kissed him, saying, "It's no secret to me that you know about the plot against me. You have been punished enough. Now confess of your own accord out of the love you owe me as your sovereign. And I swear, by the God who has made me tsar, not only to completely pardon you, but in addition, as a special mark of my clemency, to make you a colonel." This unorthodox approach so unnerved and moved the prisoner that he took the Tsar in his arms and said, "For me, this is the greatest torture of all. There is no other way you could have made me speak." He told Peter everything, and the Tsar, true to the bargain, pardoned him and promoted him to colonel.

THE SEVENTEENTH CENTURY, like all the centuries before and since, was a time of hideous cruelty. Torture was practiced in all countries and for a variety of crimes, particularly those against the sovereign or the state. Usually, since the sovereign *was* the state, any form of opposition from assassination down to the mildest grumbling against him was classified as treason and punished accordingly. But a man could also be tortured and killed for attending the wrong church or for picking a pocket.

Throughout Europe, those who touched the person or the dignity of the king suffered the full fury of the law. In France, in 1613, the assassin of Henri IV was torn to pieces by four horses in the Place de l'Hôtel de Ville in front of a huge crowd of Parisians who brought their children and their picnic lunches. A sixty-year-old Frenchman had his tongue torn out and was sent to the galleys for insulting the Sun King. Ordinary criminals in France were beheaded, burned or broken alive on the wheel. In Italy, travelers complained of the public gallows: "We see so much human flesh along the highways that trips are disagreeable." In England, the "peine forte et dur" was applied to criminals: A board was placed on the victim's chest and, one by one, weights were added until breath and life were crushed out. The penalty for treason in England was to be hanged, drawn and quartered. In 1660, Samuel Pepys wrote in his diary, "I went out to Charing Cross to see Major-General Harrison hanged, drawn and quartered, which was done there, he looking as cheerfully as any man could do in that condition. He was presently cut down and his head and heart shown to the people at which there were great shouts of joy."

Nor was cruel retribution restricted to political crimes. Witches were burned in England during Peter's lifetime and still were being hanged a century later. In 1692, six years before the Streltsy revolt, twenty young women and two dogs were hanged for witchcraft in Salem, Massachusetts. Through most of the eighteenth century, Englishmen were executed for stealing five shillings, and women were hanged for stealing a handkerchief. In the Royal Navy, infractions of discipline were commonly punished with a cat-o'-nine-tails. These floggings, which often resulted in death, were not abolished until 1881.

All this is told to provide perspective. Few of us in the twentieth century will wish to be hypocritically surprised at the barbarism of earlier times. Nations still execute traitors. Torture and mass executions still take place, both in war and in peace, made more efficient and more indiscriminate now by the instruments of modern technology. In our own time, the authorities of more than sixty nations, among them Germans, Russians, Frenchmen, Britons, Americans, Japanese, Vietnamese, Koreans, Filipinos, Hungarians, Spaniards, Turks, Greeks, Brazilians, Chileans, Uruguayans, Paraguayans, Iranians, Iraqis, Ugandans and Indonesians, have tortured on behalf of the state. Few centuries can claim a more hellish achievement than Auschwitz. Today, in psychiatric hospitals, Soviet political dissidents are tortured with destructive drugs designed not only to break down resistance but to subvert personality. And only modern technology can provide a spectacle such as the hanging of fourteen Jews in Bagdad's Liberation Square before a crowd of half a million . . . and, for those who couldn't be present, hours of television close-ups of the dangling bodies.

In Peter's time, as in ours, torture was carried out to gather information, and public execution to deter further crimes. The fact that innocent men have confessed to escape further pain has never stopped torture, nor has the execution of criminals ever stopped crime. Undeniably, the state has a right to defend itself against people who break its laws, and perhaps even a duty to try to deter future infringements, but how far into repression and cruelty can a state or society descend before the means no longer justify the end? It is a question as old as political theory, and it will not be answered here. But it should be borne in mind when we read what Peter did.

AT THE TSAR'S COMMAND, Prince Romodanovsky brought all the captured traitors to Preobrazhenskoe and constructed fourteen torture chambers to receive them. Six days a week (Sunday was a day of rest), week after week, in what became an assembly line of torture, all the surviving prisoners, 1,714 men, were examined. Half of September and most of October were spent in lashing and burning the Streltsy with knout and flame. Those who had already confessed to one charge were reinterrogated on another. As soon as

one rebel had revealed some new bit of information, all those who had already been questioned were dragged back in for reexamination on this point. Those who had lost their strength and almost their minds under torture were handed over to doctors to be restored by treatment so that they might be questioned further under new, excruciating tortures.

Major Karpakov, deeply implicated as one of the leaders of the rebellion, after being knouted and having his back roasted by fire, lost the power to speak and fainted. Worried that he might die prematurely, Romodanovsky put him in the care of Peter's personal physician, Dr. Carbonari. As soon as he was restored, he was again subjected to torture. A second officer who had also lost the power to speak was handed over to Dr. Carbonari for rehabilitation. By mistake, the doctor left his knife behind in the cell after working over the prisoner. The officer, unwilling that his life, which he knew was almost ended, be restored so that he could suffer more tortures, seized the knife and tried to cut his own throat. But he was already too weak and could not cut deeply enough. Before he could do himself fatal damage, his hand went limp and he fainted. He was discovered, partially cured and returned to torture.

All of Peter's principal friends and lieutenants were involved in the carnage. Men such as Romodanovsky, Boris Golitsyn, Shein, Streshnev, Peter Prozorovsky, Michael Cherkassky, Vladimir Dolgoruky, Ivan Troekurov, Fedor Shcherbatov and Peter's old tutor and Prince-Pope, Zotov, were chosen to participate, as a special mark of the Tsar's confidence. If the plot had spread and boyars were involved, Peter counted on these comrades to discover and faithfully report it. Peter himself, plagued by suspicion and fierce with anger, was often present and, sometimes wielding his big, ivory-handled cane, personally questioned those who seemed most guilty.

But the Streltsy did not break easily, and their sheer endurance sometimes drove the Tsar to rage. "While one accomplice or rebel was being tied to a rack," wrote Korb,

> his lamentations gave rise to a hope that truth might be pressed from him by torments; but no, for as soon as his body began to be stretched with the rope, besides the horrible cracking of his members which were being torn from their natural sockets, he remained mute, even when twenty strokes of the knout were superadded, as if the accumulation of his pain were too great to afflict the senses. All believed that the man must be crushed with excess of calamity to such a degree that he must have lost the power of moaning and of speech. So he was loosed from the infamous rack and rope, and then asked if he knew the persons present in the torture chamber. To the astonishment of all, he enumerated every one of them. But when they put a fresh question about the treason, once more he became

utterly dumb, and did not break silence during a whole quarter of an hour, while he was roasted by a fire by the Tsar's command. The Tsar, tired at last of this exceedingly wicked stubbornness, furiously raised the stick which he happened to have in his hand, and thrust it so violently into his jaws—clenched in obstinate silence—to break them open, and make him give tongue and speak. And these words too that fell from the raging man, "Confess, beast, confess!" loudly proclaimed how great was his wrath.

Although the interrogations were supposedly conducted in secret, all Moscow knew that something terrible was happening. Yet, Peter was anxious to hide the savage work, especially from foreigners; aware of the reaction that this wave of terror would produce in the Western courts he had just visited, he attempted to seal off his torture chambers from Western eyes and ears. Nevertheless, rumors provoked enormous curiosity. One group of Western diplomats ventured out to Preobrazhenskoe on horseback to see what they could learn. Passing three houses from which came appalling howls and groans, they stopped and dismounted in front of a fourth which emitted even more atrocious shrieks. Entering, they were startled to see the Tsar, Lev Naryshkin and Romodanovsky. As they retreated, Naryshkin asked them who they were and why they had come. Angrily, he ordered them to go to Romodanovsky's house so that the matter could be looked into. Mounting their horses, the diplomats refused, telling Naryshkin that if he had anything to say to them, he could come to their embassy and say it there. Russian soldiers appeared and a Guards officer attempted to drag one of the diplomats out of his saddle. Desperately, the unwelcome visitors spurred their horses and galloped to safety past the soldiers running to block their way.

Eventually, reports of the horror reached such magnitude that the Patriarch took it upon himself to go to Peter to beg for mercy. He went carrying an image of the Blessed Virgin, reminding Peter of the humanity of all men and asking for the exercise of mercy. Peter, resenting the intrusion of spiritual authority on temporal matters, replied to the churchman with great feeling: "What are you doing with that image and what business is it of yours to come here? Leave immediately and put that image in a place where it may be venerated. Know that I reverence God and His Most Holy Mother more earnestly, perhaps, than you do. But it is the duty of my sovereign office, and a duty that I owe to God, to save my people from harm and to prosecute with public vengeance crimes that lead to the common ruin." In this case, Peter continued, justice and harshness were linked, the gangrene ran deep in the body politic and could be cut out only with iron and fire. Moscow, he said, would be saved not by pity but by cruelty.

Everyone fell within the sweep of the Tsar's wrath. Priests discovered to have prayed for the success of the rebellion were condemned to execution. The wife of a minor official, passing in front of a gibbet erected before the Kremlin, said of the men hanging there, "Alas! Who knows whether you were innocent or guilty?" She was overheard and denounced as one who expressed sympathy for condemned traitors, and she and her husband were arrested and examined. Able to prove that she was only expressing compassion for all humans who suffered, the couple escaped death, but was nevertheless exiled from Moscow.

Despite the wretched forced confessions, gasped between screams or torn from groaning, half-conscious men, Peter learned little more than Shein had already learned: that the Streltsy had meant to seize the capital, burn the German Suburb, kill the boyars and ask Sophia to rule them. If she refused, they would ask the eight-year-old Tsarevich Alexis and, as a last resort, Sophia's former lover, Prince Vasily Golitsyn, "for he had always been merciful to us." Peter did learn that no boyar or important member of the government or the nobility had been involved, but the most important questions went unanswered: Had there been a plot by important persons against his life and throne? And, most importantly, had Sophia known about or encouraged the uprising in advance?

Peter was deeply suspicious of his sister and could not believe that she was not always intriguing against him. To confirm his suspicions, a number of women, including wives of the Streltsy and all of Sophia's female attendants, were examined. Two chambermaids were brought to the torture rooms and stripped naked to the waist. One had already received several blows of the knout when Peter entered. He noticed that she was pregnant and for this reason absolved her from further torture, but both women were condemned to death.

Under torture, a Streltsy, Vaska Alexeev, declared that two letters purporting to be from Sophia had been sent to the Streltsy camp and been read aloud to the soldiers. These letters supposedly urged the Streltsy to march on Moscow, seize the Kremlin and summon the Tsarevna to the throne. According to one account, the letters were smuggled out of Sophia's rooms inside loaves of bread given by Sophia to old beggar women. Other letters, less inflammatory, had been written by Sophia's sister Martha, informing Sophia that the Streltsy were marching on Moscow.

Peter went to Novodevichy himself to interrogate Sophia. There was no question of torture; according to one account, he alternated between weeping with her over the fate that had made them antagonists, and threatening her with death, using the example of Elizabeth I of England and Mary Queen of Scots. Sophia denied that she had ever written to the Streltsy. When he suggested that she might have reminded them that she could be called back to rule, she told him straightforwardly that on this

matter they needed no letter from her; they would certainly remember that she had ruled the state for seven years. In the end, Peter learned nothing from her. He spared his sister's life, but decided that she must be more closely restricted. She was forced to shave her head and take religious vows, as the nun Susanna. He confined her permanently to Novodevichy, where she was guarded by one hundred soldiers and permitted to have no visitors. She lived in this fashion for another six years and died at forty-seven in 1704. Her sisters Martha and Catherine Miloslavskaya (also Peter's half-sisters) were politically exonerated, but Martha, too, was sent to a convent for the rest of her days.

THE FIRST EXECUTIONS of the condemned Streltsy took place on October 10 at Preobrazhenskoe. Behind the barracks, a bare field rose into a steep hill, and at the top the gallows were placed. A regiment of Guards was drawn up between the execution site and the large crowd of spectators, pushing and shoving, craning their necks to see. The Streltsy, many of whom could no longer walk, arrived in a procession of small carts, each containing two men seated back to back, each holding a lighted candle. Almost without exception, the condemned men were silent, but their wives and children, running beside the carts, filled the air with shrieks and calamitous sobbing. As the carts rumbled across the brook that separated the gallows from the crowd, the individual cries rose into a loud, collective wail.

When all the carts had arrived, Peter, wearing the green Polish coat given him by Augustus, appeared with his boyars near the spot where the ambassadors of the Hapsburg empire, Poland and Denmark were watching from their carriages. As the sentence was being read, Peter shouted to the crowd to listen well. Then the guilty men began walking to the gallows, dragging logs tied to their feet to prevent escape. Each man tried to climb the gallows unaided, but some had to be helped. At the top, each made the sign of the cross in four directions and covered his own face with a piece of linen. Some put their heads in the nooses and jumped from the gallows, hoping to break their necks and find a quick end. In general, the Streltsy met death with great calm, following one another without any great sadness on their faces. Because the regular executioners were unable to handle so many, Peter ordered several military officers to mount the gallows and help with the work. That night, Korb reported, Peter went to supper at General Gordon's. He sat in gloomy silence, commenting only on the stubborn resistance of the men who had died.

This grim pageant was only the first of many similar scenes that autumn and winter. Every few days, several score or more were executed. Two hundred were hanged from the walls of the city on special beams extended out from the embrasures in the parapet, two Streltsy to each beam.

At each gate to the city, six more bodies swung from a gibbet, a reminder to all who entered of the fruits of treason. On October 11, 144 were hanged in Red Square, on beams projecting through the crenellations in the Kremlin wall. One hundred and nine were beheaded by axe and sword over an open trench at Preobrazhenskoe. Three brothers, among the most stubborn of the rebels, were executed in Red Square, two being broken on the wheel and left to die slowly while the third was beheaded before their eyes. The two survivors complained bitterly at the injustice of their brother being permitted to die so quickly and easily.

For some, there were special humiliations. For the regimental priests who had encouraged the Streltsy, a gibbet constructed in the shape of a cross was erected in front of St. Basil's Cathedral. The priests were hanged by the court jester, dressed for the occasion in clerical robes. To make the connection between the Streltsy and Sophia crystal clear, 196 were hanged from a huge square gallows erected near Novodevichy Convent, where the Tsarevna was imprisoned. Three, the supposed ringleaders, were strung up directly outside the window of Sophia's room, with one of the corpses holding a piece of paper representing the Streltsy petition asking her to rule. They remained dangling, near enough for her to touch, for the rest of the winter.

Not all the men of the four rebellious regiments were executed. Peter reduced the sentences of 500 soldiers under twenty years of age from death to branding on the right cheek and exile. Others had their noses or ears lopped off to mark them hideously as participants in treason. Throughout Peter's reign, noseless, earless, branded men, evidence of both the Tsar's wrath and his mercy, roamed the edges of his realm.

KORB REPORTED that in his vengeful fury Peter forced a number of his favorites to act as executioners. On October 23, according to Korb, the boyars who constituted the council at which the Streltsy were condemned were summoned to Preobrazhenskoe and ordered to carry out executions themselves. To each boyar a Strelets was brought and an axe was given, with the command that he decapitate the man before him. Some took the axe with trembling hands, aimed poorly and struck without sufficient force. One boyar struck far too low, hitting his victim in the middle of the back and almost cutting him in half. With the creature writhing, screaming and bleeding in front of him, the boyar could not finish his task.

In this grisly work, two apparently distinguished themselves. Prince Romodanovsky, already renowned for his relentless prosecution of the investigation in the torture chambers, beheaded four Streltsy, according to Korb. Romodanovsky's grim passion, "surpassing all the rest in cruelty," perhaps had root in the murder of his father by the Streltsy in 1682.

Alexander Menshikov, the Tsar's young favorite, eager to please, later boasted of having cut off twenty heads. Only the foreigners among the Tsar's intimates refused, saying that it was not the custom of their countries for men of their kind to act as executioners. Peter, Korb says, surveyed the whole proceeding from his saddle, frowning with displeasure when he saw a boyar, pale and trembling, reluctant to accept the axe.

Korb also says that Peter himself beheaded some of the Streltsy. The Austrian secretary declared that on the day of the first public executions at Preobrazhenskoe he was standing with a German major in Peter's army. Leaving Korb, the major pressed forward through the crowd and eventually returned to tell Korb that he had seen Peter personally decapitate five of the Streltsy. On another day later in the fall, Korb says, "it was reported by a number of persons that today again the Tsar had himself executed public vengeance upon some traitors." Most historians—Western and Russian, pre-Revolutionary and Soviet—have rejected this hearsay evidence. Those who have already found in Peter an excessive violence and brutality will have no difficulty imagining him personally wielding an executioner's axe. He did indeed become violent when he was angry, and he was enraged at these mutineers who, once again, had raised their swords against his throne; to him it was treason that was immoral, not its punishment. Those who do not wish to believe that the Tsar became an executioner can take solace in the fact that neither Korb nor his Austrian colleagues actually witnessed the event described; their evidence could not be used in a modern court.

If there is doubt on this point, there is none on the matter of Peter's responsibility for the mass tortures and death, or on the question of his presence in the torture chambers while flesh was being flayed or burned. To us this seems brutal and degrading; to Peter it seemed necessary. He was indignant, he was angry, and he wanted to hear the truth himself. "So great a distrust of his boyars had taken possession of the Tsar's mind," says Korb, "that he was afraid to entrust them with the smallest part of this examination, preferring rather to devise the interrogatories and to examine the accused [himself]." Besides, Peter never hesitated to be a participant in the enterprises he commanded, whether on the battlefield, on shipboard or in the torture chamber. He had decreed the interrogation and destruction of the Streltsy; he would not sit back and wait for someone to bring him news that his command had been obeyed.

Yet, Peter was not a sadist. He did not enjoy seeing people tortured—he did not, for instance, set bears on people merely to see what would happen, as Ivan the Terrible had done. He tortured for practical reasons of state: to extract information. He executed as punishment for treason. To him these were natural, traditional and even moral actions. Few of his seventeenth-century contemporaries, Russian or European, would have argued this

principle. In fact, at that moment in Russian history, what counted was not the morality of Peter's act but its effect. The destruction of the Streltsy inspired in the Russian people a belief in Peter's harsh, implacable will, and proclaimed his iron determination to tolerate no opposition to his rule. Thereafter, despite his Western clothes and tastes, his people knew that they had no choice except to follow. For beneath the Western clothes beat the heart of a Muscovite tsar.

This was part of Peter's plan. He did not destroy the Streltsy simply to wreak vengeance, or to expose one specific plot, but to make an example, to terrify, to force submission. The lesson of the Streltsy, burned in blood and fire, was one from which we today recoil, but it cemented Peter's reign. It gave him the power to work his reforms and—for better or worse—to revolutionize Russian society.

In the West from which Peter had so recently returned and where he hoped to build a new image of his country, the news was shocking. Even the common understanding that a sovereign could not tolerate treason was swept aside by reports of the scale of the Preobrazhenskoe tortures and executions. Everywhere, it seemed to confirm the beliefs of those who had said that Muscovy was an incorrigibly barbarous nation and its ruler a cruel Oriental tyrant. In England, Bishop Burnet recalled his appraisal of Peter: "How long he is to be the scourge of that nation, or of his neighbors, God only knows."

That Peter was aware of how the West would regard his actions was shown by his desire to conceal the tortures, if not the executions, from the foreign diplomats in Moscow. Subsequently, when Korb's diary was published in Vienna (it was printed in Latin, but translated into Russian for Peter's benefit), the Tsar reacted violently. It precipitated a serious diplomatic crisis until the Emperor Leopold I agreed to destroy all unsold copies. Even those copies that had been sold were pursued by the Tsar's agents, trying to buy back every one they could.

WHILE THE FOUR REGIMENTS of Streltsy which had rebelled were being punished, the rest of the Streltsy, including the six regiments lately sent from Moscow to garrison Azov, had become dangerously restless and were threatening to join the Don Cossacks and march on Moscow. "There are boyars in Moscow, Germans in Azov, demons in the water and worms in the earth," was the way they expressed their unhappiness with the world around them. Then came the news of the total destruction of their comrades, and the Streltsy in Azov thought better of their intended subordination and remained at their posts.

Despite this success of his grim policy, Peter decided that he could no longer tolerate the Streltsy at all. Especially after this bloody repression,

the hatred of the survivors would only increase and the state might once again be subjected to upheaval. Of the 2,000 Streltsy who had revolted, nearly 1,200 had been executed. Their widows and children were expelled from Moscow and people everywhere were forbidden to give them assistance except to employ them as servants on estates far from the capital. The following spring, Peter disbanded the remaining sixteen Streltsy regiments. Their houses and lands in Moscow were confiscated and they were sent into exile in Siberia and other distant regions to become simple villagers. They were forbidden ever to take up arms again, and the local governors were warned against trying to recruit them for military service. Later, when the Great Northern War against Sweden demanded constant replenishments of manpower, Peter reversed this decision, and several regiments of former Streltsy were formed under close control. In 1708, after a final revolt of the Streltsy stationed in the distant city of Astrachan, the organization was permanently abolished.

Thus, at last Peter was done with the turbulent, domineering Muscovite soldier-tradesmen who had so influenced and terrorized his youth. The Streltsy were swept away, and with them the only serious armed opposition to his policies and the main obstacle to his reorganization of the army. They were replaced with his own creation, the militarily up-to-date and efficient Guards regiments, trained on the Western model and imbued with support for Peter's policies. Ironically, the Russian Guards officers, recruited almost solely from the families of land-owning gentry, quickly came to play the political role to which the Streltsy had unsuccessfully aspired. As long as the sovereign's will was as strong as Peter's, they were submissive and obedient. But when the sovereign was a woman (as happened four times within the century after Peter's death) or a child (as happened twice), and in moments of interregnum when there was no sovereign and the succession was in doubt, then the Guards themselves helped to choose who would rule. The Streltsy, had they still existed, might have permitted themselves a wry laugh at this turn of events. More likely, however, nervous lest the spirit of Peter might still be watching over them, they would have held their tongues in fearful silence.

20

AMONG FRIENDS

THAT AUTUMN AND WINTER, Russia first felt the full weight of Peter's will. The torture and execution of the Streltsy were its grimmest and most dramatic manifestation, but even as the torture fires were burning, frightened Muscovites and foreign observers began to discern a common thread in all his actions. The destruction of the Streltsy, the truncating of beards and sleeves, the changes in the calendar and the money, the incarceration of the Tsaritsa, the mockery of church rituals, the ship building at Voronezh— all were part of a single purpose: to destroy the old and bring in the new; to move the huge, inert mass of his countrymen toward a more modern, more Western way of life.

Although these blows at the Old Russia have been described separately, they were taking place at the same time. From days in the torture chambers at Preobrazhenskoe, Peter went directly to nights of festivity and a succession of feasts and entertainments. Almost every night during that fearful autumn and winter, Peter attended a banquet, a masquerade, a wedding, a christening, a reception for foreign ambassadors or a mock-religious ceremony with his Drunken Synod. He did this partly to drive out his anger at the rebellion and his gloom at the terrible work of retribution and partly because he was happy, after eighteen months in the West, to be home again with friends.

On many of these occasions, Anna Mons was present. Already Peter's mistress before he left with the Great Embassy, now—with Eudoxia out of the way—the lady who described herself as the Tsar's "loyal friend" stepped forward into public recognition: on his arm, she attended the christening of the son of the Danish ambassador; on her birthday, Peter came to dine at her mother's house. Her presence and that of a small but increasing number of other women broke a precedent that carousing evenings involving Russian males should be exclusively male. Nor were these banqueters exclusively Russian. In all of these activities, the ambassa-

dors of Denmark, Poland, Austria and Brandenburg were included in Peter's company of favorites. Indeed, Peter gloried in their presence; they gave him a sense of the closeness of Western culture and they, more than his boyars, could understand his hopes and ambitions. Their presence was fortunate for history—their reports and diaries provide vivid descriptions of life at Peter's court.

The fullest and most colorful of these accounts is that of Johann-Georg Korb, secretary to a visiting Austrian ambassador. Not always reliable, often repeating hearsay, Korb was nevertheless an industrious reporter who recorded every sight he saw as well as every rumor he heard. His pages give a rich picture of Peter's life in the few years between his return from the West and his plunging into the great war which would dominate the rest of his life and reign.

The young Austrian diplomat arrived in Moscow in April 1698 when Peter was still in London. The entry of his ambassador into the Russian capital was conducted with great pomp, and the traditional formal banquet welcoming the embassy was opulent; in all, the guests counted at least 108 different dishes.

Peter received the embassy when he returned. The audience was held at Lefort's house.

Numbers of magnates were around His Majesty and amidst them all the Tsar stood preeminent, with a handsome figure and lofty look. We made our reverential obeisances which His Majesty acknowledged with a gracious nod which augured kindness. . . . The Tsar admitted the Lord Envoy and all the officials of the embassy and the missionaries present to kiss his hands.

But Korb and his colleagues quickly found that the formality of this welcome was only a façade. In fact, Peter could not tolerate official functions of this kind, and when forced to participate he became awkward and confused. Dressed in ceremonial finery, standing or sitting on the throne, listening to newly accredited ambassadors, was painful for him and he would breathe heavily, grow red in the face and perspire. He considered, as Korb was to learn, that it was "a barbarous and inhuman law enacted against kings alone that prevented them from enjoying the society of mankind." He rejected such laws and dined and talked with his companions, with German officers, with merchants, with ambassadors of foreign countries— in short, with anyone he liked. When he was ready to eat, no flourishes of trumpets sounded. Instead, someone shouted, "The Tsar wants to eat!" Then, meat and drink were placed on the table in no special order, and each reached for what he wanted.

To the Austrian visitors, accustomed to the formal banquets of the Hofburg Palace in Vienna, these Moscow banquets seemed informal and rowdy. Korb wrote:

The Tsar ordered a dinner to be prepared by General Lefort and all the ambassadors and chief boyars to be invited. The Tsar came later than usual, having been engaged in important business. Even at table, without taking notice of the presence of the ambassadors, he still continued discussing some points with his boyars, but the consultation was almost an altercation, neither words nor hands being spared, everyone excited beyond measure, each defending his own opinion with obstinacy, and with a warmth perilous beneath the eye of His Majesty. Two, whose lower rank excused them from mingling in this knotty discussion, sought favor by trying to hit one another's heads with the bread which they found upon the table; for all, in their own way, did their best to give genuine proofs of their true origin. Yet even among the Muscovite guests some there were whose more modest speech betokened high character of soul. An undisturbable gravity of manners was remarkable in the aged Prince Lev Cherkassky; ripe prudence of counsel characterized Boyar Golovin; an apt knowledge of public affairs was distinguishable in Artemonowicz. These men shone all the more as their species was evidently very rare. Artemonowicz, indignant that such a variety of madmen should be admitted to a royal banquet, exclaimed aloud in Latin, "The whole place is full of fools," that his words might more easily reach the ears of those who knew Latin.

Peter used these banquets to conduct all kinds of business:

Dancing followed immediately after the table was removed and now took place the farewell to the envoy of the Poles. The Tsar broke hastily away, quite unexpectedly from the gay crowd into a place next to the dining room where the glasses and drinking cups were kept, commanding the Polish ambassador to follow him. The whole body of guests, eager to know what was going on, crowded after them. Impeded by their own haste, they had not all got into the room when the letters of credentials had been handed back to the Polish envoy, and the Tsar, coming out of the room, bumped into those who were still pushing and shoving to get in.

For all their disdainful attitude, the Westerners sometimes behaved as badly and as childishly as the Muscovites. At one dinner for the ambassadors

of Denmark and Poland, the Polish ambassador received twenty-five dishes from the Tsar's table and the Dane merely twenty-two. The Dane was indignant, and his pique was mollified only when he was allowed to precede his Polish rival at the moment of kissing the royal hands upon departure. Thereupon, the foolish Dane so preened and strutted his minor victory that the Pole was furious. Eventually, Peter heard of the argument and, hating all protocol, cried out, "Both of them are donkeys!"

Some of the foreign ambassadors tended to make the same mistake that Peter's boyars occasionally made: having the Tsar among them as comrade and fellow carouser, they forgot who the tall man with whom they were heatedly arguing actually was. Then, suddenly, the argument would turn a corner and they would be brought up sharply with the perilous fact that they were challenging a man who was an absolute autocrat, the sole arbiter of life and death for an entire nation. Some of these arguments were relatively mild. At one dinner, Peter was telling the company that in Vienna he had been getting fat, but on his return the nature of the fare in Poland had made him quite slender again. The Polish ambassador, a man of great girth, disputed this, saying that he had been brought up in Poland and owed amplitude to the Polish diet. Peter shot back, "It was not in Poland, but here in Moscow that you crammed yourself"—the Pole, like all ambassadors, was provided with his food and expenses by the host government. The Pole, wisely, let the matter drop.

On another occasion,

> during dinner, there was discussion about the differences between countries; the one that lay next to Muscovy [Korb does not say which one] was very ill-spoken of. The ambassador who came from there replied for his part that he had noticed a great many things in Muscovy that were deserving of censure. The Tsar retorted: "If thou were a subject of mine, I would add thee as a companion to those of mine that are now hanging from the gibbet—for I well know what thy speech alludes to."
>
> The Tsar later found an opportunity of setting the same personage to dance with his fool, a laughing-stock of the court, amidst a general titter. And yet the ambassador [danced away, thinking that Peter's jest was meant as a sign of affection], not understanding what a shameful trick was played on him until the Imperial ambassador had quietly given him warning not to forget the dignity of his office.

PETER'S MOODS were strange and unpredictable, given to violent swings between elation and sudden anger. One minute he was jovial, happy to be in

the company of his friends, jesting over the surprising appearance of a newly shaven companion, yet a few minutes later he could sink into deep, irritable gloom or explode with sudden rage. At one banquet, Peter angrily accused Shein of selling offices in the army for cash. Shein denied it, and Peter stormed out of the room to question soldiers on sentry duty around Lefort's house

to learn from them how many colonels and other regimental officers the General-in-Chief had made without reference to merit, merely for money.

Continuing this account, Korb describes what happened next:

In a short time when he came back, his wrath had grown to such a pitch that he drew his sword, and facing the General-in-Chief horrified the guests with this threat: "By striking thus, I will mar thy mal government." Boiling over with well-grounded anger, he appealed to Prince Romodanovsky and to Zotov. But finding them excuse the General-in-Chief, he grew so hot that he startled all the guests by striking right and left, he knew not where, with his drawn sword. Prince Romodanovsky had to complain of a cut finger and another of a slight wound on the head. Zotov was hurt in the hand as the sword was returning from a stroke. A blow far more deadly was aiming at the General-in-Chief [Shein], who beyond doubt would have been stretched in his gore by the Tsar's right hand, had not General Lefort (who was almost the only one that might have ventured it), catching the Tsar in his arms, drawn back his hand from the stroke. But the Tsar, taking it ill that any person should dare to hinder him from the sating of his most just wrath, wheeled around upon the spot, and struck his unwelcome impeder a hard blow on the back. He [Lefort] is the only one that knew what remedy to apply; none of the Muscovites is more beloved by the Tsar than he. . . . This man [Lefort] so mitigated his [Peter's] ire, that, threatening only, he abstained from murder. Merriment followed this dire tempest. The Tsar with a face full of smiles, was present at the dancing, and to show his mirth, commanded the musicians to play the tunes to which he had danced at his most beloved lord and brother's [King Augustus] when that most august host was entertaining exalted guests. Two young ladies, departing by stealth, were, at the order of the Tsar, brought back by soldiers. Again, twenty-five great guns saluted the toasts, and the hilarity of the fete was protracted till half past five in the morning.

The following day, the promotions made by Shein were canceled, and Patrick Gordon was thereafter placed in charge of deciding which officers should be advanced in rank.

This was not the only occasion on which Lefort accepted Peter's blows or thrust himself forward between the Tsar and an intended victim of Peter's wrath. On October 18, Peter was dining again at Lefort's when, says Korb, "an inexplicable whirlwind troubled the gaieties. Seizing upon General Lefort and flinging him to the floor, His Tsarish Majesty kicked him." Lefort, however, was almost the only man who could stay Peter's wrath. At a banquet for 200 of the nobility at Lefort's house, an argument began between two of the former regents, Peter's uncle Lev Naryshkin and Prince Boris Golitsyn. Peter was so exasperated that "he loudly threatened he would cut short the dispute with the head of one or the other—whichever should be found most at fault. He commissioned Prince Romodanovsky to examine the affair and with a violent blow of his clenched fist, thrust back General Lefort who was coming up to mitigate his fury."

Korb especially disliked Prince Fedor Romodanovsky, the tall, heavy-browed Governor of Moscow and Mock-Tsar, who was also Peter's Chief of Police. Romodanovsky was a grim figure with a leaden sense of humor. He enjoyed forcing his guests to drink a large cup of pepper brandy by having the cup presented in the paws of a large, upright, trained bear; if the cup was refused, the bear proceeded to pull off the hat, wig and other articles of clothing of the reluctant guest. He disdained foreigners. Once he kidnapped a young German interpreter who worked for one of the Tsar's physicians and returned him only when the doctor complained to Lefort. Another time, he arrested a foreign physician. When, on release, the doctor "inquired of Prince Romodanovsky why he was so long kept in confinement, [he] got no answer other than that it was done to vex him."

ON OCTOBER 12, Korb reported, "The ground was covered with a dense fall of snow and everything was frozen up with the intense cold." Both the feasts and the executions went on, although Peter soon left Moscow to visit the shipyard at Voronezh. Before the holidays, however, the Tsar was back. "Today being Christmas eve," Korb's journal continued,

> which is preceded by a Russian fast of seven weeks, all the markets and public thoroughfares are seen to be filled to overflowing with meats. Here you have an incredible multitude of geese; in another place such a store of pigs already killed that you would think it enough to last the whole year. The number of oxen killed is in

proportion. Fowl of every kind looked as if they had flown together
from all of Muscovy to this one city. It was useless to attempt naming
all the varieties. It is enough to say that everything one could wish
for was to be had.

On Christmas, Korb saw the celebration of the Nativity mingled with
the horseplay of the Mock-Synod:

> The false Patriarch with his sham followers and the rest in eighty
> sledges make the round of the city and the German Suburb, carrying
> crosses, miters and other insignia of their assumed dignities. They all
> stop at the houses of the richer Muscovites and German officers and
> sing the praises of the newborn Deity in strains for which the in-
> habitants of those houses have to pay dearly. After they had sung the
> praises of the newborn Deity at his house, General Lefort received
> them all with pleasanter music, banqueting and dancing.

These raucous Christmas carolers expected a handsome reward for their
effort. When it was not sufficiently generous, the result was worse for the
householder:

> The wealthiest merchant of Muscovy, whose name is Filadilov,
> gave such offense by having only presented twelve roubles to the
> Tsar and his boyars when they sang the praises of God newborn at
> his house, that the Tsar, with all possible speed, sent off a hundred
> of the populace to the house of the merchant with a mandate to
> pay forthwith to every one of them a rouble each.

Feasting went on until Epiphany, when the traditional blessing of the
river took place beneath the Kremlin walls. Contrary to custom, the Tsar
did not seat himself with the Patriarch on his throne, but appeared in uniform at the head of his regiment, drawn up with other troops amounting to
12,000 men on the thick ice of the river. "The procession to the river, which
was frozen solid, was led by General Gordon's regiment, the exquisite red of
their new uniforms adding to their splendid appearance," wrote Korb.

> Then came the Preobrazhensky Regiment in handsome new green
> uniforms with the Tsar marching ahead as their colonel. There
> followed a third regiment, the Semyonovsky, in blue uniforms. Each
> regiment had a band of musicians. . . .
>   A place was marked off by rails on the river ice, with the regi-
> ments drawn up around it. Five hundred ecclesiastics, sub-deacons,
> deacons, priests, abbots, bishops and archbishops, robed in gold

and silver with gems and precious stones, lent an air of greater majesty. Before a splendid gold cross, twelve clerics bore a lantern with three burning wax lights. The Muscovites consider it unlawful and shameful for the cross to appear in public unattended by lights. An incredible multitude of people thronged every side. The streets were full, roofs of the houses were covered, the walls of the city were crowded with spectators.

When the clergy filled up the large space of the enclosure, the sacred ceremony began. Multitudes of wax candles were lighted. After the Almighty was invoked, the Metropolitan went around swinging his censer filled with smoking incense through the whole enclosure. In the middle, the ice was broken, allowing the water to appear like a well. Here he passed the censer three times, and hallowed the well, three times dipping the burning wax light into it. Nearby, on a pillar stood the standard bearer, holding the standard of the realm, white with a double-headed eagle embroidered in gold. It is unfurled once the clergy have entered the enclosure. Thereafter the standard bearer has to watch the ceremonies—the incensing, the blessings—each of which he indicated by waving the standard. His motions are closely observed by the regimental standard bearers, in order to wave at the same time he does.

When the benediction of the water is over, all the regimental standards approach and stand around to be duly sprinkled with the hallowed water. The Patriarch, or, in his absence, the Metropolitan, leaving the enclosure, then bestows this sprinkling on His Majesty the Tsar and all the soldiers. To complete, the artillery of all the regiments roared out, followed by a triple volley of musketry.

The bacchanals of autumn and winter reached a peak in the carnival week before the beginning of Lent. A key role in the bacchanal was played by the Mock-Synod, whose members trooped in mock-solemn procession to Lefort's palace to worship Bacchus. Korb watched them pass:

He that bore the assumed honors of the Patriarch was conspicuous with vestments proper to a bishop. Bacchus was decked with a miter and went stark naked to betoken lasciviousness to the lookers-on. Cupid and Venus were the insignia on his crozier lest there be any mistake about what flock he was pastor of. The remaining crowd of the Bacchanalians came after him, some carrying great bowls full of wine, others mead, others beer and brandy, that last joy of heated Bacchus. And as the wintry cold hindered their binding their laurel, they carried great dishes of dried tobacco leaves, with which, when ignited, they went to the remotest corners of the

palace, exhaling those most delectable odors and most pleasant incense to Bacchus from their smutty jaws. Two of those pipes through which some people are pleased to puff smoke, being set crosswise, served the scenic bishop to confirm the rites of consecration!

Many of the Western ambassadors were shocked by this parody, and Korb himself was amazed that "the cross, that most precious pledge of our redemption, was held up for mockery." But Peter saw no reason to conceal his games. During Lent, when the newly arrived ambassador of Brandenburg had presented his credentials,

the Tsar commanded him to stay for dinner which was splendid with the principal ambassadors and principal boyars present. After dinner, the Mock-Patriarch began to give toasts. He that drank did so on bended knee to revere the sham ecclesiastical dignitary and beg the favor of his benediction which he gave with two tobacco pipes in the shape of a cross. Only the Austrian ambassador withdrew furtively, saying that the sacred sign of our Christian faith was too holy to be involved in such jests. Dancing was going on in the room next to the festivities. . . . The curtains with which the place was handsomely decorated being drawn a little, the Tsarevich Alexis and [Peter's sister Natalya] were seen by the guests. The natural beauty of the Tsarevich [then nine years old] was wonderfully shown off by his civilized German dress and powdered wig. Natalya was escorted by the most distinguished of the Russian ladies. This day too beheld a great departure from Russian manners, which up to this forbade the female sex from appearing at public assemblies of men and at festive parties, for some were not only allowed to be at dinner, but also at the dancing afterward.

Meanwhile, as a grim accompaniment to this Mardi Gras, the execution of the Streltsy continued relentlessly. On February 28, thirty-six died in Red Square and 150 at Preobrazhenskoe. That same night, there was a splendid feast at Lefort's, after which the guests watched a glorious display of fireworks.

With the first week of March came Lent and, with it, an end to the twin carnivals of feasting and death. A calm descended on the city so serene that Korb noted,

The silence and modesty of this week is as remarkable as last week's tumult and fury. Neither shops nor markets are open, the courts did not sit, the judges had nothing to do. . . . With the most strict fast they

mortify the flesh on dry bread and fruits of the earth. It is such an unexpected metamorphosis that one can hardly believe one's eyes.

In the quietness of Lent, the authorities finally began to unstring the bodies of the Streltsy from the gibbets where they had hung through the winter and take them out for burial. "It was a horrible spectacle," said Korb. "Corpses lay huddled together in carts, many half-naked, all higgledy-piggledy. Like slaughtered sheep to market they were led to their graves."

Besides life at Peter's court, Korb observed many facets of ordinary life in Moscow. The Tsar decided to do something about the clamoring hordes of beggars who pursued citizens up and down the streets from the moment they left their doors until they entered another house. Frequently, the beggars managed to blend their pleas with a simultaneous deft picking of the victim's pockets. By decree, begging was forbidden and so was the encouragement of begging; anyone caught giving alms to beggars was fined five roubles. To deal with the beggars themselves, the Tsar attached a hospital to every church, personally endowed by himself, to provide for the poor. That the conditions in these hospitals may have been stark was suggested by another ambassadorial witness, who wrote, "This soon cleared the streets of those poor vagrants, many of whom chose to work rather than to be locked up in the hospitals."

Korb was astonished, even in those days of lawlessness in all countries, by the sheer number and audacity of the robbers of Moscow, who operated in packs and boldly took what they liked. Usually at night, but sometimes in broad daylight, they mugged and then frequently murdered their victims. There were mysterious, unsolved murders. A foreign sea captain dining with his wife at the house of a boyar was invited to go out for a night sleigh ride across the snow. When he and his host returned, they found that the wife's head had been cut off, and there were no clues as to the identity or motive of the assassin. Government officials were no safer than private citizens. On November 26, Korb wrote,

A courier sent off to His Majesty last night at Voronezh with letters and some valuable utensils was violently seized on the stone bridge at Moscow and robbed. The letters, with the seals broken, were found scattered on the bridge at daybreak, but where the utensils and the courier himself have been carried, there is no trace.

The courier, it was presumed, had been disposed of in the handiest way, by being "thrust beneath the ice into the waters of the river."

Foreigners had to be especially careful, as they were considered fair game not only by robbers but also by ordinary Muscovites. One of Korb's servants who knew Russian reported that he had just encountered a citizen

who mouthed a stream of oaths and threats against all foreigners: "You German dogs, you have been robbing long enough at your ease, but the day is coming when you shall suffer and pay the penalty." To catch a foreigner alone, especially if he was reeling with drink, provided some Muscovites with the rare opportunity for vindictive pleasure. Nor was it always safe to defend oneself against violence. Trying to reduce the number of deaths in the streets, Peter had made it a crime to draw a sword, pistol or knife when drunk, even if the weapon was raised in self-defense and even if it was not actually used. One night, an Austrian mining engineer named Urban was riding tipsily home from Moscow to the German Suburb when he was set upon by a Russian, first with words and then with fists. According to Korb: "Urban, losing patience, and indignant at being insulted by such a filthy rascal, and using the natural right of self-defense, drew a pistol. The ball which he wildly fired at his assailant merely grazed the fellow's head, but lest the complaints of the wounded man be fussed with a great noise to the Tsar's Majesty, Urban came to an amicable agreement with the fellow for four roubles to say nothing about it." But Peter did hear about it, and Urban was arrested and charged with a capital crime. When Urban's friends argued that the Austrian had been drunk, the Tsar replied that he would allow drunken scuffling to go unpunished, but not drunken shooting. Nevertheless, he reduced the punishment from death to knouting and, only on the continued pleas of the Austrian ambassador, finally canceled that.

Not that the robbers, when caught, were dealt with lightly. They went in batches to the rack and gallows; on a single day, seventy were hung. Still it did not stop their colleagues. For them, crime was a way of life and disobedience to the law so deeply ingrained that attempts to enforce it often aroused an indignant fury in those accustomed to breaking it. For example, although brandy was a state monopoly whose sale in private was strictly forbidden, it was being sold in a private house. Fifty soldiers were sent to seize the contraband. A battle took place, and three soldiers were killed. Far from being daunted or thinking of flight, the private brandy makers threatened even fiercer vengeance should the attempt at seizure be repeated.

In fact, the police and soldiers charged with enforcing the laws were themselves scarcely law-abiding. Korb observed that

> soldiers in Muscovy are in the habit of tormenting their prisoners in every way at their fancy, without respect of person or the matter of which they are accused. The soldiers are guilty of bruising them with their muskets and with sticks, and with thrusting them into the most beastly holes, especially the wealthy, whom they unblushingly say they will not cease from tormenting until they have paid a certain sum. Let a prisoner go willingly or unwillingly to jail, he is beaten all the same.

At one point in April 1699, the price of foodstuffs in Moscow rose precipitously. Investigation revealed that the soldiers, having been ordered to cart the bodies of the executed Streltsy out of the city before the spring thaw, had been commandeering peasant carts arriving in the city with wheat, oats and other grains, forcing the peasants to unload the food and reload their carts with bodies to carry away and bury, while the soldiers kept the food to eat or sell themselves. Faced with these thefts, the peasants had stopped bringing food into the city, and the prices of what was already there soared astronomically.

With the coming of milder weather, the foreign envoys were often invited to visit the lovely, blooming countryside outside Moscow. Korb and his ambassador were asked to a banquet at the estate of Peter's uncle Lev Naryshkin. "The rare profusion of viands," Korb said,

the costliness of the gold and silver plate, the variety and exquisiteness of the beverages, bespoke plainly the close blood relationship to the Tsar. After dinner there was an archery match. Nobody was excused because of the sport being strange to him or for his want of skill. A sheet of paper stuck on the ground was the target. The host perforated it several times amidst general applause. As the rain drove us from this pleasant exercise, we returned to the apartments. Naryshkin saluted the Lord Envoy by taking him by the hand to his wife's chambers to salute and be saluted. There is no higher mark of honor among the Russians than to be invited by the husband to embrace his wife and to receive the compliment of a sip of brandy from her hand.

On another occasion, the envoy saw the Tsar's menagerie, containing "a colossal white bear, leopards, lynxes, and many other animals that are kept merely for the pleasure of looking at them." Still later, he visited the famous New Jerusalem Monastery built by Nikon. "We saw its huge walls and the cells of the monks. A stream glides past it with wide, open fields around, affording a charming view. We amused ourselves delightfully, boating and enticing the unwary fish into the nets, a diversion all the more pleasant when we knew we should have them for supper."

The ambassadors were invited to the Tsar's estate at Ismailovo. It was July, a time of great heat in Moscow, and they found the estate "laid out most agreeably, surrounded by a grove of trees, not thickly planted but growing to a prodigious height, and affording an admirable refuge beneath the cool shade of their lofty spreading branches from the burning heat of summer." Musicians were present "to aid the gentle whisperings of the woods and winds with sweeter harmonies."

Korb's visit, tied to that of his ambassador, lasted fifteen months. In July 1699, they departed after lavish ceremonies. Peter distributed gifts, including numerous sable furs, to the envoy and his entire suite. By Peter's order, a magnificent procession was staged, and the ambassador rode in Peter's personal state carriage, with trappings of gold and silver and gems encrusting the doors and ceiling. Then the coach and the other carriages carrying the Austrian embassy were escorted out of the city by squadrons of Peter's new cavalry and detachments of his new Western infantry.

21

VORONEZH AND THE SOUTHERN FLEET

FROM THE HOUR of his return to Moscow, Peter had longed to see his ships being built at Voronezh. Even while the tortures continued at Preobrazhenskoe, while he and his friends drank through the gloomy autumn and winter nights, the Tsar desired to be on the Don, joining the Western shipwrights whom he had recruited and who even now were beginning to work in the shipyards on the riverbank.

He had made a first visit late in October. Many of the boyars, anxious to remain in the Tsar's good graces by staying close to his person, followed him south. Prince Cherkassky, the respected elder whose beard had been spared, was left behind as Prefect of Moscow, but soon discovered that his authority was not unique. Typically, Peter had confided the government not to one but to several. Before leaving, he had also said to Gordon, "To you I commit everything." And to Romodanovsky, "Meanwhile, I commit all my affairs to your loyalty." It was Peter's maxim of absentee government: By dividing power among many and confusing all as to what power each had, they would remain in constant dissent and confusion. The system was not likely to promote efficient government in his absence, but it would prevent a single regent from ever challenging his power. With the causes of the Streltsy revolt still undetermined, this was Peter's first consideration.

At Voronezh, in the shipyards sprawling along the banks of the broad and shallow river, Peter found the carpenters sawing and hammering, and he found many problems. There were shortages and great wastage of both men and materials. In haste to comply with the Tsar's commands, the shipwrights were using unseasoned timber, which would rot quickly in the water.* On arriving from Holland, Vice Admiral Cruys inspected the vessels and ordered many hauled out to be rebuilt and strengthened. The foreign

---

* The problem of using green timber was not restricted to Russian ships. In the seventeenth and eighteenth centuries, the average life of British navy ships was only about ten years, due to the use of unseasoned timber.

shipwrights, each following his own designs without guidance or control from above, quarreled frequently. The Dutch shipwrights, commanded by Peter's orders from London to work only under the supervision of others, were sullen and sluggish. The Russian artisans were in no better mood. Summoned by decree to Voronezh to learn shipbuilding, they understood that if they showed aptitude, they would be sent to the West to perfect their skills. Accordingly, many preferred to do just enough work to get by, hoping somehow to be allowed to return home.

The worst problems and the greatest sufferings were among the mass of unskilled laborers. Thousands of men had been drafted—peasants and serfs who had never seen a boat bigger than a barge or a body of water wider than a river. They came carrying their own hatchets and axes, sometimes bringing their own horses, to cut and trim the trees and float them down the rivers to Voronezh. Living conditions were primitive, disease spread quickly and death was common. Many ran away, and eventually the shipyards had to be surrounded by a fence and guards. If caught, deserters were beaten and returned to work.

Although outwardly Peter was optimistic, the slowness of the work, the sickness, death and desertion of the workers, made him gloomy and despondent. Three days after arriving, on November 2, 1698, he wrote to Vinius, "Thank God we have found our fleet in excellent condition. Only a cloud of doubt covers my mind whether we shall ever taste these fruits, which, like dates, those who plant never succeed in harvesting." Later, he wrote, "Here, by God's help, is great preparation. But we only wait for that blessed day when the great cloud of doubt over us shall be driven away. We have begun a ship here which will carry sixty guns."

Despite Peter's worries, the work moved forward although the shipyards were without machinery of any kind and all work was done with hand tools. Gangs of men and teams of horses moved the tree trunks, trimmed them to logs and pulled them through the yard and into position over pits in the earth. Then, with some men beneath the log and others leaning or sitting on it to steady it, the long planks or curved frame timbers were sawed or hewn out. There was tremendous waste, as very few planks were obtained from a single log. Once the rough board was obtained, it was turned over to more skillful artisans who worked with hatchets, hammers, mauls, augers and chisels to create the exact shapes needed. The heaviest, strongest pieces went into the keels, laid just above the earth. Then came the ribs curving out and up to be fastened together. Finally, along the sides came the heavy planks that would keep out the sea. And then work could begin on decks, interiors and all the special structures that would make the ship both a place of habitation and a machine of work.

Through the winter, ignoring the cold, Peter labored with his men. He walked through the shipyards, stepping over logs covered with snow, past

the ships standing silent in the stocks, past the workers huddled around out-door fires trying to warm their hands and bodies, past the foundry with its huge bellows driving air into the furnaces where anchors and metal fitting were being cast. He was indefatigable, pouring out his energy, commanding, cajoling, persuading. The Venetians building the galleys complained that they were working so hard they had no time to go to confession. But the fleet continued to grow. When Peter arrived in the autumn, he found twenty ships already launched and anchored in the stream. Every week, as the winter progressed, another five or six went into the water, or waited ready to be launched when the ice melted.

Not content with his overall supervision, Peter himself designed and began to build, solely with Russian labor, a fifty-gun ship called the *Predestination*. He laid the keel himself and worked on it steadily, along with the boyars who accompanied him. The *Predestination* was a handsome, three-masted ship, 130 feet long, and working on it provided Peter with the happy sensation of having tools in his hands and with the knowledge that one of the ships which would eventually sail the Black Sea would be his own creation.

IT WAS IN MARCH during his second trip to Voronezh that the Tsar was stunned by a personal blow: the death of Francis Lefort. Both times Peter went to work on his ships that winter, Lefort remained in Moscow. At forty-three, his great strength and hearty enthusiasm seemed intact. As First Ambassador of the Great Embassy, he had survived eighteen months of ceremonial banquets in the West, and his prodigious drinking capacity had not deserted him during the feasts and roaring entertainments of the fall and winter in Moscow. He still seemed gay and in high spirits when he saw Peter off for Voronezh.

But in the days before his death, while Lefort went on with his frantic life, a strange story was heard. One night when he was away from his house, sleeping with another woman, his wife heard a terrible noise in her husband's bedroom. Knowing that Lefort was not there, but "supposing that her husband might have changed his mind and come home in a great fury, she sent someone to ascertain the cause. The person came back, saying that he could see nobody in the room." Nevertheless, the uproar went on, and, if one is to believe the wife—the story is told by Korb—"the next morning all the chairs, tables and seats were scattered, topsy-turvy all about, besides which deep groans were constantly heard all through the night."

Soon afterward Lefort gave a banquet for two foreign diplomats, the ambassadors of Denmark and Brandenburg, who were departing to visit Voronezh at Peter's invitation. The evening was a great success, and the ambassadors stayed late. Finally, the heat in the room grew overpowering,

and the host led his guests, reeling, out into the frozen winter air to drink under the stars without coats or wraps. The following day, Lefort began to shiver. A fever mounted rapidly and he became delirious, raving and shouting for music and wine. His terrified wife suggested sending for the Protestant Pastor Stumpf, but Lefort shouted that he wanted no one to come near him. Stumpf came anyway. "When the pastor was admitted to see him," writes Korb,

and was admonishing him to be converted to God, they say he only told him "not to talk much." To his wife, who in his last moments asked his pardon for her past faults if she had committed any, he blandly replied, "I never had anything to reproach thee with; I always honored and loved thee." . . . He commended his domestics and their services, desiring that their wages should be paid in full.

Lefort lived for another week, solaced on his deathbed by the music of an orchestra which had been brought to play for him. Finally, at three in the morning, he died. Golovin immediately sealed the house and gave the keys to Lefort's relatives, at the same time urgently dispatching a courier to Peter at Voronezh.

When Peter heard the news, the hatchet fell from his grasp, he sat down on a log and, hiding his face in his hands, he wept. In a voice hoarse with sobbing and grief, he said, "Now I am alone without one trusty man. He alone was faithful to me. Whom can I confide in now?"

The Tsar returned immediately to Moscow, and the funeral was held on March 21. Peter took charge of the funeral arrangements himself: The Swiss was to have a state funeral grander than any in Russia except that for a tsar or a patriarch. The foreign ambassadors were invited and the boyars commanded to be present. They were instructed to assemble at Lefort's house at eight in the morning to carry the body to the church, but many were late and there were other delays and not until noon was the procession formed. Meanwhile, inside the house, Peter had observed the Western custom of laying out a sumptuous cold dinner for the guests. The boyars, surprised and pleased to find this feast before them, hurled themselves upon it.

Korb described the scene:

The tables were laid out, groaning under viands, and drinking cups in long array, and bowls with every description of wine. Mulled wine was served to those who preferred it. The Russians—for everybody of any rank or office had by the tsar's orders to be present—sat at a table ravenously devouring the viands which were

cold. There was a great variety of fish, cheese, butter, caviar and so forth.

Boyar Sheremetev, refined by much travel and dressed in the German fashion, wearing his Cross of Malta at his breast, thought it beneath his propriety to give himself up to voracity with the rest. The Tsar coming in showed many tokens of grief; fixed sorrow was in his face. To the ambassadors who paid their becoming court, bowing to the ground according to custom, the monarch replied with exquisite politeness. When Lev Naryshkin left his seat, and hastened to meet the Tsar, he received indeed his salutations graciously, but remained absent without answering for a little while, until, recollecting himself, he bent to embrace him. When the moment for removing the body came, the grief and former affection of the Tsar and some others was manifest to everybody, for the Tsar shed tears most abundantly, and in the sight of all the vast crowd of people who were assembled, he gave the last kiss to the corpse.

. . . Thus the body was conducted to the Reformed Church, where Pastor Stumpf preached a short sermon. On leaving the temple, the boyars and the rest of their countrymen disturbed the order of the procession, forcing their way with inept arrogance up to the very body. The foreign ambassadors, pretending however to take no notice of the haughty pretensions, suffered every one of the Muscovites to go on before them, even those whose humble lot and condition [did not merit this]. As they came to the cemetery, the Tsar noticed that the order was changed; that his subjects who previously had followed the ambassadors now preceded them; therefore he called young Lefort [Francis Lefort's nephew] to him and inquired: "Who disturbed the order? Why have those that followed, just now gone foremost?" And as Lefort remained prostrate without giving any answer, the Tsar commanded him to speak. And when he said that it was the Russians who had violently inverted the order, the Tsar, greatly in wrath, said: "They are dogs, not my boyars."

Sheremetev, on the contrary—and to his prudence it may be attributed—still continued to accompany the ambassadors, although all the Russians had gone on before. In the cemetery itself and on the highway there were cannon drawn up, which shook the air with a triple discharge, and each regiment also delivered a triple volley of musketry. One of the artillerymen, remaining stupidly before the cannon's mouth, had his head carried off by the shot. The Tsar went back with his troops to the house of Lefort and all followed him. Everybody that had attended the mourning was presented with a gold ring, on which was engraved the date of the death and a death's

head. The Tsar having gone out for a minute, all the boyars were hastening with anxious speed to go home. They had already gone down some steps when, meeting the Tsar returning face to face, they came back into the room. The haste of the boyars to get away gave rise to a suspicion that they were glad of the death, and it put the Tsar in such a passion that he wrathfully addressed them in the following terms. "Ho! You are made merry at his death! It is a grand victory for you that he is dead. Why can't you all wait? I suppose the greatness of your joy will not allow you to keep up this forced appearance and the feigned sorrow of your faces."

The death of this Western friend left an enormous gap in Peter's personal life. The jovial Swiss had steered his young friend and master through the early years. Lefort, the mighty reveler, had taught the youth to drink, to dance, to shoot a bow and arrow. He had found him a mistress and invented new, outrageous burlesques to amuse him. He had accompanied him on the first military campaigns at Azov. He had persuaded Peter to go to the West and then personally led the Great Embassy whose ranks included Peter Mikhailov, and the long journey had inspired Peter's effort to bring back to Russia the technology and manners of Europe. Then, almost on the eve of Peter's greatest challenge, the twenty-year war with Sweden which would convert the high-strung, enthusiastic young Tsar into the great conquering Emperor, Lefort died.

Peter understood what he had lost. All his life, he was surrounded by men trying to turn their rank and power in the state to their own personal profit. Lefort was different. Although his proximity to the sovereign had given him many opportunities to make himself rich by becoming a channel for favors and bribes, Lefort died penniless. There was so little money, in fact, that before Peter's return from Voronezh the family had to beg from Prince Golitsyn the money to buy the elegant suit in which Lefort was to be interred.

Peter kept Lefort's nephew and steward, Peter Lefort, in his service. He wrote to Geneva, asking that Lefort's only son, Henry, come to Russia, saying that he wanted someone from his friend's immediate family always to be near him. In the years afterward, Lefort's role was played by others. Peter always liked to have around him enormously powerful companion-favorites, whose devotion to the Tsar was mostly personal, and whose power came solely from their intimacy with him. Of these, the most prominent was Menshikov. But Peter never forgot Lefort. Once after a splendid party at Menshikov's palace, when Peter had been happily surrounded by cronies, he wrote to the absent host, "This was the first time I have really enjoyed myself since Lefort's death."

AND THEN, six months later, as if to make the last year of the old century an even more marked dividing point in Peter's life, he lost a second of his devoted Western counselors and friends, Patrick Gordon. The old soldier had been in failing health. On New Year's Eve 1698, he noted in his diary, "In this year I have felt a sensible failing of my health and strength. But Thy will be done, O my gracious Lord." His last public appearance had been with his soldiers in September 1699, and in October he retired permanently to his bed. Near the end of November, as Gordon's strength ebbed away, Peter visited him repeatedly. He came twice on the night of November 29, with Gordon sinking rapidly. The second time, a Jesuit priest who had already given the Last Sacrament withdrew from the bedside when the Tsar entered. "Stay where you are, Father," Peter said, "and do what you think fit. I will not interrupt you." Peter spoke to Gordon, who remained silent. Then Peter took a small mirror and held it to the old man's face, hoping to see a sign of breath. There was none. "Father," said the Tsar to the priest, "I think he is dead." Peter himself closed the dead man's eyes and left the house, his own eyes filled with tears.

Gordon also was given a state funeral attended by everyone of importance in Moscow. The Russians came willingly, for the old soldier's devotion to three Tsars and his services to the state were universally appreciated. His coffin was carried by twenty-eight colonels, and twenty ladies of the highest birth followed the widow in the mourning procession. As Gordon's coffin was placed in a vault near the altar of the church, twenty-four cannon outside fired in salute.

Peter soon felt Gordon's loss, both professionally and personally. Gordon was Russia's ablest soldier, with considerable experience in many campaigns. His value as a commander and counselor in the coming war with Sweden would have been great; had he been present, the disaster at Narva, only twelve months after his death, might never have happened. Peter also would miss the grizzled Scot at his table, where the old soldier loyally tried to please his master by matching drink for drink with men half his age. For both these reasons, a saddened Peter said at Gordon's death, "The state has lost in him an ardent and courageous servant who has steered us safely through many calamities."

BY SPRING, the fleet was ready. Eighty-six ships of all sizes, including eighteen sea-going men-of-war carrying from thirty-six to forty-six guns were in the water. In addition, 500 barges had been built for carrying men, provisions, ammunition and powder. On May 7, 1699, this fleet left Voronezh and the villagers along the Don saw a remarkable sight: a fleet of full-rigged ships sailing past them down the river. Admiral Golovin was in nominal

command, with Vice Admiral Cruys in actual command of the fleet. Peter took the role of captain of the forty-four-gun frigate *Apostle Peter*.

One day as the long procession of ships moved downriver, Peter saw a group of men on the bank preparing to cook some tortoises for dinner. To most Russians, eating tortoise was a repugnant idea, but Peter, ever curious, asked for some for his own table. His comrades dining with him tasted the new dish, not knowing what it was. Thinking it was young chicken and liking it, they finished what was on their plates, whereupon Peter ordered his servant to bring in the "feathers" of these chickens. When they saw the tortoise shells, most of the Russians laughed at themselves; two were sick.

On arriving at Azov on May 24, Peter anchored his fleet in the river and went ashore to inspect the new fortifications. There was no doubt that they were needed: Again that spring, a horde of Crimean Tatars had swept eastward across the southern Ukraine, approaching Azov itself, burning, raiding, leaving behind desolate fields, charred farms, villages in ashes and the population stricken and fleeing. Satisfied with the new defensive works, Peter moved on to visit Tagonrog, where dredging and construction were under way for the new naval base. When the ships had assembled there, Peter took them to sea, where they began to drill in signaling, gunnery and ship-handling. Through most of July the maneuvers continued, culminating in a mock sea battle of the sort Peter had witnessed on the Ij in Holland.

The fleet was ready, and now Peter faced the problem of what to do with it. It had been built for war with Turkey, to force a passage onto the Black Sea and to contest the right of the Turks to control that sea as a private lake. But the situation had changed. Prokofy Voznitsyn, an experienced diplomat, had remained in Vienna to salvage what he could for Russia from the negotiations which the allied powers, Austria, Poland, Venice and Russia, were about to begin with the partially defeated Turks. The problem was that, as the peace treaty would probably only confirm surrender of those territories actually occupied, Peter wanted the war to continue, at least for a while. It was, in fact, in order to press the war and seize Kerch, achieving entry onto the Black Sea, that he had labored so hard all winter to build his fleet.

When the peace congress finally met at Carlowitz, near Vienna, Voznitsyn urged the allied emissaries not to make peace until all of Russia's objectives were met. But the weight of other national interests was against him. The Austrians already stood to regain all of Transylvania and most of Hungary. Venice was to keep its conquests in Dalmatia and the Aegean, and Poland would keep certain territories north of the Carpathians. The English ambassador in Constantinople, instructed to do everything possible to broker a peace and free Austria for the impending contest with France, persuaded the weary Turks to be generous; grudgingly, the Turks agreed to cede Azov to Russia, but refused absolutely to yield any territory not

actually conquered, such as Kerch. Voznitsyn, isolated from his allies, could do nothing except refuse to sign the general treaty. Knowing that Peter was unready to attack the Turks on his own, he proposed instead a two-year truce, during which time the Tsar could prepare for more extensive offensive operations. The Turks agreed, and Voznitsyn wrote to Peter suggesting that the time also be used to send an ambassador directly to Constantinople to see whether Russia might gain by negotiation what she had so far failed to gain—and seemed uncertain of gaining in the future—by war.

All this happened during the winter of 1698–1699 while Peter was building his fleet at Voronezh. Now, with the fleet ready at Tagonrog and yet with the new Turkish truce making active use of it impossible, Peter decided to accept Voznitsyn's suggestion. He appointed a special ambassador, Emilian Ukraintsev, the white-haired chief of the Foreign Ministry, to go to Constantinople to discuss a permanent treaty of peace. There was even in this plan a role for the new fleet: It would escort the Ambassador as far as Kerch, from where he would sail to the Turkish capital in the biggest and proudest of Peter's new ships.

On August 5, twelve large Russian ships, all commanded by foreigners except the frigate whose skipper was Captain Peter Mikhailov, sailed from Tagonrog for the Strait of Kerch. The Turkish pasha commanding the fortress whose cannon dominated the strait which linked the Sea of Azov with the Black Sea was taken unawares. One day, he heard the salvos of Peter's saluting cannon and rushed to his parapet to see a Russian naval squadron on his doorstep. Peter's request was that a single Russian warship, the forty-six-gun frigate *Krepost* (*Fortress*), be allowed to pass through the strait bearing his ambassador to Constantinople. The pasha at first unmuzzled his guns and refused, saying that he had no orders from his capital. Peter riposted by threatening to break through by force if necessary, and his men-of-war were joined by galleys, brigantines and barges carrying soldiers. After ten days, the pasha consented, insisting that the Russian frigate submit to an escort of four Turkish ships. The Tsar withdrew, and the *Krepost* sailed through the strait. Once on the Black Sea, her Dutch captain, Van Pamburg, put on all sail and soon left his Turkish escort behind the horizon.

The moment was historic: For the first time, a Russian warship, bearing the banner of the Muscovite Tsar, was sailing alone and free on the Sultan's private lake. At sundown on September 13 when the Russian man-of-war appeared at the mouth of the Bosphorus, Constantinople was surprised and shaken. The Sultan reacted with dignity. He sent a message of welcome and congratulations and dispatched caiques to bring Ukraintsev and his party ashore. The Ambassador, however, refused to leave the ship and demanded that it be permitted to sail up the Bosphorus and carry him directly into the city. The Sultan bowed and the Russian warship moved up the Bosphorus,

finally anchoring in the Golden Horn directly in front of the Sultan's palace on Seraglio Point in full view of the Elect of God. For nine centuries, since the middle days of the great Christian empire of Byzantium, no Russian ship had anchored beneath those walls.

The Turks, staring out at the *Krepost*, were disquieted not only by the appearance but also by the size of the Russian ship—they could not understand how so large a vessel could have been built in the shallow Don—but were calmed to some extent by their naval architects, who pointed out that the vessel must be very flat-bottomed and would therefore be unstable as a gun platform in the open sea.

Ukraintsev was handsomely treated. A number of high officials waited at the dock when he came ashore, a splendid horse was provided for him and he was escorted to a luxurious seaside guest villa. Thereafter, in accordance with Peter's orders to display to the fullest Russia's new naval capacity, the *Krepost* was opened to visitors. Hundreds of boats came alongside and crowds of people of all classes swarmed aboard. The culmination was a visit by the Sultan himself, who, with an escort of Ottoman captains, inspected the ship in great detail.

The visit went peacefully, although Van Pamburg, the exuberant Dutch captain, once almost brought ruin on himself and the larger diplomatic mission. He was entertaining Dutch and French acquaintances on board and kept them until after midnight. Then, as he sent them ashore, he decided to salute them by firing all forty-six of his guns with powder but no shot. The cannonade directly beneath the walls of the palace awakened the whole city, including the Sultan, who thought it must be a signal for a Russian fleet to attack the city from the sea. The following morning, the angry Turkish authorities ordered the frigate seized and the captain arrested, but Van Pamburg threatened to blow up his ship when the first Turkish soldier set foot on it. Subsequently, with apologies and promises not to repeat the offense, the incident was smoothed over.

Meanwhile, however, the Turks were in no hurry to accommodate Ukraintsev. Not until November, three months after the Russian envoy's arrival in Constantinople, did they even consent to open negotiations. Thereafter, Ukraintsev held twenty-three meetings with his Ottoman counterparts until in June 1700 a compromise of sorts was reached. In the beginning, Peter's hopes had been ambitious. He demanded the right to keep Azov and the fortresses captured on the lower Dnieper, all already in his possession by conquest. He asked permission to sail Russian commercial (but not war) vessels on the Black Sea. He asked the Sultan to forbid the Crimean Khan to make further raids into the Ukraine, and to cancel the Khan's right to ask for annual tribute from Moscow. Finally, he asked that a Russian ambassador be permanently accredited to the Porte, as Britain,

France and other powers were so represented, and that Orthodox churchmen have special privileges at the Holy Sepulcher in Jerusalem.

For months, the Turks gave no definitive answers as wrangling, disputes and delays arose over even the smallest details of the proposed agreement. Ukraintsev sensed that the other diplomatic representatives in Constantinople —those of Austria, Venice and England as well as France—were determined to impede his mission in order to prevent Russia and the Ottoman Empire from becoming too intimate. "I get no sort of assistance and not even any information from the Emperor or from Venice," Ukraintsev complained in a report to Peter. "The English and Dutch ministers range themselves beside the Turks and have better intentions toward them than they have toward you, Sire. They hate you and envy you because you have begun to build ships and have inaugurated navigation at Azov as well as at Archangel. They fear this will hamper their maritime trade." The Tatar Khan of the Crimea was even more anxious to prevent an agreement. "The Tsar," he wrote to his master, the Sultan, "is destroying the old customs and faith of his people. He is altering everything according to German methods and is creating a powerful army and fleet, thereby annoying everyone. Sooner or later he will perish at the hands of his own subjects."

On one point the Turks were adamant and needed no bolstering from West European ambassadors or Tatar chieftains: They refused absolutely Peter's demand that Russian ships of any kind be allowed access to the Black Sea. "The Black Sea and its coasts are ruled by the Ottoman Sultan alone," they told Ukraintsev. "From time immemorial no foreign ship has sailed its waters, nor ever will sail them. . . . The Ottoman Porte guards the Black Sea like a pure and undefiled virgin which no one dares to touch, and the Sultan will sooner permit outsiders to enter his harem than consent to the sailing of foreign vessels on the Black Sea." In the end, Turkish resistance proved too strong. Although generally defeated in the war, the Turks now faced only a single enemy, Russia, and they could not be forced to give up more than they had already lost in battle. Peter, too, was anxious to conclude the negotiations, as he had more tempting prospects to the north in the Baltic. The agreement, called the Treaty of Constantinople, was not a treaty of peace but a thirty-year truce which abandoned no claims, left all questions open and assumed that on expiration, unless it was renewed, the war would begin again.

The terms were a compromise. Territorially, Russia was allowed to keep Azov and a band of territory to the distance of ten days' journey from its walls. On the other hand, the forts on the lower Dnieper, seized from the Turks, were to be razed, and the land returned to Turkish possession. A zone of unpopulated, supposedly demilitarized land was to stretch across the Ukraine from east to west, separating the lands of the Crimean Tatars

from Peter's domain. The demand for Kerch and access to the Black Sea had previously been dropped by the Russians.

In the non-territorial clauses, Ukraintsev was more successful. The Turks promised informally to assist Orthodox Christians in their access to Jerusalem. Peter's refusal to pay further tribute to the Tatar Khan was formally accepted. This infuriated the incumbent Khan, Devlet Gerey, but the ancient aggravation was finally ended and never reintroduced, even after the disaster that befell Peter eleven years later on the Pruth. Finally, Ukraintsev secured for Russia what Peter considered a major concession: the right to keep a permanent ambassador at Constantinople on equal footing with England, Holland, Austria and France. This was an important step in Peter's drive to have Russia recognized as a major European power, and Ukraintsev himself remained on the Bosphorus to become the Tsar's first permanent ambassador to a foreign power.

Ironically, the signing of a thirty-year truce with Turkey largely negated the great effort which had gone into the fleet built at Voronezh. Long before the thirty years had passed, the crews would have been dispersed and the timbers of the ships rotted away. At the time, of course, in Peter's mind the truce was only a postponement. Although his primary attention was beginning to turn to the Great Northern War with Sweden, the projects in the south, at Voronezh, Azov and Tagonrog, only slowed and did not come to a halt. Never in his lifetime did Peter give up the idea of an eventual thrust out onto the Black Sea; indeed, to the anger and despair of the Turks, the shipbuilding at Voronezh continued, new ships sailed down to Tagonrog and the walls of Azov grew higher.

As it happened, Peter's fleet was never used in battle and Azov's walls were never attacked. The fate of ships and city was decided not in a battle at sea, as Peter had hoped, but by the struggle of armies hundreds of miles to the west. And in this struggle, the ships did serve their master. When Charles XII, invading deep into Russia, bid for a Turkish alliance in the months before Poltava, the fleet at Tagonrog was one of Peter's strongest cards in persuading the Turks and Tatars not to intervene. In those critical months in the spring of 1709, Peter urgently strengthened the fleet and doubled the number of troops at Azov. In May, two months before the climactic battle at Poltava, he went himself to Azov and Tagonrog and maneuvered his fleet before a Turkish envoy. The Sultan, impressed by his envoy's report, forbade Devlet Gerey, the Tatar Khan, to take his thousands of Tatar horsemen to Charles' side. This effect of the Voronezh fleet alone justified all the effort expended on it.

Part Three

THE GREAT NORTHERN WAR

22

MISTRESS
OF THE NORTH

HE BALTIC is a northern sea, brilliant blue in sunlight, murky gray in fog and rain, and deep gold at sunset when the world turns the color of the true amber which is found only on these shores. On its northern coasts, the Baltic is fringed with pine forests, fjords of red granite, pebble beaches and a myriad tiny islands. The southern coast takes a gentler form: there, a green shore is lined with white sand beaches, dunes, marshes and low mud cliffs. Long stretches are edged with shoals and sand spits outlying shallow lagoons a dozen miles wide and fifty miles long. Through this flat and marshy country, four historic rivers make their way to the sea: the Neva, the Dvina, the Vistula and the Oder, all pouring fresh water into the sea, so that the prevailing current is out of the Baltic. For this reason, it is difficult for salt water to enter the Baltic, and there are no tides at Riga, Stockholm or the mouth of the Neva.

It is the lack of salt that brings the ice. Winter comes to the Baltic late in October with heavy frosts at night and flurries of snow. By October, in the days of sailing ships, the foreign vessels were leaving, heading down the Baltic, their holds filled with iron and copper, their decks piled high with timber. The native Baltic captains steered their ships into port, unrigged them and left the hulls locked in the ice until spring. By November, water in the bays and inlets was already covered with a thin scum of ice. By the end of the month, Kronstadt and St. Petersburg were frozen in; by December, Tallinn and Stockholm. The open sea did not freeze, but drifting ice and frequent storms made navigation difficult. The narrow sound between Sweden and Denmark was often choked by floating drift ice, and some winters the channel was sheeted over. (In 1658, a Swedish army marched across the ice to take its Danish enemy by surprise.) The northern half of the Gulf of Bothnia is solid ice from November until early May.

Spring loosens the ice and once more the Baltic comes to life. Then, in Peter's day, the fleets of merchantmen would begin arriving from Amster-

dam and London, steering through the three-mile-wide channel of the sound, with the low cliffs and the famous castle of Elsinore to starboard and the hills on the Swedish shore to port. In June, the Baltic was filled with sails: Dutch merchantmen, the cobalt-colored water creaming back from their rounded bows, the wind filling their huge mainsails; and stout, oaken-hulled English vessels, sent to load the pine masts and spars, tar and turpentine, resins, oils and flax for sails without which the Royal Navy could not survive. Through the short northern summer, under bright blue skies, ships crisscrossed the Baltic, anchored in its harbors, tied up to the quays, the captains ashore dining with merchants, the seamen drinking in bars and lying with women.

The port cities and towns of the Baltic were, and remain today, German in character, with cobbled streets and medieval stone buildings marked by high-pitched roofs, gables, turrets and battlements. The ancient town of Reval (now Tallinn), capital of Estonia, is centered on a medieval citadel perched on a great, craggy upthrust of rock. Swallows dip and soar around its high, round towers, and blond Estonian children play under the blooming chestnut trees and lilacs in the park beneath the massive walls. Riga, the capital of Latvia, is larger, more modern, but the old town on the bank of the Dvina River is also a world of cobbled streets and German drinking houses, topped by the Baroque spires of St. Peter's and St. Jacob's churches and the mighty Dom Cathedral. Outside the city, a wide white sand beach framed by dunes and pine trees runs for miles along the Gulf of Riga.

In Peter's day, the architecture, the language, the religion and the entire cultural flavor of these small states were alien to those of the colossal Russian mass adjacent to them. Ruled by the Teutonic Knights and later a German aristocracy, constituents of the Hanseatic League and the Lutheran Church, they retained their cultural and religious independence even after Peter's army marched from Poltava, captured Riga and absorbed these provinces for 200 years into the Russian empire.

To THE NORTH, in a world of forests and lakes, lies Sweden, in Peter's time at the peak of its imperial power. From the southernmost coast on the Baltic to the north beyond the Arctic Circle, Sweden stretches for a thousand miles. It is a land of evergreens and birches, of 96,000 lakes, of snow and ice. As in northern Russia, the summers are short and cool. Ice forms in November and breaks up in April, and only five months are without frost. It is a cold, sternly beautiful land, and it has bred a race of hard, uncomplaining people.

In the seventeenth century, there were scattered over all this vastness

only a million and a half people. Most were farm families, living in simple wooden cabins, using wooden plows and making their own clothes as they had for centuries. Between one farm and the next, and between the small towns and villages, travel was slow and hazardous. The roads were poor and, as in Russia, it was easier to travel in winter when a sleigh or sledge could glide over the surface of the frozen lakes. Hiding from the icy winds, Swedish peasants spent the endless winter days huddled around their warm stoves or sharing the public baths which were the most efficient means of getting the chill out of their frozen bones.

Sweden's primary exports were the products of its mines: silver, copper and iron. Iron, essential in both peace and war, was the most important, and provided half of Sweden's export trade. Most of this trade went through Stockholm, the capital, which in 1697 had a population of about 60,000. The city was located on Sweden's east coast which is fringed with a belt of islands protecting the coastline from the open sea. This belt is thickest at the point where the Gulf of Bothnia joins the Baltic. From the sea, a main channel, the Saltsjö, leads for forty-five miles through the mass of islands to Stockholm on the mainland. Here, at a juncture of lakes, rivers and the Saltsjö, medieval Stockholm was built, a little walled town of narrow, winding streets, gabled fronts and thin church spires, similar to those of other North German and Baltic towns.

In the seventeenth century, Stockholm became an important commercial port. Dutch and English merchantmen thronged the harbor and tied up at the broad shipping quay to load Swedish iron and copper. As the city's docks, shipyards, marketplaces and banking institutions grew, the town expanded to other islands. With increased wealth, the church spires and roofs of public buildings were sheathed in copper which glowed a brilliant orange when touched by the rays of the setting sun. The luxurious tastes of Versailles reached into the city's palaces and the mansions of the nobility. Ships which had sailed from Sweden carrying iron returned from Amsterdam and London bringing English walnut furniture, French gilt chairs, Dutch Delft china, Italian and German glass, gold wallpaper, carpets, linens and ornate table silver.

This wealth was built on empire as well as on iron and copper. The seventeenth century was Sweden's hour of greatness. From the accession of seventeen-year-old Gustavus Adolphus in 1611 to the death of Charles XII in 1718, Sweden stood at the pinnacle of its imperial history. The Swedish empire covered the entire northern coast of the Baltic and key territories along the southern shore. It embraced all of Finland and Karelia, Estonia, Ingria and Livonia, thus lapping completely around the Gulf of Bothnia and the Gulf of Finland. It held western Pomerania and the seaports of Stettin, Stralsund and Wismar on the North German coast. It commanded

the bishoprics of Bremen and Verden, which were west of the Danish peninsula and gave access to the North Sea. And it held most of the islands of the Baltic.

Trade was even more important than territory. Here, Sweden's supremacy was secured by the planting of her blue-and-yellow flag at the mouth of all but one of the rivers that flowed into the Baltic: the Neva, at the head of the Gulf of Finland; the Dvina, which met the sea in the marshy ground near Riga; and the Oder, which reached the Baltic at Stettin. Only the mouth of the Vistula, flowing north through Poland and emptying into the Baltic at Danzig, was not Swedish.

That these vast territories should be possessed by a crown whose own people numbered scarcely a million and a half was the achievement of Sweden's great commanders and sturdy soldiers. The first and greatest of these was Gustavus Adolphus, the Lion of the North, savior of the Protestant cause in Germany, whose campaigns led him as far as the Danube and who was killed at thirty-eight while leading a cavalry charge.* The Thirty Years' War, which continued after his death, ended with the Peace of Westphalia, which richly rewarded Sweden's efforts. Here it gained the German provinces which gave control of the mouths of the Oder, the Weser and the Elbe. These German possessions also resulted in the anomaly that Sweden, Protestant Mistress of the North, was also a part of the Holy Roman Empire and occupied seats in the Imperial Diet. More significant than this hollow power, however, was the access to Central Europe which they gave Sweden. With these territories serving as beachheads on the continent, Swedish armies could march anywhere in Europe, and that made Sweden a force to be reckoned with in every European calculation of war and peace.

Sweden, in sum, was a phenomenon—a great power, but one with weaknesses. It was not only satiated with conquest, it was over-extended. It had many advantages: hard-working people, disciplined soldiers, kings who commanded brilliantly on the battlefield. Nevertheless, to maintain its position, it also needed wisdom. The nation's strength had to be husbanded, not flung into wild, new adventures. As long as its monarchs understood

---

* Gustavus Adolphus was succeeded by his only child, a six-year-old daughter who was to become the legendary Queen Christina. Assuming full royal power at eighteen, Christina ruled Sweden for ten years from 1644 to 1654. Her passion was learning. She rose at five a.m. to begin reading. Foreign scholars, musicians and philosophers, including Descartes, were enticed to her court by tales of her genius and her largess. Then, suddenly, at twenty-eight, she abdicated, pleading that she was ill and that the burdens of ruling were too heavy for a woman. The real reason, however, was her secret conversion to the Roman Catholic Church, which was illegal in Protestant Sweden. The throne went to Christina's cousin, who became King Charles X and the grandfather of Charles XII. Christina herself left immediately for Rome, where she lived for the remaining thirty-four years of her life, a friend of four popes, a magnificent patroness of the arts and the lover of Cardinal Azzolini.

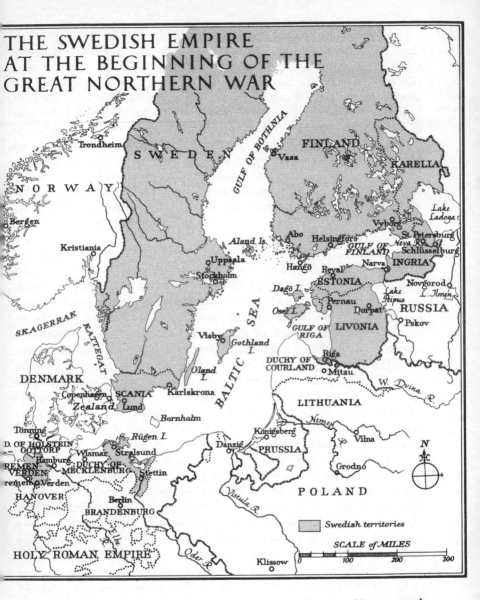

THE SWEDISH EMPIRE AT THE BEGINNING OF THE GREAT NORTHERN WAR

Swedish territories

SCALE of MILES
0   100   200   300

this and acted wisely, there was no reason that Sweden should not remain indefinitely the Mistress of the North.

THE SEEDS of the Great Northern War lay in history and economics as well as in Peter's longing for the sea. The struggle between Russia and Sweden for possession of the coastal lands on the Gulf of Finland was centuries old. Sweden had been the enemy of the city-states of Moscow and Novgorod

since the thirteenth century. Karelia and Ingria, which spread north and south of the Neva River, were ancient Russian lands; the Russian hero Alexander Nevsky won the name Nevsky ("of the Neva") by defeating the Swedes on the Neva River in 1240. During Russia's Time of Troubles following the death of Ivan the Terrible, Sweden had occupied a vast belt of territory which even included Novgorod itself. In 1616, Sweden gave up Novgorod, but kept the entire coastline anchored in such fortresses as Nöteborg on Lake Ladoga, Narva and Riga, continuing Russia's isolation from the sea. Tsar Alexis had made an attempt to regain these lands, but he had been forced to abandon it. His more important wars were with Poland, and Russia could not fight Poland and Sweden simultaneously. Swedish possession of the provinces was reconfirmed by the Russian-Swedish Peace of Kardis in 1664.

Nevertheless, in Peter's mind these were Russian lands, and Russia was suffering substantial economic loss from their being in foreign hands. Through the Swedish-held ports of Riga, Reval and Narva flowed a wide river of Russian trade, and on this trade Swedish handlers and toll collectors levied heavy duties, and the Swedish treasury fattened. Finally, of course, there was the pull of the sea. In Vienna, when he found the Emperor determined on peace, Peter understood that he could not make war alone on the Ottoman Empire, and realized that his access to the Black Sea was blocked. But here was the Baltic, its waves lapping a coast only a few miles from the Russian frontier, which could serve as a direct avenue to Holland, England and the West. Presented with a chance to repossess this territory by making war on a boy king in the company of Poland and Denmark, he found the temptation irresistible.

Yet, the war might still not have begun had fate not suddenly dispatched to the scene a dedicated man to stir the potent brew. Johann Reinhold von Patkul was a patriot without a country. He was a member of the old Livonian nobility, the hardy Germanic descendants of the Teutonic Knights, who had conquered and held Livonia, Estonia and Courland until the middle of the sixteenth century. After the severe defeats inflicted on the Knights by Ivan the Terrible, the Teutonic order was dissolved and Livonia fell into the hands of Poland. But the Poles were harsh masters, insisting on the Polish language, Polish laws and the Catholic religion, and eventually the Protestant Livonians sought the protection of Protestant Sweden. In 1660, after a long struggle, Livonia became a Swedish province and, as such, shared in the political affairs of the rest of Sweden. These included the famous and widely resisted "reduction" policy of Charles XI. After the early death of Gustavus Adolphus, the Swedish aristocracy had rapidly increased its relative power in the state, at the same time making itself hated by other classes of the population. On the accession of Charles XI, both the new King and the Swedish Parliament were determined to reduce the

influence of the aristocracy by granting the King absolute power. One effective means was to demand the return to the crown of numerous lands parceled out to the nobles for administration. (The noblemen had begun to treat these lands as their own hereditary estates.) This "reduction," begun in 1680, was applied with ruthless severity, not only to Sweden itself, but to all provinces of the Swedish empire, including Livonia. This command struck Livonia all the more painfully because only two years earlier Charles XI had solemnly affirmed the rights of the Livonian barons, expressly promising that they would not be subjected to any "reduction" which might be imposed. The barons protested the confiscation and sent emissaries to Stockholm to plead their case.

Patkul was one of these emissaries. He was a strong, handsome, cultured man who spoke numerous languages, wrote Greek and Latin and was an experienced military officer. He was also hot-tempered, single-minded and ruthless. When he spoke, his courage and fierce dedication to his cause made him a commanding, majestic figure. He pleaded his case with eloquence—Charles XI was so moved that he touched Patkul on the shoulder, saying, "You have spoken like an honest man for your fatherland. I thank you"—but the King reaffirmed reduction as a "national necessity" and declared that Livonia could not be treated differently from the rest of the realm. Patkul returned to Livonia and drafted a fiery petition which he sent to Stockholm. Its contents were deemed treasonable and he was sentenced in absentia to lose his right hand and his head. But he escaped the Swedish officers sent to arrest him and began wandering through Europe, searching for an opportunity to free his native country. For six years, he dreamed of creating an anti-Swedish coalition which might bring independence to Livonia or at least restore the power of the Livonian nobility, and when Charles XI died and a fifteen-year-old boy mounted the throne of Sweden, the opportunity seemed to present itself.

Patkul was impatient, but he was also realistic. He knew that to throw off the Swedish yoke a small province would have to accept the help and probably the sovereignty of another large power, and Poland—a republic dominated by its nobility, who elected the king—seemed a good choice. Under so loose a system, Patkul reasoned, the Livonian nobility would be more likely to maintain its rights. Further, the newly elected Polish King, Augustus of Saxony, was German and therefore could be expected to sympathize with the German nobility of Livonia.

In October 1698, Patkul secretly arrived in Warsaw and set about persuading Augustus to take the initiative in forming an anti-Swedish alliance. Patkul had already visited King Frederick IV of Denmark and found him willing. The Danes had never fully accepted the loss of territory in southern Sweden inflicted on them by Gustavus Adolphus and looked forward to restoring the days when the Oresund, the sound that separates

the Baltic from the North Sea, and Denmark from Sweden, could be looked upon as "a stream that runs through the dominions of the King of Denmark." Further, the Danes resented and feared the presence of Swedish troops on their southern border in the territory of the Duke of Holstein-Gottorp.

Augustus was intrigued by Patkul's proposition, especially by his statement that the Livonian nobles were ready to acknowledge Augustus as their hereditary king. To Augustus, this opened a glittering prospect. His ambition was to make his elective Polish crown a hereditary one. By seizing Livonia with Saxon troops and then presenting the province to the Polish nobility, he hoped to gain its support in making a permanent claim on the Polish throne. Under Patkul's spell, Augustus grew more eager. Assessing the possible reaction of the major European powers to such a war—a concern of Augustus—Patkul estimated that Austria, France, Holland and England would doubtless "make loud noises about their trade, but would probably do nothing." As a further inducement to Augustus, Patkul assured the King that the conquest of Livonia would prove easy, and he even supplied an exact description of the fortifications of Riga, the city which would be Augustus' major objective.

The result of Patkul's efforts was beyond his grandest imaginings: An offensive treaty was made between Denmark and Poland against Sweden. Frederick IV was to clear the provinces of Schleswig and Holstein of Swedish troops preparatory to an attack across the sound on Scania, the southernmost of Sweden's home provinces. Augustus was to be prepared by January or February of 1700 to march his Saxon troops into Livonia and attempt to seize Riga by surprise. Swedish forces would thus be split between North Germany, the upper Baltic and the homeland, and, in the absence of an adult king to rally the nation and lead the army, it was hoped that the Swedish empire would crumble quickly. Finally, Patkul proposed that Peter of Russia be brought into the war as an additional ally against the Swedes. Russian attacks on Ingria at the head of the Gulf of Finland would distract the Swedes. Peter might provide money, supplies and men to support the Saxon forces besieging Riga. Neither Patkul nor the others put much trust in the quality of Russian troops, but it was hoped that their quantity would make up the difference. "Russian infantry would be most serviceable for working in the trenches and for receiving the enemy's shots," Patkul suggested, "while the troops of the King [Augustus] could be preserved and used for covering the approaches"; i.e., the Russians would serve as cannon fodder.

The plotters did worry that, once Russian troops had entered the Baltic provinces, it might not be easy to persuade them to leave. "It would also be absolutely necessary," warned Patkul, "to bind the hands of the Tsar in such a way that he should not eat before our eyes the piece roasted

for us; that is, should not get hold of Livonia and should restrict his attack on Narva, for in that case he could threaten the center of Livonia and take Dorpat, Reval, and the whole of Estonia almost before it could be known in Warsaw."

Under the name Kindler and hidden in a group of twelve Saxon engineers hired by the Tsar, Patkul accompanied Augustus' personal representative, General George von Carlowitz, from Warsaw to Moscow to attempt to persuade Peter.* But in Moscow, the two conspirators found themselves in a peculiar situation. The Swedes, sensing that alliances were being formed against them, hoped to mollify Peter by sending to Moscow in the summer of 1699 a splendid embassy which would announce the accession of King Charles XII and ask for confirmation and renewal of all existing treaties, as was customary on the accession of a new monarch. The splendor of the Swedish embassy was meant to atone for the slight which the Tsar complained of having suffered when he passed through Riga in 1697. When the embassy arrived at the Russian frontier in mid-June, Peter's uncle Lev Naryshkin received them politely, but explained that they would have to await the return of the Tsar, who was with his fleet at Azov.

Peter's return to Moscow in early October was a dramatic moment. He found two embassies waiting for him: the formal Swedish embassy asking him to confirm the existing treaties of peace, and the secret Polish embassy of Carlowitz and Patkul asking him to make war on Sweden. Thereafter, for weeks, the two sets of negotiations continued side by side, the formal and unwelcome negotiations with Sweden being conducted openly at the Foreign Office, while the serious secret negotiations with Carlowitz were conducted personally by Peter at Preobrazhenskoe, with only Fedor Golovin and an interpreter, Peter Shafirov, present at the Tsar's side.

The Swedes were aware of Carlowitz' presence and knew that some kind of treaty was being discussed, but thought it was a peaceful treaty and suspected nothing of the truth. To avoid arousing suspicions, the Swedes were received with honor by Peter, to whom they presented a full-length picture of their new young King on horseback. And to bolster the deception, Peter went through the formality of confirming the previous treaties with Sweden, but, as a slight salve to his conscience, he avoided kissing the cross at the ceremony of signature. When the Swedish ambassadors noticed the omission and complained, Peter said that he had already taken an oath to observe all treaties when he came to the throne and that it was the Russian custom not to repeat it. On November 24, the Swedish ambassadors had a final audience with the Tsar. Peter was genial and gave them a formal

---

* The agreement at Rawa between Peter and Augustus had been only an exuberant burst of camaraderie. So far, there was no actual plan, either of alliance or of campaign.

letter from himself to King Charles XII confirming the treaties of peace between Sweden and Russia.

Meanwhile, the mission of Carlowitz and Patkul was proceeding successfully. Peter received Carlowitz (Patkul remained in disguise) and read the letter presented by Carlowitz but probably written by Patkul. In return for the Tsar's alliance, it offered Augustus' promise to support Russia's claims to Ingria and Karelia. Peter then called in Heins, the Danish ambassador, who was privy to the secret negotiations as Denmark had already signed its treaty of alliance with Poland. Heins endorsed the promise of the letter. Thus it was that, only three days after the Swedish embassy left Moscow, Peter signed a treaty agreeing that Russia would attack Sweden, if possible in April 1700. The Tsar carefully refused to name a specific date, and a clause stated that the Russian attack would come only *after* the signing of a peace or armistice between Russia and Turkey. Once the agreement was signed, Patkul, who until now had remained in the background, was presented to the Tsar. Two weeks later, Carlowitz left Moscow for Saxony, planning to take the road through Riga and use the opportunity to examine the city's fortifications.

PETER, having promised to attack a major Western military power within a few months, now turned to the enormous work of preparing for war. Since his return from the West, he had been primarily interested in the fleet. Overnight, he had to shift his attention from the building of ships to the accumulation of guns, powder, wagons, horses, uniforms and soldiers. With the Streltsy demoralized and only a few regiments still actually in existence, Peter's professional army consisted primarily of the four regiments of Guards, the Preobrazhensky, Semyonovsky, Lefort and Butursky. Thus, if the Tsar was to keep his promise to Augustus, an entire new army had to be raised, trained, equipped and placed on the march within three months.

Peter acted quickly. A decree was addressed to all civil and clerical landowners. Civil landowners were required to send the Tsar one serf recruit for every fifty serf households in their possession. Monasteries and other ecclesiastical landlords were more severely taxed at the rate of one recruit for every twenty-five households. Peter also asked for volunteers from among the freemen of the population of Moscow, promising good pay: eleven roubles a year plus an allowance for drink. All these men were ordered to muster at Preobrazhenskoe in December and January, and through the wintry days a stream of recruits poured into Peter's camp. Twenty-seven new infantry regiments were to be formed on the model of the four Guards regiments, with two to four battalions apiece. Now, Peter professionally felt the loss of Patrick Gordon. Lacking the Scotsman's experienced hand, Peter supervised the training himself, assisted by General

Avtemon Golovin, the commander of the Guard, and Brigadier Adam Weide. Meanwhile, Prince Nikita Repnin was sent to enlist and train men from the towns along the lower Volga.

Although the commanders of the three new army divisions, Golovin, Weide and Repnin, were Russian, all of the regimental commanders were foreigners, some of whom had seen action in the Crimean and Azov campaigns, others newly hired from the West. Peter's greatest difficulty was with the older Russian officers, many of whom had no taste whatever for going to war. To replace those who were cashiered, many courtiers were enrolled as officers. They seemed to pick up soldiering so quickly that Peter exclaimed prematurely, "Why should I spend money on foreigners when my own subjects can do as well as they?" Subsequently, nearly all the court chamberlains and other palace officials entered the army.

The new soldiers were uniformed on the German model with coats of dark-green cloth, breeches, boots and three-cornered hats. They were armed with muskets and bayonets, and a beginning was made in teaching them to march in columns, deploy into line and stand firmly side by side and fire on command. The artillery, which was numerous—thanks to 300 guns sent as a present from King Charles XII to help the Tsar fight the Turks—was under the command of Prince Alexander of Imeritia. The Prince had been Peter's companion in Holland and had devoted himself to the study of artillery at The Hague. Brigadier Weide, who had served in the Austrian army under Prince Eugene of Savoy, drew up the articles of war under which infractions of army discipline were to be severely punished.

Through the spring of 1700, Peter was caught suspended between the war he wanted to end and the war he wanted to begin. During the negotiations in February 1700, the rumors from Constantinople grew so ominous that he decided he must prepare for renewal of the war with the Sultan. He left his new regiments drilling at Preobrazhenskoe and went to Voronezh, where he worked furiously to help make his ships ready for war. Near the end of April, in the presence of his son, his sister and many boyars, he launched the sixty-four-gun ship *Predestination,* on which he himself had worked.

While Peter was at Voronezh, both of his Baltic allies struck their planned blows at Sweden. In February, without any declaration of war, 14,000 Saxon troops suddenly invaded Livonia and laid siege to the great fortress city of Riga. The Swedes counterattacked and drove them back, killing General Carlowitz in the process. Peter was disgusted, especially with Augustus; the King, he said, should have been in Livonia leading his troops himself instead of "diverting himself with women" in Saxony.

In March, the second of Peter's new allies, Frederick IV, invaded the territories of the Duke of Holstein-Gottorp, south of Denmark, with 16,000 men and laid siege to the town of Tonning. Now, if ever, was the time for

Peter to add his weight by striking at Ingria. But the Tsar's hands were tied. "It is a pity," he replied to Golovin, "but there is nothing to be done. I have not heard from Constantinople."

During the spring, rumors of Turkish preparations for war grew so strong and so disturbing to Peter that he felt it necessary to re-cement his formal good relations with Sweden. Rumors of his secret treaties with Denmark and Poland were seeping out and, to reassure the Swedes of his good intentions, he proposed sending a Russian embassy to Stockholm. Thomas Knipercrona, the Swedish ambassador in Moscow, who was entirely ignorant of the plotting which had gone on under his nose the previous autumn, was pleased by the projected embassy, and Peter deliberately played on Knipercrona's trust. On the day after his return from Voronezh, the Tsar called on Knipercrona in Moscow and jokingly rebuked the Ambassador's wife for writing to her daughter that all the Swedes in Moscow were in terror because the Russian army was about to invade Livonia. The daughter had been visiting in Voronezh and had shown the Tsar her mother's letter. "I could hardly calm your daughter, she was crying so bitterly," said Peter. "You cannot think that I would begin an unjust war against the King of Sweden and break an eternal peace which I have just promised to preserve." Knipercrona begged the Tsar to forgive his wife. Peter embraced the Ambassador affectionately and swore that if the King of Poland captured Riga from Sweden, "I will tear it from his hands." Thoroughly convinced, Knipercrona reported in his dispatch to Stockholm that the Tsar had no thought of aggression against Sweden.*

The spring passed, then June, then July, and still no word came from Constantinople. On July 15, Peter received a Saxon envoy, Major General Baron Langen. Augustus, who finally had joined his army before Riga, begged the Tsar to begin military operations. Reported Langen: "The Tsar sent his ministers out of the room, and, with tears in his eyes, said to me in broken Dutch how grieved he was at the delay in concluding a peace with Turkey. . . . [He said that] he had ordered his ambassador to conclude a peace or truce in the quickest possible time even to his own loss, in order to have his hands free to aid his allies with all his forces." Finally, on August 8, news from Constantinople arrived. The thirty-year armistice had been signed on July 3, and Ukraintsev's messenger, traveling by the fastest means, reached Moscow with the news thirty-six days later.

Free at last to act, Peter moved with great speed. On the evening of the

---

* Then, as now, morality played a peripheral role in war and diplomacy. Most states seized whatever territories or colonies they could. In Peter's view, these coastal regions were ancient Russian lands; now was simply the best time to reclaim them. Similarly, Peter's simultaneous negotiations with the Swedes and the Saxons were nothing to be ashamed of in that day. Similar charades were acted out routinely in London, Paris, Vienna and Constantinople.

day Ukraintsev's dispatch arrived, the temporary peace with Turkey was celebrated in Moscow with an extraordinary display of fireworks. The following morning, war with Sweden was declared in the manner of the old Muscovite tsars, from the Bedchamber Porch in the Kremlin. "The Great Tsar has directed," the proclamation went, "that for the many wrongs of the Swedish king, and especially because during the Tsar's journey through Riga he suffered obstacles and unpleasantness at the hands of the people of Riga, his soldiers shall march in war on the Swedish towns." The proclaimed objectives of the war were the provinces of Ingria and Karelia, "which by the Grace of God and according to law have always belonged to Russia and were lost during the Time of Troubles." That same day, Peter dispatched a handwritten letter to Augustus informing him of what had happened and saying, "We hope, by the help of God, that Your Majesty will not see other than profit."

THUS BEGAN the Great Northern War, or, as Voltaire called it, "The Famous War of the North." For twenty years, two youthful sovereigns, Peter and Charles, would wrestle for supremacy in a conflict that would settle the fate of both their empires. In the early years, 1700 to 1709, Peter would be on the defensive, preparing himself, his army and his state for the hour when the Swedish battering ram would be pointed toward his backward kingdom. In these years, amidst the storms of war, Russia would continue her transformation. Reforms would be made not as a result of careful planning and methodical execution, but rather as desperate, hurried measures dictated by the need to stave off a relentless enemy. Later, after Poltava, the tide would turn, but both sovereigns would fight on, the one enmeshed and distracted by largely useless alliances, the other burning to avenge his defeat and restore his crumbling empire.

23

LET THE
CANNON DECIDE

PETER OF RUSSIA and Charles of Sweden, Frederick of Denmark, Augustus of Poland, Louis of France, William of England, Leopold of Austria and most of the other kings and princes of the era eventually submitted their differences to the decision of war. War was the final arbiter between nations in the seventeenth and eighteenth centuries as, indeed, it has been in the twentieth. Dynastic rivalries, the drawing of frontiers, possession of cities, fortresses, trade routes and colonies, and ultimately the destinies of kingdoms and empires all were decided by war. The axiom was succinctly put by one of Louis XIV's young officers: "There is no judge more equitable than cannon. They go directly to the goal and they are not corruptible."

For fifty years, through the second half of the seventeenth century, the armies of France were the most powerful and most admired in Europe. Its forces were overwhelmingly the largest on the continent. In peacetime, it kept a standing army of 150,000, and expanded this to 400,000 in time of war. During the War of the Spanish Succession, eight large French armies, each commanded by a marshal of France, campaigned simultaneously in the Low Countries, on the Rhine, in Italy and in Spain. Thanks to the King and Louvois, France's soldiers were the best trained, the best equipped and the best supplied in Europe. Thanks to generals such as Turenne, Condé and Vendôme, they were overall also the most successful. The Duke of Marlborough's shattering defeat of Marshal Tallard at Blenheim (the Duke was aided by his companion-in-arms, Prince Eugene of Savoy) was the first great defeat of the French army since the Middle Ages.

Throughout this period, the size, firepower and destructiveness of all armies was growing rapidly. As energetic finance ministers enlarged the tax base for the support of armies, increasing numbers of troops could be put into the field. In the first half of the seventeenth century, a European battle might see as few as 25,000 troops involved on *both* sides. In 1644, at Marston Moor, the decisive battle of the English Civil War, Cromwell pitted 8,000 men against an equal number under King Charles I. Sixty-five years

later, at Malplaquet, Marlborough led 110,000 allied troops against 80,000 Frenchmen. At the peak of its strength, Sweden, with a home population of a million and a half, supported an army of 110,000. Peter, even after dismissing the disorganized, irregular mass of feudal soldiery he inherited from Sophia and Golitsyn, eventually raised and trained a completely new army of 220,000.

Although, as wars dragged on, conscription became necessary to fill the ranks, most armies in this period were made up of professional soldiers. Many of these, both officers and men, were foreign mercenaries—in that time, a soldier could join any army he liked as long as he did not fight against his own king. Frequently, kings and princes who were at peace rented out whole regiments to warring neighbors. Thus, Swiss, Scots and Irish regiments served in the French army; Danish and Prussian regiments in the Dutch army; and the Hapsburg Imperial army contained men from all the German states. Individual officers changed sides as often as modern executives change jobs, nor did their past or future employers bear them ill-will for their actions. As a twenty-four-year-old colonel, Marlborough served under Marshal Turenne against the Dutch and was personally praised at a great parade by Louis XIV himself. Later, in command of a predominantly Dutch army, Marlborough almost toppled the Sun King from his throne. For a while, both before and after Peter came to the throne, most of the senior officers in the Russian army were foreigners; without them, the Tsar could have fielded little more than a mob.

Customarily, these professional soldiers conducted warfare by accepted rules. There was a seasonal rhythm to war which was rarely broken: summer and autumn were for campaigning and battles; winter and spring were for rest, recruiting and replenishment. In the main, these rules were dictated by the weather, the crops and the state of the roads. Every year, the armies waited until the spring thaw had melted the snows and enough fresh green grass had sprouted to nourish the horses of the cavalry and baggage trains. In May and June, once the mud had dried to dust, long columns of men and wagons began to move. The generals had until October to maneuver, besiege and offer battle; by November, when the first frost appeared, the armies began going into winter quarters. These rules were almost religiously observed in Western Europe. Through ten consecutive years of campaigning on the continent, Marlborough regularly left the army in November and returned to London until spring. In the same months, senior French officers returned to Paris or Versailles. A long-vanished aspect of those civilized wars was the issuance of passports to prominent officers to travel through hostile territory on the shortest routes for winter leave. Common soldiers, of course, did not enjoy these privileges. There was no question of home leave for them until the war was over. If they were fortunate, they were confined to billets in town through the coldest months. All too often, however, they

were crowded into winter encampments of huts and hovels, prey to frostbite, disease and hunger. In the spring, the gaps chewed through their ranks by pestilence would be filled by fresh consignments of recruits.

On the march, an army of this period moved slowly, even when its passage was unopposed; few armies could move faster than ten miles a day, while the average daily march was five. Marlborough's historic march from the Low Countries up the Rhine to Bavaria before the Battle of Blenheim was considered a "lightning stroke" at the time—250 miles in five weeks. The limiting factor usually was the artillery. The horses struggling to pull the cumbersome, heavy cannon, whose wheels fearsomely rutted the roads for those that followed, simply could not move faster.

Armies marched in long columns, battalion after battalion, a screen of cavalry riding in front and on the flanks, the carts, carriages and gun caissons trundling along in the rear. Normally, an army marched at sunrise and camped in mid-afternoon. Making a new camp every night required almost as much effort as the day's march. Tents were erected in lines, baggage unpacked, cooking fires lit, water provided for men and animals, and the horses set to grazing. If the enemy was nearby, each camp had to be placed on suitable ground and prepared with temporary earthworks and wooden palisades as a potential strongpoint able to resist attack. Then, after an exhausted sleep, the men were roused, and in the pre-dawn darkness all this had to be dismantled and packed into wagons for the next day's march.

Not everything, of course, could be carried in wagons. An army of 50,000 to 100,000 men could maintain itself only by marching through fertile countryside which could supply many of its wants, or by having additional supplies brought to it by water. In Western Europe, the great rivers were the railways of war. In Russia, where the rivers flow north and south and the war between Russia and Sweden was east-west, rivers were of little value, and the consequent dependence on wagon trains and local foraging was far greater.

In Western Europe, most campaigns proceeded in a leisurely manner. Sieges were popular and much preferred to the greater risks and nasty surprises of open-field battle. Siege warfare was conducted with exquisite, almost mathematical precision; on each side, at any given moment the commander knew exactly where matters stood and what was going to happen next. Louis XIV was devoted to siege warfare; there was no risk of losing the great army which he had so carefully and expensively built. Also, it enabled him to participate safely in the Game of Mars. Besides, in Louis de Vauban, the Sun King possessed the greatest master of fortification and siege operations in the history of warfare. On behalf of his master, Vauban personally laid siege to fifty towns without a failure, and his own fortresses were the models for the age. Sometimes purely military bastions, sometimes large fortified towns or cities, they covered and protected the frontiers of

France like an interlocking web. Carefully adapted to the particular terrain, each was a work not only of supreme utility but also of art. They tended to be shaped like a gigantic star, with each rampart built so as to be protected by flanking enfilade fire from cannon or at least musketry at right angles. Each salient was a self-contained fort, with its own artillery and garrison, its own sally ports for sudden sorties by the defenders. Around these great stone ramparts ran a tracery of ditches, twenty feet deep and forty feet wide, also faced with stone—bleak and desolate places for attacking infantry to find itself. When they were built, France's armies were on the offensive, and these fortresses, their great doors decorated with gilt fleur-de-lys and opening onto buildings of severe splendor, were intended not as static defense points but as pivots on which French armies could maneuver. Later, as Marlborough's armies were battering their way toward Paris and Versailles, Vauban's fortresses saved the Sun King his throne.

Louis himself paid credit to his servant: "A town defended by Vauban is a town impregnable; a town besieged by Vauban is a town taken."* Under Vauban's direction, sieges became formal theatrical spectacles, immaculately staged and timed. Once the fortress was surrounded, Vauban began a series of trenches which zigzagged ever nearer to the fortress walls. Calculating the angles with mathematical precision, Vauban placed the trenches so that defending fire from the fortress walls could scarcely touch the infantry in the trenches digging their way ever closer. Meanwhile, the besieger's artillery fired day and night at the ramparts, silencing defending cannon, smashing holes in the parapets. When the moment of assault came, the attacking infantry stormed out of the trenches and across the ditches (which they had filled with portable fascines of tightly bound brush) and through the breaches in the pulverized walls. Few sieges, however, reached this climax. In the rigorous etiquette which governed both sides, once the defender knew that it was mathematically certain that his fortress would fall, he was free to surrender with honor; neither his own government nor the besieger expected anything less. But if, in a burst of unreasoning passion, the defender refused to surrender and the assailant was forced to go to the expense in time and lives of taking the city by storm, then, once taken, the entire city was given up to rape, sack and flames.

Although Vauban's art has never been excelled, then, as now, the greatest commanders of the era—Marlborough, Charles XII, Prince Eugene—were practitioners of the war of movement. Of these, the greatest unquestionably was John Churchill, Duke of Marlborough, who commanded the armies of Europe against Louis XIV from 1701 to 1711 and who never fought a battle he did not win or besieged a fortress he did not take. In ten years of

---

* Although when the King himself was present at a siege, the credit had to be shared. As Louis put it: "Monsieur de Vauban proposed to me the steps which I thought best."

war, fighting against one marshal of France after another, he defeated them all, and when political change in England cost him his command, he was driving relentlessly through Vauban's great fortress barrier toward Versailles itself. Marlborough was not interested in the conventional, limited warfare of the time; it was not a single town or fortress that he sought. His belief was in decisive, major action, even at great risk. His objectives were the annihilation of the French army and the humbling of the Sun King in a great open-field battle. He was ready to stake a province, a campaign, a war, even a kingdom, on the outcome of a single afternoon. Marlborough was the most successful all-round soldier of the age. He acted simultaneously as field commander, allied commander-in-chief and England's foreign minister and virtual prime minister. In terms of our own most recent major war, it was as if he combined the functions and duties of Churchill, Eden, Eisenhower and Montgomery.

But Marlborough's command always had a certain balance, a blend of grand strategy and tactical purpose. The most daring and aggressive soldier of the age was Charles XII of Sweden. Charles, it seemed to his enemies and to a watching Europe, was anxious for battle, at any time and at any odds. He was utterly devoted to rapid movement and shock tactics. His impetuosity and eagerness to attack have brought the charge of rashness, even of fanaticism, and it is true that his tactics were those of George S. Patton: Always attack! But it was not attack based on madness; rather, the Swedish attack was based on rigid training and iron discipline, on total dedication and belief in victory, and on excellent battlefield communications. Informed by drums and messengers, subordinate commanders always knew what was expected of them. Any weakness in their own army was quickly covered; any weakness in the enemy's ranks was rapidly exploited.

Charles was willing to break the seasonal tradition of warfare—the hard frozen ground was easier for his wagons and cannon, and perhaps his troops were more used to the freezing weather—and was ready to campaign in winter. Obviously, in a war of movement the army with the greater mobility had the advantage. Campaigns were as often decided by transportation and logistics as by pitched battles. Thus, anything which improved mobility was important; the French were enormously pleased by the development of a new portable baking oven which could be set up, fired and produce fresh bread within hours.

Although field commanders were always wary when an enemy army was nearby, few battles in the seventeenth and eighteenth centuries were fought unless both sides were willing to fight. It was difficult to find suitable terrain and to arrange the necessary elaborate array of men, horses and guns. A commander reluctant to fight could usually avoid battle by remaining in rough, scrubby, broken ground. Should one general begin the hours of preparation necessary to ready his lines for battle, the other, if unwilling,

could march away. Thus, two armies could exist in reasonable proximity for days without a major engagement.

When both commanders had compelling reasons to fight—to contest a river crossing or a strong position on a main road—the armies wheeled into position 300 to 600 yards apart. If there was time, the army which expected to be on the defensive—usually the Russians when confronted by Charles XII or the French when faced by Marlborough—erected barriers of sharpened stakes called chevaux de frise planted in the ground before the infantry lines to give some protection against advancing enemy cavalry. At points along the line, artillery officers sited their guns, ready to fire cannonballs weighing three, six, eight pounds or even sixteen and twenty-four pounds for the heaviest guns, 450 to 600 yards into the enemy ranks. A set-piece battle usually began with an artillery bombardment; a long pounding could be damaging, but was rarely decisive against experienced and disciplined troops. To an astonishing degree, the men simply stood waiting in ranks while cannonballs whistled through the air or bounded along the ground, tearing bloody lanes through their lines.

The greatest advances in field artillery during the seventeenth century had been made by Sweden. Gustavus Adolphus had standardized field-artillery calibers so each gun would not need its own supply of balls and, in the heat of battle, the same ammunition could feed any gun. Then, as artillery became almost an end in itself, Swedish generals realized that artillerymen often were forgetting the need to support their own infantry. To compensate, they attached light cannon directly to the infantry battalions, two guns per battalion, which could give close support by firing directly at the enemy infantry opposing that battalion. Later, Swedish artillery was attached even to cavalry. This highly mobile horse artillery could unharness, fire into enemy cavalry formations and be away in a matter of minutes.

The decisive arm, however, was not the artillery or the cavalry but the infantry, and the great battles of the age were won by infantry battalions advancing or standing in line, fighting each other with muskets, flintlocks, pikes and, later, bayonets. The seventeenth century had been a time of rapid transition in infantry equipment and tactics. For centuries, the ancient pike —a heavy steel-tipped lance fourteen to sixteen feet long—had been the all-conquering "Queen of Battles." Rows of pikemen, their long lances extended, advanced on each other, and the thrust of a wall of pikes brought the decision. But the development of firearms gradually made this famous weapon obsolete. When pikemen faced a line of musketeers, the musketeers could stand at a distance and fire musket balls into their ranks, dropping them one by one. By the end of the century, only a few pikemen still appeared on the battlefield, assigned exclusively to defending the musketeers from hostile cavalry. It still was a fearsome thing for a horseman to ride into a wall of long, sharp pikes, but when the pikeman was not under immediate

attack at close quarters, there was no one more useless or less dangerous on the battlefield. He simply stood in ranks, holding his long pike, being battered by enemy artillery and killed by enemy musket balls, while waiting for someone to approach and impale himself on his pike.

The solution was the bayonet, a device which enabled the musket to serve two purposes: It could be fired until the enemy got very close, and then, with a knife blade attached to the end, could be used as a short pike. At first, this was done by fitting a blade into the barrel. But this restricted firing and was soon succeeded by the permanent ring-held bayonet, which continued in use into the present century. The infantryman could fire until his enemy was on top of him and was still able to greet his foe with a gleaming blade. The bayonet arrived just as the Great Northern War was beginning. The Drabants, the Swedish Guards, were equipped with the bayonet in 1700, and within a few years most armies, including the Russian, had it in use.

Over the latter part of the seventeenth century, the musket itself had been greatly improved. The old matchlock was a cumbersome weapon weighing fifteen pounds or more. In order to lift and use it, the musketeer carried a long, forked stick which he planted in the ground, resting the barrel in the crotch while he aimed and fired. The process of loading and firing a single ball required twenty-two separate motions, among them loading the powder, ramming home wad and bullet, priming, raising to shoulder, aligning on the wooden stick, lighting the match and applying it to the touch hole in the weapon. All too often, because of dampness, the musketeer sighting down his long barrel and waiting for it to fire was disappointed—or worse than disappointed if enemy infantry or cavalry was fast approaching.

The replacement for the matchlock was the flintlock, in which a spark was produced automatically by a piece of steel striking against a piece of flint, the spark then dropping directly into the powder chamber. The weapon was lighter, although only relatively, weighing ten pounds, but it needed no forked stick, and the number of loading and firing motions was cut in half. A good rifleman could loose off several rounds a minute. The flintlock quickly became the standard infantry weapon in all Western armies. Only the Russians and Turks continued to issue old, heavy matchlock muskets, to the detriment of their infantry firepower.

Equipped with this new weapon—the flintlock with attached bayonet— infantry became a highly effective, dangerous and, before long, dominant force on the battlefield. The bayonet not only made two weapons of one, but made the new weapon much less clumsy than the pike, thus giving far greater battlefield mobility to infantry soldiers. The greater speed in firing muskets also demanded new tactics and new formations to make the most of this increased firepower. Cavalry, which had dominated battlefields for centuries, became secondary. Marlborough's contribution was in under-

standing and using the new firepower of the infantry. English soldiers were trained to deploy rapidly from column into line and to deliver steady, disciplined fire, platoon by platoon. As a smaller number of men could now deliver the same volume of fire, the size of battalions was reduced to make them easier to handle. Command became easier, quicker, more responsive. In order to allow larger numbers of muskets to be aimed at the enemy, and also to reduce the depth of the target presented to enemy artillery, infantry lines were extended on the flanks, thus increasing the width of the battlefield itself. Everything was practiced over and over in peacetime, in hope that by repetition it would become flawless habit. The test would come in the heart-shaking moments when the musketeers had fired, with no time for another shot before a wave of enemy horsemen, swords in hand, fell upon them.

By the beginning of the eighteenth century, the enormously increased firepower of the infantry had made the battlefield a more dangerous place than ever before. It was far easier to kill men by standing off and cutting them down with devastating volleys of musket fire than it was to move in and kill them hand to hand as had been required in all previous centuries. In earlier battles, ten percent of the armies engaged might become casualties; now the rates soared higher. Yet, despite its new predominance, infantry still depended for its own safety in battle on keeping perfect order. With their great firepower, if they could hold ranks and not be forced to break, infantrymen could inflict great damage on cavalry which came too close. But they had to depend on strict array when all around swirled enemy cavalry squadrons which, on the slightest hint of disorder, could ride them down, crumple their ranks and trample them into the dust.

The organization of a battle—keeping thousands of men in ranks, arriving in proper formations at the proper moment, under enemy fire—was in itself a stupendous task. Nature conspired against commanders; there was always a copse of trees, a ditch or even a hedge which could impede or disrupt the columns of moving men. Even so, nothing could be hurried. An advance into the most murderous enemy fire had to be slow and sure; haste could jeopardize the balance and timing of an army. Frequently, even with men dropping on all sides, an attacking column would be halted to dress the ranks into better alignment or to allow a parallel column to catch up.

With the rarest exceptions, successful commanders were those who attacked. Marlborough's unvarying tactic was to begin a battle by attacking the strongest part of the enemy line. Habitually, he used his own superbly trained, red-coated English infantry for this purpose. As the worried enemy commander fed more and more of his reserves into this area of the battle, Marlborough maintained and even increased the pressure, accepting whatever casualties he must. Then, when other segments of the enemy line were

weakened, Marlborough unleashed his own reserves, usually a mass of cavalry, against a denuded point of the enemy front. Repeatedly, a breakthrough occurred and the Duke rode a victor across the field.

In the sheer dynamism of their attack, however, the finest infantry and cavalry in Europe were not the English but the Swedes. Swedish soldiers were trained to think only in terms of attack, no matter what the odds. If an enemy somehow seized the initiative and began to advance toward Swedish lines, the Swedes immediately charged forward to break the attack with a counterattack. Unlike the English under Marlborough, whose infantry tactics were based on making the most of its devastating firepower, the basis of the Swedish attack remained the "armes blanches"—cold steel. Both infantry and cavalry deliberately sacrificed the firepower of their muskets and pistols in favor of closing with sword and bayonet.

It made an awesome sight. Slowly, steadily, silently except for the beating of their drums, the Swedish infantry advanced, holding its own fire until the last minute. At close range, the columns deployed out into a long wall of blue and yellow four ranks deep, halted, poured in a single volley and then erupted with a bayonet charge into the reeling enemy lines. It was many years before Peter's Russian levies could stand before this kind of fierce attack. The unexcelled momentum of the Swedish attack derived from two sources: religious fatalism and constant training. Each soldier was taught to share the King's belief that "God would let no one be killed until his hour had come." This produced a calm courage which was anchored in months and years of practice in marching, wheeling, halting, firing, which gave the Swedish infantry maneuverability and cohesion second to none.

Although, increasingly, infantry was the decisive arm, it still was the cavalry which provided the high drama and often, by breaking the enemy when he began to waver, carried the day. Light cavalry was used for screening the army, for reconnaissance, for foraging and for raiding. The Russians employed Cossacks for this purpose, and the Ottoman army, Tatars; the Swedes used the same horsemen in these peripheral duties and in the thick of battle. Heavy regular cavalry was organized into squadrons of 150 men, armored for battle in breastplates and backplates, and armed with swords and often pistols for use against ambush along the roads. In most modern armies of the day, the cavalry was as carefully and rigidly trained in tactical maneuver as the infantry. But there were limits on its use. One, obviously, was terrain; cavalry needed flat or gently rolling open fields. Another was the endurance of horses; even the best cavalry horses were reckoned capable of no more than five hours' fighting at a stretch. Still another was the growing destructiveness of infantry firepower. As flintlock muskets became more rapid-firing and accurate, cavalry had to beware. Neither Marlborough nor Charles XII sent cavalry into action until the climactic moment, when as a

shock force it might break a crumbling enemy line, slam down on the flank of an advancing line of infantry or, in pursuit, turn a retreat into a rout.

Despite such limitations, however, these were still the great days of cavalry (Waterloo with its massed cavalry charges was still a century away, and the charge of the Light Brigade at Balaclava a century and a half). From a quarter to a third of the men in most armies were horse soldiers, and in the Swedish army the proportion was higher. Charles trained his cavalry to attack in tight formations. The Swedish horse approached an enemy at a slow trot, riding in a wedge formation, knee to knee, one trooper locked in beside and slightly behind the next. Three ranks deep, this broad arrow bore down relentlessly on whatever opponent, mounted or on foot, its officers designated.

Seen from afar, a cavalry charge made war seem beautiful: colorful squadrons of horsemen riding across an open field, their swords and breast-plates flashing in the sun, their flags and pennants whipping in the wind, moving bravely toward an enemy line. But for those on the battlefield, it was a place of carnage, a corner of hell: cannon roaring and flashing; infantrymen struggling to keep their rigid formations and follow the commands to load and fire, while around their knees writhed the shattered bodies of comrades; men on horseback riding full tilt into a line of men on the ground; the force of impact, shouts, screams and grunts; men stumbling and falling; horsemen leaning from their saddles, slashing frantically with razor-sharp blades at everyone in sight; the men on the ground thrusting upward toward the saddles with bayonets, catching riders in the chest, the legs, the back; on both sides, the instant of terrible pain, the last flash of surprise and recognition of what was happening, the overwhelming gush of bright-red blood; running men, riderless horses and, over it all, drifting clouds of thick, blinding, choking smoke. And when the firing had ceased and the smoke had lifted, a blood-soaked field carpeted with men still screaming or gasping, or lying quietly, gazing at heaven with unseeing eyes.

Thus did the nations decide their differences.

24

CHARLES XII

THE BLOND, blue-eyed child who became King Charles XII of Sweden was born on June 17, 1682, almost exactly ten years after the birth of his great antagonist, Peter of Russia. Charles' parents were Charles XI, a stern, deeply religious man who had himself become king at the age of five, and Queen Ulrika Eleonora, a Danish princess who had managed by her warmth of character to maintain the affection of both the Danish and Swedish people, even when the two countries were at war. Seven children had been born during the first seven years and nine months of their marriage, but only Prince Charles and two sisters, Hedwig Sophia, a year older than he, and Ulrika Eleonora, six years younger than Charles, had survived. Four younger brothers died, one after another, before reaching the age of two.

Although Charles' body was frail, his boyhood was spent in rough, masculine activity. When he was only four, the people of Stockholm became accustomed to seeing his small figure in the saddle, riding behind his father at military reviews. At six, he was taken out of the care of women and installed in his own apartment with male tutors and servants. At seven he shot a fox, at eight he killed three deer in one day, at ten he killed his first wolf and at eleven his first bear. At eleven also, he lost the last element of feminine warmth in his life when his mother died at thirty-six. The Queen was beloved by her family, and at her death the King fainted and had to be bled and Prince Charles was carried to bed with a fever; soon after, he came down with smallpox, but his body was actually stronger after the disease than before. His face was pocked with deep scars, which he proudly considered marks of manliness. At fourteen, Charles had a slender, wiry body and was a superb horseman, an excellent hunter and an avid student of the military arts.

After the death of Queen Ulrika, King Charles XI spent as much time as possible with his children, who reminded him of their mother. The Prince took on as many of his father's beliefs and mannerisms as he could; his speech became brief, dry and understated, saved from being hopelessly

cryptic by occasional glimmers of sympathy and wit. Honor and the sanctity of one's word became his two cardinal principles: A king must put justice and honor ahead of everything; once given, his word must be kept.

Charles' tutors found that he had a quick intelligence and learned easily. He did not much care for the Swedish language and always spoke and wrote it unevenly. German, the court language of all the northern kingdoms, came more easily to him and he used it as his mother tongue. He became extremely proficient in Latin, speaking it and listening to university lectures in it with much enjoyment. He was taught French, but, despite his tacit alliance with Louis XIV during his years of rule, he disliked speaking it; nevertheless, he read it with ease, and admired French theater. During his fifteen years of campaigning on the continent, he read and reread Corneille, Molière and Racine. The idea of travel stirred him immensely and he devoured accounts and drawings by travelers and explorers. As a boy, he wistfully wished for a brother who might stay in Sweden to rule while he himself traveled the world. He was fascinated by history and biography, especially the lives of the military conquerors—Alexander the Great, Julius Caesar and Sweden's Gustavus Adolphus; later, he carried a biography of Alexander with him through all his campaigns, sometimes making specific comparisons between the Macedonian and his own military achievements. Charles was genuinely interested in religion. As a boy and young man, he spent an hour every morning with a bishop discussing the chapters of the Bible one by one. He was intrigued by mathematics and, like Peter, by its application to the arts of artillery ballistics and fortification. While his tutors admired his quick grasp, they worried about the strength of his will, which often seemed pure obstinacy. Once the Prince considered himself right, they discovered, it was impossible to change his mind.

Charles' education, off to a good start, was permanently interrupted when he was fourteen. On April 5, 1697, King Charles XI died at forty-two of cancer of the stomach. Traditionally, Swedish princes did not reach their majority and could not be crowned until they were eighteen, and with this in mind, the dying King appointed a council of regents, including the boy's grandmother, the Dowager Queen Hedwig Eleonora. After his father's death, Charles attended meetings of the Regency Council and at first made an excellent impression by his intelligent questions and, even more, by his willingness to remain silent and listen to the debate among his elders. He also surprised everyone by his cool behavior during a great fire which destroyed the royal palace even as his father's body lay in state inside the building. In contrast to his grandmother, who totally lost her head, the boy calmly issued orders and saved the body from the flames although the building itself was reduced to ashes.

Within six months, it became apparent that the Regency Council would not work. The Regents were divided in their opinions and often could not

reach decisions, and Charles was too intelligent and too strongly attracted to power to be left on the sidelines while others ruled his kingdom. The regents, reminded by the late King's will that they would be held responsible for their actions when young Charles reached his majority, grew eager to have his views on every subject under discussion. Increasingly, he was surrounded by those anxious to gain his favor, and the power of the regents was heavily undercut. The government of Sweden was lapsing into paralysis. The only solution, taken in November 1697, was to declare the boy, then fifteen, to be of age and to crown him King of Sweden.

To most of his countrymen, Charles' coronation ceremony was a shock. He was succeeding to the crown as the sole and absolute ruler of Sweden, unchecked by council or parliament, and he meant to drive the point home in his coronation. He refused to be crowned as previous kings had been: by having someone else place the crown on his head. Instead, he declared that, as he had been born to the crown and not elected to it, the actual act of coronation was irrelevant. The statesmen of Sweden, both liberal and conservative, and even his own grandmother were aghast. Charles was put under intense pressure, but he did not give way on the essential point. He agreed only to allow himself to be consecrated by an archbishop, in order to accede to the Biblical injunction that a monarch be the Lord's Anointed, but he insisted that the entire ceremony be called a consecration, not a coronation. Fifteen-year-old Charles rode to the church with his crown already on his head.

Those who looked for omens found many in the ceremony. By the new King's command, in respect for his father's memory, everyone present, himself included, was dressed in black; the only touch of color was the purple coronation mantle worn by the King. A violent snowstorm produced a stark contrast of black on white as the guests arrived at the church. The King slipped while mounting his horse with his crown on his head; the crown fell off and was caught by a chamberlain before it hit the ground. During the service, the archbishop dropped the horn of anointing oil. Charles refused to give the traditional royal oath and then, in the moment of climax, he placed the crown on his own head.

This astonishing scene soon was followed by further evidence of the new King's character. The nobility, hoping that Charles would mitigate the stern "reduction" decrees, was distressed to find the young monarch determined to continue his father's policy. Members of the council shook their heads over the King's self-confidence, his obstinacy, his absolute refusal to turn back or change a decision once he had made it. At meetings, he would listen for a while, then stand and interrupt the dialogue, saying that he had heard enough, that he had made up his mind and that they had his permission to depart. Too late, the Swedish statesmen repented their hasty advancement of the King's coming of age. Now, they and the greatest power

in Northern Europe were under the absolute power of a headstrong, willful adolescent. Feeling their hostility, Charles decided to downgrade, if not eliminate, the council. The old councilors and ministers were kept waiting in anterooms sometimes for hours before the King would see them—then, after listening briefly to their arguments, he would dismiss them. Only later would they learn what decisions had been taken on the gravest national matters.

Charles' formal education came abruptly to an end; his indoor hours were now completely taken up by affairs of state. But he was still a vigorously healthy adolescent, attracted by violent physical exercise and a keen wish to test his body and spirit against a whole spectrum of physical challenges. To satisfy his urge to break free of responsibility and the reproachful words and glances of older people, he began taking long rides on horseback. Determined to absorb his energy and drive away his problems by sheer physical exhaustion, he chose to concentrate on immediate challenges such as clearing a high wall on his favorite horse or beating a friend to a distant tree at a dead gallop. In the winter, accompanied only by a page and an officer of the guard, he left the palace in the darkness of early morning to ride through the forest among the lakes outside the capital. There were accidents. Once, in deep snow, his horse fell on him, pinioning him so that he could not move. As usual, he was far in advance of his companions, and by the time they found him he was nearly frozen. Another time, riding across a frozen lake, Charles had almost reached the far side when he found a fifteen-foot stretch of open water between himself and the bank. Although he could not swim, he urged his horse into the icy water and clung to its back while the animal swam across.

Every sport had to provide him the thrill of danger—and the greater the danger, the more attraction it held for him. Just to prove that he could, he rode his horse straight up a steep cliff, and both horse and rider fell over backward; the horse was injured, but not the King. He raced toboggans down icy hills. He drove sledges at breakneck speed, sometimes fastening a number of sledges together in a long train down a slope. In spring, summer and fall, he hunted, but, having decided that it was cowardly to hunt with firearms, he took only a pike and a cutlass when he went in search of bears. After a while, he decided that even the use of steel was unfair, and he went with only a strong wooden pitchfork. The sport was to taunt the cornered bear until it rose on its hind legs, then spring forward and catch it in the throat with the fork and hurl it over backward, whereupon the King's companions would hurry to bind the animal in a net.

Even more dangerous were the military games Charles loved. As Peter had done at Preobrazhenskoe, Charles divided his friends and staff into two companies, equipping them with staves and supposedly harmless hand grenades made of pasteboard which nevertheless exploded with painful

effect. While the King was storming a snowy rampart, one such blast shredded his clothing and wounded several of his friends.

The King's closest companion and greatest competitor in these martial sports was Arvid Horn, a young captain of the elite Royal Cavalry Guards, the Drabants. The Drabants were essentially a kind of cadet corps, whose ranks were filled with men who would eventually become officers of the Swedish army; indeed, each cavalryman in the ranks was already a future lieutenant and, as such, received a lieutenant's pay. With Horn at his side, Charles threw himself fervently into the vigorous and often violent training program of the Drabants. Frequently, two groups of horsemen, with Charles commanding one and Horn the other, rode at each other without saddles, using stout hazel sticks as weapons. Blows were given with maximum force; no one, not even the King, was spared. In one such fray, Charles, trading blows with Horn, lost his temper and lashed out at his adversary's face, which was not permitted. As it happened, Charles' blow landed on an already swollen boil on Horn's cheek. The Captain fell fainting from his saddle, was carried to bed and developed a fever. In an anguish of guilt, Charles visited him every day.

Sometimes the mock battles took place at sea. The royal yacht and other ships in Stockholm harbor were rigged with fire pumps and hoses to serve as cannon and maneuvered as if in battle. On one of these occasions, Horn stripped off most of his clothes and jumped from his yacht into a rowboat, rowing vigorously straight at the King. He was repelled by powerful jets of water from Charles' ship which soon filled Horn's small dinghy so that it began to sink. Horn leaped into the water and calmly swam around to the other side of the royal ship. Charles, leaning over the rail, shouted down to ask his friend whether swimming was difficult. "No," cried Horn, "not as long as you are not afraid." Stung by the challenge, Charles immediately leaped into the water. Unfortunately, he did not know how to swim. He was thrashing violently but sinking when Horn grabbed him by his clothes and towed him ashore.

To his elders, the King's behavior seemed recklessly dangerous, but Charles in fact was teaching himself the lessons of war. He set out deliberately to harden himself and to increase his resistance to fatigue. Having slept half the night in bed, he would rise and spend the rest of the night half naked on the bare floor. One week in winter, he slept three nights without undressing in a freezing stable, covered by hay. He was ashamed of any sign of weakness. He considered his delicate, fair skin to be effeminate and tried to darken it in the sun. He wore the traditional wig only until he began his first campaign against Denmark, then he threw it away and never wore another.

His older sister, Hedwig Sophia, was his closest friend as a child, but Charles saw no other girls and came to dislike the society of women. He

was cold, arrogant and violent, and there was nothing warm or inviting about his personality to attract the opposite sex—except his rank. As sovereign of the leading state in Northern Europe, Charles was of great interest to monarchs and foreign ministers eager to make alliances through royal marriages. Even in his early years, six different princesses were proposed to him. Nothing came of it, and for a long time even the mention of marriage distressed him. The only serious candidate was Princess Sophia of Denmark, five years older than Charles, who could not be considered after the Great Northern War began and Denmark became one of his enemies.

In 1698, a different impending marriage brought him a new companion when his cousin Frederick IV, Duke of Holstein-Gottorp, arrived in Stockholm to marry Hedwig Sophia. The Duke was six years older than Charles, and even more frenetically madcap. From April to August, he egged Charles into a spate of wild behavior which came in Sweden to be known as "the Gottorp Fury." Together with a suite of high-spirited young men who accompanied the Duke, the two cousins competed in wild and dangerous pranks. They raced their horses until the exhausted animals collapsed foaming to the ground. They chased a wild hare around the gallery of the Parliament building. They shattered palace windows with pistol balls and threw tables and chairs down into the palace courtyard. At dinner, it was said, they threw cherry pits in the faces of the King's ministers and knocked dishes from the servants' hands. In broad daylight, they galloped through the streets, waving naked swords and jerking hats and wigs from the heads of anyone within reach. In the middle of the night, when they came back from their little rides, galloping and shouting through the silent streets, townspeople who stumbled to their windows saw their King, his shirttails flying, riding after the Duke. Once, the King even led his Holstein comrades on horseback into a room where his grandmother, the Dowager Queen, was playing cards. The old lady collapsed in fright.

Many of the stories were exaggerated, deliberately so, to discredit the unwelcome Duke and the coming marriage. There is no firm evidence of the tales of bloody orgies at the palace in which the two young men practiced beheading sheep to determine who had the greater force of muscle and skill with a sword. But the rumors continued: The floors of the palace were said to be slippery with blood; the blood was running in rivers down the staircases; the severed heads of animals were being tossed at random out the palace windows into the street.

True or not in every detail, the reckless behavior of these two headstrong young men, to whom no one apparently had the authority to say no, greatly angered the people of Stockholm. They tended to blame the Duke, saying that he wanted to injure the King, perhaps even see him killed, so that through Charles' sister he might himself gain the throne. As the episodes continued, the murmurs grew louder. One Sunday, three Stockholm clergy-

men all preached sermons on the same theme: "Woe to thee, O Land, when thy King is a child." Charles, sincerely pious like his father, was strongly affected by these admonitions. In August 1698, when the Duke married his sister and returned to Holstein, Charles became more quiet and reflective and went back to affairs of state. He rose early every morning, spent more time at devotions and began to interest himself in architecture and theater.

There was one relapse. When Duke Frederick returned in the summer of 1699, a great drinking bout took place in which a captive bear was forced to drink so much Spanish wine that he lumbered to a window, lurched out into the courtyard below and was killed by the fall. Charles was found, his clothes in disarray, his speech slovenly, at this scene. When he realized what he had done, he was deeply ashamed and vowed to his grandmother that he would never drink alcohol again. For the rest of his life, with all the Protestant fervor of the North, he stuck to this promise. Except on two famous occasions when he was wounded or overcome with thirst in battle, he never touched another drop of strong liquor. Across Europe, he became famous as the king who drank nothing stronger than watery beer.

EIGHTEEN-YEAR-OLD Charles was deep in the forest hunting bear when he heard the news that Augustus' troops had invaded Swedish Livonia without a declaration of war. He took it calmly, smiled, turned to the French ambassador and said quietly, "We will make King Augustus go back the way he came." The bear hunt continued. But when he returned to Stockholm, Charles addressed the council. "I have resolved never to begin an unjust war," he said, "but also never to end a just war without overcoming my enemy." It was a promise which he was to pursue, beyond all normal policy, almost beyond all reason, for the rest of his life. When, a few weeks later, he heard the less surprising news that Frederick of Denmark had entered the war by marching into the territory of the Duke of Holstein-Gottorp, Charles said, "It is curious that both my cousins, Frederick and Augustus, wish to make war on me. So be it. But King Augustus has broken his word. Our cause, then, is just and God will help us. I intend to finish first one of my enemies and then will talk with the other." At this point, Charles did not know that a third enemy, Peter of Russia, was also preparing to enter the field against him.

None of his enemies took Sweden's power lightly; its military reputation was far too high. But the nation's point of weakness, as these enemies saw it, lay at the top. All responsibility and authority, military and civil, now rested on the shoulders of an eighteen-year-old King. Charles might have counselors and ministers, tutors, generals and admirals, but he was an absolute monarch, and his behavior, as had been well reported, swung between obstinate rudeness and obsessive recklessness. It seemed an unlikely

combination for leading a nation to resist the combined attack of three powerful foes.

Unfortunately for them, Charles' enemies did not and could not know the King's true character. The boy who dreamed of Julius Caesar and Alexander the Great was not afraid of the challenge; he welcomed it. He was prepared not only for war, but for fierce, desperate, far-ranging war; not for one quick battle and a petty little peace treaty, but for sweeping, radical solutions. His father's advice before his death had been to keep Sweden at peace "unless you are dragged into war by the hair." This "unjust war" thrust on Sweden by surprise brought all of Charles' stern Northern morality into play. He was not prepared, like other monarchs, to back and fill, to compromise, to outlast his enemies by intrigue, to fight one day and dance the next. He had been unjustly attacked by Augustus, and, no matter how long it took, he would not rest until Augustus was driven from his throne. In attacking Charles, the allies had unleashed a thunderbolt. Proud, rash, willful, glorying in challenge, jealous of the reputation of Sweden, anxious to test his own courage in the greatest game of all, Charles turned to war not only with determination but with glee.

WHEN CHARLES XII SAID, "I intend to finish first one of my enemies and then will talk with the other," he was describing his military strategy in a nutshell. Thereafter, no matter what was happening elsewhere in Sweden's empire, the King concentrated his attention and his forces on one enemy alone. When this enemy was totally defeated and destroyed, then he would turn to face his other foes. The first Swedish blow was to fall on the nearest of Charles' enemies, Denmark. He ignored the Saxon troops marching into Livonia across the Baltic. This province would be left to be defended by the local garrison in Riga, and the hope was that it could hold out until the Swedish field army could arrive. If not, it must fall and be avenged on a future day. But nothing must hinder the concentration of forces against the foe selected by Charles.

In his campaign against Denmark, Charles was fortunate in having the support of the two Protestant sea powers of William III, England and Holland. William, single-mindedly bent on maintaining the great coalition he had spent his life building against Louis XIV, wanted no distractions in the form of minor wars in Northern Europe. If or when Louis XIV reached out for the Spanish throne—and with it all the power and wealth of Spain and its overseas empire—William wanted Europe to be ready to resist; any new war anywhere in Europe, therefore, must be prevented or snuffed out quickly lest it spread into Germany and disrupt his grand coalition. For this reason, England and Holland needed peace in the North and had guaranteed the status quo. When Frederick of Denmark

moved troops into the Holstein-Gottorp territories at the foot of the Danish peninsula, he was in effect breaking the status quo; as Denmark was the aggressor, the two sea powers would cooperate with Sweden to defeat the Danes as quickly as possible and restore the status quo. A combined Dutch and English fleet was dispatched to the Baltic to assist the Swedes.

The Anglo-Dutch squadron was an essential factor in Charles' plans. The Swedish navy consisted of thirty-eight ships-of-the-line and twelve frigates—a formidable force in the Baltic, where Russia had neither fleet nor seacoast and Brandenburg and Poland had only negligible forces. But the Swedish fleet was second, in both size and experience, to the Danish-Norwegian navy, which was accustomed to operating not only in the Baltic but also in the North Sea and the Atlantic, and which jeeringly looked on Swedish sailors as mere "farmhands dipped in salt water." That there was some truth in this was evident from Charles' own reaction to the sea. Despite his mock sea battles in Stockholm harbor, the open waves made him seasick, and he looked upon his ships primarily as a means of transporting his soldiers from one side of the Baltic to the other. Certainly, he was not prepared to move his troops by water while a more powerful Danish fleet waited to intercept them. And he was not prepared to deal with that Danish fleet until his own navy had been reinforced by the Anglo-Dutch squadron on its way.

Through the weeks of March and April, Sweden pulsed with preparations for the coming campaign. The fleet at the main Swedish naval base, Karlskrona, was fitted out for sea. Ships were careened, their bottoms scraped, patched and retarred, their masts installed and rigging set. Cannon were trundled aboard and placed in carriages. Five thousand new seamen were recruited, raising the strength of the fleet to 16,000 men. All commercial vessels in Stockholm harbor, of both Swedish and foreign registry, were seized for use as troop transports. The training of the army was intense. Infantry and cavalry regiments were enlisted, based on the Swedish system which called for each district or town to be responsible for providing the men and equipment of a specific-sized unit. The ranks of the army grew to 77,000 men, and the men were equipped with the new muskets and bayonets so successfully used by the French, English and Dutch armies on the continent.

By mid-April, Charles was ready to depart Stockholm. On April 13, 1700, he came at night to say goodbye to his grandmother and his two sisters. It was a sad occasion, but it would have been much sadder had any of those present known what the future held. The eighteen-year-old King was leaving two of these dear relatives forever. Although Charles would live another eighteen years, he would never see his grandmother, his older sister or Stockholm, his capital, again.

The King to whom these women bade farewell had grown from an

adolescent to a young man. He was five feet nine inches—tall by the standards of the day—with broad shoulders and a narrow waist. He carried himself with almost rigid straightness, yet he was enormously supple: On horseback, he could bend down from the saddle and pick up a glove at a full gallop. His open face had a jutting nose, full lips and pink skin, although campaign life was soon to darken and harden it. His eyes were deep blue, lively and intelligent. He wore his hair short and brushed up from the sides to form a crown. Its color varied as the sun bleached it from auburn to dark blond in the summer. Over the years it turned to gray streaked with white and began to recede, exposing a full, domed forehead.

Leaving his sisters and grandmother, the King hurried south, visiting military depots along the way. On June 16, at Karlskrona, he embarked on board the *King Charles*, flagship of the Swedish Admiral Wachtmeister. The Anglo-Dutch fleet of twenty-five ships-of-the-line had now arrived off the western Swedish port of Göteborg, and as Charles set sail from Karlskrona, the allied fleet moved down the Kattegat. The two fleets were now approaching each other, but in the middle lay the formidable barrier of the sound with its three-mile-wide channel, its shoals and its defensive cannon. In addition, the Danish fleet of forty men-of-war lay at the Baltic entrance to the main channel, determined to bar the uniting of their opponents.

It was Charles who solved the problem. Standing on the deck of the flagship, he instructed Admiral Wachtmeister to take the fleet through the shallow and more treacherous subsidiary channel close to the Swedish shore. Wachtmeister was reluctant, fearing for the safety of his ships, but Charles took the responsibility, and, one by one, the great ships bearing the blue-and-yellow flag passed slowly up the channel. Three of the largest ships drew too much water and had to be left behind. Nevertheless, at a single stroke, the Anglo-Dutch and Swedish fleets had joined to make a combined force of sixty men-of-war to face the forty Danish ships. It was a superiority which the Danish admiral did not wish to challenge, and it permitted the next phase of the Swedish plan to unfold. Charles and his generals planned to move a Swedish army across the sound onto the Danish island of Zealand, on which the capital, Copenhagen, was situated. As the main Danish army was far away with King Frederick, fighting the Duke of Holstein-Gottorp, the Swedes hoped to march swiftly on Copenhagen, threaten and perhaps seize the capital and thus bring King Frederick to terms. The plan, devised by Charles' leading commander, Field Marshal Carl Gustav Rehnskjold, had the King's enthusiastic support. The Dutch and English admirals were less enthusiastic, but eventually they, too, agreed.

On July 23, the assault force of 4,000 men was embarked in transports and sailed in rain and high wind. Although the force was smaller than the 5,000 Danes defending Zealand, the Swedes had the advantage of mobility and could choose their landing spot. Feinting first to mislead the defenders,

the Swedish landing parties came ashore in small boats and found themselves opposed by only 800 men. Covered by heavy cannon fire from the men-of-war, the Swedish soldiers quickly established a beachhead. Charles himself came ashore by boat, wading the last few yards. To his chagrin, he found that by the time he arrived the enemy had already withdrawn.

The Swedish build-up was rapid. Within the following ten days, another 10,000 Swedish troops including cavalry and artillery were ferried across the sound. The outnumbered Danish forces withdrew into the city of Copenhagen, and Charles' army followed, setting siege lines around the city and beginning a bombardment. It was this dismaying situation which the King of Denmark found when he hurried back from the south: his fleet outnumbered and useless, his capital under siege, his main army engaged far to the south. Frederick knew that he was beaten and quickly came to terms. On August 18, 1700, he signed the Peace of Travendal, by which he gave back the Holstein-Gottorp territories he had taken and dropped out of the war against Sweden. Charles was satisfied—he had no designs on Danish territory, and could now turn his attention to Augustus. The English and Dutch were satisfied—the war on the boundaries of Germany and the Hapsburg empire had been snuffed out. The status quo had been restored.

Charles' first campaign of the war, thus, had been swift, successful and almost bloodless. Within two weeks, two bold decisions—to force the lesser channel with the Swedish fleet, and to land troops on the island of Zealand behind King Frederick's back—had restored the rights of his ally, the Duke of Holstein-Gottorp, and driven one enemy from the war. Not all the success in this brief, brilliant campaign can be credited to Swedish arms alone; it was the presence of the Anglo-Dutch fleet that made the descent on Zealand possible.

And so Denmark was out of the war. Charles realized that, given a promising chance, Frederick might reopen hostilities, but not for a while. At least the Swedish thrust into Zealand had gained valuable breathing time. Now, Charles could make ready to hurl himself on a second enemy. At the end of the Danish campaign, he thought that his next adversary would be Augustus of Poland. But events dictated differently. In fact, the second Swedish blow was to fall on Peter of Russia.

25

NARVA

THE TSAR'S declared objective in attacking Sweden was to seize the Baltic provinces of Ingria and Karelia. Ingria was a comparatively narrow strip of land extending seventy-five miles along the southern shore of the Gulf of Finland, from the mouth of the Neva to the town of Narva; Karelia was a much larger expanse of forest-and-lake country between the gulf and Lake Ladoga, extending as far west as Vyborg. Together, the two provinces, which had been taken from Russia during the Time of Troubles, would give Peter an adequate opening to the Baltic.

Narva, a coastal town and fortress in Estonia on the border of Ingria, had not been included in Peter's original war aims; it was part of the territory which Patkul and Augustus had designated to go to Poland. Nevertheless, Peter felt that the surest way of securing Ingria would be to capture this town. And as he studied his maps of the region, it seemed that a thrust at Narva would not be difficult; the Russian frontier lay only twenty miles to the southeast of the town, a short march for an invading army.

Peter's decision was received unhappily by Patkul and Baron Langen, Augustus' representative in Moscow. They were not eager to see Swedes replaced in Estonia by Russians, even if, for the moment, the Russians were their allies. As Baron Langen reported to Patkul, "I have done everything possible, with the help of the Danish ambassador, to distract him [the Tsar] from this intention. We found him so stubborn that we feared to touch any more on such a delicate subject and must be satisfied with the Tsar's break with Sweden in the hope that in time Narva will be in our hands." Patkul worried that, having taken Narva, Peter would move down the Baltic coast, swallowing the whole of Livonia without Augustus being able to prevent him. But there was nothing to be done; the Tsar was determined.

By mid-September 1700, Prince Trubetskoy, Governor of Novgorod, had received orders to march on Narva and invest the city with an advance guard of 8,000 men. Command of the main army was given to Fedor Golovin, who had served as ambassador, foreign minister and admiral and

now was to be a field marshal. Under Golovin, the army was divided into three divisions, to be commanded respectively by Avtemon Golovin, Adam Weide and Nikita Repnin. In all, the army totaled over 63,000 men, but the troops were widely scattered. As Trubetskoy's men were moving slowly in the direction of Narva, Repnin's division was still assembling on the Volga, a thousand miles away. By October 4, 35,000 Russians were building trenches before the town and Peter himself had arrived to oversee the siege. He was awaiting only the arrival of cannonballs and powder to begin the bombardment.

The town of Narva, built by the Danes in the thirteenth century, had been a flourishing seaport in the time of the Hanseatic League, and even in Peter's day it handled a substantial amount of Russian trade from Pskov and Novgorod. It was like many another Baltic German town, with gabled brick houses and the thin spires of Lutheran churches rising above tree-lined streets. Situated on the west bank of the River Narova on a neck of land made by a wide bend in the river, the town was in effect surrounded on three sides by water, and because it was so close to the Russian frontier, it was strongly defended. A high wall of stone laced with bastions encircled the city. Across a stone bridge was the squat, powerful castle of Ivangorod, built by the Russians in 1492 when the river was the frontier. Then, Ivangorod was intended to overawe the town of Narva, but now town and castle formed a single, integrated defense system. The garrison consisted of 1,300 infantry, 200 cavalry and 400 armed civilians.

Under the direction of Lieutenant General Ludwig von Hallart, a Saxon engineer lent to Peter by Augustus, the Russians established siege lines opposite the land walls on the western side of Narva. There, astride the only road by which a relief force could approach the town, the Russians entrenched themselves between double walls which cut off the town from the west and at the same time protected their own siege lines against attack from the rear. In time, these walls developed into earthworks four miles long, nine feet high, with a trench six feet deep in front.

The siege went more slowly than Peter had hoped. Although Narva was only twenty miles from the Russian frontier, it was well over a hundred miles from the nearest Russian cities, Novgorod and Pskov. The meager roads, sodden from the autumn rains, caused the transport wagons to mire and become bogged down. There were too few artillery harnesses, the carts went to pieces and the horses collapsed. Golovin did his best to move the soldiers quickly, seizing local horses and carts, but it was not until the end of October that most of his troops were in position.

The Russian artillery bombardment began on November 4. Meanwhile, Sheremetev was sent westward with 5,000 horsemen to report any sign of a Swedish rescue force. For two weeks, the Russian cannon battered the ramparts and towers of Narva with little success; the gun carriages were so

badly made or so damaged in transport that many fell to pieces after three or four shots. Two Russian infantry assaults on Ivangorod were easily repulsed. By November 17, there was not sufficient ammunition to continue the bombardment beyond a few days, and the guns were silenced until new supplies could arrive. At the same time, two distressing reports arrived in Peter's camp: King Augustus had given up the siege of Riga and retired into winter quarters. And King Charles XII had landed with a Swedish army at Pernau on the Baltic coast, 150 miles southwest of Narva.

ONCE THE PEACE OF TRAVENDAL was signed, the Swedish army was rapidly withdrawn from Zealand. Charles' officers were not anxious to leave their troops on the Danish island once the Dutch and English squadrons had departed for home, and these great ships were preparing to sail. True, the Danes had made peace, but who could tell what temptations might occur to them if the small Swedish expeditionary force was left alone and exposed on the wrong side of the sound. In addition, the King was eager to transfer the soldiers quickly in order to use them in a second campaign before winter. By August 24, the last Swedish soldier had been embarked and transported back to southern Sweden. During the last days of August and the first weeks of September, Charles refused to listen to any suggestions of peace, thinking only of deciding on the place where his counterblow against Augustus should fall. It was generally assumed that the army would sail for Livonia to relieve the city of Riga and drive the Saxon armies out of the province. But word began to reach him of Russian troops massing on the frontier of Ingria in such numbers that there could be little doubt of Tsar Peter's warlike intentions. And in fact, before the end of September, Charles received the Tsar's declaration of war and the news that a Russian army had crossed the frontier and appeared before the Swedish fortress of Narva.

The Swedish decision was for Livonia. Two enemies, Augustus and Peter, were attacking in that region; two major Swedish fortresses, Riga and Narva, were in danger. The king thereafter closed his mind to everything else and devoted his energy to getting his expedition under way before storms and ice on the Baltic made movement by sea impossible. In a letter from Swedish headquarters, one of Charles' officers declared, "The King is re-solved to go to Livonia. He refuses to see the French and Brandenburg ambassadors lest they be carrying peace proposals. He wishes at any price to fight with King Augustus and is annoyed at anything which seems likely to hinder his doing this."

On October 1, spurning all warnings of danger from autumn storms on the Baltic, Charles sailed from Karlskrona for Livonia. Although the troops were crowded aboard the ships, there still were only enough transports to carry 5,000 men on this first voyage. On the third day, with the fleet in mid-

Baltic, a storm swept down as predicted and scattered the ships far and wide. Some anchored and rode out the storm off the coast of Courland, others foundered and were lost. Many of the cavalry horses were crippled as the ships heaved and rolled in the waves, and Charles was desperately seasick.

On October 6, what was left of the battered Swedish fleet entered the port of Pernau at the top of the Bay of Riga. The mayor and the city council greeted the King on the quay, and an honor guard of soldiers fired its muskets in the air as he walked through the cobbled streets to his temporary lodgings. As soon as the storm damage could be repaired, the fleet was dispatched to Sweden to bring another 4,000 men, more horses and the remainder of the artillery. In Pernau, Charles heard that Augustus of Poland had lifted the siege of Riga, halted military operations and withdrawn into winter quarters. Back in mid-July, the Polish King had personally joined the siege with 17,000 Saxon soldiers, but the news of the Peace of Travendal with its sudden toppling of his once-bellicose Danish ally had surprised and disheartened him. Now, learning of the impending Swedish descent on Livonia, Augustus had prudently withdrawn to await developments. Charles received this intelligence with bitter disappointment. He had hoped to fight Augustus; he was determined to fight somebody. And, in this context, there remained a possibility. Only 150 miles away, Peter of Russia was in the field with a Russian army, besieging the fortress of Narva. Charles made his decision quickly: If the Saxons would not fight, he would fight the Russians. He would march against the Tsar to the relief of Narva.

Charles began by concentrating all his available troops. With the men he had brought and the additional soldiers sailing from Sweden, plus some of the Riga garrison now freed by Augustus' retirement, he estimated that he could amass 7,000 infantry and 8,000 cavalry by November. For five weeks, he intensively drilled the army at Wesenberg, and during this period Swedish cavalry patrols skirmished regularly with Sheremetev's horsemen along the road to Narva.

Not everyone in the Swedish camp was enthusiastic about the idea of a winter campaign against the Russians. To many of Charles' officers, the enterprise seemed extremely hazardous. The Russian army, they argued, outnumbered them four to one—some rumors said eight to one; the Russians would be defending a fortified line which the Swedes, despite their inferior numbers, would have to attack; it was a seven-day march to Narva through a burned, despoiled countryside, on dangerous, boggy roads winding through three formidable passes which the Russians would certainly defend; illness had begun to spread among the Swedish soldiers and the ranks were thinning; winter was coming and no winter quarters had been prepared.

To these arguments Charles retorted simply that they had come to fight and an enemy awaited them. If the Swedish army withdrew and Narva was

taken, the Russians would flood through Ingria, Estonia and Livonia and then all the eastern Baltic provinces would be lost. The King's optimism and energy won over some of the officers and helped improve the morale of the troops. All understood that responsibility for the campaign, its success or failure, would belong entirely to the eighteen-year-old King. "If the King succeeds," declared Rehnskjold before the march began, "there never was anyone who had to triumph over such obstacles."

At dawn on November 13, without waiting for the arrival of 1,000 cavalrymen expected from Reval, the expedition set out. The columns following the blue-and-yellow flag included every man fit to march, 10,537 in all. The conditions were, as predicted, appalling. The roads were mired by autumn rains and the men had to march and sleep in thick, syrupy mud. The ravaged country was studded with burned-out farmhouses, set alight by Russian horsemen. There was no fodder for the horses and no food for the men except what they carried in their knapsacks. Throughout the march, a steady, cold November rain drenched the men to the skin. At night, when the temperature dropped, the rain turned to flurries of snow and sleet and the ground began to freeze. The King slept with his men under the open sky, receiving the rain and snow on his face.

Despite the bad weather, the Swedish army was pleasantly surprised to find its march almost unopposed. Two of the three passes along the road were entered and occupied without any opposition at all. On the fourth day, the leading troopers of the advance Swedish cavalry screen rode into the Pyhäjöggi Pass, eighteen miles west of Narva, where the road ran alongside a stream through a deep valley surrounded by steep hills. Five thousand Russian horsemen commanded by Sheremetev waited on the far side of the stream, but the bridge across had not been cut.

Charles, riding with the advance guard, was informed of Sheremetev's presence. He ordered that eight pieces of horse artillery be brought forward. Then, at the head of a detachment of dragoons and a part of a battalion of Guards—no more than 400 men in all—the King charged down the valley. The Swedish horse artillery, screened from Russian eyes by the line of galloping dragoons and brought up unexpectedly to the very front line, was suddenly unmasked and opened fire at close range on the clusters of Russian horsemen on the opposite bank. The Russians, startled and frightened by the sudden flash and roar of cannon and having no guns of their own with which to reply, wheeled their horses and galloped away, leaving the pass undefended. Subsequently, it was learned that the Russian retreat was a planned withdrawal and not a flight, as Sheremetev had orders from Peter not to involve his troops in a fight with the main Swedish army. But by the weary Swedes, the charge of a small part of the army followed by what seemed a Russian rout was seen as a victory and provided much-needed

encouragement. A pass which, properly defended, could have cost the Swedish army heavily to force had been taken for nothing. The road to Narva lay open.

That night, still soaked with rain and covered with mud, the Swedes pitched camp on the eastern side of the Pyhäjöggi Pass. The depth of the mire forced many soldiers to spend the night standing up. The following afternoon, the 19th, hungry and half frozen, the army reached the gutted manor house and village of Lagena, about seven miles from Narva. Not knowing whether the fortress was holding out, Charles ordered the firing of a prearranged signal of four cannon shots. Soon, four dull and distant sounds replied from the beleaguered fortress. Narva was still in Swedish hands.

SHEREMETEV had been sent westward with his cavalry only to observe and not to oppose any Swedish movements. Once the Swedish army began its eastward march, he followed instructions and retreated, devastating the country, as far as the Pyhäjöggi Pass. Here, the Russian commander, believing that, if fortified, the pass could easily be defended and the Swedish advance on Narva blocked, had wanted to stop and fight. But Peter, who did not fully appreciate the geography of the area, had rejected Sheremetev's proposal. In Peter's view, the pass was too far from the main camp and he did not want to divide the army. Instead, the decision had been made to fortify the land side of the Russian camp at Narva against an attack by Charles' approaching force, while at the same time vigorously prosecuting the siege. Within the next decade, Marlborough was to take town after town in exactly this manner, first encircling the town with his army, and then fortifying the outer rim of his circular camp to hold off rescuing armies while he strangled the town or fortress within his constricting ring.

On November 17, Sheremetev led his horsemen back into camp, announcing that the Swedes had occupied the Pyhäjöggi Pass and were following close behind. Peter called his officers into council. Additional rounds of ammunition were served out and vigilance was doubled, but that night and the next passed peacefully. In fact, the Russians did not expect any sudden attack by the Swedes once Charles' army arrived. Rather, they anticipated a gradual build-up of forces, a period of reconnaissance, skirmishing and maneuver, with a battle sometime in the future.

At three a.m. on the night of November 17–18, the Tsar summoned the Duc du Croy, a nobleman from the Spanish Netherlands who was with the army as an observer on behalf of Augustus of Poland, and asked him to take command. Peter and Fedor Golovin, the nominal Russian commander-in-chief, were leaving immediately for Novgorod to speed up the reinforcements and to discuss with King Augustus the future conduct of the war.

Peter wanted Augustus' explanation of his withdrawal from Riga, a move which had aroused Peter's disappointment and suspicion, and it was for this reason that he took Golovin with him; Golovin, in addition to being commander of the army, was also minister of foreign affairs.

Some say that Peter's departure from the army the night before the Battle of Narva was an act of cowardice. The picture of a trembling Tsar fleeing in terror before the approach of Charles and leaving the unhappy Du Croy to bear the responsibility for what was to happen has been added to the story of Peter's earlier nocturnal flight to Troitsky to create an image of a man afraid of danger who panicked in moments of stress. The accusation is unfair, both generally and in this particular. Peter risked his life too many times, both on battlefields and on the decks of warships, for the charge of physical cowardice to have merit. The explanation is quite simple: Peter, the one man in Russia on whom all responsibility rested, was going where he felt he could do the most good. Accustomed to the measured pace of Russian military operations, the Tsar assumed that the Swedes would act with similar caution. No one dreamed that an army just arrived after a long, exhausting march would launch an immediate attack on an enemy four times its strength and protected by a ditch six feet wide and an earth wall nine feet high, studded with 140 cannon. Nor was anyone in the Russian camp fully aware of the impetuous character of Charles XII.

The unlucky figure in this decision was Du Croy. Charles Eugène, Duc du Croy, Baron, Margrave and Prince of the Holy Roman Empire, had served for fifteen years in the Imperial army in wars against the Turks, but had been forced to resign after he retreated before the approach of the Grand Vizier and an enormous Ottoman army. Seeking employment, he had presented himself to Peter in Amsterdam in 1698, but the Tsar did not engage him and he subsequently found work with Augustus. It was Augustus who had sent Du Croy to Peter to persuade the Tsar to send 20,000 men to help in the siege of Riga rather than embarking on his own campaign in Ingria. The Tsar followed his own plan, but took Du Croy along as an observer and advisor.

Now, suddenly, Du Croy was asked to take command. Perhaps, had Peter made his decision two weeks earlier, it might have been correct, but now it was too late. Du Croy argued that, lacking the Russian language and unfamiliar with the Russian officers, he would have difficulty issuing orders and ensuring that his commands were obeyed. And he was not happy with the disposition of the Russian troops—the line of circumvallation around the city was too long and the Russian forces were scattered too thinly along its length; a strong Swedish attack on one section of the line might easily succeed before troops from other sections could be brought to help.

Nevertheless, under strong persuasion from the Tsar, Du Croy consented. Peter gave him absolute power over the whole army. His written instruc-

tions were to postpone a battle until more ammunition could arrive, but to maintain the siege and prevent Charles' army from breaking into the town. Baron Langen, in writing to Augustus, noted wryly the change of command: "I hope when the Duc du Croy shall have the absolute command, that our affairs will take quite another turn, for he has no more wine or brandy; and being therefore deprived of his element, he will doubtless double his assaults to get nearer the cellar of the commandant." No one in the Russian camp had an inkling of what was about to happen.

AT DAWN on the morning of the 20th, the Swedish columns had been mustered at Lagena and were moving through the cold rain in the direction of Narva. By ten a.m., the vanguard of the army became visible to the watching Russians. The Duc du Croy, impressive in a red uniform and riding a gray horse, was in the middle of his morning inspection when early musket fire made him realize that the Swedes were approaching. He rode up in time to see the enemy emerging in rain-drenched columns from a wood on top of the Hermannsberg ridge. Du Croy felt no great anxiety: an assault on a fortified line of earthworks such as his was a slow and intricate procedure and he knew from experience that it would develop gradually. Nevertheless, studying the Swedish ranks through his telescope, he was surprised by their small size and he worried that this might be only the vanguard of a larger force. Even so, he would have sent part of his own army, perhaps 15,000 men, out to attack the Swedes, attempting to disrupt their formations and drive them back, had he not found his Russian officers strongly disinclined to leave the protection of their lines. Accordingly, he ordered his regiments to plant their standards along the earthworks, stand to arms and wait.

Charles and Rehnskjold meanwhile were standing on top of the Hermannsberg, sweeping their own telescopes up and down the Russian lines. The battlefield lay spread below them, bounded on both sides by the banks of the Narva River flowing in a wide curve around the town, with the Ivangorod fortress across the stream. Along the foreground lay the Russian siege line. A bridge that crossed the river behind the northern end of the Russian line was the only apparent Russian route of supply—or, should it come to that, of retreat. The defensive fortifications appeared impressive: a ditch, backed by an earth rampart studded with sharpened stakes, the chevaux de frise. Along the earthworks, separate bastions had been constructed, each lined with cannon. The Russian army inside the camp was obviously much larger than the Swedish force. Nevertheless, it was also clear from the activity that could be observed inside the Russian camp that no Russian attack was coming.

The situation Charles and Rehnskjold found themselves in was awkward; many commanders might have considered it desperate. Small and exhausted

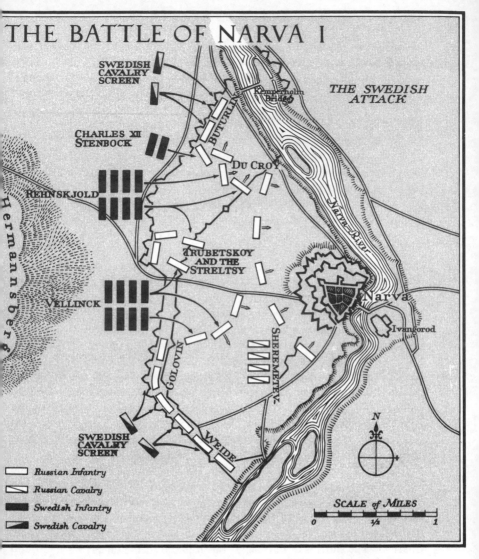

THE BATTLE OF NARVA I

SWEDISH
CAVALRY
SCREEN

Kamperholm
Bridge

THE SWEDISH
ATTACK

BUTURLIN

CHARLES XII
STENBOCK

DU CROY

Narva River

REHNSKJOLD

TRUBETSKOY
AND THE
STRELTSY

Narva

VELLINCK

Ivangorod

GOLOVIN

SHEREMETIEV

Hermannsberg

SWEDISH
CAVALRY
SCREEN

WEIDE

N

☐ Russian Infantry

◹ Russian Cavalry

■ Swedish Infantry

◣ Swedish Cavalry

SCALE of MILES

0   ½   1

armies did not normally attempt to storm fortified lines manned by a
force four times as large, but the very nakedness of the Swedish army
dictated an attack. To remain inert in the face of an enemy this size was
impossible, to retreat equally impossible; the only solution seemed to be
assault. Besides, Charles and Rehnskjold had noticed the same weakness
which Du Croy had pointed out to Peter: The Russian army was spread
along the four-mile length of the line. A concentrated assault on one
section of the line might pierce it before sufficient reinforcements could be
brought up from other sectors, and Charles trusted his disciplined Swedish
regiments, once inside the Russian camp, to exploit the chaos he hoped

would ensue. He therefore ordered Rehnskjold to attack, and the General quickly worked out a plan.

The Swedish infantry, heavily concentrated, was to deliver the main blow. Divided into two divisions, the infantry would assault the earthworks at a point near the center of the line. Once over the wall, the two divisions were to separate, one turning north, the other south, rolling up the Russian line from within and driving the Russians at each end toward the river. The Swedish cavalry would remain outside the earthworks, controlling the ground there, covering the flanks of the infantry as it advanced and dealing with any Russian sortie or escape which might be attempted. Rehnskjold would command the northern (left) wing of the Swedish infantry attack, Count Otto Vellinck would command the right. Charles himself was to command a small separate force on the far left in the company of Colonel Magnus Stenbock and Arvid Horn. As soon as the guns were unlimbered and served, the Swedish artillery opened a bombardment along the middle of the Russian line while the infantry assembled in the center and the cavalry squadrons trotted out to the wings. Thus, in a calm and orderly way, 10,000 Swedes prepared to advance on 40,000 strongly entrenched Russians.

From his position on the Russian rampart, Du Croy watched this activity with growing alarm. He had expected that, according to the rules of war, the Swedes would begin digging ditches and laying out their own fortified camps. His confusion grew when he saw that some of the Swedish soldiers were carrying fascines to use in crossing the ditch dug in front of his earthen rampart. It began to dawn on Peter's commander that, incredible as it might seem, the Swedish army was about to storm his position.

Through the morning and into the early afternoon, the Swedes calmly continued their preparations. By two p.m., when they were ready, the rain had stopped, it had grown colder and a new storm was gathering in the darkened sky. Then, just as signal rockets soared up, setting the army in motion, a blizzard roared in from behind, sweeping snow horizontally toward the Russian lines. Some of the Swedish officers hesitated, thinking it would be better to postpone the attack until the storm was over. "No," cried Charles. "The snow is at our backs, but it is full in the enemy's face."

The King was right. The Russians, with the swirling flakes biting into their eyes, fired their muskets and cannon, but most of their shots, aimed into a white void, went high and did no damage. Silently, swiftly, the Swedes advanced, suddenly looming before them out of the snow. Thirty paces in front of the earthworks, the Swedish line suddenly halted, muskets swung up to the shoulders, a single volley rang out and, on the parapet, Russians "fell like grass." Throwing their fascines into the ditch, the Swedes swarmed across on top of them. Waving swords and bayonets, they climbed over the earthworks and threw themselves on the foe. Within fifteen minutes, a fierce hand-to-hand battle was taking place inside the works. "We charged directly

sword in hand and so entered. We slew all who came at us and it was a terrible massacre," a Swedish officer wrote afterward.

At first, the Russians fought stubbornly—"They returned a heavy fire and killed many fine fellows"—but a breach had been made through which fresh Swedish infantry now poured. Precisely according to plan, the two Swedish divisions separated and began to drive the Russians back along the inside of the earthworks in opposite directions. The southern Swedish column, pressing along the left side of the Russian lines, first engaged the Streltsy regiments under Trubetskoy. These they easily routed, thus sadly confirming Peter's opinion of the value of the Streltsy in fighting a modern enemy. Farther down the Russian line, they encountered Golovin's division, which, although without its commander, put up a strong initial resistance. Then, as one regiment after another of the inexperienced Russians began to crumble, the rest fell into confusion and retreated. Sheremetev's cavalry, stationed on this wing behind the lines, should have been able to intervene, riding down on the advancing Swedish infantry, slowing or even scattering the advance by the weight of men and horses. But the Russian cavalry, made up mostly of mounted noblemen and undisciplined Cossacks, was seized with panic even before it was attacked. Seeing the determined Swedes approach, the cavalrymen wheeled their horses and galloped headlong into the river, trying to escape. Thousands of horses and a thousand men were lost in the small cataracts.

In the north, on the Russian right, the story was much the same. Attacked from behind their earthworks, the Russians attempted a stand, at first defending themselves bravely. Then, as their officers fell, panic set in and they began to flee, crying, "The Germans have betrayed us." As the Swedish advance continued northward, rolling up bastion after bastion, the mass of fleeing Russians grew to huge proportions. So many ran toward the river that soon a dense herd of terrified soldiers, artillerymen and wagoners was stampeding to escape over the single bridge. Suddenly, the bridge cracked and sagged under their weight, sending scores of men sliding and tumbling into the river.

At only one point did the Russian line hold. At the northern end, near the collapsed Kamperholm Bridge, six Russian battalions, including the Preobrazhensky and Semyonovsky Guards regiments, under Buturlin, held their ground and refused to break. Hastily creating a new strongpoint by barricading themselves behind hundreds of artillery and supply wagons, they fought back vigorously, firing with muskets and artillery at the Swedes who now swarmed around them.

Except for this single stand, the Russian army on the northern end of the line and on most of the southern end as well had been reduced to a confused, fleeing rabble. Hundreds of Russian soldiers jumped over the earthworks, trying to escape the blades of the Swedish infantry, only to be ridden down

and driven back by the Swedish cavalry. The foreign officers commanding the Russians found the situation impossible. "They ran about like a herd of cattle," said the Saxon Hallart of his men. "One regiment was mixed up with another so that hardly twenty men could be got into line." Once the Russians began to cry out against their foreign officers, there was no chance of making them obey. Seeing what was happening and hearing the threatening shouts of his own men, the Duc du Croy declared, "The Devil could not fight with such soldiers," and, along with Hallart and Langen, made his way toward the Swedish line and surrendered to Stenbock. He felt safer under Swedish guard than in command of his own undisciplined and terrified troops. Stenbock received them politely and took them to the King.

Charles' role in the action, once the attack on the earthworks had been launched, had mostly been to enjoy himself. He spent the greater part of the afternoon outside the earthworks, deliberately exposing himself to personal danger. Once, while trying to get around a mound of wounded and dying men, he fell with his horse into the ditch; he was extricated, but had to leave the animal, his sword and one of his boots behind. He mounted another horse, which was immediately killed under him, while he himself was hit by a spent ball which he found in his necktie after the battle. Seeing the King without a horse, a Swedish horseman leaped from his own mount and offered it to the King. Scrambling into the saddle, Charles said smilingly, "I see that the enemy want me to practice riding."

As darkness fell, the King appeared inside the earthworks, covered with mud and still lacking a boot. He found that although Du Croy and most of the foreign officers had surrendered and many regiments of the Russian army had disintegrated, victory was not secure. In spite of the Russian losses, there still were 25,000 Russians under arms on the scene and scarcely more than 8,000 Swedes. The native Russian generals, Prince Dolgoruky, Prince Alexander of Imeritia, Avtemon Golovin and Ivan Buturlin, had not given up so quickly as Du Croy, Hallart and Langen. They had retreated to the wagon-train barricade at the northern end of the camp, and here, around this improvised bastion, the fiercest fighting of the day was taking place. Meanwhile, on the Russian left, General Weide's division was still largely intact, having taken little part in the battle. If suddenly Weide's troops had begun to attack toward the north and the regiments inside the ring of wagons had come pouring out to attack toward the south, the thin ranks of Charles' soldiers would have been caught in between.

It seemed imperative, therefore, for Charles to capture the wagons. He brought up artillery and trained it on them, but this proved unnecessary: The spirit of the Russians inside was finally broken. Convinced that further resistance was hopeless, the Russian generals sent to make terms. Charles was secretly delighted. In the gathering darkness, his soldiers, who now completely surrounded the wagon train, had been unable to distinguish between

THE BATTLE OF NARVA II

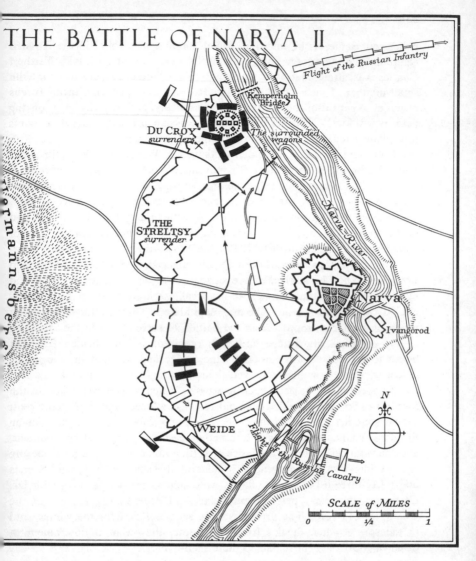

friend and foe and accidentally were firing at each other. The Russian surrender stopped this, and near eight o'clock the King gave the order to cease firing. But the Russian capitulation was less than total. At first, the Russians insisted on marching out of the redoubt with full military honors. Eventually, they settled for an arrangement which allowed the private soldiers to keep their muskets and small arms, while the officers became prisoners of war. Charles also took possession of the regimental standards and all of the artillery.

Even then, with this mass of Russians on their hands, the situation remained dangerous for the Swedes. Most of their foot regiments were totally

exhausted. Some of the men had found supplies of alcohol in the Russian camp and, drinking on empty stomachs, soon became drunk. Further, Charles was afraid that at dawn the Russians would be able to count the small number of men who had conquered and were guarding them. It was essential to get rid of the beaten Russians quickly, and to usher them off the field expeditiously. Charles ordered the Russian prisoners to get to work immediately repairing the sagging Kamperholm Bridge.

There remained also the potential danger of Weide's division, still undefeated farther down the former Russian line. Wrote one Swedish officer, "If Weide had had the courage to attack us, he would certainly have beaten us, for we were extremely tired, having scarcely eaten or slept for several days, and besides this, all our men were drunk with brandy that they had found in the Muscovite tents, so that it was impossible for the few officers that remained to keep them in order." But the Weide threat quickly evaporated. Although his troops had not been heavily engaged, Weide himself had been wounded. When he learned of the surrender of the northern wing, he had no stomach to continue alone. At daybreak, seeing himself alone and encircled by Swedish cavalry, he too capitulated. Through the rest of the morning, scattered troops across the battlefield surrendered to the Swedes.

By daybreak, the bridge had been repaired, and the beaten Russians began to cross it. Charles stood by the bridge and watched the long lines of enemy soldiers as they removed their hats, laid their banners at his feet and trudged off to the east, back to Russia. When muster was taken in the Swedish ranks, the losses were found to be 31 officers and 646 men killed, 1,205 wounded. Losses on the other side could only be estimated, even by the Russians themselves. Eight thousand at least had been killed or wounded, and the wounded stood little chance of getting home across the now freezing countryside. Ten Russian generals, including the Duc du Croy, ten colonels and thirty-three other senior officers were held as prisoners, along with Dr. Carbonari, the Tsar's personal physician, and Peter Lefort, nephew of the Tsar's dead favorite. The prisoners were sent to Reval for the winter, and in the spring, when the ice freed the Baltic, they went to internment in Sweden. Most of them remained there many years.*

---

* The Duc du Croy suffered a more curious fate. Allowed to remain at Reval after the defeat, he wrote from there to the Tsar asking for money to pay his expenses. Peter promptly sent him 6,000 roubles. In the spring of 1702, he died and was mourned by his former Russian employer. "I am sincerely sorry about the fine old man," said Peter when he heard the news. "He was in truth an able and experienced military commander. Had I entrusted the command to him fourteen days earlier, I would not have suffered defeat at Narva."

When the Duke died, he was once again insolvent. Peter was informed and intended to pay the debt, but never got around to it. Whereupon the Duke's creditors in Reval

The principal Swedish booty was the Russian artillery: 145 cannon, 32 mortars, 4 howitzers, 10,000 cannonballs and 397 barrels of powder. Peter's army was effectively stripped of the Tsar's favorite weapon. Seeing the mass of beaten Russians marching away, and contemplating the prisoners and the booty, Magnus Stenbock was moved to say, "It is God's work alone, but if there is anything human in it, it is the firm, immovable resolution of His Majesty and the ripe dispositions of General Rehnskjold."

NEWS OF THE BATTLE OF NARVA made a sensational impression throughout Europe. Accounts of the brilliant victory and glowing praise of Sweden's youthful monarch rippled westward. There was satisfaction in some quarters at Peter's humiliation and much snickering at the Tsar's "flight" on the eve of battle. A medallion struck by Charles showing a man with Peter's face running away caused much amusement. Leibniz, who earlier had shown interest in Russia, now expressed his sympathy with Sweden and expressed his wish that its "young king reign in Moscow and as far as the River Amur."

Although Rehnskjold's "ripe dispositions" and seasoned command had played an indispensable part in the successful outcome, it is also true that without the King's "firm, immovable resolution" to attack there would have been no victory at Narva. Certainly, Charles himself fully accepted the popular estimate of himself as an invincible warrior. He was exuberant— almost intoxicated with victory—when he rode over the battlefield with Axel Sparre, chattering excitedly like an adolescent boy. "But there is no pleasure in fighting with the Russians," he said disdainfully, "for they will not stand like other men but run away at once. If the river had been frozen, we should hardly have killed one of them. The best joke was when the Russians got upon the bridge and it broke under them. It was just like Pharaoh in the Red Sea. Everywhere you could see men's heads and horses' heads and legs sticking up out of the water, and our soldiers shot at them like wild ducks."

From that moment on, war became the great object of Charles' life. And in this sense, while Narva was the King's first great victory, it was also the first step toward his doom. A victory so easily won helped persuade Charles

invoked an ancient law which stated that those who died in debt could not be buried. The body was placed in a church vault, where in the dry atmosphere it did not decay but mummified. Eventually, it was taken out and placed under glass. For almost 200 years, visitors to Reval were taken to see the Duke lying before them still in his wig and uniform. A few years before the revolution, the imperial government decided that the spectacle was unseemly and the Duke was finally buried.

that he was unconquerable. Narva, added to the dramatic success of the descent on Zealand, began the legend of Charles XII—which he himself accepted—that with a handful of men he could rout vast armies. Narva also instilled in Charles a dangerous contempt for Peter and for Russia. The ease with which he had overwhelmed Peter's army convinced him that Russians were worthless as soldiers and that he could afford to turn his back on them for as long as he liked. Years later, in the summer dust of the Ukraine, the King of Sweden would pay dearly for these moments of exaltation on the snow-covered battlefield of Narva.

26

"WE MUST NOT LOSE OUR HEADS"

PETER HAD NOT GONE many miles from Narva when news of the battle overtook him. Stunned by the swiftness and magnitude of the disaster, he also understood that a far greater danger lay ahead: If Charles decided to follow up his victory and march all the way to Moscow, nothing could prevent him.

One of Peter's qualities was that when confronted with disaster he did not despair. Failure only spurred him forward; obstacles served as challenges to stimulate new effort. Whether his resilience, perseverance and determination were grounded in stubbornness, arrogance, patriotism or wisdom did not matter—he had suffered a crushing, humiliating defeat, but there were no recriminations. He kept his composure and vowed to continue. Two weeks after the battle, he wrote to Boris Sheremetev, "We must not lose our heads in misfortune. I order the work we have undertaken to go on. We do not lack men; the rivers and marshes are frozen. I will hear no excuses."

The nine years between Narva and Poltava were desperate years for Peter. He never knew how much time he had remaining. Often sick and stretched on his bed with fever, plagued by revolts among the Bashkirs and Don Cossacks behind his back, he nevertheless hurled his colossal energy into preparing Russia. He played recklessly, staking everything, impoverishing his Treasury and his people, distributing huge subsidies to keep Augustus, his one remaining ally, in the field. And always he was haunted by the knowledge that Charles might rise one morning and decide to turn his shining, invincible bayonets against Russia.

Years later, after Poltava, Peter was able to see all this in perspective. His calm, Olympian tone is that of a man looking back from the pinnacle of victory. But there is in his words an accurate assessment of the influence of Narva on himself, on the development of the Russian army and on Russia itself:

Our army was vanquished by the Swedes—that is incontestable. But one should remember what sort of army it was. The Lefort regiment was the only old one. The two regiments of Guards had been present at the two assaults of Azov, but they had never seen any field fighting, especially with regular troops. The other regiments consisted—even to some of the colonels—of raw recruits, both officers and soldiers. Besides that, there was the great famine because, on account of the late season of the year, the roads were so muddy that the transport of provisions had to be stopped. In brief, it was like child's play [for the Swedes]. One cannot, then, be surprised that against such an old, disciplined and experienced army, these untried pupils got the worst of it. The victory, then, was indeed a sad and severe blow to us. It seemed to rob us of all hope for the future, and to come from the wrath of God. But now, when we think of it rightly, we ascribe it rather to the goodness of God than to his anger; for if we had conquered then, when we knew as little of war as of government, this piece of luck might have had unfortunate consequences. . . . That we lived through this disaster, or rather this good fortune, forced us to be industrious, laborious and experienced.

THE DEFEATED RUSSIAN ARMY which had retreated from Narva under the gaze of the victorious King of Sweden straggled into Novgorod. Lacking cannon, powder, tents, baggage and, in many cases, muskets, the men were little more than a disorganized mob. Fortunately, one division of the army, that which Prince Nikita Repnin had mustered along the Volga, had not reached Narva in time to participate in the debacle, and Peter ordered Repnin to march to Novgorod and use his troops as a cadre to discipline the beaten regiments streaming into the city. Three weeks later, when the stragglers had been counted, Repnin reported to Peter that 22,967 of them had been formed into fresh regiments. Adding Repnin's own force of 10,834 men, this gave Peter an army of nearly 34,000 men. In addition, 10,000 Cossacks were on the way from the Ukraine. Peter's own first command on reaching Moscow was to instruct Prince Boris Golitsyn to raise ten new regiments of dragoons of 1,000 men each.

As commander-in-chief of the rebuilding army, Peter appointed Boyar Boris Sheremetev, who represented an unusual mixture of old and new in Peter's Russia. Twenty years older than the Tsar and a descendant of one of the nation's oldest families, Sheremetev had nevertheless been a youthful rebel against traditional Muscovite ways; once, as a young man, he was denied his father's blessing because he appeared before him with a shaven chin. Unlike most Russian noblemen, Sheremetev had traveled abroad and enjoyed the experience. In 1686, Sophia sent him on missions to King Jan

Sobieski of Poland and to the Emperor Leopold in Vienna. In 1697, at forty-five, he went abroad again, this time as a private traveler on a kind of twenty-month sabbatical from his army duties. He traveled to Vienna, Rome, Venice and Malta, and called on the Emperor, the Pope, the Doge and the Grand Master of the Knights of St. John, who made him a Knight and awarded him a Maltese Cross. Returning to Russia, Sheremetev wore his Cross so proudly that other, envious Russians took to asking snidely whether the boyar had become "the envoy of Malta." Sheremetev bore such comments serenely; Whitworth, the new English ambassador, called him "the politest man in the country."

Peter was pleased by Sheremetev's interest in Europe, but it was as a soldier rather than a diplomat that he used the boyar. Sheremetev's uncle had been commander-in-chief of the Russian army under Tsar Alexis until he was captured by the Tatars and forced to spend thirty years in captivity in the Crimea. Sheremetev himself had fought against both Poles and Tatars. In 1695 and 1696, when Peter attacked Azov, he conducted diversionary campaigns farther west that resulted in the capture of Tatar fortresses along the lower Dnieper. As a commander, Sheremetev was competent but cautious. He could be trusted to obey Peter's standing orders never to risk the army unless the odds were heavily in his favor.

While Sheremetev's new army was being assembled and re-equipped, Peter ordered the immediate construction of fortifications at Novgorod, Pskov and the Pechersk Monastery near Pskov. Women and children were harnessed along with men. Church services were halted so that the priests and monks could join the common people in moving earth. Houses and churches were pulled down to make way for the new ramparts. To set an example, Peter himself labored on the first entrenchments at Novgorod. When he left, he entrusted the effort to Lieutenant Colonel Shenshin, but Shenshin, thinking the Tsar had gone for good, quickly stopped his own manual labor. Peter returned and, discovering this, had him whipped in front of the rampart and sent him to Smolensk as a common soldier.

But Peter realized that, over the longer run, his army needed to be completely reformed as a permanent, professional body, based on a standard conscription term of twenty-five years. Even so, the first appearance of the new army in the field brought faint praise from a Russian observer in 1701:

A great number are called to serve and if they are examined closely the only result is a feeling of shame. The infantry are armed with bad muskets and do not know how to use them. They fight with their sidearms, with lances, and halberds and even these are blunt. For every foreigner killed there are three, four and even more Russians killed. As for the cavalry, we are ashamed to look at them ourselves, let alone show them to the foreigner. [They consist of]

sickly, ancient horses, blunt sabers, puny, badly dressed men who do not know how to wield their weapons. There are some noblemen who do not know how to charge an arquebus, let alone hit their target. They care nothing about killing the enemy, but think only how to return to their homes. They pray that God will send them a light wound so as not to suffer much, for which they will receive a reward from the sovereign. In battle they hide in thickets; whole companies take cover in a forest or a valley and I have even heard noblemen say, "Pray God we may serve our sovereign without drawing our swords from their scabbards."

To remedy these conditions, Peter ordered a complete overhaul in army training, with new standards of discipline and new tactics based on European models. The effort had to start from the very beginning with the creation of new training manuals, the only infantry manuals previously available in Russia being dated 1647—and these had been copied from a German manual of 1615! Peter wanted emphasis placed on training for battle; he had no use for splendidly precise parade-ground formations with soldiers who "play fencing master with their muskets and march as if they were dancing." Neither did he care for the elaborate uniforms of Western soldiers, who looked like "dressed-up dolls." His new army would be dressed in simple green cloth as fast as Russian mills could turn it out. Where possible, his soldiers would wear boots and belts and three-cornered hats. Most important, however, was that they be equipped with modern weapons. Fortunately, while in England, Peter had bought between 30,000 and 40,000 modern flintlocks with new ring bayonets, which were distributed and were used as models for a homemade version. Production at first was low—6,000 in 1701—but by 1706 Russia was producing 30,000 flintlocks a year, and by 1711, 40,000.

Modern tactics were emphasized. The men were taught to fire on command by platoons and how to use the new bayonets. The cavalry was trained to move only on command, to wheel by squadron, to attack with swords and withdraw in an orderly fashion rather than abandon the field like a fleeing herd. Finally, Peter labored to infuse a new spirit into the army: It was to fight not in "the interests of His Tsarish Majesty" but—as Peter wrote the order in his own hand—in "the interests of the Russian state."

Slowly, despite innumerable difficulties, frequent desertions, much jealousy and quarreling among officers, the new army was forged. The most serious problem in terms of equipment lay with the artillery. Almost all the cannon of the Russian army, both heavy siege mortars and field artillery, had been lost at Narva and it was necessary to start from zero. Vinius, the director of the Post Office, was placed in charge, with the title Inspector of

Artillery, and given sweeping powers. All Peter cared about was action. "For God's sake," he wrote to Vinius, "speed the artillery." The old man found that there was no time to mine and refine new metals; the new cannon would have to be cast from some more readily available materials. Peter gave the command: "From the whole of Tsardom, in leading towns, from churches and monasteries, a proportion of the bells are to be collected for guns and mortars." It was near-sacrilege, for the bells were almost as holy as the churches themselves and each played a familiar, timeworn part in people's lives. Nevertheless, by June 1701 one quarter of all the church bells in Russia were lowered from their towers, melted down and recast as cannon. Vinius had trouble with the iron founders who cast the guns, glowing red hot in the fires. They drank too much and even the knout could not force them to hurry. But behind Vinius loomed the wrath of the Tsar. "Tell the burgomasters and show them this letter," Peter wrote to Vinius, "that if through their delays the gun carriages are not ready, they will pay not only with money but with their heads."

In spite of the difficulty in finding workmen and suitable alloys for his iron, Vinius performed miracles. In May 1701, he sent twenty new cannon to the army at Novgorod, seventy-six following soon after. By the end of the year, he had produced more than 300 new guns as well as founding a school where 250 boys were learning to become cannon makers and artillerymen. Peter was pleased. "It is good work," he wrote, "and necessary, for time is like death." In 1702, despite the old man's age, Peter sent Vinius to Siberia to seek out new sources of iron and copper. Between 1701 and 1704, seven new ironworks were developed beyond the Urals, producing an ore which the English ambassador reported to be "admirably good, better than that of Sweden." The Russian artillery continued to grow, and cannon cast in the Urals began to fire at the Swedes. By 1705, the English ambassador declared that the Russian artillery was "at present extremely well served."

PETER'S ATTEMPT to protect Russia included discreet requests in two capitals, The Hague and Vienna, for help in mediating between Sweden and Russia. Both came to nothing. Andrei Matveev, the son of the statesman Matveev, had been sent to Holland as Peter's representative. There, he found William III and the States General wholly consumed by another issue. In the same month as the Battle of Narva, the event which all Europe dreaded had finally happened: Carlos II of Spain had died, leaving his throne to Philip of Anjou, grandson of Louis XIV. The Sun King had accepted on behalf of his grandson, and Europe was girding for war. In addition, Holland had no wish to take sides between Sweden, to which the

Dutch were bound by treaty, and Russia, which provided them with the lucrative Archangel trade. Matveev could manage only to buy 15,000 muskets through Witsen and send them along to Russia.

In Vienna, Prince Peter Golitsyn appeared incognito and appealed for an audience with the Emperor. He was kept waiting for seven weeks, meanwhile negotiating through the Russian-speaking Jesuit priest Father Woolf with anyone who would speak to him. Few were willing. "They all avoid me and do not want to talk to me," he reported helplessly to Golovin in Russia. So low was Russian prestige as a result of Narva that Count Kaunitz, the imperial Vice Chancellor, laughed in Golitsyn's face, and the French and Swedish ambassadors made fun of him in public. When Golitsyn finally saw the Emperor, Leopold was polite, but as he too was preparing for the great War of the Spanish Succession, he offered nothing concrete. "It is necessary to try every possible way to get a victory over the enemy," Golitsyn wrote pleadingly to Golovin. "God forbid that the present summer should pass away with nothing. . . . It is absolutely necessary for our sovereign to get even a small victory by which his name may become famous in Europe as before. Then we can conclude a peace, while now people only laugh at our troops and at our conduct of the war."

Rebuffed in his tentative diplomatic approaches, Peter made sure of the constancy of his one ally. He arranged to meet with Augustus, whom he had not seen since their first meeting in Rawa two and a half years earlier when the King-Elector first proposed this war against Sweden. Now, Augustus was nervous. Although he had not been defeated, he had seen both his allies, Denmark and Russia, swiftly and ruthlessly struck down by the young Swedish King. He had to consider whether to continue the war or come to terms with Sweden.

Peter met the King-Elector in February 1701 at Birze in an area of Livonia controlled by Saxon troops. In ten days of meetings, punctuated with banquets and celebrations, the two monarchs reconfirmed their alliance. Peter informed Augustus that, despite the defeat at Narva, Russia meant to continue the war. Augustus, as the one undefeated member of the coalition, was able to impose stiff terms on Peter. The Tsar agreed that when the spoils were divided, Livonia and Estonia should go to Poland; Ingria alone was reserved for Russia. Peter also promised 15,000 to 20,000 Russian infantrymen—to be paid, equipped and supplied by Russia—to operate under Saxon command in Livonia. Further, he agreed to pay Augustus a war subsidy of 100,000 roubles a year for three years. It was a heavy price, and once again the monasteries and merchants of Muscovy were painfully squeezed. But it was essential to Peter that Russia have an ally against the Swedes.

There were light moments during this diplomatic summit. One day the Tsar and the King-Elector held a personal artillery competition, each

firing cannonballs at a mark in an open field. To Peter's chagrin, Augustus, who had no experience with artillery, hit the mark twice, while Peter himself never hit it at all. The next day, there was a banquet which lasted all night. In the morning, Augustus was fast asleep, but Peter arose alone to go to Catholic mass. His interest in the service prompted his Catholic hosts to propose a union of the Orthodox and Catholic churches, but Peter replied, "Sovereigns have rights only over the bodies of their people. Christ is the sovereign of their souls. For such a union, a general consent of the people is necessary and that is in the power of God alone."

IN THE EXHILARATING WEEKS immediately following the Battle of Narva, Charles was preparing to do just what Peter feared: follow up his victory by invading Russia. Some of the King's counselors advised that he could easily occupy the Kremlin, unthrone Peter, proclaim Sophia and sign a new peace treaty which would add new territories to Sweden's Baltic empire. The prospect glittered before Charles' eyes. "The King thinks now about nothing except war," wrote Magnus Stenbock a few weeks after the battle. "He no longer troubles himself about the advice of other people and he seems to believe that God communicated directly to him what he ought to do. Count Piper [the King's chief minister] is much troubled about it because the weightiest things are resolved without any preparation and in general things go on in a way that I do not dare commit to paper." And in December, Karl Magnus Posse, an officer of the Guards, wrote back to Sweden, "In spite of the cold and scarcity and although water is standing in huts, the King will not let us go into winter quarters. I believe that if he had only eight hundred men left, he would invade Russia with them, without the slightest thought as to what they would live on. And if one of our men is shot, he cares no more about it than he would for a louse and never troubles himself about such a loss."

Despite Charles' impatience, large-scale pursuit into Russia at this time proved impossible. The Swedish army, victorious over its human enemies, was soon beset by more dangerous foes: hunger and disease. Livonia had been devastated by the Russians; what food there was had been eaten by Peter's soldiers. No replenishments could come from Sweden before spring, and the Swedish cavalry horses soon were gnawing bark from trees. Weakened by hunger, Charles' regiments were also ravaged by disease. Fever and dysentery ("the bloody flux") spread through the camp, and the men began to die: 400 from the Vestmanland Regiment, 270 from the Delcarlian Regiment. By spring, less than half the army was still fit for action. Reluctantly, Charles bowed to necessity and sent his regiments into winter quarters. The King himself occupied the ancient castle of Lais, near Dorpat. There, he remained for five months, passing the time with amateur

theatricals, masquerades, suppers and violent snowball fights. Magnus Stenbock organized an orchestra and played for the King music which he had composed himself.

As spring arrived in 1701, Charles still was considering the idea of invading Russia, but with less enthusiasm His contempt for the Russians as soldiers had grown and he thought them scarcely worth fighting against. Another victory over Peter would only make Europe laugh, he felt, whereas a victory over Augustus' disciplined Saxon troops would set the continent to nodding appreciatively. More practically, Charles decided that he could not march on Russia while an undefeated Saxon army was operating in his rear.

By June, 10,000 fresh recruits had arrived from Sweden, swelling Charles' army to 24,000. Leaving a detachment to face the Russians, Charles and the main army of 18,000 marched south, intending to cross the Dvina River near Riga and destroy the army of 9,000 Saxons and 4,000 Russians commanded by the Saxon General Steinau. The river was 650 yards wide, and the Swedish crossing was practically an amphibious landing. With the help of a smokescreen created by burning damp hay and manure to protect the boatloads of Swedish soldiers, and with the support of heavy guns mounted on Swedish ships anchored in the river, the assault was successful. Charles himself led the first wave of infantry, brushing aside the fears of his worried officers with the declaration that he would die only at the moment chosen by God, not before. Unfortunately for Charles, the Swedish cavalry could not cross, and the Saxon army, although badly battered, got away. The behavior of the troops which Peter had sent to aid Augustus was not auspicious. Four Russian regiments, held in Steinau's reserve, panicked and fled before even entering the battle. Charles' regard for Peter's army sank lower.

Soon after this inconclusive victory in July 1701, Charles, then nineteen years old, made a strategic decision which was to profoundly affect his own life, and Peter's: He decided to concentrate on the total defeat of Augustus before invading Russia. At the time, this decision seemed reasonable. To attack both his enemies simultaneously was impossible, and of the two, Saxony was active while Russia was inert. In addition, Saxony and even Poland were finite entities; the Elector and his armies could be pinned down and destroyed, whereas Russia was so vast that the Swedish spear might penetrate deeply and still not find the heart of the huge organism.

And there was Charles' outraged morality. Augustus, his cousin, a cultured European ruler, was a treacherous scoundrel, far worse than the Tsar. Peter at least had declared war before attacking, but Augustus had simply marched into Livonia without warning. How could Charles know that even if he made peace with Augustus, the King-Elector would not break his word and attack him again the moment the Swedes invaded Russia? In sum, Charles told a friend that he considered it "derogatory to

myself and my honor to have the slightest dealings with a man who had acted in such a dishonorable and shameful way."

Finally, Charles was baffled and worried about Augustus' relationship with the vast commonwealth of Poland, over which the Elector exercised an uneasy kingship. So far, Augustus had conducted his war against Sweden only in his capacity as Elector of Saxony. Now, the Saxon army had retreated into what was in effect the sanctuary of Poland, and Charles' army could not follow. Cardinal Radiejowski, the Primate of Poland, had insisted that the Polish commonwealth had nothing to do with the war against Sweden which King Augustus had made without its consent, and that therefore Charles must not set foot on Polish soil. In a letter to the Cardinal on July 30, 1701, Charles replied that Augustus had forfeited the Polish crown by making war without the consent of the Polish nobility and commonwealth, and the only way for Poland to ensure peace was to summon a Diet, dethrone Augustus and elect a new king. He promised that until he received the Cardinal's answer, the Swedish army would not violate the Polish frontier by pursuing Augustus onto Polish soil.

Charles had hoped that the answer would be quick, and he did not wish to press the Cardinal or the Diet. But weeks passed, summer faded into autumn and still no answer came. When the reply at last arrived, in mid-October, it was negative: the Diet requested Charles to stay away and leave Poland to manage its own affairs; no assurance was given that Poland would not allow Augustus' Saxon army to use the country as a base the following year. Charles was furious, but it was too late in the year to take action. He moved the army once again into winter quarters, this time in the neutral Duchy of Courland, which was forced to house and feed the unwelcome army at its own expense. In January, the army shifted farther south into Lithuania.

It was to this second Swedish winter camp, at Bielowice, that an unusual emissary came from Augustus, hoping to use her exceptional powers of persuasion to induce King Charles XII to peace. The lady was Countess Aurora von Königsmark, the most beautiful and most famous of Augustus' many mistresses. Aurora had golden hair, lovely eyes, a rosebud mouth, a high bosom and a slender waist; she was witty, good-natured and talented. Augustus' reasoning is not difficult to discern: If this celebrated Swedish-born beauty could spend some time with the shy, awkward King of Sweden, he might be tamed and taught to soften his rough, warlike air. The fact that Charles was nineteen and Aurora nearly thirty-nine was an advantage, not a hindrance; what was needed for a mission of this kind was beauty but also tact, maturity and experience.

The ostensible reason for Aurora's trip was to visit her many relatives among the Swedish officers in the camp. Upon arrival, she sent a flattering letter to the youthful King, asking the honor of kissing his royal hand. Charles absolutely refused to see her. Not despairing, serenely confident of

the effect of her appearance, the Countess directed her carriage to a spot on the road which the King passed on his daily rides. As Charles approached, Aurora descended from her carriage and knelt before the horseman in the muddy road. Charles, astonished, raised his hat and bowed low in the saddle, then spurred his horse and galloped away Aurora had failed; Augustus would have to find another means of distracting or deterring Charles.

A few months later, in the spring of 1702, Charles invaded Poland, marching on Warsaw and Cracow, determined to do for himself what the Poles had refused to do: remove Augustus from the Polish throne. On July 9, 1702, at the head of 12,000 Swedish troops, Charles brought 16,000 Saxons under King Augustus to battle near Klissow. Nine hundred Swedes were wounded or killed—including Charles' brother-in-law, Frederick of Holstein-Gottorp—in exchange for 2,000 Saxon casualties and 2,000 Saxon prisoners. Patkul, the Tsar's representative at Saxon headquarters, was forced to flee in a peasant cart. But Charles' victory at Klissow was incomplete; once again, Augustus' army had retreated to fight another day. And thus Charles' Polish adventure, which was becoming an obsession, continued—and was to extend itself for six more years. Despite the petitions of the Baltic Provinces, the pleas of the Swedish Parliament and even the advice of his own senior officers, Charles refused to turn on Russia until his vengeance against Augustus was total. According to one of his generals, "He believes that he is an agent of God on earth, sent to punish every act of faithlessness."

DURING THIS BREATHING SPACE while Charles turned his back on Peter to chase Augustus through the forests and marshes of Poland, Russia began to enjoy some small military successes. The first was the stand-off of a Swedish naval expedition against Archangel; then three small but significant victories won by Sheremetev in Livonia. When the Swedish King marched south against Augustus, Sheremetev initiated from his base at Pskov a series of small offensive actions against the Swedish Colonel Anton von Schlippenbach, who had been left to defend Livonia with a force of 7,000 men. On receiving the assignment, Schlippenbach had also been promoted to major general, but in surveying his mission, which was to hold off the whole of Russia for an unknown period, he wistfully told the King that rather than the promotion he would have preferred an additional 7,000 men. "It cannot be," Charles loftily replied.

In January 1702, Sheremetev won an important victory over the unfortunate Schlippenbach near Dorpat at Erestfer in Livonia. The Swedish army of 7,000 had already gone into winter quarters when Sheremetev appeared with 8,000 Russian infantry and dragoons in winter clothing, sup-

ported by fifteen cannon mounted on sledges. In a four-hour battle, the Russians not only succeeded in driving the Swedes out of their winter camp, but inflicted over 1,000 casualties by Swedish admission (the Russians claimed 3,000, and admitted losing 1,000 of their own men). More important in a symbolic sense, the Russians took 350 Swedish prisoners and sent them to Moscow. Peter was overjoyed when he heard the news, declaring, "Thank God! We can at last beat the Swedes." He promoted Sheremetev to field marshal and sent him the blue-ribboned Order of St. Andrew and his own portrait set in diamonds. Sheremetev's officers were promoted, and each of the common soldiers received one rouble of the Tsar's newly coined money. In Moscow, church bells rang, cannon fired and a Te Deum was sung. Peter gave a great banquet in Red Square and ordered fireworks. When the Swedish prisoners arrived, Peter made a triumphal entry into the capital with the captives marching in his train. Russian spirits, depressed since Narva, began to rise.

The following summer, in July 1702, Sheremetev again attacked Schlippenbach in Livonia, this time at Hummelshof, and this time the Swedish force of 5,000 men was almost annihilated. Twenty-five hundred were killed or wounded and 300 captured, along with all the artillery and standards. The Russian losses were 800.

After Hummelshof, Schlippenbach's mobile army ceased to exist and Livonia was left undefended except for the static garrisons at Riga, Pernau and Dorpat. Sheremetev's army and especially his savage Kalmuck and Cossack horsemen were able to move at will through the province, burning farms, villages and towns, taking thousands of civilian prisoners. Thus did Patkul's war for the liberation of Livonia wreak devastation on his homeland. So many civilians were crowded into Russian camps that they were being bought and sold as serfs. Sheremetev, writing to Peter, asked for instructions:

> I send Cossacks and Kalmucks to different estates for the confusion of the enemy. But what am I to do with the people I have captured? The prisons are full of them, besides all those that the officers have. There is danger besides because these people are so sullen and angry. . . . Considerable money is necessary for their support, and one regiment would be too little to conduct them to Moscow. I have selected a hundred families of the best of the natives who are good carpenters, or are skilled in some other branch of industry—about four hundred souls in all—to send to Azov."

Among the prisoners was an illiterate seventeen-year-old girl whom Sheremetev did not send to Azov but kept in his own house. In time, this girl would rise. Martha Skavronskaya, as she was born, would join the

household of the great Prince Menshikov, become the mistress of the Tsar,
Peter's wife, and, finally, sovereign in her own right, Catherine I, Empress of
Russia.

ALONG WITH HIS LAND VICTORIES, Peter, whose thoughts were never far from
the sea, imaginatively devised a new means of attacking Swedish power in
the Baltic provinces: by the use of small boats on the lakes and rivers. If
Sweden had incontestable supremacy in larger, conventional ships of war,
Peter would build swarms of smaller ships which could overwhelm the
enemy squadrons by sheer weight of numbers. He began by building small
naval craft, propelled by oars and a single sail, on Lake Ladoga, Europe's
largest lake, where Sweden maintained a naval squadron of brigantines
and galleys. On June 20, 1702, at the southern end of the lake, 400 Russian
soldiers in eighteen small boats attacked a Swedish squadron of three
brigantines and three galleys. The Swedes were caught at a disadvantage;
their ships were anchored and most of the crews were ashore pillaging a
village when the Russian boats arrived. In the ensuing fracas, the
Swedish flagship, a twelve-gun brigantine, was damaged, and the Swedes had
to retreat. On September 7, the same Swedish squadron was again attacked
near Kexholm, this time by thirty Russian boats. With the Russians harry-
ing his ships like jackals, the Swedish Admiral Nummers found his position
untenable and decided to evacuate the whole of Lake Ladoga. The withdrawal of his fleet down the Neva opened the lake to unchallenged Russian
movement and made possible an important Russian victory that autumn at
Nöteborg.

Meanwhile, Peter's men were employing the same tactics on Lake
Peipus, south of Narva. On May 31 that year, four larger Swedish vessels
were attacked by nearly a hundred Russian boats. The Swedes beat them
off and sank three, but had to withdraw to the northern half of the lake.
On June 20 and July 21, two individual Swedish ships, running supplies
and ammunition across the lake, were attacked by the Russian flotillas. One
went aground and was abandoned after the captain threw his guns over
the side. The other was boarded and then blew up. As a result, the Swedes
withdrew completely from Lake Peipus in 1702. The following year, they
returned in strength, sank twenty of the Russian boats and recaptured
mastery of the lake. But in 1704, the Russians turned the tables once and
for all. Catching the Swedish flotilla moored up the River Embach at Dorpat,
the Russians threw a boom across the mouth of the river and placed
artillery on the shore. Beyond the boom, 200 Russian boats waited for any
Swedish ship which might break through. When the thirteen Swedish ships
came down the river, the current carried them helplessly against the boom,

where the Russian shore batteries began blowing them to pieces. The Swedish crews landed, desperately stormed one of the batteries and finally fought their way back to Dorpat. But one by one the ships were destroyed and the Swedish naval presence on Lake Peipus was annihilated. Later that year, both Narva and Dorpat were captured by the Russian army.

IN THE SPRING OF 1702, Andrei Matveev picked up intelligence in Holland that the Swedes were planning a larger attack on Archangel that summer. To make sure that his country's only port remained in Russian hands, Peter resolved to go there himself. He set out with the twelve-year-old Tsarevich Alexis at the end of April on the thirty-day trip to the north, accompanied by five battalions of the Guard, 4,000 men in all. When he arrived, the defenses were put in order and the wait began. Almost three months passed while Peter occupied himself with shipbuilding, launching the *Holy Spirit* and the *Courier* and laying the keel of a new twenty-six-gun warship, the *St. Elijah*.

In August, the annual fleet of Dutch and English merchantmen arrived, far more numerous than usual, for all the trade which had previously come into Russia through the Swedish Baltic ports was now diverted to Archangel. Along with their goods, the thirty-five English and fifty-two Dutch ships brought news that the Swedes had abandoned any thought of an attack on Archangel that summer. Peter immediately departed for the south. Upon reaching the northern shore of Lake Ladoga, he signaled Sheremetev, who had just won his victory at Hummelshof in Livonia, and Peter Apraxin, who was harassing the Swedes in Ingria, to rendezvous with him and the Guards in order to seize absolute control of the lake by capturing the Swedish fortress of Nöteborg at the point where Lake Ladoga empties into the Neva River.

Nöteborg was a powerful fortress originally built by the city of Novgorod in the fourteenth century. The small island on which it was situated, just at the point where the Neva flows out of the lake and begins its forty-five-mile course to the sea, was shaped like a hazelnut; thus its Russian name, Oreshka, and its Swedish name, Nöteborg. By dominating the mouth of the river at this vital juncture, the citadel controlled all the trade which passed from the Baltic up to Lake Ladoga and through the Russian river network to the interior. Whoever controlled Oreshka controlled trade as far as the Orient. In Russian hands, it served as a barrier to shield the Russian heartland from the Swedes. When the Swedes took it in 1611, it served them as a barrier to keep the Russians away from the Baltic. Now, its thick walls and galleries of brick and stone, its six great round white towers, were studded with 142 cannon. The Swedish garrison was small, only 450 men,

but the swift current of the river made an enemy's approach by boat difficult, even without being subjected to the additional hazard of flying cannonballs. Peter was enthusiastic about the prospect of seizing the fortress. "God gives time not to be wasted," he wrote to Sheremetev, instructing him to come in a hurry. Once the Russian soldiers and siege guns were in place, the isolated fortress, which had no hope of help from a relieving army, was doomed. The lake was covered with flotillas of small Russian boats poised to carry troops into an assault. The riverbanks—the south bank was 300 yards away—were lined with heavy siege mortars planted behind earthworks. A premature Russian assault with boats and scaling ladders was beaten off, but the mortars then began a steady devastating bombardment, methodically shattering the fortress walls. On the third day of the bombardment, the wife of the Swedish commandant sent a letter to the Russian camp asking that she and the wives of the Swedish officers be allowed to depart. Peter himself replied, explaining in an ironically gallant tone that he disliked the thought of separating the Swedish ladies from their husbands; of course they could leave, he said, on condition that they took their husbands with them. A week later, after ten days of bombardment, the survivors in the fortress surrendered.

Peter was ecstatic at this capture of the first important fortress to be taken from Sweden by his new army and his new guns made from the melted-down church bells of Russia. Writing that night to Vinius, he said, "In truth, this nut was very hard, but, thank God, it has been happily cracked. Our artillery did its work magnificently." As a symbol of its importance as the key to the Neva and thus the Baltic, he fixed the key to the fort surrendered to him by the Swedish commandant to the Western bastion of the fortress and renamed the fortress Schlüsselburg, from the word "schlüssel" (key) in German. The Tsar celebrated the triumph with another entry into Moscow, three new triumphal arches and a laurel wreath laid on his own head. Meanwhile, he ordered the damage to the citadel repaired and the defenses enlarged and strengthened with outworks and quarters for up to 4,000 men. Alexander Menshikov was named governor of the rechristened fortress. Thereafter, Peter always had a special place in his heart for Schlüsselburg. Whenever he was in the vicinity on October 22, the anniversary of its capture, he took visitors, or even his entire court, to the site for celebrations and a banquet.

The fall of Nöteborg-Schlüsselburg was a blow to Sweden. It had shielded the Neva and the whole of Ingria against Russian advance from the east. Charles, at the time far way in Poland, recognized the significance when the news was brought to him by an unhappy Count Piper. "Console yourself, my dear Piper," the King said calmly. "The enemy will not be able to drag the place away with them." Nevertheless, on other occasions the King said grimly that the Russians would pay dearly for Nöteborg.

IN THE SPRING of the following year, 1703, with Charles still in Poland, Peter determined "not to lose the time granted by God" and to strike directly at establishing a Russian coastline on the Baltic. An army of 20,000 men under Sheremetev's command marched from Schlüsselburg down through the forest on the north bank of the river toward the sea. Peter followed by water with sixty boats brought from Lake Ladoga. The Neva is only forty-five miles long and is less a river than a broad, fast-flowing chute from the lake to the Gulf of Finland. Along the way, there were no serious Swedish defenses. A single Swedish settlement, Nyenskans, lay several miles upriver from the gulf. Although it was prosperous, with numerous busy mills, its fortifications were unfinished. Russian siege guns began their bombardment on May 11, 1703, and the following day the small garrison capitulated.

On the evening Nyenskans surrendered, word reached the Russian camp that a Swedish fleet was sailing up the gulf. Nine ships commanded by Admiral Nummers appeared off the mouth of the Neva and announced their arrival to their countrymen at Nyenskans by firing two signal guns. In order to deceive the Swedish seamen, the signal was answered immediately. Uncertain, Nummers sent a boat up the river to investigate. The boat was captured. Three days later, still more puzzled, Nummers ordered two of his smaller ships, a three-masted brigantine and a galley, to enter the river and find out what was happening. The two vessels moved upstream through the treacherous, fast-moving water as far as Vasilevsky Island, where they anchored for the night. Meanwhile, Peter and Menshikov had embarked two regiments of Guards in thirty large boats. Slipping down the Neva, they concealed themselves in the marshy waters among the numerous islands. At dawn on May 18, they suddenly appeared, rowing to attack the Swedish ships from all sides. The battle was fierce, with the Swedes firing their cannon to smash the Russian boats crowding around them, and the Russians replying with grenades and musket fire. Eventually, Peter and his men succeeded in boarding the two ships and capturing the few Swedes left alive. The ships and prisoners were brought up to Nyenskans, now re-named Sloteburg. Peter was elated at this first naval action in which he personally had participated, and, in consequence, both he and Menshikov were awarded the Order of St. Andrew.

With this victory, Peter gained—temporarily at least—the object for which he had declared war. He had occupied the length of the Neva River and regained access to the Baltic Sea. The province of Ingria was restored to Russia. In another triumphal entry into Moscow, one of the banners in the procession showed the map of Ingria with the inscription: "We have not taken the land of others, but the inheritance of our fathers."

What Peter had won, he set about immediately to consolidate. It was his dream to build a city on the sea, a port from which Russian ships and

Russian commerce would sail out onto the world's oceans. Thus, no sooner had he won his foothold on the Baltic than he began to build his city. To some, it seemed foolish, premature, a waste of energy. He had really only a toehold and an uncertain one at that—Charles was far away, but he had never been beaten in battle. One day, he would surely come to wrest away what Peter had taken behind his back. Then this city, so laboriously built, would be only another Swedish town on the Baltic.

Peter was right. The Swedes did return—but again and again they were beaten off. Through the centuries, none of the conquerors who subsequently entered Russia with great armies—Charles XII, Napoleon, Hitler—was able to capture Peter's Baltic port, although Nazi armies besieged the city for 900 days in World War II. From the day that Peter the Great first set foot on the mouth of the Neva, the land and the city which arose there have always remained Russian.

27

THE FOUNDING
OF ST. PETERSBURG

PERHAPS IT WAS CHANCE. Peter, at first, had no thought of building a city, much less a new capital, on the Neva. He wanted first a fort to guard the mouth of the river and then a port so that ships trading with Russia could avoid the long journey to Archangel. Perhaps if he had captured Riga first, St. Petersburg would never have been built—Riga was a flourishing port, already a great center for Russian trade, and it was free of ice for six weeks longer than the mouth of the Neva—but Riga did not fall into Peter's hands until 1710. The site of St. Petersburg was the first spot where Peter set his foot on the Baltic coast. He did not wait; who knew what the future would bring? Seizing the moment, as he always did, he began to build.

Many things about St. Petersburg are unique. Other nations, in the flush of youth or a frenzy of reform, have created new national capitals on previously empty ground: Washington, Ankara and Brasilia are examples. But no other people has created a new capital city in time of war, on land still technically belonging to a powerful, undefeated enemy. Moreover, 1703 was late in the history of Europe for the founding of a major city. By then, large towns and cities had sprung up even in Europe's American colonies: New York was already seventy-seven years old, Boston seventy-three, Philadelphia sixty. And St. Petersburg, for 200 years the capital of the Russian empire, now the second-largest city of the Soviet Union, is the northernmost of all the great metropolises of the world. Placing it at the same latitude on the North American continent would mean planting a city of three and a half million on the upper shores of Hudson Bay.

When Peter came down through the forests and emerged where the Neva meets the sea, he found himself in a wild, flat, empty marsh. At the mouth of the Neva, the broad river loops north in a backward S and then flows westward into the sea. In the last five miles, it divides into four branches which intersect with numerous streams flowing through the marshland to create more than a dozen islands overgrown with thickets and low forests. In 1703, the whole place was a bog, soggy with water. In the spring, thick

mists from melting snow and ice hung over it. When strong southwest winds blew in from the Gulf of Finland, the river backed up and many of the islands simply disappeared underwater. Even traders who for centuries had used the Neva to reach the Russian interior had never built any kind of settlement there: It was too wild, too wet, too unhealthy, simply not a place for human habitation. In Finnish, the word "neva" means "swamp."

The fort at Nyenskans was five miles upriver. Nearer the sea, on the left bank, a Finnish landowner had a small farm with a country house. On Hare Island in the center of the river were crude mud huts which a few Finnish fishermen used in the summer months; whenever the water rose, the fishermen abandoned them and retreated to higher ground. But in Peter's eyes the river sweeping past in a swift and silent flood broader than the Thames at London was magnificent. It was here that Peter decided to build a new and larger fortification to defend the newly seized mouth of the river. The first digging began on May 16, 1703, the date of the foundation of the city of St. Petersburg.*

The fortress, named after St. Peter and St. Paul, was to be large, covering the entire island, so that on all sides it would be surrounded by the Neva or its tributaries. The southern side was protected by the fast-flowing river, while the northern, eastern and western approaches were morass, criss-crossed with streams. As the island itself was low and marshy and sometimes covered by flood, the first stage of work was to bring in earth to raise the level of the island above the water's reach. The Russian workers had no tools except crude pickaxes and shovels. Lacking wheelbarrows, they scraped dirt into their shirts or into rough bags and carried it with their hands to the site of the rising ramparts.

In spite of everything, within five months the fortress began to take shape. It was in the form of an oblong hexagon, with six great bastions, each constructed under the personal supervision of one of the Tsar's closest friends and each named for its builder: the Menshikov, the Golovin, the Zotov, the Trubetskoy and the (Kyril) Naryshkin. The sixth bastion was supervised by Peter himself and named after him. The fortress was built of earth and timber; later, Peter ordered the ramparts rebuilt with higher, thicker walls of stone. They rose grim, brown, implacable, jutting up thirty feet from the Neva waves, commanded by rows of cannon. Near the end of Peter's reign, Friedrich Weber, the Hanoverian ambassador, noted that, "On

---

* There is a legend that Peter borrowed the musket of one of his soldiers and with the bayonet cut two strips of sod from the ground of Hare Island. Laying them in the form of a cross, he said, "Here shall be a town." His soldiers dug a trench in which Peter placed a box containing relics of the apostle Andrew, Russia's patron saint. At this moment, so the story goes, an eagle dipped in flight over Peter's head and alighted on top of two birch trees which had been tied together to form an arch. This arch became the position of the formal East or Peter Gateway of the future fortress.

one of the bastions they hoist every day after the Dutch manner the great flag of the fortress on a great mast. . . . On festival days they display another huge yellow flag which represents the Russian eagle grasping with his claws the four seas which touch Russia's borders, the White, the Black, the Caspian and the Baltic."

Just outside the fortress was the small one-story log house in which Peter lived while the work progressed. Constructed by army carpenters between May 24 and 26, 1703, it was fifty-five feet long and twenty feet wide and had three rooms: a bedroom, a dining room and a study. There were no stoves or chimneys, as Peter meant to occupy it only in the summer months. Its most interesting feature is the effort that the Tsar made to hide the fact that it was a log cabin: the mica windows were large and latticed in the style of Holland, the shingles on the high-angled roof were laid and painted to imitate tiles, and the log walls were planed flat and painted with a grid of white lines to give the impression of brick. (The house, the oldest building in the city, has been surrounded by a series of outer shells for preservation. There it remains to this day.)

Work on the fortress was intensive because in those early years Peter never knew when the Swedes would return. In fact, they returned every summer. In 1703, within a month of Peter's occupation of the delta, a Swedish army of 4,000 approached from the north and camped on the north bank of the Neva. On July 7, Peter personally led six Russian regiments, four dragoon and two infantry—in all, a force of 7,000—against the Swedes, defeated them and forced them to retreat. The Tsar was constantly under fire, and Patkul, who was present, was forced to remind his tall patron that "he was also mortal like all men and that the bullet of a musketeer could upset the whole army and place the country in serious danger." Throughout that first summer, too, the Swedish Admiral Nummers kept nine ships lying at anchor in the mouth of the Neva, blocking Russian access to the gulf and awaiting a chance to move against the growing Russian entrenchments upriver. Peter, meanwhile, had returned to the shipyards above Lake Ladoga to spur construction, and eventually a number of vessels, including the frigate *Standard*, arrived off the new fortress on the Neva. Unable to challenge Nummers' stronger force, the ships waited here until the approach of cold weather forced him to withdraw. Then, Peter sailed the *Standard* out into the Gulf of Finland.

It was an historic moment, the first voyage of a Russian tsar on a Russian ship on the Baltic Sea. Although skim ice was already forming over the gray waves, Peter was eager to explore. On his right, as he sailed westward away from the Neva, he could see the rocky promontories of the coast of Karelia fading away northward toward Vyborg. On his left were the low, gently rolling hills of Ingria, stretching westward to Narva, beyond the horizon. Dead ahead, just over fifteen miles from the Neva delta, he

saw the island which came to be called Kotlin by the Russians and which was to be the site of the fortress and naval base Kronstadt. Sailing around the island and measuring the depth of the water with a lead line in his own hand, Peter found that the water north of the island was too shallow for navigation. But south of the island was a channel which led all the way to the mouth of the river. To protect this passage and to install an outpost fortification for the larger work he was building on Kotlin Island, Peter ordered that a fort be constructed in the middle of the water at the edge of the channel. It was difficult work: Boxes filled with stones had to be dragged across the ice and then sunk beneath the waves to form a foundation. But by spring a small fort with fourteen cannon rose directly from the sea.

From the beginning, Peter had intended that his foothold on the Baltic would become a commercial port as well as a base for naval operations. At his instruction, Golovin wrote to Matveev in London to encourage commercial vessels to call on the new port. The first ship, a Dutch merchantman, arrived in November 1703, when the new port had been in Russian hands for only six months. Hearing of the ship's arrival at the mouth of the river, Peter went to greet her and to pilot her upstream himself. The captain's surprise at discovering the identity of his royal pilot was matched by Peter's pleasure on learning that the cargo of wine and salt belonged to his old friend Cornelius Calf of Zaandam. Menshikov gave a banquet for the captain, who was also rewarded with 500 ducats. To further honor the occasion, the ship itself was renamed *St. Petersburg*, and was granted a permanent exclusion from all Russian tolls and customs duties. Similar rewards were promised to the next two vessels to arrive in the new port, and before long a Dutchman and an Englishman anchored to claim their prizes. Thereafter, Peter did everything possible to encourage use of St. Petersburg by foreign merchantmen. He reduced the tolls to less than half what the Swedes levied in the Baltic ports they controlled. He promised to send Russian products to England at very low prices, provided the English would pick them up in St. Petersburg rather than Archangel. Later, he was to use his power as tsar to divert vast portions of all Russian trade away from its traditional path to the Arctic and toward the new ports on the Baltic.

To strengthen his grip on his new possession, Peter also made great efforts to build new ships in the Lake Ladoga yards. On September 23, 1704, he wrote to Menshikov, "Here, thanks be to God, all goes fairly well. Tomorrow and the day after, three frigates, four snows, a packet-boat and a galliot will be launched." But the Ladoga waters were stormy and treacherous, and too many of these ships were foundering or going aground on the southern shore as they approached the Schlüsselburg fortress at the Ladoga end of the Neva River. The remedy, Peter decided, was to move the main shipyard to St. Petersburg so that the Ladoga voyage could be avoided. In November 1704, he laid the foundation of a new construction

yard on the left bank of the Neva, across the river and just downstream from the Peter and Paul Fortress. Originally, the Admiralty was only a simple shipyard. A large, open rectangle was established beside the river with one side on the water and the other three made up of rows of wooden sheds which served as workshops, forges, living quarters for the workmen and storehouses for ropes, sails, cannon and timber. From the central section, which was used for offices and eventually became the headquarters of the Russian fleet, rose a tall, thin wooden spire, surmounted by a weathervane in the form of a ship.* Beneath this spire, in the open space surrounded by the sheds, Peter's ships were built. The sizable hulls were constructed beside the Neva, then slid into the river and towed to wharves for fitting out. Soon after its founding, Peter became concerned that the Admiralty was too exposed to possible Swedish attack and the three land sides were fortified with high stone ramparts, glissaded slopes and moats, giving the city a second bastion almost as powerful as the Peter and Paul Fortress.

In the years that followed, Swedish probing attacks and harassment of the new city continued, both by land and by sea. In 1705, the Russians drove tall stakes into the waters of the channel off Kotlin Island and tied ropes between them to keep Swedish craft from penetrating up toward St. Petersburg. An approaching Swedish squadron, seeing from a distance the mass of tall stakes and ropes, took them for the masts of a sizable Russian fleet and withdrew after an ineffectual long-range bombardment. In 1706, Peter himself, sailing far out in the gulf, sighted a Swedish squadron headed in his direction and returned immediately to report the news by agreed-on cannon signals to Vice Admiral Cruys, the Dutch officer in command of the Russian fleet. Cruys, however, refused to believe the Tsar's report and was convinced only when he saw the Swedish ships with his own eyes. Some time after that, Peter touched on the episode with ironic humor. Cruys, reporting on naval matters, complained to Peter of the general ignorance and insubordination of his fleet officers, saying, "His Majesty, with his skill, knows the importance of perfect 'subordination.' " Peter responded warmly, "The Vice Admiral [Cruys] is himself to blame for the want of skill of the naval officers as he himself engaged nearly all of them. . . . As concerns my skill, this compliment is not on a very firm footing. Not long ago, when I went to sea and saw the enemy's ships from my yacht and signaled according to custom the number of ships, it was thought only to be amusement or the salute for a toast, and even when I myself came on board to the Vice

---

* When the Admiralty was completely rebuilt of masonry and stone at the beginning of the nineteenth century, its rectangular shape, the central spire and the ship weathervane were retained as salient features. Today, as in the earliest days of St. Petersburg, the twin spires of the Admiralty and the fortress cathedral, facing each other across the Neva, dominate the city's skyline.

Admiral, he was unwilling to believe until his sailors had seen them from the masthead. I must therefore beg him either to omit my name from the list of those whom he judges skillful, or in future cease from such raillery." With the passage of time, Peter's vision of St. Petersburg grew broader. He began to see it as more than a fortress guarding the mouth of the Neva, or even a wharf and shipyard for commercial and naval vessels on the Baltic. He began to see it as a city. An Italian architect, Domenico Trezzini, who had built a handsome palace for King Frederick IV of Denmark, arrived in Russia at exactly this moment. His style, like that of most architects practicing then in Northern Europe, was heavily influenced by Holland, and it was this Dutch, Protestant, northern-baroque design which Trezzini brought to Russia. He had signed a contract on April 1, 1703, to become the Tsar's Master of Building, Construction and Fortification, and Peter quickly brought him to the Neva to supervise all construction there. For nine years, as the first buildings were converted from simple log structures to brick and stone, Trezzini put his stamp on the city. While laborers were still toiling on the earth foundations of the fortress, Trezzini began to build a small and functional church within its walls. Lacking elegant materials to decorate its interior, Trezzini covered the walls with yellow stucco in imitation of marble. In 1713, Trezzini began construction of the baroque Peter and Paul Cathedral, which, with numerous modifications, still stands on the site today, its Germanic golden spire soaring 400 feet into the air.

THE CEASELESS building operations required an appalling amount of human labor. To drive the piles into the marshes, hew and haul the timbers, drag the stones, clear the forests, level the hills, lay out the streets, build docks and wharves, erect the fortress, houses and shipyards, dig the canals, soaked up human effort. To supply this manpower, Peter issued edicts year after year, summoning carpenters, stonecutters, masons and, above all, raw, unskilled peasant laborers to work in St. Petersburg. From all parts of his empire an unhappy stream of humanity—Cossacks, Siberians, Tatars, Finns —flowed into St. Petersburg. They were furnished with a traveling allowance and subsistence for six months, after which they were permitted, if they survived, to return home, their places to be taken by a new draft the following summer. Local officials and noblemen charged by Peter with recruiting and sending along these human levies protested to the Tsar that hundreds of villages were being ruined by the loss of their best men, but Peter would not listen.

The hardships were frightful. Workers lived on damp ground in rough, crowded, filthy huts. Scurvy, dysentery, malaria and other diseases scythed them down in droves. Wages were not paid regularly and desertion was

chronic. The actual number who died building the city will never be known; in Peter's day, it was estimated at 100,000. Later figures are much lower, perhaps 25,000 or 30,000, but no one disputes the grim saying that St. Petersburg was "a city built on bones."

Along with human labor, the materials with which to build the city had to be imported. The flat, marshy country around the Neva delta had few large trees to supply wood and was almost devoid of rock. The first stones for the new city came from demolishing the Swedish fort and town of Nyenskans upriver and bringing its materials downstream. For years, every cart, every carriage and every Russian vessel coming into the city was required to bring a quota of stones along with its normal cargo. A special office was set up at the town wharves and gates to receive these stones, without which the vehicle was not allowed to enter the city. Sometimes, when these rocks were greatly in demand, it required a senior official to decide the fate of every stone. To conserve wood for building, it was forbidden to cut trees on the islands, and no one was allowed to heat his bath house more than once a week. Timbers were brought from the forests of Lake Ladoga and Novgorod, and newly constructed sawmills, turned by wind and water power, reduced the trunks to beams and planks. In 1714, when it developed that building in St. Petersburg was being delayed by a shortage of stonemasons, Peter decreed that until further notice, no stone house could be built in Moscow under "pain of confiscation of goods and exile." Soon after, he extended this decree to the entire empire. Inevitably, stone and brick masons throughout Russia picked up their tools and headed for St. Petersburg in search of work.

The city needed a population. Few people chose voluntarily to live there; therefore, in this matter, too, Peter employed force. In March 1708, the Tsar "invited" his sister Natalya, his two half-sisters, the Tsarevnas Maria and Feodosia Alexeevna, the two Dowager Tsaritsas, Martha and Praskovaya, along with hundreds of noblemen, high officials and wealthy merchants, to join him in St. Petersburg during the spring and no one, according to Whitworth, "was allowed to excuse themselves by age, business, or indisposition." They came unwillingly. Accustomed to an easy life in the countryside of Moscow where they had large houses and where all their provisions were brought from their own neighboring estates or bought cheaply in the flourishing Moscow markets, they were now obliged to build new houses at great expense in a Baltic marsh. They had to pay exorbitant prices for food imported from hundreds of miles away, and many calculated that they had lost two thirds of their wealth. As for amusements, they hated the water on which the Tsar doted, and none set foot in a boat except by compulsion. Nevertheless, having no choice, they came. The merchants and shopkeepers came with them and found solace in the fact that they could charge outrageous prices for their goods. Many laborers—Russian, Cossack and

Kalmuck—having served the required time in building public works, stayed on, being unwilling or unable to walk the long distance home, and were engaged by noblemen in building the private houses commanded by the Tsar. Eventually, thousands of these laborers settled and built homes for themselves in Petersburg. Peter encouraged these efforts by coming, whenever invited, to lay the first stone of any new building and to drink a glass to the success of the owner.

Neither the location nor the design of these houses was left to free will or chance. Noble families were required to build houses with beams, lath and plaster "in the English style" along the left bank of the Neva (noblemen owning more than 500 peasants were required to build two-storied houses); a thousand merchants and traders were instructed to build wooden houses on the opposite side of the river. Built in haste by unwilling labor for unhappy owners, the new houses were often flawed by leaky roofs, cracking walls and sagging floors. Nevertheless, to add to the grandeur of the city, Peter ordered that all substantial citizens whose houses were only one story high must add a second story. To aid them, he instructed Trezzini to make available free plans of different-sized houses of suitable design.

Most of the new city was built of wood, and fires broke out almost every week. Attempting to contain the damage, the Tsar organized a system of constant surveillance. At night, while the city slept, watchmen sat in church towers looking out over the silent rooftops. At the first sign of fire, the watchman who spotted it rang a bell whose signal was immediately picked up and passed along by other watchmen throughout the city. The bells woke drummers, who turned out of bed and beat their drums. Soon the streets were filled with men, hatchets in hand, running to the fire. Soldiers who happened to be in the city also were expected to hurry to the scene. Eventually, every officer, civil or military, stationed in St. Petersburg was given a special fire-fighting assignment for which he was paid an extra monthly allowance; failure to appear brought swift punishment. Peter himself had such an assignment and received a salary along with the rest. "It is a common thing," said a foreign observer "to see the Tsar among the workmen with a hatchet in his hand, climbing to the top of the houses that are all in flames, with such danger to him that the spectators tremble at the sight of it." In the winter when water was frozen, hatchets and axes were the only tools that could be used to fight fires. If the houses standing next to the house in flames could be chopped apart and dragged away quickly enough, the fire could be isolated. Peter's presence always had great effect. According to Just Juel, the Danish ambassador, "As his intelligence is extraordinarily quick, he sees at once what must be done to extinguish the fire; he goes up to the roof; he goes to all the worst danger points; he incites nobles as well as common people to help in the struggle and does not pause until the fire is put out. But when the sovereign is absent, things are very different.

Then the people watch the fires with indifference and do nothing to help extinguish them. It is vain to lecture them or even to offer them money; they merely wait for a chance to steal something."

The other looming natural danger was flood. Petersburg was built at sea level, and whenever the Neva River rose more than a few feet, the city was inundated. Peter wrote to Menshikov in 1706:

The day before yesterday the wind from west-southwest blew up such waters as, they say, have never been before. In my house, the water rose twenty-one inches above the floor; and in the garden and on the other side along the streets people went about freely in boats. However, the waters did not remain long—less than three hours. Here it was entertaining to watch how the people, not only the peasants but their women, too, sat on the roofs and in trees during the flood. Although the waters rose to a great height, they did not cause bad damage.

"On the 9th at midnight, there came out of the sea from the southwest so strong a wind that the town was completely under water," wrote an English resident in January 1711. "Many people would have been surprised and drowned if the bells had not been rung to wake them and make them go up to the roofs of their houses. The greater part of their houses and livestock were destroyed." Nearly every autumn, the Neva overflowed, cellars were swamped and provisions destroyed. So many building planks and beams drifted away that it became a capital crime to take such floating objects from the water before the owner could retrieve them. In November 1721, another tremendous southwest wind backed up the river again, carrying a two-masted schooner through the streets and leaving it stranded against the side of a house. "The damage is beyond words," the French ambassador reported to Paris. "Not a single house is left that has not had its share. Losses are reckoned at two or three million roubles. [But] the Tsar, like Philip of Spain [after the loss of the Armada], made the greatness of his soul clear by his tranquility."

EVEN FIFTEEN YEARS after its founding, as tall, windowed palaces were rising along the Neva embankments, and French gardeners were laying out formal, geometric flowerbeds, daily life in St. Petersburg remained, in one foreigner's description, a "hazardous hand-to-mouth bivouacking." One problem was that the region simply could not feed itself. The Neva delta, with its great stretches of water, forest and swamp, seldom produced good harvests, and sometimes, in wet years, crops rotted before they ripened. Wild nature was helpful; there were strawberries, blackberries and an abundance

of mushrooms, which Russians ate as a great delicacy with only salt and vinegar. There were small hares, whose gray fur turned white in winter, which provided dry, tough meat, and wild geese and ducks. The rivers and lakes teemed with fish, but foreigners were chagrined to find that they could not buy it fresh; Russians preferred fish salted or pickled. But despite what could be gleaned from soil, forest and waters, St. Petersburg would have starved without provisions sent from outside. Thousands of carts traveled from Novgorod and even from Moscow during the warmer months bringing food to the city; in winter, the lifeline was maintained on a stream of sleds. If these supplies were even slightly delayed along the way, prices immediately soared in St. Petersburg and in the villages nearby, for, in reverse of the normal process, the town supplied its satellites with food.

In the forest around St. Petersburg, an endless horizon of scraggly birches, thin pines, bushes and swamps, the traveler who ventured off the road was quickly lost. The few farms in the region lay in clearings reached by unmarked paths. And in these thickets and groves roamed bears and wolves. The bears were less dangerous, for in summer they found enough to eat and in winter they slept. But wolves were plentiful in all seasons, and in winter they appeared in aggressive packs of thirty or forty. This was when hunger drove them to enter farmyards to catch dogs and even attack horses and men. In 1714, two soldiers standing guard in front of the central foundry in St. Petersburg were attacked by wolves; one was torn to pieces and eaten on the spot, the second crawled away but died soon after. In 1715, a woman was devoured in broad daylight on Vasilevsky Island, not far from Prince Menshikov's palace.

Not surprisingly, few Russians chose to live in this wet, desolate and dangerous region. For a while, it was empty, as war and plague swept away most of the original Finnish-speaking inhabitants. Peter gave land to his noblemen and officers, and they brought families and even whole villages of peasants from the interior of Russia to settle here. These simple people, uprooted from the pleasant hills and meadows around Moscow, suffered greatly but did not complain. "It is surprising to see with what resignation and patience those people both high and low submit to such hardships," wrote Weber. "The common sort say that life is but a burden to them. A Lutheran minister related to me that on occasion when he examined some simple Russian peasants about their belief and asked whether they knew what they ought to do in order to obtain eternal salvation, they answered that it was very uncertain even whether they should go to heaven at all, for they believed that everlasting happiness was reserved for the Tsar and his great boyars."

It was not just the common people who hated St. Petersburg. Russian noblemen and foreign ambassadors grumbled and wondered how long the city would survive its founder. Tsarevna Maria declared, "Petersburg will

not endure after our time. May it remain a desert." Only a few saw more clearly. It was Menshikov who said that St. Petersburg would become another Venice, and that the day would come when foreigners would travel there purely out of curiosity and to enjoy its beauty.

THE SWEDES never understood Peter's fierce attachment to this marshy site. The Tsar's determination to keep the new city became the chief obstacle to making peace. When Russian fortunes in the war were low, Peter was willing to give up all he had conquered in Livonia and Estonia, but he would never agree to yield St. Petersburg and the mouth of the Neva. Few in Sweden understood that the Tsar had split the Swedish Baltic empire permanently, that the wedge driven between Sweden's northern and southern Baltic provinces, interrupting the lines of communication across the Neva delta, presaged their eventual total loss. Most Swedes considered the loss to be relatively minor and only temporary and thought Peter a fool. Knowing how the winds driving up the gulf piled water into the Neva delta and flooded many of the marshy islands, they assumed that wind and water would quickly destroy the fledgling town. The new settlement became the butt of jokes. The attitude of Sweden was that of its supremely confident King: "Let the Tsar tire himself with founding new towns. We will keep for ourselves the honor of taking them."

Peter called the new city St. Petersburg after his patron saint, and it became the glory of his reign, his "paradise," his "Eden," his "darling." In April 1706, he began a letter to Menshikov, "I cannot help writing you from this paradise; truly we live here in heaven." The city came to represent in brick and stone everything important in his life: his escape from the shadowy intrigue, the tiny windows and vaulted chambers of Moscow; his arrival on the sea; the opening to the technology and culture of Western Europe. Peter loved his new creation. He found endless pleasure in the great river flowing out to the Gulf, in the waves lapping under the fortress walls, in the salty breeze that filled the sails of his new ships. Construction of the city became his passion. No obstacle was great enough to prevent his carrying out his design. On it he lavished his energy, millions of roubles and thousands of lives. At first, fortification and defense were his highest considerations, but within less than a year he was writing to Tikhon Streshnev in Moscow asking for flowers to be sent from Ismailovo near Moscow, "especially those with scent. The peony plants have arrived in very good condition, but no balsam or mint. Send them." By 1708, he had built an aviary and sent to Moscow for "8,000 singing birds of various sorts."

After Peter, a succession of empresses and emperors would transform the early settlement of logs and mud into a dazzling city, its architecture more European than Russian, its culture and thought a blend of Russia and

the West. A long line of majestic palaces and public buildings, yellow, light blue, pale green and red, would rise along the three-mile granite quay which fronted the south bank of the Neva. With its merging of wind and water and cloud, its 150 arching bridges linking the nineteen islands, its golden spires and domes, its granite columns and marble obelisks, St. Petersburg would be called the Babylon of the Snows and the Venice of the North. It would become a fountainhead of Russian literature, music and art, the home of Pushkin, Gogol and Dostoevsky, of Borodin, Mussorgsky, and Rimsky-Korsakov, of Petipa, Diaghilev, Pavlova and Nijinsky. For two centuries, the city would also be the stage on which the political destinies of Russia were enacted as Russia's sovereigns struggled to rule the empire from the city Peter had created. And in this city was played the final act of the drama in which Peter's dynasty was overthrown. Even the name of the city would change as the new regime, seeking to honor its founder, decided to give Lenin "the best we had." The new name, however, still sticks in the throats of many of the city's citizens. To them, it remains simply "Peter."

28

MENSHIKOV
AND CATHERINE

DURING THESE EARLY YEARS of war, two people emerged who were to become the closest companions of Peter's life, Alexander Menshikov and Martha Skavronskaya. There were remarkable parallels between them: Both rose from obscurity; they met each other before she met Peter; they rose together, he from stable boy to mighty prince, she from orphaned peasant girl to be crowned as empress, Peter's heir and successor as Russia's sovereign. Both survived the giant Tsar who had created them, but not for long. After Peter died, the Empress Catherine quickly followed, and then the ambitious stable boy who had scaled the heights toppled dizzyingly back to earth.

THE GREAT PRINCE MENSHIKOV, the empire's mightiest satrap, Peter's "Herzenkind" (child of the heart), the human whom after Catherine he loved most, the one man who could absolutely "speak for the Tsar," who became a field marshal, First Senator, a "Serene Highness" and a Prince of Russia, as well as a Prince of the Holy Roman Empire! The best-known portrait of Menshikov shows a man with a high-domed forehead, intelligent blue-green eyes, a strong nose and a pencil-thin brown mustache. His smile is as enigmatic as the Mona Lisa's. At first, it appears blandly open and pleasant; on second glance, it seems cooler, more distant. As one considers the mouth and eyes, the smile and the general visage become decidedly calculating and unpleasant. Menshikov is dressed as the Westernized "almost sovereign potentate" which Pushkin called him. He wears a curled white wig like a grandee of Louis XIV; an armored breastplate is covered with a white robe edged in gilt, with golden tassels. Around his neck is a red silk scarf, and across his chest the wide blue ribbon of the Order of St. Andrew. The star of the order, along with the stars of the Polish Order of the White Eagle and another order, are pinned to the robe. One can tell, looking at this

painting, that here is an exceedingly clever, enormously powerful, unforgiving man.

The name and career of Alexander Danilovich Menshikov are inextricably entwined with the life of Peter the Great, yet the origins of Peter's famous lieutenant are shrouded in legend. Some have said that his father was a Lithuanian peasant who sent his son as an apprentice to a pastry cook in Moscow, where young Alexashka sold small cakes and pirozhki. In the city streets one day, so the story goes, the clever lad's perky cries as he hawked his wares attracted the attention of Lefort, who stopped to talk to him, was charmed and immediately took the boy into his personal service. Thereafter, although Menshikov could barely write his name, his wit and bold repartee sparkled so brightly that he soon was noticed by Peter. The Tsar, too, was intrigued by the intelligent, good-humored boy so near his own age, and, persuading Lefort to part with him, made Alexashka his own private servant. From this position, low in rank but at the elbow of the autocrat, Menshikov employed his great charm and his variety of useful talents to make himself one of the wealthiest and most powerful men in eighteenth-century Europe. His saucy boldness never deserted him. It led him to steal exorbitantly from the state funds entrusted to him, and then helped to shield him from the wrath of an outraged sovereign. Eventually, it is said, Peter threatened to send the mighty Prince back to selling pies in the Moscow streets. That same evening, Menshikov appeared before Peter dressed in an apron with a tray of pirozhki attached to his shoulders, calling out, "Hot pies! Hot pies! I sell fresh-baked pirozhki!" Peter shook his head in disbelief, burst out laughing and once again forgave his erring favorite.

The likelier story of the beginnings of Alexander Menshikov is only a shade less colorful. It is almost certain that Menshikov's father was a soldier who served under Tsar Alexis and became a corporal-clerk stationed at Preobrazhenskoe. Probably, the family's origins were Lithuanian: The diploma creating Menshikov a Prince of the Holy Roman Empire declared that the new Prince was descended from an ancient and noble Lithuanian family. "Ancient" and "noble" may have been added to make it easier for the rigidly conservative Hapsburg Emperor to bestow the title, but there is evidence that relatives of Menshikov were landed proprietors in the neighborhood of Minsk, at that time a part of Lithuania.

Whatever his antecedents, Menshikov was born in November 1673, a year and a half after Peter himself, and spent his childhood as a stable boy on the imperial estate at Preobrazhenskoe. From his earliest youth, he understood the value of proximity to Peter. He was one of the first boys to enroll as a play soldier in Peter's youthful military company. By 1693, he was listed as a bombardier—Peter's favorite branch of the army—in the Preobrazhensky Guards. As a sergeant, he stood next to the Tsar under the walls of Azov, and when Peter was making up his Great Embassy to

Western Europe, Menshikov was one of the first to volunteer and be chosen. By this time he had been appointed as a dentchik, one of the young men assigned as personal orderlies to the Tsar. A dentchik's duty was to attend the sovereign day and night, taking his turn sleeping in the next room or, when the Tsar was traveling, sleeping on the floor at the foot of the royal bed. At Peter's side, Menshikov worked in the shipyards of Amsterdam and Deptford. He was almost Peter's equal in ship's carpentry and the only Russian besides the Tsar who showed real aptitude for the trade. In Peter's company, Menshikov visited Western workshops and laboratories, learned to speak a smattering of Dutch and German and acquired a surface polish of polite society. Adaptable and quick to learn, he still remained a thorough Russian and, as such, was almost a prototype of the kind of man Peter wanted to create in Russia. Here was at least one subject who tried to grasp Peter's new ideas, who was willing to break with old Russian customs and who was not only intelligent enough and talented enough but actually eager to help.

On returning from Europe, Menshikov was included in the revels of Peter's Jolly Company. Six feet tall, robust, agile and good at the sports Peter liked, he became a prominent figure at Preobrazhenskoe, where he was known by his nickname, Alexashka, or his patronymic, Danilovich. He appeared in the "great company of singers who sang carols over Christmas at General Gordon's house," and he played an enthusiastic part in the execution of the Streltsy. Peter gave him a house, and on February 2, 1699, in the presence of the Tsar, it was consecrated according to the "rites of Bacchus."

Inevitably, the young man's rapid rise stirred sneers behind his back at his obscure origins and lack of education. "By birth," said Prince Boris Kurakin, "Menshikov is lower than a Pole." Korb wrote disparagingly of "that Alexander who is so conspicuous at court through the Tsar's graces" and reported that the young favorite already was selling his influence to merchants and others in need of help with various branches of the government. Whitworth, the English minister, reported in 1706, "I am credibly informed that Menshikov can neither read nor write," a charge that was only partially true. Menshikov had learned to read, but always wrote through a secretary, signing his own name in a labored and shaky hand.

Yet, despite his detractors, Menshikov continued to ascend. His tact, his optimism, his uncanny way of understanding and almost anticipating all of Peter's commands and personal moods, his acceptance and endurance of the Tsar's anger and even violent blows, made him unique. When Peter, on returning from Europe, accused General Shein of selling army commissions and at a banquet drew his sword to strike the offender, it was Lefort who deflected the blow and saved Shein's life, but it was Menshikov who grappled with and calmed the Tsar. Not long after, at a christening party for the son

of the Danish ambassador, Peter saw Menshikov wearing a sword on the dance floor. Appalled at this breach of etiquette committed in the presence of foreigners, Peter struck the offender in the face with his fist, bringing blood spurting from Menshikov's nose. The following spring in Voronezh, Menshikov bent forward to whisper something in Peter's ear and was rewarded with a burst of anger and another blow in the face, this one so powerful that it stretched the victim on the ground. Menshikov accepted this abuse not simply with resignation but with unfailing good humor. In time, his understanding of Peter's moods and his willingness to accept whatever Peter offered, be it favor or blow, made him indispensable to the Tsar. He had ceased to be a servant and become a friend.

In 1700, at the outbreak of the war, Menshikov was still attached to Peter's private household—a letter to him from Peter in that year indicates that he had special charge of the Tsar's wardrobe. But when the war began, Menshikov plunged into it, displaying a talent for military command as great as his talent for everything else. He was with Peter at Narva and left with the Tsar before the disastrous battle began. During the operations in Ingria in 1701, which Peter conducted personally, Menshikov distinguished himself as Peter's lieutenant. After the siege and capture of Nöteborg (now Schlüsselburg), Menshikov was named governor of the fortress. He participated in the advance down the Neva, the taking of Nyenskans and the ambush and capture of the Swedish flotilla at the mouth of the river. With the founding of St. Petersburg in 1703 and the building of the Peter and Paul Fortress, Menshikov was assigned responsibility for construction of the one of the six great bastions which subsequently bore his name. That same year, he became Governor General of Karelia, Ingria and Estonia. In 1703, to please the Tsar, Peter Golitsyn, envoy to the imperial court at Vienna, arranged to have Menshikov named a Count of Hungary. In 1705, the Emperor Joseph created Alexashka a Prince of the Holy Roman Empire. Two years later, after Menshikov's victory over the Swedes at Kalisz in Poland, Peter gave him the Russian title of Prince of Izhora, with large estates. Significantly, only two weeks after receiving these lands, the new Prince wrote to ascertain the number of parishes and people therein, what revenue could be collected from them, and to command that in religious services in churches in the district his name be mentioned with that of the Tsar.

Infinitely more important than titles or wealth—for both titles and wealth wholly depended on it—was Peter's friendship. The death of Lefort in 1699 left the Tsar with no close friend to whom he could reveal both his greatness and his pettiness, his visions, his hopes and his despair. Menshikov assumed this role, and during these early years of war Peter's friendship grew into deep affection. Alexashka would follow Peter anywhere and turn his hand to any enterprise the Tsar commanded. He could be the companion

of Peter's drunken orgies, the confidant of his amours, the commander of his cavalry and a minister of his government—all with equal devotion and skill. As their personal relationship grew more intimate, Peter's form of addressing Menshikov changed. In 1703, the Tsar still called him "Mein Herz" and "Mein Herzenchen." In 1704, it became "Mein Liebster Kamerad" and "Mein Liebster Freund." After that, it was "Mein Brudder." Peter ended his letters to Menshikov with the lines, "All is well. Only God grant to see you in joy again. You yourself know."*

As Menshikov's life progressed, honors and rewards continued to shower on him—and his enemies proliferated. To them he appeared obsequious, ambitious and, when he had power, despotic. He could be harsh and cruel and never forget a disservice done to him. His greatest flaw, several times his near-undoing, was avarice. Born with nothing and then surrounded by opportunities for acquiring wealth, he grabbed whatever he could. As he grew older, this trait became more pronounced—or at least less easy to hide. Peter, aware that his old friend was using his offices to amass wealth and often was stealing directly from the state, tried several times to stop him. Menshikov was hauled before courts of justice, stripped of his powers, fined, even beaten by the infuriated Tsar. But always the comradeship of thirty years intervened, Peter's anger abated and Menshikov was reinstated.

In fact, Menshikov was far more than a clever, greedy sycophant. Although he rode to the heights on Peter's back, he was indispensable to Peter as a friend. He became, as much as any man could, Peter's alter ego; he knew so well how the Tsar would react to any situation that his commands were accepted as if they were Peter's. "He does what he likes without asking my opinion," Peter once said of him. "But I for my part never decide anything without asking him his." For better or for worse, Menshikov helped Peter create a new Russia.

THE ORIGINS of Martha Skavronskaya are even more obscure than those of Menshikov. Her life before her meeting with the Tsar in 1703, when she was nineteen, is only conjecture. The likeliest story is that she was one of four children of a Lithuanian peasant, possibly a Catholic, named Samuel Skavronsky. Skavronsky had moved from Lithuania and settled in the Swedish province of Livonia, where, in 1684, in the village of Ringen near Dorpat, Martha was born. When she was still an infant, her father died of plague, followed soon after by her mother. The destitute children were

* Was there anything else? Whitworth wrote that "some have thought their intimacy rather resembled love than friendship, they having frequent jars and constant reconcilements." But there is, in fact, no evidence of any homosexual relationship between Peter and Menshikov.

scattered, and Martha was taken into the family of Pastor Ernst Gluck, a Lutheran minister of Marienburg. Although not exactly a servant, she was expected to make herself useful in the household, doing laundry, sewing, baking bread and looking after the other children. That she was not considered a full member of the family seems likely since, in this relatively well-educated household, no effort was made to educate her and she left the Gluck family unable to read or write.

In adolescence, Martha grew into a comely, sturdy girl whose warm, dark eyes and full figure attracted attention. One story is that Frau Gluck grew wary, fearing the effect of the blossoming girl on her growing sons or even on the Pastor. Martha, accordingly, was encouraged to accept the suit of a Swedish dragoon whose regiment was quartered in the neighborhood. She was betrothed to him and, according to some accounts, was actually married to him for a brief span of eight days in the summer of 1702. At this point, the rapid successes of the invading Russians suddenly compelled his regiment to evacuate Marienburg. Martha never saw her fiancé/husband again.

With the Swedish withdrawal, the district of Dorpat fell into the hands of Sheremetev's Russian army, and along with the entire population, Pastor Gluck and his family were taken prisoner. Sheremetev, a sophisticated man, received the Lutheran clergyman with kindness and accepted Gluck's offer to go to Moscow to serve the Tsar as a translator. The attractive foundling Martha, however, did not go to Moscow, but remained for six months in the domestic service of Sheremetev himself. (One tale presents the vivid picture of the girl being brought into the Field Marshal's camp wrapped only in a soldier's cloak to cover her nakedness.) Some assume that the girl became his mistress, which would not have been impossible, although nothing indicates that such a relationship actually existed between the illiterate seventeen-year-old girl and the cultivated, middle-aged Field Marshal. Later, as Peter's wife, she bore Sheremetev no ill-will, nor, on the other hand, did she especially favor him. In short, nothing except proximity suggests intimacy between them, and the likelihood is that the future Empress was a serving woman in Sheremetev's household and nothing more.

Martha's relations with her next protector, Menshikov, were closer and more complex. He was already emerging as the Tsar's favorite when, visiting Sheremetev, he spotted her. Her comeliness had increased; her hands, once red with work, had become whiter and less coarse with her new, less arduous role. She had accepted the Orthodox faith and taken the Russian name of Ekaterina (Catherine). No one knows how Menshikov persuaded Sheremetev to transfer the Lithuanian girl to his own household—some say that he simply bought her. In any case, in the autumn of 1703 he took her to Moscow.

There is the possibility that during these months the eighteen-year-old woman shared the bed of the thirty-two-year-old favorite. True or not, the bond formed at this time between them became unbreakable and lifelong. They were to be the two most powerful people in the Russian empire after the Tsar himself, yet because of their mutually humble origins, both were totally dependent on Peter. Aside from the Tsar's protection, the only separate strength either the wife or the favorite possessed was the support and alliance of the other.

In fact, there is no proof that Catherine was Menshikov's mistress, and, indeed, there is circumstantial evidence that she was not. During these years, Menshikov was strongly attached to one of a group of girls who carried the title of Boyar Maidens and whose duties consisted only of being companions to the royal ladies. In 1694, after the death of Peter's mother, the Tsar's lively younger sister, Natalya, moved in to live with him in his masculine world at Preobrazhenskoe, bringing with her a small group of such maidens, including two sisters, Darya and Barbara Arseneeva, the daughters of an official in Siberia. Menshikov, as Peter's friend, was welcomed at the feminine court around Natalya, and there soon developed an attachment between him and the beautiful Darya Arseneeva. Through his secretary, he wrote to her regularly from wherever he was and sent her rings and jewels. She wrote back and sent him dressing gowns, bed linen and shirts. In 1703, when Menshikov returned to Moscow in triumph from his military victories in Ingria, the Arseneev sisters came to live in the household which his own two sisters kept for him. It was to this same household that Menshikov brought Catherine. Although it is possible that he may, while courting a lady of higher birth, have amused himself with a Lithuanian serving girl, he was much in love with Darya, who later became his wife.

When Peter met Catherine in the autumn of 1703, she was a member of Menshikov's household with a status which, if uncertain to us, must have been quite clear to him. She was important enough to have access to the Tsar and to speak to him, although he was thirty-one and she was only nineteen, and Peter admired her. His own twelve-year relationship with Anna Mons was breaking apart.* Here before him was a sturdy, healthy, appealing girl in the full bloom of youth. She was far from a classic beauty, but her velvet black eyes, her thick blond hair (which she later dyed black

---

* Anna, feeling that Peter was straying, had attempted to re-stimulate his interest by flirting provocatively with the Prussian envoy Keyserling. The envoy over-responded by falling in love and proposing marriage. Peter's reaction was to expel Anna from her estate and his favor, reclaim his portrait set in diamonds and place her and her mother and sister under house arrest. Later, he relented, the marriage to Keyserling took place and Anna lived as the ambassador's wife, then widow, until her own death in the German Suburb in 1715.

to lighten the appearance of her sun-tanned skin) and her full, womanly bosom already had caught the eye of a field marshal and a future prince; the Tsar was no less observant.

Whatever her previous arrangements, from that time on Catherine was Peter's mistress. For convenience, she continued to live in Menshikov's house in Moscow, a dwelling which by this time was filled with women. At first, it had been kept for him by his own two sisters, Maria and Anna, but in December 1703 Anna greatly advanced the Menshikov family fortunes by marrying an aristocrat, Alexis Golovin, the younger brother of Fedor Golovin, head of the Foreign Ministry. Now it also included the two Arseneev sisters, Barbara and Darya, their aunt, Anisya Tolstoy, and Catherine.

In October 1703, Peter came to Moscow to spend five weeks with this unusual Menshikov "family"; then he departed, but returned in December to stay until March. Soon Darya and Catherine were traveling together to join Menshikov and Peter in towns near where the army was camped. For several years, this quartet was so close that whichever male was apart from the others was sad and lonely. Peter and Menshikov were often separated; Menshikov, as an increasingly successful commander of cavalry and dragoons, was constantly away in Lithuania or Poland. The two women, always traveling together for propriety's sake, could not be with both men at once; in consequence, either Peter or Menshikov was often reduced to writing mournful letters to the other three. In the winter of 1704, a son named Peter was born to Catherine, and in March 1705 Peter wrote to Catherine and Darya: "I am rarely merry here. O mothers! Do not abandon my little Petrushka. Have some clothes made for him and go as you will, but order that he shall have enough to eat and drink. And give my regards, ladies, to Alexander Danilovich. And you have shown me great unkindness in being unwilling to write to me about your health." In October 1705, a second son, Paul, was born, and in December 1706 a daughter whom they called Catherine.

Then, in the spring of 1706, a lonely Menshikov, off in the field, sent Darya a present of five lemons, all he could gather, suggesting that she share them with the Tsar. Peter wrote to thank Menshikov for the lemons, but also to summon him to Kiev. "It is very necessary for you to come by Assumption Day in order to accomplish what we have already sufficiently talked about before I go." The matter on which Peter now was sternly insisting was Menshikov's marriage to Darya, which had been on his mind for some time. He had written Menshikov from St. Petersburg, giving him a push: "As you know, we are living in Paradise, but one idea never leaves me about which you yourself know, that I place my confidence not in human will, but in divine will and mercy." Repeatedly, Menshikov had promised, but repeatedly the wedding was postponed.

Peter's insistence on this marriage stemmed from his desire to regularize the situation in which the two couples were living. It would calm the talk about the quartet—including two unmarried women—roaming shamelessly around Russia. Not that it would end such talk completely; only a marriage to Catherine, who was regularly bearing him children, would do that, but about this he hesitated while Eudoxia still lived. Nevertheless, Menshikov's marriage would be a first step—Darya would become a respectable matron with whom Catherine could properly travel. Finally, in August 1706, Menshikov bowed, and Darya became a wife who shared his thoughts and his burdens, looked after his comforts and accompanied him whenever she could on his travels and campaigns.

Once Menshikov was married, Peter began to think of taking the same step himself. In many ways, it seemed to offer more hazards than advantages. Traditional Russians would find it an act of madness for the Tsar to marry an illiterate foreign peasant. In a time of national crisis, when Peter was forcing Russians to sacrifice heavily for the state, could he inflict this outrage on them without serious disruptions? Eventually, these arguments, strong though they were, were shouldered aside by Peter's need for this extraordinary woman, and fifteen months later, in November 1707, Peter followed Menshikov's wedding with his own. The ceremony was privately performed in St. Petersburg without any of the fanfare which had surrounded the marriage of the Prince. For a while, even though Catherine had borne him three, then four, then five children, he continued to keep the marriage secret from his people and even from his ministers and some members of his family.

Catherine was content with her new status (never at any stage of her astonishing ascent did she push to go higher), but as she continued to bear his children and attach herself more deeply in his affections, Peter continued to worry about her. In March 1711, before leaving with Catherine on the Pruth campaign against the Turks, the Tsar summoned his sister Natalya, his sister-in-law, Praskovaya, and two of Praskovaya's daughters. Presenting them to Catherine, he told them that she was his wife and should be considered the Russian Tsaritsa. He planned to marry her in public as soon as he could, he said, but if he were to die first, they were to accept Catherine as his legal widow.

In February 1712, Peter kept his word and married Catherine again— this time with drums and trumpets playing, with the diplomatic corps in attendance, with a magnificent banquet and a show of fireworks in celebration. Before the ceremony, Catherine had been publicly received and baptized into the Russian church with her stepson, the Tsarevich Alexis, acting as her godfather. Thereafter, the publicly proclaimed Tsaritsa was called Catherine Alexeevna.

His new wife had qualities which Peter had never found in another

woman. She was warm, merry, compassionate, kind-hearted, generous, adaptable, comfortable, robustly healthy and possessed of great vitality. Among all of Peter's followers, she and Menshikov came closest to keeping up with the Tsar's phenomenal energy and compulsive drive. Catherine had an earthy common sense which immediately saw through flattery and deceit. The language she spoke, like Peter's own, was simple, direct and honest. In private, she alone could indulge her playful humor and treat Peter like an overgrown boy; in public, she had the tact to remain in the background. She had enough intelligence and sympathy to understand Peter's burdens as well as his character. With her own good nature, she did not take offense, no matter how gloomy his mood or outrageous his behavior. Alexander Gordon, son-in-law of Patrick Gordon, explained that "the great reason why the Tsar was so fond of her was her exceeding good temper; she was never seen peevish or out of humor; obliging and civil to all and never forgetful of her former condition."

Better than anyone else, Catherine could deal with Peter's convulsive fits. When the first symptoms of these attacks appeared, the Tsar's attendants would run for Catherine, who would come at once and firmly lay him down, take his head in her lap and gently stroke his hair and temples until the convulsions abated and he fell asleep. While he slept, she would sit silently for hours, cradling his head, soothingly stroking it when he stirred. Peter always awakened refreshed. But his need for her went far deeper than mere nursing. Her qualities of mind and heart were such that she was able not only to soothe him, play with him, love him, but also to take part in his inner life, to talk to him about serious things, to discuss his views and projects, to encourage his hopes and aspirations. Not only did her presence comfort him, but her conversation cheered him and gave him balance.

Peter was never greatly interested in women for their special and mysterious female elixir. He had no time for dallying with delicious, witty ladies in a context of court life, like Louis XIV, and he was far too busy with war and government to undertake epic campaigns of sheer physical conquest similar to those which occupied Augustus of Saxony-Poland. After his marriage to Catherine, Peter had occasional mistresses, but they barely entered his thoughts and counted for nothing. In his life, Peter cared deeply for only four women: his mother, his sister Natalya, Anna Mons and Catherine. Of these, his mother and Catherine ranked highest, and Catherine achieved this in part by becoming his second mother. The total, uncritical love she gave to Peter was similar to a mother's, constant even when the child is behaving horribly. Because of this, he trusted her completely. She—like Natalya Naryshkina or, to a lesser extent, Lefort, who also loved him without question—could approach him even in moments of ungovernable rage to quiet and soothe him. In her arms, he was able to pass peaceful nights. Often, especially in their early years, she appears in his letters as

"Moder" or "Moeder." Later, she becomes his Katerinushka. Thus, gradually, Catherine filled a larger and larger place in Peter's life and heart. There might be an occasional infidelity with some young beauty, but Catherine, quiet and secure in the knowledge that she was indispensable, only smiled. Their comradeship and love, as well as Catherine's strength and endurance, were manifested by the birth of twelve children, six sons and six daughters. Ten of these died in infancy or after only a few years of life. There is pathos in reading the names and dates, for Peter and Catherine used the same names several times, hoping that the new little Peter or Paul or Natalya would be luckier than the buried namesake.* The two of their children who lived to adulthood were Anne, born in 1708, who became Duchess of Holstein and mother of Emperor Peter III, and Elizabeth, born in 1709, who ruled as empress from 1740 to 1762. Although infant deaths were all too normal for the age, it did not lighten the burden of grief for a mother who so often endured pregnancy, labor, early hope and then a funeral.

In every arena of life, Catherine was the opposite of a terem or boudoir princess. Merging the physical stamina of a hardy peasant woman with her keen desire to stay close to her lord, she traveled constantly with Peter through Russia, to Poland, Germany, Copenhagen and Amsterdam. Twice— first against the Turks on the Pruth and then against the Persians along the Caspian—she accompanied Peter on military campaigns, enduring without complaint the hardships of the march and the noisy violence of battle. Riding two or three days on horseback, sleeping in a tent on bare ground close to the thunder of artillery, even seeing a bullet strike one of the men attending her, left Catherine unperturbed.

She was neither prudish nor delicate but a man's companion whom Peter wanted at his side even in the middle of his drunken revels. Catherine amiably obliged, although when she could do so without angering her husband, she exercised an influence for moderation. During one such orgy of excessive drinking, Catherine knocked on the door of the room in which Peter was locked with a few of his inebriated cronies. "It is time to come home," she said. The door opened and the obedient Tsar followed her home.

But Catherine was not so hardy and mannish as to lack all feminine interests. She learned to dance and executed the most complicated steps with precision and grace, a talent which she passed along to her daughter Elizabeth. Catherine loved clothes and ornamental pomp. She could be Peter's soldier-wife and sleep in a tent, but once the campaign was over, she

---

* Here is the melancholy list: Peter (b. 1704, d. 1707); Paul (b. 1705, d. 1707); Catherine (b. 1707, d. 1708); Anne (b. 1708, d. 1728); Elizabeth (b. 1709, d. 1762); Natalya (b. 1713, d. 1715); Margarita (b. 1714, d. 1715); Peter (b. 1715, d. 1719); Paul (b. and d. 1717); Natalya (b. 1718, d. 1725); Peter (b. and d. 1723); Paul (b. and d. 1724).

liked to wear jewels and magnificent gowns and to live in palaces. Peter's own tastes were simple; the smaller his house and the lower the ceiling, the happier he was. But for Catherine he built palaces and gardens in St. Petersburg, at Peterhof and in Reval. Here, at her court, the cloth tunics trimmed with simple braid which served for Peter were insufficient. Catherine's courtiers wore silk, velvet and brocade embroidered in gold and silver with delicate lace ruffles at the sleeves and diamond and pearl buttons. Most portraits of her painted after she was thirty and had been publicly acknowledged as tsaritsa show a robust, white-bosomed lady with jet-black hair, dark, almond-shaped eyes, heavy eyebrows and a winsome, well-shaped mouth. Usually, she is wearing a diadem of pearls and rubies, a brocade dress edged with lace, a lavish, ermine-tailed cape casually slipping off her right shoulder and the red sash of the Order of St. Catherine, which Peter created in her honor.

Yet, despite her love of pomp, Catherine never pretended that her origins were anything but lowly, and even as Peter's wife and tsaritsa, she always deferred to foreign royalty. A German diplomat, describing Catherine in 1717, touches on both her appearance and her manner:

> The Tsaritsa was in the prime of life and showed no signs of having possessed beauty. She was tall and strong, exceedingly dark, and would have seemed darker but for the rouge and whitening with which she covered her face. There was nothing unpleasant about her manners, and anyone who remembered the Princess's origins would have been disposed to think them good. . . . She had a great desire to do well. . . . It might fairly be said that if this Princess had not all the charms of her sex, she had all its gentleness. . . . During her visit to Berlin, she showed the Queen the greatest deference, and let it be understood that her own extraordinary fortune did not make her forget the difference between that Princess and herself.

The most graphic embodiment of the attachment between Peter and Catherine and its deepening strength as the years went by appears in their letters. Whenever they were apart, Peter wrote to her every third or fourth day, describing his loneliness, worrying about her health and reassuring her about his, sharing his anxiety when the news is bad and his elation when it is good. His only grumble is that she does not reply as often or as quickly as he would like. Catherine's answers, which had to be dictated through a secretary and therefore were not as effortlessly composed as his, are filled with cheerful affection, concern for his health, and news of their children. She never complains and never offers advice either on policies or personalities. The tone on both sides is good-natured, concerned and tender, with

private mischievous jokes, amused chiding about other romances and amorous promises between themselves. ("If you were here," Catherine writes to her husband, "there soon would be another little Shishenka [a nickname for one of their small sons]." Almost always, the letters on both sides were accompanied by small parcels of fruit, salted fish, new shirts or dressing gowns for Peter, or oysters, which she loved, for Catherine.

Peter from Lublin, August 31, 1709

Moeder: Since I left you I have no news of what I want to know, especially how soon you will be in Vilna. I am bored without you and you, I think, are the same. King Augustus has come. . . . The Poles are constantly in conference about the affairs of Ivashka Khmelnitsky [i.e., they are drinking].

—Warsaw, September 24, 1709

. . . Thanks for your package. I send you some fresh lemons. You jest about amusements [with other women]; we have none, for we are old and not that kind of people. Give my regards to Aunty [Darya]. Her bridegroom [Menshikov] had an interview day before yesterday with Ivashka [i.e., got drunk], and had a bad fall on the boat and now lies powerless; which break gently to Aunty that she does not go to pieces. . . .

—Marienwerder, October 16, 1709

. . . Give my regards to Aunty. That she has fallen in love with a monk I have already told her bridegroom, about which he is very sad, and from grief wishes to commit some follies himself.

—Carlsbad, September 19, 1711

We, thank God, are well, only our bellies are swelled up with water, because we drink like horses, and we have nothing else to do. . . . You write that on account of the cure I should not hurry to you. It is quite evident that you have found somebody better than me. Kindly write about it. Is it one of ours or a man of Thorn? I rather think a man of Thorn, and that you want to be avenged for what I did two years ago. That is the way you daughters of Eve act with us old fellows.

—Greifswald, August 8, 1712

I hear that you are bored and I am not without being bored, but you can judge that business does not leave me much time for boredom. I don't think I can get away from here to you quickly, and if the horses have arrived, come on with the three battalions that are ordered to go to Anclam. But, for God's sake, take care not to go a hundred yards from the battalions, for there are many enemy ships in the Haff and the men constantly go into the woods in great numbers and through those woods you must pass.

—Berlin, October 2, 1712

Yesterday I arrived here and I went to see the King. Yesterday morning, he came to me and last night I went to the Queen. I send you as many oysters as I could find. I couldn't get any more because they say the plague has broken out in Hamburg and it is forbidden to bring anything from there.

—Leipzig, October 6, 1712

I this moment start for Carlsbad and hope to arrive tomorrow. Your clothes and other things were bought, but I couldn't get any oysters. With this I confide you to God's keeping.

In 1716, Peter received a pair of spectacles from her. He wrote back:

Katerinushka, my heart's friend, how are you? Thanks for the present. In the same way I send you something from here in return. Really on both sides the presents are suitable. You sent me wherewithal to help my old age and I send you with which to adorn your youth.

—Pyrmont, June 5, 1716

I received your letter with the present, and I think you have a prophetic spirit that you sent only one bottle, for I am not allowed to drink more than one glass a day, so that this store is quite enough for me. You write that you don't admit my being old. In that way you try to cover up your first present [the spectacles] so that people should not guess. But it is easy to discover that young people don't

look through spectacles. I shall see you soon. The water is acting well, but it has become very tiresome here.

—Altona, November 23, 1716

Petrushka has cut his fourth tooth; God grant he cut all so well, and that we may see him grow up, thus rewarding us for our former grief over his brothers. . . .

Two years later, Catherine writes to Peter about this same son.

—July 24, 1718

I and the children, thank God, are in good health. Although on my way back to Petersburg, Petrushka was a little weak with his last teeth, yet now with God's help he is quite well and has cut three back teeth. I beg you, little father, for protection against Petrushka, for he has no little quarrel with me about you; namely, because when I tell him that Papa has gone away he does not like it, but he likes it better and becomes glad when I say that Papa is here.

—Reval, August 1, 1718

Thanks, my friend, for the figs, which came safely. I have had myself shorn here and send you my shorn locks, though I know they will not be received.

In July 1723, only eighteen months before he died, Peter wrote again from Reval, where he had built himself a small white stucco house and Catherine an ornate pink palace.

The garden planted only two years ago has grown beyond belief, for the only big trees which you saw have in some places stretched their branches across the walk. . . . The chestnuts all have fine crowns. The house is being plastered outside, but is ready within and, in one word, we have hardly anywhere such a handsome house. I send you some strawberries which ripened before our arrival, as well as cherries. I am quite astonished that things are so early here, when it is in the same latitude as Petersburg.

It is reassuring to read these letters. Not many parts of Peter's life were as unblemished and happy as his relationship with Catherine. Through

these letters, we have the satisfaction of knowing that a man whose childhood was stained with horror, whose public life was filled with struggle, and whose family life saw the appalling tragedy of the Tsarevich Alexis, did at least have moments of felicity. In Catherine, Peter found an island amidst the storms.

29

THE HAND
OF THE AUTOCRAT

IN THE EARLY YEARS of war—indeed, throughout his reign—Peter was constantly on the move. Nine years passed between the battles of Narva and Poltava; during this time, the Tsar was never more than three months in a single place. Now in Moscow, now in St. Petersburg, now in Voronezh; then on to Poland, Lithuania and Livonia, Peter traveled incessantly, everywhere inspecting, organizing, encouraging, criticizing, commanding. Even in his beloved Petersburg, he hurried back and forth between houses in different parts of the city. If he stayed under one roof for more than a week, he became restless. He ordered his carriage—he would go to see how a ship was building, how a canal was proceeding, what was being accomplished with the new harbor at Petersburg or Kronstadt. Traveling back and forth over the immense distances of his empire, the Tsar broke every precedent before the eyes of his astonished people. The time-honored image of a distant sovereign, crowned, enthroned and immobile in the white-walled Kremlin, bore no resemblance to this black-eyed, beardless giant dressed in a green German coat, black three-cornered hat and high, mud-spattered boots, stepping down from his carriage into the muddy streets of a Russian town, demanding beer for his thirst, a bed for the night and fresh horses for the morning.

Overland travel in this time was a trial for the spirit and a torment for the body. Russian roads were little more than rutted tracks across meadows or through forests. Rivers were crossed by dilapidated bridges, crude ferries or shallow fords. The human beings one encountered were impoverished, frightened and sometimes hostile. In winter, wolves prowled nearby. Because of mud and potholes, carriages moved slowly and often broke down; over some stretches, five miles was all that could be covered in a day. Inns were rare and travelers looked for beds in private houses. Horses—even when the driver carried an official order that they must be provided—were difficult to find, and usually could be used over a distance of no more than ten miles, after which they had to be unharnessed and returned to their owner while

the traveler and his driver searched for fresh animals. Under such conditions, a journey was often interrupted by long, unexpected delays. When St. Petersburg was rising, Peter ordered a new road, 500 miles long, between the new city and the old capital of Moscow. The trip between the two cities took four to five weeks. Later in his reign, the Tsar demanded a straighter road, along the line of the present railroad, which would have shortened the distance by 100 miles. Eighty miles of this new highway had been completed when the project was abandoned. The lakes, swamps and forests in the area of Novgorod made an impenetrable barrier.

In fairness, the condition of Russian roads was not unique in the early eighteenth century. In 1703, it took fourteen hours to travel from London to Windsor, a distance of twenty-five miles. Daniel Defoe, writing in 1724, declared of his country's highways, "It is a prostitution of the language to call them turnpikes." One was "vile, a narrow causeway cut into ruts"; others were "execrably broke into holes . . . sufficient to dislocate one's bones." Although stagecoaches were being introduced into Western Europe and larger cities had famous and comfortable travelers' inns like the Golden Bull in Vienna, land journeys still were difficult. To cross the Alps from Vienna to Venice during the winter, passengers had to descend from their carriages and go part of the way on foot across the snow.

The difference between Russia and Western Europe lay less in the frightful, pocked surface of the roads than in the wildness and vastness of the surrounding country. Early in April 1718, Friedrich Weber, the Hanoverian minister to Russia, set out from Moscow to St. Petersburg: "We had over twenty open rivers to pass, where there were neither bridges nor ferries," he wrote. "We were obliged to make floats for ourselves as well as we were able, the country people who were not accustomed to see travelers that way, being fled, upon our coming, with their children and horses into the woods. In all my lifetime I never had a more troublesome journey, and even some of our company who had traveled over a great part of the world protested that they never underwent the like fatigues before."

Because of the difficulty of traveling by road, Russians looked forward eagerly to the alternatives of travel by water or across the snow. The great rivers of Russia were always primary avenues of internal trade. Boats and barges carried grain, timber and flax on the broad waters of the Volga, the Don, the Dnieper, the Dvina and, later, the Neva. Travelers to and from Europe often elected to journey by sea. Before the Baltic was opened to them, Russian ambassadors sailed for Western Europe from Archangel, preferring the icebergs and storms of the Arctic Ocean to the discomforts of overland travel.

But in Peter's Russia, the most popular means of travel was by sled in winter. First, the frost froze the autumn mud and hardened the roads; then the falling snow covered everything with a smooth, slippery surface over

which a horse could pull a sled at twice the speed of a carriage in summer. Rivers and lakes, frozen hard as steel, made easy highways between the towns and villages. "Travel by sleds is certainly the most commodious and swiftest traveling in the world either for passengers or for goods," wrote John Perry. "The sleds, being light and conveniently made, and with little labor to the horses, slide smooth and easy over the snow and ice." It cost only one quarter as much to move goods on runners as on wheels. Therefore, through the autumn Russian merchants piled up their goods, awaiting the coming of winter to transport them to market. Once the blanket of snow had fallen, the sleds were loaded and every day several thousands arrived in Moscow, both horses and drivers wreathed in steaming breath, to mingle with the city's crowds.

Out in the country, the main roads were marked by high posts painted red and long avenues of trees planted on both sides of the road. "These posts and trees are useful," observed a Dutch traveler, "because in winter it would be difficult to find the way without them, all being covered with snow." Every twelve or fifteen miles, an inn had been built, at Peter's command, to provide shelter for travelers.

Noblemen and important persons traveled in closed sleds which were in fact small carriages painted red, green and gold, mounted on runners rather than wheels, and drawn by two, four or six horses. If the journey was long, the carriage-sleigh became a moving cocoon from which the traveler emerged only at the journey's end. As Weber described such travel:

> It would be impossible for a traveler to bear the immense cold in Russia, were it not for the convenient contrivance of their sleds. The upper part of the sled is so closely shut and covered that not the least air can enter. On both sides are small windows and two shelves to hold provisions and books taken along for pastime. Overhead hangs a lantern with wax candles to be lighted when night comes. In the lower part of the sled lies the bedding with which the traveler is covered night and day, having at his feet warm stones, or a pewter case filled with warm water to keep the sled warm and to preserve the adjoining box in which wine and brandy are kept against the frost. Notwithstanding all such precautions, the strongest liquors very often freeze and are spoiled. In this movable apartment a man is carried along night and day without stepping out, except in case of necessity.

In this kind of sled, Peter, by frequent changing of horses, sometimes covered as much as one hundred miles a day.

Carriage, horseback, sled, river barge and boat—these were the means by which Peter traveled across Russia. "He has," wrote Perry, "traveled twenty times more than ever any prince in the world did before him." Despite his restlessness, he did not travel for the love of travel; instead, it

was his method of governing. Always, he wanted to see what was happening and whether his orders were being carried out. Accordingly, he came, inspected, issued new orders and moved on. Riding in carriages—bouncing on inadequate springs—across roads filled with holes and ruts, his body never at ease, his backbone constantly swaying against the seat, his head bumping the leather walls when he dozed, his arms and elbows jostling against his companions, the grating noise of the wheels, the shouts of the coachmen—this was Peter's life, hour after hour, day after day, week after week. No wonder he traveled by water whenever he could. What a relief it must have been to glide along by barge or yacht, standing quietly on deck and watching villages, fields and forests slip past.

PETER'S CONSTANT MOVEMENT made administration of his government confused and difficult. The Tsar was rarely in his capital. Many of the laws of Russia were decrees written by his hand on brown paper either in his carriage or in the inn or house in which he passed the night. Whenever he set himself to work seriously at civic administration, either the war or an urgent desire to see his ships pulled him away. Meanwhile, in Moscow, the nominal seat of government until Poltava, the bureaucracy of the central government lumbered along, and gradually a number of changes in the structure of government were made. The old official hierarchy of boyars and lesser nobles was fading in importance; the men closest to Peter—Menshikov, for example—had not been made boyars at all. Menshikov was a Prince of the Holy Roman Empire and bore that title in Russia. Peter's other companions were given the Western titles of Count and Baron; indeed, boyars like Sheremetev and Golovin now preferred to be called Count Sheremetev and Count Golovin. Government officials received new Western bureaucratic titles, such as chancellor, vice chancellor and privy councilor.

Along with the titles, the men who held them were changing. When Fedor Golovin, who had succeeded Lefort as General-Admiral and also served as Chancellor (Foreign Minister), died of fever in 1706 at the age of fifty-five, the Tsar divided his titles and duties among three men: Fedor Apraxin who became General-Admiral, Gavril Golovkin who took over the foreign ministry and was appointed Chancellor after Poltava, and Peter Shafirov who became Vice Chancellor. Apraxin was well connected: he was descended from an old boyar family and he was also the brother of the Tsaritsa Martha, Tsar Fedor's wife. He was a bluff, hearty, blue-eyed man, enormously proud, who accepted insults from no one, not even the Tsar. Apraxin served Peter in many ways: as a general, a governor, a senator, but his real love—rare among Peter's subjects—was the navy. He became the first Russian admiral and commanded the new fleet at its first major victory, the Battle of Hangö.

Golovkin was a more prudent, calculating man, but he too served Peter faithfully all his life. The son of a high official of Tsar Alexis, he was a page at court and became, at seventeen, one of five-year-old Peter's gentlemen of the bedchamber. At the Battle of Narva, Golovkin displayed great bravery and was awarded the Order of St. Andrew. Most correspondence to and from Russian diplomats abroad was addressed to him and signed by him (although Peter often read and corrected the outgoing instructions). Golovkin's portrait shows a handsome, intelligent face, encased in an elegant wig; it cannot show the personal stinginess for which he was widely famous.

The most interesting of these three senior lieutenants was Peter Shafirov, raised from obscurity to become, in 1710, Russia's first baron. Shafirov was from a Jewish family that lived in the Polish frontier region around Smolensk, but his father had converted to Orthodoxy and found work as a translator in the Russian foreign office.* Peter Shafirov followed the same path, serving as a translator for Fedor Golovin whom he accompanied on the Great Embassy. His knowledge of Western languages including Latin and his skill at drafting diplomatic documents brought him promotion to private secretary in 1704, director of the foreign office under Golovkin in 1706, the Vice Chancellorship in 1709, then a barony, and the Order of St. Andrew in 1719. Shafirov was a large, double-chinned man with a contented smile and wise and watchful eyes. Over the years, Shafirov's relationship with Golovkin degenerated into mutual hatred, although Peter, needing both men, forced each to remain at his post. Foreign diplomats respected Shafirov. "It is true, he had a very hot temper," said one, "but one could always rely fully upon his word."

In addition, the names of the offices themselves were changing. There was a new Department of the Navy, a Department of Artillery and a Department of Mines. The heads of these departments, now called ministers, managed the routine business of government. Most petitions formerly addressed to the Tsar, were now addressed to the specific department or minister concerned. Peter discovered that when he was away from Moscow, the members of the old boyar council, now called the Privy Council, frequently failed to attend meetings. If, later, the Tsar criticized council decisions, these men avoided blame by saying that they had not been present. Thus, Peter demanded punctual attendance at all meetings and decreed that all decisions be signed by every member present. These papers, along with minutes of all meetings and other important papers, were sent by courier to Peter wherever he might be.

To handle these documents, Peter kept with him at all times a mobile

---

* Ivan the Terrible had banned all Jews from Russia. However, Jews who renounced their religion were free to rise in society and government in Imperial Russia.

personal chancery headed by his Cabinet Secretary, Alexis Makarov. A talented and modest man from the north, Makarov had risen on merit from a minor post in the provincial civil service to this key position in Peter's government. It was his duty not to offer advice but to see that all matters were brought to the Tsar's attention in the right sequence and at the most appropriate time. In this role, which required enormous tact and afforded enormous power, Makarov was assisted by a young German, Andrew Osterman. The son of a Lutheran pastor, Osterman was employed to translate correspondence between the Tsar and foreign courts. With the passing of time, Osterman's role was to become far greater.

Most of the business of Peter's government in those years concerned war and taxes. Peter's decrees, like his constant traveling through the country, almost invariably dealt with the enrollment of recruits or the collection of revenues. The Tsar's demands for money were insatiable. In one attempt to uncover new sources of income, Peter in 1708 created a service of revenue officers, men whose duty it was to devise new means of taxing the people. Called by the foreign name "fiscals," they were commanded "to sit and make income for the Sovereign Lord." The leader and most successful was Alexis Kurbatov, a former serf of Boris Sheremetev who had already attracted Peter's attention with his proposal for requiring that government-stamped paper be used for all legal documents. Under Kurbatov and his ingenious, fervently hated colleagues, new taxes were levied on a wide range of human activities. There was a tax on births, on marriages, on funerals and on the registration of wills. There was a tax on wheat and tallow. Horses were taxed, and horse hides and horse collars. There was a hat tax and a tax on the wearing of leather boots. The beard tax was systematized and enforced, and a tax on mustaches was added. Ten percent was collected from all cab fares. Houses in Moscow were taxed, and beehives throughout Russia. There was a bed tax, a bath tax, an inn tax, a tax on kitchen chimneys and on the firewood that burned in them. Nuts, melons, cucumbers, were taxed. There was even a tax on drinking water.

Money also came from an increasing number of state monopolies. This arrangement, whereby the state took total control of the production and sale of a commodity, setting any price it wished, was applied to alcohol, resin, tar, fish oil, chalk, potash, rhubarb, dice, chessmen, playing cards, and the skins of Siberian foxes, ermines and sables. The flax monopoly granted to English merchants was taken back by the Russian government. The tobacco monopoly given by Peter to Lord Carmarthen in England in 1698 was abolished. The solid-oak coffins in which wealthy Muscovites elegantly spent eternity were taken over by the state and then sold at four times the original price. Of all the monopolies, however, the one most profitable to the government and most oppressive to the people was the monopoly on salt. Established by decree in 1705, it fixed the price at twice the cost to the

government. Peasants who could not afford the higher price often sickened and died.

To tighten administrative control and increase the efficiency of tax collectors across the sprawling mass of the empire, Peter in 1708 divided Russia into eight giant governorships, assigning these eight provinces to his closest friends. Thus, the Moscow governorship was assigned to Boyar Tikhon Streshnev, St. Petersburg went to Menshikov, Kiev to Prince Dmitry Golitsyn, Archangel to Prince Peter Golitsyn, Kazan to Boyar Peter Apraxin, Azov to Admiral Fedor Apraxin, Smolensk to Boyar Peter Saltykov and Siberia to Prince Matthew Gagarin. Each governor was responsible for all military and civil affairs in the region, especially the production of revenue. Unfortunately, as some of the "governors" resided in the capital far from their provinces, and others had conflicting duties (Menshikov was usually with the army), their authority left much to be desired.

Nevertheless, the effort continued. The governors commanded, the fiscals schemed, the tax collectors strained and the people labored, but only so much money could be squeezed from the Russian land. More could come only from the development of commerce and industry. Peter, observing the successful practices of English and Dutch trading companies in Russia, ordered Moscow merchants to form similar associations. At first, the Dutch were worried that their own efficient trade machinery would be jeopardized, but they soon realized that these fears were groundless. "As concerns the trading business," the Dutch minister wrote reassuringly to Holland, "the matter has fallen through of itself. The Russians do not know how to set about and begin such a complex and difficult business."

No matter how much the people struggled, Peter's taxes and monopolies still did not bring in enough. The first Treasury balance sheet, published in 1710, showed a revenue of 3,026,128 roubles and expenses of 3,834,418 roubles, leaving a deficit of over 808,000 roubles. This money went overwhelmingly for war. The army took 2,161,176 roubles; the fleet, 444,288 roubles; artillery and ammunition, 221,799 roubles; recruits, 30,000 roubles; armament, 84,104 roubles; embassies, 148,031 roubles; and the court, medical department, support of prisoners and miscellaneous, 745,020 roubles.

The extraordinary demand for taxes was matched by an extraordinary demand for men. In the nine years from Narva to Poltava, Peter drafted over 300,000 men into the army. Some were killed or wounded, others died of disease, but the overwhelming proportion of the losses came from desertion. Additional drafts of peasant labor were conscripted to work on Peter's ambitious construction projects. Thirty thousand laborers a year were needed for work on the fortifications at Azov and the building of the naval base at Tagonrog. The shipyards at Voronezh and work on a never completed Don-Volga canal required more thousands. And well before Poltava, the effort to

build St. Petersburg was consuming more men than anything else. In the summer of 1707, Peter ordered Streshnev to send 30,000 laborers to St. Petersburg from the Moscow region alone. These unprecedented demands for money and men drew groans from all classes. Discontent and complaint were not new in Russia, but always the people had blamed the boyars when things went wrong, not the tsar. It was Peter himself who had shattered this image. Now, the people understood that the Tsar *was* the government, that this tall man dressed in foreign clothes was giving the orders which made their lives so hard. "Since God has sent him to be the Tsar, we have no happy days," grumbled a peasant. "The village is weighed down with furnishing roubles and half-roubles and horses' carts, and there is no rest for us peasants." A nobleman's son agreed. "What sort of tsar is he?" he asked. "He has forced us all into service, he has seized upon our people and peasants for recruits. Nowhere can you escape him. Everyone is lost. He even goes into the service himself and yet no one kills him. If they only killed him, the service would stop and it would be easier for the people."

Talk of this kind did not go far. The new Secret Office of Preobrazhenskoe had agents everywhere, watching and listening for "violent and unseemly speech." These special police were successors first to the Streltsy, who had acted as preservers of public order until their dissolution, and then to the soldiers of the Preobrazhensky Regiment, who had replaced the Streltsy as street-corner gendarmes. When the Guardsmen were called away to war, Peter created a new organization, the Secret Office. Formalized by ukase in 1702, it was given jurisdiction over all crimes and especially treason "by word or deed." Not surprisingly, the chief of this new office was Peter's comrade, the Mock-Tsar, Fedor Romodanovsky. A savage, brutal man, totally devoted to Peter, Romodanovsky dealt mercilessly with any suggestion of treason or rebellion. Through a network of pervasive eavesdropping and denunciation, followed by torture and execution, Romodanovsky and the Secret Office did their grim work well: Even under extreme oppression from tax collectors and labor conscriptors, cases of treason "by word and deed" never threatened the throne.

But the record of these years is not all cruel. In various ways, Peter made serious efforts to improve the customs and conditions of Russian life. He acted to raise the status of women, declaring that they must not remain secluded in the terem, but should be present with men at dinners and on other social occasions. He banned the old Muscovite system of arranged marriages in which bride and groom had no choice in the matter and did not even meet each other until the marriage service was being performed. In April 1702, to the immense joy of young people, Peter decreed that all marriage decisions should be voluntary, that the prospective partners should meet at least six weeks before their engagement, that each should be entirely

free to reject the other, and that the bridegroom's symbolic wielding of the whip at wedding ceremonies be replaced with a kiss.

Peter forbade the killing of newborn infants who were deformed—the custom in Moscow had been to quietly smother such children immediately after delivery—and ordered that all such births be recorded so that the authorities might oversee the continued existence of these children. He prohibited the unrestricted sale of herbs and drugs by street vendors, ordering that they be sold only at apothecary shops. In 1706, he established the first large public hospital in Moscow on the banks of the Yauza River. To make the streets safer, he forbade the wearing of daggers or pointed knives which turned drunken street brawls into bloody massacres. Dueling, largely a foreign custom, was banned. To cope with the hordes of professional beggars who besieged travelers on every street, he required beggars to go to an almshouse to do their soliciting. Later, he attacked the problem from another side by declaring that anyone caught giving alms to a beggar in the streets should himself be fined.

To encourage foreigners to serve in Russia, Peter decreed that all previous laws which had restricted the right of foreign citizens to come and go across the frontiers as they pleased were now repealed. All foreigners in Russian service were placed under the Tsar's protection, and any legal dispute affecting them was to be judged not by Russian law and Russian courts, but by a special tribunal composed of foreigners following the procedure of Roman civil law. Further, all foreigners were promised absolute religious freedom while in Russia. "We shall exercise no compulsion over the consciences of men, and shall gladly allow every Christian to care for his own salvation at his own risk," announced the Tsar.

Despite the distractions of war, Peter maintained his interest in broadening the educational horizons of his subjects. The School of Mathematics and Navigation established by Henry Farquharson and two other Scots in Moscow in 1701 flourished with 200 Russian students. These valuable investments in the future became the object of a tussle between the recruiting sergeants and Kurbatov, who stepped in to save them from conscription into the army, complaining that it was a waste of money to educate them if, after they were trained, they were to be drafted as simple soldiers. A School of Ancient and Modern Languages had been founded by Pastor Gluck, Catherine's Lutheran guardian, who had arrived in Moscow with his family in 1703; Gluck was to train future Russian diplomats in Latin, Modern Languages, Geography, Politics, Riding and Dancing. The Tsar ordered that the ancient chronicles of Russian history, especially those in the monasteries of Kiev and Novgorod, be sent to Moscow for safekeeping. He directed that the foreign books being translated into Russian and printed in Russian by the Tessing brothers of Amsterdam be exact translations, even if portions of the texts were unfavorable to Russia. The purpose, he said, "is not to flatter my

subjects, but rather to educate them by showing them the opinion entertained of them by foreign nations." In 1707, when a typefounder and two printers arrived in Moscow, Peter approved a newly revised Cyrillic type in which new books printed in Russia began to appear. The first was a manual of geometry, the second a handbook guide to the writing of letters, with instructions on how to offer compliments, issue invitations and make a proposal of marriage. Most of the volumes that followed were technical, but Peter also ordered 2,000 calendars, and histories of the Trojan War, the life of Alexander the Great and of Russia itself. The Tsar not only commissioned the books, but edited and annotated them. "We have read the book on fortifications which you translated," he wrote to one translator. "The conversations are good and clearly rendered, but in the sections teaching how to carry out fortifications, it is darkly and unintelligibly translated."

To keep his subjects abreast of the world, Peter decreed that a journal, *Vedomosti*, should be published in Moscow. All government offices were ordered to contribute news, and thus, early in 1703, the first Russian newspaper appeared under the heading *Gazette of military and other matters, meriting attention and remembrance, that have happened in the Muscovite state and in neighboring countries.* As a further means of educating and civilizing his people, Peter attempted to establish an open public theater which would stage plays in a wooden building on Red Square. A German theatrical manager and his wife arrived in Moscow with seven actors to present plays and train Russian actors. Several comedies and tragedies were produced, including Molière's *Le Médecin malgré lui* (*The Physician in Spite of Himself*).

Throughout these years, Peter attempted to change the Russian concept of the deference due a tsar. Late in 1701, he decreed that men should no longer fall on their knees or prostrate themselves on the ground in the presence of the sovereign. He abolished the requirement that Muscovites remove their hats in winter as a sign of respect when they passed the palace, whether the tsar was inside or not. "What difference is there between God and the tsar when the same respect is given to both?" asked Peter. "Less servility, more zeal in service and more loyalty to me and to the state—this is the respect which should be paid to the tsar."

FOR SOME, the burden was too heavy and the only solution to the demands of the tax collector and the work gang was escape. Perhaps hundreds of thousands of peasants simply ran away. Some faded into the forests or traveled to the north, where prosperous settlements of Old Believers already existed. Most went south to the Ukrainian and Volga steppes, the land of the Cossacks, the traditional refuge for Russian runaways. Behind, they left deserted villages and nervous governors and landlords anxiously trying to

explain why they could not fulfill the Tsar's demands for manpower. When, to check this dangerous outflow, the Tsar ordered that the runaways be returned, the response of the Cossacks was hesitation, evasion and, ultimately, defiance.

Until this century, it was in the south that the great popular rebellions of Russian history have broken out: Stenka Razin's rising against Tsar Alexis and Pugachev's revolt against Catherine the Great have passed from history into legend. In Peter's time, during the most dangerous years of the war with Charles XII, three rebellions exploded, all in the south: the revolt at Astrachan, the uprising of the Bashkirs and—most threatening to Peter's rule—the rebellion of the Don Cossacks under Bulavin.

Astrachan, which stands where the mighty Volga River flows into the Caspian Sea, seethed with disobedience and sedition. It was a place of exile for remnants of the disbanded Streltsy, and bitter memories of the executions of 1698 still burned in the hearts of Streltsy widows, sons and brothers. The Volga merchants grumbled about the new taxes, the peasants complained about the tolls on bridges, the fishermen protested the restrictions on their catch and no one liked Peter's foreign innovations. Into this flammable tinder poured incendiary rumors: The Tsar was dead, the foreigners had nailed him up in a barrel and thrown him into the sea; an impostor, perhaps even the Antichrist, now sat on the throne of Russia.

In the summer of 1705, an unusually extravagant rumor horrified the citizenry. The Tsar, it was said, had forbidden Russian men to marry for seven years so that Russian women might be married to foreigners being imported by the shipload. To preserve their young women, Astrachaners arranged a mass marriage before the foreigners could arrive, and on a single day, July 30, 1705, a hundred women were married. Many of the wine-flushed participants and onlookers rushed from the celebration to attack the local government offices, condemned and beheaded the governor and renounced the Tsar's authority by electing a new government. The new "government's" first proclamation announced that "the governor and other officers practiced all kinds of idol worship and wished to compel us to it. But we have not allowed this to happen. We have taken the idols out of the houses of the officials." In fact, these "idols" were the domed wig blocks on which Peter's Westernized officers kept their wigs. The rebels sent emissaries to other Volga towns and especially to the Don Cossacks, inviting all true Christians to join them.

Word of the uprising caused alarm in Moscow. Peter was in Courland besieging Mitau when he received the news, and, realizing the need to contain the conflagration before it spread, he dispatched Sheremetev and several regiments of cavalry and dragoons to Astrachan. As a further precaution, he ordered Streshnev to hide the state treasure and to halt temporarily all letters leaving Moscow so that news of the rebellion would not reach

Charles. To the rebels, Peter offered leniency. He invited the rebellious "government" to send deputies to Moscow, where Golovin would listen to their grievances. The deputies came, and their earnest pleading of complaints against the murdered governor made a deep impression on Golovin. "I have talked for some time with them and they seem faithful and honest people," Golovin wrote to Peter. "Deign, sir, even to force yourself to show them mercy. Even we are not without rascals." Peter agreed, and the deputies returned to Astrachan, each man with fifty roubles in his pocket for expenses, and with the promise that if the city would submit, every citizen should have amnesty. In the future, it was added, officials would collect the taxes more discreetly. Orders were sent to Sheremetev's advancing regiments to avoid bloodshed in the region.

But in these times, leniency was often seen as weakness, and the return of the deputies bearing Peter's offering of peace did not quell the revolt but rather gave encouragement to it. The citizens of Astrachan congratulated themselves: They had defied the Tsar and won. When Sheremetev sent a messenger to the city saying that his troops were about to enter and that he refused to include the leaders of the revolt in the general amnesty, rebellion flared again. The Field Marshal's messenger was roughly treated and sent back with insults to Peter and the boast that in the spring they would march to Moscow and burn the German Suburb.

But the rebels had overestimated their own strength, and no help was forthcoming. The Don Cossacks replied that they themselves had not been oppressed by the tsars and still observed all Orthodox habits. How could they wear foreign clothes, they asked, when there was not a tailor among them who knew these fashions? Astrachan was alone. Nevertheless, Sheremetev's troops were attacked when they arrived. The regular soldiers quickly defeated the rebels and entered the town. As the Russian horsemen rode by, thousands of people lay on their faces along the streets, begging for mercy. Sheremetev interrogated the leaders. "I have never seen such a tremendously crazy rabble," he wrote to Golovin. "They are puffed up with malice and believe that we have fallen away from Orthodoxy." The general amnesty was withdrawn, and hundreds of rebels were sent to Moscow or broken on the wheel. Peter, enormously relieved, rewarded Sheremetev with an increase in salary and the gift of large estates.

That same year, 1705, disturbances began among the Bashkirs, a semi-Oriental Moslem people living on the open steppe between the Volga and the Urals. They were partially nomadic, herding cattle, sheep, goats and occasionally camels, while themselves riding small but powerful horses and wearing bows and quivers of arrows across their backs. Through the seventeenth century, Russian colonists moving east had been establishing towns and farming plots on their meadowlands. And along with the pressure of Russian population came the demands of Russian tax collectors. By early

1708, the Bashkirs were in open revolt. They burned a number of new Russian villages along the Kama and Ufa rivers and advanced to within twenty miles of the large city of Kazan. Although Charles XII was approaching the Russian frontier in the west, Peter dispatched three regiments to deal with the threat. The western Bashkirs submitted peacefully and, with the exception of their leader, received amnesty, while the eastern Bashkirs continued to burn and ravage, especially when Peter recalled his regular troops to face the Swedes. But the Tsar succeeded in summoning 10,000 Buddhist Kalmucks to confront and ultimately subdue the Bashkirs.

Luck and the presence of Sheremetev's dragoons had snuffed out the Astrachan flame. The Bashkirs had lacked unity and leadership and, ultimately, they too had been put down. But the most serious upheaval of Peter's reign, coming at a time when he and his army were fully engaged with Sweden, was the revolt of the Don Cossacks under Kondraty Bulavin.

The immediate cause of the Cossack revolt was Peter's attempt to round up deserters from the army and serfs who had fled to join the Cossacks. Like the American West, the underpopulated and in many places largely empty Ukraine was a magnet for restless souls who wished to escape the restrictions and oppression of conventional society. In Russia, many of these pioneers were escaping the law: They were either serfs, legally bound to the soil by laws first made in the time of Ivan the Terrible and reinforced by Tsar Alexis, or soldiers forcibly enlisted into Peter's army to serve for twenty-five years, or laborers drafted to work in the shipyards at Voronezh or on the fortifications of Azov and Tagonrog. In the south, the Cossacks welcomed them, and demands that the fugitives be returned were generally ignored. Finally, in September 1707, Prince Yury Dolgoruky arrived on the Don with 1,200 soldiers to enforce the Tsar's decrees.

Dolgoruky's appearance frightened the Cossack elders and people. One ataman, Lukyan Maximov, received Dolgoruky respectfully and offered to help him track down the fugitives. But Kondraty Bulavin, the fiery Ataman of Bakhmut, reacted differently. On the night of October 9, 1707, his Cossacks attacked Dolgoruky's encampment on the bank of the River Aidar and slaughtered the Russians to the last man. As usual with such peasant revolts, Bulavin had no positive political program. His rising, he said, was not against the Tsar, but against all "princes and magnates, profiteers and foreigners." He called on all Cossacks "to defend the house of God's Holy Mother and the Christian Church against the heathen and Hellenic teachings which the boyars and Germans wish to introduce." Invoking the name of Stenka Razin, he declared that he would free the conscripts at Azov and Tagonrog and would, the next spring, march on Voronezh and Moscow.

Meanwhile, however, the Ataman Maximov, fearing Peter's retribution for Dolgoruky's massacre, mustered a force of loyal Cossacks and defeated Bulavin's rebels. Maximov wrote to Peter that he had exacted vengeance by

cutting off the prisoners' noses, hanging them up by their feet, whipping them and executing them by firing squads. Relieved, Peter wrote to Menshikov on November 16, 1707, that "this business, by the grace of God, is now finished." But Peter had relaxed too quickly. Bulavin himself had escaped from Maximov, gathered a new band and, in the spring of 1708, was once again roaming the Don steppe. Again, Maximov marched against the rebels, reinforced by a detachment of regular Russian troops, but this time a number of Cossacks deserted to Bulavin and the remainder were defeated in a battle on April 9, 1708.

The spreading of Bulavin's rebellion now posed a major threat. Villages as far north as Tula were burned, and Voronezh and the whole of the upper Don lay under threat. Fearing that the upheaval might reach even farther north, Peter ordered his son, the Tsarevich Alexis, to mount more cannon on the walls of the Moscow Kremlin. The Tsar also took offensive action. A force of 10,000 regular infantrymen and dragoons was placed under the command of Guards Major Prince Vasily Dolgoruky, brother of Prince Yury Dolgoruky, murdered by Bulavin the previous autumn. Dolgoruky's orders were "to extinguish this fire once and for all. This rabble cannot be treated other than with cruelty." In fact, the danger of Bulavin seizing Azov and Tagonrog so worried Peter that at one point he was about to depart for the Don himself to take command. Fortunately for Peter, Charles XII chose to rest his army in camp near Minsk for precisely the three months of greatest danger from Bulavin.

For a while, Bulavin swept all before him. He defeated Maximov again and executed him. His troops attacked Azov and captured one suburb of the town before being repulsed by the loyal garrison. Then, flushed with success, Bulavin imprudently divided his army into three divisions. On May 12, one division was defeated, and on July 1 a second division was routed by Dolgoruky's advancing regulars. Sensing the change in the wind, most of the Cossacks, even those who had supported Bulavin, drew up a petition to the Tsar promising allegiance if he would forgive them. After still another defeat of Bulavin's dwindling force, the elders decided to arrest the leader and put him to death to please the Tsar. Bulavin resisted, killing two of the Cossacks sent to arrest him, but then, seeing that all was lost, he killed himself. Gradually, the flames on the steppe died down and flickered out. In November, the remaining force of rebels was cornered by Dolgoruky, and 3,000 Cossacks died in battle. The rebellion was over. Peter commanded Dolgoruky to "execute the worst rebel leaders and send the other leaders to penal servitude; return all the remaining Cossacks to their old places, and burn the new settlements as ordered before." Two hundred rebels were hanged on gallows erected on rafts and sent floating down the Don. All who saw them drifting silently past the river towns and villages were warned that the iron hand of the autocrat reached through the breadth of his realm.

30

POLISH QUAGMIRE

CHARLES XII and the Great Northern War were Peter's main concern during these years. Having founded his new city on the Neva delta the year before, Peter moved in 1704 to control the two key Estonian towns, Dorpat and Narva, which would seal the Russian grip on Ingria and block any Swedish advance from the west against St. Petersburg. Both towns were strongly garrisoned (Narva's defenders alone numbered 4,500), but with Charles and the main Swedish army in Poland, once the cities were besieged, neither had hope of relief.

In May 1704, Russian troops appeared before Narva, occupying the same long lines of circumvallation from which they had been routed four years before. Peter himself supervised the transport of the Russian siege artillery in barges from St. Petersburg, the boats hugging the southern shoreline of the gulf so closely that cruising Swedish warships could not reach them in the shallow water. In the Russian camp at Narva, the Tsar found Field Marshal George Ogilvie, a sixty-year-old Scot who had served for forty years in the Hapsburg imperial army and now had been hired by Patkul for service in Russia. Peter was so impressed with Ogilvie's credentials that he immediately placed him in command of the Russian army before Narva. As the siege commenced, the Russians suffered losses, both from the cannon of the fortress and from Swedish sorties, but the defenders recognized the new determination of their enemies. "They seemed resolved to carry on their works, however great their loss might be," said an officer of the garrison.

Leaving Ogilvie to conduct affairs at Narva, Peter rode south to Dorpat, which Sheremetev had been besieging since June with 23,000 men and forty-six cannon. He found Sheremetev's dispositions faulty—the Russian cannon were firing at the town's strongest bastions, which meant that all their shells were wasted. Peter quickly switched the artillery to the most vulnerable wall, and a breach was made. Russian troops entered the town, and on July 13 the Swedish garrison surrendered, five weeks after

the siege began, but only ten days after the Tsar had arrived to take command. The fall of Dorpat sealed Narva's doom. Peter hurried back with Sheremetev's troops to make a combined Russian force of 45,000 men and 150 cannon. On July 30, a heavy bombardment began, continuing for ten days and lashing the fortress with more than 4,600 shells. When the wall of one of the bastions crumbled, Peter offered generous terms to Arvid Horn, the Swedish commander, as prescribed by the protocol of war. Foolishly, Horn refused, making matters worse by using insulting language about the Tsar. The assault began on August 9, and although the Swedes fought fiercely, within an hour soldiers of the Preobrazhensky Guards had entered and seized a major bastion. Immediately afterward, waves of Russian infantry poured over the walls and swept through the town. Now, too late, Horn saw that resistance was futile and tried to capitulate by beating a drum for parley with his own hands. No one listened. Russian soldiers filled the streets, slaughtering men, women and children in a mindless torrent of violence. Two hours later, when Peter rode into Narva with Ogilvie, he found the streets slippery with blood and Swedish soldiers "butchered in heaps"; of a garrison of 4,500, only 1,800 were still alive. The Tsar ordered a trumpeter to ride through the town sounding the cease-fire in every street, but many Russians still would not stop. Angrily, Peter himself slashed down one Russian soldier who refused to obey orders. Stalking into the town hall to confront the frightened town councilors, Peter threw his bloody sword on the table before them and said disdainfully, "Do not be afraid. This is Russian, not Swedish blood." But the Tsar was furious with Horn. When the enemy commander, whose wife had been killed in the assault, was brought before him, Peter demanded to know why he had not surrendered according to the rules once the first bastion had been crumbled and thus prevented all the unnecessary slaughter.

The victory at Narva had great psychological as well as strategic importance. Not only did it secure St. Petersburg from the west, but it vindicated the Russian disgrace on the same site four years before. It proved that Peter's army was no longer merely a mass of half-trained peasants. Ogilvie said that he considered the infantry better than any German infantry, and told Charles Whitworth, the English minister, that "he never saw any nation go better to work with their cannon and mortars." Peter wrote happily about the victory to Augustus, to Romodanovsky and to Apraxin. Four months later, when the Tsar returned to Moscow, the streets reverberated to the tramp of another Russian victory parade. Peter passed under seven triumphal arches at the head of his troops, while fifty-four enemy battle flags and 160 Swedish officer prisoners followed in his train.

PETER'S BALTIC VICTORIES meant little to Charles. He fully expected that when the time came he would scatter Peter's army easily and retake all former Swedish territory now in Russian hands. Far more disturbing to him was the fact that his own victories in Poland had not yet proved politically decisive. Augustus continued unwilling to concede defeat and give up the Polish throne, and the Polish Diet was still not prepared to force him to this action. Instead of an end, the victory over Augustus at Klissow was only the beginning of years of warfare in Poland, with the Swedish-Saxon struggle seesawing back and forth across the immensity of the Polish plain. The huge country with its eight million inhabitants was simply too vast for the Swedish or the Saxon army, neither of which ever numbered much more than 20,000 men, to exercise control over more than that region in which it happened to be at the moment.

Despite the political frustrations for Charles, the years in Poland, 1702–1706, were a time of great military glory, of heroic exploits, of enhancing the legend. In the autumn of 1702, for example, following the Battle of Klissow, Charles with only 300 Swedes rode up to the gates of Cracow and, from his horse, shouted loudly, "Open the gate!" The commander of the garrison opened the gate slightly and stuck out his head to see who was shouting. Charles instantly struck him in the face with his riding crop, the Swedes behind him pushed open the gate and the cowed defenders surrendered without firing a shot.

Inevitably, the war in Poland was hard on the Poles. On entering the country, Charles had promised to demand only those contributions absolutely essential to his army, but he kept this promise for merely three months. After Polish troops fought with King Augustus at Klissow, Charles resolved to take revenge by seeing that the Swedish army was wholly supported by the land. From Cracow, the Swedes extracted 130,000 thalers, 10,000 pairs of shoes, 10,000 pounds of tobacco, 160,000 pounds of meat and 60,000 pounds of bread within three weeks. As the war dragged on, Charles' instructions to his generals became more implacable: "The Poles must either be annihilated or forced to join us."

Near Cracow, Charles suffered an accident that left him with a limp for the rest of his life. He was observing cavalry exercises when his horse stumbled over a tent rope and fell on top of its rider, breaking the King's left leg above the knee. The thigh bone did not set perfectly, and one leg became slightly shorter than the other. It was several months before the King could ride again, and when the army moved north from Cracow in October, Charles was carried on a stretcher.

Year after year, the battles and victories piled up, yet final victory never seemed closer. Meanwhile came news of other victories, Russian victories, along the Baltic: the siege and fall of Schlüsselburg, the capture of the

length of the Neva River, the founding of a new city and port on the Gulf of Finland, the destruction of the Swedish flotillas on Lake Ladoga and Lake Peipus, terrible devastation of the Swedish granary province of Livonia and the seizure of whole populations of Swedish subjects, the fall of Dorpat and Narva. This grim sequence was accompanied by a stream of desperate pleas from Charles' subjects: the despairing cries of the people of the Baltic provinces, the advice and pleas of the Swedish Parliament, the unanimous request of the army generals, even the appeal of his sister Hedwig Sophia. All begged the King to give up his campaign in Poland and march north to rescue the Baltic provinces. "For Sweden, these events have a much more important significance than who occupies the Polish throne," said Piper.

Charles' reaction was the same to everyone: "Even if I should have to remain here fifty years, I would not leave this country until Augustus is dethroned." "Believe that I would give Augustus peace immediately if I could trust his word," he said to Piper. "But as soon as peace is made and we are on our march toward Muscovy, he would accept Russian money and attack us in the back and then our task would be even more difficult than it is now."

In 1704, events in Poland began to turn in Charles' favor. He seized the fortress town of Thorn with 5,000 Saxon soldiers inside it. With Augustus greatly weakened, the Polish Diet accepted Charles' thesis that Poland would be a battlefield as long as Augustus remained on the Polish throne, and in February 1704 it formally deposed him. Charles' original candidate for the throne, James Sobieski, son of the famous Polish King Jan Sobieski, had foresightedly been kidnapped by Augustus' agents and imprisoned in a castle in Saxony, so Charles chose instead a twenty-seven-year-old Polish nobleman, Stanislaus Leszczynski, whose qualifications included a modest intelligence and a sturdy allegiance to King Charles XII.

Stanislaus' election was shamelessly rigged. A rump session of the Polish Diet was rounded up by Swedish soldiery and convened on July 2, 1704, in a field near Warsaw. During the proceedings, 100 Swedish soldiers were stationed at a musket shot's distance to "protect" the electors and "to teach them to speak the right language." Charles' candidate was proclaimed King Stanislaus I of Poland.

Now that Augustus was displaced—Charles' sole objective in invading Poland—Swedes and Poles alike hoped that the King would at last turn his attention toward Russia. But Charles was not ready to leave Poland. Because the Pope had opposed Stanislaus, threatening to excommunicate anyone who participated in the election of this protégé of a Protestant monarch, and because so few of the great Polish magnates had been present at the election, the new king had at best a shaky grip on his realm. Charles resolved to remain at the side of his puppet monarch until Stanislaus was

properly crowned. More than a year later, on September 24, 1705, Stanislaus was crowned in a manner which, like the Diet's proclamation of his election, provided arguments to those who said that his sovereignty was illegitimate. The new king was crowned not in Cracow, the traditional coronation site of Polish kings, but in Warsaw, because that was where Charles and his Swedish army were. The crown placed on Stanislaus' head was not the historic crown of Poland—still in the possession of Augustus, who had not accepted his dethronement—but a new one which, along with a new scepter and new regalia, had been paid for by Charles. The Swedish King was present at the ceremony incognito, so as not to detract from the attention to be paid his new ally. But the coronation of this puppet sovereign fooled no one. Stanislaus' wife, now Queen of Poland, felt so insecure in her husband's turbulent kingdom that she chose to live in Swedish Pomerania.

Nevertheless, with a new king friendly to Sweden on the Polish throne, Charles believed that he had achieved his second objective. Soon after the coronation, he and Stanislaus signed an anti-Russian alliance between Sweden and Poland. Then, as if to release his long-pent-up feelings about Russia and relieve the huge weight of guilt which had fallen on him for failing to heed his subjects' appeals, Charles suddenly struck. On December 29, 1705, the King broke his camp in the open fields near Warsaw and marched rapidly eastward over the frozen bogs and rivers toward Grodno, where Peter's main army was massed behind the River Neman. This lunge at Grodno was not the long-awaited Swedish invasion of Russia. Charles had not done the planning or assembled the equipment and provisions for an epic march to Moscow. Nor, with Augustus still in the field and unwilling to accept his own dethronement, was Poland completely secure at Charles' rear. Thus, Charles did not take the entire army with him; Rehnskjold was left behind with 10,000 men to watch the Saxons. But with the 20,000 men who marched behind him, Charles meant to provoke a winter battle. At long last, the Tsar was to see the glint of Swedish bayonets and his soldiers were to feel the bite of Swedish steel.

AFTER THE CAPTURE of Dorpat and Narva in the summer of 1704, Peter had spent the winter in Moscow and then gone to Voronezh in March to work in the shipyards. In May 1705, he set out to join the army, but was stricken by illness and recuperated for a month at Fedor Golovin's house. In June, he reached the army at Polotsk on the Dvina, where it could be moved into Livonia, Lithuania or Poland as events required—an army which was developing into a formidable fighting force. There were 40,000 infantrymen, properly uniformed and well equipped with muskets and grenades. The cavalry and dragoons, 20,000 strong, were plentifully equipped

with muskets, pistols and swords. The artillery was standardized and numerous. Like the Swedes, the Russian army had developed a form of highly mobile gun firing a three-pound shell which would accompany infantry and cavalry to give immediate artillery support.

The problem with the army now was at the top, in the structure of command, where there was friction and jealousy between the Russian and foreign generals. The army's excellent training and overall discipline were due to Ogilvie who had taken command at the second siege of Narva and had been made the second field marshal (Sheremetev was the first) in the Russian army. Ogilvie's concern for the soldiers had made him popular with the men, but he was not well liked by the Russian officers; he did not speak Russian and was forced to deal with them through an interpreter. He had particular trouble with Sheremetev, Menshikov and Repnin. The last two were his subordinates and served under him, but Sheremetev, technically his equal in rank, was often offended. Peter, seeking a solution, first tried putting all the cavalry under Sheremetev and the infantry under Ogilvie. Sheremetev felt humiliated and complained to Peter. "I have received your letter," the Tsar replied, "and from it see how distressed you are, for which I am indeed sorry, because it is unnecessary; this was done not in any way to cause you humiliation, but to provide more effective organization. . . . However, because of your distress I have called a halt to this reorganization and ordered the old arrangement to stand until I arrive."

Peter next tried to solve the problem by splitting up the army, sending Sheremetev with eight regiments of dragoons and three of infantry—10,000 men in all—to operate in the Baltic region while Ogilvie remained in command of the main army in Lithuania. On July 16, Sheremetev attacked Lewenhaupt, the commander of Swedish forces in Livonia, and the Russians were badly defeated. Peter wrote angrily to Sheremetev, blaming the defeat on the "inadequate training of the dragoons about which I have spoken many times." Three days later, remorseful for the harsh tone of his earlier letter, he wrote again to cheer Sheremetev up: "Do not be sad about the misfortune you have had, for constant success has brought many people to ruin. Forget it and try to encourage your men."

As it happened, just at this time came news of the trouble in Astrachan, and Sheremetev and his mounted regiments were dispatched a thousand miles across Russia to deal with the revolt. With the overall strength of the army thus weakened, Peter canceled further operations and ordered the main army into winter quarters at Grodno, on the east bank of the River Neman. Nothing was expected from Charles XII until spring.

Unfortunately, even with Sheremetev gone, the friction between Peter's generals continued. Nominally, Ogilvie, as field marshal, was commander-in-chief and Menshikov and Repnin were his subordinates. Although Menshikov already possessed a growing military reputation because of his

successes on the Neva, it was not his military experience but his personal relationship to the Tsar which made him obstreperous and insubordinate. Because he was Peter's closest friend, he refused to accept the lesser military role. Often he invoked his special relationship with the Tsar to overrule the more experienced Ogilvie, saying simply, "His Majesty would not like that. He would prefer to do it this way. I know that." Further, Menshikov arranged that all of Ogilvie's letters to the Tsar should pass through his hands. Some of these he simply pocketed, later explaining to Peter that the Field Marshal was reporting news which the Tsar already knew from Menshikov himself.

This command structure, already complicated, was further confused in November 1705 when Augustus joined the Russian army. The King-Elector's fortunes were at a low ebb. Poland was now completely occupied by the troops of Charles and the newly crowned Stanislaus, and the deposed Augustus had had to make his way by a lengthy, circuitous route through Hungary, using a false name and a disguise. Nevertheless, Peter still considered him King of Poland and, in deference to this rank, granted him overall command of the army at Grodno. Ogilvie kept the senior military command. Menshikov commanded the cavalry, and both Repnin and Carl Evald Ronne, an experienced German cavalry officer, were present as subordinate commanders. It was a situation ripe for disaster.

CHARLES' MARCH to the east was rapid. The distance from the Vistula to the Neman was 180 miles; Charles covered this ground over frozen roads and rivers in only two weeks and appeared with his vanguard before Grodno on January 15, 1706. The King crossed the river with 600 grenadiers, but, seeing that the fortress was too strong for a sudden assault, he turned and made a temporary camp four miles away. When the main Swedish army of 20,000 men arrived, Charles moved fifty miles above Grodno where he could find better provisions and forage. There he made a permanent camp, waiting to see what the Russians would do. As Charles saw it, either they could come out and fight or they could wait inside their fortress and eventually starve.

With Charles nearby, the Russian commanders held a council of war presided over by Augustus. There was no question of simply marching out to attack. Although they outnumbered the Swedes by almost two to one, Peter still was far from ready to risk his carefully constructed army even at these odds and had flatly forbidden Ogilvie to offer battle in the open field. Nevertheless, Ogilvie thought his force strong enough to remain and accept a siege, and this was the course he urged. The others disagreed: if the Swedes surrounded the fortress of Grodno, the army would be cut off from Russia and nullified as a protector of the Russian frontier; and al-

though the fortifications were strong and the artillery numerous, they had not provisioned for a long siege. They urged retreat. Ogilvie was aghast, pointing to the size of the army and the superiority of the artillery. If they retreated, they would have to sacrifice the cannon, which could not be hauled without horses across the snow. They would leave the houses and barracks of a town for the bitter cold of open roads where many would perish. The Swedes would certainly pursue, and the field battle which Peter had forbidden would take place. Worse for Ogilvie would be the disgrace. A professional soldier commanding an army twice as strong as an enemy, he would abandon a strong fortress with a tremendous superiority in artillery. What would Europe say?

Augustus, caught between these opposing viewpoints and unwilling to take ultimate responsibility, dispatched an urgent messenger to Peter pleading for "an immediate, categoric and definite decision" from the Tsar. Before that decision could come, however, Augustus himself slipped out of Grodno. With Charles' departure from Warsaw, he glimpsed a chance to reoccupy the Polish capital. Taking four regiments of dragoons, he departed hastily, promising Ogilvie that he would return in three weeks bringing the entire Saxon army. Then, with a combined Russian-Polish-Saxon force of 60,000 men, they would deal with Charles' 20,000 Swedes.

Peter was in Moscow when he heard that Charles was moving toward Grodno. Skeptical of the reports, he wrote to Menshikov, "From whom did you receive this news? And can it be believed? How many reports of this kind have we had in the past?" Nevertheless, he was uneasy and declared that he would set out from Moscow on January 24. He complained of the "indescribable cold" and that his "right cheek was badly swollen," and grumbled further that

> I am mightily sorry to leave here because I am occupied with col-
> lecting taxes and other necessary things for the operations on the
> Volga. Therefore I beg you, if there is any change, to send someone
> to me, so that I may not drag myself along without reason (alas! I
> can scarcely do it). And if affairs do not change, I should like you to
> send me news every day, so that I can, if possible, hasten my
> journey.

The distance from Moscow to Grodno was 450 miles, and Peter had traveled over halfway when he was intercepted near Smolensk by Menshikov with the news that Charles had arrived and that the Tsar could not now reach his army. Worried, Peter wrote a new set of orders for Ogilvie which hinged on the promised arrival of the experienced Saxons. If the Saxons definitely were coming, Peter would permit Ogilvie to remain in Grodno, but if not, or if Ogilvie was unsure, then he was commanded to retreat to

the Russian frontier by the shortest and quickest route. "However," Peter added,

> I leave all to your judgment, for it is impossible to give an order at the distance at which we are. While we write, your time is passing. What is best for safety and profit, that do with caution. Do not forget the words of my comrade [Menshikov], who on his departure urged you to look more to the safety of the troops than to anything else. Pay no regard to the heavy guns. If it is on account of them that retreat is difficult, burst them or throw them into the Neman.

Meanwhile, inside the Grodno fortress, the situation was deteriorating. Food and forage were rapidly giving out. Then, the Russians eagerly awaiting the arrival of the Saxons received word of another blow. On February 3, 1706, at Fraustadt on the Silesian border, a Saxon army with Russian and Polish auxiliaries totaling 30,000 men was defeated by Rehnskjold's force of 8,000 Swedes. It was Rehnskjold's most brilliant victory, and Charles, on hearing of it, immediately promoted Rehnskjold to field marshal and created him a count. Peter reported the news to Golovin with anger and dismay:

> Herr Admiral: All the Saxon army has been beaten by Rehnskjold and has lost all its artillery. The treachery and cowardice of the Saxons are now plain: 30,000 men beaten by 8,000! The cavalry, without firing a single round, ran away. More than half of the infantry, throwing down their muskets, disappeared, leaving our men alone, not half of whom, I think, are now alive. God knows what grief this news has brought us. By giving money [to Augustus] we have only bought ourselves misfortune. . . . The above-mentioned calamity, as well as the betrayal of the King by his own subjects, you can tell everybody (but put it much more mildly) for it cannot remain a secret. Still, tell in detail very few.

The news of Fraustadt, further underlining the superiority of the Swedish army, sealed Peter's decision to move his own troops away from Grodno as soon as possible. He ordered Ogilvie to retreat at the first opportunity, although, with spring now coming, he recommended that the Field Marshal delay until the ice broke on the river to hinder a Swedish pursuit. On April 4, in obedience to the Tsar's orders, the Russian army pushed over 100 cannon into the Neman and began its retreat in a southeasterly direction toward Kiev around a region of forest and swamp known as the Pripet Marshes.

Charles was elated to discover that the Russians were moving out of

the Grodno fortress and ordered his army to pursue immediately. But as soon as the floating bridge which he had prepared was swung across the Neman, it was carried away by blocks of ice riding in the flooded stream. It was a week before the King could cross, and the Russian army was far ahead. Charles tried taking a short cut through the Pripet Marshes. "It is impossible to describe how men and horses suffered on this march," wrote an eyewitness. "The country was covered with marshes, the spring had thawed the ground, the cavalry could scarcely move, the wagon train got so deep in the mud it was impossible to advance. The King's carriage remained in the mire, while as to provisions, we fared so badly that everyone was happy who in that desolate country could pull a piece of dry bread out of his pocket."

Struggling ahead through the marshes, the Swedes at last reached Pinsk without catching up to the Russian troops. There, Charles climbed to the highest church tower in the town and, gazing to the south and east, saw a watery wasteland stretching to the horizon. Resigning himself to the fact that the Russians had escaped, Charles remained in the vicinity for two months, destroying towns and villages. Finally, in midsummer 1706, uncertain of his rear and unprepared for a further major campaign to the east, the King turned back toward Europe.

Peter was overjoyed to learn that his army was safe. He wrote to Menshikov from St. Petersburg on April 29,

> It is with indescribable joy that I received the . . . [news] when I was at Kronstadt on the vice-admiral's ship *Elephant* and immediately, in thanks to God, we had a triple salute from the ships and the fort. God grant to see you and the whole army again. And how glad, and then how noisy we were on account of it. . . . For, although we live in paradise, still we always had a pain in our hearts Here, praise be to God, all is well, and there is nothing new of any sort. We shall start from here next month. Don't doubt about my coming. If God send no obstacle, I shall certainly start at the end of this month. Earlier than that is impossible, alas! not because I am amusing myself, but the doctors have ordered me to keep still and take medicine for two weeks, after bleeding me, which they began yesterday. Immediately after that I shall come, for you yourself have seen in what state I was when we separated from the army.

The retreat from Grodno was the end for Ogilvie. His quarreling with Menshikov had increased during the retreat. "The general of cavalry [Menshikov] without my knowledge in the name of Your Majesty ordered the whole army to go to Bykhov, and took on himself the air of commander-in-chief," complained the exasperated Ogilvie. "He has about him

a guard of infantry and cavalry with waving banners and takes no account of me. . . . Long as I have been at war, nowhere and never have people treated me as badly as here." Pleading ill-health, he asked to be relieved of his command and allowed to leave Russia. Peter agreed, accepting Ogilvie's resignation and paying his salary in full. Ogilvie departed for Saxony, where he entered Augustus' service and served as a field marshal for four years until his death.

When Charles marched west from Pinsk rather than east, Peter knew that the threat of invasion had passed, at least for a while. But the Swedish King's thrust at Grodno had been a warning. From it, Peter understood that his army, his commanders and his country were not yet ready.

CHARLES FOLLOWED his swift lunge at Grodno with what was to be the final move of his long Polish war against Augustus. In August 1706, the King informed Rehnskjold that he had finally decided to invade Saxony itself, to strike down Augustus inside his own hereditary dominion. Four years of ricocheting around Poland in pursuit of his enemy had shown him that no decision with Augustus could be reached on Polish soil. Saxony always remained a sanctuary to which the defiant Augustus could retreat to bind up his wounds, raise new armies and await an opportune moment for reappearing in Poland.

The main diplomatic obstacle to the invasion, the opposition of the maritime powers, had now been removed by events. Marlborough's great victories at Blenheim in Bavaria and Ramillies in the Netherlands had placed Louis XIV on the defensive, and the maritime powers no longer worried that the entry of Swedish troops into the heart of Germany could tip the scales in their war against France. Charles, for his part, had offered to desist from his planned invasion of Saxony if the maritime powers could persuade Augustus to renounce his claim to the Polish throne. They had tried and failed. Therefore, seeing no other way to compel Augustus, Charles decided to go ahead. On August 22, 1706, the Swedish army crossed the Silesian frontier at Rawicz on its march toward Saxony. Charles himself swam the Oder River, which served as a border, at the head of his Guards cavalry.

Five days later, after marching through Silesia with the cheers of the Protestant Silesians ringing in their ears, the Swedish soldiers stood on the frontier of the Electorate of Saxony. There, the arrival of the Swedes produced a feeling akin to terror. Stories of Swedish plundering and ravishment during the Thirty Years' War were vividly retold. Augustus' family fled in various directions: His wife hurried to the protection of her father, the Margrave of Bayreuth; his ten-year-old son went to Denmark; his elderly mother fled to Hamburg. The state treasury and jewels were hidden in a

remote castle. Nevertheless, the Saxon Governing Council, empowered to govern in Augustus' absence, had determined not to resist the Swedish invasion and to entrust the safety of the electorate to Charles' mercy. The council had in fact had enough of their Elector's Polish ambitions; Saxony had sacrificed 36,000 troops, 800 cannon and eight million livres in the effort to keep its sovereign on the throne of Poland. Now, Saxons were weary of the struggle and determined not to sacrifice the electorate itself on Augustus' behalf.

Accordingly, Charles' regiments marched unopposed into Saxony and occupied the major cities, Leipzig and the capital, Dresden. On September 14, Charles established his headquarters at the castle of Altranstadt near Leipzig, and there he negotiated the terms of a peace treaty with two Saxon ministers. Charles demanded that Augustus give up the Polish crown forever and recognize Stanislaus in his place, as well as break his alliance with Russia and turn over to Charles all Swedish subjects employed by Augustus or fighting with the Saxon army. In return, Augustus would be allowed to keep the courtesy title of king although he could not call himself King of Poland. Finally, the Swedish army was to spend the coming winter in Saxony with all costs of supplies and provisions to be borne by the Saxon government. In Augustus' absence, the Saxon emissaries accepted these terms, and on October 13, 1706, the Treaty of Altranstadt was signed.

For Augustus, not only the terms but also the timing of the treaty were unfortunate. At exactly the moment when Charles was negotiating Augustus' abdication with the Saxon ministers, Augustus himself was moving through Poland with a large force of Russian cavalry commanded by Menshikov, bent on attacking a smaller Swedish force under Colonel Mardefelt. Augustus complained that he was so poor that he had nothing to eat, and Menshikov gave the needy King 10,000 ducats from his own pocket. The Tsar, who had invested thousands of roubles and thousands of men in propping up this Saxon ally, was disgusted when he heard about it. "You know very well that one always hears from the King, 'Give, give! Money, money!' and you also know how little money we have," he wrote to Menshikov. "However," Peter added resignedly, "if the King is always to be in this evil plight, I think it would be best to give him strong hopes of being satisfied on my arrival, and I shall try to come by the quickest route."

While he was still with the Russian army and had just accepted Menshikov's generosity, Augustus learned privately of the signing of the treaty in Saxony. He managed to keep the news from Menshikov, but still he was in an extremely awkward position. The terms of the treaty called for him to break his alliance with the Tsar and give up the war, and yet here he was, in the company of a Russian army, preparing to attack a Swedish force. Trying to avert a battle, Augustus sent secret messages to Mardefelt, the Swedish commander, informing him of the treaty and

begging him to retreat and not fight. Here, Augustus' reputation finally caught up with him. The King was so well known for duplicity and chicanery that Mardefelt assumed the message was only another of Augustus' tricks and ignored it. The result, on October 29, 1706, was the Battle of Kalisz, a three-hour fight in which the Russians, Augustus' former allies, badly defeated the Swedes with whom his ministers had just signed a treaty of peace. For Peter, it was a significant victory. Although the Russians outnumbered the Swedes two to one, Swedish soldiers had always before coped successfully with even larger odds. And it was Menshikov's first significant success as an independent commander. The Tsar was overjoyed.

Augustus, embarrassed by this Russian victory, scrambled desperately to adjust himself to his new position between Peter and Charles. He wrote to Charles apologizing for the battle and offering excuses for his inability to prevent its occurrence. In a more tangible gesture, Augustus persuaded the unwitting Menshikov to give him control of the entire body of 1,800 Swedish prisoners and promptly sent them on parole back to Swedish Pomerania, where they would be free to fight the following spring.

Meanwhile, Augustus tried not to anger Peter. He had a private conversation with Prince Vasily Dolgoruky, the Tsar's representative in Poland, and explained that he had had no choice: He could not leave Saxony to be devastated by Charles' troops, and he had seen no way to save his homeland except by stepping down from the Polish throne. He assured Dolgoruky, however, that this was only a temporary subterfuge, and that as soon as the Swedish army left Saxony, he would renounce the treaty, raise a new army and resume his place at Peter's side.

On November 30, Augustus arrived in Saxony and visited Charles at Altranstadt. He apologized personally for what had happened at Kalisz, and Charles accepted his explanation, but insisted that Augustus confirm his abdication by writing Stanislaus to congratulate him on his accession to the throne of Poland. Being completely within Charles' power, Augustus swallowed even this bitter pill. As Charles had written discreetly but serenely in a letter to Stockholm, "For the present, it is I who am Elector of Saxony."

The two Kings, first cousins (their mothers were sisters, both having been born Danish princesses), got along well together. Charles wrote to his sister that his cousin was "jolly and amusing. He is not tall, but of compact build; a little corpulent also. He wears his own hair, which is quite dark." Nevertheless, it became obvious through the winter of 1706–07 that Augustus was in no hurry to put the treaty into effect. This was especially true of Clause 11, which had been especially written to apply to the Livonian firebrand Johann Reinhold von Patkul.

The man most affected by the Treaty of Altranstadt was not Augustus but Patkul. The Livonian nobleman whose dedicated anti-Swedish efforts

had helped to bring about the Great Northern War was a special object of Charles XII's hatred. Thus, Clause 11 had been written into the Altranstadt treaty demanding that Augustus hand over to Charles all Swedish "traitors" harbored in Saxony. Patkul's name headed the list. In the affair that followed, Augustus' perfidy and Charles' vengefulness were to horrify Europe.

Patkul was a flamboyant, talented and difficult man. When the war began, he served first as a general in Augustus' army. He was wounded and, while recovering, decided to quit the King's service in disapproval "of the way the King has treated his allies." Peter, admiring Patkul's qualities, immediately invited the homeless Livonian to Moscow and persuaded him to enter Russian service as a privy councilor and lieutenant general. For the next five years, Patkul was indefatigable in Peter's service, but his imperious manner made him many enemies. He quarreled with Matveev in The Hague and Golitsyn in Vienna. Dolgoruky in Warsaw eventually refused even to exchange letters with him, and wrote to Fedor Golovin: "I think you know about Patkul. One must examine carefully not only his words but the letters in them. If he writes when he is in ill humor, he will not even give praise to God himself."

Ironically, the sequence of events which led to Patkul's downfall had its origin in a kindly element of his nature, his sympathy for the pathetic condition of the Russian troops whom Peter had sent to bolster the army of King Augustus. Eleven Russian regiments, numbering 9,000 men, and a force of Cossack cavalry, numbering 3,000 men, under command of Prince Dmitry Golitsyn, had set out from Kiev in the summer of 1704 to join Augustus in Poland. When they arrived, Patkul, as a Russian privy councilor and lieutenant general, superseded Golitsyn and took command. After a brief campaign in the autumn of 1704, Patkul was instructed by Augustus to retreat with his troops into Saxony. There, he found that no one took responsibility for his men. The ministers of the Saxon government had no use for Russian troops supplied to Augustus for his wars in Poland and refused to shelter and feed them. The men had not been paid for months; even if they had been paid, Saxon merchants would have refused their Russian money as worthless. With their thin, tattered uniforms and bare feet, the Russian soldiers were such an appalling sight that people came to stare at them. It seemed likely that during the winter ahead many of them would starve. But Patkul worked indefatigably on their behalf. He accused the Saxon ministers of acting contrary to the orders of the King-Elector in not supplying provisions and winter quarters. He wrote to Peter, to Golovin and to Menshikov, saying that the condition of the troops was bringing shame on the Tsar. They replied that the men should return to Russia—plainly impossible because the route through Poland was blocked by Swedish troops. Finally, to keep the men alive, Patkul raised large sums of money on his own personal credit. In the spring, he issued them new uniforms, and by summer

their appearance was so altered that the Saxons admitted that they looked superior to German soldiers. Still no money came from Russia, and Patkul's credit was running out.

To ensure their survival, Patkul eventually proposed to rent them for a while to the Austrian government, which would become responsible for their pay and provisions. Golovin replied that the Tsar would give his approval if it was a matter of extreme necessity. In December 1705, with the agreement of the Russian officers under him, Patkul signed the troops over to the service of the imperial government for a period of one year.

Patkul's action alarmed the Saxon ministers, who feared that both the King and the Tsar would be angry that their refusal to aid the Russians had resulted in this loss of soldiers to the common cause. Patkul had been hated for a long time in Dresden. (He was never cautious in his letters, and many of his bitter denunciations of the inefficiency and corruption of Saxon ministers made their way back to the accused.) Augustus himself was wary. "I know Patkul well," he complained to Dolgoruky, "and His Tsarish Majesty will soon learn also that Patkul has abandoned the service of his own master [Charles] only for his own plans and profit."

Scandalously, Patkul's act of mercy in signing the Russian troops over to Austria was made a charge of treason against him. Although the Saxon ministers had been informed at every stage of the negotiations, they suddenly charged him with harming Augustus' interests by signing away thousands of troops under his command. His arrest was ordered. As it happened, Patkul, tired of being caught between larger forces and despairing of his Livonian ambitions, had just become engaged and was on the point of marriage to a rich widow. He had bought an estate in Switzerland, where he intended to give up politics and live in retirement.

On his return from his betrothal, Patkul was seized, taken to the castle of Sonnenstein and put in a cell with no bed and no food for the first five days. The arrest created a sensation across Europe. A foreign ambassador in the service of a sovereign monarch had been arrested in discharge of his functions. In Dresden, the Danish and imperial ambassadors protested strongly and withdrew from the capital on grounds that they were no longer safe. The imperial ambassador rebutted the charge of treason by announcing that he personally had seen Patkul's authorization from Moscow to transfer the troops. Prince Golitsyn, now once again the senior officer of the Russian expeditionary troops, although personally antagonistic to Patkul, protested the arrest as an affront to his master the Tsar and demanded Patkul's immediate release.

Frightened that they had gone too far, the Saxon ministers sent word of their action to Augustus in Poland. Augustus wrote back that he approved what they had done and wrote briefly to Peter that, in order to protect their joint interests, his privy council had been forced to arrest Patkul. The task

of drafting the indictment was given to the King's adjutant general, Arnstedt, who did it with great reluctance and wrote secretly to Shafirov in Moscow, "I am doing everything to save him. You must work to the same end. We must not and cannot allow such a fine man to perish."

Peter agreed with Augustus that Patkul should have waited for a more definite order before signing the troops over to Austria, but he nevertheless demanded that the prisoner be sent to him immediately so that he could investigate the charges against him. Patkul was, after all, in Russian service and the troops in question were Russian troops. From Augustus came excuses and delays. In February 1706, Peter wrote again, demanding the return of Patkul. But the Swedes were then encamped near Grodno, and Augustus' Saxon ministers knew that the Tsar was physically powerless to intervene. Patkul remained a prisoner.

Then came Charles' rapid march back from Grodno, his invasion of Saxony, Augustus' capitulation and the Treaty of Altranstadt. The handing over of Patkul and other "traitors" to Sweden was a condition of the treaty. Augustus was trapped. Having failed to release Patkul sooner, he was now to be forced to deliver him to Charles. Squirming desperately, he sent Major General Goltz to assure the Tsar that Patkul would never be handed over to the King of Sweden. Peter, disbelieving these promises and fearing greatly for Patkul's life, appealed to the Emperor, to the Kings of Prussia and Denmark and to the Netherlands States General. To each, he said in essence: "We trust that the King of Sweden will willingly yield to the intercession of Your Majesty and that in doing this he may gain before the whole world the reputation of a great-hearted monarch and not be partner in a godless and barbarian business."

Augustus hesitated and delayed in carrying out this article of the treaty, but Charles was implacable. Finally, on the night of March 27, 1707, Patkul was delivered into Swedish hands. He was kept at Altranstadt for three months in a cell, fastened to a stake with a heavy iron chain. In October 1707, he stood before a Swedish court-martial which had been instructed by Charles to judge him with "extreme severity." Obediently, the Swedish court condemned him to be broken alive on the wheel, beheaded and his body quartered. Patkul's composure finally deserted him when he was tied to the wheel. The executioner, a local peasant, gave him fifteen blows with a sledgehammer, breaking his arms and legs, and then started on his chest. Patkul screamed and groaned, and then when he could cry out no longer, he gurgled, "Take off my head." The inexperienced executioner gave him four blows with a country axe before the neck was finally severed. The body was cut into quarters and exposed on the wheel, and his head was set on a post by the highway.

CHARLES IN SAXONY

THE DRAMATIC APPEARANCE of King Charles XII and his Swedish army in the heart of Germany sent powerful tremors through Europe. While in Saxony, the young monarch was visible to the continent as never before, and curiosity about him was boundless. Every move, mood and habit was scrutinized; travelers planned trips to pass by the Swedish headquarters at Altranstadt in hopes of catching a glimpse of the young King. Among the monarchs and their ministers and generals, curiosity was mingled with concern. It was understood that Charles had come to put the formal seal on his removal of Augustus of Saxony from the Polish throne, but now that this was achieved, what next? The veteran, undefeated Swedish army was camped in Central Europe only 200 miles from the Rhine. In which direction would the youthful monarch turn his invincible bayonets? Through the winter and spring of 1707, ambassadors and other emissaries flocked to the Swedish King seeking answers.

Some had specific pleas or propositions. Louis XIV's ambassador proposed uniting the Swedish army with that of France's Marshal Villiers. This would tip the balance in Germany; afterward, France and Sweden could divide up the German states between themselves. The Protestants of Silesia solicited Charles to remain in Germany as their protector against the Catholic Emperor. (By a threat to march against Vienna, Charles did win for the Silesians the right to reopen their Lutheran churches; indeed, the Emperor Joseph said that he was lucky that the King of Sweden had not demanded that he become a Lutheran himself.) But of all the visitors who made their way to Charles' castle in Saxony, the most famous was John Churchill, Duke of Marlborough, the central figure, both militarily and politically, in the allied coalition against the Sun King.

When Charles first entered Saxony, the Duke expressed alarm that the impetuous young King and his antagonism toward the Hapsburg empire could upset the delicate balance of Catholic and Protestant powers arrayed against Louis XIV's bid for European hegemony. The English minister in Charles'

camp, John Robinson, had forwarded to London a gloomy prediction as to what role a victorious Charles might play as arbiter of Europe. "That he will favor the allies is very uncertain," wrote Robinson. "That he will force them to a disadvantageous peace is not improbable; that he will act against them is possible, and if he so does . . . we must suffer what he pleases. For supposing the war in Poland and Muscovy at an end, neither the Emperor, Denmark, Prussia, nor any Prince or state in Germany will dare to appear against him. All will yield to his will and England and Holland must do so too or stand alone."

Marlborough understood that the volatile Charles would have to be handled with extreme caution. Immediately after the King's invasion of Saxony, the Duke wrote to his Dutch allies, "Whenever the States [General of Holland] or England write to the King of Sweden, there must be care taken that there be no threat in the letter, for the King of Sweden is of a very particular humor." Handling Charles would require great care and discretion as well as a nose for diplomacy and intelligence, and Marlborough proposed that he himself go to see the King. Marlborough's offer was gratefully received, and on April 20, 1707, Marlborough set off in his coach from The Hague across Germany to Altranstadt. As Marlborough, despite his towering reputation, was not a monarch, his first contact in Altranstadt was to be not with the King but with Count Piper, Charles' senior civilian advisor and de facto prime minister. When the Englishman arrived, Piper sent word that he was busy and kept Marlborough waiting in his coach for half an hour before walking down the steps to receive Queen Anne's ambassador. Marlborough was equal to the game. As the Swede came forward, the Duke stepped from his coach, put on his hat and walked past Piper without acknowledging his presence. A few feet away, with his back to the Count, the Duke peacefully urinated against a wall while Piper was left to wait. Then the Duke adjusted his dress and greeted Piper in courtly fashion, and, equality restored, together they entered the building for an hour's conversation.

The following morning, at a little after ten, the Duke called on the King. Here were the two greatest military commanders of the age: Marlborough was fifty-seven, pink-faced, and formally dressed with the blue sash and star of the Order of the Garter on his brilliant scarlet coat; Charles was twenty-five, his face darkened by sun and wind, in his customary blue coat, big boots and wearing his long sword. The two men talked for two hours until "twelve trumpets called the King to vespers," with Marlborough speaking French, which Charles understood but did not speak, and Robinson, who had served as English minister to Sweden for thirty years, translating when necessary. Marlborough presented the King with a letter from Queen Anne, written, in her words, "not from her chancery but from her heart." Marlborough elaborated: "Had her sex not prevented it,

she would have crossed the sea to visit a prince admired by the whole universe. I [Marlborough himself] am in this particular more happy than the Queen, and I wish I could serve in some campaign under so great a campaigner that I might learn what I yet want to know in the art of war." Charles was not so pleased by this flattery that he did not subsequently remark that he thought Marlborough overdressed for a soldier and his language a bit overdone.

During his two-day visit to the Swedish camp, Marlborough made no formal proposals. He simply tried to ascertain the intentions of the King and the feelings of the army. Knowing Charles' concern for the welfare of German Protestants, the Duke professed the warmest sympathy of England for this cause, but also expressed England's concern that it not be pressed against the Catholic Emperor until conclusion of the war with the more dangerous Catholic enemy, Louis XIV of France. The visitor discreetly scouted the Swedish army, noting its minimum amount of artillery and its lack of the hospital service which his own forces considered normal. He heard enough talk to conclude that a Swedish campaign against Russia was certain and that the Swedish officers expected it to be difficult and to last at least two years. Marlborough left Altranstadt relieved and pleased with his mission: "I hope that it [the visit] has entirely defeated the expectations that the French court had from the King of Sweden."

IN 1707, on the eve of his greatest adventure, the triumphant King was a different man from the eighteen-year-old youth who had sailed across the Baltic to confront his enemies more than seven years before. Charles' body still looked youthful—he was five feet nine inches tall, with slim hips rising into broad shoulders—but his face had aged considerably. Long, egg-shaped and pockmarked, it now was permanently tanned and creased by tiny squint lines. The deep-blue eyes were calmer and more quizzical; on the full lips played a constant, knowing smile as he gazed at the world around him. He wore neither beard nor mustache nor wig; his brownish-auburn hair, short, was brushed upward over his increasing baldness.

Charles took as few pains with his dress as with his person. His uniform was simple: plain dark-blue coat with high collar and brass buttons, yellow vest and yellow breeches, largely covered by thick leather riding boots with high heels, long spurs and long flaps at the knees which came over the knee and halfway up the thigh. In addition, he wore a black taffeta cravat wound several times around his neck, large, heavy deerskin gloves with broad cuffs and an outsized Swedish sword. He rarely wore his broad three-cornered hat; in summer, his hair was bleached by the sun; in fall and winter, rain and snow fell directly on his head. In cold weather, Charles threw an ordinary cavalry cape around his shoulders. Never, even in the

heat of battle, did he wear a breastplate to deflect bullet, pike or saber. On campaign, Charles often remained in these clothes for days, sleeping in them on a mattress, a heap of straw or a bare plank. Stripping off his boots, laying his sword nearby where he could reach it in the dark, wrapping himself in his cloak, he read before going to sleep from a gold-embossed Bible which he always carried with him until he lost it at Poltava, and never slept more than five or six hours.

The King ate simply—a breakfast of bread and, when it was available, butter, which he spread with his thumb. His dinner was meat with fat, coarse vegetables, bread and water. He ate silently, with his fingers, rarely taking more than fifteen minutes, and during long marches he ate in the saddle.

Even when the army was in camp, Charles wanted strenuous exercise. He kept a horse saddled in the courtyard of the Altranstadt castle so that when he felt the need, he could leap into the saddle and ride for miles, favoring days filled with storm, wind and rain. When cooped up in a room, he was restless, endlessly pacing. His literary style was rough—his letters were splotches of ink and blottings of attempted erasures—and he preferred to dictate, pacing the room, his gloved hands clasped behind his back, then seizing a pen to add in his illegible scrawl, "Charles."

For all his restlessness, he was a patient listener, sitting with a half-smile on his face, his hand resting quietly on the hilt of his long sword. If the King was on horseback when someone spoke to him, he took off his hat and tucked it under his arm for as long as the conversation lasted. His manner toward subordinates (and, with rare exceptions in his life, Charles spoke only to subordinates) was calm, reassuring and friendly but never familiar; a distance always remained between sovereign and subject. He almost never got angry, and in day-to-day matters he found it difficult to refuse his officers' requests. He liked those around him to be lively and cheerful and he would sit back, watching and listening with his quiet smile. He preferred subordinates who were forceful, direct and optimistic, and permitted those who disagreed with him great freedom of expression.

It was in adversity that Charles became more animated. Challenge brought out the steel—the streaks of hardness and ruthlessness in his character. With the approach of combat, the King stepped forward, projecting an aura of power and determination. It was then that argument stopped and the King's decisions were obeyed. Charles commanded not only by rank but by example. His officers and soldiers saw his self-discipline, his physical courage, his willingness not only to share but to exceed their own physical hardship. They not only respected him as a king, but admired him as a man and a soldier. They had come to believe implicitly in his command. They would attack wherever he pointed his sword: If he asked it, it could be done. As one victory followed another, a supreme confidence, an absolute assurance was inculcated, both in the men and in the leader. This,

in turn, reinforced Charles' superb control and ease of command, permitting him to relax and enjoy his men without lowering all the barriers between them.

Charles' strength as well as his weakness was his single-mindedness. Obstinately, he pursued his goal, neglecting all other considerations. Whether it was hunting a hare, attacking a specific piece in a game of chess or overthrowing a hostile monarch, he fixed on his objective and would consider nothing else until he had achieved this purpose. Like the other royal field commander of the age, William III, Charles was convinced that he was acting as God's instrument to punish those who had begun an "unjust" war. Prayer was part of his daily life and that of the Swedish army. In camp, his soldiers were summoned to prayer twice a day. Even on the march, the army was halted by a trumpet call at seven in the morning and at four in the afternoon. Thereupon, each soldier removed his hat, knelt in the middle of the road and said his prayers.

Because of his faith, Charles was fatalistic. He calmly accepted that destiny would watch over him only as long as he was needed to fulfill God's purpose. Although prone to accidents from his reckless behavior, he rode into battle, contemptuous of danger and death. "I shall fall by no other bullet than that which is destined for me, and when that comes, no prudence will help me," he said. But though Charles was calm at the thought of his own death and hardened to taking responsibility for the death of others, when he ordered his infantry to attack in the face of enemy fire, he was prompted by a desire for victory, not love of death. In fact, the King mourned the loss of his soldiers and once, as an alternative to this repeated carnage on the battlefield, suggested to Piper that he challenge Tsar Peter to single combat. Piper dissuaded him.

Even during this year of relative ease in Saxony, while his soldiers grew fat around him, Charles' life remained simple and dedicated to war. He lived in his castle at Altranstadt as if he were living in a tent with a battle expected the following morning. He refused permission to his two sisters who wanted to visit him in Germany, and turned a deaf ear to his grandmother's plea that he come home to Sweden, at least for a visit, saying that it would set a bad example for his soldiers.

Sexually, Charles remained chaste. "I am married to the army for the duration of the war," the King declared; he had also decided against sexual experience while the war continued. As Charles saw it, this code of asceticism and self-denial was necessary to a military commander, but it has raised the suggestion that the King of Sweden was homosexual. Charles had had little contact with women in his life. At six, he was taken from his mother and reared in the company of men. He liked to look at pretty girls, and in adolescence there was a flirtation with the wife of a concertmaster, but there were no passions. In his years in the field, Charles wrote frequently

to his sisters and his grandmother, but for seventeen years he did not see any of his female relatives, and by the time he returned to Sweden, both his grandmother and his older sister were dead. When the King met ladies in society, his manner was polite but not warm. He did not seek the companionship of women and where possible, he avoided it; it seemed to embarrass him.

As much as possible, Charles modeled the Swedish army on himself. He wanted an elite corps of unmarried men who thought only of duty and not of home, who saved their strength for battle rather than the pursuit of women and the cares of marriage. Married men with children were less likely to advance courageously across a field into a storm of enemy bullets and bayonets. Charles admired and faithfully sought to emulate the example of his father, Charles XI, who had conscientiously practiced abstinence during the years Sweden was at war.

As the years went by, the King's lack of interest in women became more pronounced. During the army's year of rest at Saxony, many Swedish-fathered babies were conceived, but there were no rumors from the headquarters of the twenty-five-year-old King. Later, when Charles spent five years as a prisoner-guest in Turkey, with long evenings devoted to plays by Molière and concerts of chamber music, still there were no whispers of women. Perhaps having denied himself both love and women so long, he simply had lost the capacity for interest in either.

And if he was not interested in women, was he therefore interested in men? There is no evidence of this. In the early years of war, Charles slept alone. Later, a page slept in his room, but an orderly slept in Peter's room and sometimes the Tsar napped with his head on this young man's stomach; this did not make either Charles or Peter homosexual.

With Charles, one can only say that the fires which burned in him had reached the point of obsession, obliterating everything else. He was a warrior. For Sweden's sake, for the sake of his army, he chose hardness. Women were soft, a distraction. He had no sexual experience; perhaps he sensed the enormity of its power and held himself in check, not daring to test it. In this respect, Charles XII was abnormal. But we already know that in many ways the King of Sweden was not like other men.

PETER'S REACTION to Augustus' dethronement and the election and coronation of Stanislaus had been to immediately crown his own court fool as King of Sweden, but he knew that the events in Poland were deadly serious for Russia. Over the years, the Tsar had come to understand that he was dealing with a fanatic; that Charles was determined to overthrow Augustus, and that the Swedish King's invasion of Russia would be postponed until this victory in Poland was achieved. Therefore, realizing his own great stake

in preserving Augustus' power, Peter had poured Russian money and soldiers into the effort to sustain the Elector of Saxony on the Polish throne. As long as the war was fought in Poland, it would not be fought in Russia.

When Augustus was forced to give up his claim, Peter searched for his own replacement as King of Poland—not a puppet but a strong, independent ruler who could both govern and command armies in the field. His first choice was Prince Eugene of Savoy, then at the peak of his reputation as one of the great commanders of the age. Eugene thanked the Tsar for the honor done him, but said that his acceptance would depend on the will of his master, the Emperor; he then wrote to the Emperor Joseph saying that, in accordance with the allegiance he had given his sovereign for twenty years, he left the decision strictly in the Emperor's hands. Joseph was torn: He could see the advantages of having so loyal and effective a subordinate on the Polish throne, but he dared not offend Charles, and he knew that Eugene's appointment would lead to war between Eugene and Stanislaus, with Charles supporting Stanislaus. Thus, he postponed a decision, writing to Peter that, as Eugene was about to embark on a new campaign, nothing could be decided until the following winter.

Peter could not wait. With Charles' army in Saxony preparing to march, if he was to have a new pro-Russian King of Poland, he needed him immediately. He approached James Sobieski, the son of the former King Jan Sobieski, who quickly declined the prickly honor. Peter negotiated with Francis Rakoczy, the Hungarian patriot who had led Hungary into revolt against the imperial crown, and Rakoczy agreed to accept the crown if Peter could persuade the Polish Diet to offer it to him. But before anything further could take place, the project was forgotten. Charles had marched out of Saxony and was advancing on Russia.

AUGUSTUS' ABDICATION removed the second of Peter's three original allies. Now, as Peter said later, "this war lay only on us." Left alone to face the Swedes, Peter intensified his efforts to offer Charles a peace settlement or, if this was impossible, to find allies who could help him avert what most of Europe regarded as his inevitable defeat.

In seeking a mediator or an ally, Peter approached both sides in the great war which had divided Europe. In 1706, Andrei Matveev proposed to the States General that if the maritime powers could persuade Sweden to accept peace with Russia, the Tsar would supply them with 30,000 of his best troops for use against France. When the Dutch did not reply, Peter approached two neutral powers, Prussia and Denmark, for help as mediators. These attempts also failed. Finally, in March 1707, Peter sent proposals to Louis XIV, promising that if the Sun King would mediate successfully between Russia and Sweden, Peter would supply him with

Russian troops to use against England, Holland and Austria. The terms which Peter offered Sweden were that he would cede Dorpat outright and pay a large sum of money to be allowed to keep Narva. He insisted only on keeping St. Petersburg and the Neva River. Louis promised to try.

Peter also approached England. As early as 1705, when Queen Anne's new ambassador, Charles Whitworth, arrived in Moscow, Peter had hoped that he could persuade his sovereign to act as mediator in the Baltic. Whitworth was favorable to Peter, but his dispatches were unable to elicit from his government any diplomatic intercession on the Tsar's behalf. At the end of 1706, Peter decided to carry the appeal directly to London and instructed Matveev to go himself from The Hague to the English capital and ask the Queen to threaten Sweden with war unless Charles made peace with Russia. Peter left the peace terms entirely up to the Queen, insisting only that he must be allowed to keep Russia's hereditary possessions on the Baltic—that is, Ingria and the course of the Neva River. Should formal negotiations fail, Matveev was to try to influence Marlborough and Sydney Godolphin, the leading English ministers, under the table. Peter was realistic about this, saying, "I do not think that Marlborough can be bought because he is so enormously rich. However, you can promise him 200,000 or more."

Before leaving Holland for England, Matveev saw Marlborough in The Hague. After the interview, the Duke wrote to Godolphin in London:

The Ambassador of Muscovy has been with me and made many expressions of the great esteem his master has for Her Majesty . . . and as a mark of it, he has resolved to send his only son into England [to be educated] . . . I hope Her Majesty will . . . [permit] it; for it is certain you will not be able to gratify him in any part of his negotiation.

Matveev's mission, thus, had little chance of success even before it began, for Marlborough's voice was authoritative. Nevertheless, the essence of diplomacy is letting each player act out his role and Marlborough not only did not dissuade Matveev from going to London but even lent the Ambassador his own yacht, *Peregrine*, to make the Channel crossing.

Matveev arrived in the English capital in May 1707, and was greeted amiably, but it was not long before he understood that nothing would happen quickly. Writing to Golovkin, who by this time had succeeded Golovin as Chancellor, he warned that progress would be slow: "Here there is no autocratic power"; the Queen could do nothing without the approval of Parliament. Finally, in September, Queen Anne gave the Russian Ambassador an audience. She was prepared, she said, to ally England with Russia by including Russia in the Grand Alliance, but first

she had to have the acquiescence of her current allies, Holland and the Hapsburg empire. During this period of further delay, Matveev's hopes were kept alive by Marlborough, who wrote from Holland that he was using all his influence to persuade the States General to agree to the Russian alliance.

The game was slipping away—Charles had marched from Saxony in August to begin his long-dreaded invasion of Russia—and Matveev's exasperation grew. "The Ministry here is more subtle than the French even in finesse and intrigue," he wrote to Moscow. "Their smooth and profitless speeches bring us nothing but loss of time." In November, Marlborough himself arrived in London. Matveev visited him the evening after his arrival and asked the Duke to say plainly, as an honest man without sweet promises, whether the Tsar could hope for anything from England. Once again, Marlborough refused to give a definite reply.

Through another source—Huyssen, who was acting as a Russian diplomatic agent on the continent—a different approach to Marlborough was under consideration. According to Huyssen, the Duke had said that he would be willing to arrange English help for Russia in return for a substantial Russian gift of money and land to him personally. When Golovkin reported this to Peter, the Tsar declared, "Tell Huyssen that if Marlborough wishes a Russian principality, he can promise him one of three, whichever he wishes, Kiev, Vladimir or Siberia. And he can promise him also that if he persuades the Queen to make a good peace for us with the Swedes, he shall receive as revenues of his principality 50,000 ducats for every year of his life, in addition to the Order of St. Andrew, and a ruby as large as any in Europe."

Neither Matveev's nor Huyssen's approach went further. As late as February 1708, with Charles XII already across the Vistula on his march to Moscow, Matveev issued a final appeal for an English alliance. The appeal was left unanswered. In April, Peter wrote to Golovkin: "Concerning Andrei Matveev, long ago we said it was time for him to depart, for all there [i.e., in London] is tales and shame."

CHARLES ADAMANTLY REFUSED to consider any negotiations for peace with Russia. He rejected the French offer of mediation, saying that he did not trust the Tsar's word; the fact that Peter had already given the title of Prince of Ingria to Menshikov was evidence that the Tsar had no intention of returning the province and therefore could not be interested in negotiating a peace. When it was suggested that Peter might compensate Sweden in order to keep a small slice of the conquered territory on the Baltic, Charles replied that he would not sell his Baltic subjects for Russian money. When Peter offered to return all of Livonia, Estonia and Ingria except St.

Petersburg and Schlüsselburg-Nöteborg and the Neva River which connected them, Charles declared indignantly, "I will sacrifice the last Swedish soldier rather than cede Nöteborg."

In this pre-invasion period of tentative peace offers by Peter and rejections by Charles, one specific and irreconcilable difference between them became clear to all: St. Petersburg. Peter would give up anything to keep the site which gave him access to the sea. Charles would give up nothing without first coming to grips with the Russian army. Therefore, on behalf of St. Petersburg—still scarcely more than a collection of log houses, an earth-walled fortress and a primitive shipyard—the war continued.

In fact, negotiation made no sense to Charles. At the pinnacle of success, with Europe paying court at his door, with a superbly trained, victorious army ready for action, with a grand strategy faithfully adhered to and successfully pursued up to this point, why should he be willing to cede Swedish territory to an enemy? It would be dishonorable and humiliating for him to give up provinces still formally Swedish by solemn treaty between his grandfather, Charles X, and Tsar Alexis—territories now temporarily occupied, as it were, behind the back of the Swedish King and army. Besides, a Russian campaign offered Charles the kind of military operation he dreamed of. Through all his years in Poland, he had been caught in the fluctuating tides of European politics. Now, with a clean stroke of the sword, he would decide everything. And if the risks of marching an army a thousand miles into Russia were great, so were the possible rewards when a King of Sweden stood in the Kremlin and dictated a peace with Russia which would last for generations. And perhaps the risks were *not* so great. Among Swedes and West Europeans in general, opinion of the Russians as warriors remained low. The effect of Narva had sunk deep, and none of Peter's subsequent successes in the Baltic had erased the impression that the Russians were an unruly mob which could not fight a disciplined Western army.

Finally, there was the Messianic side of Charles' character. In Charles' view, Peter must be punished as Augustus had been punished: The Tsar must step down from the Russian throne. To Stanislaus, who was urging peace because of the misery of the people of Poland, Charles said, "The Tsar is not yet humiliated enough to accept the conditions of peace which I intend to prescribe." Later, he again rebuffed Stanislaus by saying, "Poland will never have quiet as long as she has for a neighbor this unjust Tsar who begins a war without any good cause for it. It will be needful first for me to march thither and depose him also." Charles went on to talk of restoring the old regime in Moscow, canceling the new reforms and, above all, abolishing the new army. "The power of Muscovy which has arisen so high thanks to the introduction of foreign military discipline must be broken and destroyed," the King declared. Charles looked forward to this change, and as he was leaving on his march to Moscow, he said cheerfully to Stanislaus, "I hope

Prince Sobieski will always remain faithful to us. Does Your Majesty not think that he would make an excellent Tsar of Russia?"

CHARLES KNEW from the beginning that a Russian campaign would not be easy. It meant traversing vast expanses of rolling plain, penetrating miles of deep forest and crossing a series of wide rivers. Indeed, Moscow and the heart of Russia seemed to be defended by nature. One after another, the great north-south river obstacles would have to be crossed: the Vistula, the Neman, the Dnieper, the Berezina. Working from maps of Poland and from a new map of Russia given to Charles as a present by Augustus, Charles and his advisors plotted their march, although the actual route was so hidden in secrecy that even Gyllenkrook, Charles' Quartermaster General in charge of the maps, was not sure which one had been chosen.

The first possibility—one which most of the officers at Swedish head-quarters in Saxony assumed the King would adopt—was to march to the Baltic to cleanse these former Swedish provinces of their Russian occupiers. Such a campaign would expiate the insult of their loss, seize the new city and port which Peter was building and drive the Russians back from the sea—a powerful blow at Peter, whose passion for salt water and St. Petersburg were well known. The military advantage of such a great sweep up the Baltic coast was that Charles would be advancing with the sea close to his left flank, providing his army with easy access to sea-borne supply and reinforcement from Sweden itself. In addition, the large army he was assembling would be further augmented by forces already stationed in those Baltic regions: almost 12,000 men under Lewenhaupt at Riga and 14,000 under Lybecker in Finland already poised for a blow at St. Petersburg. But there were negative aspects to a Baltic offensive. These Swedish provinces already had suffered terribly from seven years of war. The farms were burned, the fields in weeds, the towns almost depopulated by war and sickness. If these exhausted provinces once again became a battlefield, nothing would be left. More important than his feelings of compassion, Charles also realized that even if such a campaign were wholly successful, even with the entire coast recaptured and the flag of Sweden floating over the Peter and Paul Fortress he would not have achieved a decisive victory. Peter still would be Tsar in Moscow. Russian power would be driven back, but only temporarily. Sooner or later, this vigorous Tsar would reach for the sea again.

Thus, the march to the Baltic was rejected for something bolder: a strike directly at Moscow, Russia's heart. Charles had concluded that only by a deep thrust which could place him personally inside the Kremlin could he achieve a lasting peace for Sweden.

The Russians, of course, were not to be allowed to know this. To

encourage the Tsar to believe that the objective was the Baltic, important subsidiary operations in that area were planned. Once Charles had begun to march eastward directly across Poland, and the Russians had begun to shift troops from the Baltic coast to Poland and Lithuania, the Swedish armies in the Baltic would take the offensive; the Finnish army under Lybecker would drive down the Karelian Isthmus toward Schlüsselburg, the Neva and St. Petersburg. Then, as the thrust of the main Swedish army drew Russian troops away from the force opposing Lewenhaupt near Riga, Charles would use those troops as the escort for a vast supply convoy which would move south from Riga to rendezvous with and resupply the main army for the last stage of its march to the Russian capital.

MEANWHILE, in all those towns and villages of Saxony where Swedish regiments were stationed, military preparations were moving forward. Squads and platoons were mustered from the houses and barns where they had spent the idle months. Thousands of new recruits flocked to join the ranks, many of them German Protestants. Silesian Protestants, anxious to serve a monarch who supported their cause against Catholic domination, clustered so quickly about the recruiting booths that Swedish sergeants had only to pick and choose the best.

Augmented by these new volunteers, the army which on its entry into Saxony had numbered 19,000 had now risen to more than 32,000. In addition, 9,000 fresh recruits from Sweden were drilling in Swedish Pomerania, preparing to join the main army after it had entered Poland. There, the overall strength of Charles' army would reach 41,700 men, including 17,200 infantrymen, 8,500 cavalrymen and 16,000 dragoons. Many of the dragoons were newly recruited, although not necessarily inexperienced, Germans; as dragoons, they were in effect mounted infantrymen, prepared to fight either on foot or on horseback as circumstances dictated. Finally, there were the surgeons, chaplains, officers' servants, civil officials. Not part of the army proper and thus not counted were the hundreds of civilian wagoners, locally hired to drive cartloads of supplies and ammunition over specific sections of the road.

Adding the 26,000 men under Lewenhaupt and Lybecker who waited at Charles' command in Lithuania and Finland, the grand total of the force preparing to march on Russia reached almost 70,000 men. And it was being drilled and honed into a formidable fighting machine. Foreign recruits were trained in Swedish battle drill, learned the signals of Swedish drums and were taught to use Swedish weapons. The entire army was rearmed. The so-called "Charles XII sword," a lighter and more pointed model, was issued to replace the heavier, less wieldy weapon which the King had inherited from his father's reign. Most of the battalions already carried the

modern flintlock muskets, and now the Swedish cavalry was also equipped with flintlock pistols. Large supplies of gunpowder were procured for the campaign, but the emphasis remained, as always in the Swedish army, on the attack with cold steel.

The tailors of Saxony were busy stitching these proud and well-fed soldiers into new Swedish uniforms. The Swedish veterans who had been described as looking like gypsies when they marched into Saxony in their ragged, weather-beaten uniforms were now fitted into new boots and new blue-and-yellow uniforms with cloaks of dark blue or gray. In some regiments of cavalry, cloth breeches were replaced by elkskin, better adapted to long days in the saddle. New Bibles and hymnbooks were brought from Sweden, and medical supplies accumulated. Generous amounts of food were stockpiled and distributed between the regimental wagons. Swedish soldiers were accustomed to hearty rations: almost two pounds of bread and two pounds of meat a day, along with two and a half quarts of small beer, some peas or grain, salt, butter and a weekly issue of tobacco.

By mid-August, all was ready. Charles ordered all the women who had found their way into the Swedish camp to leave, and then attended a solemn prayer service for the army. And at four o'clock in the morning on August 27, 1707, Charles XII of Sweden rode out of Altranstadt at the beginning of his greatest adventure. Behind, in a stream of cheerful men and spirited horses, marched the largest and finest army ever commanded by a King of Sweden. As the long blue-and-yellow columns moved along the dusty Saxon roads in those late August days, they made an impressive sight. "To human eyes these brave, sturdy, well-trained, well-equipped fellows look invincible," exulted one Swedish observer. "I cannot express how fine a show the Swedes make: broad, plump, sturdy fellows in blue-and-yellow uniforms," reported a Saxon. "All Germans must acknowledge that they are incomparable. And there had been a deal of grieving among the Leipzig women. They are not content to weep and cry out, but must swoon and fall down at parting. . . . It is the same in all the other small towns . . . for the freedom our Swedes have used in such matters is past belief. Some, nay all, are spoiled. Should they ever return home, I pity wives who are to welcome such pampered men; and were a girl my worst enemy, I would not counsel her to take one of these officers for a husband—no not though he were a colonel."

The first stage of the march, through Protestant Silesia, became more of a triumphal progress than the opening of an arduous campaign. The population, whose Protestant churches had been reopened thanks to Charles, regarded the King as their special savior. Crowds of people attended the daily open-air services in the army's encampments, hoping simply to catch a glimpse of their hero. The sight of Charles kneeling among his men made a deep impression, and many young men wholly untrained as soldiers sought

to accompany the army as if it had been a band of passing crusaders. Charles welcomed and even bathed in this wave of popular feeling, instructing his chaplains to choose only hymns which had been translated from German so that the population visiting the camp would recognize the music and be able to join in singing.

The campaign on which the King was embarking would be a maximum test for his superb war machine. From the beginning, it was clear that this was to be an epic march. To take an army from deep in Germany in the heart of Europe eastward more than a thousand miles to Moscow required an audacity equal to Hannibal's or Alexander's. In Marlborough's famous march up the Rhine before the Battle of Blenheim, three years before, the Englishman had moved 250 miles from the Netherlands into Bavaria. But Marlborough's men had tramped through populated regions, staying close to the great river which carried his supply barges and which, had the situation begun to deteriorate, would have provided a watery avenue on which to embark and float downstream to their original base. Charles was setting out on a journey four times as long, across plains, swamps, forests and rivers, where the roads were few and the population scarce. If misfortune or disaster struck, there was no way to retreat except to walk.

Nevertheless, Charles' own attitude was more than confident; it was light-hearted. Even as the Swedish columns of infantry, cavalry, cannon and supply wagons were rippling along the Saxon roads, Charles, accompanied by only seven Swedish officers, rode incognito into Dresden to spend an afternoon with his former enemy, the Elector Augustus. Charles' visit was so sudden that he found the Elector still in his dressing gown. The two monarchs embraced, Augustus put on a coat, and together they went for an afternoon ride along the Elbe. It was a pleasant meeting between the two first cousins and Charles bore no personal ill-will against the man who had attacked him six years before and whose dethroning he had pursued so relentlessly for so many years across the plains of Poland. Now that Augustus was punished, Charles' attitude toward him was sunny. At the end of their ride, Charles inspected the famous Green Vault collection that had so fascinated Peter nine years before, and visited his aunt, Augustus' mother, the Dowager Electress of Saxony. It was the last time the King would see either his aunt or his cousin.* Despite these pleasantries, the Swedes around Charles worried about the King's reckless decision to ride into the capital of a former enemy accompanied by only seven men. Charles later put their fears aside, smiling and saying, "There was no danger. The army was on the march."

---

* In fact, during Charles' thirty-six years of life, Augustus was the only man of kingly rank whom the King of Sweden would ever meet.

32

THE GREAT ROAD
TO MOSCOW

THAT CHARLES MEANT to march across Poland and invade Russia was no surprise to Peter. Charles had finished with Denmark and Poland; Russia was surely next. As early as January 1707, the Tsar had given orders to create a belt of devastation so that an advancing army would have difficulty living off the land. Into western Poland, which would be first to see the advancing Swedes, rode Cossacks and Kalmucks with instructions to lay waste the countryside. Polish towns were burned, bridges were broken and destroyed. Rawicz, which had been Charles' headquarters in 1705, was razed and its wells poisoned by the corpses of Poles who resisted.

Behind this shield of scorched earth, Peter worked tirelessly to expand and improve his army. New agents were sent out to bring in fresh recruits. Sometimes, potential soldiers were not easy to find and Peter needed help. A nobleman named Bezobrazov, for example, reported from his district of Bryansk that lately there had been a remarkable increase in the number of church servitors who might make excellent dragoons. Peter responded by enrolling all who could march or ride. A Swedish atrocity was used to help motivate the men. Forty-six Russian soldiers, taken prisoner by the Swedes, had had the first two fingers of their right hands cut off by their captors and had then been sent back to Russia. Peter was outraged at this cruelty perpetrated by a nation which "represents him and his people as barbarous and unchristian." Further, reported Whitworth, he meant to turn the act against the Swedes: "For he intended to place one of [the maimed soldiers] in every regiment, who might be a living remonstrance to their companions what usage they could expect from their merciless enemies in case they suffered themselves to be captured."

Preparing for the worst, the Tsar ordered new fortifications for Moscow itself. In mid-June, the engineer Ivan Korchmin arrived in the city with instructions to put its defenses, especially those of the Kremlin, in good order. Despite these efforts, the city trembled at the prospect of a Swedish occupation. "Nobody spoke of anything except of flight or death," wrote

Pleyer, the Austrian envoy in Moscow. "Many of the merchants, under pretext of going to the fair, took their wives and children to Archangel whither they had usually gone alone. The great foreign merchants and capitalists hastened to go to Hamburg with their families and property while the mechanics and artisans went into service. The foreigners, not only of Moscow but of all the neighboring towns, applied to their ministers for protection, as they feared not only the harshness and rapacity of the Swedes, but even more a general rising and massacre in Moscow, where people are already embittered by the immeasurable increase of the taxes."

In the early summer of 1707, while the fortification of Moscow was proceeding and while Charles was making his final preparations in Saxony, Peter was in Warsaw. His two months in the Polish capital were not entirely voluntary; during most of his time there, he was once again in bed with fever. At the end of August, he received word that the Swedish King was finally marching east, and, soon after, the Tsar left Warsaw, traveling slowly through Poland and Lithuania, stopping to inspect fortifications and talk to troop commanders along the way.

A council of Russian commanders joined by Peter and Menshikov generally confirmed the Tsar's defensive strategy. They decided not to risk a battle in Poland, certainly not a big, classically conducted battle in the open field, as Peter thought his Russian infantry was still not ready and he adamantly refused to endanger the army without which Russia was helpless. Accordingly, the bulk of the infantry was withdrawn from Poland and placed under Sheremetev's command near Minsk.

In line with this strategy, the Russian command in Poland was given to Menshikov, the best of Peter's native Russian cavalry commanders. Menshikov's dragoon regiments would try to delay the Swedes at the river crossings: behind the Vistula at Warsaw, on the Narew at Pultusk and on the Neman at Grodno.

Peter reached St. Petersburg on October 23 and immediately threw himself into action. He inspected the fortifications of the city itself—on the sea approaches at Kronstadt and on the Neva-Ladoga flank at Schlüsselburg. He was constantly at the Admiralty, and drew up a complete shipbuilding program for the following year. He continued to issue orders for the coming campaign and gave numerous instructions for recruiting, clothing and supplying the troops. At the same time, he found time to send condolences to the father of Prince Ivan Troekurov, killed in battle, and to write a friendly note to Darya Menshikov begging her to take better care of her husband: "Fatten him up so he looks not so thin as when he was at Meretch." He ordered Latin books sent to Apraxin to be translated into Russian and gave orders for training the puppies of his favorite dogs.

And yet, with all his work, Peter was almost overwhelmed during this autumn and early winter by feelings of anxiety and depression. He had

reason enough, for, while contemplating the Swedish invasion, he had been greeted on his arrival in St. Petersburg by news of the revolt among the Bashkirs and Don Cossacks, and an account of the massacre of Dolgoruky and his battalion by Bulavin on the River Aidar. This disaster threatened to cut short his stay in Petersburg, as he seemed urgently needed in Moscow or even on the Ukrainian steppe, but as he was preparing to leave, further news arrived that Bulavin's army had been destroyed.

In addition to these worries, Peter was never completely well during these critical months. He was in bed for weeks with attacks of fever, he was often irritable and his temper frequently flared. At one point he was angry at Apraxin for not punishing governors who sent the army fewer than the required number of recruits: "That you have done nothing to those governors who have not brought men as ordered, that you throw the blame of this on the departments of Moscow which is not to your credit, is due only to one of two causes: either to laziness or that you did not wish to quarrel with them." Apraxin was deeply hurt, and Peter, recognizing his unfairness, replied: "You feel aggrieved at what I wrote to you about the governors. But for God's sake have no grief about it, for really I bear no malice toward you, but since I have been here the slightest thing which thwarts me puts me into a passion."

Possibly because of his feelings of depression and loneliness, Peter realized his need and dependence on the one person who could truly relax him in his moments of greatest anxiety. It was in November 1707, as soon as he returned to St. Petersburg, that he finally married Catherine.

Late in November, Peter left for Moscow to pass the Christmas holidays and to visit his capital, which he had not seen for more than two years. And he was anxious to inspect the fortification which Korchmin was constructing with 20,000 men laboring day and night. The earth was frozen, and in order to thaw the ground to cut out the sods of earth used to build the ramparts, Korchmin's workers had to build great fires directly over the area to be cut. During the month he spent in Moscow, Peter also regulated the making of silver coins, and visited the printing office to see the new type which he had ordered from Holland and which had just arrived. He concerned himself with standardizing the salaries of his ambassadors and with sending more young Russians abroad. He renewed his insistence on the education of the clergy and on ensuring that clothes and hats being made in Moscow follow approved patterns. Preoccupied, he showed his annoyance with what he regarded as petty matters raised by others. When Whitworth unwisely brought up some minor grievances on behalf of English merchants in Russia, Peter replied brusquely that he would see what could be done, but not to expect much, because "God has given the Tsar twenty times more business than other people, but not twenty times more force or capacity to go through with it."

On January 6, 1708, Peter left Moscow to rejoin the army. On the road to Minsk, he learned from Menshikov that Charles was advancing swiftly across Poland, and he hurried to Grodno. The ability of the Swedish army to move rapidly in the depth of winter and strike surprise blows added to Peter's anxiety. Four days later, he wrote to Apraxin to "hasten to Vilna . . . but if you have already come to Vilna, go no further, for the enemy is already upon us."

THE SWEDISH ARMY, marching in six parallel columns, had crossed the border from Silesia into Poland at Rawicz. Here, inside the Polish frontier, King and army had their first taste of what lay ahead. The town of Rawicz was burned to the ground and corpses floated in the wells and streams; Menshikov's Cossack and Kalmuck cavalry had begun to spread a carpet of destruction before the advancing Swedish army as it marched eastward. Across Poland, the air reeked with the acrid smell of fire and smoke over farms and villages put to the torch by Menshikov's horsemen. The Russian cavalry avoided contact, staying just out of reach and withdrawing eastward toward Warsaw, where Menshikov was digging in behind the Vistula.

Screened by their own cavalry and dragoons, the Swedes advanced directly toward Warsaw at a leisurely pace. Then, west of Warsaw, Charles turned north. At Posen, the army halted and Charles established a semipermanent camp, where he remained for two months awaiting the arrival of reinforcements and an improvement in the weather. Here, Charles detached 5,000 dragoons and 3,000 infantry under Major General Krassow to remain in Poland to bolster the shaky throne of Stanislaus.

The autumn weeks passed and winter approached. With the Swedish army still inert and the Swedish King apparently lapsed into another of his long periods of lassitude, the Russians around Warsaw begun to feel more confident. Surely, with winter at hand, the Swedes would remain in their present encampment until spring. But Charles had no such intention. He had not left the comfortable quarters in Saxony at the end of the summer only to winter in a more desolate place a few miles farther east. In fact, while drilling his new troops, he was only waiting for the end of the autumn rains which had turned the roads into quagmires. Once the frost had come and the roads were hard, the King would move.

But not toward Warsaw. In the early stages of this campaign, Charles deliberately laid aside the impetuous frontal attack which was part of his reputation. He was anxious to avoid a major clash this far from his distant goal and his strategy in Poland was to allow the Russians to establish defensive positions behind a river, then himself march north, cross the stream, outflank the entrenched defenders and force them to withdraw without a battle.

The first time, it was easy. At the end of November, after two months' preparation, the Swedes broke camp at Posen and marched fifty miles northeast to a point where the Vistula curved westward in their direction. Here, the river flowed empty and wide; not a Russian soldier or Cossack horseman was to be seen anywhere on the snowy, windswept landscape. But the Swedes had to contend with nature. The snow was deep, but the river was still flowing. Because of drifting ice, it was impossible to throw a bridge across, and Charles was forced to wait impatiently another month for ice to form. On Christmas Day, the temperature dropped and the surface of the river glazed. On the 28th, the ice was three inches thick. By adding straw and boards sprayed with water and frozen into the ice, the Swedes strengthened the surface sufficiently to bear the weight of wagons and artillery, and between the 28th and the 31st, the entire army crossed the Vistula. "They have executed their design," wrote Captain James Jefferyes, a young Englishman with the army,* "without any loss other than that of two or three wagons which went to the bottom of the river."

Thus, on New Year's Day 1708, the Swedish army stood east of the Vistula. The Warsaw line was outflanked, and Menshikov evacuated the city and withdrew to new positions behind the Narew River at Pultusk. Knowing from his scouts that this position was defended, Charles again applied his strategy of moving northeast and sliding around the Russian defenses.

The second time, however, it was not so easy. North of the main road lay some of the most difficult country in Eastern Europe. The Masurian lake district was made up of bogs, marshes and thick forests, thinly populated by a wild peasantry hostile to all strangers. The roads were little more than animal trails and paths for peasant carts. Nevertheless, the King plunged forward. The march was grueling. Every night, Charles ordered huge fires to be built for each company and military music played to keep spirits up, but still the forest took its toll. Horses died, worn out from trying to pull wagons and artillery along rutted trails. In the German dragoon regiments, there were desertions; the money they were being paid

---

* Jefferyes was a soldier-diplomat with strong ties in Sweden. He was born in Stockholm during his father's long period of service to Charles XI; his elder brother was killed with the Swedish army at Narva; and Jefferyes himself had served as secretary to the British ambassador to Sweden. When he joined the Swedish army in 1707 as a "volunteer," it was a device arranged by Charles XII's Swedish ministers to get around the King's objections to having foreign diplomats accompany his army. In fact, although Jefferyes' sympathy lay with the Swedes, his real mission was to observe and report objectively to Whitehall the progress of Charles' invasion of Russia. Captured at Poltava, and allowed to return to Britain, Jefferyes reappeared briefly in Russia in 1719 as King George I's ambassador to St. Petersburg. Jefferyes' last twenty years were spent living in Blarney Castle, County Cork, Ireland, which he had inherited from his father.

was not worth this kind of warfare. Fodder was scarce. To force the peasants to give up their own carefully hoarded fodder, the Swedes threatened them in the simplest, cruelest way. A child would be taken, and before its mother's eyes, a rope would be fixed around its neck. Then a Swedish officer would ask one last time whether the mother would reveal the family cache of food. If she refused, the child was hanged. Usually, the peasants broke down and talked, although this meant starvation for all of them.

Not surprisingly, some of the inhabitants resisted. Most of the peasants were hunters who lived among bears and wolves and were trained in the use of firearms. From behind trees and thickets, they sniped at the marching columns and ambushed stragglers. Guerilla warfare quickly calls up its own grim rules. When a party of his soldiers was locked in the barn where they were sleeping and the barn burned over their heads, the King hanged ten hostages from the village as a reprisal. After the last regiment had passed through, the entire village was burned to the ground. Another day, when General Kreutz captured a band of fifty marauders, he compelled the prisoners to hang one another, with the last few being strung up by his own Swedish soldiers.

In spite of the difficulty of the march, on January 22, Charles emerged from the woods at Kolno. Russian cavalry riding up from the south found the Swedes already present in strength. There was nothing for them to do but retreat and carry the news to Menshikov.

Having achieved much by his bold stroke, Charles decided on another even more impetuous thrust at the third river line, the Neman. Before him lay the Lithuanian frontier town of Grodno, the center and key to the Neman River line, where a Russian army under Ogilvie had spent the winter two years earlier. Whatever the route of his eventual campaign, north to the Baltic or east to Moscow, both Charles and Peter understood that Charles must pass through Grodno. He needed the road; he could not march forever through forests and swamps. Because of its importance, Russian troops were moving into Grodno, and Charles decided to strike immediately in hope of capturing the town before the Russians had secured it. Leaving the main army to follow, the King rode ahead with only 600 troopers of the Guards Cavalry and Rehnskjold and Kreutz. Along the way he added fifty men of a reconnaissance troop which had been out in front. Arriving at Grodno in the afternoon, he found the bridge across the Neman still intact and guarded by 2,000 cavalrymen commanded by Brigadier Mühlenfels, one of Peter's German officers. Without hesitation, Charles launched an immediate attack to seize the bridge. Some of the Swedes rode across the river ice to come on the Russians from the rear; others charged directly onto the bridge. There was a confused melee of Russians and Swedes firing pistols and swinging swords at one another. In

the shouting mob, the King himself killed two Russians, one with a shot from his pistol, the other with a thrust of his sword. The day was short, and in the gathering gloom of the afternoon the Russians could not tell how many Swedes there were; they soon gave up the bridge and retreated into the town. Charles followed and that night camped by the river beneath the walls of the town, meanwhile sending messengers back to order the rest of the army to hurry forward. He was unaware that inside the walls of Grodno, only a few hundred yards away, was Tsar Peter himself.

Peter had arrived in Grodno to bolster the flustered Menshikov, who was confused and upset by the uncertainty of these flanking movements and sudden, rapid, unorthodox marches, and was about to withdraw his troops lest he be outflanked again. But the Tsar understood the importance of the Neman line and wanted to ensure that the river defense would not be breached as painlessly as those on the Vistula and the Narew. Neither he nor Menshikov had any idea that Charles was so close and would suddenly come galloping across the still undestroyed Neman River bridge.

When Peter and his officers inside the town heard firing and saw the cavalry action on the bridge, they were unable to tell how many Swedes were upon them. Assuming that the entire Swedish army had arrived and that the bridge was now in its hands, Peter believed that Grodno could not be held. That night, while his troops evacuated the town, he kept his own carriage near the eastern gate. Before dawn, he climbed into it with Menshikov and rolled off in the direction of Vilna and St. Petersburg. If Charles had known of Peter's presence, he surely would have made a frenzied effort to capture this towering prize and change the nature of the war at a single stroke. As it was, Charles' horsemen approached the walls of Grodno the following morning, found them deserted and entered the town. But the drama was not over. At midday, on the road to Vilna, Peter learned the true nature of the sudden Swedish onslaught: that it had been launched by a mere handful of men, that this same handful had occupied the town but had not yet been reinforced by the main Swedish army, and that among the Swedish band was Charles himself. He decided on a bold counterstroke: That night, he would launch his own surprise attack on the town to recapture it and, with luck, to seize the King of Sweden. The shamed Mühlenfels was dispatched back toward Grodno at the head of 3,000 cavalrymen with orders to attack after darkness.

Charles, with typical scorn for anything the Russians might do, had ordered that night that "all cavalrymen should off-saddle, undress and retire to rest." A watch of fifty dragoons was posted in a state of semi-alert, with horses saddled, to spend the night in houses along the road by which the Russians had evacuated Grodno, Of these fifty, a picket of fifteen men remained awake at the barrier across the road, but thirteen had dismounted and gathered around a fire to ward off the bitter cold of the

January night. Only two mounted dragoons actually stood guard over the King of Sweden and his exhausted men, now all plunged deep into sleep. After midnight, hundreds of Russian horsemen quietly approached the silent town. The sound of horses in the fields was picked up by the two dragoons on guard; they shouted to their comrades around the fire, who mounted in time to meet the first Russians at the barrier. Immediately, the other thirty-five dragoons came tumbling out of the houses, mounted their saddled horses and spurred into the fray. Although the Swedes were greatly outnumbered, the night was "so pitchy dark that none could see his hand before his face," and the Russians assumed that the force guarding the town would be much larger. Before many minutes passed, Charles and Rehnskjold both arrived, the King still in his stocking feet. They were eager to join in the melee, but unable in the darkness to distinguish friend from foe. A few minutes later, more Swedes arrived, some half dressed and riding bareback. Even in the blackness, the Russians sensed the growing reinforcement of their enemies and, unwilling to prolong the confused action, turned and retreated down the road they had come. Within an hour, Grodno was peaceful again. It was a fortunate and exhilarating night for Charles, who never stopped to ask himself what would have happened if Mühlenfels had adopted his own tactics and led 3,000 men in an impetuous dash into town, simply galloping past the two men on guard and the little group around the bonfire.

Charles remained for three days in Grodno alone with his small force of Horse Guards, but there was no further Russian attempt to retake the town. Mühlenfels, having failed twice, was arrested; the official charge was his failure to destroy the Neman bridge. When the main Swedish army began to arrive, the King put himself at the head of several elite regiments and set off in pursuit of Peter, but he was soon forced to give up the chase. His troops were too few and too tired, and the Russian scorched-earth tactics had reduced the countryside to a wintry desert.

In the days that followed, the Russian army withdrew entirely from the Neman River line, giving up its strong defense positions and its prepared winter quarters and retreating to a new line on the River Berezina. Charles followed, again riding ahead of his main army with his Guards cavalry. But the Swedish army was exhausted and needed rest. It had covered 500 miles and had already campaigned through almost three months of winter. The decisive factor was the lack of forage for the horses. The Russians had burned or the peasants had hidden what remained of the harvest; for the animals to survive, it was clear that the advance must halt until spring brought new shoots of green grass. On February 8, Charles halted, and when the main army joined him, he allowed the men to camp and rest. On March 17, he moved again, shifting the camp to Radoshkovichi, northwest

of Minsk. Here at last, in a triangle bounded by Vilna, Grodno and Minsk, the King placed the army in winter quarters.

The Polish campaign was over. On crossing the Neman at Grodno, the Swedish army entered Lithuania, the huge, sprawling, politically amorphous territory which lay between Poland, Russia and the Baltic. Three potentially formidable river barriers and the whole of Poland had been crossed with no more serious fighting than the cavalry skirmish at the Grodno bridge. The campaign had brought diplomatic as well as military fruits. In England, Queen Anne's government had been reluctant to grant recognition to Charles' puppet King of Poland, but when the news reached London of the ease with which Charles had advanced across Poland, Stanislaus was formally recognized as Augustus' successor. In Poland, those important members of the nobility who had withheld support from Stanislaus now moved to make amends. Throughout Western Europe, sovereigns and statesmen gave Peter little chance. And among the Swedish soldiers, confidence in themselves and contempt for their enemies rose higher. What could one make of a Russian army commanded by the Tsar himself which would flee from a defended river line and a fortress town at the approach of only 600 Swedish horsemen?

Confinement in winter quarters was harder on the Swedish army than campaigning in the open field. Cramped into small, poorly heated rooms, without proper food, many of the soldiers, especially the new recruits from Sweden, caught dysentery, and some died; Charles himself suffered from the disease for several weeks. Outside, beyond the camp sentry posts, there was only the howling wind, the snow, the bitter cold, the ashes of burned villages, the scorched timbers of broken bridges fallen into frozen streams. Daily, Swedish foraging parties scoured the devastated landscape in search of food. They learned the Lithuanian peasant's habit of hiding his supplies in a hole in the ground and how to detect these secret caches by such signs as the quicker melting of the snow on top because of the warmth underneath. Often these foraging patrols encountered Russian cavalry, and skirmishes were constant. Ten or twenty horsemen would be in a clearing near a peasant hut when the Cossacks or Kalmucks would stumble upon them. Then there would be sudden shouts in the brittle winter air, a spurring of horses across the snow, a few shots and sword strokes before one side or the other was gone. It was a war without quarter, and the Swedes and these Russian irregulars hated each other. If either side captured the other, it locked its prisoners in a hut and burned it to the ground.

Through the wintry days, in the building used as army headquarters, Charles and his staff huddled over their maps. One day, while Gyllenkrook, his Quartermaster General, was working on his maps, "His Majesty came

up to me and looked at my work and among other discourse he observed, 'We are now upon the great road to Moscow.' I replied that it was yet far hence. His Majesty replied, 'When we begin to march again, we shall get there, never fear.' " Gyllenkrook obediently turned back to his maps, preparing a line of march as far as Mogilov on the Dnieper, along the road to Smolensk and Moscow. To support the march, Charles summoned Count Adam Lewenhaupt, the Swedish commander in Riga, to Radoshkovichi. He ordered Lewenhaupt to scour Livonia and gather a vast amount of food, powder and ammunition along with the horses and wagons to transport it, and to be ready with his soldiers to escort this immense wagon train to a midsummer rendezvous point with the main army.

Beginning in early May, signs of impending movement multiplied in the Swedish camp. Drill intensified and the army was brought to fighting trim. Sufficient food was collected for a six-week march. With the arrival of bluer skies and warmer breezes, a tremendous spirit of optimism welled up among Charles' soldiers. Contempt for the Russians flourished. Major General Lagercrona declared that "the enemy would not dare oppose His Majesty's march to Moscow." And Major General Axel Sparre told the King that "there was an old prophecy that a Sparre should one day be Governor of Moscow, whereat the King laughed much."

AFTER THE CLASH at Grodno, Peter traveled north in his carriage to Vilna. Watching the irresistible advance of his great opponent across the rivers and plains of Poland, he had begun to despair; then, suddenly, seemingly inexplicably, the Swedish juggernaut had halted and remained inert for almost three months. In Vilna, Peter waited while he and his generals tried to discover which direction Charles would take. From Grodno, the Swedes could march in several directions. If they followed Peter north to Vilna, the Tsar would know that his enemy was marching north to free the Baltic provinces and assault St. Petersburg. If he turned east toward Minsk, it would seem certain that Moscow was his goal. Or Charles might postpone the decision and even combine the two goals by marching northeast past Lake Peipus to seize Pskov and Novgorod. From there, he would be in a position to strike at either Petersburg or Moscow.

Peter could not neglect any of these possibilities. He ordered the main army to fall back across the Dnieper although Field Marshal Goltz and 8,000 dragoons were posted at Borisov on the Berezina to oppose any attempted crossing of that stream. Menshikov was commanded to cut down trees and barricade the roads leading in all directions from the Grodno hub. A few weeks later, the Tsar grimly raised the stakes. At a council of war, Peter ordered the creation of a zone of total devastation to deny all

sustenance to the Swedes no matter which direction they marched when they broke their winter quarters. Along all roads leading north, east or south from the Swedish camp, a broad belt of total destruction 120 miles deep would be created, running from Pskov down to Smolensk. Within this zone, every building, every scrap of food and fodder was to be burned as soon as Charles was on the march. On pain of death, the peasants were commanded to remove all hay or grain from their barns and to bury it or hide it in the woods. They were to prepare hiding places for themselves and their cattle deep in the forests, far from the roads. The enemy must march into a desert of desolation.

The harshest blow fell on the town of Dorpat, which Peter had captured in 1704 and which lay directly in Charles' path if he should march to the Baltic. Peter ordered its total depopulation and destruction. To this tragedy was appended the irony that it was all in vain. Charles did not march to the north, and the ruination of Dorpat served no purpose.

When Charles went into winter quarters at Radoshkovichi, Peter decided to take advantage of the lull and return to St. Petersburg for Easter. On the eve of his departure from the army, he was again stricken by a severe fever, but left anyway. When he arrived in St. Petersburg on the last day of March, his strength was gone, and on April 6 he wrote to Golovkin:

I have always been healthy here as though in paradise and I don't know how I brought this fever with me from Poland, for I took good care of myself in the sledge and was well covered with warm clothes. But I have been racked with fever during the whole of Passion Week and even at Easter I could attend none of the services except the beginning of Vespers and the Gospel on account of the illness. Now, thanks be to God, I am getting better but still do not go out of the house. The fever was accompanied by pains in my throat and chest and ended in a cough which is now very severe.

Two days later, Peter wrote again:

I beg you to do everything that can possibly be done without me. When I was well, I let nothing pass, but now God sees what I am after this illness which this place and Poland have caused me, and if in these next weeks I have no time for taking medicine and resting, God knows what will happen.

When Menshikov sent word that the Swedes were building bridges in obvious preparation for resuming their advance, Peter answered worriedly on April 14 that he understood the gravity of the situation and would come

if it was essential. But he begged Menshikov not to summon him to the army any sooner than was absolutely necessary, as he still desperately needed further rest and treatment. He added,

> You know yourself that I am not accustomed to write in this way, but God sees how little strength I have, and without health and strength it is impossible to be of service. But if for five or six weeks from this time I can stay here and take medicine, I then hope, with God's help, to come to you well.

33

GOLOVCHIN
AND LESNAYA

THE STAGE WAS SET for a new campaign. The two armies lay opposite each other in widely dispersed encampments. The main Swedish army with Charles was in the triangle Grodno-Vilna-Minsk. Here the King had twelve regiments of infantry and sixteen regiments of cavalry and dragoons, a total of some 35,000 men; in addition, smaller Swedish armies were available on the Baltic. Lewenhaupt's 12,000 men at Riga had already been given orders to join the main army, and a separate Swedish force of 14,000 under Lybecker had been ordered to march from Finland down the Karelian Isthmus toward St. Petersburg. If completely successful, this force would take Peter's new capital; if not, it would at least provide a diversion which would occupy the Tsar's concern and resources. Finally, there were 8,000 Swedish troops in Poland under General Krassow; if Poland remained calm, they could move eastward to reinforce Charles. All told, across the entire battlefront, Charles disposed of 70,000 men.

Peter's forces were substantially larger. The main Russian army assigned by the Tsar to protect both Pskov and Moscow and commanded by Sheremetev and Menshikov was ranged in a wide arc around the triangular Swedish camp from Polotsk and Vitebsk in the north down to Mogilev and Bykhov in the south. The infantry was pulled well back and stood between the Dvina and the Dnieper. Out in front, large cavalry detachments under Goltz straddled the main Minsk-Smolensk road and patrolled along the Berezina to absorb the first shock of the Swedish advance. Farther south, another force guarded the Berezina River crossing of the southern road from Minsk to Mogilev. Altogether, in this arc Peter had twenty-six regiments of infantry and thirty-three regiments of dragoons, a total of about 57,500 men. In addition, Apraxin, whose assignment was to defend St. Petersburg, commanded 24,500 men. At Dorpat, between the Baltic and the central fronts, a third Russian force of 16,000 men was stationed under General Bauer, whose mission was to cover the Swedish army under Lewenhaupt at Riga. These forces were prepared to respond to a variety of

Swedish moves. If Charles marched toward Pskov and St. Petersburg, Menshikov and Sheremetev would shift the main Russian army north to oppose him; if the King moved directly toward Moscow, the Russian generals would fight him on the Berezina and the Dnieper. Bauer's movements were tied to Lewenhaupt's: if Lewenhaupt marched north toward St. Petersburg, Bauer would go north to reinforce Apraxin; if Lewenhaupt moved south to join the King, Bauer would shift south to bolster Sheremetev. A separate Russian force of 12,000 men under Prince Michael Golitsyn was posted near Kiev to cover the approaches to the Ukraine. At this time, that seemed the least likely direction in which the Swedes would march.

The Russian forces outnumbered the Swedes 110,000 to 70,000 (or, effectively 62,000, as Krassow's force was too far away to be of use). Disparity in numbers meant little except for the fact that in a protracted campaign the Russians could replace losses more easily than the Swedes. At Narva, the odds against Sweden had been four to one. Here they were only five to three.

By June 6, the fresh grass had pushed its way several inches above the earth and Charles decided to move. The three-month camp at Radoshkovichi was broken and the regiments converged on Minsk, the mustering point on the main Warsaw-Smolensk-Moscow highway. From Minsk, the road went east to Borisov on the Berezina River, a crossing which the Russians were prepared to defend.

At a pair of military conferences on April 26 and June 13, Sheremetev and Menshikov had decided to make their first stand against the Swedes on the Berezina. Peter was not present at either of these meetings, but he had strongly endorsed their decision to hold this river line. In May, the Russian army, its divisions commanded by Menshikov, Sheremetev, Hallart, Repnin and Goltz, moved out of its own winter quarters and took positions along a forty-mile front east of the river. Not knowing exactly where the King would strike, the Russian dispositions were kept fluid, but at the most obvious point—the crossing at Borisov—8,000 Russians under Goltz were well dug in.

Knowing this, Charles again chose to turn the flank of this enemy front, this time from the south. On June 16, after nine days' marching, the army reached the Berezina River at Berezina-Sapezhinskaya. A screening force of Cossacks and Russian dragoons retreated, Swedish engineers constructed two bridges, and the army crossed the Berezina. The success of Charles' maneuver left Minsk fifty miles to the rear and meant that the King now was leaving forever the Polish-Lithuanian area in which he had lived and campaigned the previous eight years.

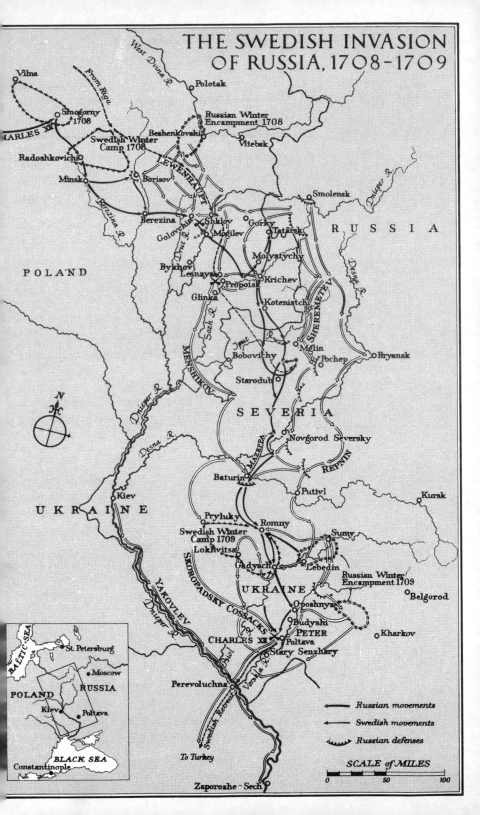

THE SWEDISH INVASION
OF RUSSIA, 1708-1709

Vilna

From Riga

West Dvina R.

Polotsk

CHARLES XII

Smogorny 1708

Radoshkovichi

Beshenkovichi

Russian Winter
Encampment 1708

Vitebsk

Swedish Winter
Camp 1708

Minsk

Borisov

LEWENHAUPT

Berezina R.

Berezina

Shklov

Golovchin

Mogilev

Gorky

Tatarsk

Smolensk

Dnieper R.

R U S S I A

Drut R.

P O L A N D

Bykhov

Lesnaya

Propoisk

Glinka

Molyatychy

Krichev

Kotenistchi

SHEREMETEV

Desna R.

Sozh R.

MENSHIKOV

Bobovichy

Mglin

Pochep

Bryansk

Iput R.

Starodub

Dnieper R.

Desna R.

S E V E R I A

N

Novgorod Seversky

MAZEPA

REPNIN

Baturin

Putivl

Kursk

U K R A I N E

Kiev

Pryluky

Romny

Swedish Winter
Camp 1709

Lokhvitsa

Sumy

Gadyach

Lebedin

Russian Winter
Encampment 1709

U K R A I N E

Belgorod

SKOROPADSKY COSSACKS

Oposhnya

YAKOVLEV

Budyshi

PETER

Kharkov

Dnieper R.

CHARLES XII

Poltava

Psiol R.

Stary Senzhary

Vorskla R.

Perevoluchna

Swedish Retreat

To Turkey

Zaporozhe - Sech

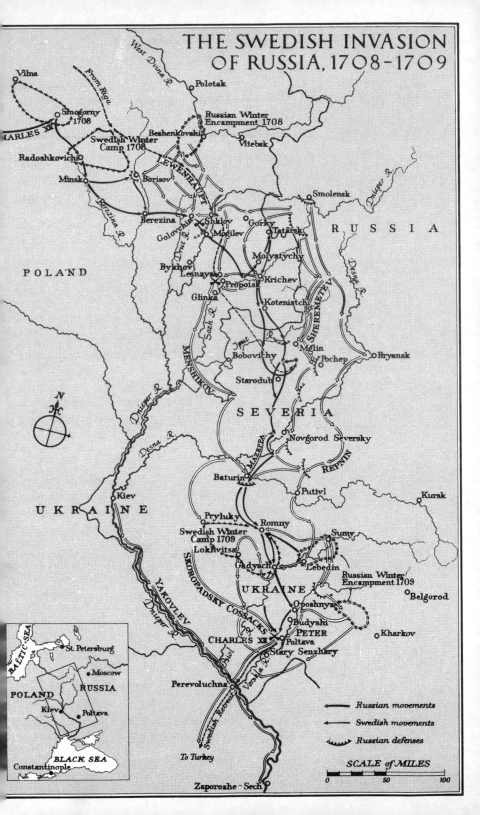

St. Petersburg

BALTIC SEA

Moscow

R U S S I A

P O L A N D

Kiev

Poltava

BLACK SEA

Constantinople

⟶ Russian movements

⟶ Swedish movements

⟿ Russian defenses

SCALE of MILES

0   50   100

Menshikov and Sheremetev were much chagrined by the relative ease with which they had been out-maneuvered, and they could guess what the Tsar's reaction to their failure would be. In a military conference at Mogilev on June 23, they agreed that they must still make a serious effort to defend the region west of the Dnieper and protect the towns of Mogilev and Shklov. Orders went out to all divisions of the army to assemble on the west bank of the River Babich, a tributary of the Drut. A battle would be offered; not a risk-everything, life-or-death battle, but a battle that would extract payment from the invaders.

Charles now thought of turning north to catch Goltz and his force guarding the Borisov crossing in the rear, but his scouts reported that the Russian army as a whole was moving south and gathering behind the River Babich near a village called Golovchin. This time the King decided not to avoid his foe. The army marched toward Golovchin. The weather became worse. Rain fell unceasingly and the earth was a sea of mud. Every few yards, the Russians cut trees to fall across the road and block the advance. Jefferyes wrote to London: "I cannot on this occasion pass by the praises due to the Swedish troops, for whether I consider the great hardship which they have been obliged to undergo by forcing their way through places almost impassable, and by wading through morasses up to their middle, or I consider their patience in suffering hunger and thirst, they being for the most part reduced to bread and water, I must conclude they are as good subjects as any prince in Europe can boast of."

On June 30, the King himself arrived at Golovchin, which lay in front of the swampy and shallow Babich. He found the Russian army drawn up in strong positions across the river in a line extending for six miles along the Babich's rain-swollen marshy banks. It took several days for a substantial part of the Swedish army to come up, while across the river the Russian forces also were being continually reinforced by fresh arrivals of infantry and cavalry. Meantime, Charles examined the terrain and worked out a plan of battle, and his Swedish veterans grew restless. The river was shallow and easily fordable—why didn't they just go and scatter the Russian rabble? Charles understood that it might not be so easy. The Russians were dug into strong positions behind ditches and trenches with chevaux de frise placed in front. Their army was divided into two central divisions: to the north, thirteen regiments of infantry and ten regiments of cavalry under Sheremetev and Menshikov; to the south, nine regiments of infantry and three dragoon regiments under Repnin. The two divisions were separated in the center by a marshy, wooded area through which a tributary stream ran down into the Babich. Farther along on either flank were still more Russian troops: to the north of Sheremetev, beyond a deeper and more extensive swamp, was more Russian infantry and cavalry

under Hallart; to the south of Repnin was Goltz with ten regiments of dragoons numbering 10,000 men, plus Cossack and Kalmuck cavalry.

In fact, the Russians, after repeated experience of being outflanked, had spread themselves thin to prevent it happening again, and Charles determined to use the over-extension of his opponents' line to his own advantage. While his forces were assembling, he marched detachments of troops up and down the bank, feinting here and there, encouraging the Russians to keep their forces strong on the outer wings. In this way, Hallart's Russian corps was kept far to the north and never entered the subsequent battle at all.

But this time there was not to be a flanking movement. Charles had detected the most vulnerable point in the long Russian line: It lay in the center, between the two divisions commanded by Sheremetev and Repnin, in the area of the tributary and marsh. If Charles attacked at this point, the marsh would prevent or hinder one Russian division from coming to assist the other. The King decided that the blow would fall on Repnin, south of the marsh. In the assault, he personally would lead the infantry against Repnin's Russian infantry. Rehnskjold would lead the cavalry which would grapple with Goltz's horsemen.

By July 3, Charles had assembled 20,000 men, more than half his total force, and at midnight his regiments were alerted and ordered to prepare for battle. That night, the river and the opposite bank were concealed by a thick mist rising from the stream, and behind this natural screen Charles quietly brought up artillery, rolling it efficiently into previously chosen sites. By two a.m., he had placed eight of his heaviest cannon in position to fire at close range directly across the stream. At daybreak, as the sun's first rays were filtering through the mist, the Swedish artillery suddenly thundered at the surprised Russians and Charles plunged into the river at the head of 7,000 Swedes.

The water reached to their chests, sometimes their shoulders, and Russian fire was heavy, but, holding their weapons aloft, the Swedes advanced calmly and steadily as they had been trained to do. As soon as they climbed the opposite bank, the troops halted to regroup. Charles walked along the lines, calmly dressing the ranks, and then led them forward through the marsh. The going was difficult, and the Russians, to Charles' surprise, did not break and run, but stayed to fight, firing at the Swedes from thirty to forty paces, retiring more or less in order, reloading and running forward to fire again at the oncoming Swedish line. They were not willing, however, to stand and grapple with the Swedish infantry in a clash of cold steel, and although their firing took its toll, it had little effect on the steady advance of the Swedish veterans.

As the Swedes, maintaining ranks, recognized the Russian pattern, they

began to fall in with it themselves. The Swedish lines halted to load, and those whose weapons would fire fired back at the Russians. This exchange was unique in the battles of Charles XII. Wrote Jefferyes, "The battle grew so hot that in a whole hour's time nothing was heard but the continual firing of musketry on both sides."

By seven a.m., Repnin began to understand that he was taking the full force of the Swedish attack. On his plea, 1,200 men of Goltz's Russian dragoons advanced from the south, trying to assist the hard-pressed Russian infantry by riding down the Swedish infantry on its right flank. Charles was saved by Rehnskjold, who, waiting across the stream with the still uncommitted Swedish cavalry, saw the movement of the Russian horse. With four squadrons—600 men—of the Guards cavalry, he galloped across the river and engaged the Russian cavalry before it could fall on the Swedish infantry. The impact between the opposing horsemen was bloody as the Swedes repeatedly repulsed a force twice their number. Gradually, as additional squadrons of Swedish cavalry crossed the river and rode into the fray, the Russians were forced to check their attack and retire into the woods.

Meanwhile, the failure of the Russian cavalry to break through and attack the Swedish infantry left the Russian infantry alone to cope with Charles' assault. The Swedish advance continued implacably as fresh Swedish infantry crossed the river and, as Charles had known it would, this furious, concentrated pressure on a single section of the Russian line finally forced it to break. Repnin's forces fell back, rallied, wavered and finally broke. The Russian left wing abandoned its camp and its artillery, dispersed into company-sized units and retreated through the woods.

It was now eight a.m. Charles' sudden, determined attack had defeated Repnin's division, but Sheremetev's division to the north, on the opposite side of the marsh, remained uninvolved. At first, hearing the firing and seeing the Swedes crossing to attack Repnin, Sheremetev had attempted to send troops to assist his colleague, but, as Charles had anticipated, the morass made this difficult, and when Charles turned to meet Sheremetev, he found it was not necessary. The Russian Field Marshal, mindful of Peter's admonition not to risk everything, was already in retreat toward Mogilev and the Dnieper.

The Battle of Golovchin was the first serious engagement between Russian and Swedish troops since Charles had begun his long march from Saxony almost a year before. By the classical definition of victory, the Swedes had won. They had attacked and gained a strong position. The Swedish cavalry had fought brilliantly and repulsed a much larger Russian force. The King had been in the thick of the fight, performing with great personal bravery, and had remained untouched. The Russians had once

again retreated. The road to the Dnieper lay open. All the legends were intact.

Yet, there were factors which were not displeasing to Peter, who arrived late and heard about the battle in Gorky from Menshikov. Although worried that his army had been forced to abandon another river line, he took solace in the fact that only one third of the Russian forces present had actually been engaged, and that these regiments had taken the whole weight of the famous Swedish attack led by the King of Sweden himself. Through four hours of heavy fighting, they had not collapsed, but had retreated in good order, fighting every step, and when they finally abandoned the field, it was not as a disorderly mob but in units which could be reassembled to fight again. The Russian casualties were 977 dead and 675 wounded, the Swedes had 267 dead and over 1,000 wounded. But there was an important difference. Peter's losses could be replaced; when one of Charles' soldiers fell, the King's army was permanently decreased by one.

Peter ordered investigations into which regiments had stood and which had broken; he was angry at certain officers, and there were punishments. Repnin was court-martialed and temporarily relieved of his command. Four days after the battle, a conference was held at Shklov and it was decided not to attempt to defend Mogilev on the Dnieper but to fall back farther to Gorky along the road to Smolensk. But not before the Cossacks and Kalmucks had done their terrible work. The region had been doomed by the Tsar's order, and Charles' victorious army would advance through utterly barren lands.

Although Charles, too, was pleased and the news went back to Stockholm and spread through Europe that Sweden had won another victory, the King was aware of a change in his Russian adversaries. The Battle of Golovchin opened his eyes to the fact that the Russian army was no longer the same disorderly mob which had fled at Narva. Here, in a battle in which the numbers of men actually engaged were almost equal, the Russians had fought well. Jefferyes admitted, "The Muscovites have learned their lesson much better and have made great improvements in military affairs and if their soldiers had shown but half the courage their officers did (which for the most part are foreigners) they had probably been too hard for us in the late action."

Along the road to Mogilev, the Swedish army advanced between smoldering houses and barns. On July 9, the army reached the town on the River Dnieper, then the frontier of Russia itself. Without a shot being fired, the King sent troops across, although the main body remained on the western bank. Everyone assumed that the halt would be only temporary, a brief rest while supplies were gathered for the final stage of the march. The campaign was now practically over. All the great river barriers had been

crossed. Smolensk was 100 miles to the northeast, and 200 miles beyond Smolensk lay Moscow.

AT MOGILEV, Charles sent detachments across the Dnieper, laid bridges across the river and then—to the surprise of both the Swedish army and the watching Russian patrols—failed to cross. For an entire month—from July 9 to August 5—the 35,000 men of the Swedish army waited on the western bank of the Dnieper for Lewenhaupt's force from Riga to join them. Count Adam Ludwig Lewenhaupt, General of Infantry, whose pedantic scholarship had prompted Charles to dub him "the little Latin colonel," was a meticulous, melancholy man, overly sensitive to the opinions of those around him, finding rivals and plots on every side, but was nevertheless a brave and skillful officer with rare devotion to orders. No matter how small the formation of infantry he commanded, no matter how large or well entrenched the opposing enemy force, if Lewenhaupt had explicit orders, he would dress ranks and advance with absolute serenity into murderous enemy fire. His tragedy—and Charles' mistake—was that he was given a command which called for a wide latitude of personal initiative and improvisation.

Lewenhaupt was military governor of Courland and what remained of the Swedish Baltic provinces. In and around the fortress city of Riga, he commanded 12,500 troops. In March, when he visited Charles at Radoshkovichi, the King had given him simple, uncomplicated orders: He was to use his troops at Riga to collect supplies, gather a huge wagon train, load it with enough food and ammunition to last his own men for three months and the entire army for six weeks, and then escort this wagon train through the Lithuanian countryside to join the main army. His wagons would replenish the army for the final phase of the march on Moscow, while his soldiers would substantially augment the King's combat strength. Although the route chosen from Riga to Mogilev was 400 miles, it was calculated that if he left early in June, he would complete the journey in two months.

These assumptions were wrong. Lewenhaupt returned to Riga early in May and set about collecting supplies, but the sheer task of assembling 2,000 wagons and 8,000 horses to pull them, as well as the supplies themselves, delayed him. On June 3, as Charles' army was preparing to break camp at Radoshkovichi, Lewenhaupt received orders to leave Riga for the Berezina River, but he reported that he could not possibly start before the end of the month. And, indeed, not until the last days of June were the long supply column and its escort of 7,500 infantry and 5,000 cavalry on the road. Lewenhaupt himself remained in Riga another month and did not join his command until July 29, when, according to the original plan, it

should have been approaching its junction with the main army. In fact, his men had crawled only 150 miles and still were to the north of Vilna, while Charles' main army had moved on to Mogilev, over 250 miles away.

For Peter, the news that Lewenhaupt's army was leaving Livonia and Courland and moving south, away from the Baltic, was cause for enormous relief. It indicated with reasonable certainty that the Swedish King's ultimate objective was not St. Petersburg, that there would be no combined attack on the Neva by Lewenhaupt from the south and Lybecker from Finland. And with Lewenhaupt out of the picture, Apraxin had enough men to deal with whatever Lybecker might attempt. Accordingly, General Bauer's Russian force of 16,000 men—whose mission had been to watch Lewenhaupt—was now ordered to move south.

Charles' plans now hinged on Lewenhaupt. Critics have blamed Lewenhaupt harshly for his excessive delays, but he could not control the weather. Moving his heavy supply wagons with their great wheels churning in the mud proved almost impossible in the rain, although fascines of brush, branches and wooden boards were laid down. Lewenhaupt was even carrying a portable bridge, the pride of his engineering corps, held together with flexible strips of leather which became so sodden that thirty-two men had to carry each section, and they could carry it only twenty paces before setting it down to rest. In a month, the army moved only 143 miles, an average of less than five miles a day. July stretched out into August and then into September, and still Lewenhaupt slowly rumbled and churned his way forward.

TWO PRECIOUS MONTHS, July 8 to September 15, the best campaigning days of midsummer, passed while Charles waited. It was not that the supplies themselves were urgently needed yet, but Charles felt that he could not move too far ahead of Lewenhaupt lest the Russian army slip into the gap between the two Swedish armies and catch the smaller force exposed and unsupported. At first, the King had hoped to rendezvous with Lewenhaupt at Mogilev on the Dnieper before the main army crossed the river, and from reports of the lumbering supply column's progress, Charles, pacing impatiently, believed that it must arrive by August 15. But that date came and went and Lewenhaupt still had not appeared. Meanwhile, the army was stagnant and restless. The Golovchin wounded were well again, but the countryside around Mogilev had been eaten bare as thousands of horses grazed the pastureland.

Charles decided that offensive operations must be resumed: not the bold, deep thrust at Moscow that he had planned, but something closer to the Dnieper which would perhaps provoke a battle with the Russians and

still, somehow, cover Lewenhaupt. He began a series of maneuvers, marching short distances each day, changing direction—first south, then north—hoping to confuse the Tsar and catch part of his army off guard.

Between August 5 and 9, the Swedish army at last crossed the Dnieper and began moving southeast toward the southern flank of the position Peter had taken on the Smolensk road. On August 21, Charles' army reached Cherikov on the Sozh River to find Menshikov's cavalry already in position on the opposite bank and the mass of the Russian infantry coming closer. With the two opposing armies now in close proximity, their patrols were in constant contact and there were frequent skirmishes. On August 30, a battle of sorts took place. It was not the battle that Charles had hoped for or even expected. The King had camped his army along a branch of the stream Chornyaya Natopa, which bordered a marsh. Roos, commanding the rear guard, was camped on the edge of a marsh three miles away. The marsh was difficult but not impassable, and the Tsar and his officers had quickly learned the lesson of Golovchin: that a marsh could be crossed. At dawn on August 30, 9,000 Russian infantry and 4,000 dragoons commanded by Prince Michael Golitsyn crossed the marsh in a dense morning mist and attacked Roos' camp. The Swedes were taken by surprise, having never before been subjected to a Russian infantry attack. Two hours of fierce hand-to-hand combat ensued before reinforcements from the main Swedish camp arrived and the Russians withdrew, fading back across the marsh. When Charles heard the firing, he assumed that Peter desired a major battle, and the following day the entire Swedish army was drawn up in battle formation. But no attack came, and when Rehnskjold's cavalry reconnoitered the silent Russian positions, he found them empty. The last of the Russian rear guard was just retreating, setting fire to villages and fields as it rode away.

Although this battle near Molyatychy was a minor action and Russian casualties were twice as heavy (700 Russians killed and 2,000 wounded to 300 Swedes killed and 500 wounded), Peter was elated. For the first time, Russian infantry had taken the initiative and a Swedish division had been isolated and attacked. The Russian troops had fought bravely, then successfully broken off the action and retreated in good order. Golitsyn received the Order of St. Andrew. To Apraxin, the Tsar wrote exuberantly: "I assure you that since I began to serve, I have never seen such fire or such orderly conduct on the part of our soldiers. The Swedish King himself has not seen such an action in the course of this war. O God, do not take your mercy from us for the future."

Charles resumed his slow march to the north and on September 11, the Swedish army arrived at Tatarsk on the Russian border, the most northeastern point in Russia that he would reach. From here, the road went to Smolensk, but the view down that road was a grim one: Day and night, the

horizon glowed in a red haze. Charles had seen the devastation of Poland and the Lithuanian provinces adjacent to Russia, but he had not believed that the Tsar would wreak the same policy on his own Russian lands. The sight gave Charles pause. No matter how stubbornly he pursued the foe, he could never catch up. His soldiers drew up in line of battle only to find themselves standing in ranks facing an empty wilderness. And every day the supplies of food collected at Mogilev were running lower. The food itself was wretched, and although the King refused to eat any food better than his common soldiers were eating, the hired German soldiers and even some of the Swedish veterans were grumbling. Always they marched over charred ground. Always the clouds of smoke from burning villages and smoldering fields hung on the horizon, sometimes so thick that it dimmed the sun. And always the trailing squadrons of Kalmucks and Cossacks waited pitilessly to cut down stragglers. Mournfully, Jefferyes reported, "We are now forced to live off what we find buried [by peasants] under the ground, but should a sudden frost deprive us of that expedient, instead of a formidable army, I fear His Majesty would bring into Russia a parcel of starved beggars."

The key was Lewenhaupt. Had the main Swedish army possessed the supplies he was bringing, it might have pierced through the devastated regions ahead and reached the more fertile region near Moscow. At Swedish headquarters, while the King and his officers stared eastward at the smoke of burning villages, they also looked anxiously over their shoulders. Where was Lewenhaupt?

With every day that passed, the problem facing Charles grew more acute. The army was poised, ready for the last great thrust that would end the war, yet it couldn't move forward without Lewenhaupt because the Tsar had scorched the earth bare in the regions ahead. And because of the lack of food, it couldn't simply stand where it was. This left two choices, the first being to retreat to the Dnieper and wait for Lewenhaupt there. Charles rejected this idea. To retrace his steps was repugnant to him—it would confirm publicly that the entire summer campaign had been a failure. Although uncertain as to Lewenhaupt's exact position, Charles believed that he was approaching and that, despite the delays, the rendezvous would soon take place. The second alternative was bolder and therefore more to Charles' liking: a march south, away from Smolensk and Moscow, into the Russian province of Severia. This would maintain the momentum of the Swedish offensive and, at the same time, bring the army into a rich area still untouched by Peter's ravaging, where the fields were just being harvested. Replenished in Severia and reinforced by Lewenhaupt, Charles could then march on Moscow.

After prolonged discussions with Rehnskjold and Piper at Tatarsk, Charles decided to take this course. Once decided, it was urgent that the move be made swiftly and secretly to ensure that the Swedes would arrive

in Severia before the Russians. The Swedes had the advantage: Charles was nearer and had the more direct route. If he turned his back on the Russians now and marched rapidly south, he would leave them behind and get there first. Thus, at Tatarsk, new orders were issued to the Swedish army. A special mobile vanguard of 2,000 infantry and 1,000 cavalry—the best of the Guards and other elite regiments—was issued two weeks' rations so it could move rapidly and not have to waste time foraging. Placed under the command of General Anders Lagercrona, it was ordered to hurry by forced marches and seize the towns and river crossings which would open Severia to the Swedes and block it to the Russians. Lagercrona was informed of the overall plan and knew that the objective of the operation was the seizure of the provincial capital, Starodub. The distance from Tatarsk to Starodub as the crow flies was 125 miles. That same night, three separate couriers were dispatched to Lewenhaupt telling him of the change of plan and ordering him to change the direction of his march toward Starodub. The three couriers were sent at intervals during the night to ensure the arrival of at least one.

On the early morning of September 15, the march to the south began, a march fateful in the life of Charles XII and in the history of Peter and of Russia. The advance on Moscow was turned aside—as it happened, for good. Charles' decision at Tatarsk also marked a turn in Sweden's fortunes. In the previous fall and winter, he had marched halfway across Europe, brilliantly maneuvering his enemy out of a series of formidable river barriers. Yet in the summer of 1708, Charles' strategic planning had gone badly awry: he had allowed himself to be chained to the arrival of Lewenhaupt and the supplies. Lewenhaupt had not arrived, and the summer and the advance on Moscow had both been lost. Nevertheless, in September 1708, when Charles stood at Tatarsk and decided to turn south, he still held the initiative. His army was intact. He turned toward Severia with optimism and hope that, if the Moscow campaign had failed, the setback was only temporary.

In fact he was on the brink of a series of disasters which for him would end in ruin.

THE FIRST CONSEQUENCE of Charles' move fell on Lewenhaupt. On September 15, the day Charles broke camp at Tatarsk and marched south, Lewenhaupt was still thirty miles west of the Dnieper. Charles' position at that moment was sixty miles east of the river. Peter immediately saw his opportunity: The ninety-mile gap left the wagon train exposed. The Tsar dispatched his main force southward with Sheremetev to shadow Charles, but he held aside ten battalions of his best infantry, including the Preobrazhensky and Semyonovsky Guards. Mounting these infantrymen on horse-

back and supplementing them with ten regiments of dragoons and cavalry, he created a new, highly mobile "flying corps" of 11,625 men of which he took personal command. With Menshikov at his side, Peter rode directly west to intercept Lewenhaupt. Although the Tsar did not know Lewenhaupt's strength, reports reaching Russian headquarters placed it at around 8,000. Actually, it was 12,500. As a precaution, Peter ordered an additional 3,000 dragoons under Bauer to ride west to join his force. Thus, 14,625 Russians were moving to intercept 12,500 Swedes.

Meanwhile, Lewenhaupt's weary column, still lumbering forward after three months on the road, finally reached the Dnieper on September 18. Here, Lewenhaupt received the King's three messengers commanding him to cross the river and turn south toward the new rendezvous point, Starodub. For three days, the tired soldiers trundled their wagons across the river. As the last companies were crossing on the 23rd, Lewenhaupt became aware that a Russian force was moving against him; red-coated Russian cavalry began appearing on the fringes of the forest. Doggedly, he hurried on, making for the town of Propoisk on the River Sozh. Once across that stream, he would have a fair chance of reaching the main army intact.

It became a race. Lewenhaupt was desperately trying to reach Propoisk, but the muddy roads bogged his heavy wagons. On the morning of the 27th, the leading Russian cavalry caught up, and skirmishing with the Swedish rear guard began. Realizing that a major action was imminent, Lewenhaupt faced a choice: He could either leave his rear guard to hold off his pursuers as long as possible, sacrificing it if necessary, while pushing his main force and the baggage wagons forward in an effort to reach the Sozh, or he could halt his flight, stand and, with his whole force, fight. Being Lewenhaupt, he chose the second course. He sent the wagons ahead and brought the main body of his infantry and cavalry back down the road, drew them up in battle formation and awaited a Russian attack. There they stood through the morning and early afternoon of the 27th. Late in the afternoon, when it became clear that no Russian attack was coming, Lewenhaupt dissolved his battle line and fell back several miles along the road, then again drew up in line. His men stood in formation through the night.

The following morning, the 28th, when no attack had yet come, the Swedes again fell back, their columns skirmishing with the Russian horsemen who were all around them. They arrived at the village of Lesnaya, a short day's march from Propoisk. Now, the loss of time—almost the entire day of the 27th—revealed its importance. But for this fruitless day, the main body might have reached and crossed the Sozh to safety.

Nevertheless, with the Russians clustered thickly around him, Lewenhaupt realized that he could not reach the river, and that he would have to fight. He sent 3,000 cavalrymen ahead to Propoisk to secure the river crossing and with the remaining 9,500 prepared for battle. He ordered a weeding

out of the wagon train: Colonels could keep four wagons, majors three, and so on.

On the opposite side, Peter dismounted his troops, dragoons and mounted infantry alike, and deployed them on the edges of the forest with Menshikov commanding the left wing with eight regiments, and Peter him self commanding the Preobrazhensky and Semyonovsky Guards and three dragoon regiments on the right wing. At one p.m. on the 28th, the battle began. It raged all afternoon, and, in Peter's words, "all day it was impossible to see where victory would lie." At one point, when Menshikov's troops were wavering, Peter reinforced him with the Semyonovsky Guards whose desperate counterattack restored the crumbling Russian line. Soon after four p.m., Bauer arrived with his 3,000 dragoons to bolster the Russians, but this was balanced on the Swedish side by the return of the 3,000 cavalrymen who had been sent ahead to secure the ford and then been recalled. The battle continued until nightfall, when a sudden snowstorm, unusual for this early in autumn, obscured the combatants and brought the fighting to a halt. Although his lines were unbroken, Lewenhaupt ordered a retreat and the wagons burned. Like bonfires on wheels, the cartloads of supplies so laboriously pulled from Riga through 500 miles of mud and rain-soaked forest blazed through the night. The brass-and-iron cannon were lifted from their carriages and buried in pits dug in the earth to prevent the Russians from finding and capturing them. In the eerie light of the blazing wagons, confusion took hold and Swedish discipline disintegrated. Soldiers began plundering the wagons of officers' possessions and brandy. Units lost cohesion and stragglers stumbled off into the forest. Some of the infantry rode off on the horses freed from wagon yokes to Propoisk to cross the river to safety. When the surviving regiments arrived at Propoisk at dawn, they found the bridges burned. The few remaining wagons could not cross and they, too, were burned on the riverbank. At this point, a swarm of pursuing Cossacks and Kalmucks caught part of the disorderly Swedish mass on the riverbank and killed another 500 Swedes.

Morning broke over a Swedish disaster. The battle and the chaos of the night had cut Lewenhaupt's force in half. Of 2,000 cavalry, 1,393 remained; of 2,500 dragoons, 1,749 still were present; but of 8,000 infantry, only 3,451 remained. The total loss was 6,307 men; of these, over 3,000 were taken prisoner. Others wandered off into the forest alone or in small bands. Many died or were eventually captured. A thousand actually found their way back across Lithuania to Riga. All the supplies, clothes, food, ammunition, medicines which Charles so desperately needed were lost. On the Russian side, 1,111 were killed and 2,856 wounded. Each side had approximately 12,000 engaged; the Russians lost about one third, but the Swedes lost half.

Lewenhaupt led the bedraggled Swedish survivors—6,000 in all, now mounted on the wagon horses—down the road toward Severia. Peter, busy

claiming the battlefield, did not pursue him, and ten days later Lewenhaupt finally joined the King. But what a disparity between what was expected and what arrived! Instead of a huge train of supplies to nourish the army, and 12,500 troops to reinforce it, Lewenhaupt brought 6,000 exhausted, nearly starving men, without artillery or supplies, straggling into camp. The cavalry units were kept together, but the infantry regiments were so shattered that they could no longer be maintained. They were disbanded, and the men used as replacements to fill gaps in the regiments of the main army.

On seeing the new arrivals, fresh gloom spread over the Swedish camp. The Battle of Lesnaya gave further evidence of the new fighting quality of the Russian army. The two sides had been almost equal in numbers, and the Swedes had lost. Nevertheless, Charles reacted to the defeat with equanimity. He did not criticize Lewenhaupt either for the slowness of his march or for the defeat. In fact, the King realized that he himself shared the blame: Having waited too long for Lewenhaupt, in the end he had not waited long enough.

ON THE RUSSIAN SIDE, there was jubilation. The Russians believed that the Swedish force had been somewhat larger than their own—thus, that they had not only triumphed, but had triumphed against numerical odds. Peter, writing later, saw the importance in terms of the self-confidence of his men: "This victory may be called our first, for we have never had one like it over regular troops and then with numbers inferior to those of the enemy. Truly, it was the cause of all the subsequent good fortune of Russia and it put heart into our men, and was the mother of the Battle of Poltava."

For Peter, all these actions were stages in his larger effort to create an effective Russian army. Even when his troops were defeated, he was vitally interested in how they had behaved under fire and if they had retreated in good order. From the battlefield of Lesnaya, he wrote to his friends and even to Augustus. He sent descriptions and diagrams of the battle to the Tsarevich in Moscow with instructions that they be printed, both in Russian and in Dutch: The news of his victory over the supposedly invincible Swedes was to be circulated not only in Russia but across Europe. After the battle, Peter led the "flying corps" to Smolensk, where he staged a triumphal parade, marching to the thunder of cannon salutes, with Swedish prisoners and captured colors following in his train.

Peter was still in Smolensk in mid-October when more good news arrived from the north. As one part of his overall strategy, Charles had planned that Lybecker's force of 14,000 men in Finland should attack St. Petersburg. Although the attack was intended to be diversionary, drawing the Tsar's

attention and army away from the main Swedish attack on Moscow, Charles naturally hoped that Lybecker might succeed in capturing the new city at the mouth of the Neva.

Lybecker began his march down the Karelian Isthmus and on August 29, he succeeded in reaching and crossing the Neva River above St. Petersburg. Here, however, false information planted by Apraxin convinced him that the fortifications of the city were too strong, and rather than attacking, Lybecker continued his march in an arc south and west of the city through the Ingrian countryside. Again, Peter's grim order to destroy the landscape bore fruit; the Swedes soon exhausted their own provisions and, unable to find anything on the land, began killing their own horses for food. Without cannon, Lybecker could not attack walled cities, and he wandered aimlessly through Ingria, finally reaching the coast near Narva, where a Swedish naval squadron took the soldiers but not the horses aboard. Six thousand animals were either killed or hamstrung to prevent the Russians from using them, and the Swedish squadron returned to Vyborg in Finland. Lybecker's force had thus made a complete circle of Peter's city with no achievement other than the loss of 3,000 Swedish soldiers. Even as a diversionary tactic, the expedition failed: not a single Russian soldier in the main army facing Charles was transferred north.

Peter remained in Smolensk for three weeks before starting off to rejoin Sheremetev and the army. He found high spirits at Russian headquarters, as news of the victory at Lesnaya and of Apraxin's success in Ingria had filled both officers and men with excitement and growing confidence.

It was at this point that fortune, which had not been kind to Russia in the early years of war but which now seemed to be swinging fast in the Tsar's direction, once again reversed itself and gave the jubilant Peter what seemed a staggering blow. On October 27, with Charles' army deep inside Severia and marching rapidly toward the Ukraine, Peter received an urgent message from Menshikov: Mazeppa, Hetman of the Ukrainian Cossacks, loyal to Moscow for twenty-one years, had betrayed the Tsar and allied himself with Charles.

34

MAZEPPA

MAZEPPA'S DEFECTION is better understood in the light of Charles' decision in mid-September to turn south. General Anders Lagercrona's vanguard of 3,000 men and six cannon had been sent ahead to seize the crossings on the Sozh and Iput rivers and to march on the fortified town of Mglin and the pass at Pochep. These two positions were vital to Charles: If his army was to seize Severia and its capital, Starodub, intact before the Russians could arrive, it was essential to occupy these two sites—in effect, the gates to the province—and close them in Peter's face.

Lagercrona's mobile force set out with maps prepared by the Swedish quartermaster staff. Before reaching the Iput, however, it encountered other, unmarked roads which seemed better and more direct than those indicated on their Swedish maps, and Lagercrona took them. But instead of heading southeast toward Mglin and Pochep, he was heading directly south for Starodub itself. He would miss the two gateway points he was supposed to seize, and the gates themselves would be left open.

Meanwhile, Charles followed with the main army. He reached Krivchev on the Sozh on September 19, and his troops crossed on bridges built by Lagercrona's advance party and moved southward into a tract of primeval forest between the Sozh and the Iput. Men and horses, enfeebled by weeks of hunger, stumbled, fell and died. Dysentery was raging in the Swedish ranks and the toll was high. "Tis thought we have lost more in this ramble than if we had given the enemy a battle," wrote Jefferyes. On emerging from the woods, the army was heading in the direction of Mglin when Charles learned that Lagercrona had proceeded directly south, and that Mglin and Pochep therefore were presumably unoccupied. Seeing the danger, Charles hastily picked a second advance guard, the fittest of the exhausted men who stumbled from the woods behind him, and, with himself at their head, set off to seize the two positions. After enormous exertions he arrived at Kotenistchi, a village about six miles short of the town of Mglin, where he discovered that Mglin was filled with Russian troops. Peter, in establishing a

defensive position on the Smolensk road, had left a detachment under General Nicholas Ifland to guard Severia, and this force had already occupied both Mglin and Pochep. Charles' small detachment might have attacked Mglin, but to dislodge an enemy from a fortified town he needed cannon, and his cannon were far away. Lagercrona's force had six cannon, but Lagercrona was nowhere to be seen. Thus, having lost the race to bar the gates, Charles halted his men, who were too fatigued to move farther anyway. Charles now realized that Lagercrona's mistake might provide a new opportunity to seize Severia, for, having turned south, Lagercrona was heading directly for Starodub, the capital and main road junction of the province. If Lagercrona occupied Starodub, the failure to take Mglin and Pochep would be more than compensated for. Messengers were sent racing after Lagercrona to instruct him to occupy the town.

In fact, Lagercrona had already reached Starodub, but had not captured it. He was embarrassed and irritated to find that he had taken the wrong road and was beneath the walls of the wrong town, but he refused to accept his colonels' urgent pleas that he occupy Starodub. He had been given orders first to seize Mglin and Pochep and *then* to occupy Starodub, and he meant to do things in exactly that sequence. Although he was camped beneath the walls of Starodub, he denied his men permission to enter the town even to find food and shelter, and the next day Ifland's Russian troops secured the town. When Charles heard what had happened, he burst out, "Lagercrona must be mad!"

Charles realized that he was now in serious difficulty. Starodub as well as Mglin and Pochep were in enemy hands. As the last detachments of the army emerged from the forest and joined the troops before Mglin, Charles, moving among them, saw that they were in no shape to attack Ifland. The men were hungry, eating roots and berries to supplement their rations. There, on October 7, the King learned of Lewenhaupt's defeat. The news reached the Russians in Mglin first, and the Swedes camped nearby heard the firing of Russian guns in celebration of the Tsar's victory. On October 11, the remnants of Lewenhaupt's force began to arrive in camp. The wagons, of course, were gone, and instead of 12,500 fresh Swedish faces, Lewenhaupt brought half that number, gray with fatigue, hunger and defeat.

Severia was lost; Sheremetev's army was pouring into the province through the open Pochep pass; the Kalmucks were ranging across the province, ravaging and burning. Charles had no choice; he must continue south. On October 11, the King broke camp and marched south toward the River Desna, which forms the boundary between the Russian province of Severia and the Ukraine.

The fertile Ukraine, rich in cattle and grain, offered Charles what the Swedish army needed: refuge, rest and potential reinforcement. Here, if Charles could persuade the Cossack Hetman Mazeppa to join his cause, the

Swedish army could winter in security. Here he might obtain thousands of Cossack horsemen who would make up the losses of the year's campaign. And Baturin, Mazeppa's capital, was stocked with gunpowder. For all these reasons, on the day after news of Lewenhaupt's defeat had been received, Charles sent an express courier to Mazeppa to ask for winter quarters. It was taken for granted that Mazeppa would reply positively: For many months, Mazeppa had been actively and secretly negotiating a Swedish alliance.

To speed his crossing of the Desna into the Ukraine, Charles dispatched an advance guard under Kreutz to secure the town of Novgorod-Seversky and its bridge across the river. Kreutz marched day and night, arriving on October 22, but he was too late: The Russians had been there first and the bridge was destroyed. Now, for the first time, the Russians were gaining the upper hand. They had excellent reconnaisance; they seemed to know which way the Swedes would move; and themselves got there first. It was worrying, even ominous. But still the Swedes marched hopefully and confidently toward, in Jefferyes' words, "a country flowing with milk and honey," the homeland of General Ivan Mazeppa, Hetman of the Ukrainian Cossacks.

THROUGH THE SPRING and summer of 1708, the Cossack Hetman had struggled with a desperate dilemma. A subject of Tsar Peter, caught geographically between forces stronger than his own—the Russians to the north, the Poles to the west, the Tatars to the south—Mazeppa still dreamed the old Cossack dream of independence. He was anxious to insure against all risks and, at the same time, to prepare for all opportunities. And now the advance of the Swedish army and the almost certain defeat of Tsar Peter made the opportunities seem greater than the risks. For the famous Cossack chief, renowned for his exploits in love and war, who had survived for twenty-one years as leader of his tumultuous people, it was the supreme moment of decision. Now sixty-three and stricken with gout, Mazeppa was shrewd, calculating and captivatingly charming. His life had spanned an era of Cossack history.

Ivan Stepanovich Mazeppa was born in 1645, the son of a petty nobleman in Podolia, a part of the vast Ukrainian borderland west of the Dnieper then held by the Poles. Podolia's Polish masters were Catholic, and Mazeppa's family were Orthodox; one defiant relative had been roasted alive by the Poles half a century before Mazeppa's birth. But the path of advancement in those years lay through Catholic schools and the Polish court, and Mazeppa was enrolled at a Jesuit academy and learned to speak fluent Latin, although he never gave up his Orthodox religion. A handsome and intelligent boy, he was accepted as a page at the court of King Jan Casimir of Poland, where he was subjected to frequent jibes and taunts by

his Catholic comrades because of his religion and place of birth. One day, stung to fury, Mazeppa drew his sword. This act inside the palace was a capital offense, but the King moderated the punishment because of the circumstances. Mazeppa was exiled to his mother's estate in Volynia, where, one story goes, he attracted the eye of a local nobleman's wife and subsequently was caught in flagrante by the outraged husband. Stripped naked, tarred and feathered, the intruder was bound to his horse, which was then sent galloping through woods and thickets with its helpless burden on its back. When the animal finally brought its master home, the young man was so cut and torn that he was scarcely recognizable. Unable to return to Polish society after this humiliation, Mazeppa took refuge among the Cossacks of his homeland, the classical haven for society's outcasts.

The Cossacks' hetman was quick to recognize the young man's talents— he was clever and brave, fluent in Polish, Latin, Russian and German—and he became an assistant to the hetman and rose to the position of secretary general of the Cossacks. While still young, he served as emissary from the Cossacks who lived on the Polish side of the Dnieper to those on the Russian side, and also made a diplomatic mission to Constantinople. On the way home, he was captured by the Zaporozhsky Cossacks, who were loyal to Tsar Alexis, and sent to Moscow for questioning. His interrogator was none other than Artemon Matveev, the chief minister and friend of Alexis, who was impressed by Mazeppa, especially when the young man declared himself favorable to Russian interests. Released and honored by an audience with the Tsar, Mazeppa was sent back to the Ukraine. During the rule of Sophia, Mazeppa ingratiated himself with Prince Vasily Golitsyn, who was as captivated by Mazeppa's charm and education as Matveev had been. In 1687, when the Cossack hetman Samoyovich was deposed as one of the scapegoats for Golitsyn's unsuccessful march to the Crimea, Golitsyn chose Mazeppa as his successor.

In the main, his years of leadership had been successful. He understood and followed faithfully the single most important precept necessary to maintain his position: always to be on the side of the ruling party in Moscow. Two years after his own appointment, during the final trial of strength between Sophia and Peter, he managed to tread the line with superb timing and luck. He had set out for Moscow in June 1689 to declare his support for the Princess and Golitsyn, but, arriving at exactly the moment when it became clear that Peter was going to win, Mazeppa hurried to the Troitsky Monastery to declare his fealty to the youthful Tsar. Although the Cossack chief was one of the last important figures in the realm to side with Peter, he quickly ingratiated himself. The charm of Mazeppa's manner soon inspired Peter with an affection for, and confidence in, the lively and amusing Hetman which remained unshaken despite rumors and accusations against him. In Moscow, Mazeppa ranked with the highest in Peter's court. He was

one of the first to receive the coveted Order of St. Andrew, and Peter had arranged for Augustus to award him the Polish Order of the White Eagle. Despite the confidence shown in him by Peter, the official position of hetman was far from easy. Torn between resentment against and dependence on Moscow, the Cossacks were also split between a new class of landowners, which had scrambled into the positions left behind by the departing Poles, and the simple rank and file, who disliked the newly successful upper class. They dreamed of the free-loving Cossack bands such as the Zaporozhe, who lived the old, true Cossack life below the Dnieper rapids and whose example was a constant stimulant to restlessness. The landowners and townspeople of the Ukraine, however, were uneasy with this lingering frontier spirit and wanted more stable conditions so that they could trade and prosper in peace. Just as the simpler Cossacks grumbled that the Hetman now was only Moscow's puppet and yielded too much to the Tsar, so the Cossack townspeople and upper classes now looked to him and the Tsar to control this restlessness and provide order and stability.

With his Polish education and manners, Mazeppa was inclined to favor the landowning class of which he himself was a member, and over the years he had successfully balanced and blended its interests with Moscow's and his own. As hetman, he had amassed great wealth and authority—he even dreamed of making the office of hetman hereditary rather than elective— but in his heart Mazeppa was ambivalent. Allegiance to the Tsar and maintenance of Moscow's confidence and support was the cornerstone of his policy, but his secret desire was that of his people: Ukrainian independence. The union with Russia had laid heavy burdens on the Ukraine, especially during the long years of war. Taxes had increased, new fortifications had been built and large Russian garrisons had been stationed on Cossack territory. Food and wagons were arbitrarily requisitioned and moved in constant convoys across the steppe to Russian strongholds. The Tsar's officers took recruits, willing or not, from the villages. There were constant protests that the Russians were pillaging Cossack homes, stealing provisions, raping wives and daughters. Mazeppa was blamed by his people for such outrages and for all of Moscow's increasing demands and encroachments. He hated his puppet role, was bitter and jealous of the men around Peter and especially feared Menshikov, who had humiliated him on more than one occasion and who, it was rumored, wanted to become hetman himself. Moreover, Mazeppa, who in cultural and religious matters was an arch-conservative and strictly Orthodox, was frightened and dismayed by Peter's Westernizing policies.

But, caught in many currents, surrounded by enemies actual, potential and imagined, Mazeppa had clung to power by supporting Peter. In the long run, if he supported the Tsar, the Tsar would support him, and that was what would make or break a Cossack hetman. During his long years in

office, Mazeppa had given many demonstrations of loyalty, most recently by keeping the Zaporozhsky Cossacks quiet during the Bulavin revolt. In the light of such fresh proofs of service, Peter's faith in him was firm and stubbornly held. Although from time to time he heard that Mazeppa was plotting treason and was in correspondence with Stanislaus or even with Charles himself, Peter steadfastly refused to listen, dismissing the accusations as the work of Mazeppa's enemies trying to make trouble by undermining his faith in the loyal hetman.

In fact, the accusations were true. Mazeppa's sole motivation was to be on the winning side. If Charles marched to Moscow and dethroned the Tsar, what would be the future of the Cossacks and their Hetman if he had maintained his loyalty to Peter too long? When Charles placed a new tsar on the Russian throne as he had placed a new king on the Polish throne, might he also place a new hetman over the Ukrainian Cossacks? On the other hand, if Mazeppa declared for Charles at the right moment and Charles was victorious, what new possibilities might open up for an independent Cossack state? And for an hereditary hetman?

Exploring these possibilities, Mazeppa had been in secret contact with Peter's enemies for almost three years. At first, when Stanislaus made approaches, Mazeppa rejected them. In 1705, when a Polish envoy came to the Cossack leader, Mazeppa sent the envoy in chains to Peter, writing flamboyantly:

> For I, the Hetman and faithful subject of Your Tsarish Majesty, by my duty and my oath of loyalty confirmed on the Holy Gospels, as I served your father and your brother, so now I serve you truly, and as up to this time I have remained before all temptations like a column immovable and like a diamond indestructible, so now I humbly lay my unworthy service at your sovereign feet.

As long as Charles was far away, Mazeppa's loyalty to Peter remained hard as a diamond. But as Charles' seemingly invincible army came closer, Mazeppa grew excited and uneasy. Along with most of Europe, he took it for granted that the Swedish King could defeat the Tsar if he decided to do so. Yet if he declared for Charles too soon, a Russian army might descend on the Ukraine and annihilate him.

During the spring of 1708, an episode occurred which, springing from the Hetman's colorful character, almost upset his political intrigues. Mazeppa was as charming among women as men and had, in fact, a lifelong reputation as a seducer. Fiery and amorous all his life, at sixty-three he had fallen in love with his godchild, a beautiful Cossack girl, Matrena Kochubey, who returned his love with wild abandon. Mazeppa proposed marriage, which

scandalized her parents, and the desperate girl ran away from home and sought refuge with the Hetman. Mazeppa sent her back, telling her that "although I love no one on earth as much as you, and it would have been for me a happiness and joy to have you come and live with me," the opposition of the church and the enmity of her parents made the situation impossible. Matrena's father, Judge-General of the Cossacks, was horrified and enraged. Believing that his daughter had been ravished and disgraced, he set his heart on destroying the Hetman. He had heard that Mazeppa was plotting with the Poles and Swedes against Peter and he made public these rumors, which, early in March 1708, reached Peter's ears. Still trusting his Hetman, the Tsar was angry at Kochubey's denunciations, considering them a mischievous and dangerous attempt to stir up unrest in the Ukraine at a time of external peril. He wrote to Mazeppa assuring him that he did not believe the accusations and was resolved to end them. Kochubey was arrested, interrogated and, being unable to substantiate his charges with specific proof, he was handed over to Mazeppa. With great relief—although to the horror of Matrena—Mazeppa beheaded her father on July 14, 1708.

At that very moment, Mazeppa was reaching his final decision to throw in his lot with the Swedes. Charles had promised to stay out of the Ukraine if possible and not to make a battleground out of Cossack territory, but he did not promise, as Mazeppa hoped he ultimately would, independence for the Ukraine. Charles wanted to keep a middle position between the Cossacks and Poles. Poland still had claims on the western region of the Ukraine, and Charles did not want to alienate one ally by prematurely satisfying another.

Despite the execution of Kochubey, rumors of these contacts continued to leak, and Peter commanded the Hetman to come before him and explain. Mazeppa was not afraid to go—he still believed in his ability to charm the Tsar—but he wanted to delay until he could better estimate the outcome of the war. If the Tsar seemed the likely victor, the agreement with Sweden could be quietly scuttled. To gain time, he made excuses, feigned serious illness and, to allay the suspicions of Peter's messengers who had been sent to fetch him, even took to what he called his "deathbed" and ordered a priest to give him the Last Sacrament. Meanwhile, he was sending two sets of letters: pledges of allegiance to Peter with appeals for help against the Swedish invader, and pledges of faith to Charles with appeals for help against the Tsar.

Charles' sudden decision in September to enter the Ukraine was a monumental blow to Mazeppa. The Hetman had assumed—and Charles had promised—that the Tsar would be unseated by a direct march on Moscow. When he realized that the King was on the road to the Ukraine, that finally he was faced with the need to commit himself irrevocably to one side or the other and that, whatever happened, war would roll over his people and his

lands, Mazeppa was filled with consternation. Two powerful monarchs, both with large armies, were moving in his direction. He was pledged to both. If, in this final moment of choice, he chose the wrong side, he was lost.

EARLIER IN THE SUMMER, Peter had ordered Mazeppa to prepare his Cossacks for battle and lead them across the Dnieper to attack the Swedish army in the rear. Mazeppa had replied that he was too ill to lead his troops himself and that he dared not leave the Ukraine—he must remain behind to hold the region firmly for Peter. The Tsar accepted these excuses; he, too, was worried about the unsettling effect of the Swedish advance on the restless Cossacks.

On October 13, Peter again summoned Mazeppa to appear before him, this time at Starodub. Once again, the Hetman made excuses, and Peter agreed that he should remain at Baturin, the Cossack capital, for, as the Tsar wrote to Menshikov, "his great value is in keeping his own people in check, rather than in the war."

But now thousands of soldiers in torn, mud-stained uniforms—the Russians in green and red, the Swedes in blue and yellow—with muskets on their shoulders or slumped in their saddles, moved in columns along the roads to the south. Sheremetev and the main Russian army were moving parallel to Charles, prepared to block any Swedish move to the east, and farther west an independent cavalry force under Menshikov was moving in the same direction. As this cavalry would pass close by Baturin, Peter, believing Mazeppa's lies about being on his "deathbed," asked Menshikov to see the Hetman and consult with the Cossack elders about the election of a loyal successor. Accordingly, Menshikov sent a message to Mazeppa that he was on his way to pay a visit. When the Hetman learned that Menshikov, whom he hated and feared, was coming to see him, he grew convinced that the Tsar knew his plans and that the Prince intended to arrest or kill him. Mazeppa was seized by panic.

In retrospect, perhaps the wisest thing he could have done, having made up his mind to join Charles, would have been to remain at Baturin until Charles' army could arrive. Even when Menshikov appeared, there was little he and his unsupported cavalry could have done against a fortress protected by cannon. But Mazeppa did not know how many Russians were approaching. He *did* know and fear Menshikov, and he feared even more Peter's reaction to the news of his betrayal. Deciding that the game was up, he mounted his horse, gathered 2,000 men around him, posted another 3,000 to guard Baturin, commanding them not to admit Menshikov to the town, and galloped north to throw in his lot with the King of Sweden. For Peter, the situation was saved by Menshikov's swift and decisive movements. The Prince arrived at Baturin on October 26 to find that Mazeppa

had vanished and that those Cossacks still inside the town refused to permit his men to enter. Surprised and suspicious, he questioned people in the countryside and learned that Mazeppa had ridden by with a large number of horsemen on his way to cross the Desna. The ominous implications of this news were confirmed when a party of Cossack officers asked Menshikov for protection against their Hetman, who, they said, had gone to join the Swedes and betray the Tsar.

Realizing that Peter must immediately learn what had happened, Menshikov left Prince Golitsyn with a force of cavalry outside Baturin to screen the town while he himself galloped to the Tsar, who was accompanying Sheremetev's army. When Peter heard of Mazeppa's betrayal, he was stunned, but he did not lose his head. The greater danger—to be prevented at all costs—was the spreading of Mazeppa's treason.

The Tsar reacted vigorously to prevent this chain reaction. The night he heard of Mazeppa's betrayal, he ordered Menshikov to dispatch dragoon regiments to block any movement by the nearest bands of Ukrainian and Zaporozhsky Cossacks to join Mazeppa in the Swedish camp. The following day, October 28, Peter issued a formal proclamation to the people of the Ukraine. Declaring Mazeppa's treachery, he appealed to their Orthodox faith: Mazeppa had deserted to the Swedes, he said, "in order to put the land of Little Russia [the Ukraine] as before under the dominion of Poland and to turn the churches and monasteries over to the Catholics." Circulating the proclamation in all the towns and villages of the Ukraine and the lower Volga, he called on the Cossacks to support a new hetman in their fight against the Swedish invader who was the ally of their traditional enemy, the Poles. On a less exalted level, he appealed to the well-known cupidity of the freebooter Cossacks, offering rewards for Swedish prisoners: 2,000 roubles would be paid for a captured Swedish general, 1,000 for a colonel and five for an ordinary soldier. A dead Swede was worth three roubles.

Peter quickly turned to the immediate military situation. It seemed clear that Charles would head for Mazeppa's fortified capital, Baturin, where, it was common knowledge, there were large stores of powder and food. A hastily convened war council decided that Menshikov must return to Baturin with a strong force, including artillery, and assault the town before the Swedes and Mazeppa could reach it. Peter, knowing that the Swedes were about to cross the Desna, was nervous. Repeatedly, as Menshikov was making ready, the Tsar urged him to hurry and to be firm and merciless.

The race for Baturin was on.

DURING THESE LAST DAYS of October, as Charles' army approached the Desna, the Swedish soldiers were cheered by the arrival of Mazeppa and his strange-looking Cossacks. They had hoped that there would be more

Cossacks, but these were promised once the army reached Baturin. And for both officers and men, the imminent prospect of reaching a friendly, fortified town where permanent quarters, good food and plenty of powder were waiting was sufficient to lift their spirits. Thus, despite the fact that the Russians had seized the crossing at Novgorod-Seversky and that the Swedes would be forced to cross the river in open country against a Russian force under Hallart, Charles' men were cheerful. The crossing was not easy; the Desna was a broad, fast-flowing stream with high banks, and the first freezing days of winter had already filled the river with drifting ice. On November 3, with Mazeppa at his side, Charles employed his favorite tactic. He feinted a crossing upstream to confuse the Russians, then launched a powerful assault directly across the river at the enemy's center. Late in the afternoon, having overcome the determined opposition of a smaller Russian force, the King of Sweden stepped onto the soil of the Ukraine. His objective now was clear. Baturin was to the south and the road to the Cossack capital lay open. But, unknown to Charles, on the very day the King crossed the river and set foot in the Ukraine, Baturin had ceased to exist.

MENSHIKOV HAD WON THE RACE. With a force of cavalry and mounted infantry, he arrived back at Baturin on November 2 to find the Cossacks inside caught between loyalties to their Hetman and to the Tsar. Their first response to Menshikov's demands was that the Russians could not enter until a new hetman had been elected and given them orders. Menshikov, knowing that the enemy was pressing forward, renewed his demand for immediate entry. Again the garrison refused, insisting, however, that it was faithful to the Tsar and would permit his troops to enter after a three-day wait to allow it to withdraw freely. Menshikov rejected the delay, countering that if the garrison came out at once, no harm would be done to it. Forced to a decision, the Cossacks hardened and sent the messenger back with a defiant cry: "We will all die here, but we will not allow the Tsar's troops to come in."

At dawn the following morning, November 3, Menshikov's troops stormed Baturin, and after a two-hour battle the fortress capitulated (some say a gate was opened to the Russians by a disaffected Cossack). Peter had left to Menshikov's discretion what to do with the town. As Menshikov saw it, he had no choice. The main Swedish army and Mazeppa were approaching rapidly; he had no time and too few men to prepare the town's defenses for a siege; he could not allow Baturin and its supplies of food and ammunition to be captured by Charles. Accordingly, he ordered the city demolished. His troops slaughtered all the 7,000 inhabitants, soldiers and civilians alike, except for a thousand who fought their way free. Everything movable was distributed among Menshikov's soldiers, the supplies so

desperately needed by the Swedes were destroyed and the whole town razed to the ground by fire. Baturin, the ancient stronghold of the Cossacks, disappeared.

The fate of Baturin, Peter believed, would serve as an example to others contemplating treason. And indeed, from his viewpoint, the town's cruel destruction had a salutary effect. It was a brutal stroke, a summary punishment which Cossacks understood, demonstrating to them where the greatest power to punish lay. To further circumscribe the effect of Mazeppa's betrayal, Peter immediately summoned the Cossack elders and officers. His candidate—the Cossack colonel of Starodub, Skoropadsky—was elected hetman to succeed Mazeppa. The following day, the Metropolitan of Kiev and two archbishops arrived. With full church ceremonial, they publicly excommunicated Mazeppa and pronounced the curse of anathema on him. To make the impression even more vivid, Mazeppa's portrait was dragged through the streets, then swung from a rope on a gallows next to the dangling bodies of the leaders of the Baturin garrison. A similar ceremony of anathema was repeated in Moscow and in all the churches of Russia and the Ukraine, and a proclamation promised a similar fate to all other traitors to the Tsar.

Thus, Peter successfully snuffed out the flame of Mazeppa's revolt before it could spread. Thereafter, instead of Mazeppa's leading the whole Ukrainian people into the Swedish camp, a split developed between the minority who followed him and the majority who remained loyal to Peter. Charles' promise to take the Cossacks under his protection had little effect. The Ukrainian people stood by the Tsar and their new Hetman, hiding their horses and provisions from the Swedes and turning over captured Swedish stragglers for the reward. Delightedly, Peter wrote to Apraxin, "The people of Little Russia stand with God's help more firmly than was possible to expect. The King sends enticing proclamations, but the people remain faithful and bring in the King's letters."

The loss of Baturin's storehouses and magazines—and of Lewenhaupt's wagons—left Swedish reserves of food and gunpowder dangerously low. Deep inside Russia, Charles now had no way to replenish his meager, dwindling stock of powder. Worse was the loss of the hope of a mass Ukrainian revolt. Far from finding refuge in a secure region, the invading army was once again surrounded by bands of ravaging and burning enemy cavalry. And there was also a growing shortage of manpower.

The effect of these events on Mazeppa was catastrophic. Instead of brilliantly casting his lot with the victors, he had chosen destruction. He had seen his capital razed, his title taken, his followers desert. At first he told Charles that Menshikov's brutality would only enrage the Cossacks, but this proved illusory, and overnight the proud Cossack Hetman was reduced to being a defeated old man, little more than a fugitive protected by

the Swedish army. Charles now became Mazeppa's sole hope—only if the Swedish King won a conclusive victory and overthrew the Tsar could Mazeppa's fortunes be restored. Until the end of his life, Mazeppa remained in Charles' camp. He was no longer a potent ally, but Charles was loyal to him for what he had risked. Charles also enjoyed the wit and vivacity of the wiry little man, who, despite his age, was still full of fire and life and spoke Latin as fluently as the King himself. Through the remainder of the Russian campaign, Mazeppa's sagacity and his intimate knowledge of the country made him a valuable counselor and guide. And he and his several thousand horsemen remained loyal to Charles, inspired in their devotion by the knowledge of what would happen to them if they fell into Russian hands. But there is evidence that Mazeppa never completely gave up his scheming ways. A Cossack officer who had gone over with Mazeppa to the Swedes came back to Peter bearing an oral message supposedly from the old Hetman, offering to deliver Charles into Peter's hands if the Tsar agreed to pardon him and restore him to his rank and office of hetman. Peter sent the messenger back with a favorable reply, but nothing more was ever heard.

35

THE WORST WINTER
WITHIN MEMORY

ON NOVEMBER 11, Charles XII and the advance regiments of his army arrived at Baturin. The ruins were still smoldering and the air was heavy with the stench of half-burned corpses. Following the advice of the heart-broken Mazeppa, the Swedes continued south in the direction of Romny in a district lying between Kiev and Kharkov which abounded in rich grasslands and grainfields and supported many flocks and herds. Now, as winter was approaching, the sheds and barns were filled with corn, tobacco, sheep and cattle and there was an abundance of bread, beer, honey, hay and oats. Here, at last, both men and animals could eat and drink their fill. Gratefully, the Swedes settled into a broad square of territory bounded by the towns of Romny, Pryluky, Lokhvitsa and Gadyach, dispersing the regiments into companies and platoons and taking up quarters in houses and huts throughout the area. Although they were isolated deep in the Ukraine, so far from Sweden and Europe "as it had been outside the world," here they believed they were safe and could rest.

Meanwhile, parallel to the Swedes but some miles to the east, Peter and Sheremetev with the main Russian army had also been moving south, always covering the Swedes and screening them from Moscow more than 400 miles to the northeast. When the Swedes settled down for the winter, Peter established his own winter headquarters in the town of Lebedin and distributed his forces in a northwest-southeast arc, taking positions in the towns of Putivl, Sumy and Lebedin, blocking the Kursk-Orel road to Moscow. To prevent a Swedish thrust east to Kharkov or west to Kiev, he put garrisons in other towns and villages east, south and west of the Swedish encampments. One of these towns was named Poltava.

Skirmishing continued, but increasingly the military pattern of the two armies was being reversed. Charles, who normally favored aggressive winter campaigning, was on the defensive, while Russian patrols constantly harried and provoked the extended perimeters of the Swedish camp. Peter's purpose was not to fight a general battle but simply to maintain pressure, to

whittle away at the isolated Swedes, to deplete them, wear them down and demoralize them before spring. Time, Peter knew, was on his side.

The Tsar thus initiated new tactics designed to keep his enemies off balance, to deny them rest and a chance to spend the winter in bed with their boots off. The approaching winter was already colder than usual, and Russian irregular cavalry could cross the frozen rivers and streams with ease at any point. Because of this new mobility, the Swedish regiments found it more difficult to guard the edges of their encampments. The Russians also kept the Swedes off balance with a series of feints and diversions. Peter's tactic was to send a substantial force into the vicinity of the Swedish camp and tempt Charles to muster his troops and move out toward it, whereupon Peter's men would withdraw. This happened on November 24 at Smeloye, where Charles' troops, fully mobilized and prepared for battle, found the Russians vanishing before them. Enraged, the King gave his frustrated men permission to loot the town—systematically, with each regiment allowed a section—and burn it to the ground.

As the Russians persisted, Charles' anger grew, and in hopes of a general battle to deal a blow to the Russians and end these harassments, he fell into a trap which Peter had prepared for him. Three Swedish regiments were quartered along with some of Mazeppa's Cossacks, in Gadyach, about thirty-five miles east of Romny. On December 7, Peter moved a substantial part of his army southeast as if to attack the town. Meanwhile, he sent Hallart with another corps toward Romny itself with instructions to attack and occupy it if the main Swedish army marched out to the relief of Gadyach. His objective was to force the Swedes to abandon their hearthsides and march out into the freezing countryside and then to steal Romny out from under them.

When Charles heard that the Russians were swarming on the outskirts of Gadyach, his combative instincts were aroused. In vain, his generals advised him to remain where he was and let the troops in Gadyach beat off any Russian assault. Despite their advice and the fearful cold, on December 19 Charles ordered the entire army to march. He himself set out first with the Guards, hoping to catch the Russians by surprise as he had at Narva. Peter, learning that Charles' army was on the march, ordered his troops to maintain their positions near Gadyach until the Swedes were close, and then to withdraw. The Russians actually held until the Swedish advance guard was only half a mile away, and then, as planned, they simply melted away, retreating to Lebedin, where the Tsar had his headquarters. Meanwhile, once the Swedes were gone, Hallart's men stormed into Romny, occupying it without difficulty, just as Peter had anticipated.

Now, as Peter had hoped, with the Swedish army strung out on the road between Gadyach and Romny, an enemy worse than the Russians swept down on Charles and his soldiers. All over Europe, the winter that year

was the worst in memory. In Sweden and Norway, elk and stags froze to death in the forests. The Baltic was choked and often solid with ice, and heavily laden wagons passed from Denmark across the sound to Sweden. The canals of Venice, the estuary of the Tagus in Portugal, even the Rhône were sheeted with ice. The Seine froze at Paris so that horses and wagons could pass across. Even the ocean froze in the bays and inlets along the Atlantic coast. Rabbits froze in their burrows, squirrels and birds fell dead from the trees, farm animals died rigid in the fields. At Versailles, wine froze in the cellars and glazed with ice on the tables. The courtiers put fashion aside, layered themselves in heavy clothes and huddled around the great chimneys where logs blazed day and night, trying to warm the icy rooms. "People are dying of the cold like flies. The windmill sails are frozen in their sockets, no corn can be ground, and thus many people are dying of starvation," wrote Louis XIV's sister-in-law, the Princess Palatine. In the vast, empty, windswept, unprotected spaces of the Ukraine, the cold was even more intense. Through this icy hell, the ragged, freezing Swedish army was marching to the relief of a garrison which was no longer even in danger.

The futility of the effort was compounded by a cruel fate which awaited the army at Gadyach. The Swedes struggled forward, arriving at evening, hoping to reach shelter and warmth. But they found that the only entrance to the town was a single, narrow gate, which soon was jammed and blocked by a mass of men, horses and wagons. Most of the Swedes had to spend one night, and some two or three nights, camped outside the town in the open air. The suffering was extreme. Sentries froze to death at their posts. Frostbite furtively stole noses, ears, fingers and toes. Sledgeloads of frostbitten men and long lines of wagons, some of whose passengers were already dead, crawled slowly through the narrow gate into the town. "The cold was beyond description, some hundred men of the regiment being injured by the freezing away of their private parts or by loss of feet, hands, noses, besides ninety men who froze to death," wrote a young Swedish officer who participated. "With my own eyes, I beheld dragoons and cavalrymen sitting upon their horses stone-dead with their reins in their hands in so tight a grip that they could not be loosened until the fingers were cut off."

Inside the town, nearly every house became a hospital. The patients were crowded onto benches near a fire or laid side by side on the floor covered by a layer of straw. Amid the stench of gangrene, the surgeons worked, crudely lopping off frozen limbs, adding to the piles of amputated fingers, hands and other parts accumulating on the floor. The carnage inflicted on the Swedish army during the nights among the snowdrifts under the open sky was more terrible than any which might have come from the battle Charles had sought. Over 3,000 Swedes froze to death, and few escaped being maimed in some way by frostbite. Out of ignorance, most refused to rub their frozen extremities with snow in the manner of the Cossacks.

Charles himself was caught by frostbite on the nose and cheeks and his face began to turn white, but he quickly followed Mazeppa's advice and restored himself by rubbing his face with snow.

The cold reached its peak at Christmas, normally the most festive time in the Swedish church calendar. During these days, Charles rode from regiment to regiment inspecting the men crowded twenty and thirty into small cabins. All church services and sermons, including one on Christmas Day itself, were canceled to avoid calling the men out into the open. Instead, simple morning and evening prayer services for each group were led by an ordinary soldier. Two days after Christmas, the cold was at its worst. The third day, it was a little warmer, and by December 30 the men began to move outside again. Charles consoled himself with the assumption that if the winter had been hard on his own men, it must have been equally hard on the Russians. In fact, although Peter's troops had also suffered, they were in general more warmly clothed and their losses were comparatively lighter.

Astonishingly, despite the widespread suffering and partial destruction of his army, Charles could not suppress the impulse to attack which had allowed the army to be lured to Gadyach in the first place. "Although Earth, Sky, and Air were now against us," exclaimed the young Prince Max of Württemberg, "the king's designs had to be accomplished." The loss of Romny to Hallart grated on him, and he wished to regain the initiative. On top of a hill only eight miles from Gadyach there was a small, fortified Cossack village called Veprik. Charles disliked having a Russian position so close, and decided to take it. But Veprik had been strongly garrisoned by Peter with 1,100 Russians and several hundred loyal Cossacks, the whole commanded by an English officer of Peter's army. On taking command, this energetic officer had raised the level of the village walls by piling baskets filled with earth on top of them. These earth ramparts had then been made even more difficult to climb by pouring water over the surface, which, when the temperature plunged, made them palisades of solid ice. The village gates were blocked in similar fashion with cartloads of dung covered with a layer of ice. Thus ingeniously prepared, the English officer was undismayed when Charles arrived on January 7 and demanded his immediate surrender. When the King threatened to hang the Englishman and all his garrison from the walls, the commander calmly refused and, instead, prepared his men to receive an assault. Knowing that the Swedish officers would be out in front leading their men up his ice-covered ramparts, he ordered his soldiers to aim especially at the Swedes who came first.

Charles' assault force consisted of six of his depleted infantry battalions and two dragoon regiments, a total of 3,000 men for what seemed a simple operation. He would sweep the walls clear of defenders with artillery, and then three columns of infantry would storm over the walls and into the town. The attack was begun with great resolution by the Swedish veterans. Under

the roar of cannon, the three assault columns approached the walls carrying ladders. But the artillery failed. The guns were too few and the fire too sparse. The defenders were able to maintain their places on the walls and to shoot down many of the men carrying the ladders before they could be put in place. When the remaining ladders were in position and the infantry began to mount them, the walls were found to be too slippery and the ladders too short. Cossack and Russian marksmen poked their barrels over the top, shooting first, as instructed, at the Swedish officers. Other Russians threw logs, boiling water and even hot porridge down on the assailants.

Although Swedish bodies were piling up at the foot of Veprik's ice ramparts, Charles refused to admit that he could be held off by such a "hovel." Once again, the attack was launched, and again it was beaten off with heavy casualties. Rehnskjold, who had been in the middle of the action, was hit by splinters from an exploding grenade and received a wound in the chest from which he never completely recovered. Still the fort was holding out when darkness forced the Swedes to abandon the attack. Luckily for Charles, the commander of the garrison did not know how heavily the Swedes had suffered and, fearing that his men could not withstand a third assault, sent a messenger after dark to arrange a surrender on honorable terms. Charles agreed, and the garrison marched out, surrendering 1,500 men and four cannon. But Charles' losses had been severe. In two hours on a short winter afternoon, 400 Swedes had died and 800 had been wounded —more than a third of the attacking force and a serious drain on the dwindling strength of the Swedish army.

The town was taken, but no major advantage had been gained.

FROM MID-JANUARY to mid-February, the Swedish army once again was on the move. Charles was mounting a limited offensive, moving generally eastward across the frozen streams and untrodden snows. Peter watched uneasily; Kharkov, the major city of the eastern Ukraine, was less than a hundred miles from the Swedish vanguard. Worse from the Tsar's point of view, the King might be marching toward the precious dockyards at Voronezh on the Don. To protect this place on which so much effort had been lavished was worth any sacrifice, even a major battle. Accordingly, as the Swedes began to lap around his southern flank, Sheremetev, with the main Russian army, began shifting southward. His course lay parallel to and west of the Swedes, constantly interposing him between the invader and the shipyards. Meanwhile, Menshikov and the bulk of the Russian horsemen, both cavalry and dragoons, slipped south of the Swedish advance, screening Charles from the Vorskla and standing ready to oppose any Swedish crossing of the river.

On January 29, Charles struck at Menshikov. As the Prince was finishing

dinner in Oposhnya on the Vorskla, there was a sudden alarm and Charles burst upon him with five cavalry regiments. It was the kind of action which the King loved, a repeat of the dashing sortie at the Grodno bridge the year before. Charles, sword in hand, was riding with the Drabants as they attacked. Menshikov himself escaped, but his seven dragoon regiments were chased out of town and pursued until the Swedes were finally stopped by deep snow. When Charles gave the order to withdraw, he had inflicted 400 casualties at the cost of only two men killed.

Throughout this offensive, Charles ravaged and destroyed. He was applying the tactics which Peter had taught him: to shield his army by laying down a belt of devastation through which enemy penetration would be painful and difficult. By mid-February, Charles had turned southeast toward Kharkov, and on the 13th he reached Kolomak on a small river of the same name. This was the most easterly point, the deepest penetration, of the Swedish invasion of Russia. Just then, however, Charles' month-long offensive was halted by a new factor: another great turn in the Russian weather. The intense cold suddenly gave way to sweeping thaw. Crashing thunderstorms and a torrential downpour were followed by a rapid melting of masses of snow. Rivers and streams overflowed, the Swedish soldiers sank in the mud, and water and melted snow poured in over their boot tops. Further military operations were paralyzed, and Charles had no choice but to order a withdrawal. With great effort, artillery and wagons were dragged through the mire. On the 19th, the Swedes were back at Oposhnya on the Vorskla. By the middle of March, the thaw was over and the ground hard and passable again. Taking advantage of the moment, the Swedes with all their baggage and most of their Cossack allies moved even farther south to new positions between the Psyol and the Vorskla, both tributaries of the Dnieper. There, the regiments were strung out along a forty-mile north-south line along the west bank of the Vorskla. Near the southern end of this line lay the town of Poltava, still strongly held by a Russian garrison. In this freshly occupied, relatively untouched region, the Swedish army waited through the rest of March and April. Behind them to the north, the land of milk and honey was now a ruined earth of plundered towns and burned villages.

Charles was able to inspect and assess the damage inflicted on the army during the winter. The situation was alarming. Frostbite, fever and battle casualties had taken a heavy toll, shoes and boots were worn through, uniforms were frayed and ragged. There was enough to eat, but the entire Swedish artillery now consisted of only thirty-four cannon, and the powder was wet and deteriorated. "The campaign is so difficult and our condition so pitiful," Count Piper wrote to his wife, "that such great misery cannot be described and is beyond belief." A little later, he wrote, "The army is in an indescribably pitiful state."

Charles, however, seemed determined not to notice. On April 11, he wrote to Stanislaus, "I and the army are in very good condition. The enemy has been beaten and put to flight in all the engagements." His determination to remain positive, to stiffen morale and encourage optimism is illustrated by a meeting with a wounded young officer, Ensign Gustav Piper of the Guards. Piper had resisted the surgeon's desire to amputate both his legs, but had nevertheless lost some toes and both heels. Crippled and unable to walk, he was traveling in one of the baggage wagons when the King came up.

I saw His Majesty King Charles XII a great way off, with a suite of some fifty horsemen, riding along a column of wagons; and since I lay unclothed in nought but a white undershirt, bedded in an ammunition wagon with half the lid open to shade me from the sun and admit fresh air, I thought it not decent to see the King in such a posture. Therefore, I turned about with my back to the opening and feigned sleep. But His Majesty continuing straight forward along the line of wagons, he came at last to mine and inquired who I was. The colonel replied, "This is the unfortunate Ensign Piper of the Guards, whose feet were frostbitten." His Majesty then rode up close beside the wagon, inquiring of the groom, "Is he asleep?" The groom answered, "I don't know. He was awake but now." And the King staying beside the wagon, I thought it not fitting to keep my back to him and so turned. He asked me, "How is it with you?" I replied, "Ill enough, Your Majesty, for I cannot stand upon either foot." His Majesty asked, "Have you lost part of your feet?" I told him that heels and toes were gone, and to this he said, "A trifle. A trifle," and resting his own leg upon the pommel of his saddle, he pointed to half the sole, saying, "I have seen men who lost this much of their foot and when they had stuffed their boot [to support the missing part], they walked as well as before." Turning then to the colonel, His Majesty asked, "What does the surgeon say?" The colonel answered, "He believes he may do something for the feet." His Majesty said: "Perhaps he will run again?" The colonel replied, "He may thank his God if he can so much as walk; he must not think of running." And as His Majesty rode away, he said to the colonel, who afterward told me, "He is to be pitied, for he is so young."

Charles himself was then twenty-six.

THE DECLINING STATE of the Swedish army and its exposed position on the steppe led Count Piper and Charles' officers to a single urgent conclusion:

The King must withdraw from the Ukraine, retreat across the Dnieper in the direction of Poland, seeking reinforcement from the armies of Stanislaus and Krassow in Poland. Thus augmented, he might renew his invasion of Russia, although many wondered whether further pursuit of the elusive and dangerous Tsar would ever bring the decisive, overwhelming triumph to which the King had obsessively committed himself.

Charles flatly refused to give up his campaign and to retreat, saying that a withdrawal would look like a flight and only make Peter bolder. Instead, he told his dismayed senior advisors that he intended to remain where he was and press on in his duel with the Tsar. He admitted that, in its diminished state, his Swedish army alone, even with Mazeppa's men, was now too small to reach Moscow unaided. Accordingly, while holding his advanced position, he would seek reinforcements. Already in December, he had ordered Krassow in Poland to join with Stanislaus' Polish royal army, and to march from Poland to Kiev and then eastward to unite with the main army. Further, he hoped to recruit additional allies among the Cossacks of the Ukraine. Mazeppa had assured him that many of these people would willingly join the Swedish King once his army came near enough to offer them protection from the Tsar's retribution. Finally, the grandest dream of all: Charles hoped to persuade the Crimean Tatars and perhaps their overlords, the Ottoman Turks, to break the armistice signed in 1700 and join with him in a mighty coalition. With himself as its commander, with his Swedish veterans as its steely core, a vast allied army would march irresistibly on Moscow from the south. Then, with the King in the Kremlin, Russia would be carved up and each of the invading parties—Swedes, Cossacks, Tatars and Turks—would take that slice which it found most desirable. But none of this was possible, Charles insisted, unless the army remained where it was to provide the nucleus and launching point for this next phase of his great enterprise.

According to Mazeppa, Charles' closest and most immediate source of new allies lay among the Zaporozhsky Cossacks, a wild people who lived on a cluster of thirteen fortified islands below the rapids of the Dnieper River. They formed a fellowship of river brigands, owing allegiance to no one except their Hetman, Konstantin Gordeenko and, among the Cossacks, they were reputed to be the fiercest warriors. When the Tatars and the Turks had impinged upon their grazing grounds and constructed river forts to block their boats, they had fought the Tatars and the Turks. Now it was the Russians who were closing in on them, curtailing their freedom; therefore, now they would fight the Russians. Mazeppa, who had been negotiating with Gordeenko, was aware of their inclination to do so, and the shift of the Swedish army south to the region of Poltava was partly intended to encourage the Zaporozhsky to believe that it was safe to declare against Tsar Peter.

On March 28, Gordeenko and 6,000 of his men joined the Swedes,

manifesting their new allegiance by attacking a small force of Russian dragoons which garrisoned the town of Perevoluchna, an important crossroads where the Vorskla flows into the broad Dnieper. Once Perevoluchna was taken, the Zaporozhsky Cossacks moved their entire fleet of boats north and moored them in rows along the shore. These boats, capable of carrying 3,000 men in a single trip, were more important to Charles than the additional horsemen, for the Dnieper was wide and swift, there were no bridges and only on such boats could the armies of Krassow and Stanislaus be transported across once they came to join him.

On March 30, Gordeenko arrived at Charles' headquarters to formalize his bargain with the King of Sweden. A treaty, to which Charles, Mazeppa and Gordeenko all were signatories, bound the King not to make peace with Peter until full independence of both the Ukrainian and the Zaporozhsky Cossacks had been obtained. Charles also promised to move his army out of the Ukraine, ending its use as a battlefield, as soon as militarily possible. For their part, the two Cossack leaders agreed to fight beside the King and to persuade other Cossack and Ukrainian people to join against the Tsar. Eventually, their appeals did bring an additional 15,000 unarmed Ukrainian recruits into the Swedish camp, but as neither Charles nor the Cossack Hetmen had any surplus muskets with which to arm these peasants, they effected almost no increase in the King's combat potential. Charles' puritanical nature also suffered from their presence, for the new recruits brought their women with them, and soon the camps of the Swedish battalions were swarming and overrun with "the wanton sluts" of the Zaporozhsky Cossacks.

Far worse for Charles were the results of a sudden, brilliant stroke on Peter's part which, within two weeks of Charles' treaty with the Zaporozhsky Cossacks, obliterated its major advantage. Peter had been well aware of the danger of Gordeenko's defecting, and had never counted on his loyalty. Accordingly, he ordered Colonel Yakovlev to embark a force of 2,000 Russian troops in barges at Kiev and set off down the river toward Perevoluchna and the Zaporozhe Sech. While the Hetman Gordeenko and his followers were still with Charles, negotiating terms, Yakovlev's force arrived and destroyed the Cossacks at Perevoluchna. A few weeks later, the same Russian force stormed ashore on the Zaporozhsky Cossacks' island base. The town was taken and razed, many Cossacks were killed and others captured and executed as traitors. This victory had several significant effects. The strength of the once-feared band of Cossacks was diminished. And, as in the case of the destruction of Mazeppa's capital at Baturin, Peter had demonstrated the terrible cost of alliance with his enemy. It not only quieted the rest of the Cossacks, but gave all the border peoples food for thought. Finally, the Russian victory had purely military value for Peter. Having taken Perevoluchna and the Sech, Yakovlev's men put every Cossack boat

on the river to the torch. At one stroke, Charles' floating bridge across the Dnieper was destroyed.

EVEN THE LOSS of the boats and of the prospect of additional Cossack soldiers would not have mattered had Charles been successful in reaching agreement with a more powerful potential ally, the fiery Russophobe Khan of the Crimean Tatars, Devlet Gerey. For nine years, the restless Khan had been held in check by Peter's armistice in 1700 with the Khan's overlord, the Sultan. But Devlet's hatred of the Russians had not softened, and as Charles' army had seemed to be marching on Moscow, he had anxiously urged the Porte in Constantinople to seize the opportunity. In the spring of 1709, in response to an invitation from Count Piper, the eager Khan sent two Tatar colonels to the Swedish camp to open negotiations, the agreement, of course, being subject to final approval from Constantinople. Devlet's terms included the demand that Charles pledge not to make peace with Peter until all Tatar, as well as Swedish, objectives had been achieved. Normally, Charles would never have considered such a commitment, but, torn between the weakness of his own army and his obsession to finish Peter, he began to negotiate. Just at that moment arrived the news of the destruction of the Sech. Disturbed, the Khan's representatives withdrew to consult with their master.

Meanwhile, both Charles and Stanislaus were making appeals for an alliance directly to the Sultan in Constantinople. Essentially, their argument was the same as Devlet Gerey's: What better time than now, with a veteran Swedish army already deep inside Russia, to reverse the results of Peter's Azov campaigns, regain the city, destroy the naval base at Tagonrog, burn the fleet based there, push the impudent Tsar back across the steppe and restore the Black Sea once and for all to the state of "a pure and immaculate virgin."

Peter was aware that these temptations would be put before the sultan, and he moved, by diplomatic and military means, to counter them. In 1708, Golovkin had instructed Peter's ambassador in Constantinople, the wily Peter Tolstoy, to do whatever was necessary to keep the Turks quiet during the Swedish invasion. Early in 1709, Tolstoy reported that the Grand Vizier had promised that the Turks would maintain the armistice and would not permit the Tatars to march. Nevertheless, in April of that year, new Tatar emissaries arrived in Constantinople to urge a Swedish alliance. Using all his arts, Tolstoy strove to thwart this mission. He spread dismal information about the state of the Swedish army. He let it be known that the Russian fleet at Tagonrog was being powerfully reinforced. Gold—always a powerful influence at the Ottoman court—was lavishly distributed among Turkish courtiers and statesmen. Tolstoy also dangled false rumors that Peter and

Charles were on the verge of concluding a peace. It was almost settled, he declared, and would be announced with the news that Peter's sister Natalya was to marry Charles and become the Queen of Sweden. Tolstoy had few equals in deviousness, and his campaign had its effect. In the middle of May, the Sultan sent orders forbidding the Khan to join the Swedes. Tolstoy was handed a copy of the letter.

Despite Tolstoy's estimate that the Turks would abide by the armistice at least for a while, and despite the weakening of the Swedish army and its isolation on the steppe, Peter knew that Charles was still planning an offensive. The Tsar also knew, however, that without reinforcements Charles was no longer in a position to deal Russia a fatal blow, and Peter's major objective during the winter and spring of 1709 was to prevent reinforcements reaching Charles. As early as December, Peter had detached a large, mobile force from the main army and sent it under Goltz's command to operate west of Kiev along the Polish frontier, its purpose to intercept and block any relieving army under Krassow and Stanislaus. Far more dangerous, however, was the possibility of the Turks and Tatars joining his enemy. Vast numbers of Tatar cavalry and Turkish infantry joined to the veteran battalions of Swedes would create an irresistible force. Preventing this junction was a matter of convincing the Sultan and the Grand Vizier that war with Russia would not be profitable, and the point on which the Sultan and his ministers were most sensitive was the specter of the Russian fleet. Therefore, to use as a deterrent or, if war came, as a weapon, Peter resolved to prepare his fleet and sail it that summer on the Black Sea.

Through the winter, Peter was anxious about his ships. In January, when Charles began his limited offensive to the east, Peter feared that the King meant to march to Voronezh to burn the wharves and shipyards as a service to the Sultan and a demonstration of what an alliance with Sweden could bring. In February, he wrote to Apraxin, ordering him to Voronezh to ready the ships for the trip down the Don to join the fleet at Tagonrog. Then, he himself hurried to Voronezh, along the way dispatching a flurry of letters and instructions. He ordered Apraxin to send a good gardener to Tagonrog with plenty of seeds and plants. Learning that there was to be an eclipse of the sun on March 11, he asked that Western mathematics teachers in Moscow calculate the extent and duration of the eclipse in Voronezh and send him a diagram. He read a Russian translation of a Western manual on fortification and sent it back for rewriting. In Belgorod, he stopped long enough to become the godfather of Menshikov's newborn son.

The Tsar found that many of the older ships in Voronezh were rotted beyond saving, and he ordered them broken up so that some of the rigging and materials could be salvaged. Once again taking a hammer in his hand, he worked on the ships himself. The problems of carpentering and the fatigue of physical effort were a balm after the anxieties which had been weighing

on him through the year of invasion just passed. Catherine, his sister Natalya, and his son Alexis were there to cheer him. Menshikov left the army twice to visit. In April, when the ice on the river had melted, Peter sailed down the Don to Azov and Tagonrog, where he saw the fleet being prepared for sea. He was prevented from going on the first maneuvers by a fever which kept him in bed from the end of April to the end of May, and by then Tolstoy had received the Sultan's assurance in Constantinople that the Turkish and Tatar armies would not march. The fleet was held in readiness as a guarantor of this promise, but Peter was eager to return to the army. On May 27, he was finally well enough, and he set off by carriage. Summer was coming on the steppe, and the climax with Charles was approaching.

36

THE GATHERING
OF FORCES

EARLY IN APRIL, winter was finally coming to an end in the Ukraine. The snow had gone, the mud was drying out, the grass was beginning to grow and wild crocuses, hyacinths and tulips were blooming in the rolling meadowlands and along the riverbanks. In this atmosphere of spring, Charles was optimistic. He was negotiating with the Crimean Tatars and with the Sultan; at the same time, he was awaiting the fresh regiments of Swedes and of the Polish royal army. So confident did he feel that he rejected out of hand a tentative Russian offer of peace. A Swedish officer captured at Lesnaya had arrived with Peter's proposal that the Tsar "was inclined to make peace, but could not be persuaded to quit Petersburg." Charles made no reply to Peter's offer.

While he waited for his negotiations with the Tatars and the Turks to bear fruit, Charles resolved to move farther south to a position nearer the expected reinforcements from Poland and the south. Poltava was a small but important commercial town 200 miles southeast of Kiev on the Kharkov road. Its site was the crest of two high bluffs overlooking a wide, swampy area of the Vorskla River, a major tributary of the Dnieper. Poltava was not in the European sense an effective fortress; its ten-foot earth ramparts topped by a wooden palisade had been built to resist marauding bands of Tatars and Cossacks rather than a modern European army equipped with artillery and professional siege engineers. Had Charles marched on Poltava the previous autumn, the town would have fallen easily, but at that time the King disliked the idea of establishing winter quarters in so large a place. Since then, the Russians had improved the defenses, studding the walls with ninety-one cannon and reinforcing the garrison to 4,182 soldiers, and 2,600 armed residents of the city, all under the command of an energetic Colonel O. S. Kelin.

Nevertheless, Charles now decided to seize the town. The technical arrangements for the siege were entrusted to Gyllenkrook, the Quartermaster General, who was an authority on mining and other aspects of

siege warfare. "You are our little Vauban," the King told Gyllenkrook, urging him to use all the refinements of the French master. Gyllenkrook began, although he warned the King in advance that the army lacked one essential prerequisite of any successful siege: sufficient power to conduct a sustained artillery bombardment. Eventually, he believed, Charles would have to storm the walls with foot soldiers, in which case, he said, "Your Majesty's infantry will be ruined. Everybody will believe that it was I who advised Your Majesty to make this siege. If it should miscarry, I humbly beg you not to put the blame on me." "No," Charles replied cheerfully, "you are not to blame for it. We take the responsibility on ourself."

The first trenches were dug, and on May 1 the bombardment began. Gradually, the trenches advanced toward the walls, and yet to some of the Swedes, especially Gyllenkrook, it seemed that less was being done than was possible. The cannon fired steadily all day, pouring red-hot shot into Poltava, but at eleven p.m. the King suddenly ordered a halt. Gyllenkrook protested, pleading that if he could only bombard the town for six more hours, Poltava would be at the King's mercy. But Charles insisted, and the guns were silenced. Thereafter, the bombardment was limited to five shots per day, which was meaningless except as harassment. Swedish powder was short, but not that short.

Gyllenkrook and others did not understand Charles' strange behavior or, indeed, the purpose of the siege. Why, for the first time on this Russian campaign, had the King who was the master of campaigning in the field undertaken a siege? And why, having undertaken a siege, was he pursuing it in so lackadaisical a fashion? Puzzled and worried, Gyllenkrook asked Rehnskjold. "The King wishes to have a little amusement until the Poles come," was the Field Marshal's reply. "It is a costly pastime which demands such a number of human lives," observed Gyllenkrook. "If His Majesty's will is so, we must be content with it," declared Rehnskjold and terminated the interview by riding away.

Many of Charles' officers, as perplexed as Gyllenkrook, believed that the siege was only an elaborate lure to tempt Peter to commit the main Russian army to battle. If this was Charles' purpose, the Russian garrison made it easier for him. The town was effectively defended, repelling assaults, sending out sorties, destroying the mines which Gyllenkrook pushed ever nearer the walls. Charles himself was astonished at the vigorous defense. "What! I really believe the Russians are mad and will defend themselves in a regular way."

For six weeks, the siege dragged on into the summer heat of the Ukraine. Charles was always in the thick of the action. To encourage his men, he took up quarters in a house so close to the fortress that its walls were riddled with bullets. Gradually, the Swedish trenches came closer to the ramparts, although accurate Russian musket fire picked off the Swedish sapper and

engineer officers supervising the work. As the heat became more oppressive, the wounded began to die when their wounds putrefied with gangrene. Food grew scarce as the Swedish foraging parties rode again and again through the district, stripping farms and villages which had already been plucked clean a week before. Soon, nothing was left to eat except horse-flesh and black bread. Powder was scarce, and what there was had deteriorated because of the dampness of melting snow and rain. The firing of a cannon sounded no louder than a clapping of hands. Bullets fired from Swedish muskets fell to the ground scarcely twenty yards away. And there were so few musket balls that Swedish scavenging parties were sent outside the trenches around the fortress to collect and pick up spent Russian balls and bring them in for re-use.

MEANWHILE, across the river on the east bank of the Vorskla, Russian forces were gathering. Menshikov, the most aggressive of Peter's generals, commanded these troops from his headquarters in the village of Krutoy Bereg, while Sheremetev with the main army was approaching from the northeast. Menshikov's orders were to observe the Swedes across the river and to do what he could to assist the garrison inside Poltava. The latter mission was not easy. Between the low east bank where the Russians were and the steep west bank which rose more than 200 feet to the walls of the town, the river wandered through a maze of marshes impassable to a large army and difficult even for small parties. Several times the Russians tried to send reinforcements directly across to Poltava, even attempting to build a road with sacks of sand, but these efforts failed. The communication problem was finally solved by putting messages inside hollow cannonballs and firing them back and forth across the river between Menshikov and Colonel Kelin.

The river war continued. Parties of horsemen, Russians and Swedes, rode along the opposite sides of the river, patrolling and watching for any sign of movement on the other bank, trying to snatch prisoners from whom they could gain some intelligence. At the end of May, Sheremetev arrived in the Krutoy Bereg camp with his masses of Russian infantry, but, despite their numerical superiority, the Russian generals were uncertain what to do. They learned from Colonel Kelin that his supply of gunpowder was danger-ously low, that Swedish mining under his walls was about complete, that he estimated he could not hold out beyond the end of June. Menshikov and Sheremetev did not want the town to fall, but were not prepared to provoke a general engagement. Certainly, nothing so dramatic and decisive as an attempted mass crossing of the Vorskla in the teeth of determined Swedish opposition had any appeal. Nevertheless, knowing that the decisive moment was approaching, Menshikov sent word to Peter, who was on his way from

Azov across the steppe, to hurry. The Tsar replied on May 31 that he was coming as fast as he could, but that rather than lose an advantage which might present itself, the army should if necessary fight without him. As Poltava still held out, the Russian generals decided to wait a little longer.

On June 4, Peter arrived and while his habit had been to appoint one of his generals as commander-in-chief and to take only subordinate rank himself, he now assumed supreme command. Peter brought with him 8,000 new recruits to add to the troops now preparing for battle. His arrival infused new spirit into the soldiers who were skirmishing vigorously at all points along the river. On June 15, a surprise Russian attack on Stary Senzhary inside the Swedish-occupied region freed 1,000 Russian prisoners taken the previous winter at Veprik, and Cossack horsemen loyal to the Tsar broke in and plundered a section of the Swedish baggage train.

Now, the great trial of arms was drawing near. The two armies were in close proximity, each commanded by its monarch. Both realized that the climax was at hand. Charles, confined in an ever narrowing space, would eventually have to try to break out. Peter understood and accepted this. The Tsar, who in the past had been unwilling to risk everything on a single battle, was steeling himself to meet the final test. His strategy had borne fruit. The enemy was isolated. Across Charles' line of retreat to Poland lay Field Marshal Goltz with a powerful force which could either prevent the advance of any relieving force or cut off the retreat of Charles himself. And Peter's army on the Vorskla was now twice as strong as Charles'. It was therefore with grim optimism that Peter wrote to Apraxin on June 7, after joining the army, "We have gathered close to our neighbors and, with God's help, we shall certainly this month have our affair with them."

Within a few days of his arrival, Peter summoned all his generals to his tent and together they examined the facts. It was only a matter of time before Poltava fell. In Swedish hands, the city would serve as a rallying point for the potential reinforcements which Charles hoped—and Peter feared— might join the Swedish King and even at this late date open the road to Moscow. These stakes were high enough to force Peter and his generals to a climactic decision: To relieve pressure on the Poltava garrison and prevent the city's fall, the main Russian army would have to be brought into play. A major, and very possibly a decisive battle would have to be fought no later than June 29 in order to save Poltava. By the 29th, Peter expected to have concentrated all his forces; not only Skoropadsky's Cossacks would be present, but 5,000 Kalmucks riding behind their khan Ayuk. But the army could not be used as long as it remained on the east bank of the Vorskla; it would have to cross to the west bank. Once on the same side of the river as the Swedes, Peter could launch a flank attack on the Swedish lines besieging the city. At the very least, even if a major battle was not joined, the presence of the Russian army would force the Swedes to divert much of

their strength from their positions before Poltava and thus relieve the pressure on the city. In addition, a position on the Swedish flank would permit the Tsar to bring to bear the considerable Russian field artillery. His guns, now silent and useless across the river, would be able to fire into the Swedish camp.

Peter next had to determine where and when to cross. There was no thought of attempting to force a passage across the wide, marshy river in the teeth of strong opposition, as Charles had frequently done. Instead, Peter decided to mount diversionary feints all along the river front both north and south of Poltava to distract the Swedes, while the main army would cross at Petrovka, seven miles north of the town where there were places shallow enough for horsemen to ride across. Ronne would cross first with ten regiments of cavalry and dragoons, followed by ten regiments of infantry under Hallart. Once this force had cleared a bridgehead and successfully entrenched itself in a camp at Semenovka a mile below the ford, Peter would bring the main army across. Ronne and Hallart quickly moved their troops into position and, on the night of June 14, they attempted a crossing, which was repulsed. But the Tsar was not to be denied. From Poltava, Colonel Kelin sent word that he could not hold out much longer and Peter decided to try again immediately.

THE SWEDES were fully aware of the impending crossing at Petrovka. On the nights of June 15 and 16, the Swedish army remained at battle stations. Rehnskjold was in command of the Swedish forces—ten cavalry regiments and sixteen infantry battalions—which would meet the Russians as they crossed the river. His tactics would be to permit a part of the Russian army to cross and then, while the Swedes still enjoyed a numerical advantage, attack and drive the Russian vanguard back into the river. Charles remained in command of the troops before Poltava and along the river south of the city. His intention was to wait there until the battle began and he had determined that no major Russian force was crossing south of the city; then, he would ride north to join Rehnskjold at Petrovka. It was a logical formula for victory. But before this Swedish plan could be executed, disaster struck.

June 17, 1709, was Charles XII's twenty-seventh birthday. In his nine years of active campaigning, the King had led a charmed life relative to injury in battle. Although he had been hit by a spent bullet at Narva and had broken his leg in Poland, he had never been seriously wounded. Now, at the most critical moment of his military career, his luck suddenly deserted him.

At daybreak that morning, the King rode to the village of Nizhny Mliny south of Poltava to inspect the Swedish and Cossack positions along the

Vorskla. He had good reason: The battle portending north of the city when the Russians would draw most of the Swedish army in that direction. Before permitting this maneuver, Charles wanted to make sure that the river defenses to the south were sufficiently strong to repel any crossing in that region. On the opposite bank, as part of Peter's diversionary tactics, a Russian cavalry force was doing its best to keep the Swedes distracted. One Russian attempt to cross had already been repulsed.

Charles arrived around eight a.m. with a squadron of Drabants and began riding along the bank at the water's edge to inspect the men and their positions. Some of the Russians from the force which had been driven back remained on one of the numerous islands in midstream, and they began to fire at the party of Swedish officers across the water. The musket range was short and a Drabant was shot dead in his saddle. Charles, without the slightest care for his own safety, continued his slow ride at the water's edge. Then, his inspection finished, he turned his horse to ride back up the bank. His back was to the enemy, and at that moment he was hit in the left foot by a Russian musket ball.

The ball struck his heel, piercing the boot, plunging forward through the length of the foot, smashing a bone and finally passing out near the big toe. Count Stanislaus Poniatowski, a Polish nobleman accredited to Charles XII by King Stanislaus, who was riding next to the King, noticed that he was hurt, but Charles commanded him to keep quiet. Although the wound must have been excruciatingly painful, the King continued his tour of inspection as if nothing had happened. It was not until eleven a.m., almost three hours after being hit, that he returned to his headquarters and prepared to dismount. By this time, the officers and men near him had noticed his extreme pallor and the blood dripping from his torn left boot. Charles tried to dismount but the movement caused such agony that he fainted.

By then, the foot had swollen so much that the boot had to be cut off. The surgeons examining him found that the ball, which had come out of the foot, was resting in the King's stocking near his big toe. Several bones had been crushed and there were splinters in the wound. The doctors hesitated to make the deep incision necessary to remove the splinters, but Charles, coming out of his faint, was adamant. "Come! Come! Slash away! Slash away!" he said and, grasping his own leg, held his foot up to the knife. Throughout the operation, he watched, stubbornly suppressing all signs of pain. Indeed, when the surgeon approached the lips of the wound, swollen, inflamed and sensitive, and shrank from cutting them away, Charles took the scissors himself and coolly removed the necessary flesh.

News that Charles was wounded quickly spread through the Swedish camp, a shattering blow to the soldiers; the cornerstone of the Swedish army's morale was its belief that their King was not only invincible but personally invulnerable. Charles had plunged into the thick of countless battles and

never been touched, as if God were protecting him with a special shield, and believing this, the soldiers had been able to follow him anywhere. Charles instantly realized the threat to morale. When Count Piper and the generals galloped up in a state of great agitation, he calmly assured them that the wound was slight, that it would heal quickly and that he would soon be back on horseback.

But the wound began to fester rather than heal. Charles developed a high fever and the inflammation began to spread, eventually reaching the knee. The surgeons thought that amputation might be necessary, but feared to act, knowing what the psychological effect on Charles would be. For two days, between the 19th and the 21st, it seemed almost too late, and Charles hovered between life and death; on the 21st, the surgeons thought that he might die within two hours. During these feverish days, the King had his old personal servant sit by his bed and tell childhood fairy tales, old Northern sagas of hero princes who successfully battle an evil foe and claim beautiful princesses as their brides.

The King's illness immediately affected the tactical situation of the two armies maneuvering around Poltava. On the 17th, after Charles was wounded but before he was overcome by fever, he placed the decision whether to fight at Petrovka in Rehnskjold's hands. The Field Marshal's troops were already poised, waiting for the Russian squadrons and battalions massing across the river. But on hearing of Charles' wound, Rehnskjold immediately left the northern front and returned to headquarters to learn the gravity of the sovereign's injury and to discover what changes, if any, the King wished to make in their overall plan of battle. When Charles instructed him to take command, Rehnskjold consulted with his fellow officers and decided not to attack in the north as originally planned. Officers and men were still too badly shaken by the wounding of the King.

By the evening of the 17th, Peter knew that the King had been wounded. His decision to cross the river had been made hesitantly; he had, in effect, intended to put one toe on the western bank to see what would happen. Now, hearing that Charles was injured, Peter immediately ordered the entire army to move. On June 19, Ronne's cavalry and Hallart's infantry crossed the Vorskla unmolested and quickly entrenched themselves at Semenovka. That same day, the main army broke camp at Krutoy Bereg and marched north to the Petrovka ford, the Guards Brigade in the van, then Menshikov's division, the artillery and supply train, and Repnin's division in the rear. For two days, between the 19th and the 21st—the same days that Charles lay near death—the river was filled with lines of men and horses, cannon and wagons, as Russian infantry and cavalry regiments moved across from the eastern to the western bank. Once they reached the opposite side, a battle became inevitable. Confronting each other at

such close quarters, surrounded by river barriers, neither side could easily withdraw. Indeed, to retreat in the presence of so much enemy strength at such proximity would be extremely dangerous. On the western bank, finding themselves unchallenged, the Russians continued entrenching themselves with their backs to the river, preparing for the Swedish attack which they were sure was coming. But it did not come.

By the 22nd, the Swedes had reconstituted themselves. Charles still was gravely ill, but his fever had broken and he was no longer in danger of dying. Rehnskjold drew his army up in line of battle in a field northwest of Poltava, offering a battle to the Russians if Peter wished it. Charles himself appeared, carried in front of the soldiers in a stretcher slung between horses, in order to cheer the troops. But Peter, still busy entrenching, had no intention of coming out to fight. By drawing the Swedish army away from Poltava, he had already achieved his immediate purpose: to relieve the pressure on the town. Seeing that the Russians were not attacking, Charles ordered Rehnskjold to disperse his men. It was at this moment, as the King lay on a stretcher in the field surrounded by his troops, that the long-awaited messengers from Poland and the Crimea arrived with news of the long-awaited reinforcements.

From Poland, Charles learned that Stanislaus and Krassow were not coming. It was the old, familiar Polish story of intrigue, jealousy and hesitation. Stanislaus felt insecure on his shaky throne and was unwilling to march to the east, leaving his new, unstable kingdom behind him. He and Krassow had quarreled, and Krassow had retreated with all his troops to Pomerania to train the new recruits arriving from Sweden before marching to join Charles in the Ukraine. Now, Krassow could not possibly arrive before late summer. The second messenger was from Devlet Gerey. The Khan confirmed that because the Sultan had denied permission for him to join the King against Peter, he could not send troops; he promised friendship. Thus Charles, lying on his stretcher, learned that his policy of waiting at Poltava for reinforcements had failed. His dream of a great allied thrust as Moscow from the south was in vain.

The King passed the news to his advisors, who received it gloomily. The practical Piper urged him to abandon the whole Russian campaign immediately, raising the siege of Poltava and retreating across the Dnieper to Poland, thus saving himself and the army for the future. In addition, he advised more energetic pursuit of diplomatic negotiations with the Tsar. He pointed out that Menshikov had recently written to him proposing a visit to the Swedish camp in person if Charles would grant him safe-conduct. Even if he signed a peace with Russia, Piper counseled, Charles could always renew the war later on more favorable terms. But Charles refused either to retreat or to negotiate.

Meanwhile, his situation was slowly, inexorably deteriorating. The army was being nibbled away; irreplaceable men were being killed and wounded every day in minor skirmishes. Food was low, as the region had been stripped bare; powder was damp and there were not enough musket balls; uniforms were patched and feet were showing through the soldiers' boots. The conviction that the Russians would not come out and fight had depressed the men, while the whole army was caught in torpor and lassitude caused by the intense heat. Charles himself, lying day after day on his sickbed, was racked by a strange blend of boredom and anxiety. Knowing that something must be done, he suffered the frustration of being unable to do anything physical himself. As one hope after another failed, as the Swedish position before Poltava became increasingly untenable, he longed to strike a sudden blow which would end all his troubles. The only way he knew was battle—a battle would salvage honor, no matter what the outcome. If he won, a victory might revitalize the hopes which had just collapsed. The Turks and Tatars might be happy to join a victorious Swedish army in its final march on Moscow. And if, because of the odds, a total victory was not won, another stand-off such as Golovchin would clear the way for realistic negotiations and permit a return with honor to Poland.

Thus, Charles decided on battle. He would hurl his army upon the enemy with all the strength it still possessed. He would strike, the sooner the better. And if it was possible, the Swedish attack would be a surprise.

For Peter, the arguments in favor of a battle were less persuasive than they were for Charles. Charles' situation would be saved only if he brought the Russian army to battle and won at least a partial victory. Peter, on the other hand, was already achieving his purpose by relieving the pressure on Poltava and by sealing off the isolated Swedish army from any hope of reinforcement. The Tsar had no need of an actual battle unless it could be contrived that the Russian army's superiority should be further enhanced by forcing the Swedes to assault a heavily fortified Russian defensive position. This situation Peter now proceeded to arrange.

On the night of June 26, the Russian army moved south from the Semenovka camp and established a new main camp near the village of Yakovtsy, only four miles north of the walls of Poltava. Here, Russian soldiers, working feverishly through the night, threw up a large square earth entrenchment. Peter was still respectful of his Swedish adversary, but by this movement, although not attacking, he was coming closer—inviting, tempting, almost forcing an attack on his own new earth ramparts and entrenched army. The rear of the new Russian camp overlooked the bluff of the Vorskla at a point where the bank was so steep and the river so broad

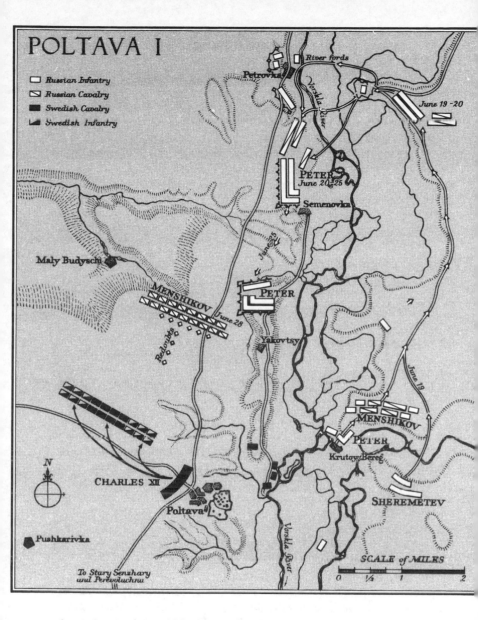

and marshy that it would be impossible for large numbers of men to cross in either direction. Thus, the only retreat for an army in this position would be north, back to the ford at Petrovka.

Nevertheless, the site was well chosen. To the south, the ground between the camp and the town was heavily forested and too slashed by ravines and gullies to be suitable for maneuver by large bodies of men. To the north,

thick woods made passage by troops and especially by cavalry impossible. Only from the west, where a broad plain was ringed by patches of woodland, could the camp be approached. The camp was fortified on all four sides, but, naturally, the western rampart was most heavily fortified. Here, a trench six feet deep ran in front of an earth rampart which mounted seventy Russian cannon. Behind these walls, the Russian infantry, fifty-eight battalions, totaling 32,000 men, pitched their tents and waited. Close at hand, in the plain beyond the ramparts, seventeen Russian cavalry and dragoon regiments totaling 10,000 horsemen picketed their horses and waited.

But even this deep entrenchment and numerical superiority were not enough for Peter. Having learned over nine years of the Swedish army's taste and talent for sudden, surprise attacks, Peter had taken further precautions. Any Swedish attack on the Russian camp would have to come up the road from Poltava. About a mile south of the camp, the plain narrowed and the road passed between an area cut by forest and ravines to the east and a wooded swampy area to the west. Across this gap, Peter threw up a line of six earth redoubts at a distance of a musket shot (about 300 feet) apart. Each redoubt was about 100 feet on each of its four sides and, when the earthworks were garrisoned by two battalions of the Belgorodsky Regiment and part of the Nekludov and Nechaev regiments, each redoubt was defended by several hundred soldiers and one or two cannon. Behind this line of redoubts, Peter positioned seventeen dragoon regiments with thirteen pieces of horse artillery, under the command of Menshikov, Ronne and Bauer. Together, this combination of field fortification and heavy concentration of horsemen would give warning and a first line of opposition to any Swedish advance out onto the broader part of the plain.

On June 26, Peter issued a proclamation to his army: "Soldiers: the hour has struck when the fate of the whole motherland lies in your hands. Either Russia will perish or she will be reborn in a nobler shape. The soldiers must not think of themselves as armed and drawn up to fight for Peter, but for tsardom, entrusted to Peter by his birth and by the people." He concluded, "Of Peter it should be known that he does not value his own life, but only that Russia should live in piety, glory and prosperity."

37

POLTAVA

JUNE 27 WAS A SUNDAY. Late that afternoon, after prayers, Charles summoned the Swedish generals and colonels to his bedside to tell them that he planned to force a battle the following day. Peter had more troops, he declared, but this superiority could be overcome if daring tactics were employed. The Swedes seemed to have the Russians where they wanted them. Peter's army had boxed itself into a position with the river and steep bluff behind it and only the ford at Petrovka open as a line of retreat. If Charles' army could cut that line, the Russians would be trapped. At long last, there was a chance of the victory against Peter which Charles had always sought. And as the Tsar himself was with his army, they might be fortunate enough to seize an even greater prize.

In actual numbers, the Swedish army now preparing for battle was little more than half the force that had marched from Saxony two years before. Now there were twenty-four infantry battalions and seventeen regiments of cavalry, a total of 25,000 men, although some of them were badly crippled by wounds and the frostbite of the winter before. Lewenhaupt, who would command the infantry, wanted to throw every available Swede at the Russians, but Charles refused. Two thousand infantrymen were left in the siege works before Poltava to ensure against a sortie by the garrison. Another 2,500 cavalrymen were assigned to guard the Swedish baggage train. A further 1,500 Swedes, mixed infantry and cavalry, were left scattered at various points along the Vorskla below the town to bolster the Cossacks patrolling against a Russian crossing in that region. The 6,000 Cossacks under Mazeppa and Gordeenko did not figure in Charles' plans and were to be kept well clear of the main Swedish army during the battle. The King felt that their undisciplined behavior could only confuse and entangle the well-drilled maneuvers of his Swedish veterans. In all, the Swedish force going into battle against 42,000 Russians totaled 19,000 men.

Although Charles himself would be with the army, his role was to be largely symbolic and inspirational. The King would be with the infantry,

carried on a litter between two horses. In case the horses became restless or unmanageable, or if one happened to be shot, a platoon of twenty-four Guardsmen was assigned to accompany the King and, if necessary, carry the litter. Thus, although the King's physical presence on the battlefield was important—the soldiers attacking against great odds would know that the King was with them—Charles would in fact be helpless. Lying on his back, he would not be able to see anything except the sky and the nearby treetops. There was no possibility of following or controlling the movements of a field army in a great battle.

With Charles an invalid, physically unable to sit in his saddle, authority had to be delegated. Command of the army went, naturally, to Rehnskjold, the senior military officer of Sweden after the King. He was, in fact, Charles' own instructor as well as his most experienced and trusted subordinate. Indeed, Rehnskjold was a superb commander, the victor of Fraustadt, the brilliant cavalry leader at Klissow and Golovchin. But now he was assuming command of the King's own army—with the King still present. It was a difficult role, and it was made more difficult by the personalities of the leading soldiers in the Swedish camp.

The first of these difficult personalities was Rehnskjold's own. Now fifty-eight years old—more than thirty years older than Charles—he was a powerful, hot-tempered, physically impressive man with a huge capacity for work and intense loyalty and devotion to Charles. Subordinates sometimes complained that the Field Marshal was haughty and rude. Rehnskjold's tongue could lash—but there were reasons. At an age when most soldiers retired, he had been campaigning in the field for nine years without rest. Like the King, he had campaigned through every summer and autumn and remained in camp through every winter with no thought of furlough. He had had little sleep, poor food, had been under constant strain and was understandably irritable and nervous. He lacked the soft words and smile with which Charles administered reproofs so that the delinquent would outdo himself to please the King thereafter.

Rehnskjold's irritability was especially aggravated by two men who stood close to him. He resented Piper, the senior civilian official of the field chancery. Piper's presence in military discussions, his constant raising of diplomatic and other non-military considerations, hugely annoyed Rehnskjold. In addition, the Field Marshal knew that if something happened to the King, Piper would rightfully assume leadership of the government in the field and become Rehnskjold's superior.

But, more particularly, Rehnskjold did not like Lewenhaupt. The commander of the ill-fated baggage train was a moody, intractable man whose touchiness was exacerbated when Rehnskjold impatiently shouted at him. On the battlefield, Lewenhaupt was a steady commander whose courage never deserted him. After Charles himself, he was the King's finest

general of infantry, just as Rehnskjold was Sweden's finest general of cavalry. It was natural, therefore, that Charles should appoint these two to command at Poltava. But he mistakenly ignored their clashing personalities. As he worked out plans for the battle with Rehnskjold, he assumed that the Field Marshal would communicate them to Lewenhaupt, who would be both commanding the infantry and acting as deputy commander, and would need to know the overall plan so that he could follow it and adapt it if conditions changed in the heat of battle. But Rehnskjold decided not to tell Lewenhaupt anything, because he disliked even speaking to him. Lewenhaupt had a way of receiving orders with a haughty, disdainful look, as though only loyalty to Charles could force him to listen to this foolish Rehnskjold. This infuriated the Field Marshal, which is why, on the eve of Poltava, he simply did not tell Lewenhaupt what he proposed to do on the following day.

The resulting confusion proved fatal on the battlefield. It stemmed from the absence of the one commanding figure who rose above such jealousies and who was implicitly obeyed. Lewenhaupt himself recognized this after the battle. "Would to God our gracious King had not been wounded," he said, "for then it had never gone as it did."

THE SWEDISH PLAN worked out by Charles and Rehnskjold was to attack with great speed just before dawn, taking the Russians by surprise, and move rapidly past the redoubts, ignoring any fire that might come from the defenders. Once through the redoubts, the Swedish columns would swing left and break out onto the broad plain in front of the main Russian camp. The infantry would march down the western edge of the plain to a position northwest of Peter's entrenched army while the Swedish cavalry swept the field clear of Peter's horsemen. Having reached the desired position between the Russians and the ford at Petrovka, the entire Swedish army would wheel to the right and form a line of battle. If the maneuver worked, the Russians would find themselves pinned into their camp against the riverbank with the steep bluff behind them and the Swedish army ready for battle standing astride their escape route to Petrovka. If they were unwilling to accept Charles' challenge to fight, they would be welcome to stay inside their entrenchments and eventually starve.

Lewenhaupt's infantry, whose total strength was only 7,000 men, was divided into four columns—two on the left comprising ten battalions, and two on the right comprising eight battalions. The King and his stretcher would be with the first column on the left wing, composed entirely of Guards. The second column on the left would be commanded by Major General Karl Gustav Roos, the two on the right by Generals Berndt Stackelberg and Axel Sparre. The cavalry squadrons were divided into six columns, under the overall command of Kreutz. Of the thirty pieces of

Swedish artillery still operable, most were left behind in the siege works or with the baggage. This was partly Rehnskjold's decision. He had a cavalry-man's distaste for artillery and believed that to drag cannon past the redoubts would reduce the rapid movement he demanded. Further, there would be no time to position the guns and begin a bombardment; besides, the powder was largely spoiled by the wet weather of the previous winter. Accordingly, the Swedes took only four cannon with them. The final decision, Rehnskjold hoped, would be reached with the steel of sword and bayonet.

At eleven p.m. on that short summer night, darkness fell and the Swedish infantry quietly broke camp and began moving forward to assembly points. Charles had his wounded foot freshly bandaged and himself dressed in full uniform with a high, spurred boot on his unharmed right leg. Beside him in his litter he laid his naked sword. The litter was carried forward through the long lines of marching men to the position where the Guards battalions were assembling. Here he found Rehnskjold, Piper, Lewenhaupt and his other generals wrapped in their cloaks, talking quietly and waiting. There was little moon and the brief night was relatively dark for a Ukrainian summer evening.

At midnight, when the short darkness was most intense, the soldiers who had been sitting or lying on the ground began to form ranks. There was some confusion in the darkness as battalions sorted themselves out and formed into columns. Uniforms were old, faded and patched after two years of campaigning, and some were scarcely identifiable. To distinguish himself from his enemies, each Swedish soldier took a wisp of straw and fixed it to his cap. In addition, a password was circulated among the troops: "With God's help" was to be shouted in Swedish in case of confusion. When the four columns were formed, the men were given permission to sit again to rest while waiting for the cavalry to arrive. This delay was longer than expected. Normally, the cavalry squadrons were expertly managed and led by Rehnskjold, but he was not with them, having been given command of the entire army, and the saddling of the horses at Pushkarivka and the forming of six columns of horsemen fell behind schedule.

As they were waiting, the Swedish generals heard a new sound from the Russian lines, a sound of "knocking and hewing," which showed that men were working not far away, much closer to them than the line of the first six Russian redoubts. It was obvious that Russian working parties were up to something in this no-man's-land. But what? To find out, Rehnskjold himself rode out to investigate.

In the dim light, the Field Marshal made an alarming discovery. During the night, the Russians had been furiously throwing up earth to construct a new line of four redoubts on a line at right angles to the previous six. These new redoubts extended straight forward down the Poltava road in the direc-

tion of the Swedish camp and would force a split of any Swedish advance into two separate wings, passing by either side of the redoubts and permitting the Russians to pour a flanking fire into the Swedish columns as they swept past. As Rehnskjold stared, he realized that the last two redoubts, the ones nearest to him, were still only partially finished. At the same moment, the men working on them saw him and his party of horsemen. There was a shout, a pistol shot, other shots, and then inside the Russian lines a warning drum began to beat. Rehnskjold hurried back to where Charles lay on his stretcher, and a council of war was held. The light was growing fast. The cavalry had now arrived, but the element of surprise was rapidly vanishing. Time was extremely short. Rehnskjold wanted to seize the moment and order the attack as planned; otherwise, he would have to give up the assault and the entire plan of battle would have to be canceled.

Charles, although unable to reconnoiter personally, was always an advocate of attack. He agreed, and orders were quickly issued. The infantry battalions reformed into five columns with the commanders of four instructed to move quickly past the new redoubts, ignoring their fire, and then form into line of battle on the plain according to the original plan. The fifth column, consisting of four battalions, was to envelop and attack the four new redoubts. Thus, the Swedish advance was to be split by the projecting line of redoubts like a stream divided by a series of large rocks, and flow past them, while the central wave was to dash against and if possible flood over the new obstacles.

As the Swedish generals urgently issued fresh commands, the darkness was turning to gray. The Swedish infantry was still reforming when Russian cannon in the forward redoubts opened fire. Cannonballs plowed into the massed, stationary Swedish ranks, decapitating a captain, two grenadiers and four musketeers. It was essential to move. At four a.m., just as the sun peeked up over the trees to the east, the Swedish redeployment was finished and Rehnskjold gave the order to advance. The Battle of Poltava had begun.

SEVEN THOUSAND Swedish foot soldiers, massed in oblong blocks of blue, purposefully fixed their bayonets and advanced across the field toward the Russian redoubts. Behind the columns on the left came the files of Swedish cavalry, some in blue coats trimmed in yellow, a few in yellow coats trimmed with blue. The horsemen reined their mounts and slowed the pace so as not to outrun the infantry, but amidst the leading squadrons the early rays of sun already glinted upon unsheathed steel. Most of the army ignored the redoubts, but as the central column of infantry reached the first redoubt, the Swedish grenadiers stormed over the unfinished earthwork, bayoneting the defenders in a fierce hand-to-hand struggle. It fell quickly. The second redoubt met the same fate as the Swedish infantry climbed into the earth-

work, firing and bayoneting. Some of the companies which had captured the two redoubts then fell back into the lines of men flowing past the redoubts to the left while others prepared for assault on the third redoubt, which was already under attack by two battalions under Roos.

It was in the attack on the third and fourth redoubts that a dangerous problem developed. The third redoubt was bravely defended, and the first Swedish assault was rebuffed. More troops were committed, and eventually six battalions of Swedish troops piled up before this obstacle. It was as if, in rushing past the redoubts, the Swedes had snagged a piece of clothing on a nasty bramble and, once entangled, had tried unsuccessfully to free themselves, all the while becoming more and more diverted from their original purpose.

The trouble lay in the secrecy which Rehnskjold had employed to keep his plan of attack from his subordinates. Roos never understood that his primary objective was simply to mask the redoubts while the rest of the army streamed past on both sides. What Roos should have done when repulsed was to withdraw and move past to the assembly point on the far side. Instead, he grimly reformed ranks and tried again. Repulsed a second time, he stubbornly added strength until six battalions—2,600 men—of the precious Swedish infantry were impaled on this unimportant obstacle. Taking the redoubt became Roos' sole ambition; he had not the least idea what was happening to the rest of the army or even where it was. So, in the first stage of the Swedish attack, a fundamental error was committed. Later, assessing what happened, Lewenhaupt said that the entire army, Roos included, should have avoided the central redoubts completely and simply swept past them. Rehnskjold later, as a prisoner of war in Russia, admitted the same mistake, saying, "One mistake can darken all previous gloire." Even Charles, who refused to criticize his generals after the battle, admitted ruefully, "Here the reconnaissance was not well done."

Suddenly, as the battle raged around the redoubts, two crowded lines of Menshikov's Russian dragoons issued from between the redoubts and charged the Swedish infantry. Seeing them coming, a cry of "Advance cavalry" arose from the Swedish infantry and the Swedish horsemen formed into wedges, knee to knee, and advanced at a trot to meet the oncoming Russian dragoons. Twenty thousand naked swords flashed in the sunlight as the two masses of cavalry clashed in the intervals between the Russian redoubts. Clouds of dust mingled with the roar of cannon, the report of pistols and the clang of steel on steel. For almost an hour, the melee continued with both Russians and Swedes refusing to retreat. Menshikov, exhilarated, sent fourteen captured Swedish standards and banners to Peter in the camp, along with the urgent advice that the Tsar immediately advance with all his forces and fight the battle on the line of the redoubts. Peter, still wary of Swedish prowess and scarcely believing that Menshikov's men could

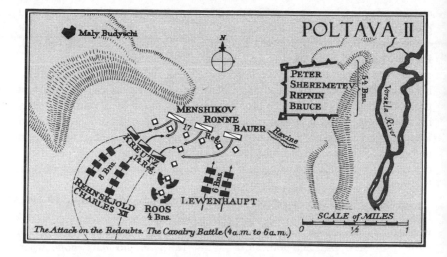

The Attack on the Redoubts. The Cavalry Battle (4 a.m. to 6 a.m.)

be doing so well, twice ordered his headstrong lieutenant to break off action and withdraw. Reluctantly, the Prince finally complied, wheeling his squadrons to the north, dispatching the larger part of the force under Bauer (Ronne had been severely wounded) to the northern flank of the Russian camp, and retreating himself with a smaller group to the camp's left flank. From the camp itself, Russian cannon along the ramparts laid down a protective curtain of fire, screening the withdrawing Russian horsemen and discouraging the Swedish cavalry from serious pursuit.

Meanwhile, Rehnskjold's failure to brief his subordinate commanders fully was leading to confusion elsewhere on the battlefield. The six Swedish infantry battalions on the right wing, personally commanded by Lewenhaupt, whose purpose was simply to march past the redoubts and join the main Swedish army in the field beyond, became confused in the smoke and dust raised by the cavalry battle and, at the same time, began taking destructive musket and cannon fire from the redoubts. To save his men, Lewenhaupt moved the line of march even farther to the right, away from the haze and out of range of the Russian fire. As he pulled off to the east, drifting farther and farther to the right, Lewenhaupt opened a wide gap in the Swedish line of battle. In fact, Lewenhaupt, uninformed and unconcerned about Rehnskjold's overall purpose, desired only to lead his column of infantry forward and attack the main enemy army. Forgetting or ignoring the Field Marshal's basic order to remain parallel, he swung off even farther to the right after passing the last line of redoubts because the ground there seemed easier to cross. With every step, he and his six battalions were marching farther away from the main body of troops. In fact, Lewenhaupt was

enormously pleased to be off by himself away from Rehnskjold, who, he grumbled, had treated him "like a lackey."

Now, the direction of Lewenhaupt's march lay straight toward the main Russian fortified camp. The large camp was by this time very wide awake, and as he marched forward, Russian artillery on the rampart opened fire on his men. But Lewenhaupt, now happily independent, was undeterred by the prospect of leading his six battalions against the entire Russian army, and his ranks went forward in textbook formation. Within musket range of the Russian entrenchment, he discovered that his advance was blocked by an unexpected ravine. Undaunted, he began to move his soldiers around this obstacle, still cheerfully preparing to storm over the Russian rampart at the head of 2,400 men into the midst of 30,000.

Meanwhile, to the left of the redoubts on the far side of the field from Lewenhaupt, the main Swedish force was the only one of three divisions which had followed the original plan, no doubt because it was commanded by Rehnskjold himself. Once the Russian cavalry had departed the field, the two infantry columns of this force hurried past the redoubts as envisaged, taking casualties from the flanking fire but penetrating quickly into the field beyond. It was here that the entire Swedish infantry of eighteen battalions had been scheduled to rendezvous in preparation for the attack on the Russian camp. For the moment, the officers with Rehnskjold were jubilant; everything seemed to be going according to plan. As the six battalions of the left reached the rendezvous point and wheeled into position, officers came up to congratulate the King, who had been carried on his stretcher through the redoubts with the infantry and was now sipping water while his wounded foot was redressed.

Unfortunately, as Rehnskjold looked around for the remainder of his infantry, there was nothing to be seen. Twelve battalions—the forces assigned to Lewenhaupt and Roos—were missing. Within moments, Lewenhaupt's six battalions were located: Far out in front and to the right, they were heard being fired upon as they worked their way around the ravine at the southwest corner of the Russian camp. Rehnskjold urgently dispatched a messenger, ordering Lewenhaupt to abandon his approach to the camp from that direction and immediately rejoin the main force waiting for him at the western edge of the field. When Lewenhaupt received the order, he was furious. Although he had only infantry—his force lacked even a single piece of artillery—he had already overrun two of the Russian redoubts blocking his path, and he was at the point of storming over the southern rampart of the Russian camp with sword and bayonet. This southern rampart was weakly defended, and Lewenhaupt with his 2,400 men was about to achieve the classic Swedish objective in battle: to bear down with momentum on a weak point in the enemy line, break through and then roll

up the opposing army, using panic and confusion as allies. Whether by breaking over the wall into Peter's camp his tiny force would actually have been able to panic Peter's army is questionable. These Russians were not the raw recruits of Narva, but disciplined veterans. In addition, Peter was already moving the army to the front of the camp and assembling it for battle, which is why Lewenhaupt found the southwest corner thinly defended. Had his fiery Swedes actually come over the wall and found themselves confronted by ten times as many Russians prepared for battle, they might have had initial success, but, unsupported, they soon would have been engulfed. In any case, to Lewenhaupt's dismay, they were commanded to withdraw, and they withdrew.

It was now six a.m. There was a lull in the fighting as far as most of the Swedish army was concerned. The main body, with Rehnskjold, the King, the cavalry and one third of the infantry, had moved northwest past the front of the Russian camp to the pre-planned position from where it could strike either at the camp or at the Petrovka river crossing. Lewenhaupt's six battalions, retiring from the camp's southern wall, were making their way toward Rehnskjold; when they reached the main body and fell into place, Rehnskjold would have twelve of his eighteen infantry battalions. But where were the other six?

They were in fact still south of the cross line of six redoubts, which were for the most part still in Russian hands, and still struggling under Roos' command to take the third and fourth of the forward redoubts by assault. The effort was gallant and at the same time pathetically irrelevant. The only purpose in attacking the protruding redoubts had been to mask the march-past of the main army; that done, the assault battalions had been supposed to abandon the effort and hurry to rejoin the main body. But no one had told Major General Roos, and this gallant officer was still trying to do what Swedish officers were supposed to do: capture the objective in front of him.

The battle at the redoubts did not last much longer. Three times Roos assaulted the redoubts, and three times he was repulsed. Finally, with forty percent of his men killed or wounded, he decided to withdraw. His intention then was to join the main army, but he had no idea where it had gone. Needing time to reform his shattered force into companies and battalions, he began to retreat into a wood east of the redoubts. Many of his wounded men tried to follow, crawling on their hands and knees.

Meanwhile, Peter was standing on the western rampart of his camp and looking out over the field. He saw that the Swedish army had passed through the redoubts and now was massing to his right on the northwest. At the same time, watching Lewenhaupt's withdrawal, he saw that a clear path was open from his camp to the redoubts which had resisted Roos. At once, the Tsar ordered Menshikov with a powerful force—five battalions of infantry drawn from the main camp and five regiments of his own dragoons,

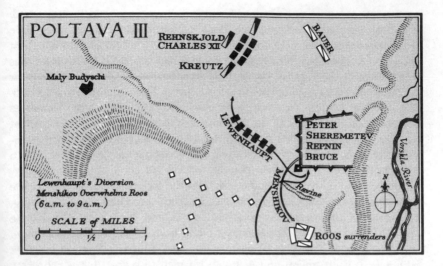

6,000 men in all—to find Roos in the woods, attack and destroy him. This force would also be available to reinforce Poltava, the road to which now lay open. As Menshikov's first squadrons approached them, Roos' beleaguered men took them for Swedish reinforcements. Almost before they discovered their mistake, the Russians were upon them. Under the fire of the advancing Russian cavalry and infantry, Roos' shattered ranks crumbled completely. In fierce hand-to-hand fighting, most of his men were killed or captured. Roos himself escaped with 400 men, fleeing south with Menshikov's horsemen close behind. Near Poltava, the Swedes threw themselves into an abandoned trench, but once again the Russians closed in. At last, mauled, pursued, outnumbered, Roos had no choice but to surrender. Just as he was led away, the sound of cannon to the northwest began in earnest. The first shots of the real battle were being fired, but Roos and his men would not be there. Before the main Battle of Poltava had begun, six battalions, one third of the Swedish infantry, had been annihilated to no purpose. The disaster can be blamed on Roos for persisting too long, or on Rehnskjold for not trusting his officers and briefing them more thoroughly before the battle began. But the real fault was that the brain of the Swedish army was missing. The clear, unhurried, commanding mind which all Swedes obeyed without question simply was not functioning at the Battle of Poltava.

AS SOON AS REHNSKJOLD, waiting with the King and other officers, discovered the absence of Roos' force, he sent a messenger back to find out what had happened. The messenger returned to report that Roos was still attack-

ing the first redoubts and was in difficulty. Rehnskjold hurriedly dispatched two cavalry regiments and two additional infantry battalions to Roos' aid. Meanwhile, the main body of the Swedish army could only wait. The Swedes were standing within cannon range about one mile from the northwest corner of the Russian camp, fully exposed to the enemy. Inevitably, the Russian artillery shifted its fire onto them. The cannonballs began to take a toll of heads, arms, legs; one ball killed two Guardsmen standing near the King. Another ball hit the King's stretcher. For the officers in the vicinity, this was an added concern; in addition to their other worries and responsibilities, they were forced to worry about the King's safety. Under this fire, some of the Swedish infantry was moved south into the wooded terrain of Maly Budyschi to find cover from the Russian guns. It was at this point that Lewenhaupt and the others fervently regretted the decision to leave most of the meager Swedish artillery behind. The Swedes had only four field guns to answer the seventy cannon firing from the Russian camp.

After an hour had passed, Sparre, who had led the two Swedish infantry battalions to Roos' relief, returned with his men to report that it had been impossible to break through the large Russian force which surrounded Roos. Accordingly, he had followed his orders and returned.

Rehnskjold was now in an increasingly perilous situation. He had stormed through the redoubts as planned. In a major cavalry action, his squadrons had triumphed and driven the Russian cavalry from the field. But now the tide had begun to shift. The momentum of his initial charge had been expended, and surprise was lost. For two hours, he had been forced to wait under heavy enemy fire for two wandering divisions of infantry, Lewenhaupt's and Roos', to join the main body. Lewenhaupt's had now arrived, but Roos' men apparently were lost. To fill the gap, Rehnskjold sent messengers back to the main Swedish camp before Poltava, ordering the reserve battalion guarding the baggage to hasten forward, bringing artillery. But these messengers never got through. There were no reinforcements, either for the depleted Swedish infantry or for the four Swedish cannon.

It was nearing nine a.m., and Rehnskjold had to make a decision. He had waited two hours for reinforcements which apparently were not coming. He could not stay where he was; he had to move. Three choices were open to him. He could move north, attack the Russian cavalry again, attempt to break through and seize the Petrovka ford, hold it and starve the Russians out of their camp. The flaw in this plan was that his small force, already vastly outnumbered, would be divided between Petrovka and Poltava without hope of mutual reinforcements; should Peter decide to go over to the offensive, he could move against one of these Swedish forces without the intervention and possibly even the knowledge of the other. Another choice was to carry out the original plan and attack the entrenched Russian army still waiting untouched behind the earth ramparts of its camp. But this meant

that the dwindling Swedish army would have to attack straight across the plain, into the mouths of dozens of Russian cannon which were already cutting through the Swedish ranks. Once over the trench and onto the ramparts, the Swedes would have to deal with 30,000 Russian infantrymen who were waiting inside.

The third alternative was the one that Rehnskjold chose: to retreat. His strength was too small and the odds too great. He meant to go back through the redoubts, relieving Roos and adding his strength as he passed through the redoubts, and as he moved back to the original launching point of the dawn attack, he would summon the battalions guarding the baggage train, those in the trenches before Poltava and those patrolling the river crossings below the city. Then, with the Swedish infantry back to twenty-four battalions instead of the twelve he now commanded, he would decide where next to fight the Tsar.

But just as Rehnskjold's men were starting to execute these orders, abandoning their long line of battle and forming into marching columns, an astonishing thing began to happen. Swedish officers watching the Russian camp noted that the whole Russian army seemed to be in motion. The entrances to the camp were open, the bridges over the defensive trench were down, and over these bridges Russian infantry in great strength was pouring out of the entrenchments and forming up in order of battle in front of the camp. For the first time in this war, the main Russian army was preparing to fight the main Swedish army in the presence of both Peter and Charles.

The Russian movement proceeded swiftly and smoothly, evidence of the training and discipline which now marked Peter's army. When the deployment was completed, a long, thick, shallow crescent containing tens of thousands of men and horses faced westward against the Swedes. On the Russian right, Bauer now commanded the Russian cavalry, eighteen regiments of dragoons, in uniforms of red and green. At the opposite tip of the crescent were six more dragoon regiments commanded by Menshikov, who typically had singled himself out by wearing white. In the center of the line stood the massed battalions of green-coated Russian infantry under Sheremetev and Repnin. General Bruce, commander of the Russian artillery, had divided his guns. Some remained on the earth rampart of the camp to fire over the heads of the Russian army, while other cannon served by red-coated artillerymen were wheeled into the front rank of the Russian line to greet any Swedish attack with devastating close-range fire.

Peter was on horseback with the infantry of the Novgorod regiment on the Russian left. He rode his favorite horse, a dun-colored Arabian that had been sent to him by the Sultan. His saddle that day was green velvet over leather, embroidered with silver thread; his reins and tack were of black leather and gold fittings. The Tsar's uniform was similar to that of many of his officers: a black, three-cornered hat, high black boots and the

bottle-green coat of the Preobrazhensky Regiment with red sleeves and trim. Only the blue silk ribbon of the Order of St. Andrew distinguished the sovereign. The troops around Peter, three veteran battalions of Novgorodians, were wearing gray coats and black hats. This was a ruse, proposed by the Tsar. Normally, gray coats were worn only by inexperienced troops, but Peter had chosen to dress several of his best battalions in gray that day, hoping to fool the Swedes into attacking that part of the Russian line.

The new position of the Russian army in front of its camp posed a further dilemma for Rehnskjold. The Swedish infantry had already moved out of its line of battle and was in column formation, preparing to march back south in search of Roos. If he began to move in this formation and the Russians attacked, it would be not a battle but a massacre. It was impossible to ignore the possibility, and Rehnskjold quickly decided to halt his withdrawal, turn and fight. Once more, the Swedish infantry wheeled to form a line of battle against the Russians.

Rehnskjold and Lewenhaupt then consulted and went to report to Charles that Peter was bringing out his infantry. "Would it not be best if we attacked the cavalry first and drove that off?" Charles asked. "No," Rehnskjold replied, "we must go against the infantry." The King was lying down and unable to see. "Well," he said, "you must do as you think best."

By ten a.m., the Swedish army had deployed into a battle line against the Russians. The Swedish cavalry was placed behind the infantry, not on the wings as Peter's cavalry was stationed. Lewenhaupt's infantry force now numbered only twelve battalions, scarcely 5,000 men. Opposite them stood two packed lines of Russian infantry, each one longer and stronger than his single line. The first Russian line consisted of twenty-four battalions, 14,000 men; the second line was made up of eighteen battalions, 10,000 men. (Nine infantry battalions remained as a reserve inside the Russian camp.) The superiority in numbers and firepower made the contest seem absurd: 5,000 infantry exhausted by hunger and fatigue, with no artillery, about to attack 24,000 men supported by seventy cannon. Lewenhaupt's only hope was the old tactic of delivering a hard blow on a single part of the Russian line, hoping to break through, spread confusion and thus roll up the far larger force.

At this moment, the old quarrel between the two principal Swedish commanders came to an end. Rehnskjold rode up to Lewenhaupt, who had to lead the attack in the face of almost hopeless odds. Taking him by the hand, the Field Marshal said, "Count Lewenhaupt, you must go and attack the enemy. Bear yourself with honor in His Majesty's service." Lewenhaupt asked whether it was Rehnskjold's command that he begin the attack immediately. "Yes, at once," the commander-in-chief replied. "In God's name, then, and may His grace be with us," said Lewenhaupt. He gave the

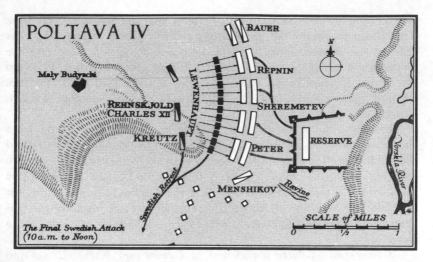

POLTAVA IV

BAUER

Maly Budyschi

LEWENHAUPT

REPNIN

REHNSKJOLD
CHARLES XII

SHEREMETEV

KREUTZ

PETER

RESERVE

Swedish Retreat

MENSHIKOV

Ravine

Vorskla River

SCALE *of* MILES

The Final Swedish Attack
(10 a.m. to Noon)

0   ½   1

signal to move forward. With drums beating, the famous Swedish infantry marched into its last battle. The force was pitifully small: twelve battalions strung out side by side in a thin line with gaps between the battalions to make the advancing line as wide as possible.

Ignoring the odds, the blue-clad Swedish line briskly advanced across the field. As it approached, the Russian artillerymen doubled their rate of fire, sending their whistling cannonballs to chop bloody holes in the Swedish ranks. Still the Swedes came forward, following their blue-and-yellow flags. As they got closer, the Russian infantry began firing volleys of musket balls into the shredded Swedish line; nevertheless, the unflinching Swedes kept coming, without returning a single shot. Led by the Guards, the Swedish battalions on the right finally reached and violently assaulted the first Russian rank. With stabbing swords and thrusting bayonets, the Swedes broke through, driving the Russians before them, capturing the forward Russian cannon which had been firing at them as they advanced across the field. Within a few minutes, the guns were turned and firing into the confused, wavering—and now retreating—Russian first line.

At this stage, having achieved his first objective and pierced a part of the enemy line, Lewenhaupt looked around for the Swedish cavalry which should have come up quickly to exploit his breakthrough. But no Swedish cavalry was to be seen. Instead, through the haze of smoke which covered the battlefield, Lewenhaupt could see that the Swedish battalions on his left wing were in grave difficulty. There, the Russian artillery, concentrated earlier in this sector to provide protective fire for the Russian cavalry massed to the north, had leveled the muzzles of its cannon directly at the advancing

Swedes. The fire was so intense and deadly that the Swedish ranks were simply shot to pieces; half the men were scythed down before they even reached the Russian infantry. Between this faltering left wing and the battalions on the right—which were still pressing ahead, preparing to attack the second Russian line of infantry—a gap opened. And the farther the Swedish right wing advanced, plunging forward toward the second Russian line, the wider the gap became.

Standing with the Novgorod regiment at exactly this point on the field, Peter also saw what was happening. He observed that the Swedish army had divided into two separate armies: the left wing held at bay, suffering terribly from his artillery, and in no position to threaten the Russian right wing; and the Swedish right, still plunging forward, deeper into his lines, about to reach the waiting second line of Russian infantry. Even as he watched, the gap grew wider. Into this gap, Peter dispatched his own infantry in overwhelming numbers.

It happened as Peter hoped and as Lewenhaupt feared. It was the Swedish line which now was broken; it was the Russian infantry which would advance and roll up the broken enemy line in a sweeping counter-blow. Unhindered by the presence of any Swedish cavalry, the Russian infantry began to envelop the Swedish right wing. The momentum of the Swedish attack actually helped Peter's strategy: As the thrust of the Swedish charge carried it forward, plunging deeper into the Russian mass, other Russian battalions moving through the gap in the Swedish line simply flowed around and to the rear. The farther the Swedes pressed forward, the more hopelessly engulfed they became in the sea of Russian soldiers. Eventually, the forward momentum of the Swedish charge was broken, its shock absorbed by the sheer mass of Russian soldiers.

Swedish cavalry finally arrived, but not the full weight of Rehnskjold's disciplined squadrons. Only fifty Swedish horsemen appeared, troopers of the Household Cavalry, who rode with flashing swords into the middle of the Russian infantry. All were quickly shot, speared or dragged from their saddles. Engulfed and overwhelmed, the Swedes attempted to retreat, at first with stubborn discipline and then, as panic spread, in wild disorder. With most of his officers dead or dying, Lewenhaupt rode up and down his crumbling Swedish line, trying to make his men stand fast. "I begged, threatened, cursed and hit out, but all was in vain," he remembered later. "It was as if they neither saw nor heard me."

Throughout this part of the battle, the tall figure of Peter was conspicuous among the Russian troops. Although his height made him an obvious target, he ignored the danger and spent his energies directing and encouraging his men. That he was not wounded was remarkable, for he was hit three times during the battle. One musket ball knocked his hat off,

another lodged in his saddle, while the third actually struck him in the chest but was deflected by an ancient silver icon which he wore on a chain around his neck.

Within a few minutes, the Swedish attack had dissolved, although separate units continued to fight. The Swedish Guards battled with their usual doggedness. They died where they stood, and the Russian torrent poured over them. Whole companies of Swedes were surrounded and fell together as the Russians rushed over them, killing with pike, sword and bayonet and leaving them piled in heaps.

Where was the Swedish cavalry? Again, perhaps, it missed the touch of its master, Rehnskjold, now trying to command the entire army. On the Swedish right, the cavalry was late in deploying and Lewenhaupt's infantry began to advance before the cavalry was ready to follow up. Then, as the squadrons began moving forward, their movement was obstructed by difficult terrain. On the left, the Swedish cavalry was distracted by its assignment to screen the battlefield from the mass of Russian cavalry poised to the north. When some of the Swedish cavalry regiments finally came to the aid of the hard-pressed infantry, they found that, rather than giving help, they soon needed it themselves. The regiments charging the Russian lines were cut to ribbons by the same enormous volume of Russian cannon and musket fire which had decimated the infantry.

And so, for another half an hour, it continued—glorious for Peter, disastrous for Charles. Most of the Swedish infantry which had crossed the field into the Russian lines was simply destroyed. Rehnskjold, seeing what was happening, shouted to Piper, "All is lost!" Plunging into the thickest area of the fight, he was soon made prisoner.

Charles himself was in the midst of the disaster. When the collapse came, the King did his best to rally the panicking Swedes, but his thin cry of "Swedes! Swedes!" went unheeded. The Russian fire was so intense that "men, horses and boughs of trees all fell to the ground." Twenty-one of the King's twenty-four litter-bearers were cut down and the stretcher itself was hit and shattered. For a moment, with no bearers, it looked as if the King would be captured. Then, an officer dismounted and Charles was lifted into the saddle. The bandage on his foot came loose and blood dripped from the reopened wound. The horse was shot from under him and another supplied. Thus, the King made his way back to the Swedish lines with his wounded foot bleeding profusely, resting on the horse's neck. Presently, the King fell in with Lewenhaupt. "What are we to do now?" Charles asked. "There is nothing to do but try to collect the remains of our people," replied the General. Under his direction, the remnants of the infantry, covered by the cavalry, which still was relatively intact, retreated south through the redoubts to the temporary safety of the camp at Pushkarivka. As the shattered army

withdrew, the reserve regiments and the artillery as well as Mazeppa's and Gordeenko's Cossacks were placed in defensive positions around the camp to ward off any Russian pursuit. By noon, most of the beaten army had reached camp and the exhausted men could rest. Lewenhaupt, parched and hungry, ate a piece of bread and drank two glasses of beer.

To the north, on the battlefield, the last shots had been fired and the field had fallen silent. Peter, exuberant, had given thanks in a service on the battlefield and then had gone to dinner. The Battle of Poltava was over.

38

SURRENDER
BY THE RIVER

THE BATTLEFIELD was a place of carnage. The Swedish army which had begun the battle 19,000 strong had left 10,000 men on the field, including 6,901 dead and wounded and 2,760 prisoners. Among these losses were 560 officers—300 dead and 260 captured, the latter including Field Marshal Rehnskjold, Prince Max of Württemberg, four major generals and five colonels. Count Piper, who was with the King all day, became separated from him in the final melee and wandered about the battlefield with two secretaries until finally he made his way up to the gates of Poltava and surrendered.

Russian losses were relatively light—not surprisingly, as the Russians had fought most of the battle from defensive positions inside the redoubts and their entrenched camp while their cannon worked havoc on the advancing Swedes. Of 42,000 engaged, Peter lost 1,345 killed and 3,290 wounded. In its casualty figures as well as its outcome, it was a reversal of every previous battle between Peter and Charles.

As the Swedes retreated toward Pushkarivka, the Russians did not pursue. The climax of the battle had been hand-to-hand combat, and by the end, Peter's infantry was as disorganized as Charles'. Not completely convinced by its success, it advanced with caution. More important, however, was Peter's overwhelming desire to celebrate. After a thanksgiving service, he went to his tent inside the camp, where he and his generals sat down to dinner. The Russians were tired, hungry and exultant. After many toasts, the captured Swedish generals and colonels were brought in and seated around him. It was a supreme moment in Peter's life. A nine-year burden of anxiety had fallen away, and the despair with which the Tsar had watched the irresistible advance of his great antagonist had vanished. Yet, in his excitement, Peter was not overbearing. He was considerate, even kindly, to his prisoners, especially Rehnskjold. When, during the long afternoon, Count Piper was brought in from Poltava, he, too, was seated next to the Tsar.

Peter kept looking around, fully expecting that at any moment the King also would be brought in. "Where is my brother Charles?" he asked repeatedly. When, with great respect, he asked Rehnskjold how he dared invade a huge empire with a handful of men, Rehnskjold replied that the King had commanded it and it was his first duty as a loyal subject to obey his sovereign. "You are an honest fellow," said Peter, "and for your loyalty I return you your sword." Then, as the cannon on the ramparts roared another salute, Peter stood holding a glass and proposing a toast to his teachers in the art of war. "Who are your teachers?" asked Rehnskjold. "You are, gentlemen," said Peter. "Then, well have the pupils returned thanks to their teachers," said the Field Marshal wryly. Peter remained excitedly talking to his prisoners and celebrating through most of the afternoon, and it was five p.m. before anyone thought of pursuing the beaten Swedish army. Then, the Tsar commanded Prince Michael Golitsyn with the Guards and General Bauer with dragoons to follow Charles south. On the following morning, Menshikov led more Russian cavalry to join the pursuit.

That night, when the celebrations were over, Peter took time in his tent to record the day's events. To Catherine, he wrote:

> Matushka [Little Mother], good day. I declare to you that the all-merciful God has this day granted us an unprecedented victory over the enemy. In a word, the whole of the enemy's army is knocked on the head, about which you will hear from us.
>
> Peter
>
> P.S. Come here and congratulate us.

Longer letters, fourteen in all, "from the camp at Poltava," were sent to Romodanovsky (now elevated for the occasion from Mock-Tsar to Mock-Emperor), Buturlin, Boris, Peter, and Dmitry Golitsyn, Apraxin, Peter Tolstoy, Alexander Kikin, the head of the Church Stephen Yavorsky, his sister Princess Natalya, the Tsarevich Alexis and others. The text in all cases was practically the same:

> This is to inform you that, by God's blessing and the bravery of my troops, I have just gained a complete and unexpected victory without much effusion of blood. These are the particulars of the action.
> This morning the enemy's cavalry and infantry attacked my cavalry, which gave way with considerable loss, after a brave resistance.
> The enemy formed themselves in line of battle exactly opposite

our camp. I drew immediately our infantry out of the entrenchments to oppose the Swedes, and placed our cavalry on the two wings. The enemy, on seeing this, made a movement to attack us. Our troops advanced to meet them, and received them in such a manner that the enemy deserted the field of battle after little or no resistance, leaving us in possession of a number of cannon, colors and standards. Field Marshal General Rehnskjold, Generals Schlippenbach, Stackelberg, Hamilton and Roos are among the prisoners, as are also Count Piper, prime minister, secretaries Imerlin and Cederheilm and several thousand officers and soldiers.

I will send you in a little time a more circumstantial account; at present I am too busy to satisfy your curiosity entirely. In a few words, the enemy's army has met with the fate of Phaeton. I can give you no account of the King, not knowing whether he be in the number of the living or gone to sleep with his fathers. I have sent Prince Golitsyn and Bauer with part of the cavalry in pursuit of the runaways. I congratulate you on this good news and beg all the magistrates and officers of my empire to consider it a happy omen.

Peter

It was in a final footnote to this letter to Apraxin that Peter expressed most succinctly his great joy and the ultimate significance of Poltava: "Now, with God's help, the final stone in the foundation of St. Petersburg has been laid."

THUS, IN A SINGLE MORNING, the Battle of Poltava terminated the Swedish invasion of Russia and permanently shifted the political axis of Europe. Until that day, statesmen in every country had waited expectantly for the news that Charles had triumphed once again, that his famous army had entered Moscow, that the Tsar had been replaced and perhaps killed in the general turmoil and insurrection that must arise among the leaderless Russian masses. A new tsar would be proclaimed and become a puppet like Stanislaus. Sweden, already Mistress of the North, would become Empress of the East, arbiter of everything that happened between the Elbe and the Amur. Servile Russia would shrink as Swedes, Poles, Cossacks and perhaps Turks, Tatars and Chinese carved out generous portions. St. Petersburg would vanish from the Russian landscape, the Baltic coast would be sealed off and Peter's awakening people would be halted in their tracks, turned around and marched like prisoners back into the shadowy world of old Muscovy. These dream castles fell with a crash. Between dawn and dinner, the conqueror had become a fugitive.

Poltava was the first thunderous announcement to the world that a new

Russia was being born. In the years that followed, European statesmen who theretofore had paid scarcely more attention to the affairs of the Tsar than to those of the Shah of Persia or the Mogul of India learned to reckon carefully the weight and direction of Russia's interests. The new balance of power established that morning by Sheremetev's infantry, Menshikov's cavalry and Bruce's artillery, under the eyes of their six-foot-seven-inch lord, continued and developed through the eighteenth, nineteenth and twentieth centuries.

THE SWEDISH ARMY was defeated, but it had not surrendered. In early afternoon, while Peter was sitting at dinner with his Swedish guests, the surviving remnants of the Swedish army dribbled back into the camp at Pushkarivka. Added to the troops in the siege trenches before Poltava and the detachments guarding the baggage train and the crossings on the lower Vorskla, the total came to more than 15,000 Swedes plus 6,000 Cossacks still under arms, awaiting the command of the King and his generals. Some of these were freshly wounded, others were still invalided from battles or frostbite the previous winter. Only a few of those remaining were foot soldiers; most of the survivors were cavalrymen.

Charles was among the last to reach Pushkarivka. While his foot was again rebandaged and he ate a piece of cold meat, he asked for Rehnskjold and Piper and it was then that he learned they were missing. Lewenhaupt was now the senior general of this Swedish army, and it was on the "little Latin colonel" that the wounded King would now have to rely.

There was no question what must be done. The Swedes must get away before the Russians fully realized the extent of their success and began to pursue. Nor was there any question about which way to go. North, east and west lay divisions of Peter's victorious army. Only the road to the south lay open. This was the best and most direct path to the Tatar lands where they might find sanctuary under the protection of Devlet Gerey. Charles was realistic enough to understand that his arrival would be received far differently now that his army was only a shattered fragment, but he hoped that the Khan would offer sanctuary long enough for the beaten troops to rest and gather strength before beginning the long march through the Tatar and Turkish borderlands back to Poland.

Thus, the immediate decision was to march south down the west bank of the Vorskla toward Perevoluchna eighty miles away, the point at which the Vorskla flows into the Dnieper. Along the way, there were several fords known to the Cossacks, and if the army crossed the river to the east bank, it could then join the road which ran from Kharkov to the Crimea. This road was clear, and led through several Cossack towns along the way which could help feed and succor the army.

The order was given to march that same afternoon. The retreat from Pushkarivka was orderly, with the artillery and baggage wagons going ahead. Kreutz, in command of the rearguard, abandoned and set fire to the heavier wagons, taking the wagon horses and giving them to the infantry to make for greater mobility. As the hastily reorganized columns began to move, they were not in headlong flight; this was a disciplined army defeated in battle but still conducting a properly structured retreat. There were still many thousands of veteran soldiers who, if called upon to fight, could wage a formidable battle.

Yet the Swedes, both officers and men, were in a state of fatigue. They had not slept the night before—only eighteen hours earlier, the army had been assembling for the dawn assault on the redoubts. Toward evening, the soldiers were stumbling, blindly following their officers, spurred mainly by the desire to get away. Charles' own condition had deteriorated. Exhausted by lack of sleep, weakened by the reopening of his wound, stricken by the shock of the disaster, the somber uncertainties of the future and the stifling heat, he had lain in a wagon until he fell asleep. When he awoke, the army in motion, his mind was clouded and he had no clear idea as to what was happening. He asked again for Piper and Rehnskjold; when told that they were not there, he lay back and said, "Yes, yes, do what you will."

The following day, June 29, the march south continued through the oppressive heat. Propelled by the fear that the Russians were pursuing, the army marched past first one, then a second and then a third of the Vorskla fords without giving a serious thought to crossing. It was easier to keep going south on land than to stop and ford a river. Behind loomed the specter of the Russians, a specter made real at four a.m. on the 30th when Kreutz caught up with the main body and reported that the Russian pursuit had started; not just Cossacks, but regular Russian troops were following.

For two days, the Swedish columns straggled into the tip of land at the junction of the Vorskla and Dnieper. On the evening of the 29th, the artillery, the remaining wagons and the mass of men began to pour into Perevoluchna at the point where the two rivers joined. Here there were no fords, and as the soldiers looked out over the broad Dnieper, a feeling of panic gripped them. The town itself and the hundreds of boats assembled there by the Zaporozhsky Cossacks had been burned by Peter's lightning raid in April. Obviously, the army was far too numerous to cross in the remaining boats; only a few would make it before the Russians caught up. Conceivably, the whole force could march back north to cross the Vorskla, but the Russians there must be drawing closer. To the south, east and west lay the two rivers. The Swedish army was trapped.

It was a moment of decision: A few could cross the Dnieper. Who should go? Lewenhaupt and Kreutz dropped to their knees and begged the King to grasp this chance to escape. At first, Charles refused, insisting on

staying with the army and sharing its fate. Then, as pain and fatigue overwhelmed him, he agreed to go. Subsequently, there were those who said
that Charles abandoned his army to save himself, knowing that his flight
would mean death or captivity for the men who had followed him so
bravely. But Charles' decision was based on legitimate reasoning. He was
wounded. The army faced a long march south, probably under close
pursuit from a strong, victorious enemy. Most of the men were mounted now
and could ride fast, but Charles, lying in a wagon, would be no more than
a worry and a hindrance to the officers who exercised command. And
Charles was King of Sweden. If he was captured the Tsar might humiliate
him by parading him through the streets. More certainly, in Russian hands,
he would be a huge liability in any peace negotiations with Russia. To
obtain freedom for its monarch, Sweden would have to pay dearly in
Swedish territory.

There were other reasons for Charles to escape. If he went with the
army to the Crimea, then, even if the march was successful, he would be
cut off from his homeland at the opposite end of Europe, totally unable to
influence events. Further, he knew that the continent would soon be ringing
with news of Peter's triumph. He wanted to reach a place from which he
could rebut Peter's boasts and promote Sweden's side of the story. Then,
too, if he reached the Ottoman dominions, he might persuade the Turks to
make an alliance, provide him with a new army and enable him to
continue the war. Finally, there were the Cossack followers of Mazeppa and
Gordeenko to be considered. They were now Charles' responsibility. If
Charles or his Swedes were captured, the Cossacks would be treated as
traitors and tortured and hung. It would be a stain on Swedish honor to
permit these allies to fall into Russian hands.

For all these reasons, it was decided that the King, with as many
wounded Swedes as possible, plus an escort of fighting soldiers, would go
with the Cossacks straight across the steppe to the Bug River, the boundary
of the Ottoman Empire. There they would ask for sanctuary and wait for
their wounds to heal and for the rest of the army to join them. The army
itself would go north to the Vorskla fords, cross the river and march south
along the Dnieper to the Khan's dominions, to rejoin the King at Ochakov
on the Black Sea. Reunited, the entire force would return to Poland.

That very night, Charles was ferried across the Dnieper on a stretcher.
His coach was brought after him, its weight distributed between two boats
lashed together. Through the night, small fishing boats were rowed back and
forth, carrying wounded officers and men. With him, the King took the
survivors of the Drabant Corps, now only eighty strong, about 700 cavalrymen and some 200 infantrymen, plus members of his household and
chancery staffs. Many of Mazeppa's Cossacks who were expert swimmers
swam the river holding on to the tails of their horses. The boats also brought

over part of the Swedish army treasury and two barrels of gold ducats which Mazeppa had carried with him from Baturin. In all, about 900 Swedes and 2,000 Cossacks crossed the river. At dawn, before departing, Charles looked back and felt uneasy at seeing no sign of movement from the army still camped along the water's edge. Some Swedes saw clouds on the horizon which they thought might be dust from a mass of approaching horsemen. Lewenhaupt took command of the army. This was as he wished; the moody General had specifically volunteered to stay behind and share the fate of the troops. He and Kreutz discussed with Charles the route the army would take and the projected rendezvous point at Ochakov. Lewenhaupt promised the King that if the Russians pursued him, he would fight. Here, as subsequent events were to prove, there was a grave misunderstanding. Charles assumed that Lewenhaupt had promised unconditionally, but Lewenhaupt understood that he had bound himself to fight only after he got the army away from Perevoluchna. "If, with the grace of God, we are spared onslaught of a strong enemy force with infantry for this night and the morrow, I believe there may yet be some hope of saving the troops." In any case, only the two of them were able to interpret the discussion of Charles' orders and Lewenhaupt's promises; no one else was present. As Charles later admitted when accepting partial responsibility for what happened, "I was guilty . . . I forgot to give the other generals and colonels who were there the orders of which Lewenhaupt and Kreutz alone had knowledge." Once again, it was the story of Roos and the redoubts at Poltava. Ignorance of the overall plan left the other officers and the army helpless.

Lewenhaupt's first objective was to get away from Perevoluchna. This meant retracing his steps by marching north to one of the fords across the Vorskla. But as the troops were exhausted and many of the officers who had spent the night getting the King and his party across the Dnieper even more so, Lewenhaupt gave the order for the men to rest and be prepared to start at dawn.

During the night, preparations were made to travel fast and light. The money remaining in the regimental chests was distributed among the troops, each man to be responsible for his own share thereafter. Ammunition and provisions were similarly distributed, with each man taking only the amount he could carry on horseback; the rest was to be abandoned. Any remaining baggage and supply wagons which could impede the march were to be left behind. An attempt would be made to take the artillery, but if it became a hindrance, it, too, would be abandoned.

The passage of the night worked further damage on the Swedish army. Discipline frayed. It was obvious to the soldiers that safety lay across the broad Dnieper. The word that in the morning they were to march north again was sullenly received. Lewenhaupt himself was exhausted, a condition

made worse by a bad case of diarrhea. Overcome by fatigue, he lay down for a few hours' rest.

At dawn the next morning, July 1, the two Generals arose, the army stirred, the men began saddling their horses and preparing to march. Then, at eight a.m., just as the columns were forming and about to march, figures appeared on the heights above the river. There were more and more every minute; soon the heights were swarming with horsemen. It was Menshikov, with 6,000 dragoons and 2,000 loyal Cossacks. The Prince sent a trumpeter and an aide-de-camp to the Swedish camp to parley. Lewenhaupt ordered Kreutz to ride back to discover what terms Menshikov offered. Menshikov offered normal surrender terms, and Kreutz reported them to Lewenhaupt. The weary commander decided to consult his colonels. The colonels asked what the King's last orders had been. Suppressing details of the proposed march to Tatary and the Ochakov rendezvous, Lewenhaupt said that Charles had asked only that the army "defend itself as long as it could." The colonels went back to the soldiers to ask whether they would fight. The soldiers, also unwilling to take responsibility, replied, "We will fight if the others do."

Once these parleys and discussions were begun, the temptation to surrender became irresistible. Although the Swedes and Cossacks outnumbered the Russians on the scene by almost three to one, the Swedes were beaten men. Their King had fled, and they were isolated, facing a long march into unknown regions. To some, the prospect of an end to fighting after nine long years seemed welcome. Among the officers, there was the hope of speedy repatriation to Sweden in exchange for captured Russian officers. Defeatism was in the air, perhaps helped psychologically by the fact that the Russians were above them, looking down from the heights above the river. Finally, there was the effect of Poltava. The legend of invincibility had been shattered. The Swedish army had become a collection of lost, weary and frightened men.

At eleven a.m. on the morning of July 1, Lewenhaupt capitulated without a fight. The army he surrendered included 14,299 men, thirty-four cannon and 264 battle flags. Together with the 2,871 Swedes captured on the field at Poltava, Peter now held over 17,000 Swedish prisoners.

The Swedes became prisoners of war, but the 5,000 Cossacks who had remained with Lewenhaupt were not so fortunate. Menshikov offered them no terms. Many simply mounted their horses, rode off and escaped, but some were ridden down and captured. Their mutilated bodies were hung from the gallows to proclaim the fate of traitors.

MEANWHILE, on the far side of the Dnieper, Mazeppa took charge of the escape. Before dawn on July 1, he had sent Charles ahead in a coach escorted by 700 Swedes led by Cossack guides. Mazeppa, himself confined

to a carriage by illness, divided the remainder of the Swedes and Cossacks into separate parties and sent them to the southwest by different trails, hoping to confuse the Russians if they tried to follow. By evening, all who had crossed the river had departed the western bank and moved into the tall grass of the steppe. That same night, Mazeppa caught up with Charles and urged the King and his escort to move faster.

The steppe through which the escapees were hurrying was a no-man's-land of tall grass between the Dnieper and Bug rivers, deliberately left unpopulated to serve as a buffer between the empires of the Tsar and the Sultan. There were no trees, no houses, no cultivation—nothing but the grass growing higher than a man on foot. There was little food and water came only from small, muddy streams running through the grass. The heat was so intense that the party was forced to halt for several hours at midday.

By July 7, the Swedes had reached the eastern bank of the Bug and could stare across the river at the place of sanctuary. Here, another obstacle arose. For two days, the Swedes were forced to wait on the wrong side of the river while they negotiated the price of boats and asylum with the Sultan's representative in this territory, the Pasha of Ochakov. This haggling continued until the potentate had been sufficiently bribed and boats were provided. The Swedes began to cross, but there were not enough boats, and at the end of the third day, when the Russians finally caught up, 300 Swedes and 300 Cossacks were still stranded on the wrong side of the river.

As soon as Lewenhaupt's surrender at Perevoluchna was signed, Menshikov dispatched Volkonsky with 6,000 horsemen to cross the Dnieper and pursue and capture the King and Mazeppa. The Cossack feints threw them off, but when they did find the trail, they rode swiftly, racing the fugitives to the Bug. They arrived to find their principal quarry escaped, but 600 men still remaining on the east bank. The Russians attacked, and the 300 Swedes quickly surrendered. The Cossacks knew that no quarter would be given them and they fought to the last man. Helplessly, from across the river, Charles watched the hopeless struggle.

This massacre was the final battle in the Swedish invasion of Russia. In the twenty-three months since Charles had left Saxony, a great army had been destroyed. Now, the King of Sweden stood with 600 survivors inside the Black Sea borders of the Ottoman Empire, on the outer rim of the European world.

39

THE FRUITS
OF POLTAVA

FOR PETER, the triumph at Poltava was so immense that, long after his victory dinner, he remained in a mood of intense excitement and festivity. It scarcely seemed possible that the perils which so long had threatened Russia had suddenly vanished as if the Ukrainian earth had simply opened up and swallowed them. Two days after the battle, the Tsar entered Poltava with his generals. He found the town in a grim condition after its two-month siege, its walls shattered and its 4,000 defenders exhausted and hungry. With the gallant Colonel Kelin, commander of the garrison, at his side, Peter gave thanks and celebrated his Name Day at the Spasskaya Church.

When Menshikov returned in triumph from the Swedish mass surrender at Perevoluchna, Peter began a distribution of rewards and decorations to the victorious army. Menshikov was promoted to the rank of field marshal; Sheremetev, already a field marshal, was given larger estates. All the generals of the Russian army received promotions or new estates, and each was subsequently presented with a portrait of Peter set in diamonds. The Tsar himself, who up to that time had held the rank of colonel in the army and captain in the navy, also allowed himself to be promoted: He now became a lieutenant general in the army and a rear admiral in the navy.

In granting these rewards and promotions, the charade with Romodanovsky was continued. Peter thanked the new Mock-Tsar for his promotion:

Sir:

The gracious letter of Your Majesty and the decree to His Excellency the Field Marshal and Cavalier [Knight of St. Andrew] Sheremetev by which I have been given in your name the rank of Admiral in the fleet and of Lieutenant General on land, have been announced to me. I have not deserved so much, but it has been given

to me solely by your kindness. I therefore pray God for strength to be able to serve such honor in the future.

Peter.

Across Russia, there were celebrations; in Moscow, the citizens wept for joy. Poltava meant delivery from the foreign invader and, it was hoped, an end to the crushing taxes imposed by the war and to the prolonged absence of husbands, fathers, sons and brothers. A formal celebration in the capital was postponed until the arrival of the Tsar with part of the army, but meanwhile the nineteen-year-old Tsarevich Alexis, acting in his father's place, gave a huge banquet for all foreign ambassadors at Preobrazhenskoe. Peter's sister, Princess Natalya, gave a great banquet for the important ladies of the capital. Tables loaded with free beer, bread and meat were placed in the street so that all could celebrate. For an entire week, church bells rang incessantly from morning to night and volleys of cannon thundered from the Kremlin walls.

By July 13, the army at Poltava had ended its celebrations. The bodies of the Russian and Swedish dead had been collected and buried in separate mass graves on the battlefield. The army was rested and it must now be moved: The region around the city had been stripped bare of provisions. (Eight days after the battle, 12,000 Kalmuck horsemen had arrived to reinforce the Russian army. They were too late to fight but they, like the rest of the army, still had to be fed.) Besides, with the Swedish army annihilated and the warrior King in flight, this was the moment to reap the harvest of victory. Two great regions, which had stubbornly thwarted the Tsar's ambitions, the Baltic and Poland, now lay all but naked before him. At a council of war in the Poltava camp that lasted from July 14 to 16, the army was divided in two. Sheremetev with all of the infantry and part of the cavalry was to march north to the Baltic and seize the great fortress port of Riga. Menshikov with most of the cavalry would move westward into Poland to operate with Goltz against the Swedes under Krassow and those Poles who supported King Stanislaus.

Peter himself went from Poltava to Kiev. In the Ukrainian capital, he attended a service of thanksgiving in Santa Sophia Cathedral, an architectural masterpiece of layered domes, interlocking arches and glowing interior mosaics. The prefect of the cathedral, Feofan Prokopovich, preached a great, rolling panegyric to Peter and to Russia which so pleased the Tsar that he marked the priest for higher service; later, Prokopovich was to become the primary instrument of Peter's reform of the Russian church.

Peter had not meant to remain in Kiev, but on August 6 he wrote to Menshikov that he had a fever:

For my sins, sickness has stricken me. It's really an accursed illness, for although not now accompanied by shivering and temperatures but with nausea and pain, it lays me low unexpectedly, and so I do not think I will be able to leave here because of weakness earlier than the 10th or on the holy day of the Assumption.

PETER WANTED all the world to know of his triumph. From the camp at Poltava, the Tsar sent letters to his envoys in foreign capitals, giving them details of the battle to pass along. At the Tsar's command, Menshikov wrote a special letter, sent by the swiftest couriers, to the Duke of Marlborough. The West, accustomed to hearing of an unbroken string of Swedish triumphs, now received a deluge of letters and messages from the East, all describing the "complete victory" of the Tsar and the "total defeat" of Charles XII. From Flanders, where he had received the first news of the battle even before the arrival of Menshikov's letter, Marlborough wrote to Godolphin in London:

> We have no confirmation as yet of the battle between the Swedes and Muscovites, but should it be true of the first being so entirely beaten as is reported, what a melancholy reflection it is that after constant success for ten years, he [Charles XII] should in two hours' mismanagement and ill success, ruin himself and his country.

On August 26, Menshikov's letter arrived, and Marlborough wrote to Sarah, his Duchess:

> This afternoon I have received a letter from Prince Menshikov, favorite and general of the Tsar, of the entire victory over the Swedes. If this unfortunate King had been so well advised as to have made peace the beginning of the summer, he might, in great measure, have influenced the peace between France and the Allies, and have made his kingdom happy; whereas now he is entirely in the power of his neighbors.

As news of the victory spread across the continent, opinion in Europe, previously hostile to and even contemptuous of Peter and Russia, began to change. The philosopher Leibniz, who after Narva had announced his hope of seeing Charles rule over Muscovy as far as the Amur, now proclaimed that the destruction of the Swedish army was one of the glorious turning points of history:

> As for me, who am for the good of the human race, I am very glad that so great an empire is putting itself in the ways of reason

and order, and I consider the Tsar in that respect as a person whom God has destined to great works. He has succeeded in having good troops. I do not doubt that . . . he will succeed in also having good foreign relations, and I shall be charmed if I can help him make science flourish in his country. I maintain even that he can do in that respect finer things than all other princes have done.

Leibniz suddenly became a bubbling fountain of ideas and suggestions for this potential new patron. Offering his services, he stressed his readiness to draw up plans for an academy of science, for museums and colleges and even for designing medals to commemorate Poltava.

In hurrying to adjust to the Tsar's new influence, Leibniz was doing what all Europe was about to do. The diplomatic turn-around came quickly. Proposals for new arrangements and new treaties came flocking to Peter. The King of Prussia and the Elector of Hanover both signaled their desire for Russian ties. The Russian ambassador in Copenhagen, Prince Vasily Dolgoruky, was informed that Louis XIV would be glad to make an alliance with the Tsar: France proposed to guarantee Russian conquests on the Baltic in order to injure British and Dutch trade. With Charles humbled, Sweden's enemies hastened back into the field. King Frederick IV of Denmark proposed to Dolgoruky a new Danish-Russian alliance against Sweden. This was very pleasant and ironic for Dolgoruky, who had already spent many months trying in vain to negotiate exactly such an alliance. Peter agreed, and that month Danish troops crossed the sound and invaded southern Sweden while the satisfied Dolgoruky observed the landing from a ship in the invasion fleet.

The most immediate impact of Poltava was on events in Poland. As soon as news of the battle arrived, Augustus of Saxony issued a proclamation repudiating the Treaty of Altranstadt by which he had been forced to give up the Polish crown, and, with a Saxon army of 14,000, he entered Poland and summoned his Polish subjects to renewed allegiance. The Polish magnates, without Charles' army there to compel their acceptance of Stanislaus, welcomed Augustus back. Stanislaus fled, first to Swedish Pomerania, then to Sweden, and finally to Charles' camp inside the Ottoman Empire.

In late September, Peter, recovering from his illness in Kiev, began a long, circular journey which would last three months and take him from the Ukrainian capital to Warsaw, East Prussia, Riga, St. Petersburg and, finally, to Moscow. Early in October, after passing through Warsaw, he sailed down the Vistula, meeting Augustus on board the Polish King's royal barge near Thorn. Augustus was nervous; the two monarchs had not met since he had broken his vows to Peter by signing the treaty with Charles, withdrawing from the war and leaving Russia to face Sweden alone. But the Tsar was gracious and good-humored, telling Augustus to forget the past; he under-

stood that Augustus had been forced to do what he had done. Nevertheless, at dinner Peter could not resist an ironic thrust at Augustus' faithlessness. "I always wear the cutlass you gave me," Peter said, "but it seems you do not care for the sword I gave you as I see you are not wearing it." Augustus replied that he prized Peter's gift but that somehow in the haste of his departure from Dresden he had left it behind. "Ah," said Peter, "then let me give you another." Whereupon he handed to Augustus the same sword he had given him before, which had been discovered in Charles' baggage at Poltava.

It was sufficient revenge. On October 9, 1709, Peter and Augustus signed a new treaty of alliance in which the Tsar once again promised to help Augustus gain and hold the throne of Poland, while Augustus again committed himself to fight against Sweden and all the Tsar's enemies. The two agreed that their objective was not to destroy Sweden but simply to force Charles back into Swedish territory and render him powerless to attack their neighbors. Peter's part of the bargain was carried out almost before the treaty was signed. By the end of October, Menshikov's troops had secured the greater part of Poland without a fight. Krassow, the Swedish general, had decided that his small force could not engage the Russian army and had retreated to the Baltic coast, taking refuge in the fortified towns of Stettin and Stralsund in Swedish Pomerania. Stanislaus accompanied him as a refugee, and thereafter for many years the fiction that Stanislaus was King of Poland was maintained only in his presence.

From Thorn, Peter sailed farther down the Vistula to Marienwerder to meet King Frederick I of Prussia, who was alarmed by the emergence of Russia's new power in Northern Europe but was eager to acquire any Swedish territories in Germany which might now be attainable. Peter understood that the King's intention was to collect spoils without doing any fighting, and he behaved coolly. Nevertheless, the meeting was successful: A treaty was signed establishing a defensive alliance between Russia and Prussia, and Menshikov, who was present, was awarded the Prussian Order of the Black Eagle.

In his meeting with Frederick, Peter also arranged a marriage. This was the second foreign marriage Peter was then negotiating for a member of the Russian royal house, and both represented a drastic change in Russian policy. Traditionally, Russian princes married only Russian women, avoiding the contamination of bringing non-Orthodox believers into the royal line. From the time of the Great Embassy, Peter had wanted to change this, but no foreign monarch had seen much profit in marrying a relative into the Muscovite dynasty which was considered a negligible force in European affairs. Since 1707, Peter had been dickering with the minor German House of Wolfenbüttel, hoping to persuade the Duke to permit his daughter

Charlotte to marry the Tsarevich Alexis. Negotiations had dragged, as the Duke was in no hurry to marry a daughter to the son of a tsar on the verge of being toppled from his throne by the King of Sweden. Obstacles to the marriage suddenly disappeared after Poltava, and dynastic links with Moscow now seemed highly attractive. Even before the Duke of Wolfenbüttel could signal his change of mind, a messenger from Vienna arrived with the Emperor's offer of his youngest sister, Archduchess Magdalena, as a potential bride for the Tsarevich. Peter continued to negotiate with the Duke, however, and a marriage contract was drawn up.

The second foreign marriage Peter arranged was between his niece Anne, daughter of his half-brother, Ivan, and the young Duke Frederick William of Courland, a nephew of Frederick of Prussia. As part of the arrangement, Peter agreed that the Russian troops occupying the Duchy of Courland, a small principality south of Riga, would be withdrawn and that Courland would be allowed to remain neutral in future wars. Frederick of Prussia was pleased by this, as it placed a buffer between himself and the Russians on his Baltic frontier. For Peter, Anne's marriage was important. She was the first Russian princess to marry a foreigner in more than 200 years. Her acceptance was a sign of Europe's recognition of Russia's new status and signaled that thereafter Peter and subsequent tsars could use marriageable Russian princesses to intervene in the complicated dynastic affairs of the German states.*

Leaving East Prussia, Peter traveled north through Courland to join Sheremetev, whose troops had completed the siege works around Riga but who had delayed opening the bombardment until the Tsar could be present. On November 9, Peter arrived and on the 13th with his own hands fired the first three shells from the mortars into the city. This act assuaged his festering sense of grievance over his treatment by Riga when he passed through thirteen years before at the start of the Great Embassy. Riga resisted fiercely, however, and before departing the Tsar instructed Sheremetev not to leave his men in the trenches through the rigors of the Baltic winter, but simply to blockade the city and put the troops in winter quarters.

From Riga, Peter continued northeast to St. Petersburg, his "paradise" now secure. He did not stay long, taking time only to issue orders for building a new church in honor of St. Samson, the saint on whose day the Battle of Poltava had been fought, to lay the keel of a new warship to be called *Poltava* and to give instructions for the design and embellishment of public gardens. Then he traveled south to Moscow to celebrate his triumph. He

*Anne's marriage was celebrated a year later in St. Petersburg. Unfortunately, her nineteen-year-old bridegroom drank himself into illness during the celebrations and died on the journey home. Anne remained Duchess of Courland until 1730 when she was summoned to St. Petersburg to become Empress Anne of Russia.

arrived at Kolomenskoe on December 12, but had to wait there for a week until the two Guards regiments which were to participate in the parade could arrive and the final decorations and arrangements could be completed. On December 18, everything was ready and the huge parade was beginning when Peter learned that Catherine had just given birth to a baby girl. Instantly, he postponed the parade and hurried with his friends to see the child, who was named Elizabeth.

Two days later, the victory celebration began. Beneath classical Roman arches trotted squadrons of Russian cavalry and horse-drawn artillery, followed by the foot soldiers of the Guards, the Preobrazhensky Regiment in bottle-green coats, and the Semyonovsky Regiment in blue. Then came Peter, his sword drawn, riding an English horse given to him by Augustus, and wearing the same colonel's uniform he had worn at Poltava. As he passed, women threw flowers. Behind the Russian leaders were 300 captured Swedish battle flags, reversed and trailing in the dirt, then the defeated generals walking in single file, led by Field Marshal Rehnskjold and Count Piper, and finally long columns of soldiers—more than 17,000—marching as prisoners through the snowy Moscow streets. The following day, Peter attended a Te Deum mass in the Assumption Cathedral. The crowd was enormous, and the Tsar stood in the middle of the church pressed on all sides by people.

The formal announcement of victory and the presentation of awards took place with Romodanovsky on the throne. One by one, the two field marshals, Sheremetev and Menshikov, followed by Peter as a colonel promoted to lieutenant general, approached the throne and reported their victories to the seated Mock-Tsar. Sheremetev described and was given credit for the victory at Poltava and Menshikov for the capture of the Swedes at Perevoluchna. Peter described and was given credit only for his victory at Lesnaya. On hearing their reports, Romodanovsky thanked them formally and confirmed their previously announced promotions and rewards. When Rehnskjold, Piper and the other Swedish generals were brought in, they were astonished to see on the throne, not the tall man who had been their host at dinner after the battle and had led them through the streets of Moscow, but a round-shouldered, older man whom they didn't recognize. A row of tall screens on one side of the hall was removed, revealing tables set with silver plate and candelabra. Hundreds of candles were lighted to dispel the winter gloom, and the crowd swarmed to take seats, regardless of rank. Romodanovsky sat on a dais attended by the two Field Marshals, Chancellor Golovkin and the Tsar. The Swedish generals had a separate table. Each time a toast was proposed, the master of ceremonies, standing behind Peter's armchair, fired a pistol shot out the window as a signal to the artillery and musketeers outside. A few minutes later, as glasses were raised, the walls shook with the thunder of the cannon. The day ended with a brilliant fire-

works display which, according to the Danish ambassador, was far superior to one he had witnessed in London which "had cost seventy thousand pounds sterling."

THE SWEDISH PRISONERS—those taken at Poltava and the much larger number captured at Perevoluchna—had finally reached their destination, Moscow, not as conquerors but as part of a triumphal procession led by the Tsar. The senior generals were treated with courtesy; several were allowed to return to Stockholm carrying terms of peace proposed by Peter and an offer to exchange prisoners of war. Young Prince Max of Württemberg was released unconditionally, but died of fever on his way home; Peter gave him a military funeral and sent his body back to his mother in Stuttgart. Those Swedish officers who were willing, Peter enrolled in his own army. Once they had taken the required oath of allegiance, he awarded them the same rank they had held in the Swedish army and gave them command of Russian squadrons, battalions and regiments. None was asked to serve against his own king or compatriots in the Great Northern War. Instead, they were posted to garrisons in the south or east, where they patrolled the frontiers, holding the line against incursions by the Kuban Tatars, the Kazaks and other Asiatic peoples. The rest of the officers were dispersed as internees into all corners of Russia. At first, they were allowed considerable freedom of movement, but some who had been given permission to return on parole to Sweden never came back, and a few who had entered Russian service used their Russian rank to escape. After this abuse of trust, the rest were severely restricted.

As the years passed, these Swedish officers, scattered through all the provinces of the Russian empire, often lived in want, as they had no money. The Swedish common soldiers received small allowances from their government at home, but nothing was sent to the officers. Of the 2,000 officers, only 200 received money from their families; the rest were obliged to learn a trade in order to feed themselves. In time, these former warriors, hitherto knowledgeable only in the art of soldiering, developed an astonishing number of talents. In Siberia alone, a thousand Swedish officers turned themselves into painters, goldsmiths, silversmiths, turners, joiners, tailors, shoemakers, makers of playing cards, snuffboxes and excellent gold and silver brocade. Others became musicians, innkeepers and one a traveling puppeteer. Some who were unable to learn a trade became woodsmen. Still others set up schools, teaching the children of their fellow prisoners (some had summoned their wives from Sweden to join them; others had married Russian women). These children were better educated than most in Russia, learning mathematics, Latin, Dutch and French as well as Swedish. Soon, Russians in the neighborhood were sending their own children to the

foreign schoolmasters. Some of the officers embraced the Russian religion and joined the Orthodox Church, while others held fast to their Protestant religion and built their own churches in the wilderness. Although Siberia generally was a bleak and joyless landscape, the Russian governor, Prince Matthew Gagarin, had a reputation for generosity, and Swedish officers living under his jurisdiction praised his warm and forgiving nature. In time, as the Westernizing of the state administration developed, Peter needed skilled administrators and bureaucrats. A number of former Swedish officers were offered positions and came to St. Petersburg to work in the newly established Colleges (Ministries) of War, the Admiralty, Justice, Finance and Mines.

The common Swedish soldiers, over 15,000 of them, were treated more severely. They, too, were offered a chance to enter Peter's service (an entire regiment of 600 Swedish dragoons served under a German colonel against the Kuban Tatars). But many refused and were sent to do forced labor. Some worked in the mines in the Urals and others were employed in the dockyards or on the fortifications of St. Petersburg. Although records were kept of the whereabouts of interned officers, none were kept of the common soldiers. Many were in towns or on the estates of the Russian nobility, and married and settled down to life in the Russian church and Russian society. When peace finally came in 1721, twelve years after Poltava, and the Swedish prisoners were allowed to go home, only about 5,000 of Charles' proud grenadiers, the remnant of an army of 40,000, could be found to return to the towns and villages of their native Sweden.

IN THE SPRING OF 1710, Peter plucked the military fruits of Poltava. Russian armies, unopposed by any Swedish army in the field, swept irresistibly through Sweden's Baltic provinces. While Sheremetev with 30,000 men besieged Riga to the south, Peter sent General-Admiral Fedor Apraxin, newly made a Count and a Privy Councilor, with 18,000 men to besiege Vyborg in the north. This town at the head of the Karelian Isthmus, seventy-five miles northwest of St. Petersburg, was an important fortress and an assembly point for Swedish offensive threats against St. Petersburg. A Russian attempt on Vyborg from the land side in 1706 had failed, but now there was something new in Peter's favor. His growing Baltic fleet, consisting of frigates and numerous galleys, the latter craft propelled by a combination of sails and oars and ideally suited for maneuvering in the rocky waters of the Finnish coast, was available both to transport men and supplies and to keep Swedish naval squadrons at bay. As soon as the Neva was clear of ice, in April, Russian ships sailed from Kronstadt with Vice Admiral Cruys in command and Peter, in his new rank as rear admiral, as Cruys' deputy. The ships made their way through the ice floes in the Gulf of Finland and

arrived off Vyborg to find Apraxin's besieging army cold and hungry. The fleet brought provisions and reinforcements, raising Apraxin's strength to 23,000. Peter, after studying the siege plans and instructing Apraxin to take the town no matter what the cost, returned to St. Petersburg in a small vessel, narrowly escaping capture by a Swedish warship. During the following month, in St. Petersburg, the Tsar again was ill. At the beginning of June, learning that the siege of Vyborg was nearing an end, he wrote to Apraxin, "I hear that you intend making the assault today. If this has already been ordered, God aid you. But if it is not fixed for today, then put it off till Sunday or Monday when I can get there, for this is the last day that I take medicine and tomorrow I shall be free."

On June 13, 1710, Vyborg with its garrison of 154 officers and 3,726 men fell to Apraxin. Peter arrived just in time to witness the surrender. The subsequent clearing and permanent occupation of Kexholm and all the Karelian Isthmus provided a northern buffer one hundred miles thick for St. Petersburg, meaning that Peter's "holy paradise" would no longer be subjected to surprise attacks by Swedish armies from the north. Relieved and happy, the Tsar wrote from Vyborg to Sheremetev, "And thus through the taking of this town, final safety has been gained for St. Petersburg." To Catherine, he wrote, "Now, by God's help, it is a strong cushion for St. Petersburg."*

All the Swedish citadels on the southern coast of the upper Baltic surrendered during the summer of 1710. On July 10, the great city of Riga with its garrison of 4,500 fell to Sheremetev after an eight-month siege. The city had been pounded by 8,000 Russian mortar shells and the garrison was decimated by hunger and disease which Peter called "the wrath of God." Although Peter's agreement with Augustus had assigned Livonia and Riga to Poland, Peter now decided that the city and the province had been bought with Russian blood at Poltava at a time when Augustus was no longer King of Poland and a Russian ally. The Tsar therefore determined to

* Through the years, Russians have continued to try to protect St. Petersburg, now Leningrad, from threats from this direction. For 109 years, while Finland was an Imperial Russian grand duchy, the threat was non-existent, but in 1918, Finland gained independence and Vyborg and Karelia were attached to the new state. The Soviet government felt keenly the naked exposure of Leningrad, its second largest city, now only twenty miles from the Finnish frontier, and desired, as Peter had, a larger "cushion." In 1940, the Soviet Union attacked Finland primarily to regain this buffer territory. At first, the "Winter War" went badly for the Soviets. The Finns fought gallantly and attracted the admiration of the West. The Soviet army, its officer corps riddled by Stalin's purges, was stopped in its tracks. Eventually, sheer weight of numbers had an effect and the Red Army ground its way through the Finnish Mannerheim Line. The peace which followed established a new frontier in approximately the same place as in Peter's day. This extra buffer helped save Leningrad during the 900-day siege of the city between 1941 and 1943 by the Nazi and Finnish armies.

keep them. Of these territories, he was to become a tolerant overlord. Although requiring an oath of allegiance from the Baltic nobility and Riga merchants, he promised to respect all of their former privileges, rights, customs, possessions and immunities. The churches were to remain Lutheran, and German was to remain the language of provincial administration. For many years, the essential problem in these provinces was simple survival, the war having reduced the land and towns to a semi-desert, but the nobility and gentry were not displeased to exchange a Swedish master for a Russian one.

Three months after the fall of Riga, Reval—the last of the fruits of Poltava—capitulated. Peter was overjoyed. "The last town has surrendered and Livonia and Estonia are entirely cleared of the enemy," he wrote. "In a word, the enemy does not now possess a single town on the left side of the Baltic, not even an inch of land. It is now incumbent upon us to pray the Lord God for a good peace."

Part Four

ON THE
EUROPEAN
STAGE

40

THE SULTAN'S WORLD

I T WAS extraordinarily fortunate for Peter that while he was tsar Russia never had to fight two enemies simultaneously. Poland, Moscow's traditional enemy, had been transformed into an ally by the treaty of 1686. The war with Turkey, reignited by Peter's two campaigns to seize Azov, had been suspended by a thirty-year armistice signed in August 1700, after which Peter could join Poland and Denmark in an attack on Sweden. Through the perilous years before Poltava when Charles XII seemed invincible and a Turkish-Swedish alliance would have sealed Russia's fate, the Sultan kept the peace. Only after Poltava, when the Swedish army had disintegrated into a column of prisoners, did the Ottoman Empire ponderously decide to make war on the Tsar. Even then, because of over-optimism on Peter's part and betrayal by one of his new Balkan Christian allies, this campaign had near-catastrophic results for Russia.

THE OTTOMAN EMPIRE, every hectare conquered by the sword, stretched over three continents. The sweep of the sultan's rule was greater than that of a Roman emperor. It embraced the whole of southeastern Europe. It stretched westward across the entire coast of Africa to the Moroccan border. It touched the shores of the Caspian Sea, the Red Sea and the Persian Gulf. The Black Sea was an Ottoman lake. Great cities as distant and as different as Algiers, Cairo, Bagdad, Jerusalem, Athens and Belgrade were ruled from Constantinople. Twenty-one modern nations have been created from the former territories of the Ottoman Empire.*

Within this immense sweep of mountains, deserts, rivers and fertile

---

* Turkey, Greece, Bulgaria, Romania, Yugoslavia, Hungary, Albania, Syria, Lebanon, Jordan, Israel, Aden, Kuwait, Egypt, Sudan, Libya, Iraq, Yemen, Tunisia, Algeria, Cyprus, not to mention huge stretches of the Soviet Ukraine, Crimea, the Caucasus, Armenia and Georgia.

valleys lived some twenty-five million people, a huge number in that day, almost twice the population of any European empire or kingdom except France. The empire was Moslem; it surrounded, in the heart of Arabia, the holy cities of Mecca and Medina, whose sacred shrines it was the sultan's personal responsibility as caliph to protect. Among the Moslem peoples, the Ottoman Turks were the dominant minority, but there were also Arabs, Kurds, Crimean Tatars, Circassians, Bosnians and Albanians. The sultan also ruled over millions of Christian subjects: Greeks, Serbs, Hungarians, Bulgars, Walachians and Moldavians.

Almost necessarily, the political bonds that tied such a polyglot of peoples and religions were flexible and loose. From Constantinople, the sultan ruled, but his rule was administered locally by a bevy of pashas, princes, viceroys, beys, khans and emirs, some of them autonomous in all but name. The Christian princes of the rich Balkan provinces of Walachia and Moldavia, lying between the Danube and the Carpathians (present-day Romania), were personally chosen by the sultan, but once in office, their allegiance was manifested solely by payment of annual tribute. Every year, wagons loaded with gold and other tax monies arrived from the north before the gates of the Sublime Porte in Constantinople. The Tatar Khan of the Crimea ruled his peninsula as an absolute lord from his capital, Bakhchisarai, owing only the duty to bring himself and 20,000 to 30,000 horsemen when summoned to the sultan's wars. Twelve hundred miles to the west, the Barbary states of Tripoli, Tunis and Algeria obliged their Ottoman master in war by diverting their fast corsair ships, normally engaged in lucrative peacetime piracy against all nations, to attack the fleets of the great Christian naval powers, Venice and Genoa.

In the sixteenth century, under Sultan Suleiman the Magnificent (1520–1566), the Ottoman Empire had reached its zenith. This was a golden age for Constantinople, when great wealth poured into the city, a dozen beautiful imperial mosques were built and sparkling pleasure palaces sprang up along the shores of the Bosphorus and the Sea of Marmara. Suleiman himself was a patron of literature, the arts and science; he loved music, poetry and philosophy. But first he was a warrior. Along the great military road that led north to Belgrade, Buda and finally Vienna, the Ottoman armies marched, leaving mosques and minarets scattered across the Balkan hills and valleys. Outraged by these visible signs of Moslem occupation, the Christian kingdoms of the West saw the Turks as oppressors of the Greeks and other Christian peoples of the East. But the Ottoman Empire, more generous in this respect than most Western kingdoms, tolerated religions other than its own. The Sultan formally recognized the Greek Church and acknowledged the jurisdiction of its patriarch and archbishops, and Orthodox monasteries retained their property. The Turks preferred to rule through local political

institutions, and in return for tribute, Christian provinces were permitted their own systems of government, rank and class structure.

In a curious way, the Ottoman Turks paid the highest compliment to their Christian subjects: They recruited them to fill the ranks of their own central imperial administration and to form the special regiments of the sultan's guard, the Janissaries. In the subject Balkan provinces, conversion to the Moslem faith was the key to success for bright young Christian boys who were sent—at first by force—to Moslem schools, and given a rigorous education designed to purge every memory of mother, father, brothers and sisters, and to eradicate every trace of the Christian religion. Their only allegiance was to the Koran and the sultan, and they became a corps of fearless and devoted followers, available for any service. The most intelligent might serve as pages in the palace or apprentices in the civil service and might rise to the very top of the imperial administration. Many distinguished men followed this path, and the mighty Ottoman Empire was often administered by men who had been born as Christians.

But most of these young men entered the regiments of guards, the Janissaries. As boys, and later as soldiers, they lived all their lives in barracks, forbidden to marry or have children, so that their total devotion might be given to the sultan. In status, the Janissary was a slave; the barracks was his home, the Koran his religion, the sultan his master and fighting his profession. In the early centuries of the empire, Janissaries were like an order of fanatical military monks, pledged to fight the enemies of Allah and the sultan. They provided the Ottoman armies with a steely corps of superbly trained and dedicated infantry, superior to any military force in Europe until the advent of the new French army of Louis XIV.

A company of Janissaries made a colorful sight. They wore red caps embroidered in gold, white blouses, baggy pantaloons and yellow boots. The Janissaries of the sultan's personal guard were distinguished by their red boots. In time of peace, they carried only a scimitar, but when he went into battle, each Janissary was allowed to arm himself with the weapons he liked best: javelin, sword, arquebus or, later, a musket.

In the fourteenth century, there were 12,000 Janissaries; in 1653, a count produced 51,647. As the centuries passed, older Janissaries were allowed to retire, marry and have families. Moslem as well as Christian families begged to have their sons enrolled in the corps and, in time, the privilege was restricted to the children or relations of former Janissaries. The Janissaries became a free-born, privileged, hereditary caste. In peacetime, they took up trades, like the Streltsy. Ultimately, as with regiments of imperial guards in many countries, they became a greater danger to their own master than to his enemies. Grand viziers and even sultans rose and fell at the whim of the Janissaries until finally, in 1826, they were abolished.

APPROACHED FROM THE SEA, the historic city of Constantinople seemed like an immense, flowered pleasure garden. Rising from the blue waters of the Bosphorus and the Sea of Marmara, its domes and minarets set amidst dark-green cypresses and flowering fruit trees, it was one of the most beautiful cities in the world. Today, as Istanbul, it is vividly alive, but is no longer a capital; the republican government of Turkey, to cleanse itself of the city's sins, has removed itself to the austere, modern purity of Ankara in the center of the Anatolian plateau. But in the seventeenth century, Constantinople was the capital of the Moslem world, the military, administrative, commercial and cultural hub of the mighty Ottoman Empire. With a population of 700,000, larger than any city in Europe, blending many races and religions, it was studded with great mosques, colleges, libraries, hospitals and public baths. Its bazaars and wharves were piled with merchandise from every corner of the world. Its parks and gardens were filled with flowers and fruit trees. In the spring, wild roses bloomed and nightingales sang in the hedgerows.

Overlooking the great city from a high point of land where the Golden Horn separates the Bosphorus from the Sea of Marmara was the Topkapi Palace, the seraglio of the sultan. Here, behind high walls, lay dozens of buildings: barracks, kitchens, mosques, gardens with bubbling fountains and long avenues of cypress trees bordered with beds of roses and tulips. A city within a city, existing entirely for the pleasure of a single man, the Seraglio made huge demands on the outside world. Every year, from all provinces of the empire came shiploads and cartloads of rice, sugar, peas, lentils, pepper, coffee, macaroons, dates, saffron, honey, salt, plums in lemon juice, vinegar, watermelons and, in one year alone, 780 cartloads of snow. Inside this city 5,000 servants fulfilled the sultan's needs. The sultan's table was presided over by the Chief Attendant of the Napkin, assisted by the Senior of the Tray Servers, the Fruit Server, the Pickle Server and the Sherbet Maker, the Chief of the Coffee Makers and the Water Server (as Moslems, the sultans were teetotalers). There were also the Chief Turban Folder and the Assistants to the Chief Turban Folder, the Keeper of the Sultan's Robes, the Chiefs of the Laundrymen and Bathmen. The Chief of the Barbers had on his staff a Manicurist who pared the sultan's nails every Thursday. Besides these, there were pipe lighters, door openers, musicians, gardeners, grooms and even a collection of dwarfs and mutes whom the sultan used as messengers, the latter being especially useful for attending the sultan during confidential moments.

Hidden though it was from the eyes of his subjects, the Seraglio was in fact but the outer shell of an inner, even more closely guarded private world, the harem. The Arabic word "harim" means "forbidden," and the sultan's harem was forbidden to all but the sultan himself, his guests, the women who lived there and the eunuchs who guarded them. It could be approached

from the Seraglio only by passing down a single passage through four locked doors, two of iron and two of bronze. Each door was guarded day and night by eunuchs who kept the only keys. At the end of this passage lay an intricate maze of luxurious apartments, corridors, staircases, secret doors, courtyards, gardens and pools. Because many rooms were surrounded on all sides by other rooms, light filtered down through stained glass in skylight domes and windows. In the royal apartments, the walls and ceilings were covered with intricate patterns in blue and green Nicean tiles. The floors were spread with glowing Turkish carpets and low sofas on which the inhabitants could sit cross-legged while sipping Turkish coffee and eating fresh fruit. In rooms where the sultan might wish to speak confidentially to an advisor, there were fountains so that the sound of running water would keep the wrong ears from hearing what was said.

The harem was a closed world of veils, gossip, intrigue and—at any moment of the sultan's choosing—sex. But it was also a world rigidly ruled by protocol and rank. Until the time of Suleiman the Magnificent, sultans had married; the Moslem religion permitted them four wives. But Suleiman's wife, a red-haired Russian woman named Roxelana, had interfered so much in matters of state that thereafter Ottoman sultans did not marry. The sultan's mother, therefore, became the ruler of the harem. The Turks believed that "heaven lay under the feet of the mother," that no matter how many wives or concubines a man might take, he had only one mother, who held a unique place in his life. Sometimes, when the sultan was young or weak, his mother issued orders in his name directly to the grand vizier. Beneath the sultan's mother ranked the mother of the heir apparent if there was one, and then the other women who had borne the sultan's male children. Finally, there came the odalisques, or concubines. All of these women, technically at least, were slaves, and, as Moslem women could not be enslaved, it followed that all the harem women were foreigners: Russians, Circassians, Venetians, Greeks. From the end of the sixteenth century, most came from the Caucasus, because the blue-eyed women of that region were renowned for beauty. Once she passed through the harem doors, a woman remained for life. There were no exceptions.

On entering the harem, usually at the age of ten or eleven, a girl was rigorously schooled in feminine charm by experienced older women. Fully trained, the hopeful girl awaited the moment of preliminary approval when the sultan tossed a handkerchief at her feet and she became "gozde" ("in the eye"). Not every gozde reached the supreme moment when she was summoned and became "ikbal" ("bedded"), but those who did received their own apartments, servants, jewels, dresses and an allowance. As all the women in the harem were totally dependent on how well the sultan was pleased, all were eager for opportunities to reach his bed and, once in it, desperate to please. So much so that several sultans, surfeited with endless

days and nights of passion supplied by platoons of eager, adoring women, went, quite simply, insane.*

Into this private world of women, no male except the sultan was allowed to penetrate. So exclusive was the harem that, according to a Turkish saying, if the sun had not been female, even she would never have been allowed to enter. To ensure this exclusivity was the duty of the harem eunuchs. Originally, the eunuchs had been white, mostly brought, like the harem women, from the Caucasus. But by the beginning of the seventeenth century, the 200 eunuchs who guarded the harem were black. Most were bought as children in the annual slave caravans from the upper Nile and were castrated near Aswan as they came down the river. Ironically, as the Moslem religion forbade castration, the deed was performed by Copts, a Christian sect living in the region. These mutilated children were then presented as gifts to the sultan from his governors and viceroys in lower Egypt.

In theory, the eunuchs were slaves, and servants of the slaves who were the harem women. But the eunuchs often gained great power because of their proximity to the sultan. In the ceaseless round of court intrigue, the alliance of women and eunuchs could heavily influence the flow of favors and public positions. Eventually, the Chief of the Black Eunuchs, known as the Aga of the Women or the Aga of the House of Felicity, often played a great role in affairs of state, becoming tyrant of the whole Seraglio and sometimes ranking third in power in the empire, after the sultan and the grand vizier. The Aga of the Black Eunuchs always lived grandly, having many privileges and a large staff which included a number of his own slave girls, whose duties, it must be said, are difficult to imagine.

Within the harem, as everywhere in his empire, the sultan was treated as a demi-god. No woman was allowed to meet him unsummoned. At his approach, those in his path had to hide quickly; one sultan, in order to give warning of his approach, wore slippers with silver soles to make a clatter on the stone passageways. When he wanted to bathe, the sultan went first to his undressing room, where his clothes were removed by young female slaves; next to a massage room, where his body was oiled and rubbed; then to a bath chamber with a marble tub, fountains of hot and cold running water and gold faucets, where, if he desired, his body was washed, an assignment usually given to rather elderly women; finally, he would be dressed and perfumed, again by younger females. When the sultan wished festivity, he repaired to his audience hall, a large, blue-tiled chamber spread with

---

* Some of the Ottoman sultans kept boys as well as women in their harems. But while it is true that certain Turkish sultans had homosexual tastes, as did some Christian kings, most Ottoman sultans preferred women. The harem was overwhelmingly a reservoir of females.

crimson carpets. There, he sat on his throne while his mother and his sisters and daughters sat on sofas, and the ikbal and godze sat on cushions on the floor in front of him. If there were dancing girls and music, the court musicians might be required to attend, but on these occasions they were carefully blindfolded to protect the harem women from their eyes. Later, a balcony for the musicians was built above the audience hall, with walls so high that only the music could pass over.

It was in this audience hall that the sultan occasionally received a foreign ambassador. At these moments, he sat on his marble throne, wearing a long robe of golden cloth trimmed with sable and a white turban with a black-and-white aigrette and a giant emerald. Always, he sat with his face in profile, so that no infidel might gaze on the full countenance of the Shadow of God on Earth.

THROUGHOUT ITS HISTORY, the Ottoman Empire remained a warrior state. All power lay in the hands of the sultan. When the sultan was strong and gifted, the empire prospered. When he was weak, the empire decayed. Not surprisingly, life in the harem, surrounded by adoring women and conniving eunuchs, took much of the fiber out of a race which had begun with warrior conquerors. A second circumstance tended, as the history of the empire unfolded, to degrade the quality of ruling sultans. Ironically, it had begun with an act of mercy. Until the sixteenth century, it had been an Ottoman tradition that, of the sultan's many sons, the one who succeeded to the throne would immediately have all his brothers strangled, to remove any threat to his position. Sultan Murad III, who ruled from 1574 to 1595, sired more than a hundred children and was survived by twenty sons. The eldest, succeeding to the throne as Mehmet III, strangled his nineteen brothers and also, to be certain of liquidating any possible competition, murdered seven of his father's concubines who happened to be pregnant. In 1603, however, the new sultan, Ahmed I, ended this terrible rite by refusing to strangle his brothers. Instead, to keep them innocuous, he walled them up in a special pavilion called "The Cage," where they lived cut off from all communication with the outside world. Henceforth, all Ottoman princes idled away their lives in this place, in the company of eunuchs and of concubines, who, to prevent the birth of children, were required to be beyond the age of childbearing. If, by mistake, a child was born, the infant was not allowed to complicate the royal genealogical tree by remaining alive. Thus, when a sultan died or was deposed without a son, a brother would be summoned from seclusion and proclaimed the new Shadow of God on Earth. Amidst this collection of ignorant, unaggressive royal males, neither the Janissaries nor the grand viziers could often find a man with the intellectual development or political knowledge to rule an empire.

At all times, but especially when the sultan was weak, the Ottoman Empire was actually administered by the grand vizier. From a vast building erected in 1654 near the Seraglio and known to Europeans as the Sublime Porte, the grand vizier controlled the administration and armed forces of the empire—everything, in fact, except the Seraglio. In theory, the grand vizier was the servant of the sultan. His appointment was symbolized by his acceptance from the sultan's hands of a signet ring; his dismissal was signaled by the recall of this imperial seal. In practice, however, the grand vizier ruled the empire. In peacetime, he was the chief executive and chief magistrate. In war, he commanded the Ottoman army in the field, assisted by the Janissary Aga and the Captain Pasha of the Navy. He presided over his council, the Divan, in a large, domed audience chamber whose walls were adorned with mosaics, arabesques and blue-and-gold hangings. Here, on a bench circling the perimeter, sat the great officers of the Porte, the colors of their fur-trimmed, wide-sleeved robes—green, violet, silver, blue, yellow—denoting their rank. In the center sat the grand vizier, wearing a robe of white satin and a turban bound with gold.

The office of grand vizier carried enormous power—on occasion, grand viziers could arrange the fall of sultans—but it also entailed enormous risks and offered little prospect of a peaceful death. Defeat in war was blamed on the grand vizier and was followed inevitably by dismissal, exile and, not infrequently, strangulation. Only a master of intrigue could attain the office. Between 1683 and 1702, twelve grand viziers came and went from the Divan and the Sublime Porte.

Nevertheless, earlier in the seventeenth century, it had been the grand viziers who saved the empire while the sultans sat in their harems indulging their tastes and fantasies.* Outside, Ottoman power had declined so greatly that Venetian ships cruised off the Dardanelles while Cossack "seagull" corsairs from the Dnieper raided the western entrance of the Bosphorus. The empire, bubbling with corruption and dissolving into anarchy, was rescued by the skill of what amounted to a dynasty of grand viziers: father, son and brother-in-law.

In 1656, with the empire near collapse, the harem hierarchy reluctantly named as grand vizier a stern, seventy-one-year-old Albanian, Memmed Korpulu, who solved problems ruthlessly: Between 50,000 and 60,000

---

* One sultan, Ibrahim the Mad, encased his beard in a network of diamonds and passed his days tossing gold coins to the fish in the Bosphorus. He wanted to see and feel nothing but fur, and levied a special tax for the import of sables from Russia so that he might cover the walls of his apartments with these precious furs. Deciding that the bigger a woman was, the more enjoyable she would be, he had his agents search the empire for the fattest woman they could find. They brought him an enormous Armenian woman, who so fascinated the Sultan that he heaped riches and honors upon her and finally made her Governor General of Damascus.

executions purged the Ottoman administration of graft and corruption. By the time he died, five years later, the decline in the empire's fortunes had been halted. Under his son Ahmed Korpulu and later his brother-in-law, Kara Mustapha, a brief revival of Ottoman power occurred. The fleets and armies of the Christian powers, Austria, Venice and Poland, were driven back. In 1683, responding to a Hungarian appeal for aid against the Emperor Leopold, Kara Mustapha decided to capture Vienna. An army of over 200,000 men under a banner with horsehair plumes, commanded by Kara Mustapha himself, marched up the Danube, conquered all of Hungary and, for the second time in Ottoman history, stood before the walls of Vienna. Through the summer of 1683, Europe watched anxiously. Regiments of soldiers from the German states enlisted under the Hapsburg Emperor's banner to fight the Turks. Even Louis XIV, normally the enemy of the Hapsburgs and secret ally of the Turks, could not afford not to help save the great Christian city. On September 12, 1683, an allied relieving army fell on the Turkish siege lines from the rear and drove the Turks in flight down the Danube. By order of the Sultan, Kara Mustapha was strangled.

The years that followed the repulse from Vienna were disastrous for the Turks. Buda and then Belgrade fell, and the Austrian armies even neared Adrianople. The great Venetian admiral Francesco Morosini captured the Peloponnesus, advanced across the isthmus of Corinth and laid siege to Athens. Unfortunately, during his bombardment one of his shells hit the Parthenon, which the Turks were using as a powder magazine. On September 26, 1687, the building, then still largely intact, blew up and was reduced to its present state.

In 1703, Sultan Mustapha II was deposed by the Janissaries in favor of his thirty-year-old brother Ahmed III, who came to the throne from the seclusion of "The Cage" and ruled for twenty-seven years. An esthete, unstable, morose, greatly influenced by his mother, he liked women, poetry and painting flowers. He had a passion for architecture and built beautiful mosques to please his people and beautiful gardens to please himself. Along the Golden Horn, he erected a series of luxurious pleasure pavilions, some in Chinese design, some in French, where he would sit in the shade of a tree and, in the company of his favorite concubines, listen to poetry. Ahmed loved theatrical entertainment; in winter, elaborate Chinese shadow plays were performed, followed by a distribution of jewels, sweets and robes of honor. In summer, elaborate mock sea battles and firework displays were staged. Tulipmania possessed his court. In the spring evenings, in gardens hung with lanterns or drenched with moonlight, the Sultan and his court, accompanied by musicians, would stroll, stepping carefully over hundreds of turtles that crawled among the tulips and through the grass with lighted candles on their backs.

In this secluded, scented environment, Ahmed III lived out the same

years which saw the active, turbulent reign of Peter of Russia. Although Ahmed's reign outlasted Peter's, its end had a distinctly Ottoman flavor. In 1730, with the empire once again in turmoil, Ahmed thought to appease his enemies by ordering the current grand vizier, who happened also to be his brother-in-law, strangled and his body given to the mob. This only temporarily postponed Ahmed's own fate. Soon after, he was deposed and succeeded by his nephew, who had him poisoned.

41

LIBERATOR OF THE BALKAN CHRISTIANS

IN THE SECOND HALF of the seventeenth century, a new and quite un-expected danger appeared in the north to threaten the Ottoman Empire. Muscovite Russia waxed in power and portended menace for the throne of the Shadow of God. Traditionally, the Turks had regarded the Muscovites with disdain; it was not they, but their vassals the Crimean Tatars who dealt with the Muscovites. Indeed, such was the order of ascendancy that the Crimean Tatars, the sultan's tributaries, themselves received tribute from the tsar. For the Crimean khans, Muscovy was a harvest ground for slaves and cattle taken in the great annual Tatar raids into the Ukraine and southern Russia.

That the Ottoman Empire had been able to display this indifference toward the Russian tsardom was due to Moscow's involvement with its other enemies. The two most numerous Christian people of Eastern Europe, the Orthodox Russians and the Catholic Poles, had been fighting each other for generations. But in 1667 a change disagreeable to the sultan occurred: Russians and Poles resolved their differences at least temporarily to unite against the Turks. And it was in 1686 that King Jan Sobieski of Poland, anxious to fight the Ottoman Empire, surrendered temporarily (the transfer became permanent) the city of Kiev to the Regent Sophia in return for Russian adherence to a Polish-Austrian-Venetian alliance against Turkey.

Prodded by her allies, Russia finally initiated military action in this war. The offensives launched against the Crimean Tatars in 1677 and 1689, both commanded by Sophia's favorite, Vasily Golitsyn, ended in failure. In Constantinople, the insignificance of Russian military power seemed further confirmed, while in Moscow, Golitsyn's failures precipitated a shift in power. The revelation of Sophia's weakness led to the Regent's downfall and the assumption of power by the Naryshkin party in Peter's name. Thereafter, while the youthful Tsar was drilling soldiers, building boats and visiting Archangel, relations between Russia and Turkey remained quiet. Technically, they were still at war but in fact there was no fighting.

As Peter came of age, he discovered in the anti-Turkish alliance and the never ended war the opportunity to realize a personal dream: to break through to the south and sail a fleet on the Black Sea. The two summer campaigns of 1695 and 1696 against Azov were the first Russian assaults not on Tatars but on a Turkish fortress manned by Turkish soldiers. Peter's success in his second attempt alarmed the sultan's government: Russian warships seemed more dangerous than Russian soldiers. Now, the Tsar had cleared the mouth of the Don and was massing a fleet at Tagonrog and Azov, but—fortunately, from the Turkish point of view—Ottoman fortresses still commanded the Strait of Kerch and prevented these ships from sailing on the Black Sea.

Officially, of course, it was to reignite the war, to invigorate his allies and perhaps to find new ones that Peter set out on his Great Embassy in 1697. As we have seen, he failed in this purpose, and once his allies signed a treaty of peace at Carlowitz, Russia, a minor combatant, was left to make the best peace it could with the Turks. Denied the fruits for which he hungered, the Tsar never forgave the Austrians for deserting him at Carlowitz. "They take no more notice of me than they do a dog," he complained bitterly. "I shall never forget what they have done to me. I feel it and am come off with empty pockets."

Despite the incompleteness of Peter's gains, Azov was to have far-reaching consequences. The first Russian victory over the Turks, it demonstrated at least a local and temporary superiority over a power which the Muscovites had always before treated with circumspection. It was fortunate for Russia that no great sultan or grand vizier like those of the Ottoman past rose up in Peter's day. The vast power to Russia's south was somnolent, but it remained colossal in size, still possessed of immense resources, and, when provoked, could bring crushing weight to bear on its neighbors.

It was this lethargic but still formidable giant that Peter challenged in 1711 with his march into the Balkans.

By 1710, the thirty-year truce with Turkey, signed on the eve of the Great Northern War, had lasted for ten years; even when Peter had seemed most vulnerable, the truce had been maintained. For this good fortune, the man most responsible was Peter's—and Russia's—first permanent ambassador at Constantinople, Peter Tolstoy. A portrait of Tolstoy depicts a man with shrewd blue eyes, bushy black eyebrows, a high forehead and a gray Western wig. His clean-shaven face is serene. Everything about the man radiates vigor, tenacity, self-confidence and success.

Tolstoy had needed these qualities plus a great deal of luck to skirt the pitfalls already encountered in a long and remarkable career. Born in 1645 into a landed family of the lesser aristocracy, he had initially favored the

Miloslavskys and ardently supported the Regent Sophia in her climactic confrontation with the young Tsar Peter in 1689, but had switched to the winning side just before the end. Peter, not fully trusting this new adherent, sent him to govern the distant northern province of Ustiug. There, as governor, it fell to Tolstoy to entertain the Tsar during the summers of 1693 and 1694 when he was traveling to and from Archangel. Tolstoy made a good impression, which he reinforced by serving capably in the second campaign against Azov. Finally, in 1696, he established himself in Peter's favor when, although fifty-two and the father of a family, he volunteered to travel to Venice to study shipbuilding and navigation. He learned something of these trades and cruised the Mediterranean, but a more important consequence was that he learned to speak Italian and to understand something of Western life and culture, both useful in his subsequent career as diplomat. Shrewd, cool-headed, opportunistic, a man who by Russian standards was cultured and sophisticated, Tolstoy became immensely useful to the Tsar. Recognizing his qualities, Peter entrusted Tolstoy with two of the most difficult assignments of his reign: the long mission to Constantinople and, later, the luring back to Russia of the Tsarevich Alexis. Prizing this talented and useful servant, Peter gave Tolstoy the hereditary rank of count, but he never completely forgot the older man's earlier opposition. Once, when this dark thought flitted across his mind, the Tsar took the older man's head between his two powerful hands and said, "Oh, head, head! You would not be on your shoulders now if you were not so wise."

Tolstoy's character and experience suited him admirably for his assignment as Russia's first resident ambassador at the sultan's court. His instructions, when he arrived near the end of 1701, were those of diplomats since time immemorial: to preserve the truce between Turkey and Russia, to do what he could to stir up trouble between Turkey and Austria, to gather and forward to Moscow information on the foreign relations and internal politics of the Ottoman Empire, to pass along his judgments of the men in power and those likely to come to power, and to learn what he could about Turkish military and naval tactics and the strength of Turkish fortresses on the Black Sea. It was a challenging assignment, made all the more so because the Turks did not really want a Russian ambassador in Constantinople. Other foreign ambassadors were stationed in the Ottoman capital to facilitate commerce, but trade did not flow between Russia and Turkey, and the Turks, accordingly, were suspicious of Tolstoy's presence.

At first, he was placed under something close to house arrest. As he wrote to Peter:

> My residence is not pleasant to them because their domestic enemies, the Greeks, are our co-religionists. The Turks are of the opinion that, by living among them, I shall excite the Greeks to rise

against the Mohammedans, and therefore the Greeks have been forbidden to have intercourse with me. The Christians have been so frightened that none of them dare even pass by the house in which I live. . . . Nothing terrifies them so much as your fleet. The rumor has circulated that seventy great ships have been built at Archangel and they think that when it is necessary these ships will come around from the Atlantic Ocean into the Mediterranean Sea and will sail up to Constantinople.

Despite these hardships, Tolstoy had considerable success. He managed to build up an intelligence network based partly on the organization of the Orthodox Church within the Ottoman Empire (Dositheus, the Patriarch of Jerusalem, was especially helpful) and partly with the assistance of the Dutch, who had much experience in the maze of Turkish court politics.

During Tolstoy's years, this maze was particularly complex. Grand vizier followed grand vizier. Some were more tolerant of Tolstoy than others, but his position was never comfortable. In 1702, the Grand Vizier Daltaban Mustapha came to power, determined to back the Tatar Khan in his desire to renew the war with Russia. By generous bribery, Tolstoy managed to bring the Vizier's scheme to the attention of the Sultan's mother, and Daltaban was deposed and beheaded. The next vizier handled Tolstoy more carefully, but two Janissaries still guarded his door and watched his movements.

In 1703, when Sultan Mustapha II was replaced by his brother Ahmed III, Tolstoy at first was allowed to go where he pleased; then came a new grand vizier and again he was restricted. Despairingly, the ambassador wrote to Moscow: "The new Vizier is very ill-disposed to me, and my wretched situation, my troubles and fears are worse than before. Again no one dares to come to me and I can go nowhere. It is with great trouble that I can send this letter. This is the sixth Vizier in my time and he is the worst of all." The sixth vizier was soon replaced by the seventh, but Tolstoy's situation remained bleak.

In part, the ill-treatment of Tolstoy was due to the complaints of a Turkish envoy to Moscow about *his* treatment by the Russians. The Turkish ambassador sent to announce the accession of Ahmed III had been politely received, but had been made to wait a long time before seeing the Tsar. This delay was deliberate: Peter had wanted to gain time and impress on the envoy the power of the Russian Tsar. In addition, Peter fended the envoy away from what he most wanted to see: the Russian fleet base at Azov and its building site at Voronezh. Peter wrote to the governor of Azov, "Do not go near Voronezh. Be as slow on the road as possible, the longer, the better. Do not allow him to see Azov on any account."

All of this rebounded on Tolstoy's head when the envoy sent a letter

home describing his treatment in Russia. "What he [his counterpart, the Turkish ambassador in Russia] has written, I do not know," said Tolstoy, "but they ill-treat me in a frightful way, and they shut us all up in our house and allow no one either to go out or to come in. We have been some days almost without food because they let no one out to buy bread, and it was with difficulty that I succeeded by great presents in getting permission for one man to go out to buy victuals."

Tolstoy also worried that one of his own staff would convert to Mohammedanism and then betray his intelligence service. Eventually, such a case did occur, and the Ambassador dealt with it summarily:

I am in great fear of my attendants [he wrote to Moscow]. As I have been living here for three years they have gotten acquainted with the Turks and have learned the Turkish language. Since we are now in great discomfort, I fear that they will become impatient on account of the imprisonment and will waver in their faith because the Mohammedan faith is very attractive to thoughtless people. If any Judas declare himself, he will do great harm because my people have seen with which of the Christians I have been intimate and who serves the Tsar . . . and if any one turns renegade and tells the Turks who has been working for the Tsar, not only will our friends suffer, but there will be harm to all Christians. I follow this with great attention and do not know how God will turn it. I have had one affair like this. A young secretary, Timothy, having got acquainted with the Turks, thought of turning Mohammedan. God helped me to learn about this. I called him quietly and began to talk to him and he declared to me frankly that he wished to become a Mohammedan. Then I shut him up in his bedroom till night, and at night he drank a glass of wine and quickly died. Thus God kept him from such wickedness.

As time went on, Tolstoy had other troubles. His salary failed to arrive, and in order to make ends meet, he was forced to sell some of the sable skins he had been given to use as gifts. He wrote to the Tsar begging for his pay and also for permission to resign and come home. Peter wrote back refusing, telling him that his services were essential. Tolstoy struggled along, bribing, intriguing, doing his best. In 1706, he reported that "two of the most prudent pashas have been strangled at the instigation of the Grand Vizier, who does not like capable people. God grant that all the rest may perish the same way."

During Bulavin's Cossack rebellion on the Don and the Swedish invasion of Russia, Peter feared that the Sultan might be tempted to try to retake Azov. His instinct was to appease, and he gave orders to be sure that no

Turk or Tatar prisoners were still being held in Russian prisons. Tolstoy disagreed with this approach. He felt that the better policy was to be forceful, even threatening, with the Turks, in order to keep them quiet. Events seemed to bear him out. In 1709, the spring and summer of Poltava, the Turks not only failed to intervene on the side of Sweden, but talk of war with Russia and rumors of the appearance of a Russian fleet at the mouth of the Bosphorus caused panic in the streets of Constantinople.

Thus, for eight difficult years Tolstoy successfully upheld his master's interests and preserved the peace between Russia and Turkey. Then, in 1709, Charles XII, fleeing Poltava, arrived within the Sultan's dominions. Thereafter, four times within three years, the Sultan declared war on Russia.

WHEN CHARLES XII crossed the Bug River and entered the territory of the Ottoman Empire, he became the Sultan's guest. The King and the Cossack Hetman Mazeppa had sought asylum within the Sultan's dominions; this, according to the religion of Islam, imposed on Ahmed III the duty to receive and protect them. So strongly was this obligation felt that when word reached Constantinople of the delaying tactics of the local pasha which had resulted in the massacre of the stranded Cossacks on the far side of the river, the Sultan contemplated sending the pasha a silken cord.

Once he knew that the King of Sweden was within his empire, the Sultan moved quickly to make amends. Within a few days, the Seraskier of Bender, Yusuf Pasha, arrived with a formal welcome and a wagon train of special provisions. Soon, the famished Swedish survivors were feasting on melons, mutton and excellent Turkish coffee. Yusuf Pasha also brought the Sultan's suggestion, tinged with the weight of command, that his guests move to Bender on the Dniester River, 150 miles farther southwest. At this new site, Charles pitched camp in a row of handsome Turkish tents set in a meadow lined with fruit trees along the bank of the Dniester. In this pleasant country, now called Bessarabia, the restless King of Sweden was to spend three years.

At the time he moved there, Charles could have no inkling of this future. The King's intention had been to return to Poland and take command of the armies of Krassow and Stanislaus as soon as his foot was healed. In Poland, he also hoped to rendezvous with the troops under Lewenhaupt which he had left behind at Perevoluchna. In addition, he had sent orders to the governing Council in Stockholm to raise new regiments and send them across the Baltic. Nature and politics conspired against him. The wound healed slowly, and it was another six weeks before the King was able to mount a horse. During this recuperation, he learned that his eldest sister, the widowed Duchess of Holstein, Hedwig Sophia, had died in Stockholm during an epidemic of measles. For days, the bachelor King could not stop

weeping. Shutting himself in his tent, he refused to see even his closest comrades; for a while he even refused to believe the report, although the news had been transmitted in an official letter of condolence from the Swedish Council. To his younger sister, Ulrika, he wrote that he hoped that the "too terrible, quite unexpected rumor which totally numbed me" would be contradicted. Later, he wrote to Ulrika that he would have been happy if he had been the first of the three to die, and prayed now that at least he would be the second.

Another sorrow quickly followed. Mazeppa, the aging Hetman who had ruinously cast his lot with Charles before Poltava, had been carried from Charles' camp to a house in the town of Bender, where during the hot summer days his condition worsened. Charles remained faithful: When an offer from Peter arrived, suggesting that the Tsar would free Count Piper if Charles would hand over Mazeppa, the King refused. On September 22, 1709, Mazeppa died, and Charles hobbled on crutches to attend the funeral.

Blow followed upon blow. In quick succession, Charles learned that Lewenhaupt had surrendered at Perevoluchna, that Russian troops under Menshikov were flooding Poland, that Stanislaus and Krassow had retreated, that Augustus had broken the Treaty of Altranstadt and invaded Poland to reclaim his crown, that Denmark had reentered the war against Sweden and that Sweden itself was invaded by a Danish army. Meanwhile, Peter's Russian troops were marching through the Baltic provinces, occupying Riga, Pernau, Reval and Vyborg. Why did Charles not return to Sweden to take command? The journey would not have been easy. Bender was 1,200 miles south of Stockholm. The route through Poland was closed by the soldiers of Peter and Augustus. A recurrence of the plague had caused the Austrians to seal all their frontiers. Louis XIV repeatedly offered a ship to bring Charles home—the Sun King was eager to have the Swedish thunderbolt making mischief again in Eastern Europe behind the backs of his English, Dutch and Austrian opponents—but Charles worried about being seized by pirates. And if he accepted passage from the French—or even from the English or Dutch—what would be the price? Almost certainly, it would mean choosing sides in the War of the Spanish Succession.

In fact, once his disappointment at being unable to leave immediately for Poland had passed, Charles actually preferred to stay in Turkey. As he saw it, his presence inside the Ottoman Empire provided him with an impressive new opportunity. If he could arouse the Sultan to make war on the Tsar and join him in one successful southern offensive, Peter might still be beaten and all that Sweden had lost might be regained. Beginning in the autumn of 1709, Charles' agents, Poniatowski and Neugebauer, plunged into the murky politics of Constantinople, toiling to undo Tolstoy's work.

Their task was not easy. The Turks did not want to fight. This general feeling was reinforced by the news of Poltava, which had made an enormous

impression in Constantinople: How long now would it be before the Tsar's fleet appeared at the mouth of the Bosphorus? Faced with these dangers, many of the Sultan's advisors would have been happy to do as Peter demanded and expel the Swedish troublemaker from their empire. "The King of Sweden," reads a contemporary Turkish document, "has fallen like a heavy weight on the shoulders of the Sublime Porte." On the other hand, there were parties inside the Ottoman Empire who were eager for war with Russia. The most prominent was the violent Russophobe Khan of the Crimea, Devlet Gerey, who had been stripped of his right to tribute from Russia by the treaty of 1700. He and his horsemen were thirsting for a chance to renew the great raids on the Ukraine which had been so lucrative in booty and prisoners. In addition, Neugebauer was so fortunate as to gain the ear of Sultan Ahmed's mother. This lady's imagination had already been captured by the hero legend of Charles XII; now Neugebauer made her see how her son could help her "lion [Charles] devour the Tsar."

Another element was necessary to Charles' plan. It was not enough simply to induce the Sultan to go to war; the campaign must be successfully fought and the right objectives achieved. Charles understood that in order to have a voice in these matters, he needed to command a fresh Swedish army on the continent. Even as the Ottoman army was mobilizing, Charles was writing urgently to Stockholm "to ensure the safe transport into Pomerania of the aforesaid regiments in good time, that our part in the forthcoming campaign may not fall to the ground."

In Stockholm, the Council was astonished, even aghast, at this request. Already in November 1709, after Poltava, a newly emboldened Denmark had broken the Peace of Travendal and reentered the war against Sweden. Danish troops had invaded southern Sweden. To the Swedish Council, confronting immediate threats to the homeland along with the crushing burden of paying for a war which seemed already lost, the King's command that another expeditionary force be sent to Poland seemed madness. A message was sent to Charles that no troops could be spared.

In the end, ironically, Neugebauer and Poniatowski were successful in Constantinople while Charles XII failed in Stockholm. The Ottoman Empire was persuaded to go to war, but none of the proud Swedish regiments which might have steeled the ranks of the Turkish army and given weight to the voice of the Swedish King were present. Although he was incontestably the greatest commander within the empire, and although the Turkish army in general and the Janissaries in particular idolized the warrior King, Charles was not a formal ally of the Turks and played no active part in the coming military campaign. Because of this, his last and perhaps his greatest opportunity to defeat Peter crumbled into dust.

It was not only the Turks who were concerned about the presence of

Charles XII in the Ottoman Empire. Ever since the King's arrival, Peter had pressed through Tolstoy for Charles' surrender or expulsion. As the months passed, the tone of his messages became increasingly peremptory, and this played directly into the hands of the war party in Constantinople and Adrianople. The Tsar's categorical demand that the Sultan reply by October 10, 1710, to his request that Charles be expelled from Turkey was considered insulting to the dignity of the Shadow of God. This, following the persuasions of the Khan, the Swedes, the French and the Sultan's mother, tipped the balance. On November 21, in a solemn session of the Divan, the Ottoman Empire declared war on Russia. Tolstoy was the first to suffer. Under Turkish law, ambassadors had no immunity in wartime, and Tolstoy was seized, stripped of half his clothes, set on an aged horse and paraded through the streets to confinement in the Seven Towers.

With the declaration of war came a new Grand Vizier, Mehemet Baltadji, appointed for the express purpose of making war on Russia. He was a curious choice, described by a contemporary as a dull-witted, blundering old pederast who had never been a serious soldier. Yet he decided on an offensive campaign. That winter, as soon as the Khan's horsemen could make ready, a mobile Tatar army would strike north from the Crimea into the Ukraine to harry the Cossacks and reap the rewards in prisoners and cattle which ten years of peace had denied them. In the spring, the main body of the Ottoman army would march northeast from Adrianople. The artillery and supplies would go by sea to the Danube town of Isaccea to rendezvous with the army. There, the Tatar cavalry would join them to form a combined force of almost 200,000 men.

In January, the Tatars struck, ravaging the area between the middle Dnieper and the upper Don. They met heavy resistance from Peter's new Cossack Hetman, Skoropadsky, and were forced to withdraw without having created the major diversion for which the Grand Vizier had hoped. At the end of February, the horsetails signifying war were raised in the Court of the Janissaries and the elite corps of 20,000, shouldering its polished muskets and ornamental bows, marched north. The main army moved slowly, reaching the Danube only at the beginning of June. Here, the cannon were unloaded from ships and placed in gun carriages, the supply trains organized, and the entire army transferred to the east bank of the river.

While the Turks were assembling on the Danube, the Grand Vizier sent Poniatowski, who had been representing Charles at the Sultan's court, to Bender to invite the King to join the campaign, but only as a guest of the Grand Vizier. At first, the King was strongly tempted, but he decided against it. As a sovereign, he could not join an army he did not command, especially an army commanded by one lower in rank than himself. In retrospect, it appears a fatal mistake.

THE WAR OF 1711, which led to the campaign on the Pruth, was not of Peter's asking; it was Charles who had instigated this fight between Russia and the Ottoman Empire. Nevertheless, once war came, Peter, still flushed with his success at Poltava, accepted the challenge with confidence and took rapid steps to prepare. Ten regiments of Russian dragoons were dispatched from Poland to watch the Ottoman frontier. Sheremetev with twenty-two regiments of infantry was ordered to march from the Baltic to the Ukraine. A new, exceptionally heavy tax was levied to support the coming military operations.

On February 25, 1711, a great ceremony was held in the Kremlin. The Preobrazhensky and Semyonovsky Guards regiments stood in ranks in Cathedral Square before the Assumption Cathedral, their red banners bearing a cross inscribed with the ancient watchword of the Emperor Constantine: "By this sign you shall conquer." Inside the cathedral, Peter solemnly proclaimed a holy war "against the enemies of Christ." The Tsar meant to lead the Turkish campaign personally, and on March 6 left Moscow with Catherine at his side. But he became ill, and his letters carried a tone of resignation and despair. "We have before us this uncertain road which is known to God alone," he wrote to Menshikov. To Apraxin, who had been given command of all the lower Don, including Azov and Tagonrog, and who had written asking for instructions as to where to place his headquarters, the Tsar replied, "Do as is most convenient to you, for all the country is entrusted to you. It is impossible for me to decide as I am so far off, and, if you will, in despair, being scarcely alive from illness, and affairs change from day to day."

Peter's illness was severe. To Menshikov, he wrote that he had suffered one seizure lasting a day and a half and had never been so sick in his life. After several weeks, he began to feel better and moved along to Yavorov. There, he was pleased that Catherine was received with dignity and addressed as "Your Majesty" by the local Polish noblemen. Catherine herself was delighted. "We here are often at banquets and soirees," she wrote on May 9 to Menshikov, who had been left behind to defend St. Petersburg. "Three days ago we visited the Hetman Sieniawski and yesterday were at Prince Radziwill's, where we danced a good bit." Then, turning to some imagined slight, she soothed the worried Prince: "I beg your Highness not to be troubled by believing any stupid gossip coming from here, for the Rear Admiral [Peter] keeps you in his love and kindest remembrance as before."

Peter had traveled to Yavorov to sign the marriage treaty which would link his son Alexis to Princess Charlotte of Wolfenbüttel. Schleinitz, the ambassador of the Duke of Wolfenbüttel, wrote to his master describing the Russian royal couple at this moment:

The next day about four o'clock the Tsar sent for me again. I knew that I should find him in the room of the Tsaritsa and that I should give him great pleasure if I congratulated the Tsaritsa on the publication of her marriage. After the declaration made on this subject by the King of Poland and the hereditary prince, I did not consider it out of place and besides I knew that the Polish minister gave the Tsaritsa the title of Majesty. When I went into the room I turned, notwithstanding the presence of the Tsar, and congratulated her in your name on the announcement of her marriage, and entrusted the Princess [Charlotte] to her friendship and protection.

Catherine was delighted and asked Schleinitz to thank the Duke for his good wishes. She said that she was eager to see and embrace the princess who was to become her stepdaughter-in-law and asked whether the Tsarevich seemed as much in love with Charlotte as people said. While Catherine was talking with the Ambassador, Peter was examining some mathematical instruments on the other side of the room. When he heard Catherine speak of Alexis, he laid these down on a table and walked over, but did not break into the conversation.

"I had been warned," Schleinitz continued in his letter to the Duke,

that as the Tsar knows me very slightly, it was incumbent on me to address him first. I therefore told him that Her Majesty the Tsaritsa had asked me whether the Tsarevich was very much in love with the Princess. I declared that I was sure that the Tsarevich awaited with impatience the consent of his father in order to be fully happy. The Tsar replied through an interpreter: "I do not wish to put off the happiness of my son, but at the same time I do not wish entirely to deprive myself of my own happiness. He is my only son and I desire to have the pleasure at the end of the campaign of being personally present at his marriage. His marriage will be in Brunswick." He explained that he was not entirely his own master, for he had to do with an enemy who was strong and rapid in his movements, but he would try and arrange it to take the waters at Carlsbad in the autumn and then go to Wolfenbüttel.

Three days later, the marriage contract arrived, signed without alteration by the Duke of Wolfenbüttel. Peter summoned Ambassador Schleinitz and greeted him in German with the statement, "I have some excellent news to give you." He produced the contract, and when Schleinitz congratulated the Tsar and kissed his hand, Peter kissed him three times on the forehead and cheeks and ordered that a bottle of his favorite Hungarian wine be brought.

They clinked glasses and Peter talked excitedly for two hours about his son, the army and the coming campaign against the Turks. Afterward, a pleased Schleinitz wrote to the Duke: "I cannot sufficiently express to Your Highness with what clearness of judgment and what modesty the Tsar spoke about everything."

Peter's confidence that the campaign against Turkey would be swiftly concluded so that he could take the waters at Carlsbad and then attend his son's wedding was further reflected in an interview he had at this time with Augustus. The Elector of Saxony had once again entered Warsaw and claimed the crown of Poland, while his rival, Stanislaus, had fled with the retreating Swedes to Swedish Pomerania. Augustus intended to pursue these enemies and besiege the Swedish-held Baltic port of Stralsund. To support this effort, Peter pledged 100,000 roubles and placed 12,000 Russian soldiers under Augustus' command.

Against the Turks, Peter's plan, bold to the point of recklessness, was to march to the lower Danube, cross the river just above the place where it flows into the Black Sea and proceed southwest through Bulgaria to a point where he could threaten the Sultan's second capital, Adrianople, and even the fabled city of Constantinople itself. The Russian army he would take with him would not be large—40,000 infantry and 14,000 cavalry—compared to the vast array which the Sultan could put in the field. But Peter expected that once he entered the Christian provinces of the Ottoman Empire bordering on Russia, he would be welcomed as a liberator and reinforced by 30,000 Walachians and 10,000 Moldavians. Then, his army would number 94,000.

The offensive plan had been conceived partly as a means of keeping war away from the Ukraine, devastated by the Swedish invasion and the defection of Mazeppa, and now quiet, at least for the moment. If an Ottoman army invaded the Ukrainian steppes, who knew which way the volatile Cossacks would go? By thrusting into the Ottoman Empire, Peter could at least lay these concerns to rest. Better for him to stir up trouble among the Sultan's restless vassals than the other way around.

Peter's expectation of help once his army arrived in the Christian provinces was not unfounded. Throughout his reign, he had received constant appeals from representatives of the Orthodox peoples of the Balkans: the Serbs, Montenegrins, Bulgars, Walachians and Moldavians. His partial defeat of the Sultan in 1698 and his capture of Azov had encouraged their dreams of liberation and exaggerated their promises. Once a Russian army appeared in their midst, they pledged, native troops would join it, supplies would be plentifully available and whole populations would rise. Between 1704 and 1710, four Serbian leaders arrived in Moscow to stir the Russians to action. "We have no other tsar than the Most Orthodox Tsar Peter," they said.

Before Poltava, Peter, wary of any behavior which might cause the Sultan to break the truce of 1700, responded discreetly to these appeals. After Poltava, however, Tolstoy and other Russian agents inside the Ottoman Empire began to prepare the ground for an uprising. Now, in the spring of 1711, the hour had struck. In the Kremlin ceremony before he left Moscow, Peter issued a proclamation, openly presenting himself as the liberator of the Balkan Christians. He called on all of them, Catholic as well as Orthodox, to rise against their Ottoman masters and ensure that "the descendants of the heathen Mohammed were driven out into their old homeland, the sands and steppes of Arabia."

42

FIFTY BLOWS
ON THE PRUTH

THE KEY to Peter's campaign lay in the two Christian principalities, Walachia and Moldavia. Lying south of the Carpathians and north of the Danube, these regions today make up a sizable piece of the southeastern Soviet Union and a large part of present-day Romania. In the fifteenth and sixteenth centuries, seeking security, they placed themselves under the suzerainty of the Sublime Porte, retaining their internal autonomy but agreeing to pay the sultan an annual tribute in return for protection.

With the passage of time, however, the Porte began assuming the right to appoint and dismiss their native princes. Anxious to make their offices hereditary, the princes secretly began looking elsewhere for protection. During the reign of Tsar Alexis, there were preliminary discussions with Moscow about Russia assuming suzerainty, but the Tsar was still too heavily involved with Poland.

In 1711, Walachia, the stronger and richer of the two principalities, was ruled by a prince (the local title was hospodar) named Constantine Brancovo, wily and flexible, who had come to office by poisoning his predecessor and had used his talents not only to cling to his title for twenty years but to build a powerful army and great personal wealth. From the Sultan's viewpoint, Brancovo was much too rich and powerful for a satellite prince, and the hospodar was marked for replacement once an opportunity arrived. Inevitably, Brancovo sensed this feeling and, convinced after Poltava that Peter's star was ascending, he made a secret treaty with the Tsar. In case of a Russian war with Turkey, Walachia would side with the Tsar, putting 30,000 troops in the field and furnishing supplies for Russian troops who reached Walachia—supplies to be paid for, however, by Peter. In return, Peter promised to guarantee the independence of Walachia and the hereditary rights of Brancovo, and he made Brancovo a Knight of the Order of St. Andrew.

Moldavia was weaker and poorer than Walachia, and its rulers had changed rapidly. The latest, Demetrius Cantemir, in 1711 had been in office

for less than a year, appointed by the Sultan with the understanding that he would help the Porte seize and overthrow his neighbor Brancovo, for which service he would become hospodar of both Walachia and Moldavia. Arriving in his new capital, Jassy, however, Cantemir also sniffed a shift in fortune and began negotiating in utmost secrecy with Peter. In April 1711, he signed a treaty with the Tsar, agreeing to assist a Russian invasion and furnish 10,000 troops. Moldavia, in return, was to be declared an independent state under Russian protection. No tribute would be paid, and the Cantemir family would rule as a hereditary dynasty.

It was with the promise of help from these two ambitious princes, each of whom hated the other, that Peter launched his campaign against the Turks.

CANTEMIR'S DECISION was popular in Moldavia. "You have done well in inviting the Russians to free us from the Turkish yoke," his nobles told him. "If we had found out that you intended to go meet the Turks, we had resolved to abandon you and surrender to the Tsar Peter." But Cantemir also knew that the Ottoman army was on the march and that, as the Grand Vizier drew closer, it would become obvious that he and his province had deserted to the Tsar. Accordingly, he sent messages to Sheremetev, who commanded the main Russian army, urging the Field Marshal to hurry. If the main body could not move faster, Cantemir pleaded for at least an advance guard of 4,000 men to shield his people from Ottoman vengeance. Sheremetev was also receiving commands to hurry from Peter, who wanted him to reach and cross the Dniester by May 15 to protect the principalities and encourage the Serbs and Bulgars to rise.

To ensure that the Moldavians would look on this arrival of foreign troops as a blessing, Sheremetev had been equipped with printed messages from the Tsar to all Balkan Christians:

> You know how the Turks have trampled into the mire our faith, have seized by treachery all the Holy Places, have ravaged and destroyed many churches and monasteries, have practiced much deceit, and what wretchedness they have caused, and how many widows and orphans they have seized upon and dispersed as wolves do the sheep. Now I come to your aid. If your heart wishes, do not run away from my great empire, for it is just. Let not the Turks deceive you, and do not run away from my word. Shake off fear, and fight for the faith, for the church, for which we shall shed our last drop of blood.

Peter also gave his Field Marshal strict orders about the behavior of Russian troops during their march across Moldavia: They were to observe decorum and pay for everything they took from Christians; any pillaging was to be punished by death. Once Cantemir declared for the Russians and the

first Russian troops began to appear, the Moldavians flung themselves on the Turks in their midst, first in Jassy, then throughout the principality. Many were killed; others lost their cattle, sheep, horses, clothes, silver and jewels.

Originally, Peter's plan had been for Sheremetev to march south straight down the east bank of the Pruth River to its junction with the Danube and there to deny passage to the Turks. However, on May 30, when Sheremetev arrived on the Dniester near Soroka (two weeks behind Peter's schedule), Cantemir begged him to march directly to Jassy, the Moldavian capital. Sheremetev yielded, and on June 5 his army camped near Jassy on the west bank of the Pruth. Sheremetev's excuse for disregarding Peter's order was that the army had suffered greatly crossing the steppe under the hot sun and needed replenishment. The animals had had a minimum of forage, the grass having been burned by Tatar horsemen who hovered on his flanks. Further, Sheremetev realized that he probably was already too late to prevent the Turks crossing the Danube and that by crossing the Pruth he would be in a better position to protect Moldavia from the Grand Vizier.

Peter, reaching Soroka behind Sheremetev, was angry at his Field Marshal and wrote that the old general had let the Turks outmarch him. Nevertheless, once Sheremetev had changed the original plan, the Tsar, following behind, had no choice but to accept the new route; anything else would have divided the army. Peter's own force had suffered greatly on the march, and the men were exhausted when they reached the Pruth on June 24. Leaving them there, the Tsar rode ahead, crossing the river and entering Jassy for a conference with Cantemir. He was received with regal pomp and a huge banquet. The hospodar made a good first impression: "a man very sensible and useful in council" was the Tsar's appraisal. While in Jassy, Peter received two emissaries bearing an offer of peace from the Grand Vizier. The offer was indirect, but it reflected the Vizier's—and behind him, the Sultan's—reluctance to fight a battle and provoke the Russians into sending a fleet out onto the Black Sea. Peter rejected the offer. Surrounded by his army, with assurances of Moldavian and Walachian support, and hearing reports that the Grand Vizier was reluctant to fight, the Tsar felt confident of victory. In this happy mood, Peter took Cantemir to visit the Russian army camped on the Pruth. There, with Catherine and his guests beside him, he celebrated the second anniversary of Poltava, the great victory which had made all this possible.

Even as the Tsar was celebrating, his military situation was deteriorating. The Grand Vizier had completed the crossing of the Danube at Isaccea and, informed of Peter's rejection of peace, was marching north with an army of 200,000 men. Moreover, there was an ominous absence of news from Walachia, which, in the long run, was far more important to Peter's campaign than Moldavia. Everything in Walachia depended on the Hospodar Bran-

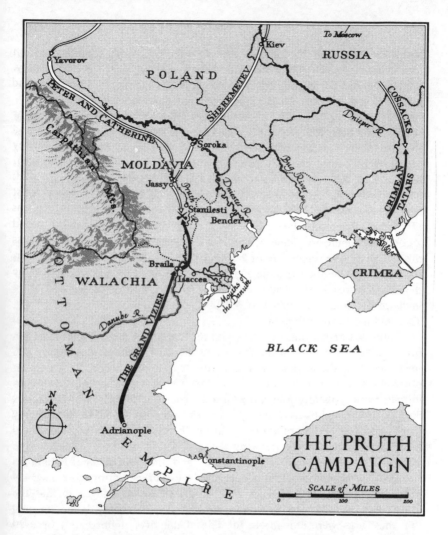

THE PRUTH CAMPAIGN

SCALE of MILES

0   100   200

covo. Until he raised his princely banner for the Tsar in public, the nobility and the common people could hardly be expected to follow Peter's call to rise against the Turk. But Brancovo was fearful and therefore cautious. Knowing that a huge Turkish army was in the field, knowing also what would happen if the Turks won and he was on the losing side, he held back from public support of the Russians. His boyars agreed. "It is dangerous to declare for Russia until the Tsar's army crosses the Danube," they advised. When the Turkish army crossed the Danube first, Brancovo made his choice. Just as the Grand Vizier, informed of the Hospodar's treason, was ordering his arrest, Brancovo suddenly switched sides again. Using as a pretext a letter from Peter whose tone he said offended him, Brancovo announced that he no longer considered himself bound by his secret treaty

with the Tsar, and he handed over to the Turks the supplies he had amassed for the Russian army with Peter's money. This betrayal had an immediate and devastating effect on the Russian campaign. The provisions had vanished, and the Moldavians could not make up the deficit. Nevertheless, Peter did not give up the campaign. He was told that large supplies had been collected for the Turks and lay without guard on the lower Pruth near its junction with the Danube. As the main Turkish army had crossed the Danube and was marching north up the east bank of the Pruth to meet him, the Tsar decided to cross to the west bank and move south. If he succeeded, he would outflank the Grand Vizier, capture the Turkish supplies and cut the Ottoman army off from its base. To increase the chance of success, Peter detached Ronne with the whole of the Russian cavalry, 12,000 horsemen, to plunge ahead down the west bank of the Pruth into the Ottoman rear, capturing or burning the magazines and storehouses at Braila on the Danube. On June 27, the cavalry rode off, and three days later the infantry crossed the Pruth and began moving south down the west bank in three divisions. The first was led by General Janus, the second by the Tsar and the third by Repnin.

Janus was first to make contact with the Turks. As the Russians marched south on the west bank of the Pruth and the Turks advanced north on the opposite bank, the advance guards of the two armies caught sight of each other across the river on July 8. Both sides were startled to find themselves in such close proximity. When the Grand Vizier was told, he was frightened and his first thought was to retreat. "For as he had never before seen enemy troops and was by nature a great poltroon, he at once conceived himself as lost," wrote Poniatowski, traveling with the Ottoman army. Together, the Tatar Khan Devlet Gerey, Poniatowski and the Aga of the Janissaries steadied his courage, and the next day the Turkish army continued its march northward. Turkish engineers rapidly threw up bridges so that the army could cross back to the western bank to meet its enemy. Peter, learning that the Turks were crossing to his side of the river, immediately ordered Janus to fall back and rejoin the main army.

Peter was holding a position behind a marsh south of Stanilesti, and Janus' tired men fell back into these entrenchments. They got little rest. The following day, a Sunday, the Turks, who had come up quickly behind, launched repeated attacks. Cantemir's Moldavians, despite their inexperience, stood well, and the Russians as a whole held their ground. But the Tsar's urgent messages to Repnin to bring the third division forward to relieve the other two were fruitless. Repnin's men were pinned down by Tatar cavalry at Stanilesti and could advance no farther.

That evening, after a long day of Turkish assaults mounting in strength, and with the Tsar alarmed by the absence of Repnin's men and the lack of provisions, a Russian council of war was held. It had little choice: Retreat

was imperative. The withdrawal began during the night and continued through the following morning in the direction of Repnin's division at Stanilesti. The retreat was a nightmare. The Turks pressed closely behind, launching continual attacks on the Russian rear guard. Tatar squadrons galloped in and out among the Russian wagons, and most of the Russian baggage train with the remaining provisions was lost. The Russian infantry was exhausted and preoccupied by thirst. Companies and battalions formed squares and marched in this formation to the riverbank, where, by sections, some drank while others beat off the Tatar horsemen. Only late on Monday afternoon, July 9, was all the Russian infantry reunited at Stanilesti, where on a promontory they began digging shallow trenches to make a stand against the horsemen who swarmed around them.

Before dark, long lines of Turkish infantry including the Janissaries began to arrive, and, in the presence of the Grand Vizier, the Ottoman elite guards launched a major attack on the sketchily constructed Russian camp. Russian discipline held as Peter's men poured heavy fire into the advancing ranks of Janissaries. Its first attack broken, the Turkish infantry fell back and began, in its turn, to throw up a line of entrenchments completely hemming in the Russian camp. The Turkish artillery arrived and the guns were rolled into place in a great crescent; by nightfall, 300 cannon pointed their muzzles at the Russian camp. Thousands of Tatar horsemen, together with Poles and Cossacks provided by Charles, patrolled the opposite riverbank. There was no escape: The Tsar and his army were surrounded.

The strength of the Turks was overwhelming: 120,000 infantry and 80,000 cavalry. Peter's strength was only 38,000 infantry; his cavalry was far to the south with Ronne. He was pinned down against a river and ringed by 300 cannon which could sweep his camp with shot and shell. Most important, his men were so exhausted by hunger and heat that some of them could no longer fight. It was difficult even to draw water from the river; the men sent for the purpose came under intense fire from the Tatar horsemen massed on the opposite bank. His own earthworks were scanty, and one entire section was covered only by the bodies of dead wagon horses and makeshift chevaux de frise. In the center of the camp, a shallow pit had been dug to protect Catherine and her women. Surrounded by wagons and shielded from the sun by an awning, it was a frail barrier against Turkish cannonballs. Inside, Catherine waited calmly, while around her the other women wept.

Peter's situation was impossible. That night he could look out all around him on the thousands of campfires of the huge Ottoman army sparkling in the low-lying hills on both sides of the river as far as the eye could reach. In the morning, when the Turks undoubtedly would attack, he would be doomed. He, the Russian Tsar, the victor of Poltava, would be overwhelmed and perhaps pulled through the streets of Constantinople in a cage. The

fruits of twenty years of arduous, colossal toil were about to evaporate in a day. Could it have come to this? Yet, why not? Had not exactly the same thing happened to his enemy Charles? And for an identical reason: Too proud, too sure of his destiny, he had ventured too far onto enemy ground. Actually, the situation was much worse than Charles' at Perevoluchna. There, the Swedish army had not been surrounded by superior forces, and the King himself had found a way to escape. But here the Turks held every card: They could take the Russian army, the new Tsaritsa and, most important, the man on whom everything else rested, the Tsar himself. What would he have to give up, what huge sacrifices in territory or treasure would Russia have to pay to win his freedom?

There is a story that at this moment the Tsar asked whether Neculce, the commander of the Moldavian troops, could somehow escort Catherine and himself to the Hungarian frontier. Neculce refused, knowing that even if he were somehow able to pass through the surrounding lines, the whole of Moldavia was now swarming with Tatar horsemen. Some have said that this request showed cowardice on Peter's part. But when the battle was lost and the army on the verge of surrender, the chief of state had to think of saving the nation. Peter knew that at this time he was Russia. He knew what a blow it would be to Russia if, along with the army he had so carefully built, he himself was taken prisoner. In time, the lost army could be replaced—if he was free to do it. But his own loss would be irreparable.

The next morning, Tuesday, the 10th, it should have ended. The Turkish artillery opened fire and the Russians prepared for a final stand—but the Janissaries did not attack. As a measure of desperation, Peter ordered a sortie, and thousands of weary Russians rose from their trenches and flung themselves on the first lines of Ottomans, inflicting heavy losses before they were forced to retreat. During the sortie, the Russians took prisoners, and from one of these Peter learned that the Janissaries had suffered heavily in the previous day's fighting and were disinclined to make another full-scale attack on the Russian lines. At the very least, this might give the Tsar a little maneuverability in negotiating the terms of his surrender.

During the lull, Peter proposed to Sheremetev and his Vice Chancellor, Shafirov, that he send an envoy to the Grand Vizier to see what terms the Turks might offer. Sheremetev, clearly appraising the military situation, bluntly told his master that the proposal was ridiculous. Why would the Turks be willing to consider anything except surrender? The cat does not negotiate with the mouse. But Catherine was present at this council, and she encouraged her husband to proceed. Sheremetev was ordered to draft a proposal in his own name as commander of the Russian army.

In preparing the offer, Peter viewed his prospects with gloomy realism. Knowing that Charles was a guest and now an ally of the Sultan, he assumed that any peace would have to include a settlement of his disputes with

Sweden as well as Turkey. He assumed that his concessions would have to be drastic. Ultimately, although this was not contained in his first proposal, he was prepared to surrender Azov, dismantle Tagonrog and give up everything he had won from the Turks over twenty years. To the Swedes, he would restore Livonia, Estonia, Karelia—everything he had taken in war except St. Petersburg, his "beloved paradise." If this was not enough, he would trade away the ancient Russian city of Pskov and other territories. In addition, he was prepared to allow Charles to return home to Sweden, to recognize Stanislaus as King of Poland and to promise to cease his own intervention in Polish affairs. To tempt the Grand Vizier and other Turkish officers, he would offer large bribes: 150,000 roubles was the gift he suggested for the Grand Vizier. By afternoon, the proposals were drafted, and Shafirov was sent with a trumpeter under a white flag to present them to the Grand Vizier.

Unknown to the Russians, Shafirov's arrival in the Grand Vizier's camp produced a profound relief in that hesitant warrior. In his multi-chambered silken tent, the elderly Baltadji had been greatly perplexed and ill at ease. His best troops, the Janissaries, were grumbling about renewing the assault. A further attack against even a weakened Russian camp might severely deplete their numbers at a time when Hapsburg Austria was rumored to be mobilizing for another war. Further, the Grand Vizier possessed a piece of news which Peter had not yet learned: Ronne's Russian cavalry had captured Braila, seized many of the Turkish army's supplies and burned some of its powder magazines. At his elbow, Poniatowski and the Tatar Khan were urging him to deliver a final attack and finish at one stroke the battle, the war and the Tsar. Reluctantly, Baltadji was about to agree and give the orders for a grand assault when Shafirov was brought into his tent. The Russian Vice Chancellor handed over the letter from Sheremetev which suggested that war was not in the true interests of either party and had been brought about by the intrigues of others. The two generals, therefore, should stop the bloodshed and investigate possible terms of peace.

The Grand Vizier saw the hand of Allah. He could be a victor and a hero without risking further battle. Overriding the anguished pleas of Poniatowski and the Khan, Baltadji ordered the bombardment halted and sat down happily with the Russian envoy. The negotiations continued through the night. The following morning, Shafirov sent back word that although the Grand Vizier was anxious for peace, the discussions were dragging. Impatiently, Peter instructed his envoy to accept any terms that were offered "except slavery," but to insist on an immediate agreement. The Russian troops were starving, and if peace was not to come, Peter wanted to use their last strength in a desperate break-out attack on the Turkish trenches.

Spurred by this threat of renewed fighting, Baltadji itemized his terms.

In relation to the Turks, they were what Peter had expected: the Tsar was to give up all the fruits of his 1696 campaign and the 1700 treaty. Azov and Tagonrog were to be returned, the Black Sea fleet was to be abandoned, the lower-Dnieper forts destroyed. In addition, Russian troops were to evacuate Poland, and the Tsar's right to keep a permanent ambassador at Constantinople would be canceled. As for Sweden, King Charles XII was to be granted free passage home and the Tsar was "to conclude a peace with him if agreement can be reached." In return for these commitments, the Ottoman army would stand aside and permit the encircled Russian army to return peacefully to Russia.

When Peter heard these terms, he was astonished. They were not light—he would lose everything in the south—but they were far milder than he had expected. Nothing had been said about Sweden and the Baltic except that Charles should go home and that Peter should try to make peace. Under the circumstances, it was a deliverance. The Turks added one further demand: Shafirov and Colonel Michael Sheremetev, the son of the Field Marshal, must remain in Turkey as hostages until the Russians carried out their promises to return Azov and the other territories.

Peter was eager to sign before the Grand Vizier changed his mind. Shafirov took young Sheremetev and returned immediately to the Turkish camp, where the treaty was signed on July 12. On the 13th, the Russian army, still keeping its arms, formed columns and began to march out of the ill-fated camp on the Pruth. Before Peter and the army could leave, however, they passed unknowingly through one final, potentially disastrous crisis.

THROUGHOUT BALTADJI'S NEGOTIATIONS with Shafirov, Poniatowski had done his best to delay. Charles XII's agent had seen that Peter was trapped and that the Tsar would have to accept almost any terms dictated by the Grand Vizier. If his own master's needs were not ignored, Sweden might regain all it had lost, perhaps more. Thus, as soon as Shafirov arrived in the Grand Vizier's tent, Poniatowski rushed out and scribbled a letter to Charles, handed it to a courier and sent him galloping to Bender.

Poniatowski wrote the note at noon on July 11. The horseman arrived in Bender on the evening of the 12th. Charles reacted instantly. His horse was saddled, and at ten p.m. he was galloping through the darkness toward the Pruth fifty miles away. At three p.m. on the 13th, after a continuous seventeen-hour ride, Charles appeared suddenly on the perimeter of the Grand Vizier's camp. He rode through the lines to look down on the makeshift Russian fortifications. Before him, the last of the Russian columns were marching out unhindered, escorted by squadrons of Tatar horsemen. The king saw everything: the dominating position of the Turkish cannon, the

ease with which, without even the necessity of an assault, a few days' wait would have brought the starving Russians out as prisoners.

No one knows what feelings of regret Charles, studying the panorama before him, may have had about his decision not to accompany the Turkish army. Had he been there to add his forceful voice to that of the Tatar Khan (who had wept in frustration when the Grand Vizier signed the peace treaty), a different decision might have been reached. He rode silently through the watching Turkish soldiers to the tent of the Grand Vizier. With Poniatowski and an interpreter at his side, he entered rudely, still wearing his spurs and dirty boots, and flung himself exhausted on a sofa near the sacred green banner of Mohammed. When the Grand Vizier came in, accompanied by the Khan and a crowd of officers, Charles asked that they withdraw so that he could speak to Baltadji in private. The two men drank a ceremonial cup of coffee in silence and then Charles, making an extreme effort to control his feelings, asked why the Grand Vizier had let the Russian army go. "I have won enough for the Porte," replied Baltadji calmly. "It is against Mohammed's law to deny peace to an enemy who begs it." Charles asked whether the Sultan would be satisfied with so limited a victory. "I have command of the army and I make peace when I will," answered Baltadji.

At this point, unable to contain his frustration, Charles rose from his seat and made a final appeal. As he had not been a party to the treaty, would the Grand Vizier lend him a fraction of the Turkish army and a few cannon so that he might pursue the Russians, attack and win far more? Baltadji refused, declaring that the Faithful must not be led by a Christian.

The game was over and Charles was beaten. From that moment, he and Baltadji were mortal enemies and each worked mightily to get rid of the other. The Grand Vizier stopped payment of the Swedish daily allowance, forbade merchants to sell provisions to the Swedes and intercepted the King's mail. Charles retaliated by complaining bitterly to the Sultan about Baltadji's behavior. In particular, he set his agents in Constantinople to spreading the rumors that the real reason the Grand Vizier had let the Tsar and his army escape was that he had been massively bribed.

The story took root in Russia, too. One version was that Catherine—some say without the knowledge of her husband, others say with Peter's private consent—had ordered Shafirov to promise the Grand Vizier a vast sum, including her own jewels, to secure the Tsar's freedom.

In retrospect, the story seems exaggerated. Baltadji was promised 150,000 roubles, which is a large sum, but that this was the reason he made peace on relatively mild terms seems unlikely. He had other reasons: He was not primarily a warrior, his troops were reluctant to fight, he feared a new war with Austria and was glad to end this war with Russia, he disliked the fanatical Russophobia of the Khan Devlet Gerey and wanted him

leashed. Further, he had undoubtedly been told that messages had been sent to Charles XII and that at any minute the Swedish King might ride into camp, demanding a battle of annihilation. Indeed, should Charles arrive and Peter be captured, he would be in the complicated position of having two of the greatest sovereigns in Europe, both without their armies and powerless, as his "guests." The diplomatic implications were unthinkable. And, from the Ottoman point of view, Baltadji had achieved all his objectives. The territory Russia had taken from the Sultan was now fully restored. What more should one ask from a treaty of peace?

None of this was solace for Charles. A unique opportunity, a moment when overwhelming power could be applied against an almost helpless foe, had been lost—and not just lost, but deliberately thrown away. Thereafter, although Charles worked hard and helped incite three more brief wars between the Tsar and the Ottoman Empire, the opportunity never returned. Poltava remained decisive in Peter's war against Charles; the Pruth did not upset this. Peter realized this as well as Charles. "They had the bird in their hand there," he said later, "but it will not happen again."

THE GRAND VIZIER had won the Battle of Pruth, although no one, especially the Sultan, was to thank him. Peter and Charles both lost, the former less than he might have, the latter because he gained nothing where he might have gained everything. Peter's allies, the hospodars of Moldavia and Walachia, also lost: one his lands, the other his head.

The handing over of Cantemir, Prince of Moldavia, was one of the Grand Vizier's original conditions for peace. The Hospodar had hidden under the baggage of the Tsaritsa Catherine in one of the wagons, and only three of his men knew where he was. Shafirov was therefore able to tell the Grand Vizier truthfully that it was impossible to surrender Cantemir as, since the first day of the battle, no one had seen him. The Grand Vizier waved the matter aside, declaring contemptuously, "Well, let us speak no more about it. Two great empires should not prolong a war for the sake of a coward. He will soon enough meet with his deserts."

Cantemir escaped with the Russians, collected his wife and children in Jassy and, along with twenty-four leading Moldavian boyars, returned to Russia with the Tsar's army. There, Peter showered favors on him, giving him the title of Russian prince and granting him large estates near Kharkov. His son entered diplomatic service and became Russian ambassador to England and France. Cantemir's principality, Moldavia, was not so lucky. Baltadji gave the Tatars permission to ravage the towns and villages by fire and sword.

The fate of Brancovo, Hospodar of Walachia, who had first betrayed the Sultan and then betrayed the Tsar, had an appropriate twist: The Turks

never trusted him again. Although he was warned that a tide of disfavor was running against him in Constantinople, and although he began sending large sums of money to Western Europe to prepare for a comfortable exile, Brancovo delayed his own departure. In the spring of 1714, he was arrested and sent to Constantinople. There, on his sixtieth birthday, together with his two sons, he was beheaded.

THE TREATY signed on the Pruth ended the war, but did not bring peace. Peter, heartsick at having to hand over Azov and Tagonrog, procrastinated until Charles XII should be sent out of Turkey. Shafirov, now superseding Tolstoy as senior Russian diplomat in Constantinople, urgently pressed the Grand Vizier to expel the Swedish King. Baltadji tried. "I wish the Devil would take him because I now see that he is king only in name, that he has no sense in him and is like a beast," the Grand Vizier told Shafirov. "I will try to get rid of him somehow or other." Baltadji failed because Charles flatly refused to go. Meanwhile, the King's agents in Constantinople were working actively to undermine Baltadji himself. Peter continued to delay, sending orders to Apraxin not to destroy the fortifications at Azov just yet, but to await further instructions. When, under pressure, Shafirov promised the Turks that Azov would be surrendered within two months, Peter again wrote to Apraxin, telling him to level the walls of the fortress, but not to damage the foundations, and to keep exact plans so that, if some new change occurred, the fortress could quickly be rebuilt.

In November, five months after the Pruth signing, Azov and Tagonrog still had not been given up. Charles' agents used this fact, skillfully blended with rumors that the Grand Vizier had let the Tsar escape because carts loaded with Russian gold had rumbled up to his tent on the Pruth, to procure the fall of Baltadji. He was replaced by Yusuf Pasha, the Janissary Aga, who, to Charles' satisfaction, used the non-surrender of Azov and Tagonrog as a pretext for declaring a new war on Russia. Shafirov, Tolstoy and young Sheremetev were sent back to the Seven Towers. Tolstoy, at this point, wrote Peter begging to be allowed to return to Russia. He had been in Turkey under painful conditions for ten years, and the negotiations he had been conducting had now been taken over by Shafirov, his superior. Peter agreed, but the Turks did not, informing the aging diplomat that he must wait until a final treaty had been signed, whereupon he could return with Shafirov.

There was no fighting in this new war, and it ended quietly when, in April 1712, Peter finally surrendered Azov and Tagonrog. In fact, Apraxin was on such good terms with the Turkish pasha who came to occupy the forts that he managed to sell all the guns, powder, supplies and four of the Russian ships which remained, all for a handsome price, even though one

Russian captain later assured Whitworth that the vessels sold were so rotten that they would "fall to pieces in the first storm." This peace agreement quickly came to naught when Yusuf Pasha was overthrown and succeeded by Suleiman Pasha, who listened to Charles' continuing complaints that the Tsar still had not removed his troops from Poland. On December 10, 1712, the Turks declared war a third time to enforce this article of the treaty. Again, Shafirov, backed by the envoys of Britain and Holland, successfully smoothed matters over before actual fighting began. "This war," Shafirov wrote to Golovkin, "is disliked by the whole Turkish people and is begun by the sole will of the Sultan, who from the very beginning was not content with the Peace on the Pruth and raged greatly against the Grand Vizier because he did not profit as he ought by fortunate circumstances."

In April 1713, Ahmed III assembled his army, declared war a fourth time and, with Poniatowski at his elbow, drew up new and even more devastating terms of peace to be imposed on Russia: The entire Ukraine was to be ceded to Turkey; all of Peter's conquests, including St. Petersburg, were to be returned to Sweden. Peter met this threat by simply refusing to send a new envoy empowered to discuss the matter. As time passed, the Sultan's ardor for war passed. He began to doubt the wisdom of invading Russia, and he began to see Charles as the source of many of his difficulties. The Pasha of Bender was instructed to increase the pressure on the King of Sweden to depart the Ottoman Empire and go home. Negotiations with Russia continued; grand viziers came and went—Suleiman Pasha was succeeded by Ibrahim Pasha, then by Damad Ali Pasha, the Sultan's favorite son-in-law. Finally, on October 18, 1713, this fourth war in three years ended when the Sultan ratified the Treaty of Adrianople. Shafirov, Tolstoy and Michael Sheremetev were kept in prison, however, until the final designation of the Russian-Turkish frontier. In December 1714, the envoys were at last released and allowed to go home. The months of incarceration and suspense had overcome young Michael Sheremetev, who went mad in the Seven Towers and died on the way home; Shafirov and Tolstoy were to continue to play major roles in the reign of Peter the Great.

LOOKING BACK on the Pruth disaster, it was not difficult for Peter to understand his mistakes. He had abandoned his normally cautious tactics, the waiting game which had been so successful against Charles XII. Instead, he had adopted Charles' role and plunged impetuously into the Ottoman Empire, trusting for support and provisions from an ally who proved unfaithful. He had been misinformed about the strength of the Turkish army, and he had miscalculated the speed with which the Grand Vizier could move. He had continued his advance even after learning that the Turkish army was across the Danube and marching north. Later, he explained that

he had felt compelled to continue "in order not to place in despair the Christians who implored [my] aid." In fact, the Christians most important to his campaign, the Walachians, had betrayed him.

Nevertheless, although it failed, Peter's march to the Pruth heralded the opening of a new avenue in Russian history. A Russian tsar had invaded the Balkans; Russian infantry had marched to within forty miles of the Danube; Russian cavalrymen had watered their horses in the Danube 500 miles southwest of Kiev. A further presage was Peter's summons to the Balkan Christians to rise against the infidel and welcome his Russians as liberators. This dramatic appeal planted a hardy seed and the idea that Russia would act as Orthodox champion of the Balkan Slavs took root and grew.

DEFEAT ON THE PRUTH and his final treaty with the Sultan ended forever Peter's southern ambitions. With the hauling down of the Russian flag and the destruction of the forts at Azov and Tagonrog, the dream of his youth and the work of sixteen years came to an end. "The Lord God drove me out of this place like Adam out of paradise," said Peter of Azov. During his lifetime, there would be no Black Sea fleet. The mouth of the Don remained closed, and all Russian ships would continue to be forbidden on the sea, which would remain the Sultan's private lake. Not until the time of Catherine the Great would Russia conquer the Crimea, open the Don, force the Strait of Kerch and finally achieve what Peter had begun.

Russia simply was not strong enough to accomplish simultaneously everything that Peter wanted. He was still at war with Sweden, he was building St. Petersburg and he was trying, through sweeping reforms and reorganization, to reshape the Muscovite tsardom into a new, technologically modern European state. In this last, overriding purpose, the Baltic and St. Petersburg were more important than the Black Sea and Azov. If Peter had chosen differently, if he had stopped the building on the Neva, if he had poured that energy and labor and money into colonizing the Ukraine, if he had withdrawn his soldiers and his seamen from Poland and the Baltic and sent them all against the Turks, then a Russian fleet flying Peter's flag might have sailed the Black Sea in his lifetime. He chose differently. The south was abandoned for the west, the Baltic took priority over the Black Sea. The ultimate direction of Russia under Peter the Great was to be toward Europe, not toward the Ottoman Empire.

Peter himself was candid about his loss and clear about its implications: He wrote to Apraxin:

> Although it is not without grief that we are deprived of those places where so much labor and money have been expended, yet I

hope that by this very deprivation we shall greatly strengthen ourselves on the other side [the Baltic], which is incomparably of greater
gain to us.

Later, Peter gave an even more succinct appraisal of what had happened
to him on the Pruth: "My 'good fortune' consisted in having received only
fifty blows when I was condemned to receive a hundred."

43

THE GERMAN CAMPAIGN
AND FREDERICK WILLIAM

LEAVING THE PRUTH BEHIND, Peter and Catherine traveled north into
Poland. There and in Germany, Peter's objective was to pick up the momentum of Poltava and resume the war against Sweden. The first step was to
reassure his allies, Augustus of Poland and Frederick IV of Denmark,
that the disaster on the Pruth had not shaken his resolve to force Charles
XII to an acceptable peace. More immediately, Peter meant to visit Germany
in order to take a cure at Carlsbad and to witness the marriage of his son
Alexis to Princess Charlotte of Wolfenbüttel. All of these projects and even
Peter's travel route had been made possible by Poltava; before the destruction of the Swedish army, Charles XII had dominated Poland and made it
physically impossible for the Tsar to pass through Poland into Germany.
Now, the Swedes had vanished and Charles was far away in Turkey. For the
rest of his life, Peter traveled through the German states almost as frequently
and securely as he traveled through Russia.

Peter needed to rest and recover from the exhaustion, depression and
illness which had attended his disastrous summer in the Balkans. Even as
he traveled by water down the Vistula to Warsaw, where he spent two days,
then farther to Thorn, where he left Catherine, the Tsar was sick. In Posen,
he had a violent colic and remained in bed for several days before continuing on to Dresden and Carlsbad where he was to take the waters. This
was a dreary process of drinking mineral water that was supposed to clear
out the system; often it did so unpleasantly, and Whitworth, who was
accompanying Peter, faithfully informed his masters in London that the Tsar
was suffering "a violent looseness." Peter found it dull from the beginning
and complained to Catherine:

> Katerinushka, my friend, how are you? We arrived here well, thank
> God, and tomorrow begin our cure. The place is so merry you might
> call it an honorable dungeon, for it lies between such high mountains
> that one scarcely sees the sun. Worst of all, there is no good beer.

However, we hope God will give us health from the waters. I send you herewith a present, a new-fashioned clock, put under glass on account of the dust. . . . I could not get more [because] of my hurry, for I was only one day in Dresden.

From Carlsbad, Peter went back to Dresden, remaining a week. He stayed at the Golden Ring Inn, rather than at the royal palace, and at the inn he chose the low-ceilinged room of the porter rather than one of the main guest suites. He went to a tennis court, took a racquet and played. Twice he visited a paper factory and made sheets of paper with his own hands. He called on Johann Melchior Dinglinger, the court jeweler, whose gorgeous constructions in jewels, precious metals and enamel were famous throughout Europe. (A year later, visiting Dresden, Peter insisted on spending a week living in Dinglinger's house.) He passed three hours with Andrew Gartner, the court mathematician and mechanician, who was famous for his inventions. Peter was especially interested in a machine which Gartner had designed to carry people or objects from one floor of a house to another: in short, an elevator. In gratitude for his visit, the Tsar gave Gartner an armful of sables, suggesting that he make himself a warm coat for the winter.

On October 13, Peter arrived at Torgau, the castle of the Queen of Poland, where his son was to be married. This site, rather than Dresden, had been chosen so that the ceremony could be private, without the necessity of inviting the King of Prussia, the Elector of Hanover and other German princes, thus avoiding problems of protocol and saving time for the Tsar and money for the bride's father, the Duke of Wolfenbüttel. The wedding took place on Sunday, October 14, 1711, in the great hall of the palace. In order to increase the illuminated brilliance of the occasion, the windows were covered and the walls hung with mirrors to reflect the light of thousands of candles. The Orthodox service was performed in Russian, except that the bride, who had been converted from Lutheranism to become the consort of a future tsar, was ritually questioned in Latin. A marriage supper in the Queen's apartments was followed by a ball, after which, reported a contemporary chronicler, "His Great Tsarish Majesty gave his fatherly blessing in a most touching manner to the newly married pair and himself conducted them to their bedchamber." That same night, before retiring, Peter managed to write to Menshikov:

I will answer your letter later. I have no time now because of the marriage of my son, which was celebrated today, thank God, in a good way, with many notable people present. The marriage took place in the house of the Queen of Poland and the watermelon sent

by you was put upon the table, which vegetable is a mighty wonder here.

In Torgau, Peter finally met Gottfried von Leibniz. Ever since Peter's first visit to Germany at the time of the Great Embassy, the famous philosopher and mathematician had waited for a chance to get the Tsar's ear and to urge on him new institutions for learning and research. When he finally met Peter, Leibniz achieved at least a partial success. The Tsar did not turn over to him the future of Russian culture and education, but the following year he did appoint Leibniz a Councilor of Justice, assign him a salary (never paid) and ask him to draw up a list of proposed educational, legal and administrative reforms. As Leibniz described their next meeting, at Carlsbad in 1712, to the Electress Sophia:

I found His Majesty on the point of finishing his cure. He nevertheless desired to wait some days before leaving here, because last year he found himself unwell from having begun to travel immediately after his cure. . . . Your Electoral Highness will find it extraordinary that I am to be in a sense the Solon of Russia, although at a distance. That is to say that the Tsar has told me through Golovkin, his Grand Chancellor, that I am to reform the laws and draw up some regulations for the administration of justice. As I hold that the best laws are shortest, like the Ten Commandments or the Twelve Tables of Ancient Rome, and as this subject is one of my earliest studies, this will scarcely keep me long.

The Duke of Wolfenbüttel, a regular correspondent of Leibniz', jokingly warned the "new Solon" that he might receive little for his efforts other than the Cross of St. Andrew. Leibniz replied, disparaging his new assignment:

I am very glad to have made Your Highness laugh a little at my Russian Solon. But a Russian Solon does not need the wisdom of the Greeks and can get along with less. The Cross of St. Andrew I should like very well if it were set in diamonds, but these are not given in Hanover, but only by the Tsar. Still my promised five hundred ducats were very acceptable.

At the end of December 1711, Peter returned to St. Petersburg after an absence of almost a year. Once there, he threw himself into the administration of domestic affairs which had languished while he was on the Pruth and in Germany. He gave instructions for the expansion of trade with

Persia, formed a company of merchants to trade with China and, in April 1712, commanded his newly established Russian Senate to move from Moscow to St. Petersburg. His presence spurred much new construction along the Neva, and, in May, Peter laid the cornerstone for the new Cathedral of Peter and Paul which Trezzini was to erect within the fortress.

That spring was a worrisome time for Peter—he still had not evacuated his garrisons in Azov and Tagonrog and the Turks had declared war a second time—but he was reassured by an unusual vision which he described to Whitworth and which the ambassador faithfully reported to London:

> Some nights ago the Tsar dreamed: he saw all sorts of wild beasts fighting together, from among which a fierce tiger made at him with open jaws and put him into such confusion that he could neither defend himself nor retreat. But a voice, he could not tell from whence it came, called out to him several times that he should not fear, and the tiger stopped short of a sudden without any further attempt [to harm him]. Then four people appeared in white and, advancing into the middle of the wild beasts, their rage immediately ceased and all separated in peace. The dream has made such an impression on his [the Tsar's] fancy that he noted it down in his table book with the day of the month. I find it has really increased his confidence.

On February 19, 1712, Peter formalized and publicly proclaimed his marriage to Catherine. The ceremony, which took place at \seven a.m. in Prince Menshikov's private chapel, was intended to clarify her position as his wife and official consort to those who said that their private marriage in November 1707 was insufficient for a tsar and tsaritsa. It also was a mark of Peter's gratitude to this calm, devoted woman whose sturdy courage during the Pruth campaign had helped carry him through that disastrous episode. Peter was married in the uniform of a rear admiral, with Vice Admiral Cruys acting as his sponsor, and other naval officers acting as witnesses. Returning to his own palace in sledges between lines of trumpeters and drummers, Peter halted his sledge before he reached his front door so that he could go inside and hang over the dinner table his wedding gift to Catherine. It was a six-branched candelabrum of ivory and ebony which he himself had made in two weeks of work. That evening, wrote Whitworth, "the company was very splendid, the dinner magnificent, the wine good, from Hungary, and what was the greatest pleasure, not forced on the guests in too large quantities. The evening was concluded with a ball and fireworks." Peter was in a jolly mood; at one point in the festivity, he confided to Whitworth and the Danish ambassador that it was "a fruitful wedding, for they already had had five children."

Two years later, Peter further honored Catherine by creating a new

decoration, the Order of St. Catherine, her patron saint, which consisted of a cross hanging on a white ribbon inscribed with the motto, "Out of Love and Fidelity to My Country." The new order, Peter declared, commemorated his wife's role in the Pruth campaign, where she had behaved "not as a woman, but as a man."

AT THE BEGINNING OF 1711, even before the ill-fated campaign on the Pruth, Peter's interest was to make peace with Sweden. He had richly achieved his war aims. St. Petersburg had been given its "cushion" to the north by the capture of Vyborg and the province of Karelia. It was secured from the south by the occupation of Ingria and Livonia. Two additional seaports, Riga and Reval, along with St. Petersburg, had opened Russia's Baltic "Window on the West" as wide as could conceivably be needed. There was nothing more that Peter wanted, and he sincerely desired peace.

The governing Council and the people of Sweden also wanted peace. Sweden was defeated, the war was ruinous and the only realistic prospect was that if it continued, it would get worse. In the summer of Poltava, 1709, the harvest in Sweden failed. That autumn, emboldened by the Russian victory, Denmark reentered the war. In 1710 and 1711, the plague swept across Sweden; Stockholm lost one third of its population. Now, at the end of 1711, as the Tsar roamed freely through Germany meeting kings and princes and taking the waters, Sweden was exhausted. It had no allies, while ranged against it was the formidable coalition of Russia, Denmark, Saxony and Poland. Before long, Hanover and Prussia would also enter the anti-Swedish alliance.

If reason dictated peace, why did peace not come? Primarily, because the King of Sweden forbade it. To Charles, Poltava was only a temporary setback. New Swedish armies could be raised to replace the one lost in the Ukraine. His flight and exile in Turkey could be transformed into a brilliant opportunity if he could persuade the Sultan and the vast Ottoman army to join him in a march to Moscow. Certainly, there was no question of concluding a peace which would leave an inch of Swedish territory in Russian hands. Everything, including the Tsar's new capital on the Neva, must be returned. As the Tsar would not surrender it any other way, it must be wrenched back with the sword. Peter, accepting his opponent's stubbornness, was equally determined not to give up St. Petersburg. And so the war continued.

In 1711 and 1712, the new Russian and allied offensives against the crumbling Swedish empire were directed against the Swedish possessions in North Germany. These territories—Pomerania with its seaports of Stralsund, Stettin and Wismar; and Bremen and Verden on the Weser—were Sweden's entry ports into the continent, the springboards used by her armies.

Naturally, the disposition of these territories became a matter of keenest interest for all the states on which they bordered—Denmark, Prussia and Hanover—and eventually all three became Peter's allies. The attack on Swedish Pomerania began in the summer of 1711. Even as Peter, Catherine, Sheremetev and the main body of the Russian army were marching south to the Pruth, another Russian army of 12,000 men was moving westward through Poland to attack this Swedish territory north of Berlin. It was to be an allied effort, and in mid-August 12,000 Russian, 6,000 Saxon and 6,000 Polish troops passed through Prussia within a few miles of Berlin. A Danish contingent joined them, and together the multinational army besieged Stralsund and Wismar. Unfortunately, because of disagreements between commanders and a lack of siege artillery, nothing was achieved. Autumn came, the siege was lifted and the troops remained in Pomerania for the winter. In the spring of 1712, they moved on to besiege Stettin. Once again, the confusion of allied purposes and lack of artillery led to failure. The Russian army, now commanded by Menshikov, invested the fortress port, but could not mount an effective siege. King Frederick IV of Denmark had promised to supply the artillery, but was actually using the guns in an attempt to seize the—to him—juicier Swedish plums on the opposite side of the Danish peninsula, Bremen and Verden. The Danes protested to Menshikov that it was the duty of the Poles to supply the artillery.

This was the situation which Peter found when he arrived with Catherine before Stettin in June 1712. The Tsar was exasperated. "I consider myself very unfortunate to have come here," he wrote to Menshikov. "God sees my good intentions and the crooked dealings of others. I cannot sleep at night on account of the way I am treated." Peter also wrote to Frederick of Denmark, complaining of the wastage of another summer. Angry as he was, Peter could do no more than complain. The Danish fleet was an essential ingredient in the allied effort; no other Baltic power had a naval force capable of dealing with the Swedish fleet and cutting off the Swedish army on the continent from its homeland base. Nevertheless, Peter's tone was tart:

> I think Your Majesty knows that I have not only furnished the number of troops agreed upon last year . . . with the King of Poland, but even three times as many, and besides that, for the common interest, I have come here myself, not sparing my health with the constant fatigue and long journey. But on my arrival here I find the army idle, because the artillery promised by you has not come, and when I asked your Vice Admiral Segestet about it, he replied that it could not be given without your particular order. I am greatly at a loss to understand why these changes are made and why favorable time is thus being wasted, from which, besides the loss of money and

to the common interests, we shall gain nothing except the ridicule of our enemies. I have always been, and am, ready to help my allies in everything that the common interest demands. If you do not comply with this request of mine to [send the artillery], I can prove to you and the whole world that this campaign has not been lost by me, and I shall then not be to blame if, as I am inactive here, I am obliged to withdraw my troops, because on account of the expense of things here it is a waste of money, and I cannot endure being dishonored by the enemy.

Peter's letter did no good; the Danish artillery continued to batter at Bremen, not Stettin. In this frustrated mood, Peter left the army at the end of September 1712 to return for the third straight autumn to take the waters at Carlsbad. On the way, passing through Wittenberg, he visited the grave of Martin Luther and the house in which Luther had lived. In the house, the curator showed him an ink spot on the wall which supposedly dated to the moment when Luther had seen the Devil and thrown his inkpot at him. Peter laughed and asked, "Did such a wise man really believe that the Devil could be seen?" Asked to sign the wall himself, Peter chidingly wrote, "The ink spot is quite fresh, so the story obviously is not true."

Traveling to Carlsbad, Peter also passed through Berlin and called on the elderly King Frederick I of Prussia and his son Frederick William, the Prince Royal. "The Tsar arrived here last Tuesday at seven p.m.," wrote a member of the Prussian court.

We were in the tabiage [smoking room] when the Field Marshal came to inform the King, who asked me how the Tsar had been received in Dresden. I said that although the King [Augustus] was absent, all sorts of honors had been offered to him, but he had accepted nothing and had lodged in a private house. His Majesty replied that he would likewise offer him everything. . . .

The Tsar went to the palace and going up the private staircase surprised the King in his bedroom playing chess with the Prince Royal. The two Majesties stayed half an hour together. Then the Tsar looked at the apartments in which the King of Denmark had stayed, admired them, but refused to occupy them. A supper was given by the Prince Royal, there being eight at the table besides the Tsar, who allowed no toasts, ate though he had already supped, but did not drink. . . .

Yesterday the Tsar went to the King in the tabiage, put on a fine red coat embroidered with gold, instead of his pelisse, which he found too hot, and went to supper. He was gallant enough to give his hand to the Queen, after having put on a rather dirty glove. The

King and all the royal family supped with him. . . . The Tsar surpassed himself during all this time. He neither belched, nor farted, nor picked his teeth—at least I neither saw nor heard him do so—and he conversed with the Queen and with the Princesses without showing any embarrassment. The crowd of spectators was very great. He embraced the King for goodbye, and, after making a general bow to all the company, went off with such long strides that it was impossible for the King to keep up with him.

Five months later, on his way back to Russia, Peter again passed through Berlin. King Frederick I had just died and the twenty-five-year-old Prince Royal now sat on the throne as King Frederick William I. "I have found the new King very pleasant," Peter wrote to Menshikov, "but cannot decide him on any action. As far as I can understand from two reasons: first, because he has no money, and second, because there are still here many dogs of Swedish heart. The King himself is unskilled in political matters and when he asks his Ministers for advice, they help the Swedes in every way. . . . The Court here is not so grand as it was before." As for joining an active alliance against Sweden, the new King of Prussia said that he needed at least a year to put his army and finances in order.

THE LIFETIME of Peter the Great and the rise of Russia also saw the emergence of a new, highly disciplined military state in North Germany, the kingdom of Prussia. It sprang from the electorate of Brandenburg, whose ruling house, the House of Hohenzollern, had descended from the Teutonic Knights. Its capital, Berlin, was still only a town in Peter's day, with a population in 1700 of 25,000. Its people were Protestant, frugal and efficient, with a capacity for organization, a willingness to sacrifice and a belief that duty was the highest call. Other Germans—Rhinelanders, Bavarians, Hanoverians and Saxons—thought of Brandenburgers as semi-feudal, less civilized and more aggressive than themselves.

The weakness of the state was geographical. A product of dynastic marriages and inheritances, it was scattered in unconnected fragments all across the Northern European plain. Its westernmost territory, the duchy of Cleves, lay on the Rhine near the point where the great river flows into Holland; its easternmost fief, the duchy of East Prussia, lay on the Neman, over 500 miles east of Cleves. The Treaty of Westphalia in 1648, which ended the Thirty Years' War, had left the state of Brandenburg with gloomy prospects. It was cut off from the sea. It lacked natural resources; because of its poor soil, it was called "the sandbox of the Holy Roman Empire." Its countryside had been ravaged and depopulated by the constant passage of foreign Protestant and Catholic armies. In 1640, however, the ancient

House of Hohenzollern, which had ruled Brandenburg since 1417, had produced a remarkable ruler, the Elector Frederick William. Although his territories were scattered and impoverished, he dreamed of a new Hohenzollern state which should be independent, united and powerful. Frederick William, who came to be called the Great Elector, created the machinery which was to raise Prussia to the front rank of European states. He organized an efficient, centralized government with a disciplined civil service, a postal system, a graduated income tax. And by 1688, after forty-eight years as ruler, the Great Elector had given Brandenburg, which had a population of only one million people, a modern, standing army of 30,000 men.

The Great Elector's descendants built faithfully on his foundations. By 1701, the power of the Prussian state had grown to the point that the Great Elector's son Frederick was no longer content with the title of elector. He wanted to be a king. The Emperor in Vienna, who awarded such titles, was reluctant; if he made Frederick a king, then the electors of Hanover, Bavaria and Saxony would also want to be kings. But in this case the Emperor had no choice. About to enter what he knew would be a long and difficult war with France (the War of the Spanish Succession), he badly needed the Prussian regiments which Frederick was only too happy to rent to him—if he could become a king. The Emperor bowed, and on January 18, 1701, Frederick placed a crown on his own head in Königsberg to become King Frederick I of Prussia.

He was succeeded in 1713 by twenty-five-year-old King Frederick William I, who became the friend and ally of Peter of Russia. Even more single-mindedly than his father or grandfather, Frederick William I set as the unique purpose for the Prussian state the achievement of maximum military power. Everything was bent toward it: a sound economy which would support a larger army; an efficient bureaucracy which would make it easier to collect taxes to pay for more soldiers; an excellent system of public education which would create more intelligent soldiers. In contrast to France, where national wealth was poured into public architectural grandeur, Prussian buildings were constructed exclusively for military purpose: powder mills, cannon factories, arsenals, barracks. The King of Prussia's goal was a professional army of 80,000 men. Yet, despite this waxing military power, Prussian diplomatic policy was cautious. Like his father, Frederick William I coveted new territories and new seaports, but he did not rush to seize them. Prussian troops fought in Hapsburg imperial armies in Flanders and Italy, but always under contract; Prussia itself was never at war. In its dealings with the participants in the Great Northern War, which raged around its frontiers, Prussia was especially careful. During all the years that Charles XII was marching back and forth in Poland, Prussia remained neutral. Only after Poltava, when Sweden had dropped to its knees, did Prussia join Hanover to declare war and pick up the spoils.

In his personal life, Frederick William I was a curious and unfortunate man. Eccentric, homely, apoplectic, a martinet, he hated everything his father had loved, especially everything French. Frederick William despised the people, the language, the culture and even the food of France. When criminals were hanged, the King first had them dressed in French clothes. On the surface, Frederick William was a plain Protestant monarch, a faithful husband, a stodgy, bourgeois father. He stripped his court of frills, selling most of his father's furniture and jewels and dismissing most of his courtiers. He fell in love with and married his Hanoverian first cousin, Sophia Dorothea, the daughter of the future King George I of England. He referred to her as "my wife" instead of "the Queen" and his son as "Fritz" instead of "the Heir to the Throne." Every night, he ate dinner with his family.

What spoiled this pretty domestic scene were Frederick William's violent rages. Quite suddenly, he would flare out brutally at his children or anyone near him. Triggered by small, harmless remarks or even looks, he would begin to swing his wooden cane, hitting people in the face, sometimes breaking their noses or teeth. When he did this in a Berlin street, there was nothing the victim could do; to resist or strike back at the enraged monarch was punishable by death. The explanation, apparently, was porphyria, the disease supposedly descended from Mary Queen of Scots which later afflicted King George III. A derangement of the metabolism whose symptoms are gout, migraines, abscesses, boils, hemorrhoids and terrible pains in the stomach, the disease plunged the King into agony and tinged him with insanity. He became very fat, his eyes bulged and his skin glistened like polished ivory. Seeking distraction from these miseries, Frederick William learned to paint and signed his canvases "FW in tormentis pinxit." Every evening after dinner, he convoked his ministers and generals to drink tankards of beer and smoke long pipes. At these crude, masculine gatherings, the leaders of the Prussian state delighted in teasing and tormenting a pedantic court historian, whom they once actually set on fire.

The King's most famous obsession was his collection of giants, for which he was renowned throughout Europe. Known as the Blue Prussians or the Giants of Potsdam, there were over 1,200 of them, organized into two battalions of 600 men each. None was under six feet tall, and some, in the special Red Unit of the First Battalion, were almost seven feet tall. The King dressed them in blue jackets with gold trim and scarlet lapels, scarlet trousers, white stockings, black shoes and tall red hats. He gave them muskets, white bandoleers and small daggers, and he played with them as a child would with enormous living toys. No expense was too great for this hobby, and Frederick William spent millions to recruit and equip his giant grenadiers. They were hired or bought all over Europe; especially desirable specimens, refusing the offer of the King's recruiting agents, were simply

kidnapped. Eventually, recruiting in this way became too expensive—one seven-foot-two-inch Irishman cost over 6,000 pounds—and Frederick William tried to breed giants. Every tall man in his realm was forced to marry a tall woman. The drawback was that the King had to wait fifteen to twenty years for the products of these unions to mature, and often as not a boy or girl of normal height resulted. The easiest method of obtaining giants was to receive them as gifts. Foreign ambassadors advised their masters that the way to find favor with the King of Prussia was to send him giants. Peter especially appreciated his fellow sovereign's interest in nature's curios, and Russia supplied the Prussian King with fifty new giants every year. (Once, when Peter recalled some of the Russian giants lent to Frederick William and replaced them with men who were a trifle shorter, the King was so upset that he could not discuss business with the Russian ambassador; the wound in his heart, he said, was still too raw.)

Needless to say, the King never risked his cherished colossi in the face of enemy fire. In turn, they provided the ailing monarch with his greatest delight. When he was sick or depressed, the entire two battalions, preceded by tall, turbaned Moors with cymbals and trumpets and the grenadiers' mascot, an enormous bear, would march in a long line through the King's chamber to cheer him up.

Not surprisingly, Frederick William's Queen, Sophia Dorothea, was unhappy with this strange man. She wanted more grandeur, more courtiers, more jewels, more balls. Especially after her father became King of England and a potentate on a par with the Emperor in Vienna, she looked down on the House of Hohenzollern and this frugal little court in Berlin. Nevertheless, she bore her husband fourteen children and protected them by hiding them in her private rooms when her enraged husband was chasing them through the palace with his stick. Their two firstborn were sons, both named Frederick, and both died quickly. The third, also named Frederick, survived, along with nine younger brothers and sisters. He was a delicate, polite little boy who loved everything French—the language, clothes, even hair styles— and whose tongue was so quick he could run circles around his father in an argument. Despite his sensitive nature, he was brought up as a warrior prince, the heir to a military state. His father gave him his own toy regiment, the Crown Prince Cadets, made up of 131 little boys whom the Prince could command and play with as he liked. At fourteen, the small boy (he never grew to be more than five feet seven inches) was made a major of the giant Potsdam Grenadiers, and on the parade ground he commanded these titans, who towered over him.

Relations worsened between father and son. The King, who was often in a wheelchair suffused with agony, treated his son contemptuously. At the same time, realizing what he was doing, the King told Frederick, "If my

father had treated me as I treat you, I wouldn't have put up with it. I would have killed myself or run away."

In 1730, at the age of eighteen, Frederick did run away. He was quickly recaptured, and the King treated his son and Frederick's companion, the esthetic Hans Hermann von Katte, a Francophile and the son of a general, as deserters from the army. They were imprisoned, and one morning the Prince awoke to see Von Katte led into the prison courtyard and beheaded by a saber stroke.

In 1740, the disintegrating King Frederick William died, and Prince Frederick, at twenty-eight, succeeded to the Prussian throne. Within several months, he had put the Prussian war machine so carefully created by his father and grandfather into motion. To the astonishment of Europe, he invaded Silesia, provoking war with the Hapsburg Empire. It was the first of the brilliant military campaigns which were to proclaim the military genius of the slight young monarch and earn him the title of Frederick the Great.

IN THE AUTUMN OF 1712, while Peter's army was mired before Stettin and the Tsar himself was traveling between Dresden, Carlsbad and Berlin, Sweden, incredibly, was preparing a final offensive on the continent. Charles XII had commanded that still another army be raised and sent to North Germany. Its mission was to march south through Poland to rendezvous with him and an Ottoman army to pursue his dream of invading Russia. The poverty-stricken Swedes heard this command with despair. "Tell the King," wrote one of his officials, "that Sweden can send no more troops to Germany, if she has to defend herself against Denmark and especially against the Tsar, who has already conquered the Baltic provinces and part of Finland and now threatens to invade the country and lay Stockholm in ashes. The patience of Sweden is great but not so great as to wish to become Russian." Nevertheless, the King's command was finally obeyed, and with great difficulty a new army was raised. Magnus Stenbock landed in Swedish Pomerania with a mobile field army of 18,000 men. Stenbock's mission was badly damaged from the beginning when the Danish fleet intercepted a convoy of Swedish cargo ships, their holds crammed with provisions, ammunition and powder needed by his troops, and sent thirty of the ships to the bottom. Even so, Stenbock's landing caused great concern among the allies, and the destruction of his force became an urgent priority for their combined armies. From Dresden, where he was resting after his cure, Peter urged Frederick of Denmark to lead his troops from Holstein against the Swedes: "I hope Your Majesty recognized the necessity of such action. I beseech you in the most friendly and brotherly way, and at the same time I declare that although

my health demands repose after my cure, yet, seeing the urgent need, I will not neglect this profitable affair and will go to the army." To Menshikov, Peter was even more insistent: "For God's sake, if there be a good opportunity, even if I do not succeed in getting to you, do not lose time, but in the Lord's name attack the enemy."

Faced by converging forces of Danes, Saxons, and Russians, Stenbock decided to attack the Danes separately before the Tsar with the main Russian and Saxon armies could arrive. Marching through a snowstorm on December 20, 1712, he caught 15,000 Danes in their camp at Gadebusch and severely mauled them, almost capturing King Frederick IV. But his victory had limited results; his force was reduced to 12,000, and he was soon being pursued by 36,000 Saxons, Russians and Danes. Still waiting for fresh supplies and reinforcements from Sweden, he saw the ice crusting in the Baltic harbors and realized that no help would come from home that winter. Seeking refuge, he marched west toward Hamburg and Bremen. He demanded of Altona, a town near Hamburg, a ransom of 100,000 thalers for his expenses, and when the town could raise only 42,000 thalers, Stenbock's men burned it to the ground, leaving only thirty houses. Two days later, a Swedish detachment came back and burned twenty-five of the thirty. Peter, reaching Altona with his pursuing army eight days later, was shaken by the sight of the refugees without shelter among the ruins, and distributed a thousand roubles among them. Stenbock's retreat eventually came to an end in the fortress of Tonning on the North Sea coast, where he was surrounded and closed in for the winter by allied troops.

On January 25, 1713, with no further military action possible until spring, Peter left the army, giving command of the Russian troops to Menshikov and leaving the allied force under the command of the King of Denmark. From Tonning, Peter traveled to Hanover to meet the Elector George Louis, soon, on the death of Queen Anne, to become King George I of England. Peter wanted not only to persuade Hanover to enter the war against Sweden but, through the Elector, to determine the attitude of England. After his visit, Peter wrote to Catherine, "The Elector appeared very favorably inclined and gave me much advice, but does not wish to do anything actively."

The Tsar then returned to St. Petersburg, and four months later, in May 1713, Stenbock capitulated at Tonning. Menshikov led the Russian army back to Pomerania, along the way threatening Hamburg and extracting a 100,000-thaler "contribution" from the free city to punish it for its highly profitable trade with Sweden. Peter was delighted with this action and wrote to Menshikov, "Thanks for the money which was taken from Hamburg in a good manner and without loss of time. Send the greater part of it to Kurakin [in Holland]. It is very necessary for the purchase of ships." From

Hamburg, Menshikov marched eastward and besieged Stettin. This time, he was equipped with Saxon siege artillery, and on September 19, 1713, Stettin fell. As agreed, Stettin was then turned over to Frederick William of Prussia, who so far had not been required to fire a shot.

Now, of all Charles' once-great empire south of the Baltic Sea, only the ports of Stralsund and Wismar remained under the blue-and-yellow flag of Sweden.

44

THE COAST
OF FINLAND

PETER RETURNED to St. Petersburg on March 22, 1713, but spent only one
month in his beloved city. During April, he learned from Shafirov in Turkey
that, despite damaging Tatar raids in the Ukraine, the Ottoman Turks had
no intention of making serious war in the south. The Tsar therefore was able
to devote all his attention to readying the fleet and army to conquer the
north shore of the upper Baltic.

Once the surrender of Stenbock, penned up in the fortress of Tonning,
seemed inevitable, Peter turned to the opposite end of the Baltic, resolving
to drive the Swedes out of Finland. He did not intend to keep the province,
but any territory he took in Finland beyond Karelia would be useful for
bargaining when peace negotiations began. It could, for example, be used
to balance those Swedish territories such as Ingria and Karelia which Peter
did intend to keep. There was another advantage to a Finnish campaign:
He would be on his own, without wrangling allies to hinder his operations.
After the agonizing delays in Pomerania over the delivery of artillery and
the necessity of pleading with other monarchs to live up to their promises, it would be a relief to conduct a campaign exactly how and where he
wished.

In fact, Peter had not waited until that spring to decide on this campaign.
Already in the previous November, he had written from Carlsbad ordering
Apraxin to intensify the preparation of troops and fleet for an advance into
Finland. "This province," Peter wrote, "is the mother of Sweden as you
yourself are aware. Not only meat, but even wood is brought from it, and if
God let us get as far as Abo [a town on the east coast of the Gulf of
Bothnia, then the capital of Finland] next summer, the Swedish neck will
be easier to bend."

The Finnish campaign that summer and the next was swift, efficient and
relatively bloodless. For this brilliant success, the new Russian Baltic fleet
was almost wholly responsible.

DURING PETER'S REIGN, there was a radical shift in warship design and naval tactics. In the 1690's, the term "ship-of-the-line" first appeared when the confused melee of individual ship-to-ship duels was replaced by the "line" tactic—two rows of warships sailing on parallel courses and pounding each other with heavy artillery. The "line" imposed standards of design; a capital ship had to be powerful enough to lie in the line of battle, as compared to the smaller, faster frigates and sloops used for reconnaissance and commerce raiding. The qualifications were strict: stout construction, fifty or more heavy cannon and a crew trained in expert seamanship and accurate gunnery. In all these respects, Englishmen excelled.

The average ship-of-the-line carried from sixty to eighty heavy cannon placed in rows on two or three gundecks and divided, port and starboard, so that even a full broadside meant that only half the guns aboard a ship could fire at an enemy. Some men-of-war were even bigger, goliaths of ninety or one hundred guns, whose crews, including marine sharpshooters posted in the rigging to pick off officers and gunners on the enemy decks, reached more than 800 men.

Apart from damage inflicted in battle, the effectiveness of warships was limited by the damage caused by time and the elements. Leaking hulls, loose masts, tattered rigging and parted lines were commonplace in ships at sea. For serious repairs, ships had to come into port, and the bases to support them were an essential element of seapower.

In winter—especially in the Baltic, where ice made naval operations impossible—fleets went into hibernation. The ships were brought alongside a quay, where sails, rigging, topmasts, spars, cannon and cannonballs were carried off and laid in rows or stacked in pyramids. At the Baltic naval bases—Karlskrona, Copenhagen, Kronstadt and Reval—the great hulls were lined up side by side like sleeping elephants, frozen into the ice for winter. In the spring, one by one, the hulls were careened—that is, rolled on one side so that rotten or damaged bottom planks could be replaced, barnacles scraped, seams recalked and tarred. This done, the ships went back to the quay, and the procedure of the previous autumn was reversed: Cannon, spars, rigging all came back on board and the hull became once more a warship.

Relative to England's Royal Navy with its 100 ships of the line, the Baltic powers had smaller fleets, intended mainly for use against each other within the confines of that enclosed sea. Denmark was almost an island kingdom whose capital, Copenhagen, was wholly exposed to the sea. The Swedish empire when Charles XII came to the throne was also a maritime entity, its integrity resting on secure communications and freedom to move troops and provisions between Sweden, Finland, Estonia, Livonia and North Germany. From her new, strategically placed naval base built at Karlskrona in 1658 to curb the Danes and protect her sea communications with her

German provinces, Sweden was able to control all the middle and upper Baltic. Even after Poltava had humbled the previously invincible Swedish army, the Swedish navy remained formidable. In 1710, the year after Poltava, Sweden had forty-one ships-of-the-line, Denmark had forty-one, Russia had none. The senior Swedish admiral, Wachtmeister, was primarily occupied against the Danes, but powerful Swedish squadrons still cruised in the Gulf of Finland and off the Livonian coast.

Against the Russians, the Swedish fleet was able to do little. It could ensure the arrival of supplies and reinforcements, but once an army was committed to action on land, a fleet was not much help. At the time the Russians were besieging Riga, the entire Swedish fleet assembled off the mouth of the Dvina, but could contribute nothing to the town's defense, and eventually Riga capitulated. In the later phase of the Great Northern War, however, seapower became increasingly important. The only way to force an obdurate Sweden to make peace, Peter realized, was to reach across the Baltic Sea to threaten the Swedish homeland. One invasion avenue was directly across from Denmark to Sweden, a massive landing to be supported and covered by the Danish fleet; this projected assault occupied the Tsar during the summer and autumn of 1716. The other approach lay along the coast of Finland, then across the Gulf of Bothnia into the Aland Islands and thence toward Stockholm. It was this approach which Peter tried first, in the summers of 1713 and 1714.

Peter would have preferred to make this effort at the head of a powerful Russian sea-going battle fleet of fifty ships-of-the-line. But to lay the great keel beams in place, then add the ribs and planking, to cast the cannon, set the rigging, recruit and train the crews to sail and fight them so that they would do more damage to the enemy than to themselves, was a gigantic task. Despite the hiring of foreign shipwrights, admirals, officers and seamen, the project moved slowly. The herculean effort expended at Voronezh, Azov and Tagonrog was now fruitless; the construction of a new fleet on the Baltic had to begin from scratch.

Gradually, through 1710 and 1711, the big ships accumulated, but Peter still possessed too few to challenge the Swedish navy in a classic sea battle for control of the upper Baltic. Besides, once he had spent the immense effort in time and money necessary to build and equip the ships, he wanted to preserve them. Accordingly, he had given an order absolutely forbidding his admirals to risk the ships-of-the-line and frigates in battle unless the odds were overwhelmingly favorable. Thus, for the most part, the new big ships of Peter's Baltic fleet remained in the harbor.

Although Peter continued to build ships-of-the-line at home and to order them from Dutch and English shipyards, the brilliant success of the Tsar's naval campaigns in 1713 and 1714 in the Gulf of Finland was due to his employment of a class of ship never seen before in the Baltic, the galley.

Galleys were hybrid ships. Usually around eighty to a hundred feet long, a typical galley possessed a single mast and a single sail, but also numerous benches for oarsmen. Thus equipped, it combined the qualities of sailing ships and rowed vessels and could move in wind or calm. For centuries, galleys had been used in the enclosed waters of the Mediterranean, where the wind was freakish and unreliable. Even in the eighteenth century, on these sun-baked bays and gulfs, the naval tradition of the Persian emperors and Roman republic survived. A few small cannon had been added, but the galleys were too small and unstable to carry the heavy naval guns of larger ships. Accordingly, eighteenth-century galleys fought using the tactics developed in the days of Xerxes and Pompey: They rowed toward their enemy and grappled with him, deciding the issue with a hand-to-hand infantry battle conducted on crowded, violent, slippery decks.

In Peter's time, the Ottoman navy was made up mostly of galleys. Officered by Greeks, manned by slaves, they were behemoths, the biggest carrying as many as 2,000 men divided between two decks of oarsmen and ten companies of soldiers. To fight the Turks in the confined waters of the Aegean and the Adriatic, the Venetians also built galleys, and it was to Venice that Peter sent numerous young Russians to learn the art of galley building. France kept some forty galleys in the Mediterranean, rowed by convicts sent to the galleys for life in lieu of execution. Surrounded by stormy seas, Britain had no use for galleys.

Peter had always been interested in galleys. They could be built quickly and inexpensively, of pine rather than hardwood. They could be manned by inexperienced seamen, soldiers who could double as naval infantrymen to board and attack an enemy. The largest would carry 300 men and five guns, the smallest 150 men and three guns.* Peter had constructed galleys first at Voronezh, then at Tagonrog, and those built on Lake Peipus were used in the campaigns of 1702, 1703 and 1704 to drive a Swedish flotilla from the lake. Galleys would be perfect to circumvent the Swedish advantage in big men-of-war in the Baltic. Given the nature of the Finnish coast, studded with myriad rocky islands and fjords fringed with red granite and fir trees, Peter could neutralize the Swedish fleet simply by conceding to it the open water while his more maneuverable shallow-draft galleys moved in the inshore coastal waters that the larger Swedish ships would not dare enter. Cruising along the coast, the Russian galleys could carry supplies and troops, almost invulnerable to the larger Swedish ships outside. And if the Swedes came in to meet them, the big ships might easily founder on the rocks, or if the wind

---

* A model of a Russian galley, the *Dvina,* built in 1721, is in the Russian Navy Museum in Leningrad today. It models a ship 125 feet long and 20 feet wide, and each of its 50 benches could accommodate four or five men, pulling an oar 43.5 feet in length.

dropped and left them becalmed, the Swedes would lie helpless before the Russian galleys rowing to attack.

For Sweden, Russia's surprising appearance as a Baltic naval power and Peter's heavy reliance on galleys created a painful dilemma. Traditionally, Swedish admirals were accustomed to maintain a regular fleet of modern, heavy ships-of-the-line ready to confront their traditional adversaries, the Danes. When Peter's galleys began splashing down from the construction ways, Sweden faced an entirely different kind of naval warfare. Already financially exhausted, Sweden lacked the means simultaneously to maintain its fleet against the Danes and to build a huge galley fleet to combat Russia. Thus it was that Swedish admirals and captains could only watch helplessly from their larger ships outside as Peter's oar-driven, shallow-draft galley flotillas moved inshore along the coastline, swiftly and efficiently conquering the coast of Finland.

The overall commander in these successful naval campaigns was General Admiral Fedor Apraxin, who usually also took personal command of the galley fleet. Vice Admiral Cornelius Cruys, the Dutch officer who had helped Peter build his fleet and train his seamen, customarily flew his flag on one of the ships-of-the-line, while the Tsar himself, always insisting on calling himself "Rear Admiral Peter Alexeevich" when afloat, switched back and forth between commanding squadrons of larger ships and flotillas of galleys. Apraxin impressed his foreign officers with his manner and skill. One of his English captains described him as a man "of moderate height, well-made, inclining to feed, careful about his hair which is very long and now grey; and generally wears it tied up in a ribbon. A widower of long date, without issue, yet you observe an incomparable economy, order and decency in his house, gardens, domestics and dress. All unanimously vote in behalf of his excellent temper; but he loves to have men comport themselves according to their rank." Apraxin's relations with Peter, ashore and afloat, were conducted with a delicate blend of dignity and circumspection. At court, having given his word, and convinced of the merit of his case, Apraxin continued "even if opposed by the Sovereign's absolute will to maintain the justice of his demand until the Tsar, in a passion, by his menaces enforces silence." But at sea Apraxin would not give way to Peter. The General Admiral had never been abroad and had not himself been trained in seamanship and naval tactics until he was well along in years. Nevertheless he refused to submit

> even when the Tsar, as junior flag officer, differing in opinion, will endeavor to invalidate the General Admiral's opinion by alleging his inexperience as never having seen foreign navies. Count Apraxin will instantly overrule the same invidious charge, to the utmost provoca-

tion of the Tsar; though afterwards he will submit with the following statement: "Whilst I as Admiral argue with Your Majesty in quality of flag officer, I can never give way; but if you assume the [rank of] Tsar I know my duty."

BY THE SPRING OF 1713, the galley fleet was ready. At the end of April, only a month after his return from Pomerania, Peter sailed from Kronstadt with a fleet of ninety-three galleys and 110 other large boats carrying between them more than 16,000 soldiers. Apraxin commanded the whole fleet; the Tsar commanded the vanguard. The campaign was an overwhelming success. Using the galleys to leapfrog the troops from one point on the coast to another, the Russian army worked its way steadily westward along the Finnish coast. It was a classic example of amphibious warfare: Whenever the Swedish General Lybecker positioned his force in a strong defensive position, the Russian galleys, hugging the coastline, would slip around behind him, row into a harbor and disembark hundreds or thousands of men, unfatigued by marching, with cannon and supplies. There was nothing the Swedes could do to stop them and nothing Lybecker could do except retreat.

Early in May, dozens of Russian ships filled with soldiers appeared off Helsingfors (now Helsinki), a prosperous town with an excellent deep-water harbor. Faced with thousands of Russians suddenly arriving from the sea, the defenders could only burn their stores and abandon the town. Peter sailed immediately for the nearby port of Borga, and Lybecker abandoned it as well. Lybecker was never popular in Stockholm and had been the subject of constant complaints, but the Council had not dared remove him, as he had been personally appointed by the King. Now, however, the argument was heard that "It is a question of whether we shall get rid of Lybecker or of Finland."

By September 1713, the Russian amphibious advance had carried as far as Abo. Lybecker was recalled and replaced by General Karl Armfelt, a native Finn. On October 6, Armfelt's troops took a stand in a narrow pass near Tammerfors. The Russians attacked, defeated them badly and drove them out of the pass. Thereafter, a small Swedish army remained in Finland to the north of Abo, but all Swedish civilian officials, all official papers and the library of the provincial government were removed to Stockholm. Much of the Finnish population fled across the Gulf of Bothnia and took refuge in the Aland Islands. Thus, in a single summer, without the aid or encumbrance of any foreign ally, Peter had conquered all of southern Finland.

At sea, however, the Swedish fleet remained supreme. In the open water, the Swedish ships-of-the-line could stand off and pound the Russian galleys

to pieces with their heavy guns. The galleys' only chance would be to tempt the bigger ships close inshore and then catch them there when the wind had dropped. This was exactly the fortuitous situation presented to Peter at the Battle of Hangö in August 1714.

In preparation for the naval campaign of 1714, Peter had nearly doubled the size of his Baltic fleet. During March alone, sixty new galleys were completed. Three ships-of-the-line purchased in England arrived at Riga, and another built in St. Petersburg anchored at Kronstadt. By May, twenty Russian ships-of-the-line and almost 200 galleys were ready for action.

On June 22, 100 galleys, mostly commanded by Venetians and Greeks who had had experience in the Mediterranean, sailed for Finland with Apraxin again in overall command and Peter as rear admiral serving as his deputy. Through the midsummer weeks, the Russian ships cruised off the coast of southern Finland, but did not dare venture beyond the rocky promontory of Cape Hangö at the western end of the gulf lest they encounter a formidable Swedish fleet which waited for them on the horizon. This was a major squadron including sixteen ships-of-the-line, five frigates and a number of galleys and smaller vessels under the Swedish commander-in-chief, Admiral Wattrang, whose mission was to bar passage any farther westward in the direction of the Aland Islands and the Swedish coast.

For several weeks, this impasse continued. Wattrang had no intention of fighting a battle inshore, and the Russian galleys, unwilling to submit themselves to Wattrang's big guns on open water, remained anchored at Tvermine, six miles east of Cape Hangö. Finally, on August 4, Wattrang's ships moved in toward the Russians and then, seeing the vast number of Russian sails, turned back to the open sea. The Russian galleys quickly pursued, hoping to catch at least some of the Swedish ships if the wind should drop. In the maneuvering that followed, most of the Swedish ships managed to withdraw out of reach.

But the following morning what Peter had hoped for finally happened. The wind died, the sea was becalmed, and on the glassy surface lay a division of the Swedish fleet commanded by Admiral Ehrenskjold. The Russians moved quickly to seize the advantage. At dawn, twenty Russian galleys left the protective waters of the coast and rowed outside to seaward of the motionless Swedish vessels. Realizing what was happening, Ehrenskjold's ships lowered small boats, which under oars tried to tow their ships away. But the power of a few oarsmen in small boats could not match the coordinated strokes of the oarsmen in the Russian galleys. That night, Apraxin's main force, over sixty galleys, slipped between the Swedes and the coast, moving out to sea between the squadrons of Wattrang and Ehrenskjold. For refuge, Ehrenskjold withdrew up a narrow fjord and formed his ships into a line, head to stern, from one side of the fjord to the other. The following day,

with the Swedish squadron isolated, Apraxin was ready to attack. First, he sent an officer on board the Swedish flagship to offer Ehrenskjold honorable terms if he would surrender. The offer was refused, and the battle began. It was a strange and extraordinary contest between warships of two different kinds, one ancient and one modern. The Swedes had superiority in heavy cannon and skilled seamen, but the Russians had an overwhelming advantage in numbers of ships and men. Their smaller, more maneuverable galleys, decks loaded with infantry, simply charged the Swedish ships en masse, taking what losses they had to from Swedish cannon fire, closing in and boarding the immobile Swedish vessels. Indeed, Apraxin launched his ships less like an admiral than a general sending in waves of infantry or cavalry. At two p.m. on August 6, he sent in the first wave of thirty-five galleys. The Swedes held their fire until the galleys were close, then raked their decks with cannon fire, forcing the galleys to fall back. A second attack by eighty galleys was also repulsed. Then, Apraxin's combined fleet attacked, ninety-five galleys in all, concentrating on the left side of the head-to-stern line. Russian boarding parties swept over the Swedish vessels; one Swedish vessel capsized from the sheer weight of the men struggling on its deck. Once the Swedish line was broken, the Russians rowed through the gap, swarming along the remainder of the line, attacking from both sides at once and seizing ship after ship of the immobile Swedish line. The battle raged for three hours with heavy casualties on both sides. In the end, the Swedes were overwhelmed, 361 were killed and more than 900 became prisoners. Ehrenskjold himself was captured, along with his flagship, the frigate *Elephant*, and nine smaller Swedish ships.

There is a disagreement as to Peter's whereabouts during the battle. Some have said that he commanded the first division of Apraxin's galleys; others, that he watched the action from the shore. Hangö was not a classic naval action, but it was Russia's first victory at sea, and Peter always considered it a personal vindication of his years of effort to build a navy, and a victory equal in importance to Poltava.

Elated, he meant to celebrate in the grandest style. Sending the bulk of the galley fleet westward to occupy the now unprotected Aland Islands, Peter returned with his Swedish prizes to Kronstadt. He remained for several days while Catherine was in childbirth, delivering their daughter Margarita. Then, on September 20, he staged his triumph, leading the captured frigate and six other Swedish ships up into the Neva River while cannon boomed a 150-gun salute. The ships anchored near the Peter and Paul Fortress, and both Russian and Swedish crews came ashore for the victory procession. The parade was led by the Preobrazhensky Guards and included 200 Swedish officers and seamen, the flag of the captured Admiral and Admiral Ehrenskjold himself, wearing a new suit laced in silver which was a present from the Tsar. Peter appeared in the green uniform of a

Russian rear admiral laced with gold. A new triumphal arch had been erected for the occasion, adorned with a Russian eagle seizing an elephant (an allusion to the captured Swedish frigate) and the inscription, "The Russian Eagle catches no flies." From the arch, victors and vanquished marched to the fortress, where they were greeted by Romodanovsky, seated on a throne in his role as Mock-Tsar and surrounded by the Senate. Romodanovsky summoned the tall Rear Admiral before him and accepted from Peter's hands a written account of the battle at sea. The account was read aloud, after which the Mock-Tsar and senators questioned Peter on several points. After brief deliberation, they unanimously proclaimed that in consideration of his faithful service, the Rear Admiral was promoted to Vice Admiral, and the crowd broke into cheers of "Health to the Vice Admiral!" Peter's speech in thanks called his comrades' attention to the changes wrought in only two decades: "Friends and Companions: Is there any one among you who, twenty years ago, would have dared to conceive our covering the Baltic with ships built with our own hands or living in this town built on soil conquered from our enemies?"

When the ceremony ended, Peter boarded his own sloop and hoisted the flag of vice admiral with his own hands. That night, Menshikov's palace was the scene of a huge banquet for Russians and Swedes alike. Peter, rising and turning to his Russian followers, praised Admiral Ehrenskjold. "Here you see a brave and faithful servant of his master who has made himself worthy of the highest reward at his hands and who shall always have my favor as long as he is with me, although he has killed many a brave Russian. I forgive you," he said directly to Ehrenskjold, "and you may depend on my good will."

Ehrenskjold thanked the Tsar and replied, "However honorably I may have acted with regard to my master, I did only my duty. I sought death, but did not meet it, and it is no small comfort to me in my misfortune to be a prisoner of Your Majesty and to be used so favorably and with so much distinction by so great a naval officer and now worthily a vice admiral." Later, talking to the foreign envoys present, Ehrenskjold declared that the Russians had indeed fought skillfully, and that nothing but his own experience could have convinced him that the Tsar could make good soldiers and sailors out of his Russian subjects.

The victory at Hangö cleared not only the Gulf of Finland but the eastern side of the Gulf of Bothnia of Swedish ships. Admiral Wattrang now quit the upper Baltic entirely, being unwilling to risk his big ships against the unorthodox tactics of the Russian galleys. Thus, the way was open for the Russian flotillas to continue their westward advance. In September, a fleet of sixty galleys landed 16,000 men in the Aland Islands. Soon afterward, the larger Russian ships returned to Kronstadt, but Apraxin's galleys kept working their way up into the Gulf of Bothnia. On September 20, he

reached Wasa, and from there he sent nine galleys across the gulf to attack the coast of Sweden, burning the Swedish town of Umean. As some galleys were lost and the winter ice was coming, Apraxin put his fleet in winter quarters, at Abo on the Finnish coast and across the Gulf of Finland at Reval.

The success of the Finnish campaigns spurred Peter to increase his shipbuilding program. Later, near the end of the Tsar's reign, the Baltic fleet consisted of thirty-four ships-of-the-line (many of them sixty- and eighty-gun vessels), fifteen frigates and 800 galleys and smaller ships, manned by a total of 28,000 Russian seamen. This was a gigantic achievement; to complain that Peter's fleet was still smaller than Great Britain's is to overlook the fact that Peter began without a single ship; with no tradition, shipwrights, officers, navigators or seamen. Before the end of Peter's life, some Russian ships were equal to the best in the British navy and, said an observer, "were more handsomely furnished." The only weakness that Peter could never overcome was his countrymen's lack of interest in the sea. Foreign officers—Greeks, Venetians, Danes and Dutchmen—continued to command the ships; the Russian aristocracy still hated the sea and resented the imposition of naval service almost more than any other. In his love of blue waves and salt air, Peter remained unique among Russians.

45

THE KALABALIK

BITTERLY FRUSTRATED by his failure to prevent the peace made on the Pruth, Charles XII had worked doggedly to undo it. To some extent, the three subsequent short "wars" a year or two apart between Russia and the Ottoman Empire had been his work, although Peter's unwillingness to hand over Azov and to withdraw his troops from Poland had also been responsible. A promising opportunity had come with the third of these wars, declared by the Turks in October 1712. Then, a huge Ottoman army had assembled at Adrianople under the personal command of the Sultan. As part of a joint war plan, Ahmed III had agreed to send Charles XII north into Poland with a strong Turkish escort so that the King could rendezvous with a new Swedish expeditionary force under Stenbock's command. But when Stenbock landed in Germany, he moved west, not south, and he was eventually captured in the fortress of Tonning. Charles remained a king without an army, and the Sultan, reflecting on the uncertainties of invading Russia alone, had decided to make peace and return to his harem.

Thus, by the winter of 1713, Charles XII had been in Turkey for three and a half years. Moslem hospitality notwithstanding, most Turkish officials had grown weary of him. He was indeed a "heavy weight on the Sublime Porte." The Sultan wanted to make a permanent peace with Russia, but Charles' constant intrigues had made this difficult. It was decided, one way or another, to send Charles home.

Out of this decision developed a plot. Devlet Gerey, the Tatar Khan, had originally been an admirer of Charles, but his feelings had changed when the King refused to join the Turkish army marching to the Pruth. Now the Khan made contact with Augustus of Poland and worked out a plan whereby the King of Sweden would be offered a strong escort of Tatar cavalry ostensibly to cross Poland and return to Swedish territory. Once under way, the escort would be progressively weakened as parts of the force were detached under various pretexts. Across the Polish frontier, the group would be confronted by a strong force of Poles, and the diminished

escort, too weak to resist, would surrender and hand over the Swedish King. Thus, both sides would profit: The Turks would get rid of Charles, and Augustus would have him.

This time, however, fortune was with Charles. A body of his men, disguised as Tatars, intercepted the messengers and brought the correspondence between Augustus and the Khan to the King at Bender. Charles learned that both the Khan and the Seraskier of Bender were involved in the plot; as best he could determine, the Sultan was not. For years, Charles had been trying to get away from Turkey, but now he made up his mind not to go. He tried to contact Ahmed III to tell him of the plot, but he found that all communication between Bender and the south had been cut. None of the messages he sent, even by roundabout routes, arrived.

In fact, the Sultan was anxious to see the last of Charles, but had worked out a different solution. On January 18, 1713, he gave orders to abduct the King, by force if necessary, but without harming him, and take him to Salonika, where he would be put on board a French ship which would carry him back to Sweden. Ahmed did not believe that force would be required. He did not know of the Khan's plot, and of course he did not know that Charles was aware of it. From this tangle of plots, partial knowledge and misunderstandings arose the extraordinary episode known by its Turkish name as the Kalabalik (tumult).

THE SWEDISH CAMP at Bender had greatly changed in three and a half years. Tents had been replaced by permanent barracks built in rows as in a military camp, with glass windows for the officers and leather-covered windows for the common soldiers. The King lived in a large, new, handsomely furnished brick house which, with a chancery building, officers' quarters and a stable, formed a semi-fortified square in the center of the compound. From the balconies of his upper windows, he had an excellent view of the whole Swedish encampment and the surrounding cluster of coffee houses and small shops in which merchants sold figs, brandy, bread and tobacco to the Swedes. The settlement, called New Bender, was a tiny Swedish island lost in a Turkish ocean. But it was not a hostile ocean. The Janissary regiment posted to guard the King watched over him with an admiring eye. Here was a hero of the kind that Turkey desperately lacked. "If we had such a king to lead us, what could we not do?" they asked.

Despite these friendly feelings, when the Sultan's orders arrived in January 1713, the air around the Swedish camp began to fill with tension. Charles' officers watched from the balconies as thousands of Tatar horsemen rode in to join the Janissaries. To confront this force, Charles had fewer than a thousand Swedes and no allies; seeing the massing of the Turkish forces, the Poles and Cossacks nominally under Charles' command had

quietly drifted away and placed themselves under Turkish protection. Undeterred, the King began preparations to resist; his men began collecting provisions to last six weeks. To stiffen Swedish morale, Charles one day rode alone and unmolested through the waiting ranks of the Tatar army standing thickly "like organ pipes so close together on all sides."

On January 29, Charles was warned that an attack would come the following day. He and his men spent the night trying to build a wall around the camp, but the frozen earth made digging impossible. Instead, they created a barricade of wooden carts, wagons, tables and benches, and shoveled piles of dung between the wagons. What happened the following day was one of the most bizarre martial episodes in European history. As the dramatic tale resounded through Europe, people shook their heads, but of course, at the time, none who heard the tale knew that Charles intended simply to make a token stand to foil the plot to carry him off and betray him in Poland. Unable to inform the Sultan of this plot, he hoped by his stand to force the Khan and the Seraskier to pull back, wait and ask for new instructions from their master, Ahmed III.

THE "TUMULT" began on Saturday, January 31, when Turkish artillery opened fire with a salvo of cannonballs at the Swedish makeshift fortress. Twenty-seven cannonballs hit the King's brick house, but the powder charges were light and the bombardment did little damage. Thousands of Turks and Tatars massed to attack. "The whole host of Tatars advanced toward our trench and made a halt within three or four steps of it, which was very frightful to see," wrote a Swedish participant. "At ten in the forenoon, there appeared several thousand Turkish horse, after that several thousand Janissaries on foot from Bender. These were drawn up in order as if they were to attack us presently."

The attack was ready, but for some reason it never came. According to one account, the Turkish soldiers were reluctant to attack the Swedish King, whom they admired, and demanded to see a written order from the Sultan commanding them to do so. Another story is that fifty or sixty Janissaries carrying only white staves marched up to the Swedish camp and entreated Charles to place himself in their hands, swearing that not a hair of his head would be touched. Supposedly, Charles refused, warning, "If they do not go away, I will singe their beards," whereupon all the Janissaries threw down their weapons, declaring they would not attack. Finally, there is a story that, just before the assault, three rainbows, one on top of the other, appeared over Charles' house. The astonished Turks refused to attack, saying that Allah was protecting the Swedish King. The most likely reason is that the Seraskier and the Khan had simply staged the bombardment and the massing of troops to cow Charles into submission without violence. In

any case, the Turkish army stood silent and still, the cannonade stopped and the ranks eventually broke up.

On the morning of the following day, Sunday, February 1, the view from the Swedish camp was depressing: "Such a vast number of these infidels that when we were on top of the Royal House we could not see over them." Small red, blue and yellow flags fluttered along the waiting lines of Turks, and on a hill behind was a huge red standard, "planted to signify that they were going to push the Swedes to the last drop of blood." Shaken by this sight, some of the Swedish soldiers and junior officers, not understanding that all this was a game and seeing themselves as the prospective victims of a massacre, began to trickle out across the barricades to place themselves under the protection of the Turks. To stiffen their courage, Charles ordered his trumpeters to blow and his kettledrummers to beat their drums on top of his house. To halt the desertions, he sent a promise and a threat to all his men: "That His Majesty did assure every one from the highest to the lowest who should stand with him for two hours longer and not desert, should be rewarded by him in the kindest manner. But whoever should desert to the infidels he would never see more."

As it was Sunday, the King went to a church service in his house, and he was listening to the sermon when the air was suddenly filled with the thunder of cannon and the whistling of cannonballs. The Swedish officers, rushing to the upper windows of the house, saw a mass of Turks and Tatars, swords in hand, running toward their camp, shouting, "Allah! Allah!" At this, the Swedish officers on the barricade called to their men, "Don't shoot! Don't shoot!" A few men fired their muskets, but most of the men on the barricades surrendered quickly. This act, even against hopeless odds, was so unlike the normal behavior of Swedish soldiers that it strongly implies a royal order to avoid bloodshed.

Similarly, on the other side, the Khan and the Seraskier apparently gave equivalent instructions. Although a "cloud of arrows" fell on the compound, few hit anything. The cannonballs directed at the King's house either "flew over the house and did no hurt" or, fired with a minimum charge of powder, bounced harmlessly off the walls.

Nevertheless, although the original intention on both sides may have been to stage a battle rather than to fight one, a drama involving cannonballs, musket shots and naked swords is difficult to keep entirely peaceful. Very soon, tempers became inflamed and blood began to flow. With most of the Swedes scarcely resisting, the Turks swarmed into Charles' house and began looting. The great hall of the house filled with Turks taking everything in sight as plunder. This insult was more than Charles could stand. In a rage, with a sword in his right hand and a pistol in his left, the King threw open the doors and rushed into the hall, followed by a band of Swedes. There were pistol volleys on both sides, and the room filled with the dense

smoke of gunpowder. Through the swirling haze, Swedes and Turks, choking and coughing, thrust and parried in hand-to-hand combat. As so often on the battlefield, the impetus of the Swedish charge had its effect; besides, in the house itself, the numbers of Swedes and Turks were more nearly equal. The hall and house soon were cleared; the last Turks jumped out the windows.

At this point, one of Charles' Drabants, Axel Roos, looked around and did not see the King. He dashed through the house and found Charles in the High Steward's Chamber, "standing betwixt three Turks, both arms raised in the air, sword in the right hand. . . . I shot down the Turk with his back to the door. . . . His Majesty lowered his sword arm and stabbed the second Turk through the body and I was not slow in shooting the third Turk dead." "Roos," cried the King through the smoke, "is it you who have saved me?" When Charles and Roos stepped over the bodies, the King's face was bleeding from nose, cheek and the lobe of an ear where bullets had nicked him. His left hand was badly sliced between thumb and forefinger where he had warded off a Turkish sword by grasping the enemy blade barehanded. The King and Roos rejoined the others, who had driven the Turks out of the house and were firing at them from the windows.

The Turks wheeled up cannon, which began to boom at close range. The balls shattered the masonry, but the thick walls held up. Charles filled his hat with musket balls and toured the house, parceling reserves of powder and ammunition to the men stationed at the windows.

By now, dusk was falling. The Turks understood the absurdity of trying to storm a house containing less than a hundred men with an army of 12,000, particularly when they were under orders not to kill the hundred. They decided to try a new tactic to force the Swedes into the open. Tatar archers fastened burning straw to their arrows and shot them at the wood-shingled roof of the King's house. At the same time, a group of Janissaries rushed to a corner of the house with bales of hay and straw, which they piled up and set afire. When the Swedes attempted to push the burning bundles away with iron bars, the Tatar archers, aiming accurately, forced them back. Within minutes, the roof was ablaze. Charles and his comrades rushed into the attic to fight the flames from below. Using swords, they hacked at the roof, tearing away as much as possible, but the fire spread rapidly. The burning beams, roaring with flames, forced the King and his followers to retreat down the staircase with coats over their heads to protect themselves from the scorching heat. On the ground floor, the exhausted men drank brandy, and even the King, equally parched, was persuaded to swallow a glass of wine. It was the first time since leaving Stockholm thirteen years before that Charles had touched alcohol.

Meanwhile, burning shingles were falling from the roof onto the top floors, spreading the flames. Suddenly, what remained of the roof fell, and the whole upper half of the house became a furnace. At this point, some of

the Swedes, seeing nothing to be gained by being burned alive, proposed surrender. But the King, in great excitement, possibly inspired by his unaccustomed gulps of wine, refused to yield "until our clothes begin to burn."

Still, they obviously could not remain. Charles agreed to a proposal that they dash to the chancery building, which was still untouched fifty paces off, and renew the struggle from there. The watching Turks, wondering if the King were still alive, amazed that men could survive in the furnace before their eyes, suddenly saw King Charles, sword and pistol in hand, emerge at the head of his small band and run through the night, silhouetted against the blazing building. The Turks dashed forward. It was a race. Unfortunately, as Charles rounded a corner of the building, he tripped over one of the spurs he always wore and fell headlong.

Before he could rise, the Turks were upon him. One of his followers, Lieutenant Aberg, threw himself on top of the King to protect his master from Turkish steel. Aberg received a saber blow in the head and was dragged off, bleeding. Two Turks then hurled themselves on the King to wrench his sword from his hand. Their weight inflicted on Charles his most serious wound of the day: Two bones in his right foot were broken. Unnoticing, the Turks began tearing the King's coat to shreds; the man who could deliver the Swedish King alive had been promised six ducats, and the coat would be proof of who made the capture.

Despite the pain in his foot, Charles rose. He was not otherwise harmed, and the Swedes behind him, seeing that the King had given up, themselves surrendered immediately. They were stripped on the spot of their watches, money and the silver buttons on their coats. Charles was bleeding from nose, cheek, ear and hand, his eyebrows were singed off, his face and clothes were black with gunpowder and reeking with smoke, and his coat was torn into strips, but he resumed his usual air of calm, almost amused unconcern. He had done what he had set out to do and had resisted not for two but for eight hours. Satisfied, he allowed himself to be carried to the house of the Seraskier of Bender. Charles entered ragged, blood-stained, his face caked with blood and dirt, but with imperturbable serenity. The Seraskier received him politely with apologies for the misunderstanding that had led to the fight. Charles sat down on a couch, asked for water and a dish of sherbet, refused the supper that was offered to him and promptly fell asleep.

The following day, Charles and all who had fought with him were escorted to Adrianople. Some who saw him go were distressed by the sight. Jefferyes wrote to London: "I cannot express to Your Excellency what a melancholy spectacle this was to me, who had formerly seen this prince in his greatest glory and terror, now to see him so low as to be the scorn and derision of the Turks and infidels." But others thought that Charles seemed cheerful. "In as good a humor as in the days of his luck and liberty," said

one, and to another he seemed as pleased with himself "as if he had all the Turks and Tatars in his power." Certainly, he had succeeded in his objective: After a battle on this scale, the Khan and the Seraskier would not be carrying him off to Poland.

Ironically, on the day after the Kalabalik, new orders from the Sultan arrived in Bender countermanding the permission he had given to use force to abduct Charles. An emissary of the Sultan met the King and pleaded that "his Great Master was an utter stranger to these hellish conspiracies."

In Adrianople, Charles was received with honor and installed in the stately castle of Timurtash, where he lay for weeks, waiting for his foot to heal. In punishment for the Kalabalik, both the Khan and the Seraskier were deposed. Three months later, the Ottoman Empire embarked on a fourth brief war with Russia. Charles' action had been a temporary success on all points.

Throughout Europe, the Kalabalik caused a sensation. Some saw it as heroism: Like a legendary hero, the King had fought in personal combat against overwhelming odds. But many saw it as sheer insanity. How could the King so offend the Sultan's hospitality? This was Peter's attitude when he heard the news: "I now perceive that God has abandoned my brother Charles, inasmuch as he has taken it upon himself to attack and irritate his only friend and ally."

And, in fact, was it such a heroic story? On the surface, 100 Swedes with muskets, pistols and swords defended themselves against 12,000 Turks equipped with cannon. Stories circulating in Europe told of Turks falling in droves, of bodies piling up in heaps in front of the King's house. Actually, forty men were killed on the Turkish side, while the Swedes lost twelve. Even this loss was unnecessary, for the Janissaries had used great forbearance. Had the Turks not burst into Charles' house and begun wild-eyed looting, most of those who died would have remained alive. The truth was that the Kalabalik was a charade turned bloody, played for political reasons, to prevent the King's deportation and capture. But it was also a game which Charles desperately enjoyed and allowed to continue. He had not had a fight for' over three years; he had suffered the humiliation of the Pruth; here at least he could wield his sword. The Kalabalik took place because Charles XII loved the heady excitement of battle.

For twenty months after the Kalabalik, Charles remained in Turkey, installed as the Sultan's guest at the castle of Timurtash with its handsome park and beautiful gardens. It took many weeks for the bones in his foot to heal completely, and it was ten months before he could walk or ride. Meanwhile, in Europe, events had been moving swiftly. In April 1713, the signing of the Treaty of Utrecht finally ended the twelve-year War of the Spanish Succession. Nobody had won. The Sun King's grandson Philip de Bourbon sat on the Spanish throne as Louis XIV had wished, but the kingdoms of

France and Spain were carefully separated by the terms of the peace treaty. At seventy-one, Louis himself was two years away from death and France was impoverished by war. The other claimant to the Spanish crown, Charles of Austria, now occupied a different throne, having become the Holy Roman Emperor on the death of his older brother, in 1711.

During these years, Russia and Turkey at last made a permanent peace. After the Pruth and the three bloodless wars which followed, Peter finally gave up Azov and withdrew his troops from Poland. The Turks were anxious for peace; the end of the war in Western Europe had freed the Austrian army for possible action against Turkey in the Balkans, and the Sultan wished to be ready. On June 15, 1713, the Treaty of Adrianople was signed, pledging peace for twenty-five years.

It was this treaty which ultimately made it impossible for Charles XII to remain any longer in the Ottoman Empire. The Turks, who had harbored the King for four years, were now at peace with his enemies. Somehow, therefore, Charles must leave. With the continent at peace, the road across Europe lay open. Charles could not go through Poland, as he had originally planned, because his enemy Augustus was on the throne. But he could travel through Austria and the German states. Indeed, the new Emperor, Charles VI, was eager to see the King of Sweden return to North Germany. The kings and princes in that region were preparing to swallow up all of Sweden's territory in the Holy Roman Empire; the Emperor preferred to see the status quo maintained and a balance preserved. The Emperor therefore not only agreed that Charles should pass through the empire, but urged the King to come to Vienna and be received officially. Charles refused the second request, insisting that he be allowed to pass without formalities or recognition of any kind. If this was denied, Charles declared that he would accept the invitation of Louis XIV to travel home in a French ship. The Emperor agreed.

Charles decided to travel incognito. Traveling as fast as horses could gallop, he might ride ahead of the news and arrive on the Baltic coast before Europe knew that he had left Turkey. At the end of the summer of 1714, Charles began to train for the ride, exercising himself and his horses, preparing for long days in the saddle. By September 20, he was ready to leave. The Sultan sent farewell gifts: splendid horses and tents, a jeweled saddle. Escorted by an honor guard of Turkish cavalry, the King and the 130 Swedes who had been with him since the Kalabalik rode north through Bulgaria, Walachia and the Carpathian passes. At Pitesti, on the frontier of the Ottoman and Austrian empires, Charles and his small group met the larger number of Swedes who had remained behind at Bender after the Kalabalik. Riding along and planning to make the entire trip were dozens of creditors who had decided to accompany the Swedes across Europe in hopes that once the King reached Swedish soil, he would be able to pay them what

he owed. While this group was assembling, Charles exercised his horses even harder, galloping them around posts, over crossbars, swinging down from the saddle at a gallop to pick up a glove on the ground. When all the Swedish exiles had assembled, there were 1,200 men and almost 2,000 horses with dozens of wagons. Such a convoy would have to move slowly and would attract the eye of everyone for miles around. Charles was anxious to move quickly, not only to avoid capture by Saxon, Polish or Russian agents, but to avoid embarrassing demonstrations in his favor by Protestants in the empire who still looked on the King of Sweden as their champion. The King, therefore, decided to go alone.

Along with speed, Charles would rely on disguise. As his ascetic personal habits were known across Europe, one member of his party joked that the King could establish an impenetrable disguise if he wore a curled court wig, stayed in the most luxurious inns, drank heavily, flirted with every girl, wore slippers most of the day and slept until noon. Charles would not go this far, but he did grow a mustache, wear a dark wig, a brown uniform and a hat lined with gold braid, and carried a passport made out in the name of Captain Peter Frisk. He and his two companions were to ride ahead of the convoy, giving the impression that they were an advance party sent ahead to order horses and accommodations for the royal convoy following behind. Among those in the main body was an officer dressed in Charles' clothes and wearing his gloves and sword, whose role was to impersonate the King. Along the way, one of Charles' two escorts was left behind, so that the King of Sweden actually rode across Europe with a single companion.

The farther he went, the more impatient he became. He stopped briefly at staging posts—Debrecen in Hungary, Buda on the Danube—nowhere for more than an hour. He rarely slept in an inn, preferring to spend the night as a passenger in a fast postal coach, curling up to sleep on the straw on the floor of the bouncing carriage. At a gallop he passed from Regensburg to Nürnberg to Kassel and north. On the night of November 10, the guard of the city gate at Stralsund on the Baltic, in Swedish Pomerania, opened to an insistent knocking. Outside, he found a figure with a large hat curled over a dark wig. Progressively more senior officers were summoned until at four a.m. the Governor of Stralsund rose grumbling from his bed and went to confirm the astonishing report: After fifteen years, the King of Sweden stood once again on Swedish territory.

The ride made another astonishing story. In less than fourteen days, the King had traveled from Pitesti in Walachia to Stralsund on the Baltic, a distance of 1,296 miles. Of this, 531 miles had been traveled in post coaches, the rest on horseback. His average pace was more than 100 miles a day, and during the last six days and nights from Vienna to Stralsund, when the waxing moon aided him by lighting the roads, his speed was even greater: Charles covered 756 miles in six days and nights. He traveled without once

removing his clothes or boots; when he arrived in Stralsund, the boots had to be cut from his feet.

The famous ride seized the imagination of Europe. Once again, the King of Sweden had done the dramatic and unpredictable. In Sweden, the news was received with "indescribable joy." After fifteen years, a miracle had happened: The King was back. Perhaps, despite all the disasters that had struck in the five years since Poltava somehow the King would now turn everything around. In churches across Sweden, there were services of thanksgiving. But elsewhere Charles' ride to Stralsund created anxiety rather than thanksgiving. Now that the warrior King was back on Swedish soil, what new drama was about to begin? For those who had fought him so long—Peter of Russia, Augustus of Saxony, Frederick of Denmark—and for those who had joined to pluck the spoils—George Louis of Hanover and Frederick William of Prussia—this sudden event cast all in doubt. But a single dramatic exploit could not overturn the vast assembly of forces which, sensing the kill, mobilized against him.

Although after his ride everyone in Sweden and in Europe expected that Charles would immediately board a ship and return to his homeland, the King once again upset all expectations. He rested, summoned a tailor and had himself measured for a new uniform with a plain blue coat, white waistcoat, buckskin breeches and new boots, and then announced that he intended to remain in Stralsund, the last outpost of Swedish territory on the continent. There was logic in this. Stralsund, the strongest Swedish bastion in Pomerania, was sure to be attacked by the growing number of enemies closing in on Sweden. By conducting the defense himself, the King might distract his enemies from moving across the Baltic to attack Sweden. Besides, it would give him another chance to smell gunpowder.

Charles ordered fresh troops and artillery from Sweden. The Council, unable to resist his command now that he was on Swedish territory and so close to home, scraped up 14,000 men to garrison the town. Just as Charles expected, in the summer of 1715 a Prussian-Danish-Saxon army appeared before the town. It numbered 55,000.

The lifeline of the besieged town was the sea lane to Sweden. As long as the Swedish fleet could convoy supplies and ammunition, Charles had a chance to prevent its fall. Then, on July 28, 1715, the Danish fleet appeared and the two squadrons engaged in an intense six-hour cannonade. At the end, both fleets were badly damaged and had to limp home for repairs. But six weeks later the Danish fleet, reinforced by eight large British warships, reappeared. The Swedish admiral, complaining of adverse winds, remained in port.

With the sea lane closed, the fall of Stralsund became inevitable. Danish troops first took the island of Rügen, which lay to seaward of Stralsund. Charles was present, and with a force of 2,800 men he attacked and tried

to dislodge 14,000 entrenched Danes and Prussians. The attack was beaten off, the King hit in the chest by a spent musket ball but not badly hurt, and the Swedish troops gave up the island. The siege continued through the autumn, with Charles constantly exposing himself to harm both on land and at sea.* Finally, on December 22, 1715, the defenses were breached and the city fell.

Just before the garrison surrendered, the King left Stralsund in a small, open boat. For twelve hours, his sailors struggled in wintry seas amidst floating ice floes to reach a Swedish ship waiting offshore to carry the King to Sweden. He made it safely, and two days later, at four a.m. on December 24, 1715, fifteen years and three months after his departure, the King of Sweden stood in darkness and icy rain on the soil of his homeland.

* At one point, deciding to reconnoiter an enemy position by boat, Charles took a small rowing skiff whose helmsman was a master shipwright named Schmidt. Once in range of the Prussians, the boat was enveloped in a cloud of musket balls. Schmidt crouched as low in the boat as possible; Charles, seeing him, stood up, exposing himself fully, and waved at the enemy with his right hand. He was not hit, and when he had seen enough, he ordered Schmidt to steer for safety. Not proud of his conduct, Schmidt apologized by saying, "Your Majesty, I am no helmsman but Your Majesty's shipwright, whose business is to build ships by day and beget children at night." Charles replied good-humoredly that his service at the helm that day had not disabled him for either occupation.

VENICE OF THE NORTH

THERE IS A LEGEND that the city of St. Petersburg was completely constructed in the airy blue heavens and then lowered in one piece onto marshes of the Neva. Only thus, the legend explains, can the presence of so beautiful a city on so bleak a site be accounted for. The truth is only slightly less miraculous: The iron will of a single man, the skills of hundreds of foreign architects and artisans, and the labor of hundreds of thousands of Russian workers created a city which admiring visitors later described as the "Venice of the North" and the "Babylon of the Snows."

The building of St. Petersburg began in earnest in the years after the 1709 victory at Poltava had, in the words of its founder, "laid the foundation stone" of the city. It was spurred the following year by Russia's capture of Riga and Vyborg, "the two cushions on which St. Petersburg now can rest in complete tranquillity." Thereafter, although Peter was absent from his "paradise" for months at a time (and sometimes a year or more), construction never ceased. Wherever he was, whatever else was demanding his attention, Peter's letters were filled with questions and orders relating to the building of embankments, palaces and other buildings, the digging of canals, the design and planting of gardens. In 1712, although no decree on the subject was ever issued, St. Petersburg became the capital of Russia. Autocratic government centered on the Tsar, and the Tsar preferred St. Petersburg. Accordingly, government offices transferred themselves from Moscow, new ministries sprang up there and very soon the simple fact of Peter's presence transformed the raw city on the Neva into the seat of government.

In the first decade of its existence, St. Petersburg grew rapidly. By April 1714, Weber reported, Peter had taken a census and counted 34,500 buildings in the city. This figure must have included every possible dwelling with four walls and a roof, and even then it was doubtless exaggerated. Nevertheless, not only the quantity but the quality of the new buildings in St. Petersburg was impressive. Architects from many countries had arrived

and gone to work. Trezzini, the first Architect General, had been in Russia for almost ten years; he was succeeded in 1713 (although Trezzini remained and continued to raise buildings) by a German, Andreas Schlüter, who brought with him a number of his countrymen and fellow architects.

In 1714, the nucleus of the new city was still on Petrograd Island, a few yards east of the Peter and Paul Fortress. The center was Trinity Square, which faced the river embankment near Peter's original three-room log cabin. Around the square, a number of larger structures had been erected. One was the wooden Church of the Holy Trinity, built in 1710, in which Peter attended regular services, celebrated his triumphs and mourned his dead. The main building of the State Chancellery, the Government Printing Office (where Bibles and scientific and technical books were printed on type and presses imported from the West) and the city's first hospital were on the square, along with the new stone houses of Chancellor Golovkin, Vice Chancellor Shafirov, Prince Ivan Buturlin, Nikita Zotov (now created a count) and Prince Matthew Gagarin, Governor of Siberia. Nearby, the famous Four Frigates Tavern continued to offer a comfortable retreat where government officials including the Tsar himself, foreign ambassadors, merchants and decently dressed people from the street could stop in and refresh themselves with tobacco, beer, vodka, wine and brandy.

Not far from Trinity Square stood the city's single market, a large, two-storied wooden building enclosing three sides of a wide courtyard. Here, in hundreds of shops and stalls, merchants and traders of a dozen nations displayed their wares. All of them paid rent to the Tsar, who preserved his monopoly on trade by allowing no selling of goods in any other part of the city. Close by, in another large wooden building, was the market for food and housewares, where peas, lentils, cabbages, beans, oatmeal, flour, bacon, wooden utensils and earthen pots were sold. In the back streets, the Tatar flea market, a hodge-podge of tiny stalls, offered used shoes, pieces of old iron, old rope, old stools, used wooden saddles and hundreds of other items. In the congested mass of humanity, elbowing and pushing each other around these stalls, pickpockets found rich plucking. "The crowd is so dense that one has to take real care of one's purse, one's sword and one's handkerchief," wrote Weber. "It is wise to carry everything in one's hand. I once saw a German officer, a grenadier, return without his wig and a lady of quality without her bonnet." Tatar horsemen had galloped past, snatched off both wig and bonnet and then, to the laughter of the crowd, offered the stolen objects for sale still within sight of their bareheaded victims.

Once Poltava had dissipated the Swedish threat, the city spread from its original center east of the fortress to other islands and to the mainland. Downstream, on the north side of the main branch of the Neva, lay the largest island of the river delta, Vasilevsky Island, whose leading inhabitant was Prince Menshikov, the city's governor general, to whom Peter had

given most of the island as a present. In 1713, on the embankment facing the river, Menshikov had begun construction of a massive stone palace three stories high, with a roof of iron plates painted bright red. This palace, designed by the German architect Gottfried Schädel, remained the largest private house in St. Petersburg throughout Peter's life, and was richly decorated with elegant furniture, ornate silver plate and many articles which, the Danish ambassador commented dryly, appeared "to have been removed from Polish castles." Its spacious main hall was the principal site of the city's great entertainments, weddings and balls. Peter used Menshikov's palace much as he had used the large house built earlier in Moscow for Francis Lefort, preferring himself to live more simply in houses with no chamber sufficiently large for mass entertaining. Sometimes, when Menshikov was receiving for the Tsar, Peter would look across the river from his own smaller house, see the lighted windows of Menshikov's great palace and say to himself with a chuckle, "Danil'ich is making merry."

Behind Menshikov's house were the Prince's private church, with a bell tower and a soft chime, and a large, formal garden with latticed walls, hedges and a grove of trees, houses for his gardeners and a farm with chickens and other animals. Being on the north side of the river, the garden made the most of the southern exposure, and, shielded from the wind by trees and hedges, produced fruits and even melons. The rest of the island contained a few wooden houses and grazing fields for horses and cattle, but most of Vasilevsky Island was still covered with forest and bushes.

Always, the heart of the city was the great river, a deep torrent of cold water sweeping silently and swiftly down from the inland sea of Lake Ladoga, past the fortress, past Menshikov's great red-roofed mansion and out through the islands, flowing so vigorously into the Gulf of Finland that the current was still visible a mile from shore. The tremendous surging power of the current, the pressure of winter ice and the crunch of ice floes in springtime all would have made it difficult to build a bridge in Peter's time; but these were not the reasons that no bridge was built. Peter wanted his subjects to learn seamanship and sailing, so he insisted that they cross the Neva by boat—without oars. For those who could not afford a private boat, twenty government-authorized ferryboats were permitted, but the boatmen, most of them ignorant peasants, were often confounded by the rapid current and by strong gusts of wind. Only after the Polish ambassador, a major general and one of the Tsar's own doctors had drowned in successive sailing accidents did Peter relent and allow the ferrymen the use of oars. For the general population, crossing remained risky; if a storm came up, people might be detained on the wrong side of the river for several days. In winter, citizens could easily walk across the ice, but in summer when there were storms, in autumn or spring when the ice was forming or melting, the people on the islands in the Neva were virtually cut off from the rest of

Russia. (In April 1712, Peter devised a way to cross the river without much danger from falling through the thinning ice: he had a four-oared rowboat put upon a sled and he sat in the boat; horses and sled might go through the ice, but boat and tsar would float.)

Because of this isolation, government buildings and private mansions began to spring up along the south bank of the river, which was the mainland. The largest of these was the thirty-room palace of General-Admiral Apraxin, which stood next to the Admiralty on a corner of the site now occupied by the 1,100-room Winter Palace built by Rastrelli for Empress Elizabeth. Upriver along the southern embankment were the houses of Attorney General Yaguzhinsky, Vice Admiral Cruys and the Winter Palace of Peter himself, standing on the ground which Catherine the Great's small Hermitage occupies today. Peter's palace was made of wood, two stories high, with a central building and two wings, but, except for a naval crown over the doorway, it was undistinguished from other mansions along the river. The Tsar felt ill at ease in spacious chambers and preferred small, low-ceilinged rooms, but in order to present a symmetrical line in the façades of the palaces along the river, he was forced to make each story of his own house higher than he liked. His solution was to install a false lower ceiling beneath the upper one in all the rooms he inhabited. The first Winter Palace was torn down in 1721 to be replaced by a larger structure of stone.*

In 1710, a mile upstream from the Admiralty, at the point where the Fontanka River flows into the Neva, Trezzini began to construct a beautiful Summer Palace, with wide-latticed windows looking out over water on two sides, with two solid Dutch chimneys and a steep gabled roof crowned by a gilded weathervane in the form of St. George on horseback. Peter and Catherine lived here together, and its fourteen light and airy rooms were divided equally between husband and wife, Peter occupying the seven rooms on the ground floor and the seven rooms on the floor above belonging to Catherine. His chambers reflected his own modest taste and practical interests; hers displayed her desire to frame herself in royal luxury and grandeur. The walls of Peter's study and reception room, for example, were covered to window level with hundreds of blue Dutch tiles, each depicting a view of ships or a nautical or pastoral scene. The ceilings of his reception room and small bedroom were decorated with paintings of winged cherubs celebrating "The Triumph of Russia." On the Tsar's desk was an ornate ship's clock and compass of brass and engraved silver, presented to him by King George I of England. Peter's canopy bed, covered with red cut velvet, was large but not large enough for the Tsar to stretch out on; in the eight-

---

* The second Winter Palace also vanished, and today it is the fifth Winter Palace which occupies the site and, transformed into the Hermitage Museum, has become the city's center.

eenth century, people slept propped up by pillows. The most interesting room on Peter's floor was the Turning Room, where the Tsar kept lathes to use in his spare time. Against a wall of this room stood the carved wood frame, twelve feet high, of a special instrument made for Peter by Dinglinger in Dresden in 1714. Three large dials, each three feet in diameter, showed the time and, by means of rods connected to the weathervane on the roof, the direction and force of the wind. Peter's dining room was large enough only for his family and a few guests; all public banquets were held at Menshikov's palace. Peter's kitchen walls were covered with blue tiles with different floral designs. Water was brought to its black marble sink by the first system of water pipes in St. Petersburg. Most important, a window from the kitchen opened directly into the dining room; Peter liked hot food and hated those large palaces in which food grew cold wending its way from the oven to the table.

On the floor above, Catherine had a reception room, a throne room and a dancing room as well as a bedroom, a nursery with a crib carved as a boat, and her own kitchen. Her rooms had painted ceilings, parquet floors, walls hung with Flemish and German tapestries or Chinese silk wallpaper woven with gold and silver thread, drapes, carpets, furniture inlaid with ivory and mother of pearl, and Venetian and English mirrors. Today, this little palace, superbly restored and filled with original or period objects, decorated with numerous portraits of Peter's family and lieutenants, is— along with the little pavilion Mon Plaisir at Peterhof—the place where one can most intimately sense the lingering presence of Peter himself.

IN 1716, another foreign architect arrived in St. Petersburg to leave a permanent mark on Peter's "paradise." This was the French architect Alexandre Jean Baptiste LeBlond. A Parisian and a pupil of the great Le Notre who had designed the gardens at Versailles, LeBlond was only thirty-seven, but was already well known in France for his buildings in Paris and for books he had written on architecture and formal gardens. In April 1716, LeBlond signed an unprecedented contract to come to Russia for five years as Architect General at a guaranteed salary of 5,000 roubles a year. He was also to be given a state apartment and permission to leave Russia at the end of his five-year term without having to pay duty on any of his possessions. In return, LeBlond promised to do his best to pass along his knowledge to the Russians who would work with him.

En route to his new appointment, LeBlond passed through Pyrmont, where Peter was taking the waters, and the two men talked about the Tsar's plans and hopes for his new city. Peter was delighted with his new employee and, on LeBlond's departure, wrote enthusiastically to Menshikov in St. Petersburg:

Welcome LeBlond in a friendly manner and respect his contract, for he is better than the best and a veritable prodigy, as I could see in no time. Besides he is an energetic and intelligent man and highly respected in the ateliers of France, so that we can, through him, engage whomsoever we wish. Therefore, all our architects must be told that from now on they are to submit all their plans for new construction to LeBlond for approval, and, if there is still time, carry out his instructions for correcting the old ones.

Armed with his title of Architect General, his princely contract and the glowing commendation of the Tsar, LeBlond arrived in Russia intending to take charge. In his train, he brought not only his wife and six-year-old son but several dozen French draftsmen, engineers, joiners, sculptors, stonemasons, bricklayers, carpenters, locksmiths, chiselers, goldsmiths and gardeners. Immediately, he established a new Chancellery of Building, an administrative office through which all plans for building would have to pass for his approval. Then, on the basis of his talks with Peter, he began to draft an overall plan which would dictate the major development of the city for years to come.

The most ambitious part of this new scheme was to be the creation of a city of canals, modeled after Amsterdam, on the eastern half of Vasilevsky Island. This would be a rectangular grid of parallel streets and intersecting canals cut through the low-lying marshy ground. Two main canals would run the length of the island and twelve smaller canals would cross it, and even the smaller canals would be wide enough for two boats to pass. Every house was to have a courtyard, a garden and a dock for the householder's boat. In the center of this great watery checkerboard, the Tsar was to have a new palace with an extensive formal garden.

LeBlond began as soon as he arrived in August 1716, using poles driven into the marshy ground to mark the outlines of his new town. That autumn and the following spring, digging of the canals was begun and the first new householders, sternly commanded by Peter's order, commenced construction of their dwellings. All did not go well, however. In wielding his new power, LeBlond had impinged on both the prerogative and the possessions of an even more powerful Petersburger, Menshikov, who was both governor general of the city and the owner of a large part of Vasilevsky Island, some of which was to be taken for LeBlond's new city of canals. Menshikov did not dare oppose directly a plan which Peter had approved, but the Tsar would be away for many months and in the meantime the Governor General would be in overall command of every activity in the city—including the new construction. Menshikov's retaliation came in a typical way. The canals were built, but they were narrower and shallower than LeBlond had called for; two boats could not pass each other, and soon the shallow

waterways began to silt up with mud. When Peter returned and went to look at the new construction, he was pleased to see the new houses rising along the canals, but, noticing the dimensions of the waterways, he was astonished and enraged. LeBlond, who by this time knew better than to challenge Menshikov directly, remained silent. With his architect beside him, Peter walked across the island and then, turning to LeBlond, asked him, "What can be done to carry out my plan?"

The Frenchman shrugged. "Raze, sire, raze. There is no other remedy than to demolish all that has been done and dig the canals anew." This, however, was too much, even for Peter, and the project was abandoned, although from time to time Peter would go to Vasilevsky Island to look at the canals and come home sorrowfully without uttering a word. On the south bank, however, LeBlond built the city's main boulevard, the great Nevsky Prospect, cutting straight through two and a half miles of meadows and forests from the Admiralty to the Alexander Nevsky Monastery. The Nevsky was constructed and paved by gangs of Swedish prisoners (who were also ordered to clean it every Saturday) and soon became the most famous street in Russia.

LeBlond also made a remarkable contribution to another famous St. Petersburg landmark, the Summer Garden. Even before Poltava, Peter had begun the garden, which spread over thirty-seven acres behind his Summer Palace at the junction of the Neva and the Fontanka. At the height of his worry about the Swedes, the Tsar constantly issued orders about the garden. Moscow was commanded to send "seeds and roots, together with thirteen young lads to train as gardeners." Books on the gardens of France and Holland were sought. Trees were ordered to line the avenues: lime and elm trees from Kiev and Novgorod, chestnuts from Hamburg, oaks and fruit trees from Moscow and the Volga, cypresses from the south. Flowers arrived from everywhere: tulip bulbs from Amsterdam, lilac bushes from Lubeck, lilies, roses and carnations from other parts of Russia.

LeBlond's contribution to the Summer Garden was water. "Fountains and water are the soul of a garden and make the principal ornament of it," he had written. He pumped water from the Fontanka (the name derives from Fountain) into a new water tower, from which elevation the pressure would cause his new fountains to jet and spray. There were fifty fountains scattered through the garden: grottoes, cascades, plumes of water spouting from the mouths of dolphins and horses. In the basins beneath these fountains, creatures real and mythical—stone gargoyles, real fish and even a seal—swam or splashed. Nearby, rare birds sang in cages shaped like pagodas, a blue monkey chattered and a porcupine and sables stared morosely back at human sightseers.

Using the lessons he had learned from Le Notre, LeBlond created for

Peter a true French formal garden. He traced parterres of flower, shrubs and gravel in intricate curving lines. He pruned the crowns of trees and shrubs into spheres, cubes and cones. He built a glassed conservatory and installed orange, lemon and bay trees and even a small tree of cloves. Italian sculptures were placed at the intersections of all the walks and along the avenues; eventually, sixty white marble statues depicting scenes from Aesop's fables were set in place along with other sculptures titled "Peace and Abundance," "Navigation," "Architecture," "Truth" and "Sincerity."

When Peter was in St. Petersburg, he came often to the Summer Garden. There the Tsar would sit on a bench and drink beer or play draughts with his friends while Catherine and her ladies walked along the paths. The garden was open to the public, and society came to stroll during the afternoons, or to sit by its fountains during the long white nights of June and July. In 1777, a terrible flood wreaked fearful damage on the Summer Garden, uprooting trees and shattering the fountains, and afterward, Catherine the Great reconstructed the garden on different lines, preferring the less formal English garden to the French style; she did not rebuild the fountains, and the trees and shrubs were allowed to grow normally. But the Summer Garden maintained its charm and appeal. Pushkin lived nearby and often came to walk there; Glinka and Gogol were constant visitors to Peter's Summer Garden. As old as the city itself, the Summer Garden still renews itself every spring and remains as young as the newest leaf and the tenderest bud.

Menshikov was increasingly jealous of LeBlond's favor with the Tsar and used the Summer Garden as another means of striking at the Frenchman. In 1717, he wrote to Peter that LeBlond was cutting down the Summer Garden trees of which he knew the Tsar was extremely proud—in fact, LeBlond had only lopped some branches to improve the view and shape the trees according to French concepts. When Peter returned and encountered LeBlond, he flew into a rage, thinking of his lost trees. Before he knew what he was doing, he had struck the architect with his cane, sending LeBlond to bed with shock and fever. Peter then went to see the garden and realizing that the trees had only been trimmed, hastily sent apologies to LeBlond and instructions that the Architect General should be specially cared for. Soon after, the Tsar met Menshikov on a stairway. Seizing him by the collar and pushing him up against the wall, Peter shouted, "You alone, you rascal, are the cause of LeBlond's illness!"

LeBlond recovered, but a year and a half later he contracted smallpox. In February 1719, at thirty-nine, he died, having spent only thirty months in Russia. Had he lived and continued to wield the great power of Peter's favor, the face of St. Petersburg would have been far more French. One

glorious example of this architecture-that-might-have-been actually exists. Before his death, LeBlond had chosen the site, prepared the drawings and laid out the gardens for the fabled summer estate and palace by the sea that is known as Peterhof.

PETERHOF WAS CONCEIVED long before LeBlond came to Russia; its origins were linked with Kronstadt. In 1703, within a few months of his conquest of the Neva delta, Peter sailed out on the Gulf of Finland and first saw Kotlin Island. Soon afterward, he decided to build a fortress there to protect St. Petersburg from the sea. Once work was under way, the Tsar visited the island often to observe its progress. At times, and especially in autumn when there were frequent storms, he could not sail directly from the city. On these occasions, he went by land to a point on the coast just south of the island and made the shorter journey by boat, and there he built a small landing wharf and a two-room cottage on the shore where, if necessary, he could wait until the weather improved. This cottage was the genesis of Peterhof.

Once the victory at Poltava had ensured possession of Ingria, Peter divided the land along the south coast of the Gulf of Finland outside St. Petersburg into tracts which he distributed among his chief lieutenants. Many built palaces or mansions along the fifty- or sixty-foot ridge which ran about a half-mile from the shore. The largest and finest of this semi-circular row of great country houses looking out on the gulf belonged to Menshikov, for whom Schädel erected an oval-shaped palace, three stories high, which Menshikov named Oranienbaum.

Peter's first summer house by the gulf, built at a place called Strelna, did not rival the magnificent palace of the Serene Prince. Strelna was only a large wooden cottage whose most distinctive feature was a treehouse which the Tsar could reach by ladder. In the evening, Peter would smoke his pipe and gaze out contentedly at the boats on the bay. Eventually, he wanted something grander, and it was to LeBlond that he entrusted the task of building a palace to rival Oranienbaum, a Versailles-by-the-Sea: Peterhof.

LeBlond's grand palace, a large, two-storied structure handsomely decorated and furnished, opened onto a wide, formal French garden behind the palace. But it was far smaller and less ornate than either Versailles or the enlarged and remodeled palace which Rastrelli was to create for Empress Elizabeth on the same site a generation later. The glory of Peterhof— and it is LeBlond's masterpiece—is in the use of water. Water soars high in the air at Peterhof; it plumes and sprays from dozens of imaginative fountains; it splashes over statues of men and gods, horses and fish and unidentifiable creatures which neither man nor god has ever seen; it glides in mirror-like sheets over the edge of marble steps; it runs deep and dark

in basins, pools and canals. The great cascade in front of the palace flows down giant twin marble stairways which flank a deep grotto, opening out into a wide central basin. Along the stairs, gilded statues flash in the sunlight; in the center of the basin, bathed in the jets of myriad water spouts, stands a dazzling golden Samson prying open the jaws of a golden lion. From the basin, the water flows toward the sea through a long canal wide enough to bring small sailing ships up to the foot of the palace. Cutting straight through the center of the lower garden, the great canal is flanked by more fountains, statues and rows of trees. The water to supply these fountains came not from the gulf but through wooden pipes from a source on higher ground thirteen miles away.

In this lower garden, between the palace and the sea, crisscrossed by avenues and paths, studded with fountains and white marble statues, LeBlond also created three exquisite summer pavilions which stand to this day—the Hermitage, Marly and Mon Plaisir. This Hermitage is a tiny, elegant structure surrounded by a little moat over which a drawbridge leads to the single door. It is two stories high, the ground floor being occupied by a kitchen and an office, the upper floor by a single, airy room with tall windows opening onto balconies. This room was used solely for private dinner parties. In the center of the room, a huge oval table, seating twelve, incorporated a spectacular French mechanical surprise: When the host rang a bell between courses, the central part of the table was lowered to the first floor, where dishes were removed and the next course was served, after which the table would rise back into position. In this way, the diners were never embarrassed by the presence of servants.

Marly was named after the private retreat of Louis XIV, but it "in no way resembles Your Majesty's," the French ambassador reported to Paris. Peter's Marly was a simple Dutch house with oak-paneled rooms and Dutch tiles, set at the edge of a quiet lake.

The most important of these pavilions was Mon Plaisir, which Peter preferred to all his other country houses. It is a one-story red-brick house in Dutch style, perfectly proportioned, set right by the sea, and in its way it is a second jewel to match the Tsar's small Summer Palace in the Summer Garden. Tall French windows made it possible to step directly from any room onto a brick terrace a few feet above the water. Inside, a central hall and reception room is lined with dark oak in the Dutch fashion, with paintings of Holland, especially Dutch ships, set in the panels. The ceiling is painted in gay French arabesques, while the floor is set with large black and white tiles to form a human-sized checkerboard.

Today, Mon Plaisir is almost as it was when Peter lived there. The furniture, decorations and household articles are period, if not actually the Tsar's possessions. On one side of the central hall is Peter's study overlooking the gulf, his desk covered with nautical instruments, the walls faced

to window level with blue Dutch tiles depicting ships, and wood-paneled above. The next little room is Peter's bedroom, and from his bed he could watch the sea. On the other side of the hall is the blue-tiled kitchen, only one step from the dining table. A curiosity is the elegant little Chinese room, completely decorated in red-and-black lacquer. Each side of the house is flanked by a handsome gallery with tall, wide windows, those in front opening onto the sea, those in back onto a garden filled with tulips and fountains; between the windows, more Dutch paintings, mostly seascapes, were mounted. Peter loved this little house and liked to live here even when Catherine was in residence in the Grand Palace on the ridge above. From here, he could look at the water or lie in bed by an open window and hear the waves. More than anywhere else, in the later part of his life the restless monarch found tranquillity at Mon Plaisir.

47

AN AMBASSADOR REPORTS

WHEN PETER MOVED HIS COURT, his government and his noblemen from Moscow to St. Petersburg, the foreign ambassadors accredited to the Tsar were also forced to settle along the Neva. Many of these diplomats left accounts of their service, among them Whitworth of England, Campredon of France, Juel of Denmark and Bergholz of Holstein. But the richest eyewitness picture of the later years at Peter's court comes from Friedrich Christian Weber, the ambassador of Hanover, whose description of life at court in St. Petersburg complements the description of life at court in Moscow presented by the Austrian Johann Korb twenty years before. Weber arrived in Russia in 1714 and spent seven years in St. Petersburg before returning to his homeland and publishing his lengthy memoir. He was a dignified, relatively open-minded man who admired Peter and was interested in everything he saw, although he saw some things of which he did not approve.

At his very first public function, the stolid Hanoverian envoy received an indication of the talents required of an ambassador to the court of the Tsar. "I had hardly arrived," Weber begins, "when Admiral Apraxin gave a magnificent entertainment to the whole court and, by His Tsarish Majesty's order, caused me to be invited." At the door, however, the new Ambassador had trouble with the guards: "They used foul language to me, they kept putting their halberds across the door, then, with greater rudeness, they turned me down the stairs." Finally, through the intervention of a friend, Weber was admitted. He had learned his first lesson about life in Russia. It was:

that I ran great hazard of exposing myself to the like treatment in the future unless I changed my plain, though clean, dress and appeared all trimmed with gold and silver, and with a couple of footmen walking before me and bawling out "Clear the way!" I was soon

made more sensible that I had a great many more things to learn. After having gulped down at dinner a dozen bumpers of Hungary wine, I received from the hands of the Vice Tsar Romodanovsky a full quart of brandy, and being forced to empty it in two draughts, I soon lost my senses, though I had the comfort to observe that the rest of the guests lying asleep on the floor were in no condition to make reflections on my little skill at drinking.

In his first days, Weber's dignity was subjected to other strains:

I went, according to the custom of all polite countries, to pay my respects to the chief nobility of the Russian court in order to get acquainted with them. As it was not the custom to send word ahead . . . I was obliged to wait in the cold until his lordship came out. Having made my compliments to him, he asked whether I had anything else to say; upon my answering in the negative, he dismissed me with this reply: "I have nothing to say to you either." I ventured to go a second time to visit another Russian. But as soon as he heard me mentioning my own country, he cut me short and flatly told me, "I know nothing of that country. You may go and apply to those to whom you are directed." This put an end to my desire of making visits and I firmly resolved never to go any more to any Russians without being invited except to the ministers with whom I had business, who indeed showed me all imaginable civility. A week after, I met those impolite courtiers at court and as they had observed His Tsarish Majesty discoursing with me for a considerable while and treating me with a great deal of favor, and besides that he had given Admiral Apraxin to see me well entertained, they now both came up to me and in a very mean and abject manner asked my pardon for their fault, almost falling down to the ground, and very liberally offering me all their brandy to oblige me.

During Peter's absence with his fleet, his sister, Princess Natalya, gave a banquet which provided Weber with another opportunity to observe Russian customs:

The toasts are begun at the very beginning of the meal, in large cups and glasses in the form of bells. At the entertainment of people of distinction no other wine is given but that of Hungary. . . . All the beauties of Petersburg appeared at this entertainment, they were already at that time in the French dress, but it seemed to fit very

uneasy upon them, particularly the hoop petticoats, and their black teeth were a sufficient proof that they had not yet weaned themselves from the notion so fast riveted in the minds of the old Russians, that white teeth only become blackamoors and monkeys.

The custom of blackening the teeth faded quickly, and by 1721, when he was writing his account, Weber assured his readers that this and other primitive habits "have since been so far removed that a stranger who comes into a polite assembly at Petersburg will hardly believe he is in Russia, but rather, as long as he enters into no discourse, think himself in the midst of London or Paris."

Among his fellow ambassadors in St. Petersburg, Weber was especially intrigued by the representatives of the Kalmuck and Uzbeki khans. One morning, Weber recalled,

I had the honor to meet an ambassador of the Khan of Kalmucks at the Chancery Office for Foreign Affairs. He was a man of frightful and fierce aspect. His head was shaved all over except a lock of hair which hung from the crown down to the neck according to the custom of that nation. He delivered on the part of his master, who is the Tsar's vassal, a roll of paper. Then he threw himself down to the ground, muttering for a long while something between his teeth. Which compliment, being interpreted to the Grand Chancellor Golovkin, he had this short answer: that it was very well. This ceremony over, the ambassador resumed his fierce air.

Later that year, another ambassador arrived from the Kalmuck Khan bearing an odd commission. Some time before, Weber wrote, Prince Menshikov had "made a present of a handsome coach of English make to the Khan. Now, one of the wheels being broken, this ambassador was sent to ask the Prince to let him have another wheel. The ambassador told us that his master gave audience to the envoys of his neighbors in this coach and that on solemn days he dined in it."

On May 17, 1714, an ambassador of the Khan of Uzbek arrived in St. Petersburg. Among the ambassador's commissions was an offer from his master to the Tsar of

a passage through his dominions for the Tsar's yearly caravans to China, an incredible advantage, considering that the caravans were at that time obliged to make their journey to Peking with great inconvenience and in a year's time, through the whole extent of Siberia, following the windings and turnings of the rivers, there being

no beaten road, whereas they might go thither through his master's dominions on a good road in four months.

He afterward laid many silks and other Chinese and Persian goods together with rare furs at the Tsar's feet as a present from his master, adding that he left some Persian horses and beasts behind at Moscow and expressing his concern that a fine leopard and an ape had died on the road. In this speech, he never styled the Tsar other than the Wise Emperor, which with them is the highest title of honor. The ambassador was . . . about fifty years of age, of a lively and venerable aspect. He wore a long beard and on his turban he wore an ostrich feather, which he reported only princes and lords of the first rank were allowed to wear in his country.

Weber described Easter, the greatest of all Russian religious holidays.

The festival of Easter was celebrated with particular pomp, when large amends were made for the severe and pinching abstinence to which the Russians are kept during the preceding Lent. Their mirth, or rather madness in those days, is inexpressible, it being their opinion that he who has not been drunk at least a dozen times has shown but little of Easter devotion. Their singers in church are so extravagant as any of them, and it was little surprise to me to see two parties of them who fell out among themselves at a public house come to blows and beat each other with great poles so furiously that several of them were carried off for dead. The most remarkable ceremony in the said holidays is that the Russians of both sexes present each other with painted eggs, giving the Kiss of Peace, the one saying "*Christos voskres*, Christ is risen," and the other answering "*Voistino voskres*, verily He is risen," whereupon they exchange eggs, and so part. For this reason many persons, particularly foreigners, who delight in that way of kissing the women, are seen rambling up and down with their eggs the whole day long.

IN PETER'S TIME, dwarfs and giants were much valued throughout Europe as exotic decorations in royal and noble households. King Frederick William of Prussia had collected most of the giants on the continent, although Peter kept Nicholas Bourgeois, the seven-foot-two-inch giant he had found in Calais. For years, Nicholas stood behind Peter's table, and in 1720 the Tsar married him to a Finnish giantess in hopes of producing oversized offspring. Peter was disappointed; the couple remained childless.

Dwarfs were more evenly distributed. Every Infanta of Spain was accompanied by a court dwarf to underscore whatever beauty she possessed. In Vienna, the Emperor Charles VI kept a famous Jewish dwarf, Jacob Ris, as a kind of ex-officio counselor at the Imperial court. More often, dwarfs were kept as human pets whose antics and droll appearance were even more amusing and diverting than talking parrots or dogs that could stand on their hind legs. In Russia, dwarfs were especially prized. Every great noble wanted a dwarf as a symbol of status or to please his wife, and competition among the nobility for their possession became intense. The birth of a dwarf was considered good luck and dwarfs born as serfs were often granted their freedom. To encourage the largest possible population of dwarfs, Russians took special care to marry them together in hopes that a dwarf couple would produce dwarf children.

It was a lavish gift when a dwarf or, even more, a pair of dwarfs was given away. In 1708, Prince Menshikov, a particularly keen collector of dwarfs, wrote to his wife: "I send you a present of two girls, one of whom is very small and can serve as a parrot. She is more talkative than is usual among such little people and can make you gayer than if she were a real parrot." In 1716, Menshikov appealed to Peter: "Since one of my daughters possesses a dwarf girl and the other does not, therefore I beg you kindly to ask Her Majesty the Tsaritsa to allow me to take one of the dwarfs which were left after the death of the Tsaritsa Martha."

Peter was enormously fond of dwarfs. They had been around him all his life. As a child, he went to church walking between two rows of dwarfs carrying red silken curtains; as tsar, he kept at court a large population of dwarfs to amuse him and to play prominent roles on special occasions. At banquets, they were placed inside huge pies; when Peter cut into the pastry, a dwarf popped out. He liked to combine their strange shapes with the mock ceremonies in which he reveled. Dwarf weddings and even dwarf funerals, closely aping the ceremonies his own court performed, set Peter to laughing so hard that tears rolled down his cheeks.

In 1710, two days after the marriage of Peter's niece Anne to Duke Frederick William of Courland, a marriage of two dwarfs was celebrated with exactly the same ceremony and pomp as the marriage of the royal couple. On the basis of accounts from others, Weber described this festivity, which was attended by seventy-two dwarfs:

A very little dwarf marched at the head of the procession, as being the marshal . . . conductor and master of the ceremony. He was followed by the bride and bridegroom neatly dressed. Then came the Tsar attended by his ministers, princes, boyars, officers and others; next marched all the dwarfs of both sexes in couples. They were in

all seventy-two, some in the service of the Tsar, the Tsarina Dowager, the Prince and Princess Menshikov, and other persons of distinction, but others had been sent for from all parts of Russia, however remote. At the church, the priest asked the bridegroom whether he would take his bride to be his wife in a loud voice. He answered in a loud voice, addressing himself to his beloved, "You and no other." The bride being asked whether she had not made any promise of marriage to another than her bridegroom, she answered, "That would be very pretty, indeed." However, when the main question came to be asked, whether she would have the bridegroom for her husband, she uttered her "Yes" with such a low voice as could hardly be heard, which occasioned a good deal of laughter to the company. The Tsar, in token of his favor, was pleased to hold the garland over the bride's head according to the Russian custom. The ceremony being over, the company went by water to the Prince Menshikov's palace. Dinner was prepared in a spacious hall, where two days before the Tsar had entertained the guests invited to the Duke's marriage. Several small tables were placed in the middle of the hall for the new-married couple and the rest of the dwarfs, who were all splendidly dressed after the German fashion. . . . After dinner the dwarfs began to dance after the Russian way, which lasted till eleven at night. It is easy to imagine how much the Tsar and the rest of the company were delighted at the comical capers, strange grimaces, and odd postures of that medley of pygmies, most of whom were of a size the mere sight of which was enough to provoke laughter. One had a high bunch on his back, and very short legs, another was remarkable by a monstrous big belly; a third came waddling along on a little pair of crooked legs like a badger; a fourth had a head of prodigious size; some had wry mouths and long ears, little pig eyes, and chubby cheeks and many such comical figures more. When these diversions were ended, the newly married couple were carried to the Tsar's house and bedded in his own bedchamber.

Perhaps the Tsar's own abnormal height fed this taste for reveling with the physically deformed; in any case, it included not only giants and dwarfs, but all who were handicapped or afflicted by age or illness. On January 27 and 28, 1715, for example, the whole court joined in a two-day masquerade, preparations for which had been under way for three months. The occasion was the wedding of Nikita Zotov, who forty years before had been Peter's tutor and now, having served as Mock-Pope, was in his eighty-fourth year. The bride was a buxom widow of thirty-four.

"The nuptials of this extraordinary couple were solemnized by the court in masks," reported Weber.

The four persons appointed to invite the guests were the greatest stammerers that could be found in all Russia. Old decrepit men who were not able to walk or stand had been picked out to serve for bridesmen, stewards and waiters. There were four running footmen, the most unwieldy fellows, who had been troubled with gout most of their lifetime, and were so fat and bulky they needed others to lead them. The Mock-Tsar of Moscow, who represented King David in his dress, instead of a harp had a lyre covered with a bearskin to play upon. He was carried on a sort of pageant [float], placed on a sled, to the four corners of which were tied as many bears, which, being pricked with goads by fellows purposely appointed for it, made such a frightful roaring as well suited the confused and horrible din raised by the disagreeing instruments of the rest of the company. The Tsar himself was dressed like a Boor of Frizeland, and skillfully beat a drum in company with three generals. In this manner, bells ringing everywhere, the ill-matched couple were attended by the maskers to the altar of the great church, where they were joined in matrimony by a priest a hundred years old who had lost his eyesight and memory, to supply which defect a pair of spectacles were put on his nose, two candles held before his eyes, and the words sounded into his ears so that he was able to pronounce them. From the church the procession went to the Tsar's palace, where the diversions lasted some days.

Weber's memoir, of course, ranges wider than his descriptions of the people and activities of Peter's court. He was fascinated by Russia and the Russian people. He admired the calm endurance of the average man and woman, while at the same time he was often appalled by what he described as their "barbarous customs." In the following description of Russian baths, for example, amazement is mingled with a touch of admiration. (Weber fails to mention, however, that the Russian custom of a weekly bath kept the Russian people far cleaner than most Europeans, who sometimes went weeks or months without taking a bath.)

The Russian way of bathing, which they make use of for a universal medicine against any indisposition, includes four different sorts of baths out of which they choose one which they think to be proper against their particular distemper.

Some sit naked in a boat, and having brought themselves by violent rowing into a great sweat, suddenly throw themselves into the river and after having swum for some time, they get out and dry themselves either by the sun or with their shirts. Others leap cold into the river and afterward lie close to a fire which they make on the shore, rubbing themselves over the whole body with oil or grease,

and then turn themselves so long about the fire till it is chafed in; which in their opinion renders their limbs supple and nimble.

The third sort is the most common: along a little river are built upwards of thirty bagnios, one half for men and the other half for women. Those who have a mind to bathe, undress under the open sky, and run into the bagnio; after having sufficiently sweated and got cold water poured upon them, they go to bask and air themselves, and run up and down through the bushes sporting with one another. It is astonishing to see not only the men, but also the women un-married as well as married . . . running about to the number of forty or fifty, and more together, stark naked, without any sort of shame or decency, so far from shunning the strangers who are walking thereabouts that they even laugh at them. The Russians in general both men and women use this sort of bathing both winter and summer twice a week at least; they pay one kopek a head, the bagnios belong-ing to the Tsar. Those that have bagnios in their houses pay yearly something for it; which universal bathing throughout Russia brings considerable revenue into the Tsar's coffers.

There is a fourth sort of bathing which is their most powerful remedy to the greatest distempers. They cause an oven to be heated as usual, and when the heat is somewhat abated (yet still so hot that I was not able to hold my hand on the bottom a quarter of a minute), five or six Russians, more or less, creep into it and having stretched themselves out at their full length, their companion who waits without shuts the hole so fast that they can hardly breathe within. When they can endure it no longer they call, upon which he that is upon the watch lets the sick come out again, who after having breathed some fresh air, creep into the oven again and repeat this operation till they are almost roasted, and coming out, their bodies being ruddy like a piece of red cloth, throw themselves in the summertime into the water, or in winter, which they love best, into the snow, with which they are covered all over, leaving only the nose and eyes open, and so they lie buried for two or three hours according to the state of their distemper; this they count an excellent method for the recovery of their health.

Weber also witnessed Russians at sports and recreation. In a large, grassy field on the south side of the Neva, peasants, laborers and common people of all sorts gathered on Sunday afternoons after drinking in the taverns. Men and boys divided into groups to box and fight for fun, screaming and shouting. Foreigners were appalled by these dusty, drunken melees, reporting that when the combat was over "the ground lies full of blood and hair, and many had to be carried away."

In the height of summer, the heat in St. Petersburg was almost intolerable; not even during the few hours of night when the sun disappeared below the horizon did the air become really cool. For some Russians, beer was a solution. But one visit to a Russian taphouse to see how the beer was dispensed was enough to put most foreigners off Russian beer forever. As Weber described this scene:

> The liquor stands there in an open tub or cooler to which the common people crowd, taking it out with a wooden dipper and drinking it, holding their mouths over the tub that nothing may be spilled, so that if by any chance any of it misses their mouths, it runs down their beards and falls again into the tub. If a customer happens to have no money, he leaves his old fur coat, a shirt, a pair of stockings or some other part of his wearing apparel, to pawn until the evening when he receives his wages. In the meantime, those filthy pledges [the clothing] hang on the brim round the tub, nor does it matter much whether they are pushed in and float there for some time.

While his people were brawling in the fields and cooling themselves with beer, Peter's favorite summer relaxation was to sail on the Gulf of Finland. Sometimes, when he sailed to Kronstadt or Peterhof, he invited foreign ambassadors to accompany him. Weber's account of one such excursion presents a graphic picture of what it was like to spend a weekend in the country as a guest of Peter the Great:

> On June 9, 1715, the Tsar went to Kronstadt, where we also followed in a galley, but in consequence of a great storm, we were obliged to remain at anchor in this open boat for two days and two nights without lights, without beds, without food and drink. When at last we arrived at Kronstadt, the Tsar invited us to his villa at Peterhof. We went with a fair wind, and at dinner warmed ourselves to such a degree with old Hungarian wine, although His Majesty spared himself, that on rising from the table, we could scarcely keep our legs, and when we had been obliged to empty a bowl holding a quart apiece from the hands of the Tsaritsa, we lost our senses, and in that condition they carried us out to different places, some to the garden, some to the woods, while the rest lay on the ground here and there.
>
> At four o'clock in the afternoon, they woke us up and again invited us to the summer house, where the Tsar gave us each an axe and bade us follow him. He led us into a young wood, where he pointed out trees which it was necessary to fell in order to make an *allée* straight to the sea about a hundred paces long, and told us to

cut down the trees. He himself began to work on the spot (there were seven of us besides the Tsar) and although this unaccustomed work, especially when we had not half recovered our senses, was not at all to our liking, we nevertheless cut boldly and diligently, so that in about three hours the *allée* was ready and the fumes of wine had entirely evaporated. None of us did himself any harm except a certain ambassador who hacked at the trees with such fury that by the fall of one, he was hit, knocked down, bruised, and badly scratched. After verbal thanks, we received our real recompense after supper in a second drink, which was so strong that we were taken to our beds unconscious.

We had hardly succeeded in sleeping an hour and a half before the Tsar's favorite appeared at midnight, pulled us out of our beds and dragged us willing or unwilling to the bedroom of a Circassian prince, asleep there with his wife, where by their bedside they plied us with so much wine and vodka that on the following day none of us could remember how we got home.

At eight o'clock in the morning we were invited to the palace for breakfast, which instead of coffee or tea as we expected, consisted of a good glass of vodka. Afterward we were taken to the foot of a little hill and made to mount eight wretched country nags without saddles or stirrups and ride about in review for an hour in the sight of Their Majesties, who leaned out the window. A certain Russian of distinction led the vanguard, and by the help of switches or sticks we made our jades mount uphill as best we could. After having taken a turn for an hour in the wood and refreshed ourselves with hearty draughts of water, we had a fourth drinking bout at dinner.

As the wind was strong we were put in the Tsar's covered boat, in which the Tsaritsa with her maid of honor had occupied the cabin, while the Tsar stood with us on the open deck and assured us that in spite of the strong wind we should arrive at Kronstadt at four o'clock. But after we had been tacking back and forth for two hours, we were caught by such a frightful squall that the Tsar, leaving aside all his jokes, himself took hold of the rudder, and in that danger displayed not only his great skill in working a ship, but an uncommon strength of body and undauntedness of mind. The Tsaritsa was laid on high benches in the cabin, which was full of water, the waves beating over the vessel, and violent rains falling, in which dangerous condition she also showed a great deal of courage and resolution.

We all gave ourselves up wholly to the will of God, and consoled ourselves with the thought that we should drown in such noble company. All effects of the drink disappeared very quickly, and we were filled with thoughts of repentance. Four smaller boats on which

were the court of the Tsaritsa and our servants were tossed about on the waves and driven ashore. Our boat, which was strongly built and crewed with experienced sailors, after seven dangerous hours reached the harbor of Kronstadt, where the Tsar left us saying: "Good night to you, gentlemen. This was carrying the jest too far."

Next morning, the Tsar was seized with a fever. We on our part, being thoroughly soaked, having for so many hours sat in water up to the middle, made haste to get ashore on the island. But not being able to get either clothes or beds, our own baggage being gone another way, we made a fire, stripped stark naked, and wrapped our bodies up again in the coarse covers of sleds which we had borrowed from the peasants. In this condition we passed the night, warming ourselves at the fire, moralizing and making grave reflections on the miseries and uncertainties of human life.

On the 16th of July, the Tsar put to sea with his fleet, which we had not the good fortune to see, being all of us ill with fevers and other indispositions.

48

THE SECOND
JOURNEY WEST

PETER'S SECOND HISTORIC JOURNEY to the West, in 1716–1717, came nineteen years after the Great Embassy of 1697–1698. The curious and
enthusiastic young Muscovite giant who insisted on anonymity while he
learned to build ships and who was regarded in Europe as something
between a bumpkin and a barbarian had now become a powerful and
victorious monarch, forty-four years old, whose exploits were known and
whose influence was felt wherever he traveled. This time, of course, the Tsar
was a familiar figure in many of the places he visited. In 1711, 1712 and
1713, Peter had visited the towns and princely courts of the North
German states, and the outlandish stories about his appearance and behavior
were disappearing. Still, he had never been to Paris; Louis XIV had been
a friend of Sweden, and it was not until the Sun King died in September
1715 that the Tsar felt free to visit France. Ironically, Peter's visit to Paris,
the most memorable event in this second journey, was not on his itinerary
when he left St. Petersburg. His trip had three purposes: to try to improve
his health, to attend a royal marriage and to attempt a final blow at Charles
XII and end the war with Sweden.

Peter's doctors had long insisted that he go. For a number of years, the
Tsar's health had given them concern. It was not his epileptic convulsions
that bothered them; they were of short duration, and a few hours after they
had passed, Peter seemed quite normal. But fevers—sometimes as a result
of unrestricted drinking, sometimes because of the fatigue of travel and
worry, sometimes from a mixture of these causes—kept him in bed for
weeks. In November 1715, after a drinking bout at Apraxin's house in
St. Petersburg, Peter became so ill that the Last Sacrament was given to him.
For two days, his ministers and senators remained in an adjacent room,
fearing the worst. But within three weeks the Tsar was on his feet and able
to go to church, although his face was pale and shrunken. During this illness,
one of Peter's physicians went to Germany and Holland for consultation,
and returned with the opinion that the patient should travel as soon as

possible to Pyrmont near Hanover, where the mineral waters bubbling out of the earth were thought to be milder than the waters of Carlsbad, which Peter had visited previously.

Peter was also going to oversee the marriage of his niece Catherine, the daughter of his half-brother, Ivan. Ivan's wife, Tsaritsa Praskovaya, was devoted to Peter and had allowed her daughters, Anne and Catherine, to be used as marriage partners to promote his German alliances. Anne had married the Duke of Courland in 1709 only to be widowed two months later. Now, Catherine, at twenty-four the older of the two, was to wed the Duke of Mecklenburg, whose small duchy lay on the Baltic coast between Pomerania, Brandenburg and Holstein.

Peter's third purpose in traveling west was to meet his allies, Frederick IV of Denmark, Frederick William of Prussia and George Louis of Hanover, who since September 1714 was now also King George I of England. Peter's ambassador in Copenhagen, Prince Vasily Dolgoruky, had been urging King Frederick IV to join Peter in an allied invasion of the Swedish province of Scania, which lay three miles across the Oresund from the Danish coast of Zealand. Frederick was hesitating, and Peter believed that only by going in person would he be able to persuade the Danes to take what now seemed the only step that could force Charles to end the war.

On January 24, 1716, the royal party left St. Petersburg. With Peter were the senior officials of the Foreign Ministry, Golovkin, Shafirov and Tolstoy, and the rising second-level men, Osterman and Yaguzhinsky. Catherine would look after Peter's health, leaving her little son, Peter Petrovich, three months old, and his sisters, Anne, now eight, and Elizabeth, seven, in the care of the Tsaritsa Praskovaya, who every day wrote a brief but affectionate account of the health and progress of the children. Praskovaya, in turn, was trusting her daughter "Katusha" (Catherine, the intended bride) to Peter's care.

Peter arrived in Danzig on February 18, a Sunday, just in time to attend a church service, accompanied by the Burgomeister. During the sermon, feeling a draft, Peter reached over, removed the Burgomeister's wig and put it on his own head. At the end of the service, he returned the wig with thanks. It was later explained to the startled official that it was Peter's habit, when his head was cold, to borrow a wig from any nearby Russian; in this case, the Burgomeister's had been the handiest.

Although all parties were on hand to celebrate the marriage in Danzig, the terms of the settlement had not yet been worked out. Duke Karl Leopold of Mecklenburg has been described as "a tyrannical boor and one of the most notorious little despots that only the decay of the German constitution at that time had allowed to grow up." Mecklenburg was small and weak and needed a powerful protector; marriage to a Russian princess would bring the Tsar's support. Knowing that two daughters of Tsar Ivan V were

available, not caring which he received, he sent a betrothal ring to St. Petersburg with a letter of proposal in which the name of the recipient had been left blank. Catherine had been chosen. The wedding took place on April 8, with Peter and King Augustus both present. The bridegroom was dressed in a Swedish-style uniform, with a long Swedish sword, but he forgot to wear his cuffs. At two o'clock, the Tsar's carriage arrived to bring Karl Leopold and his chief minister, Baron Eichholtz, to Peter's house. In front of a crowd of people filling the square before the house, the Duke stepped out of the carriage—and his wig caught on a nail. Bareheaded, he stood in front of the crowd while the faithful Eichholtz scrambled up and detached the wig from the nail. Then, with the bride, who wore the crown of a Russian grand duchess, the party walked through the streets to a small Orthodox chapel which Peter had had built especially for the service. The Orthodox ceremony, performed by a Russian bishop, lasted two hours, during which time Peter moved freely through the congregation and the choir, prompting in the Psalter and helping with the singing. After the service, as the wedding party again walked through the streets, people in the crowd cried out, "Look! The Duke has no cuffs on!"

In the evening, there was a fireworks display on the square in front of the house where the Duke was staying. Peter led Augustus and the new bridegroom through the crowd, personally setting off the rockets. So long did this last that at one o'clock in the morning Eichholtz had to remind his master that his bride had gone to bed three hours earlier. Karl Leopold departed, but even here Eichholtz had to worry. The bridal chamber had been decorated with many lacquered objects, including a lacquered bed. The Duke hated the sharp odor and Eichholtz feared that he would be unable to sleep on it, but the Duke managed, and the next day the newly married pair and the entire wedding party dined with a satisfied and happy Peter. The festivities ended badly, however, when officials in both parties fell to squabbling over the exchange of commemorative gifts. The Duke had made handsome presents to the Russian ministers, but the Mecklenburgers received nothing—"not even a crooked pin." Worse, Tolstoy, who was used to the exchange of fabulous stones in Constantinople, complained that the ring he received was less valuable than those presented to Golovkin and Shafirov. Osterman, a junior diplomat in the Russian party, tried to calm Tolstoy's wrath by giving him also the small ring with which *he* had been presented, but Tolstoy continued to complain that he had been insulted.

To Peter's chagrin, the marriage caused grave complications with his North German allies, especially Hanover, which, with Prussia, had joined Russia, Denmark and Poland against Sweden. The common motive of these new allies was to expel Charles XII from the continent and to pick up and distribute among themselves the pieces of former Swedish territory

inside the Holy Roman Empire. Increasingly, however, they began to realize that the destruction and disappearance of Swedish power was being accompanied by the rise of a new and greater power, that of the Russian Tsar. Until the Mecklenburg marriage, the suspicions of the North German princes remained beneath the surface. In July 1715, the Danish and Prussian troops besieging Stralsund had even asked for Russian help. Sheremetev's army lay in western Poland and could easily have marched, but Prince Gregory Dolgoruky, the experienced Russian ambassador in Warsaw, feared that the situation in Poland was still too volatile and insisted that Sheremetev stay where he was. Accordingly, Stralsund fell without the participation of a single Russian soldier. When he heard the news, Peter was furious at Dolgoruky: "I am truly astonished that you have gone out of your mind in your old age and have let yourself be carried away by these constant tricksters and so have held these troops in Poland."

As Peter feared, a few months later when it came the turn of Wismar, the last Swedish port on the continent to be besieged, Russian troops were deliberately excluded. Wismar, a Pomeranian coastal town which Peter had specifically promised to Duke Karl Leopold of Mecklenburg as part of Princess Catherine's dowry, was invested by Danish and Prussian troops. When Prince Repnin arrived with four Russian infantry regiments and five regiments of dragoons, he was told to take them away. An argument broke out and the Russian and Prussian commanders almost came to blows, but the Russians withdrew. When Peter heard, he was chagrined, but he kept his temper, as he needed allied help for his sea-borne invasion of Sweden.

Shortly afterward, the situation worsened. A Prussian detachment passing through Mecklenburg was intercepted by a larger Russian force and conducted forcibly to the frontier. Frederick William of Prussia was outraged, declaring that his men had been treated "as if they were enemies." He canceled a meeting with the Tsar and threatened to withdraw completely from the alliance. "The Tsar must give me complete satisfaction," he fumed, "or I shall immediately concentrate my army, which is in good condition." To one of his ministers, he sputtered on, "Thanks be to God I am not in need like [the King of Denmark], who has let himself be cozened by the Muscovites. The Tsar may know that he has to do with no King of Poland or Denmark but with a Prussian who will break his pate for him." Frederick William's anger passed quickly, as did most of his rages. Beneath the surface, his annoyance and suspicion of Hanover were greater than his fear of Russia, and he soon agreed to meet Peter in Stettin, where he handed over the port of Wismar to the Duke of Mecklenburg. First, he insisted that the fortifications of the town be razed, for, he said, to give it to Karl Leopold with its ramparts intact "would be like putting a sharp knife in the hands of the child."

One of Frederick William's reasons for turning Wismar over to the

Duke of Mecklenburg was that he thought it would irritate the Hanoverians, and he was right. Here in Hanover lay a deeper and more suspicious antagonism toward Peter and the Russian presence in North Germany. In part, it was personal: Bernstorff, the leading Hanoverian minister of King George I, was a native Mecklenburger and a member of the aristocratic party which was strongly hostile to Duke Karl Leopold. From his position at King George's elbow, he was able to insinuate his prejudices into the King's ear. Why was the Tsar establishing such close dynastic relations with a small duchy deep in the heart of North Germany? Why were ten Russian regiments to be permanently stationed there? Was not the Tsar's demand that Wismar be turned over to Mecklenburg as part of his niece's dowry simply a clever way of establishing a Russian base in the western Baltic? If more Russian troops were coming, supposedly to participate in an invasion of Sweden, who could say what use would be found for them once they were in North Germany? To all these prejudices and suspicions, George I listened with a ready ear, for he was himself worried about the growing Russian influence and the prospect of large numbers of Russian troops being quartered so close to Hanover. Had Peter been properly informed and counseled regarding these Hanoverian suspicions, he might have acted differently in regard to Mecklenburg. But Peter was already in Danzig, the marriage agreement was already drawn, and although he was eager to maintain an alliance with Hanover and gain an alliance with England, the Tsar refused to go back on his word.

After three weeks in Pyrmont drinking the waters and taking his cure, Peter returned to Mecklenburg, where he had left the Tsaritsa Catherine with Duke Karl Leopold and his bride, Catherine. It was now midsummer, and during the visit Peter preferred to dine in the garden of the Duke's palace, looking out over a lake. Karl Leopold insisted that to give the scene the proper formality, a number of his tall guardsmen, all of whom possessed giant mustaches, must stand at attention around the table, with drawn swords. Peter, who liked to relax at dinner, found this ridiculous and repeatedly asked that the guardsmen be dispensed with. Finally, one evening, he suggested to his host that they might all be more comfortable if the guardsmen would lay down their swords and use their large mustaches to swat the gnats which swarmed over the table.

AGAINST A BACKDROP of suspicion and dissension between allies, Peter went ahead with his plans for a joint invasion of Sweden in the summer of 1716. Obstinate "Brother Charles" showed no sign of making peace; on the contrary, the Charles who returned to Sweden after the fall of Stralsund was busily raising a new army and preparing once again to attack. Rather than leave the initiative to his enemies, he had already, in February, lashed out at

his nearest enemy, Denmark. If the ice had frozen the Oresund that winter, he would have marched across into Zealand and stormed the city of Copenhagen with an army of 12,000 men. The ice formed, but broke up in a storm, and Charles marched his army instead into southern Norway, then still a province of Denmark. He swept through the mountain passes, quickly overcoming the rocky fortresses and occupying the city of Kristiania (now Oslo) before being forced to retreat because of inadequate supplies.

To Peter, Charles' offensive demonstrated that the only way to end the war was to invade Sweden and defeat Charles XII on his home ground. To do this, Russia needed allies. Even despite his commanding position on the upper Baltic, Peter did not dare risk a large-scale, water-borne invasion of Sweden with only the Russian fleet to protect his troopships; the Swedish navy was still too strong. Thus it was that in the spring of 1716, while Peter was overseeing a marriage in Mecklenburg and taking the waters at Pyrmont, the Russian galley fleet began moving westward down the southern coast of the Baltic, first to Danzig, then to Rostock. Stopping in Hamburg before taking the waters, Peter had met King Frederick IV of Denmark and worked out a general plan for the invasion. It called for a combined Russian-Danish landing in Scania, the southernmost province of Sweden, while simultaneously a strong entirely Russian force would land on the Swedish east coast, thus forcing Charles to fight on two fronts. Both invasion forces would be covered by the Russian and Danish fleets, acting as a unit under the Danish Admiral Gyldenløve. England also would contribute a powerful squadron, although neither Peter nor Frederick was certain that the English would actually fight if a naval battle occurred. Peter agreed to supply 40,000 Russian soldiers including infantry and cavalry, plus his entire Russian fleet, both galleys and men-of-war. The Danes would contribute 30,000 men, most of the artillery and ammunition for the entire army, and the whole of the Danish navy. To transport the huge number of men and horses and their equipment across the Oresund, Frederick IV also agreed to commandeer the Danish merchant fleet for the entire summer. Frederick William I of Prussia declined to participate in the actual invasion, but did agree to supply twenty transport ships for use in convoying the Russian infantry assembled at Rostock to Copenhagen, the jumping-off point for the Scania invasion. On paper, at least, it seemed a formidable aggregation, especially against a supposedly helpless Sweden. One part of the plan, devised to satisfy the egos of Frederick and Peter, appeared unwise: Supreme command of the expedition was to be divided, with the two monarchs assuming control in alternate weeks.

After three weeks in Pyrmont, Peter went to Rostock, where his troops were concentrated, and, leaving Catherine, set out with a flotilla of forty-eight galleys for Copenhagen, arriving in the harbor on July 6. He was received with thunderous honors and wrote to Catherine, "Let me know when you will be here, so that I can meet you, for the formalities here are inde-

scribable. Yesterday, I was at such a ceremony as I have not seen for twenty years."

Despite this welcome, time was passing. July slipped away and Peter wrote to Catherine, "We are only chattering in vain." The main problem was that the Danish fleet, necessary to cover the invasion force, was still cruising off the coast of Norway, watching over the withdrawal of the Swedish force which had captured Kristiania. This fleet did not return to Copenhagen until August 7, and even then the transports were not ready for the troops to board. Meanwhile, with the arrival of Admiral Norris and an English squadron of nineteen ships-of-the-line, a gigantic combined fleet had assembled at Copenhagen. In the interim until the armies could be embarked, Admiral Norris proposed a cruise of the joint fleets in the Baltic. Peter, tired of doing nothing, consented. As neither Norris nor the Danish Admiral Gyldenløve would consent to serve under the other, the Tsar was named as commander-in-chief. On August 16, Peter hoisted his flag on the Russian ship-of-the-line *Ingria* and signaled the fleet to weigh anchor. It was the noblest fleet of sail ever to appear in the Baltic: sixty-nine men-of-war—nineteen English, six Dutch, twenty-three Danish and twenty-one Russian warships—and more than 400 merchantmen, all under the command of a self-made sailor whose country had not possessed a single ocean-going ship twenty years before.

Yet, for all its majesty and overwhelming strength, it achieved little. The Swedish fleet, its twenty ships-of-the-line outnumbered three to one, remained in Karlskrona. Norris wanted to brave the fortress guns, enter the harbor and try to sink the fleet at its moorings, but the Danish Admiral, partly out of jealousy and partly because his government had secretly instructed him to withhold the fleet from risky action, declined. Peter was frustrated and, after returning to Copenhagen, went back to the Swedish coast with two small frigates and two galleys to reconnoiter. He found that Charles XII had not wasted the time provided him by the allied delays; as Peter's ships edged in close to shore to get a better look, cannon balls hit his ship. Another Russian ship suffered more serious damage. A troop of Cossacks landed from the galleys and captured some prisoners, who declared that the King of Sweden had an army of 20,000 men.

In fact, Charles had worked wonders. He had garrisoned and provisioned all the fortresses along the coast of Scania. At inland towns, reserves of infantry and cavalry were gathered, ready to counterattack an enemy bridgehead. A large reserve of artillery was held at Karlskrona, awaiting the King's command. Charles had only 22,000 men—12,000 cavalry and 10,000 infantry—but he knew that not all the invaders could be brought across at once, and his hope was to attack and defeat the vanguards before they could be reinforced. If he himself was forced to retreat, he was prepared to follow Peter's example and burn all the villages and towns of southern

Sweden, confronting the invaders with a blackened desert. (It helped, in forming this plan, that Scania had been Danish until the mid-seventeenth century.)

In Zealand, through the early days of September, the preparation went ahead. Seventeen regiments of Russian infantry and nine regiments of Russian dragoons, totaling 29,000 men, had been brought from Rostock. Added to 12,000 Danish infantrymen and 10,000 Danish cavalry, the combined allied force totaled 51,000. The landing date, September 21, was fixed.

Then on September 17, just before the regiments were to move to their embarkation sites, Peter suddenly announced that the invasion had been called off. It was too late in the year, he declared; the assault would have to wait until the following spring. Both George I of England and Frederick IV of Denmark, as well as their ministers, admirals and generals, were stunned by this unilateral decision. Frederick protested that postponement meant cancellation, as he could not possibly commandeer the merchant fleet of Denmark for two years in a row.

Nevertheless, Peter remained adamant. His allies had lost the summer through procrastination, he argued, and now the arrival of autumn made the expedition hazardous. He understood that Charles would meet the first invaders ashore with a pulverizing counterblow and explained that to repulse this stroke and gain a secure foothold which could be held through the winter, a large number of troops would have to be landed very quickly, a successful battle fought and at least two towns, Malmö and Landskrona, besieged and taken. If this operation failed, he asked, where were his troops to spend the icy winter? The Danes replied that the soldiers could shelter in pits dug in the earth. Peter replied that this would kill more men than a battle. And how could his men find food and forage in the unfriendly province of Scania? "Thirty thousand Swedish troops are sitting at that table," Peter said, "who will not easily give place to uninvited guests."

The Danes argued that provisions could be brought across the Danish islands. "Soldiers' bellies," said Peter, "are not satisfied with empty promises and hopes but they demand ready and real storehouses." Further, he asked, how could the allies prevent Charles from burning and ravaging the country as he retreated north? How could they force him to stand and give battle? Might the allied armies not find themselves dwindling away in a hostile country in the dead of winter, just as Charles' own army had dwindled away in the Russian winter? Instead of delivering the coup de grâce to Sweden, might they not be courting a disaster for themselves? Peter understood and had great respect for Charles. "I know his way of making war. He would give us no rest, and our armies would be weakened." No, he repeated decisively, given the lateness of the season and the strength of the enemy, the invasion must be postponed until the following spring.

Peter's decision caused a diplomatic storm. Abandonment of the expedition seemed to confirm the worst suspicions of his allies. Cleverly, Peter had brought 29,000 Russian soldiers to Copenhagen not to invade Sweden but to occupy Denmark, seize Wismar and dictate the politics of North Germany. Frederick IV of Denmark was apprehensive about the numerous Russian regiments camped in the suburbs of his capital; he was also angry that Peter's sudden decision had robbed him of certain victory over Sweden. The English were worried about the effect a powerful Russian army and fleet stationed at the entrance to the Baltic would have on English trade in that sea. But it was the Hanoverians who were most violently distressed by this Russian "plot." Bernstorff, their chief minister, went to see the English General Stanhope, who was then in Hanover with King George I, and hysterically proposed that England "crush the Tsar immediately and secure his ships, even seize his person" as a means of ensuring that all Russian troops would evacuate Denmark and Germany. Stanhope refused, and Bernstorff thereupon sent an order directly to Admiral Norris at Copenhagen to seize the Tsar and the Russian ships. Norris prudently refused also, saying that he took orders from the government of England, not of Hanover.

While all these accusations flew behind his back, Peter remained at Copenhagen, where he continued to be honored by the Danes. The Tsar was especially pleased by the treatment accorded Catherine. She was accepted as his wife and Tsaritsa, and in acknowledgment of her rank, the Queen of Denmark paid a formal call to welcome her to the capital. Admiral Norris was respectful and amiable to his fellow admiral, the Tsar. On the anniversary of the Battle of Lesnaya, the victory for which Peter had taken personal credit, all the ships of the English squadron thundered a salute.

In fact, the suspicions of the Tsar's allies were groundless. Peter's intention had been to invade Sweden in order to end the war. When the invasion attempt seemed too risky, he canceled it, but immediately he began looking for another means to achieve his purpose. As early as October 13, he had written to the Senate in St. Petersburg, explaining what he had done and declaring that the only possibility remaining would be to attack the Swedish homeland from a different direction: across the Gulf of Bothnia from the Aland Islands. He ordered such an attack prepared. As for the threat to Denmark and Hanover, it melted away even as Bernstorff was proclaiming doom. The Russian battalions quietly returned to Mecklenburg and thence —with the exception of a small force of infantry and one cavalry regiment —to Poland. The Russian fleet sailed north for its winter harbors, Riga, Reval and Kronstadt. On October 15, Peter and Catherine also left the Danish capital, traveling slowly through Holstein to meet King Frederick William of Prussia at Havelsberg.

Frederick William disliked Hanover, although both his wife and his

mother were Hanoverian princesses. When Bernstorff accused the Russians of wishing to occupy Lübeck, Hamburg and Wismar, Frederick William stood by Peter. "The Tsar has given his word that he will take nothing for himself from the empire," the Prussian King pointed out. "Besides, part of his cavalry is marching toward Poland, and it would be impossible for him to take those three cities without artillery which he does not possess." To a report from his own minister, Ilgen, on the Hanoverian insinuations, the King replied, "Tomfoolery! I shall refuse and sit fast by brother Peter." Not surprisingly in view of Frederick William's attitude, the Tsar's meeting with the King went well. As tokens of friendship, the two monarchs exchanged gifts: Peter promised more Russian giants for the Potsdam Grenadiers, while Frederick William presented the Tsar with a yacht and a priceless amber cabinet.

IT WAS WINTER in Northern Europe. Darkness came early, the air had a chilling edge, the roads were hardening into ruts. Soon, snow would cover everything. Catherine was in advanced pregnancy and the long journey back to St. Petersburg would not be easy. Peter decided, accordingly, not to return to Russia for the winter, but to travel farther westward and pass the coldest months in Amsterdam, which he had not seen for eighteen years. Leaving Catherine to follow more slowly, he traveled through Hamburg, Bremen, Amersfoort and Utrecht, arriving in Amsterdam on December 6. Even on these relatively well-traveled roads, conditions were primitive. Peter wrote to warn Catherine:

> What I have written before I now confirm, not to come by the way which I came, for it is indescribably bad. Do not bring many people, for life in Holland has become very expensive. As to the church singers, if they have not already started, half of them will be enough. Leave the rest in Mecklenburg. All who are with me here sympathize with you about your journey. If you can endure it, you had better stay where you are, for the bad roads may be dangerous to you. However, do as you please, and for God's sake do not think that I do not want you to come, for you know yourself how much I wish it, and it is better for you to come than to be lonely and sad. Still, I could not desist from writing and I know that you will not endure being left alone.

Catherine started, but after a difficult journey she was forced to halt at Wesel, near the Dutch frontier. Here, on January 2, 1717, she gave birth to a son, whom they had agreed should be called Paul. The Tsar, who was

once again lying in bed with a six-week bout of fever, wrote to her enthusiastically:

> I received yesterday your delightful letter in which you say that the Lord God has blessed us by giving us another recruit . . . for which praise be to him and unforgetting thanks. It delighted me doubly, first about the newborn child, and that the Lord God has freed you from your pains, from which also I became better. Ever since Christmas I have not been able to sit up as long as yesterday. As soon as possible, I will immediately come to you.

The following day, Peter received a shock: His son was dead and his wife was very weak. Peter, who had already sent couriers to Russia to announce the birth, tried to be helpful to Catherine.

> I received your letter about what I knew before, the unexpected occurrence which has changed joy to grief. What answer can I give except that of the long-suffering Job? The Lord has given and the Lord has taken away; Blessed be the name of the Lord. I beg you to reflect on it in this way; I do as far as I can. My illness, thank God, lessens from hour to hour, and I hope to soon go out of the house. It is now nothing but irritation. Otherwise, I praise God I am well, and should long ago have gone to you if I could have gone by water, but I fear the shaking up of land traveling. Besides, I am waiting for an answer from the English King, who is expected here in these days.

Although Peter tried to cast off his unhappiness at losing a son and thought for the moment that he was getting better, little Paul's death seemed to aggravate his fever and he remained in bed for another month. Catherine found him there when she arrived in Amsterdam. Because of this illness, Peter did not meet the stolid Hanoverian who had become England's King. When George I passed through Holland to board his ship for England, Peter sent Tolstoy and Kurakin to call on him, but the Russian envoys were not received. Later, George I apologized, saying that he had been already on board his ship and had had to sail with the tide.

When he began to feel better, Peter enjoyed his stay in Holland. Catherine was with him, and he devoted himself to revisiting and showing her the places where he had been happy as a young man. He returned to Zaandam with Catherine and saw again the East India Company wharf where he had built a frigate. He journeyed to Utrecht, the Hague, Leyden and Rotterdam. And in the spring, if his plans worked out, he would at last visit Paris and see the city renowned throughout the world for its culture, its elegant society and its architectural splendor.

49

"THE KING
IS A MIGHTY MAN..."

THE FRANCE which Peter proposed to visit in 1717 was like a vast, intricately complex system of orbiting spheres whose sun, once the source of warmth, life and meaning for the whole, was now extinct. On September 1, 1715, Louis XIV, the Sun King, died at the age of seventy-six, after a reign which had lasted seventy-two years. For thirty-five of those years, Louis' reign had run parallel to that of Peter, the other great monarch of the time. But Louis and Peter were of different generations, and as Peter's influence and Russia's power had grown, the Sun King's glory had begun to fade.

Louis' last years were blighted by domestic tragedy; his only surviving legitimate child, his heir, the colorless Grand Dauphin, who was terrified of his father, died in 1711. The new Dauphin, the dead man's son and the King's grandson, was the Duc de Bourgogne, a handsome, charming, intelligent young man who embodied France's hopes for the future. His beautiful wife, Marie Adelaide of Savoy, was almost more brilliant than he. Brought as a child bride to Versailles, she grew up in the presence of the aging King, who doted on her. It was said that of all the women he had ever loved, he never loved any as much as his grandson's bride. Suddenly, in 1712, both the new Dauphin and his gay young wife were gone, dead of measles within a week of each other, he at thirty, she at twenty-seven. Their eldest son, Louis' great-grandson, became the next Dauphin. Within a few days, he died of the same disease.

There remained to the seventy-five-year-old King only one great-grandson, a pink-cheeked child of two, the last surviving infant in the direct line. He, too, had measles, but he survived the disease because his governess locked the doors and would not permit the doctors to touch him with their bleedings and emetics. This new little Dauphin remained miraculously alive and lived to rule France for fifty-nine years as Louis XV. On his deathbed, Louis XIV called for his great-grandson and heir who by then was five. Face to face, these two Bourbons who between them ruled France for 131

years regarded each other. Then the Sun King said, "My child, you will one day be a great king. Do not imitate me in my taste for war. Always relate your actions to God and make your subjects honor Him. It breaks my heart to leave them in such a state."

ON THE SUN KING'S DEATH, Versailles was quickly deserted. The great rooms were stripped of furniture, the magnificent court was dissolved. The new King lived in the Tuileries in Paris, and sometimes strollers in the garden could see him, a chubby, pink-cheeked boy with long, curling hair, long eyelashes and a lengthening Bourbon nose.

The ruling power in France had passed into the hands of a regent—Louis XIV's nephew, Philippe, Duc d'Orléans, who was the First Prince of the Blood and the direct heir to the throne after the boy King. In 1717, Philippe was forty-two, small, robust and a heroic womanizer: noblewomen, girls from the opera, girls from the street. He savored whores especially and liked to try out new young girls as soon as they arrived in Paris. He cared not a whit whether the women were beautiful or ugly. His mother admitted, "He is quite crazy about women. Provided they are good-tempered, indelicate, great eaters and drinkers, he troubles little about their looks." Once when she said something to Philippe about this last point, he countered amiably, "Bah, Maman, at night all cats are gray."

The Regent's private suppers at the Palais Royal were the talk of France. Behind barricaded doors, he and his friends lay on couches and dined with women from the opera ballet who wore flimsy, transparent dresses and later danced naked. The Regent not only cared nothing for convention; he delighted in shocking it. His language at the table was so gross that his wife refused to invite anyone to dinner. He scorned religion and once brought a book by Rabelais to mass and read from it ostentatiously during the service. His wife, a daughter of Louis XIV and Madame de Montespan, bore him eight children and spent most of her time locked in her room, suffering from migraines.

Under the circumstances, many in France feared for the life of the young King Louis XV. For if something happened to the boy, the Regent would become king. In fact, these fears were groundless. Philippe d'Orléans, for all his grossness, had many good qualities. He was humane and compassionate as well as sensual, and his sins did not include personal envy or ambition. He had great charm of voice and smile, and when he wished, his manners and gestures were graceful and eloquent. He was fascinated by science and art. His suite in the Palais Royal was hung with Titians and Van Dycks, and he wrote chamber music which still is played today. He was completely devoted to the small boy placed in his charge, and desired only to protect the throne until the King reached his majority. He

began work at six a.m., no matter how hard he had debauched the night before. None of his co-hedonists, male or female, had the slightest effect on his decisions or policy. He saw clearly the desperate state of poverty to which his glorious uncle's martial adventures had reduced his country. During the eight years of Philippe's regency, except for a single brief fracas with Spain, French soldiers stayed in their barracks. Philippe's foreign policy was based on peace. Even more incredible to all of Europe, the cornerstone of this new French policy was friendship with England.

SHORTLY BEFORE PETER'S VISIT to Paris, the pattern of many years in Western Europe had been broken by a series of dramatic events. The fall of the Whig ministry in England had stripped Marlborough of his power, and the Anglo-Dutch invasion of northern France had ground to an inconclusive halt. The new Tory ministry was anxious for peace, and the exhausted, aging Sun King had been happy to agree. Peace was signed in 1713 with the Treaty of Utrecht, and the great War of the Spanish Succession, which had engulfed all the kingdoms and empires of Western Europe, ended. Soon after, the Sun King himself was gone. In England, too, a royal death occurred. Queen Anne died, leaving no Protestant Stuart heir, all sixteen of her children having died in infancy or childhood. In order to ensure the Protestant succession, as agreed by Parliament in advance, the Elector of Hanover, George Louis, ascended the throne of England as King George I while retaining his rule over Hanover.

Taken as a whole, these events created an entirely new diplomatic landscape in Europe. With peace among themselves, the nations of the West could devote more attention to what, for them, had been a secondary theater: the War in the North. England, which had emerged from the War of the Spanish Succession virtually unchallenged in its supremacy at sea, was concerned that the growing power of Russia in the Baltic might affect British trade in that area, and powerful British naval squadrons began to appear in that northern sea. Hanover was also hostile to Peter, fearing the Tsar's new presence in northern Germany. Three times the King-Elector refused Peter's overtures for a meeting, demanding first that all Russian troops be evacuated from Germany.

Meanwhile, the foreign policy of France had done a revolutionary flip-flop. Instead of hostility to England and support for the Catholic Jacobites, France, under the regency of Philippe, sought friendship with England and guaranteed the rights of the Protestant Hanoverian dynasty. France's long support of Sweden also seemed ready for change. For years, the Sun King had subsidized the Swedes and used them as a counterpoise to keep the Austrian emperor distracted in Germany. Now, with the Swedes defeated and driven completely out of Germany, and with the power of the

Hapsburg Emperor greatly enhanced, France needed a new ally in the East. Peter's Russia, which had soared to prominence within the past decade, was a natural possibility. Through diplomatic channels, various hints and overtures began to pass. And Peter was eager to listen. Although throughout his reign France had opposed him in Poland and in Constantinople, he knew that the structure of Europe was changing. An alliance or an understanding with France would be a balance to his increasingly difficult relations with Hanover and England. Even more, he saw France's help as a possible way of ending the Northern War. France was still paying monthly subsidies to Sweden; if these could be cut off and France's diplomatic support of Sweden withdrawn, Peter felt that he might at last persuade an isolated Charles XII that Sweden must make peace.

Peter's proposal to France, when it came, was a bold one: that France take Russia instead of Sweden as her ally in the East. In addition, Peter suggested that he could bring Prussia and Poland into the arrangement. Aware that France's treaties with England and Holland would be a stumbling block, Peter argued that the new alliance would not threaten the earlier one. Specifically, he proposed that, in return for Russian guarantees of the Treaty of Utrecht, France halt its subsidies to Sweden and instead pay to Russia 25,000 crowns a month for the duration of the Northern War—which, with France behind him, he hoped would be short. Finally, Peter proposed a personal link between the two nations. To seal the alliance and to mark Russia's emergence as a great power, he would marry his eight-year-old daughter Elizabeth to the seven-year-old King of France, Louis XV.

Such proposals were not unattractive to the Regent of France, but to the decisive power in French foreign policy, the Abbé Guillaume Dubois, they were unwelcome. The new alliance with England was his handiwork, and he feared that any arrangement with Russia would throw the whole thing off balance. In a letter to the Regent advising against the Russian proposal, Dubois said, "If, in establishing the Tsar, you chase the English and the Dutch from the Baltic Sea, you will be eternally odious to these two nations." Further, Dubois warned, the Regent might be sacrificing England and Holland in return for only a short-term relationship with Russia. "The Tsar has chronic maladies," he pointed out, "and his son will support nothing."

Peter, excited by his own proposal, and deciding that he might accomplish more by seeing the Regent in person, decided to go to Paris. Besides, he had seen Amsterdam, London, Berlin and Vienna, but never Paris. Through Kurakin, his ambassador in Holland, he informed the Regent that he would like to make a visit.

There could be no question of refusing, although the Regent and his advisors had misgivings. Following diplomatic custom, the host country paid the expenses of the guest, and for the Tsar and his suite, this expense would be enormous. Further, Peter had a reputation as an impetuous

monarch, sensitive to insult and quick to anger, and the men of his suite were said to be of similar character. Nevertheless, the Regent made ready; the Tsar was to be received as a grand European monarch. A cavalcade of carriages, horses, wagons and royal servants under the command of Monsieur de Liboy, a gentleman of the King's household, was sent to Calais to escort the Russian guests to Paris. Liboy was to honor Peter, wait upon him and pay all his expenses. In Paris, meanwhile, the apartments of the Sun King's mother, Anne of Austria, in the Louvre were prepared for the guest. At the same time, Kurakin, knowing Peter's tastes, suggested that his master might be happier in a smaller, more private place. Accordingly, a handsome private mansion, the Hôtel Lesdiguières, was also prepared. On the chance that the Tsar would choose it, the hôtel was handsomely furnished from the royal collection. Magnificent armchairs, polished desks and inlaid tables were carried there from the Louvre. Cooks, servants and fifty soldiers were assigned to provide the Tsar with nourishment, comfort and security.

Meanwhile, Peter and his party of sixty-one persons, including Golovkin, Shafirov, Peter Tolstoy, Vasily Dolgoruky, Buturlin, Osterman and Yaguzhinsky, traveled slowly through the Low Countries. As was his custom, the Tsar stopped often to visit towns, examine curiosities and study the people and their way of life. Although he had again adopted the partial façade of traveling incognito to minimize the time wasted in official ceremonies, he was pleased to hear church bells rung and cannon fired in his honor as he passed by. Catherine accompanied him as far as Rotterdam; to simplify the journey, she would wait at The Hague while he visited France. He felt that her presence would demand additional time-consuming ceremonies which by himself he could avoid.

From Rotterdam, Peter traveled by boat to Breda and up the Scheldt to Antwerp, where he climbed the cathedral tower to gaze out over the city. In Brussels, he wrote to Catherine: "I wish to send you lace for *fontange* and *engageants* [that is, lace ribbons to be clustered in the hair and across the bodice—the latest style in Paris], for the best lace in all Europe is made here, but they make it to order only. Therefore, send the pattern and what name or arms you wish worked on it." From Brussels, Peter moved on to Ghent, Bruges, Ostend and Dunquerque, finally reaching the French frontier at Calais, where he rested for nine days to observe the last week of Lent and to celebrate Russian Easter.

At Calais, the Russian travelers met Liboy and the French welcoming escort. For Liboy, this first exposure to the Russian character was traumatic. The guests complained about the carriages to which they were assigned, and they spent freely, every écu of which had to be paid by Liboy. In desperation, he urged Paris that the Tsar and his suite be put on a fixed daily allowance, not to be exceeded, allowing them to argue among themselves how the sum should be spent.

Liboy had been ordered to report to Paris on the habits of the visitors and to ascertain the purpose of their visit. He found it impossible to understand Peter, who, instead of doing anything serious, seemed only to be idly amusing himself, ambling along, examining things which, in Liboy's eyes, were irrelevant. "This little court," he wrote of the Russian party of twenty-two persons of rank and thirty-nine orderlies, "is very changeable and irresolute and from the throne to the stable, very subject to anger." The Tsar, he reported, "is of very great stature, a little stooped, with the habit of holding his head down. He is dark and there is a fierceness in his expression. He appears to have a lively mind and a ready understanding, with a certain grandeur in his movements, but with little restraint." Elaborating in a subsequent report, Liboy continued:

In the Tsar, one does indeed find seeds of virtue, but they are wild and very mixed with failings. I believe that he lacks most of all uniformity and constancy of purpose and that he has not arrived at that point where one can rely on what would be concluded with him. I admit that Prince Kurakin is polite; he appears to be intelligent and to desire to arrange everything to our mutual satisfaction. I do not know if it is by temperament or through fear of the Tsar, who appears, as I have said, very hard to please and quick-tempered. Prince Dolgoruky appears a gentleman and to be much esteemed by the Tsar; the only inconvenience is that he understands absolutely no language but Russian. In this respect allow me to remark that the term "Muscovite" or even "Muscovy" is deeply offensive to all this court.

The Tsar rises very early, dines about ten o'clock, sups about seven and retires before nine. He drinks liquors before meals, beer and wine in the afternoon, sups very little and sometimes not at all. I have not been able to perceive any sort of council or conference for serious business, unless they discuss affairs while tippling, the Tsar deciding alone and promptly whatever is presented. This prince varies on all occasions his amusements and walks and is extraordinarily quick, impatient and very hard to please. . . . He likes especially to see the water. He lives in the great apartments and sleeps in some out-of-the-way room if there be any.

To counsel the French maîtres d'hôtel and chefs who would be preparing food for the Russian visitor, Liboy forwarded specific recommendations:

The Tsar has a head cook who prepares two or three dishes for him every day and who uses for this purpose enough wine and meat to serve a table of eight.

He is served both a meat and a Lenten dinner on Fridays and Saturdays.

He likes sharp sauces, brown and hard bread, and green peas.

He eats many sweet oranges and apples and pears.

He generally drinks light beer and dark vin de nuits without liquor.

In the morning he drinks aniseed water [kümmel], liquors before meals, beer and wine in the afternoon. All of them fairly cold.

He eats no sweetmeats and does not drink sweetened liquors at his meals.

On May 4, Peter left Calais on the road to Paris, characteristically refusing to follow the expected route. A formal reception had been prepared for him at Amiens; he skirted the city. At Beauvais, where he saw the nave of the largest cathedral in France, still unfinished since the thirteenth century, he spurned a banquet which was offered. "I am a soldier," he told the Bishop of Beauvais, "and when I find bread and water I am content." Peter was exaggerating; he still liked wine, although he preferred his favorite Hungarian Tokay to the French varieties. "Thanks for the Hungarian wine, which here is a great rarity," he wrote to Catherine from Calais. "But there is only one bottle of vodka left. I don't know what to do."

At noon on May 7, at Beaumont-sur-Oise, twenty-five miles northeast of Paris, Peter found the Marshal de Tessé waiting for him with a procession of royal carriages and an escort of red-coated cavalry of the Maison du Roi. Tessé, standing beside the Tsar's carriage, made a deep, low bow, flourishing his hat, as Peter stepped out. Peter greatly admired the Marshal's carriage and chose to ride in it as he entered the capital through the Porte St. Denis. But he did not want Tessé in the carriage with him, preferring instead three of his own Russians. Tessé, whose duty was to please, followed in another carriage.

The procession arrived at the Louvre at nine p.m. Peter entered the palace and walked through the late Queen Mother's apartments which had been prepared for him. As Kurakin had predicted, the Tsar found them too magnificent and too brilliantly lighted. While there, Peter looked at a dinner table which had been superbly set for him and sixty people, but he only nibbled some bread and radishes, tasted six kinds of wine and drank two glasses of beer. Then he returned to his carriage and, with his suite following, drove to the Hôtel Lesdiguières. Peter liked this better, although here, too, he found the rooms assigned to him to be too large and luxuriously furnished and ordered his own camp bed to be placed in a small dressing room.

The next morning, the Regent of France, Philippe d'Orléans, came to pay his official welcoming call. As the Regent's carriage entered the courtyard of the Hôtel Lesdiguières, it was met by four noblemen of the Tsar's suite, who conducted the Regent into the reception hall. Peter emerged from

his private chamber, embraced the Regent and then turned and walked into the private chamber ahead of Philippe, leaving him and Kurakin, who was to serve as interpreter, to follow. The French, noting every nuance of protocol, were affronted by Peter's embrace and his walking ahead of the Regent; these acts, they said, displayed "a haughty air of superiority" and were "without the slightest civility."

In Peter's room, two armchairs had been placed facing each other, and the two men sat down with Kurakin nearby. For nearly an hour they talked, devoting themselves entirely to pleasantries. Then the Tsar walked out of the room, the Regent once again behind him. In the reception hall, Peter made a deep bow (rendered in mediocre fashion, says Saint-Simon), and left his guest at the same spot where he had met him on entering. This precise formality was unnatural for Peter, but he had come to Paris on a mission and he thought it important to comply with the demands of his etiquette-conscious hosts.

The remainder of that day and the day following (a Sunday), Peter remained cloistered in the Hôtel Lesdiguières. Anxious as he was to get out and see Paris, he forced himself to observe protocol and remain secluded until he had received the formal visit of the King. As he wrote to Catherine during this weekend:

For two or three days, I must stay in the house for visits and other ceremonies and therefore I have as yet seen nothing. But tomorrow or the day after I shall begin sightseeing. From what I could see on the road, the misery of the common people is very great.

P.S. I have this moment received your letter full of jokes. You say that I'll be looking about for a lady, but that would not be at all becoming to my old age.

On Monday morning, King Louis XV of France arrived to greet his royal guest. The Tsar met the King as he stepped down from his carriage and, to the astonishment of the French party, he took the little boy in his arms, lifted him into the air until their faces were at the same level, and hugged and kissed him several times. Louis, although unprepared for this display, took it well and showed no fear. The French, once having overcome their shock, were struck by Peter's grace and by the tenderness he showed the boy, somehow establishing their equality of rank while at the same time recognizing the difference in their ages. After embracing Louis again, Peter returned him to the ground and escorted him into the Tsar's reception chamber. There, Louis made a short speech of welcome, filled with memorized compliments. The remainder of the conversation was furnished by the Duc du Maine and Marshal de Villeroy, with Kurakin

again interpreting. After fifteen minutes, Peter rose and, again taking Louis in his arms, escorted him to his carriage.

The next afternoon at four, Peter went to the Tuileries to return the King's visit. The courtyard was filled with companies of the red-coated Maison du Roi, and as the Tsar's carriage approached, a line of military drummers began to beat. Seeing little Louis waiting to meet his carriage, Peter jumped out, picked the King up in his arms and carried him up the palace steps for a meeting which also lasted only fifteen minutes. Describing these events to Catherine, Peter wrote: "Last Monday the little King visited me, who is only a finger or two taller than our Luke [a favorite dwarf]. The child is very handsome in face and build and very intelligent for his age, which is only seven." To Menshikov, Peter wrote: "The King is a mighty man and very old in years, namely seven."

Peter's formal call on the King at the Tuileries fulfilled the requirements of protocol. At last, the Tsar was free to go out and see the great city of Paris.

50

A VISITOR IN PARIS

IN 1717 AS TODAY, Paris was the capital and the center of everything that matters in France. But Paris, with its 500,000 citizens, was only the third largest city in Europe; both London (750,000) and Amsterdam (600,000) were larger. In relation to total national populations, Paris was even smaller. In Britain, one man in ten was a Londoner, in Holland one man in five was from Amsterdam, while in France only one Frenchman in forty lived in Paris.

To those who know it now, the Paris of 1717 seems small. The great palaces and squares which today lie in the heart of Paris—the Tuileries, the Luxembourg, the Place Vendôme, the Invalides—were then on the city's fringes. Beyond Montparnasse were fields and pastures. The Tuileries looked through its splendid gardens to the wilder part of the Champs-Elysées rising up to the wooded hill where the Arc de Triomphe now stands. To the north, a single road ran through the meadows up to the ridge of Montmartre.

The Seine was the heart of the city. The river was not confined by its present granite quays, and along its muddy banks women did their washing, oblivious to the unpleasant odors of slaughterhouse and tannery wastes poured directly into the stream. Passing through the city, the river flowed beneath five bridges. The two most recent, the magnificent Pont Royal and the Pont Neuf, were open-sided; the others were lined by four- and five-story buildings. The Paris of wide, tree-lined boulevards did not exist; the city in 1717 was a jumble of narrow streets and four- and five-story buildings with pointed roofs. The great twin towers of Notre Dame rose above the city, but the world-famous view of the cathedral façade was unavailable because the plaza was a cluster of tiny streets crowded with buildings. Louis XIV had begun to change the face of the medieval city. Early in his reign, he had ordered the city's fortified ramparts destroyed and boulevards planted with trees laid out where the walls had been. Only one great square, the elegant Place Royale (now Place des Vosges), had been in existence when the Sun King reached the throne. During Louis' reign, he added the

Place des Victoires, the Place Vendôme and the immense church and esplanade of the Invalides.

Each section of the city had a special flavor. The Marais attracted the aristocracy and the higher bourgeoisie. Wealthy financiers built their houses at the other end of the city, around the new Place Vendôme. Foreigners and foreign embassies preferred the quarter surrounding St. Germain des Prés, where the streets were wider and the air was said to be purer. Travelers were also advised that the best hotels were available near St. Germain des Prés, but a visitor could find a room in many private mansions; even the highest members of the aristocracy rented their top floor to a paying guest. The Latin Quarter then, as now, was for students.

During the day, the people of Paris swarmed through the streets. Pedestrians were in constant danger as horses, carriages and carts tried to thrust themselves through narrow passageways already jammed with people. The noise of iron-rimmed wheels and shouting men was deafening; the smells from human excrement dumped from the windows, from piles of manure and from the courtyards where butchers slaughtered their animals were dreadful. To reduce the noise and give traction to the wheels, as well as to maintain a modicum of cleanliness, fresh straw was laid down daily, the dirty straw being swept up and dumped in the river. To avoid the dangers and inconvenience of walking in these streets, those who could afford them used private carriages which they owned or rented by the day or month. Others used closed sedan chairs carried by two men.

The Pont Neuf and the Place Dauphine on the tip of the Ile de la Cité swarmed with itinerant vendors, quack doctors, marionette shows, stilt walkers, street singers and beggars. Pickpockets waited outside the doors of fashionable hotels to brush against unwary foreigners. It was easy to find women. The most desirable, the girls of the Opéra and the Comédie, were generally reserved for the French aristocracy, but the streets were crowded with parading prostitutes. Visitors were warned, however, that they risked their health if not their lives.

At night, the streets were relatively safe until around midnight. Paris in 1717 was the best-lighted city in Europe with 6,500 candle lamps suspended over the streets. Replaced each day and lighted at dark, the fat tapers cast a murky glow over the vicinity. But at midnight, when the candles guttered out one by one and the city was plunged into darkness, all who wished to see morning were behind a door.

The Opéra and the Comédie were always crowded. Molière was still the favorite, but people also wanted to see Racine, Corneille and the newly fashionable Marivaux. After the theater, cafés and cabarets remained open until ten or eleven o'clock. Society flocked to the 300 new coffee houses clustered near St. Germain des Prés or the Faubourg St. Honoré, to drink tea, coffee or chocolate. For many, the best recreation was a stroll in a park

or garden. The most elegant strollers favored the long Cours la Reine, a walk along the right bank of the Seine which extended from the Tuileries down the river as far as the present Place de l'Alma. This flowered walk was so popular that its use was extended into the evening by placing torches and lanterns along the path. Other gardens open to the public were the garden of the Palais Royal, the Luxembourg Gardens and the Jardin du Roi, now known as the Jardin des Plantes.

Then, as now, the most famous garden in Paris was the Jardin des Tuileries. There, in the afternoon and evening, one met the greatest personages of the kingdom, even the Regent himself, strolling along. Beyond the Tuileries lay the Champs-Elysées, flanked by symmetrical rows of trees. Here people exercised on horseback and opened the windows of their carriages to enjoy the fresh air. Still farther west, beyond the village of Passy, lay the wood later turned into the park of the Bois de Boulogne. The wood was filled with deer, which riders and dogs hunted for sport, but it was also a place where, on warm Sunday and holiday afternoons, Parisians spread themselves on the grass to picnic and sleep. The wood was also a place for love affairs, which took place inside carriages with the curtains drawn, the coachman sitting impassively atop the carriage, the reins loose, the horses peaceably munching the grass.

When the boy King left Versailles and moved back to Paris, most of the aristocracy followed, building or refurbishing its mansions (*hôtels particuliers*) in the fashionable section of the Marais on the eastern edge of the city, or across the river in the Faubourg St. Germain. The Hôtel Lesdiguières, in which Peter was living during his six weeks in Paris, was one of the grandest of the mansions of the Marais* with gardens spreading over a large block. Its walls, filled with sheds and stables, touched the Rue St. Antoine, and behind lay the Cerisaie, the King's cherry orchard with rows of handsome little trees.

The Bastille stood directly adjacent to the hôtel, and its eight thin gray stone towers towered directly over the garden wall. While strolling, the Tsar had only to raise his eyes to see the legendary stronghold. In fact, the fourteenth-century fortress has been the most unjustly maligned of all the castles of France. Depicted as a grim, gigantic symbol of the oppression of the French monarchy, it was actually rather small: seventy yards long and

---

* Many of the splendid mansions of the Marais still stand, but the Hôtel Lesdiguières has disappeared. In 1866, its grounds were pierced when the engineer Baron Georges Haussmann, then driving his broad boulevards through Paris at the command of Emperor Napoleon III, laid the Boulevard Henri IV through the hôtel garden. Thereafter, the mansion survived only a few years and was torn down in 1877. Today, there remains only a plaque commemorating Peter's visit on the wall above No. 10 Rue de la Cerisaie. Across the street at No. 11, in a house which was standing there during Peter's visit, the author lived for three of the years he was writing this book.

thirty yards wide (although a dry moat with drawbridges and an outer courtyard surrounded by guard buildings made the space it occupied seem larger). The furious Paris mob which tore it down on July 14, 1789, and the happy crowds of Frenchmen who still celebrate Bastille Day every July 14, have imagined the Bastille as a mournful den where a tyrant wreaked his will on the suffering people of France. Nothing could be further from the truth. The Bastille was the most luxurious prison which has ever existed. Imprisonment there carried no dishonor. With rare exceptions, its occupants were aristocrats or gentlemen who were received and treated according to their rank. The King could order troublesome nobles put there until he or they changed an opinion. Fathers could send unruly sons to the Bastille for several months to cool their foolishness. Rooms were furnished, heated and lighted according to the means and tastes of the prisoners. A servant could be kept, and guests could be invited for dinner— Cardinal de Rohan once gave a banquet for. twenty. There was competition for the more favorable rooms; those at the tops of the towers were the least desirable, being coldest in winter and hottest in summer. Nothing was required of the prisoner. He could play his guitar, read poetry, exercise in the governor's garden and plan menus to please his guests.

Many a famous man spent time in the Bastille. The most mysterious was the Man in the Iron Mask, whose identity was ornamented by Alexandre Dumas into a twin brother of Louis XIV. Like most stories about the Bastille, this one was mostly imaginary; the famous mask was not of iron, but of black velvet, although even the governor of the Bastille was not allowed to lift it, and the prisoner died, still unknown, in 1703. During the weeks Peter spent in Paris, another famous Frenchman was locked in the Bastille, and it is possible that this prisoner looked down from a tower window into the garden of the Hôtel Lesdiguières to see the Tsar strolling among the trees. This was twenty-three-year-old François-Marie Arouet, a waspish young epigrammist whose suggestive verses about the relations between the Regent and his daughter the Duchesse de Berri had inspired the Regent to lock him up. Forty years later, using the name Voltaire, the prisoner would write a *History of the Russian Empire under Peter the Great*.

BEFORE COMING TO PARIS, Peter had made a list of everything he wanted to see, and the list was long. Once the welcoming ceremonies were over, he asked the Regent that all protocol be dispensed with; he wanted to be free to visit whatever he liked. Subject to his insistence that the Tsar be always escorted by the Marshal de Tessé or some other member of the court, and that Peter allow himself to be accompanied by a bodyguard of eight soldiers of the royal guard whenever he went out, the Regent agreed.

Peter began his sightseeing by rising at four a.m. on May 12 and walk-

ing in the early light down the Rue St. Antoine to visit the Place Royale and see the sun reflected in the great windows which looked down on the royal parade ground. That same day, he visited the Place des Victoires and the Place Vendôme. The next day, he crossed to the Left Bank and visited the Observatory, the factory of the Gobelins, famous for tapestries, and the Jardin des Plantes, which had over 2,500 species. In the days that followed, he visited the shops of artisans of every kind, examining everything and asking questions. One morning at six a.m., he was in the Grand Gallery of the Louvre, where the Marshal de Villars showed him the enormous models of Vauban's great fortresses which guarded the frontiers of France.* Then, leaving the Louvre, he walked in the Tuileries Garden, where the usual crowd of strollers had been asked to leave.

A few days later, Peter visited the vast hospital and barracks of the Invalides, where 4,000 disabled soldiers were housed and cared for. He tasted the soldiers' soup and wine, drank to their health, clapped them on their backs and called them his "comrades." At the Invalides, he admired the famous dome of the church, recently completed, towering 345 feet and considered to be the marvel of Paris. Peter sought out interesting people. He met the refugee Prince Rakoczy, the Hungarian leader who had rebelled against the Hapsburg Emperor and whom Peter had once proposed to make King of Poland. He dined with the Marshal d'Estrées, who came for him at eight one morning and talked to him the entire day about the French navy. He visited the house of the director of the Post Office, who was a collector of all kinds of curiosities and inventions. He spent an entire morning at the Mint and watched a new goldpiece being struck. When it was taken and placed, still warm, in Peter's hand, he saw to his surprise that on the coin were his own face and the inscription "Petrus Alexievitz, Tzar, Mag. Russ. Imperat." He was solemnly received at the Sorbonne, where a group of Catholic theologians gave him a plan for the reunion of the Eastern and Western churches (Peter took it back with him to Russia, where he ordered his Russian bishops to study it and give him an opinion). He visited the Academy of Science, and on December 22, 1717, six months after his departure from Paris, the Tsar was formally elected a member of the Academy.

As Paris began to see him frequently, reports and impressions circulated rapidly. "He was a very tall man," wrote Saint-Simon,

---

* These astonishing exact-scale models, created by order of Louis XIV, including mountains, rivers and details of cities as well as of the fortifications, were gigantic, some as large as 900 square feet. Considered secrets of war, they were kept under guard in the Grand Gallery of the Louvre until 1777, when they were transported to the top floor of the Invalides. There, they have remained for 200 years and can be seen today by anyone willing to climb the stairs.

well proportioned, rather thin with a roundish face, a broad forehead and handsome, sharply defined eyebrows, a short, but not-too-short nose, large at the end. His lips were rather thick, his complexion a ruddy brown, fine black eyes, large, lively and piercing, and well apart. When he wished, his look was majestic and gracious, at other times it was fierce and severe. He had a nervous, twitching smile which did not come often, but which contorted his face and his whole expression and inspired fear. That lasted but a moment, accompanied by a wild and terrible look, and passed away as quickly. His whole air showed his intellect, his reflection and his greatness, and did not lack a certain grace. He wore only a linen collar, a round brown wig without powder which did not touch his shoulders, a brown tight-fitting coat, plain with gold buttons, a waistcoat, breeches, stockings, and no gloves or cuffs. He wore the star of his order on his coat and the ribbon underneath; his coat was often quite unbuttoned, his hat was always on a table and never on his head even out of doors. With all this simplicity, and in whatever bad carriage or company he might be, one could not fail to perceive the air of greatness that was natural to him.

Peter's visiting was conducted at a headlong pace. Only when he had a bout of fever and was forced to cancel a dinner with the Regent did the Tsar briefly slow down. The poor Marshal de Tessé and the eight French body-guards did their best to keep up, often with no success. Peter's combination of curiosity and impetuosity, along with his disdain for majesty, astonished the French. Every action was precipitous. He wanted to be free to go from place to place in the city without ceremony; therefore, he often took a rented carriage or even a hackney cab instead of waiting for the royal carriage assigned to him. More than once, a French visitor who called on a member of the Russian party at the Hôtel Lesdiguières came to the door to find his carriage gone. The Tsar, striding out of the house, would jump into the first carriage he saw and calmly drive away. Often, he escaped in this manner from the Marshal de Tessé and his soldiers.

Inside the Hôtel Lesdiguières, Verton, one of the royal maîtres d'hôtel assigned to running the Tsar's kitchen and table, was doing his best to feed Peter and his Russians. Verton was a man of spirit, good cheer and self-possession, and before long Peter and all his party liked him enormously. Through Verton and others, stories filtered out as to what went on at this Russian table in the French capital. Wrote Saint-Simon:

What he [Peter] drinks and eats in two regular meals is incredible, without adding what he swallowed of beer, lemonade and other drinks

between meals. As for his suite, they drank even more: a bottle or two of beer at least, and sometimes more of wine, and liquors after the end of the meal. This was normal for every meal. He ate at eleven o'clock in the morning, and eight o'clock at night.

Peter's relations with the Regent were excellent, in part because it amused Philippe to make himself agreeable. One night, the two men went together to the Opéra, where they sat alone in the front row of the royal box in full view of the audience. During the performance, Peter became thirsty and asked for a glass of beer. A large goblet was brought on a saucer, and the Regent stood up, took it and himself presented it to the Tsar. Peter accepted the glass with a smile and a nod, drank the beer and put the goblet back on the saucer. Then Philippe, still standing, placed a napkin on a plate and presented it to the Tsar. Peter, still without rising, used it to dry his mouth and mustache and replaced it. Throughout the performance, with the Regent of France acting like a servant, the audience watched in fascination. During the fourth act, Peter wearied and left the box to go to supper, declining Philippe's offer to escort him and insisting that his host remain until the end.

Everywhere, the Tsar was received with respect. Most members of the royal family and ranking aristocracy were excited by his presence among them and determined to meet him, among them the current first lady of France, "Madame," the Regent's mother, a bosomy, gossipy German lady of sixty-five. The Regent brought the Tsar to her one day after first showing his guest the palace and gardens at St. Cloud. "Madame" received her visitor at the Palais Royal, where she lived with her son, and the lady was charmed. "Received a great visit today, that of my hero, the Tsar," she wrote. "I find that he has very good manners . . . and is not in the least affected. He has much judgment. He speaks bad German, but still makes himself understood without trouble and talks very freely. He is polite toward everyone and is much liked."

Not to be outdone by her grandmother, the Regent's scandalous daughter, the Duchesse de Berri, sent her compliments to Peter and asked whether he would visit her. Peter agreed and came to the Luxembourg Palace and afterward walked in the Luxembourg Gardens. But disputes over etiquette prevented him from seeing some of the great ladies of Paris. Several Princes of the Blood refused to call on Peter unless he promised to return the calls and meet their wives. Peter found this petty and absurd and simply refused. He preferred, in any case, to visit people of merit rather than people of blood.

On May 24, two weeks after his first visit to the Tuileries, Peter returned to visit the King. He arrived at an early hour before the boy was awake, so Marshal de Villeroy took him to see the French crown jewels. Peter found

them more numerous and more beautiful than he had expected, although he said he did not know much about jewels. In fact, he told Villeroy, he was not much interested in objects, no matter how beautiful or valuable, which had no practical utility. From there, he went to see the King, who was just coming to find him in Marshal de Villeroy's apartments. This was purposely done so that their meeting would be not a formal visit but seemingly by chance. Meeting Peter in an office, the King held in his hand a roll of paper which he gave to the Tsar, telling him that it was a map of his dominions. Louis' politeness charmed Peter, who treated the boy with a skillful blend of affection and royal respect.

Villeroy, writing to Madame de Maintenon, had the same impression: "I cannot express to you the dignity, the grace and the politeness with which the King received the visit of the Tsar. But I must tell you that this Prince, said to be barbarous, is not so at all. He displayed sentiments of grandeur and generosity which we never expected."

That night, Peter drove to Versailles, where the royal apartments had been prepared for him. His Russian companions, given rooms nearby, had brought from Paris a collection of young women, who were installed in the former chambers of the puritanical Madame de Maintenon. Reported Saint-Simon: "Blouin, Governor of Versailles, was extremely scandalized to see thus profaned this temple of prudery."

In the morning, the Tsar rose early. His escort at Versailles, the Duc d'Antin, going to find him, discovered that the Tsar had already walked among the clipped hedges and stylized flower beds of the palace gardens and was at that moment rowing a boat on the Grand Canal. That day, Peter inspected all of Versailles, including the great fountains which had been the Sun King's special pride, and the pink marble Trianon. Regarding the great palace itself with its small central château of Louis XIII and the monumental wings added by Louis XIV, Peter declared that it seemed to him "a pigeon with the wings of an eagle." Leaving Versailles, he returned to Paris in time to see the Whitsunday procession the following morning. Tessé took him to Notre Dame, where, beneath the great rose windows of the cathedral, Peter observed a mass being celebrated by Cardinal de Noailles.

A visit to Fontainebleau, the other majestic royal château outside Paris, was less successful. The Tsar's host, the Comte de Toulouse, one of Louis XIV's legitimized bastards by Madame de Montespan, urged him to go on a stag hunt, and Peter agreed. For Frenchmen of blood, the chase was the noblest of outdoor sports. They swept through the forests with sword or spear in hand, their horses hurtling fallen trees and streams at a mad gallop, following the sounds of the baying dogs and hunting horns, until the pursued stag or wolf or wild boar turned at bay and was pulled down in a bloody melee among the moss and ferns of the virgin forest. Peter had no stomach for this kind of thing, and, unused to the breakneck pace of the riders, he

nearly fell off. He returned to the château angry and humiliated, swearing that he did not understand the sport, did not like it and found it too violent. He refused to dine with the Count, instead eating only with three members of his Russian suite. Soon after, he left Fontainebleau.

Returning to Paris by boat down the Seine, he glided past the lovely château of Choisy and asked to visit it. By chance, he met its owner, the Princesse de Conti, one of the Princesses of the Blood whom etiquette had barred from meeting him before. Arriving in Paris, Peter was so pleased to be once more on the water that, instead of disembarking on the eastern edge of the city and returning directly to the Hôtel Lesdiguières, he ordered the boatmen to continue downstream so that he could float under all the five bridges of Paris.

On June 3, Peter returned to Versailles to sleep in the Trianon and to spend several nights at Marly, the country pavilion which Louis XIV had built to escape the ponderous etiquette of Versailles. While staying there, Peter drove to St. Cyr to visit Louis XIV's widow, Madame de Maintenon, in the convent she had established, and to which she had retired after the King's death. Everyone was surprised when the Tsar expressed a wish to see her. "She has much merit," he explained. "She has rendered great service to the King and nation."

Not surprisingly, the elderly woman was enormously flattered at the prospect of a visit from the man about whom all Paris was talking. "The Tsar . . . seems to me a very great man since he has inquired about me," she wrote before his visit. To conceal her age and put on her best appearance, she received the Tsar at twilight, sitting in her bed with all the curtains drawn except one which let in a single shaft of light. When Peter entered, he went straight to the windows and dramatically opened the curtains to let in the light. Then, he pulled back the curtains around her canopy bed, sat down at the end of the bed and silently looked at her. According to Saint-Simon (who was not present), the silence continued with neither saying a word until Peter rose and left. "I know that she must have been greatly astonished and even more humiliated, but the Sun King is no more," Saint-Simon wrote. From a sister of the convent, there is a kinder version, according to which Peter asked Madame what her illness was. "Old age," she replied. She then asked him why he had come to see her. "I came to see everything of note that France contains," he answered. At this, it was reported, a ray of her former beauty lighted up her face.

It was not until the very end of Peter's visit to Paris that Saint-Simon met the Tsar in person:

> I entered the garden where the Tsar was walking. The Marshal de Tessé, who saw me from afar, came to me, expecting to present

me to the Tsar. I begged him not to do it and not to notice me in his presence because I wished to observe him at my leisure . . . and get a good look at him, which I would not be able to do if I was known. . . . With this precaution, I satisfied my curiosity completely at my leisure. I found him rather affable, but behaving always as if he were everywhere the master. He walked into an office where D'Antin showed him different maps and several documents on which he asked several questions. It was there that I saw the tic of which I have spoken. I asked Tessé if this happened often; he said several times a day, especially when he did not take care to control it.

After six weeks in Paris, the visit was now coming to a close. He revisited the Observatory, climbed the tower of Notre Dame and went to a hospital to watch a cataract operation. In the Champs-Elysées, he sat on horseback and reviewed two regiments of the elite Maison du Roi, both cavalry and musketeers, but the heat and dust and enormous crowd were so great that Peter, who loved soldiers, scarcely looked at them and left the review early.

There was a round of farewell calls. On Friday, June 18, the Regent came early to the Hôtel Lesdiguières to bid the Tsar goodbye. Once again, he spoke privately to Peter with only Kurakin present to interpret. The Tsar returned for a third visit to the Tuileries to take his leave of Louis XV. The visit was informal, as Peter had insisted it be. Once again, Saint-Simon was charmed: "One could not show more spirit, more grace and tenderness for the King than the Tsar displayed on all these occasions, and the next day when the King went to the Hôtel Lesdiguières to wish the Tsar a good trip, once again everything passed with great charm and gentleness."

On all sides, the visit was now acclaimed a triumph. Saint-Simon, who had seen the Sun King on his throne, described the lasting impression the Tsar had made:

This was a monarch who compelled admiration for his extreme curiosity about everything that had any bearing on his views of government, commerce, education, police methods, etc. His interests embraced each detail capable of practical application and disdained nothing. His intelligence was most marked; in his appreciation of merit, he showed great perception and a most lively understanding, everywhere displaying extensive knowledge and a lively flow of ideas. In character, he was an extraordinary combination: he assumed majesty at its most regal, most proud, most unbending; yet, once his supremacy had been granted, his demeanor was infinitely gracious and full of discriminating courtesy. Everywhere and at all times he

was the master, but with degrees of familiarity according to a person's rank. He had a friendly approach which one associated with freedom, but he was not exempt from a strong imprint of his country's past. Thus his manners were abrupt, even violent, his wishes unpredictable, brooking no delay and no opposition. His table manners were crude, and those of his staff still less elegant. He was determined to be free and independent in all that he wished to do or see. . . .

One might go on forever describing this truly great man with his remarkable character and rare variety of extraordinary talents. They will make him a monarch worthy of profound admiration for countless years, despite the large flaws in his own education and his country's lack of culture and civilization. Such was the reputation he gained everywhere in France, where he was considered a veritable prodigy.

On Sunday afternoon, June 20, Peter left Paris quietly and unescorted. Traveling eastward through France, he stopped at Rheims, where he visited the cathedral and was shown the missal on which for centuries the kings of France had sworn their coronation oaths. To the astonishment of the French priests present, Peter was able to read to them the mysterious characters with which the missal was inscribed. The language was old church Slavonic; in all probability, the missal had been brought to France in the eleventh century by the Kievan princess Anna Yaroslavna, who married King Louis I and became Queen of France.*

Although Peter left Shafirov, Dolgoruky and Tolstoy behind in Paris to negotiate with the French, the visit bore no diplomatic fruit beyond a meaningless treaty of friendship. The Regent was interested in the Tsar's proposal of an alliance between France and Russia, but the Abbé Dubois remained actively hostile to the idea. By now, the antagonism between King George I of England and Tsar Peter was too great to permit a treaty with both; Dubois chose England over Russia. Indeed, the hopelessness of Peter's case was later confirmed by Tessé, who revealed that throughout the negotiations with the Russians, Dubois had secretly disclosed everything to the English. "The government," Tessé later admitted, "had no intention other than to amuse the Tsar as long as he stayed without concluding anything." With the idea of an alliance discarded, the marriage which was to have been its seal was also dropped. Peter's daughter Elizabeth remained in Russia to rule as empress for twenty years, and Louis XV eventually

---

* It required some sacrifice for a princess of Kiev to leave her native city, then at the height of its civilization, to marry into the cruder culture of France. The relative levels of their cultures are suggested by the fact that Anna could read and write and signed her name to the marriage document, whereas Louis I could only scrawl an X.

married the daughter of Charles XII's puppet King of Poland, Stanislaus Leszczynski.

As he traveled again through the French countryside, Peter remarked, as he had on his way to Paris, on the poverty of the French peasants. The comparison between the luxury he found in the capital and what he saw outside surprised him and he wondered aloud to his friends how long this system could last.

FROM RHEIMS, Peter went slowly down the Meuse by boat, first to Namur and Liège and then to the health resort of Spa. This region, now part of Belgium, was then divided between Holland and the Hapsburg Empire, and along the route both Dutch and imperial officials in the river towns competed to pay him honor. Peter remained at Spa for five weeks, drinking the waters and taking a cure. Catherine still waited for him in Amsterdam, and his letters to her suggest his impatience and fatigue:

> Yesterday, I received your letter of the 11th in which you write of the illness of our daughters [Anne and Elizabeth both had smallpox] and that the first, thank God, is getting better while the other has taken to her bed, about which Alexander Danilovich also writes me. But your changed style has made me very sad, as the bringer of this letter will tell you. For your letter was very differently written from usual. God grant we can hear the same about Anushka as about Lisenka. When you write for me to come quickly and that you are very lonesome, I believe you. The bringer of this will tell you how lonely I am without you and I can say that except those days when I was in Versailles and Marly twelve days ago, I have had no great pleasure. But here I must stay some days and when I finish drinking the water I will start that very day, for there are only seven hours by land and five days by water. God grant to see you in joy which I wish from all my heart.
>
> P.S. I received this morning the glad news that Anushka is better and therefore began to drink the water more joyously.

Soon after, he wrote again:

> I congratulate you on this triumphal day of the Russian resurrection [it was the anniversary of Poltava], only I am sorry that we celebrate apart, as well as tomorrow's day of the Holy Apostle, the name day of your old man [Peter himself] and the boy [their son Peter Petrovich]. God grant that these days pass quickly and that I can be with you sooner. The water, thank God, acts well and I hope to

finish the cure in a week from St. Peter's day. Today I put on for the first time your camisole and drank your health, but only very little, because it is forbidden.

P.S. [after acknowledging a letter and two bottles of vodka] You write that you sent little because I drank little at the waters, which is true. I do not drink altogether more than five times a day and spirits only once or twice, and not always, partly because it is strong, and partly because it is scarce. I think it is very tiresome that we are so near and cannot see each other. God grant soon. On finishing this, I drink once again to your health.

While at Spa, the Tsar sat for the Dutch painter, Karl Moor, and this painting and the one Kneller had done almost two decades before became the Tsar's favorite portraits of himself.

On July 25, Peter began an eight-day boat journey down the Meuse (in Holland, the Maas), and finally, on August 2, he was reunited with Catherine in Amsterdam. He remained in Holland for a month and on September 2, he departed Amsterdam and Holland for the last time, traveling up the Rhine to Nimwegen, Cleves and Wesel and then on to Berlin. Along the way, he left Catherine behind to follow him. They often separated on the road like this, because it was difficult to find enough horses to service both their suites and also simply because she did not like to travel as rapidly as her husband.

Two days after Peter's arrival, Catherine caught up with him in Berlin. It was her first visit to the Prussian capital, and although by now Peter was familiar, his wife was an object of much curiosity. But Catherine was well received and dinners and balls were given in her honor, so that she and Peter departed for Russia in good spirits. By October, the Tsar was back in St. Petersburg. There, Peter had to face the climax of a personal and political tragedy which ran deeper than any other in his reign.

51

THE EDUCATION
OF AN HEIR

On October 11, 1717, Peter returned to St. Petersburg. "The two princesses, his daughters [Anne and Elizabeth, then nine and eight], waited for him in front of the palace, dressed in Spanish costumes," Monsieur de La Vie, the French envoy, reported to Paris, "and his son, the young Prince Peter Petrovich, greeted him in his room where he was riding a tiny Icelandic pony." But his joy at seeing his children quickly faded. While he was away, the government of Russia had functioned badly. Maladministration, jealousies and corruption everywhere had all but swamped the governmental system he had tried to erect; men who were supposed to be the leaders of the state were quarreling like children, frantically accusing one another of political and financial misdeeds. Peter plunged into this confusion and tried to straighten it out. Every morning, at six a.m., he convened the Senate and sat in person to hear the accusations and defenses of the contending parties. Finally, realizing that the complaints were too widespread and the corruption too deep, he created a special court of justice with separate investigating commissions, each consisting of a major, a captain and a lieutenant of the Guards, who were to examine the cases and render judgment according to "common sense and equity." "And so it came to pass in Russia," wrote Weber, "that members of the venerable Senate, composed of the heads of the greatest families in the Tsar's dominions, were obliged to appear before a lieutenant as their judge and be called to account for their conduct."

But these trials were only a preliminary to something far more serious, something that threatened the whole future of Peter's Russia. For it was at this time that Peter was forced to make a final decision in the case of his son, the Tsarevich Alexis.

Alexis was born in February 1690, not long after the eighteen-year-old Tsar's marriage to the meek, sad, reclusive Eudoxia. At Alexis' birth, Peter was enormously proud, giving court banquets and fireworks displays in honor of the new Prince. Yet, as the years went by, the Tsar saw little of his son. Absorbed by shipbuilding, by Lefort and Anna Mons, by the Azov

campaigns and the Great Embassy, Peter left Alexis in the company of Eudoxia. Visiting his son meant seeing the boy's mother, toward whom he was openly contemptuous, and Peter preferred to avoid them both. Naturally, Alexis sensed the breach between his parents and understood that in his father's mind he was identified with his mother. Thus, in his earliest, formative years, Alexis saw Peter as disapproving, perhaps even a threat, an enemy. Growing up in his mother's care, he took her part and adopted her ways.

Then, suddenly, when Alexis was a thin eight-year-old boy with a high forehead and dark, serious eyes, Peter wrenched his little world apart. In 1698, when the Tsar returned from the West to suppress the Streltsy, he sent Eudoxia to a convent. Alexis was installed in his own house in Preobrazhenskoe and confided to the general supervision of his aunt, Peter's sister Natalya. His education, which until that time had consisted mainly of readings from the Bible and other religious lessons, was placed in the hands of Martin Neugebauer of Danzig, who had been recommended by Augustus of Saxony. Neugebauer had a Germanic character—he was orderly and prompt—and he soon came into conflict with the Russian temperament. There is a story of a meal which the twelve-year-old Tsarevich was sharing with Neugebauer, his earlier teacher Nikifor Viazemsky and Alexis Naryshkin. They were eating chicken, and the Tsarevich having finished his piece, took another. Naryshkin instructed him first to empty his plate by putting his bones back into the serving dish. Neugebauer, shocked, declared that this was ill-bred. Alexis looked at Neugebauer and whispered to Naryshkin; Neugebauer declared that whispering also was ill-bred. The two men began to argue, and Neugebauer exploded: "None of you understand anything! When I get the Tsarevich abroad, then I shall know what to do!" Russians, he shouted, were all barbarians, dogs and pigs, and he would demand the dismissal of all of Alexis' Russian household. Throwing down his knife and fork, he stormed out of the room. It was Neugebauer, however, who was dismissed. Unable to find any work in Russia, he returned to Germany, became a secretary to King Charles XII of Sweden and functioned for many years as Charles' advisor and expert on Russian affairs.

Meanwhile, to replace Neugebauer, Peter had followed Patkul's advice and chosen a German doctor of laws, Heinrich von Huyssen, who submitted a plan for the education of a future tsar which Peter approved. Alexis was to study French, German, Latin, mathematics, history and geography. He was to read foreign newspapers and to continue intensive study of the Bible. In his spare time, he was to look at atlases and globes, train with mathematical instruments and exercise by fencing, dancing, riding and playing games involving throwing or kicking balls. Alexis was intelligent and made good progress. In a letter to Leibniz, Huyssen reported,

The Prince lacks neither capacity nor quickness of mind. His ambition is moderated by reason, by sound judgment, and by a great desire to distinguish himself and to gain everything which is fitting for a great prince. He is of a studious and pliant nature, and wishes by assiduity to supply what has been neglected in his education. I notice in him a great inclination to piety, justice, uprightness and purity of morals. He loves mathematics and foreign languages and shows a great desire to visit foreign countries. He wishes to acquire thoroughly the French and German languages and has already begun to receive instruction in dancing and military exercises, which give him great pleasure. The Tsar has allowed him not to be strict in the observance of fasts, for fear of harming his health and bodily development, but out of piety he refuses any indulgence in this respect.

Alexis was also influenced during these adolescent years by Menshikov, who was appointed the official governor to the Tsarevich in 1705. Menshikov's duties were a general supervision of the education, finances and the overall training of the heir to the throne. To many, the largely illiterate confidant of Peter's loves and wars seemed a strange trustee for the guidance and preparation of the heir. But it was precisely because of their intimacy that Peter chose his friend. He disliked the results of the years his son had spent with his mother, and he was suspicious of the foreign tutors who still surrounded the boy. He wanted one of his own men, the comrade who was closest to him, who thought as he did and whom he trusted completely, to oversee the training of the boy who would be tsar. But Menshikov, like Peter, was away with the army for most of the years of Alexis' youth, and the Serene Prince mainly exercised his duties from afar. There were stories of rough treatment when ward and governor met; Pleyer, the Austrian minister, reports an episode (which he did not witness) in which Menshikov dragged Alexis across the ground by the hair while Peter looked on unprotestingly. Whitworth recorded a more dignified scene, with Menshikov giving a dinner for the heir who, the ambassador informed London, was "a tall, handsome prince about sixteen years old who speaks pretty good High Dutch." Mostly, as we know from Alexis' letters to Menshikov, it was with a mixture of awe and distaste that the boy regarded the rough figure whom his father had set over him, and later Alexis blamed Menshikov for many of his failings. In his final break with Peter, when he appealed for asylum in Vienna, the Tsarevich claimed that Menshikov had made him a drunkard and was even trying to poison him.

The root of the problem, of course, was not Menshikov but Peter; as always, Menshikov was only reflecting the attitude and will of his master.

And Peter's attitude was strangely inconsistent. A moment of pride in the Tsarevich would be followed by a long period of indifference. Then would come a sudden demand that his son join him immediately to experience some event important for a future tsar. In 1702, when Peter left for Archangel with five battalions of the Guards to defend the port from a rumored Swedish attack, he took Alexis, then twelve, with him. The boy was a thirteen-year-old bombardier in an artillery regiment at the siege of Nyenskans which broke the Swedish grip on the Neva delta. A year later, at fourteen, Alexis was present at the storming of Narva.

Like many a strong father whose strength and qualities have made him respected, successful and admired by the world, Peter was trying to force his son to follow in his footsteps. Unfortunately, a father like Peter with a strong sense of duty or mission, desiring to inculcate the same sense of purpose in his son, may instead become a crushing weight on the fledgling personality.

Alexis' presence at Archangel, Nyenskans and Narva suggests the extent to which the boy's education was interrupted by war. Then, in 1705 his tutor Huyssen was sent abroad on diplomatic missions which kept him away from Russia for three years. During this period, when father, governor and tutor were all away, no one took much notice of the Tsarevich.

It was extraordinary that the heir to Peter's throne was brought up this way. The Tsar was keenly aware of the defects in his own early education and had struggled all his life to catch up, and one would have expected him to devote extra attention to his son's training in order to make sure that he had groomed a successor who would complete his work. In fact, over the course of Alexis' youth and young manhood, Peter was primarily interested in schooling his son for war. After taking the young Alexis along to participate in campaigns and sieges, he assigned him independent military tasks to carry out as heir to the throne. At sixteen, in 1706, Alexis was sent for five months to Smolensk with orders to gather provisions and recruits for the army. Returning to Moscow, he was next commanded to see to the defense of the city. The seventeen-year-old Tsarevich was slow and defeatist in carrying out this order. To his confessor, the priest Ignatiev, he expressed his doubt as to the value of fortifying Moscow at all. "If the Tsar's army cannot hold back the Swedes," he sighed, "Moscow will not stop them." Peter heard of the remark and was furious, although when he learned that the defenses actually had been substantially strengthened, his anger subsided.

Unfortunately, try as he would, Peter never succeeded in interesting his son in war. Assigned military tasks, Alexis usually showed himself to be unwilling or incapable. Eventually, discouraged and disgusted, as well as caught up in the ever increasing tempo of the war, Peter turned his atten-

tion away from his son, leaving the youth to himself in Moscow and Preobrazhenskoe. This respite delighted the Tsarevich. He loved Moscow. The quiet, religiously passionate youth and the old city with its innumerable cathedrals, churches and monasteries, adorned with gold and jewels and filled with history and legend, perfectly suited each other. In the old capital, now increasingly abandoned in favor of St. Petersburg, Alexis was thrown into the company of those who preferred the old order and feared the reforms and innovations of the Tsar. There were Miloslavskys who still sympathized with their sister Sophia, who had died in her cell in 1704, and their sister Martha, who died in a convent in 1707. There were the Lopukhins, the brothers and family of Alexis' mother, the repudiated Eudoxia, who regarded Alexis as the vehicle for their eventual return to power. There were the old aristocratic families, indignant that they had been passed over in favor of Westerners and upstart Russians. Most of all, there were members of the old Orthodox clergy, who regarded Peter's works as those of Antichrist, and saw in Alexis, the heir, the last chance for saving the true religion in Russia.

The leader of this intimate clerical circle around the Tsarevich was Alexis' confessor, Jacob Ignatiev. Ignatiev came from Suzdal, where the Tsaritsa Eudoxia was incarcerated in a convent. The priest was in contact with the former Tsaritsa, and in 1706, when Alexis was sixteen, he took the boy to see his mother. Peter, learning of this visit from his sister Natalya, was furious with Alexis and warned him never to go there again.

Although Ignatiev encouraged Alexis' interest in the Orthodox religion, he also encouraged him in different ceremonies as well. For although Alexis was very different from Peter in many ways, he resembled his father in one: He liked to drink. Together with Ignatiev and certain monks and priests and others, the Tsarevich formed a "company" like the intimate circle of Peter's youth, with different political ideas but the same love of drinking and carousing. Like Peter's, Alexis' company was a special society: Each member had a name such as Hell, Benefactor, Satan, Moloch, the Cow, Judas or the Dove. The group even had a secret code for private correspondence.

As the climax of the war approached, the Tsarevich was once more summoned to the army. In the autumn of 1708, Peter ordered his son to recruit five regiments in the Moscow region and bring them to the Ukraine as soon as possible. Alexis complied and delivered the troops to Peter and Sheremetev in mid-January 1709. This was during the fiercest days of the coldest winter within memory and, having completed his mission, the Tsarevich became ill. His condition was serious, and Peter, who had planned to go to Voronezh, remained for ten days until his son was out of danger. When Alexis was better, he joined Peter in Voronezh and then

returned to Moscow. He missed the Battle of Poltava, but when news of the great victory was received, Alexis arranged the triumphal program and served as host in the celebrations.

AFTER POLTAVA, Peter made two decisions regarding his son: The Tsarevich should have a Western education and he should have a Western wife. Both would help pull him away from the old Muscovite orbit into which he had been falling. Earlier, the old Hapsburg Empress, who remembered Peter favorably from his visit to Vienna, had urged that Alexis be sent to her to be educated there; the Tsarevich, she promised, would be treated by the Emperor and herself as one of their own children. This project never materialized, but another early promise did bear fruit. Twelve years before, on Peter's first meeting with Augustus of Saxony, the Elector had pledged to look after the education of Peter's heir. Now that Alexis was nineteen, Peter remembered and sent his son to the beautiful Saxon capital Dresden to study under the protection of Augustus' family.

The Tsarevich's marriage was also to have a Saxon connection. Long before, Peter had decided to ally himself with a powerful German family by marrying his son to a German princess, and the one chosen for Alexis, after long negotiations, was Charlotte of Wolfenbüttel. The family was excellently connected, being a branch of the House of Hanover. In addition, Charlotte's sister Elizabeth was married to the Archduke Charles of Austria, at that moment a claimant to the throne of Spain, but subsequently the Emperor Charles. As Charlotte was living at the Saxon court under the watchful eye of her aunt the Queen of Poland, both projects —Alexis' education and his marriage—centered on Dresden. Charlotte was sixteen years old, tall and plain but with a fresh, sweet-natured charm, and bred to the manners and customs of a Western court. This was what Peter was seeking for his son. He hoped that by putting Alexis into an intimate relationship with a princess of refinement, he could counteract and rub away the primitive edges of the company the Tsarevich had been keeping.

Alexis was aware that these negotiations were going on and that it was his father's wish that he marry a foreigner. In the winter of 1710, at Peter's command, the Tsarevich went to Dresden, then moved on to the spa at Carlsbad, and, in a village nearby, he met for the first time his intended bride, Princess Charlotte. The meeting went well. Both Alexis and Charlotte understood the purpose of their meeting and, given the circumstances of that time of arranged marriages, neither was desperately unhappy with the other. Alexis, in a letter to his confessor Ignatiev soon after the meeting, wrote that Peter had asked his reaction to Charlotte.

So now I know that he wishes to marry me not to a Russian, but to one of these people according to my choice. I wrote to him that if it is his will that I should marry a foreigner, I will marry this princess whom I have seen and who pleases me and who is a good person and better than whom I cannot find. I beg you to pray for me if it is the will of God that this be accomplished; if not, that it be hindered, for my hope is in Him. What He wishes will happen. Write to me how your heart feels about this matter.

Charlotte, for her part, liked the Tsarevich, telling her mother that he seemed intelligent and courteous and that she felt honored that the Tsar had chosen her for his son. In the end, the courtship bore fruit when Alexis went twice to Torgau and the second time formally asked the Queen of Poland for Charlotte's hand.

The marriage was deferred until Peter could be present. Meanwhile, Alexis passed the time with his studies in Dresden and his education there was as Western as his father could have wished. He took dancing lessons and fencing lessons, he developed a talent for drawing and he improved his German and French. He shopped for books in old bookstalls and bought old engravings and medallions to take back to Russia. The Tsar would have been less happy, however, to know that his son was spending a great deal of time reading books on church history, studying the relationship between temporal and spiritual powers and the history of disputes between the church and state. In fact, throughout this period of Western schooling, despite his Western dance steps and work with the epée, Alexis was deeply concerned that he had no contact with any Orthodox priest. Writing to Ignatiev, he asked his confessor to send him a priest

capable of keeping a secret. He must be young, unmarried, and unknown to everyone. Tell him to come to me in great secrecy, to lay aside all marks of his condition, to shave his beard and his hair, and to wear a wig and German clothes. He should come as a courier and for that he should be able to write. Let him not bring anything incumbent on a priest, or a missal, only a few bits of communion bread. I have all the books necessary. Have pity on my soul and do not let me die without confession. I shall tell no one that he is a priest. He will appear to be one of my servants. Do not let him have any doubt about shaving his beard. It is better to commit a small sin than to ruin my soul without repentance.

Ignatiev found and sent a priest who not only could give the Tsarevich confession but who also joined the royal student and his small Russian

circle in drunken evenings. During the course of one of these, Alexis scrawled another letter to Ignatiev:

> Most honorable father, salutation to you. I wish you very long life, that we should see each other in joy in a short time. On this letter wine has been poured out, so that after receiving it you may live well and drink strongly and remember us. God grant our desires to meet soon. All the orthodox Christians here have signed this, Alexis the sinner, the priest Ivan Slonsky, and have certified it with cups and glasses. We have kept this festival for your health, not in German wise but in Russian style.

At the end of the letter, Alexis added an almost indecipherable postscript begging Ignatiev's pardon if the letter was illegible, explaining that when he was writing, everyone, including himself, was drunk.

ALEXIS REMAINED in Dresden while his father suffered the disaster of Pruth, but Peter quickly recovered from this blow and moved ahead with all his plans, including his son's marriage on October 14, 1711, to Princess Charlotte. Charlotte's grandfather, the reigning Duke of Wolfenbüttel, had asked Peter if the newlyweds might be permitted to pass the winter together in his dukedom, but Peter replied that he now needed his son's services in the war against Sweden. Thus, a brief four days after his wedding, Alexis was ordered to leave Charlotte and go to Thorn to oversee the forwarding of food supplies for the Russian troops who were to winter in Pomerania On appeal, Peter delayed the departure a few days and then Alexis obediently set out, leaving his new bride alone. Six weeks later, she joined him in Thorn, but it was a dismal place for a honeymoon. Charlotte wrote miserably to her mother of the desolation created by war and winter: "The houses opposite are half-burned and empty. I myself live in a monastery." She complained about the lack of society caused by the local nobility's habit of sticking close to the land and refusing to congregate in the larger towns: "For that reason it is impossible even in the largest towns to find a single person of quality."

During the first six months of marriage, Alexis was devoted to his young wife and Charlotte told everyone that she was happy. But the affairs of the royal household were haphazard, even chaotic. When Menshikov visited in April, he was shocked by Alexis' and Charlotte's penury. He wrote urgently to the Tsar saying that he had found Charlotte in tears because of money, and that to alleviate the situation he had lent her 5,000 roubles from army funds. Peter sent money, and he and Catherine visited the little court after Alexis had left to join the army in Pomerania. Like

most young wives, Charlotte was highly sensitive to the relationship between her new husband and his family, and she wrote to her mother of her worry at the way Peter spoke of and treated his son. Once, hoping to help, she pleaded with Catherine to act as an advocate with the Tsar on behalf of Alexis.

In October 1712, at the end of a year of marriage during which her husband had been mostly away with the army, Charlotte was suddenly commanded by Peter to go to St. Petersburg to establish herself and wait for her husband. The seventeen-year-old girl was terrified—she had heard frightening things about Russians and was afraid to go to Russia without her husband to introduce and protect her—and, disobeying Peter's order, she fled home to Wolfenbüttel.

The Tsarevich did not react, but his father did. Peter wrote to Charlotte criticizing her behavior, but adding gently, "We would never have thwarted your wish to see your family if only you had informed us of it beforehand." Charlotte apologized and asked forgiveness. Peter came to see her, gave her his blessing and a sum of money, and she agreed to leave soon after for St. Petersburg. As the old Duke wrote to Leibniz, "The Tsar has been with us this week. . . . He was very kind to the Tsarevna, gave her large presents and begged her to hasten her journey. Next week she is really going to start and to all appearances leave Europe forever."

When Charlotte arrived in St. Petersburg that spring of 1713, Alexis had left the capital to join his father on the galley expedition along the coast of Finland. He returned at the end of the summer to the small house in which she was living on the left bank of the Neva. Meeting after a separation of almost a year, the couple was at first affectionate, but things soon went wrong. Alexis began to drink heavily again with his friends, returning home to treat his wife abusively in front of the servants. Once, when drunk, he vowed to be revenged on Chancellor Golovkin, who had negotiated his marriage, by one day cutting off the heads of the Chancellor's sons and setting them up on stakes.

Sometimes, the morning after, Alexis remembered these horrible scenes and tried to atone for them by renewed tenderness. Charlotte would forgive him, but every recurrence deepened the wound. Then, after a winter of heavy drinking, the Tsarevich became ill. His doctors diagnosed tuberculosis and prescribed a cure at Carlsbad. Charlotte, eight months pregnant, was the last to know he was leaving; she learned it only as he walked out the door to take his seat in a carriage, saying, "Goodbye. I am going to Carlsbad." During the six months of his absence, she heard nothing from him—not a single letter. On July 12, 1714, five weeks after his departure, she gave birth to a daughter, Natalya, but Alexis failed to respond to this news. In November, the desperate nineteen-year-old mother wrote to her parents: "The Tsarevich has not yet come back. No one knows where he is, whether

he is dead or alive. I am in frightful uneasiness. All the letters that I have written to him in the last six or eight weeks have been sent back to me from Dresden and Berlin because no one knows where he is."

In the middle of December 1714, Alexis returned to St. Petersburg from Germany. At first, he behaved decently to Charlotte and was delighted with his daughter. Later, however, Charlotte wrote to her parents that her husband had reverted to his former conduct except that she rarely saw him any more. The reason was Afrosina, a Finnish girl captured during the war, who had been taken into the household of his teacher, Viazemsky. Blindly infatuated with her, Alexis took her openly into a wing of his own house, where he lived with her as his mistress.

Alexis' treatment of Charlotte grew progressively worse. He took no interest in her. In public, he never spoke to her, but went out of his way to avoid her, moving to the opposite side of the room. Although they shared their house, he had his apartment in the right wing, where Afrosina lived with him; Charlotte and her child lived in the left wing. He saw her once a week, coming grimly to make love in hopes of fathering a son to secure his own succession to the throne. The rest of the time, he was invisible to her. He left her without money. He cared so little about her welfare that the house was in terrible repair, and rain fell through the roof into Charlotte's bedroom. When this news reached Peter, the Tsar, angry and disgusted, upbraided his son for his neglect of his wife. Although it was not Charlotte who had told Peter, Alexis believed that it was, and the Tsarevich angrily accused his wife of maligning him to his father. Through all these episodes, through increasingly horrendous bouts of drunkenness and flaunting of Afrosina, Charlotte lived in silence and resignation, weeping in her bedroom, with no friends other than the single German lady-in-waiting who had come with her.

As time passed, Alexis' health deteriorated. He was almost constantly drunk. In April 1715, he was carried unconscious from a church, so sick that no one dared to bring him across the Neva to his home and he had to spend the night in a foreigner's house. Charlotte went to him and later wrote pitifully, "I ascribe his illness to the fast and to the great quantity of brandy which he drinks daily, for he is usually drunk."

Nevertheless, there were occasional moments of happiness. Alexis was fond of his daughter, and every mark of love he showed the child warmed the heart of the mother. On October 12, 1715, the determined love-making bore fruit: A second child was born, this time a son, whom Charlotte named Peter in fulfillment of a promise to her father-in-law. But this birth, thus apparently securing her husband's right to the throne, was the last service performed for Russia and her husband by this unhappy German Princess. Weakened by pregnancy and grief, she had stumbled and fallen before her delivery. Four days after her son was born, she came down with fever.

Charlotte realized that she was dying and asked to see the Tsar. Catherine could not come, but Peter, although sick, came in a wheelchair. Weber describes Charlotte's death:

> The Tsar being arrived, the Princess took her leave of him in the most moving expressions and recommended her two children and servants to his care and protection. Whereupon, she embraced her two children in the most tender manner imaginable, almost melting away in tears, and delivered them to the Tsarevich, who took them in his arms and carried them to his apartments, but never returned afterward. Then she sent for her servants, who lay prostrate on the ground in the antechamber, praying and calling to heaven to assist their dying mistress in her last minutes. She comforted them, gave them several admonitions and, at her last blessing, desired to be left alone with the minister. The physicians were trying to persuade her to take some medicines, but she flung the vials behind the bed, saying with some emotion, "Do not torment me any more but let me die in quiet, for I will live no longer." At length, on October 21, having continued all that day in fervent devotion until eleven at night, she departed an unfortunate life, after having endured for the last five days the most acute pains, in the twenty-first year of her age, having been married four years and six days. Her corpse was, according to her desire, interred without being embalmed in the great church of the fortress, whither it was carried with a funeral pomp becoming her birth.

Charlotte was not long mourned. The day following her funeral, the Tsaritsa Catherine gave birth to a son. Thus, within a week, Peter had acquired two potential heirs, both named Peter—a grandson, Peter Alexeevich, and his own new son, Peter Petrovich. At the birth of this second little Peter, the Tsar's joy and pride immediately washed away any grief for the wife of his heir. He wrote exuberantly to Sheremetev, "God has sent me a new recruit," and he began a round of celebrations that lasted eight days. On November 6, the new Prince was baptized, his godfathers being the Kings of Denmark and Prussia. The celebrations, according to Weber, included a dinner at which "a pie was served up on the table of the gentlemen, which being opened, a well-shaped woman dwarf stepped out of it being stark naked except for her headdress and some ornaments of red ribbons. She made a well-set speech to the company, filled some glasses of wine which she had with her in the pie, and drank several healths." On the ladies' table, a man dwarf was served up in similar manner. In the dusk of the evening, the company broke up and went to the islands, where magnificent fireworks were set off in honor of the young Prince.

In all this merriment, the death of Princess Charlotte and the birth of her son were largely ignored. In the long run, however, the quiet German Princess had a kind of recompense. The much-hailed and adored Peter Petrovich, child of Peter and Catherine, lived only to be three and a half, whereas Peter Alexeevich, Charlotte's son, became Peter II, Emperor of Russia.

52

A PATERNAL ULTIMATUM

IN THE AUTUMN OF 1715, when his son was born and his wife died, the Tsarevich Alexis was no longer a youth. He was twenty-five years old and physically a lesser man than his father. The Prince was six feet tall, an unusual height for that time, but Peter at six feet seven inches towered over him as he did over everyone else. Peter Bruce, a foreign officer in Russian service, described Alexis in these years as being "very slovenly in his dress, tall, well made, of a brown complexion, black hair and eyes, of a stern countenance and strong voice." His eyes, closer together than Peter's, often flickered with anxiety and fear.

The two were wholly opposite. Alexis grew up a man of considerable intellectual background and capacity. He was intelligent, fond of reading, curious about theological questions and had an ease with foreign languages. Physically lazy, he loved a quiet, contemplative life and had little inclination to go out into the world and use his education in a practical way. All this was directly contrary to Peter's character and training. The Tsar had had only limited formal education. At the age when Alexis was reading and reflecting over works like *The Divine Manna, The Wonders of God* and Thomas à Kempis' *Imitation of Christ*, Peter was drilling soldiers, building boats and firing skyrockets. Most of all, Alexis lacked altogether the titanic energy, the burning curiosity and the compulsive drive which were the sources of Peter's greatness. He was bookish rather than active, cautious rather than bold, preferred the old to the new. It seemed almost as if the son were of an older generation than the father. As the offspring of another tsar—say, his own grandfather Tsar Alexis, or his uncle Tsar Fedor—Alexis' character might have been more appropriate and the story of his life might have been different. Whatever he might have been, however, he was spectacularly ill-suited to be the son—and the heir—of Peter the Great.

Although the differences between father and son were always tacit (the Tsarevich never publicly raised his voice to oppose the Tsar), they were

always there, and both men felt them keenly. In his younger years, he tried desperately to please Peter, but a sense of inferiority weakened all his efforts. The more Peter upbraided him, the more incompetent he became and the more he grew to loathe and fear his father, his father's friends and his father's ways. He retreated and evaded, and the more Peter was enraged by this, the more reticent and frightened Alexis became. There seemed to be no solution.

To overcome his fears and weakness, Alexis drank more heavily. To avoid the responsibilities that he could not face, he pretended that he was sick. When Alexis returned from Germany in 1713, after his year of study in Dresden, Peter asked what he had learned in geometry and fortifications. The question frightened Alexis; he was afraid that his father would ask him to execute a drawing before his eyes and that he would be unable to do it. Returning to his house, the Tsarevich took a pistol and tried to maim himself by firing the ball through his right hand. His hands were shaking and he missed, but the powder flash burned his right hand badly. When Peter asked what had happened, Alexis said that it had been an accident.

This was not an isolated episode. Having no interest in soldiers or ships, new buildings, docks, canals or any of Peter's projects or reforms, he sometimes took medicines to make himself ill so that he might avoid public appearances or duties. Once when required to be present at the launching of a ship, he said to a friend, "I would rather be a galley slave or have a burning fever than be obliged to go there." To another, he said, "I am not a stupid fool, but I cannot work." As his mother-in-law, the Princess of Wolfenbüttel, said, "It is quite useless for his father to force him to attend to military matters, as he would rather have a rosary than a pistol in his hand."

As Alexis' dread of his father deepened, he found that he was scarcely able to face the Tsar. Once, he admitted to his confessor that he had frequently wished for his father's death. Ignatiev replied, "God will forgive you. We all wish for his death because the people have to bear such a heavy burden."

Involuntarily, but also inevitably, Alexis became the focus of serious opposition to the Tsar. All who opposed Peter looked to Alexis as the hope of the future. The clergy prayed that Alexis as tsar would restore the church to its former power and majesty. The people believed that he would lighten their burdens of labor, service and taxation. The old nobility hoped that when he sat on the throne, Alexis would restore their former privileges and dismiss the upstart newcomers like Menshikov and Shafirov. Even many of the noblemen whom Peter trusted showed their sympathy for the Tsarevich privately. The Golitsyns, the Dolgorukys, Prince Boris Kurakin and even Field Marshal Boris Sheremetev were among these. Senator

Prince Jacob Dolgoruky warned Alexis, "Do not say any more, they are watching us." Prince Vasily Dolgoruky told Alexis, "You are wiser than your father. Your father is wise, but he has no knowledge of men. You will have more knowledge of men."

Despite these sentiments and a general current of discontent at Peter's rule, there was no conspiracy. The only policy of Alexis' adherents was to wait until the son succeeded the father, which, given the precarious state of Peter's health, seemed unlikely to be long. One of Alexis' closest advisors, Alexander Kikin—one of Peter's new men, who had accompanied the Tsar on the Great Embassy and been promoted to head of the Admiralty— secretly counseled the Tsarevich to think of leaving Russia, or, if he happened to be in a foreign country, to remain there. "After your recovery [in Carlsbad]," Kikin had told Alexis before he left, "write to your father that you will be obliged to take medicines again in the spring, and in the meantime you may go to Holland, and afterward to Italy, after the cure in the spring. At this rate, you may make your absence last two or three years."

As for Peter, his feelings for his son were a blend of frustration and anger. Years before, when he had ignored his infant son, it was because Alexis was Eudoxia's child and because he himself was scarcely more than an adolescent. Then, as the boy grew older and the flaws in his character became more evident, Peter tried to strengthen him by treating him roughly, with almost Spartan harshness, rather than with warmth and understanding. Repeatedly, through the governorship of Menshikov, through his own letters and talks with his son, and by employing him on various public assignments and governmental missions, Peter tried to instill in Alexis a sense of duty to the state and participation in the reforms he was forcing on Russia. By sending him to the West for schooling, by marrying him to a German princess, Peter hoped to change his son. On Alexis' return to St. Petersburg in 1713, Peter waited hopefully to observe the results of the Tsarevich's foreign travel and study. But when the Tsar asked Alexis for a demonstration of his new knowledge, his reward was that the Tsarevich tried to shoot himself in the hand.

More and more, as Peter saw it, his son rejected all the responsibilities of being heir to the throne, preferring to hang back and turn away from every challenge. Rather than taking up his natural role in Peter's work, Alexis surrounded himself with people who opposed everything Peter stood for. To certain parts of his son's personal life, Peter did not object: He did not mind Alexis' drinking, or his charades with his own little "Exotic Company" or his taking a Finnish serf as a mistress—all these traits had parallels in Peter's own life. What the Tsar could not accept was his son's continual rejection of what he saw as the Tsarevich's duty. Peter was willing to be tolerant of all those who tried to carry out his orders, but he was furious

when he met resistance. How else could he react when his own son, who at twenty-five should have been the leading exemplar of the Tsar's concepts of duty and service, refused any part in Peter's life work except when he was driven to it? In the winter of 1715–1716, Peter decided that he must get things in order; the passive, lazy and frightened man who had no interest in military affairs or ships and the sea, no sympathy for reforms and no wish to build on the foundations laid by his father, must change himself once and for all. What Peter was demanding was a complete re-creation of personality. Unfortunately, the time for this had passed; the son, like the father, now was set in his temperament for life.

ON THE DAY of Princess Charlotte's funeral, the Tsarevich was handed a letter which Peter had written sixteen days earlier, before Charlotte's death and the births of the two male infants named Peter. This letter reveals the hopes Peter had for Alexis, how desperately he wished the Tsarevich to pick up the mantle and prepare himself, and his growing dismay that Alexis was unable or unwilling to do this:

A Declaration to My Son:
    You cannot be ignorant of what is known to all the world, to what degree our people groaned under the oppression of the Swedes before the beginning of the present war.
    By the usurpation of so many maritime places so necessary to our state, they had cut us off from all commerce with the rest of the world. . . . You know what it has cost us in the beginning of this war (in which God alone has led us, as it were, by the hand, and still guides us) to make ourselves experienced in the art of war and to put a stop to those advantages which our implacable enemies obtained over us.
    We submitted to this with a resignation to the will of God, making no doubt that it was He who put us to that trial till He might lead us into the right way and we might render ourselves worthy to experience that the same enemy who at first made others tremble, now in his turn trembles before us, perhaps in a much greater degree. These are the fruits which, next to the assistance of God, we owe to our own toil and to the labor of our faithful and affectionate children, our Russian subjects.
    But at the time that I am viewing the prosperity which God has heaped on our native country, if I cast an eye upon the posterity that is to succeed me, my heart is much more penetrated with grief on account of what is to happen, seeing that you, my son, reject all

means of making yourself capable of governing well after me. I say your incapacity is voluntary because you cannot excuse yourself with want of natural parts and strength of body, as if God had not given you a sufficient share of either; and though your constitution is none of the strongest, yet it cannot be said that it is altogether weak.

But you even will not so much as hear warlike exercises mentioned; though it is by them that we broke through that obscurity in which we were involved, and that we made ourselves known to nations whose esteem we share at present.

I do not exhort you to make war without lawful reasons; I only desire you to apply yourself to learn the art of it. For it is impossible to govern well without knowing the rules and disciplines of it, be it for no other end than for the defense of the country.

I could place before your eyes many instances of what I am proposing to you. I will only mention to you the Greeks [the Byzantine Empire, whose capital, Constantinople, fell to the Turks in 1453], with whom we are united by the same profession of faith. What occasioned their decay but that they neglected arms? Idleness and repose weakened them, made them submit to tyrants and brought them to that slavery to which they are now so long since reduced. You mistake if you think it is enough for a prince to have good generals to act under his orders. Everyone looks upon the head; they study his inclinations and conform themselves to them. All the world knows this. My brother [Fedor] during his reign loved magnificence in dress and great equipages of horses. The nation was not much inclined that way, but the Prince's delight soon became that of his subjects, for they are inclined to imitate him in liking a thing or disliking it.

If the people so easily break themselves of things which only concern pleasure, will they not forget in time, or will they not more easily give over the practice of arms, the exercise of which is the more painful to them the less they are kept to it?

You have no inclination to learn war, you do not apply yourself to it and consequently you will never learn it. And how then can you command others, and judge of the reward which those deserve who do their duty, or punish others who fail of it? You will do nothing, nor judge of anything, but by the eyes and help of others, like a young bird that holds up his bill to be fed.

You say that the weak state of your health will not permit you to undergo the fatigues of war. This is an excuse which is no better than the rest. I desire no fatigues but only inclination, which even sickness itself cannot hinder. Ask those who remember the time of my brother. He was of a constitution weaker by far than yours. He was

not able to manage a horse of the least mettle, nor could he hardly mount it. Yet he loved horses, hence it came that there never was, nor is there actually now in the nation, a finer stable than his was.

By this you see that good success does not always depend on pains, but on the will.

If you think there are some [monarchs] whose affairs are successful though they do not go to war themselves, it is true. But if they do not go themselves, yet they have an inclination for it and understand it.

For instance, the late King of France [Louis XIV] did not always take the field in person, but it is known to what degree he loved war and what glorious exploits he performed in it, which made his campaigns to be called the theater and school of the world. His inclinations were not confined solely to military affairs, he also loved mechanics, manufactures and other establishments, which rendered his kingdom more flourishing than any other whatsoever.

After having made to you all those remonstrances, I return to my former subject which regards you.

I am a man and, consequently, I must die. To whom shall I leave after me to finish what I have partly recovered? To a man who like the slothful servant hides his talent in the earth—that is to say, who neglects making the best of what God has entrusted to him?

Remember your obstinacy and ill-nature, how often I reproached you for it and for how many years I almost have not spoken to you. But all this has availed nothing, has effected nothing. It was but losing my time, it was striking the air. You do not make the least endeavors, and all your pleasure seems to consist in staying idle and lazy at home. Things of which you ought to be ashamed (forasmuch as they make you miserable) seem to make up your dearest delight, nor do you foresee the dangerous consequences of it for yourself and for the whole state. St. Paul has left us a great truth when he wrote: "If a man know not how to rule his own house, how shall he take care of the church of God?"

After having considered all those great inconveniences and reflected upon them, and seeing I cannot bring you to good by any inducement, I have thought fit to give you in writing this act of my last will with this resolution, however: to wait still a little longer before I put it in execution to see if you will mend. If not, I will have you know that I will deprive you of the succession, as one may cut off a useless member.

Do not fancy that, because I have no other child but you, I only write this to terrify you. I will certainly put it in execution if it please God; for whereas I do not spare my own life for my country

and the welfare of my people, why should I spare you who do not render yourself worthy of either? I would rather choose to transmit them to a worthy stranger than to my own unworthy son.

Peter

Alexis' reaction to this letter was the opposite of that his father had hoped for. Terrified by Peter's summons, he rushed to his most intimate confidants and begged for advice. Kikin advised him to renounce his rights to the throne on the ground of ill-health. "You will at last be able to rest if you cut yourself off from everything. I know that otherwise, with your weakness, you cannot hold out. But it is a pity you did not stay away when you were [in Germany]." Viazemsky, his first teacher, concurred that he should declare himself unfit to bear the heavy burden of the crown. Alexis spoke also to Prince Yury Trubetskoy, who told him, "You do well not to aspire to the succession. You are not proper for it." The Tsarevich then pleaded with Prince Vasily Dolgoruky to persuade the Tsar to let him resign the succession peacefully and live the rest of his life on an estate in the country. Dolgoruky promised to speak to Peter.

Meanwhile, three days after he received his father's declaration, Alexis wrote his reply:

Most Clement Lord and Father:
I have read the paper Your Majesty gave me on the 16th of October 1715 after the funeral of my late consort.

I have nothing to reply to it but that if Your Majesty will deprive me of the succession to the crown of Russia by reason of my incapacity, your will be done. I even most urgently beg it of you because I do not think myself fit for government. My memory is very much weakened and yet it is necessary in affairs. The strength of my mind and of my body is much decayed by sicknesses which I have undergone and which have rendered me incapable of governing so many nations. This requires a more vigorous man than I am.

Therefore I do not aspire after you (whom God preserve many years) to the succession of the Russian crown, even if I had no brother as I have one at present whom I pray God preserve. Neither will I pretend for the future to that succession, of which I take God to witness and sear it upon my soul, in testimony whereof I write and sign this present with my own hand.

I put my children into your hands, and as for myself, I desire nothing of you but a bare maintenance during my life, leaving the whole to your consideration and to your will.

Your most humble servant and son, Alexis.

After Peter had received Alexis' letter, he saw Prince Vasily Dolgoruky, who relayed to Peter his own conversation with Alexis. Peter seemed agreeable, and Dolgoruky told Alexis, "I have spoken to your father about you. I believe he will deprive you of the succession, and he seems content with your letter. I have saved you from the block by speaking to your father." If Alexis was reassured by the sum of this message, he cannot have been cheerful to hear that there had been talk of the scaffold.

In fact, Peter was far from content. His warning to the Tsarevich had provoked the wrong reaction, and Alexis' letter of submission and renunciation seemed far too prompt and sweeping. How could a serious man lay aside a throne so easily? Was the renunciation sincere? And even if it were, how could the heir to a great throne simply retire and live in the country? As a farmer or a country squire, would he not remain—perhaps even involuntarily—a rallying point for opposition to his father?

For a month, Peter pondered these questions and did nothing. Then, fate intervened and almost settled the matter. Attending a drinking party at Admiral Apraxin's, the Tsar suffered a violent convulsion and became dangerously ill. For two days and nights, his chief ministers and the members of the Senate remained in a room just outside his bedchamber, and on December 2 his condition became so critical that the Last Rites were administered. Then Peter rallied and began very slowly to improve. For three weeks, he remained in bed or in his house and finally was able to go to church on Christmas Day, where people saw that he was very thin and pale. During the illness, Alexis remained silent and visited his father only once. Perhaps this was because Kikin had warned Alexis to beware a trick: Peter, he suggested, might be only pretending to be sick, or at least exaggerating his illness by receiving the Last Rites, in order to see how everyone around him—and especially Alexis—would react to his imminent death.

As he recovered, Peter was pondering his next step. Alexis had sworn before God and "seared it on his soul" that he would never seek the succession, but Peter feared the influence on him of "great beards"—that is, the priests—once he himself was gone. Further, Peter still earnestly desired the active help of a son playing a full role as heir to the throne. Thus he decided: Alexis must join him or renounce the world completely by entering a monastery. On January 19, 1716, the Tsarevich received a second letter from his father with a demand for an immediate reply:

My Son:

My last sickness has hindered me until now from explaining myself to you about the resolution I have taken upon your letter which you wrote to me in answer to my first. At present I answer that I observe you talk of nothing in it but of the succession, just as if I needed your consent to do in that affair what in fact depends solely

on my will. But whence comes it that in your letter you say nothing of that incapacity wherein you voluntarily put yourself and of that aversion you have for state affairs, which I touched on in mine, and instead stress only the ill state of your health? I also remonstrated with you about the dissatisfaction your conduct has given me for so many years, and you pass all that over in silence, though I strongly insisted upon it. Thence I judge that those paternal exhortations have no weight with you. I have therefore taken a resolution to write to you once more by this letter, which shall be the last. If you reject the advice I give you in my lifetime, how will you value it after my death?

Can one rely on your oaths when one sees you have a hardened heart? King David said, "All men are liars." But supposing you have at present the intention of being true to your promises, those great beards may turn you as they please and make you break them.

Because at present their debauches and sloth keep them out of posts of honor, they are in hopes that one day or other their condition will mend by you who already show much inclination for them.

I do not see that you are sensible of the obligations you have to your father, to whom you owe your very being. Do you assist him in his cares and pains since you have attained the years of maturity? Certainly in nothing; all the world knows it. Quite contrary, you blame and abhor all the good I do at the hazard and expense of my own health for the sake of my people and for their welfare. And I have all the reasons in the world to believe that you will be the destroyer of it, if you outlive me. And so I cannot resolve to let you live on according to your own free will, like an amphibious creature, neither fish nor flesh. Change therefore your conduct and either strive to render yourself worthy of the succession or turn monk. I cannot be easy on your account, especially now that my health begins to decay. On sight therefore of this letter, answer me upon it, either in writing or by word of mouth. If you fail to do it, I will treat you as a criminal.

Peter

This ultimatum fell on the Tsarevich like a thunderbolt: Transform himself into the son Peter demanded or become a monk! Alexis could not do the former; he had tried for twenty-five years and failed. But to become a monk? It meant giving up everything of the world, including Afrosina. At this point, Kikin stepped in with some cynical advice. "Become a monk as your father commands," he counseled. "Remember that they do not nail the cowl to a man's head. One can always slip it off again and throw it away." Alexis eagerly accepted this solution. "Most Clement Lord and

Father," he wrote to Peter, "I received this morning your letter of the 19th. My indisposition hinders me from writing to you more at length. I will embrace the monastical state and desire your gracious consent to it. Your servant and unworthy son, Alexis."

Once again, Peter was taken aback by the suddenness and totality of Alexis' submission. Besides, the Tsar was on the point of leaving Russia on the long journey to the West and the time before his departure was too short to resolve an issue of this importance and complexity. Two days before he left, Peter visited Alexis at the Tsarevich's house, where he found his son shivering in bed. Again, Peter asked Alexis what he had chosen to do. Alexis swore before God that he wished to become a monk. But at this, Peter stepped back, deciding that perhaps his ultimatum had been too harsh and that he should give his son more time to think. "Becoming a monk is not easy for a young man," he said gently. "Think about it a little more. Do not hurry. Then write to me what you have decided. It would be better to follow the straight road than to become a monk. Anyway, I will wait another six months." As soon as Peter left the house, an overjoyed Alexis threw off his bedclothes, got up and went to a party.

When Peter departed St. Petersburg for Danzig and the West, Alexis was enormously relieved—his father was gone and the great shadow over his life had receded. He remained heir to the throne and for six months need not think of any other choice. Six months seemed an eternity. In that time, with a man as mercurial or as subject to illness as his father, everything might change. Meanwhile, the Tsarevich could enjoy himself.

SIX MONTHS can flash by when one is postponing an unpleasant choice. So it was with Alexis during the spring and summer of 1716. As autumn approached, Peter's six-month deadline had passed and the Tsarevich still procrastinated. He had written to his father, but his letters mentioned only his health and daily routine. Then, early in October came the letter from Peter which Alexis dreaded. It was written on August 26 from Copenhagen, where preparations for the allied invasion of Scania were reaching a climax. The letter was the final ultimatum from father to son; the Tsarevich was to return his answer by the same courier.

My Son:

I have received your letter of the 29th of June and the other of the 30th of July. Seeing that you talk of nothing in it but only of the state of your health, I write to you now to tell you that I demanded your resolution concerning the succession when I bade you farewell. You answered me then as usually, that you did not judge yourself capable of it by reason of your infirmity and that you had rather

retire into a convent. I tell you to think once more seriously upon it, and afterward to write to me what resolution you have taken. I have expected it this seven months past, and you send me no word at all about it; therefore upon the receipt of my letter, choose one or the other. In case you determine for the first, which is to apply yourself in order to be capable of the succession, do not delay above a week to repair hither, where you may arrive in time enough to be present at the operations of the campaign. But if you resolve on the other side, let me know where, what time and even the day you will execute your resolution, that my mind may be at rest and that I may know what I am to expect from you. Send your final answer back to me by the same courier who is to deliver you this letter.

In the first case, mark to me the day when you intend to set out from Petersburg, and in the second when you will put it in execution. I repeat it to you that I absolutely will have you resolve on something, for otherwise I must judge that you only seek to gain time to pass it in your usual idleness.

Peter

Holding this letter in his hand, Alexis at last made up his mind. His decision was to take neither of the two courses Peter offered, but to flee, to find some place where the towering figure of his father could not reach him. Only two months earlier, as Kikin departed to escort Alexis' aunt the Tsarevna Maria to Carlsbad, he had whispered to the Tsarevich, "I am going to look for some place for you to hide." Kikin had not returned, and Alexis did not know where to go, but in his mind there burned only a single, overwhelming idea: to escape the iron hand which now reached out for him.

Alexis acted swiftly and with subterfuge. He went immediately to Menshikov in St. Petersburg, declared that he was leaving for Copenhagen to join his father and needed 1,000 ducats to pay for his trip. He visited the Senate, asked his friends there to remain faithful to his interests and received a further 2,000 roubles for his expenses. In Riga, he borrowed 5,000 gold roubles and 2,000 roubles in other coins. When Menshikov asked him what he was going to do about Afrosina while he was gone, Alexis replied that he would take her with him as far as Riga and then send her back to Petersburg. "You will do better to take her with you all the way," suggested Menshikov.

Before leaving St. Petersburg, Alexis confided his real intentions only to his manservant Afanasiev. But along the road, a few miles outside Libau, he met the carriage of his aunt Tsarevna Maria Alexeevna returning from her cure at Carlsbad. Although sympathetic to Alexis and the old ways, she was too frightened of Peter to offer any spoken opposition. Alexis sat in her carriage, telling her first that he was obeying his father's command and was

on his way to join the Tsar. "Good," replied the Tsarevna, "it is necessary to obey him. That is pleasing to God." But then Alexis broke into tears and weepingly told his aunt that he wished to find some place to hide from Peter. "Where could you go?" asked the horrified Tsarevna. "Your father would find you no matter where." Her advice was to endure, hoping that in the end God would solve his problems. Meanwhile, she said, Kikin was in Libau and perhaps he could give better advice.

In Libau, Kikin advised that Vienna might be safe, as the Emperor was Alexis' brother-in-law. Alexis seized the suggestion and he continued in his own coach as far as Danzig. There, dressed as a Russian officer and taking the name Kokhansky, accompanied by Afrosina disguised as a boy page, and with three Russian servants, he set off by way of Breslau and Prague for Vienna. Before he left, Kikin had given him urgent parting advice: "Remember, if your father sends somebody to persuade you to return, do not do it. He will have you publicly beheaded."

53

FLIGHT
OF THE TSAREVICH

ON THE EVENING of November 10, 1716, Count Schönborn, Vice Chancellor of the Imperial court in Vienna, was already in bed when a servant entered his chamber to announce that the heir to the Russian throne, the son of Tsar Peter of Russia, was in an anteroom demanding to see him. The astonished Schönborn immediately began to dress, but before he could finish, the Tsarevich burst into the room. In a state of near-hysteria, pacing rapidly from one side of the room to the other, Alexis poured out his appeal to the amazed Austrian. He had come, he said, to beg the Emperor to save his life. The Tsar, Menshikov and Catherine wished to deprive him of the throne, send him to a monastery and perhaps even to kill him. "I am weak," he said, "but I have sense enough to rule. Besides," he added, "God, not man, gives kingdoms and appoints heirs to a throne."

Schönborn stared at the frantic young man, who was looking from left to right almost as if he expected his tormentors to pursue him right into the room. Raising his hand for calm, the Vice Chancellor offered a chair. Alexis swallowed hard, sank into the chair and asked for beer. Schönborn had no beer, but he offered his visitor a glass of Moselle wine and then, in a friendly and reassuring way, began asking questions to convince himself that this really was the Tsarevich.

When this was done, Schönborn explained to the sobbing Prince that the Emperor could not be roused that night, but would be informed the following morning. Meanwhile, it would be best for the Tsarevich to return to his inn and remain in concealment until it had been decided what to do. Alexis agreed and, after expressing his gratitude with another gush of tears, he left.

Alexis' arrival put Emperor Charles VI in a delicate position. To step between father and son was risky. If there was rebellion or civil war in Russia, no one could tell who would win, and if Austria had backed the loser, who could say what form the winner's revenge might take? In the end, it was decided expedient not to receive Alexis officially or take public notice of his presence in imperial territory. On the other hand, Alexis'

appeal to his brother-in-law would not be totally rejected. Retaining his incognito, the Tsarevich would be hidden within the empire until he effected a reconciliation with his father or some further development occurred.

Two days later, in great secrecy, Alexis and his small party (including Afrosina, whose disguise as a boy had not been penetrated) were escorted to the castle of Ehrenberg in the remote Tyrolean valley of the Lech River, where they lived under conditions of highest security. The commandant was not told the identity of his guest and believed him to be an important Polish or Hungarian nobleman. The soldiers of the garrison were restricted to the castle for the entire length of the Tsarevich's stay; none was to go on leave and none was to be replaced. The visitor was to be treated as a guest of the Imperial court, served respectfully, and his table furnished with a lavish allowance of 300 florins a month. All mail coming to or from the guest was to be intercepted and forwarded to the Imperial Chancery in Vienna. Most important, no strangers were to be allowed anywhere near the castle. Anyone coming near the gate or attempting to speak to the guards was to be arrested immediately.

Enclosed by thick walls, lost in the high mountains and deep snows of the Alps, Alexis at last felt safe. Afrosina was with him, along with four Russian servants and many books. His only need was an Orthodox priest—an impossibility while he maintained his incognito, but he implored Schönborn to send one should he become ill or reach the point of death. During these five months, his contact with the world was through Count Schönborn and the Imperial Chancery in Vienna. From time to time, the Count would send him news. "People are beginning to say that the Tsarevich has perished," ran one communication from Schönborn. "According to some, he has run away from the severity of his father; according to others, he has been put to death by his father's orders. Others say that, while traveling, he was assassinated by robbers. Nobody knows exactly where he is. I enclose as a matter of curiosity what has been written from St. Petersburg. The Tsarevich is advised in his interest to keep himself well concealed, because active search will be made for him as soon as the Tsar's return from Amsterdam."

On the Russian side, awareness of the Tsarevich's disappearance came more gradually than one would suppose. The Tsar's family was dispersed: Peter was in Amsterdam, Catherine was in Mecklenburg, and travel in that time was slow and uncertain. Alexis supposedly was making his way over winter roads from St. Petersburg down the Baltic to join the army which was in winter quarters in Mecklenburg; travel conditions alone could explain a delay of weeks. Nevertheless, in time, people began to worry. Twice, Catherine wrote to Menshikov asking about Alexis. One of the Tsarevich's servants, sent by Kikin to follow his master, lost the trail in North Germany and came to Catherine in Mecklenburg to report that he had traced Alexis as far as Danzig, where the Tsarevich appeared to have vanished. It was

during these early weeks that Count Schönborn sent to the fugitive hidden in the Tyrol a letter written in January from St. Petersburg by the Austrian representative, Pleyer:

As no one up to this time had shown special attention to the Crown Prince, no one thought much about his departure. But when old Princess Maria [to whom Alexis had admitted his desire to flee] returned from the baths [Carlsbad] and visited the house of the Crown Prince and began to cry, "Poor orphans, who are without father and mother, how sorry I am for you!" and besides this, news was received that the Tsarevich had gone no further than Danzig, everyone began to inquire about him. Many high personages secretly sent to me and to other foreigners to ask if we had not received in our letters some news of him. Two of his servants came to me also with questions. They wept bitterly and said that the Tsarevich had taken here a thousand ducats for his journey and in Danzig two thousand more and had sent them an order to secretly sell his furniture and pay the drafts, and since then they had no news of him. Meanwhile, they say in whispers that he was seized near Danzig by the Tsar's people and carried off to a distant monastery, but it is not known whether he is alive or dead. According to others, he has gone to Hungary or some other land of the Emperor.

Then Pleyer, who hated Peter, began to exaggerate. "Everything here is ripe for rebellion," he told Vienna. He wrote of a plot which rumor said would kill Peter, imprison Catherine, free Eudoxia and set Alexis on the throne. He went on to catalogue the complaints of the nobility, to whom he had obviously been talking. "High and low talk of nothing else except the contempt shown to them and their children who are obliged to be sailors and shipbuilders, although they have been abroad to learn languages and have spent so much money; of the ruin of their property by taxes and by their serfs being carried off to build fortresses and harbors." Pleyer's letter, which Alexis gave to Afrosina to keep with her belongings, and which later turned up in the hands of his inquisitors in Moscow, was to do the Tsarevich great harm.

For Peter, spending the winter in Amsterdam before his visit to Paris, the rumors that his son had disappeared were alarming, and when they turned to fact, the Tsar was overcome with anger and shame. The flight alone was bad enough for Peter's pride; worse was the fact that the defiance of the heir would stimulate and encourage all those dissident elements who hoped one day to overturn the Tsar's reforms. It was imperative, therefore, to find the Tsarevich. In December, General Weide, commanding the Russian army in Mecklenburg, was ordered to search throughout North Germany. On the

chance that the fugitive might be in the Hapsburg Emperor's dominions, Abraham Veselovsky, the Tsar's resident in Vienna, was summoned to meet Peter in Amsterdam. There, Peter ordered him to begin a discreet search within the imperial territories and handed him a letter addressed to Charles VI, requesting that if the Tsarevich did appear either openly or secretly in the Emperor's lands, Charles would send Alexis back to his father under armed escort. Humiliated by having to write such a letter, Peter told Veselovsky not to give it to the Emperor unless evidence developed that Alexis actually was in imperial territory.

Grimly accepting the role of sleuth, Veselovsky went from Amsterdam to Danzig to pick up the Tsarevich's trail. From Danzig, it led down the road to Vienna, and Veselovsky discovered that a man named Kokhansky, fitting the Tsarevich's description, had passed that way from posthouse to posthouse several months before. In Vienna, the trail faded, and in interviews with Count Schönborn, with Prince Eugene and even with the Emperor himself, the detective could learn nothing. Reinforcement arrived in the person of Captain of the Guards Rumyantsov, a giant of a man, almost as big as Peter himself, who was a personal aide to the Tsar. Rumyantsov's orders were to assist Veselovsky in seizing Alexis by force if necessary to bring him home.

By the end of March 1717, the efforts of Veselovsky and Rumyantsov began to produce results. A bribed clerk in the Imperial Chancery indicated that a search in the Tyrol might prove fruitful. Rumyantsov traveled there and learned that a mysterious stranger was rumored to be hidden in the castle of Ehrenberg. He prowled as close to the castle as he could, returned repeatedly and eventually caught a glimpse of a man who he was sure was the Tsarevich. Armed with this information, Veselovsky returned to Vienna and delivered the Tsar's letter from Amsterdam to the Emperor. Alexis had been positively identified at Ehrenberg, Veselovsky declared, and it was obvious that he was living there with the knowledge of the Imperial government. His Imperial Majesty was respectfully requested to deal frankly with the Tsar's request concerning his son. Charles VI hesitated, still uncertain how to deal with this unwanted entanglement. He told Veselovsky that he doubted the accuracy of his information from the Tyrol, but would investigate. He then sent an imperial secretary straight to the Tsarevich to tell him what had happened, show him Peter's letter and ask whether he was now prepared to go back to his father. Alexis' response was to break into hysterics. Running from room to room, weeping, wringing his hands, wailing aloud in Russian, he made it plain to the secretary that he would rather do anything than return. The secretary then announced the Emperor's decision: that, as his present hiding place had been discovered and the Tsar's demands could not be summarily rejected, the Tsarevich would be transferred to

another place of refuge within the empire: the city of Naples, which had come to the Imperial crown four years earlier through the Treaty of Utrecht. Alexis gratefully agreed. In great secrecy, he was conducted through Innsbruck and Florence to southern Italy, taking with him his "page" Afrosina and his servants, who called attention to themselves by getting drunk. Writing to Count Schönborn, the imperial secretary noted that "as far as Trento suspicious people followed us; all was well, however. I used all possible means to hold our company from frequent and excessive drunkenness, but in vain." Early in May, the fugitive party arrived in Naples, and after a dinner at the Trattoria of the Three Kings, the Tsarevich's coach rolled into the courtyard of Castle St. Elmo. The massive brown walls and towers of this fortress looking out over the blue Bay of Naples toward Mount Vesuvius were to be Alexis' home for the next five months. He settled down in the warm sunshine and began writing letters to Russia, telling the clergy and the Senate that he was still alive and explaining his reasons for his flight. With the passage of time, Afrosina's swelling body made plain the sex of the "page." As Count Schönborn joked in a letter to Prince Eugene: "Our little page has at last been acknowledged as a female. She is declared to be a mistress and indispensably necessary."

Unfortunately for the lovers, their belief that their hiding place remained secret was false. The "suspicious people" spotted by the secretary as they traveled south were none other than Rumyantsov and his men, who followed the Tsarevich through Italy and entered Naples on his heels. As soon as they were certain that the fugitives were settling into Castle St. Elmo for an extended stay, a courier hurried north to inform Tsar Peter. The messenger found him at Spa, where he was resting and taking the waters after his Paris visit.

When Peter heard the news, he was extremely angry. Nine months had passed since the Tsarevich's flight, and throughout that time, as the Tsar passed through foreign territories and visited Western courts, he had borne the humiliation of his son's defection. Now, in addition, he knew that not only had the Emperor lied to him about Alexis' presence within his dominions, but that, as indicated by the move to a new asylum in Naples, Austria did not mean to give the Tsarevich up. Grimly, Peter wrote again to the Emperor, this time demanding the return of his renegade son.

To carry this ultimatum to Vienna, Peter had selected the most skillful diplomat in his service, Peter Tolstoy. The clever old fox, with his bushy black eyebrows and cold, impressive face, was now seventy-two. He had survived his original support of the Tsarevna Sophia in the struggle between brother and sister years before. He had survived twelve years as Russian ambassador in Constantinople and numerous incarcerations in the Seven Towers. Now, returning with Peter from Paris, Tolstoy was chosen for a

final mission: He was to go to Vienna and inquire of the Emperor why a disobedient son had been given refuge. He was to hint to Charles VI the possible consequences of this unfriendly action. Further, if he could gain access to the Tsarevich, he was to present to Alexis a letter written by Peter, promising the son his father's forgiveness if he returned. Meanwhile, locked in his own breast, Tolstoy carried Peter's real orders: The Tsarevich was to be brought back to Russia, no matter what the means.

TOLSTOY ARRIVED in Vienna and immediately went with Veselovsky and Rumyantsov to an audience with the Emperor. There, he presented the Tsar's letter, which declared that he knew exactly where Alexis was and that both as a father and as an autocratic sovereign he had a complete right to the restitution of his son. Charles listened and said little, but promised a quick reply. Tolstoy next went to the Princess of Wolfenbüttel, Alexis' mother-in-law, who happened to be in Vienna visiting her daughter, the Empress. He begged her, in the interest of her grandchildren, the son and daughter of the Tsarevich, to exert her influence on behalf of the refugee's return. She agreed, for she was well aware that if the Tsarevich did not submit to the Tsar, little Peter Alexeevich might be removed from the line of succession.

On August 18, the Imperial Council met to consider the dilemma. Alexis could not be summarily dispatched back to Peter; if the Tsar's protestations of mercy later proved false, Austria would then be accused of having played a part in Alexis' death. On the other hand, a large Russian army was stationed in Poland and North Germany. Such was Peter's character, it was believed, that if thwarted he might divert his troops from the war against Charles XII to march on Silesia and Bohemia. The solution eventually reached was to reply to Peter's letter that the Emperor had actually been performing a service for the Tsar by attempting to preserve the affection between father and son and by not allowing Alexis to fall into the hands of a hostile nation. The Emperor insisted to Tolstoy that Alexis was not a prisoner in Naples: He was and always had been free to go where he liked. Meanwhile, the Emperor instructed his viceroy in Naples that the Tsarevich was not to be forced into anything and that precautions were to be taken to make sure the Russians did not assassinate the fugitive.

On September 26, 1717, Alexis was invited to the Viceroy's palace in Naples. Led into a chamber, he saw, to his horror, Tolstoy and Rumyantsov standing beside the Viceroy. The Tsarevich trembled; the Viceroy, Count Daun, had not told him of their presence, suspecting that if he had known, he would not have come. Alexis, aware that the giant Rumyantsov was an intimate of his father's, expected the sudden flash of a sword blade. Gradually, Tolstoy, speaking in his most reassuring tones, persuaded the young

man that they had come only to deliver a letter from Peter, to listen to his thoughts and to wait for his reply. Still trembling, the Tsarevich took the letter and read it.

My Son:

Your disobedience and the contempt you have shown for my orders are known to all the world. Neither my words nor my corrections have been able to bring you to follow my instructions, and last of all, having deceived me when I bade you farewell and in defiance of the oaths you made, you have carried your disobedience to the highest pitch by your flight and by putting yourself like a traitor under a foreign protection. This is a thing hitherto unheard of, not only in our family, but among our subjects of any consideration. What wrong and what grief have you thereby occasioned to your father, and what shame have you drawn upon your country!

I write to you for the last time to tell you that you are to do what Messrs. Tolstoy and Rumyantsov will tell you and declare to be my will. If you are afraid of me, I assure you and I promise to God and His judgment that I will not punish you. If you submit to my will by obeying me and if you return, I will love you better than ever. But if you refuse, then I as a father, by virtue of the power I have received from God, give you my everlasting curse; and as your sovereign, I declare you traitor and I assure you I will find the means to use you as such, in which I hope God will assist me and take my just cause into His hands.

As for what remains, remember I forced you to do nothing. What need had I to give you a free choice? If I had wished to force you, was it not in my power to do it? I had but to command and I would have been obeyed.

Peter

Finishing the letter, Alexis told the two envoys that he had put himself under the Emperor's protection because his father had decided to deprive him of the crown and put him in a monastery. Now that his father promised pardon, he said, he would reflect and reconsider; he could not answer immediately. Two days later, when Tolstoy and Rumyantsov returned, Alexis told them that he was still afraid to go back to his father and would continue to ask the hospitality of the Emperor. Hearing this, Tolstoy put on a different face. Roaring with anger, storming about the room, he threatened that Peter would make war on the empire, that the Tsar eventually would take his son dead or alive as a traitor, that wherever he might flee, there would be no escape because Tolstoy and Rumyantsov had orders to remain close by until they took him.

His eyes staring with fright, Alexis grasped the Viceroy by the hand, pulled him into an adjoining room and begged Count Daun to guarantee the Emperor's protection. Daun, whose orders were to facilitate the interviews while at the same time preventing violence, suspected his master's dilemma. Believing that if he could help persuade the Tsarevich to return voluntarily he would be doing a service to all parties, he calmed Alexis. But he began to work with Tolstoy.

Meanwhile, Tolstoy turned his fertile mind to other intrigues worthy of his years in Constantinople. With 160 ducats, he bribed the Viceroy's secretary to whisper in the Tsarevich's ear that he had heard that the Emperor had decided to return the son to the angry father. Next, speaking again to Alexis himself, Tolstoy lied, saying that he had received a new letter from Peter announcing that he was coming to seize his son by force and that the Russian army soon would be marching toward Silesia. The Tsar- himself meant to come to Italy, Tolstoy went on. "And when he is here, who can prevent him from seeing you?" he asked. At the thought, Alexis turned pale.

Finally, Tolstoy's relentless mind located the key to Alexis' decision: It was Afrosina. Observing the Tsarevich's almost desperate need for the serf, he told the Viceroy that she was a major cause of the rift between father and son. Further, he suggested, Afrosina was still encouraging Alexis not to return home because there her own status would be questionable. At Tolstoy's urging, Count Daun issued orders to remove the girl from Castle St. Elmo. When Alexis heard this, his defenses crumbled. He wrote to Tolstoy, begging him to come alone to the castle so that they might work out an agreement. His battle almost won, Tolstoy then persuaded Afrosina, with promises and gifts, to urge her lover to return home. She did as she was asked, begging her lover in tears to give up his last desperate idea: a flight to the Papal States to put himself under the protection of the Pope.

Alexis was now emotionally and psychologically battered to the point of submission. His choice lay between returning to Russia in the company of his mistress to receive his father's pardon, or the removal of Afrosina and of the Emperor's protection, leaving him at the mercy of Tolstoy and Rumyantsov or, worse, Peter himself. The choice was obvious, and when Tolstoy arrived, the Tsarevich quickly capitulated. Although hesitant and filled with fear and misgiving, he told the Ambassador: "I will go to my father on two conditions: that I may be allowed to live quietly in a country house and that Afrosina will not be taken away from me." Tolstoy, mindful of Peter's command to get the Tsarevich back to Russia by any means, instantly agreed; indeed, he promised Alexis that he would write personally to the Tsar asking permission for the Tsarevich to marry Afrosina immediately. Cynically, Tolstoy explained in his letter to Peter that this marriage would demonstrate that Alexis had fled not for serious political

reasons but simply for frivolous love of a peasant girl. This in turn, Tolstoy added, would strip away any last sympathy the Emperor might have for his erstwhile brother-in-law.

Alexis wrote begging the Tsar's forgiveness and entreating that the two conditions to which Tolstoy had agreed might be carried out. On November 17, Peter replied: "You ask for pardon. It has already been promised to you orally and in writing by Messrs. Tolstoy and Rumyantsov, and I now confirm it, of which you can be fully assured. As regards certain other wishes expressed by you [marriage to Afrosina], they will be allowed to you here." To Tolstoy, Peter explained that he would permit the marriage if Alexis still wished it on his return, but that it must take place either on Russian soil or in one of the newly conquered Baltic territories. Peter also promised to grant Alexis' wish to live in peace in a country house. "Perhaps he may doubt whether he will be allowed to do this," the Tsar wrote to Tolstoy, "but let him reason thus: when I have pardoned such a great crime, why should I not allow this little matter?"

Once Alexis had agreed to return and had written this to the Emperor in Vienna, there could be no question of detention by the imperial authorities. The Tsarevich left Castle St. Elmo with Tolstoy and Rumyantsov, and, traveling slowly and feeling more relaxed, he made a pilgrimage to Bari to visit the shrine of St. Nicholas, the miracle worker. From there, he went to Rome, where he visited the holy shrines in a Vatican carriage and was received by the Pope. In a cheerful mood, he reached Venice, where he was persuaded to leave Afrosina behind so that she would not have to cross the Alps in winter in her delicate state.

For the Tsarevich's wary escorts, Tolstoy and Rumyantsov, and for Veselovsky, who was waiting for them near Vienna, the passage through the Imperial capital posed something of a gauntlet to be run. Alexis was asking that the party halt in Vienna so that he could call on the Emperor and thank him for his hospitality. Tolstoy, however, was afraid that one or both of the brothers-in-law might have a change of mind which would upset the success of his mission. Accordingly, he arranged for Veselovsky to spirit the little party through Vienna in a single night. By the time the Emperor heard about it, the Tsarevich and his escorts were already north of the city in the town of Brünn in the imperial province of Moravia.

Charles was alarmed and indignant. He had suffered needles of conscience over what he had permitted to take place in Naples. To reassure himself, he had resolved to interview his brother-in-law in Vienna to make sure that the Tsarevich truly was returning to Russia voluntarily. The Emperor hoped, of course, that this was so; repatriation of the embarrassing guest would remove a large thorn from his own foot. But honor required that Alexis consent; the imperial dignity could not permit the Tsarevich to be dragged away by force. Thus, a meeting of the Council was hastily

convened and a messenger dispatched to Count Colloredo, Governor of Moravia, commanding him to detain the Russian party until Alexis had personally assured the Governor that he was traveling freely at his own wish. Tolstoy, finding his inn surrounded by soldiers, denied that the Tsarevich was in the party. He threatened to use his sword to prevent anyone from entering Alexis' room, and promised that the episode would summon the vengeance of Tsar Peter. The Governor, taken aback, sent to Vienna for new instructions, and again he was ordered not to permit Tolstoy's party to leave Brünn until he had seen and talked with the Tsarevich; if necessary, he was to use force to achieve this. This time, Tolstoy backed down. The interview was permitted, although the Governor's request to speak to Alexis alone was ignored; Tolstoy and Rumyantsov remained in the room. Under the circumstances, Alexis spoke only in monosyllables, saying that he was anxious to return to his father and that he had not stopped to call on the Emperor because he lacked court clothes and a suitable carriage. The game was over. The forms of propriety and diplomatic etiquette had been observed. The Governor and, through him, the Emperor had discharged their obligations; permission to depart was granted. Within a few hours, Tolstoy had secured new horses and the Russian party was gone. It reached Riga in Russian-occupied territory on January 21, 1718. From there, Alexis was taken to Tver near Moscow, to await his father's summons.

Afrosina remained in Venice, intending to travel in better weather and at a more leisurely pace. As he journeyed farther from her, Alexis wrote to her constantly, expressing his love and concern: "Do not trouble yourself. Take care of yourself on the road. Go slowly because the road in the Tyrol is stony, as you know. Stop where you want as many days as you like. Do not consider the money expense. Even if you spend much, your health is dearer to me than anything." He counseled her on places to buy medicines in Venice and Bologna. From Innsbruck, he wrote, "Buy either here or somewhere else a comfortable carriage." To one of her servants, he pleaded, "Do all you can to amuse Afrosina so that she will not be unhappy." Arriving in Russia, his first concern was to send her some women servants and an Orthodox priest. His last letter, written from Tver, where he was awaiting his father's summons, was optimistic: "Thank God, all is well. I expect to be rid of everything so as to live with you, if God allow, in the country, where we will not have trouble about anything."

While Alexis was pouring his heart out to her, his beloved Afrosina was enjoying her new status as the favorite of both the son and—through her aid to Tolstoy—the father. She amused herself in Venice, riding in a gondola and buying cloth of gold for 167 ducats, a cross, earrings and

a ruby ring. Most of her letters lack the urgency and passion displayed by her lover; indeed, they were written by a secretary, with the uneducated mistress usually adding a few lines in her large, ill-formed scrawl, begging Alexis to send her some caviar, smoked fish or kasha by the next courier. In Russia, news of the Tsarevich's return stirred mixed feelings. No one knew quite how to receive him: Was it the heir to the throne or a traitor to Russia who now waited outside Moscow to see his father? De la Vie, the French commercial agent, expressed this strange, uneasy mood: "The arrival of the Tsarevich caused as much joy to some as grief to others. Those who took his part were glad before his return in hope that some revolution would take place. Now all is changed. Policy takes the place of discontent and everything is quiet while waiting for the result of the affair. His return is generally disapproved, for it is believed that he will have the same fate as his mother." Some observers, especially those who had hoped that the heir would outlast and succeed his father, were angry and disgusted. Said Ivan Naryshkin: "That Judas of a Peter, Tolstoy, has delivered the Tsarevich." Said Prince Vasily Dolgoruky to Prince Gagarin: "Have you heard that that fool of a Tsarevich is coming here because his father has allowed him to marry Afrosina? He will have a coffin instead of a wedding!"

54

THE FUTURE
ON TRIAL

ON WINTER MORNINGS in Moscow, a pale sun emerges to cast a hazy light on the snow-covered rooftops of the ancient city. At nine o'clock on such a morning, February 3, 1718, the great men of Russia were assembled in solemn conclave in the Great Audience Hall of the Kremlin. Ministers and other officials of the government, the highest dignitaries of the clergy and the leading members of the nobility had gathered to witness a historic act: the disinheritance of a Tsarevich and the proclamation of a new heir to the throne of Russia. To underscore the drama and its potential dangers, three battalions of the Preobrazhensky Regiment had been brought into the Kremlin and stationed around the palace with muskets loaded.

Peter arrived first and took his place upon the throne. Then Alexis was escorted in by Tolstoy. The status of the Tsarevich was clear to everyone: He lacked his sword and therefore came as a prisoner. Alexis confirmed this instantly by going straight to his father, falling on his knees, acknowledging his guilt and begging pardon for his crimes. Peter ordered his son to rise while a written confession was read aloud:

> Most Clement Lord and Father: I confess once more at present that I have swerved from the duties of a child and of a subject in evading and putting myself under the Emperor's protection and by applying to him for support. I implore your gracious pardon and your clemency. The most humble and incapable servant, unworthy to call himself son, Alexis.

The Tsar then denounced his son formally, condemning him for repeatedly ignoring his father's commands, for his neglect of his wife, for his relations with Afrosina, for his desertion from the army and, finally, for his dishonorable flight to a foreign country. Speaking loudly, Peter announced that the Tsarevich begged only for his life and was ready to renounce the inheritance. Out of mercy, Peter continued, he had assured Alexis of his

pardon, but only on condition that the whole truth of his past conduct and the names of all who had been his accomplices be revealed. Alexis agreed and followed Peter into a small nearby chamber, where he swore that only Alexander Kikin and Ivan Afanasiev, the Tsarevich's valet, had known that he planned to flee. Father and son then returned to the Audience Hall, where Vice Chancellor Shafirov read a printed manifesto listing the offenses of the Tsarevich, declaring that he had been both pardoned and disinherited, and proclaiming that Catherine's son, the two-year-old Tsarevich Peter Petrovich, was now the heir to the throne. From the palace, the entire assembly walked across the Kremlin courtyard to the Assumption Cathedral, where Alexis, kissing the Gospel and a cross, swore before the holy relics that when his father died, he would bear faithful allegiance to his little half-brother and never attempt to regain the succession for himself. Everyone present took the same oath. That night, the manifesto was published, and over the next three days all citizens of Moscow were invited to visit the cathedral and swear the new oath of allegiance. At the same time, messengers were dispatched to Menshikov and the Senate in St. Petersburg, ordering them to administer the oath of allegiance to Peter Petrovich as heir to the throne to the whole of the garrison, the nobility, the townspeople and the peasants.

The two public ceremonies in Moscow and St. Petersburg seemed to bring the affair to an end. Alexis had resigned his claim to the throne; a new heir had been proclaimed. What more was necessary? A great deal more, as it turned out. For the terrible drama was only beginning.

PETER'S DECREE in the Kremlin ceremony, making his pardon conditional on Alexis' revealing the names of all his advisors and confidants, introduced a new element into the affair between father and son. This was, in fact, a betrayal by the Tsar of the promise given the Tsarevich by Tolstoy at Castle St. Elmo. There, Alexis had been promised an unconditional pardon if he would return to Russia. Now, it was demanded that he name all his "accomplices" and not conceal even the slightest detail of the "conspiracy."

The reason, of course, was Peter's gnawing curiosity to know how far the threat to the throne and perhaps his life had gone, and his growing determination to know who among his subjects—and perhaps even among his advisors and intimates—had secretly sided with his son. He could not believe that Alexis would have fled without assistance and without some conspiratorial purpose. Thus, as Peter saw it, this was no longer merely a family drama, but a political confrontation involving the permanence of the achievements of his reign. He had settled the succession on another son, but Alexis remained alive and free. How could Peter be sure that, after his own death, the same nobles who had so speedily signed the oath to two-year-

old Peter Petrovich would not equally hastily overturn their vows and rush to support Alexis? Above all, how could he continue to surround himself with familiar faces, not knowing which among them had been false? Tormented by these questions, Peter decided to get to the bottom of what had happened. The first investigation began immediately at Preobrazhenskoe. Holding Alexis to his promise to reveal everything, Peter drew up in his own hand a list of seven questions which Tolstoy presented to the Tsarevich, along with the Tsar's warning that a single omission or evasion in his answers could cost him his pardon. In reply, Alexis wrote a long, rambling narrative of the events of his life during the preceding four years. Although he insisted that only Kikin and Afanasiev had possessed foreknowledge of his flight, he also mentioned a number of other people with whom he had spoken about himself and his relations with his father. Among those named were Peter's half-sister, the Tsarevna Maria Alexeevna; Abraham Lopukhin, who was the brother of Peter's first wife, Eudoxia, and thereby Alexis' uncle; Senator Peter Apraxin, brother of the General-Admiral; Senator Samarin; Semyon Naryshkin; Prince Vasily Dolgoruky; Prince Yury Trubetskoy; the Prince of Siberia; the Tsarevich's tutor, Viazemsky; and his confessor, Ignatiev.

The only person whom Alexis attempted to exempt from all blame was Afrosina. "She carried [my] letters in a box, but she had not the least knowledge of them," he declared. As to advance knowledge of his flight, he explained, "I carried her along with me by a stratagem when I had taken the resolution to fly. I told her that I would only take her as far as Riga, and from thence I carried her further, making her as well as those of my retinue believe that I had orders to go to Vienna to make an alliance against the Ottoman Porte and that I was obliged to travel in private that the Turks might not get notice of it. That is all [she and] my servants knew of it."

With the names supplied by Alexis before him, Peter wrote urgent orders to Menshikov in St. Petersburg, where most of the accused lived. As soon as the couriers arrived, the city gates were closed and no one was allowed to leave for any reason. Peasants bringing food into market were searched on leaving to prevent anyone from escaping concealed in a simple sledge. Apothecaries were forbidden to sell arsenic or other poisons lest some of the accused attempt that form of escape.

Once the city was sealed off, Peter's agents struck. At midnight, Kikin's house was quietly surrounded by fifty soldiers of the Guards. An officer entered, found him in bed, took him in his dressing gown and slippers, fettered him in chains and an iron collar and carried him away before he could say more than a word to his beautiful wife. In fact, Kikin had almost escaped. Realizing that he was in danger, he had bribed one of Peter's confidential orderlies to warn him of any move the Tsar might make against him. When Peter was writing his orders to Menshikov, the orderly was

standing behind the Tsar and read the message over Peter's shoulder. The orderly left the house immediately and sent a messenger riding to Kikin in St. Petersburg. His message arrived only minutes after Kikin had been arrested.

Menshikov also received orders to arrest Prince Vasily Dolgoruky, a lieutenant general, a Knight of the Danish Order of the Elephant and the director general of the commission established by Peter to look into the mismanagement of state revenues. Supposedly, he was still high in Peter's favor, for he had only just returned with the Tsar from Peter's eighteen-month journey to Copenhagen, Amsterdam and Paris. Menshikov surrounded Dolgoruky's house with soldiers, then entered and announced his orders to the Prince. Dolgoruky handed over his sword, declaring, "I have a good conscience and but one head to lose." He was fettered and taken to the Peter and Paul Fortress. That same evening, Menshikov visited and arrested Senator Peter Apraxin, Abraham Lopukhin, Senator Michael Samarin and the Prince of Siberia. In addition, all of Alexis' servants and nine others were chained and made ready to travel as prisoners to Moscow.

Through February, the net continued to widen. Both in Moscow and St. Petersburg, new persons were arrested daily. Dositheus, the Bishop of Rostov, one of the most famous and powerful churchmen in Russia, was arrested and accused of having publicly prayed in his church for Eudoxia and of having prophesied the death of Peter. Eudoxia herself and Peter's only surviving half-sister, Maria, were arrested and brought to Moscow for questioning. Peter was deeply suspicious of his former wife. She had been in communication with Alexis, and she had much to gain if her son were to sit on the throne. On the day Alexis was removed from the succession, Peter sent Guards Captain Gregory Pisarev to the convent in Suzdal where Eudoxia had been living for nineteen years. Arriving there, Pisarev found that Eudoxia had long before laid aside the veil of a nun and put on the robes of a royal lady. He found on the convent altar a tablet which contained "A Prayer for the Tsar and Tsaritsa," citing the names of Peter and Eudoxia as if the Tsar had not divorced his wife. Finally, Pisarev discovered that the former wife and former nun had taken a lover, Major Stephen Glebov, the captain of her guards.

Eudoxia, now forty-four years old, trembled to imagine how the giant man who had been her husband would react to all this. As she was being taken to Moscow, she wrote a letter and sent it ahead so that it should reach Peter before she did. "Most Gracious Sovereign," she pleaded,

Many years ago, which year I do not remember, I went to Suzdal Convent, taking the vows as I had promised, and was given the name of Helen. After becoming a nun, I wore monastic dress for half a year. But not greatly desiring to be a nun, I gave it up and abandoned

the dress, staying on quietly at the convent as a lay person in disguise. My secret has been revealed by Gregory Pisarev. Now I rely on the humane generosity of Your Majesty. Falling at your feet, I beg mercy for my crime, and forgiveness, that I may not die a useless death. And I promise to go back to the life of a nun and remain in it till my death, and will pray to God for you, Sovereign. Your most humble slave, your past wife, Eudoxia.

Although the original charge against Eudoxia seemed to have little weight—communications between Alexis and his mother were rare and harmless—Peter was now aroused by his former wife's behavior and determined to ferret out the details of the situation in Suzdal. Glebov was arrested, along with Father Andrew, the chief priest of the convent, and a number of nuns. It was difficult to believe that Eudoxia's way of life had gone completely unnoticed and unreported to Moscow for twenty years, or that Peter's anger now was directed solely at the offense against his honor. Rather, what stimulated his rage was his belief that a conspiracy existed, and the possibility that its threads ran through the convent in Suzdal.

As prisoners flowed into Moscow from St. Petersburg, Suzdal and other parts of the country, huge crowds stood at the Kremlin gates to see what they could and to catch the latest rumor. The heads of the clergy, the members of Peter's court, his generals and administrative officers and most of the nobility of Russia had been summoned, and the daily processions of coaches carrying great noblemen and churchmen accompanied by their servants made a rich spectacle.

The churchmen were there to attend the trial of their colleague Dositheus, Bishop of Rostov. Judged guilty, he was stripped of his ecclesiastical robes and delivered to the secular authorities for interrogation under torture. While being disrobed, he turned and shouted to his fellow bishops who had judged him, "Am I then the only one guilty in this matter? Look into your own hearts, all of you. What do you find there? Go to the people. Listen to them. What do they say? Whose name do you hear?" Put to torture, Dositheus admitted nothing except a general sympathy for Alexis and Eudoxia; no act of defiance or rebellious words could be extracted or proved. And yet, just as with the Streltsy two decades before, the very vagueness of these replies tended to anger Peter and spur his determination to dig deeper.

The dominant figure in the inquisition was Peter himself, dashing from the palace through the city, accompanied only by two or three servants. Contrary to the custom of all previous Muscovite tsars, he appeared not only as judge, dressed in jewels and ancestral robes, seated in honor and wisdom on his throne, but as chief prosecutor, in Western dress—breeches, frock coat, stockings and buckled shoes—demanding judgment from the dignitaries of the realm, temporal and spiritual. Standing in the Great Kremlin Hall, lift-

ing his voice in anger, he argued the danger to which his government had been exposed and the horrors of the crime of treason against the state. It was Peter who presented the case against Dositheus, and when the Tsar was finished, the Bishop of Rostov was doomed.

Late in March, the Moscow phase of the inquisition came to an end when the Council of Ministers, sitting as a temporal High Court of Justice, handed down its verdict. Kikin, Glebov and the Bishop of Rostov were condemned to die a lingering, painful death; others were condemned to die more simply. Many more were publicly knouted and sent into exile. The lesser of the women, including some nuns of the Suzdal convent, were publicly whipped and transferred to convents on the White Sea. The Tsaritsa Eudoxia was not touched physically, but she was moved to a remote convent on Lake Ladoga, where she remained under strict supervision for ten years until the accession of her grandson, Peter II. She then returned to court and lived there until 1731, when she died in the time of Empress Anne. The Tsarevna Maria, Peter's half-sister, was judged to have encouraged opposition to the Tsar and was imprisoned in Schlüsselburg fortress for three years. In 1721, she was released and returned to St. Petersburg, where she died in 1723.

A number of the accused were completely exonerated or dealt with mildly. The Prince of Siberia was exiled to Archangel; Senator Samarin was acquitted. The charge against Senator Peter Apraxin was that he had advanced 3,000 roubles to the Tsarevich upon his departure from St. Petersburg for Germany. When it developed in the investigation that Apraxin had assumed Alexis was going to join the Tsar and had had no means of knowing that the Tsarevich intended to flee, he was completely exonerated.

Prince Vasily Dolgoruky, who admitted sympathy for the Tsarevich, was saved from execution by the pleas of his relatives, especially his older brother, Prince Jacob, who reminded the Tsar of the Dolgoruky family's long record of faithful service. Nevertheless, Vasily was stripped of his rank of general, his Danish Order of the Elephant was sent back to Copenhagen, and he was exiled to Kazan. Leaving St. Petersburg with a long beard and a shabby black coat, he obtained permission to say goodbye to the Tsaritsa Catherine. Once in her presence, he delivered a long speech justifying his behavior and at the same time complaining that he possessed nothing in the world except the clothes on his back. Catherine, soft-hearted as usual, sent him a present of 200 ducats.

The executions of those condemned to a cruel death took place on March 26 in Red Square under the Kremlin walls before a huge crowd of spectators which foreigners estimated at 200,000 to 300,000. The Bishop of Rostov and three others were broken with hammers and left to die slowly on the wheel. A worse fate was reserved for Glebov, Eudoxia's lover. He was first beaten with the knout and burned with red-hot irons and glowing coals. Then he

was stretched on a plank with spikes puncturing his flesh and left there for three days. Still he refused to confess treason. Finally, he was impaled. There is a story that as he suffered his excruciating final agonies with the sharp wooden stake in his rectum slowly gouging him to death, Peter approached. If Glebov would confess, the Tsar offered to release him from this torture and have him killed at once. Glebov, according to the story, spat in Peter's face, and the Tsar coolly walked away.

Similarly, Kikin, who had admitted advising the Tsarevich to seek refuge with the Emperor, was slowly tortured to death, being revived and rested at intervals so that he might suffer more. On the second day of his agony, Peter came up to him also. Kikin, still alive on the wheel, begged the Tsar to pardon him and allow him to become a monk. Peter refused that, but, with a kind of mercy, ordered him beheaded at once.

Nine months later, the second phase of this grim retribution took place in Red Square. Prince Shcherbatov, who had been friendly to the Tsarevich, was publicly knouted and then his tongue was cut out and his nose sliced off. Three others were knouted, including a Pole who had served as Alexis' interpreter. Unlike the Russians, who submitted to their fate with great resignation, the Pole underwent his punishment with great reluctance, refusing to undress and face the knout; his clothes were pulled off him by force. These men all lived, but then five more were brought forward to die. They were Abraham Lopukhin, Eudoxia's brother; Ignatiev, Alexis' confessor; Afanasiev, his valet; and two men of Alexis' household. All were condemned to be broken on the wheel, but at the last minute the sentence was mitigated to simple beheading. The priest died first, then Lopukhin, then the others, with the last being obliged to lay their heads on the block in the blood of those who had died before.

While all this blood was flowing, Peter waited, still unconvinced that all the opposition had been identified, but certain that what he had done so far was right and necessary. Congratulated by a foreign diplomat on having discovered a conspiracy and beaten down his enemies, the Tsar nodded in agreement. "If a fire meets with straw and other light stuff, it soon spreads," he said. "But if it finds iron and stone in its way, it is extinguished of itself."

AFTER THE TRIALS and the bloody executions in Moscow, it was generally hoped that the affair of the Tsarevich was over. The major threads of the conspiracy, if such there may have been, had now been identified and rooted out. When Peter left Moscow for St. Petersburg in March 1718, he took Alexis with him. Traveling together, father and son led observers to believe that the breach between them was repaired. Yet, Peter's mind still seethed with suspicions and fears and the nation sensed his irresolution. "The more I consider the confused state of affairs in Russia," de la Vie wrote to Paris,

"the less I see how these disorders will be brought to an end." Most people, he continued, "still wait and hope only for the end of his [Peter's] life to plunge into the slough of sloth and ignorance." The Tsar's immediate dilemma was that no real conspiracy had been found, but neither had the Tsarevich been proved a faithful son, nor had all those close to the throne revealed themselves as loyal subjects. Above all, nothing had been done to solve the problem that troubled Peter most. A dispatch from Weber enlarged on this dilemma:

> Now comes the question: What shall be done further with the Tsarevich? It is said that he is going to be sent to a very distant monastery. This does not seem probable to me, for the further the Tsar removes him, the greater opportunity does he give to the restless mob for liberating him. I think that he will be brought here again and kept in the neighborhood of St. Petersburg. I will not decide here whether the Tsar is right or wrong to exclude him from the succession and give him his paternal curse. This is sure: the clergy, the nobility, and the common people respect the Tsarevich like a god.

Weber's guess was accurate. Although nominally free, Alexis was required to live in a house next to Catherine's palace and scarcely allowed out of Peter's sight. The Tsarevich, meanwhile, was cowed and seemingly uncaring. Without protesting, he had watched his mother, his tutor, his confessor and all his friends and adherents arrested. As they were interrogated, tortured, exiled, flogged and executed, he meekly stood by, grateful that he himself was not being punished. His only thought seemed to be to marry Afrosina. At the Easter service, Alexis formally congratulated Catherine in the traditional manner, then fell on his knees before her and begged her to influence his father to allow him to marry Afrosina soon.

The young woman arrived in St. Petersburg on April 15, but instead of being received into the waiting arms of her impatient lover, she was immediately arrested and taken to the Fortress of Peter and Paul.* Among her belongings were found drafts of two letters from Naples written in Alexis' hand, one to the Russian Senate, the other to the archbishops of the Russian Orthodox Church. To the Senate, he had written:

> Gentlemen Most Excellent Senators:
>   I believe you will be no less surprised than all the world at my going out of the country and at my residing in a place unknown at

---

* The fate of her child by the Tsarevich is unknown. According to some accounts, the child was born in Riga as Afrosina traveled home. Other stories say that she delivered the infant in the fortress. In any case, the child disappeared from history.

present. The continued ill-usage and the disorders have obliged me to quit my dear native country. They designed to shut me up in a convent in the beginning of the year 1716, though I had committed nothing that had deserved it. None of you can be ignorant of it. But God, full of mercy, saved me by presenting to me last autumn an opportunity of absenting myself from my dear country and you, whom I could not have resolved to leave had I not been in the case where I found myself.

At present I am well and in good health, under the protection of a certain High Person [the Emperor], till the time when God who preserved me shall call me to return to my dear native country.

I desire you not to forsake me then, and as for the present, to give no credit to the news that may be spread of my death, or otherwise out of the desire they have to blot me out of the memory of mankind, for God keeps me in His guard and my benefactors will not forsake me. They have promised me not to forsake me, even not for the future, in case of need. I am alive and I shall always be full of good wishes for Your Excellencies and for the whole country.

The letter to the archbishops was very similar, except that Alexis added that the idea of shutting him up in a convent "proceeded from the same persons who used my mother in like manner."

Four weeks passed before the next act of this drama took place. In the middle of May, Peter decided to question the two lovers separately and then confront them with each other. He took Alexis with him to Peterhof, and two days later Afrosina was brought across the gulf from the fortress in an enclosed boat. In Mon Plaisir, Peter questioned them both, first the girl, then his son.

And here at Peterhof, Afrosina betrayed and doomed Alexis. Without torture, she confessed, responding to her royal lover's passion for her, his attempt to protect her, his willingness to give up a throne in order to marry and live quietly with her, by fatally incriminating him. She described the intimate details of their daily life during the time they were abroad. Through her mouth, all of the Tsarevich's fears and bitterness about his father came pouring out. Alexis, said Afrosina, had written several times to the Emperor complaining about his father. When he read in Pleyer's letter rumors of mutiny among the troops in Mecklenburg, and that there had been a rebellion in the towns near Moscow, he said to her happily, "Now, you see how God acts in His own way." When he read in a newspaper that the Tsarevich Peter Petrovich was ill, he rejoiced. He spoke to her constantly about the succession to the throne. When he became tsar, he told her, he would abandon St. Petersburg and all of Peter's foreign conquests and make Moscow his capital.

He would dismiss Peter's courtiers and appoint his own. He would ignore the navy and allow the ships to rot. He would reduce the army to a few regiments. There would be no more wars with anyone, and he would content himself with Russia's old frontiers. The ancient rights of the church would be restored and respected.

Afrosina also recast her own role; only because of her continual urging, she said, had Alexis agreed to return to Russia. Further, she declared that she had accompanied him on his flight only because he had drawn a knife and threatened to kill her if she refused. Even when she slept with him, she declared, it had been the result of threats and force.

Afrosina's testimony strengthened many of Peter's suspicions. Writing later to the Regent of France, Peter declared that his son had "admitted nothing of his designs" until he was confronted with the letters found in the hands of his mistress. "By these letters, we have known clearly about the rebellious designs of a conspiracy against us, all the circumstances of which the said mistress has publicly, voluntarily confessed without much examination."

Peter's next move was to summon Alexis and confront him with his lover's accusations. The scene at Mon Plaisir is portrayed in the famous nineteenth century painting by Nikolai Ge: The Tsar, wearing boots which are still in the Kremlin, is seated at a table on the black-and-white-tiled floor of the main hall. His face is stern, yet an eyebrow is raised; he has asked a question and is waiting for an answer. Alexis stands before him, tall, thin-faced, dressed in black like his father. He is worried, sullen and resentful. He looks not at his father but down to the floor while his hand, resting on the table, gives him support. It is a moment of decision.

Under his father's gaze, Alexis struggled to get free of the coils slowly crushing him: He had written to the Emperor complaining of his father, he admitted, but he had not sent the letter. He also admitted writing to the Senate and the archbishops, but declared that he had been forced to do so by the Austrian authorities on threat of expulsion from their protection. Peter then brought in Afrosina, and, to the Tsarevich's face, she repeated her accusations.* As his world crumbled around him, Alexis' explanations became feebler. It was true, he admitted, that the letter to the Emperor *had* been sent. He had spoken ill of his father, but he had been drunk. He had spoken about the succession and about returning to Russia, but only after his father's natural death. This he explained at length: "I believed my father's death was near when I heard that he had had a sort of epilepsy. As they said

---

* Afrosina was released, pardoned, and Peter allowed her to keep an assortment of his son's possessions. She lived her remaining thirty years in St. Petersburg, where she eventually married an officer of the Guards.

that older people who have had it can hardly live long, I believed he would die in two years at the furthest. I thought that after his death I might go out of the Emperor's dominions to Poland and from Poland into the Ukraine, where I did not question but everyone would declare for me. And I believed that at Moscow the Tsarevna Maria and the greater part of the archbishops would do the same. And as for the common people, I heard many persons say that they loved me.

"As for what remains, I was resolved absolutely not to return in my father's lifetime, except in the case I did; that is, when he recalled me."

Peter was not satisfied. He remembered that Afrosina had told him that Alexis had rejoiced when he heard rumors of a Russian army revolt in Mecklenburg. This suggests, the Tsar went on, that if the troops in Mecklenburg really had revolted, "you would have declared for the rebels even in my lifetime."

Alexis' answer to this question was disconnected but honest, and it did enormous damage: "If this news had been true and if they had called me, I would have joined the malcontents, but I had no formed design whether I should go and join them or not unless I was called. On the contrary, if they had not sent for me, I should have been afraid of going thither. But if they had, I would have gone.

"I believed they would not call for me but when you were no more, because they designed to take away your life, and I did not believe that they would dethrone you and let you live. But if they had called me, even in your lifetime, probably I should have gone, if they had been strong enough."

A few days later, a further piece of damning evidence was laid before the Tsar. Peter had written to Veselovsky, his ambassador in Vienna, to demand of the Emperor why his son had been forced to write to the Senate and the archbishops. On May 28, Veselovsky's answer came. There had been a major uproar at the Austrian court. The Vice Chancellor, Count Schönborn, had been examined about the matter in the presence of the entire ministry, after which Prince Eugene of Savoy had reported to Veselovsky that neither the Emperor nor Count Schönborn had ever ordered the Tsarevich to write the letters. The truth was that Alexis had written them himself and sent them to Count Schönborn for forwarding to Russia. Schönborn, in his discretion, had not forwarded the letters, and they remained in Vienna. In sum, the Tsarevich had lied and in this lie had involved the Imperial court.

Peter needed to hear no more. The Tsarevich was arrested and placed in the Trubetskoy Bastion of the Peter and Paul Fortress. Two high courts of justice, one ecclesiastical, the other secular, were convoked to consider what should be done with the prisoner. The ecclesiastical court was to consist of all the leaders of the Russian church, the secular court of all ministers, senators, governors, generals and many officers of the Guards. Before the two courts began their sessions, says Weber, Peter spent several hours a day, for

a period of eight days, on his knees praying to God to instruct him what his honor and the welfare of the nation required. Then, on June 14, the proceedings began in the Senate Hall in St. Petersburg. Peter arrived accompanied by the ecclesiastical and secular judges, and a solemn religious service was held, asking for divine guidance. The whole assembly took places at a row of tables, and the doors and windows were flung open. The public was invited to enter; Peter wanted the affair to be heard by everyone. The Tsarevich was brought in under guard of four young officers, and the proceedings against him commenced.

Peter reminded his listeners that over the years he had never sought to deny the succession to his son; on the contrary, he had tried "by powerful exhortations to force [Alexis] to lay claim to it by endeavoring to make himself worthy of it." But the Tsarevich, turning his back on his father's efforts, had "made his escape and fled to the Emperor for refuge, claiming his assistance and protection in succoring and assisting him even with armed force . . . [to gain] the crown of Russia." Alexis, said Peter, had admitted that if rebellious troops in Mecklenburg had summoned him to be their leader, he would have gone to them even in his father's lifetime. "So that one may judge by all those circumstances that he had a mind for the succession, not in the manner his father would leave it to him, but in his own way, by foreign assistance or by the strength of rebels, even in his father's lifetime." Further, throughout the investigations Alexis had continually lied and evaded telling the whole truth. As the pardon promised by the father had been conditional on total and honest confession, this pardon was now invalid. At the end of Peter's denunciation, Alexis "confessed to his father and his lord, in the presence of the whole assembly of the states ecclesiastical and secular, that he was guilty of everything described."

Peter asked the ecclesiastical court—three metropolitans, five bishops, four archimandrites and other high churchmen—to advise him what a royal father ought to do with this modern Absalom. Desperately, the churchmen tried to avoid giving a direct answer. The case, they argued, was inappropriate for an ecclesiastical court. Pressed by Peter for a more substantial answer, they proceeded to show that if the Tsar desired to punish his son, he had the authority of the Old Testament to do so (Leviticus xx: "Everyone that curseth his father or his mother shall be surely put to death," and Deuteronomy xxi: "If a man have a stubborn and rebellious son which will not obey the voice of his father . . . then shall his father . . . lay hold on him and bring him out unto the elders of his city. . . . And all the men of his city shall stone him with stones, that he die.") On the other hand, the churchmen said, if the Tsar wished to be merciful, there were many examples in the teachings of Christ, most notably the parable of the Prodigal Son.

Still not content with this pallid verdict, Peter turned to the 127 members of the secular court. He ordered them to judge his son fairly and objectively,

"without flattering us, or being apprehensive. Do not be moved by the fact that you are to judge the son of your sovereign. For we swear to you by the Great God and His judgments that you have absolutely nothing to fear." On June 16, Peter specifically passed to the court the power to proceed against Alexis as it would against any other subject accused of treason, "in the form required and with the necessary examination"—i.e., torture.

Given these commands and assurances, the court summoned the Tsarevich to the Senate Hall and announced to him that "though they were much grieved by his past conduct, yet they were obliged to obey their orders and, without regard for his person and his being the son of their most clement sovereign, interrogate him." First came examination under torture. On June 19, Alexis received twenty-five blows of the knout. No new confession was wrung from him by this pain, and on June 24 torture was applied again. With fifteen more strokes of the knout tearing the flesh off his back in bloody ribbons, Alexis admitted that he had told his confessor, "I wish for my father's death!" In that abject state, ready to admit anything, he told his interrogator, Tolstoy, that he would even have been willing to pay the Emperor to supply him with foreign troops to use in seizing the Russian throne from his father.

This was sufficient. That same evening, June 24, the high court, unanimously and without discussion, "with afflicted hearts and eyes full of tears," pronounced sentence. Alexis was to die for the "design of rebellion, the like of which was hardly ever heard of in the world, joined to that of a horrid double patricide, first against the Father of his country and next against his Father by nature." The signatures that followed constituted an almost complete roster of Peter's lieutenants: Menshikov's name came first, followed by General-Admiral Fedor Apraxin, Chancellor Golovkin, Privy Councilors Jacob Dolgoruky, Ivan Musin-Pushkin and Tikhon Streshnev, Senator Peter Apraxin, Vice Chancellor Shafirov, Peter Tolstoy, Senator Dmitry Golitsyn, Generals Adam Weide and Ivan Buturlin, Senator Michael Samarin, Ivan Romodanovsky, Alexis Saltykov, Prince Matthew Gagarin, Governor of Siberia, and Kyril Naryshkin, Governor of Moscow.

The sentence now lay in Peter's hands; it could not be carried out without his approval and signature. Peter hesitated to sign, but very soon thereafter events were lifted beyond his control. An account of the final day is given by Weber:

> The next day being Thursday, the 26th of June, early in the morning, the news was brought to the Tsar that the violent passions of the mind and the terrors of death had thrown the Tsarevich into an apoplectic fit. About noon, another messenger brought advice that the Prince was in great danger of his life, whereupon the Tsar sent for the principal men of his court, and caused them to stay with him until he was

informed by a third messenger that the Prince, being past hopes, could not outlive the evening, and that he longed to see his father.

Then the Tsar, attended by the aforesaid company, went to see his dying son, who, at the sight of his father, burst into tears, and with his hands folded spoke to him to this effect: That he had grievously and heinously offended the Majesty of God Almighty and of the Tsar, that he hoped he would die of this sickness, and that even if he lived, he was unworthy of life, therefore he begged his father only to take from him the curse he laid upon him at Moscow; to forgive him all his heavy crimes, to give him his paternal blessing, and to cause prayers to be said for his soul.

During these moving words, the Tsar and the whole company almost melted away in tears; His Majesty returned a pathetic answer, and represented to him in a few words all the offenses he had committed against him, and then gave him his forgiveness and blessings, after which they parted with an abundance of tears and lamentations on both sides.

At five in the evening came a fourth messenger, a major of the Guards, to tell the Tsar that the Tsarevich was extremely desirous once more to see his father. The Tsar at first was unwilling to comply with his son's request, but was at last persuaded by the company, who represented to His Majesty how hard it would be to deny that comfort to a son who, being on the point of death, might probably be tortured by stings of guilty conscience. But when His Majesty had just stepped into his sloop to go over to the Fortress, a fifth messenger brought the news that the Prince had already expired.

How, IN FACT, did Alexis die? No one knew, and no one knows today. The death of the Tsarevich provoked rumor and controversy first in St. Petersburg, then across Russia and Europe. Peter, concerned about the unfavorable impression which this mysterious demise would create abroad, ordered a lengthy official explanation sent to all the courts of Europe. Especially worried about the court of France, which he had so recently visited, he sent a courier to Paris with a letter addressed to his ambassador, Baron de Schleinitz, for delivery to the King and the Regent. After giving a history of the affair and the trial, he concluded:

The secular court, according to all the laws divine and human, were obliged to condemn him [Alexis] to death, with the restriction that it depended on our sovereign power and our paternal clemency whether to pardon him his crimes or to execute the sentence. And of this we notified the Prince, our son.

Nevertheless, we were still undecided, and did not know how to determine an affair of such great importance. On one side paternal tenderness inclined us mostly to pardon him his crimes, on the other we considered the evils into which we would replunge our state and the misfortunes which could arrive if we gave grace to our son.

In the midst of uncertain and distressing agitation, it pleased Almighty God, whose Holy Judgments are always just, to deliver by His divine grace our person and all our empire from all fear and danger and to end the days of our son Alexis, who died yesterday. As soon as he had convinced himself of the great crimes he had committed against us and all our empire, and had received the sentence of death, he was struck with a kind of apoplexy. When he recovered from this attack, having still his spirit and free word, he begged us to come to see him, which we did, accompanied by our ministers and senators, in spite of all the wrong he had done us. We found him with his eyes bathed in tears and marking a sincere repentance. He told us that he knew that the hand of God was on him and that he was at the point of accounting for all the actions of his life, and that he did not believe he would be able to be reconciled with God if he was not reconciled with his Sovereign Lord and father. After that he entered into new details of all that had passed, feeling himself guilty, confessed, received the Holy Sacraments, demanded our benediction and begged us to pardon all his crimes. We pardoned him as our paternal duty and the Christian religion obliged us to do.

This unexpected, sudden death has caused us a great sadness. However, we have found solace in believing that Divine Providence has wished to deliver us from all anxiety and to calm our empire. Thus we have found ourselves obliged to render thanks to God and to comport ourselves with all Christian humility in this sad circumstance.

We have judged it wise to give you knowledge of everything that has happened by express courier so that you will be sufficiently informed of it and that you will communicate it in the accustomed manner to His Most Christian Majesty [King Louis XV] and to his Royal Highness the Duke of Orléans, Regent of the Kingdom.

In case also that anyone wished to publish this event in an odious manner, you will have in hand what is necessary to destroy and solidly refute any unjust and unfounded tales.

Weber and De la Vie accepted the official explanation and reported to their capitals that the Tsarevich had died from a stroke of apoplexy. But other foreigners were dubious, and a number of lurid accounts began to circulate. Pleyer first reported that Alexis had died of apoplexy, but three

days later he informed his government that the Tsarevich had been beheaded with a sword or an axe (one account, many years later, depicted Peter himself beheading his son); a woman from Narva was said to have been brought into the fortress to sew the head back onto the body so that it could lie in state. The Dutch resident, De Bie, reported that Alexis had been bled to death by the opening of his veins with a lancet. Later, there were rumors that Alexis had been smothered with pillows by four Guards officers, including Rumyantsov.

The daily log of the St. Petersburg garrison states that at about eight a.m. on June 26, the Tsar, Menshikov, and eight others gathered in the fortress to attend a new interrogation at which torture was administered—on whom is not specified. "By eleven a.m. they had all departed," the log continued. "The same day at six o'clock in the evening, the Tsarevich Alexis Petrovich, who was under guard in the Trubetskoy Bastion, died." Menshikov's diary says that on that morning he went to the fortress, where he met the Tsar, then went to the Tsarevich Alexis, who was very ill, and remained there for half an hour. "The day was clear and bright with a light wind. On that day the Tsarevich Alexis Petrovich passed from this world into eternal life."

The truth is that none of these suggested causes—beheading, bleeding, smothering or even apoplexy—is required to explain Alexis' death. The simplest explanation is the most likely: Forty strokes of the knout were sufficient to kill a robust, healthy man; Alexis was not robust, and the shock and wounds caused by forty lashes across his thin back could easily have killed him.

No matter exactly how Alexis died, Peter's contemporaries held the Tsar responsible. And although many were shocked, there was also a widespread belief that Alexis' death was the most satisfactory solution to Peter's problem. As Monsieur de la Vie reported to Versailles, "The death of the Prince leaves no reason to doubt that all seeds of rebellion and conspiracy are totally extinguished. A death never occurred more opportunely in the reestablishment of public tranquillity and in dissipating our fears of the ominous events that threatened us." A few days later, the Frenchman added, "It is impossible to praise the conduct of the Tsar too highly."

Peter did not evade the charge against him. Although he said that it was God who ultimately had taken Alexis' life, he never denied that it was he who had brought his son to a trial which had led to a sentence of death. He had not signed his approval of the sentence, but he was fully in accord with the verdict of the judges. Nor did he bother afterward to make a false display of grief. The day after the Tsarevich's death was the anniversary of the Battle of Poltava, and nothing was postponed or muted because of the tragedy. Peter celebrated a Te Deum for the victory and attended a banquet and a ball in the evening. Two days later, on the 29th, a ninety-four-gun ship, the

Lesnaya, built according to Peter's own design, was launched at the Admiralty. Peter was present with all his ministers, and afterward, says one account, "there was great merrymaking." Nevertheless, the ceremonies surrounding the Tsarevich's body reflected Peter's conflicting emotions. Although Alexis had died a condemned criminal, the services of mourning were conducted according to his rank. It was almost as if, now that Alexis was no longer there to threaten his father, Peter wanted him treated as properly befitted a tsarevich. On the morning after Alexis' death, his body was carried from the cell in which he died to the house of the governor of the fortress, where it was laid in a coffin and covered with black velvet and a pall of rich gold tissue. Attended by Golovkin and other high officials of state, it was carried to the Church of the Holy Trinity, where it lay in state, with the face and right hand uncovered in normal Orthodox fashion so that all who wished could kiss the hand or forehead in farewell. On June 30, the funeral and burial took place. In keeping with Peter's instructions, none of the gentlemen present wore mourning clothes, although some ladies were dressed in black. Foreign ambassadors were not invited to this strange royal funeral and were advised not to wear mourning, as the sovereign's son had died a criminal. Nevertheless, the preacher chose for his text the words of David, "O Absalom, my son, my son!" and some of those attending declared that Peter wept. Afterward, the coffin was borne from Trinity Church back to the fortress, with Peter and Catherine and all the high officers of state (most of whom had voted to condemn Alexis) following in a procession carrying lighted candles. In the fortress cathedral, the coffin was placed in the new vault of the Tsar's family, resting beside the coffin of the Tsarevich's wife, Charlotte.

At the end of the year, Peter had a medal struck, almost as if he were commemorating a victory. On the medal, clouds have parted and a mountaintop is bathed in rays of sunlight. Beneath the scene is the inscription: "The horizon has cleared."

ULTIMATELY, what can one say about this tragedy? Was it simply a family matter, a clash of personalities, the awful, bestriding father relentlessly tormenting and eventually killing the pitiable, helpless son?

Peter's relationship with his son was an inseparable blend of personal feelings and political realities. Alexis' character helped stimulate the antagonism between father and son, but at the root of the trouble lay the issue of sovereign power. There were two sovereigns—the sovereign on the throne and the sovereign in waiting—with different dreams and different goals for the state. In achieving those dreams, however, each faced a gnawing frustration. As long as the reigning monarch was on the throne, the son had to

wait, and yet the sovereign knew that, once he had departed, his dreams could be undone, his goals overturned. Power lay only in the crown.

There is, of course, a long history of dissension in royal families, of clashing temperaments, suspicion and maneuvering for power between generations, of the impatience of the young for the older generation to die and yield power. There are also many stories of kings and princes condemning their own kin for opposition to the crown, or, on the losing side, fleeing their homelands to seek refuge at a foreign court. In Peter's time, Princess Mary, daughter of King James II of England, helped to drive her father from the throne. James fled to France to wait for better times; when he died, his son twice landed in Britain attempting to claim his father's throne. Who here was the traitor? Invariably, history bequeaths this title to the loser.

In earlier times, the path to royal thrones was deeply stained with family blood. Plantagenets, Tudors, Stuarts, Capetians, Valois and Bourbons all killed royal kinsmen for reasons of state. The fabled Gloriana, Elizabeth I of England, kept her cousin Mary Queen of Scots in prison for twenty-seven years while life and beauty wasted away and then, still unable to accept the fact that Mary would succeed her on the throne, had the prisoner beheaded. Amidst all this, Mary's son, King James VI of Scotland, gladly accepted his mother's death; her removal cleared his own path as Elizabeth's chosen heir.

Killing one's own royal children is a rarer crime. One must search back to the Greeks, whose tragedies revolve around dim figures, half myth, half god, or to imperial Rome, where naked personal ambition and court depravity made anything acceptable. In Russia, Ivan the Terrible killed his son with his iron staff, but Ivan was raging and half mad. To us, the most unsettling thing about Alexis' death is that it came as a result of a cool, supposedly objective judicial proceeding. That a father could stand by and permit his son to be tortured seems to us an incredible blot, the most brutal of all the violent episodes of Peter's life.

To Peter, however, the judicial proceeding was the final, legal step required in his legitimate defense of the state and his life work. That it was prompted by political necessity rather than personal rancor he felt was obvious. In Peter's eyes, he had overindulged his son. No other subject would have received letter after letter, plea after plea, urging him to accept his responsibilities and the sovereign's will. This was his concession to the personal relationship between them.

The trials had revealed treasonable words and widespread hope for Peter's death. Many had been punished; was it possible to condemn these peripheral figures and leave the central figure untouched? This was the choice Peter faced and which he put to the judicial tribunal. Peter himself, torn between paternal feeling and preserving his life work, chose the latter. Alexis was condemned for reasons of state. As with Elizabeth I of England,

it was a grim decision by a monarch determined to preserve the nation which he or she had spent a lifetime to create.

Did Alexis actually pose a threat to Peter while the father lived? Given the character of the two men, any real danger seems remote. The Tsarevich had neither the energy nor the desire to put himself at the head of a revolt. True, he wanted to succeed to the throne and he wished for Peter's death, but his only program was to wait, believing that he was popular far and wide in Russia—"and of the simple people I have heard that many loved me." And if Alexis had succeeded Peter, would all that Peter feared have taken place? This, too, seems unlikely. Alexis would not have carried through all of Peter's reforms, and some things would have slipped backward. But, overall, not much would have changed. For one thing, Alexis was not a medieval Muscovite prince. He had been raised by Western tutors, he had studied and traveled often in the West, he had married a Western princess, his brother-in-law was the Holy Roman Emperor. Russia would not have hurtled back to the caftans, the beards and the terem. History may slow its pace, but it does not move backward.

Finally, it seems that at the end Alexis himself accepted the judgment of the court and of his father. He confessed and asked for pardon. His feeble, almost involuntary challenge to the towering Tsar had failed, his beloved Afrosina had betrayed and deserted him, he had been weakened by torture. Perhaps he simply withdrew from life as he had wished to withdraw from government into the country, too weary to continue, unable to go on with an existence dominated by this overwhelming man who was his father.

55

CHARLES'
LAST OFFENSIVE

WHEN PETER CALLED OFF the allied invasion of Sweden in September 1716, Charles XII could not know whether the landing had been permanently canceled or merely postponed until spring. Accordingly, he remained through the winter in the southernmost tip of Sweden, at Lund near Malmö, just across the sound from Copenhagen. The house in which he stayed belonged to a professor; to suit the King's taste, some of the rooms were enlarged and painted in the Swedish colors of blue and yellow. In the spring, a new well was dug, fresh vegetables were planted and two pools were created to be filled with fish fresh for Charles' table.

In this house, Charles was to live and work for almost two years. In the summer, his day began at three a.m., when the sun was already up and the sky filled with light. Until seven, he worked with his secretaries or received visitors. Then, whatever the weather, the King mounted his horse and rode until two, visiting and inspecting the numerous regiments stationed along the southern coast. Dinner, in mid-afternoon, was short and simple. Homemade marmalade was Charles' only delicacy, and this was regularly supplied by his younger sister, Ulrika, who made most of it herself. The table service was pewter, the silver service having long before been sold to raise money for the war. At nine p.m., the King lay down to sleep on a straw mattress.

During these quiet months, Charles had time to indulge his peaceful interests and curiosities. He attended lectures and enjoyed discussions with professors of mathematics and theology at the University of Lund. With his court architect, Tessin, he planned new palaces and public buildings to be constructed in the capital once peace had come. He designed new flags and uniforms for some of his regiments, prohibiting the color green—perhaps because that was the color worn by Peter's Russian soldiers. People found the King enormously changed from the headstrong, impetuous youth who had scandalized Sweden with his adolescent escapades; this was a gentler, more serene man who, at thirty-four, showed a wide tolerance of human

faults and weaknesses. And yet, in one overwhelmingly important matter, the King had not changed: Charles XII remained determined to continue the war.

Because of this, many Swedes found the King's return an unfortunate blessing. When Stralsund and Wismar fell, they were almost relieved, believing that the loss of these last fragments of empire meant that at last the war would end. Their desire for glory and even commercial profit had long since given way to an overpowering desire for peace. The King, aware of these feelings, explained his plans to Ulrika, herself torn between a desire for peace and loyalty to her brother: "This does not mean that I am against peace. I am in favor of a peace that is defensible in the eye of posterity. Most states are willing to see Sweden weaker than she was. We must rely on ourselves first and foremost." More war meant more men and more money, yet Sweden was devastated. Half the farmland was out of cultivation because there were no laborers. Fisheries were abandoned. Foreign trade was ruined by the blockade of the allied fleets; the number of Swedish merchant ships fell from 775 in 1697 to 209 in 1718.

In these circumstances, Charles XII's plans for a new military offensive sent men fleeing into the woods to avoid military service. They were dragged from church in the middle of services, brought up from the mines, carried off from public taverns. University students, even schoolboys, were conscripted. Some cut off a finger or shot themselves in a foot to avoid service, but a new edict decreed that they should be given thirty lashes and forced to serve anyway. (If they succeeded in disabling themselves beyond use as soldiers, they were given sixty lashes and assigned to compulsory labor as convicts.) As a result, a Dutch traveler in Sweden in 1719 found himself driven only by gray-haired men, women, or boys under twelve. "In the whole of Sweden, I have not seen a man between twenty and forty," he said. Old taxes were increased and new taxes were created. The tax on land was doubled and trebled, the tax on the post was increased and the tax on all luxuries—tea, coffee, chocolate, lace, silk, gold and silver ornaments, fur robes, smart hats and carriages—made them almost nonexistent.

It seemed impossible that even a king like Charles could extract the fresh reserves of money and manpower he was demanding from his exhausted and sullen country. That Charles was able to, was due to the appearance at his side of an extraordinary man who served him both as administrator at home and as diplomat overseas, the brilliant, unscrupulous, much maligned and eventually ill-fated Baron Georg Heinrich von Goertz, an audacious international adventurer without real ties of nationality but with a taste for power and a passion for intrigue. He had a complex, versatile intellect which allowed him to work on several divergent, even contradictory

schemes simultaneously. It has been said of him that "he achieved twenty times as much as Talleyrand or Metternich while working with less than one twentieth of their resources."

For four years—from 1714 to 1718—Goertz, armed with the power of the king, loomed over Sweden. In person, he was a dramatic figure, tall, handsome (in spite of an artificial eye, made of enamel, which replaced one lost in a student duel), charming and a brilliant conversationalist. Born in South Germany into a noble Franconian family, he studied at the University of Jena and then, seeking a situation in which his adventurous spirit could flower, he attached himself to the court of the young Duke Frederick IV of Holstein-Gottorp who had been Charles' madcap companion and had married Charles' sister, Hedwig Sophia. Shortly before the Duke went off to war at Charles' side, Hedwig Sophia produced a son, Charles Frederick. In 1702 at the Battle of Klissow, still at Charles' side, the Duke was killed, leaving his two-year-old son as his successor and Georg Heinrich von Goertz as the real ruler of Holstein-Gottorp. More important, until Charles XII married and produced a child, the infant Charles Frederick was the male heir to the throne of Sweden.

Goertz conducted all the duchy's affairs. He toured Europe, calling on the Tsar, Queen Anne, the King of Prussia and the Elector of Hanover. In 1713, he proposed to strengthen the duchy's position by a Russian alliance, the seal to be a marriage between the twelve-year-old Duke and Peter's oldest daughter, five-year-old Anne. Goertz once proposed to Menshikov the idea of cutting a ship canal through Holstein at the base of the Danish peninsula, thus giving Russian ships an exit from the Baltic into the North Sea without having to pass through the sound and subject themselves to Danish tolls or cannon.* It was Goertz who arranged for Magnus Stenbock's Swedish army, victorious at Gadebusch but being pursued by larger Saxon, Danish and Russian forces, to be admitted into the Holstein fortress of Tonning. And it was also Goertz who, five months later, when the besieged army could hold out no longer, arranged the terms of its surrender.

Successful though he was, in time Goertz came to feel that the little duchy of Holstein-Gottorp was too narrow an arena for his abilities. He had long admired Charles XII, the legendary uncle of his own young master, and when Charles appeared at Stralsund in November 1714 after his ride across Europe, Goertz hurried to meet him. In a single long conversation, he won Charles' favor and emerged an unofficial advisor. Before much more time had passed, Charles relied on him totally. He admired Goertz' energy, his breadth of vision, his analytical capacity and his willingness to attempt, like Charles himself, vast, grand-scale schemes and radical solutions even with limited resources. As Charles saw it, Goertz applied in administration

---

* One hundred and seventy-four years later, in 1887, the Kiel Canal was built.

and diplomacy the same dash and reckless bravado which the King employed in war.

Thereafter, until Charles' death, Goertz was indispensable to him. He took absolute control of Sweden's finances and all the great domestic departments of state. He became the King's voice, if not his brain, in Swedish diplomacy. By February 1716, he was describing himself as Director of the Finances and Commerce of Sweden. In effect, he became Charles' prime minister, although he held no actual rank or title in Sweden and was still nominally the servant of Charles' nephew, the Duke of Holstein-Gottorp.

Goertz knew how to deal with the King. As a condition for accepting service, he had won Charles' promise that all communications should be between themselves and not through intermediaries. He knew it was best not to bother Charles with details in areas in which the King was not interested. He found that if the King did not agree with him when presented with an oral argument, he could put his views in writing in his clear, incisive style and usually get his way.

As Sweden felt the resourceful, ruthless hand of Baron von Goertz, hatred of the King's foreign advisor spread through every class. Bureaucrats hated him because he exercised power outside the normal channels of administration. The Hessian party, formed around Charles' sister, Ulrika, and her husband, Frederick of Hesse, hated him because they imagined him working to ensure the succession for his young Holstein master, to their own exclusion. And Swedes everywhere hated him for the enthusiasm and ingenuity with which he set to work to wring more men and money from the exhausted nation to continue the war. He issued paper currency. He raised taxes higher and then higher still. He was accused of lining his own pockets, but these accusations were untrue—in money matters, Goertz was totally honest. He even spent his own small income in an effort to achieve more efficiency in mobilizing Swedish resources for the new war effort. In his commanding role, Goertz was called by furious Swedes "the Grand Vizier." Although he was known to be only a creature of the King, he was clothed in the King's power. For as long as Charles stood behind him, Goertz was invincible.

ALTHOUGH it was Goertz' domestic policies which infuriated the average Swede, he was even more useful to the King as a diplomat. He was a master of this subtle art, and Charles gave him a free hand to perform his juggling tricks all over Europe. This was Goertz' analysis of Sweden's situation: As Sweden could not possibly defeat all her enemies, she must make peace, and perhaps even an alliance, with one in order to fight the others. Either Charles could make peace with Russia and concentrate his efforts against Denmark, Prussia and Hanover, or he could make peace with Den-

mark, Prussia and Hanover and renew his attack on the Tsar in the upper Baltic. Goertz preferred the first alternative—peace with Russia. It meant sacrificing the provinces of Ingria, Karelia, Estonia, Livonia and possibly Finland, as well as acquiescence in a major Russian naval and commercial presence on the Baltic, but it would free Charles to win back the lost German provinces of Pomerania, Bremen and Verden and allow him perhaps to seize Mecklenburg and Norway as well. Goertz' preference may have been partly due to the fact that a reassertion of Swedish power in North Germany would be useful to his youthful master in Holstein-Gottorp, but Goertz was also now inclined to rate Peter's power and resolve as much greater than those of Russia's allies. Peter had demonstrated his tenacious determination to hold and expand his window on the Baltic. The growth of his fleet, the far-flung operations of his army and the Tsar's implacable will combined to suggest that even an enormous Swedish effort would not easily dislodge the Russians from their entrenched position on the Baltic coast.

Most leading Swedes, however, disagreed with Goertz. They were not unhappy to see the former German possessions go; they had always believed Sweden's position in the empire to be a source of weakness. If there had to be continued war, they preferred to make peace in Germany and to regain the Baltic provinces. The rich farmland of Livonia, called "the corn barn of Sweden," and the great port of Riga with its rich customs tolls from the Russian trade were assets which could be used directly to make up the great losses of wealth which Sweden had suffered in the war.

No matter which direction the Swedish offensive eventually took, the important thing was that simply by raising the idea of separate peace treaties and new alliances Goertz had placed the balance of power in the Baltic back in Charles' hands. As the months progressed, Goertz skillfully exploited this new situation, making it clear that from then on anything might be expected of Sweden in the way of new alignments and combinations. He negotiated with every one of Sweden's enemies except Denmark, for ultimately the Holsteiner meant to make Denmark pay the bill. It was a virtuoso performance. Overnight, his diplomacy transformed Sweden from a victim about to be overpowered by a grand coalition of powers into the initiator of events, able to choose which of the allies it would favor with peace and which would become the targets of its renewed offensive. Not since Poltava had Sweden held such power in Europe.

Already Goertz had tested the bonds of the anti-Swedish alliance and found them remarkably weak. All of Peter's allies were apprehensive about Russia's growing strength, but the weakest point in the coalition lay in the personal antagonism between Peter and King George I of England, who was also Elector of Hanover. Knowing this, Goertz began negotiating simultaneously with both, aware that when one monarch heard he was treating with the other, it would automatically improve Goertz' hand with both. He

went first to Peter, meeting the Tsar in Holland in June 1716. Peter respected him, although when Goertz was directing only the affairs of tiny Holstein, his dreams of turning kingdoms and empires around his finger made the Tsar laugh; to the Holstein envoy Bassewitz, Peter once said, "Your court, directed by the vast schemes of Goertz, seems to me like a skiff carrying the mast of a man-of-war—the least side-wind will upset it." But the same man managing the diplomacy of Sweden was a different matter. At their meeting, Peter and Goertz discussed the idea of a new balance in Northern Europe based on an alliance between Sweden and Russia, to be guaranteed by France. In the peace, Russia would restore Finland to Sweden but keep all her other conquests, while Sweden would be free to regain whatever she could from Denmark and Hanover. Goertz knew that Charles would never cede as much territory as Peter demanded; nevertheless, he was pleased by the Tsar's willingness to negotiate at all, and before their conference ended, they had agreed that a formal peace conference should be convened as soon as possible in the Aland Islands in the Gulf of Bothnia, islands being thought more inaccessible to spies.

News of this interview was diligently spread by Goertz' agents through Europe. Both George I of England and Frederick IV of Denmark were alarmed, although George claimed that Peter would never make peace without keeping Riga and he thought it impossible that Charles XII would agree to give it up. Nevertheless, as Goertz had foreseen, all of Sweden's enemies were now eager to come to terms. George I dispatched an envoy to Charles at Lund declaring that if Sweden would cede Bremen and Verden to Hanover, he would help Charles drive the Russians out of the Baltic. Charles refused.

The proposed invasion of Scania suspended the idea of direct negotiations between Russia and Sweden, but once the invasion had itself been suspended, Goertz proceeded with his plan. He discussed it with Prince Kurakin in Holland in the summer of 1717, and the Russian confirmed the Tsar's willingness to go ahead. In fact, Peter wanted the negotiations to begin as soon as possible, although during the winter and spring of 1718 the most dangerous and important problem facing Peter was not the negotiations with Sweden but his relationship with his son, a drama which deeply overshadowed the effort to bring the war to an end. Partly for this reason, it was not until May that the two sides faced each other across a table.

The Aland Islands, a group of 6,500 red-granite islets in the middle of the Gulf of Bothnia, are carpeted with pine forests and grassy meadows. On Lofo, two large barns were built to house the two delegations. Originally, Peter had suggested that the negotiations be conducted informally, with no ceremonies and modest accommodations; he even suggested that the two sides live in a single house, each side having a room but with no wall

between them so that they could work efficiently. This was not at all what the Swedes had in mind, and Goertz arrived on Lofo with a suite of gentlemen, secretaries, servants and soldiers and a table service and silver borrowed from the Duke of Holstein.

The Swedish delegation was led by Goertz and Count Gyllenborg, the Swedish ambassador in London. Across the table, the Russians were led by General James Bruce, a Scot who had proved himself in the Finnish campaign and by the Councilor for Foreign Affairs, Andrew Osterman. Osterman, a Westphalian brought to Russia by Vice Admiral Cruys, was one of the ablest of all the foreigners who made their careers in Russia during Peter's reign. He spoke German, Dutch, French, Italian and Latin as well as Russian; he had accompanied Shafirov and Peter on the Pruth expedition and assisted in the negotiations with the Grand Vizier; in 1714, he had journeyed to Berlin to help persuade the Prussians to join the alliance against Sweden.

Now it was a major test of his skill to be pitted against Goertz (although Bruce was nominally the leader of the Russian delegation, Osterman provided the real diplomatic skills). In a sense, it was ironic: Here were two Germans—Osterman born in Westphalia and Goertz born in Franconia—sitting across a table bargaining on behalf of Russia and Sweden. Goertz, at fifty-one, was the older and more experienced, but he represented the waning power of Sweden, whereas Osterman, thirty-two but no less skillful, represented the waxing power of Russia.

The basis of the negotiations as understood by both sides was that Goertz would seek a peace with Russia which would enable Sweden to regain some of its territories lost to Peter while freeing it to act against its adversaries in North Germany. Peter was generally agreeable; he had seized more Swedish territory than he needed or desired and was willing to give some of it back in return for a peace treaty which would confirm his right to keep the rest. Despite this general agreement, the specific proposals and instructions from their monarchs which the two negotiating teams carried in their pockets were so far apart that, unless a diplomatic miracle occurred, there could be no treaty. Thus, as a preliminary condition for negotiations Bruce and Osterman demanded Swedish cession of Karelia, Estonia, Ingria and Livonia; only Finland west of Vyborg was negotiable. Goertz had heard these conditions the previous summer from Kurakin in Holland, but, knowing what Charles' reaction would be, he had never dared present them to the King; his tactic, instead, was to persuade Charles first to agree to negotiations and then lead him gradually into whatever concessions were necessary. In fact, when he arrived at Lofo, Goertz brought signed instructions from Charles XII which, had he laid them on the table, would have terminated the peace conference immediately. For Charles de-

manded that Russia not only restore all conquered provinces to Sweden in exactly the state in which they had been before the war began, but also pay to Sweden an indemnity for having begun an "unjust war."

In these opening sessions, Goertz played his weak hand brilliantly. By the princely pomp with which he surrounded himself, by the nonchalance with which he affected to listen to Russian proposals as if Charles rather than Peter were the victor, he established a strong psychological base from which to present his case. Further, he skillfully exploited the fact that Sweden was now the crux of all diplomacy in the North. Bruce and Osterman knew that, concurrently with the negotiations in the Aland Islands, Charles was also negotiating with George I. Goertz insinuated that those negotiations, which could only have an anti-Russian outcome, were rapidly approaching a favorable conclusion. Under this kind of pressure, the Russian negotiators backed away from their own preconditions and Osterman offered a modified settlement in which Russia would restore all of Livonia and Finland, being allowed to keep only Ingria, Karelia and Estonia. At the end of this first round of talks, the dispute had narrowed to the issue of the port of Reval (Tallinn); the Swedes insisted it be returned as necessary to control Finland, and the Russians equally firmly refused to return it, saying that without this port which commanded the entrance to the Gulf of Finland, the Tsar's fleet and merchant trade would be at Sweden's mercy.

In the middle of June, as Goertz was returning to Sweden to consult with Charles, Osterman, on Peter's instructions, privately promised Goertz that if a treaty was worked out which the Tsar could sign, Peter's gratitude would take the form of the finest sable cloak anyone had ever seen plus 100,000 thalers. Goertz reported to Charles, who, as he expected, rejected the terms as much too favorable to Russia and sent him back to Lofo to reopen negotiations.

Goertz returned in mid-July bearing a set of new and astonishing proposals which, it turned out, came only from Goertz, not from Charles. As he explained his scheme privately to Osterman, Sweden would cede Ingria and Livonia to Russia and Karelia and Estonia would be discussed later. The other ingredient of the plan was a new Swedish-Russian military alliance in which the Tsar should help the King to conquer Norway, Mecklenburg, Bremen, Verden and even parts of Hanover. For Peter, this would mean war with Denmark and Hanover. Osterman's initial reaction was that the Tsar would not fight as an open ally of Sweden; however, in return for Swedish territorial concessions, he might provide 20,000 men and eight men-of-war to Charles as "auxiliaries." Interestingly, Osterman added that should such a plan be agreed on, Peter would want a special clause inserted in the treaty by which Charles bound himself not to expose

his person to danger in military campaigns, as the success of the plan obviously depended on the Swedish King being able to command. Goertz went jubilantly back to Charles, while Osterman returned to St. Petersburg to consult with the Tsar. But Goertz' triumph was brief. Charles serenely rejected all that Goertz and Osterman had tentatively agreed to, on the grounds that the Baltic provinces could not be ceded for such uncertain and illusory gains in Germany. At last, making a slight concession to Goertz, the King declared that while he might permit the Tsar to keep Karelia and Ingria, which had once belonged to Russia, Peter must "naturally give up Livonia, Estonia and Finland, which had been conquered in an unjust war." "Good," said Goertz in a bitter aside to another Swedish minister, "but there is one little difficulty—that the Tsar will never give them back." Once again, Charles sent Goertz back to negotiate, with almost nothing to offer. "My mission," he said as he departed, "is to fool the Russians if they are big enough fools to be fooled."

Goertz' position was becoming increasingly vulnerable. His plan had been based on the assumption of a speedy and acceptable peace with either Russia or Hanover or both, which the majority of Swedes would accept; otherwise, as he well knew, he personally would be blamed for the resumption of the war. Returning to Lofo, Goertz heard Peter's reply to his own earlier offer: The Tsar would not change any of his earlier territorial demands, and he refused to join Sweden in any alliance against Frederick IV of Denmark or Frederick William of Prussia. He would be willing to supply Charles with 20,000 Russian soldiers and eight men-of-war to serve under Swedish colors in a campaign against Hanover. Finally, Osterman told Goertz that the Tsar was wearying of Swedish procrastination and had declared that if a treaty were not arranged during the month of December, the peace conference would be terminated. Goertz, pledging his word of honor that he would return within four weeks, went again to consult with Charles, who by this time was with his army in Norway.

Four weeks passed, but Goertz did not reappear. In the final days of December, a courier arrived from Stockholm with news that plunged the Swedish delegation into confusion and dismay: Goertz had been arrested; all ships in Stockholm harbor were forbidden to leave, and all correspondence abroad was being held. Ten days passed without further news. Then, on January 3, a Swedish captain arrived, and the following morning the Swedish delegates informed Osterman and Bruce that while besieging a town in Norway, King Charles XII had been killed.

FROM LOFO, Osterman had written to Peter, putting his finger on a major potential flaw in the negotiations: the possibility that Charles might not be

there to sign any treaty. The King, Osterman feared, "through his fool-hardy actions some time or other will either be killed or break his neck riding at a gallop." Osterman's worries were well grounded. The truth was that during the summer of 1718, even as Goertz shuttled back and forth to the Aland Islands bearing offers and counter-offers to the Russians, making peace with Peter was far from Charles' mind. As always, the King relied on his sword far more than on the diplomatic intrigues of Goertz to break out of the impasse in which he found himself. For Charles, therefore, the Aland talks were valuable primarily as a device for gaining time; by conducting negotiations, Charles made sure that the Russians would not attack his coast that summer and drain away the strength of his new army in efforts to repulse these raids.

In planning his strategy, Charles accepted the fact that, for the moment, Russia was too strong—no frontal attack on the Russian Baltic could dislodge the Tsar from these conquered territories. The first opponent would be Denmark. He would begin with a campaign to seize southern Norway, then cross to Zealand and Jutland to knock Denmark out of the war. From there, his army would pass south to reconquer Bremen and Verden and his 50,000 Swedes would be joined by 16,000 Hessians, supplied by his brother-in-law, Frederick of Hesse. At the head of this force, he would either impose a peace on, or invade, Hanover, Prussia and Saxony, according to the preference of their rulers. Finally, with the Swedish position in Germany once more secure, he could march again on Russia—unless, of course, the Tsar desired to give back the lands he had unjustly taken. All of this, Charles said, might take "forty years of war," but "it would be much more harmful to Sweden to agree to a hard and insecure general peace than to accept a long war conducted outside the frontiers of Sweden proper."

The first objective was Norway, and 43,000 troops were designated for this campaign. An invasion force thrust toward Trondheim in August 1718, and the King marched on Kristiania (Oslo) in October. Moving through the hilly, sparsely populated country west of the Swedish border, the army waded or swam the rivers and stormed the hastily erected defenses thrown up by the Norwegians in the mountain passes. By November 5, the main army had arrived before Frederiksten, a strongly held fortress on the road to Kristiania. Charles brought up his heavy cannon, and a classical siege operation began.

From the beginning of the campaign, Charles was aware that this was his last army and he spared nothing, least of all his own comfort or personal safety, to inspire in his men a courageous fatalism and a willingness to obey any command that was given. Charles resolved to ask nothing of his officers and men which he was not willing to do himself; if the King was seen taking dire risks, every man would follow. Thus, on November 27, the King himself led 200 grenadiers up storm ladders to capture Gyldenløve, an

outwork of the Frederiksten fortress. Thereafter, he remained with the front-line troops. Although the main headquarters of the Swedish army was at Tistedal, Charles ate and slept in a small wooden hut near Gyldenløve, just behind the first trenches.

On the afternoon of November 30, Charles rode to army headquarters. Staff officers at Tistedal noticed that he seemed preoccupied and sad, and that he burned some of the papers he sorted. He put on fresh linen, a clean uniform, boots and gloves, and at four p.m. swung back into the saddle, waved his hat in farewell and returned to the front. His servant Hultman brought his supper, and Charles seemed relaxed. "Your food is so good, I'll promote you to Master Cook," he bantered. The easy relationship between the two permitted the cook to say, "I'll have that in writing, Sire."

After supper, Charles returned to the front-line trench to observe the digging of further assault trenches which was going on steadily every night, using darkness to shield the diggers from the enemy. A party of 400 soldiers had begun at dusk, working with spades and picks, and carrying bundles of twigs for protection. The Norwegians hung out wreaths of burning pitch on the fortress ramparts and shot fire bombs from their cannon to light the surrounding landscape. By this illumination, sharpshooters on the fortress walls kept up a steady fire at the Swedish soldiers toiling before the trenches, well within musket range. Their fire was accurate; between six o'clock and ten o'clock they killed seven Swedish soldiers and wounded fifteen.

At about nine-thirty p.m. Charles, who was in the deep front-line trench with some of his officers, decided to climb up the side to see what was happening. He kicked two footholds into the earth of the side of the trench and clambered up until his arms rested on the parapet. His head and shoulders were above the breastwork, exposed to the musket balls whistling about. His aides, standing below in the trench, their heads on a level with the King's knees, were worried. "It is not a fit place for Your Majesty," said one, urging him to come down. But those who knew him best hushed the others, saying, "Let him be. The more you warn him, the more he will expose himself."

The night was thick and cloudy, but the flares burning on the fortress walls and the frequent Norwegian fire bombs gave some light. Charles, leaning on the top of the trench, his shoulders wrapped in his cloak, his head supported by his left hand on his cheek, was clearly visible to the Swedish working party out in front of the trench. He remained in this position a long time while his officers debated how to get him down. But the King was in a good mood. "Don't be frightened," he said and stayed where he was, looking out over the top of the trench.

Suddenly, the men below heard a special sound, as if "a stone had been thrown with great force into mud," or "the sound one hears when one slaps two fingers sharply against the palm of one's hand." Afterward, there was no

movement from Charles except that his hand fell from his left cheek. He remained above them, supported by the breastwork. Then, an officer below realized that something had happened. "Lord Jesus," he cried, "the King is shot!" Charles was lowered into the trench, where the horrified officers found that a musket ball had pierced the King's left temple, traveled through the skull and exited from the right side of his head. He had died instantly.

To give themselves time to think, the officers posted guards at the entrances to the trench. A stretcher was brought and the body placed on it with two cloaks spread over the corpse to hide its identity. Twelve guardsmen, unaware of the importance of their burden, carried the King out of the trench and down a road to the rear, but one of the guardsmen stumbled, the stretcher tipped and the cloak over the upper part of the body fell off. Just at that moment, the clouds parted overhead and the moon shone through onto the dead face. The horrified soldiers instantly recognized their King.

Charles' death had an immediate, decisive effect not only on the siege, but on the entire war plan of which the Norwegian campaign was to have been only a prologue. Even the Norwegian defenders of Frederiksten realized that something had happened. "Immediately everything became so quiet not only the whole night through, but even the next day," said one. In fact, once the stunned Swedish commanders met at Tistedal headquarters later that night, there seemed nothing to do; without Charles, his leadership and inspiration, even the war seemed meaningless. Two days later, the generals solemnly abandoned the Norwegian campaign. The soldiers were withdrawn from the trenches, and the supply wagons, one carrying the King's body, rumbled back across the hills into Sweden. After an absence of eighteeen years, Charles XII finally returned to Stockholm. The body was embalmed and lay in state at the Carlberg Palace.

He had been away so long and was responsible for so many burdens of war that the general population did not mourn. But those who knew him were brokenhearted. His nephew, Duke Charles Frederick of Holstein, wrote to the Council in Stockholm, "This nearly unbearable sorrow touches my heart [so deeply that] I can write no more." The King's tutor and comrade-in-arms, Field Marshal Rehnskjold, recently returned to Sweden in an exchange of officers, described "this inimitable king" filled with wisdom, courage, grace and gentleness, who had died so young. "We shall miss him when success comes," said Rehnskjold. "To see him lie dead before our eyes is grief indeed."

The funeral was held in Storkyrkan, the cathedral in which Charles had been crowned, and then the body was transferred to the Riddarhom Church, the burial place of Swedish kings and queens. He lies there now in a black

marble sarcophagus covered with a bronze lion's skin and surmounted by a crown and a scepter. Opposite Charles, on the other side of the church, is the Italian marble sarcophagus of Sweden's other legendary military hero, Gustavus Adolphus. Over their heads, the church is hung with hundreds of military standards and banners captured in their wars, now faded and slowly crumbling into dust.

56

KING GEORGE
ENTERS THE BALTIC

PETER WAS STANDING with a group of officers when he heard the news of the death of his great antagonist. His eyes filled with tears; wiping them away, he said, "My dear Charles, how much I pity you," and ordered the Russian court into mourning for a week. In Sweden, the succession was quickly resolved. Had she lived, the King's older sister, Hedwig, Duchess of Holstein, would have succeeded him, but Hedwig had died in 1708 and her claim had passed to her son, the young Duke Charles Frederick, who was eighteen at his uncle's death. The other claimant was Charles' younger sister, Ulrika Eleonora, now thirty years old and married to Frederick, Duke of Hesse. For several years, as young Charles Frederick grew older, the two parties had been antagonistic, each trying to position itself favorably in case anything should happen to the King.

As long as he lived, the King had steadfastly refused to choose between his nephew and his sister and proclaim an heir. He may have believed, of course, that one day he would marry and beget an heir. Meanwhile, he wished to have the affection and support of both Ulrika and Charles Frederick. He kept the young Duke at his side and took special care to train him in the military arts. He wrote regularly to Ulrika and designated her husband as one of his principal advisors and commanders. Time enough in the future to make a choice which would painfully alienate one of these beloved kinsmen.

Frederick of Hesse, Ulrika's husband, was more realistic. Before the Norwegian campaign, he had given his wife a list of the actions she was to take if the King should suddenly die: Ulrika was to proclaim herself queen, have herself crowned and ruthlessly arrest any who opposed her. And so it happened. Charles Frederick, like Frederick of Hesse, was with the King in Norway when the fatal bullet struck, and Ulrika mounted the throne unopposed. At first, young Charles Frederick was too brokenhearted to resist or even to greatly care and when he awoke to consider his situation, events had passed him by. Thereafter, the older and more experienced

Frederick of Hesse easily convinced him that his duty lay in allegiance to his Aunt Ulrika, now Queen of Sweden.

The figure most abruptly and drastically affected by the King's death was Goertz. The morning after Charles fell, Frederick of Hesse dispatched two officers to arrest Goertz "in the King's name." Goertz, who had the same day returned from the Aland Islands with news of his latest negotiations with the Russians, was astonished, asking, "Does the King still live?" His papers and money were seized and, for fear that he might attempt suicide, he was not allowed a knife and fork. He passed the night reading and wrote a short letter to his relatives declaring his innocence.

For six weeks, with Goertz imprisoned, articles of impeachment were carefully drawn to make sure there was no possibility of escape. His captors feared that if he were tried for treason before the regular high court of justice, he might win acquittal by arguing that the court had no jurisdiction as he was not a Swedish subject. Further, Goertz could argue truthfully that as a servant of the King, not of the state, he had acted by the absolute authority of Charles himself. He could also argue that nothing he had done had been on his own behalf; he had not enriched himself by so much as a penny.

Nevertheless, Sweden was determined to destroy him. A special extra-judicial commission was appointed to try him. He was charged with a crime new in Swedish law: "having alienated the late King's affection from his people." He was accused of misusing the King's confidence by suggesting to Charles measures harmful to Sweden, such as continuing the war. From the beginning, Goertz was doomed; in vain, he protested the lack of jurisdiction of the special commission. His claim that he was an alien and untouchable was rejected. His petition to have legal counsel was refused as unnecessary. He was not allowed to call his own witnesses or to confront hostile witnesses. He was not allowed to develop his defense in writing or to bring notes into the courtroom. He was given only a day and a half to prepare his reply, which permitted him time to read only one fifth of the evidence presented against him. Inevitably, he was found guilty, and unanimously he was condemned to be beheaded and his body buried under the scaffold, a mark of special contempt. He received the sentence with composure, but petitioned that his body might be spared this final disgrace. Grimly, Ulrika ordered the entire sentence carried out. Goertz mounted the scaffold with courage and dignity and said, "You bloodthirsty Swedes, take then the head you have thirsted for so long." As he laid his head on the block, his last words were, "Lord, into thy hands I commend my spirit." His head fell at the first blow, and his body was buried on the spot.*

* In life, Goertz shared many qualities with the other great international adventurer of the age, Patkul. Both came from obscure backgrounds, possessed enormous talents

With the sudden, violent elimination of both Charles XII and Goertz from the helm of the Swedish state, many in Sweden and elsewhere quite naturally expected a radical change. It was true that the King's death had led to a swift termination of the Norwegian campaign, and presumably to the vast continental enterprises of which Charles XII had dreamed. But, strangely, as the weeks and months went by, the end of the Great Northern War seemed no closer. On ascending the throne, the new Queen, Ulrika Eleonora, wrote to Peter that she desired peace. The Tsar replied that although he would not give up his earlier demand to keep Livonia, he was now prepared to pay a million roubles to Sweden in return for cession of the province. Ulrika rejected this offer and presented new demands. On this note, the negotiations foundered, and Bruce and Osterman withdrew from the Aland Islands conference.

Behind this continued reticence in the Swedish monarchy over making peace lay a rising hope that Sweden might win back by diplomacy some of what she had lost in war. In the shadows, only dimly perceived from St. Petersburg, which had deliberately been kept uninformed, a whole new structure of Baltic alliances was taking shape. Goertz had participated in these negotiations and Charles XII had approved them. Now, both the warrior and the diplomat were dead, but the diplomatic game continued. And the chief player was the hard-headed, obstinate German, King George I of England—brave, shy, some said stupid, but a man who, when he had fixed on an object, would go to any lengths to achieve it. Peter had met him twenty years before during his Great Embassy and several times in the years that followed, and did not much like him, but he could never ignore him. For during the final years of the Great Northern War, the key to ending the struggle lay—or at least seemed to lie—in George's pudgy hands.

THE FOG ON THE THAMES was so thick on the morning of September 29, 1714, that the new King of England could not sail up the river and step ashore in his new capital. Instead, his ship, flanked by English and Dutch men-of-war, anchored below Greenwich, and George was rowed ashore through the blinding, wet mist. There, standing before the colonnade of Wren's magnificent Royal Naval Hospital, the noble personages of England, Whig and Tory alike, waited for him in their best velvet and satin. The

---

and were willing to take great risks. As a result, each played a distinctive role in the history of their time. Their allegiances were different: Patkul was the adroit and hated enemy of Charles XII; Goertz was the King's devoted minister and servant. But they shared the same end: Both died in degradation under a Swedish axe.

King stepped from the boat and greeted his new subjects, a ceremony complicated by the fact that the new monarch spoke no English and few of his subjects spoke German. To the Duke of Marlborough, humiliated by Queen Anne and her Tory ministers, the King made a special effort to be gracious. "My dear Duke," he said in French, which Marlborough also spoke, "I hope now you have seen the end of your troubles."

The arrival of a foreign prince to mount the throne was becoming almost routine in England. Three times it had happened in scarcely more than a century as James I, William III and now George I had been imported to preserve the Protestant religion.* George Louis' claim to the English throne traced back through his mother, a granddaughter of James I, but the truth is that he came reluctantly. As Elector of Hanover, he governed one of the principal German states of the Holy Roman Empire, rich in agriculture and minor industry. Hanover was only one tenth as large as Great Britain both in area and in population. Its army had been hardened in eleven years of war against the French, and the Elector had served with Marlborough and Prince Eugene as one of the principal allied commanders. In the scales of European power, Hanover weighed about as much as Denmark, Prussia or Saxony. It was a thriving, pleasant, proud little state.

George Louis accepted the English throne for much the same reason that the Prince of Orange had accepted it twenty-six years before: to ensure English support for his own continental ambitions. As Elector of Hanover, George Louis was a significant personage in Europe, but as King of England, he would be one of Europe's overlords, more powerful than his nominal master, the Hapsburg Emperor.

Two days after his landing at Greenwich, when George I made his public entry into London, the people of England got a look at their new King. He was a short man, fifty-four years old, with the white skin and the bulging blue eyes which were to mark many of his royal descendants over the next two centuries. Bred a soldier, a brave and competent if not brilliant commander, his habits were those of the army, his tastes simple and homey. He disliked his new subjects. Unlike the docile Germans, the English were proud, touchy, argumentative and held stubbornly to the belief that their monarchs must share power with Parliament. As often as he could, George left England for Hanover, and once there, to the distress of his English ministers, he stayed for months at a time. Deliberately, he showed his disdain for his new subjects by never troubling to learn their language. The English, for their part, disliked George, complaining about

---

* "England," said Viscount Bolingbroke, "would as soon have a Turk as a Roman Catholic for its king."

his dullness, his coldness, his German ministers and his ugly mistresses. Only his religion appealed to them, and even here he was Lutheran, not Anglican.

In London, the King avoided ceremony whenever possible. He lived in two rooms, where he was looked after by two Turkish servants whom he had captured in his campaigns as an imperial general. His favorite companions were his two German mistresses, one tall, thin and bony, the other so corpulent that the London crowd dubbed them "The Elephant and Castle." He was fond of cards and often went to the house of a friend where he could play in private with his few cronies. He loved music and was an enthusiastic admirer of George Frederick Handel, who emigrated from Germany to England largely at the urging of this royal patron.

He hated his son. The King's eyes blazed with fury and his face turned purple whenever the Prince of Wales appeared. By every possible means, he directed snubs toward his heir. Such treatment reduced the Prince to paroxysms of rage, but all he could do was to wait. Meanwhile, the King seized his son's children and forbade him to appear at court. The go-between for these two irreconcilable men was the King's daughter-in-law, Caroline of Anspach, Princess of Wales, a blue-eyed, flaxen-haired beauty with a superb and ample figure, great intelligence and earthy wit. She was the kind of woman whom the King most admired, and the fact that she was married to his hated son only deepened his antipathy toward the younger man.

Upon ascending the English throne, George I had every intention of using the great power of England to serve the purposes of Hanover. He had long looked with envy at the Swedish-held duchies of Bremen and Verden, which commanded the estuaries of the Elbe and Weser rivers and thus cut his Hanoverian dominions off from the North Sea. Now, with the Swedish empire seeming on the verge of collapse, he wanted to be present when the spoils were divided. Thus it was that in 1715, Hanover—but not England—entered the anti-Swedish alliance. As Vasily Dolgoruky, Peter's ambassador in Copenhagen, explained this confusing situation to the Tsar: "Although the English King has declared war on Sweden, it is only as Elector of Hanover, and the English fleet has sailed [to the Baltic] only to protect its merchants. If the Swedish fleet attacks the Russian fleet of Your Majesty, it is not to be thought that the English will engage the Swedes."

Despite this qualification, Peter, whose policy for years had been to bring both Hanover and England into the war against Sweden, was delighted. And when he heard that the British Admiral Sir John Norris had arrived in the Baltic commanding eighteen ships-of-the-line escorting 106 merchantmen, the Tsar was overjoyed. On Norris' first call at Reval, the Tsar was at Kronstadt, but, hearing of the British visit and that Norris would be back, Peter hurried to Reval with a Russian squadron. When the

British Admiral returned, he found Peter there with nineteen Russian ships-of-the-line. Norris remained for three weeks while the admirals and officers of the two fleets entertained each other with gala festivities. Catherine and most of Peter's court were also present and dined with Norris aboard his flagship. During the visit, Peter examined the British ships from keel to topmast and Norris was allowed to freely inspect the Russian vessels. He saw three new sixty-gun ships built in St. Petersburg which he described as "in every way equal to the best of that rank in our country and more handsomely furnished." At the end of the visit, Peter enthusiastically offered Norris command of the Russian navy, and although the Admiral declined, the Tsar gave his visitor his royal portrait set in diamonds.

Every summer thereafter until the death of Charles XII (in all, the summers of 1715, 1716, 1717 and 1718), Norris returned to the Baltic with a British squadron and the same orders: not to engage the Swedes unless British ships were attacked. In 1716, Norris' squadron was part of the combined allied fleet assembled to cover the invasion of Scania, and if the Swedish fleet had appeared, British cannon would have opened fire. But the Swedish fleet remained in port, and in September Peter postponed the invasion.

As seen from London, Charles' death in November 1718 created an entirely new situation in the Baltic. Until then, George I's interest had been permanent Hanoverian possession of Bremen and Verden, and the British Cabinet had been concerned about protection of British merchant trade and an assured flow of naval supplies from the Baltic. Both parties had also worried about the possibility of Charles XII offering support to a Jacobite uprising in England against the Hanoverian King. But Charles' death eliminated these fears and enabled the King and his ministers to reassess the underlying change which was taking place in the North: the decline of the Swedish empire and its replacement in the Baltic by the growing power of Russia.

King George I conceived a plan which, if successful, would profit both England and Hanover; the Baltic would be made safe for British trade and the continued, unmolested flow of naval stores and also the possession of Bremen and Verden would be guaranteed to Hanover not just by right of conquest but by formal cession from the Swedish crown. George's goal was the preservation of sufficient Swedish power "so that the Tsar should not grow too powerful in the Baltic." His means was to be a complete reversal of the alliance system in the Baltic. Sweden in 1718 stood alone against a powerful assembly of states: Russia, Poland, Denmark, Hanover and Prussia. This alignment would now be reversed. First, Sweden would be induced to make peace with all of her enemies in the lower Baltic, then a general league of Germanic powers would together march on the Tsar and drive him away from the northern sea. Initially, the peace would be

expensive for Sweden: All of its German possessions would be divided among Hanover, Prussia, Denmark and Poland. In return, however, these states would become Sweden's allies, helping it to recover all it had lost to the Tsar. Sweden was to receive back Livonia, Estonia and Finland, giving up only St. Petersburg, Narva and Kronstadt. If Peter refused these terms, still harsher ones would be imposed: He would be deprived of all his conquests and, in addition, forced to cede Smolensk and Kiev to Poland. In sum, Russia, until then the apparent victor in the war, having gained the most territory, would now become the loser and would pay for the peace. Hanover and Prussia, which had entered the war late and done almost no fighting, would become the real victors.

In its initial stages, George I's plan was brilliantly successful. One by one, through skillful diplomacy, Peter's allies were stripped away, bribed or pressured into making a separate peace with Sweden. Fittingly, Hanover was the first in this parade. On November 20, 1719, George I, as Elector of Hanover, signed a formal treaty of peace with Sweden. By the treaty, Hanover obtained permanent cession of Bremen and Verden on payment of one million thalers. Two months later, as King of England, the same George I signed an alliance with Sweden by which England was to pay a subsidy of 300,000 thalers per year for as long as the war with Russia lasted, to assist Sweden with a British fleet in the Baltic, and to help Sweden reach a favorable peace with Russia.

King Frederick William of Prussia was highly uncomfortable about the English proposition, as he considered himself a friend of the Tsar and had only recently—in August 1718—signed a new alliance with Peter. But he was strongly, and in the end decisively, tempted by the promise of permanent cession of the port of Stettin, which gave his kingdom access to the sea, plus a piece of Swedish Pomerania. As a salve to his conscience, Frederick William kept the negotiations completely aboveboard. He informed the Russians of every detail of his discussions with the English, and endeavored to convince Golovkin and, later, Tolstoy, whom Peter sent especially to Berlin, that the new treaty would not be harmful to Russia. Even after a treaty of peace was finally signed between Prussia and Sweden on January 21, 1720, the King signed a declaration that he would never act against the interests or territory of his friend Peter.*

---

* Frederick William's distress at the role he found himself playing is displayed in an emotional memorandum he wrote before the treaty was signed: "Would to God that I had not promised to conclude the treaty. It is an evil spirit which has moved me. Now we shall be ruined, which is what my false friends wish. May God take me from this evil world before I sign it, for here on earth there is nothing but falsehood and deceit. I will explain to Golovkin that I must wear the cloak on both shoulders. To have the Tsar at my hand is my interest and if I give him money I can have as many troops as

Denmark was cajoled into peace with Sweden by the combined influence of English money and the Royal Navy. An armistice was signed on October 19, 1719, and a Swedish-Danish peace treaty on July 3, 1720. Sweden agreed henceforth to pay tolls for Swedish ships passing through the sound and to give up all support for the Duke of Holstein-Gottorp. Then, King Augustus, who had helped instigate the Great Northern War and whose persuasion had turned the Tsar against Sweden, signed a treaty of peace with Sweden on December 27, 1719. No territory changed hands, but by its terms Augustus was confirmed in his title of King of Poland, while Stanislaus, the other candidate for that title, was allowed to wander about Europe calling himself King Stanislaus.

To Russia, King George I and his English ministers explained all these changes as merely the results of a British effort to mediate peace in the North. The Russians understood better. In the summer of 1719, Fedor Veselovsky, the Tsar's ambassador in London, called on General Lord James Stanhope, who conducted the foreign policy of the British government. Speaking bluntly, Veselovsky warned Stanhope that any alliance, even defensive in nature, between England and Sweden would be regarded as an English declaration of war against Russia. Stanhope protested that Russia should show more appreciation for the important services which England had rendered to the Tsar during the war.

"What services has England rendered to Russia in the present war?" retorted Veselovsky.

"England," said Stanhope, "has allowed the Tsar to make great conquests and establish himself on the Baltic and besides has sent her fleet and assisted his undertakings."

"England," replied Veselovsky, "allowed His Majesty to make conquests because she had no means of preventing him, though she had no wish to aid him and from circumstances was obliged to remain neutral. She sent her fleet to the Baltic for the protection of her own trade and to defend the King of Denmark in consequence of treaty obligations to him."

The primary means of executing England's new anti-Russian policy was to be the presence of a strong British fleet in the Baltic. The commander of the fleet would be the same Admiral Sir John Norris who for

---

I wish. The Tsar will make just such a treaty with me. With the English everything is deceit, just as in the most rascally way they deceived me in 1715. I pray God to stand by me if I must play an odd part, but I play it unwillingly for it is not one for an honest man." The King concluded that his predicament should "teach my successors to guard against accepting such friends, and not to follow my wicked, Godless maxims in this treaty, but to stick to friends that one once has, and to turn away from false friends. Therefore, I exhort my posterity to keep a still stronger army than I have; on this I shall live and die."

four years had commanded the British squadron in those waters. Now Norris' orders were to reverse course and switch friendships. The Admiral's secret instructions from Stanhope were to offer the mediation of Great Britain between the warring parties, Russia and Sweden.

In July 1719, Admiral Norris' great ships sailed through the sound into the Baltic, steering northeast for Stockholm, entering the Skargard and anchoring off the Swedish capital. Norris went ashore with letters for the Queen, and on July 14 Queen Ulrika dined aboard Norris' flagship. On this occasion she informed the Admiral that Sweden accepted the British offer.

The Russians, naturally, viewed the arrival of this British fleet with suspicion and apprehension. When it appeared in the Baltic, Peter inquired as to its purpose and demanded that Norris assure him he had no hostile intentions, otherwise British ships would not be permitted to approach the Russian coastline. The English purpose became clearer when letters from Norris and Lord Carteret, the English ambassador in Stockholm, addressed to the Tsar, were delivered. These English letters all but commanded the Tsar to make peace with Sweden, announcing that the British fleet was in the Baltic not only to protect trade but to "support mediation." Bruce and Osterman, finding the language of the English Minister and Admiral "unusual and insolent," refused to forward the letters to the Tsar, suggesting that in a matter of such importance King George should write to Peter himself. Hearing of the letters, Peter was indignant. He had no intention of accepting the mediation of a monarch who, as Elector of Hanover, was now an active ally of Sweden. To manifest his displeasure, the Tsar ordered both James Jefferyes, now English ambassador to Russia, and Weber, the Hanoverian representative, to leave St. Petersburg.

WHILE the complicated diplomatic maneuvers of George I and his English ministers were taking place behind his back, Peter proceeded straightforwardly to try to beat the Swedes on the field of battle. Charles XII was dead and the Aland Islands negotiations had borne no fruit; Sweden, therefore, needed to be reminded that the war was not yet over. The main effort of the 1719 campaign was to be a powerful amphibious attack on the homeland coast of Sweden along the Gulf of Bothnia. The weapons were to be the same as those which had been so effective in the conquest of Finland: fleets of galleys carrying thousands of soldiers into shallow waters where big ships could not go. In May, 50,000 Russian troops marched from their winter quarters to assembly points at St. Petersburg and Reval to be moved by sea to western Finland, from where the attacks would be launched. Apraxin was to be in overall command of the Russian fleet of 180 galleys and 300 flat-bottom boats, convoyed by twenty-eight ships-

of-the-line. On June 2, Peter himself left St. Petersburg for Peterhof and Kronstadt, commanding a flotilla of thirty galleys carrying 5,000 men. Already that summer, Peter's fleet had had a success. On June 4, a squadron of seven Russian men-of-war sailing from Reval had intercepted three smaller Swedish ships in the open sea. Outnumbered and heavily outgunned, the Swedish ships tried running for the Stockholm Skargard, the archipelago of islands and islets which screen the Swedish capital from the sea. The Russian ships overtook them, however, and after an eight-hour fight all three Swedish ships, including the fifty-two-gun *Wachtmeister*, were captured. The return of this squadron with its prizes to Reval was deeply satisfying to Peter. Here was a deepwater victory, unlike the galley action at Hangö.

On June 30, Peter and the Kronstadt squadron arrived at Reval with the largest Russian men-of-war, including the ninety-gun *Gangut*, the seventy-gun ships *St. Alexander, Neptunus* and *Reval* and the sixty-four-gun *Moscow*. Meanwhile, Admiral Norris had entered the Baltic with a squadron of sixteen ships-of-the-line. Despite the potentially menacing presence of this English fleet, Peter's men-of-war sailed toward Sweden on July 13, followed a few days later by 130 galleys filled with soldiers. On the 18th, the entire Russian naval force anchored at Lemland in the Aland Islands, and on the evening of the 21st they put to sea. Fog and calm seas forced the big ships to anchor, but the galleys proceeded under oars and, with Apraxin in command, reached the first islands of the Stockholm Skargard on the afternoon of the 22nd.

For the next five weeks, Apraxin's ships and the 30,000 men they carried wreaked havoc on the eastern coast of Sweden. Finding himself unopposed at sea, Apraxin divided his force, sending Major General Lacy with twenty-one galleys and twelve sloops north up the coast, while moving the main body south. He landed a force of Cossacks to raid Stockholm, but their assault was repulsed—the Skargard was difficult, its narrow channels well defended, and a force of four men-of-war and nine frigates in the Stockholm harbor kept the Russian galleys at bay. Moving south, Apraxin again divided his ships into smaller squadrons to work along the coasts, burning small towns, industries and ironworks and capturing coast shipping. On August 4, the southernmost Russian ships reached Nykoping, and on the 10th they were at Norrkoping, where a number of Swedish merchant ships were captured, some of them loaded with copper ore taken from the nearby mines. These were sent back to Russia. In one cannon foundry, 300 cannon still undelivered to the Swedish army were seized and hauled away. On August 14, Apraxin's fleet turned north, stopping to pick up other landing detachments along the coast. Arriving again off the Stockholm Skargard, he attempted another assault on the capital, but again was beaten off. On August 21, twenty-one Russian sloops and twenty-one

galleys forced one channel in the face of heavy fire from Swedish forts and ships, but then fell back.

Meanwhile, to the north, Lacy's force had been moving with similar devastating effect along the upper coast. He had destroyed factories and ironworks, storehouses and mills, and had burned three towns. The troops had fought three small battles, winning two and being repulsed in a third, at which point he turned back. A large quantity of iron, forage and provisions was seized, some taken aboard, and that which could not be carried away was thrown into the sea or burned. By August 29 Lacy and Apraxin were both back in the Aland Islands, and on the 31st they departed for home, the galley fleet heading for Kronstadt and the men-of-war for Reval.

That autumn, hoping that the lesson of the summer attacks had made itself felt, Peter sent Osterman to Stockholm under a flag of truce to see whether the Swedes were now any more ready for peace. Osterman returned to the Tsar with a letter in which Queen Ulrika offered to cede Narva, Reval and Estonia, but still demanded the return of all of Finland and Livonia. In Stockholm, Osterman reported, the Swedes were embittered by the Russian raids, unwilling to talk peace while Cossacks rode within a few miles of their capital. Nevertheless, an extraordinary shift in power had been made plain that summer. Ten years before, Charles XII had been fighting one thousand miles away in the heat and dust of the Ukraine. Now, Peter's Cossack horsemen rode within sight of the steeples of the capital of Sweden.

57

VICTORY

OUTWARDLY AT LEAST, the spring of 1720 seemed to bring a grave deterioration in Peter's position relative to Sweden. All of Russia's allies had been stripped away by the efforts of King George I. Formidable squadrons of the British navy were entering the Baltic to hinder and overawe the Tsar. In March of that year, after a reign of only seventeen months, Queen Ulrika Eleonora of Sweden abdicated her crown in favor of her husband, Frederick of Hesse, who was vigorously anti-Russian and determined to prosecute the war.

In May 1720, Sir John Norris appeared in the Baltic with a more powerful British fleet than ever before, twenty-one ships-of-the-line and ten frigates. His orders this year were clearly hostile. On April 6 in London, Stanhope had once again offered Veselovsky England's services as a "mediator" between Russia and Sweden, and Veselovsky had curtly refused. In any case, Stanhope had continued magisterially, when Norris arrived in the Baltic, it would be up to the Russians to decide how they would treat him: They could recognize him as a friend by making peace with Sweden, or as an enemy by continuing the war.

Norris arrived in Stockholm on May 23 and went ashore to receive further written orders from young Lord Carteret, then on a special mission to Copenhagen and the Swedish capital. Carteret's instructions were fervent:

Sir John Norris: It is now in your power by the help of God to do the most signal piece of service to your country that any man has done in this age. The scales of the North are in your hand. . . . If the Tsar refuses the King's mediation, as he probably will, a mark of which will be his continuing hostility against Sweden, I hope you will by force of arms bring him to reason and destroy that fleet which will disturb the world. . . . God bless you, Sir John Norris. All honest and good men will give you just applause. Many persons will envy

you and nobody will dare say a word against you. Every Englishman will be obliged to you if you can destroy the Tsar's fleet, which I don't doubt you will do.

While Norris was in Stockholm, he also paid his respects to the new King, Frederick I, who asked the Admiral to cruise in the sea area between the Hangö peninsula and the Aland Islands to prevent the passage of Russian galleys into the Gulf of Bothnia and a repetition of the preceding summer's devastating raids against the coast of Sweden. But Norris had no more desire to clash with Peter's galleys in these dangerous waters than the Swedish admirals had displayed. There were myriad rocks, ledges, fogs, fickle winds, poor charts and no pilots. An admiral who took big, ocean-going ships into such a maze would have half his bottoms ripped out by granite and lose the rest when the wind died and his becalmed behemoths faced a legion of Russian galleys rowing to the attack. Accordingly, Norris suggested firmly that he take his ships in a different direction to see whether an attack might be made on Reval, now, like Kronstadt, a main base of the Russian Baltic fleet. With a combined fleet of twenty English and eleven Swedish men-of-war, Norris cruised off Reval, making an impressive naval demonstration, and sent a letter ashore addressed to the Tsar, again offering England's mediation. The letter was returned unopened; Peter, understanding that Britain was now siding openly with his enemy, had left instructions not to accept any further communications from Norris or Carteret. Apraxin further warned the British Admiral to keep his ships out of range of the guns of Russian coastal fortresses. Faced with this rebuff, and deciding that the defenses of Reval were too strong, Norris disappeared over the horizon.

Meanwhile, as Norris was parading off Reval, Apraxin's galleys had already outmaneuvered him and descended once again on the Swedish coast. Eight thousand men, including Cossacks, moved down the coast without opposition and penetrated as far as thirty miles inland, leaving behind towers of smoke from burning towns, villages and farmhouses. Summoned by a desperate appeal from Frederick I, Norris hurried from Reval to inter-cept the Russian galleys, but they were already gone, slipping through the rocky islands and along the inshore waters of Finland where Norris dared not follow. The one exception had just the result Norris had feared. A Swedish flotilla of two ships-of-the-line and four frigates caught up with a force of sixty-one Russian galleys. Pursuing the galleys, trying to bring them within range before the smaller ships could reach the safety of the coast, all four Swedish frigates ran aground and were captured. The Tsar was delighted by this sea victory and rejoiced in the impotence of the British fleet. Writing to Yaguzhinsky, he said, "Our force under the command of Brigadier von Mengden has invaded Sweden and has safely returned to our shores. It is

true that no very great loss was inflicted on the enemy, yet thank God it was done under the eyes of their allies, who could do nothing to prevent it." In retrospect, there seems something strange about the operations of Norris' fleet. Although his ships in the Baltic were in a state of armed hostility, no British ship ever fired at a Russian ship. If Norris' powerful men-of-war had ever caught Peter's galley flotillas in the open sea, the British ships with their greater speed and overwhelming gun power would have massacred the Russians. But the English, despite Norris' orders from his civilian masters, were content to support Sweden merely by their presence, showing the flag in Swedish harbors and cruising in the central Baltic. It is hard to believe that an aggressive British admiral leading the finest seamen in the world could not have drawn some blood if he had wished to. It leaves a suspicion that Norris preferred not to engage the ships of the Tsar, whose admiration and generosity he had personally enjoyed when they had met five years before. For George I, Norris' failure was a serious embarrassment. Despite his maneuvers in isolating Russia and plucking away her allies, despite his employment of the British navy in the Baltic, neither his diplomacy nor his fleet had succeeded in helping Sweden or harming Russia. While British ships-of-the-line cruised the Baltic or lay in Swedish harbors, Russian galley flotillas roved up and down the Swedish coastline, supporting landing parties which burned and ravaged where they chose. In England, the King's opponents laughed at the fleet which was sent to defend Sweden but which somehow never managed to be present at the right time or place.

By the middle of the summer of 1720, George I's anti-Russian policy was on the verge of failure. Most people in England realized that Peter and Russia could not be defeated without a far greater effort than they were willing to consider making. Veselovsky reported from London that eight out of every ten Members of Parliament, both Whig and Tory, believed that war with Russia would be contrary to the best interests of England. Peter, wisely, had always made it abundantly clear that his quarrel was not with the English people or English merchants but only with the King. Thus, although the Tsar had broken off diplomatic relations and expelled both the English and Hanoverian ministers from St. Petersburg, he had never allowed any break in commercial relations. Before his departure, Jefferyes had attempted to order home English shipwrights and naval officers in the service of the Tsar, but most were Peter's favorites who enjoyed many privileges in Russia, and few heeded Jefferyes' demand. Similarly, the Tsar personally told English merchants in Russia that they were welcome to stay under his protection. Veselovsky passed the same message to those trading companies in London which traded with Russia. Soon afterward, Peter lifted his blockade of Swedish ports in the Baltic, allowing free passage of

Dutch and English commercial shipping. In every way, the Tsar emphasized that his quarrel was not with England but with the King's policy of using England to advance the interests of Hanover.

Finally, in September 1720, the likelihood of any serious British military involvement in the Baltic was terminated by an event in Britain which distracted attention from everything else, the bursting of the South Sea Bubble. Shares in the South Sea Company, chartered to trade with South America and the Pacific and enjoying the governorship of the King, had stood at 128.5 in January 1720, rose to 330 in March, 550 in April, 890 in June and 1,000 in July. In September, the bubble burst and shares plummeted to 175. Speculators from all levels of society were ruined, there was a rash of suicides, and an angry roar of indignation rose up against the company, the government and the King.

In this crisis, Sir Robert Walpole emerged to save the King and secure his own position for the next twenty years. Walpole was the living embodiment of the educated eighteenth-century English country squire; his private language was that of the barnyard, and his rhetoric in the House of Commons was superb. Short, weighing 280 pounds, with a heavy head, a double chin and strong black eyebrows, he had the habit of munching little red Norfolk apples during a debate. Walpole had invested in the company and had suffered losses, but had retired both from the company and from the government before it was too late. Summoned back, he worked out a scheme to restore confidence by transferring large blocks of South Sea stock to the Bank of England and the East India Company. In parliament, he vigorously defended the government and the crown from charges of scandal. By so doing, he earned the gratitude not only of George I but also of George II, both of whom passed into his hands more responsibility for administering the realm than any king had previously given up to one of his ministers. It is for this reason that Walpole is often called "the first Prime Minister."

Having steered the King to safety, Walpole took charge of British policy. A Whig to his eyebrows, Walpole believed in avoidance of war and encouragement of trade. This teasing, dangerous semi-war with Russia had no part in his view of the future prosperity of England. The subsidies paid to Sweden and the costs of sending the fleet could be better spent elsewhere. With Walpole at the helm, it became British policy to end the war as speedily as possible. The King was chagrined, but even the King could see that his plan to roll Peter back from the Baltic coast was not succeeding.

It did not take Frederick of Sweden long to realize where matters stood. Disillusioned by the impotence of George I's support, and aware that continuation of the struggle meant further Russian attacks along his coasts, Frederick decided to face the fact that the war was lost. This decision was spurred by the arrival in St. Petersburg of Duke Charles Frederick of

Holstein-Gottorp seeking asylum. Reports reached Stockholm that the Duke had been magnificently received by the Tsar, and that Peter proposed to marry him to one of his own daughters. This attention to Charles Frederick, implying Russian support to the Holstein faction in the struggle for the Swedish throne, was a well-aimed stroke by Peter. It clearly implied that only by signing a peace treaty with the Tsar which incorporated Russian acquiescence in Frederick I's possession of the Swedish throne would the new King ever be easy in his new title.

Frederick informed Peter that he was ready to reopen negotiations, and a second peace conference was convened on April 28, 1721, in the town of Nystad on the Finnish coast of the Gulf of Bothnia. Again, the Russian representatives were Bruce, now a count, and Osterman, now a baron. In the opening sessions, the Russians were astonished to find that the Swedes expected easier terms than those they had been offered at Aland. The Swedes in turn were dismayed to learn that Peter now demanded permanent cession of Livonia, whereas previously he had been content with a "temporary" occupation of forty years. "I know my interest," the Tsar now declared. "If I leave Sweden in Livonia, I would harbor a serpent in my bosom."

Great Britain's new desire for peace in the North did not entail a total abandonment of its Swedish ally. In April 1721, King George I wrote to King Frederick I that, in accordance with treaty obligations, a British fleet would enter the Baltic that summer. But George I begged that Sweden attempt to conclude a peace with Russia. The cost of sending a fleet every summer was prohibitive, George explained; the sum expanded on the present squadron came to 600,000 pounds. A few weeks later, Norris' twenty-two ships-of-the-line appeared, but throughout the summer the British squadron lay anchored in Stockholm Skargard, completely idle.

Meanwhile, with the negotiations at Nystad deadlocked over Livonia and no military truce arranged, Peter once again launched his galley fleet against the Swedish coast. Five thousand soldiers under Major General Lacy landed one hundred miles north of Stockholm and attacked the fortified town of Gefle, but the town was too strong for Lacy's strength and the Russian troops moved south, leaving a swath of destruction. Sundeval and two other towns were burned, along with nineteen parishes and 506 villages. Lacy defeated the Swedish force sent against him, while his galleys burned six Swedish galleys. On June 24, having ravaged 400 miles of Swedish coastline, Lacy was ordered to withdraw.

Lacy's raid, although on a smaller scale than those of the preceding summers, appeared to be the last straw for Sweden. Frederick I finally yielded Livonia. The main articles of the peace treaty granted Peter the territories he had so long desired. Livonia, Ingria and Estonia were ceded "in perpetuity" to Russia, along with Karelia as far as Vyborg. The re-

mainder of Finland was to be restored to Sweden. As compensation for Livonia, Russia agreed to pay two million thalers over four years, and Sweden was granted the right to purchase Livonian grain without paying duty. All prisoners of war on both sides were to be freed. The Tsar pledged that he would not interfere in Swedish domestic politics, thus confirming Frederick I's right to the throne.

It was on September 14, 1721, when Peter had left St. Petersburg for Vyborg to inspect the new frontier which would be drawn by the treaty, that a courier arrived from Nystad with the news that the treaty had actually been signed on September 10. The Tsar was exuberant. When a copy of the treaty was placed in his hands, he wrote joyfully, "All scholars in arts usually finish their course in seven years. Our school has lasted three times that long. However, thank God, it is so well finished that better would have been impossible."

News that peace had come after twenty-one years of war was received with jubilation in Russia. Peter was beside himself with excitement, and the celebrations which took place were prolonged and prodigious. St. Petersburg first realized that something extraordinary had happened when on September 15, the Tsar's yacht was unexpectedly seen sailing back up the Neva, returning from his visit to Vyborg far sooner than expected. That the news was good was signaled by repeated firing of salutes from the three small cannon on board the yacht and, as the vessel grew nearer, by the sound of trumpeters and drummers on deck. A crowd quickly gathered at the wharf on Trinity Square, swelled every minute by the arrival of more government officials, for there could only be one reason for this behavior on the approaching ship. When Peter stepped ashore and confirmed the news, people in the crowd wept and cheered. Peter walked from the wharf to Trinity Church to pray and give thanks. After the service, General-Admiral Apraxin and the other senior officers and ministers present, knowing what reward would most please their master, asked him to accept promotion to admiral.

Meanwhile, tubs of beer and wine were being set in the middle of streets packed with excited people. Peter mounted a small, makeshift platform in the square outside the church and shouted to the crowd, "Rejoice and thank God, you Orthodox people, that Almighty God has put an end to this long war lasting twenty-one years, and given us a happy and eternal peace with Sweden!" Taking a cup of wine, Peter toasted the Russian nation while the ranks of soldiers fired their muskets in the air and the guns of the Peter and Paul Fortress thundered a salute.

A month later, Peter gave a masquerade party that continued for days. Forgetting his age and his various ailments, he danced on tabletops and sang at the top of his lungs. Tiring suddenly in the middle of a banquet, he

rose from the table, ordered his guests not to go home and went to sleep on his yacht anchored in the Neva. When he returned, the celebration continued, with rivers of wine and prodigious noise. For an entire week, thousands of people remained masked and in fancy dress, dining, dancing, walking in the streets, rowing on the Neva, going to sleep and rising to begin again.

The celebration reached a peak on October 31 when Peter appeared in the Senate to declare that, in gratitude for God's mercy in giving Russia victory, he would pardon all imprisoned criminals except murderers, ¡and that he would annul all debts to the government and arrears of taxes accumulated over eighteen years from the war's beginning to 1718. In that same session, the Senate resolved to offer Peter the titles of Peter the Great, Emperor and Father of His Country. This resolve, in which the Holy Synod joined, was put in the form of a written petition and taken to the Tsar by Menshikov and a delegation of two senators and the Archbishops of Pskov and Novgorod. Peter promised to consider the petition.

A few days before, Campredon, the French ambassador, who had helped urge the Swedes toward peace, had arrived at Kronstadt aboard a Swedish frigate. Breaking all the laws of protocol the happy Tsar himself went on board the frigate, embraced the envoy on deck and took him to visit the six large Russian men-of-war then anchored in the port. Returning to the capital, and walking through the streets, Peter kept the astonished Campredon with him throughout the festive week. In the Trinity Church, Peter placed Campredon in a position of honor, abruptly shoving aside a nobleman who obscured the Frenchman's view. During the service, Peter himself directed the liturgy, sang with the priests and helped beat time. At the end of the regular service, the terms of the treaty and its ratification were read to the congregation. Peter's favorite churchman, Archbishop Feofan Prokopovich, delivered an oration praising the Tsar and was followed by Chancellor Golovkin, who addressed Peter directly:

"By your tireless labors and leadership alone, we your loyal subjects have stepped from the darkness of ignorance into the theater of fame of the whole world, and, so to speak, have moved from non-existence to existence, and have joined in the society of political peoples. For that and for winning a peace so renowned and so rewarding, how can we render our proper gratitude? And so that we may not be with shame before the whole world, we take it upon ourselves in the name of the Russian nation and of all ranks of the subjects of Your Majesty, humbly to pray you to be gracious to us and agree, as a small mark of our acknowledgment of the great blessings that you have brought to us and to the whole nation, to take the title: Father of the Fatherland, Peter the Great, Emperor of All Russia."

With a brief nod of his head, Peter indicated that he would accept the

titles.* "Vivat! Vivat! Vivat!" shouted the senators. Inside and outside the church, the crowd roared, trumpets sounded and drums beat, echoed by the clanging and thundering of all the church bells and cannon in St. Petersburg. When the tumult subsided, Peter responded, "By our deeds in war we have emerged from darkness into the light of the world, and those whom we did not know in the light now respect us. I wish our entire nation to recognize the direct hand of God in our favor during the last war and in the conclusion of this peace. It becomes us to thank God with all our might, but while hoping for peace, we must not grow weaker in military matters, so as not to have the fate of the Greek monarchy [the Eastern empire of Constantinople]. We must make efforts for the general good and profit which may God grant us at home and abroad and from which the nation will receive advantage."

Leaving the church, Peter led a procession to the Senate palace, where tables for a thousand guests were set in a large hall. There he was congratulated by Duke Charles Frederick of Holstein-Gottorp and the foreign ambassadors. A banquet was followed by another ball and by fireworks which Peter himself had designed. Again the cannon boomed and the ships on the river were illuminated. In the hall, an enormous basin of wine—"a true cup of grief," one participant called it—was passed among the guests,

---

* The idea of awarding the title of emperor to the Tsar was not, of course, wholly spontaneous on the part of the Senate. Four years earlier, in 1717, when Michael Shafirov, brother of the Vice Chancellor, was rummaging among old records and papers in the archives, he found a letter written in 1514 by the Holy Roman Emperor Maximilian to Tsar Vasily Ivanovich (father of Ivan the Terrible). In the letter, Maximilian, urging Vasily to join him in an alliance against the King of Poland and Grand Prince of Lithuania, addressed the Tsar as "Great Lord, Vasily, Emperor and Dominator of All the Russias." When Shafirov showed Peter the letter, which was written in German, the Tsar immediately had it translated into all languages and gave copies to all foreign ambassadors in St. Petersburg. Simultaneously, through Russian diplomats and agents, he had the letter published in newspapers throughout Western Europe along with the notice, "This letter will serve to maintain without contestation the said title to the monarchs of all Russia, which high title was given them many years past and ought to be valued so much the more because it was written by an emperor who by his rank was one of the first monarchs of the world."

In Europe, acceptance of the Russian title came only in stages. Holland and Prussia immediately recognized Peter as Emperor of Russia. Other states delayed, chiefly because they were unwilling to antagonize the Holy Roman Emperor, who was jealous of the uniqueness of his ancient title. Sweden, however, recognized Peter as emperor in 1723, and the Ottoman Empire recognized Empress Anne in 1739. King George I always refused to give his old enemy Peter the imperial title, and English recognition waited until 1742, fifteen years after the King's death. In this same year, the Hapsburg Emperor recognized his Russian counterpart as an equal. France and Spain accepted the imperial title in 1745 and Poland in 1764.

The imperial title remained in use from Peter's proclamation in 1721 until the abdication of Emperor Nicholas II in 1917.

carried on the shoulders of two soldiers. Outside, fountains of wine burbled at the street corners and whole oxen were roasted on a platform. Peter came out and carved the first pieces with his own hands, distributing them among the crowd. He ate some himself and then lifted his cup to drink the health of the Russian people.

Part Five

THE NEW
RUSSIA

58

IN THE SERVICE
OF THE STATE

ETER HAD BEEN SITTING at dinner one night in 1717 surrounded by friends and lieutenants when the talk turned to Tsar Alexis and the achievements and disappointments of his reign. Peter had mentioned his father's wars against Poland and his struggle with the Patriarch Nikon, when Count Ivan Musin-Pushkin suddenly declared that none of Tsar Alexis' accomplishments had measured up to Peter's and that most of Alexis' successes had actually been due to the work of his ministers. Peter's reaction was icy. "Your disparagement of my father's achievements and your praise of mine are more than I can listen to," he said. The Tsar got up and walked over to the seventy-eight-year-old Prince Jacob Dolgoruky, sometimes called the Russian Cato. "You criticize me more than anybody else and plague me with your arguments until I sometimes feel I could lose my temper with you," said Peter. "But I know that you are sincerely devoted to me and to the state and that you always speak the truth, for which I am deeply grateful. Now, tell me how you estimate my father's achievements and what you think of mine."

Dolgoruky looked up and said, "Pray be seated, Sire, while I think a moment." Peter sat down and Dolgoruky was quiet for a while, stroking his long mustache. Then he replied, "It is impossible to give a short answer to your question since you and your father were occupied with different matters. A tsar has three main duties to perform. The most important is the administration of the country and the dispensation of justice. Your father had enough time to attend to this, while you have had none, which is why your father accomplished more than you. It is possible that when you do give some thought to this matter—and it is time you did—you will do more than your father.

"A tsar's second duty is to the organization of the army. Here again, your father is to be praised because he laid the foundations of a regular army, thereby showing you the way. Unfortunately, certain misguided men undid all his work, so that you had to start all over again, and I must admit

that you have done very well. Even so, I still do not know which of you has done better; we will only know that when the war is over.

"And, finally, we come to a tsar's third duty, which is building a fleet, making treaties and determining our relationship with foreign countries. Here, and I hope you will agree with me, you have served the country well and have achieved more than your father. For this, you deserve much praise. Somebody tonight said that a tsar's work depends on his ministers. I disagree and think the opposite, since a wise monarch will choose wise counselors who know their worth. Therefore, a wise monarch will not tolerate stupid counselors because he will know their quality and be able to distinguish good advice from bad."

When Dolgoruky finished, Peter stood up and said, "Faithful, honest friend," and embraced Dolgoruky.

The "administration of the country and the dispensation of justice" were much on Peter's mind during these later years. Victory at Poltava had given him more time and freedom to consider domestic matters; his actions were no longer hasty improvisations made under the threat of imminent invasion. In the years after Poltava, Peter turned his attention from organizing armies and building fleets to a basic remodeling of the structure of civil and church administration, to modernizing and changing the economic and social patterns of the nation, and even to rechanneling the age-old trade routes of the Russia he had inherited. It was in the second half of the reign, the years between 1711 and 1725, that the fundamental Petrine reforms were fashioned. Alexander Pushkin, Russia's greatest poet, compared the later fundamental reforms with the early wartime decrees: "The permanent laws were created by a broad mind, full of wisdom and kindness; the earlier decrees were mostly cruel and self-willed and seemed to have been written with a knout."

The nature and sequence of Peter's early reforms were dictated by war and the need for money to pay for it. For a while, as Pushkin wrote, the state was ruled primarily on the basis of Peter's decrees, hastily scribbled on pieces of paper. Traditionally in Russia, the tsar had ruled with the advice of an ancient, consultive council of boyars, and beneath it, the administration of the laws was carried out by a number of government offices, or prikazi. For the first two decades of Peter's reign, 1689–1708, there had been no change in this structure. The youthful Tsar attended meetings when he was in Moscow and delegated power when he was absent—thus, when Peter went abroad in 1697–1698, he made Prince Fedor Romodanovsky president of the council and ordered other members to accept his leadership. As Peter grew older and grasped the reins of government more firmly, he used the council little, and his opinion of it became openly contemptuous. In 1707, he ordered the council to keep minutes of its meetings, which were to be

signed by all members. "No resolution shall be taken without this," he instructed, "so that the stupidity of each shall be evident."

In 1708, when Charles XII was marching on Russia, the central government had seemed unable to cope with the crisis. To raise money and find recruits, both desperately needed, Peter ordered a sweeping decentralization of government administration. The nation was divided into eight huge provinces or governments—Moscow, Ingermanland (later called St. Petersburg), Kiev, Smolensk, Archangel, Kazan, Azov and Siberia—endowed with wide powers, especially in the areas of revenue collection and army recruiting. To underline the importance of these new regional governments, Peter had assigned his most senior lieutenants as governors. But this new system did not work. Most of the governors lived in St. Petersburg, too far from the regions they supposedly governed to control them effectively. Some of the governors, such as Menshikov and Apraxin, had more pressing duties with the army or the fleet. In February 1711, Peter was ready to admit defeat. He wrote to Menshikov, "Up to now, God knows in what grief I am, for the Governors follow the example of crabs in transacting their business. Therefore, I shall not deal with them with words, but with hands." Menshikov himself was criticized. "Inform me what merchandise you have, how much has been sold, when and where the money had gone," commanded the anguished Tsar, "for we know no more about your government than about a foreign country."

The failure of the provincial governments left only Peter at the center of government along with the crumbling boyar council and the increasingly ineffective, overlapping administrative offices. Although Peter attempted to overcome inefficiency and inertia by his own enormous energy, often even he had not enough. In frustration and despair, he wrote to Catherine, "I can't manage with my left hand, so with my right hand alone I have to wield both the sword and the pen. How many there are to help me you know yourself."

In time, Peter realized that he himself was part of the problem. All power was concentrated in his person, which, as he was so often on the move, made administration difficult. Further, he was completely absorbed by military affairs and foreign policy and had no time for domestic matters. To discover what laws were necessary, to formulate the legislation, to administer the laws and government and to judge violations, Peter needed a new institution more powerful and more efficient than the boyar council.

The Senate was created in February 1711, on the eve of Peter's departure for the disastrous campaign on the Pruth, and was intended as a temporary institution to govern during the months he was away. The short decree establishing the Senate was specific on this point: "We appoint the governing Senate to administer in our absence." Because the new body of

nine senators would rule in place of the Tsar, it was granted wide powers: It was to oversee the provincial governments, act as the highest court of justice, take charge of all state expenditures and, above all, "to collect money as much as possible, for money is the artery of war." Another decree proclaimed that all officials, civil and clerical, and all institutions were under pain of death to obey the Senate as they would the Tsar.

When Peter returned from the Pruth, the Senate did not disappear but gradually became the chief executive and legislative organ of the central government of Russia. Nothing could be done without the command or consent of the Senate; in the absence of the Tsar, it *was* the government of Russia. Yet, for all Peter's effort to enhance its power, no one was fooled. The Senate's power was mostly hollow, its grandeur mostly façade. In fact, the Senate remained a body for transmitting and administering the will of the autocrat and had no independent will of its own. It was an instrument, its powers were those of an agent, its jurisdiction touched only on domestic matters—all questions of foreign policy and peace or war were reserved to the Tsar. The Senate helped Peter by interpreting and clarifying his hastily, cryptically written instructions and transforming them into legislation. But in the eyes of the people and in its own mind, the Senate knew it was the creature and servant of an unchallengeable master.

The subordinate status was made plainer by the fact that none of Peter's principal lieutenants—Menshikov, Apraxin, Golovkin, Sheremetev—was included in the Senate. These "Supreme Lords" or "Principals," as they were called, could send the Senate instructions "by order of His Majesty." And yet, at the same time, Peter instructed Menshikov that he and the others must obey the Senate. In fact, Peter wanted both the assistance of his powerful, loyal lieutenants and the aid of a powerful, central administrative body. He would not choose one definitely over the other, and therefore he left the situation confused, with opposing methods and systems of government functioning in contradiction to each other. Inevitably, the "Supreme Lords" and "Principals" bridled and refused to accept the authority of this fledgling body.

Nor was Peter himself always pleased with the Senate's behavior. He wrote regularly to the senators, scolding them as if they were thoughtless children, telling them that they had made themselves a laughingstock, which he said was doubly infamous "for the Senate represents the person of His Majesty." He ordered them not to waste time in meetings talking about matters unrelated to business, and not to chatter and joke, because "loss of time is like death, as hard to return as a life that has ended." He ordered them to transact no business at home or in private, and commanded that every discussion must be written down. Yet, the Senate still moved too slowly for Peter. On one occasion, he summoned it to tell him "what has

been done and what has not been done and the reason for it." Repeatedly, he threatened the senators with punishment. "You have nothing else to do except to govern," he declared, "and if you do not do this conscientiously, you will answer to God and also will not escape justice here below." "You have acted in a contemptible way, accepting bribes according to ancient and stupid customs," he thundered on another occasion. "When you come before me, you will be called to account in a different way."

In November 1715, attempting to discipline the Senate and make it more effective, Peter created the supervisory post of Inspector General of Decrees to sit "in the same place as the Senate, to take note of the Senate's decrees, to see that they are enforced, and to denounce and fine negligent senators." Vasily Zotov, the foreign-educated son of his old tutor, was the first Inspector General, but he had little success, and soon it was he who was complaining to Peter that the Senate paid no attention to his wishes, failed to hold the required sessions three days a week, and had left one and a half million roubles of state revenue uncollected.

In 1720, detailed new rules of Senate procedure were promulgated. Meetings were to be conducted "without shouting and other manifesta- tions. . . . The business is to be stated and is to be thought about and dis- cussed for half an hour. If, however, it be complicated and more time is asked for, then it is to be postponed until the following day. If the business is urgent, extra time up to three hours will be granted for further delibera- tions, but as soon as the hourglass shows that time has run out, paper and ink are to be handed out and every senator is to note down his opinion and sign it. If a senator fails to do this, business is to be stopped while some- body runs to tell the Tsar, wherever he may be."

Eventually, when it became clear that even the Inspector General could not keep order in the Senate, officers of the Guards were assigned for a month at a time to police the senators. If a senator misbehaved, he was to be arrested and confined in the Peter and Paul Fortress until the fact could be reported to the Tsar.

As it was, the Senate functioned as well as it did only because of Prince Jacob Dolgoruky, the First Senator, who had served in many capacities over many decades. He was the first Russian ambassador to the court of Louis XIV, and it was on this mission in 1687 that he purchased an astro- labe to bring back to the fifteen-year-old Peter. At the age of sixty-two, he was present at the Battle of Narva, was captured and spent eleven years in a Swedish prison. In 1712, at seventy-three, he escaped and made his way back to Russia, where he was appointed First Senator. A portrait of Dol- goruky shows a powerful man with a double chin and a shaggy mustache, a man who looks unkempt, shrewd and fierce. He was also brave, obstinate, strong-willed and liked to have his way; when he could not impose his

wishes by force of logic or force of character, he simply shouted at his opponent at the top of his lungs. Only Menshikov, permanently armored in the Tsar's favor, could stand up to him. Dolgoruky always dared to tell Peter the truth. Once, late in the reign, Dolgoruky actually tore up a decree because he believed that the Emperor had not reflected on it. The decree had commanded all landowners in the governments of St. Petersburg and Novgorod to send serfs to dig the Ladoga Canal. Dolgoruky had been absent on the day the decree was signed, and the following morning, when he read it, he protested loudly. The other senators looked uncomfortable, but warned that it was too late to object, as the Emperor had already signed it. Whereupon, in a spasm of disgust, Dolgoruky ripped the edict in half. Stunned, the other senators stood up, demanding to know if he realized what he had done. "Yes," said Dolgoruky passionately, "and I will answer for it before God, the Emperor and my country."

At this moment, Peter walked into the room. Surprised to see the entire Senate standing, he asked what had happened. In a trembling voice, one member told him. His expression grim, Peter turned to the eighty-three-year-old Dolgoruky and demanded an explanation. "It is my zeal for your honor and the good of your subjects," Dolgoruky replied. "Do not be angry, Peter Alexeevich, that I have too much confidence in your wisdom to think you wish, like Charles XII, to desolate your country. You have not reflected on the situation of the two governments your decree regards. Do you not know that they have suffered more in the war than all the provinces of your empire together, that many of their inhabitants have perished, and are you unacquainted with the present miserable state of the people? What is there to hinder you from taking a small number of men from each province to dig this canal, which is certainly necessary? The other provinces are more populous than the two in question and can easily furnish you with laborers. Besides, have you not Swedish prisoners enough to employ without oppressing your subjects with works like these?"

Peter listened to Dolgoruky's appeal and then turned calmly to the other senators. "Let the decree be suspended," he said. "I will consider this matter further and let you know my intentions." Soon after, several thousand Swedish prisoners were transferred to work on the Ladoga Canal.

Nevertheless, despite the presence of Dolgoruky, Zotov and the Guards officers, the Senate failed to perform as Peter wished. In time, he came to realize that force or the threat of force exercised from above was insufficient and often counterproductive. The Senate could not be disciplined roughly and peremptorily, as the Tsar was accustomed to doing, and still maintain its dignity and authority in the eyes of the public. In addition, it was overloaded with work. Inefficiency, quarrels among its members and

unwillingness to take responsibility caused a huge and growing backlog of work which at one point reached 16,000 unresolved cases and decisions.

Thus, in 1722, Peter resolved to create a new managerial office, that of the Procurator General, who was to be the Emperor's personal representative in the Senate. "Here is my eye through whom I will see everything," Peter declared when he presented his Procurator General to the senators. "He knows my intentions and wishes. What he considers to be for the general good, you are to do. Although it may seem to you that what he does is contrary to the advantage of me and of the state, you should nevertheless carry it out and, having notified me, await my orders." The Procurator General's duty was to direct the Senate and superintend its work. Although he was not a member of the body and could not vote, he was in fact President of the Senate, responsible for maintaining order during sessions, for initiating legislation and bringing it to a vote (using an hourglass to limit discussion), and for seeing that, once passed, new legislation was sent to the Emperor for approval. When administrative offices were unable to understand the language or meaning of a Senate decree or discovered difficulty in administering one, they were to notify the Procurator General, who would ask the Senate to rewrite the decree in clearer language.

Peter's choice for this important role was Pavel Yaguzhinsky, one of his low-born "fledglings." Yaguzhinsky was eleven years younger than the Emperor, born of Lithuanian parents in Moscow, where his father was the organist in a Lutheran church. Peter liked him from the first, enrolled him in the Guards, and, charmed by the good humor and intelligence of the stalwart young man, made him a field orderly to his own person. Yaguzhinsky was promoted rapidly. Peter used him on diplomatic missions and took him along to Paris, where the French described him as Peter's "favorite." Yaguzhinsky was excitable, he enjoyed drinking, and he made and forgot new enemies every week. But he was unquestioningly loyal, he was almost completely honest and he was decisive, qualities which Peter found lacking in many senators.

Even before the appointment of Yaguzhinsky, Peter had altered the Senate's role. From 1711 to 1718, the Senate had been responsible for administration as well as for legislation, but Peter realized that the state needed a new executive machinery, separate from the Senate, which would permit the Senate to concentrate on legislative matters. It was this realization which led him to begin his experiment with a new government institution imported from Europe, the system of colleges or ministries.

From his own travels and from reports of foreign ambassadors and his agents, the Tsar had learned that colleges were the basic working institutions of government in Denmark, Prussia, Austria and Sweden. Even in England, the semi-autonomous, college-like Board of the Admiralty was charged with

administering all the affairs of the Royal Navy. Leibniz, whom Peter had consulted, reported: "There cannot be good administration except with colleges. Their mechanism is like that of watches whose wheels mutually keep each other in movement." The college system in Sweden had the highest reputation in Europe; it functioned so well that the Swedish government continued to administer the country smoothly despite the absence of its sovereign for fifteen years, the loss of armies, the conquest of its empire and a devastating plague. Peter, admiring both Charles and Swedish efficiency and, having no qualms about borrowing from his enemy, decided to use the Swedish colleges as models for his own.

By 1718, his new system was ready. The old-fashioned prikazi, or government offices, now thirty-five in number, were superseded by nine new colleges: Foreign Affairs, Revenue Collection, Justice, Expenditure, Financial Control, War, Admiralty, Commerce, and Mining and Manufacturing. The presidents of these colleges were to be Russians (in fact, they were all Peter's close friends and chief lieutenants) and the vice presidents foreigners. Two exceptions were the College of Mining and Manufacturing, of which General Bruce, a Scot, was appointed president, and the College of Foreign Affairs, whose president, Golovkin, and vice president, Shafirov, were both Russians. All nine college presidents simultaneously became members of the Senate, which had the effect of transforming that body into a council of ministers.

To help make these foreign institutions work, Peter imported foreign experts. Russian agents circulated through Europe inviting foreigners to come to the new Russian colleges. Even Swedish prisoners of war who had learned Russian were invited to the colleges. (Weber thought that some would not accept, "considering that they are apprehensive of a troublesome inquiry at home into their behavior.") In the end, enough foreigners were found, and Weber was to describe the humming activity at the College of Foreign Affairs in glowing terms: "Hardly any foreign office in the world issues dispatches in so many languages. They have sixteen interpreters and secretaries: Russian, Latin, Polish, High Dutch, Low Dutch, English, Danish, French, Italian, Spanish, Greek, Turkish, Chinese, Tatar, Kalmuck and Mongolian."

Yet, even with foreigners working at several levels in the new machinery, the college system began jerkily. The foreign lawyers, administrators and other experts had difficulty explaining the new system to their Russian colleagues, and the translators brought in to help were tongue-tied by their own ignorance of Swedish terminology and administrative affairs. Explanation of the new system and procedures to local officials in the provinces was even more difficult, and uncomprehending provincial clerks sent reports to the capital which could not be categorized, understood or even read in the new offices in St. Petersburg.

In addition, several of the college presidents treated their new assignments lackadaisically, and Peter once again was forced to lecture them like children. They must appear at their colleges every Tuesday and Thursday, he commanded, and while there and in the Senate must act with decorum. "There should be no unnecessary talking or chatter, but only talk of the matter in hand. Moreover, if someone begins to speak, another shall not interrupt but shall allow him to finish, behaving like orderly people and not like market women."

Peter had hoped that including the new college presidents as members of the Senate would enhance the efficiency of that body, but there were such antagonisms and jealousies among these potentates that putting them all in the same room without the Tsar to enforce order led to violent quarrels and even brawls. The aristocratic senators Dolgoruky and Golitsyn disdained the low-born Menshikov, Shafirov and Yaguzhinsky. Golovkin, president of the College of Foreign Affairs, and Shafirov, its vice president, hated each other. The quarrels became more strident, senators openly accused one another of being thieves, and while Peter was away on the Caspian Sea, a resolution was passed reporting Shafirov to the Emperor for outrageous, illegal behavior in the Senate. On Peter's return, a special high court composed of senators and generals was summoned to Preobrazhenskoe and, on hearing the evidence, sentenced Shafirov to death. On February 16, 1723, Shafirov was brought into the Kremlin in a common sledge. The sentence was read to him, his wig and tattered sheepskin coat were taken away and he mounted the scaffold. Crossing himself repeatedly, he knelt and placed his head on the block. The executioner lifted the axe—and at this moment Peter's Cabinet Secretary, Makarov, stepped forward and announced that, in consideration of Shafirov's long record of service, the Emperor had granted him life and sentenced him instead to exile in Siberia. Shafirov got to his feet and climbed down from the scaffold, his eyes filled with tears. He was taken to the Senate, where his former colleagues, shaken by the experience, congratulated him on his reprieve. To calm his nerves, the doctors bled him, and Shafirov, contemplating his dismal future, said to them, "You had better open my largest vein and thus relieve me of my torments." His exile to Siberia was further commuted to confinement with his family in Novgorod. Two years later, on Peter's death, Catherine pardoned Shafirov, and under Empress Anne he returned to the Senate.

Peter's hopes for his new administrative machinery often went unfulfilled. The institutions were alien to Russian practice, the new administrators were insufficiently trained and motivated, and the looming, mercurial presence of the Tsar himself did not contribute to initiative and decisiveness on the part of his subordinates. On the one hand, Peter commanded them to assume responsibility and act boldly; on the other, he punished them if the move they made was the wrong one. Naturally, this made them excessively

cautious, "as if a servant, seeing his master drowning, would not save him until he had satisfied himself as to whether it was written down in his contract that he should pull him out of the water."

As Peter grew older, he seemed to grasp this problem. He began to understand the importance of government by laws and institutions rather than by the arbitrary power of individuals, including himself. Instead of being commanded from above, the people were to be taught, guided and persuaded. "It is necessary to explain just what are the interests of the state," he said, "and to make them comprehensible to the people." After 1716, his major decrees usually were prefaced by pedagogical explanations of the need for this legislation, citation of historical parallels, appeals to logic and promises of utility.

On balance, Peter's new governmental system was an improvement. Russia was changing, and the Senate and the colleges administered this new state and society more efficiently than would have been possible under the old boyar council and government prikazi. Both Senate and colleges endured until the end of the dynasty, although the colleges were changed into ministries and the Senate was renamed the Council of the Empire. In 1720, the architect Trezzini set to work on an immensely long red-brick building on the Neva embankment on Vasilevsky Island to house the colleges and the Senate. This building, which now houses Leningrad University, is the largest surviving edifice of Peter's St. Petersburg.

PETER'S REFORMS affected individuals as powerfully as institutions. Russian society, like that of medieval Europe, was based on obligations of service. The serf owed service to the landowner, the landowner owed service to the tsar. Far from breaking or even loosening these bonds of service, Peter twisted them tight to extract every last degree of service from every level of society. There were no exceptions and no mitigations. Service was the motive force of Peter's life, and the Tsar thrust his energy and power into making sure that every Russian served as efficiently as possible. Noblemen serving as officers in the new Russian army or navy must know how to fight with modern weapons and tactics; those entering the growing Westernized central administration must have the training and skills necessary to manage their new assignments. The concept of service was broadened to include the duty of becoming educated.

Peter began this program pragmatically with his first impulsive dispatch of young Russians to the West in 1696, on the eve of the Great Embassy. After Poltava, the effort became more serious, more inclusive and more institutionally structured. In 1712, a decree ordered all sons of landowners to report to the Senate. They were divided into age groups; the youngest were sent to Reval to study seamanship, the middle group went to Holland

for naval training and the eldest marched directly into the army. In 1714, the dragnet was extended: All young noblemen between ten and thirty not already registered or in service were commanded to report to the Senate for service during the winter.

Peter intended the army to be wholly officered by professionally trained Russian noblemen who had begun their twenty-five years of service at the age of fifteen when they entered the Guards or a line regiment as private soldiers. From that lowest rank, each nobleman was to work his way up on the basis of merit. In February 1714, Peter categorically prohibited the commissioning of any officer, no matter what his title, who had not come up through the ranks. At one point, 300 princes of the noblest families of Russia were serving as private soldiers, receiving the minimum in pay, food and comfort. According to Prince Kurakin, it was not uncommon for Petersburgers to see a Prince Golitsyn or Prince Gagarin with a musket on his shoulder doing sentry duty in front of his barracks.

Instruction for these young men, however, went far beyond how to handle firearms and conduct military drill. As more and more of them passed through these training years, the regiments became not only nurseries for officers but academies for service to the state in a variety of fields. Some young men would learn gunnery, some engineering, some navigation, some languages—one was sent to Astrachan to learn about salt mining. In time, the officers of Peter's Guards became a pool from which Peter could draw for almost any service. The watchdogs whom the Tsar set on his Senate were Guards officers; these same officers made up the majority of the civil tribunal which condemned the Tsarevich Alexis.

Although most of the young noblemen went into the army, this was not the preferred avenue of state service; the civil service was growing rapidly, and its entry doors were always crowded as work in government offices was less dangerous, less arduous and potentially far more lucrative. To narrow the stream of candidates flowing in this direction, Peter decreed that no more than one third of the members of a family could serve in civil government; two thirds must serve in the army or the navy.

The navy, a body wholly alien and repugnant to most Russians, was even more intensely and universally unpopular than the army. When a son had to go into service, the father struggled to enter him anywhere other than in the navy. Nevertheless, in 1715, when the School of Mathematics and Navigation was transferred from Moscow to St. Petersburg, its classrooms were filled. "This summer the Naval Academy was opened," wrote Weber in 1715. "I daresay that there was not one noble family within the boundaries of the vast Russian empire but what was obliged to send thither one or more sons above ten and under eighteen. We saw swarms of these young plants arriving from all parts of Russia at St. Petersburg. So that this academy at present contains the flower of the Russian nobility who for these four

years past have been instructed in all the sciences belonging to navigation, besides which they are taught languages, fencing and other bodily exercises."

Russian nobles did not bow easily to Peter's disposition of their sons or themselves. Although Peter's first decree in 1712 was simply an effort to bring the lists of noblemen up to date and register them for future service, the Tsar knew he could not easily uproot these young men from their comfortable lives in the provinces. Accordingly, he accompanied the order with the threat that failure to report would be punished by fines, corporal punishment and confiscation of property. He added that anyone accurately identifying a nobleman who failed to report would receive all of that nobleman's wealth, even if the informer was "a runaway serf."

This threat often failed. Noblemen dreamed up endless deceptions and explanations, business and travels, visits abroad and to monasteries, to avoid registering for service. Some simply disappeared into the vast emptiness of the Russian land. A clerk or soldier would arrive to investigate and find a deserted house; oddly, no one in the village would know where the master had gone. Some escaped service by pretending illness or feigning holy foolishness: "He jumped into the lake and stood there with the water lapping at his beard." When one group of young noblemen enrolled in a Moscow theological seminary to evade service, Peter swiftly drafted all these novice monks into the navy, packed them off to the Naval Academy in St. Petersburg and, as further punishment, sent them to drive piles along the Moika Canal. General-Admiral Apraxin, offended by this humiliation of the honor of old Russian families, went to the Moika, stripped off his admiral's uniform with its blue ribbon of the Order of St. Andrew and hung it on a pole, and began to drive piles beside the young men. Peter came up and asked with astonishment, "How is it, Fedor Matveevich, that you, a general-admiral, are driving piles?" Forthrightly, Apraxin replied, "Sire, these laborers are my nephews and grandchildren. Who am I then and by what right should I be privileged?"

In time, Peter was forced to decree that all noblemen who failed to report for service were outlaws. This meant that they could be robbed or killed with impunity, and that anyone bringing in such an outlaw would receive half of the outlaw's property. Finally, in 1721, also to limit evasion, Peter established the office of Herald, whose duty was to keep up-to-date lists of the nobility, recording the names of all male children and the place and capacity in which these sons were meeting their obligation of state service.

Education, in Peter's mind, was simply the first rung on the ladder of state service, and he tried to place every child on that ladder at a tender age. In 1714, along with his plan for compulsory enrollment of all noblemen into the army at fifteen, he decreed that their younger brothers must enroll in

secular schools at the age of ten. For five years, until they were ready for the army, they were to learn to read and write and do elementary arithmetic and geometry; until a young man had a certificate stating that he had finished this course, he was forbidden to marry. Landowners deeply resented this disruption of their traditions, and two years later, in 1716, Peter admitted defeat and revoked his decree. His effort to insist on compulsory education for children of the middle class also met with such widespread resistance and evasion that Peter was forced to give it up.

Once noblemen or others were enrolled in the service of the state, whether in military, naval or civil administration, their promotion supposedly was based on merit. A different and potentially far-reaching reform incorporating the principle of meritocracy was the Tsar's overthrowing of the time-honored Muscovite law of inheritance. Traditionally, when a father died, his landed estate and other immovable property was equally divided among his sons. The result of this continual subdivision into smaller and smaller plots was the impoverishment of the gentry and the drying up of sources of tax revenue. Peter's decree of March 14, 1714, declared that a father must pass his undivided estate to only one son—and that this son need not be the eldest. (If there were no sons, the same rules should be applied to daughters.) In England, Peter had been impressed by the system in which the eldest son inherited both title and land and the younger sons were expected to go into the army, the navy or some form of commerce. But Peter rejected primogeniture and chose inheritance by merit, which he thought would be even more productive than the English system: The ablest son would inherit, the land would be kept whole, thus preserving the wealth and distinction of the family (and facilitating the collection of taxes), the serfs would be better cared for, and the disinherited sons would be free to find some useful occupation in the service of the state. Unfortunately, no decree of Peter the Great was more unpopular; it produced family quarrels and violent feuds, and in 1730, five years after Peter's death, it was repealed.

Throughout his life, merit, loyalty and dedication to service were the only criteria by which Peter chose, judged and promoted men. Nobleman or "pie seller," Russian, Swiss, Scot or German, Orthodox, Catholic, Protestant or Jew, the Tsar heaped titles, wealth, affection and responsibility on anyone who was willing and competent to serve. Sheremetev, Dolgoruky, Golitsyn and Kurakin were illustrious names long before their bearers devoted themselves to Peter's service, but they owed their success not to blood but to merit. Menshikov's father, on the other hand, was a clerk, Yaguzhinsky's a Lutheran organist, Shafirov's a converted Jew and Kurbatov's a serf. Osterman and Makarov began as secretaries; Anthony Devier, the first Police Commissioner of St. Petersburg, began as a Portuguese

Jewish cabin boy whom Peter found in Holland and brought back to Russia. Nikita Demidov was a hard-working illiterate metalworker in Tula until Peter, admiring his energy and his success, gave him huge land grants to develop mines in the Urals. Abraham (or Ibrahim) Hannibal was a black Abyssinian prince brought as a slave to Constantinople where he was bought and sent as a present to Peter. The Tsar set him free and made him his godson, sent him to Paris to be educated, and eventually promoted him to General of the Artillery.* These men—Peter's eagles and eaglets, in Pushkin's phrase—began with nothing, but when they died, they were princes, counts and barons, and their names were inseparably entwined with Peter's in the history of Russia.

There is no better example of Peter's promotion by merit than the career of Ivan Neplyuev, one of Peter's most famous "fledglings." Neplyuev, the son of a small landowner in the Novgorod region, was summoned into service in 1715, when he was already twenty-two years old and the father of two children. He was sent to school in Novgorod to learn mathematics, then to the navigation school in Narva, then to the Naval Academy in St. Petersburg. In 1716, he was one of thirty midshipmen serving with the Russian fleet in Copenhagen. From there, Neplyuev followed the Tsar to Amsterdam, whence Peter sent him to Venice to train aboard Venetian galleys. After two years fighting the Turks in the Adriatic and Aegean seas, Neplyuev went on to Genoa, Toulon, Marseilles and Cadiz, where he served six months in the Spanish navy. When he returned to St. Petersburg in June 1720, he was ordered to come to the Admiralty for examination by the Tsar. "I do not know how my comrades received this news," wrote Neplyuev in his memoirs, "but I did not sleep the whole night and prepared myself as for the Day of Judgment."

When his turn came, Peter was kindly and, extending his hand to be kissed, said, "You see, brother, that I am tsar, yet there are callous places on my hands, because I wished to give you an example." As Neplyuev knelt, Peter said, "Stand up, brother, and answer the questions. Do not be afraid. If you know, say so. If you do not know, say so, too." Neplyuev survived the examination and was given command of a galley.

Almost immediately, however, he was transferred and placed in charge of ship construction in St. Petersburg. Upon taking the assignment, Neplyuev had been advised, "Always speak the truth and never lie. Even though things may be bad for you, the Tsar will be much angrier if you lie." It was not long before the young shipbuilder had occasion to test this advice.

---

* After his death, Hannibal gained immortality when he became the maternal grandfather of Alexander Pushkin and the central figure in Pushkin's novel (only a forty-page fragment of which was completed) *The Negro of Peter the Great*.

Arriving late at work one morning, he found Peter already there. He considered running home and sending word that he was sick, but then he remembered the advice and walked directly up to Peter. "You see, my friend, that I am here before you," said Peter, looking up. "I am to blame, Sire," replied Neplyuev. "Last night, I was with people and I stayed up very late and I was late getting up." Peter seized him by the shoulder and squeezed it hard. Neplyuev was convinced that he was doomed. "Thanks, my boy, for telling the truth," said the Tsar. "God will forgive you. All of us are human."

But Neplyuev was not long in this assignment either. Because of his language skills, he was frequently used as a translator, and in January 1721, still only twenty-eight, he was sent as Russian ambassador to Constantinople, returning home in 1734 to enjoy the estates which Peter had granted him in his absence. Eventually he became a senator. In 1774, during the reign of Catherine the Great, he died at the age of eighty.

Near the end of his reign, in 1722, Peter embodied his passionate belief in meritocracy in a permanent institutional framework, the famous Table of Ranks of the Russian Empire, which set before all young men entering service three parallel ladders of official ranks in the three branches of state service—military, civil and court. Each ladder had fourteen ranks, and each rank had a corresponding rank in the other two. Everyone was to begin his service on the bottom rung, and promotion was to depend not on birth or social status, but strictly on merit and length of service. Thereafter, at least in theory, nobility was of no importance in Russia, and honors and office were open to everyone. The noble titles of Old Russia were not abolished, but they carried no special privileges or distinctions. Commoners and foreigners were encouraged to apply for higher service, and soldiers, sailors, secretaries and clerks who merited notice were given appropriate positions on the Table of Ranks, where, once included, they competed, supposedly on equal terms, with Russian noblemen. Commoners who reached the lowest rank—i.e., the fourteenth on the military table, or the eighth on the civil or court ladder—were granted the status of "hereditary nobleman," with the right to own serfs and to pass along to their sons the right to enter state service at the bottom rank.

Thus, Peter, who had always given more weight to ability than to birth and who himself had worked his way up through the ranks in the army and the navy, passed his belief along to succeeding generations. This reform endured, and, despite subsequent alterations and inevitable corrosion by special favors and promotions won by bribes, it remained the basis of class structure in the Russian empire. Position on the Table of Ranks largely displaced birth as the measure of a man's worth, new blood was constantly brought into the army and the bureaucracy, and a man whose father had been a poor landowner or even a serf-soldier from the faraway Volga might

find himself rubbing elbows with men who bore the oldest names in Russian history.*

ON PAPER, as written in the decrees which flowed from Peter's pen, the reforms in administration might conceivably have made the Russian government function like the wheels of a watch. That it did not function this way was due not only to slowness to grasp or unwillingness to change, but also to many layers of corruption in government. Corruption affected not only the finances of the state but its basic efficiency. It made the imported administrative systems, already awkward to understand, almost impossible to operate.

Bribery and embezzlement were traditional in Russian public life, and public service was routinely looked upon as a means of gaining private profit. This practice was so accepted that Russian officials were paid little or no salary; it was taken for granted that they would make their living by accepting bribes. In Peter's time, only a handful of men in government were said to be honest and imbued with the idea of conscientious service to the state —Sheremetev, Repnin, Rumyantsov, Makarov, Osterman and Yaguzhinsky. The others were loyal to Peter personally, but regarded the state as a cow to be milked.

As a result, the majority of administrators were motivated less by a sense of service to the state than by desire for private gain, mingled with the effort to escape detection and punishment. Thus, two powerful negative motives, greed and fear, became the predominant features of Peter's bureaucrats. There were chances for immense riches—the vast wealth of Menshikov was an example; there was also a very good chance of torture, the scaffold or the wheel. Yet, whatever Peter did—urge, persuade, cajole, threaten, punish—seemed to make little difference. He realized that force was not enough. "I can turn dice not too badly with my chisel," he said sadly, "but I cannot turn mules with my cudgel."

Disappointment followed disappointment, not only at the highest levels. Once, Peter elevated an honest lawyer to a judgeship. In this new position,

---

* Ironically, under the Table of Ranks, Lenin, born Vladimir Ilych Ulyanov, was an hereditary Russian nobleman. This title was inherited from his father, Ilya, the son of a serf, who had gone to Kazan University and become an educator. Taking over responsibility for primary education in Simbirsk province on the Volga in 1874, he raised the number of primary schools in the province from 20 to 434 in fourteen years. For this achievement, he was promoted to the rank of Actual State Councilor in the civil service, the fourth rank from the top and the equivalent of a major general in the army. When Lenin's elder brother Alexander Ulyanov was executed in 1887 for attempting to assassinate Tsar Alexander III, the title passed automatically to the future founder of the Soviet state. In 1892, when Lenin, at twenty-one, applied to St. Petersburg for permission to take examinations in law, he signed himself "Nobleman Vladimir Ulyanov."

where his decision could become an object of bribery, the new judge became corrupt. When Peter found out, he not only absolved the judge, but doubled his salary to prevent further temptation. At the same time, however, the Tsar promised that if the judge ever again betrayed his trust, he would surely hang. The judge fervently promised that Peter's faith was justified—and soon afterward accepted another bribe. Peter hanged him.

The Tsar accepted that he could not enforce complete honesty at every level of government, but he was determined to suppress all forms of corruption which drained the national Treasury. In 1713, a decree called on all citizens to report to the Tsar himself any case of government corruption. The reward of the informer was to be the property of the accused, providing the informer's charge turned out to be accurate. This seemed too dangerous for most people, and what resulted was a torrent of anonymous letters, many of them maliciously inspired by a wish to pay off personal scores. Peter promulgated another decree, condemning anonymous letters by those who "beneath a show of virtue put out their venom." He promised his protection to accurate informers, saying, "Any subject who is a true Christian and an honorable servant of his sovereign and his fatherland may without any misgiving report orally or by letter to the Tsar himself." Eventually, an anonymous letter arrived which accused some of the highest officials of government of corruption on a grand scale. The writer was persuaded to stand up, and a dramatic trial ensued.

Over the years, the system by which villages were required to raise provisions for the army and deliver them to St. Petersburg and other towns through the newly conquered territories created a heavy burden because of transportation difficulties. To deal with these problems, middlemen stepped forward who agreed to make the required deliveries in return for the right to charge a higher price. This practice became a source of innumerable frauds. A number of key figures in the government were involved, conspiring with the deliverers and sometimes taking delivery of the provisions themselves under borrowed names. Although the scandal was widely known, nobody dared to challenge the noblemen and high officials involved by breaking the matter to Peter. Finally, so great was the misery of the people who were being taxed twice to pay for the stolen provisions that one man decided he must inform the Tsar. At the same time, he attempted to save his own neck by remaining anonymous and leaving unsigned letters of accusation in places where Peter went. Peter read one and offered the author not only his protection but a large reward if he would make himself known and could prove what he had charged. The informer appeared and provided the Tsar with unimpeachable evidence that his chief lieutenants were engaged in fraud.

A great investigation commenced early in 1715. Those involved included Prince Menshikov; General-Admiral Apraxin; Prince Matthew

Gagarin; Master of the Artillery General Bruce; Vice Governor of St. Petersburg Korsakov; First Lord of the Admiralty Kikin; First Commissioner of the Artillery Sinavin; Senators Opukhtin and Volkonsky, and a large number of civil servants of lesser ranks. The investigation was thorough and turned up much evidence. Apraxin and Bruce, brought before a commission, defended themselves by saying that they had rarely been in St. Petersburg, being mostly at sea or with the army in the field; accordingly, they had been unaware of actions taken behind their backs by their servants. Menshikov, who also had been away for many months commanding the army in Pomerania, was accused of financial dishonesty in his administration of that assignment, of making unlawful profits on government contracts and of wasting over one million roubles of government money and property.

Because Menshikov was so generally hated and because the commission of inquiry was headed by his bitter enemy, Prince Jacob Dolgoruky, the accusations were brought in an exaggerated, vengeful form which made them easier for Menshikov to moderate and partially disprove. Under scrutiny, what turned up was not sheer avarice; a considerable portion of bad management and confusion was blended in and there were many instances of irregularity in which there had been no intention of cheating. Menshikov's lawful income from his various estates was very large. Frequently, his own revenues had been applied to government uses and, also frequently, he had used public money for his own needs. Much of the irregularity consisted of diverting funds from one purpose to another without keeping proper accounts. Menshikov, for example, had been Governor of St. Petersburg since its founding, a period of more than ten years. During this time, he had received no salary and had repeatedly used his own money for government affairs. Because Peter disliked large palaces and huge receptions, Menshikov had built his grand palace and acted as host at innumerable public and diplomatic functions costing huge sums. Often he was not reimbursed for these expenses, yet Peter expected him to continue in this role. In addition, he had sometimes taken money from his own pocket to deal with state emergencies. In July 1714, Admiral Apraxin had written urgently from Finland that his troops were starving. As Peter was away, Menshikov demanded action by the Senate, but the senators refused to accept any responsibility, whereupon Menshikov boldly requisitioned 200,000 roubles' worth of supplies on his own account, loaded them aboard ships and sent them to succor Apraxin's forces.

Nevertheless, there were irregularities which could not be explained away. He was found to owe 144,788 roubles on one account and 202,283 roubles on another. These sums were assessed against him as fines. Menshikov paid the fines in part, but, on petitioning the Tsar, part was forgiven.

Apraxin and Bruce also escaped with heavy fines in recognition of their

past services to the nation. But for the others involved, the punishments were grim. The two convicted senators, Volkonsky and Opukhtin, who had incriminated not only themselves but tarnished the reputation of the newly formed Senate, were publicly knouted and had their tongues seared with hot iron for breaking their oaths. Korsakov, the Vice Governor of St. Petersburg, was publicly knouted. Three others had their noses slit after a knouting and then went to the gallows, while eight others, convicted of lesser offenses, were stretched on the ground to be beaten with batogs by soldiers. When Peter ordered them to stop, the soldiers shouted, "Father, let us beat them a little more, for the thieves have stolen our bread!" Some were exiled to Siberia. Kikin, who had been a special favorite of Peter's, was condemned to exile and his property was confiscated, but Catherine interceded for him, and both his office and his property were restored to him. Four years later, Kikin was tried again, this time for his role in the affair of the Tsarevich Alexis, and this time he lost his head.

ANONYMOUS LETTERS and public denunciations were a haphazard means of rooting out corruption, and in March 1711 Peter created a bureau of official informers called fiscals. They were to be headed by a chief, the Ober-Fiscal, whose assignment was to track down and report to the Senate all offenders, no matter what their rank. This kind of systematic, official informing was new to Russia. Previously, Russian law had permitted arrest and trial on the basis of a private accusation, but accusation was a double-edged weapon. The accuser had to present himself and prove his charges, and if the charges turned out to be false, the accuser rather than the accused was tortured and punished. Now, however, the accusers were permanent officers of the law, safe from revenge. Naturally, accusations multiplied, and soon the 500 fiscals were the most hated men in Russia. Even the members of the Senate, their nominal employers, feared these diligent spies. In April 1712, three senior fiscals complained to Peter that senators deliberately ignored their submitted reports, that Senators Jacob Dolgoruky and Gregory Plemyannikov had described them as "Antichrists and rogues" and that they dared not even physically approach most senators. Later in 1712, the Metropolitan, Stephen Yavorsky, denounced the fiscals in a sermon, declaring that they held everyone at their mercy while they themselves were above the law. Yet, Peter did not intercede, and the fiscals continued their hated work.

The most dedicated of the fiscals was Alexis Nesterov, who eventually became the Ober-Fiscal. This zealot labored with a fury, poking into every aspect of government, denouncing his victims with fanatical malice and at one point even bringing his own son to judgment. Nesterov's most prominent prey was Prince Matthew Gagarin, who since 1708 had been the

Governor of Siberia. Because of the great distance of his province from the capital, Gagarin ruled almost as a monarch beyond the Urals. Among his responsibilities was supervision of the China trade which passed through Nerchinsk and which was now a government monopoly. Nesterov, through his network of spies, discovered that Gagarin was cheating the government of revenue by allowing private merchants to trade illegally and by trading illegally himself. By this means, he had amassed an enormous fortune; his table was set every day for dozens of guests, and near his bed hung an icon of the Virgin decorated with diamonds worth 130,000 roubles. The record was not all black; on the contrary, Gagarin had made a substantial contribution to the development of Siberia by promoting industry and trade and opening up the mineral resources of the vast region. In addition, Gagarin was highly popular throughout the province for the mildness of his rule. When he was arrested, 7,000 Swedish prisoners working in Siberia petitioned the Tsar to pardon him.

Nesterov's first report on Gagarin's dishonesty was submitted to Peter in 1714, but the Tsar refused to pursue the matter. In 1717, Nesterov presented a more incriminating dossier, and Peter appointed a commission of Guards officers to investigate. Gagarin was arrested and confessed to irregularities and even illegalities, begging pardon and permission to end his days doing penance in a monastery. Everybody believed that Peter would pardon the Governor in recognition of his influence and services. But the Tsar, furious that his repeated decrees about honesty had been flouted, determined to make an example. Gagarin was condemned and publicly hanged in St. Petersburg in September 1718.

Nesterov wielded his power for almost ten years. Then the Ober-Fiscal himself was caught receiving presents which, although almost inconsequential in size, attracted the eye of his many ill-wishers. Quickly, the accumulated weight of enmity crushed him. He was tried, convicted and condemned to be broken alive on the wheel. The sentence was carried out in the square opposite Trezzini's new building for the colleges on Vasilevsky Island. By then, Nesterov was an old man with white hair. As he lay on the wheel, still alive, Peter, who happened to be visiting the colleges, went to the window and looked out. Seeing Nesterov and pitying him, the Tsar ordered the Ober-Fiscal's head to be cut off immediately so that he would not suffer longer.

The worst offender, whom even Nesterov had never dared to accuse, was Menshikov. Again and again, the Prince presumed on the indulgence of his long-suffering master. He knew that Peter needed him; for any man who occupies the lonely pinnacle of power, such a friend is essential. He was Peter's confidant, the interpreter of his thoughts and executor of his decisions, his closest companion for drinking, the governor of Peter's son, his cavalry commander, his right arm. In public, he was careful to treat the

Tsar with exaggerated respect; in private, he knew exactly how near the line he could go. If he passed it unwittingly, he received a blow from Peter's fist or cudgel. He accepted these with good humor and never sulked, which further endeared him. Yet, behind Peter's back, Menshikov showed a different face. To inferiors, he was domineering; to rivals, insolent. He had boundless ambition, his manners were coarse, he was an implacable enemy and he was bitterly hated as well as widely feared.

As Peter's reign progressed, the power of this royal favorite steadily grew, and after Poltava it knew few bounds. Menshikov was Governor General of St. Petersburg, First Senator, Knight of the Order of St. Andrew, Prince of the Holy Roman Empire, and bore titles from the Kings of Poland, Denmark and Prussia. It was commonly said that he could travel across the empire from Riga on the Baltic to Derbent on the Caspian and always sleep on one of his own estates. His palace on the Neva housed a glittering court of gentlemen, chamberlains, pages and Parisian cooks who prepared dinners of 200 dishes served on golden plates. Making his way through the streets in a fan-shaped carriage with his coat of arms emblazoned in gold on the door and a golden crown on the roof, drawn by six horses caparisoned in red and gold, he was always accompanied by liveried servants, musicians and an escort of dragoons to clear a way through the crowds. Yet, although Peter in affection and gratitude had endowed Menshikov with enormous wealth, it was never enough. Like many another man raised from nothing to vast power, he cared greatly for the trappings which would display that power. When not enough came in as bribes and gifts, he stole rapaciously. Despite the huge fines fixed on him by Peter, he was always rich and, after a brief period of disgrace, always returned to renewed favor. To the foreign ambassadors, expecting that each successive scandal would be Menshikov's last, then seeing him rise again, radiant and awesome, the Prince seemed a phoenix.

Often, Peter simply overlooked Menshikov's behavior. At one point, the Senate found evidence of irregularity in Menshikov's purchases of ammunition. They asked the Prince for an explanation, but Menshikov arrogantly brushed them aside, refusing to answer in writing or sign his name to anything, sending instead a junior officer with an oral reply. The senators then drew up a list of the principal charges and evidence against Menshikov and placed the paper on a table in front of the Tsar's chair. When Peter came in, he picked up the paper, ran his eye quickly over it and put it back on the table without a word. Finally, Tolstoy dared to ask what his reaction was. "Nothing," replied Peter. "Menshikov will always be Menshikov."

Nevertheless, Peter's indulgence had limits. Once, when he had deprived Menshikov temporarily of his immense estates in the Ukraine and compelled him to pay a fine of 200,000 roubles, Menshikov retaliated by taking down all the brocade and satin hangings and removing all the elegant furni-

ture from his palace on the Neva. A few days later, when Peter came to visit, he was surprised to find the house almost empty. "What does this mean?" he asked. "Alas, Your Majesty, I was obliged to sell everything in order to settle with the Treasury," said Menshikov. Peter stared at him for a minute. "I know better," he roared. "None of these games with me. If when I come back in twenty-four hours your house is not furnished as becomes a Serene Prince and Governor of St. Petersburg, the fine will be doubled!" On Peter's return, the palace was furnished more magnificently than before.

Peter's first warning to Menshikov came in 1711 after the Prince was accused of extortion during his command of the army in Poland. (Menshikov excused himself by arguing that he had taken only from the Poles.) "Mend your ways or you will answer to me with your head," Peter threatened, and for a while Menshikov obeyed. In 1715, he was charged again, and again he escaped by paying a fine. Nevertheless, after the 1715 trial Peter exhibited a new coolness toward his old friend. He continued to go to Menshikov's house and wrote him amiable, even affectionate, letters, but never fully trusted him again. Menshikov circumspectly adjusted to this new relationship. In his own letters, he dropped the familiar forms of address he had always used to Peter and switched to a more formal, respectful style as became a subject addressing an autocrat. He was abjectly apologetic, invoking Peter's old friendship and his own past services whenever the Tsar's mood darkened. The Prince had a powerful protector in Catherine, who was always ready to intercede on his behalf. On one of these occasions, Peter acceded to his wife's pleas, but warned her for the future: "Menshikov was conceived in iniquity, brought into the world in sin and will end his life in deceit. Unless he reforms, he will surely lose his head."

Menshikov was not out of trouble for long. At the beginning of January 1719, new charges were brought against him. He was summoned before a military court-martial, along with General-Admiral Apraxin and Senator Jacob Dolgoruky, and charged with maladministration of Ingria and embezzlement of 21,000 roubles meant for the purchase of cavalry horses. Menshikov admitted taking the money, but explained in his defense that the government still owed him 29,000 roubles which he had never been able to collect; therefore, when this money came into his hands, he had pocketed it in partial repayment. The court accepted the extenuating circumstances, but still condemned him for violating military laws. Both he and Apraxin were sentenced to the loss of all their estates and honors, and ordered to give up their swords and confine themselves in their homes until confirmation of the sentences by the Tsar. Both men went home to await the blow. Peter first confirmed the sentences and then, a day later, to everyone's surprise, canceled them in recognition of former services. Both men were restored to full rank. They paid severe fines, but nothing more. Peter simply could not afford to lose them.

For the time, it seemed, Menshikov was subdued. Soon after, the Prussian minister wrote, "The good Prince Menshikov has been well plucked. The Tsar asked him how many peasants he possessed in Ingria. He confessed to seven thousand, but His Majesty, who was much better informed, told him he was welcome to keep his seven thousand but he must give up all above that figure—in other words, eight thousand more. Menshikov, from anxiety and wondering what will happen to him next, has grown quite ill and as lean as a dog, but he has saved his neck once more and been pardoned till Satan tempts him again."

Nevertheless, true to Peter's prediction that "Menshikov will always be Menshikov," the Prince continued to swindle his master. In 1723, he was caught again and brought before an investigatory commission. He had been granted Mazeppa's estates near Baturin, and in 1724 he was accused of having concealed there over 30,000 serfs who had either fled the obligation of military service or run away from their landowners. Menshikov relied again on the advocacy of the good-natured Tsaritsa and presented a petition to Catherine at her coronation in which he laid the blame on Mazeppa, saying that the concealment of serfs had been done before he inherited the estates. Again, he was forgiven in greater part, but investigations were still continuing when Peter died, after which they were quashed by Catherine.

Peter, a man of simple tastes, was distressed and disgusted by the shameless rapacity of his lieutenants clutching at every opportunity to rob the state. On all sides, he saw bribery, embezzlement and extortion, and the Treasury's money "flowing from everybody's sleeves." Once, after hearing a Senate report listing further corruption, he summoned Yaguzhinsky in a rage and ordered the immediate execution of any official who robbed the state of even enough to pay for a piece of rope. Yaguzhinsky, writing down Peter's command, lifted his pen and asked, "Has Your Majesty reflected on the consequences of this decree?" "Go ahead and write," said Peter furiously. "Does Your Majesty wish to live alone in the empire without any subjects?" persevered Yaguzhinsky. "For we all steal. Some take a little, some take a great deal, but all of us take something." Peter laughed, shook his head sadly and went no further.

Yet he persevered to the end. Now and then, as with Gagarin, he made an example of a prominent delinquent, hoping to deter the smaller ones. Once when Nesterov asked, "Are only the branches to be cut off or are the roots to be cut out?" Peter replied, "Destroy everything, roots and branches alike." It was a hopeless task; Peter could not compel honesty. In this sense, the Tsar's admiring contemporary Ivan Pososhkov was right when he wrote, "The great monarch works hard and accomplishes nothing. The Tsar pulls uphill alone with the strength of ten, but millions pull downhill."

59

COMMERCE BY DECREE

In Russia, before Peter's time, there was little that could be called industry. Scattered through the towns were small factories and workshops for household implements, handicrafts and tools which met the needs of tsar, boyars and merchants. In the villages, the peasants made everything for themselves.

Upon his return from the West in 1698, Peter determined to change this and for the remainder of his life he labored to make Russia richer and its economy more efficient and productive. At first, with his country plunged into a major war, Peter's attempt to build industry related entirely to the needs of war. He developed cannon foundries, powder mills, factories to make muskets, leatherworks for saddles and harness, textile mills to weave woolen cloth for uniforms and make sails for the fleet. By 1705, the state-owned textile factories in Moscow and Voronezh were doing so well that Peter wrote to Menshikov: "They are making cloth and God gives excellent results, so that I have made a caftan for myself for the holidays."

After Poltava, the emphasis changed. As the demands of war diminished, Peter became more interested in other kinds of manufacturing, those designed to raise Russian life to the level of the West and at the same time to make Russia less dependent on imports from abroad. Aware that large sums were being drained out of the country to pay for imports of silk, velvet, ribbon, china, and crystal, he established factories to make these products in Russia. To protect the fledgling industries, he placed high import duties on foreign silk and cloth which doubled their price for Russian buyers. Basically, his policy was similar to that of other European states at the time, which can generally be described as mercantilism: to increase exports in order to earn foreign currency, and decrease imports in order to stem the flow of Russian wealth abroad.

Peter's industrialization policy had a second purpose, equally important. His tax collectors were already wringing the Russian people lifeless to finance the war. The only long-term way to extract more revenue from his people, Peter realized, was to increase the production of national wealth,

thus increasing the tax base. To achieve this goal, the Tsar hurled himself and the power of the state into every aspect of developing the national economy. Peter viewed himself as personally responsible for the strengthening of the national economy, but at the same time he understood that private enterprise and initiative were the true sources of national wealth. His goal was to create a class of Russian entrepreneurs who would assist and eventually replace the sovereign and the state as producers of this wealth. It was not an easy task. By tradition, Russian noblemen looked disdainfully on any involvement in trade and industry and were determined not to invest their capital in commercial enterprises. Peter employed a combination of persuasion and force, preaching the dignity and usefulness of commerce and making trade and industry an honorable form of state service—like service in the army, navy or civilian bureaucracy. The government, through the College of Mining and Manufacturing, provided initial capital in the form of loans and subsidies, granted monopolies and tax exemptions, and sometimes simply erected factories at Treasury expense and leased them to private individuals or companies. These arrangements often were compulsory. In 1712, the state constructed a group of cloth factories to be managed by private merchants. "If they do not wish to do this of their own free will," declared the order, "then they must be forced. Grant them facilities to defray the cost of the factory so that they may take pleasure in trading."

Not all of the new enterprises flourished. A silk company formed by Menshikov, Shafirov and Peter Tolstoy was granted generous privileges and subsidies and still managed to fail. Menshikov quarreled with his partners and resigned, to be replaced by Admiral Apraxin. Eventually, having swallowed all of its original capital, the company was sold to private merchants for 20,000 roubles. Menshikov had better luck with a company formed to fish for walrus and cod in the White Sea.

The most productive partnership between state and private industry was in mining and heavy industry. When Peter came to the throne, Russia possessed some twenty small state and private iron foundries around Moscow, in Tula and at Olonets on Lake Onega. Declaring that "our Russian state abounds in riches more than many other lands and is blessed with metals and minerals," Peter began early in his reign to develop these natural resources. Among the foreigners employed by the Great Embassy for service in Russia were numerous mining engineers. Once the war began, the ironworks at Tula, founded by the Dutch father of Andrew Vinius and owned in part by the crown and in part by the ironmaster Nikita Demidov, were expanded to provide muskets and cannon for the entire army. The city of Tula became an immense arsenal, its various suburbs populated by different categories of armorers and smiths. After Poltava, Peter sent prospectors throughout the Urals looking for new deposits. In 1718, he estab-

lished a College of Mining and Manufacturing, to encourage location and development of new mineral sites. In December 1719, a decree threatened with the knout any landowner who concealed mineral deposits on his lands or who obstructed prospecting by others. The rolling hills of the Urals, especially in Perm province, revealed themselves to be astonishingly rich in high-grade ores: the ore taken from the ground produced almost half its weight in pure iron. To help develop these rich veins, Peter turned again to Nikita Demidov. By the end of Peter's reign, a vast industrial and mining complex consisting of twenty-one iron and copper foundries had risen in the Urals, centering on the town of Ekaterinburg, named in honor of Peter's wife.* Nine of these works were owned by the state and twelve by private individuals, including Demidov, who owned five. Their production constantly increased, and by the end of the reign more than forty percent of all Russian iron was coming from the Urals. Within Peter's lifetime, Russian output of pig iron equaled that of England, and in the reign of Catherine the Great, Russia supplanted Sweden as the largest producer of iron in Europe. These flourishing mines and foundries made the state strong (16,000 cannon were in the arsenals at Peter's death) and Demidov enormously rich. On the birth of the Tsarevich Peter Petrovich, Demidov presented the infant with 100,000 roubles as "tooth-cutting money." In 1720, the infant's proud father made Demidov a count, a title which lasted until the end of the dynasty.

To facilitate trade, Russia needed more circulating currency. New Russian coins had been minted since Peter's return from the West with the Great Embassy, but coins were so scarce that merchants in Petersburg, Moscow and Archangel borrowed them at fifteen percent interest simply to keep their businesses operating. One reason for this scarcity was the ingrained habit of all Russians, from peasant to noble, of quickly hiding any money on which they could lay their hands. As a foreign visitor explained, "Among the peasants, if by chance one happens to gain a small sum, he hides it under a dunghill, where it lies dead to him and to the nation. The nobility, being afraid of making themselves noticed and obnoxious to the court by the show of their wealth, commonly lock it up in coffers to molder there, or those more sophisticated send it to banks in London, Venice or Amsterdam. Consequently, with all the money thus concealed by nobility and peasants, it has no circulation and the country reaps no benefit from it." At the beginning of the war, a decree declared that "the hoarding of money is forbidden. Informers who discover a cache are to be rewarded with one third of the money, the remainder to go to the state."

---

* In 1918, Ekaterinburg was the site of the murder of the family of the last Russian Emperor, Nicholas II. Today, the city is named Sverdlovsk.

Another reason for the scarcity of coinage was an insufficiency of precious metals. Gold- and silversmiths who came to Russia became discouraged and went home, and many freshly coined roubles were defective as to both alloy and weight of metal. Peter knew this and it worried him, but as the mines simply were not producing enough gold and silver, he was forced to allow the debasement to continue. In 1714, to preserve the nation's economy, Peter forbade the export of silver. In 1718, merchants leaving Russia were searched and any gold, silver or copper coins found were confiscated. On the least suspicion, customs officers would dismantle the carriages or sledges in which merchants were traveling. In 1723, this regulation was strengthened by adding the death penalty for anyone caught exporting silver. On the other hand, the import of gold and silver was vigorously encouraged; there was no duty on these metals. And when Russians sold their goods to foreigners, they were not permitted to accept Russian money in payment, but had always to receive foreign money.*

Peter's commands, issued impatiently from above, often were received without the slightest understanding of what was wanted or why. This compelled the Tsar not only to supervise everything closely himself, but also to employ force to get things done. Traditionally conservative, Russians balked at innovations, and Peter told his ministers, "You know yourselves that anything that is new, even if it is good and necessary, our people will not do without being compelled." He never apologized for using force. In a decree in 1723, he explained that "our people are like children who never want to begin the alphabet unless they are compelled to by the teacher. It seems very hard to them at first, but when they have learned it, they are thankful. So in manufacturing affairs, we must not be satisfied with the proposing of the idea only, but we must act and even compel."

Commerce is a delicate mechanism, and state decrees are not usually the best way to make it work. In Peter's case, it was not simply the element of compulsion that detracted from the success of his efforts—he himself was not always sure what he wanted. When his attention wandered or he was distracted, those below him, uncertain as to his desires, did nothing and all activity stopped. Peter's methods were strictly empirical. He tried this or that, ordering and countermanding, seeking a system that worked, sometimes without thoroughly understanding what was needed or the nature of the obstacles confronting him. His constant changes in direction, his minute regulations leaving no scope for local adjustment, confused and drained initiative from Russian merchants and manufacturers. Once, when the Dutch ambassador was pressing for Russian approval of a new commercial treaty

---

* All this has a familiar ring to foreigners who live or travel in the Soviet Union today.

and had been frustrated by repeated delays, he was told by Osterman, "Between ourselves, I will tell you the truth. We have not a single man who understands commercial affairs at all."

There were occasions when enterprises foundered simply because Peter was not present to give instructions. His temper could be so fierce and unpredictable that, in the absence of specific orders, people were unwilling to take initiative and simply did nothing. In Novgorod, for example, a large number of leather saddles and harnesses had been stored for the army. The local authorities knew that they were there, but because no order to distribute them had come down from above, they were left until "eventually, moldy and rotten, they had to be dug up with spades." Similarly, in 1717, many oak trunks brought from central Russia through the canals to Lake Ladoga for use in building the Baltic fleet were left to wash up on the shores and bury themselves in mud, simply because Peter was away in Germany and France and had not left specific instructions for their use.

To bridge the gap between the innovative Tsar who, despite his consuming interest, was often occupied with other matters, and the uncomprehending, unwilling nation, there were the foreigners. None of Peter's work in developing the national economy would have been possible without the foreign experts and craftsmen who poured into Russia between the time of Peter's return from the West in 1698 and his death in 1725. The Tsar engaged more than a thousand foreigners during his first visit to Amsterdam and London, and thereafter Russian envoys and agents at foreign courts were urgently commissioned to search out and persuade local artisans and technicians to enter Russian service.

Foreign craftsmen, foreign ideas and foreign machines and materials were at work in every sphere of industrial, commercial and agricultural activity. Vines, brought from France, were planted near Astrachan to produce wine which a Dutch traveler pronounced as "red and pleasant enough." Twenty shepherds, arriving from Silesia, were sent to Kazan to shear the sheep and teach the Russians there how to make wool so that it would no longer be necessary to buy English wool to clothe the army. Peter saw better horses in Prussia and Silesia and ordered the Senate to establish stud farms and import stallions and mares. He observed Western peasants reaping grain with a long-handled scythe rather than the short-handled sickle which Russian peasants had always bent to use, and decreed that his people must adopt the scythe. Near Petersburg was a factory which turned Russian flax into a linen as fine in every respect as linen from Holland. The flax was spun in a workhouse where an old Dutch woman was teaching eighty Russian women how to use the spinning wheels, which were little known in Russia. Not far off was a paper mill run by a German specialist. Throughout the land, foreigners were teaching Russians how to build and operate glass factories, brick kilns, powder mills, saltpeter works, ironworks

and paper mills. Once in Russia, foreign workers enjoyed numerous special privileges, including free houses and exemption from taxes for ten years. Surrounded by suspicious and xenophobic Russians, they lived under the Tsar's personal protection, and Peter sternly warned his people not to harm or take advantage of them. Even when a foreigner failed, Peter usually treated him with kindness and sent him home with a sum of money.

Behind this policy was not a frivolous love of everything foreign. Instead, Peter had a single, firm purpose: to use foreign technicians to help build a modern Russia. Foreigners were invited and privileges granted to them on a single condition which was part of every contract: "that they instruct our Russian people properly and conceal nothing." Occasionally, foreign experts did attempt to conceal trade secrets. In one such case, English tobacco curers, departing from Russia, used violent means to prevent their special technology from falling into Russian hands. Astonishingly, Charles Whitworth, the English ambassador, not only countenanced this violence, but committed it himself:

> The great secret which the Muscovites desire to know is the liquor for preparing and coloring the tobacco. . . . The Russian laborers were dismissed and the same evening I went to the workhouse together with Mr. Parsons, my secretary, and four of my servants. We spent the best part of the night in destroying the several instruments and materials, some of which were so strong that they obliged us to make a great noise in pulling them to pieces. There were cloven barrels about a quarter full of the tobacco liquor which I caused to be let out. . . . I likewise broke the great spinning wheel, and above three score reels for rolling; I then destroyed three engines already set up for cutting tobacco and took away the plates and cranes for two more; several engines for pressing the tobacco into form have been pulled to pieces, their screws split, the wooden moles broken, the copper carried away, and about 20 fine sieves cut to pieces. . . . The next day my servants returned and burned all that remained of wood.

Had Peter discovered the ambassador's role in this violent, nocturnal episode, Whitworth's stay in Russia would certainly have been cut short.

On another occasion, however, a Russian outwitted a secretive foreigner. Peter had established a ribbon factory near Petersburg, staffing it with young Russian apprentices; the master was a foreigner. At the end of a year, Peter found that one young man, the most skilled of the young Russians, could make any kind of ribbon once the materials were set upon the loom, but that neither he nor his companions could begin unaided because the master always placed the work upon the loom himself and forbade anyone to watch during this operation. Peter instructed the Russian apprentice to discover

this secret and promised a reward if he succeeded. Accordingly, the apprentice bored a small hole in the ceiling of the workshop and lay quietly on his stomach, observing the master as he set the looms. Having learned the technique, he informed the Tsar, who had set up a loom in his presence in the palace. When the apprentice succeeded, Peter kissed him, gave him money and made him the new master.

HAVING CONSTRUCTED a new capital on the Neva, Peter was determined that it should be more than an administrative hive for his bureaucrats and a parade ground for his Guards regiments; he meant St. Petersburg to be a great port and commercial center. To endow it with importance and build it into a major commercial center, he took steps to divert trade to the Neva from other ports, in particular from the lengthy, circuitous Archangel route. This arbitrary commercial upheaval was achieved only by overriding the pleas and cries of many—Russians and foreigners alike—who had invested heavily in that route. Nevertheless, Peter gradually increased the pressure. The struggle continued until 1722, when he finally forbade the shipping of any goods from Archangel other than those actually produced in that province or along the banks of the Dvina. That year, St. Petersburg finally prevailed over Archangel and became the leading port on Russian soil, although its trade was still not as large as Riga's. By the end of Peter's reign, the volume of Russia's foreign trade exceeded the wildest of Peter's early dreams. Overall seaborne commerce had quadrupled in value. In 1724, 240 Western merchant ships arrived in St. Petersburg, while 303 visited Riga. In 1725, 914 foreign ships called at Russian Baltic ports.

But Peter failed in another objective: the creation of a Russian merchant marine. He had hoped that Russian goods could be carried to the West in Russian merchant ships, but this effort ran into an old prejudice, long inflicted by Western maritime nations. In the time of Novgorod, when Russian merchants had desired to export their produce in their own ships, the merchants of the Hanseatic League had joined against them to insist that they would buy Russian goods only in Novgorod and then be responsible for shipping them themselves. At a later time, an enterprising merchant of Yaroslavl took a cargo of furs to sell in Amsterdam, but, by concerted arrangement among Dutch buyers, he was unable to sell a single fur and had to carry them back to Archangel. There, they were bought immediately at a good price by the Dutch merchant who owned the vessel which had carried the furs back to Russia.

Early in his reign, Peter resolved to change this pattern and instructed Apraxin, as Governor of Archangel, to build two small Russian ships which would sail to the West carrying Russian cargoes under the Russian flag. Knowing that their arrival would provoke opposition, he pondered where

to send them. Dutch and English merchants would be vigorously opposed, while in France, the Tsar felt, the Russian flag might not be respected. At last the ships *were* dispatched to France, but already Peter had retreated: They sailed under the Dutch rather than the Russian flag. One of the ships was confiscated by the French, and its return became the subject of a lengthy argument. In general, Peter never succeeded in this effort, and in shipping—and even in the handling of foreign commerce in Russian ports—Dutch and English merchants retained their virtual monopoly.

Despite this failure, Peter bore no grudge against foreign captains or seamen. On the contrary, he was delighted when foreign merchant ships arrived in Russian ports, welcoming them grandly and treating the captains as brother mariners. As soon as a foreign ship appeared in the harbor of Kronstadt or St. Petersburg, Peter arrived on board to walk its decks, examine its structure and rigging and look for new developments in its construction. His visits were so common, especially among the Dutch captains who came annually to St. Petersburg, that they looked forward to sitting down with the Tsar in their cabins with brandy, wine, cheese and biscuits to answer his questions about their voyages. In return, Peter invited them ashore to attend his court and all its celebrations; it was seldom that they returned sober to their ships. As one observer noted: "It is easy to conceive how much this reception was to the taste of people in that line of life and with how much pleasure they steered their course for St. Petersburg."

Nothing was allowed to spoil this relationship. In 1719, when new customs regulations were drawn up for the port of St. Petersburg, the first draft presented to Peter for approval declared that ships that carried contraband or concealed dutiable goods should be confiscated. Peter struck out this article, explaining that it was much too early in the life of the port for such drastic action; he had no desire to frighten ship captains and merchants away.

The Emperor allowed visiting captains to speak to him on terms of familiarity which shocked his Russian favorites. When one Dutch captain said he still preferred Archangel to St. Petersburg and the Tsar asked why, the captain cheekily replied that there were no pancakes in St. Petersburg. "Come to court tomorrow," Peter replied, "and you will have your fill of pancakes."

When foreign seamen became embroiled in disputes with Russians, Peter hurried to the defense. Once, a Dutch merchant vessel, maneuvering into the crowded harbor of Kronstadt, accidentally rammed a Russian frigate, breaking its accommodation ladder. The Russian captain was furious, although the apologetic Dutch captain offered to pay for the damage. Unappeased, the Russian sent a guard of Russian soldiers and sailors on board the merchantman and demanded ten times the appropriate sum. Peter was at Kronstadt and, hearing of the commotion, rowed out to the frigate to

inspect the damage. Seeing that no harm had been done except to the ladder, which could be repaired in a few hours, he became enraged at his frigate captain. "In three hours," he said, "I will return and I expect to see the ladder of your ship repaired." Three hours later, the Tsar returned to find the ladder repaired but unpainted. "Paint the ladder red," he commanded, "and in the future, let foreigners receive nothing at your hands but marks of politeness and friendship."

IT WAS TYPICAL of Peter's character that in the middle of a war, with a new army, a new navy, a new capital and a new national economy all under construction, he should also begin to dig a new system of canals at different points in Russia. It was not that they were unneeded. The distances in Russia were so vast and the roads so poor that commercial goods as well as individual travelers faced almost insurmountable obstacles in moving from place to place. This problem had always bedeviled the effort to bring products from deep inside the giant nation to the seaports for export; now, it presented itself even more acutely in the form of transporting the quantities of grain and other foodstuffs which were needed to feed St. Petersburg. The solution had been provided in large part by nature, which had equipped Russia with a magnificent network of rivers—the Dnieper, the Don, the Volga and the Dvina. Although all these rivers except the Dvina flowed south, it still remained possible to haul goods northward, upstream, by the sheer brute force of human and animal labor. What remained was to connect this far-flung tracery of natural water routes with a system of canals which linked the rivers at vital points.

Peter's first herculean effort was to try to link the Volga with the Don and thus, by his possession of Azov at the mouth of the Don, give most of the Russian heartland access to the Black Sea. For more than ten years, thousands of men labored to dig a canal and build stone locks, but the project was abandoned when Peter was forced to return Azov to the Turks. The growth of St. Petersburg inspired a second vision: linking the whole of Russia to the Baltic by connecting the Volga to the Neva. By extensive surveying, Peter located in the region of Tver and Novgorod a tributary of the Volga which ran within less than a mile of another stream which flowed, through many lakes and rivers, into Lake Ladoga, which emptied into the Neva. The key was a small canal at Vyshny-Volochok. It took 20,000 men four years to dig the canal with the necessary locks, but when it was finished, the Caspian Sea was linked by water with St. Petersburg, the Baltic and the Atlantic Ocean. Thereafter, a stream of flat-bottomed barges loaded with grain, oak timbers and other products of southern and central Russia, along with the goods of Persia and the East, moved slowly but continuously across the face of Russia.

Naturally, there were difficulties and opposition. Prince Boris Golitsyn, assigned to oversee the first of these projects, grumbled that "God made the rivers go one way and it was presumption in man to think to turn them another." The flow of river traffic was sometimes impeded when the stone locks of Vyshny-Volochok canal silted up and had to be redredged. But this was a minor obstacle compared to the hazards faced on Lake Ladoga. The surface of this mighty inland lake, the largest in Europe, was sometimes whipped by wind into a violence worthy of an ocean, and often the waves overwhelmed the unwieldy, flat-bottomed river barges which had to have an exceptionally shallow draft to pass through the Vyshny-Volochok canal. When storm winds howling down from the north caught these clumsy river craft on the open lake, the boats either capsized or were driven onto the southern shore of the lake and broken in pieces. Every year, gale winds sank or drove ashore hundreds of barges, with the loss of their cargoes. Peter ordered the construction of a special fleet of lake boats with hulls and keels deeper than the shallow barges, to be used for the passage across Lake Ladoga. But this required unloading and reloading which were far too expensive and time-consuming with cargoes such as grain, hay and timber. His next move was to look for a way of avoiding the lake passage. In 1718, he decided to cut a canal through the swampy land along the southern shore of the lake from the River Volkhov to the mouth of the Neva at Schlüsselburg. The total distance would be sixty-six miles.

The project was first entrusted to Menshikov, who knew nothing of engineering, but was anxious to accept any assignment which might win him favor with Peter. Menshikov spent more than two million roubles and squandered the lives of 7,000 workmen, who died of hunger and disease because of bad administration. A great deal of needless work was done even before the basic decision had been made whether it was better to dig the canal in the earth behind the shoreline or to try to wall off part of the lake with dikes. The Tsar was on the point of abandoning the work when he encountered a German engineer, Burkhard Christopher von Munnich, who had had extensive experience building dikes and canals in North Germany and Denmark. Once Munnich took over, the work proceeded more efficiently, and in 1720 Weber wrote: "I am credibly informed that this work is in such an advanced state as to be ready next summer and that consequently the trade between the Baltic and the Caspian Sea, or between all Russia and Persia, will be upon a sure foot, though still with the inconvenience that ships coming from Kazan might be near two years on their way." Weber was badly misinformed, and by 1725, when Peter died, the Emperor had seen only twenty miles of the great canal (it was seventy feet wide and sixteen feet deep) actually dug. After Peter's death, Menshikov frowned on the engineer, and it was not until 1732, in the reign of Empress Anne, that the canal was finished and Munnich triumphantly escorted the

Empress in a procession of state barges along the entire length of the prodigious waterway.

Today, the great canal system of Russia initiated by Peter forms a giant artery of commerce for the Soviet Union. The canals permit large ships to pass to and fro, up and down the rivers of Russia from the Black Sea and the Caspian to the White Sea and the Baltic. During the White Nights in Leningrad, one can sit on the Neva embankment and, after midnight, when the city's bridges have gone up, watch a long procession of ocean-sized cargo ships pass like silent mammoths up the river, bound for the interior of Russia a thousand miles away.

EVERYTHING had to be paid for. Relentlessly and remorselessly, the war and the great construction projects sucked up the lifeblood and treasure of Russia. Although Peter repeatedly emphasized to his officials that taxes should be levied "without unduly burdening the people," his own constant demand for funds overruled this sentiment. Taxes crushed every article and activity of daily life, yet the state never collected enough money to pay its mounting expenses. In 1701, the army and navy swallowed up three quarters of the revenues; in 1710, four fifths; and in 1724, even though the war was over, two thirds. When money was short, Peter slashed the salaries of all officials, temporal and spiritual, excepting only those most necessary to the realm: "foreign artisans, soldiers and sailors." In 1723, there was so little cash that some government officials were paid in furs.

The only solution, until growing commercial and industrial activity could expand the tax base, was to lay still heavier taxes on the burdened nation. Hitherto, the basic tax had been the old household tax, determined by a census taken in 1678 during the reign of Tsar Fedor. This tax was laid on every village and landowner according to the number of houses and farms possessed (and made for crowded living because, to avoid taxation, as many families and people as possible crowded under one roof). In 1710, believing that the population must have increased, Peter ordered a new census. To his astonishment, the new census showed that in thirty years the number of households had decreased by from one fifth to one quarter. There was some real justification for this: Peter had drained off hundreds of thousands of men into the army, the shipyards at Voronezh, the work on the canals and the building of St. Petersburg, while thousands more had fled into the forest or to the frontier. But the new low figures also represented the helplessness of the government to overcome the stratagems of both nobility and peasants who were determined to evade taxes. Bribing the commissioners who counted the houses was a preliminary gambit. If this failed, the peasants simply removed their houses from the commissioners' sight. Russian peasant houses were largely made of logs or timbers notched at four corners. Thus,

they could be un-notched in a few hours and either removed to the forest or scattered about. The census takers and tax collectors knew the trick, but there was little they could do about it.

Upon his return from France, Peter decided to approach the problem differently, replacing the household tax with a version of the individual head tax he had observed in France. The tax-paying unit of this new poll tax was to be the "soul": that is, every male from infant to grandfather in every village, town or peasant commune. But before the new tax could be levied, a new census was required. On November 26, 1718, a decree ordered that every Russian male except noblemen, churchmen and certain privileged merchants (all of whom were taxed differently) be inscribed. Again, opposition was intense but by 1722, a census had been compiled, listing 5,794,928 male "souls" and in 1724 the soul tax was collected for the first time. Peasants were assessed at 74 kopeks or 114 kopeks per year, depending on whether they worked on private or state land. In terms of revenue, the tax was an enormous success, producing half of the state income that year and continuing in use through most of the nineteenth century until 1887, when it was abolished by Alexander III.

The soul tax solved Peter's problem of revenue, but at the cost of placing an even heavier burden on the peasants and strengthening the bonds of the serfdom that tethered them to the land. In earlier times, Russian peasants had been free to move where they wished, a right that made it difficult and sometimes impossible for landowners to meet their needs for labor. This crisis intensified in the middle of the sixteenth century when Ivan the Terrible conquered Kazan and Astrachan, opening to Russian colonization vast regions of virgin black earth previously inhabited by nomads. By the thousands and hundreds of thousands, Russian peasants abandoned the forest to the north and poured into this flat, rich country. Farms and villages in central Russia were left uninhabited; whole provinces were semi-deserted. Landowners, threatened with ruin, appealed to the state, and the state, unable to collect taxes from empty villages, reacted. Beginning in the 1550's, decrees forbidding peasants to leave the land were issued. Runaway peasants were pursued, and in 1649 it was declared that any person who harbored them was liable to their landlord for his losses. In Peter's time, over ninety-five percent of the people were serfs; some were state peasants and some belonged to private landlords, but all were bound for life to the land they worked.

Peter's new soul tax placed the peasants even more firmly in the hands of the landowners. Once the population of a district had been counted by the census, the landowners and local authorities were responsible to the state for producing the tax revenue based on that population; actual collection of the money was left up to them. To assist landowners in keeping track of their peasants and extracting these taxes, Peter decreed in 1722 that serfs

could not leave a landowner's estate without his written permission. This was the origin of the internal-passport system which continues in use in the Soviet Union today. Eventually, the power placed in the hands of the landowners—to collect taxes, to control movement, to dictate work, to punish infractions—made each landowner a little government unto himself. Where his ability to enforce was threatened, he was supported by the intervention of army regiments permanently billeted throughout the countryside. In time, to increase the controls on peasant movement, any serf wanting to leave the land was required to get not only the landowner's written permission, but written permission from the army as well. The result was a hereditary, all-embracing system of permanent servitude.

Most Russian serfs were bonded to the land, but not all. One great obstacle to persuading Russian noblemen and merchants to open new factories had been the difficulty of finding labor. To overcome this, Peter decreed in January 1721 that factory and mine owners could have factory serfs—that is, laborers permanently attached to the factory or mine in which their labor took place. Underscoring the key importance of building new industry, the Tsar also waived the strict rules about returning runaway serfs. Those serfs, he declared, who had fled their landowners to find work in factories should not be returned, but should remain where they were as permanent industrial serfs.

In the end, Peter's tax policies were a success for the state and a massive burden for the people. When the Emperor died, the state did not owe a kopek. Peter had fought twenty-one years of war, constructed a fleet, a new capital, new harbors and canals without the aid of a single foreign loan or subsidy (indeed, it was he who paid subsidies to his allies, especially Augustus of Poland). Every kopek was raised by the toil and sacrifice of the Russian people within a single generation. He did not float internal loans so that future generations could help to pay for his projects, nor did he devalue the currency by issuing paper money as Goertz had done on behalf of Charles XII of Sweden. Instead, he laid the entire burden on his contemporary Russians. They strained, they struggled, they opposed, they cursed. But they obeyed.

60

SUPREME UNDER GOD

IN MATTERS OF RELIGION, Peter was an eighteenth- rather than a seventeenth-century man, secular and rationalist rather than devout and mystical. He cared more about trade and national prosperity than about dogma or interpretations of Scripture; none of his wars was fought over religion. Yet, personally, Peter believed in God. He accepted God's omnipotence and saw His hand in everything: life and death, victory and defeat. His letters are studded with the phrase "Thanks be to God"; every victory was promptly celebrated with a Te Deum. He believed that tsars were more responsible to God than commoners were, as tsars were entrusted with the duty to rule, but he did not enshrine the role of monarchy in anything so theoretical or philosophical as the Divine Right of Kings. Peter simply approached religion as he approached everything else: What seemed reasonable? What was practical? What worked best? The best way to serve God, he believed, was to work for the strength and prosperity of Russia.

Peter enjoyed going to church. As a child, he was thoroughly drilled in the Bible and the liturgy, and as tsar he made an effort to spread accurately written Bibles throughout his realm. He loved choral singing, the only music of the Orthodox Church, and it was his lifelong habit to push his way forward through the standing crowd and take his place to sing with the choir. Orthodox congregations are less disciplined than those of other faiths: People stand through the service and move about, coming and going, signaling, whispering and smiling among themselves. Peter accepted this, but he would not tolerate people talking openly during a service. When he heard such an offender, he immediately collected a fine of one rouble. Later, he erected a pillory in front of a church in St. Petersburg for those who spoke during the service.

Respect for the service was more important to Peter than the form of the service. To the despair of many of his countrymen—especially the leaders of the Russian church—Peter's tolerance of other Christian sects was

greater than ever experienced before in Holy Orthodox Russia. Peter had early understood that if he was to recruit foreigners in sufficient numbers, he would have to permit them to worship according to their own traditions. This view was reinforced in 1697 by his first visit to Amsterdam, which allowed people of all nations to practice any form of religion as long as they did not disturb the established church or the churches of other foreigners. "It is our belief that the religious ceremonies of those who have come to reside among us are of little consequence to the state, providing that they contain nothing contrary to our laws," Witsen had explained. This toleration, Peter noted later, "contributed greatly to the influx of foreigners and consequently increased public revenues," adding, "I intend to imitate Amsterdam in my city of St. Petersburg."

As much as possible, he did so. Foreigners in Russia were permitted to have their own councils to rule on marriages and other ecclesiastical matters without being subject to Russian laws or the control of the Russian church. Late in his reign, Peter issued decrees recognizing the validity of Protestant and Catholic baptisms and permitting marriages between Russian Orthodox believers and members of other faiths, providing the children were brought up as Orthodox. Both these laws eased the path of Swedish prisoners now settled in Russia who desired to marry Russian women. Toleration was also state policy toward members of other religions, Christian or non-Christian, in other parts of the Russian empire. In the Baltic provinces conquered from Sweden, Peter agreed that the Lutheran religion should be preserved as the state church, and this guarantee became an article in the Treaty of Nystad. In the vast khanate of Kazan and other regions where the majority of the people were Moslem, Peter made no effort to convert them to Christianity; he knew that such an effort would probably fail and might provoke rebellion.

To a considerable degree, Peter was even tolerant of Old Believers, whom the church vociferously condemned and persecuted. For Peter, the crucial point was whether their religious beliefs helped or harmed the state; their desire to cross themselves with two fingers instead of three mattered little to him. Thousands of Old Believers, fleeing persecution, had formed new settlements in the forests of northern Russia. In 1702, when Peter was traveling south from Archangel with five battalions of the Guard, he was to pass through this region, and the Old Believers, assuming that they were to be attacked, gathered in their wooden churches, locked the doors and prepared to burn themselves to death rather than recant. But Peter had no such intention. "Let them live as they like," he said, and moved south to fight the Swedes. Subsequently, when iron ore was discovered nearby in the vicinity of Olonets, a number of Old Believers went to work in the mines and forges and proved to be good workmen. This was even more to Peter's liking; it was a useful fruit of toleration. "Let them believe what they like,

for if reason cannot turn them from their superstitions, neither fire nor sword can do it. It is foolish to make them martyrs. They are unworthy of the honor and would not in this way be of use to the state."

Granted this latitude, the Old Believers continued to live quietly in remote regions, refusing to submit to church authority, but paying taxes and living irreproachable lives. In time, however, as the war made huge demands on Russian labor, Peter began to see their withdrawal into the forests not just as religious conservatism but also as political opposition. In February 1716, he decreed that a census of Old Believers be taken, that they be subjected to a double tax and that, in order to encourage public derision and shame them back into the arms of the established church, they be required to wear a bit of yellow cloth on their backs. Inevitably, the result was that the Old Believers exhibited the badge proudly, their numbers increased and, to escape taxes, they fled even farther from the reach of government control. Toward the end of his life, Peter's tolerance of them had largely faded. In an exasperated effort to diminish their numbers, he began sending them to Siberia, then rescinded that order because "there are enough of them there already." In 1724, all Old Believers except peasants who wished to keep their beards were required to wear a copper medallion that depicted a beard—and for this medallion they paid handsomely.

Although Peter tolerated a wide variety of religious worship in Russia, there was one Christian order which he disliked: the Jesuits. (Other brotherhoods of Catholic priests and monks were welcome in Russia; the Franciscans and the Capuchins even possessed small monasteries.) Originally, the Jesuits also had been free to hold services in Moscow and to travel freely through Russia on their way to the court of the great Manchu Emperor of China, K'ang-hsi. In time, however, Peter began to suspect that their religious zeal was largely a façade behind which they were reaching for political power. Confirmation of Jesuit worldliness, in Peter's view, came from the close relationship between the order and the Imperial government in Vienna, and eventually he decreed that "all Jesuits are earnestly commanded by virtue of these Letters Patent to quit the Russian dominions within four days after notice having given them, the world being sufficiently apprised of their dangerous machinations, and how common it is for them to meddle with politic affairs." Yet, Peter did not demand the closing of the Catholic church in St. Petersburg. He permitted the parish to send for replacement priests, insisting only that they not be Jesuits and that they not claim protection from the court of Austria.

In other countries, Peter's well-known tolerance inspired in the heads of other churches the hope that, through him, their own faith might gain a foothold or even predominance in Russia. There was no possibility of this. Peter's interest in other Christian faiths was a matter of curiosity about the service and the institutions of administration. He never considered any form

of religious conversion. Nevertheless, in 1717, while Peter was in Paris, a group of divines at the Faculty of Divinity at the Sorbonne proposed uniting the churches of Rome and Moscow by "observing a certain moderation of doctrine on both sides." The project worried some of the Protestant envoys in St. Petersburg because of the political implications of any such unity. Thus, it was with satisfaction that Weber reported that the proposal stood little chance. "Neither is it probable that the Tsar, after having suppressed the Patriarchal Authority in Russia, will subject himself and his dominions to a far greater dependency on the Pope. . . . It is needless to mention that difficulty concerning the marriage of priests which is looked upon in Russia as sacred, and other controverted points, about which both churches are never likely to agree."

In preserving the predominance of Orthodoxy in Russia, Peter demanded of the church that it make itself useful to society. In his view, the most useful thing that Russian priests could do, besides saving souls, was to teach. There were no schools, and priests were the only channel by which enlightenment could come to the Russian peasantry scattered across the immense land. But, for this purpose, the clergy seemed a woefully inadequate instrument. Many priests were hopelessly ignorant and unshakably lazy. Some were as super-stitious as their parishioners. Few had any knowledge of how to preach, and therefore such education and morality as they did possess could not be transmitted. Attempting to overcome this deficiency, Peter sent a number of country priests to Kiev and other theological schools to learn not just theology, but how to speak in public.

Beyond what might be called the innocent ignorance of the Russian clergy, there was another failing which drove the Tsar into a rage. This was the widespread superstition of the Russian people and the playing on this trait by certain unscrupulous people, including members of the clergy. The common people believed in everyday miracles—believed that by the inter-cession of a specific icon of Christ, the Virgin Mary or one of the special Russian saints, a miraculous personal advantage might be obtained. Un-questioning belief made fertile ground for charlatans. When Peter came upon this kind of unscrupulous priest, his anger flared. One priest in St. Petersburg, for example, persuaded the people that a picture of the Virgin Mary which he kept in his house could work miracles, but only those who could pay were allowed access. "Though he carried on this trade with great circumspection in the nighttime and took all imaginable care in recommend-ing secrecy to his customers, yet the Tsar got information of it," said Weber. "The priest's house was searched and the miraculous image fetched away, which the Tsar caused to be brought to him in order to see whether it could perform miracles in His Majesty's presence. But the priest, at the sight of it, threw himself at the Tsar's feet and confessed his imposture, for which he was carried to the fortress and suffered heavy corporal punishment, and was after-

ward degraded from his office in order to be made an example to his brethren."

Not surprisingly, the impostures which angered Peter most were those which challenged or threatened his own will. On one occasion, a peasant who disliked being forced to live in St. Petersburg prophesied that the following September the Neva would flood so high that it would cover an ancient and lofty ash tree which stood near a church. People immediately began to move themselves and their belongings to higher ground. Peter, furious at this interruption of his plans for the city, ordered the tree cut down and the peasant imprisoned until September. At the end of that month, when no sign of the threatened inundation had appeared, the population was summoned to the site of the tree stump, on which a scaffold had been built. The rustic seer was brought, lifted onto the scaffold and given fifty lashes with the knout while the crowd was lectured on the foolhardiness of listening to false prophets.

A more sophisticated religious hoax simultaneously provoked Peter's wrath and stimulated his curiosity. In 1720, an icon of the Virgin Mary in a church in St. Petersburg was said to be shedding tears because she was obliged to live in so dismal a part of the world. Chancellor Golovkin heard the report and went to the church, forcing his way through a dense crowd which had gathered to marvel at the phenomenon. Golovkin immediately sent for Peter, who was a day's journey away, inspecting the Ladoga Canal. Peter came at once, traveling all night, and went directly to the church. The priests took him to the miraculous icon, which at that moment was dry-eyed, although numerous spectators assured him that they had seen tears. Peter stared up at the icon, which was covered with paint and thick varnish, and decided that something about it looked suspicious. He ordered it lifted down from its elevated position and brought to his palace, where in the presence of the Chancellor, many noblemen, the leaders of the clergy and the priests who had been present when the icon was taken down, he proceeded to examine it. He soon found several tiny holes in the corners of the eyes which the shadows created by the curve of the eyes made invisible from below. Turning the icon around, he stripped away the cloth that covered it behind. A little cavity had been hollowed out of the wooden plank, and in it was a small residue of congealed oil. "Here is the source of the miraculous tears," Peter declared, summoning everyone present to come close and see for themselves. The congealed oil remained solid as long as the icon was in a cold place, he explained, but during a service, when the surrounding air was heated by the burning candles placed before the icon, the oil became fluid and the Virgin "wept." Peter was delighted with the ingenuity of the mechanism and kept the icon for his Cabinet of Curiosities. But he was extremely angry at the charlatan who had invoked superstition to threaten his new city. The perpetrator was found

"and so severely chastised that no one afterward thought proper to attempt anything of a similar nature."

Along with tightening discipline among the priesthood and stamping out charlatanism and superstition, Peter set himself to bring piety and utility to Russian monasteries. The Tsar himself was not opposed to the monastic ideal of poverty, scholarship and devotion to God. As a young man, he had paid a respectful visit to the great Solovetsky Monastery on the White Sea, and in 1712 he had founded the Alexander Nevsky Monastery in St. Petersburg. What distressed him was the extent to which Russian monasteries had strayed from their ideal. There were more than 557 monasteries and convents in Russia in Peter's day, housing more than 14,000 monks and 10,000 nuns, and some of these institutions possessed great wealth. In 1723, the 151 monasteries in the vicinity of Moscow owned 242,198 male serfs—Troitskaya Sergeeva, the richest of them, owned 20,394 peasant houses—and the number was constantly growing, as Russian noblemen and wealthy merchants competed to give money and land to monasteries in order to assist their own salvation.

For all their wealth, little that Peter found useful emerged from these retreats. No notable scholarship or learning was being produced in monasteries in Peter's time, and the charity dispensed under their walls simply attracted swarms of army deserters, runaway serfs, "hale and lazy beggars, enemies to God and useless hands," in Peter's scornful words. The Tsar considered many of the monks to be parasites, sunk in sloth and superstition, whose growth in number and decline in holiness threatened the state.

Peter began to restrict the role of Russian monasteries soon after the death of the Patriarch Adrian in 1700. Administration of these institutions was turned over to a new state office, the Monastery Office, headed by a layman, Boyar Ivan Musin-Pushkin. All money and property belonging to the monasteries were to be managed by this office "in order to enable the monks and nuns to better fulfill their religious duties." The number of new monks was drastically limited by forbidding the taking of holy vows by noblemen, officials of the government, minors and anyone who could not read or write. In time, any person desiring to take holy orders had to receive permission from the Tsar. Simultaneously, all monasteries containing fewer than thirty monks were closed and converted into parish churches or schools. The monks from these small institutions were transferred to larger houses.

As RULER OF THE STATE, Peter was basically concerned with the structure and role of the church as an institution and the relation of that institution to the state. Despite the blow at church independence struck by Tsar Alexis

when he removed the Patriarch Nikon, the Patriarchy still wielded considerable autonomous power when Peter came to the throne. It possessed its own administrative, judicial and fiscal offices. It taxed the inhabitants of its immense landholdings. It judged all questions of marriage, adultery, divorce, wills and inheritance, as well as disputes between husbands and wives, parents and children, laity and clergy. The Patriarch Adrian, who took office when Peter was eighteen, was not as strong a personality as Nikon, but as an arch-conservative he was constantly interfering in Peter's personal life: protesting the time he spent with foreigners, demanding that Peter change the Western clothes he preferred, insisting that he spend more time with Eudoxia. Not surprisingly, the young Tsar wished that he might somehow be rid of both the personal irritation and the conservative policies which the Patriarch embodied.

As it happened, Adrian died suddenly in October 1700 while Peter was with the army besieging Narva. The Tsar had given no thought to the choice of a successor; he knew only that he wanted a man who could not challenge his own supreme power and who would support the changes he might wish to make in the structure and authority of the church. No such candidate seemed available, and he lacked time to make a search. Rather than appoint the wrong man, and unwilling to risk confusing and dividing the country by doing away with the office, Peter compromised. He preserved the office of Patriarch, but declared the throne "temporarily vacant." To provide the church with interim leadership, he appointed a "temporary" guardian whose indefinite status would not permit him to become a true focus of power. Then, satisfied with this arrangement, he simply let the matter drift. Whenever the clergy urged, as it did strongly and repeatedly, that a new Patriarch be appointed, Peter replied that he was too busy with the war to give the choice the deep thought necessary.

Peter had chosen as temporary Guardian Exarch the forty-two-year-old Metropolitan of Ryazan, Stephen Yavorsky, a Ukrainian monk trained in the Jesuit-inspired Orthodox academy in Kiev, where the level of church scholarship and general culture was higher than among the purely Muscovite Orthodox clergy. As professor of theology at the academy and a frequent orator in the city's great Santa Sophia Cathedral, Yavorsky made an impressive figure. His deep, sonorous voice, his dramatic gestures, his skillful blend of scholarship and anecdote moved his large audiences easily from laughter to tears. Peter had never heard such oratory in a Russian church, and whenever possible—at church ceremonies, public dedications or military triumphs—he asked that Yavorsky preach. But in giving office to Yavorsky, Peter did not equip him even temporarily with all the authority formerly held by the Patriarch. The actual administration of church properties, as well as the taxing of all inhabitants of ecclesiastical lands, was turned over to the new Monastery Office headed by Musin-Pushkin. There-

after, most church income went directly into the state Treasury, which, in turn, paid the salaries of church officials.

Yavorsky was never really happy in his office. He was not ambitious, and soon he was looking back wistfully on the calmer, more reclusive life he had led in Kiev. In 1712, he begged Peter to release him from his assignment. "Where shall I go from your spirit and how shall I flee from your face?" he wrote despairingly to the Tsar. "I will not go to a foreign realm, for your power is given to you by God. In Moscow or in Ryazan— everywhere your sovereign power reigns over me. It is impossible to hide from it." Peter, having no one to replace him with, always refused Yavorsky's appeals until, with the passage of time, Yavorsky began to grow stronger in his office; he began to support his fellow churchmen in their confrontation with civilian authorities; he began to protest the extent to which church revenues were being diverted from religious purposes to support the army and the war. Even his sermons began to take a turn which Peter did not like: He preached against husbands who had persuaded their wives to enter a convent so that the husbands could remarry—a thrust whose most prominent target was obvious to all. In 1712, Yavorsky used the occasion of the Feast of St. Alexis to speak of the Tsarevich Alexis as "our only hope." Peter was not present, but a copy of the sermon was brought to him. He read it carefully, annotating it with his pen. Unwilling to make Yavorsky a martyr, he did not retaliate, but sent word to the churchman that he should not admonish in public before doing so in private. Yavorsky apologized, "writing with tears, not with ink," and remained in office, although for a while Peter forbade him to preach.

Thereafter, Peter found a new instrument with which to reform the church. This was another Ukrainian monk from Kiev, much younger than Yavorsky, more sophisticated, more practical and infinitely more forceful. Feofan Prokopovich was a modern eighteenth-century man who happened to be a cleric. He was an administrator, a reformer, a polemicist, even a propagandist, and he concurred completely in Peter's desire to modernize and secularize the Russian church. For a Russian churchman, Prokopovich was a man of extraordinary learning—he had read Erasmus, Luther, Descartes, Galileo, Kepler, Bacon, Machiavelli, Hobbes and Locke. An orphan in childhood, Prokopovich was educated by his uncle, a learned monk and rector of the academy in Kiev, and went on to Jesuit colleges in Poland and then to a special college in Rome. There, he studied theology, took Catholic orders and, in 1700 at the age of twenty-two, witnessed the coronation of Pope Clement XI. The effect of his three years in Rome, however, was to instill in Prokopovich a permanent dislike of the Papacy and the Roman church. Returning to the Kiev academy, he taught philosophy, rhetoric, poetics and literature, lecturing to his students in Latin. He pioneered in introducing arithmetic, geometry and physics into the curriculum. While

still in his twenties, he wrote a five-act play in verse, dramatizing the theme of the bringing of Christianity to Russia in the tenth century by Vladimir, Prince of Kiev. In 1706, Peter visited Kiev and heard Prokopovich preach in Santa Sophia. In the crisis of 1708, when Mazeppa betrayed the Tsar in favor of Charles XII, Prokopovich quickly took Peter's side. Prince Golitsyn, Governor of Kiev, responded to Peter's question about the loyalty of the higher clergy in the city by saying, "All the monks avoid us. In all of Kiev I have found only one man, the prefect of the academy [Prokopovich], who is well disposed toward us." In 1709, following the Russian victory at Poltava, the Tsar returned to Kiev, where Prokopovich welcomed him as "His Most Sacred Majesty, the Tsar of All the Russias" and preached a sermon filled with superlatives. In 1711, Prokopovich accompanied Peter on the disastrous campaign on the Pruth, and later that year, at the age of thirty-one, he was appointed rector of the Kiev academy. In 1716, the Tsar summoned him to St. Petersburg, and Prokopovich left Kiev, never to return.

Unlike Yavorsky, Prokopovich firmly supported Peter's attempts to subordinate the church to the state. Vockerodt, secretary to the Prussian minister Mardefelt, commented that he found in Prokopovich, apart from wide learning, "an ardent concern for the good of the country, even at the expense of the clergy's interests." Prokopovich's antagonism toward the "beards of the church" was further stimulated by their support of the Tsarevich Alexis, and on Palm Sunday, April 6, 1718, as the leaders of the church were being asked to judge the Tsarevich, Prokopovich thundered from the pulpit on the power and glory of the tsar and the holy duty of all subjects to obey the temporal power. "The supreme authority is established and armed with the sword of God, and to oppose it is a sin against God himself," he cried. He dealt harshly with the idea that the clergy was exempt from loyalty and service to the sovereign: "The clergy, like the army, the civil administration, doctors and artisans, is subject to the state. The clergy is another order of rank of the people and not a separate state." Naturally enough, the rest of the clergy accused Prokopovich of sycophancy, opportunism, hypocrisy and ambition. When Peter nominated him as Archbishop of Pskov and Narva, the Moscow clergy accused him of heretical Protestant leanings. Yavorsky joined this attack until Peter asked for evidence; unable to document his charge, the Exarch was obliged to retract it.

As the war with Sweden drew to a close, Peter's thoughts turned toward a permanent structure for governing the church. Yavorsky's temporary assignment had stretched into eighteen years. Repeatedly and urgently, the bishops begged the Tsar to name a new patriarch. At last Peter responded, but in a manner very different from that which they expected. In the years since the last patriarch had died, Peter had traveled abroad and seen much of other religions in both Catholic and Protestant countries. The Roman

church, of course, was administered by a single man, but in Protestant lands the churches were administered by a synod or assembly or board of administrators, and this idea appealed to Peter. Having already reformed his civil administration by putting government in the hands of ministries or colleges, he was ready to impose a comparable structure on the church. In the latter part of 1718, Peter entrusted to Prokopovich the drafting of a church charter called the Ecclesiastical Regulation, which was to promulgate a new administrative structure for the Russian Orthodox Church. Prokopovich worked for many months, and the document is his most important achievement, but every section was read, revised and sometimes rewritten by Peter himself.

In 1721, the Ecclesiastical Regulation was enacted by decree. It struck hard at those features of the old Muscovite church which so angered Peter. Ignorance and superstition were to be rooted out, not only among the parishioners but among the clergy. "When the light of learning is lacking," read the Regulation, "it is impossible that the church should be well run." Bishops were ordered to establish training schools for priests; forty-six such schools opened their doors within four years. Priests were to learn theology; "he who would teach theology must be learned in Holy Scripture and be able to corroborate all the dogmas with scriptural evidence," declared the Ecclesiastical Regulation. On Prokopovich's insistence, priests also had to study history, politics, geography, arithmetic, geometry and physics. Parishioners were required to attend church, and those who failed to appear or who talked in church were fined.

The most notable feature of the new Regulation was the abolition of the Patriarchate as the governing body of the church, and its replacement with a bureaucratic institution called the Holy Governing Synod. In effect, the Synod was organized on the same model as the colleges of the civil government; it had a president, a vice president and eight members. In fact, Peter wished it to be apart from and superior to the colleges, equal to the Senate. Like the Senate, the Synod had a civilian watchdog administrative officer, the Chief Procurator of the Holy Synod, whose job it was to oversee church administration, settle quarrels and deal with negligence and absenteeism. In effect, the Holy Synod, which was responsible for all spiritual as well as temporal affairs of the church, became a Ministry of Religious Affairs, and the Chief Procurator, the Minister of Religion.

In a lengthy preamble, Prokopovich (and, through him, Peter) explained the decision to abolish the one-man rule of the Patriarchate and replace it with collective administration:

> From collegiate government in the church there is much less danger to the country of sedition and disorder than may proceed from rule by a single spiritual ruler. For the common people do not un-

derstand the difference between the spiritual power and that of the autocrat. Instead, dazzled by the splendor and glory of the highest clergyman, they think that he is a second sovereign equal to or even greater than the autocrat, and that the spiritual power is of another and better realm. If then there should be any dispute between the patriarch and the tsar, they might take the part of the patriarch in the belief that they were fighting for God's cause.

For the next two centuries, until 1918, the Russian Orthodox Church was governed by the principles set down in the Ecclesiastical Regulation. The church ceased to be an institution independent of government; its administration, through the office of the Holy Synod, became a function of the state. The rule of the autocrat in all matters except doctrine was supreme and absolute; ordained priests were required to swear an oath pledging themselves "to defend unsparingly all the powers, rights and prerogatives belonging to the High Autocracy of His Majesty." In return, the state guaranteed to Orthodoxy the role of state religion within the Russian empire.

Although Yavorsky was strongly opposed to the new institution, Peter installed him in the leading post as president of the Holy Synod, deciding that he would be far less dangerous enmeshed in the new machinery than in opposition to it. Yavorsky tried to decline, asking to be allowed to finish his days in a monastery, but, over his objections, he was appointed and remained in the post a year until his death in 1722.

Prokopovich, despite his relative youth (he was forty-one in 1721) and junior position in the church hierarchy, was appointed to the third-ranking position in the Holy Synod, second vice president. From this office, he effectively administered the church along the lines he himself had drawn, surviving Peter by ten years and continuing to dominate the Holy Synod under the Emperor's successors until eventually he was appointed to the prestigious post of Archbishop of Novgorod.

By abolishing the Patriarchate and transforming the administration of the church into a branch of the secular government, Peter had achieved his goal. There was no further danger from a second competitive focus of power in the land; how could there be when the church bureaucracy was actually administered by his own lieutenants? Some improvement in the education and discipline of priests resulted, although Russian village priests in the eighteenth and nineteenth centuries never became paragons of learning. The most striking feature of the Ecclesiastical Regulation was that it met no opposition, either within the church or among the people. In large part, this was because Peter had not tampered with the elements which mattered most in the Russian church, the sacred ritual and dogma. Who administered the church was of overriding concern to Peter; the form of the liturgy and sacraments did not interest him, and so he did not touch it.

In time, however, the assumption of state control over the church had an injurious effect on Russia. Individual parishioners could seek salvation and find solace from life's burdens in the glory of the Orthodox service and its choral liturgy, and in the warm communality of human suffering found in a church community. But a tame church which occupied itself with private spiritual matters and failed to stand up against successive governments on behalf of Christian values in questions of social justice soon lost the allegiance of the most dynamic elements of Russian society. The most fervent peasants and simple people seeking true religion gravitated toward the Old Believers and other sects. Students, educated people and the middle classes disdained the church for its conservative anti-intellectualism and slavish support of the regime. The church, which might have led, simply followed, and ultimately the entire religious bureaucracy established by Peter followed the imperial government over the cliff; the Holy Synod was abolished in 1918 along with all the other governing institutions of the imperial regime. Lenin reestablished the Patriarchate, but it was a puppet Patriarchate, more controlled by the state than the Holy Synod ever was. Not once in its existence has this new Patriarchate uttered a word of criticism against the regime it serves. It was the continuing passivity and servitude of the Russian church which Alexander Solzhenitsyn was regretting when he declared that the history of Russia would have been "incomparably more humane and harmonious in the last few centuries if the church had not surrendered its independence and had continued to make its voice heard among the people, as it does, for example, in Poland."

THE EMPEROR
IN ST. PETERSBURG

THE EMPEROR, noted one foreigner, "could dispatch more affairs in a morning than a houseful of senators could do in a month." Even in winter, when the sun in St. Petersburg does not rise until nine in the morning, Peter awoke at four and immediately, still wearing his nightcap and a billowing old Chinese dressing gown, received reports or held conferences with his ministers. After a light breakfast, he went to the Admiralty at six, worked there for at least an hour, sometimes two, then went to the Senate. He returned home at ten to work for an hour at his lathe before dinner at eleven. After dinner, he lay down for his regular two-hour nap, which he took wherever he was. At three, Peter made a tour around the city or worked in his office with Makarov, his private secretary. He carried a tablet or notebook in his pocket to write down ideas or suggestions which struck him during the day, and if he had no tablet, he scribbled notes in the margin of the first piece of paper he could lay his hands on. In the evening, he visited friends in their houses or attended one of the new public assemblies which he had instituted after his return from France.

The schedule varied, of course. There were times when he was rarely indoors, and other times when he scarcely went out—the winter of 1720, for example, when he worked by himself in his office fourteen hours a day, for five months, writing and revising drafts of his new *Maritime Regulations*. At such times, the Emperor stood at a walnut writing desk made specifically for him in England. Its writing surface was five feet six inches above the floor.

When he sat down to dinner, Peter brought a sailor's appetite. He preferred hearty, simple fare. His favorite dishes were cabbage soup, stew, pork with sour-cream sauce, cold roast meat with pickled cucumbers or salted lemons, lampreys, ham and vegetables. For dessert, he avoided sweets and ate fruit and cheese, being especially partial to Limburger cheese. He never ate fish, believing that it disagreed with him. On fast days, he lived on whole-meal bread and fruit. Before dinner, he took a little aniseed water,

and after the meal he drank kvas or Hungarian wine. Whenever he went out in his carriage, he always carried some cold provisions with him, as he was likely to get hungry at any time. When he dined out, an orderly always brought his wooden spoon mounted with ivory and his knife and fork with green bone handles, for Peter never used any table implements other than his own.

No ceremony attended Peter's private meals. He and Catherine often dined alone, with Peter in shirt sleeves and only a young page and a favorite maid of honor to wait on them. When he had several ministers or generals at his table, he was attended only by his chef and maître d'hôtel, an orderly and two pages, and they had strict orders to retire as soon as dessert was put on the table and a bottle of wine had been set before each guest. "I don't want them to observe me when I am speaking freely," Peter explained to the Prussian ambassador. "Not only do they spy on me, but they understand everything erroneously." There were never more than sixteen places set at Peter's table, which were filled at random by those who sat down first. Once he and the Empress had taken their chairs, he said, "Gentlemen, please take your places as far as the table will hold. The rest will go home and dine with their wives."

In public, the Emperor liked to listen to music while he ate. When he dined at the Admiralty on naval rations of smoked beef and small beer, a fife-and-drum band played from the central tower. When he ate in his palace with his generals and ministers, army musicians played military music on trumpets, oboes, French horns, bassoons and drums.

Peter's cook was a Saxon named Johann Velten, who had come to Russia to serve the Danish ambassador. Peter tasted his cooking in 1704 and persuaded Velten to come to him, first as one of his cooks, then as chief cook and finally as maître d'hôtel. Velten was gay and cheerful, and Peter was enormously fond of him, although the cook was often chastised. ("His cane," Velten said later, "often danced on my back.") One such episode occurred when Velten served Peter a Limburger cheese which the Tsar found especially tasty. He ate a piece and then took out his compass, carefully measured the amount remaining and wrote down the dimensions on his note pad. Then he summoned Velten and said, "Put this cheese away and don't let anyone else taste it because I wish to finish it myself." The following day, when the cheese reappeared, it seemed much smaller. To verify this impression, Peter took out his compass and measured it, comparing his calculations with the note in his pocket. The cheese was smaller. Peter called for Velten, displayed his notes, pointed out the discrepancy, stroked the cook with his cane and then sat down and finished the cheese with a bottle of wine.

Peter had an aversion to pomp and lived simply and frugally. He preferred old clothes, well-worn shoes and boots, and stockings which had

been darned and mended in several places by his wife and daughters. He rarely wore a wig until near the end of his life, when he had his head shaved in summer for coolness and had a wig made from his own hair. In summer, he never wore a hat. In the colder months, he wore the black three-cornered hat of the Preobrazhensky Regiment and an old greatcoat into the commodious pockets of which he habitually stuffed state papers and other documents. He owned elegant long Western coats with wide sleeves and wide lapels—green with silver thread, light blue with silver thread, brown velvet with gold thread, gray with red thread, red with gold thread—but he rarely put them on. To please Catherine, at her coronation he wore a coat which she had embroidered with her own hands in gold and silver, although he protested that the expense of the garment might have gone to better use in the support of several soldiers.

Peter's preference for simplicity was evident also in the size and upkeep of his personal court. He had no chamberlain or footman; his personal attendants were only two valets and six dentchiks, or orderlies, who waited on him, two by two, in relays. The dentchiks were young men, usually from the petty nobility or merchant class, who served the Emperor in countless ways, acting as messengers, waiting on his table, riding behind his carriage and guarding him while he slept. When Peter was traveling, he took his midday nap lying upon straw, using a dentchik's stomach as a pillow. The dentchik, according to one who had served in this capacity, was "obliged to wait patiently in this posture and not make the least motion for fear of waking him, for he was as good-humored when he had slept well as he was gloomy and ill-tempered when his slumber had been disturbed." Becoming a dentchik could be the first rung on a ladder to success; both Menshikov and Yaguzhinsky had been dentchiks. Usually, Peter kept a dentchik near him for about ten years and then assigned him an office in either the civil or military administration. Some had no higher ambitions. One young dentchik, Vasily Pospelov, was "a poor young fellow in the Tsar's choir, and as the Tsar himself is a singer and every feast day stands in the same row with the common choristers and sings with them in church, he [Peter] took such a great liking to him [Pospelov] that he can scarcely live an instant without him. He seizes him by the head perhaps a hundred times a day and kisses him, and even lets the highest ministers stand and wait while he goes and talks to him."

It was Peter's belief that magnificence of ornament and display had nothing to do with greatness. He always remembered the simplicity of the royal palaces in England and Holland and the restraint and modesty shown by William III, who was the ruler of two of the wealthiest nations in Europe. Nor did Peter care for bombastic flattery. When two Dutchmen toasted him overlavishly, Peter laughed. "Bravo, my friends. Thank you," he said, shaking his head. In his relations with people of all ranks, Peter's manners

were free and easy. He rarely observed protocol. He hated long, ceremonial banquets; such occasions, he said, had been invented "to punish the great and rich for their sins." At official banquets, he always gave the place of honor to Romodanovsky or Menshikov and seated himself near the end of the table in order to be able to escape. When he rode through the streets, it was in a small, open, two-wheeled carriage, like a Victorian love-seat on wheels, with room only for himself and one other passenger (one foreigner declared scornfully that no respectable Moscow merchant would set foot in so petty a vehicle). In winter, he used a simple one-horse sledge with a single attendant, who sat beside him. Peter still preferred walking to riding—on foot, he could see more and could stop to take a second look. He spoke to everyone he met.

Peter's habit of walking freely among his people carried personal danger. There were reasons enough for an assassin to strike; indeed, many believed he was the Antichrist. One summer when Peter was attending a meeting in his Summer Palace on the Fontanka, a stranger quietly stole into the palace antechamber. In his hand, he carried a small colored bag similar to those in which secretaries and clerks brought papers for the Tsar to sign. The man waited quietly, attracting no attention, until Peter walked into the room, escorting his ministers to the door. At this point, the stranger stood up, drew something from his bag, wrapped the bag around it to conceal it and moved toward Peter. The Tsar's attendants did not block him, assuming that he was an orderly or servant of one of the ministers. At the last minute, however, a dentchik stepped forward and took the stranger's arm. A scuffle followed and, as Peter turned, a knife with a six-inch blade fell to the floor. Peter asked the man what he had meant to do. "To assassinate you," the stranger replied. "But why? Have I done you any harm?" Peter asked. "No, but you have done harm to my brethren and religion," said the man, declaring that he was an Old Believer.

Assassins did not frighten Peter, but there were creatures before which he trembled: cockroaches. When he traveled, he never entered a house until he had been assured that no cockroaches were present and his own room had been carefully swept by his own servants. This followed an episode in which Peter, as a guest at dinner in a country house, asked if his host ever had cockroaches. "Not many," the host replied, "and to chase them away, I have pinned a living one to the wall." He pointed to the place where the insect was pinned, still squirming, not far from the Tsar. With a roar, Peter leaped from the table, gave his host a tremendous blow and rushed out of the house.

Peter's hasty temper and his habit of disciplining subordinates with a stick or his fists never left him. No one close to the Tsar was immune, although usually, once the blows had been delivered, calm quickly returned. A typical incident occurred one day in St. Petersburg when Peter was

driving in his small gig with Lieutenant General Anthony Devier, the Commissioner of Police in St. Petersburg, in which capacity he was responsible for the condition of roads and bridges in the capital. On this day, Peter's carriage was crossing a small bridge over the Moika Canal when the Tsar noticed that several planks were missing and others loose. Stopping the carriage, Peter jumped out and ordered the dentchik accompanying him to repair the bridge at once. While the planks were being fastened in place, Peter took his cane to Devier's back. "This is a punishment for negligence," he said. "It will teach you to make the rounds and be sure that everything is safe and in good condition." Once the bridge was repaired, Peter turned to Devier and said in a pleasant tone, "Get in, brother. Sit down," and the two drove off as if nothing had happened.

Peter's blows fell equally on great and small. Once, when his yacht was becalmed for an entire day between Kronstadt and St. Petersburg, the Tsar went down to his cabin to sleep after midday dinner. Before his two hours were up, he was awakened by noises on deck. Furious, he went topside and found the deck deserted except for a small black page sitting quietly on the stair ladder. Peter grabbed the boy and caned him, saying, "Learn to be more quiet and not wake me when I sleep." But the boy had not been guilty; the noise had been made by the Tsar's doctor, an engineer and two naval officers, who had fled and hid when they heard Peter mounting the ladder. After the caning, they crept back and warned the boy against telling the truth, on pain of another beating. An hour later, Peter reappeared on deck, now cheerful from his rest. Astonished to see the boy still weeping, he asked him why. "Because you have chastised me cruelly and unjustly," the boy replied, naming those who had actually been responsible for the noise. "Well," said Peter, "since I have punished you this time undeservedly, the next folly you commit shall be pardoned." A few days later, when Peter was about to cane the boy again, the page reminded him of his statement. "True," said the Tsar. "I remember and forgive you this time, as you have been punished by anticipation."

His outbursts could be terrifying. One day, Peter was working in the Turning Room of the Summer Palace, making a large ivory chandelier in the company of his chief turner Andrei Nartov and a young apprentice whom Peter liked for his gaiety and forthrightness. The apprentice had orders to quietly remove the Emperor's hat whenever Peter sat down without taking it off. This time, grabbing the hat in haste, the apprentice pulled a lock of hair. Roaring with anger, Peter leaped to his feet and chased the young man, threatening to kill him. The apprentice escaped by hiding, and the next day Peter, his anger forgotten, returned to the lathe. "That cursed boy had no mercy on me," he laughed, "but he hurt me more than he intended, and I am very glad that his flight was quicker than my pursuit." Several more days passed and Peter noticed that the apprentice still had not

returned to work. He told Nartov to look for him and assure him that he could return without fear, but the young man still could not be found, even by the police. In fact, he had fled St. Petersburg, first to a little village on Lake Ladoga and then to Vologda on the Dvina River, where he pretended to be an orphan and was taken in by a glazier, who taught him his trade. Ten years later, on Peter's death, the young man dared to reveal his real name and return to St. Petersburg. Nartov told him of the Tsar's pardon and rehired him, and he worked at court through the reigns of Empresses Anne and Elizabeth.

With the passage of time, Peter tried to correct his temper, and although he never fully succeeded, he was aware of it as a flaw. "I am sensible that I have my faults," he said, "and that I easily lose my temper. For which reason I am not offended with those who are on familiar terms with me when they tell me of it and remonstrate with me, as does my Catherine."

Indeed, it was Catherine who could best—and sometimes only—deal with Peter's temper. She was not afraid of him, and he knew that. Once, when she persisted in mentioning a subject which irritated him, he flew into a rage and smashed a handsome Venetian mirror, shouting ominously, "Thus can I destroy the most beautiful object in my palace!" Catherine understood the threat, but looked him in the eye and replied calmly, "And have you made the palace more beautiful by doing so?" Wisely, she never opposed her husband directly, but searched for a way to make him look at matters from a new angle. On one occasion, she used his favorite dog, Lisette, to mollify his anger. Wherever he went at home, this small dun-colored Italian greyhound followed, and during his afternoon nap she always lay at his feet. It happened that Peter was furious at a member of the court whom he thought guilty of corruption and who was in grave danger of the knout. Everyone at court, including Catherine, was convinced of the unhappy courtier's innocence, but all appeals to the Tsar had only made him angrier. Finally, to obtain peace around him, Peter had forbidden everyone, including the Tsaritsa, to present any petition or speak to him on the subject. Catherine did not give up. Instead, she composed a short, pathetic petition in the name of Lisette, presenting strong evidence of the innocence of the accused and begging, on the ground of Lisette's total fidelity to her master, for a pardon. Then she tied the petition to Lisette's collar. On Peter's return from the Senate, the faithful Lisette leaped joyfully about him as usual. Peter saw the petition, read it, smiled wearily and said, "Well, Lisette, as this is the first time *you* have asked, I grant your prayer."

Although he hated formality, there were some ceremonies which Peter enjoyed hugely, and others which he accepted dutifully as obligations of the ruler of the state. Above all, he loved the launching of a new ship; generally frugal, he did not mind spending large sums to celebrate this kind of event, and crowds flocked to the Admiralty to share in his largess. The occasion

always demanded an enormous banquet on the decks of the new vessel, and the Tsar, his face shining, his voice excited, could be found at the center of all activity, accompanied by his family, including his daughters and even the aging Tsaritsa Praskovaya, who never missed a launching and its attendant rivers of alcohol. These parties inevitably ended with General-Admiral Apraxin bursting into tears and moaning that he was a lonely old man and with the mighty Prince Menshikov drunk and inert under the table, whereupon his servants would send for his wife, Princess Darya, and her sister, who came to revive him with smelling salts, massage and cold water, "and then would get permission from the Tsar to take him home."

Life in St. Petersburg revolved around weddings, baptisms, christenings and funerals. Peter and the members of his family were always willing to appear as witnesses at a wedding, and he was frequently a godfather, often holding over the baptismal font the children of common soldiers, artisans, and lower-ranking officials. Peter did this cheerfully, but the family could not expect a lavish present; all that was given was a kiss for the mother and a rouble slipped under the baptismal pillow in the old Russian fashion. After the ceremony, if the weather was warm, Peter would take off his caftan and sit down in the first empty seat. When he served as Marshal of Ceremonies at a wedding, he fulfilled his duties rigorously, then put down his marshal's rod, moved to the table, took a hot roast of meat in his hands and began to eat.

Winter scarcely slowed Peter's incessant activity. On days when Jefferyes was writing to London that "one can hardly put one's nose out of doors without running the risk of losing it in the cold," Peter, Catherine and members of the court drove forty miles to the village of Dudderoff, where— reported the startled ambassador—they enjoyed "the diversion of what they call the *catat*, or the driving in sledges full speed down a steep mountain." Another winter sport, ice-boating, attracted the Tsar even more. "In winter when both the river Neva and . . . [the Gulf] are frozen over, then he has his boats . . . ingeniously fixed for sailing upon the ice," wrote Perry. "Every day when there is a gale of wind, he sails and plies to windward upon the ice, with Jack-Ensign and Pennant flying in the same manner as upon the water."

During the summer months, Peter delighted in opening the Summer Garden for receptions and celebrations. The anniversary of the Battle of Poltava on June 28 was always memorable: the Preobrazhensky Guards in their bottle-green uniforms and the Semyonovsky Guards in dark blue were massed in ranks in an adjacent field, and Peter himself handed wooden beakers of wine and beer to his soldiers to toast the victory. Catherine and their daughters, Anne and Elizabeth, dressed in elegant gowns, with jewels and pearls in their hair, stood in the center of the garden receiving guests, surrounded by the court and by LeBlond's bubbling fountains and cascades.

Nearby, like two stiff little wax dolls, stood Peter's two grandchildren, Peter and Natalya, the orphaned son and daughter of the Tsarevich Alexis. Having paid their respects, the guests sat down around wooden tables placed among the groves, none of them happier than the bearded bishops and other clergy devotedly drinking their fill.

On one of these occasions, gaiety turned to alarm, especially among the foreigners and some of the ladies, when they observed six brawny Guardsmen advancing toward them carrying huge buckets of corn brandy to be consumed in serious toasting. Guards having been posted at all the gates to prevent anyone from leaving, a stampede began in the direction of the river, where several galleys had been moored. The bishops, however, made no attempt to flee, but sat at their tables, smelling of radishes and onions, their faces wreathed in smiles, drinking toast after toast. Later, the Tsaritsa and the Princesses led the company in dancing on the decks of the galleys, and fireworks lit up the sky over the river. Some continued dancing and drinking into morning, but many simply sank down where they were in the garden and drifted into sleep.

Members of the imperial family as well as those who had faithfully served the Emperor were buried with pomp. A number of Peter's older lieutenants had fallen. Romodanovsky died in 1717 and his offices passed to his son. Sheremetev followed in 1719 at sixty-seven, a few years after marrying a cultured young widow who had lived in England. Jacob Dolgoruky died in 1720 at eighty-one. To old and loyal foreigners who had spent many years—in some cases, most of their adult lives—in his service, Peter responded with special generosity. While still in service, they received estates; when they retired, they received pensions, which were continued for their widows or orphaned children. Nor would Peter permit the reduction of an official's income when he went into retirement. When one aging foreigner retired after thirty years' service, the College of Financial Control proposed a pension equal to half his salary. Peter was distressed. "What?" he asked. "Shall a man who has spent his youth in my service be exposed to poverty in his old age? No, give him the whole of his pay as long as he lives, without requiring anything from him, since he is unable to serve. But take his advice in whatever relates to his profession and profit from his experience. Who would sacrifice the most valuable years of his life if he knew that he was doomed to poverty in his old age and that he to whom his youth was devoted would neglect him when he was worn out?"

FOR A MAN as impatient and charged with energy as Peter, relaxation was difficult. "What do you do at home?" he once asked those around him. "I don't know how to stay at home with nothing to do." He eschewed the favorite sport of many monarchs by refusing to hunt. Although his father

had spent every free moment hunting with falcons, and the royalty of France reveled in the pursuit of stags through forests, Peter disliked such sports. "Hunt, gentlemen," he said one day in reply to an invitation to join a hunting party near Moscow, "hunt as much as you please, and make war on wild beasts. For my part, I cannot amuse myself that way while I have enemies to encounter abroad and constant and refractory subjects to deal with at home." Peter's favorite game was chess and, so that he could play at any time or place with anyone, he carried with him a folding leather chessboard with black and white squares. He did not object to gambling and played a Dutch card game for money, but mainly to enjoy the comradeship and conversation of the sea captains and shipbuilders who were his fellow players. Among his soldiers or the sailors of his fleet, he made a strict rule: No man's loss could amount to more than a rouble. As Peter saw it, serious gamblers had no taste for anything really useful and thought of nothing but devising ways of fleecing each other.

Peter relaxed best when he was working with his hands: wielding a hatchet at the Admiralty shipyard, bent over his lathe turning objects in wood or ivory, or hammering out iron bars next to a forge. The Emperor enjoyed visiting iron foundries—he liked the pumping of the bellows, the glowing of the metal in the fires, the clang of hammers on the anvils—and he had learned the basic skills of the blacksmith's trade. Once he spent a month working in the forges of a master blacksmith named Werner Muller. Peter worked hard, forging 720 pounds of iron bars in a single day, and when he asked for his pay, Muller lavishly overpaid him. Peter refused the excess, accepting only the wage of an average smith, then taking the sum to a shop where he bought a pair of shoes. Afterward, he showed his new shoes proudly to everyone saying, "I have earned them by the sweat of my brow with a hammer and an anvil."

As always, Peter's greatest pleasure was to be on the water. Even when he was ashore, he had a standing arrangement that upon the firing of three cannon shots from the Peter and Paul Fortress, all ships in the river between the fortress and the Winter Palace were obliged to exercise their crews by running up sails, hoisting anchors and tacking to and fro. The Tsar, standing at a window of the Winter Palace, observed all this activity with a keen eye and much pleasure. In summer, he spent as much time as possible on board a boat or ship. He relished general boating excursions on the Neva, which he announced by having special flags hung at street inter- sections throughout the city. On the appointed day, all citizens who owned boats assembled on the river in front of the fortress. On Peter's signal, the flotilla set off downstream with the Tsar in the van, standing at the tiller of his own boat. Many of the noblemen brought musicians, and the peals of trumpets and oboes sounded across the water. Near the mouth of the river, boats usually turned into a small canal which led to Catherine's little

country palace, Ekaterinhof. Here, the guests moved to tables placed under the orchard trees and quenched their thirst drinking glasses of Tokay wine. Peter's joy was to sail on the Gulf of Finland between St. Petersburg and Kronstadt. In fine weather, out on the water, with the deep blue of the sky above him, the bright sun beating down, the gentle murmur of the waves slapping against the side of the boat and his own hand on the tiller, the Tsar was at peace. Sailing alone, he had a fine view of the coastline, of wooded hills climbing back from the water and, on the crest, the summer palaces beginning to rise. Returning across the gulf to Petersburg, he saw first the river mouth and surrounding forest; then, rising above the treetops, the spires and steeples of the churches, covered with tin and brass and, occasionally, with gilt, then the palaces and buildings along the embankments. After such a day, Peter always stepped ashore and returned to everyday life with a reluctant sigh.

As MUCH AS Peter loved simplicity, Catherine loved luxury. During the later years, Peter established for his wife a brilliant court that offered a striking contrast to his own style of living. The Tsaritsa was fond of dresses and jewels, perhaps to drown in glitter the memories of her humble origins. Catherine's household included pages in green uniforms faced with red and trimmed with gold lace and a private orchestra in green uniforms. The Empress' favorite companion, surprisingly, was Matrena Balk, a sister of Anna Mons, Peter's German mistress in the years before he met Catherine. Her court also included a daughter of the Pastor Gluck, who had sheltered Catherine as an orphan; Barbara Arseneeva, sister of Darya Arseneeva, who was Menshikov's wife and Catherine's early friend; Anisya Tolstoya, who had known Catherine since she first met Peter; Princess Cantemir of Moldavia; Countess Osterman, wife of the Vice Chancellor; Countess Anna Golovkina, daughter of the Chancellor, who became the second wife of Yaguzhinsky; the daughter of Anthony Devier, the Police Commissioner of St. Petersburg; and Marie Hamilton, a relation of the Scottish wife of Andrei Matveev.

The most outspoken of these ladies was Catherine's inseparable friend, the old Princess Anastasia Golitsyna, who accompanied the Tsaritsa to Copenhagen and Amsterdam, was implicated in the affair of the Tsarevich Alexis and publicly whipped, and soon after regained her position at court. One of her letters to the Tsar from Reval in 1714 gives a glimpse of Catherine's court:

> Sire: I desire your presence here quickly. If Your Majesty delays, really, Sire, my life will be hard. The Tsaritsa is never willing to go to sleep before three o'clock in the morning and I have to sit

constantly by her while Kyrilovna dozes as she stands by the bed. The lady Tsaritsa deigns to say, "Aunt, are you dozing?" and she replies, "No, I am not dozing. I am looking at my slippers," while Marie Hamilton walks about the room with a mattress which she spreads in the middle of the floor, and Matrena Balk walks through the rooms and scolds everybody. With your presence, I shall get freedom from bedroom service.

In April 1719, fate dealt Peter and Catherine a devastating blow. The death of the Tsarevich Alexis had clarified, albeit grimly, the problem of the succession. There remained two young males in Peter's line: Peter Petrovich, his son by Catherine; and Peter Alexeevich, his grandson, the son of Alexis and Princess Charlotte. But the uncle, Peter Petrovich, was never as healthy as his nephew, who was four weeks older. The child was the apple of his parents' eyes, and careful efforts were made with his health and education. He appeared from time to time at court celebrations riding a tiny pony, but he was backward and often ill. In every aspect of childhood development, he fell further and further behind his active, aggressive nephew, the little Grand Duke Peter Alexeevich.

In February 1718, when Peter Petrovich was two, Alexis was stripped of the succession, and the nobility and clergy of Russia swore allegiance to Peter's and Catherine's little son as heir to the throne. Fourteen months later, this little boy, only three and a half, followed his half-brother Alexis to the grave.

The death of this favorite child, in whom Peter had placed his hopes for the future of the dynasty, overwhelmed him. He rammed his head against a wall so hard that he went into a convulsion; then for three days and nights, he shut himself up in his room and refused to come out or even to speak to anyone through the door. During all this time, he remained stretched on his couch without eating. The business of government came to a halt, the war with Sweden was ignored, messages and letters went unanswered. Catherine, overcoming her own grief, became alarmed at her husband's obsessive despondency and knocked at his door and called to him, but no answer came, and she retired, weeping, to beg for help from Prince Jacob Dolgoruky. The aged First Senator calmed the frightened Tsaritsa and summoned the entire Senate to meet outside Peter's door. Dolgoruky knocked. There was no answer. Knocking again, Dolgoruky called out to the Tsar that he was there with the entire Senate, that the country needed its Tsar, and that if Peter did not open the door immediately, he would be obliged to break it down and carry the sovereign away by force as the only means of saving the crown.

The door opened and a pale and haggard Peter stood before them. "What is the matter?" he asked. "Why do you come to disturb my repose?"

"Because your retirement and your excessive and useless sorrow are the cause of the disorder that prevails in the country," replied Dolgoruky. Peter bowed his head. "You are right," he said, and went with them to Catherine. He embraced her gently and said, "We have afflicted ourselves too long. Let us no longer murmur against the will of God."

The death of little Peter Petrovich left Peter and Catherine with three children living, all daughters. In 1721, Anne and Elizabeth were thirteen and twelve respectively, and Natalya was three. The two older girls already were attracting favorable notice from foreign diplomats, always on the lookout for a useful match. "Princess Anne," said Bergholz, whose master, the Duke of Holstein, was eventually to marry this daughter, "is a brunette and as pretty as an angel with a charming complexion, arms and a figure very much like her father and rather tall for a girl, even a little inclined to be thin and not as lively as her younger sister Elizabeth, who was dressed like her. The dresses of the two princesses were without gold or silver, of pretty, two-colored material, their heads ornamented with pearls and precious stones in the latest French fashion, in a way which would have done honor to the best French hairdresser."

Three years later, when Anne was sixteen, her charms were praised by Baron Mardefelt, the Prussian minister and a skillful painter of miniatures who had done portraits on ivory of all members of the Russian imperial family. Of Anne, he wrote: "I do not believe that there is today in Europe a Princess who can dispute the palm with her majestic beauty. She is taller in figure than any lady in her court, but her waist is so slender, so graceful, her features so perfect, that the antique sculptors would have had nothing left to desire. Her bearing is without affectation, equable, serene. Above all amusements, she prefers the reading of historical and philosophical works."

As for Elizabeth at fifteen, "She is a beauty the like of which I have never seen," said the Spanish ambassador, the Duke of Liria. "An amazing complexion, glowing eyes, a perfect mouth, a throat and bosom of rare whiteness. She is tall in stature and her temperament is very lively. One senses in her a great deal of intelligence and affability, but also a certain ambition."

Both Anne and Elizabeth were receiving the education of European princesses, which consisted mainly of languages, manners and dancing. They already spoke High Dutch and were becoming fluent in French. When Peter asked their tutors why French was necessary, whether the German language was not broad enough to enable one to express oneself fully, the tutors replied that it was, but that all civilized men, including Germans, wished to learn French. Anne, the more apt pupil, apparently learned a little Italian and Swedish also. To display her progress, she wrote to her father and mother in German while they were abroad. To one of these letters, Catherine replied in 1721:

As I know from the letters of your tutor, as well as of M. Devier, you, my heart, are learning with diligence. I am very glad and send you as a present, to stimulate you to do better, a diamond ring. Choose one of them for yourself, whichever pleases you, and give the other to your dear sister, Elizabeth, and kiss her for me. I send you also a box of fresh oranges and lemons which have just come from the ships. Pick out some dozens and send them as from yourself to the Serene Prince [Menshikov] and to the Admiral [Apraxin].

Many years later, the Empress Elizabeth recalled the keen interest her father had taken in the education of his daughters. He came frequently to their rooms, she said, to see how they were passing their time, and "he often required an account of what I had learned in the course of the day. When he was satisfied, he gave me commendations accompanied by a kiss and sometimes by a present." Elizabeth also remembered how greatly Peter regretted the neglect of his own formal education. "My father often repeated on this subject," she said, "that he would have given one of his fingers that his education had not been neglected. Not a day passed in which he did not feel his deficiency."

The third daughter, little Princess Natalya Petrovna, born in 1718, did not live to begin serious schooling. In appearance, she was a blend of her two parents, with a wide face, black hair curled on her forehead in imitation of her mother, black eyes and a little red rosebud mouth. But she died in 1725. Of the twelve children of Catherine and Peter, six boys and six girls, only Anne and Elizabeth lived beyond the age of seven.

One of the great characters of Russian society at this time was the gouty old Tsaritsa Praskovaya, the widow of Peter's half-brother and co-tsar, Ivan V. A widow since 1696, Praskovaya was always fiercely loyal to Peter and had given him two of her three daughters, Anne and Catherine, to marry off to European princelings in furtherance of the Tsar's foreign policy. Although she much preferred her own country villa, the Ismailovsky Palace in the rolling meadowland outside Moscow, she dutifully moved to Petersburg. Carried to banquets and balls in her chair, she was always seated at the side of the Tsaritsa Catherine, from which vantage she observed and commented acidly on whatever was happening. Her desire to please the Tsar extended even to traveling with him to Olonets to take the iron waters, although most of those around her felt that she left these cures in poorer health than when she arrived. As Praskovaya grew older, she became irascible and quarreled often with her older daughters, both of whom returned to Russia; Catherine, the gay and lively Duchess of Mecklenburg, returned for good in 1722, and Anne, Duchess of Courland, traveled home frequently for visits until her permanent return in 1730, when she was crowned as Empress Anne. After one ferocious argument,

Praskovaya placed her formal curse on Anne and withdrew it only in the final moments before she died.

During the summer and autumn of 1722, while Peter and Catherine were away on the Caspian Sea, the court transferred itself to Moscow. Catherine of Mecklenburg was living with her mother at the Ismailovsky Palace, and she often invited people out from Moscow for entertainment. They came over the muddy country roads to be served with cups of vodka by the Duchess' own hand, be fed a badly cooked dinner and dance until midnight. When the heat of bodies and candles in the small drawing room became too great, the dancers moved into the bedroom where the crippled Tsaritsa Praskovaya was lying, or into the bedroom of the Duchess. The house was poorly designed, with bedrooms scattered between drawing room and dining room, and, in any case, Praskovaya cared little about appearances. When Peter returned from the Caspian, Bergholz hurried out in the middle of the night to be the first to bring the news to the Tsaritsa. He found everyone in bed, but Catherine of Mecklenburg was delighted and took Bergholz to announce the news to her mother, her sister and their maids of honor, who were all undressed. The Holsteiner was surprised by the small size and poor condition of the Tsaritsa's house. "In general, this nocturnal visit did not make a favorable impression on me," he noted in his diary, "although I had the luck to see many bare necks and bosoms."

In 1718, Peter instituted his new assemblies, or evening parties, which were held two or three times a week during the long winter. They were the most important part of the Tsar's effort to bring the two sexes together and give Petersburg a taste of the genteel social intercourse which he had witnessed in the salons of Paris. Because this idea was a novelty in Russia, Peter issued regulations, spelling out to his subjects exactly what the new assemblies were meant to be and how they were to be performed. His explanation, typically, has the sound of a teacher lecturing pupils:

Regulation for Keeping Assemblies at Petersburg

Assembly is a French term which cannot be rendered in a single Russian word: It signifies a number of persons meeting together, either for diversion or to talk about their own affairs. Friends may see each other on that occasion, to confer together on business or other subjects, to inquire after domestic and foreign news, and so to pass their time. After what manner we will have those assemblies kept may be learned from what follows:

1. The person at whose house the assembly is to be in the evening

is to hand out a bill or other sign to give notice to all persons of either sex.

2. The assembly shall not begin sooner than four or five in the afternoon, nor continue later than ten at night.

3. The master of the house is not obliged to go and meet his guests, to conduct them out, or to entertain them; but though he himself is exempt from waiting on them, he ought to find chairs, candles, drink and all the other necessaries asked for, as also to provide for all sorts of gaming and what belongs thereto.

4. No certain hour is fixed for anybody's coming or going; it is sufficient if one makes his appearance at the assembly.

5. It is left to everyone's liberty to sit, walk or play, just as he likes, nor shall anybody hinder him or take exception at what he does, on pain of emptying the Great Eagle [a bowl filled with wine or brandy] to be swallowed as punishment. As for the rest, it is enough to salute at coming and going.

6. Persons of rank, as for instance noblemen, and superior officers, likewise merchants of note, and headmasters (by which are chiefly understood shipbuilders), persons employed in the Chancery, and their wives and children shall have the liberty of frequenting the assemblies.

7. A particular place shall be assigned to the footmen (those of the house excepted) that there may be sufficient room in the apartments designed for the assembly [that is, so that the rooms would not be clogged with footmen hanging about and mingling with guests].

Although the host was not asked to prepare anything more than tea or cold water for his guests, nothing prevented him from furnishing a large supper and plenty to drink. Yet no one was forced to drink, and, in contrast to Peter's famous all-male banquets, heavy drinking and drunkenness at the assemblies were severely frowned upon. Peter himself kept the list of hosts and designated the host whose turn it was; and although he still refused to give formal parties at his own palace, he readily agreed to act as host for an assembly when his name came up on the list.

Before long, St. Petersburg society flocked to these receptions. In one room there would be dancing, in another people playing cards, in a third a group of men solemnly smoking their long clay pipes and drinking from earthenware mugs, and in a fourth men and women laughing, gossiping and enjoying one another in a way hitherto unknown in Russia. Peter was always there, merry and talkative, moving from room to room or sitting at a table, smoking a long Dutch pipe, sipping Hungarian wine and studying his next move in a game of draughts or chess. The course of these assemblies did

not always run smoothly. Prince Gregory Dolgoruky and the younger Prince Romodanovsky, old enemies from a divorce suit, got into a fist fight at the supper table; on another occasion, a guest climbed onto the table and, walking along it, stumbled into a pie. But in general, the level of behavior was pleasing to the watchful eye of the imperial mentor who had performed this miracle of blending the society of Old Russia with the society of Europe. Most ladies in St. Petersburg society, once exposed to Peter's mixed assemblies, rushed to embrace the change. Instead of remaining in the reclusive world of their own households, they now stepped forward into a new, more exciting life. Young, unmarried girls now had a place to meet a wide range of young, unmarried men. It was delicious to be able to dress, to dance, to display their charms in public. Extravagant new dresses, glorious in color and style, appeared, and, reported Bergholz, "all the ladies here use rouge as much as the French." However, they were still unwilling to spend hours preparing the lavish coiffures of the ladies of Western courts. "It is still too hard for them to make a sacrifice of their accustomed love of ease," said Bergholz. "Russians think too much of their ease and coif themselves very unwillingly."

With Western manners in vogue, Russian mothers hurried to bring their daughters up in the style of Germany or France. "One must do the parents here justice," said Bergholz, "to say that they spare nothing to have their children well educated, so that it is with astonishment that one sees the great changes which have been made in this nation in such a short time. There is no more trace of the rude and displeasing behavior they had not long ago." Some of these young women had a special advantage gained in a somewhat ironic way. General Trubetskoy, who had been held prisoner in Stockholm with his wife and daughters, was exchanged in 1718 for Field Marshal Rehnskjold. When the family returned from Sweden, his three daughters, who had been in Stockholm "with their father from their tender years, had so much improved by a good education that upon their return to Russia they distinguished themselves far above any other ladies of their own country."

The gentlemen as well as the ladies of St. Petersburg rushed to adorn themselves. Instead of the traditional single fine robe worn on state occasions and passed down from father to son, Russian gentlemen now ordered numerous rich new coats, embroidered with gold. One foreigner, watching a group of Russians covered with furs coming into a house on a cold winter night, declared, "On entering any house, some of the servants immediately untie your fur shoes and divest you of your pelisse; nor is it unamusing to see fine gentlemen, adorned with silver and gold and purple, and precious stones, starting forth from their rough external guise like so many gaudy butterflies, bursting suddenly free from their winter encrustations."

The extravagance in clothes was accompanied by extravagance in other aspects of living. Russians kept regiments of servants and clothed them in splendid liveries. They ordered exquisite furniture, elegant carriages and rare foreign wines. Banquets, balls and other entertainments displayed their wealth, although all too often the wealth disappeared as expenses ate up the fortune. Debts and ruin were frequent, and impoverished officers and officials begging for a new position with a handsome salary were often to be seen in the offices of government.

Another result of the sudden emancipation of Russian women after centuries of sequestration was a general easing of morality, or what Prince Mikhail Shcherbatov later described as "a depravation of morals." Peter's personal behavior in this area remains obscure. Anna Mons and Catherine were his mistresses at different times. Catherine's maids of honor Marie Hamilton and Marie Cantemir were rumored to have received his favors, and several eighteenth-century writers wrote rollicking accounts of Catherine traveling through Europe accompanied by a suite of ladies, each one carrying her baby by Peter in her arms. One presumes that Peter was not chaste and that the stories of a liaison with an actress in London or a lady in Paris may be true. It is clear, however, that these affairs, if they took place, were episodes to which Peter gave little thought and attached no importance. Catherine understood this and frequently teased him in her letters. Peter's assurances that no other woman would be interested in "an old fellow like me" were good-humored but sometimes a little red-faced.

Catherine could tease him, but others could not. In Copenhagen in 1716, King Frederick IV turned to him smiling and with an eyebrow raised. "Ah, my brother," he said, "I hear you also have a mistress." Peter's face instantly darkened. "My brother," he snapped, "my harlots do not cost me much, but yours cost you thousands of pounds which could be better spent."

Essentially, Peter's attitude toward morality in relations between men and women was based on a utilitarian social ethic. He was indulgent toward behavior and indiscretions which did no harm to society. Prostitutes enjoyed "perfect liberty in Russia," reported Weber, except in the case of one who had "peppered some hundreds of the Preobrazhensky Guards who, being unable to march on their duty with the rest, were obliged to remain behind at Petersburg in order to be cured"; this woman was knouted for having harmed state interests. In general, the Tsar refused to defend chastity or punish adultery. Told that the Emperor Charles V had forbidden adultery under pain of death, he asked, "Is it possible? I should have thought that so great a prince had more judgment. Without a doubt he fancied that his people were too numerous. It is necessary to punish disorders and crimes, but we ought to spare the lives of our people as much as possible." Unmarried women, when pregnant, were encouraged to bear their infants.

Once, when Peter found a pretty girl barred from the company of other maidens because she had an illegitimate son, he said, "I forbid her to be excluded from the company of other women and girls." The girl's son was placed under the Tsar's protection.

Peter's court was filled with examples of men and women who had profited from or been saved by the Tsar's leniency in these matters. He encouraged Yaguzhinsky to divorce his first wife, who was making his life miserable, and to marry Countess Golovkin, "one of the most agreeable and well-educated ladies in Russia," according to Bergholz. Although her face was scarred by smallpox, she had a splendid figure, spoke French and German fluently, danced exquisitely and was always cheerful. He denied Prince Repnin permission to take his Finnish mistress as his fourth wife (the Orthodox church permitted only three in sequence), but legitimized their children under the name Repninsky. When his favored dentchik Vasily Pospelov married a lady flute player, Peter not only attended their wedding but was present at the baptism of their baby the following morning. He supported General Anthony Devier in his suit for the hand of Menshikov's sister. Having been refused by the Prince, who hoped for a better match, Devier and the lady nevertheless conceived a child. Devier appealed again to Menshikov on the grounds that the child should be born legitimate, to which Menshikov responded by kicking Devier down the stairs. Peter intervened on Devier's appeal and the marriage was celebrated, although after the Emperor's death Menshikov exiled his brother-in-law to Siberia.

But if Peter was tolerant of indiscretion, he was implacable in criminal matters. Prenatal abortion or the murder of an unwanted infant after birth was punishable by death. The most dramatic example of the Tsar's unwavering stand on this issue came with the case of Marie Hamilton. This young woman, one of the Tsaritsa Catherine's favorite maids of honor, was, in the language of the day, "much addicted to gallantry." In consequence, she bore three illegitimate children. The first two were murdered in such secrecy that no one at court suspected, but the third dead infant was discovered and the mother arrested. In prison, she confessed that this was the third time this mournful event had occurred. To her surprise, for she believed that the friendship and favor of the Tsar and the Tsaritsa would win her a pardon, she was sentenced to death. On the day of the execution, the prisoner appeared on the scaffold in a white silk gown trimmed with black ribbons. Peter climbed the structure to stand beside her and spoke quietly into her ear. The condemned woman and most of the spectators assumed that this would be her last-minute reprieve. Instead, the Tsar gave her a kiss and said sadly, "I cannot violate the laws to save your life. Support your punishment with courage, and, in the hope that God may forgive you your sins, address your prayers to him with a heart full of faith

and contrition." Miss Hamilton knelt and prayed, the Tsar turned away and the headsman struck.

DURING THE FINAL YEARS of his reign, Peter turned his attention to bringing to St. Petersburg some of the institutional refinements of civilized society: museums, an art gallery, a library and even a zoo. Like almost everything new in Russia created by the Tsar's effort, these institutions strongly reflected his own taste. He had little inclination for theater (his preference ran to the crude masquery of his Mock-Synod) and none whatsoever for instrumental music. The only theatrical performances to which Russian society had access were those arranged by Peter's sister Princess Natalya, who established a small theater of her own, taking a large empty house and fitting it out with a stage, pit and boxes. Weber, who attended a performance, was not enthusiastic. "The actors and actresses, ten in number, were all native Russians who had never been abroad, so that it is easy to imagine their ability," he wrote. The play he saw, a tragedy written by the Princess herself and performed in Russian, was a moralistic tale of rebellion in Russia and the horrors proceeding from that unhappy event. And if Weber found the actors bad, he found the orchestra worse. "The orchestra was composed of sixteen musicians, all Russians," he wrote. "They are taught music as well as other sciences with the help of batogs. If a general pitches upon some spare fellow in a regiment who he decides should learn music, notwithstanding the soldier has not the least notion of it nor any talent that way, he is sent out to a master who gives him a certain time for learning his task; first, learning the handling of the instrument, then to play some Lutheran hymns or some minuet and so on. If the scholar has not learned his lesson during the term prefixed, the batogs are applied and repeated till such time as he is master of the tune."

Even this small theater disappeared in 1716 when Princess Natalya died. Later, in Moscow, the Duchess of Mecklenburg established a small theater at Ismailovo with herself as director, ladies of her court as actresses and the male roles being taken mostly by servants. Despite the distance from Moscow, many people came to see these performances, although some in the audience may have attended for mixed motives. Bergholz grumbled that on his first visit he was robbed of his snuffbox and that on another occasion the pockets of many Holstein gentlemen were picked of their silk handkerchiefs. In time, Peter made arrangements for a professional theatrical company to come from Hamburg, but it never arrived. For two or three years, a small, wretched theater existed in St. Petersburg on the banks of the Moika Canal, doing bad imitations of French plays and poor translations of German farces. But with the Tsar uninterested, his subjects also showed

little interest. Like Peter himself, they preferred more popular spectacles, such as juggling and rope dancing. A special favorite of the Tsar's was the celebrated German strongman Samson, who arrived in Russia in 1719. Irritated by those, especially among the clergy, who said that Samson performed his feats by magic, witchcraft or trickery rather than by strength, the Tsar stood beside Samson and called some of the principal clergymen upon the stage to witness the performance at close range. Samson lay down across two chairs supported only under his head and feet; Peter placed an anvil on his chest, and then broke several large pieces of iron upon the anvil with a sledgehammer. Samson next placed a stick between his teeth, which the Tsar tried with both hands to pull out; he failed not only to move the stick but even to move Samson from his place. The strongman's power, Peter triumphantly announced to everyone present, lay solely in his sheer physical strength.

On his second visit to the West in 1716–1717, Peter went earnestly and regularly to see scientific collections and public and private collections of paintings, and brought many paintings home with him. Hoping that one day not all the paintings in Russia would be the work of foreigners, Peter sent a number of young Russian artists to Holland and Italy to study. The Tsar was even prouder of his new scientific collections. In 1717, he had purchased the entire collection of the celebrated Dutch anatomist Professor Ruysch, whose lecture hall and dissecting room the Tsar often had visited on his first trip twenty years before. The collection, which had been forty years in forming, came with an illustrated catalog titled *Thesaurus Anatomicus*. Peter also purchased the collection of the Dutch apothecary Seba, consisting of all known land and sea animals, birds, reptiles and insects of the East Indies. These two celebrated collections were the foundation of the Museum of the Academy of Science, which Peter established in a large stone building on Vasilevsky Island across from the Admiralty. It was his custom to go to the museum at dawn two or three times a week to study the exhibits before he went to the Admiralty. He enjoyed being there so much that on one occasion he decided to hold an audience with the Austrian ambassador in the museum. The Chancellor asked whether the Summer Palace would not be more appropriate. "The ambassador is accredited to me, not to one of my palaces," Peter replied, and he received the ambassador at the museum at five a.m. on a subsequent morning.

At Peter's insistence, the museum was open to the public and guides were provided to explain the exhibits. When Yaguzhinsky suggested that a rouble be charged for admission to defray expenses, Peter objected that this would keep people away. Instead, he said that the museum should not only be free, but that people should be tempted to come by offering in the

Tsar's name a dish of coffee or a glass of wine as refreshment. These expenses were paid from Peter's pocket.

To the collections purchased abroad were added curios such as elephants' teeth found near Voronezh which Peter speculated were relics of the passage of Alexander the Great, and antiquities found among the ruins of a pagan temple near the Caspian Sea—images, vessels and several parchments in an unknown language. Similarly, while digging for gold near Samarkand, prospectors had found a number of ancient brass figures, which were sent to Prince Gagarin, the Governor of Siberia, and by him to the Tsar. They included brass idols, minotaurs, oxen, geese, deformed old men and young women. The mouths of the idols were hinged so that they could move; Peter, ever wary of religious superstitions, speculated that "it is likely the priests made use of this to impose on the people by speaking through them."

Peter also attempted to broaden the knowledge of his subjects through the use of books and libraries. The Tsar himself had collected books all his life, and especially on his visits to Germany, France, Holland and other countries in the West. His personal library included works on a wide range of subjects, including military and naval affairs, science, history, medicine, law and religion. Peter's books were first kept in the Summer Palace; then, as their number grew, they were moved to the Winter Palace, Peterhof and other sites. After his death, his library became the nucleus of the library of the Russian Academy of Science. In 1722, Peter sent orders to the principal ancient monasteries of Russia to make a search for old manuscripts, chronicles and books, and to send those that were found to Moscow, whence they were forwarded to Peter's private study in St. Petersburg. Upon the Emperor's death, most of these invaluable documents also were transferred to the library of the Academy of Science.

Peter had admired the zoo in Paris and on his return from France immediately established a menagerie in St. Petersburg. Apes and monkeys, lions and leopards and even an elephant from India were installed, but all had difficulty surviving the frigid months of winter. Although Peter had a special house built for the elephant, with fires burning night and day to warm the beast, it lived only a few years. A different kind of exhibition was that displayed by the colony of Samoyeds, a tribe of savage Laplanders from the Arctic coast, who came every winter, bringing their reindeer and dogs, to camp on the ice in the Neva. There, inside an enclosure, they lived in a model of one of their native villages, accepting the alms-giving of a curious crowd. The Russians did not go too close, however, as the Samoyeds were reputed to "bite strangers on the face and ears."

The new collections and the buildings that housed them were products of Peter's insatiable curiosity and his desire to teach his subjects what he had learned. Every journey in Russia and, even more so, every journey abroad resulted in the acquisition of more oddities, instruments, books,

models, paintings and animals. On arriving in even a small town when traveling, Peter always asked to see whatever was remarkable or different in that place. When told that there was nothing unusual, he replied, "Who knows? If it not be so for you, perhaps it will be for me. Let me see everything."

One of the most extraordinary of these acquisitions was the Great Globe of Gottorp. While traveling in Schleswig in the duchy of Gottorp in 1713, Peter had discovered this remarkable scientific and mechanical device. It was a huge, hollow globe, eleven and a half feet in diameter, made in 1664 for the ruling Duke of Holstein. The external surface was a globular map of the earth, while on the inside was a chart of the heavens. Viewers could climb inside by ascending several steps, then sit at a round table circled by benches for ten or twelve people. A winch could be turned which would make the heavens revolve around the audience. Naturally, Peter was intrigued and delighted by the globe, and when the administrator for the young Duke Charles Frederick offered it as a gift in the name of the state, Peter accepted with joy, declaring that the people of Holstein could not have made a more acceptable present. Menshikov, commanding the Russian army in Germany, was ordered to take personal charge of packaging and shipping the globe. Special permission was obtained from the Swedes for its unhindered passage by ship up the Baltic to Reval. In the winter of 1715, the enormous sphere was transported by sledges and rollers over the snows to St. Petersburg. Because the globe was so large and Peter would not risk it being dismantled, in many places the road had to be widened, branches lopped off or even whole trees felled so that the globe could pass. When it arrived, Peter placed it in the house he had built for the now deceased elephant, and he went to look at it for several hours every day.

Peter's most important and lasting contribution to intellectual activity in Russia was his foundation of the Academy of Science.* The project had been suggested by Leibniz, who had already founded the Prussian Academy of Science in Berlin, but who died in 1716 before Peter was ready to act. The Tsar's interest was further stimulated by his own election to the French Academy after his visit to Paris. His letter accepting this honor shines with almost childish delight: "We are very delighted that you have honored Us in this way, and we would like to assure you that we shall accept the position you have given Us with great pleasure, and that it is our fervent wish to apply Ourself assiduously in order to contribute as much as possible to science and therefore to demonstrate that we are a worthy member of your association." As an initial contribution, the new member forwarded

---

* Which, after two hundred fifty years, remains the nation's preeminent intellectual institution.

a new map of the Caspian Sea. He signed his letter "Affectionately yours, Peter I."

On January 28, 1724, a year before his death, the Tsar issued the decree founding the Russian Academy. Typically, it also contained an explanation so that Russians would understand what it was that was being founded:

Usually two kinds of institutions are used in organizing arts and sciences. One is known as a University; the other as an Academy of arts and sciences. A University is an association of learned individuals who teach young people. . . . An Academy, on the other hand, is an association of learned and skilled people who do research and inventions.

In this case, however—so the decree continued—because learned men were rare in Russia, Academicians would teach as well as do research. An annual grant of 25,000 roubles, drawn from the customs tolls at the Baltic ports, was assigned to support the institution.

Peter died before the Academy began to function, but in December 1725, its doors first opened. Seventeen Academicians had been lured from France, Germany, and Switzerland, including philosophers, mathematicians, historians, an astronomer, and doctors of anatomy, law, and chemistry, many of them scholars of first rank. Unfortunately, there were no Russian students qualified for university classes so that eight German students also had to be imported. Even so, audiences for lectures were smaller than the number required by charter so that Academicians occasionally had to attend each others' lectures.

The irony of a learned academy functioning in a country that lacked any significant number of elementary or secondary schools was not lost on contemporaries, but Peter, looking into the future, thrust all objections aside. Using a metaphor, he explained:

I have to harvest big stooks [shocks of grain], but I have no mill; and there is not enough water close by to build a water mill; but there is water enough at a distance; only I shall have no time to make a canal for the length of my life is uncertain. And therefore I am building the mill first and have only given orders for the canal to be begun, which will the better force my successors to bring water to the completed mill.

62

ALONG THE CASPIAN

WITH THE SIGNING of the Treaty of Nystad, Russia was finally at peace. Now, it seemed, the colossal energies which had been poured into military campaigns from Azov to Copenhagen could at last be turned toward Russia itself. Peter did not wish to be remembered in history as a conqueror or a warrior; he saw his place as a reformer. Yet, the celebrations in St. Petersburg hailing the Peace of Nystad were still in progress when Peter ordered his army to prepare for a new campaign. The following spring, the army would march into the Caucasus against Persia. And, once again, the army would be personally led by the Emperor.

Although its announcement came as a surprise, this march to the south was no sudden whim. For most of his life, Peter had heard stories of the East, the empire of Cathay, the wealth of the Great Mogul of India, the richness of the trade which passed over caravan routes through Siberia to China, and from India through Persia to the West. These tales had come from travelers passing through Russia who stopped long enough in the German Suburb to stir the imagination of the youthful Tsar. They came from Nicholas Witsen, Burgomaster of Amsterdam and expert on the geography of the East, who spent many hours in conversation with Peter during the Tsar's first winter in Holland. Now, at last, Peter meant to carry out these youthful dreams.

He had already attempted to reach out toward China by extending the existing trade in tea, furs and silk and by establishing a permanent Russian mission in Peking. But the Chinese were proud and suspicious. The militant Manchu Dynasty was at the peak of its power in Peking. The great Emperor K'ang-hsi, who had come to the throne at the age of seven in 1661 and ruled until his death in 1722, had made peace with all his neighbors and embarked on a reign distinguished for its patronage of painting, poetry, porcelain and learning; dictionaries and encyclopedias published with his encouragement remained standard for generations. K'ang-hsi tolerated foreigners at his court, but Peter's efforts to improve relations with China

made slow progress. In 1715, a Russian priest, the Archimandrite Hilarion, was received at Peking and given the rank of Mandarin, Fifth Class. Finally, in 1719, Peter appointed Captain Lev Ismailov of the Preobrazhensky Guards as his envoy extraordinary to Peking and sent with him as a present for the emperor four ivory telescopes which Peter had made himself. Ismailov was received on a friendly and dignified footing at the Chinese court, but he outreached himself. He asked that all restrictions on trade between Russia and China be lifted, that permission be given for construction of a Russian church in Peking, and that Russian consulates be established in important towns in China to facilitate trade. To this, the Chinese replied loftily, "Our Emperor does not trade and has no bazaars. You value your merchants very highly. We scorn commerce. Only poor people and servants occupy themselves in that way with us, and there is no profit at all to us from your trade. We have enough of Russian goods even if your people did not bring them." Ismailov departed, and thereafter Russian caravans were hindered more severely. K'ang-hsi died in 1722, and his son Yung Cheng was even more hostile to Christians in general; thus, the avenue to trade with China was narrowed rather than broadened in Peter's final years.

Far to the north, along the desolate shores of the Sea of Okhotsk and the northern Pacific, there was no one to bar the Russian advance. It was under Peter that the huge Kamchatka Peninsula and the Kurile Islands were claimed by Russia. In 1724, shortly before he died, Peter summoned a Danish-born captain in his fleet, Vitus Bering, and assigned him the task of leading an expedition to the periphery of the Eurasian continent a thousand miles beyond Kamchatka, to determine whether Eurasia and North America were joined by land. Bering found the strait, fifty-three miles wide and only 144 feet deep, which subsequently was named after him.*

A year before Bering set out, Peter had dispatched two frigates to the opposite end of the earth, to carry his fraternal greetings "to the illustrious King and Owner of the glorious island of Madagascar." The inhabitants of that gigantic island had a poor record of hospitality to Western visitors: French traders and colonists were massacred in 1674, and through most of the eighteenth century the only Westerners who set foot on the island were pirates such as Captain Kidd. Peter's motive in sending this expedition was

* In the years that followed, Russian explorers and settlers crossed the strait, and a string of Russian forts and trading posts sprang up along the Alaska coast. Eventually, these Russian settlements reached as far south as San Francisco, where, in 1806, a little over eighty years after Peter's death, a Russian fur-trading center was established. For more than a century, Alaska—known then as Russian America—was controlled by the state-owned Russian-American Company. In 1867, the vast area which became America's forty-ninth state was sold by Tsar Alexander II for $7,000,000. Today, the only point on the globe where the frontiers of the United States and the Soviet Union actually meet is across the fifty-three miles of the Bering Strait.

not really to establish a foothold in Madagascar. His ships were ordered to stop there and conclude a treaty if possible, then to sail on to their real destination, India. Peter dreamed of a trade agreement with the Great Mogul and also wanted some teakwood on which he could exercise his talent for carpentry. As it happened, the ships reached neither India nor Madagascar; they never left the Baltic. One of the frigates sprang a leak a few days after sailing, and both ships returned to Reval. Peter was disappointed, but he died before the project could be renewed.

It was not the sea route to India, in any case, but the land routes through Persia and Central Asia which attracted him. The Central Asian caravans came over the Khyber Pass from India, passed through Kabul, crossed the jagged peaks of the Hindu Kush and traversed a thousand miles of desert inhabited by Kazaks and Kalmucks before reaching Astrachan and the lower Volga. In Peter's time, there was more turbulence than usual among these desert people. Two rival Moslem khans, the rulers of Khiva and Bokhara, were struggling for predominance, and each sometimes turned to the Russians for assistance.* Peter, because of his war with Sweden, had been unable to respond to these appeals, but his interest in the desert lands had been aroused.

Peter's interest in all the regions to the east and south had also been stimulated by reports of gold. There were pebbles of gold in the rivers of Siberia, veins of gold along the shores of the Caspian, golden sands in the deserts of Central Asia—such stories circulated freely in St. Petersburg. In 1714, 1716 and 1719, Peter sent expeditions into Siberia and Central Asia in search of the precious metal. They ended without gain, although the first expedition, during its withdrawal, constructed a fort at the juncture of the Irtysh and Om rivers which grew into the town of Omsk.

The 1716 expedition ended in spectacular tragedy. Hearing stories of gold along the Amu Darya River, which ran through the lands of the Khan of Khiva, Peter resolved to send congratulations to the new Khan on his accession to the throne and an offer of Russian protection if he would accept the Tsar's suzerainty. Along the way, the expedition was also to build a fort at the mouth of the Amu Darya, reconnoiter the length of the river and send merchants and engineers to the head of the river, across the mountains and down into India. Once their reports were in hand and the Khans of Bokhara and Khiva had given allegiance, Peter could begin the development of the permanent trade route which was his ultimate objective.

---

* Weber describes an unusual kind of help which the Khan of Bokhara asked of Peter. The Khan's ambassador in Petersburg, says Weber, "begged of the Tsar a number of Swedish girls to go along with him, or to give him leave to buy some, his master having heard that the Swedes were a very warlike nation, which made him desirous to have some of their race in his dominions." This request met with a repulse; however, he found means to get two Swedish girls, whom he carried along with him.

Unfortunately, Peter chose the wrong man to lead this expedition. Prince Alexander Bekovich Cherkassky had been born a Circassian Moslem prince named Devlet Kisden Mirza. His father's lands in the Caucasus lay within the empire of the Shah of Persia. One day, the Shah happened to see the beautiful wife of Cherkassky's father and ordered his vassal to send to him this exquisite piece of property. The father refused, and fled with his family to Moscow for protection. There, his son converted to Christianity, became a captain of the Guard and served as an officer in Astrachan and along the Caucasus frontier. Peter, thinking Cherkassky's background ideally suited him for dealing with the Moslem khans, summoned him to Riga for final instructions and sent him on his way.

In the summer of 1716, Cherkassky left Astrachan with 4,000 regular soldiers and detachments of Cossacks, engineers and surveyors. He built two forts on the eastern side of the Caspian Sea, long considered the territory of the Khan of Khiva. In the spring of 1717, despite reports of the Khan's anger at this action, he began his march toward Khiva, 300 miles across empty, waterless desert. One hundred miles from Khiva, the Khan's army appeared and a three-day battle ensued. Cherkassky was victorious, and the Khan asked for peace, which he and his elders swore on the Koran to uphold. Then, he invited his conqueror to enter Khiva, suggesting that, for greater convenience and ease of provisioning, the Russian force divide itself into five detachments, each to be stationed in a separate town. Cherkassky foolishly agreed, and shortly thereafter the Khan's army marched from one town to another, compelling the surrender of the Russian detachments one by one. Every officer was slaughtered and every soldier sold into slavery. Cherkassky himself was carried into the Khan's tent, where a piece of red cloth, the sign of blood and death, was spread on the ground. Cherkassky refused to kneel on the cloth before the Khan, whereupon the Khan's guards slashed the calves of his legs with their scimitars, pitching him involuntarily on the ground before their master. Afterward, the unfortunate Circassian-Russian was beheaded, his skin was stuffed, and, thus transformed, he was exhibited in a courtyard of the Khan's palace.

Frustrated in his hope of reaching India through Central Asia, Peter pressed ahead with his efforts to open the land route through Persia. He was also anxious to persuade the Shah to divert the lucrative silk trade so that it should pass from Persia north into the Caucasus to Astrachan and thence along the Russian rivers to St. Petersburg, rather than following its traditional route west from Persia through Turkey to the Mediterranean. Peter did not think that this would be difficult; his relations with the incumbent Shah had always been amicable. This monarch was, according to Weber, writing in 1715, "a prince of forty years of age, of a very indolent temper, giving himself wholly up to pleasures, adjusting his difference with the Turks, Indians and other neighbors by the interposition of his governors

and by dint of money; that though he called himself the Shah-in-Shah, or Emperor of Emperors, yet he dreaded the Turk . . . and notwithstanding the Turks have in the space of eighty years conquered from the Persians many kingdoms, viz, Media, Assyria, Babylon and Arabia, yet they [the Persians] always avoided making war against the Porte."

To seek this agreement, Peter appointed one of his most aggressive "fledglings," Artemius Volynsky, a young nobleman who had served as a dragoon in the army and as a diplomatic assistant to Shafirov in negotiations with the Turks. Volynsky's assignment, written in Peter's own hand, was to study the "true state of the Persian empire, its forces, fortresses and limits." He was to try especially to learn "whether there is not some river from India that flows into the Caspian Sea."

Volynsky arrived in Isfahan, the ancient capital of Persia, in March 1717 and soon found himself under house arrest. This had nothing to do with his own behavior; rather, the Shah and his vizier had learned of Cherkassky's construction of forts on the eastern Caspian and his disastrous campaign against the Khan of Khiva. They accurately saw in Volynsky the first tentative probe against Persia by the outreaching Russian Emperor. Accordingly, to prevent him from observing the general weakness and vulnerability of Persia, Volynsky was confined to his house. But they could not prevent the envoy from making a personal assessment when he was received at court. "Here," reported Volynsky, "there is now such a head that he is not over his subjects but the subject of his subjects, and I am sure that it is rarely one can find such a fool, even among common men, not to say crowned heads. For this reason [the Shah] never does any business himself, but puts everything on his vizier, who is stupider than any cattle, but is still such a favorite that the Shah pays attention to everything that comes out of his mouth and does whatever he bids."

Despite the restrictions placed on his movements, Volynsky managed to conclude a commercial treaty giving Russian merchants the right to trade and buy raw silk throughout Persia. He also saw enough to report to Peter that the state of decay in Persia was so far advanced that the Shah's Caspian provinces must be ripe for plucking. As Volynsky journeyed home, an emissary of the Prince of Georgia visited him secretly, pleading that the Tsar march south to aid the Christian people who lived on the southern side of the snow-capped Caucasian peaks.*

On his return, Volynsky was rewarded by appointment as Governor of Astrachan and Adjutant General of the Tsar. From Astrachan, Volynsky was tireless in urging that Peter seize the opportunity offered by the crumbling of the Persian empire. In addition to describing the prizes available

* The huge, volcanic mountains of the Caucasus are higher than the Alps. Mount Elbrus rises 18,481 feet, Dykh-Yau 17,054 and a number of others are over 16,000. It was to one of these mighty peaks that Prometheus was said to have been chained.

to even a small army, he constantly warned that the Turks were advancing, and that if the Tsar did not take the Caucasus soon, the Sultan surely would do so. Peter delayed until the war with Sweden was over. Then, at almost the moment the Treaty of Nystad was signed, an incident occurred which offered an excuse for intervention. A tribe of Caucasian mountaineers who had already proposed themselves as allies of Russia against the Persians decided not to wait and attacked the Persian trading center of Shemaha. At first, the Russian merchants in the town were unconcerned, having been promised that they and their shops and warehouses would not be touched. But the mountain tribesmen began looting indiscriminately, killing several Russians and carrying off half a million roubles' worth of goods. Volynsky immediately wrote to Peter that here was a perfect opportunity to move, on the grounds of protecting Russian trade and assisting the Shah to restore order in his dominions. Peter's reply answered Volynsky's prayers:

> I have received your letter in which you wrote about the affair of Daud Bek and that now is the very occasion for what you were ordered to prepare. To this opinion of yours I answer that it is very evident we should not let this occasion slip. We have ordered a considerable part of our forces on the Volga to march to winter quarters, whence they will go to Astrachan in the spring.

Volynsky also urged that this was the time to stir up the Christian princes in Georgia and elsewhere in the Caucasus against their Persian overlord. But here Peter was more cautious. He had no wish to repeat his experience of eleven years before with the Christian princes of the Ottoman provinces of Walachia and Moldavia. His objective here was the silk trade, the land route to India and the peaceful control of the western shore of the Caspian Sea to facilitate this project. Thus he declined to issue any religious proclamation or pose as a liberator before embarking on this new campaign. Instead, he wrote to Volynsky, "As to what you write about the Prince of Georgia and other Christians, if any of these should be desirable in this matter, give them hopes, but on account of the habitual fickleness of these people, begin nothing until the arrival of our troops, when we will act according to best counsel."

While Peter waited in Moscow for the coming of spring, further reports from Persia stimulated his anxiety. The Shah had been deposed in the face of an Afghan revolt; the new ruler was the Shah's third son, Tahmasp Mirza, who was struggling against the Afghan leader Mahmud to keep his throne. The danger was that the Turks, who had clearly evident designs on the western Caucasus, might see the collapse of authority in Persia as an opportunity to seize the eastern Caucasus as well—and these provinces along the Caspian were precisely those which Peter had it in mind to pluck.

Peter dispatched the Guards regiments from Moscow on May 3, 1722, and ten days later he followed with Catherine, Admiral Apraxin, Tolstoy and others. At Kolomna on the Oka River, they embarked in galleys, sailing down the Oka and the Volga to Astrachan. The journey, even traveling downstream and with the rivers high because of the melting snows, took a month, because of Peter's insatiable curiosity. He stopped at every town to make an inspection, examine objects of interest, receive petitions and ask questions about local administration and revenues. Nothing escaped his notice, and every day decrees flowed from his pen on subjects from improving the cottages of peasants to changing the design of barges along the Volga. In Kazan, ancient capital of the Tatar kingdom conquered by Ivan the Terrible, Peter was the first tsar since Ivan to visit the city, and he was anxious to see not only its shipbuilding yards, churches and monasteries, but also the sections of the city still inhabited by Tatars. Inspecting a government-owned textile mill, he observed that it was languidly producing shoddy materials while, not far away, a privately owned mill was flourishing. On the spot, Peter simply gave the government mill to the private owner. At Saratov, the Emperor met Ayuk Khan, the seventy-year-old chief of the Kalmucks. On board the Imperial galley, Catherine presented the Khan's wife with a gold watch set with diamonds. The Khan immediately responded by ordering five thousand Kalmuck horsemen to join the Emperor's campaign.

In Astrachan, Peter spent a month making final preparations for the campaign. An army of 61,000 men was assembling: 22,000 Russian infantrymen, 9,000 cavalry and 5,000 sailors, plus auxiliary forces of 20,000 Cossacks and 5,000 Kalmucks. Meanwhile, he observed the fishing for the great eighteen-foot beluga, whose delicious gray caviar the Russians kept for themselves, and the equally large sturgeon whose slightly less tasty black caviar they exported in large quantities to Europe.

On July 18, he embarked with the Russian infantry at Astrachan and sailed 200 miles down the west coast of the Caspian Sea, while the huge mass of cavalry was sent by land across the semi-desert Terek steppe. The sea was rough and the voyage took a week, but eventually a landing was made on a small bay north of the town Derbent. Peter was the first to land on the shallow beach, although he arrived sitting on a board, carried by four sailors. Immediately, he decided that every one of his officers who had not previously bathed in the Caspian should go for a swim. Some of the older officers, unable to swim, complied with reluctance. Peter himself went happily, but, rather than swimming, he had himself let down into the water on his board.

When the Russian cavalry arrived, although both men and horses had suffered from "lack of water and bad grass" on their overland march, the advance on Derbent began. The route lay along the coast down the narrow

strip between the mountains and the sea, but only once was there any armed resistance. On this occasion, a local chief horribly murdered three Cossacks ("cutting open their breasts while they were yet alive, and taking out their hearts") sent to him with a letter from Peter. Reprisal was swift and the offending village was burned to the ground. Peter was surprised by the individual courage of these mountain people. "When they are together, they do not hold at all, but run away," he said, "while separately each man resists so desperately that when he has thrown away his musket as if he were going to surrender, he begins to fight with his dagger."

Elsewhere, the Russian Emperor and Empress were received as honored guests. At Tarku, the local Moslem Prince brought his wives and concubines to visit the Russian camp. The Moslem women were seated cross-legged "on cushions of crimson velvet, laid on Persian carpets" in the Empress's tent, whereupon—reported Captain Peter Bruce—Catherine invited all the Russian officers to come into the tent in relays "to gratify their curiosity" as to "these incomparably beautiful, most lovely creatures." Peter and Catherine attended mass at a chapel built by the Preobrazhensky Guards, after which each of them placed a stone on the site, and then every soldier in the army also placed a stone, so that a pyramid was raised to commemorate the mass said on the spot for the Emperor of Russia.

Peter's first important objective was Derbent, a town supposedly founded by Alexander the Great. Derbent's significance was both commercial and military: It was an important trading center, and it also occupied a strategic position on the north-south road along the shore of the Caspian. It was here that the mountains came down closest to the sea; thus, the town situated in this narrow passage controlled all movement, military or commercial, to the north or south, and was called the Eastern Iron Gates. Derbent surrendered without a fight; indeed, as Peter approached, he found the governor waiting to present him "with the golden keys to the town and the citadel on a cushion of rich Persian brocade."

Peter's plan, now that Derbent was occupied, was on a typically grand scale. He meant to continue down the coast and seize Baku, 150 miles to the south. Then, he intended to found a new commercial city still farther south, at the mouth of the Kura River, which would become an important center on his proposed new overland trade route between India, Persia and Russia. That done, he would move up the Kura to the Georgian capital, Tiflis, there to cement the proposed alliance with the Christian Prince Vakhtang. Finally, from Tiflis, he would recross the great Caucasus Mountains to the north, returning to Astrachan through the lands of the Terek Cossacks. "Thus, in these regions," he wrote to the Senate, "we will have gained a foothold."

Unfortunately, events were moving against him. The Persian governor of Baku refused to accept a Russian garrison, which meant that the city could

be taken only by a major military effort. Although Peter's army seemed sufficiently large to overcome any military opposition, he was worried about supplies. A provisioning fleet from Astrachan had encountered a disastrous storm on the Caspian and never arrived at Derbent; supplies locally available were vanishing rapidly the longer the army stayed. Further, the August heat along the coast was taking a toll of men and horses. Soldiers had been eating the fruits and melons for which the Caucasus has always been famous, but in such quantities as to become sick, and many of the regiments were decimated. To cope with the sweltering heat, Peter had his head shaved and during the day wore a wide-brimmed hat over his naked skull. In the cool of the evening, he covered himself with a wig made from his own shorn hair. The Empress copied her husband, shaving off her own hair, while at night covering her head with the cap of a grenadier. More concerned than Peter about the suffering of his troops in this oppressive heat, she even dared on one occasion to countermand his military orders. The Emperor had commanded the army to march and then retired to his tent to sleep. When he awoke, he found the soldiers still in camp. What general, he asked angrily, had dared to overrule his orders? "I did it," said Catherine, "because your men would have died of heat and thirst."

As he considered the situation of his army, Peter grew uneasy. He was a long way from the nearest Russian base at Astrachan, his seaborne supply line was not functioning, a number of potentially hostile tribesmen inhabited the mountains along his northern flank and there was always the danger that the Turks—who, unlike the Persians, constituted a serious military opponent—might march to protect their own interests in the Caucasus. Peter did not wish to repeat the experience on the Pruth. Thus, at a council of war, the decision was made to withdraw. A garrison was left behind at Derbent, and the main body of the army retreated north by land and water to Astrachan.

Peter reached the mouth of the Volga and Astrachan on October 4. He remained for a month, looking after the welfare of his troops, arranging for care of the sick and winter quarters for the rest. Part of this time, Peter was severely ill with an attack of strangury and stone, a disease of the urinary tract. Before leaving Astrachan, Peter made it clear that, despite the abandonment of that summer's campaign, he was not abandoning Russian ambitions on the Caspian Sea. In November, he sent a combined naval and military expedition to capture the port of Resht, 500 miles away on the south shore of the Caspian. In July of the following summer, a Russian force captured Baku, thus securing the entire western coast of the great inland sea. Negotiations with the now helpless Shah resulted in Persia ceding Derbent to Russia along with three seaboard provinces of the eastern Caucasus. As Peter explained it to the Persian ambassador, if the Shah did not give up the provinces to Russia, which was his friend, then

he would certainly lose them to Turkey, which was his enemy. The Shah was in no position to argue against this Russian logic.

THE DISINTEGRATION of the Persian empire and Peter's military campaign along the Caspian Sea threatened once again to bring Russia into collision with the Ottoman Empire. The Porte had always been particularly interested in the Transcaucasus—that is, the Persian provinces of Georgia and Armenia, lying south of the mighty Caucasus mountain range. The Turks coveted them not because they were Christian, but because they were on the Turkish frontier and because they lay on the Black Sea. The Sultan was quite willing that Peter take the Persian provinces on the Caspian side of the Caucasus, but he must not approach the Black Sea, which, since Azov had been returned to Turkey, was once again the Sultan's private lake. Eventually, the Tsar and the Sultan amicably settled the matter by dividing up the Caucasus provinces of Persia. Inconveniently, the Persians did not accept this settlement, and continued intermittently fighting with both their powerful neighbors. In 1732, Empress Anne, tired of the constant drain on her resources by these Caspian provinces (up to 15,000 Russian soldiers were dying every year of disease in the unfamiliar climate) and restored them to Persia. It was not until the reign of Catherine the Great that the northern Caucasus was designated a Russian province, and not until 1813, in the time of Catherine's grandson Alexander I, that Persia permanently ceded to Russia the coastal territories along the Caspian through which Peter the Great had marched on his final campaign.

63

TWILIGHT

THE SNOW BEGAN to fall before Peter and Catherine started for Moscow from Astrachan late in November 1722. Along the way, the cold grew more intense. A hundred miles below Tsaritsyn, the Volga was covered with ice and Peter's boats could go no farther. There was trouble finding sledges suitable for the imperial party, and, as a result, the journey took a month.

Once back in Moscow, Peter plunged into the atmosphere of the season. During the week of Carnival, the procession outdid those of any previous year. The Saxon ambassador reported:

> The procession consisted of sixty sledges, each constructed to appear as a boat. On the first of these boat-sledges rode Bacchus— appropriately portrayed, as the player representing him had been kept drunk for three days and three nights. Then came a sledge drawn by six bear cubs, a sledge drawn by four hogs and a sledge drawn by ten dogs. The College of Cardinals came next, fully robed, but mounted on oxen. After them followed the great sledge of the Mock-Pope, surrounded by his archbishops, making signs of blessing right and left. Next, the Mock-Tsar, accompanied by two bears. The triumph of the procession was a miniature two-decked, three-masted frigate under full sail, thirty feet long, with thirty-two guns; standing on her deck, maneuvering the sails, was the Emperor dressed as a navy captain. This astounding sight was followed by a hundred-foot sea serpent with the tail supported on twenty-four small sledges linked together to undulate across the snow. After the serpent came a large gilded barge on which Catherine rode, dressed as a Frisian peasant woman, accompanied by her court made up as blacks. Then in succession came Menshikov dressed as an abbot, General-Admiral Apraxin dressed as the Burgomeister of Hamburg and other notables costumed as Germans, Poles, Chinese, Persians, Circassians and Siberians. The foreign envoys appeared together dressed in domino

suits of blue and white, while the Prince of Moldavia was dressed as a Turk.

Before leaving Moscow for St. Petersburg in early March 1723, Peter invited his friends to another astonishing spectacle: the burning of the wooden house at Preobrazhenskoe in which he had first secretly planned the war against Sweden. With his own hand, the Emperor filled shelves and closets with inflammable colored chemicals and fireworks and then he put the house to the torch. Many small explosions and brilliantly colored flames erupted from the burning structure, and for some time before it collapsed, the heavy log frame of the house stood silhouetted against an incandescent rainbow. Later, when only the blackened, smoking rubble was left, Peter turned to the Duke of Holstein, nephew of Charles XII, and said, "This is the image of war: brilliant victories followed by destruction. But with this house in which my first plans against Sweden were worked out, may every thought disappear which can arm my hand against that kingdom, and may it always be the most faithful ally of my empire."

In the warmer months, Peter spent much of his time at Peterhof. On his doctors' recommendation, he drank mineral waters and took exercise, including mowing grass and taking hikes with a knapsack on his back. To be on the water was still his greatest pleasure, and the Prussian minister reported that even his own ministers were unable to reach him. "The Emperor is so occupied with his villas and sailing on the gulf," he reported, "that none had the heart to interrupt him."

In June 1723, the entire court—including even the Tsaritsa Praskovaya, now suffering intensely from her gout—moved with Peter to Reval, where he had constructed an elegant pink palace for Catherine and a small three-room house nearby for himself. Catherine's palace was surrounded by an extensive garden with fountains, pools and statues, but when the Emperor went for a walk on its broad paths, he was surprised to find himself alone. The reason, he quickly discovered, was a locked main gate guarded by a sentry whose standing orders were to keep the public out. Peter immediately reversed the order, explaining that he would never have built so large and expensive a garden only for himself and his wife, and the following day drummers were sent through the town to announce that the garden was open to all.

In July, Peter sailed with his fleet for maneuvers on the Baltic. In August, he returned with the fleet to Kronstadt, where a ceremony had been arranged to honor the little boat which Peter had found rotting at Ismailovo with Karsten Brandt and in which he had taken his first lessons in sailing on the Yauza River. Now known as the "Grandfather of the Russian Navy," the boat had been brought to Kronstadt. There, the Emperor boarded the little vessel, now flying the imperial standard, and with Peter at the tiller and four senior admirals at the oars, the boat passed in front of

twenty-two Russian ships-of-the-line, and 200 galleys anchored in columns. On a signal from Peter, cannon aboard all the ships roared out salutes; soon, a heavy smoke hung over the water, and only the topmost spars of the biggest ships could be seen. A feast of ten hours followed and Peter declared that the guest who did not get drunk that day would not merit his friendship. The ladies remained, and the young Princesses Anne and Elizabeth stayed to pass around glasses of Hungarian wine. The Duchess of Mecklenburg became drunk, and other distinguished guests were tipsy, weeping, embracing and kissing, then later quarreling and thumping each other. Even Peter, who now drank far less than in his youth, took many glasses.

In the autumn, another public masquerade celebrated the second anniversary of the Peace of Nystad. Peter was costumed first as a Catholic cardinal, then as a Lutheran minister, having borrowed his collar from the Lutheran pastor in St. Petersburg, and finally as an army drummer, beating his drum almost as well as a professional drummer. This was the last great party for the Tsaritsa Praskovaya, who died soon after.

To purge his system after these bacchanals, Peter now took his cures drinking the newly discovered "iron waters" at Olonets. The Emperor went often in winter, when he could travel across the lake by sledge, sometimes accompanied by Catherine; he argued that these Russian mineral waters were superior to any he had drunk in Germany. Not everyone agreed with him, and some worried that continued drinking of these heavily ferrous waters would damage rather than aid his health. Peter's unwillingness to obey his doctor's prescriptions was another problem; sometimes he would drink as many as twenty-one glasses of mineral water in a morning. He was forbidden to eat raw fruit, cucumbers, salted lemons or Limburger cheese while taking a cure. Yet, one day, immediately after drinking the waters, he ate a dozen figs and several pounds of cherries. To break the monotony of drinking the waters, Peter worked at his lathe for hours every day, turning objects in wood and ivory. When he felt strong, he visited forges in the neighborhood and hammered out bars and sheets of iron.

PETER'S TWO OLDEST DAUGHTERS were reaching marriageable age (Anne was fourteen in 1722 and Elizabeth, thirteen), and, like any sensible monarch, he was looking for matches to bolster his country's diplomacy. From the time of his visit to France, his hope had been to marry one of his daughters, presumably Elizabeth, to the boy King, Louis XV. Not only would immense prestige accrue to Russia from a link with the House of Bourbon, but France would be a useful ally in Western Europe to counterbalance the hostility of England. If marriage to the King was impossible, Peter hoped at least to marry Elizabeth to a French prince of the royal house and make

the pair King and Queen of Poland. Immediately after the signing of the Peace of Nystad and his own proclamation as emperor, he had broached the subject to Paris. The French minister in Petersburg, Campredon, added his own enthusiastic endorsement, "To put the Tsaritsa entirely in our interest, it would be desirable to assure a marriage between the younger daughter of the Tsar, who is very amiable and has a pretty figure, and some French prince who could easily and surely, through the power of the Tsar, be made King of Poland."

Philippe, Duc d'Orléans, Regent of France, was tempted. Poland would be a useful ally for France in Austria's rear. If the Emperor were indeed to use his power to put a French prince on the throne of Poland, it might well be worth marrying that prince to the Emperor's daughter. Philippe had certain hesitations: the Empress Catherine's obscure origins and the mystery surrounding the date of her marriage to Peter raised questions as to Elizabeth's legitimacy. But he overcame his doubts and even proposed that the French prince best suited to become the bridegroom—and thus the King of Poland—was his own son, the youthful Duc de Chartres. When Peter returned from Persia and heard that de Chartres was being proposed by France, his face broke into a smile. "I know him and esteem him highly," he said to Campredon.

Unfortunately for the negotiating parties, there was an important obstacle over which they had no control: Augustus of Saxony, now fifty-three and ill, still occupied the Polish throne. Although he and Peter were now neither friends nor allies, the Emperor had no intention of actually pushing Augustus off the throne. His proposal was that the Duc de Chartres should marry his daughter immediately and then wait for Augustus to die, when the Polish throne would become vacant. The French preferred to wait until the Duke was elected King of Poland before performing the marriage, but Peter refused to wait. What would happen, he asked, if Augustus should live another fifteen years? Campredon insisted that this could not possibly happen. "The King of Poland needs only a new, witty and vivacious mistress to render the event near," he said.*

Eventually, Campredon accepted Peter's view and tried to persuade his government to proceed with the match immediately. He wrote to Paris praising Elizabeth's qualities. "There is nothing but what is agreeable in the person of the Princess Elizabeth," he said. "It may be said indeed that she is a beauty in her figure, her complexion, her eyes and her hands. Her defects, if she has any, are on the side of education and manners, but I am assured that she is so intelligent that it will be easy to rectify what is lacking by the care of some skillful and experienced person who should be placed near her if the affair should be concluded."

---

* In fact, Augustus did live another ten years, dying in 1733 at the age of sixty-three.

In the end, the affair was prevented by the objections of Peter's old enemy, George I of England. The Regent of France and his chief minister, the Abbé Dubois, had made friendship with England the pivot of France's new foreign policy. So close were the two former enemies that, because England now had no diplomatic representation in Russia, Dubois sent Campredon's dispatches from St. Petersburg in the original to King George, who returned them to Paris with marginal comments in his own handwriting. George I had no desire to see Russian influence grow greater. Dubois accommodated him and refused for a while even to answer Campredon's messages. When he did reply, it was to say that England had raised objections and that his envoy was to await instructions. Before the close of 1723, both Dubois and the Regent had died and Louis XV had attained his majority as King of France. The Duc de Chartres eventually married a German princess. Peter's daughter Elizabeth never married officially (although it is possible that she secretly married her charming lover Alexis Razhumovsky, whom she raised from a commoner to count); and instead of becoming Queen of Poland, she remained at home to rule as Empress of Russia for twenty-one years.

Peter's plans for his eldest daughter, Princess Anne, bore more immediate fruit. Years before, the fertile mind of Goertz had hatched the idea of marrying his young master, Duke Charles Frederick, to Anne. Goertz had mentioned the plan to Peter, with whom it had taken root. In the intervening years, the youthful Duke's fortunes had soared and plunged. He was the only nephew of the childless King Charles XII, who had kept the young man close to him, and many in Sweden still believed that Charles Frederick should have succeeded to the throne instead of his aunt Ulrika Eleonora and her husband, Frederick of Hesse. In 1721, Charles Frederick traveled secretly to Russia, hoping to win Peter's support for his claim to the Swedish succession and perhaps to seal it by marrying one of the Russian Emperor's daughters. Once in Russia, he nicely served Peter's purposes. Ulrika Eleonora and Frederick saw the young man's presence in St. Petersburg as an implied threat, and this further incentive to peace helped lead to the Treaty of Nystad in 1721, one clause of which was a Russian guarantee not to support the Duke's claims to the Swedish throne. Despite this disappointment, Charles Frederick stayed on in Russia. Catherine liked him, he had a place at all public celebrations and his little refugee court became a rallying point for a number of Swedish officers who had married Russian wives whom they were forbidden to take back to Sweden. Before long, as these homeless souls met every day to expand and refine their taste for vodka, the only nephew of Charles XII, who had fought at his uncle's side and wept at his death, was in danger of being reduced to nothing more than a tame poodle at the Russian court.

Nevertheless, Charles Frederick persisted in his hope of marrying

Princess Anne, who was tall, dark-haired and handsome like her mother. She was also intelligent, well mannered and high-spirited, and when she appeared in court dress with her hair dressed in European fashion and set with pearls, foreign envoys were impressed. Charles Frederick's chances improved greatly when a Russian-Swedish defensive alliance was signed in 1724. He was granted the title of Royal Highness and a Swedish pension, and Russia and Sweden agreed to attempt to persuade Denmark to restore lost territory to Holstein. The Duke's position was now thoroughly regularized, and in December 1724 he was pleased to receive a message from Osterman asking him to draw up a marriage contract between himself and Princess Anne. Part of the arrangement, it was understood, was to be the appointment of Charles Frederick as Governor General of Riga.

The betrothal ceremony was grandly celebrated. On the evening before, the Duke's private orchestra serenaded the Empress beneath the windows of the Winter Palace. The following day, after a service at Trinity Church and a dinner with the imperial family, the Duke was betrothed to Anne when Peter himself took rings from each prospective partner and exchanged them. The Emperor shouted "Vivat!" and the betrothal party moved on to a supper, a ball and a display of fireworks. At the ball, Peter, feeling ill, refused to dance, but Catherine, entreated by young Charles Frederick, danced a polonaise with him.

Anne lived only four years after her marriage and died when she was twenty. But fate used her and her husband to continue Peter's line on the Russian throne. They returned to Holstein, where at Kiel, shortly before her death, Anne gave birth to a son whose name became Karl Ulrich Peter. In 1741, when this boy was thirteen, his Aunt Elizabeth became empress. Unmarried and needing to designate an heir, she brought her nephew back to Russia and changed his name to Peter Fedorovich. In 1762, on Elizabeth's death, he succeeded to the throne as Emperor Peter III. Six months later, he was deposed and murdered by supporters of his German wife. This vigorous lady then seized the throne, was crowned Empress Catherine II and became known to the world as Catherine the Great. The son, grandsons and further descendants of Peter III and Catherine the Great occupied the Russian throne until 1917, all of them ultimately tracing their ancestry back through Princess Anne and Charles Frederick of Holstein, nephew of Charles XII, to Peter the Great.

PETER'S EFFORTS to marry both his daughters to foreign princes suggested that he did not envision either of them as his successor on the Russian throne. Indeed, no woman had ever sat on that throne. But the death of Peter Petrovich in 1719 left only one remaining male in the House of Romanov—Peter Alexeevich, son of the Tsarevich Alexis. Many Russians

regarded him now as the legitimate heir, and Peter was well aware that the traditionalists looked upon the young Grand Duke as their future hope. This hope he was determined to thwart.

But if not Peter Alexeevich, who was to succeed? More and more, as he pondered the problem, the emperor's thoughts turned to the person closest to him: Catherine. Over the years, the passion which had first attracted Peter to this simple, robust young woman had ripened into love, trust and mutual contentment. Catherine was a partner of enormous energy and remarkable adaptability; although she loved luxury, she was equally good-humored in primitive circumstances. She traveled with Peter devotedly even when pregnant, and he often told her that her stamina was greater than his. They had bonds of joy in their daughters and shared grief over the numerous infants they had lost. They took pleasure in each other's company and were melancholy when apart. "Praise God, all is merry here," wrote Peter from Reval in 1719, "but when I come to a country house and you are not there, I feel so sad." Again, he wrote, "But when you state that it's miserable walking alone, although the garden is pleasant, I believe you, for it's the same for me; only pray God that this is the last summer we'll spend apart, and that we may always be together in the future."

It was during one of Peter's lengthy wartime absences that Catherine had prepared a surprise which had particularly delighted her husband. Knowing how much pleasure he took in new buildings, she secretly constructed a country palace about fifteen miles southwest of St. Petersburg. The mansion, built of stone, two stories high, and surrounded by gardens and orchards, was situated on a hill which looked back over the immense, flat plain stretching to the Neva and the city. When Peter returned, Catherine mentioned to him that she had found a charming deserted spot "where Your Majesty would not dislike to build a country house, if you would but take the trouble to go and see it." Peter immediately promised to go and "if the place really answers your description," to build any house she wished. The following morning, a large party set out, accompanied by a wagon carrying a tent under which Peter suggested they might eat. At the foot of the hill, the road began to climb and suddenly, at the end of an avenue of linden trees, Peter saw the house. He was still astonished when he arrived at the door and Catherine said to him, "This is the country house I have built for my sovereign." Peter was overjoyed and embraced her tenderly, saying, "I see that you wish to show me that there are beautiful places around Petersburg even though they are not on the water." She led him through the house, finally bringing him into a large dining room where a handsome table had been laid. He toasted her taste in architecture, and then Catherine raised her glass to toast the master of the new house. To his further astonishment and delight, the minute the glass touched Catherine's lips, eleven cannon hidden in the garden thundered a salute. When night fell, Peter said that he

could never remember a day as happy as this one. In time, the estate came to be known as Tsarskoe Selo, the Tsar's Village, and Empress Elizabeth commanded Rastrelli to begin a gigantic new palace on the site. The magnificent Catherine Palace, which still stands, was named after her mother, the Empress Catherine I.

Peter's respect and gratitude to Catherine had been deepened by her participation in the military campaigns on the Pruth and in Persia. He had acknowledged these feelings publicly by their remarriage and by establishing the Order of St. Catherine in her honor. She already carried the courtesy title of empress as the wife of the Emperor, but now, as he faced the future without a son, he decided to go further. His first step, taken in February 1722 before he and Catherine departed for the Caucasus, was to issue a general decree concerning the succession. It declared that the ancient, time-honored rule by which the throne of the grand dukes of Muscovy and later the Russian tsars had been handed down from father to son, or occasionally from elder brother to younger brother, was no longer valid. Henceforth, Peter decreed, every reigning sovereign would have absolute power to designate his or her successor. "Thus," he concluded, "children or children's children will not be tempted to fall into the sin of Absalom." The new decree also required all officials and subjects to swear an oath to accept the Emperor's choice.

Revolutionary though it was, the February 1722 ukase was only a preliminary step to a still more sensational act: Peter's declaration that he had decided to formally crown Catherine as empress. A decree of November 15, 1723, declared that whereas

> our best beloved Spouse, Consort, and Empress Catherine has been a great support to us, and not only in this, but also in many military operations, putting aside womanly weakness, of her own will she has been present with us and has helped in every way possible . . . for these labors of our Spouse we have decided that by virtue of the supreme power given us by God, she shall be crowned, which, God willing, is to take place formally in Moscow in the present winter.

Peter was treading on dangerous ground. Catherine was a Lithuanian servant girl who had come to Russia as a captive. Was she now to wear the imperial crown and sit on the throne of the Russian tsars? Although the manifesto proclaiming the coronation did not specifically name Catherine as heir, on the night before the coronation Peter told several senators and a number of important church dignitaries at the house of an English merchant that Catherine was being crowned in order to give her the right to rule the state. He waited for objections; he heard none.

The coronation ceremony was to be on the grandest scale. Peter, who

was always careful about spending money on himself, commanded that no expense be spared. An imperial coronation mantle was ordered from Paris, and a St. Petersburg jeweler was commissioned to make a new imperial crown more magnificent than any previously worn by a Russian sovereign. The ceremony would be held not in Peter's city, the new capital of St. Petersburg, but in Holy Moscow, inside the Kremlin, according to the traditions of the ancient tsars. Stephen Yavorsky, president of the Holy Synod, and the indefatigable Peter Tolstoy were sent to Moscow six months early with orders to make the ceremony glorious. The Senate, the Holy Synod and every official and nobleman of rank was commanded to be present.

Peter was delayed by a bout of strangury at the beginning of March 1724 and went to Olonets to drink the waters and try to improve his health. By March 22, he was sufficiently recovered, and he and Catherine set out together for Moscow. At dawn on May 7, a signal cannon was fired from the Kremlin. The procession outside the Kremlin included 10,000 soldiers of the Imperial Guard and a squadron of booted horse guards whose passage was watched somewhat sourly by certain Moscow merchants whose noblest steeds had been appropriated by Tolstoy for the ceremony. At ten o'clock, as every bell in Moscow pealed and every cannon in the city thundered, Peter and Catherine appeared at the top of the Red Staircase, escorted by all the officials of the realm, the members of the Senate, generals of the army and great officers of state. The Empress was dressed in a purple gown embroidered in gold, and needed five ladies in waiting to carry her train. Peter was wearing a sky-blue tunic embroidered in silver and red silk stockings. Together, the couple stood looking out over the crowd in Cathedral Square from exactly the spot where, forty-two years before, ten-year-old Peter and his mother had looked out over the raging Streltsy and their forest of glittering halberds. Then, they descended the Red Staircase, walked across Cathedral Square and entered the Cathedral of the Assumption. In the center, a platform had been constructed, and on it, beneath a canopy of velvet and gold, two chairs encrusted with precious stones waited for Peter and Catherine.

At the door of the cathedral, Yavorsky, Feofan Prokopovich and the other high clergymen, dressed in their clerical robes, met the imperial couple. Yavorsky presented the cross for them to kiss, then conducted them to the thrones. The service began while Peter and Catherine sat side by side in silence. At the climax of the ceremony, Peter rose and Yavorsky presented him with the new imperial crown. Peter took it and, turning to the audience, declared in a loud voice, "It is our intention to crown our beloved consort." Peter himself placed the crown on Catherine's head. He then handed her the orb, but, significantly, he kept the scepter, the emblem of ultimate power, in his own hand. The crown was studded with 2,564 diamonds, pearls and other

precious stones, and an enormous ruby as large as a pigeon's egg was set immediately beneath a cross of diamonds, at the apex of the crown.

As Peter placed the crown on her head, Catherine, overcome with emotion, tears streaming down her cheeks, knelt before him and tried to kiss his hand. He pulled it away and she tried to embrace him around his knees, but Peter lifted her up. Then, prayers were solemnly chanted, cannon thundered and the bells of Moscow pealed.

After the service, Peter returned to the palace to rest, but Catherine, wearing her crown, walked alone at the head of a procession from the Assumption Cathedral to the Cathedral of the Archangel Michael to pray at the tombs of the tsars, according to custom. The imperial mantle, made in France and encrusted with hundreds of golden double-headed eagles, was now on her shoulders, and its great weight, even borne in part by attendants, forced her to stop and rest several times. As she walked, Menshikov followed slightly behind, scattering handfuls of gold and silver among the watching crowd. At the foot of the Red Staircase, the Duke of Holstein waited to conduct her to the Terem Palace, where a magnificent banquet had been prepared. During the banquet, Menshikov distributed medals bearing a portrait of Peter and Catherine on one side and, on the reverse, a depiction of Peter placing the crown on Catherine's head and the words "Crowned in Moscow 1724." The feasting and celebration went on in the city for days. In Red Square, two huge oxen had been roasted and stuffed with game and poultry, while two fountains, one running with red wine and the other with white, splashed nearby.

Catherine's powers and the Emperor's long-range intent were unspecified. As a sign that she exercised some aspects of sovereignty, Peter allowed her to create old Peter Tolstoy a count, a title which all his descendants, including the great novelist Lev Tolstoy, have worn. By her command, Yaguzhinsky was made a Knight of the Order of St. Andrew, and Prince Vasily Dolgoruky, disgraced and exiled in the affair of the Tsarevich Alexis, was allowed to return to court. But her powers even in this respect were limited. She pleaded in vain for a pardon for the exiled former Vice Chancellor Shafirov. What Peter actually intended, no one was sure. It is possible that he had not made up his mind even as he lay on his deathbed. But it is certain that he wanted to ensure Catherine's importance—perhaps to act as regent for one of his daughters if not actually to wear the crown. Peter knew that the throne of Russia could not be bestowed simply as a reward for faithful and loving service. The wearer of the crown had to be a person of energy, wisdom and experience. Catherine's qualities were somewhat different. Still, she had been anointed, and Campredon, the French envoy, concluded that Peter wanted her thus to be "recognized as regent and sovereign after the death of her husband."

After her coronation, more than ever the path to favor lay through

Catherine. Yet, within a few weeks of this triumph, Catherine found herself teetering on the brink of personal disaster, looking down at the possibility of utter ruin. Among Catherine's attendants was a handsome young man named William Mons, the younger brother of Anna Mons, who had been Peter's mistress twenty-five years earlier. Mons was a foreigner, a German born in Russia with one foot well placed in each world. Elegant, gay, clever, ambitious and opportunistic, he had chosen his patrons shrewdly, worked hard and risen to the rank of chamberlain and the post of secretary and confidant to Catherine. The Empress enjoyed his company, for he was, in the words of a French observer, "One of the best-made and most handsome men that I have ever seen." Mons' sister Matrena had achieved equal success. She was married to a Baltic nobleman named Fedor Balk, a major general who was Governor of Riga, while she herself was a lady in waiting and the closest confidante of the Empress Catherine.

Gradually, between them, on the pretense of assisting the Empress and looking after her interests, brother and sister contrived to gain control of access to Catherine. Through Mons and Matrena Balk, messages, petitions and appeals were most likely to be presented favorably to Catherine; indeed, without their help, such messages were unlikely to reach her at all. And since Catherine's influence over her husband was known to be great, the Mons channel became immensely valuable. Government ministers, foreign ambassadors, even foreign princes and members of the Emperor's family approached the zealous and handsome German with a petition in one hand and a bribe in the other. No personage was too august—the Tsaritsa Praskovaya and her daughters, the Duke of Holstein, Prince Menshikov, Prince Repnin and Count Tolstoy—or too humble—a peasant who was supposed to return to his village bribed Mons to arrange permission to remain in Petersburg. Mons arranged his "fees" according to the importance of the service and the wealth of the petitioner. Besides the wealth gained by these activities, Mons and his sister received estates, serfs and money directly from the Empress. Deferred to by the highest in Russia, with Menshikov calling him "brother," Mons concluded that "William Mons" was too simple a name for such a magnifico, and changed his name to Moens de la Croix. Obligingly, everyone called him by his new name—except Peter, who did not know either of the transformation or of the reason for the new importance of the former William Mons.

Gossip said there were other things that Peter did not know about William Mons. It was whispered in Petersburg, and soon after in Europe, that the Empress had taken the handsome young chamberlain as a lover. Lurid stories circulated, including one that Peter had found his wife with Mons one moonlit night in a compromising position in her garden. No evidence of any kind was cited. The moonlit-garden tale is disposed of by the fact that Peter first learned of Mons' fiscal offenses in November,

when the moonlit garden would have been deep in snow. More important, the nature of Catherine's character argues against such a liaison. The Empress was generous, warm-hearted and earthy, but she was also intelligent. She knew Peter. Even if her own affection for him had cooled (which is unlikely, especially at the moment when he had just crowned her empress), she certainly understood the impossibility of keeping an intrigue with Mons a secret and the horrible consequences when it was found out. That Mons, following an ancient tradition of bold and successful adventurers, may have wished to seal his success by presuming on the Emperor's marital rights is possible; that Catherine would have become involved in such folly is not.

Even without this ultimate insult, it seems strange that Peter should so long have remained ignorant of Mons' corruption. It is a sign of his growing weakness, abetted by illness, that Peter did not know what was an open secret to everyone else in Petersburg. When the Emperor did discover the truth, retribution was swift and deadly. Exactly who told Peter is unknown. Some believe that it was Yaguzhinsky, who had been stung by Mons' pretensions. Others say that the informer was one of Mons' own subordinates. Once he knew, Peter's first move was to forbid anyone to petition him for a pardon on behalf of criminals. Then, while the suspense and alarm stimulated by this decree began to mount, he waited. On the evening of November 8, he returned to the palace without a sign of anger, supped with the Empress and his daughters and had a trivial conversation with William Mons. Then, saying that he felt tired, he asked Catherine the hour. She looked at a Dresden watch which he had given her and replied, "Nine o'clock." Peter nodded and said, "It is time for everyone to go to bed." All rose and went to their rooms. Mons went home, undressed and was smoking his pipe before retiring when General Ushakov entered and arrested him on a charge of receiving bribes. Mons' papers were seized, his room was sealed and he himself was taken away in chains.

The following day, Mons was brought into Peter's presence. According to the official minutes of the inquiry, he was so frightened that he fainted; once revived, he confessed to everything he was accused of. He admitted taking bribes, he admitted taking revenue from the Empress' estates for his own use and he admitted that his sister Matrena Balk was involved. He did not confess to any improper relations with Catherine because he was not asked any such question—further evidence, it would seem, of the groundlessness of the rumors. Nor did Peter seek to conduct the inquiry in private. On the contrary, he issued a proclamation ordering that everyone who had given a bribe to Mons or knew of such a bribe should step forward. For two days, a town crier walked through the streets of Petersburg calling out this proclamation and threatening dire punishment to those who withheld information.

Mons was doomed—any one of the charges against him was enough to

condemn him—and on November 14 he was sentenced to death. Catherine did not believe, however, that he would die. Confident of her power to influence her husband, she first sent word to Matrena Balk not to worry about her brother, and then she went to Peter to ask for pardon for her handsome chamberlain. Here, she misjudged her husband. The avenging fury that had struck down a Gagarin and a Nesterov and humbled a Menshikov and a Shafirov would not turn aside to spare a William Mons. Mons received no reprieve, but the night before his death Peter went to his cell to say that he was sorry to lose such a talented man, but that the crime demanded the punishment.

On November 16, 1724, William Mons and Matrena Balk were taken in sledges to the execution site. Mons behaved courageously, nodding and bowing to friends he saw in the crowd. Mounting the scaffold, he calmly took off his heavy fur coat, listened to the reading of the sentence of death and laid his head on the block. After his death, his sister received eleven blows of the knout, very lightly administered so that not much harm was done, and was exiled for life to Tobolsk in Siberia. Her husband, General Balk, was given permission to marry again if he wished.

Not surprisingly, this ordeal strained the relations between Peter and Catherine. Although her name had never been mentioned either by Mons or his accusers and no one dared charge her with taking bribes herself, it was widely suspected that she had known what Mons was doing and had ignored it. Peter himself seemed to link her with Mons by issuing on the day of the execution a decree addressed to all officers of state. Written in his own hand, it declared that because of abuses which had taken place in the Empress' household without her knowledge, they were forbidden to obey any future order or recommendation she might make. Simultaneously, the conduct of her financial affairs was removed from her control.

Catherine bore these blows with courage. On the day of Mons' execution, she summoned her dancing master and, with her two eldest daughters, practiced the minuet. Knowing now that any expression of interest in Mons could dangerously affect herself, she steeled her emotions. But she did not easily forgive Peter, and a month after the execution an observer noted, "They hardly speak to each other; they no longer eat or sleep together." By mid-January, however, the tension was ebbing away. "The Empress has made a long and ample genuflection before the Tsar to obtain remission of her faults," wrote the same observer. "The conversation lasted three hours and they even supped together."

Whether this reconciliation would have been permanent, we can never know. Throughout the affair of William Mons the Emperor was ill, and he had grown worse. Less than a month after Catherine's genuflection, Peter was dead.

AFTER THE PEACE OF NYSTAD and the coronation of Catherine, Peter, in the eyes of the world, stood at the summit of his power. Yet to those inside Russia, and especially those close to the Emperor, there were disquieting signs. The harvest was poor two years in a row; grain was bought from abroad, but not enough to make up the deficit. New accusations of corruption had been brought against the highest in the land. Shafirov had been condemned, reprieved and exiled, and now Menshikov was removed as president of the College of War. Nothing seemed to move unless Peter was there personally to make certain that it did. In the palace at Preobrazhenskoe, the servants even neglected to bring in wood to burn in the fireplaces in winter until the Emperor commanded them to do it.

This gradual decline in the general condition of the state was paralleled by a deterioration in Peter's health and state of mind. Sometimes, he worked with his customary energy and enthusiasm. One of his last projects was the planning of a large new building to house his projected Academy of Science, and he was also thinking of establishing a new university in the capital. But, more often, he was moody and apathetic. In these periods of depression, he would let things slide, sitting and sighing, and refusing to act until the last minute. When the Emperor was so withdrawn and aloof, few of those around him dared speak to him even when matters were pressing. Reflecting this atmosphere, Mardefelt, the Prussian minister, wrote to his master, King Frederick William, "No expressions are strong enough to give Your Majesty a just idea of the unendurable negligence and confusion with which the most important affairs are treated here, so that neither foreign envoys nor Russian ministers know where to turn. The answers which we get from the Russian ministers are only sighs, and they confess themselves in despair about the difficulties that they have with regard to every proposition. This is no feint but the real truth. Here nothing is considered important until it stands on the edge of the precipice."

What lay behind all this, only gradually realized even by those who were close to him, was the fact that Peter was seriously ill. His previous disorder still afflicted him, the tremors still shook his giant but weakening frame, and only Catherine, taking his head in her lap, could bring him peace. In recent years, he had suffered from a new, troublesome malady. As Jefferyes described it to London:

His Majesty has for some time had a weakness in his left arm which was occasioned at first by his being let blood by an unskilled surgeon, who, missing the vein, made an incision in the nerve that lies by it. This accident has obliged him ever since to wear a furred glove on his left hand, in which, as well as in the arm, he is often troubled with pains, and sometimes loses feeling in it.

And the years had taken their toll. In 1724, Peter was only fifty-two, but his huge exertions, his ceaseless motion, the violent excesses of drink in which he had indulged in his youth, had severely undermined his once magnificent constitution. At fifty-two, the Emperor was an old man. Beyond these afflictions, he had a new illness, the one which eventually was to kill him. For some years, he had suffered from an infection of the urinary tract, and in 1722, during the summer heat of the Persian campaign, the symptoms reappeared. His doctors diagnosed strangury and stone, a blockage in the urethra and bladder caused by muscle spasms or infection. During the winter of 1722–1723, the pain in the urethra returned. At first, Peter mentioned it to no one except his valet, and continued to drink and carouse in his normal way, but soon the pain grew stronger and he had to consult his doctors. For the next two years, he was constantly in and out of pain. He followed the doctors' advice, swallowing their drugs and limiting his drinking to a little kvas and a very occasional glass of brandy. Some days he suffered and could scarcely attend to business; then for a while he would enjoy a period of respite when he could resume his normal activity.

Near the end of the summer in 1724, the disease reappeared and this time the symptoms were much worse. Unable to pass urine, Peter was in agony. His personal physician, Dr. Blumentröst, summoned a consulting physician, Dr. Horn, an English surgeon. To facilitate a passage, Horn inserted a catheter, repeatedly attempting to penetrate the bladder but obtaining only blood and pus. Eventually, with great difficulty, he managed to extract about half a glass of urine. During this probing, unattended by anesthesia, Peter lay on a table, holding the hand of one doctor on each side of him. He was trying to be still, but so great was his pain that the two hands he held were almost crushed. Eventually, a giant stone was passed and the pain abated. Within a week, his urine began to pass in an almost normal way. He remained in bed for many more weeks, however, and not until the end of September was he beginning to walk around his room and impatiently awaiting the moment when he could resume his normal life.

At the beginning of October, the sky outside Peter's window was blue and the air was crisp, and he ordered his yacht to be moored in the Neva where he could see it. A few days later, despite his doctors' warning that he should not exert himself, he went out of doors. He went first to Peterhof to see the new fountains which had been installed in the park. Then, while the doctors protested even more loudly, he set off on a long and arduous tour of inspection. He began at Schlüsselburg to celebrate the anniversary of the fall of that key fortress twenty-two years before. Then he proceeded to the ironworks at Olonets, where he was already strong enough to hammer out with his own hands a sheet of iron weighing more than a hundred pounds. From there, he went to observe the work on the Ladoga Canal, now proceeding rapidly under the direction of the German Munnich.

The tour lasted almost the whole month of October, and during it Peter felt twinges of pain and other symptoms of the disease, but they did not slow his progress. On November 5, he returned to Petersburg, but decided almost immediately to travel by boat to visit another ironworks and armament factory at Systerbeck on the Gulf of Finland. The weather was typical of early winter in the North: gray skies, high winds and rough, icy seas.

Beyond the mouth of the Neva, Peter's yacht was approaching the fishing village of Lakhta when in the distance he saw a boat carrying twenty soldiers swept out of control by the wind and waves. As Peter watched, the boat was driven aground on a shoal. There, its keel stuck in the sand and the waves pounding its side, the little vessel began rolling back and forth, threatening to capsize. Those inside, obviously unable to swim, seemed incapable of doing anything to save themselves. Peter sent a skiff from his own yacht to assist, but his sailors were unable to refloat the grounded boat; the men inside, meanwhile, did little to help, being almost paralyzed by fear of drowning. Watching impatiently, the Emperor ordered his own skiff to take him alongside the grounded boat. Unable to come close because of the waves, the Emperor suddenly jumped into the sea, plunging into the shallow icy water up to his waist and wading to the stranded boat. His arrival and presence galvanized the desperate men. Responding to his shouts, they caught lines thrown from the other boat, and, with the help of other sailors now in the water beside the Emperor, the stranded boat was pulled and dragged off the shoal. Blessing themselves for their salvation, the survivors were taken ashore to recover in the houses of the local fishermen.

Peter returned to his yacht to strip off his wet clothes and dress in something warm before anchoring at Lakhta. At first, although he had been immersed in the icy water for a considerable time, it did not appear that this exposure had affected him. Enormously pleased at his exploit in saving lives and refloating the boat, he went to sleep at Lakhta. During the night, however, he came down with chills and fever, and within a few hours the pain in his intestine reappeared. He canceled his trip to Systerbeck and sailed back to St. Petersburg, where he went to bed. From that moment on, the disease never relinquished its fatal grip.

For a while, it seemed that Peter was once again recovering. At Christmas, he was well enough to make his traditional tour of the major houses of St. Petersburg in the company of his band of carolers and musicians. On New Year's Day, he was present at the customary fireworks, and on Epiphany he went out onto the ice of the Neva River for the traditional Blessing of the Waters, catching another cold during the ceremony. During these weeks, he also participated one final time in the celebration of the Drunken Synod, which assembled to elect a successor to the recently deceased "Mock-Pope" Buturlin. The election of a new "Pope" demanded the summoning of a conclave of "cardinals" to a hall presided

over by Bacchus seated on a cask. Peter himself sealed up the "cardinals" in a separate room, forbidding them to emerge until they had chosen a new "Pope." To aid their deliberations, each "cardinal" was required to swallow a large spoonful of whiskey every fifteen minutes. The process took all night, and when the conclave stumbled out the following morning, an obscure officer had been chosen. That evening, this newly elevated dignitary celebrated at a banquet at which the guests were served the flesh of bears, wolves, foxes, cats and rats.

By mid-January, the coolness which had developed between Peter and Catherine because of the Mons affair appeared to have vanished. The Emperor and his wife went together to a harlequin wedding of a servant of one of his dentchiks. Later in the month, Peter attended assemblies at the houses of Peter Tolstoy and Admiral Cruys. But on January 16, the disease returned and compelled him to take to his bed. Dr. Blumentröst again called other doctors, including Horn. Probing gently, they found that Peter had an inflammation of the bladder and intestine so severe that they believed gangrene was present. Knowing no treatment which could arrest an inflammation so advanced, Blumentröst and his colleagues sent urgent couriers to two famous European specialists, Dr. Boerhaave in Leyden and Dr. Stahl in Berlin, describing Peter's symptoms and appealing desperately for advice.

At first, resting in bed, Peter seemed to rally. He continued to work, summoning Osterman and other ministers to his bedside, where they remained in discussions an entire night. On January 22, he spoke to the Duke of Holstein and promised to accompany him to Riga as soon as he was well. The following day, he suffered a relapse and, calling a priest, received the Last Rites. Tolstoy, Apraxin and Golovkin were admitted to his bedside, and in their presence Peter ordered the pardoning and release of all state prisoners except murderers, and granted an amnesty to young noblemen being punished for not presenting themselves for service. He also commanded Apraxin, who was weeping, and the other ministers to protect all foreigners in St. Petersburg in case he should die. Finally, still typically attentive to detail, he signed decrees regulating fishing and the sale of glue.

By evening on the 26th, the Emperor seemed a little stronger and the doctors began to talk of letting him get up and walk about the room. Encouraged, Peter sat up and ate a little oatmeal gruel. Immediately, he was stricken with such violent convulsions that those in the room thought the end had come. The ministers, the members of the Senate, the senior officers of the Guard and other officials were hastily summoned to the palace to begin a vigil. Soon, the surges of pain through Peter's body became so great that Osterman begged him to think only of himself and forget all matters of business. In agony, crying out loudly from the intensity of the pain, Peter repeatedly expressed contrition for his sins. Twice more, he received the Last Rites and begged for absolution. On the 27th, the priest was Feofan

Prokopovich, in whose presence Peter said fervently, "Lord, I believe. I hope." Soon after, he said, as if speaking to himself, "I hope God will forgive me my many sins because of the good I have tried to do for my people."

Through his ordeal, Catherine never left her husband's bedside, day or night. At one point, telling him that it would help him make his peace with God, she begged Peter to forgive Menshikov, still in disgrace. Peter consented, and the Prince entered the room to be pardoned for the last time by his dying master. At two o'clock on the afternoon of the 27th, perhaps thinking of the succession, the Emperor asked for a writing tablet. One was given to him, and he wrote, "Give all to . . ." Then the pen dropped from his hand. Unable to continue, meaning to dictate, he sent for his daughter Anne, but before the Princess arrived, he had become delirious.

He never recovered consciousness, but sank into a coma, moving only to groan. Catherine knelt beside him hour after hour, praying incessantly that he might be released from his torment by death. At last, at six o'clock in the morning of January 28, 1725, just as she was pleading, "O Lord, I pray Thee, open Thy paradise to receive unto Thyself this great soul," Peter the Great, in the fifty-third year of his life and the forty-third year of his reign, entered eternity.

EPILOGUE

THE CAUSE of Peter's death has never been fully described in medical terms. Professor Hermann Boerhaave, the eminent physician in Leyden, received the urgent communication of the Emperor's symptoms sent by Horn and Blumentröst, but before he could write out his prescription, a second courier arrived with the news that the patient was dead. Boerhaave was stunned. "My God! Is it possible?" he exclaimed. "What a pity that so great a man should have died when a pennyworth of medicine might have saved his life!" Later, talking to other court physicians, Boerhaave expressed his belief that if the disease had not been concealed for so long and if he had been consulted earlier, he might have cured Peter's illness and allowed the Emperor to live for many years. But Boerhaave never told his nephew, who later became physician to Peter's daughter Empress Elizabeth and who was responsible for passing this account along, what medicines he would have prescribed or what illness he would have been treating. Some doubt may be cast on the Professor's optimism by the facts that he never saw the patient and that, on autopsy, the area around Peter's bladder was found already to be gangrenous and his sphincter muscle so swollen and so hard that only with difficulty could it be cut with a knife.

The succession was quickly settled in favor of Catherine. While Peter still drew his last breaths, a group from the Emperor's inner circle of favorites, among them Menshikov, Yaguzhinsky and Tolstoy—all of them "new men" created by Peter, all with much to lose if the old nobility came back to power—had moved decisively to support Catherine. Guessing rightly that the Guards regiments would make the ultimate decision on the succession, they summoned these troops into the capital and massed them near the palace. There, the soldiers were reminded that Catherine had accompanied them and her husband on military campaigns. All arrears in military pay were swiftly paid in the name of the Empress. The Guards regiments were devoted to the Emperor, and Catherine was already popular

with both officers and men; with these new inducements, they readily pledged their support.

Even with these precautions, the succession of the Lithuanian peasant girl, mistress and eventually wife and consort of the autocrat, was far from certain. The other serious candidate was the nine-year-old Grand Duke Peter, son of the Tsarevich Alexis. According to Russian tradition, as grandson of the dead Emperor he was the direct male heir, and the vast majority of the aristocracy, the clergy and the nation at large regarded him as the rightful successor. Through the young Grand Duke, old noble families such as the Dolgorukys and the Golitsyns hoped to restore themselves to power and reverse Peter's reforms.

The confrontation came on the night of January 27, a few hours before the Emperor's death, when the Senate and leading men of state assembled to decide the succession. Prince Dmitry Golitsyn, a member of the old nobility who had spent many years abroad and advocated a sharing of monarchical power with the aristocracy, proposed a compromise: young Peter Alexeevich should become emperor, but Catherine should be regent, assisted by the Senate. Peter Tolstoy, whose name was prominently linked with the prosecution and death of the Tsarevich Alexis and who therefore greatly feared the accession of Alexis' son, objected that rule by a minor was dangerous; the state needed a strong, experienced ruler, he insisted, and it was for this reason that the Emperor had trained and crowned his wife. When Tolstoy spoke, a number of officers of the Preobrazhensky and Semyonovsky Guards who had filtered into the room shouted their agreement. At the same time, a roll of drums in the courtyard below brought the statesmen to the windows. Looking out into the darkness, they made out the thick ranks of the Guard drawn up around the palace. Prince Repnin, commander of the Petersburg garrison and a member of the aristocratic party, flew into a rage and demanded to know why the soldiers were there without his orders. "What I have done, Your Excellency," stonily replied the commander of the Guard, "was by the express command of our sovereign lady, the Empress Catherine, whom you and I and every faithful subject are bound to obey immediately and unconditionally." The soldiers themselves, many of them in tears, cried out, "Our father is dead, but our mother still lives!" Under the circumstances, Apraxin's proposal "that Her Majesty be proclaimed Autocrat with all the prerogatives of her late consort" was quickly accepted.

The following morning, the forty-two-year-old widow came into the room weeping and leaning on the arm of the Duke of Holstein. She had just sobbed that she was now "a widow and an orphan" when Apraxin knelt before her and declared the decision of the Senate. Those in the room cheered, and the acclamation was taken up by the Guardsmen outside. A

manifesto issued that day announced to the empire and the world that the new Russian autocrat was a woman, the Empress Catherine I.

Peter's body was embalmed and placed on a bier in a room hung with French tapestries presented to the Emperor on his visit to Paris. For over a month, the public was allowed to file past and pay their respects. Then, on March 8, in the middle of a snowstorm, the coffin was carried to the cathedral of the Peter and Paul Fortress. Catherine walked at the head of the cortege, followed by 150 court ladies and a huge procession of courtiers, government officials, foreign envoys and military officers, all bareheaded under the snow. In the cathedral, Feofan Prokopovich preached the funeral sermon. Comparing Peter to Moses, Solomon, Samson, David and Constantine, he articulated the general disbelief that the familiar towering figure was really gone forever. "O men of Russia," he asked, "what do we see? What do we do? This is Peter the Great whom we are committing to the earth!"

CATHERINE'S REIGN was brief. On taking the throne, she declared that she would adhere faithfully to Peter's policies and reforms. Ever practical, she quickly consolidated her rule in the quarter where it counted most by abolishing army labor on the Ladoga Canal, keeping the soldiers paid on time, issuing new uniforms and holding numerous military reviews. She remained friendly, open and generous, so much so that court expenses quickly tripled. She put on no airs about her sudden elevation to the pinnacle of power. She spoke frequently about her common origin and extended her own good fortune to all members of her family. She found her brother, Carl Skavronsky, serving as a groom in a post station in Courland, brought him to St. Petersburg, educated him, and then created him Count Skavronsky. Her two sisters and their families were also summoned to the capital. The elder sister had married a Lithuanian peasant named Simon Heinrich, the younger, a Polish peasant, named Michael Yefim. The families were established in St. Petersburg and their names changed to Hendrikov and Yefimovsky. Catherine's generous daughter, Empress Elizabeth, created the two former peasants, her uncles, Count Hendrikov and Count Yefimovsky.

The real ruler of the state during Catherine's reign was Menshikov. On February 8, 1726, a year after her accession, a new governing body, the Supreme Privy Council, was created "to lighten the heavy burden of government for Her Majesty." Collectively, the six original members—Menshikov, Apraxin, Golovkin, Osterman, Tolstoy and Prince Dmitry Golitsyn—exercised near-sovereign power, including the issuing of decrees. Menshikov dominated this body as he did the Senate, now reduced in function. He met

opposition in either forum simply by rising and declaring that the views he expressed were those of the Empress.

Menshikov's policies contained elements of prudence. He understood that the weight of taxation was crushing the peasantry, and he told the Empress, "The peasants and the army are like soul and body; you cannot have one without the other." Accordingly, Catherine agreed to a reduction of the soul tax by one third, along with a concomitant reduction by one third in the size of the army. In addition, all arrears in the tax were canceled. Nor did Menshikov wield wholly unrestricted power. Catherine's favorite, Charles Frederick of Holstein, married the Empress' daughter Anne on May 21, 1725, and the following February, over Menshikov's opposition, he was appointed to the Supreme Privy Council.

Catherine's death, brought about by a series of chills and fevers, came only two years and three months after her accession. In November 1726, a storm backed up the Neva, forcing the Empress to flee her palace in her nightdress "in water up to her knees." On January 21, 1727, she participated in the ceremony of the Blessing of the Waters on the Neva ice. Afterward, with a white plume in her hat and holding a marshal's baton, she remained in the winter air for many hours to review 20,000 troops. This outing put her in bed for two months with fever and prolonged bleeding from the nose. She rallied and relapsed. Near the end, she named the young Grand Duke Alexeevich as her successor, with the entire Supreme Privy Council to act as regents. Her two daughters, Anne, seventeen, now Duchess of Holstein, and Elizabeth, sixteen, were named to the council as regents.

Ironically, the accession of Peter II, the hope of the old nobility and the traditionalists, was engineered by Menshikov, the supreme example of the commoner raised from the ranks. His motives, of course, were self-preservation and further advancement. While Catherine was alive, Menshikov calculated the chances of her two daughters, Anne and Elizabeth, against those of Peter and concluded that the young Grand Duke was the stronger candidate. Accordingly, he switched sides and used his formidable powers to urge the Empress along the path which eventually she took: that is, naming Peter as heir, with her daughters joining the regency council. Nor had Menshikov forgotten his own family. Before persuading Catherine to make Peter emperor, he obtained her consent to marry the eleven-year-old boy to his sixteen-year-old daughter Maria.

Menshikov's sudden reversal of loyalty startled and frightened other members of the old circle of favorites, most notably Tolstoy. The grizzled fox, now eighty-two, understood clearly that a new Emperor Peter II would inevitably reach out to settle the score with the man who had lured his father back from Italy to death. Tolstoy appealed to other members of the circle, but found limited support. Osterman had joined Menshikov, Yaguzhinsky

was in Poland, the others preferred to wait and see. Only Anthony Devier, Menshikov's brother-in-law, and General Ivan Buturlin of the Guards resisted Menshikov. It was too late. Catherine was dying, and Menshikov had taken care to surround her with his own people and make it impossible for others to approach. Invulnerable to attack, he now lashed out. Devier, against whom Menshikov had vowed vengeance for marrying the Serene Prince's sister, was arrested, knouted and sent to Siberia. Tolstoy was banished to an island of whale fisheries in the White Sea, where he died in 1729 at the age of eighty-four.

Once Catherine was dead and Peter II proclaimed as emperor, Menshikov moved swiftly to reap his rewards. Within a week of his accession, the boy Emperor was bodily transferred from the Winter Palace to Menshikov's palace on Vasilevsky Island. Two weeks later, young Peter's engagement to Maria Menshikova was celebrated. The Supreme Privy Council was filled with Menshikov's new aristocratic allies, the Dolgorukys and Golitsyns. As a further gesture, Menshikov had the aging Tsaritsa Eudoxia, Peter the Great's first wife and grandmother of the new Emperor, transferred from the lonely fortress of Schlüsselburg to Novodevichy convent near Moscow where she would be more comfortable.

The Duke of Holstein, whom Catherine had installed on the Supreme Privy Council against Menshikov's wishes, saw the handwriting on the wall and applied for permission to leave Russia with his wife, Princess Anne. Menshikov gladly saw them return to Kiel, the ducal seat, and sweetened the Duke's departure with a generous Russian pension. It was in Kiel, on May 28, 1728, that Princess Anne died, shortly after giving birth to a son, the future Emperor Peter III. A ball given in her honor to celebrate the birth had been followed by a display of fireworks. Although the Baltic weather was cold and damp, the happy young mother insisted upon standing on an open balcony to get a better view. When her ladies worried, she laughed and said, "I am Russian, remember, and used to a much worse climate than this." Within ten days, this eldest daughter of Peter the Great was dead. Now, only one child of Peter and Catherine, the Princess Elizabeth, remained.

The new Emperor was handsome, physically robust and tall for his age. Osterman, who had taken virtually sole charge of Russian foreign policy, now took on additional duties as young Peter's tutor. His high-spirited pupil was not much interested in books; he preferred to ride and hunt, and when Osterman remonstrated with him for his lack of application, the eleven-year-old sovereign replied, "My dear Andrei Ivanovich, I like you, and as my Minister of Foreign Affairs, you are indispensable, but I must request you not to interfere in future with my pastimes." Peter's closest companions were his sister Natalya, only a year older than himself, his blonde eighteen-year-old aunt, Princess Elizabeth, who was not interested in government but cared

only about riding, hunting and dancing, and nineteen-year-old Prince Ivan Dolgoruky.

For those few months in the summer of 1727, Menshikov stood alone at the summit; "Not even Peter the Great," declared the Saxon ambassador, "was so feared or so obeyed." He was the unchallenged ruler of Russia and the prospective father-in-law of the Emperor; all future Russian monarchs would carry his blood in their veins. Assured of his preeminence, Menshikov's manner became insupportable; he issued orders in a lordly fashion even to the Emperor—he intercepted a sum of money Peter had been given and chastised the Emperor for accepting it, then he took away a silver plate which Peter had presented to his sister Natalya. Stung, the boy said ominously to Menshikov, "We shall see who is emperor, you or I."

In July 1727, Menshikov had the misfortune to fall ill. While his grip on the reins of power was briefly relaxed, Peter, Natalya and Elizabeth moved to Peterhof. People at court began to comment that affairs of state seemed to progress satisfactorily even without the presence of Prince Menshikov. When he recovered, Menshikov appeared at Peterhof, but, to his amazement, Peter turned his back on him. To his equally astonished companions, the Emperor said, "You see, I am at last learning how to keep him in order." Menshikov's fall came a month later, in September 1727. Arrested, deprived of his offices and stripped of his decorations, he and his family— including his daughter Maria—were exiled to an estate in the Ukraine. This stage of his fall was cushioned: He left St. Petersburg with four six-horse carriages and sixty wagons of baggage.

Peter II now passed into the hands of the Dolgorukys. Prince Alexis Dolgoruky, father of the Emperor's friend Ivan, and Prince Vasily Dolgoruky were appointed to the Supreme Privy Council, and late in 1729 the Emperor's betrothal to Prince Alexis' seventeen-year-old daughter Catherine was announced. The Dolgorukys completed the destruction of Menshikov. In April 1728, the great Prince was accused of treasonable contacts with Sweden, his huge wealth was confiscated and he was exiled with his family to Berezov, a tiny village above the tundra line in northern Siberia. In this place, in November 1729, he died at the age of fifty-six, followed to the grave a few weeks later by his daughter Maria.

Increasingly, under Peter II, Moscow began to resume its ancient role as the center of Russian life. After his coronation in January 1728, Peter refused to go back to St. Petersburg, complaining "What am I to do in a place where there's nothing but salt water?" Naturally, the court remained with him, and as the months passed, a number of government offices began to move back to the older city. But the reign of Peter II was destined to be only a few months longer than the reign of Catherine I. Early in January 1730, the fourteen-year-old Emperor became ill. His condition was diagnosed

as smallpox, he worsened rapidly and on January 11, 1730, the day fixed for his wedding, he died.

Death came too quickly and unexpectedly for Peter II to follow the procedure established by his grandfather and nominate a successor. Accordingly, it devolved upon the Supreme Privy Council, now dominated by Prince Dmitry Golitsyn, to choose a sovereign. The pleasure-loving Princess Elizabeth, last child of Peter the Great, was considered too frivolous, and Catherine of Mecklenburg, the eldest daughter of Tsar Ivan V (Peter the Great's afflicted half-brother and co-Tsar) and Tsaritsa Praskovaya, was thought to be too much under the influence of her husband, the Duke of Mecklenburg. The choice therefore fell on the second daughter of Ivan V: Anne, Duchess of Courland, who had been a widow since a few months after her marriage in 1711. The offer made to Anne carried many restrictive conditions. She was not to marry and not to appoint her successor. The council would retain approval over war and peace, the levying of taxes and expenditure of money, the granting of estates and the appointment of all officers above the rank of colonel. Anne accepted the conditions, arrived in Russia and, with the support of the Guards regiments and the service gentry, immediately tore up the conditions, abolished the Supreme Privy Council and reestablished the power of the autocracy. Having lived in Courland for most of eighteen years, the new Empress had Western inclinations, and the court moved back to St. Petersburg. Her government was dominated by a trio of Germans: Ernst Biron, her First Minister in Courland, now made a Russian count; Osterman, who continued to manage foreign policy; and Munnich, the builder of the Ladoga Canal, who took command of the army and became a field marshal.

Empress Anne died in 1740, leaving the throne to the grandson of her elder sister, Catherine of Mecklenburg. This child, Ivan VI, scarcely knew he was emperor; he inherited the throne at the age of two months and was dethroned at the age of fifteen months to be held as a secret state prisoner for the remaining twenty-two years of his life. His successor was Elizabeth, now thirty-one, still pleasure-loving and beloved by the Guards Regiment with whose help she seized the throne, primarily because she feared she was to be sent to a convent by the adherents of Ivan VI. Elizabeth's reign lasted twenty-one years (1741–1762), then followed the brief reign of Peter III and the thirty-four-year reign of Catherine the Great.

Thus, Peter the Great's overturning of the laws of succession and his proclamation that every sovereign should have the right to designate the heir led to an anomaly in Russian history: Since the distant days of the Kievan state, no woman had reigned in Russia; after his death in 1725, four empresses reigned almost continuously for the next seventy-one years. They were Peter's wife (Catherine I), his niece (Anne), his daughter (Elizabeth) and his grandson's wife (Catherine the Great). The reigns of three pitiable

males (Peter the Great's grandsons Peter II and Peter III and his brother's great-grandson Ivan VI) were interspersed among these women, but their three reigns encompassed only forty months. Upon the death of Catherine the Great, her son Paul, who hated his mother, became emperor. On the day of his coronation, he upset Peter the Great's decree on the succession and established hereditary primogeniture in the male line. Thereafter, Russia's sovereigns were again all male: Paul's sons Alexander I and Nicholas I, his grandson Alexander II, his great-grandson Alexander III and his great-great-grandson Nicholas II.

THE BODY of Peter the Great had been committed to earth, but his spirit continued to bestride the land. Immediately after his death, Russians diligently began to collect every object connected with his life and put them on display: his formal court coats, the blue-green uniform of the Preobrazhensky Regiment which he had worn at Poltava, his hat, his enormous black boots, pairs of shoes worn out but newly soled, his sword, his ivory-headed cane, his nightcap, his stockings mended in several places, his desk, his surgical, dental, and navigational instruments, his turning lathe, his saddle and his stirrups. His little dog Lisette and the horse he had ridden at Poltava were stuffed and exhibited. A life-size wax figure of a seated Peter was molded by the elder Rastrelli; the figure was dressed in the clothes which the Emperor had worn at Catherine's coronation, and in the wig of Peter's own hair which had been cut off during the campaign along the Caspian Sea. All of these mementoes have been carefully preserved and can still be seen at the Hermitage or in other Russian museums.

To those who had been close to Peter, his loss seemed irreparable. Andrei Nartov, the young lathe turner with whom Peter had worked almost every day in his last years, declared, "Although Peter the Great is no longer with us, his spirit lives in our souls and we who have had the honor to be near the monarch will die true to him and our warm love for him will be buried with us." Neplyuev, the young naval officer whom Peter had sent as ambassador to Constantinople, wrote, "This monarch has brought our country to a level with others. He taught us to recognize that we are a people. In brief, everything that we look upon in Russia has its origin in him, and everything which is done in the future will be derived from this source."

As the century progressed, veneration of Peter became almost a cult. Mikhail Lomonosov, Russia's first notable scientist, described Peter as "a God-like man" and wrote, "I see him everywhere, now enveloped in a cloud of dust, of smoke, of flame, now bathed in sweat at the end of strenuous toil. I refuse to believe that there was but one Peter and not several." Gavril Derzhavin, Russia's finest eighteenth-century poet, wondered, "Was it not God Who in his person came down to earth?" The clever German

Empress Catherine the Great, desiring to identify herself more closely with her giant Russian predecessor, commissioned a heroic bronze statue by the French sculptor Falconet. A miniature cliff of 1,600 tons of granite was dragged to the bank of the Neva to form a pedestal. The Emperor, wearing a cape and crowned with laurel, sits firmly astride a fiery, rearing stallion which is trampling a snake beneath its hooves; Peter's right arm is flung out, pointing imperiously across the river to the Peter and Paul Fortress—and to the future. The figure, which captures Peter's exuberance, vitality and absolute authority, immediately became the most famous statue in Russia. When Alexander Pushkin wrote his immortal poem "The Bronze Horseman," the statue found a permanent place in literature.

There were, of course, dissenting views. The hope of the common people that Peter's death would mean a lifting of their heavy burdens of service and taxation expressed itself in a popular lithograph titled "The Mice Bury the Cat." This sly work depicts an enormous whiskered cat with a recognizable face, now trussed on a sledge with its paws in the air, being dragged away by a band of celebrating mice. In the nineteenth century, traditionalists who believed in the inherent values of Muscovite culture blamed Peter as the first to open the door to Western ideas and innovations. "We began [in Peter's reign] to be citizens of the world," said the conservative historian Nikolai Karamzin, "but we ceased in some measure to be citizens of Russia." A grand-scale historical and philosophical debate evolved between two schools: the "Slavophiles" who deplored the contamination and destruction of old Russian culture and institutions, and the "Westernizers" who admired and praised Peter for suppressing the past and forcing Russia onto the road of progress and enlightenment. The arguments often became heated, as when the influential literary critic Vassarion Belinsky described Peter as "the most extraordinary phenomenon not only in our history but in the history of mankind . . . a deity who has called us into being and who has breathed the breath of life into the body of ancient Russia, colossal, but prostrate in deadly slumber."

Soviet historians have not had an easy time coping with the figure of Peter the Great. Required to write history within the framework not only of general Marxist theory and terminology but also of the current party line, they sway back and forth between portraying Peter as irrelevant (individuals play no part in historical evolution), as an exploitative autocrat building "a national state of landowners and merchants," and as a national hero defending Russia against external enemies. A small but graphic example of this ambivalence is the treatment of Peter at the Poltava Battlefield Museum. A large statue of the Emperor stands in front of the museum, and the visual exhibits inside all emphasize the presence and role of Peter. But the written material in captions and booklets obediently ascribes the victory to the efforts of "the fraternal Russian and Ukrainian peoples."

Peter himself was realistic and philosophical about the way he was seen and would be remembered. Osterman recalled a conversation with a foreign ambassador in which Peter asked what the opinion was of him abroad.

"Sire," replied the ambassador, "everyone has the highest and best opinion of Your Majesty. The world is astonished above all at the wisdom and genius you display in the execution of the vast designs which you have conceived and which have spread the glory of your name to the most distant regions."

"Very well, very well, that may be," said Peter impatiently, "but flattery says as much of every king when he is present. My object is not to see the fair side of things, but to know what judgment is formed of me on the opposite side of the question. I beg you to tell it to me, whatever it may be."

The ambassador bowed low. "Sire," he said, "since you order me, I will tell you all the ill I have heard. You pass for an imperious and severe master who treats his subjects rigorously, who is always ready to punish and incapable of forgiving a fault."

"No, my friend," said Peter, smiling and shaking his head, "this is not all. I am represented as a cruel tyrant; this is the opinion foreign nations have formed of me. But how can they judge? They do not know the circumstances I was in at the beginning of my reign, how many people opposed my designs, counteracted my most useful projects and obliged me to be severe. But I never treated anyone cruelly or gave proofs of tyranny. On the contrary, I have always asked the assistance of such of my subjects as have shown marks of intelligence and patriotism, and who, doing justice to the rectitude of my intentions, have been disposed to second them. Nor have I ever failed to testify my gratitude by loading them with favors."

The arguments about Peter and the controversies over his reforms have never ended. He has been idealized, condemned, analyzed again and again, and still, like the broader issues of the nature and future of Russia itself, he remains essentially mysterious. One quality which no one disputes is his phenomenal energy. "Eternal toiler upon the throne of Russia," Pushkin described him. "It is an age of gold in which we are living," Peter himself wrote to Menshikov. "Without loss of a single instant, we devote all our energies to work." He was a force of nature, and perhaps for this reason no final judgment will ever be delivered. How does one judge the endless roll of the ocean or the mighty power of the whirlwind?

GENEALOGY
ACKNOWLEDGMENTS
BIBLIOGRAPHY
NOTES
INDEX

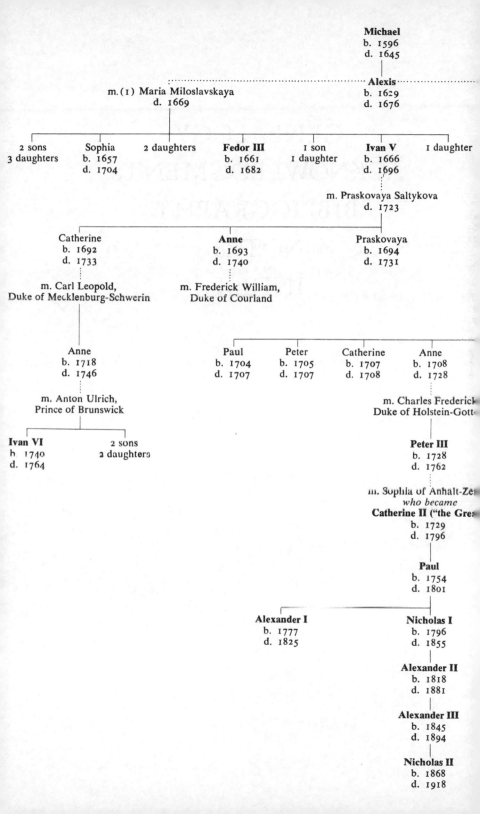

Michael
b. 1596
d. 1645

m.(1) Maria Miloslavskaya   Alexis
d. 1669   b. 1629
                                  d. 1676

2 sons   Sophia   2 daughters   Fedor III   1 son   Ivan V   1 daughter
3 daughters   b. 1657   b. 1661   1 daughter   b. 1666
              d. 1704   d. 1682   d. 1696

                                                        m. Praskovaya Saltykova
                                                           d. 1723

        Catherine   Anne   Praskovaya
        b. 1692   b. 1693   b. 1694
        d. 1733   d. 1740   d. 1731

     m. Carl Leopold,   m. Frederick William,
Duke of Mecklenburg-Schwerin   Duke of Courland

        Anne   Paul   Peter   Catherine   Anne
        b. 1718   b. 1704   b. 1705   b. 1707   b. 1708
        d. 1746   d. 1707   d. 1707   d. 1708   d. 1728

     m. Anton Ulrich,   m. Charles Frederick
     Prince of Brunswick   Duke of Holstein-Gott

Ivan VI   2 sons   Peter III
b. 1740   2 daughters   b. 1728
d. 1764   d. 1762

                                                 m. Sophia of Anhalt-Zer
                                                     who became
                                                 Catherine II ("the Grea
                                                     b. 1729
                                                     d. 1796

                                                     Paul
                                                     b. 1754
                                                     d. 1801

                Alexander I   Nicholas I
                b. 1777   b. 1796
                d. 1825   d. 1855

                                                     Alexander II
                                                     b. 1818
                                                     d. 1881

                                                     Alexander III
                                                     b. 1845
                                                     d. 1894

                                                     Nicholas II
                                                     b. 1868
                                                     d. 1918

m.(2) Natalya Naryshkina
b. 1651
d. 1694

Eudoxia Loupkhina	Peter I ("the Great")	m.(2) Martha Skavronskaya	Natalya
b. 1669	b. 1672	*who became*	b. 1673
d. 1731	d. 1725	Catherine I	d. 1716
		b. 1684	
		d. 1727	

‹is   Alexander
590   b. 1691
718   d. 1692

narlotte of Brunswick-Wolfenbüttel

lya   **Peter II**
714   b. 1715
728   d. 1730

beth	Natalya	Margarita	Peter	Paul	Natalya	Peter	Paul
709	b. 1713	b. 1714	b. 1715	b. 1717	b. 1718	b. 1723	b. 1724
762	d. 1715	d. 1715	d. 1719	d. 1717	d. 1725	d. 1723	d. 1724

GENEALOGY
OF THE ROMANOV DYNASTY
1613–1917

boldface = Tsars, Emperors and Empresses

Acknowledgments

IN WRITING THIS BOOK, I worked in the Frederick Lewis Allen Room of the New York Public Library, the Butler Library of Columbia University, the Firestone Library of Princeton University, the British Museum Library in London and the Bibliothèque Nationale in Paris. I am grateful to the staffs of all of these institutions for their assistance and courtesy.

I am greatly indebted to my friends, Janet Kellock, Edward Kline and Juan de Beistegui, whose encouragement was constant and whose reading of the manuscript provided many wise and helpful suggestions.

For specific help in working with parts of the manuscript or for assistance in obtaining not easily available materials, I wish to thank Valery and Galina Panov, Constantine Kuzminsky, the late Max Hayward, Helen Semmler, Marilyn Swezey, Valery and Irina Kuharets, George Riabov, Nikita Romanov, Dr. Ismail Amin, Professors John Malmstad, Andrew Blane, Elizabeth Valkenier and Zoya Trifunovich, as well as Professor Martin Bos of the University of Utrecht and Vice Admiral H. Bos of the Royal Netherlands Navy. I am especially grateful to the late Prince Paul of Yugoslavia and to Princess Olga of Yugoslavia who provided me with rare materials from their private library. For their support and guidance in a time of troubles, I would like to thank Nicholas A. Robinson and Charles H. Miller.

In writing this book, I made many trips to the Soviet Union. In museums, libraries and at historical sites, I was always made to feel welcome. This was particularly true in Leningrad when people learned that my subject was the founder of their beloved city. For reasons that would seem exaggerated to most Western readers, but that Soviet citizens will abundantly understand, I prefer not to give the names of those who helped me. They know who they are and I thank them.

Some years ago, I mentioned to a friend who is a distinguished French editor that I was working with Robert Gottlieb of Knopf on this book. I said that I thought that Bob was the best editor in New York, but my friend

corrected me; "In the world," he said. Truly, Bob Gottlieb's combination of dedication to his authors, enthusiasm for their work, skill in seeing how a book should be constructed and precisely where it should be cut must be unique. I am fortunate and grateful.

Few readers are aware of the endless, essential details of transforming a long manuscript into a printed book. Katherine Hourigan of Knopf has been superb at this, working with problems of text, pictures, maps and many other things, never losing her serenity or her smile.

There were others at Knopf who helped to create this book: Martha Kaplan, Lesley Krauss, Virginia Tan, William Luckey, Nina Bourne, Anne McCormick, William Loverd, Jane Becker Friedman, Eleanor French, and Toinette Lippe. The House of Knopf is like a family, and for six months, while I worked there almost daily, I was made by everyone to feel a member of the family. Now that this book is finished, I must look for new excuses to visit.

My children, Bob, Susanna and Elizabeth, have given me their love, their encouragement and above all their patience for many years. When I began working on this book, they were quite young; now they have reached or are approaching adulthood. All this while, they have had faith that "Dad's book" would someday appear.

Authors usually thank their wives, but how does one thank a wife who is also an author? While I have been writing this book, Suzanne Massie has written two of her own books, at the same time caring for our home and children, and never failing her myriad of friends, East and West. To this extraordinary woman, I express my gratitude and admiration.

Selected Bibliography

ADLERFELD, M. GUSTAVUS, *The Military History of Charles XII*, 3 vols. London, J. and P. Knapton, 1740.

ALLEN, W. E. D., *The Ukraine: A History*. Cambridge, Cambridge University Press, 1940.

ANDERSON, M. S., *Britain's Discovery of Russia, 1553–1815*. London, Macmillan, 1958.

———, *Peter the Great*. London, Thames and Hudson, 1978.

ANDERSON, R. C., *Naval Wars in the Baltic During the Sailing Ship Epoch, 1522–1850*. London, C. Gilbert-Wood, 1910.

ANDREEV, A. I., editor, *Peter the Great: A Collection of Essays (Petr Veliky: Sbornik statei)*. Moscow-Leningrad, 1947.

AVVAKUM, *The Life of the Archpriest Avvakum by Himself*, translated by Jane Harrison and Hope Mirrlees. London, Published by Leonard and Virginia Woolf at The Hogarth Press, 1924.

BAIN, R. NISBET, *Charles XII and the Collapse of the Swedish Empire*. New York, G. P. Putnam, 1895.

———, *The Pupils of Peter the Great*. London, Constable, 1897.

BELL, JOHN, *Travels from St. Petersburg in Russia to Various Parts of Asia*. Edinburgh, 1806.

BENGTSSON, FRANS G., *The Life of Charles XII*, translated by Naomi Walford. London, Macmillan, 1960.

BILLINGTON, JAMES J., *The Icon and the Axe*. New York, Alfred A. Knopf, 1966.

BLACK, CYRIL E., *Rewriting Russian History*. New York, Vintage Books, 1962.

BOGOSLOVSKY (Bogoslovskii), M. M., *Peter I: Materials for a Biography (Petr I: Materialy dlya biografii)*, 5 vols. Moscow, 1940–1948.

BOWEN, MARJORIE, *William Prince of Orange*. New York, Dodd, Mead, 1928.

BRIDGE, VICE ADMIRAL CYPRIAN A. G., editor, *History of the Russian Fleet During the Reign of Peter the Great by a Contemporary Englishman*. London, The Navy Records Society, 1899.

BROWNING, OSCAR, *Charles XII of Sweden*. London, Hurst and Blackett, 1899.

BRUCE, PETER HENRY, *Mémoires*. London, 1782.

BURNET, GILBERT (Bishop of Salisbury), *History of His Own Time*, 6 vols. Edinburgh, Hamilton, Balfour and Neill, 1753.

The New Cambridge Modern History, Volume VI: The Rise of Great Britain and Russia, 1688–1725, edited by J. S. Bromley. Cambridge, Cambridge University Press, 1970.

CARR, FRANK G. G., *Maritime Greenwich*. London, Pitkin, 1969.

CARR, JOHN LAURENCE, *Life in France Under Louis XIV*. New York, G. P. Putnam's Sons, 1966.

CASSELS, LAVENDER, *The Struggle for the Ottoman Empire, 1717–1740*. London, John Murray, 1966.

CHANCE, JAMES FREDERICK, *George I and the Northern War*. London, Smith, Elder & Co., 1909.

CHURCHILL, WINSTON S., *Marlborough: His Life and Times*, 6 vols. New York, Charles Scribner's Sons, 1933–1938.

CLARK, G. N., *The Later Stuarts, 1660–1714*. Oxford, Oxford University Press, 1934.

Collection of the Imperial Russian Historical Society (Sbornik Imperatorskago Russkago Istoricheskago Obshchestva), 148 vols. St. Petersburg, 1867–1916.

COLLINS, SAMUEL, *The Present State of Russia*. London, Printed by John Winter for D. Newman, 1671.

CRACRAFT, JAMES, *The Church Reform of Peter the Great*. London, Macmillan, 1971.

———, "Feofan Prokopovich," in *The Eighteenth Century in Russia*, edited by J. G. Garrard. Oxford, The Clarendon Press, 1973.

CRULL, JODOCUS, *The Ancient and Present State of Muscovy*. London, A. Roper, 1698.

DE GRUNWALD, CONSTANTIN, *Peter the Great*, translated from the French by Viola Garvin. London, Saunders, MacGibbon & Kee, 1956.

DE JONG, ALEX, *Fire and Water: A Life of Peter the Great*. London, Collins, 1979.

DMYTRYSHYN, BASIL, editor, *Modernization of Russia Under Peter I and Catherine II*. New York, John Wiley & Sons, 1974.

DURUKAN, ZEYNEP M., *The Harem of the Topkapi Palace*. Istanbul, Hilal Matbaacilik Koll., 1973.

EVELYN, JOHN, *The Diary of John Evelyn*, with an Introduction and Notes by Austin Dobson, 3 vols. London, Macmillan, 1906.

FEDOTOV, G. P., *The Russian Religious Mind*. Cambridge, Mass., Harvard University Press, 1966.

FISCHER, LOUIS, *The Life of Lenin*. New York, Harper and Row, 1964.

FISHER, H. A. L., *A History of Europe*, Vol I. London, Fontana Library, 1960.

FLORINSKY, MICHAEL T., *Russia: A History and an Interpretation*, 2 vols. New York, Macmillan, 1953.

GASIOROWSKA, XENIA, *The Image of Peter the Great in Russian Fiction*. Madison, University of Wisconsin Press, 1979.

GEYL, PIETER, *History of the Low Countries: Episodes and Problems*. The Trevelyan Lectures, 1963. London, Macmillan, 1964.

GIBB, HAMILTON, and HAROLD BOWEN, *Islamic Society and the West*. London and New York, Oxford University Press, 1950.

GOOCH, G. P., *Louis XV: The Monarchy in Decline*. London, Longmans, 1956.

GORDON, ALEXANDER, *History of Peter the Great*, 2 vols. Aberdeen, F. Douglass and W. Murray, 1755.

GORDON OF AUCHLEUCHRIES, GENERAL PATRICK, *Passages from the Diary of, 1635–1699*. Aberdeen, Printed for The Spalding Club, 1859.

GRAHAM, STEPHEN, *Peter the Great*. New York, Simon and Schuster, 1929.

GREY, IAN, *Peter the Great*. Philadelphia, Lippincott, 1960.

HATTON, RAGNILD M., *Charles XII of Sweden*. London, Weidenfeld and Nicolson, 1968.

———, *Europe in the Age of Louis XIV*. London, Thames and Hudson, 1969.

HINGLEY, RONALD, *The Tsars: Russian Autocrats, 1533–1917*. London, Weidenfeld and Nicolson, 1968.

JEFFERYES, JAMES, *Captain James Jefferyes's Letters from the Swedish Army, 1707–1709*, edited by Ragnild Hatton. Stockholm, Kungl. Boktryckeriet, P. A. Norstedt & Söner, 1954.

JOLLIFFE, JOHN, "Lord Carlisle's Embassy to Moscow," in *The Cornhill*, Autumn 1967.

KAFENGAUZ, B. B., *Russia Under Peter the First (Rossiya pri Petre Pervom)*. Moscow, 1955.

KLUCHEVSKY, VASILY O., *Peter the Great*, translated by Liliana Archibald. New York, Vintage Books, 1958.

KORB, JOHANN GEORG, *Diary of an Austrian Secretary of Legation at the Court of Tsar Peter the Great*, translated and edited by the Count Mac-Donnel, 2 vols. in one. London, Frank Cass & Co., 1968.

KUNSTLER, CHARLES, *La Vie quotidienne sous la Régence*. Paris, Hachette, 1960.

MALAND, DAVID, *Europe in the Seventeenth Century*. London, Macmillan, 1968.

MANSTEIN, C. H., *Memoirs of Russia, 1727–1744*. London, 1773.

MARSDEN, CHRISTOPHER, *Palmyra of the North: The First Days of St. Petersburg*. London, Faber & Faber, 1942.

MAVOR, JAMES, *An Economic History of Russia*, 2 vols. New York, E. P. Dutton, 1914.

MAZOUR, ANATOLE G., *Modern Russian Historiography*. Princeton, Van Nostrand, 1958 ed.

MILUKOV, PAUL, and others, *History of Russia*, Vol. 1. New York, Funk & Wagnalls, 1968.

MITCHELL, R. J., and M. D. R. LEYS, *A History of London Life*. London, Penguin Books, 1968.

MITFORD, NANCY, *Frederick the Great*. New York, Harper and Row, 1964.

O'BRIEN, C. BICKFORD, *Russia Under Two Tsars, 1682–1689: The Regency of Sophia*. Berkeley, University of California Press, 1952.

OGG, DAVID, *Europe of the Ancien Regime, 1715–1783*. London, Collins, 1967.

OKENFUSS, MAX J., "The Jesuit Origins of Petrine Education," in *The Eighteenth Century in Russia*, edited by J. G. Garrard. Oxford, The Clarendon Press, 1973.

———, "Russian Students in Europe in the Age of Peter the Great," in *The Eighteenth Century in Russia*, edited by J. G. Garrard. Oxford, The Clarendon Press, 1963.

OLEARIUS, J. ALBERT DE M., *The Voyages and Travels of the Ambassadors Sent by Frederick Duke of Holstein to the Great Duke of Muscovy and the King of Persia*, translated by John Davies. London, 1669.

OLIVA, L. JAY, *Peter the Great*. Englewood Cliffs, Prentice-Hall, 1970.

PARES, BERNARD, *A History of Russia*. New York, Alfred A. Knopf, 1960.

PAUL OF ALEPPO, *The Travels of Macarius: Extracts from the Diary of the Travels of Macarius, Patriarch of Antioch, written by his son, Paul, Archdeacon of Aleppo, 1652–1660*, translated by F. C. Balfour. London, Oxford University Press, 1936.

PAVLENKO, N. I., NIKIFOROV, L. A., and VOLKOV, M. I., *Russia in the Period of the Reforms of Peter I (Rossiia v period reform Petra I)*. Moscow, "Nauka," 1973.

PENZER, N. M., *The Harem*. London, Spring Books, 1965.

PEPYS, SAMUEL, *The Diary of Samuel Pepys*, 3 vols., edited by Robert Latham and William Matthews. Berkeley, University of California Press, 1970.

PERRY, JOHN, *The State of Russia Under the Present Tsar*. Printed for Benjamin Tooke at the Middle Temple Gate, Fleet Street, 1716.

PETER THE GREAT, *Letters and Papers (Pisma i Bumagi Imperatora Petra Velikogo)*. St. Petersburg-Moscow, 1887–   . (Twelve volumes have so far been published. The most recent, Vol. 12, carries the work through 1712.)

PIPES, RICHARD, *Russia Under the Old Regime*. New York, Charles Scribner's Sons, 1974.

PLATONOV, SERGEI F., *History of Russia*. New York, Macmillan, 1929.

PLUMB, J. H., *The First Four Georges*. London, Collins-Fontana Library, 1968.

POKROVSKY, MICHAEL N., *History of Russia: From the Earliest Times to the Rise of Commercial Capitalism*, translated and edited by J. D. Clarkson and M. R. M. Griffiths. New York, International Publishers, 1931.

Poltava: A Collection of Articles on the Two Hundred Fiftieth Anniversary of the Battle (Poltava: k 250 letiyu Poltavskogo srazheniya, Sbornik statei). Moscow, 1959.

Portraits of Peter's Time: The Exhibition Catalogue (Portret Petrovskogo vremeni: katalog vystavki). Leningrad, 1973.

PREDTECHENSKY, A. B., editor, *Petersburg of Peter's Time: Studies (Petersburg Petrovskogo vremeni: ocherki).* Leningrad, 1948.

PUTNAM, PETER, *Seven Britons in Imperial Russia, 1698–1812.* Princeton, Princeton University Press, 1952.

RAEFF, MARC, *Origins of the Russian Intelligentsia: The Eighteenth Century Nobility.* New York, Harcourt, Brace, 1966.

———, editor, *Peter the Great: Reformer or Revolutionary?* Boston, D. C. Heath, 1966.

Relation fidèle de ce qui s'est passé au sujet du Jugement rendu contre le Prince Alexei, et des circonstances de sa mort. From the Library of the Palazzo de San Donato, Florence, Italy.

RIASONOVSKY, NICHOLAS V., *A History of Russia.* New York, Oxford University Press, 1963.

RUNCIMAN, STEVEN, *The Fall of Constantinople, 1453.* Cambridge, Cambridge University Press, 1969.

The Russian Primary Chronicle, translated and edited by Samuel H. Cross and Olgerd P. Sherbowitz-Wetzor. Cambridge, Mass., The Medieval Academy of America, 1953.

SAINT-SIMON, LE DUC DE, *Mémoires,* 6 vols. Paris, Bibliothèque de la Pléiade, Editions Gallimard, 1965.

SCHELTEMA, M. J., *Anecdotes historiques sur Pierre le Grand et sur ses voyages en Hollande et à Zaandam.* Lausanne, Marc Ducloux, 1842.

SCHUYLER, EUGENE, *Peter the Great,* 2 vols. New York, Charles Scribner's Sons, 1884.

SHAFIROV, P. P., *A Discourse Concerning the Just Causes of the War Between Sweden and Russia: 1700–1721.* Dobbs Ferry, N.Y., Oceana Publications, 1973.

SHCHERBATOV, M. M., editor, *Journal de Pierre le Grand depuis l'année 1698 jusqu' à la conclusion de la paix de Neustadt.* Berlin, 1773.

SOLOVEV, S. M., *History of Russia from Earliest Times (Istoriya Rossii s drevneishikh vremen),* 15 vols. Moscow, 1960–1966.

STAEHLIN VON STORCKSBURG, *Original Anecdotes of Peter the Great.* London, J. Murray, 1787.

STOYE, JOHN, *Europe Unfolding, 1648–1688.* London, Collins-Fontana Library, 1969.

SUMNER, B. H., *Peter the Great and the Emergence of Russia.* New York, Collier Books, 1965.

———, *Peter the Great and the Ottoman Empire.* Hamden, Conn., Archer Books, 1965.

TARLE, E. V., *The Russian Fleet and the Foreign Policy of Peter I (Russkii flot i vneshnyaya politika Petra I).* Moscow, 1949.

———, *The Northern War (Severnaya Voina).* Moscow, 1958.

TREASURE, G. R. R., *Seventeenth Century France.* London, Rivingtons, 1966.

TREVELYAN, G. M., *The English Revolution, 1688–89.* Oxford, Oxford University Press, 1938.

USTRYALOV, N. G., *History of the Reign of Peter the Great (Istoriya tsarstvovuniya Petra Velikago),* 6 vols. St. Petersburg, 1858–1863.

VOYCE, ARTHUR, *Moscow and the Roots of Russian Culture.* Norman, University of Oklahoma Press, 1964.

WALISZEWSKI, KASIMIERZ, *Peter the Great.* New York, Appleton, 1897.

WEBER, FRIEDRICH CHRISTIAN, *The Present State of Russia,* 2 vols. London, W. Taylor, 1723.

WHITWORTH, CHARLES, *An Account of Russia as It Was in 1710.* Strawberry Hill, 1758.

WILLIAMS, BASIL, *The Whig Supremacy: 1714–1760.* Oxford, Oxford University Press, 1962.

WILLIAMS, NEVILLE, *Chronology of the Expanding World, 1492–1762.* London, Cresset Press, 1969.

WILSON, FRANCESCA, *Muscovy: Russia Through Foreign Eyes, 1553–1900.* London, Allen & Unwin, 1970.

WITTRAM, R., *Peter I, Tzar und Kaiser,* 2 vols. Göttingen, 1964.

WOLF, JOHN B., *Louis XIV*. London, Victor Gollancz, 1968.

WOODWARD, DAVID, *The Russians at Sea: A History of the Russian Navy*. New York, Frederick A. Praeger, 1966.

ZIEGLER, GILETTE, *At the Court of Versailles: Eye-Witness Reports from the Reign of Louis XIV*. New York, E. P. Dutton, 1966.

Notes

Abbreviations Used in Notes

P&B   Letters and Papers of Emperor Peter the Great, St. Petersburg–Leningrad, 1887–1975.

Sbornik, I.R.I.O.   Collection of the Imperial Russian Historical Society, St. Petersburg, 1867–1916.

Manifesto   Manifesto of the Criminal Process of the Czarewitz Alexei Petrowitz, The Hague, 1718. (Printed in Volume II of *The Present State of Russia* by Friedrich Christian Weber)

Chapter 1: Old Muscovy

3 MOST RICH AND BEAUTIFUL: Perry, 263.
4 ANOTHER COMMODITY: Olearius, 43.
5 THESE VILLAINS: Weber, I, 128.
5 THE AUTUMNAL RAINS: Paul of Aleppo, 63.
8 THE EARTH SHOOK: Ibid., 26.
9 LIKE A SPARKLING SUN: Jolliffe, 217.
10 WE HUMBLY BESEECH YOU: O'Brien, 6.
10 'TIS DEATH: Collins, 117.
10 TUFTS OF DIAMONDS: Paul of Aleppo, 88.
10 HIS IMPERIAL MAJESTY: Collins, 44.
10 SEVERE IN HIS CHASTISEMENTS: Ibid., 110.
11 BRIGHT EYES OF THE TSAR: Crull, 170.
11 IF HE BE WELL: Collins, 122.
11 BUT THREE MEALS A WEEK: Ibid.
12 n. THE DISCONSOLATE WIDOW: Wilson, 66.
16 THEIR HAIR IS CROPT: Weber, I, 120.

Chapter 2: Peter's Childhood

20 YOUNG MEN COME: Staehlin, 15.
22 OFFENDERS FOR THE FIRST: Voyce, 93.
22 A FLIGHT OF SCREECH OWLS: Collins, 33.
23 A GOOD AND CLEAN WOMAN: Schuyler, I, 16.
25 THE DOOR OPENED: Ibid., 17.
25 DRAWN BY FOUR DWARF PONIES: Bogoslovsky, I, 30.
27 MADAM, IT IS TIME: Kluchevsky, 2.
27 YOU ARE A GOOD MAN: Ibid., 4.
29 WHICH OF THE TWO: Schuyler, I, 37.

Chapter 3: "A Maiden of Great Intelligence"

32 MY DAUGHTER: Korb, II, 213.
33 BY USING THE WHIP: De Grunwald, 21.

33 SOME OF THESE BARBARIANS:
Collins, 9.
36 A MAIDEN OF GREAT INTELLIGENCE:
O' Brien, 49.
36 THIS ELECTION IS UNJUST: Ibid., 21.
37 THE DEAD SHOULD BURY THE DEAD:
Schuyler, I, 38.
37 YOU SEE HOW OUR BROTHER: Ibid.

Chapter 4: The Revolt of the Streltsy

39 BROTHERS, WHY DO YOU: Schuyler,
I, 44.
40 BEAT THEM HARDER: Ustryalov, I, 24.
41 EVERYBODY CALLS YOU A FOOL:
Schuyler, I, 35.
42 THE NARYSHKINS HAVE MURDERED:
Ibid., 49.
43 WE ARE GOING TO THE KREMLIN:
Ibid.
43 WE WANT TO PUNISH: Ibid., 50.
44 HERE IS THE LORD TSAR: Ibid.
46 HERE COMES THE BOYAR: Ibid., 54.
47 IF YOU FASTEN THE DOOR: Ibid., 60.
47 YOUR BROTHER WILL NOT ESCAPE:
Bogoslovsky, I, 44.
48 GO ON QUICKLY: Schuyler, I, 61.
48 WHAT'S THE USE: Ibid., 62.
48 WE ARE NOW CONTENT: Ibid.

Chapter 5: The Great Schism

56 AS YOUR FIRST SHEPHERD:
Billington, 133.
56 n. ALL THEIR CHURCHES: Paul of
Aleppo, 19, 20, 26, 29, 64, 68, 70.
57 A GREEN VELVET MANDYA: Ibid., 30.
57 A HABIT OF ATTENDING: Ibid., 32.
57 THE EMPEROR TOOK: Ibid., 74.
58 NIKON'S JANISSARIES: Ibid., 36.
59 WHEN THE COUNCIL MET: Ibid., 35.
59 STUPID CLOWN: Ibid., 85.
59 OF HIS OWN WILL: Ibid., 118.
60 TO REVIEW AND CONFIRM: Ibid., 119.
60 HAST THOU NOT LEARNED: Pipes, 235.
61 I KNOW NEITHER THE OLD NOR THE
NEW: Billington, 145.
61 I AM RUSSIAN: Paul of Aleppo, 37.
61 THOU SIMPLE, IGNORANT AND
HUMBLE RUSSIA: Billington, 141.

62 WE SHALL BE BURNED AT THE STAKE:
De Grunwald, 63.
62 A WOMAN CAME: Avvakum, 44.
62 THEY PAINT THE IMAGE: Ibid., 23.
63 BURNING YOUR BODY: Ibid., 22.
63 THERE IS TERROR: Ibid., 21.

Chapter 6: Peter's Games

65 BOTH THEIR MAJESTIES SAT:
Bogoslovsky, I, 53–5.
66 THEN I KISSED THE RIGHT HAND:
Schuyler, I, 106.
66 THE YOUNG TSAR: Ibid.
66 THE NATURAL LOVE AND INTELLI-
GENCE: Ibid., 103.
72 WHAT KIND OF BOAT IS IT?:
Ustryalov, II, App. i, 399.
73 AND MIGHTY PLEASANT IT WAS:
Schuyler, I, 112.
73 n. BRING THE BOAT TO SCHLÜSSEL-
BURG: Museum of the Navy,
Leningrad.
74 YES, WE CAN BUILD BOATS HERE:
Schuyler, I, 113.
77 TO MY BELOVED: P&B, I, No. 6.
77 SECOND LETTER: Ibid., I, No. 7.
78 I WISH TO HEAR ABOUT YOUR HEALTH:
Ibid., No. 9.
78 I SALUTE MY LORD: Museum,
Pereslavl-Zalessky.

Chapter 7: The Regency of Sophia

79 HER MIND AND HER GREAT ABILITY:
Schuyler, I, 170.
81 PEOPLING THE DESERTS: De
Grunwald, 64.
89 OH, MY JOY: Ustryalov, I, 238.
89 20,000 KILLED: Schuyler, I, 166.
90 EVERYONE SAW PLAINLY: Ibid., 168.
90 WITHERED, FALLEN APPLES:
Ibid., 173.
91 WE ALWAYS HAVE SORROW:
Ibid., 158.
91 TALLER THAN HIS COURTIERS: De
Grunwald, 71.
94 THE HEAT AND BITTERNESS:
Bogoslovsky, I, 80.
94 RUMORS UNSAFE: Ibid.

Chapter 8: Sophia Overthrown

97 EXCEPT FOR MY PRECAUTIONS:
Schuyler, I, 175.
97 LET HIM RUN: Ibid., 176.
100 I SHALL CERTAINLY GO: Ibid., 179.
100 THEY ALMOST SHOT ME: Ibid.
101 HOW DARE YOU: Ustryalov, II, 70.
101 EVIL-MINDED PEOPLE: Schuyler,
I, 180.
102 A LONG AND FINE SPEECH: Ibid., 181.
103 YOU HAD BETTER FINISH: Ibid., 182.
105 THIS SHAMEFUL THIRD PERSON: *P&B,*
I, No. 10.
106 SUCH WISE GOVERNMENT: O'Brien, ix.
107 A PRINCESS ENDOWED: Weber, I, 138.

Chapter 9: Gordon, Lefort and the Jolly Company

110 IGNORANCE AND SIMPLICITY:
Schuyler, I, 197.
110 THE TSAR TOLD US: Ibid.
116 MY HEART IS WHOLLY IN MOSCOW:
De Grunwald, 77.
117 EXCEEDINGLY BEAUTIFUL: Grey, 199.
118 THE JOY OF THE RUSSES: *Primary
Chronicle,* 97.
118 HANDSOMELY FUDDLED: Collins, 63.
118 WOMEN ARE OFTEN THE FIRST:
Korb, I, 100.
118 NEVER OVERCOMES HIM: Schuyler,
I, 281.
120 THE PROCESSION WAS: Ibid., 219.

Chapter 10: Archangel

124 FOR SOME YEARS: Schuyler, I, 227.
126 YOU HAVE WRITTEN, O LADY: *P&B,*
I, No. 14.
126 IF YOU ARE GRIEVED: Ibid., Nos. 15,
16.
128 I DUMBLY TELL: Ibid., No. 21.
131 WHAT I HAVE SO LONG: Ibid., No. 29.
133 I BELIEVE: Schuyler, I, 240.

Chapter 11: Azov

136 THERE WAS TALK OF A JOURNEY:
Schuyler, I, 240.
137 THE CRIMEAN TATARS ARE BUT A

HANDFUL: Sumner, *Ottoman,* 17.
138 AT KOZHUKHOVO WE JESTED:
Ustryalov, II, 228.
138 FULL OF FLOWERS AND HERBS:
Schuyler, I, 245.
139 MOST OF ALL THE DELAY: *P&B,*
I, No. 38.
139 WE SOMETIMES ACTED: Schuyler,
I, 245.
140 SUCH WAS THE RESULT: Gordon, 184.
141 GREAT QUANTITIES OF PROVISIONS:
Schuyler, I, 248.
144 ACCORDING TO THE DIVINE DECREE:
P&B, I, No. 72.
145 OUT OF DANGER: Schuyler, I, 256.
145 IT IS NOT I WHO GO NEAR: *P&B,*
I, No. 99.
146 ANY HEALTHY GOOD SENSE: Ibid.,
No. 108.
146 CUT OFF MY HEAD: Schuyler, I, 258.
147 WHEN YOUR LETTER CAME:
Ibid., 261.
147 IF "THE LABORER IS WORTHY": *P&B,*
I, No. 122.
150 THE SOVEREIGN HAS DIRECTED:
Bogoslovsky, I, 367.

Chapter 12: The Great Embassy to Western Europe

155 MERELY A CLOAK: Ustryalov, II,
App. xi, 640.
156 HE TURNED HIS WHOLE MIND:
Schuyler, I, 265.
157 HIS SLIGHTEST GESTURE: Gooch, 2.
157 I NEVER TREMBLED: Ibid., 3.
161 I HAVE OFTEN SEEN THE KING: Ziegler,
163.
161 I HAVE NEVER: Ibid., 150.
161 KINGS WHO HAVE A DESIRE: Ibid., 163.
164 DETERMINED THE COURSE: Basil
Williams, 378.
166 THEIR DIGNITY AS AMBASSADORS:
Sbornik, I.R.I.O., XXXIV, 17.

Chapter 13: "It Is Impossible to Describe Him"

169 A MERRY NIGHT HAS BEEN SPOILED:
Schuyler, I, 277.
172 THUS THE LORD GOD: Solovev, VIII,
285.

172 OPEN TABLES: Grey, 101.
173 BAPTIZED BEARS: Ibid.
174 THE ELECTOR IS VERY GOOD:
Bogoslovsky, II, 101.
176 I DON'T KNOW: Ibid., 115–16.
176 THESE GERMAN WOMEN: Schuyler,
I, 286.
176 A NATURAL, UNCONSTRAINED AIR:
Ibid., 285.
177 THE TSAR IS VERY TALL: Ibid.

Chapter 14:
Peter in Holland

181 GERRIT . . . STOP LYING: Scheltema,
89.
181 CERTAINLY, IT IS THE TSAR: Ibid., 91.
182 BRAVO! MARSJE: Schuyler, I, 289.
182 TOO MANY PEOPLE: Ibid.
186 CARPENTER PETER: Scheltema, 112.
187 SOMETIMES FROM WEARINESS:
P&B, I, No. 191.

Chapter 15:
The Prince of Orange

192 I NOW POSSESS: Bowen, 166.
192 DIE IN THE LAST DITCH:
Churchill, I, 86.
195 GOD HELP ME!: Ibid., 257.
196 I AM SURE THAT THIS PEOPLE:
Geyl, 133.
196 I WISH I WERE A BIRD: Ibid., 132.
198 I'LL PUT HIM ON MY KNEES:
Scheltema, 159.
199 QUICKLY, QUICKLY: Ibid., 141.
199 THEY ARE LATE: Ibid., 142.
201 THE TSAR WAS IN A STATE: Ibid., 110.

Chapter 16:
Peter in England

204 SALUTING EACH OTHER: Mitchell &
Leys, 163.
209 RIGHT NASTY: Evelyn, III, 334–5.
209 AS IF A REGIMENT: Kluchevsky, 29.
210 TO OFFER HIM SUCH INFORMATION:
Burnet, IV, 322.
210 I WAITED OFTEN ON HIM: Ibid.

211 WHOEVER COULD LIVE: Schuyler,
I, 305.
212 ON YOUR ORDERS: Grey, 120.
212 ONE OF THE MOST SUBLIME:
Carr, 18.
212 IF I WERE TO ADVISE: Staehlin, 40.
213 HE WOULD THROW IT: Grey, 458.
214 TODAY, I HAVE SEEN THE RAREST
THING: Schuyler, I, 304.
214 IT IS GOOD TO HEAR: Kluchevsky, 28.
214 THE COURT HERE: Ibid.
215 MORE THAN THEY DESERVED:
Grey, 459.
215 THE IMPERIAL CROWN: Ibid.
216 IF HE HAD NOT COME TO ENGLAND:
Perry, 165.
216 AN ADMIRAL IN ENGLAND: Ibid., 164.
216 THE ENGLISH ISLAND: Andreev, 88.

Chapter 17:
Leopold and Augustus

218 WITH A PERFECTION: Schuyler, I, 311.
218 I THANK GOD: Ibid., 312.
224 HERE HE APPEARS: Bogoslovsky,
II, 475.
224 THE KEYS WOULD BE BESTOWED:
Waliszewski, 98.
224 A TALL YOUNG MAN: Schuyler, I, 315.
225 I BELIEVE YOU KNOW THE TSAR:
De Grunwald, 93.
226 THE TURKS ARE NOT ACCUSTOMED:
Schuyler, I, 316.
227 THE SEED OF IVAN MIKHAILOVICH:
P&B, I, No. 252.
228 THIS UNSETTLED NATION: Sbornik,
I.R.I.O., XXXIX, 222.
231 I CANNOT BEGIN TO DESCRIBE TO YOU:
Bogoslovsky, II, 558–9.
231 I PRIZE HIM MORE THAN THE WHOLE
OF YOU: Korb, I, 156.

Chapter 18: "These
Things Are in Your Way"

234 THE PROMPTITUDE OF THEIR
OBSEQUIOUSNESS: Korb, I, 155.
235 TO SHAVE THE BEARD: Maland, 435.
235 GOD DID NOT CREATE MEN BEARDLESS:
Ustryalov, II, 193–4.

236 IN A MERRY HUMOR: Perry, 196.
236 THE TSAR CAME: Ibid.
236 SEEING AT A GLANCE: Korb, I, 157.
237 HIS GUMS SWOLLEN: Ibid., 170.
238 SUCH A BRAINLESS ASS: Ibid., 196.
238 THESE THINGS ARE IN YOUR WAY:
Ibid., 257.
239 MANY HUNDREDS OF COATS:
Perry, 198.
239 IN ALL THIS GREAT CITY: *Sbornik,
I.R.I.O.,* XXXIX, 60.
242 VIEW THE MAP: Perry, 235.
242 DISPLAY THEIR HAPPINESS:
Dmytryshyn, 10.

Chapter 19:
Fire and Knout

245 TODAY FOR THE FIRST TIME: Korb,
I, 121.
246 THEY HAD BEEN ORDERED: Schuyler,
I, 324.
247 I USED ALL THE RHETORIC:
Gordon, 190.
250 KEEPING TIME: Perry, 217.
250 SO MANY STROKES ON THE BARE BACK:
Ibid., 218.
251 HANDS AND FEET ARE TIED: Ibid.
251 IF ONE IS PERFORMED: Lebrun, in
Weber, II, 403.
251 THE SHARPEST PAIN: Korb, I, 204.
252 IT'S NO SECRET TO ME: Ibid., 202.
252 WE SEE SO MUCH: Wolf, 173.
252 I WENT OUT TO CHARING CROSS:
Pepys, I, 265.
254 WHILE ONE ACCOMPLICE: Korb,
I, 243.
255 WHAT ARE YOU DOING WITH THAT
IMAGE: Ibid., 180.
256 ALAS! WHO KNOWS: Ibid., 136.
259 IT WAS REPORTED: Ibid., 187.
259 SO GREAT A DISTRUST: Ibid., 178.
260 HOW LONG: Burnet, IV, 324.

Chapter 20:
Among Friends

263 NUMBERS OF MAGNATES: Korb,
I, 161.
263 A BARBAROUS AND INHUMAN LAW:
Ibid., II, 158.

263 THE TSAR WANTS TO EAT!: Ibid., 157.
264 THE TSAR ORDERED: Ibid., I, 200.
264 DANCING FOLLOWED: Ibid., 201.
265 BOTH OF THEM: Ibid., 163, 171–2.
265 IF THOU WERT A SUBJECT: Ibid., 198.
266 TO LEARN FROM THEM: Ibid., 164.
267 AN INEXPLICABLE WHIRLWIND:
Ibid., 188.
267 CUT SHORT THE DISPUTE: Ibid., 216.
267 INQUIRED OF PRINCE ROMODANOVSKY:
Ibid., 236.
267 THE GROUND WAS COVERED:
Ibid., 217.
268 THE FALSE PATRIARCH: Ibid., 223.
268 THE WEALTHIEST MERCHANT OF
MUSCOVY: Ibid.
268 THE PROCESSION TO THE RIVER:
Ibid., 224–8.
269 HE THAT BORE THE ASSUMED HONORS:
Ibid., 255.
270 THE CROSS: Ibid., 256.
270 THE TSAR COMMANDED HIM TO STAY:
Ibid., 264.
270 THE SILENCE AND MODESTY:
Ibid., 265.
271 IT WAS A HORRIBLE SPECTACLE:
Ibid., 267.
271 A COURIER SENT OFF: Ibid., 208.
272 YOU GERMAN DOGS: Ibid., 248.
272 URBAN, LOSING PATIENCE: Ibid., 172.
272 SOLDIERS IN MUSCOVY: Ibid., 297.
273 THE RARE PROFUSION: Ibid., II, 36.
273 A COLOSSAL WHITE BEAR: Ibid.,
I, 210.
273 WE SAW ITS HUGE WALLS: Ibid.,
II, 16.
273 LAID OUT MOST AGREEABLY: Ibid., 25.

Chapter 21: Voronezh
and the Southern Fleet

275 TO YOU I COMMIT EVERYTHING:
Korb, II, 3.
276 THANK GOD WE HAVE FOUND OUR
FLEET: *P&B,* I, No. 255.
276 HERE, BY GOD'S HELP: Ibid., No. 256.
277 SUPPOSING THAT HER HUSBAND:
Korb, I, 272.
278 WHEN THE PASTOR WAS ADMITTED:
Ibid., 268.
278 NOW I AM ALONE: Ibid., 272.

278 THE TABLES WERE LAID OUT: Ibid., 274–9.
280 THIS IS THE FIRST TIME: *P&B*, VI, No. 2081.
281 IN THIS YEAR I HAVE FELT: Gordon, 193.
281 STAY WHERE YOU ARE, FATHER: Korb, II, 232–5.
281 THE STATE HAS LOST IN HIM: De Grunwald, 98.
285 I GET NO SORT: Ibid., 93.
285 THE TSAR IS DESTROYING: Ibid.
285 FROM TIME IMMEMORIAL: Ustryalov, III, 551–2.

Chapter 22: Mistress of the North

295 YOU HAVE SPOKEN LIKE AN HONEST MAN: Adlerfeld, II, 367.
296 A STREAM THAT RUNS THROUGH THE DOMINIONS: Hatton, *Europe,* 109.
296 RUSSIAN INFANTRY: Schuyler, I, 369.
296 IT WOULD ALSO BE: Ibid.
299 DIVERTING HIMSELF WITH WOMEN: Bogoslovsky, IV, 366.
300 IT IS A PITY: Schuyler, I, 376.
300 I COULD HARDLY CALM YOUR DAUGHTER: Bogoslovsky, IV, 405–6.
300 THE TSAR SENT HIS MINISTERS: Schuyler, I, 376.
301 THE GREAT TSAR: Grey, 171.
301 OTHER THAN PROFIT: *P&B,* I, No. 325.

Chapter 23: Let the Cannon Decide

302 NO JUDGE MORE EQUITABLE: Wolf, 211.
305 n. MONSIEUR DE VAUBAN PROPOSED: Churchill, I, 94.
310 GOD WOULD LET NO ONE BE KILLED: Hatton, *Charles,* 116.

Chapter 24: Charles XII

316 NOT AS LONG AS YOU ARE NOT AFRAID: Hatton, *Charles,* 101.

318 WOE TO THEE: Schuyler, I, 386.
318 WE WILL MAKE KING AUGUSTUS GO BACK: Hatton, *Charles,* 118.
318 I HAVE RESOLVED: Bain, *Charles,* 55.
318 IT IS CURIOUS: Hatton, *Charles,* 118.
319 DRAGGED INTO WAR: Ibid., 100.
319 I INTEND TO FINISH: Ibid., 128.
320 FARMHANDS DIPPED IN SALT WATER: Ibid., 129.

Chapter 25: Narva

323 I HAVE DONE EVERYTHING POSSIBLE: Ustryalov, IV, ii, App. ii, No. 1.
325 THE KING IS RESOLVED: Schuyler, I, 396.
327 IF THE KING SUCCEEDS: Hatton, *Charles,* 151.
332 THE SNOW IS AT OUR BACKS: Bain, *Charles,* 75.
332 FELL LIKE GRASS: Bengtsson, 87.
332 WE CHARGED DIRECTLY: Ibid.
333 THEY RETURNED A HEAVY FIRE: Ibid.
333 THE GERMANS HAVE BETRAYED US: Schuyler, I, 397.
334 THEY RAN ABOUT LIKE A HERD OF CATTLE: Ibid., 398.
334 THE DEVIL COULD NOT FIGHT: Ibid., 397.
334 I SEE THAT THE ENEMY: Adlerfeld, I, 57.
336 IF WEIDE HAD HAD THE COURAGE: Schuyler, I, 398.
336 n. I AM SINCERELY SORRY: Ustryalov, IV, i, 59.
337 IT IS GOD'S WORK: Bain, *Charles,* 77.
337 AS FAR AS THE RIVER AMUR: Schuyler, I, 402.
337 THERE IS NO PLEASURE: Ibid., 403.

Chapter 26: "We Must Not Lose Our Heads"

339 WE MUST NOT LOSE OUR HEADS: De Grunwald, 108.
340 OUR ARMY WAS VANQUISHED: Shcherbatov, 30.
341 THE POLITEST MAN: Whitworth, 72.
341 A GREAT NUMBER ARE CALLED: Kluchevsky, 87.

342 PLAY FENCING MASTER: Sumner,
Emergence, 58.
342 THE INTERESTS OF HIS TSARISH
MAJESTY: Ibid.
342 THEY ARE ARMED: Schuyler, I, 411.
343 SPEED THE ARTILLERY: *P&B*, I,
No. 369.
343 FROM THE WHOLE OF TSARDOM:
Ustryalov, IV, i, 70.
343 TELL THE BURGOMASTERS: *P&B*, I,
No. 374.
343 IT IS GOOD WORK: Ibid., No. 370.
343 EXTREMELY WELL SERVED: Sumner,
Emergence, 57.
344 THEY ALL AVOID ME: Ustryalov, IV,
ii, App. ii, No. 94, 207.
344 TRY . . . TO GET A VICTORY: Ibid.,
No. 83, 201.
345 SOVEREIGNS HAVE RIGHTS: Grey, 191.
345 THE KING THINKS NOW ABOUT
NOTHING: Schuyler, I, 403.
345 IN SPITE OF THE COLD: Ibid.
346 DEROGATORY TO MYSELF: Schuyler,
II, 13.
348 HE BELIEVES: Sumner,
Emergence, 61.
349 THANK GOD!: Ustryalov, IV,
i, 106–7.
349 I SEND COSSACKS: Schuyler, I, 420.
352 GOD GIVES TIME: *P&B*, II, No. 452.
352 THIS NUT WAS VERY HARD: Ibid.,
No. 462.
352 CONSOLE YOURSELF: Schuyler, I, 424.

Chapter 27:
The Founding of St. Petersburg

357 ON FESTIVAL DAYS: Weber, I, 304.
358 HERE, THANKS BE TO GOD: *P&B*,
III, No. 723.
359 HIS MAJESTY, WITH HIS SKILL:
Schuyler, II, 5.
361 ALLOWED TO EXCUSE THEMSELVES:
Sbornik, I.R.I.O., L, 2.
362 AS HIS INTELLIGENCE: De
Grunwald, 170.
363 THE DAY BEFORE YESTERDAY: *P&B*,
IV, i, No. 1349.
363 ON THE 9TH AT MIDNIGHT: *Sbornik,
I.R.I.O.*, L, 401.
363 THE DAMAGE IS BEYOND WORDS:
Ibid., LX, 348–9.

364 IT IS SURPRISING: Weber, I, 191.
364 PETERSBURG WILL NOT ENDURE:
Ustryalov, IV, i, 274.
365 LET THE TSAR: Schuyler, II, 6.
365 I CANNOT HELP WRITING YOU:
Grey, 227.
365 ESPECIALLY THOSE WITH SCENT:
Sumner, *Emergence*, 59.
365 8,000 SINGING BIRDS: *Sbornik,
I.R.I.O.*, L, 6.

Chapter 28:
Menshikov and Catherine

368 HOT PIES!: Ustryalov, IV, i, 208.
369 LOWER THAN A POLE:
Kluchevsky, 11.
369 THAT ALEXANDER: Korb, II, 6.
369 NEITHER READ NOR WRITE: *Sbornik,
I.R.I.O.*, XXXIX, 125.
371 HE DOES WHAT HE LIKES: De
Grunwald, 196.
371 n. SOME HAVE THOUGHT:
Whitworth, 64.
374 I AM RARELY MERRY HERE: Schuyler,
I, 437.
374 IT IS VERY NECESSARY: Ibid., 439.
374 WE ARE LIVING IN PARADISE: Ibid.
376 THE GREAT REASON WHY: Alexander
Gordon, II, 258.
378 THE TSARITSA WAS IN THE PRIME:
Waliszewski, 271.
379 IF YOU WERE HERE: Ibid., 277.
379 LETTER FROM PETER OF AUGUST 31,
1709: *P&B*, IX, i, No. 3397
(Schuyler, I, 441).
379 LETTER OF SEPTEMBER 24, 1709:
Ibid., No. 3429; (ibid.).
379 LETTER OF OCTOBER 16, 1709: Ibid.,
No. 3464 (ibid., 442).
379 LETTER OF SEPTEMBER 14, 1711:
Ibid., XI, ii, No. 4746 (ibid.).
379 LETTER OF SEPTEMBER 19, 1711:
Ibid., No. 4763 (ibid.).
380 LETTER OF AUGUST 8, 1712: Schuyler,
I, 442.
380 LETTER OF OCTOBER 2, 1712: Ibid.,
443.
380 LETTER OF OCTOBER 6, 1712:
Ibid.
380 KATERINUSHKA: Ibid.
380 LETTER OF JUNE 5, 1716: Ibid.

381 LETTER OF NOVEMBER 23, 1716:
Ibid., 444.
381 LETTER FROM CATHERINE OF JULY
24, 1718: Ibid.
381 LETTER OF AUGUST 1, 1718: Ibid.
381 LETTER OF JULY 1723: Ibid.

Chapter 29:
The Hand of the Autocrat

384 IT IS A PROSTITUTION: Basil
Williams, 103.
384 WE HAD OVER TWENTY: Weber,
I, 224.
385 TRAVEL BY SLEDS: Perry, 244.
385 THESE POSTS AND TREES ARE USEFUL:
Lebrun, in Weber, II, 408.
385 IT WOULD BE IMPOSSIBLE FOR A
TRAVELER: Weber, I, 114.
385 HE HAS TRAVELED: Perry, 279.
389 AS CONCERNS THE TRADING BUSINESS:
Schuyler, II, 139.
390 SINCE GOD HAS SENT HIM: Solovev,
VIII, 98.
390 WHAT SORT OF TSAR IS HE?: Ibid.
391 WE SHALL EXERCISE NO COMPULSION:
Ibid., 76.
391 NOT TO FLATTER MY SUBJECTS:
Staehlin, 219.
392 WE HAVE READ THE BOOK: Solovev,
VIII, 334.
392 WHAT DIFFERENCE IS THERE?:
Ibid., 88.
393 THE GOVERNOR AND OTHER OFFICERS:
Schuyler, II, 157.
394 I HAVE TALKED FOR SOME TIME WITH
THEM: Ibid., 158.
394 SUCH A TREMENDOUSLY CRAZY
RABBLE: Ibid., 159.
395 DEFEND THE HOUSE: Ibid., 161.
396 THIS BUSINESS . . . IS NOW FINISHED:
P&B, VI, No. 2068.
396 EXTINGUISH THIS FIRE: Solovev,
VIII, 183.
396 EXECUTE THE WORST: P&B, VII, i,
No. 2553.

Chapter 30:
Polish Quagmire

397 THEY SEEM RESOLVED: Adlerfeld,
II, 13.

398 THIS IS RUSSIAN . . . BLOOD: Staehlin,
49; Weber, I, 96.
398 NEVER SAW ANY NATION GO BETTER:
Sbornik, I.R.I.O., XXXIX, 56.
399 "OPEN THE GATE": Adlerfeld, I, 168.
399 THE POLES MUST EITHER BE AN-
NIHILATED: Schuyler, II, 18.
400 FOR SWEDEN: Ibid., 19.
400 EVEN IF I SHOULD HAVE TO REMAIN:
Ibid., 17.
400 I WOULD GIVE AUGUSTUS PEACE:
Hatton, Charles, 187.
400 TEACH THEM . . . THE RIGHT
LANGUAGE: Ibid., 199.
402 I HAVE RECEIVED YOUR LETTER: P&B,
III, No. 788.
402 INADEQUATE TRAINING: Ibid.,
No. 862.
402 DO NOT BE SAD: Ibid., No. 864.
404 FROM WHOM DID YOU RECEIVE:
Ibid., No. 1005.
405 I LEAVE ALL TO YOUR JUDGMENT:
Ibid., IV, i, Nos. 1064, 1067.
405 ALL THE SAXON ARMY HAS BEEN
BEATEN: Ibid., No. 1117.
406 IT IS IMPOSSIBLE TO DESCRIBE:
Adlerfeld, II, 218.
406 IT IS WITH INDESCRIBABLE JOY: P&B,
IV, i, No. 1212.
406 THE GENERAL OF CAVALRY: Schuyler,
II, 44.
408 YOU KNOW VERY WELL: Ibid., 50.
409 FOR THE PRESENT, IT IS I:
Bengtsson, 232.
409 JOLLY AND AMUSING: Hatton,
Charles, 215.
410 I THINK YOU KNOW ABOUT PATKUL:
Schuyler, II, 55.
411 I KNOW PATKUL WELL: Ibid.
412 I AM DOING EVERYTHING TO SAVE HIM:
Ustryalov, IV, i, 424.
412 WE TRUST THAT THE KING OF
SWEDEN: P&B, V, Nos. 1690–3.
412 TAKE OFF MY HEAD: Schuyler, II, 60.

Chapter 31:
Charles in Saxony

414 THAT HE WILL FAVOR THE ALLIES:
Hatton, Charles, 225.
414 WHENEVER THE STATES OR ENGLAND:
Churchill, V, 252.

414 TWELVE TRUMPETS: Adlerfeld,
II, 329.
414 HAD HER SEX NOT PREVENTED IT:
Churchill, V, 252.
415 I HOPE THAT IT HAS ENTIRELY DE-
FEATED: Hatton, *Charles*, 226.
417 I SHALL FALL BY NO OTHER BULLET:
Browning, 357.
417 I AM MARRIED TO THE ARMY: Hatton,
Charles, 210.
419 THIS WAR LAY ONLY ON US: *P&B*, V,
No. 1490.
420 I DO NOT THINK THAT MARLBOROUGH
CAN BE BOUGHT: Ibid., IV, i, No.
1401.
420 THE AMBASSADOR OF MUSCOVY:
Grey, 271.
420 HERE THERE IS NO AUTOCRATIC
POWER: Ibid.
421 THE MINISTRY HERE IS MORE SUBTLE:
Schuyler, II, 68.
421 TELL HUYSSEN: *P&B*, V, No. 1551.
421 CONCERNING ANDREI MATVEEV:
Solovev, VIII, 256.
422 I WILL SACRIFICE THE LAST . . .
SOLDIER: Schuyler, II, 66.
422 THE TSAR IS NOT YET
HUMILIATED: Ibid.
422 POLAND WILL NEVER HAVE QUIET:
Sumner, *Emergence*, 61.
422 THE POWER OF MUSCOVY: Ibid.
422 I HOPE PRINCE SOBIESKI: Schuyler,
II, 66.
425 TO HUMAN EYES: Bengtsson, 242.
425 I CANNOT EXPRESS: Ibid.
426 THERE WAS NO DANGER: Ibid., 247.

Chapter 32: The Great Road to Moscow

427 BARBAROUS AND UNCHRISTIAN:
Sbornik, I.R.I.O., XXXIX, 80.
427 NOBODY SPOKE OF ANYTHING:
Schuyler, II, 76.
428 FATTEN HIM UP: *P&B*, VI, No. 2050.
429 THAT YOU HAVE DONE NOTHING:
Ibid., No. 1885.
429 YOU FEEL AGGRIEVED: Ibid., No.
1977.
429 GOD HAS GIVEN THE TSAR: *Sbornik,
I.R.I.O.*, XXXIX, 448–9.

430 HASTEN TO VILNA: Solovev,
VIII, 199.
431 THEY HAVE EXECUTED THEIR DESIGN:
Jefferyes, 35.
433 ALL CAVALRYMEN SHOULD OFF-
SADDLE: Bengtsson, 253.
434 SO PITCHY DARK: Ibid.
435 HIS MAJESTY CAME UP TO ME:
Ibid., 256.
436 THE ENEMY WOULD NOT DARE:
Hatton, *Charles*, 255.
436 AN OLD PROPHECY: Ibid.
437 I HAVE ALWAYS BEEN HEALTHY:
Solovev, VIII, 200.
437 I BEG YOU TO DO EVERYTHING:
Ibid., 201.
438 YOU KNOW YOURSELF: Schuyler, II,
84.

Chapter 33: Golovchin and Lesnaya

442 I CANNOT ON THIS OCCASION:
Jefferyes, 47.
444 THE BATTLE GREW SO HOT: Ibid., 51.
445 THE MUSCOVITES HAVE LEARNED:
Ibid., 53.
448 I ASSURE YOU: *P&B*, VIII, i, Nos.
2616, 2619.
449 WE ARE NOW FORCED: Jefferyes, 61.
452 ALL DAY IT WAS IMPOSSIBLE: *P&B*,
VIII, i, No. 2681.
453 THIS VICTORY MAY BE CALLED OUR
FIRST: *Poltava*, 39.

Chapter 34: Mazeppa

455 TIS THOUGHT: Jefferyes, 63.
456 LAGERCRONA MUST BE MAD: Hatton,
Charles, 271.
457 MILK AND HONEY: Jefferyes, 63.
460 FOR I, THE HETMAN: Solovev,
VIII, 213.
461 ALTHOUGH I LOVE NO ONE ON EARTH:
Schuyler, II, 101.
462 HIS GREAT VALUE: Solovev, VIII, 241.
463 IN ORDER TO PUT THE LAND:
Ibid., 245.
464 WE WILL ALL DIE HERE: Schuyler,
II, 107.

465 THE PEOPLE OF LITTLE RUSSIA:
Solovev, VIII, 252.

Chapter 35: The Worst
Winter Within Memory

467 AS IT HAD BEEN OUTSIDE THE WORLD:
Bengtsson, 317.
469 THE COLD WAS BEYOND DESCRIPTION:
Ibid., 319.
470 ALTHOUGH EARTH, SKY, AND AIR:
Bain, *Charles*, 178.
472 THE CAMPAIGN IS SO DIFFICULT:
Schuyler, II, 113.
473 I AND THE ARMY ARE IN VERY GOOD
CONDITION: Ibid.
473 I SAW HIS MAJESTY KING CHARLES XII:
Bengtsson, 329.

Chapter 36:
The Gathering of Forces

479 INCLINED TO MAKE PEACE: Hatton,
Charles, 285.
480 YOU ARE OUR LITTLE VAUBAN:
Schuyler, II, 114.
480 THE KING WISHES TO HAVE A LITTLE
AMUSEMENT: Ibid., 116.
480 I REALLY BELIEVE: Ibid.
482 WE HAVE GATHERED CLOSE: Solovev,
VIII, 270.
484 COME! COME! SLASH AWAY!:
Adlerfeld, II, 118.
489 SOLDIERS: THE HOUR HAS STRUCK:
P&B, IX, i, No. 3251.

Chapter 37: Poltava

492 WOULD TO GOD: Bengtsson, 353.
495 ONE MISTAKE: Hatton, *Charles*, 297.
495 HERE THE RECONNAISSANCE: Ibid.
502 WOULD IT NOT BE BEST: Ibid., 299.
502 YOU MUST GO AND ATTACK THE
ENEMY: Bengtsson, 366.
504 I BEGGED, THREATENED, CURSED:
Hatton, *Charles*, 299.
505 ALL IS LOST!: Bengtsson, 370.
505 WHAT ARE WE TO DO NOW?: Bain,
Charles, 189.

Chapter 38:
Surrender by the River

508 WHERE IS MY BROTHER CHARLES?:
Bain, *Charles*, 189.
508 YOU ARE AN HONEST FELLOW: Bain,
Charles, 190.
508 WHO ARE YOUR TEACHERS?: Solovev,
VIII, 274.
508 MATUSHKA, GOOD DAY: P&B, IX, i,
No. 3266.
508 THIS IS TO INFORM YOU: Ibid.,
No. 3252.
509 THE FINAL STONE: Ibid., No. 3259.
511 DO WHAT YOU WILL: Bengtsson, 375.
513 IF, WITH THE GRACE OF GOD:
Ibid., 382.
513 I WAS GUILTY: Hatton, *Charles*, 305.
514 WE WILL FIGHT IF THE OTHERS DO:
Ibid.

Chapter 39:
The Fruits of Poltava

516 SIR: THE GRACIOUS LETTER: P&B, IX,
i, No. 3318.
518 FOR MY SINS: Solovev, VIII, 280.
518 WE HAVE NO CONFIRMATION:
Churchill, VI, 119.
518 THIS AFTERNOON: Ibid., 120.
518 FOR THE GOOD OF THE HUMAN RACE:
Schuyler, II, 127.
520 I ALWAYS WEAR THE CUTLASS:
Ibid., 126.
523 SEVENTY THOUSAND POUNDS
STERLING: De Grunwald, 113.
525 I HEAR THAT YOU INTEND: P&B, X,
No. 3793.
525 AND THUS THROUGH THE TAKING OF
THIS TOWN: Ibid., No. 3818.
525 A STRONG CUSHION: Ibid., No. 3814.
526 THE LAST TOWN HAS SURRENDERED:
Ibid., No. 4059.

Chapter 41: Liberator
of the Balkan Christians

540 THEY TAKE NO MORE NOTICE OF ME:
Sbornik, I.R.I.O., LXI, 2, 35.
541 OH, HEAD, HEAD: Schuyler, II, 173.

541 MY RESIDENCE IS NOT PLEASANT: Ibid.
542 THE NEW VIZIER IS VERY ILL-DISPOSED: Ibid., 176.
542 DO NOT GO NEAR VORONEZH: Ibid.
543 WHAT HE HAS WRITTEN: Ibid., 177.
543 I AM IN GREAT FEAR: Ibid.
543 TWO . . . PASHAS HAVE BEEN STRANGLED: Ibid., 179.
545 TOO TERRIBLE, QUITE UNEXPECTED: Hatton, *Charles*, 313.
546 THE KING OF SWEDEN: Sumner, *Emergence*, 37.
546 HER "LION": Ibid., 38.
546 ENSURE THE SAFE TRANSPORT: Bengtsson, 411.
548 THIS UNCERTAIN ROAD: Schuyler, II, 187.
548 DO AS IS MOST CONVENIENT: Ibid.
548 WE HERE ARE OFTEN AT BANQUETS: Solovev, VIII, 374–5.
549 THE NEXT DAY ABOUT FOUR O'CLOCK: Schuyler, II, 189.
550 I CANNOT SUFFICIENTLY EXPRESS: Ibid., 190.
550 WE HAVE NO OTHER TSAR: Sumner, *Ottoman*, 45.
551 THE DESCENDANTS OF THE HEATHEN: Ibid., 46.

Chapter 42: Fifty Blows on the Pruth

553 YOU KNOW HOW THE TURKS: Schuyler, II, 192.
554 A MAN VERY SENSIBLE AND USEFUL: Ibid., 193.
555 IT IS DANGEROUS TO DECLARE: Sumner, *Ottoman*, 44.
556 A GREAT POLTROON: Bengtsson, 414.
561 I HAVE WON ENOUGH FOR THE PORTE: Ibid., 418.
562 THEY HAD THE BIRD IN THEIR HAND: Ibid., 419.
563 I WISH THE DEVIL WOULD TAKE HIM: Schuyler, II, 202.
564 FALL TO PIECES: *Sbornik, I.R.I.O.,* LXI, 74.
564 THIS WAR IS DISLIKED: Schuyler, II, 204.
565 NOT TO PLACE IN DESPAIR: Sumner, *Ottoman*, 42.

565 NOT WITHOUT GRIEF: Solovev, VIII, 389–90.
566 MY "GOOD FORTUNE": Schuyler, II, 212.

Chapter 43: The German Campaign and Frederick William

567 A VIOLENT LOOSENESS: *Sbornik, I.R.I.O.,* LXI, 12.
567 KATERINUSHKA, MY FRIEND: Schuyler, I, 442.
568 HIS GREAT TSARISH MAJESTY: Ibid., 216.
568 I WILL ANSWER YOUR LETTER: Ibid.
569 I FOUND HIS MAJESTY: Ibid., 230.
569 I AM VERY GLAD: Ibid.
570 THE TSAR DREAMED: *Sbornik, I.R.I.O.,* LXI, 167.
570 THE COMPANY WAS . . . SPLENDID: Ibid., 143–6.
572 I CONSIDER MYSELF VERY UNFORTUNATE: Schuyler, II, 226.
572 I THINK YOUR MAJESTY KNOWS: Ibid.
573 DID SUCH A WISE MAN: Staehlin, 143.
573 THE TSAR ARRIVED: Schuyler, II, 231.
574 I HAVE FOUND THE NEW KING: Ibid., 237.
577 IF MY FATHER HAD TREATED ME: Mitford, 47.
578 TELL THE KING: Schuyler, II, 235 n.
578 I HOPE YOUR MAJESTY RECOGNIZED: Ibid., 229.
579 FOR GOD'S SAKE: Ibid.
579 THE ELECTOR APPEARED VERY FAVORABLY INCLINED: Ibid., 236.
579 THANKS FOR THE MONEY: Ibid., 241.

Chapter 44: The Coast of Finland

581 THE MOTHER OF SWEDEN: Schuyler, II, 245.
585 MODERATE HEIGHT: Bridge, 77.
585 EVEN WHEN THE TSAR: Ibid., 79.
586 GET RID OF LYBECKER: Schuyler, II, 245.
589 FRIENDS AND COMPANIONS: Staehlin, 349.

589 A BRAVE AND FAITHFUL SERVANT:
Weber, I, 37.

Chapter 45: The Kalabalik

592 IF WE HAD SUCH A KING: Bain,
Charles, 198.
593 LIKE ORGAN PIPES: Hatton,
Charles, 356.
593 THE WHOLE HOST: Ibid., 357.
594 A VAST NUMBER OF THESE INFIDELS:
Ibid., 358.
594 HIS MAJESTY DID ASSURE EVERY ONE:
Ibid.
595 STANDING BETWIXT THREE TURKS:
Bengtsson, 428.
596 I CANNOT EXPRESS TO YOUR EX-
CELLENCY: Hatton, *Charles*, 363.
596 IN AS GOOD A HUMOR: Ibid., 364.
597 THESE HELLISH CONSPIRACIES: Ibid.
597 GOD HAS ABANDONED MY BROTHER
CHARLES: Bain, *Charles*, 218.
601 n. I AM NO HELMSMAN:
Bengtsson, 454.

Chapter 46:
Venice of the North

603 THE CROWD IS SO DENSE: Weber,
I, 318.
604 POLISH CASTLES: De Grunwald, 161.
604 DANIL'ICH IS MAKING MERRY:
Schuyler, II, 430.
607 WELCOME LEBLOND: Marsden, 61.
608 RAZE, SIRE, RAZE: Staehlin, 202.
608 SEND "SEEDS AND ROOTS": Sumner,
Emergence, 59.
608 FOUNTAINS AND WATER: Marsden, 65.
609 YOU ALONE, YOU RASCAL:
Staehlin, 312.
611 IN NO WAY RESEMBLES YOUR
MAJESTY'S: *Sbornik, I.R.I.O.*,
XLIX, 372.

Chapter 47:
An Ambassador Reports

613 I HAD HARDLY ARRIVED: Weber, I, 4.
614 I WENT, ACCORDING TO THE CUSTOM:
Ibid., 6.

614 THE TOASTS ARE BEGUN: Ibid., 26.
615 AN AMBASSADOR OF THE . . .
KALMUCKS: Ibid., 5.
615 A HANDSOME COACH: Ibid., 83.
615 A PASSAGE THROUGH HIS DOMINIONS:
Ibid., 20.
616 THE FESTIVAL OF EASTER: Ibid., 9.
617 A PRESENT OF TWO GIRLS: Schuyler,
II, 437 n.
617 SINCE ONE OF MY DAUGHTERS: Ibid.
617 A VERY LITTLE DWARF: Weber,
I, 285.
618 THE NUPTIALS OF THIS EXTRAORDI-
NARY COUPLE: Ibid., 89.
619 THE RUSSIAN WAY: Ibid., 31.
620 THE GROUND LIES FULL OF BLOOD:
Ibid., 328.
621 THE LIQUOR STANDS THERE:
Ibid., 179.
621 ON JUNE 9, 1715, THE TSAR WENT TO
KRONSTADT: Ibid., 92–5.

Chapter 48:
The Second Journey West

625 A TYRANNICAL BOOR: Schuyler,
II, 282.
626 THE DUKE HAS NO CUFFS ON:
Ibid., 287.
626 NOT EVEN A CROOKED PIN: Ibid., 288.
627 I AM TRULY ASTONISHED: Solovev,
IX, 44.
627 THE TSAR MUST GIVE ME . . .
SATISFACTION: Schuyler, II, 289.
627 A SHARP KNIFE: Ibid., 290.
629 LET ME KNOW WHEN YOU WILL BE
HERE: Solovev, IX, 53.
630 CHATTERING IN VAIN: Ibid.
631 THIRTY THOUSAND SWEDISH TROOPS:
Schuyler, II, 294.
631 SOLDIERS' BELLIES: Ibid.
631 I KNOW HIS WAY OF MAKING WAR:
Hatton, *Charles*, 427.
632 CRUSH THE TSAR IMMEDIATELY:
Schuyler, II, 294.
633 THE TSAR HAS GIVEN: Ibid., 297.
633 TOMFOOLERY!: Ibid.
633 WHAT I HAVE WRITTEN BEFORE:
Solovev, IX, 57.
634 I RECEIVED YESTERDAY: Ibid.
634 CHANGED JOY TO GRIEF: Schuyler,
II, 299.

Chapter 49: "The King Is a Mighty Man . . ."

636 MY CHILD . . . ONE DAY: Gooch, 26; Wolf, 618.
636 HE IS QUITE CRAZY ABOUT WOMEN: Gooch, 31.
638 IF, IN ESTABLISHING THE TSAR: Schuyler, II, 305.
639 I WISH TO SEND YOU LACE: Ibid., 307 n.
640 THIS LITTLE COURT: *Sbornik, I.R.I.O.*, XXXIV, 145, 150–3, 164, 174–5.
640 THE TSAR HAS A HEAD COOK: Ibid., 184.
641 I AM A SOLDIER: Cracraft, *Church Reform*, 6 n.
641 THANKS FOR THE HUNGARIAN WINE: Schuyler, II, 310.
642 A HAUGHTY AIR OF SUPERIORITY: Saint-Simon, V, 667.
642 FOR TWO OR THREE DAYS: Solovev, IX, 68.
643 LAST MONDAY THE LITTLE KING: Ibid.
643 THE KING IS A MIGHTY MAN: Schuyler, II, 312.

Chapter 50: A Visitor in Paris

648 HE WAS A VERY TALL MAN: Saint-Simon, V, 666.
649 WHAT HE DRINKS: Ibid., 667.
650 RECEIVED A GREAT VISIT TODAY: Schuyler, II, 312.
651 I CANNOT EXPRESS TO YOU THE DIGNITY: *Sbornik, I.R.I.O.*, XXXIV, xxv.
651 BLOUIN, GOVERNOR OF VERSAILLES: Saint-Simon, V, 671.
651 A PIGEON WITH THE WINGS: Marsden, 35.
652 SHE HAS MUCH MERIT: Staehlin, 57.
652 THE TSAR . . . SEEMS TO ME: Schuyler, II, 315 n.
652 SHE MUST HAVE BEEN GREATLY ASTONISHED: Saint-Simon, V, 672.
652 OLD AGE: Staehlin, 57.
652 I ENTERED THE GARDEN: Saint-Simon, V, 673.

653 ONE COULD NOT SHOW MORE SPIRIT: Ibid., 674.
653 THIS WAS A MONARCH: Ibid., 665, 675.
654 THE GOVERNMENT HAD NO INTENTION: Schuyler, II, 318.
655 YESTERDAY, I RECEIVED YOUR LETTER: Ibid., 316.
655 I CONGRATULATE YOU: Ibid.

Chapter 51: The Education of an Heir

657 THE TWO PRINCESSES: *Sbornik, I.R.I.O.*, XXXIV, 255.
657 AND SO IT CAME TO PASS IN RUSSIA: Weber, I, 193.
658 NONE OF YOU UNDERSTAND ANYTHING: Schuyler, II, 261.
659 THE PRINCE LACKS NEITHER: Ibid.
659 A TALL, HANDSOME PRINCE: *Sbornik, I.R.I.O.*, XXXIX, 43.
660 IF THE TSAR'S ARMY: Solovev, IX, 117.
663 SO NOW I KNOW: Schuyler, II, 266.
663 CAPABLE OF KEEPING A SECRET: Ibid.
664 MOST HONORABLE FATHER: Ibid., 267.
664 THE HOUSES OPPOSITE ARE HALF-BURNED: Ibid., 268.
665 WE WOULD NEVER: Solovev, IX, 125.
665 THE TSAR HAS BEEN WITH US: Schuyler, II, 237.
665 GOODBYE. I AM GOING: Ibid., 269.
665 THE TSAREVICH HAS NOT YET COME BACK: Ibid., 270.
666 I ASCRIBE HIS ILLNESS: Ibid.
667 THE TSAR BEING ARRIVED: Weber, I, 107.
667 GOD HAS SENT ME A NEW RECRUIT: Staehlin, 305.
667 A PIE WAS SERVED UP ON THE TABLE: Weber, I, 108.

Chapter 52: A Paternal Ultimatum

669 VERY SLOVENLY IN HIS DRESS: Bruce, 101.
670 I WOULD RATHER BE A GALLEY SLAVE: Manifesto, 141.
670 IT IS QUITE USELESS: Schuyler, II, 271.

670 GOD WILL FORGIVE YOU: Solovev, IX, 114.
671 DO NOT SAY: Ustryalov, VI, 54.
671 YOU ARE WISER THAN YOUR FATHER: Schuyler, II, 272.
671 AFTER YOUR RECOVERY [IN CARLSBAD]: Manifesto, 120.
672 A DECLARATION TO MY SON: Ibid., 97–102.
675 YOU WILL AT LAST BE ABLE TO REST: Ibid., 116.
675 YOU DO WELL NOT TO ASPIRE: Ibid., 118.
675 MOST CLEMENT LORD AND FATHER: Ibid., 102.
676 I HAVE SPOKEN TO YOUR FATHER: Ibid., 115.
676 MY LAST SICKNESS: Ibid., 103.
677 BECOME A MONK: Ibid., 116.
677 MOST CLEMENT LORD AND FATHER: Ibid., 105.
678 NOT EASY FOR A YOUNG MAN: Ustryalov, VI, 52.
678 PETER'S LETTER: Manifesto, 107–8.
679 I AM GOING TO LOOK: Ibid., 114.
679 YOU WILL DO BETTER: Ustryalov, VI, 53.
680 IT IS NECESSARY TO OBEY HIM: Ibid., 54.
680 REMEMBER, IF YOUR FATHER SENDS SOMEBODY: Manifesto, 126.

Chapter 53: Flight of the Tsarevich

681 I AM WEAK: Ustryalov, VI, 64–69.
682 PEOPLE ARE BEGINNING TO SAY: Manifesto, 135.
683 NO ONE UP TO THIS TIME: Schuyler, II, 329.
685 AS FAR AS TRENTO: Ustryalov, VI, 87.
685 OUR LITTLE PAGE: Ibid., 383.
687 YOUR DISOBEDIENCE AND THE CONTEMPT: Manifesto, 108.
688 AND WHEN HE IS HERE: Ustryalov, VI, 116.
688 I WILL GO TO MY FATHER: Ibid., 117.
689 YOU ASK FOR PARDON: Solovev, IX, 165–6.
689 PERHAPS HE MAY DOUBT: Ibid., 166.
690 DO NOT TROUBLE YOURSELF: Ustryalov, VI, 422–3.
690 DO ALL YOU CAN: Ibid., 135.

690 THANK GOD, ALL IS WELL: Ibid., 437.
691 THE ARRIVAL OF THE TSAREVICH: Sbornik, I.R.I.O., XXXIV, 304.
691 THAT JUDAS OF A PETER: Solovev, IX, 168.
691 A COFFIN INSTEAD OF A WEDDING: Ibid.

Chapter 54: The Future on Trial

692 I CONFESS: Manifesto, 110.
694 SHE CARRIED [MY] LETTERS: Ibid., 117.
695 BUT ONE HEAD TO LOSE: Weber, I, 204.
695 MOST GRACIOUS SOVEREIGN: Graham, 269.
696 AM I THEN THE ONLY ONE: Schuyler, II, 340.
698 IF A FIRE MEETS WITH STRAW: Weber, I, 220.
699 NOW COMES THE QUESTION: Schuyler, II, 341.
699 GENTLEMEN MOST EXCELLENT SENATORS: Manifesto, 136.
700 PROCEEDED FROM THE SAME PERSONS: Ibid., 139.
700 NOW, YOU SEE HOW GOD ACTS: Ibid., 143.
701 BY THESE LETTERS, WE HAVE KNOWN: Relation fidèle, 5.
701 I BELIEVED MY FATHER'S DEATH: Manifesto, 150.
702 YOU WOULD HAVE DECLARED FOR THE REBELS: Ibid., 154.
702 IF THIS NEWS HAD BEEN TRUE: Ibid.
703 BY POWERFUL EXHORTATIONS TO FORCE: Ibid., 158.
703 EVERYONE THAT CURSETH HIS FATHER: Ibid., 172.
704 WITHOUT FLATTERING US: Ibid., 165.
704 THOUGH THEY WERE MUCH GRIEVED: Ibid., 169.
704 I WISH FOR MY FATHER'S DEATH: Ibid., 189.
704 WITH AFFLICTED HEARTS: Ibid., 200.
704 THE NEXT DAY BEING THURSDAY: Weber, I, 228.
705 THE SECULAR COURT: Relation fidèle, 8.
707 BY ELEVEN A.M.: Solovev, IX, 188.

707 THE DAY WAS CLEAR AND BRIGHT:
Schuyler, II, 345 n.
707 THE DEATH OF THE PRINCE:
Sbornik, I.R.I.O., XXXIV, 354.
708 THERE WAS GREAT MERRYMAKING:
Waliszewski, 541.

Chapter 55:
Charles' Last Offensive

712 THIS DOES NOT MEAN: Hatton,
Charles, 375.
712 IN THE WHOLE OF SWEDEN: Bain,
Charles, 305.
713 TWENTY TIMES AS MUCH AS . . .
METTERNICH: Ibid., 278.
716 A SKIFF CARRYING THE MAST:
Schuyler, II, 250.
719 THERE IS ONE LITTLE DIFFICULTY:
Ibid., 406.
720 FOOLHARDY ACTIONS: Sumner,
Emergence, 103.
720 FORTY YEARS OF WAR: Hatton,
Charles, 475.
721 YOUR FOOD IS SO GOOD: Ibid., 502.
721 IT IS NOT A FIT PLACE: Bain,
Charles, 298.
721 DON'T BE FRIGHTENED:
Bengtsson, 476.
721 A STONE: Hatton, *Charles,* 503.
722 THE KING IS SHOT: Ibid.
722 IMMEDIATELY EVERYTHING BECAME
SO QUIET: Ibid., 497.
722 THIS NEARLY UNBEARABLE SORROW:
Ibid., 520.
722 WE SHALL MISS HIM: Ibid., 521.

Chapter 56: King
George Enters the Baltic

724 MY DEAR CHARLES: Staehlin, 248.
725 DOES THE KING STILL LIVE?:
Schuyler, II, 408.
725 YOU BLOODTHIRSTY SWEDES:
Ibid., 409.
727 MY DEAR DUKE: Plumb, 40.
727 n. ENGLAND WOULD AS SOON HAVE A
TURK: Basil Williams, 151.
728 THE ELEPHANT AND CASTLE:
Ibid., 152 n.
728 ALTHOUGH THE ENGLISH KING:
Solovev, IX, 40.

729 IN EVERY WAY EQUAL: Chance, 92.
729 SO THAT THE TSAR SHOULD NOT
GROW: Sumner, *Emergence,* 105.
730 n. WOULD TO GOD: Schuyler, II, 418.
731 WHAT SERVICES HAS ENGLAND
RENDERED: Ibid., 413.
732 UNUSUAL AND INSOLENT: Solovev,
IX, 270.

Chapter 57: Victory

735 SIR JOHN NORRIS: Chance, 361.
736 OUR FORCE UNDER THE COMMAND:
Solovev, IX, 273.
739 I KNOW MY INTEREST: Sumner,
Emergence, 106.
740 ALL SCHOLARS IN ARTS: Schuyler,
II, 424.
740 REJOICE AND THANK GOD: Grey, 379.
741 BY YOUR TIRELESS LABORS: Solovev,
IX, 321.
742 BY OUR DEEDS IN WAR: Grey, 380.
742 n. GREAT LORD: Weber, I, 257–63.
742 A TRUE CUP OF GRIEF: Schuyler,
II, 426.

Chapter 58: In the
Service of the State

747 YOUR DISPARAGEMENT OF MY
FATHER'S ACHIEVEMENTS:
Kluchevsky, 52.
748 THE PERMANENT LAWS: Gasiorowska,
21.
749 NO RESOLUTION SHALL BE TAKEN:
Kluchevsky, 184.
749 UP TO NOW, GOD KNOWS: Ibid., 199.
749 I CAN'T MANAGE WITH MY LEFT
HAND: Sumner, *Emergence,* 112.
749 WE APPOINT THE GOVERNING
SENATE: Kluchevsky, 200.
750 MONEY IS THE ARTERY: Ibid., 157.
750 LOSS OF TIME IS LIKE DEATH:
Schuyler, II, 349.
750 WHAT HAS BEEN DONE:
Kluchevsky, 201.
751 YOU HAVE NOTHING ELSE TO DO:
Ibid.
751 YOU HAVE ACTED IN A CONTEMPTIBLE
WAY: Ibid., 218.
751 SIT "IN THE SAME PLACE AS THE
SENATE": Ibid., 219.
751 WITHOUT SHOUTING: Ibid., 220.

752 I WILL ANSWER FOR IT BEFORE GOD: Staehlin, 325.
753 HERE IS MY EYE: Kluchevsky, 221.
754 THEIR MECHANISM IS LIKE THAT OF WATCHES: Sumner, *Emergence*, 114.
754 APPREHENSIVE OF A TROUBLESOME INQUIRY: Weber, I, 267.
754 HARDLY ANY FOREIGN OFFICE: Ibid., 46.
755 NO UNNECESSARY TALKING: Schuyler, II, 352.
755 OPEN MY LARGEST VEIN: Solovev, IX, 464.
756 AS IF A SERVANT: Sumner, *Emergence*, 122.
757 SWARMS OF THESE YOUNG PLANTS: Weber, I, 180.
758 HE JUMPED INTO THE LAKE: Kluchevsky, 95.
758 HOW IS IT, FEDOR MATVEEVICH: Ibid., 97.
760 NEPLYUEV'S STORY: Solovev, IX, 552.
762 I CAN TURN DICE: Sumner, *Emergence*, 113.
762 n. NOBLEMAN VLADIMIR ULYANOV: Fischer, 19.
763 ANY SUBJECT WHO IS A TRUE CHRISTIAN: Solovev, VIII, 491.
765 FATHER, LET US BEAT THEM: Schuyler, II, 360.
767 MENSHIKOV WILL ALWAYS BE MENSHIKOV: Staehlin, 83.
768 WHAT DOES THIS MEAN?: Bain, *Pupils*, 46.
768 MENSHIKOV WAS CONCEIVED IN INIQUITY: Kluchevsky, 244.
769 THE GOOD PRINCE MENSHIKOV: *Sbornik, I.R.I.O.*, XV, 200.
769 HAS YOUR MAJESTY REFLECTED?: Staehlin, 159.
769 ONLY THE BRANCHES: Kluchevsky, 245.
769 THE TSAR PULLS UPHILL: Ibid., 95.

Chapter 59:
Commerce by Decree

770 THEY ARE MAKING CLOTH: Schuyler, II, 375.
771 IF THEY DO NOT WISH TO DO THIS: Kluchevsky, 145.
771 OUR RUSSIAN STATE ABOUNDS: Solovev, VIII, 474.
772 HOARDING OF MONEY IS FORBIDDEN: Kluchevsky, 146.
773 YOU KNOW YOURSELVES: Sumner, *Emergence*, 144.
773 OUR PEOPLE ARE LIKE CHILDREN: Ibid.
774 BETWEEN OURSELVES: Schuyler, II, 372.
774 EVENTUALLY, MOLDY AND ROTTEN: Kluchevsky, 147.
774 RED AND PLEASANT: Lebrun, in Weber, II, 421.
775 THE GREAT SECRET: *Sbornik, I.R.I.O.*, XXXIX, 137.
777 IT IS EASY TO CONCEIVE: Staehlin, 106.
777 COME TO COURT TOMORROW: Ibid., 108.
778 IN THREE HOURS: Ibid., 132.
779 GOD MADE THE RIVERS: Perry, 7.
779 I AM CREDIBLY INFORMED: Weber, I, 290.
780 WITHOUT UNDULY BURDENING: Florinsky, I, 358.

Chapter 60:
Supreme Under God

784 IT IS OUR BELIEF: Staehlin, 173.
784 LET THEM BELIEVE WHAT THEY LIKE: Sumner, *Emergence*, 127.
785 THERE ARE ENOUGH OF THEM THERE: Schuyler, II, 401.
785 ALL JESUITS: Weber, I, 268.
786 NEITHER IS IT PROBABLE: Ibid., 282.
786 THOUGH HE CARRIED ON: Ibid., 235.
787 HERE IS THE SOURCE: Staehlin, 124.
788 HALE AND LAZY BEGGARS: Sumner, *Emergence*, 133.
788 IN ORDER TO ENABLE THE MONKS: Schuyler, II, 145.
790 WHERE SHALL I GO?: Cracraft, *Church Reform*, 1; Grey, 486.
790 WRITING WITH TEARS: Grey, 398.
791 ALL THE MONKS AVOID US: Cracraft, "Prokopovich," 90.
791 AN ARDENT CONCERN: Ibid., 92.
791 THE SUPREME AUTHORITY: Ibid., 93.
792 WHEN THE LIGHT OF LEARNING: Ibid., 90.

792 FROM COLLEGIATE GOVERNMENT IN
THE CHURCH: Ibid., 102.
793 TO DEFEND UNSPARINGLY: Pipes, 241.
794 INCOMPARABLY MORE HUMANE:
Ibid., 245.

Chapter 61:
The Emperor in St. Petersburg

795 MORE AFFAIRS IN A MORNING:
Bell, 562.
796 I DON'T WANT THEM TO OBSERVE ME:
Staehlin, 147.
796 DINE WITH THEIR WIVES: Bell, 566.
796 HIS CANE OFTEN DANCED:
Staehlin, 275.
797 OBLIGED TO WAIT: Ibid., 233.
797 A POOR YOUNG FELLOW: Schuyler,
II, 434.
797 BRAVO, MY FRIENDS: Staehlin, 239.
798 TO PUNISH THE GREAT AND RICH:
De Grunwald, 174.
798 TO ASSASSINATE YOU: Staehlin, 257.
798 I HAVE PINNED A LIVING ONE:
Ibid., 87.
799 A PUNISHMENT FOR NEGLIGENCE:
Ibid., 113.
799 LEARN TO BE MORE QUIET: Ibid., 221.
799 THAT CURSED BOY: Ibid., 268.
800 I AM SENSIBLE: Ibid., 266.
800 THUS CAN I DESTROY: Schuyler,
II, 503.
800 WELL, LISETTE: Staehlin, 308.
801 ONE CAN HARDLY PUT ONE'S NOSE:
Sbornik, I.R.I.O., LXI, 480.
801 THE DIVERSION OF . . . THE CATAT:
Ibid., 358.
801 IN WINTER: Perry, 263.
802 SHALL A MAN WHO HAS SPENT HIS
YOUTH: Staehlin, 180.
802 WHAT DO YOU DO AT HOME?: M. S.
Anderson, Peter, 157.
803 HUNT, GENTLEMEN: Staehlin, 115.
803 I HAVE EARNED THEM: Ibid., 24.
804 SIRE, I DESIRE YOUR PRESENCE:
Schuyler, II, 436.
805 WHAT IS THE MATTER?: Staehlin, 304.
806 PRINCESS ANNE . . . IS A BRUNETTE:
Schuyler, II, 438.
806 I DO NOT BELIEVE THERE IS . . . IN
EUROPE A PRINCESS: Sbornik,
I.R.I.O., XV, 239–40.

806 SHE IS A BEAUTY: Ibid.
807 AS I KNOW FROM THE LETTERS:
Schuyler, II, 439.
807 HE OFTEN REQUIRED AN ACCOUNT:
Staehlin, 295.
808 I HAD THE LUCK: Schuyler, II, 446.
808 THE ASSEMBLY REGULATIONS:
Weber, I, 186–8.
810 ALL THE LADIES HERE USE ROUGE:
Schuyler, II, 444.
811 MY HARLOTS DO NOT COST ME MUCH:
Ibid., 323.
811 PERFECT LIBERTY: Weber, I, 277.
811 IS IT POSSIBLE?: Staehlin, 325.
812 I FORBID HER: Ibid., 328.
812 ONE OF THE MOST AGREEABLE:
De Grunwald, 198.
812 I CANNOT VIOLATE THE LAWS:
Staehlin, 279.
813 THE ACTORS AND ACTRESSES: Weber,
I, 188.
814 THE AMBASSADOR IS ACCREDITED TO
ME: Staehlin, 94.
815 IT IS LIKELY THE PRIESTS: Weber,
I, 112.
815 BITE STRANGERS: Ibid., 27.
816 WHO KNOWS?: Staehlin, 141.
816 WE ARE VERY DELIGHTED:
Dmytryshyn, 13.
817 USUALLY TWO KINDS: Ibid., 14.
817 I HAVE TO HARVEST: Sumner,
Emergence, 181.

Chapter 62:
Along the Caspian

819 OUR EMPEROR DOES NOT TRADE:
Schuyler, II, 458.
819 TO THE ILLUSTRIOUS KING: Sumner,
Emergence, 152.
820 n. A NUMBER OF SWEDISH GIRLS:
Weber, I, 223.
821 A PRINCE OF FORTY YEARS OF AGE:
Ibid., 92.
822 THE "TRUE STATE OF THE PERSIAN
EMPIRE": Weber, I, 100.
822 THERE IS NOW SUCH A HEAD:
Schuyler, II, 464.
823 THE AFFAIR OF DAUD BEK: Solovev,
IX, 374.
825 CUTTING OPEN THEIR BREASTS:
Bruce, 277.

825 WHEN THEY ARE TOGETHER:
Schuyler, II, 472.
825 CUSHIONS OF CRIMSON VELVET:
Bruce, 273.
825 GRATIFY THEIR CURIOSITY . . . MOST
LOVELY CREATURES: Ibid., 271,
273–4.
825 THE GOLDEN KEYS: Bell, 553.
825 THUS, IN THESE REGIONS: Solovev,
IX, 379.
826 I DID IT: *Sbornik, I.R.I.O.,*
XLIX, 287.

Chapter 63: Twilight

828 THE PROCESSION CONSISTED OF SIXTY
SLEDGES: *Sbornik, I.R.I.O.,*
III, 342–3.
829 THIS IS THE IMAGE OF WAR: Schuyler,
II, 485.
829 THE EMPEROR IS SO OCCUPIED:
Ibid., 486.
831 TO PUT THE TSARITSA ENTIRELY IN
OUR INTEREST: *Sbornik, I.R.I.O.,*
XL, 304.
831 I KNOW HIM AND ESTEEM HIM
HIGHLY: Schuyler, II, 495.
831 A NEW, WITTY AND VIVACIOUS
MISTRESS: Ibid., 496.
831 THERE IS NOTHING BUT WHAT IS
AGREEABLE: *Sbornik, I.R.I.O.,*
XLIX, 324.
834 PRAISE GOD, ALL IS MERRY: Solovev,
VIII, 519.
834 THIS IS THE COUNTRY HOUSE:
Staehlin, 208.
835 THUS CHILDREN OR CHILDREN'S
CHILDREN: Bain, *Pupils,* 59.
835 OUR BEST BELOVED SPOUSE:
Grey, 431.
836 IT IS OUR INTENTION: Bain,
Pupils, 62.
837 RECOGNIZED AS REGENT: De
Grunwald, 210.
838 ONE OF THE BEST-MADE . . . MEN:
Ibid., 211.
839 IT IS TIME . . . TO GO TO BED: *Sbornik,
I.R.I.O.,* III, 391.
840 THEY HARDLY SPEAK TO EACH OTHER:
Ibid., 394.
840 A LONG AND AMPLE GENUFLECTION:
Ibid., 396.

841 NO EXPRESSIONS ARE STRONG
ENOUGH: Schuyler, II, 488.
841 HIS MAJESTY HAS FOR SOME TIME:
Sbornik, I.R.I.O., LXI, 486.
845 LORD, I BELIEVE: Bain, *Pupils,* 68.
845 GIVE ALL TO: Pares, 225.
845 RECEIVE . . . THIS GREAT SOUL:
Sbornik, I.R.I.O., III, 399.

Epilogue

846 MY GOD! IS IT POSSIBLE?:
Staehlin, 365.
847 WHAT I HAVE DONE, YOUR EX-
CELLENCY: Bain, *Pupils,* 76.
847 OUR FATHER IS DEAD: *Sbornik,
I.R.I.O.,* III, 400, also LII, 430.
847 HER MAJESTY BE PROCLAIMED
AUTOCRAT: Bain, *Pupils,* 77.
848 O MEN OF RUSSIA: Cracraft, *Church
Reform,* 304.
848 TO LIGHTEN THE HEAVY BURDEN:
Bain, *Pupils,* 85.
849 THE PEASANTS AND THE ARMY:
Pares, 230.
849 WATER UP TO HER KNEES: *Sbornik,
I.R.I.O.,* III, 454.
850 I AM RUSSIAN, REMEMBER: Bain,
Pupils, 125.
850 MY DEAR ANDREI IVANOVICH:
Ibid., 139.
851 SO FEARED OR SO OBEYED: *Sbornik,
I.R.I.O.,* III, 478.
851 WE SHALL SEE: Ibid., 491.
851 YOU SEE, I AM AT LAST LEARNING:
Ibid., 490.
851 WHAT AM I TO DO IN A PLACE:
Bain, *Pupils,* 148.
853 HIS SPIRIT LIVES IN OUR SOULS:
Kluchevsky, 248.
853 THIS MONARCH: Ibid., 253.
853 A GOD-LIKE MAN: Ibid., 248; De
Grunwald, 215.
853 WAS IT NOT GOD: Kluchevsky, 249.
854 WE BEGAN TO BE CITIZENS OF THE
WORLD: Ibid.
854 THE MOST EXTRAORDINARY PHE-
NOMENON: Florinsky, I, 428.
855 EVERYONE HAS THE HIGHEST AND
BEST OPINION: Staehlin, 291.
855 ETERNAL TOILER: De Grunwald, 179.
855 AN AGE OF GOLD: Ibid.

Index

Academy of Science of France:
Peter elected member, 648, 816
Academy of Science of Russia:
building planned by Peter, 841
founding, 816–17
library, 815
museum, 814
Adrian, Patriarch:
beard spared, 234
death (1700), 788
election (1690), 110
and Peter, 120–1, 147
and torture of Streltsy (1698), 255
Adrianople, Treaty of (1713), 564, 598
Affray of 1713 (Kalabalik), 592–6
consequences, 597
Afrosina, mistress of Tsarevich Alexis,
666, 680, 682, 685, 688–9, 690–1,
694, 699, 700–701
Ahmed III, Sultan, 537–8, 542
Aland Islands, 589
peace negotiations at (1718), 716–19,
726, 732
Alexis, Tsarevich, 375, 517, 656–710
and Afrosina, 666, 680, 682, 685,
688–9, 690–1, 694, 699, 700–701
arrest and trial (1718), 702–704
birth (1690), 76, 109–10, 657
in care of Natalya Alexeevna, 241,
658
and Charles VI, 681–90 *passim*
and Charlotte of Wolfenbüttel, 520–1,
548–50, 568, 662–3, 664, 665–6

childhood and youth, 657–60
children, 665, 666; *see also* Peter II,
Emperor
and Church, 661, 663–4
death (1718), 704–707
disinheritance (1718), 692–3
drinking and drunkenness, 661, 664,
665, 666, 670
education, 658–9, 660
as fugitive from Russia (1716–18),
679–90
funeral, 708
and Menshikov, 659, 679
personality and characteristics, 659
and Peter, 656–710
correspondence, 672–9 *passim*, 687
physical appearance, 270
Alexis (Mikhailovich), Tsar:
achievements compared to Peter's,
747–8
conflict with Archpriest Nikon, 59–60
death (1676), 25
exalted status, 9–10
lifestyle, 10–12
piety, 55
Altranstadt, Treaty of (1706), 408, 410,
412
repudiated by Augustus (1709), 519
Amsterdam:
description, 183–4
Peter's visits:
(1697–8), 184–8, 217
(1716–17), 633–4
amusements, *see* entertainments

Anne (Petrovna), Duchess of Holstein-
  Gottorp, 377, 806–807
  death (1728), 833, 850
  marriage to Charles Frederick, 832–3,
    849
  son (Peter III) born (1828), 833, 850
Anne (Ivanovna), Empress:
  later life, 521 n.
  marriage arranged, 521
  and Praskovaya, 807–808
  reign (1730–40), 852
Apraxin, (General-Admiral) Fedor
    Matveevich, 386, 585
  in Amsterdam (1697), 186
  Baltic campaigns (1719–21), 732–4,
    736, 739
  corruption charges (1715), 763–5, 768
  Finnish naval campaigns (1713–14),
    585–90
  Battle of Hangö (1714), 386, 587–8
  Order of St. Andrew, 758
  and Peter, 585–6
  at Vyborg (1710), 524–5
Apraxin, (Senator) Peter:
  arrested in Tsarevich conspiracy, 695
  exonerated, 697
Archangel:
  description, 124–5
  Peter's summer visits (1893–4), 124–7,
    129–32
architecture:
  Amsterdam, 183–4
  ecclesiastical, 58, 204
  France (Versailles), 158–60
  London, 204
  Moscow, 4–8, 82–3
  St. Petersburg, 360, 362, 602–12,
    834–5
Army of Russia, see Russia: army
Army of Sweden, see Sweden: army
Arseneeva, Darya, 373
  and Menshikov, 373, 374–5
assemblies (evening parties), 808–10
Assumption Cathedral (Uspensky Sobor),
  Moscow, 6–7
Astrachan uprising (1705), 393–4
Augustus II, King of Poland, 217, 227,
    831
  appearance and character, 230–1
  and Charles XII, 346–7, 400, 407–409,
    420
  as contender for Polish throne, 174,
    296

deposed (1704), 400
  effect on Peter, 419
  election as King of Poland, 175,
    229–30
  and Patkul, 295–7
  and Peter, 230 1, 299, 300, 344 5,
    519–20, 550, 831
  reinstated as King (1709), 519
  confirmed by Sweden (1720), 731
Avvakum, Archpriest, 55, 62–4
  martyrdom, 63
  awards of merit, 243, 759–60, 802
  after Hangö, 589
  Order of St. Andrew, 243
  Order of St. Catherine, 570–1, 835
  after Poltava, 516, 522
  see also meritocracy; Peter the Great:
    trappings of office
Azov:
  campaign and siege:
    (1695), 136–42
    (1696), 144–7; consequences, 148;
      victory celebration, 147–8
  ceded to Russia (1699), 282, 285
  description, 139
  as Russian fortress, 286
  surrendered to Turks (1712), 563

Baku, 825–6
Balk, Matrena, 804
  bribery scandal, 838–40
  execution, 840
Balkan Christians:
  Peter and Russians as liberators of,
    551, 565
Baltadji Mehemet Pasha, Grand Vizier,
  547, 554, 556, 559–63
Baltic Sea:
  description, 288, 290
  English fleet in (1715–20), 729, 731–3,
    735–7
  (1721), 739
  Russian naval power in, 357–8, 581–90,
    720–2, 732–7, 739
  see also Great Northern War: Baltic
    phase
banquets, see entertainments
Bashkirs:
  revolt (1708), 394–5
Bastille, the, Paris, 646–7
bathing, 619–20
batog (instrument of torture), 250

battles:
Azov (1696), 144–8
Fraustadt (1706), 405
Golovchin (1708), 442–4
Hangö (1714), 587–8
Kalisz (1706), 409
Klissow (1702), 348
Lesnaya (1708), 451–3
Molyatychy (1708), 449
Narva (1700), 330–7
Poltava (1709), 494–510
Pruth (1711), 557–62
Baturin, 462, 463–5
destruction of, 464–5
beards in Russia:
bans against, 234–6, 785
beer, 621
beggars, 271, 391
bells of Moscow, 7–8
Bender:
"the Tumult" at (1713), 592–6
Berezina River:
Swedish army crossing (1708), 440,
442
Bering, Vitus, 819
Bering Strait, 819 *n.*
Blue Prussians (Giants of Potsdam),
576–7
Bono Tower, Moscow, 7
books, printing, and libraries, 187, 391–2,
429, 815
Bourgeois, Nicholas, 616
boyars, 12
changing role, 386, 748–9
at Lefort's funeral, 279–80
and precedence system, 28–9
resistance to Sophia and Golitsyn,
90, 92
and Streltsy, 40–1
and Western dress, 237–9
Brancovo, Constantine, Hospodar of
Walachia, 552, 555
defection to Turks, 555–6
execution (1714), 563
Brandt, Karsten, 73–5
bribery, *see* corruption in government
Bruce, (General) James, 717–19
Bruce, (Captain) Peter, 825
Brunswick-Wolfenbüttel, Charlotte, *see*
Charlotte, Princess of Wolfenbüttel
Bulavin, Kondraty, 395–6
Burnet, Gilbert, Bishop of Salisbury, 210
Buturlin, (General/Vice-Admiral) Ivan:

and Menshikov, 850
at Narva, 333
as naval officer, 129, 132
as the "Polish King" in Jolly Company,
119
in Sophia's overthrow, 100
in war games, 122, 132

calendar reform, 241–2
canals in Russia, 607–608, 778–80
Cantemir, Demetrius, 552–3, 562
Carlowitz, (General) George von, 297–8
death, 299
Carlowitz, Treaty of (1699), 282–3, 540
Carmarthen, Peregrine Osborne, Marquis
of, 208, 212, 213, 215–16
Casimir, Frederick, Duke of Courland,
172
Caspian Sea, 824–7
Castle St. Elmo, Naples:
Tsarevich Alexis takes refuge in
(1717), 658–9
Cathedral of the Annunciation,
Moscow, 7
Cathedral of the Archangel Michael,
Moscow, 7
Cathedral of St. Peter and St. Paul, St.
Petersburg, 570
Catherine (Ivanovna), Princess:
marriage to Duke of Mecklenburg,
625–7
and Praskovaya, 807–808
Catherine I, Empress, 371–82
accession to throne (1725), 846–8
in battle zone, 557
character, *see* Catherine I: personality
and characteristics
compassion for soldiers, 826
coronation (1724), 835–7
court, 804–805
death (1727), 849
designated Peter's heir, 834–7
and Menshikov, 367, 372–3, 769,
848–9
origins, 371–2
personality and characteristics, 375–8
and Peter, 373–82, 549, 570–1, 605–
606, 834–5
and (his) anger, 800
children, 374, 377, 522, 588, 625,
633–4, 805–807; list, 377 *n.*
and (his) convulsions, 136, 376, 841

Catherine I, Empress (*continued*)
  correspondence, 378–82, 655–6
  at (his) deathbed, 844–5
  marriage: 1st (1707), 375, 429; 2nd
    (1712), 375, 570–1
  meeting, 373
  and Mons affair, 840, 844
  travel together, 377, 567, 625, 632,
    634, 824
  physical appearance, 373–4, 378
  reign (1725–7), 848–9
  taken captive by Sheremetev (1702),
    349–50, 372
Catholic Church, *see* Roman Catholic
  Church
Caucasus:
  mountains, 822 *n.*
  Russian claims in, 818–27 *passim*
ceremonies, *see* entertainments; rituals
  and ceremonies
Charles VI, Holy Roman Emperor:
  and Tsarevich Alexis, 681–90 *passim*
Charles XI, King of Sweden, 83
  death (1697), 231, 313
Charles XII, King of Sweden:
  and Augustus II, 346–7, 400, 407–409,
    420
  childhood, 312–13
  coronation, 314
  in danger:
    in battle: at Dvina River, 346; at
      Frederiksten, 720–2; at Narva,
      334; at Perevoluchna, 511–12; at
      Poltava, 500, 505; at Stralsund,
      601 *n.*
    as youth, 315–18
    see also Charles XII: injuries
  death, 719–22
    political consequences, 729
  and Devlet Gerey, 590
  and drinking, 318
  at Bender (1713), 595
  education, 313, 315
  and Frederick IV, King of Denmark,
    317–18
  injuries, 399, 483–5; *see also* Charles
    XII: in danger
  invincibility ascribed to, 337–8, 416,
    484–5
  and Kalabalik (1713), 592–6
    consequences, 597
  lifestyle, 416, 417
  and Marlborough, 413–15
  and Mazeppa, 454, 461, 462–6, 514–15
  as military leader, 306, 319, 416–17
  morality, 318, 319, 346, 475
  at Narva (1700), 330, 334
  effect of battle, 337–8
  Norwegian campaigns (1716, 1718),
    628–9, 720–2
  at Perevoluchna (1709), escape, 511–
    12
  personality and characteristics, 313–19,
    415–18, 422
  and Peter:
    at Charles's death, 724
    at Grodno (1708), 433
    after Poltava (1709), 508
  physical appearance:
    (1700), 321
    (1707), 415–16
  in Poland:
    (1702–1706), 399–401
    (1707–1708), 430–5
  at Poltava, 490–1, 494, 500, 505
  return to Sweden (1714), 598–601
  Russian campaign, 431–515
  in Saxony (1706–1708), 408, 413, 424,
    425–6
  and Tatars, 476–7
  in Turkey, 515, 544–7, 560–3
    departure from (1714), 598–9
    Kalabalik, the, 591–7
  war games, 315–16
  and women, 316–17, 347–8, 417–18
Charles Frederick, Duke of Holstein-
  Gottorp:
  and Charles XII's death, 722
  departure from Russia (1728), 850
  marriage to Princess Anne (1725),
    832–3, 849
  in Russia, 738–9, 832
  son (Peter III) born (1828), 833
  and succession to Swedish throne,
    724–5
Charles-Leopold, Duke of Mecklenburg,
  see Mecklenburg, Karl Leopold,
  Duke of
Charlotte, Princess of Wolfenbüttel:
  and (Tsarevich) Alexis, 520–1, 548–50,
    568, 662–6
  birth of daughter Natalya (1714), 665
  birth of son Peter (1715), 666
  death (1715), 667
Cherkassky, (Prince) Alexander Bekovich,
  821

Cherkassky, (Prince) Michael:
beard spared, 234
and Golitsyn, 90–1
in Peter's service, 117
as Prefect of Moscow, 275
and Streltsy revolt (1682), 43
China:
Russian boundary with, 84–5 *n.*
Russian trade with, 570, 818–19
Church, *see* Balkan Christians; Orthodox
Church; Peter I, the Great, Tsar:
and the Church; Roman Catholic
Church
Churchill, John, *see* Marlborough, John
Churchill, Duke of
clothing, *see* dress
coinage, *see* currency reform
college system of administration, 753–6
conscription, *see* recruitment
Constantinople:
description, 532
Treaty of (1699), 285–6
Conti, François Louis de Bourbon,
Prince de, 175, 229
corruption in government, 762–9
Cossacks, 13, 15, 458–9
in Azov campaigns (1695–6), 141,
144–5, 146
at Perevoluchna (1709), 479–80
revolt (1707–1708), 395–6
and Swedish army, 463–6, 512–13, 514
treaty with Sweden (1709), 475
Zaporozhsky, 459, 474–5
Courland, Duchy of:
Peter's visit (1697), 172–3
crime:
London, 204
Moscow, 5, 271–2
punishments for, 251–3, 272
Crimea:
first Russian campaign to (1687),
86–7
second Russian campaign to (1689),
87–9
Crimean Tatars, *see* Tatars
Cross, Laetitia, 208
Cruys, (Vice-Admiral) Cornelius, 201,
217, 275, 359–60
currency reform, 213, 242, 772–3

decorations and awards of merit, *see*
awards of merit

Demidov, Nikita, 146, 760, 771–2
Denmark:
alliance with Russia against Sweden:
(1709), 519
(1716), 629
attacked by Sweden (1716), 628–9
in Great Northern War, 299, 318,
319–20, 321–2
defeat, 322
naval fleet, 572, 578
opposition to Sweden (1698), 295–6
peace treaty with Sweden (1720), 731
treaty with Poland against Sweden
(1699), 296
dentchiks (orderlies), 797
Derbent, 824–6
Devier, (General) Anthony, 812, 849–50
Devlet Gerey, Khan of the Crimea, 546,
556
and Charles XII, 590
and Treaty of Constantinople (1699),
286
Devlet Kisden, Mirza, 821
divorce, 33
Dnieper River:
Charles XII's escape across (1709),
511–12
crossed by Swedish army (1708),
445–6
Dolgoruky, (Prince) Gregory, 627
Dolgoruky, (Prince) Jacob, 166–7, 169,
751–2, 805–806
(his) assessment of Peter's achievements, 747–8
death (1720), 802
and Menshikov, 764
pleads for brother Vasily (1718), 697
Dolgoruky, (Prince) Michael, 45
Dolgoruky, (Prince) Vasily:
as ambassador to Denmark, 625, 728
exiled to Kazan (1718), 697
and Tsarevich Alexis conspiracy, 694
arrest, 695
Dolgoruky, (Prince) Yury, 39, 395–6
Don Cossacks, *see* Cossacks
Donskoy Monastery, 95
Dorpat:
birthplace of Catherine I, 371
Russian naval victory near (1702),
348–9
Russian victory at (1704), 397–8
Swedish army winter quarters at, 345
in zone of devastation (1708), 437

Dosithius, Bishop of Rostov, 695–7
Dresden:
  occupied by Sweden (1706), 408
  Peter's visit (1698), 217–18
dress:
  of boyars, 237–9
  of Russian peasants, 16
  of Russian women, 31
  Western, 237–9, 429, 810
drinking and drunkenness, 118–19, 172–3,
  830
  at assemblies, 809
  see also Alexis, Tsarevich: drinking
    and drunkenness; Charles XII:
    and drinking; Jolly Company,
    the; Peter I, the Great: drinking
    and drunkenness
Drunken Synod (Mock Synod), 119–21,
  268, 269–70, 843–4; see also Jolly
  Company, the
Dubois, (Abbé) Guillaume, 638, 654,
  832
Du Croy, Charles Eugène, Duc:
  death and burial, 336–7 n.
  at Narva, 328–30, 332, 334
  taken prisoner, 334, 336
Dutch East India Company, 179, 184
dwarfs, 617–18

Easter, 616
Ecclesiastical Regulation (1721), 792–3
education in Russia, 391–2, 756–9, 817
  of clergy, 429, 786, 792
  of women, 806, 810
Ehrenskjold, (Admiral) Johan Eriksson,
  587–8
  as prisoner, 588–9
Ekaterina, Empress, see Catherine I,
  Empress
Ekaterinhof, 804
Elizabeth (Petrovna), Empress, 377,
  806–807
  birth, 522
  heir (Peter III) designated, 833
  later life, 832
  marriage plans:
    to Duc de Chartres, 831–2
    to Louis XV, 638, 654, 830
  reign (1741–62), 852
embezzlement, see corruption in government

England:
  alliance with Sweden (1720), 730
  and Holland, 205–206
  Peter's visit (1698), 206–16
  political situation (1698), 205–206
  see also George I, King of England;
    William III, King of England
entertainments, 262, 264–5, 273
  assemblies (evening parties), 808–10
  Christmas and New Years, 828
  fireworks, 121
  New Years, 237
  Poltava victory and anniversary
    celebrations, 517, 801–802
  at ship launchings, 800–801
  Treaty of Nystad celebrations, 740–3
  at Versailles, 160–1
  see also sports and recreation; war
    games
Eudoxia, Tsaritsa, see Lopukhina,
  Eudoxia (Fedorovna)
Eugene, Prince of Savoy, 222–3, 225
Europe:
  culture, 18th century, 162–5; see also
    Western cultural influence on
    Russia
  Russian shipbuilders trained in, 149–
    50, 156–7, 185, 200, 201–202,
    232, 584
  Russian travels in:
    (1697–8), see Great Embassy
    (1716–17), 624–56
Europeans in Russia, see foreigners in
  Russia
evasion of service, 758; see also
  recruitment
Evelyn, John, 208–209

Fedor III (Alexeevich), Tsar, 25–6, 28–9
  burial site, 7
  death, 29
  funeral, 36–7
  as heir to throne, 18
Finland:
  campaigns (1713–14), 581–90
    Battle of Hangö (1714), 587–8
  fiscals (informers), 765–6
Flam, (Captain) Jan, 131, 132
foreigners in Russia:
  at Academy of Science, 817
  and college system of administration,
    754

danger to, 271–2
diplomats, 262–3, 265, 615–16; *see
also* Korb, Johann-Georg; Weber,
Friedrich Christian
and economy, 774–6
military officers, 70, 102, 141, 245,
299, 334
mining engineers, 771
and Peter, 109, 112–13
religious freedom of, 784
Swedish prisoners of war, 523–4, 754,
784
tsar's protection of, 391, 775
see also Moscow: German Suburb
France:
Academy of Science:
Peter elected member, 648, 816
alliance with Russia refused (1717),
638
foreign policy, early 18th century,
637–8
political situation (1717), 635–7
see also Louis XIV, King of France;
Louis XV, King of France;
Versailles palace
Fraustadt, Battle of (1706), 405
Fray of 1713 (Kalabalik), 592–7
Frederick I, King of Prussia, 520, 573,
574, 575
Frederick I, King of Sweden, 724–5
accession to throne (1720), 735
peace negotiations with Russia (1721),
739–40
Frederick III, Elector of Brandenburg,
173–4
Frederick IV, Duke of Holstein-Gottorp,
317
death of, 348
and the "Gottorp Fury," 317
marriage to Charles XII's sister, Hedwig
Sophia, 318
Frederick IV, King of Denmark, 295,
296, 519
and Charles XII, 317–18
and Peter, 629
Frederick Augustus, Elector of Saxony,
see Augustus II, King of Poland
Frederick, the Great, 577–8
Frederick William, the Great Elector,
575
Frederick William I, King of Prussia:
accession to throne (1713), 573–5
in conflict between Russia and England
(1720), 730 and *n.*
death (1740), 578
foreign policy, 575, 627–8
and Giants of Potsdam, 576–7
personality and characteristics, 576–7
and Peter, 632–3, 730 and *n.*, 731 *n.*

Gadyach, 468–9
Gagarin, (Prince) Matthew, 763–4,
765–6, 769
galley (ship), 583–4
gambling, 803
Ge, Nikolai:
painting of Peter and the Tsarevich,
701
George I, King of England (George
Louis, Elector of Hanover), 726–8
and Peter, 579, 654, 715
physical appearance, 727
and Russian influence in Europe, 628,
716
anti-Russian policy (1719–20), 729–
32, 737, 739, 831–2
and succession to English throne, 637,
727
George II, King of England, 176
Gerey, Devlet, *see* Devlet Gerey, Khan of
the Crimea
German Suburb of Moscow, 19, 110–12
and Peter, 109, 112–13
see also foreigners in Russia
Giants of Potsdam, 576–7
Glebov, (Major) Stephen, 695–6, 697–8
Glorious Revolution, the (1688), 195–6
Goertz, (Baron) Georg Heinrich von,
712–19
negotiations with Russia (1718),
716–19
and Patkul, 725–6 *n.*
trial and execution, 725
gold:
search for (1714–19), 820
shortage of in Russia, 773
Golitsyn, (Princess) Anastasia, 804–805
Golitsyn, (Prince) Boris:
and Peter's anger, 267
in Peter's government, 109
governs in Peter's absence, 169
and Sophia's overthrow, 96, 97, 102,
103–104
Golitsyn, (Prince) Michael, 448

Golitsyn, (Prince) Vasily Vasilievich,
    80–3, 112
  exile (1689), 104
  and Mazeppa, 458
  negotiates Polish cession of Kiev
    (1686), 84
  and opposition to Sophia, 94, 99,
    102–104
  and Peter, 89–91, 93
  and Sophia, 78, 81, 89
  and Streltsy revolt (1682), 41, 43
  and war with Ottoman Empire
    (1687–9), 85–90
Golovchin, Battle of (1708), 442–5
Golovin, Avtemon, 298–9
  at Narva, 324
Golovin, (Count) Fedor Alexeevich:
  in Azov campaign (1695), 138, 140
  death, 386
  on Great Embassy, 150, 168, 227
  at Narva, 322–3
  Order of St. Andrew, 243
  as Peter's companion, 117
Golovkin, Gavril, 386, 387
  on Western journey (1716–17), 625
Gordeenko, Konstantin, Hetman of the
    Zaporozhsky Cossacks, 474–5
Gordon, (General) Patrick, 112
  allegiance to Peter (1689), 102–103,
    115
  in Azov campaigns (1695–6), 138–9,
    140, 146
  death (1699), 281
  early career, 113–14
  as naval officer, 129, 132
  received at court, 66, 109–10
  and Streltsy uprising (1698), 245–8
  wounded in war games (1691), 122
"Grandfather of the Russian Navy"
    (boat), 73 n., 829
grand vizier, 536
Granovitaya Palata (Palace of Facets),
    Moscow, 8
Great Embassy, the, 150–1, 155–7, 168–
    232
  assessment, 231–2
  diplomatic efforts, 173–4, 197–8, 215,
    225–6, 231–2
  in Dresden, 217–18
  in England, 206–16
  personnel, 168
  in Poland, 230–1
  reasons for, 155–7

  in Riga, 170–2
  in Vienna, 223–7
Great Globe of Gottorp, the, 816
Great Northern War:
  Baltic phase (1711–21), 572–90, 600–
    601, 628–32, 720–2, 732–7, 739
  battles:
    Fraustadt (1706), 405
    Golovchin (1708), 442–4
    Kalisz (1706), 409
    Klissow (1702), 348
    Lesnaya (1708), 451–3
    Molyatychy (1708), 449
    Narva (1700), 330–7
    Poltava (1709), 494–510
  beginning, 299–301
  campaign of 1700, 299–301; Danish
    invasion of Holstein-Gottorp, 318–
    19; Swedish offensive in Denmark,
    Peace of Travendal, 321–2; Rus-
    sian siege of Narva, 323–4;
    Swedish offensive in Livonia,
    325–6; Battle of Narva, 327–37
  campaign of 1701, 346
  campaign of 1702: Sweden attacks
    Poland, 348; Swedish victory at
    Klissow, 348; Russian victories in
    Livonia, 348–50; Russian naval
    victories on Lake Ladoga, Lake
    Peipus, at Nöteborg, 350–2
  campaign of 1703: Russian naval vic-
    tory at Nyenskans, 353; Sweden
    threatens St. Petersburg, 357
  campaign of 1704: Russian victory at
    Dorpat, 397–8; Swedish offensive
    in Poland, 399–401
  campaign of 1705/1706: Swedish vic-
    tory at Grodno, 403–406; Swedish
    victory at Fraustadt, 405; Swedish
    army leaves Poland, invades Sax-
    ony, 407; Treaty of Altranstadt,
    408; Russian victory at Kalisz,
    409
  campaign of 1707: Swedish invasion of
    Russia, 421, 431; Swedish army in
    Silesia, 425–6; Swedish army in
    Poland, 430–1
  campaign of 1708: Swedish stand at
    Grodno, 432–4; Swedish victory at
    Golovchin, 442–4; Russian victory
    at Lesnaya, 451–3; Swedish threat
    to St. Petersburg, 453–4; Sweden

invades Ukraine, 456–7, 461, 464;
destruction of Baturin, 464–5
campaign of 1708/1709: Russia occupies Romny, 468; Swedish victories at Veprik, Oposhnya, 470–2;
Russian victory at Perevoluchna,
474–5; Poltava, 479–510; Swedish
withdrawal from Ukraine, 510–15;
Russian victories in Poland, 520;
Russian siege and victory at Riga,
521, 524
campaign of 1710: Russian sieges and
victories at Vyborg, Riga and
Reval, 524–6
campaign of 1711/1712: allied invasion
of Pomerania, 572; Danish fleet
attacks Bremen, 572–3; allied attack on Stettin, 572, 578; Sweden
attacks Danish army at Gades-
busch, 579; Danish army retreats
to Tonning, 579
campaign of 1713/1714: Danish army
surrenders at Tonning, 579; Russian army invades Pomerania, 579;
Stettin falls to Russia, 580;
Finnish campaign (Baltic fleet),
581, 583, 586–90; Russian naval
victory at Hangö, 587–8; Danish
fleet victorious over Swedish
fleet at Stralsund, 600–601
campaign of 1716: Sweden attacks
Denmark in Norway, 628–9;
effort for allied attack on Sweden,
629–32
campaign of 1718: Sweden attacks
Denmark in Norway, 720; siege of
Kristiania, 720–1; Norwegian campaign abandoned at Charles XII's
death, 722
campaign of 1719: English fleet at
Stockholm, 732; Russian naval
victories in Baltic, 732–4
campaign of 1720: English fleet in
Baltic, 735–6; Russian naval victories on Swedish coast, 736–7
campaign of 1721: Russian naval victories on Swedish coast, 739
causes, 231, 293–8
conclusion:
Treaty of Nystad (1721), 739–40
naval aspects, *see* Great Northern War:
Baltic phase; Russia: naval fleet:
in Baltic

peace negotiations:
at Lofo (1718), 716–19, 726
(1719), 734
at Nystad (1721), 739; Treaty,
739–40
Polish phases, 348, 399–401, 405–407,
430–1
Russian phase (1708–1709), 431–515
Ukrainian phase (1708–1709), 456–7,
461, 464–5, 467–515
Great Schism, 53–64
Griboyedov, Semyon, 39
Grodno:
Swedish offensive:
(1706), 401, 403–407
(1708), 532–5
Guards, *see* Russian Imperial Guards
Gulf of Finland naval campaigns (1713–
14), 581–90
Battle of Hangö (1714), 587–8
Gustavus Adolphus, King of Sweden,
291, 292, 723

Hallart, (General) Ludwig von:
at Narva, 324
taken prisoner, 334
Hamilton, Marie, 804
execution, 812–13
Hamilton, Mary, 19–20, 112
Hangö, Battle of (1714), 587–8
Hannibal, Abraham, 760 and *n.*
Hapsburg, House of, 218–21
Hare Island, 356 and *n.*
harem, the, 532–4
health and hygiene, 18th century, 165
Hedwig Sophia, Princess of Sweden
(Duchess of Holstein-Gottorp),
316–17, 724
Hermitage, the (pavilion, Peterhof), 611
Hofburg Palace, Vienna, 221
Hohenzollern, House of, 173, 575
Holland:
description, 178–9
and England, 190–1, 205–206
Peter's visit (1697), 197–202
Holstein, (Duke) Charles Frederick, *see*
Charles Frederick, Duke of
Holstein-Gottorp
Holstein, (Prince) Karl Ulrich Peter,
see Peter III, Emperor
Holy Roman Empire, 219
Holy Synod, 792–3

Horn, (Count) Arvid Bernard:
  at Battle of Narva (1700), 332
  Charles XII's youthful companion, 316
  surrender of Narva (1704), 398
hunting:
  Peter and, 68, 177, 651-2, 803
Huyssen, Heinrich von, 421, 658, 660

Ignatiev, Jacob, 661, 663-4, 694
  execution, 698
industry in Russia, *see* Russia: trade and
  industry
informers (fiscals), 765-6
Ingria:
  description, 323
  as Peter's objective in Great Northern
    War, 301
  retaken by Russian fleet (1703), 353
intermarriage of dynasties, 18-19; *see also*
  individual arranged marriages, by
  name(s)
inventions, European, 163
Istanbul, *see* Constantinople
Ivan V (Alexeevich), Tsar:
  burial site, 7
  coronation, 50-1
  as co-tsar with Peter, 49-50, 65-7, 77,
    82, 129
  death (1696), 143
  as heir to throne, 18, 29-30
  personality and characteristics, 18, 29

Janissaries, 531
  at the Pruth (1711), 557-8
  in war with Russia, 547
Jefferyes, (Captain) James, 431 and *n.*
  deported from Russia (1719), 732, 737
Jensen, Jacob, 139-40, 146, 148
Jesuits:
  in Hapsburg empire, 220
  in Russia, 81
    expulsion from, 109, 785
Jews in Russia, 387 *n.*
Joachim, Patriarch:
  and Church-State relations, 61
  death, 110
    effects of, 112
  defection from Sophia to Peter, 99-100
  power during Peter's reign, 108-109
  in selection of tsar, 29-30
Jolly Company, the, 117-21, 148

Drunken (Mock) Synod of, 119-21,
  268, 269-70, 843-4
  see also individual members

Kalabalik (1713), 592-6
  consequences, 597
Kalisz, Battle of (1706), 409
Kamchatka Peninsula, 819
Kara Mustapha, Grand Vizier, 85
Kardis, Treaty of (1661), 83
Karl Leopold, Duke of Mecklenburg:
  marriage to Catherine (Ivanovna),
    625-7
Karl Ulrich Peter, Prince of Holstein,
  see Peter III, Emperor
Khovansky, (Prince) Ivan, 41, 49, 50, 53
Kikin, Alexander Vasilievich:
  and (Tsarevich) Alexis, 671, 675, 677,
    679, 680, 692
  arrest (1718), 694-5
  corruption charges, 764, 765
  death (1718), 697, 698
Kiev, 83-4
"King of Pressburg," *see* Romodanovsky,
  (Prince) Fedor
Kist, Gerrit, 180, 181
Klissow, Battle of (1702), 348
Kneller, (Sir) Godfrey, 207
Knipercrona, Thomas, 300
knout (instrument of torture), 250-1
Kolomenskoe palace, 24-5
Königsmark, Aurora, Countess von,
  347-8
Korb, Johann-Georg:
  reports of Russia, 263-74
Kremlin, the, Moscow, 3, 6-9
Kurile Islands, 819

Lacy, (Major General) Peter, 733-4, 739
Lagercrona, (General) Anders, 436, 450,
  455-6
Lake Ladoga, 350-2
  shipyards at, 350, 357, 358
    moved to St. Petersburg, 358-9
land, Russian, 9-10
Langen, Major General, Baron, 300, 323
  taken prisoner at Narva, 334
law and order, *see* crime
LeBlond, Alexandre Jean Baptiste,
  606-10
Lefort, Francis, 89

in Azov campaigns (1695-6), 138, 140,
144
death and funeral, 277-80
drinking, 118, 173, 277-8
early career, 115-16
on Great Embassy, 150, 168, 227
personality and characteristics, 116
and Peter, 266-7, 278-9
Lefort, Peter, 279, 336
Leibniz, Gottfried von, 163, 754, 816
and Peter, 569
response to Narva, 337
response to Poltava, 518-19
and Sophia Charlotte, 176
Leningrad, *see* St. Petersburg
Leopold I, Holy Roman Emperor:
career, 220
court life, 221
and Peter, 223-5
politics and administration, 221-2
Lesnaya, Battle of (1708), 451-3
Leszczynski, Stanislaus, *see* Stanislaus
I, King of Poland
Lewenhaupt, (Count) Adam Ludwig,
446-53, 513-15
career, 446
at Lesnaya, 451-3
at Perevoluchna, 514-15
at Poltava, 491-2, 496-8
and Rehnskjold, 491-2, 502-503
libraries, printing, and books, 187, 391-2,
429, 815
life span, 18th century, 164-5
Livonia:
Saxon invasion of (1700), 299
Sheremetev's victories in (1702), 348-9
Swedish offensive in (1700), 325-6
as Swedish province, 294-6
see also Narva; Riga
Lofo:
peace negotiations at (1718), 716-19,
726, 732
London:
description, 203-205
Peter's visit (1698), 206-16
Lopukhina, Eudoxia (Fedorovna),
Tsaritsa:
and (Tsarevich) Alexis, 658
arrested (1718), 695-6
later life, 697, 850
and Peter, 76, 78, 129, 225, 239-41,
658
at Pokrovsky Monastery, 241, 695-6

Lopukhin family, 109, 661
Louis XIV, King of France, 155-6,
157-62
death (1715), 624, 635-6
late years, 635
and Paris, 52 *n.*
physical appearance, 158
social life, 161
see also Versailles palace
Louis XV, King of France:
at Louis XIV's death, 635-6
and Peter, 642-3, 650-1, 653

Macarius, Patriarch of Antioch, 56-7,
59, 60
Madagascar, 819-20
Makarov, Alexis, 388
manufacturing in Russia, *see* Russia:
trade and industry
Maria (Alexeevna), Tsarevna:
arrested in Tsarevich conspiracy
(1718), 695
death (1723), 697
imprisoned at Schlüsselburg (1718-21),
697
Maria (Miloslavskaya), Tsaritsa:
death (1669), 18
Marlborough, John Churchill, Duke of,
302-305 *passim*
and Charles XII, 413-15
defection to William of Orange (1688),
195
descent from power, 637, 727
and Eugene of Savoy, 222
and George I, 727
and Matveev's peace effort (1706-
1707), 420-1
military genius of, 305-306
response to Poltava, 518
victories in War of the Spanish
Succession, 205
Marly (pavilion, Peterhof), 611
marriage:
arranged:
banned, 390-1
as instrument of diplomacy, 18-19
see also divorce
Matveev, Andrei Artemonovich, 343-4,
351
on Great Embassy, 168
peace mission to Sweden (1706-1707),
419-21

Matveev, Artemon Sergeevich, 19–21
death, 45–6
imprisonment (1676), 26, 41
as interrogator of Mazeppa, 458
as potential regent, 29
and Streltsy revolt (1682), 41–6 *passim*
Maximov, (Ataman) Lukyan, 395–6
Mazeppa, (General) Ivan Stepanovich,
Hetman of the Cossacks, 454–66
birth and youth, 457–8
and Charles XII, 454, 461, 462–6
directs Charles's escape at Perevoluchna (1709), 514–15
death (1709), 545
Order of St. Andrew, 243, 459
and Peter, 459–60, 462–3, 465
seeks asylum from Sultan, 544
Mecklenburg, (Duke) Karl Leopold:
marriage to Catherine (Ivanovna),
625–7
Medvedev, Sylvester, 80, 92, 100, 102
torture and death, 105
Mehemet Baltadji, *see* Baltadji Mehemet
Pasha
Menshikov, Alexander Danilovich,
367–71
and (Tsarevich) Alexis, 659, 679
avarice and corruption of, 371, 763–4,
766–9
career, 368–9, 370
and Catherine, 367, 372–3, 769
power during her reign, 848–9
and Darya (Arseeneva), 373, 374–5
death (1729), 851
defection to Peter II, 849–50
detractors, 369
and Devier, 812, 849–50
and execution of Streltsy, 259
exiled (1727, 1728), 851
as Governor of Schlüsselburg, 352, 370
on Great Embassy, 168
household, 373, 374
at Kalisz, 409
and Lefort, 280, 368
at Oposhnya, 471–2
Order of St. Andrew, 353, 767
palace on Vasilevsky Island, 603–604
and Peter, 369–71, 402–403, 766–9
physical appearance, 367–8
in Poland (1709), 517, 520
at Poltava, 495–6, 498–9
and Swedish surrender, 514–15

and Preobrazhenskoe war games, 68,
368
meritocracy, 759–61
Mglin, 455–6
Michael, Tsar, 8, 21, 30
Mikhailov, Peter, *see* Peter I, the Great:
incognito travel
Miloslavskaya, Maria, Tsaritsa:
death (1669), 18
Miloslavsky, Ivan, 26
coffin opened, 169–70
as potential regent, 29
and Sophia's regency, 80
and Streltsy revolt (1682), 41
Miloslavsky family, 18, 20, 21
and (Tsarevich) Alexis, 661
ascendency with Fedor's tsardom, 26
support of Ivan's claim as tsar, 29,
66–7
mining in Russia, 771–2, 773
Mitchell, (Sir) David, 202, 206, 207, 216
mock battles, *see* war games
Mock Synod (Drunken Synod), 119–21,
268, 269–70, 843–4
Moens de la Croix, William, *see* Mons,
William
Mogilev, 445–6
Moldavia, 552–4
Molyatychy, Battle of (1708), 449
monasteries:
books and manuscripts procured from,
815
Donskoy, 95
governmental regulation, 788, 789–90
Pechersk, 341
Pertominsk, 130
Pokrovsky (Suzdal), 241, 695–6
reform of, 788
of the Resurrection ("The New
Jerusalem"), 58, 61
description by Korb, 273
Patriarch Nikon in residence, 59, 60
Streltsy rebellion (1698) at, 246
Solovetsky, 62, 129, 130
Troitsky, 96–7
see also Novodevichy Convent
Monomakh, Cap of, 51, 92
Mon Plaisir (pavilion, Peterhof), 611–12
Mons, Anna, 116–17, 234, 240, 262, 373
and *n.*, 811
Mons, William:
bribery scandal, 838–40
execution, 840

Moor, Carl, 656
Moscow:
  bells of, 7–8
  description, 3–8
  fires, 5, 82–3
  fortifications, 427–8
  German Suburb, 19, 110–12
    and Peter, 109, 112–13
    see also foreigners in Russia
  River:
    blessing of, 25, 268–9
  social life and customs, 82, 271–3;
    see also Russia: social life and
    customs
Munnich, Burkhard Christopher von,
    779–80, 852
Musin-Pushkin, Ivan Alexeevich, 788,
    789–90
Mustapha, Kara, Grand Vizier, 85

Naples:
  (Tsarevich) Alexis takes refuge in
    (1717), 685–9
Narva:
  Battle of (1700), 281, 330–7
    consequences, 337–8
    effect on Charles XII, 337–8
    effect on Peter, 339–40
    Russian surrender, 334–6
  description, 324
  Russian siege:
    (1700), 323–4
    (1704), 397–8
Naryshkin, Ivan, 37, 46–8, 169
Naryshkin, Kyril, 19, 23, 48–9
Naryshkin, Lev Kyrilovich, 96, 97
  as Director of Foreign Affairs, 108–
    109
  and Peter's anger, 267
Naryshkina, Natalya, 19–22
  marriage, 21
Naryshkin family, 26
  and Sophia's regency, 67
  and Streltsy, 40–1
Natalya (Alexeevna), daughter of
  (Tsarevich) Alexis, 665
Natalya (Alexeevna), Peter's sister:
  birth, 25
  in charge of (Tsarevich) Alexis, 241
  and Peter, 129, 145
  at St. Petersburg, 361
  theatrical interests, 813

Natalya (Naryshkina), Tsaritsa, 19–22,
    108
  death (1694), 128–9
  marriage, 21
  and Peter, 77–8, 126–7, 128
  political exile under Sophia, 67
  and Streltsy revolt (1682), 43–9 *passim*
  theatrical interests, 22
Natalya (Petrovna), Princess, 806
  death (1725), 807
naval fleet of Russia, see Russia: naval
  fleet
naval warfare and battles, see Great
  Northern War: Baltic phase;
  Russia: naval fleet
Nechaev, (Colonel) Ivan, 101, 102
Nemetskaya Sloboda, see Moscow:
  German Suburb
Neplyuev, Ivan, 760–1
Nerchinsk, Treaty of (1689), 85 *n.*, 117,
    168
Nesterov, Alexis, 765–6
Netherlands, see Holland
Neugebauer, Martin, 658
Neva River, 355–6, 604–605
  blessing of, 849
  Swedish forces cross it, 454
Nevsky Prospect, St. Petersburg, 608
"New Jerusalem" monastery, 58, 61
  description by Korb, 273
  Patriarch Nikon in residence, 59, 60
  site of Streltsy rebellion (1698), 246
Newton, (Sir) Isaac, 163–4
Nikon, Patriarch, 55–61
  conflict with Alexis, 59–60
  reforms, 55–7, 61, 62, 64
  as regent, 58–9
  trial, 60
Norris, (Sir) John, Admiral
  in Baltic (1715–21), 729, 731–3,
    735–7, 739
Nöteborg, 351–2
Novodevichy Convent:
  Sophia's exile in, 105–106, 257
  Streltsy executions at, 258
  Tsaritsa Eudoxia moved to, 851
Nyenskans, 353
Nystad, Treaty of (1721), 818, 832
  anniversary celebration (1723), 830
  Russian celebrations, 740–3
  terms, 739–40
  religious freedom, 784

Ogilvie, (Field Marshal) George, 397–8, 402–407
Old Believers, 53, 61–4, 392, 784–5, 794
Order of St. Andrew, 243; *see also* under individual recipients
Order of St. Catherine, 570–1, 835
Oreshka (Nöteborg), 351–2
Orléans, Philippe, Duc d':
    foreign policy of, 637–8
    and Peter, 641–2, 650, 653
    proposes son's marriage to Peter's daughter Elizabeth, 831–2
    as Regent of France, 636–7
Orthodox Church:
    conservatism of, 54
    Easter festival, 616
    Ecclesiastical Regulation, 792–3
    Great Schism, 53–64
    Holy Synod, 792–3
    mockery of, 119–21, 268–70
    Old Believers, *see* Old Believers
    Patriarchy, 789–94
    elections: (1690), 110; (1700–21), 789–93
    reforms of Nikon, 55–7, 61, 62, 64
    reforms of Peter, 783–94
    and Streltsy, 53
    teaching function, 786
    and temporal power, 61, 64, 232, 345, 789–94
    on tobacco, 211–12
    see also Balkan Christians
Osborne, Peregrine, Marquis of Carmarthen, 208, 212, 213, 215–16
Osterman, Andrew (Heinrich), 850, 852
    as assistant to Makarov, 388
    at peace negotiations (1718), 717–19
    and peace offer to Sweden (1719), 734
    on Western journey (1716–17), 625
Ottoman Empire:
    administration, 530
    armistice with Russia (170), 300
    early history, 536–7
    extent, 528, 530
    population, 530
    war with Russia:
        (1687–9), 84–9
        (1695), first Azov campaign, 136–42
        (1696), second Azov campaign, 144–7
        (1710–11), 546–7, 553–66
        (1712), 564
        (1713), 564–5

    see also individual battles and campaigns, e.g. Pruth

Palace of Facets, Moscow, 8
pardons and reprieves (general):
    on Peter's deathbed, 844
    after Treaty of Nystad, 741
Paris:
    description, 644–7
    and Louis XIV, 52 *n.*
    and Peter's visit (1717), 647–54
passport system, 782
Patkul, Johann Reinhold von, 294–8, 357, 409–12
    arrest and death, 411–12
    and Goertz, 725–6 *n.*
peace treaties, *see* treaties
peasants, 781–2
    dress, 16
    runaways, 392–3, 781
Pechersk Monastery, 341
Perevoluchna, 479–80
Perry, (Captain) John, 213, 236
Persia, 821–7
    campaign (1722), 824–6
    trade with, 570
Pertominsk Monastery, 130
Peter and Paul Cathedral, St. Petersburg, 360
Peter and Paul Fortress, St. Petersburg, 356–7
Peterhof, 610–11, 829
Peter Alexeevich, Grand Duke, *see* Peter II, Emperor
Peter Fedorovich, *see* Peter III, Emperor
Peter Petrovich, Prince, 625
    birth (1704), 374, 667–8
    death (1719), 805
        Peter's grief, 805–806
    named heir to throne (1718), 692–3
Peter I, the Great, Tsar:
    achievements compared to Alexis's, 747–8
    administration of government, *see* Peter I: governance and administration
    and (Tsarevich) Alexis, 656–710
    anger, *see* Peter I: moods and anger
    as Antichrist, 120, 661, 798
    appearance, *see* Peter I: physical appearance
    and (General-Admiral) Apraxin, 585–6

ascent to power, 89–106
and Augustus II, 230–1, 299, 300,
  344–5, 519–20, 550, 831
birth (1672) and christening, 22–3
and boats, *see* Peter I: nautical interests
and Catherine, *see* Catherine I, Empress: and Peter
character of, *see* Peter I: personality
  and characteristics of
and Charles XII, 433, 508, 724
childhood, 23–30
children of, 374, 377, 522
  list, 377 *n.*
  see also Alexis, Tsarevich
and the Church:
  early education, 27, 783
  faith (personal) of Peter, 783
  mockery of Church by Jolly
    Company, 119–21
  and Patriarch Adrian, 110, 121, 789
  and Patriarch Joachim, 109–10
  and Protestants in England, 209–11
  reforms, 783–94
  religious toleration, 189, 783–4
  and Roman Catholic Church, 224,
    648, 785, 786; *see also* Jesuits
  and temporal power, 61, 64, 232,
    345, 789–94
clothing of, 796–7
coronation, 50–1
as co-tsar with Ivan, 65–7, 77, 82, 129
  coronation, 50–1
  ends at Ivan's death (1696), 143
  request by Streltsy, 49–50
courage of, 329; *see also* Peter I: in
  danger
curiosity of, 70–1, 815–16, 824
  on European travels, 187–8, 198,
    207–208, 212–13, 218, 232, 568,
    649, 652
in danger:
  of assassination, 798
  in battle, 129, 357; at Poltava, 501–
    502, 504–505
  capsized boat, Zaandam (1697), 200
  storm at sea (1694), 130
death, 844–5
  causes, 846
  lying-in-state and funeral, 848
drinking and drunkenness, 118–19, 830
  abroad, 172–3, 208
  Catherine's influence on, 377
  effect on health, 135, 624

early years of reign (1689–94), 108–23
education:
  formal, 26–8, 71
  informal, at Preobrazhenskoe, 67–73
  election as tsar (1682), 30
  in England (1698), 206–16
epilepsy, *see* Peter I: health
and Eudoxia, 76, 78, 129, 225, 239–41
food and meals, 640–1, 795–6
  quantity of, 172, 649–50
  in France (1717), 638–55
  and Frederick I, King of Prussia, 520
  and Frederick William I, 632–3, 730
    and *n.*, 731 *n.*
  and George I, 579, 654, 715
  and the German Suburb, 109, 112–13
  and Vasily Golitsyn, 89–91, 93
governance and administration, 429,
  569–70, 747–69, 795
  on travels, 186–7, 386, 387–8
  see also Peter I: reforms
and the handicapped, 618–19
health, 122, 624, 830
  convulsions and tremors, 134–6, 224,
    376, 548, 652, 841; during conflict with (Tsarevich) Alexis, 676;
    at Peter Petrovich's death, 805
  cures: at Carlsbad, 567–8, 573; at
    Olonets, 830, 836; at Pyrmont,
    625, 628, 629; at Spa, 655
  fevers, 135, 428, 429, 437–8, 478,
    517–18, 624, 633–4
  final illness, 840–5
  strangury and stone, 826, 836, 842–6
  see also Peter I: drinking and
    drunkenness
and hunting, 68, 177, 651–2, 803
incognito travel, 155, 157, 172, 180–2,
  199, 207
journeys to Western Europe:
  (1697–8), *see* Great Embassy
  (1716–17), 624–56; reasons for
    going, 624–5
  and (F.) Lefort, 266–7, 278–9
  and Leibniz, 569
  and Leopold I, 223–5
  and Louis XV, 642–3, 650–1, 653
manual labor of, 177, 210, 803
  in Amsterdam, 185–6, 199, 201
  at Archangel, 125, 127
  at Lake Pleschev, 74, 77
  at Voronezh, 143–4, 276–7, 477–8
  see also Peter I: nautical interests

Peter I, the Great, Tsar (*continued*)
and Mazeppa, 459–60, 462–3, 465
and Menshikov, 369–71, 402–403,
766–9
moods and anger, 174, 210, 265–7,
640, 798–800, 841
morality, 811–12
and Narva:
effect of battle on Peter, 339–40
and Natalya (Alexeevna, his sister),
129, 145
and Natalya (Tsaritsa, his mother),
77–8, 126–7
response to her death, 128
nautical interests, 136, 777, 803–804,
829
at Archangel (1693–4), 126, 127,
131–2
galleys, 584
sailing with guests, 621–3
in storm at sea (1694), 130
youthful, 72–5, 77, 122–3, 829
see also Russia: naval fleet; shipbuilding
and (Admiral) Norris, 728–9
Order of St. Andrew, 353
and (Philippe d') Orléans, 641–2, 650,
653
personality and characteristics of:
(1683–4), 65–6
(1697), 177
(1698), 210–11
(1700), 339
(1717), 640–1, 653–4
see also specific aspects under Peter
I, e.g. courage; curiosity; moods
and anger
physical appearance of:
(1683–4), 65–6
(1694), 134
(1697), 176–7
(1698), 207, 224
(1717), 640, 648–9, 656
likenesses: portrait by Sir Godfrey
Kneller, 207; portrait by Carl
Moor, 656; statue by Falconet,
853–4
at Poltava, 501–502, 504–505, 507–
509
effects and consequences, 516–26
and Quakers, 211
reforms of, 234–9, 241–3, 262
church, 783–94

economic, 770–82
fundamental (1711–25), 748
in government and military, 749–69
and St. Petersburg, 365, 422, 509
and ships, see Peter I: nautical interests
skills of, 187–8, 207–208, 213, 568;
see also Peter I: manual labor
and Sophia, 78, 89–94, 107
Streltsy uprising (1698), 256–7
and Streltsy:
revolt (1682), 44, 45–6, 47, 52
treason (1697), 169
uprising (1698) and aftermath,
244–61
and trappings of office, 797–8
military rank, 69–70, 119, 148
titles, 741–2, 742 n.
see also Peter I: incognito travel
travel, 383, 385–6; see also Catherine I,
Empress: and Peter: travels together; Peter I: incognito travel;
Peter I: journeys to Western
Europe
veneration of, 853
at Versailles (1717), 651, 652
war games:
and decision to attack Azov, 137
Kozhukhovo maneuvers (1694),
132–3
at Preobrazhenskoe, 67–70, 121–2
and Western culture, 854
early exposure to, 74–5, 109, 112–13
Great Embassy and westernizing
influence, 157, 232–3
interest in Western technology, 187–8
(Tsaritsa) Natalya's response, 75
see also Peter I: reforms
and William III, 148, 197–8, 199–200,
202, 207, 214–15
and women, 116, 175, 376; see also
Catherine I; Cross, Laetitia;
Lopukhina, Eudoxia; Mons, Anna
Peter II (Alexeevich), Emperor:
accession to throne (1727), 849
birth (1715), 666
death (1730), 851
and succession to throne, 686, 805
Peter III, Emperor:
birth (1728), 833
later life, 833, 852
Philippe, Duc d'Orléans, see Orléans,
Philippe, Duc d'
Piper, (Count) Carl:

counsels abandoning Russian campaign, 486
and Marlborough, 414
at Poltava, 507
and Rehnskjold, 491
Pokrovsky (Suzdal) Monastery, 241, 695–6
Poland:
army, 228–9
invasion by Sweden (1702), 348
Peter's visit (1698), 230–1
political and geographic situation (1698), 227–30
treaty with Denmark against Sweden, 296
see also Augustus II, King of Poland
police in Russia, 390
Poltava, Battle of (1709), 494–506
anniversary celebrations, 801–802
conclusion, 505–506
consequences, 509–10, 516–26
losses sustained (both sides), 507
preliminaries to, 481–94
reasons for, 487
Russian camp, 487–9
Swedish plan, 492–3
Swedish siege, 479–80
victory celebrations, 517
Pomerania, 571–2
Poniatowski, Stanislaus, 545, 547, 556, 560
Praskovaya, Tsaritsa:
cares for Peter's children, 625
later years, 807–808, 829, 830
in Peter's care, at Ivan's death, 143
at St. Petersburg, 361
precedence, system of, 28–9
Preobrazhenskoe:
and (Tsar) Alexis's falconry, 12, 22
burning of wooden house at (1723), 829
Peter's flight from (1689), 96–7
effect on Peter, 135
Peter's youth at, 67–70
Streltsy executions at (1698–9), 257–9
Streltsy interrogation at (1698), 249, 253–7
theater at, 22
war games at, 67–70, 121–2
Preobrazhensky Regiment:
in Azov campaigns (1695–6), 138, 144
ceremonial function, 268
founding, 68

at Narva (1700), 333
and Streltsy uprising (1698), 246
and succession to throne, 692, 846–7
war games, 121–2, 132–3
Pressburg, 70
"King of," *see* Romodanovsky, (Prince) Fedor
prikazy (departments), 12
"Prince Caesar," *see* Romodanovsky, (Prince) Fedor
printing, books and libraries, 187, 391–2, 429, 815
Prokopovich, Feofan, Archbishop of Novgorod:
administers Last Rites to Peter, 844–5
career, 790–1
at Catherine's coronation, 836
as Guardian Exarch, 791–2
in Holy Synod, 793
oration on Treaty of Nystad, 741
preaches in Kiev (1709), 517, 791
preaches Peter's funeral sermon (1725), 848
prostitutes in Russia, 811
Prussia:
defensive alliance with Russia (1709), 520
description, 574–5
peace treaty with Sweden (1720), 730
Pruth (River):
campaign of 1711, 557–62
consequences, 565–6
peace treaty, 558–61
punishment for crime, 251–3, 272
executions in England, 204
see also batog; knout; torture
Pyhäjöggi Pass, 327–8

Rastrelli, Bartolomeo Francesco, 835
Razhumovsky, Alexis, 832
rebellions in Russia (1705–1708), 393–6
effect on Peter, 429
recreation and sports, 620, 801
in London, 204
see also entertainments; hunting
recruitment:
of laborers:
for construction projects, 360–1, 389–90
for Voronezh shipyards, 276, 389
of shipwrights and naval officers, 156, 212, 213, 217, 232

recruitment (*continued*)
  of soldiers:
    for Russian army, 298–9, 340, 389
    for Swedish army, 546, 578, 600,
      712
Red Square, Moscow, 4
Rehnskjold, (Field Marshal) Carl Gustav,
    321, 491
  and Charles XII's death, 722
  at Fraustadt (1706), 405
  at Narva (1700), 330–2, 337
  at Poltava, 483, 485, 491–2, 494–505
    passim
    captured, 507
  and Lewenhaupt, 491–2, 502–503
  wounded at Veprik (1709), 471
Repnin, Nikita:
  court-martialed after Golovchin
    (1708), 445
  and Narva, 324, 340
Reval (Tallinn):
  capitulates to Russian siege (1710),
    526
  Catherine's palace at, 829
  description, 290
  as issue in peace talks (1718), 718
  Peter's house at, 381
Riga:
  description, 290
  Peter's visit (1697) and consequences,
    170–2, 297, 301
  sieges of:
    (1700), 299, 325
    (1709–10), 521, 524
rituals and ceremonies, 267–70, 801
  blessing of rivers, 25, 268–9, 849
  Christmas, 267–8, 828
  Easter, 616
rivers of Russia, 13, 288, 292, 778
  blessing of, 25, 268–9, 849
  see also individual rivers
Roman Catholic Church:
  mocked by Drunken Synod, 121
  and Peter, Vienna (1898), 224
  tolerated, 785
  see also Jesuits
Romanov family:
  burial sites, 7
  succession to throne, 29, 75, 833
Romny, 468, 470
Romodanovsky, (Prince) Fedor, 267
  beard spared, 234
  death (1717), 802

and Jolly Company, 119
  as naval officer, 129, 132
  and Peter, 117, 240
  and Secret Office, 390
  and Streltsy (1698), 253–4, 258
  as Viceroy of Russia, 169, 275
  in war games, 122, 132
  and Western dress, 238
Roos, (General) Karl Gustav:
  at Chornyaya Natopa, 448
  at Poltava, 492, 495, 498–9
  surrender, 499
Russia:
  Academy of Science:
    building planned by Peter, 841
    founding, 816–17
    library, 815
    museum, 814
  architecture:
    ecclesiastical, 58
    Moscow, 4–8, 82–3
    St. Petersburg, 360, 362, 602–12,
      834–5
  army:
    artillery, 342–3
    assessments: (1701), 341–2; (1705),
      401–402
    battles, *see* battles
    command problems, 140, 142, 402–
      403
    foreign officers, 70, 102, 141, 245,
      299, 334
    preparation for Swedish invasion
      (1707), 427–8
    promotions, 266–7, 757, 759–61
    recruitment, 298–9, 340, 389
    reform of (1700–1701), 341–3
    training of, 236–7, 298–9, 342–3;
      see also war games
  boundaries, 13, 15
  bureaucracy, 386–9
    college system of administration,
      753–6
    precedence system, 28–9
    prikazy, 12
  canals in, 607–608, 778–80
  civil service, 757; *see also* meritocracy
  College of Mining and Manufacturing,
    772
  college system of administration, 753–6
  currency reform, 213, 242, 772–3
  description, 12–17, 384
  economy, 770–82

education in, 391–2, 756–9, 817
of clergy, 786, 792
of women, 806, 810
fleet, *see* Russia: naval fleet
government and administration, 386–90
college system, 753–6
corruption, *see* corruption in government
reform of, 748–56
Senate, 749–56
see also Russia: bureaucracy; Russia: civil service
Inspector General of Decrees, 751
land, 9–10
merchant marine, 776–7
mining in, 771–2, 773
Monastery Office, 788, 789–90
naval fleet:
Admiralty, St. Petersburg, 359 and *n*.
in (2nd) Azov campaign (1696), 144–5
in Baltic: (1702), 350–1; (1703), 357–8; (1710), 524–5, 590; (1713–14), 581–90; Battle of Hangö (1714), 587–8; (1719), 732–4, 736; (1721), 739
base at Tagenrog, 147, 149
beginnings, 129, 131
cost of, 149
as deterrent force (1709), 477
drilling and maneuvers, 282
escorts Ukraintsev to Constantinople (1699), 283–4
flag, 131 *n*.
growth, 277, 281–2
see also Russia: navy; shipbuilding
navy, 757–8
nobility, *see* boyars; meritocracy
police, 390
population, 13
Procurator General, 753
prostitution in, 811
rebellions (1705–1708), 393–6
effect on Peter, 429
rivers, 13, 288, 292, 778
blessing of, 25, 268–9, 849
see also individual rivers
School of Mathematics and Navigation (Naval Academy), 757
seasons, 16–17
Secret Office, 390
Senate, 749–56
changing role, 753

creation of (1711), 749–50
move to St. Petersburg (1712), 570
new rules (1720), 751
quarrels in, 657, 752, 755
social hierarchy, 12, 756
social life and customs, 619–23; *see also* Moscow: social life and customs
Supreme Privy Council, 848, 849
trade and industry, 770–82
war with Sweden, *see* Great Northern War
Western cultural influence on, *see* Western cultural influence on Russia
women in:
arranged marriages banned, 390–1
dress, 239, 810
education of, 806, 810
lifestyle, 31–5
in male society, 262, 270, 390, 810
ruling, 106–107, 852–3; *see also* individual rulers, e.g. Elizabeth (Petrovna), Empress
Russian Imperial Guards:
in Azov campaigns (1695–6), 138, 144
ceremonial function, 268
founding, 68–9
at Narva (1700), 333
and Streltsy uprising (1698), 246
and succession to throne, 692, 846–7
war games, 121–2, 132–3
Russian Orthodox Church, *see* Orthodox Church
Russians in foreign countries, 165–7; *see also* Europe: Russian travels in; Great Embassy
Ruysch, Fredrik, 187, 814
Ryswick, Treaty of (1697), 197, 206

St. Petersburg, 355–66
canals, 607–608
as commercial center, 776, 777
construction of, 356–61, 602–12
cultural life, 813–14
fires, 362–3
floods, 363
food supply, 363–4, 778
fortifications (1707), 428
Peter's feelings for, 365, 422, 509
population, 361–2, 364
Senate relocated in (1712), 570

St. Petersburg (*continued*)
 site, 355-6
 Swedish threats to, 357, 359, 453-4,
  525
 see also individual landmarks, e.g.
  Nevsky Prospect
Savoy, (Prince) Eugene of, 222-3, 225
Schey, Gilles, 200, 201
Schleinitz, Johann Christoph, 548-50
Schlippenbach, (Colonel) Anton von,
 348-9
Schlüsselburg (Nöteborg), 351-2
School of Mathematics and Navigation
 (Naval Academy), 757
schools, *see* education in Russia
seasonal rituals and ceremonies, *see*
 rituals and ceremonies
Semyonovsky Regiment:
 in Azov campaigns (1695-6), 138, 144
 ceremonial function, 268
 founding, 69
 at Narva (1700), 333
 and Streltsy uprising (1698), 246
 and succession to throne, 846-7
 war games, 121-2, 132
serfs, *see* peasants
Shafirov, Peter, 297, 386, 387
 imprisoned in Constantinople, 560,
  563
 as negotiator (1711), 559-60
 Order of St. Andrew, 387
 trial and exile (1723), 755
  pardon (1725), 755
  pardon appeal fails, 837
 on Western journey (1716-17), 625,
  654
Shaklovity, Fedor, 80, 90, 92-3
 death, 105
 and Sophia's downfall, 94-105 *passim*
Shein, Alexis, 169, 234
 at Azov (1696), 144, 146, 148
 and Streltsy uprising (1698), 226-7,
  245-8
Sheremetev, (Count and Field Marshal)
 Boris:
 in Azov campaign (1695), 138, 141
 (sent to) Baltic (1709), 517
 career, 340-1
 death (1719), 802
 in Livonia, 348-50
 and Narva (1700), 324, 327-8, 333
  (1704), 397-8

Order of St. Andrew, 243, 349
 in Peter's early regime, 109
 and Streltsy revolt (1682), 42-4
Sheremetev, (Colonel) Michael Boriso-
 vich, 560, 563, 564
shipbuilding:
 in Amsterdam, 184-6
 Baltic fleet, 590
 English, 216
 at Lake Ladoga, 350, 357, 358
 at St. Petersburg, 358-9
 training in Europe for, 149-50, 156-7,
  185, 200, 201-202, 232, 584
 at Voronezh, 142-4, 149, 275-7
 in Zaandam, 179-80
 see also Russia: naval fleet
ships, eighteenth century, 582
 galley, 583-4
Skavronskaya, Martha, *see* Catherine I,
 Empress
Skoropadsky, Ivan Ilich, Hetman of the
 Cossacks, 547
Sloteburg (Nyenskans), 353
smoking and tobacco, 211-12
Sobieski, James, 400, 419
Sobieski, Jan, King of Poland, 84, 87,
  539
 death (1696), 155
Solovetsky Monastery, 62, 129, 130
Sophia, Electress of Hanover, 175-7
Sophia (Alexeevna), Tsarevna and
 Regent:
 achievements, 106-107
 ascent to power, 49-50
 as autocrat, 92
 early life, 35-7
 education, 26, 36
 exile to Novodevichy Convent, 105-
  106, 257
 and Old Believers, 63
 and Peter, 78, 89-94, 107, 256-7
 physical appearance, 79-80
 regency (1682-9), 79-94
  ending of, 95-107
 and Streltsy, 41-2, 47-50, 92, 94,
  95-103
Sophia Charlotte, Electress of Brandenburg, 175-6
Sophia Dorothea, Queen of Prussia, 577
soul tax, 781, 849
South Sea Bubble, 738
sports and recreation, 620, 801

in London, 204
see also entertainments; hunting
Stanilesti, *see* Pruth
Stanislaus I, King of Poland, 400–401
flees Poland (1709), 519, 520
sovereignty recognized by England, 435
Starodub, 455–6
Stenbock, (Colonel) Magnus:
at Narva (1700), 332, 334, 336
in Pomerania (1712–13), 578–9
surrender at Tonning, 579
Stettin, 571, 572, 573
surrender to Russia (1713), 580
Stockholm, 291
Stralsund:
Charles XII's return to, from Turkey (1714), 599–600
siege and surrender of (1715), 600–601
Streltsy, 38–50
in Azov campaign (1st, 1695), 138, 139, 244
in Azov as military colonizers, 149, 244
and the Church, 53
disbanded (1708), 261
formation, 38–9
at Narva (1700), 333
and Peter, 44–7, 52, 169, 244, 259–61
refuge at Astrachan, 393
revolt (1682), 39–49
effect on Peter, 135
and Sophia, 92, 94, 95–103
uprising (1698), 107, 226–7, 245–9
executions. 257–9, 270; Western reaction to, 260
interrogation, 249, 253–7
Streshnev, Tikhon, 109, 234
Sublime Porte, Constantinople, 85, 536
sultans, 532, 534–5
Summer Garden, St. Petersburg, 608–609, 801–802
Summer Palace, St. Petersburg, 605–606
"Sun King," the, *see* Louis XIV, King of France
superstition, 786–7
Suzdal (Pokrovsky) Monastery, 241, 695–6
Sweden:
army:
artillery, 307

battles, *see* Great Northern War: battles
command conflicts, 491–2, 502–503, 513
conscription, 546, 578, 600, 712
disease and hunger: (1701), 345; (1708), 435, 449, 455
disintegration after Poltava, 513–14, 515
freezing (winter 1708–1709), 469–70, 472
infantry, 310
preparation for Russian campaign (1707), 424–5
as prisoners of war in Russia, 523–4, 754, 784
strength and reputation, 292, 318
in Ukraine, 456–7, 461, 464–5, 467–515
defensive fortifications, 630
description, 290–2
invasion of Russia (1707–1709), 431–515; plans for, 423–4; reasons for, 421–2
naval fleet, 320
engagements with Russian fleet: (1702), 350–1; (1713–14), 581–90
succession to throne, 724–5
war with Russia, *see* Great Northern War

Table of Ranks of the Russian Empire, 761
Tagenrog harbor and fort, 147, 282
surrendered to Turks (1712), 563
Tallinn, *see* Reval
Tatars, 15, 85–6, 88–9, 539–40
and Charles XII, 476–7
raids on Ukraine, 15, 85–6, 109, 137, 282, 546, 580, 581
see also Devlet Gerey
taxes, 388–9, 548
as exemption from beard ban, 235–6
household, 780–1
increased base for, 770–1
Peter's tax policy, 780–2
soul tax, 781, 849
in Sweden, 712, 714
terem, the, 35, 390
Terem Palace, Moscow, 8–9

theater:
in France, 645
in Russia, 813–14
at Preobrazhenskoe, 22
public, 392
Timmerman, Franz, 71–5, 216 n.
titles, see awards of merit; meritocracy;
Peter I: trappings of office
tobacco and smoking, 211–12
Tolstoy, Peter Adreevich:
and (Tsarevich) Alexis, 685–91
as ambassador to Constantinople,
541–4, 563
imprisoned (1710), 547, 564
early career, 540–1
exile and death, 850
naval training, 150
opposes Menshikov (1727), 849
prevents Swedish-Tatar alliance (1709),
476–7
on Western journey (1716–17), 625,
654
Topkapi Palace, Constantinople, 532
torture, 249–56
by fire, 251
societies, 251–2
of Streltsy (1698), 249, 253–7
Tower of the Patriarch Philaret,
Moscow, 7
travel conditions, 383–5
roads, 383–4
by sled, 384 5
Travendal, Peace of (1700), 322, 325
and Augustus II, 326
broken by Denmark (1709), 546
treaties:
Adrianople (1713), 564, 598
Altranstadt (1706), 408, 410, 412, 519
Carlowitz (1699), 282–3, 540
Constantinople (1699), 285–6
Kardis (1661), 83
Nerchinsk (1689), 85 n., 117, 168
Nystad, 739–43, 784, 818, 830, 832
Ryswick (1697), 197, 206
Travendal (1700), 322, 325, 326, 546
Utrecht, 597–8, 637
Trezzini, Domenico, 360, 362, 603, 605,
756
Troitskaya-Sergeeva (Laurel of St.
Sergius under the Blessing of the
Holy Trinity) Monastery, 96–7
tsarevnas, 34–5
tsaritsas, 34

tsars:
changing role of, 342–3, 390, 392
duties of, 747–8
exalted status of, 9–10, 392; see also
Peter I: trappings of office
title of Emperor, 742 n.
see also individual tsars
Tsarskoe Selo, 834–5
Tsykler, Ivan, 98, 169, 249
Tumult of 1713, 592–7
Turgenev, Jacob, 120, 235
Turkey, see Ottoman Empire

Ukraine:
description, 15
Swedish army in (1708–1709), 456–7,
461, 464–5, 467–515
Tatar raids on, 15, 85–6, 109, 137, 282,
546, 580, 581
Ukraintsev, Emilian Ignatievich, 109,
146, 283–6
Ulrika Eleonora, Queen of Sweden:
abdication (1720), 735
accession to throne (1718), 724–5
Urals, 771–2
Uspensky Sobor (Assumption Cathedral),
Moscow, 6–7
Utrecht, Treaty of (1713), 597–8, 637

Vauban, Louis de, 304–305
Venice, and shipbuilders, 143, 584
Veprik, 470–1
Versailles palace, 158–62, 636
architectural influence of, 159 60
entertainments at, 160–1
gardens, 159
Peter's visits (1717), 651, 652
Veselovsky, Abraham, 731
and (Tsarevich) Alexis, 684, 686, 689
Viazemsky, Nikifor, 658
Vienna:
description, 219
Peter's visit (1698), 223–7
Vinius, Andrew, 109, 113, 342–3
Vistula River, Swedish crossing (1708),
431
Volynsky, Artemius, 822–3
Voronezh shipyards, 142–4, 149, 275–7;
see also Russia: naval fleet
Vorskla River, Russian army crosses,
482–3, 485

Voznitsyn, Prokofy, 150, 168, 227, 282–3
Vyborg, 524–5
Vyshny-Volochok canal, 778–9

Wachtmeister, (Count) Hans, 583
Walachia, 552, 554–6
Walpole, (Sir) Robert, 738
war, ca.1700, 302–11
    artillery, 307
    battle deployment, 306–307
    cavalry, 310–11
    conscription for, 303; *see also* recruitment: of soldiers
    infantry, 307–10
    mobility of armies, 304
    seasonal aspect, 303–304
    sieges, 304–305
    size of armies, 302–303
    tactics, 309–11
    weapons, 307–309
war games:
    of Charles XII, 315–16
    in England (1698), 213–14
    in Holland (1697), 200–201
    of Peter, 67–70, 121–2, 132–3
War of the Spanish Succession, 197, 302, 343–4, 597–8
warships, *see* Russia: naval fleet; shipbuilding; ships; Sweden: naval fleet
Weber, Friedrich Christian:
    reports of Russia, 613–23
Weide, (General) Adam, 299, 324, 334
Western cultural influence on Russia, 80–1, 162–6
    changes effected in Russia, 234–9, 241–3, 262, 808–17
    in German Suburb, 111–12
    and Great Embassy, 157, 232–3
    see also Peter I: reforms
Westerners in Russia, *see* foreigners in Russia
William III, King of England:
    ascent to throne, 194–6
    and Azov, 148
    and Great Northern War, 319
    life/career, 191–7

personality and characteristics, 193–4
Peter's visit (1897), 197–8, 199–200, 202
    (1898), 207, 214–15
Winter Palace, St. Petersburg, 605
Wismar, 627–8
Witsen, Nicholas, 127, 131, 148, 185, 187
Wolfenbüttel, Charlotte, *see* Charlotte, Princess of Wolfenbüttel
women:
    in the Ottoman Empire, 532–4
    in Russia:
        arranged marriages banned, 390–1
        dress, 239, 810
        education, 806, 810
        lifestyle, 31–5
        in male society, 262, 270, 390, 810
        ruling, 106–107; *see also* individual rulers, e.g. Elizabeth (Petrovna), Empress

xenophobia, *see* foreigners in Russia

Yaguzhinsky, Pavel:
    career, 753
    marriage to Countess Golovkin, 812
    and Mons bribery scandal, 839
    Order of St. Andrew, 837
    as Procurator General, 753
    on Western journey (1716–17), 625
Yavorsky, Stephen, Metropolitan of Ryazan, 789–90, 793

Zaandam, Holland, 179–83
Zaporozhsky Cossacks, 459, 474–5
zoos, 815
Zotov, Nikita:
    at Azov victory celebration, 148
    as Inspector General of Decrees (1715), 751
    as Peter's tutor, 27–8
    as "Prince-Pope" of Drunken Synod, 120–1
    and torture of Streltsy (1698), 254
    wedding (1715), 618–19

EUROPE IN THE TIME OF PETER THE GREAT

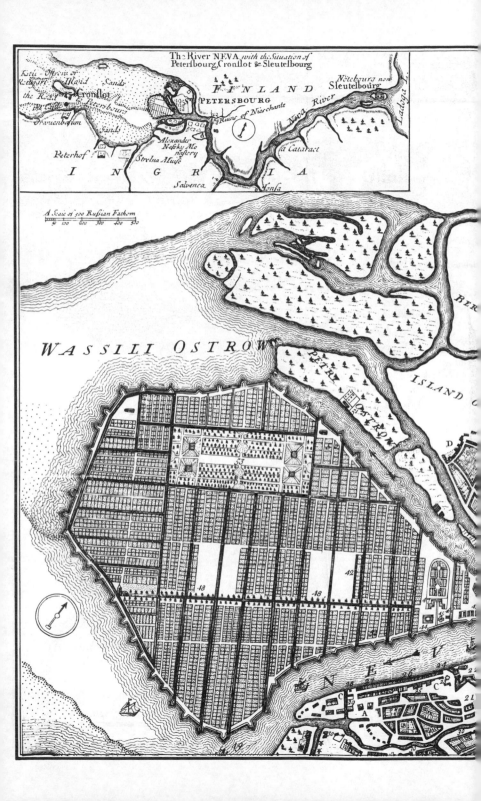

The River NEVA with the Situation of
Peterfbourg, Cronflot & Sleutelbourg

FINLAND

Noteburg non
Sleutelbourg

Katti Ostrow or
Retclaff Illand Sands
the R.
the Castle

Cronflot

PETERSBOURG

Neva River

Ladoga

Peterburg

Ruins of Nieschantz

Grauenboum Sands

Alexander
Nefsky Mo
nastery

a Cataract

INGRIA

Peterhof

Strelna Muifo

Salvenca

Monfa

A Scale of 500 Ruffian Fathom
50 100   200   300   400   500

WASSILI OSTROW

PETRI OSTROW

BER

ISLAND O

D

48

42

48

N E V

Питербурхъ.
A Plan of the City of
ST. PETERSBOURG
as it stood in the Year 1716.
With A Map of its Harbour, the River
Neva and the Neighbouring Country,
And the Prospect of the Castle of
Cronslot.

CRONSLOT КРОНЗШЛОТ

PETERSBOURG

RIVER

PART OF

FINLAND

**PHOENIX
PRESS**

GENERAL EDITORS:
SIMON SCHAMA AND ANTONIA FRASER

*Phoenix Press publishes and re-publishes hundreds of the very best new
and out of print books about the past. For a free colour catalogue listing
more than 400 titles please*

telephone: +44 (0) 1903 828 503
fax: +44 (0) 1903 828 802
e-mail: mailorder@lbsltd.co.uk
or visit our website at www.phoenixpress.co.uk

The following books might be of particular interest to you:

The Fall of the Russian Monarchy

BERNARD PARES

The foremost expert on Russian history of his generation, Pares
tells the story of the Russian Revolution from the point of view of
the Romanovs, beginning with Nicholas II's accession in 1894 and
ending with his and his family's murder at Ekaterinburg in 1918.

Paperback £12.99   528pp + Maps   1 84212 114 6

The Life of Lenin

LOUIS FISCHER

Lenin was revolution: his absolute determination can truly be said
to have changed the course of world history. No-one else of his
time could have overcome the chaos in Russia, the foreign intervention, and the economic ruin without losing control of the
revolution. Fischer knew Lenin personally and was given privileged access to his archives to create this landmark biography.

Paperback £16.99   720pp + 16pp b/w   1 84212 230 4

Roots of Revolution
INTRODUCED BY ISAIAH BERLIN
FRANCO VENTURI

Venturi offers nothing less than a history of the populist and socialist movements in 19th-century Russia that spawned the events of 1917 that shook the world. Isaiah Berlin, who was himself uprooted by that Revolution, contributes an introduction, and a later essay by the author on Russian Populism is also included.

Paperback
UK: £18.99   960pp   1 84212 253 3

On Sledge and Horseback to Outcast Siberian Lepers
KATE MARSDEN

Kate Marsden recounts her extraordinary journey, sponsored by Queen Victoria, from Constantinople to Yakutsk in north-east Siberia in the 1890s. A fervent Christian, Marsden was driven to research leprosy and its then widely differing treatments from the Middle East to Siberia. Illustrated with some of the author's own photographs and drawings.

Paperback
UK: £12.99   272pp + 24pp b/w   1 84212 397 1

The History of Pugachev
ALEXANDER PUSHKIN

A history of Russia's greatest peasant rebellion by its greatest national poet. With a new introduction by Orlando Figes.

Paperback
UK: £9.99   160pp   1 84212 418 8

Catherine the Great

HENRI TROYAT

The Prix Goncourt-winning French historian reveals the true nature of the ambitious and ruthless despot. 'Theoretically straightforward biography, it illuminates far more than the life of that amazing woman; a brilliant court, Russian itself, sparkle before our eyes'
Antonia Fraser, *The Good Book Guide*
Paperback: £14.99   400pp + 16pp b/w   1 84212 029 8

Ivan the Terrible

HENRI TROYAT

Outstanding popular biography of one of the most violent and demented rulers in history, by the author of *Catherine the Great*.
UK: £14.99   304pp + 20pp b/w + Map   1 84212 419 6

Journey for our Time

THE JOURNALS OF THE MARQUIS DE CUSTINE

The 'de Tocqueville of Russia' provides a timeless insight into the divisions and distempers of one of the world's most enigmatic nations. With a new introduction by Simon Sebag Montefiore.
Paperback
UK: £9.99   240pp   1 84212 436 6

Peasant Russia, Civil War

THE VOLGA COUNTRYSIDE IN REVOLUTION 1917–21

ORLANDO FIGES

Britain's most celebrated historian of Russia investigates why and how the October Revolution occurred.
Paperback
UK: £14.99   432pp + 8pp b/w + Maps   1 84212 419 6